Comprehensive Model of the

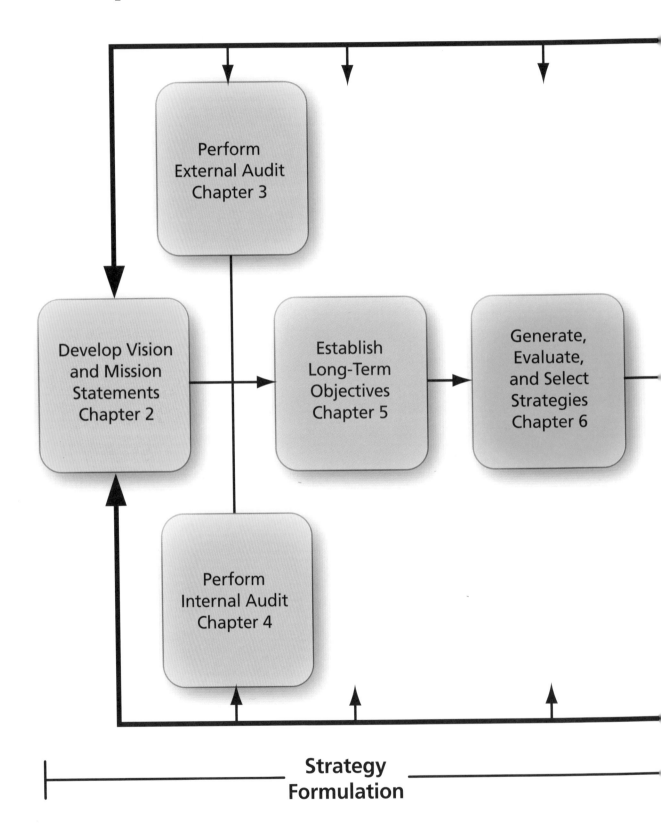

Perform
External Audit
Chapter 3

Develop Vision
and Mission
Statements
Chapter 2

Establish
Long-Term
Objectives
Chapter 5

Generate,
Evaluate,
and Select
Strategies
Chapter 6

Perform
Internal Audit
Chapter 4

Strategy
Formulation

**USED WIDELY AMONG BUSINESSES
AND ACADEMIA WORLDWIDE**

Strategic Management Process

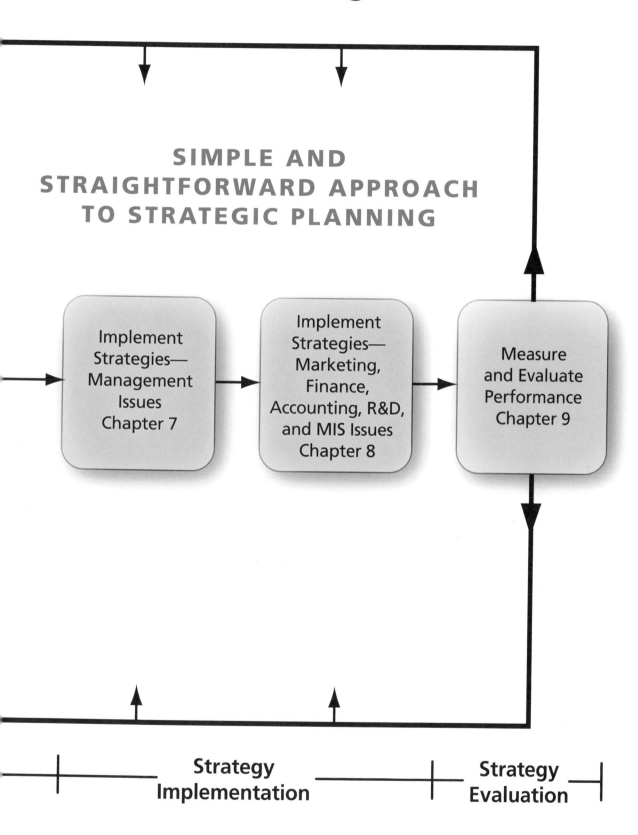

SIMPLE AND STRAIGHTFORWARD APPROACH TO STRATEGIC PLANNING

Implement Strategies—Management Issues Chapter 7

Implement Strategies—Marketing, Finance, Accounting, R&D, and MIS Issues Chapter 8

Measure and Evaluate Performance Chapter 9

Strategy Implementation

Strategy Evaluation

USED TO INTEGRATE AND ORGANIZE ALL CHAPTERS IN THIS TEXT

Strategic Management

• CONCEPTS AND CASES

twelfth edition

Strategic Management

• CONCEPTS AND CASES

Fred R. David
FRANCIS MARION UNIVERSITY
FLORENCE, SOUTH CAROLINA

PEARSON

Prentice
Hall

PEARSON EDUCATION INTERNATIONAL

To Joy, Forest, Byron, and Meredith—
my wife and children—
for their encouragement and love.

Editor-in-Chief: David Parker
Product Development Manager: Ashley Santora
Assistant Editor: Kristen Varina
Editorial Assistant: Elizabeth Davis
Marketing Manager: Nikki Jones
Marketing Assistant: Ian Gold
Associate Managing Editor: Suzanne DeWorken
Project Manager, Production: Ann Pulido
Permissions Project Manager: Charles Morris
Senior Operations Supervisor: Arnold Vila
Senior Art Director: Janet Slowik
Interior Design: Liz Harasymczuk
Director, Image Resource Center: Melinda Patelli
Manager, Rights and Permissions: Zina Arabia
Manager: Visual Research: Beth Brenzel
Manager, Cover Visual Research & Permissions: Karen Sanatar
Image Permission Coordinator: Ang'John Ferreri
Composition: Laserwords
Full-Service Project Management: Thistle Hill Publishing Services, LLC
Printer/Binder: Quebecor World Color/Versailles
Typeface: 10/12 Times

Credits and acknowledgments borrowed from other sources and reproduced, with permission, in this textbook appear on the appropriate page within text.

Pearson Education LTD.
Pearson Education Singapore, Pte. Ltd
Pearson Education, Canada, Ltd
Pearson Education–Japan

Pearson Education Australia PTY, Limited
Pearson Education North Asia Ltd
Pearson Educación de Mexico, S.A. de C.V.
Pearson Education Malaysia, Pte. Ltd.

10 9 8 7 6 5 4 3 2 1
ISBN-13: 978-0-13-501320-5
ISBN-10: 0-13-501320-8

Brief Contents

Contents

Cases

Manufacturing Firms

Service Firms

Preface

The business world today is considerably different and more complex than it was just two years ago when the previous edition of this text was published. Today, we experience private-equity firms acquiring hundreds of companies, rising consumer and business concern about global warming and pollution, high oil and gasoline prices, extensive outsourcing, a migration of work to China and India, more attention on business ethics, ballooning federal budget deficits, continued globalization, consolidation within industries, a European Union in dispute over its constitution, and intense rivalry in almost all industries. E-commerce continues to alter the nature of business to its core.

Thousands of strategic alliances and partnerships, even among competitors, formed in recent years. Hundreds of companies have declared bankruptcy and corporate scandals have highlighted the need for improved business ethics and corporate disclosure of financial transactions. Downsizing, rightsizing, reengineering, and countless divestitures, acquisitions, and liquidations have permanently altered the corporate landscape in the last two years. Thousands of firms have begun global operations and thousands more have merged. Thousands have prospered and yet thousands more have failed in the last two years. Many manufacturers have become e-commerce suppliers and long-held competitive advantages have eroded as new ones have formed.

Both the challenges and opportunities facing organizations of all sizes today are greater than ever. Illegal immigration across the U.S–Mexico border has reached emergency levels. There is less room than ever for error today in the formulation and implementation of a strategic plan. This textbook provides a systematic effective approach for developing a clear strategic plan.

Changes made in this twelfth edition are aimed squarely at illustrating the effect of this new world order on strategic-management theory and practice. Due to the magnitude of the changes affecting companies, cultures, and countries, every page of this edition has been updated. The first edition of this text was published in 1986 and since that time it has grown to be one of, if not the most widely read strategic management books in the world. This text now is published in nine languages other than English. All 31 of the case companies in this twelfth edition are brand new, having not appeared in the prior edition.

This twelfth edition provides updated coverage of strategic-management concepts, theory, research, and techniques in the chapters. Every sentence and paragraph has been scrutinized, modified, clarified, deleted, streamlined, updated, and improved to enhance the content and caliber of presentation. The structure of this edition parallels the last, with nine chapters and a Cohesion Case, but the improvements in readability and coverage are dramatic. Every chapter features strategic-management concepts and practices presented in a clear, focused, and relevant manner with hundreds of new examples integrated throughout.

The skills-oriented, practitioner perspective that historically has been the foundation of this text is enhanced and strengthened in this edition. New and expanded coverage of strategic-management theories and research herein reflect companies' use of concepts such as value chain analysis (VCA), Balanced Scorecard, resource-based view (RBV), benchmarking, restructuring, and outsourcing. To survive and prosper in the new millennium, organizations must build and sustain competitive advantage. This text is now trusted around the world to provide future and present managers the latest skills and concepts needed to effectively formulate and efficiently implement a strategic plan—a game plan if you will—that can lead to sustainable competitive advantage for any type of business.

Our mission in preparing the twelfth edition of *Strategic Managemen: Concepts and Cases* was "to create the most current, well-written strategic management textbook on the market—a book that is exciting and valuable to both students and professors." Based on comments from 49 reviewers of the prior edition, new strategic-management research and practice, such as the Industrial Organizational (I/O) Model, Market Commonality, Value Chain Analysis, Balanced Scorecard, and First Mover Advantages, are incorporated and supported by hundreds of new practical examples. There is a brand-new Cohesion Case on Walt Disney—2008 which replaces the prior Google case. Nearly all of the twelfth edition Experiential Exercises have been revamped, replaced, or improved.

The time basis for all cases included in this edition is 2007 since year-end 2006 or 2007 financial statements are provided in all of the cases. This case lineup represents the most up-to-date compilation of cases ever assembled in a strategic management text. There are more cases on technology companies this time, more nonprofit companies, and more global companies. The cases are paired up within industries. The 31 cases in this edition represent a totally fresh beginning for this text and all the cases focus on well-known, student-exciting companies and organizations.

The 49 reviewers (on pp. 22–23) and I believe you will find this edition to be the best strategic management textbook available for communicating both the excitement and value of strategic management. Concise and exceptionally well organized, this text is now published in English, Chinese, Spanish, Thai, German, Japanese, Farsi, Indonesian, Indian, and Arabic. A version in Russian is being negotiated. On five continents, this text is widely used in colleges and universities at both the graduate and undergraduate levels. In addition, thousands of companies, organizations, and governmental bodies use this text as a management guide, making it perhaps the most widely used strategic planning book in the world.

This textbook meets all AACSB-International guidelines for the business policy and strategic-management course at both the graduate and undergraduate levels, and previous editions have been used at more than 500 colleges and universities. Prentice Hall maintains a separate Web site for this text at www.prenhall.com/david. The author maintains the Strategic Management Club Online at www.strategyclub.com, which offers many benefits for strategic-management and business policy students.

Chapter Themes

As listed below, two themes permeate all chapters in this edition and contribute significantly to making it timely, informative, exciting, and valuable. Boxed insert "Perspectives" in each chapter link concepts being presented to each theme. Nearly all of the boxed inserts are new to this edition.

1. **Global Factors Affect Virtually All Strategic Decisions** The global theme is enhanced in this edition because doing business globally has become a necessity, rather than a luxury in most industries. Nearly all strategic decisions today are affected by global issues and concerns. There is new global coverage in each chapter consistent with the growing interdependence among countries and companies worldwide. The dynamics of political, economic, and cultural differences across countries directly affect strategic-management decisions. Doing business globally is more risky and complex than ever. The global theme illustrates how organizations today can effectively do business in an interlocked and interdependent world community.

2. **Preserving the Natural Environment Is a Vital Strategic Issue** Unique to strategic-management texts, the natural environment theme is strengthened in this edition in order to promote and encourage firms to conduct operations in an environmentally sound manner. This theme now includes social responsibility, sustainability, and business ethics issues. Countries worldwide have enacted laws to curtail the pollution of streams, rivers, the air, land, and sea. Global warming is now undeniable, and even oil companies are supporting emission restrictions as consumers are demanding responsible action from companies and politicians. Thousands of companies are "going green." The strategic efforts of both companies and countries to preserve the natural environment are described herein. More and more businesses are issuing Sustainability Reports to detail their efforts to curb global warming and operate in an environmentally-friendly manner. Respect for the natural environment has become an important concern for consumers, companies, society, and AACSB-International.

Twelfth Edition Design Features

There are some nice design features in this edition. For the first time ever, four photos in vivid color are present in each chapter and are tied directly to (1) chapter opening, (2) global perspective, (3) natural environment perspective, and (4) Walt Disney end-of-chapter experiential exercises. These four photos per chapter make the twelfth edition much more visually appealing. In the prior edition, only chapter opening photos were present.

The comprehensive strategic-management model is displayed on the inside front cover of the text. At the start of each chapter, the section of the comprehensive strategy model covered in that chapter is highlighted and enlarged so students can see the focus of each chapter in the basic unifying comprehensive model.

A new Case Information Matrix and Case Description Matrix are provided in the Preface to reveal (1) topical areas emphasized in each case and (2) contact and location information for each case company. These matrices provide suggestions on how the cases deal with the two themes and the nine chapters. For example, the Case Information Matrix provides details regarding which cases can be used to highlight mission/vision and which ones are best for strategy implementation.

Time-Tested Features

This edition continues to offer many special time-tested features and content that have made this text so successful for nearly twenty years. Historical trademarks of this text that are strengthened in this edition include:

Chapters: Time-Tested Features

- This text meets AACSB-International guidelines which support a practitioner orientation rather than a theory/research approach. It offers a skills-oriented approach to developing a vision and mission statement; performing an external audit; conducting an internal assessment; and formulating, implementing, and evaluating strategies.
- The global and natural environment themes permeate all chapters and examine strategic-management concepts in these important perspectives.
- The author's writing style is concise, conversational, interesting, logical, lively, and supported by numerous current examples throughout.
- A simple, integrative strategic-management model appears in all chapters and on the inside front cover of the text. This model is widely utilized for strategic planning among consultants and companies worldwide. One reviewer said: "One thing I have admired about David's text is that he follows the fundamental sequence of strategy formulation, implementation, and evaluation. There is a basic flow from mission/purposes to internal/external environmental scanning to strategy development, selection, implementation, and evaluation. This has been, and continues to be, a hallmark of the David text. Many other strategy texts are more disjointed in their presentation, and thus confusing to the student, especially at the undergraduate level."
- A Cohesion Case follows Chapter 1 and is revisited at the end of each chapter. This Cohesion Case allows students to apply strategic-management concepts and techniques to a real organization as chapter material is covered, which readies students for case analysis in the course.
- End-of-chapter Experiential Exercises effectively apply concepts and techniques in a challenging, meaningful, and enjoyable manner. Eighteen exercises apply text material to the Cohesion Case; ten apply textual material to a college or university; another ten exercises send students into the business world to explore important strategy topics. The exercises are relevant, interesting, and contemporary.
- There is excellent pedagogy in this text, including Notable Quotes and Objectives to open each chapter, and Key Terms, Current Readings, Discussion Questions, and Experiential Exercises to close each chapter.

- There is excellent coverage of strategy formulation issues such as business ethics, global versus domestic operations, vision/mission, matrix analysis, partnering, joint venturing, competitive analysis, governance, and guidelines for conducting an internal/external strategy assessment.
- There is excellent coverage of strategy implementation issues such as corporate culture, organizational structure, outsourcing, marketing concepts, financial analysis, and business ethics.
- A systematic, analytical approach is presented in Chapter 6, including matrices such as the SWOT, BCG, IE, GRAND, SPACE, and QSPM.
- The chapter material is again published in four-color.
- "Visit the Net" Internet exercises are available online at www.prenhall.com/david or at the www.strategyclub.com Web site and in the page margins of the text. This feature reveals the author's recommended Web sites for locating additional information on the concepts being presented, and greatly enhances classroom presentation in an Internet environment since the recommended sites have been screened closely to assure that each is well worth visiting in class. This feature also provides students with substantial additional material on chapter concepts.
- The Web site, www.prenhall.com/david, provides chapter and case updates and support materials.
- The nine chapters are organized in the same manner as the previous edition.
- A chapters-only paperback version of the text is available.
- Custom-case publishing is available whereby an instructor can combine chapters from this text with cases from a variety of sources, or select any number of cases you desire from the 31 cases in the full text.
- For the chapter material, the outstanding ancillary package includes a comprehensive *Instructor's Manual,* computerized test bank, and PowerPoints.

Cases: Time-Tested Features

- This edition contains the most current set of cases in any strategic-management text on the market. All cases include year-end 2006 or 2007 financial data and information.
- The cases focus on well-known firms in the news making strategic changes. All cases are undisguised and most are exclusively written for this text to reflect current strategic-management problems and practices. These are all "student friendly" cases.
- Organized conveniently by industry (usually two competing firms per industry), the cases feature a great mix of small business, international, and not-for-profit firms.
- All cases have been class tested to ensure that they are interesting, challenging, and effective for illustrating strategic-management concepts.
- All the cases provide complete financial information about the firm, an organizational chart, and a vision and mission statement for the organization if those were available.
- Customized inclusion of cases to comprise a tailored text is available to meet the special needs of some professors.
- For the cases, the outstanding ancillary package includes an elaborate *Case Solutions Manual,* PowerPoint, and support from the www.strategyclub.com Web site.
- All of the cases are comprenhensive in the sense that each provides a full description of the firm and its operations rather than focusing on one issue or problem such as a plant closing. Each case thus lends itself to students preparing a three-year strategic plan for the firm.

What's New to This Edition in the Chapters

In addition to the special time-tested trademarks described above, this edition includes some exciting new features, changes, and content designed to position this text as the clear leader and best choice for teaching business policy and strategic management.

First of all, the new Cohesion Case on the Walt Disney Company features one of the most successful, well-known, best managed, and largest family entertainment companies in the world. In addition to its theme parks worldwide, Disney owns Touchstone Pictures, Miramax Films, Pixar, ESPN Zone, 17 hotels at the Walt Disney World Resort, ABC News, Disney Channel, and more. It is a fun company and real challenge for students to address strategic issues facing Disney.

Experiential Exercises at the end of each chapter apply concepts to the Disney Cohesion Case and ready students for case analysis when they complete the chapter material. Over the past twenty years, the Cohesion Case for this text has changed from Ponderosa Steakhouse in the first and second editions, to Hershey Foods in the third through seventh editions, to AOL in the eighth edition, to American Airlines in the ninth edition, Krispy Kreme in the tenth, Google in the eleventh, and now Walt Disney, which is a great company for students to focus upon throughout the semester.

In this edition, new features, changes, and content common to all nine chapters include the following:

- New Global and Natural Environment boxed inserts.
- New examples throughout.
- New Visit the Net (VTN) Web sites provided in the page margins. Many universities now teach in Internet-ready classrooms and utilize Web sites during lectures. These sites are hot-linked at the www.prenhall.com/david and www.strategyclub.com Web sites.
- Improved coverage of global issues and concerns.
- Expanded coverage of business ethics.
- All new current readings at the end of each chapter reveal new, relevant strategic-management research.
- More international flavor than ever. There is excellent new coverage of cultural and conceptual strategic-management differences across countries.
- New research and theories of seminal thinkers in strategy development such as Ansoff, Chandler, Porter, Hamel, Prahalad, Mintzberg, and Barney are included. Scholars such as these have brought strategic management to its present place in modern business. Practical aspects of strategic management are still center-stage and the trademark of this text.
- Substantial new material on business ethics throughout. Corporate fraud, scandals, and illegalities are numerous, so we in academia must be certain to emphasize that "good ethics is good business." This notion is tied to the natural environment theme in this edition.

In addition to the changes listed above, some specific chapter by chapter changes in this twelfth edition are:

Chapter 1

- There is a new Global Perspective boxed insert regarding the extent that U.S. firms dominate industries.
- There is a new Strategies in Action Table featuring McDonalds and American General.
- Experiential Exercises 1A and 1B have been overhauled.
- There are new examples throughout.

Chapter 2

- Eight new vision statements are provided along with new "Author's Comments" about each one.
- Six new mission statements are provided along with new "Author's Comments" about each one.
- Updated Global Perspective is provided.

- Updated Natural Environment Perspective is provided.
- Experiential Exercises 2A and 2B have been overhauled.
- New examples throughout.

Chapter 3

- New Natural Environment Perspective on climate change.
- New Global Perspective on auto producers in China.
- Deleted section on "The U.S.–Mexico Border."
- Deleted section on "Russia's Economy."
- Deleted section on "China: Opportunities and Threats."
- New EFE Matrix on ten-theatre cinema complex.
- New examples throughout.
- Experiential Exercises 3A, 3D, and 3E have been overhauled.

Chapter 4

- New Natural Environment Perspective on EU use of chemicals.
- New Global Perspective on work week variation across countries.
- New IFE Matrix on a retail computer store.
- New examples throughout.
- Experiential Exercise 4A has been overhauled.

Chapter 5

- New heading and material on private-equity firm acquisitions.
- New Global Perspective on joint venturing in India.
- Over 80 new examples.
- New material on joint ventures.
- New material on cooperating with rival firms.
- Deleted section on "Joint Ventures in Russia."
- Experiential Exercises 5A and 5C overhauled.

Chapter 6

- New Natural Environment Perspective on developing a Sustainability Report.
- New SWOT Matrix for a retail computer store.
- New Global Perspective on comparing corporate tax rates worldwide.
- New strategy detail provided to support SPACE Matrix and BCG Matrix.
- New BCG, IE, and QSPM Matrices.
- New examples thoughout.
- All Experiential Exercises updated.

Chapter 7

- New coverage of Six Sigma, the quality-boosting process improvement technique.
- New coverage of ESOPs, including a new table listing the eight largest in the United States.
- New coverage on women's issues, including a new table listing the ten best firms for women to work for.
- Deleted the section "The Russian Culture."
- Revised Natural Environment Perspective on environmental training of students in colleges and universities.
- New examples throughout.
- Experiential Exercise 7A has been overhauled.

Chapter 8

- Substantially more information is provided on "How to Develop Projected Financial Statements," including a full new example of this concept worked out in detail for Mattel, Inc. Many students have trouble with these financial concepts, yet they need to show what impact their recommended strategies would have on this firm's financial future.
- New coverage and examples on calculating a company's worth, including use for the first time of Yahoo's Enterprise Value technique.
- New Natural Environment Perspective on "Strategic Management of Your Health." This is the author's favorite new Boxed Insert in this edition and it focuses on "wellness campaigns" at companies.
- All Experiential Exercises fully updated.
- New examples throughout.

Chapter 9

- New Natural Environment Perspectve on the pollution situation in China.
- Revised/updated Global Perspective on use of atomic energy.
- Fully updated Experiential Exercises.
- New examples throughout.

What's New to This Edition in the Cases

Rather than 41 cases as in prior editions there are 31 cases included herein. None appeared in the prior edition, so this is indeed a fresh start. However, the following ten popular cases from two editions ago (the tenth edition text) are fully updated and included:

Revlon

Krispy Kreme Doughnuts

Pilgrim's Pride

Anheuser-Busch

Winnebago Industries

E*Trade Financial

Amazon.com

Southwest Airlines

Carnival Cruise Lines

Riverbanks Zoo

Also among the cases in this edition, three feature companies headquartered outside the United States:

Waterford Wedgwood, PLC in Dublin, Ireland

Skoda Automobile Company in Mladá Boleslav, Czech Republic

Compass Group PLC in Chertsey, London, United Kingdom

The twelfth edition cases are mostly organized into pairs of rivals competing within various industries, such as cases on:

Estée Lauder and Revlon

Continental Airlines and Southwest Airlines

Wendy's International and McDonald's Corporation

Included in the case lineup is a nice mix of cases on not-for-profit organizations, including:

Miami University

Wesley United Methodist Church

Riverbanks Zoo

Also among the cases are several hospitality cases, including:

MGM Mirage

Marriott International

Starwood Hotels

Facts About the Twelfth Edition Lineup of Cases

- The new mix of thirty-one cases includes sixteen service companies and fifteen manufacturing companies.
- The time setting of all the cases is early 2007, making them exceptionally up-to-date.
- All the cases contain year-end 2006 financial statements, so students can project financial implications of their recommendations for 2007 and beyond.
- All of the cases are "comprehensive" in the sense that each focuses on multiple business functions, rather than addressing one particular business problem or issue. Students are generally asked to prepare a three-year strategic plan for each case company, rather than being asked to solve a particular business problem.
- The new mix of cases includes two purely e-commerce cases—E*trade Financial and Amazon.com.
- The new mix of cases includes four small business cases – S/W Printing Company, Waterford Wedgwood PLC, Toll Brothers, and Cellox.
- In support of the global theme, every single one of the case firms has a Web site and does business globally, which provides students ample opportunity to evaluate and consider international aspects of doing business.
- All the cases are undisguised and feature real organizations in real industries using real names and real places. Nothing is fictitious in any case in any way in this edition.
- All the cases feature an organization "undergoing strategic change," thus offering students specific issues to evaluate and consider.
- All the cases feature organizations in familiar or interesting settings.
- All the cases provide excellent coverage of a firm's internal weaknesses and external threats, rather than focusing on the organization's strengths and opportunities.
- All the cases are written in a lively, concise writing style that captures the reader's interest and establishes a time setting, usually in the opening paragraph.
- The cases provide excellent quantitative information such as numbers, ratios, percentages, dollar values, graphs, statistics, and maps so students can prepare a more specific, rational, and defensible strategic plan for the organization.
- Each case provides excellent information about the industry and competitors.
- Each case includes the organization's existing vision statement and mission statement, if available.
- Each case is supported by an excellent teacher's note.
- A new running update of the Walt Disney Cohesion Case is provided at www.prenhall.com/david. The Disney case is kept fully updated online for both professors and students. Scores of excellent hot links for the Disney case are provided at www.prenhall.com/david.

Instructor's Resource Center

At **www.prenhall.com/irc**, instructors can access a variety of print, digital, and presentation resources available with this text in downloadable format. Registration is simple and gives you immediate access to new titles and new editions. As a registered faculty member, you can download resource files and receive immediate access and instructions for installing course management content on your campus server.

If you ever need assistance, our dedicated technical support team is ready to help with the media supplements that accompany this text. Visit **www.247.prenhall.com** for answers to frequently asked questions and toll-free user support phone numbers.

The following supplements are available to adopting instructors (for detailed descriptions, please visit **www.prenhall.com/irc**):

- **Instructor's Resource Center (IRC) on CD-ROM**—ISBN: 0-13-813210-0
- **Printed Instructor's Manual with Test Item File**—ISBN: 0-13-813217-8
- **Printed Case Instructor's Manual** —ISBN: 0-13-813209-7
- **PowerPoints** – available on the IRC (both online and on CD-Rom)
- **TestGen Test Generating Software**—Available at the IRC Online.
- **Custom Videos on DVD**—ISBN: 0-13-813212-7

Companion Website

This text's Companion Website at www.prenhall.com/david contains valuable resources for both students and professors, including an interactive student study guide.

Special Note to Students

Welcome to business policy or strategic management, whichever title this course has at your university. This is a challenging and exciting course that will allow you to function as the owner or chief executive officer of different organizations. Your major task in this course will be to make strategic decisions and to justify those decisions through oral and written communication. Strategic decisions determine the future direction and competitive position of an enterprise for a long time. Decisions to expand geographically or to diversify are examples of strategic decisions.

Strategic decision making occurs in all types and sizes of organizations, from Exxon and IBM to a small hardware store or small college. Many people's lives and jobs are affected by strategic decisions, so the stakes are very high. An organization's very survival is often at stake. The overall importance of strategic decisions makes this course especially exciting and challenging. You will be called upon in this course to demonstrate how your strategic decisions could be successfully implemented.

In this course, you can look forward to making strategic decisions both as an individual and as a member of a team. No matter how hard employees work, an organization is in real trouble if strategic decisions are not made effectively. Doing the right things (effectiveness) is more important than doing things right (efficiency). For example, ineffective strategies led to revenue declines of 71 percent and 10 percent in 2006 for Avis Budget Group and American Express, respectively. Boston Scientific and the *New York Times* had profit declines of 670 percent and 309 percent, respectively that year. Even well known firms such as Nortel, Circuit City, Eastman Kodak, La-Z-Boy, Citigroup, New Century Financial, Cadbury Schweppes, and Motorola are struggling with ineffective strategies. Many American newspapers are faltering as consumers increasingly switch to interactive media for news.

You will have the opportunity in this course to make actual strategic decisions, perhaps for the first time in your academic career. Do not hesitate to take a stand and defend specific strategies that you determine to be the best based on tools and concepts in this textbook. The rationale for your strategic decisions will be more important than the actual decision, because no one knows for sure what the best strategy is for a particular organization at a given point in time. This fact accents the subjective, contingency nature of the strategic-management process.

Use the concepts and tools presented in this text, coupled with your own intuition, to recommend strategies that you can defend as being most appropriate for the organizations that you study. You will also need to integrate knowledge acquired in previous business courses. For this reason, strategic management is often called a capstone course; you may want to keep this book for your personal library.

This text is practitioner-oriented and applications-oriented. It presents techniques and content that will enable you to formulate, implement, and evaluate strategies in all kinds of profit and nonprofit organizations. The end-of-chapter Experiential Exercises allow you to apply what you've read in each chapter to the new Walt Disney Cohesion Case and to your own university.

Definitely visit the Strategic Management Club Online at www.strategyclub.com. The templates and links there will save you time in performing analyses and will make your work look professional. Work hard in policy this term and have fun. Good luck!

Acknowledgments

Many persons have contributed time, energy, ideas, and suggestions for improving this text over twelve editions. The strength of this text is largely attributed to the collective wisdom, work, and experiences of business policy professors, strategic-management researchers, students, and practitioners. Names of particular individuals whose published research is referenced in this edition of this text are listed alphabetically in the Name Index. To all individuals involved in making this text so popular and successful, I am indebted and thankful.

Many special persons and reviewers contributed valuable material and suggestions for this edition. I would like to thank my colleagues and friends at Auburn University, Mississippi State University, East Carolina University, and Francis Marion University. These are universities where I have served on the management faculty. Scores of students and professors at these schools helped shape the development of this text. Many thanks go to the following 49 reviewers of the prior edition whose comments shaped this twelfth edition:

Joseph Adamo, Cazenovia College

Asad Aziz, University of Colorado

John Bade, Washington University

Henry Beam, Western Michigan University

James Beierlein, Penn State University

Carl Broadhurst, Campbell University

Doug Cannon, Lindenwood University

Val Calvert, San Antonio College

Debi Cartwright, Truman State University

Ronald Decker, University of Wisconsin at Eau Claire

Jonathan Elimimian, Albany State University

Monique Forte, Stetson University

Charles Forrest, Lindenwood University

Mike Frandsen, Albion College

John Frankenstein, Brooklyn College/City University of New York

Steven Frankforter, Winthrop University

Jeff Furman, Boston University

Debbie Gilliard, Metropolitan State College of Denver

George Gresham, Texas A&M University at Kingsville

Robert Gulbro, Athens State University

Carol Himelhoch, Siena Heights University

Gordon Holbein, University of Kentucky

Phillip Jutras, Regis College

David Kimball, Elms College

Robert Ledman, Georgia Southwestern State University

Ugbo Mallam, Paul Quinn College

William Martello, St. Edward's University

Brenda McAleer, University of Maine at Augusta

Norman McElvany, Johnson State College

Joe Mosca, Monmouth University

Richard Mpoyi, Middle Tennessee State University

Carolyn Mueller, Stetson University

Carl Nelson, Polytechnic University

James O'Connor, University of Texas at El Paso

Don Okhomina, Fayetteville State University

David Olson, California State University at Bakersfield

Jeffrey Parker, Jacksonville State University

James Schiro, Central Michigan University College of Professional Studies

Mike Schraeder, Troy University

Karen Silva, Johnson & Wales

James Smith, Dana College

William Tita, Northeastern University

David Vequist, University of the Incarnate World

Richard Weaver, National University

Morrison Webb, Manhattanville College

Michael Welch, Loyola University Chicago

Kenneth Wendeln, Kelley School of Business, Indiana University at Indianapolis

Floyd Willoughby, Oakland University

Nancy Wyant, International College

Individuals who develop cases for the North American Case Research Association Meeting, the Midwest Society for Case Research Meeting, the Eastern Case Writers Association Meeting, the European Case Research Association Meeting, and Harvard Case Services are vitally important for continued progress in the field of strategic management. From a research perspective, writing strategic management cases represents a valuable scholarly activity among faculty. Extensive research is required to structure business policy cases in a way that exposes strategic issues, decisions, and behavior. Pedagogically, strategic management cases are essential for students in learning how to apply concepts, evaluate situations, formulate a "game plan," and resolve implementation problems. Without a continuous stream of updated business policy cases, the strategic-management course and discipline would lose much of its energy and excitement.

Professors who teach this course supplement lecture with simulations, guest speakers, experiential exercises, class projects, and/or outside readings. Case analysis, however, is typically the backbone of the learning process in most strategic-management courses across the country. Case analysis is almost always an integral part of this course.

Analyzing strategic-management cases gives students the opportunity to work in teams to evaluate the internal operations and external issues facing various organizations and to craft strategies that can lead these firms to success. Working in teams gives students practical experience solving problems as part of a group. In the business world, important decisions are generally made within groups; strategic-management students learn to deal with overly aggressive group members and also timid, noncontributing group members. This experience is valuable as strategic-management students near graduation and soon enter the working world on a full-time basis.

Students can improve their oral and written communication skills as well as their analytical and interpersonal skills by proposing and defending particular courses of action for the case companies. Analyzing cases allows students to view a company, its competitors, and its industry concurrently, thus simulating the complex business world. Through case analysis, students learn how to apply concepts, evaluate situations, formulate strategies, and resolve implementation problems. Instructors typically ask students to prepare a three-year strategic plan for the firm. Analyzing a strategic-management case entails students applying concepts learned across their entire business curriculum. Students gain experience dealing with a wide range of organizational problems that impact all the business functions.

The following individuals wrote cases that were selected for inclusion in this twelfth edition. These persons helped develop the most current compilation of cases ever assembled in a strategic-management text:

Dr. Joe Aniello, Francis Marion University

Dr. M. Jill Austin, Middle Tennessee State University

Dr. Alen Badal, The Union Institute

Dr. Mernoush Banton, Florida International University

Dr. Gene Bland, Texas A&M University – Corpus Christi

Dr. Rochelle R. Brunson, Alvin College

Dr. Clare Burns, Lamar University

Dr. Charles M. Byles, Virginia Commonwealth University

Forest R. David, MBA, Francis Marion University

Dr. James Harbin, Texas A&M University – Texarkana

Dr. Randall D. Harris, California State University

Dr. Lester A. Hudson, Jr., Queens University of Charlotte

William James, MBA, Francis Marion University

Dr. Joe W. Leonard, Miami University

Dr. John Marcis, Coastal Carolina University

Dr. Lisa D. McNary, NC State University

Mario Musa, MBA, Francis Marion University

Dr. Vijaya Narapareddy, University of Denver

Dr. Tim O. Redmer, Regent University

Dr. John Ross III, Southwest Texas State University – San Marcos

Sherry Ross, Southwest Texas State University – San Marcos

Brandan Still, Harvard Law School

Dr. Marlene M. Reed, Baylor University

Dr. Amit J. Shah, Frostburg State University

Dr. Carolyn Stokes, Francis Marion University

Dr. A. Gregory Stone, Regent University

Dr. Sharynn M. Tomlin, Angelo State University

Dr. Anne M. Walsh, La Salle University

Brianna Zhang, MBA, Francis Marion University

I especially appreciate the wonderful work completed by the twelfth edition ancillary authors as follows:

Case Instructor's Manual—Forest David, Francis Marion University

Instructor's Manual—Tracy Ryan, Virginia Commonwealth University

Test Item File and PowerPoints—Charles Seifert, Siena Collega

Internet Study Guide—Amit J. Shah, Frostburg State University

Following is a small sampling of schools that have used the eleventh edition of this textbook.

Alabama University – Birmingham	Bob Jones University
Albany State University	California State–Long Beach
American University	Carnegie Mellon University
Arizona State University	Central Michigan University
Auburn University at Montgomery	College of Charleston

Colorado State University–Pueblo

Delaware State University

Eastern Michigan University

Eastern Oregon University

Fordham University–Rose Hill

Hofstra University

Humboldt State University

Indiana State University

Indianan University–Kokomo

Iona College

Jackson State University

Johns Hopkins University

Johnson & Wales University

Kentucky State University

La Salle University

Loyola–Chicago

Loyola College

Marshall University

Maryland College Park University

Millsaps College

Mississippi State University

Murray State University

New Mexico State University

New York University

Niagara University

Nicholls State University

North Carolina Wesleyan College

Norfolk State University

Oakland University

Oral Roberts University

Pennsylvania State University–University Park

Philadelphia University

Rider University

Rochester College

Saint Xavier University

Saint Bonaventure University

Saint Leo University

Saint Louis University

Saint Mary's University

Saint Thomas University

Sam Houston State University

Seton Hall University

Southern Wesleyan University

Stetson University

Tennessee State University–Main Campus

Texas Tech University

Texas Wesleyan University

Trinity University

Troy University–Main Campus

University of Missouri–Kansas City

University of Alabama–Huntsville

University of California–Riverside

University of Colorado–Boulder

University of Hawaii–Manoa Campus

University of Maine at Augusta

University of Memphis

University of Miami

University of Minnesota–Minneapolis

University of Minnesota–Saint Paul

University of Mobile

University of Nebraska–Lincoln

University of Nevada–Las Vegas

University of Nevada–Reno

University of New Mexico

University of New Orleans

University of North Dakota

University of San Francisco

University of Tennessee–Chattanooga

University of Texas–El Paso

University of Texas–Pan American

University of Texas–San Antonio

University of Toledo

University of Wisconsin–Green Bay

Virginia Commonwealth University

Virginia State University

Virginia Union University

Voorhees College

Washington University

Western Kentucky University

Winona State University

Wright State University

West Virginia University at Parkersburg

Scores of Prentice Hall employees and salespersons have worked diligently behind the scenes to make this text a leader in the business policy market. I appreciate the continued hard work of all those persons.

I also want to thank you, the reader, for investing the time and effort to read and study this text. It will help you formulate, implement, and evaluate strategies for any organization with which you become associated. I hope you come to share my enthusiasm for the rich subject area of strategic management and for the systematic learning approach taken in this text.

Finally, I want to welcome and invite your suggestions, ideas, thoughts, comments, and questions regarding any part of this text or the ancillary materials. Please call me at 843–661–1431, fax me at 843–661–1432, e-mail me at strategy29@aol.com, or write me at the School of Business, Francis Marion University, Florence, South Carolina 29501. I sincerely appreciate and need your input to continually improve this text in future editions. Your willingness to draw my attention to specific errors or deficiencies in coverage or exposition will especially be appreciated.

Thank you for using this text.

Fred R. David

About the Author

Dr. Fred R. David is the sole author of three mainstream strategic-management textbooks: (1) *Strategic Management: Concepts and Cases*, (2) *Strategic Management Concepts*, and (3) *Strategic Management Cases*. These texts have been on a two-year revision cycle since 1986, when the first edition was published. They are among the best if not the best-selling strategic-management textbooks in the world and are used at more than 500 colleges and universities. Prestigious universities that have used these textbooks include Harvard University, Duke University, Carnegie-Mellon University, John Hopkins University, the University of Maryland, University of North Carolina, University of Georgia, Florida State University, San Francisco State University, and Wake Forest University.

This strategic-management textbook has been translated and published in Chinese, Japanese, Farsi, Spanish, Indonesian, Indian, Thai, and Arabic, and is widely used across Asia and South America. It is the best-selling strategic-management textbook in Mexico, China, Peru, Chile, Japan, and number two in the United States. Approximately 90,000 students read Dr. David's textbook annually as well as thousands of businesspersons. The book has led the field of strategic management for more than a decade in providing an applications/practitioner approach to the discipline.

A native of Whiteville, North Carolina, Fred R. David received a B.S. degree in Mathematics and an MBA from Wake Forest University before being employed as a bank manager with United Carolina Bank. He received a PhD in Business Administration from the University of South Carolina where he majored in Management. Currently the TranSouth Professor of Strategic Management at Francis Marion University (FMU) in Florence, South Carolina, Dr. David has also taught at Auburn University, Mississippi State University, East Carolina University, the University of South Carolina, and the University of North Carolina at Pembroke. He is the author of 150 referred publications, including 39 journal articles, 53 proceedings publications, and 58 business policy cases. David has articles published in such journals as *Academy of Management Review*, *Academy of Management Executive*, *Journal of Applied Psychology*, *Long Range Planning*, and *Advanced Management Journal*. He serves on the Editorial Review Board of the *Advanced Management Journal*.

Dr. David has received a Lifetime Honorary Professorship Award from the Universidad Ricardo Palma in Lima, Peru. He delivered the keynote speech at the twenty-first Annual Latin American Congress on Strategy hosted by the Centrum School of Business in Peru. Dr. David recently delivered an eight-hour Strategic Planning Workshop to the faculty at Pontificia Universidad Catolica Del in Lima, Peru, and an eight-hour Case Writing/Analyzing Workshop to the faculty at Utah Valley State College in Orem, Utah. He has received numerous awards, including FMU's Board of Trustees Research Scholar Award, and the university's Award for Excellence in Research given annually to the best faculty researcher on campus, and the Phil Carroll Advancement of Management Award, given annually by the Society for the Advancement of Management (SAM) to a management scholar for outstanding contributions in management research. He has given the graduation commencement speech at Troy University for the last two years.

David served for three years on the Southern Management Association's Board of Directors. Through his Web site, www.checkmateplan.com, Dr. David actively assists businesses across the country and around the world in doing strategic planning. He has developed and markets the CheckMATE Strategic Planning Software, which is an industry-leading business planning software package (www.checkmateplan.com).

Case Information Matrix

Manufacturing Firms	Stock Symbol	Headquarters	Web Site Address	# of Employees	2006 Revenues in Millions
Cosmetics					
1. Estée Lauder, Dr Sharynn Tomlin, Angelo State University	EL	New York, NY	www.ELcompanies.com	26,200	6,336.3
2. Revlon, Dr. M. Jill Austin, Middle Tennessee State University	REV	New York, NY	www.revlon.com	6,800	83.7
Food					
3. Krispy Kreme Doughnuts, Forest David and Mario Musa, Francis Marion University	KKD	Winston-Salem, NC	www.krispykreme.com	5,733	543.4
4. Pilgrim's Pride, Dr. Jim Hardin, Texas A&M University at Texarkana	PPC	Pittsburg, TX	www.pilgrimspride.com	40,550	5,666.3
Beverages					
5. Coca-Cola Company, Dr. Alen Badal, The Union Institute	KO	Atlanta, GA	www.coca-cola.com	55,000	24,088.0
6. Anheuser-Busch Companies, Inc., Dr Alen Badal, The Union Institute	BUD	St. Louis, MO	www.anheuser-busch.com	31,485	15,035.7
Computers					
7. Hewlett-Packard, Dr. Mernoush Banton, Florida International University	HPQ	Palo Alto, CA	www.hp.com	150, 000	91,658.0
8. IBM Corporation, Dr. Vijaya Narapareddy, University of Denver	IBM	Armonk, NY	www.ibm.com	366,345	22,618.0
Automotive					
9. Ford Motor Company, Dr. Alen Badal, The Union Institute	F	Dearborn, MI	www.ford.com	300,000	37,110.0
10. Winnebago Industries, Dr. Gene Bland, Texas A&M–Corpus Christi and Dr. John Marcis, Coastal Carolina University	WGO	Forest City, IA	www.winnebagoind.com	3,610	864.4
11. Skoda Auto (a division of Volkswagen), Dr. Marlene Reed, Baylor University and Dr. Rochelle R. Brunson, Alvin College	na	Mladá Boleslav, Czech Republic	www.skoda-auto.com/global	26,738	189,816
Small Business					
12. Southwest Printing Company, Dr. Joe Aniello and Brianna Zhang, Francis Marion University	na	Florence, SC	www.swprinting.com	8	0.762
13. Waterford Wedgwood PLC, Brandan Still at Harvard Law School, Dr. Lisa McNary, NC State University, Clare Burns at Lamar University in Texas	WATFF (London)	Dublin, Ireland	www.waterfordwedgwood.com	9,606	772.6 E
14. Toll Brothers, Dr. Randy Harris, California State University, Stanislaus	TOL	Horsham, PA	www.tollbrothers.com	5,581	6,123.5
15. Cellox, Dr. Greg Stone and Dr. Tim Redmer, Regent University	na	Reedsburg, WI	www.celblox.com/www.cellox.com	20	3.4

(continued)

Case Information Matrix (continued)

Manufacturing Firms	Stock Symbol	Headquarters	Web Site Address	# of Employees	2006 Revenues in Millions
E-Commerce					
16. E-Trade Financial, Dr. Amit Shah, Frostburg State University	ETFC	New York, NY	www.etrade.com	4,126	2,770
17. Amazon.com, Dr. M. Jill Austin, Middle Tennessee State University	AMZN	Seattle, WA	www.amazon.com	12,000	10,711.0
Retailing					
18. Zale Corporation, Dr. Sharynn Tomlin, Angelo University	ZLC	Irving, TX	www.zalecorp.com	16,300	2,439.0
19. The Gap, Inc., Dr. Sharynn Tomlin, Angelo University	GPS	San Francisco, CA	www.gap.com	153,000	16,023.0
Restaurants					
20. Wendy's International, Dr. Vijaya Narapareddy, University of Denver	WEN	Dublin, OH	www.wendys.com	57,000	3,783.1
21. McDonald's Corporation, Dr. Vijaya Narapareddy, University of Denver	MCD	Oak Brook, IL	www.mcdonalds.com	447,000	21,586.4
22. Compass Group PLC, Dr. Les Hudson, Jr. and William Garcia, Queens University of Charlotte	CPG	Chertsey, United Kingdom	www.compass-group.com	410,074	22,390.8
Travel – Air and Sea					
23. Continental Airlines, Dr. Charles Byles, Virginia Commonwealth University	CAL	Houston, TX	www.continental.com	42,200	13,128.0
24. Southwest Airlines, Dr. Amit Shah, Frostburg State University	LUV	Dallas, TX	www.southwest.com	31,729	9,086.0
25. Carnival Cruise Lines, Dr. Mernoush Banton, Florida International University	CCL	Miami, FL	www.carnivalcorp.com	71,200	11,839.0
Hospitality					
26. MGM Mirage, Dr. John Ross III and Sherry Ross, Southwest Texas State University – San Marcos	MGM	Las Vegas, NV	www.mgmmirage.com	45,000	6,482.0
27. Marriott International, Dr. Vijaya Narapareddy, University of Denver	MAR	Bethesda, MD	www.marriott.com	143,000	12,160.0
28. Starwood Hotels, Dr. Anne Walsh, La Salle University	HOT	White Plains, NY	www.starwoodhotels.com	145,000	5,979
29. Miami University Dr. Joe Leonard, Miami of Ohio Univ.	na	Oxford, Ohio	www.miami.muohio.com	355	626.6
Not-for-Profit					
30. Wesley United Methodist Church, William James, Francis Marion University	na	Hartsville, SC	www.wesleyhartsville.com	12	0.315
31. Riverbanks Zoo, Dr. Carolyn Stokes, Francis Marion University and Dr. Eugene Bland, Texas A&M University – Corpus Christi	na	Columbia, SC	www.riverbanks.org	160	6.36

Case Description Matrix

Topical Content Areas (Y = Yes and N = No)

	1	2	3	4	5	6	7	8	9	10	11	12	13	14
Cohesion Case – Walt Disney	Y	Y	Y	Y	Y	Y	Y	Y	Y	N	N	Y	Y	N

Cohesion Case - Walt Disney Company

Manufacturing Firms

Cosmetics

	1	2	3	4	5	6	7	8	9	10	11	12	13	14
1. Estée Lauder Companies	Y	Y	Y	Y	Y	Y	Y	Y	Y	N	N	Y	Y	N
2. Revlon	Y	Y	Y	Y	Y	Y	Y	Y	Y	Y	Y	Y	Y	N

Food

3. Krispy Kreme Doughnuts	Y	N	Y	Y	Y	Y	Y	Y	Y	Y	N	Y	Y	N
4. Pilgrim's Pride	Y	Y	Y	Y	Y	Y	Y	Y	Y	Y	Y	Y	Y	N

Beverages

5. Coca-Cola Company	Y	Y	Y	N	Y	Y	Y	Y	Y	N	N	Y	Y	N
6. Anheuser-Busch Companies, Inc.	Y	Y	Y	N	Y	Y	Y	Y	Y	N	N	Y	Y	N

Computers

7. Hewlett-Packard	Y	Y	Y	N	Y	Y	Y	Y	Y	N	N	Y	Y	N
8. IBM Corporation	Y	Y	Y	N	Y	Y	Y	Y	Y	N	N	Y	Y	N

Automotive

9. Ford Motor Company	Y	Y	Y	N	Y	Y	Y	Y	Y	Y	Y	Y	Y	N
10. Winnebago Industries	Y	Y	Y	Y	Y	Y	Y	Y	Y	N	Y	Y	Y	N
11. Skoda Auto	Y	Y	Y	Y	Y	Y	Y	Y	N	N	Y	Y	Y	Y

Small Business

12. S/W Printing Company	Y	Y	N	Y	Y	Y	Y	Y	Y	N	N	Y	Y	N
13. Waterford Wedgwood PLC	Y	Y	Y	Y	Y	Y	Y	Y	Y	Y	N	Y	Y	Y
14. Toll Brothers	Y	N	Y	Y	Y	Y	Y	Y	Y	Y	Y	Y	Y	N
15. Cellox	Y	Y	N	Y	Y	Y	Y	Y	Y	N	Y	Y	Y	N

Service Firms

E-Commerce

16. E*Trade Financial	Y	Y	Y	Y	Y	Y	Y	Y	Y	N	N	Y	Y	N
17. Amazon.com	Y	Y	Y	Y	Y	Y	Y	Y	Y	N	Y	Y	Y	N

Retailing

18. Zale Corporation	Y	Y	Y	N	Y	Y	Y	Y	Y	Y	N	Y	Y	N
19. Gap, Inc.	Y	Y	Y	Y	Y	Y	Y	Y	Y	Y	Y	Y	Y	N

Food Service

20. Wendy's International	Y	Y	Y	N	Y	Y	Y	Y	Y	Y	Y	Y	Y	N
21. McDonald's Corporation	Y	Y	Y	N	Y	Y	Y	Y	Y	N	N	Y	Y	N
22. Compass Group PLC	Y	Y	Y	Y	Y	Y	Y	Y	Y	Y	Y	Y	Y	Y

Travel – Air or Sea

23. Continental Airlines	Y	N	Y	N	Y	Y	Y	Y	Y	N	N	Y	Y	N
24. Southwest Airlines	Y	Y	Y	Y	Y	Y	Y	Y	Y	N	N	Y	Y	N
25. Carnival Corporation	Y	Y	Y	Y	Y	Y	Y	Y	Y	N	N	Y	Y	Y

Hotel/Motel

26. MGM Mirage	Y	Y	Y	Y	Y	Y	Y	Y	Y	N	N	Y	Y	N

(continued)

Case Description Matrix (continued)

	1	2	3	4	5	6	7	8	9	10	11	12	13	14
27. Marriott International	Y	N	Y	N	Y	Y	Y	Y	Y	N	Y	Y	Y	N
28. Starwood Hotels	Y	Y	Y	Y	Y	Y	Y	Y	Y	N	N	Y	Y	N
Nonprofit Organizations														
29. Miami of Ohio University	Y	N	Y	Y	Y	N	Y	Y	N	N	N	Y	Y	N
30. Wesley United Methodist Church	Y	Y	Y	Y	Y	N	Y	Y	Y	Y	Y	Y	Y	N
31. Riverbanks Zoo	Y	Y	Y	Y	Y	Y	Y	Y	Y	N	Y	Y	Y	N

1. Year-end 2006 Financial Statements Included?

2. Is Organizational Chart Included?

3. Does Company Do Business Outside the United States?

4. Is a Vision or Mission Statement Included?

5. E-Commerce Issues Included?

6. Natural Environment Issues Included?

7. Strategy Formulation Emphasis?

8. Strategy Implementation Included?

9. By-segment Financial Data Included?

10. Firm has Declining Revenues?

11. Firm has Declining Net Income?

12. Discussion of Competitors is Provided?

13. Case Appears in Text for the First Time Ever?

14. Is Firm Headquartered Outside the United States?

Strategic Management

• CONCEPTS

Part 1 • Overview of Strategic Management

1 The Nature of Strategic Management

"notable quotes"

If we know where we are and something about how we got there, we might see where we are trending—and if the outcomes which lie naturally in our course are unacceptable, to make timely change.

ABRAHAM LINCOLN

Without a strategy, an organization is like a ship without a rudder, going around in circles. It's like a tramp; it has no place to go.

JOEL ROSS AND MICHAEL KAMI

Plans are less important than planning.

DALE McCONKEY

The formulation of strategy can develop competitive advantage only to the extent that the process can give meaning to workers in the trenches.

DAVID HURST

Most of us fear change. Even when our minds say change is normal, our stomachs quiver at the prospect. But for strategists and managers today, there is no choice but to change.

ROBERT WATERMAN, JR.

If business is not based on ethical grounds, it is of no benefit to society and will, like all other unethical combinations, pass into oblivion.

C. MAX KILLAN

If a man takes no thought about what is distant, he will find sorrow near at hand. He who will not worry about what is far off will soon find something worse than worry.

CONFUCIUS

Graduation Day. *Source:* Bryan David.

chapter objectives

After studying this chapter, you should be able to do the following:

1. Describe the strategic-management process.

2. Explain the need for integrating analysis and intuition in strategic management.

3. Define and give examples of key terms in strategic management.

4. Discuss the nature of strategy formulation, implementation, and evaluation activities.

5. Describe the benefits of good strategic management.

6. Explain why good ethics is good business in strategic management.

7. Explain the advantages and disadvantages of entering global markets.

8. Discuss the relevance of Sun Tzu's *The Art of War* to strategic management.

9. Discuss how a firm may achieve sustained competitive advantage.

10. Explain ISO 14000 and 14001.

This chapter provides an overview of strategic management. It introduces a practical, integrative model of the strategic-management process; it defines basic activities and terms in strategic management; and it discusses the importance of business ethics.

This chapter initiates two themes that permeate all the chapters of this text. First, *global considerations impact virtually all strategic decisions*! The boundaries of countries no longer can define the limits of our imaginations. To see and appreciate the world from the perspective of others has become a matter of survival for businesses. The underpinnings of strategic management hinge upon managers' gaining an understanding of competitors, markets, prices, suppliers, distributors, governments, creditors, shareholders, and customers worldwide. The price and quality of a firm's products and services must be competitive on a worldwide basis, not just on a local basis. A "Global Perspective" box is provided in each chapter of this text to emphasize the importance of global factors in strategic management.

A second theme is that *the natural environment has become an important strategic issue.* Global warming, bioterrorism, and increased pollution suggest that perhaps there is now no greater threat to business and society than the continuous exploitation and decimation of our natural environment. Mark Starik at George Washington University says, "Halting and reversing worldwide ecological destruction and deterioration . . . is a strategic issue that needs immediate and substantive attention by all businesses and managers." According to the International Standards Organization (ISO), and in this textbook, the word *environment* refers to the natural environment and is defined as "surroundings in which an organization operates, including air, water, land, natural resources, flora, fauna, humans, and their interrelation." A "Natural Environment Perspective" box is provided in each chapter to illustrate how firms are addressing natural environment concerns.

What Is Strategic Management?

Once there were two company presidents who competed in the same industry. These two presidents decided to go on a camping trip to discuss a possible merger. They hiked deep into the woods. Suddenly, they came upon a grizzly bear that rose up on its hind legs and snarled. Instantly, the first president took off his knapsack and got out a pair of jogging shoes. The second president said, "Hey, you can't outrun that bear." The first president responded, "Maybe I can't outrun that bear, but I surely can outrun you!" This story captures the notion of strategic management, which is to achieve and maintain competitive advantage.

Defining Strategic Management

Strategic management can be defined as the art and science of formulating, implementing, and evaluating cross-functional decisions that enable an organization to achieve its objectives. As this definition implies, strategic management focuses on integrating management, marketing, finance/accounting, production/operations, research and development, and computer information systems to achieve organizational success. The term *strategic management* in this text is used synonymously with the term *strategic planning.* The latter term is more often used in the business world, whereas the former is often used in academia. Sometimes the term *strategic management* is used to refer to strategy formulation, implementation, and evaluation, with *strategic planning* referring only to strategy formulation. The purpose of strategic management is to exploit and create new and different opportunities for tomorrow; *long-range planning,* in contrast, tries to optimize for tomorrow the trends of today.

The term *strategic planning* originated in the 1950s and was very popular between the mid-1960s and the mid-1970s. During these years, strategic planning was widely believed to be the answer for all problems. At the time, much of the business world was "obsessed" with strategic planning. Following that "boom," however, strategic planning was cast aside during the 1980s as various planning models did not yield higher returns. The 1990s, however, brought the revival of strategic planning, and the process is widely practiced today in the business world.

A strategic plan is, in essence, a company's game plan. Just as a football team needs a good game plan to have a chance for success, a company must have a good strategic plan to compete successfully. Profit margins among firms in most industries have been so reduced that there is little room for error in the overall strategic plan. A strategic plan results from tough managerial choices among numerous good alternatives, and it signals commitment to specific markets, policies, procedures, and operations in lieu of other, "less desirable" courses of action.

The term *strategic management* is used at many colleges and universities as the subtitle for the capstone course in business administration—Business Policy—which integrates material from all business courses. The Strategic Management Club Online at www.strategyclub.com offers many benefits for business policy and strategic management students.

Stages of Strategic Management

The *strategic-management process* consists of three stages: strategy formulation, strategy implementation, and strategy evaluation. *Strategy formulation* includes developing a vision and mission, identifying an organization's external opportunities and threats, determining internal strengths and weaknesses, establishing long-term objectives, generating alternative strategies, and choosing particular strategies to pursue. Strategy-formulation issues include deciding what new businesses to enter, what businesses to abandon, how to allocate resources, whether to expand operations or diversify, whether to enter international markets, whether to merge or form a joint venture, and how to avoid a hostile takeover.

Because no organization has unlimited resources, strategists must decide which alternative strategies will benefit the firm most. Strategy-formulation decisions commit an organization to specific products, markets, resources, and technologies over an extended period of time. Strategies determine long-term competitive advantages. For better or worse, strategic decisions have major multifunctional consequences and enduring effects on an organization. Top managers have the best perspective to understand fully the ramifications of strategy-formulation decisions; they have the authority to commit the resources necessary for implementation.

Strategy implementation requires a firm to establish annual objectives, devise policies, motivate employees, and allocate resources so that formulated strategies can be executed. Strategy implementation includes developing a strategy-supportive culture, creating an effective organizational structure, redirecting marketing efforts, preparing budgets, developing and utilizing information systems, and linking employee compensation to organizational performance.

Strategy implementation often is called the "action stage" of strategic management. Implementing strategy means mobilizing employees and managers to put formulated strategies into action. Often considered to be the most difficult stage in strategic management, strategy implementation requires personal discipline, commitment, and sacrifice. Successful strategy implementation hinges upon managers' ability to motivate employees, which is more an art than a science. Strategies formulated but not implemented serve no useful purpose.

Interpersonal skills are especially critical for successful strategy implementation. Strategy-implementation activities affect all employees and managers in an organization. Every division and department must decide on answers to questions, such as "What must we do to implement our part of the organization's strategy?" and "How best can we get the job done?" The challenge of implementation is to stimulate managers and employees throughout an organization to work with pride and enthusiasm toward achieving stated objectives.

Strategy evaluation is the final stage in strategic management. Managers desperately need to know when particular strategies are not working well; strategy evaluation is the primary means for obtaining this information. All strategies are subject to future modification because external and internal factors are constantly changing. Three fundamental strategy-evaluation activities are (1) reviewing external and internal factors that are the bases for current strategies, (2) measuring performance, and (3) taking corrective actions.

VISIT THE NET

Provides nice narrative regarding strategy formulation and implementation at Southern Polytechnic State University. (www.spsu.edu/planassess/ strategic.htm)

Strategy evaluation is needed because success today is no guarantee of success tomorrow! Success always creates new and different problems; complacent organizations experience demise.

Strategy formulation, implementation, and evaluation activities occur at three hierarchical levels in a large organization: corporate, divisional or strategic business unit, and functional. By fostering communication and interaction among managers and employees across hierarchical levels, strategic management helps a firm function as a competitive team. Most small businesses and some large businesses do not have divisions or strategic business units; they have only the corporate and functional levels. Nevertheless, managers and employees at these two levels should be actively involved in strategic-management activities.

Business expert and icon Peter Drucker says the prime task of strategic management is thinking through the overall mission of a business:

> . . . that is, of asking the question, "What is our Business?" This leads to the setting of objectives, the development of strategies, and the making of today's decisions for tomorrow's results. This clearly must be done by a part of the organization that can see the entire business; that can balance objectives and the needs of today against the needs of tomorrow; and that can allocate resources of men and money to key results.[1]

Integrating Intuition and Analysis

The strategic-management process can be described as an objective, logical, systematic approach for making major decisions in an organization. It attempts to organize qualitative and quantitative information in a way that allows effective decisions to be made under conditions of uncertainty. Yet strategic management is not a pure science that lends itself to a nice, neat, one-two-three approach.

Based on past experiences, judgment, and feelings, most people recognize that *intuition* is essential to making good strategic decisions. Intuition is particularly useful for making decisions in situations of great uncertainty or little precedent. It is also helpful when highly interrelated variables exist or when it is necessary to choose from several plausible alternatives. Some managers and owners of businesses profess to have extraordinary abilities for using intuition alone in devising brilliant strategies. For example, Will Durant, who organized General Motors Corporation, was described as "a man who would proceed on a course of action guided solely, as far as I could tell, by some intuitive flash of brilliance. He never felt obliged to make an engineering hunt for the facts. Yet at times, he was astoundingly correct in his judgment."[2] Albert Einstein acknowledged the importance of intuition when he said, "I believe in intuition and inspiration. At times I feel certain that I am right while not knowing the reason. Imagination is more important than knowledge, because knowledge is limited, whereas imagination embraces the entire world."[3]

Although some organizations today may survive and prosper because they have intuitive geniuses managing them, most are not so fortunate. Most organizations can benefit from strategic management, which is based upon integrating intuition and analysis in decision making. Choosing an intuitive or analytic approach to decision making is not an either–or proposition. Managers at all levels in an organization inject their intuition and judgment into strategic-management analyses. Analytical thinking and intuitive thinking complement each other.

Operating from the I've-already-made-up-my-mind-don't-bother-me-with-the-facts mode is not management by intuition; it is management by ignorance.[4] Drucker says, "I believe in intuition only if you discipline it. 'Hunch' artists, who make a diagnosis but don't check it out with the facts, are the ones in medicine who kill people, and in management kill businesses."[5] As business consultant Bruce Henderson notes:

VISIT THE NET

Reveals that strategies may need to be constantly changed. (www. csuchico.edu/mgmt/strategy/ module1/sld041.htm)

> The accelerating rate of change today is producing a business world in which customary managerial habits in organizations are increasingly inadequate. Experience alone was an adequate guide when changes could be made in small increments. But intuitive and experience-based management philosophies are grossly inadequate when decisions are strategic and have major, irreversible consequences.[6]

In a sense, the strategic-management process is an attempt both to duplicate what goes on in the mind of a brilliant, intuitive person who knows the business and to couple it with analysis.

Adapting to Change

The strategic-management process is based on the belief that organizations should continually monitor internal and external events and trends so that timely changes can be made as needed. The rate and magnitude of changes that affect organizations are increasing dramatically. Consider, for example, e-commerce, laser surgery, the war on terrorism, the aging population, the Enron scandal, and merger mania. To survive, all organizations must be capable of astutely identifying and adapting to change. The strategic-management process is aimed at allowing organizations to adapt effectively to change over the long run. As Waterman has noted:

> In today's business environment, more than in any preceding era, the only constant is change. Successful organizations effectively manage change, continuously adapting their bureaucracies, strategies, systems, products, and cultures to survive the shocks and prosper from the forces that decimate the competition.[7]

E-commerce and globalization are external changes that are transforming business and society today. On a political map, the boundaries between countries may be clear, but on a competitive map showing the real flow of financial and industrial activity, the boundaries have largely disappeared. The speedy flow of information has eaten away at national boundaries so that people worldwide readily see for themselves how other people live. People are traveling abroad more: 10 million Japanese annually travel abroad. People are emigrating more: Germans to England and Mexicans to the United States are examples. We have become a borderless world with global citizens, global competitors, global customers, global suppliers, and global distributors!

As the Global Perspective indicates, U.S. firms are challenged by large rival companies in many industries. General Motors' sales decreased 16.6 percent in early 2007 while Ford Motor's sales decreased 19 percent during the same time that Toyota Motor's sales rose 9.5 percent and Honda Motor's sales rose 2.4 percent. To say U.S. firms are being challenged in the automobile industry is an understatement. But this situation is true in many industries. Citigroup cut nearly 17,000 jobs in 2007 in a major restructuring, striving to compete. Westinghouse Electric is one of many landmark American firms that have recently been acquired by companies located outside the United States. Now owned by Japan's Toshiba, Westinghouse in 2007 won a $5.3 billion contract to build four nuclear power plants in China. This was the largest nuclear reactor contract ever for any firm. Based in Nagoya, Japan, that country's largest car maker, Toyota, surpassed General Motors in 2007 as the world's top producer of cars. GM is in the midst of a painful restructuring and has recently incurred billion-dollar annual losses.

The need to adapt to change leads organizations to key strategic-management questions, such as "What kind of business should we become?" "Are we in the right field(s)?" "Should we reshape our business?" "What new competitors are entering our industry?" "What strategies should we pursue?" "How are our customers changing?" "Are new technologies being developed that could put us out of business?"

Key Terms in Strategic Management

Before we further discuss strategic management, we should define nine key terms: competitive advantage, strategists, vision and mission statements, external opportunities and threats, internal strengths and weaknesses, long-term objectives, strategies, annual objectives, and policies.

Competitive Advantage

Strategic management is all about gaining and maintaining *competitive advantage*. This term can be defined as "anything that a firm does especially well compared to rival firms."

VISIT THE NET

Reveals that actual strategy results from planned strategy coupled with reactive changes. (www.csuchico.edu/mgmt/strategy/module1/sld032.htm)

GLOBAL PERSPECTIVE
The Largest Companies in the World

*F*orbes magazine's annual ranking of the world's largest companies reveals that U.S. firms are being challenged in many industries. The world's largest thirty companies are listed here. Note that only twelve U.S. companies are in the top 30 in sales worldwide.

Rank	Company	2006 Sales ($mil.)	Country
1	Wal-Mart Stores	348,650	USA
2	ExxonMobil	335,086	USA
3	Royal Dutch Shell	318,845	Netherlands
4	BP	265,906	United Kingdom
5	General Motors	207,349	USA
6	DaimlerChrysler	199,985	Germany
7	Chevron	195,341	USA
8	Toyota Motor	179,024	Japan
9	Total	175,051	France
10	ConocoPhillips	167,578	USA
11	General Electric	163,391	USA
12	Ford Motor	160,123	USA
13	ING Group	153,439	Netherlands
14	Citigroup	146,558	USA
15	Allianz	125,329	Germany
16	HSBC Holdings	121,508	United Kingdom
17	Fortis	121,186	Netherlands
18	Bank of America	116,574	USA
19	ENI	113,595	Italy
20	American Intl Group	113,194	USA
21	Volkswagen Group	112,610	Germany
22	Siemens Group	110,819	Germany
23	UBS	105,587	Switzerland
24	JP Morgan Chase	99,302	USA
25	Sinopec-China Petrol	99,026	China
26	AXA Group	98,845	France
27	Berkshire Hathaway	98,539	USA
28	Carrefour	97,726	France
29	Dexia	95,785	Belgium
30	Deutsche Bank	95,496	Germany

Source: Adapted from Scott DeCarlo, "2000 World Leaders: The World's Biggest Public Companies," *Forbes* (April 16, 2007): 143.

When a firm can do something that rival firms cannot do, or owns something that rival firms desire, that can represent a competitive advantage. Getting and keeping competitive advantage is essential for long-term success in an organization. The Industrial/Organizational (I/O) and the Resource-Based View (RBV) theories of organization (as discussed in Chapters 3 and 4, respectively) present different perspectives on how best to capture and keep competitive advantage—that is, how best to manage strategically. Pursuit of competitive advantage leads to organizational success or failure. Strategic management researchers and practitioners alike desire to better understand the nature and role of competitive advantage in various industries.

Normally, a firm can sustain a competitive advantage for only a certain period due to rival firms imitating and undermining that advantage. Thus it is not adequate to simply obtain competitive advantage. A firm must strive to achieve *sustained competitive advantage* by (1) continually adapting to changes in external trends and events and internal capabilities, competencies, and resources; and by (2) effectively formulating, implementing, and evaluating strategies that capitalize upon those factors. For example, newspaper circulation in the United States is steadily declining. Most national newspapers are rapidly losing market share to the Internet, cable, radio, television, magazines, and other media that consumers use to stay informed. Daily newspaper circulation in the United States totals about 55 million copies annually, which is about the same as it was in 1954. Strategists ponder whether the newspaper circulation slide can be halted in the digital age. The six U.S. broadcast networks—ABC, CBS, Fox, NBC, UPN, and WB—are being assaulted by cable channels, video games, broadband, wireless technologies, satellite radio, high-definition TV, and TiVo. The three original broadcast networks captured about 90 percent of the prime-time audience in 1978, but today their combined market share is less than 50 percent.[8]

An increasing number of companies are gaining a competitive advantage by using the Internet for direct selling and for communication with suppliers, customers, creditors, partners, shareholders, clients, and competitors who may be dispersed globally. E-commerce allows firms to sell products, advertise, purchase supplies, bypass intermediaries, track inventory, eliminate paperwork, and share information. In total, e-commerce is minimizing the expense and cumbersomeness of time, distance, and space in doing business, thus yielding better customer service, greater efficiency, improved products, and higher profitability.

The Internet and personal computers are changing the way we organize our lives; inhabit our homes; and relate to and interact with family, friends, neighbors, and even ourselves. The Internet promotes endless comparison shopping, which thus enables consumers worldwide to band together to demand discounts. The Internet has transferred power from businesses to individuals. Buyers used to face big obstacles when attempting to get the best price and service, such as limited time and data to compare, but now consumers can quickly scan hundreds of vendor offerings.[9] Both the number of people shopping online and the average amount they spend is increasing dramatically. Online shopping is expected to increase from 7 percent of all shopping today to an eventual peak of 15 percent in ten years, because shoppers still enjoy touching and viewing merchandise. Apparel is expected to become the largest product category of online sales by 2009. Most traditional retailers have learned that their online sales can boost in-store sales as they utilize their Web sites to promote in-store promotions.

Consumers spent more money online for clothes than computers in 2006 for the first time ever. U.S. apparel sales should hit $22.1 billion in 2007 with computer hardware/software at $20.1 billion, followed by autos and auto parts ($19.6 billion), and home furnishings ($12.3 billion).[10] Ten percent of all clothing sales in 2007 were purchased online, a dramatic shift in how people shop. The top three online apparel retailers are Victoria's Secret, L.L. Bean, and Gap.

The Internet has changed the very nature and core of buying and selling in nearly all industries. It has fundamentally changed the economics of business in every single industry worldwide. Broadband, e-trade, e-commerce, e-business, and e-mail have become an integral part of everyday life worldwide. Business-to-business e-commerce is five times greater than consumer e-commerce.

Strategists

Strategists are the individuals who are most responsible for the success or failure of an organization. Strategists have various job titles, such as chief executive officer, president, owner, chair of the board, executive director, chancellor, dean, or entrepreneur. Jay Conger, professor of organizational behavior at the London Business School and author of *Building Leaders,* says, "All strategists have to be chief learning officers. We are in an extended period of change. If our leaders aren't highly adaptive and great models during this period, then our companies won't adapt either, because ultimately leadership is about being a role model."

Strategists help an organization gather, analyze, and organize information. They track industry and competitive trends, develop forecasting models and scenario analyses, evaluate corporate and divisional performance, spot emerging market opportunities, identify business threats, and develop creative action plans. Strategic planners usually serve in a support or staff role. Usually found in higher levels of management, they typically have considerable authority for decision making in the firm. The CEO is the most visible and critical strategic manager. Any manager who has responsibility for a unit or division, responsibility for profit and loss outcomes, or direct authority over a major piece of the business is a strategic manager (strategist). In the last five years, the position of chief strategy officer (CSO) has emerged as a new addition to the top management ranks of many organizations, including Sun Microsystems, Network Associates, Clarus, Lante, Marimba, Sapient, Commerce One, BBDO, Cadbury Schweppes, General Motors, Ellie Mae, Cendant, Charles Schwab, Tyco, Campbell Soup, Morgan Stanley, and Reed-Elsevier. This new corporate officer title represents recognition of the growing importance of strategic planning in the business world.[11]

Strategists differ as much as organizations themselves, and these differences must be considered in the formulation, implementation, and evaluation of strategies. Some strategists will not consider some types of strategies because of their personal philosophies.

Strategists differ in their attitudes, values, ethics, willingness to take risks, concern for social responsibility, concern for profitability, concern for short-run versus long-run aims, and management style. The founder of Hershey Foods, Milton Hershey, built the company to manage an orphanage. From corporate profits, Hershey Foods today cares for over one thousand boys and girls in its School for Orphans.

Vision and Mission Statements

Many organizations today develop a *vision statement* that answers the question "What do we want to become?" Developing a vision statement is often considered the first step in strategic planning, preceding even development of a mission statement. Many vision statements are a single sentence. For example, the vision statement of Stokes Eye Clinic in the southeastern United States, is "Our vision is to take care of your vision." The vision of the Institute of Management Accountants is "Global leadership in education, certification, and practice of management accounting and financial management."

Mission statements are "enduring statements of purpose that distinguish one business from other similar firms. A mission statement identifies the scope of a firm's operations in product and market terms."[12] It addresses the basic question that faces all strategists: "What is our business?" A clear mission statement describes the values and priorities of an organization. Developing a mission statement compels strategists to think about the nature and scope of present operations and to assess the potential attractiveness of future markets and activities. A mission statement broadly charts the future direction of an organization. An example of a mission statement is Microsoft's:

> Microsoft's mission is to create software for the personal computer that empowers and enriches people in the workplace, at school and at home. Microsoft's early vision of a computer on every desk and in every home is coupled today with a strong commitment to Internet-related technologies that expand the power and reach of the PC and its users. As the world's leading software provider, Microsoft strives to produce innovative products that meet our customers' evolving needs. At the same time, we understand that long-term success is about more than just making great products. Find out what we mean when we talk about Living Our Values (www.microsoft.com/mscorp).

External Opportunities and Threats

External opportunities and *external threats* refer to economic, social, cultural, demographic, environmental, political, legal, governmental, technological, and competitive trends and events that could significantly benefit or harm an organization in the future. Opportunities and threats are largely beyond the control of a single organization—thus the word *external*. The wireless revolution, biotechnology, population shifts, high gas prices, changing work values and attitudes, illegal immigration issues, and increased competition from foreign companies are examples of opportunities or threats for companies. These types of changes are creating a different type of consumer and consequently a need for different types of products, services, and strategies. Many companies in many industries face the severe external threat of online sales capturing increasing market share in their industry.

Other opportunities and threats may include the passage of a law, the introduction of a new product by a competitor, a national catastrophe, or the declining value of the dollar. A competitor's strength could be a threat. Unrest in the Middle East, rising energy costs, or the war against terrorism could represent an opportunity or a threat.

A basic tenet of strategic management is that firms need to formulate strategies to take advantage of external opportunities and to avoid or reduce the impact of external threats. For this reason, identifying, monitoring, and evaluating external opportunities and threats are essential for success. This process of conducting research and gathering and assimilating external information is sometimes called *environmental scanning* or industry analysis. Lobbying is one activity that some organizations utilize to influence external opportunities and threats.

Internal Strengths and Weaknesses

Internal strengths and *internal weaknesses* are an organization's controllable activities that are performed especially well or poorly. They arise in the management, marketing, finance/accounting, production/operations, research and development, and management information systems activities of a business. Identifying and evaluating organizational strengths and weaknesses in the functional areas of a business is an essential strategic-management activity. Organizations strive to pursue strategies that capitalize on internal strengths and eliminate internal weaknesses.

Strengths and weaknesses are determined relative to competitors. *Relative* deficiency or superiority is important information. Also, strengths and weaknesses can be determined by elements of being rather than performance. For example, a strength may involve ownership of natural resources or a historic reputation for quality. Strengths and weaknesses may be determined relative to a firm's own objectives. For example, high levels of inventory turnover may not be a strength to a firm that seeks never to stock-out.

Internal factors can be determined in a number of ways, including computing ratios, measuring performance, and comparing to past periods and industry averages. Various types of surveys also can be developed and administered to examine internal factors such as employee morale, production efficiency, advertising effectiveness, and customer loyalty.

Long-Term Objectives

Objectives can be defined as specific results that an organization seeks to achieve in pursuing its basic mission. *Long-term* means more than one year. Objectives are essential for organizational success because they state direction; aid in evaluation; create synergy; reveal priorities; focus coordination; and provide a basis for effective planning, organizing, motivating, and controlling activities. Objectives should be challenging, measurable, consistent, reasonable, and clear. In a multidimensional firm, objectives should be established for the overall company and for each division.

Strategies

Strategies are the means by which long-term objectives will be achieved. Business strategies may include geographic expansion, diversification, acquisition, product development, market penetration, retrenchment, divestiture, liquidation, and joint ventures. Strategies currently being pursued by some companies are described in Table 1-1.

Strategies are potential actions that require top management decisions and large amounts of the firm's resources. In addition, strategies affect an organization's long-term

TABLE 1-1   Example Strategies in Action in 2007

McDonald's Corp.

The world's largest restaurant chain by number of outlets, Big Mac is doing fantastic both in the United States and abroad. In recent months, McDonald's began opening drive-through restaurants in China, closed twenty-five sites in the United Kingdom, and disposed of a supply-chain operation in Russia. Big Mac in 2007 is opening 800 new restaurants in China, Japan, and Russia. Shares of McDonald's stock increased 42 percent in 2006 as sales for the year eclipsed $41 billion. Big Mac is working to eliminate trans fats from its food (New York City is requiring this of all restaurants in 2007). McDonald's plans in 2008 to turn ownership of about 2,300 restaurants in Canada and the United Kingdom over to licensees.

American General

A Fortune 500 company based in Piscataway, New Jersey, American General split into three businesses in 2007: air-conditioning systems, bath-and-kitchen business, and vehicle-control systems. The firm also is renaming itself Trane, after its flagship air-conditioning brand name. The company plans to divest the bath-and-kitchen division and to spin off its vehicle-control division into a publicly traded company named Wabco. Led by CEO Fred Poses, American General employs about 62,000 persons and has manufacturing operations in twenty-eight countries.

prosperity, typically for at least five years, and thus are future-oriented. Strategies have multifunctional or multidivisional consequences and require consideration of both the external and internal factors facing the firm.

Annual Objectives

Annual objectives are short-term milestones that organizations must achieve to reach long-term objectives. Like long-term objectives, annual objectives should be measurable, quantitative, challenging, realistic, consistent, and prioritized. They should be established at the corporate, divisional, and functional levels in a large organization. Annual objectives should be stated in terms of management, marketing, finance/accounting, production/operations, research and development, and management information systems (MIS) accomplishments. A set of annual objectives is needed for each long-term objective. Annual objectives are especially important in strategy implementation, whereas long-term objectives are particularly important in strategy formulation. Annual objectives represent the basis for allocating resources.

Policies

Policies are the means by which annual objectives will be achieved. Policies include guidelines, rules, and procedures established to support efforts to achieve stated objectives. Policies are guides to decision making and address repetitive or recurring situations.

Policies are most often stated in terms of management, marketing, finance/accounting, production/operations, research and development, and computer information systems activities. Policies can be established at the corporate level and apply to an entire organization at the divisional level and apply to a single division, or at the functional level and apply to particular operational activities or departments. Policies, like annual objectives, are especially important in strategy implementation because they outline an organization's expectations of its employees and managers. Policies allow consistency and coordination within and between organizational departments.

Substantial research suggests that a healthier workforce can more effectively and efficiently implement strategies. No-smoking policies in workplaces are usually derived from annual objectives that seek to reduce corporate medical costs associated with absenteeism and to provide a healthy workplace. Ireland recently banned smoking in all pubs and restaurants. A no-smoking ban went into effect on January 1, 2007 in all restaurants in Belgium, Hong Kong, Alberta (Canada), Thailand, and Louisiana. Also on that date, Washington, DC's smoking ban extended to bars, and many other cities banned smoking in public places, too.

The Strategic-Management Model

The strategic-management process can best be studied and applied using a model. Every model represents some kind of process. The framework illustrated in Figure 1-1 is a widely accepted, comprehensive model of the strategic-management process.[13] This model does not guarantee success, but it does represent a clear and practical approach for formulating, implementing, and evaluating strategies. Relationships among major components of the strategic-management process are shown in the model, which appears in all subsequent chapters with appropriate areas shaped to show the particular focus of each chapter.

Identifying an organization's existing vision, mission, objectives, and strategies is the logical starting point for strategic management because a firm's present situation and condition may preclude certain strategies and may even dictate a particular course of action. Every organization has a vision, mission, objectives, and strategy, even if these elements are not consciously designed, written, or communicated. The answer to where an organization is going can be determined largely by where the organization has been!

FIGURE 1-1

A Comprehensive Strategic-Management Model

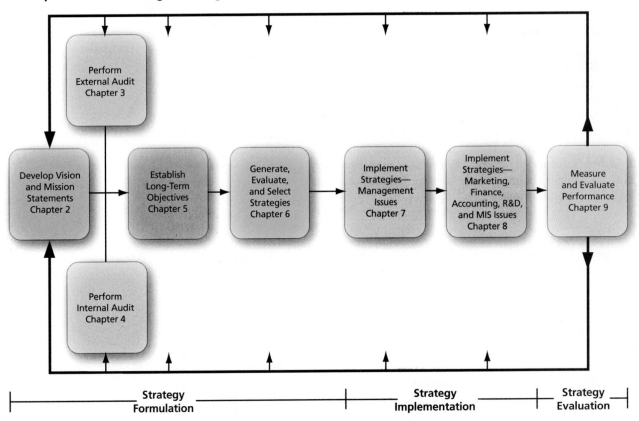

Source: Fred R. David, "How Companies Define Their Mission," *Long Range Planning* 22, no. 3 (June 1988): 40.

The strategic-management process is dynamic and continuous. A change in any one of the major components in the model can necessitate a change in any or all of the other components. For instance, a shift in the economy could represent a major opportunity and require a change in long-term objectives and strategies; a failure to accomplish annual objectives could require a change in policy; or a major competitor's change in strategy could require a change in the firm's mission. Therefore, strategy formulation, implementation, and evaluation activities should be performed on a continual basis, not just at the end of the year or semiannually. The strategic-management process never really ends.

The strategic-management process is not as cleanly divided and neatly performed in practice as the *strategic-management model* suggests. Strategists do not go through the process in lockstep fashion. Generally, there is give-and-take among hierarchical levels of an organization. Many organizations semiannually conduct formal meetings to discuss and update the firm's vision/mission, opportunities/threats, strengths/weaknesses, strategies, objectives, policies, and performance. These meetings are commonly held off-premises and are called *retreats*. The rationale for periodically conducting strategic-management meetings away from the work site is to encourage more creativity and candor from participants. Good communication and feedback are needed throughout the strategic-management process.

Application of the strategic-management process is typically more formal in larger and well-established organizations. Formality refers to the extent that participants, responsibilities, authority, duties, and approach are specified. Smaller businesses tend to be less formal. Firms that compete in complex, rapidly changing environments, such as technology companies, tend to be more formal in strategic planning. Firms that have many divisions, products, markets, and technologies also tend to be more formal in applying strategic-management concepts. Greater formality in applying the strategic-management process is usually positively associated with the cost, comprehensiveness, accuracy, and success of planning across all types and sizes of organizations.[14]

Benefits of Strategic Management

Strategic management allows an organization to be more proactive than reactive in shaping its own future; it allows an organization to initiate and influence (rather than just respond to) activities—and thus to exert control over its own destiny. Small business owners, chief executive officers, presidents, and managers of many for-profit and nonprofit organizations have recognized and realized the benefits of strategic management.

Historically, the principal benefit of strategic management has been to help organizations formulate better strategies through the use of a more systematic, logical, and rational approach to strategic choice. This certainly continues to be a major benefit of strategic management, but research studies now indicate that the process, rather than the decision or document, is the more important contribution of strategic management.[15] *Communication is a key to successful strategic management.* Through involvement in the process, managers and employees become committed to supporting the organization. Dialogue and participation are essential ingredients.

The manner in which strategic management is carried out is thus exceptionally important. A major aim of the process is to achieve the understanding of and commitment from all managers and employees. Understanding may be the most important benefit of strategic management, followed by commitment. When managers and employees understand what the organization is doing and why, they often feel that they are a part of the firm and become committed to assisting it. This is especially true when employees also understand linkages between their own compensation and organizational performance. Managers and employees become surprisingly creative and innovative when they understand and support the firm's mission, objectives, and strategies. A great benefit of strategic management, then, is the opportunity that the process provides to empower individuals. *Empowerment* is the act of strengthening employees' sense of effectiveness by encouraging them to participate in decision making and to exercise initiative and imagination, and rewarding them for doing so.

More and more organizations are decentralizing the strategic-management process, recognizing that planning must involve lower-level managers and employees. The notion of centralized staff planning is being replaced in organizations by decentralized line-manager planning. For example, Walt Disney Co. recently dismantled its strategic-planning department and gave those responsibilities back to the Disney business divisions. Former CEO Michael Eisner had favored the centralized strategic-planning approach, but new CEO Robert Iger dissolved Disney's strategic-planning department within weeks of his taking over the top office at Disney. The process is a learning, helping, educating, and supporting activity, not merely a paper-shuffling activity among top executives. Strategic-management dialogue is more important than a nicely bound strategic-management document.[16] The worst thing strategists can do is develop strategic plans themselves and then present them to operating managers to execute. Through involvement in the process, line managers become "owners" of the strategy. Ownership of strategies by the people who have to execute them is a key to success!

Although making good strategic decisions is the major responsibility of an organization's owner or chief executive officer, both managers and employees must also be involved in strategy formulation, implementation, and evaluation activities. Participation is a key to gaining commitment for needed changes.

An increasing number of corporations and institutions are using strategic management to make effective decisions. But strategic management is not a guarantee for success; it can be dysfunctional if conducted haphazardly.

VISIT THE NET

Explains in detail how to develop a strategic plan and compares this document to a business plan. (www.planware.org/strategy. htm#1)

VISIT THE NET

Provides excellent narrative on the "Benefits of Strategic Planning," "Pitfalls of Strategic Planning," and the "Steps in Doing Strategic Planning." (www.entarga.com/stratplan/index.htm)

Financial Benefits

Research indicates that organizations using strategic-management concepts are more profitable and successful than those that do not.[17] Businesses using strategic-management concepts show significant improvement in sales, profitability, and productivity compared to firms without systematic planning activities. High-performing firms tend to do systematic planning to prepare for future fluctuations in their external and internal environments. Firms with planning systems more closely resembling strategic-management theory generally exhibit superior long-term financial performance relative to their industry.

High-performing firms seem to make more informed decisions with good anticipation of both short- and long-term consequences. On the other hand, firms that perform poorly often engage in activities that are shortsighted and do not reflect good forecasting of future conditions. Strategists of low-performing organizations are often preoccupied with solving internal problems and meeting paperwork deadlines. They typically underestimate their competitors' strengths and overestimate their own firm's strengths. They often attribute weak performance to uncontrollable factors such as a poor economy, technological change, or foreign competition.

The credit reporting company Dun & Bradstreet reports that more than 100,000 businesses in the United States fail annually. Business failures include bankruptcies, foreclosures, liquidations, and court-mandated receiverships. Although many factors besides a lack of effective strategic management can lead to business failure, the planning concepts and tools described in this text can yield substantial financial benefits for any organization. An excellent Web site for businesses engaged in strategic planning is www.checkmateplan.com.

Nonfinancial Benefits

Besides helping firms avoid financial demise, strategic management offers other tangible benefits, such as an enhanced awareness of external threats, an improved understanding of competitors' strategies, increased employee productivity, reduced resistance to change, and a clearer understanding of performance–reward relationships. Strategic management enhances the problem-prevention capabilities of organizations because it promotes interaction among managers at all divisional and functional levels. Firms that have nurtured their managers and employees, shared organizational objectives with them, empowered them to help improve the product or service, and recognized their contributions can turn to them for help in a pinch because of this interaction.

In addition to empowering managers and employees, strategic management often brings order and discipline to an otherwise floundering firm. It can be the beginning of an efficient and effective managerial system. Strategic management may renew confidence in the current business strategy or point to the need for corrective actions. The strategic-management process provides a basis for identifying and rationalizing the need for change to all managers and employees of a firm; it helps them view change as an opportunity rather than as a threat.

Greenley stated that strategic management offers the following benefits:

1. It allows for identification, prioritization, and exploitation of opportunities.
2. It provides an objective view of management problems.
3. It represents a framework for improved coordination and control of activities.
4. It minimizes the effects of adverse conditions and changes.
5. It allows major decisions to better support established objectives.
6. It allows more effective allocation of time and resources to identified opportunities.
7. It allows fewer resources and less time to be devoted to correcting erroneous or ad hoc decisions.
8. It creates a framework for internal communication among personnel.
9. It helps integrate the behavior of individuals into a total effort.
10. It provides a basis for clarifying individual responsibilities.
11. It encourages forward thinking.
12. It provides a cooperative, integrated, and enthusiastic approach to tackling problems and opportunities.
13. It encourages a favorable attitude toward change.
14. It gives a degree of discipline and formality to the management of a business.[18]

Why Some Firms Do No Strategic Planning

Some firms do not engage in strategic planning, and some firms do strategic planning but receive no support from managers and employees. Some reasons for poor or no strategic planning are as follows:

- *Poor reward structures*—When an organization assumes success, it often fails to reward success. When failure occurs, then the firm may punish. In this situation, it is better for an individual to do nothing (and not draw attention) than to risk trying to achieve something, fail, and be punished.
- *Firefighting*—An organization can be so deeply embroiled in crisis management and firefighting that it does not have time to plan.
- *Waste of time*—Some firms see planning as a waste of time because no marketable product is produced. Time spent on planning is an investment.
- *Too expensive*—Some organizations are culturally opposed to spending resources.
- *Laziness*—People may not want to put forth the effort needed to formulate a plan.
- *Content with success*—Particularly if a firm is successful, individuals may feel there is no need to plan because things are fine as they stand. But success today does not guarantee success tomorrow.
- *Fear of failure*—By not taking action, there is little risk of failure unless a problem is urgent and pressing. Whenever something worthwhile is attempted, there is some risk of failure.
- *Overconfidence*—As individuals amass experience, they may rely less on formalized planning. Rarely, however, is this appropriate. Being overconfident or overestimating experience can bring demise. Forethought is rarely wasted and is often the mark of professionalism.
- *Prior bad experience*—People may have had a previous bad experience with planning, that is, cases in which plans have been long, cumbersome, impractical, or inflexible. Planning, like anything else, can be done badly.
- *Self-interest*—When someone has achieved status, privilege, or self-esteem through effectively using an old system, he or she often sees a new plan as a threat.
- *Fear of the unknown*—People may be uncertain of their abilities to learn new skills, of their aptitude with new systems, or of their ability to take on new roles.
- *Honest difference of opinion*—People may sincerely believe the plan is wrong. They may view the situation from a different viewpoint, or they may have aspirations for themselves or the organization that are different from the plan. Different people in different jobs have different perceptions of a situation.
- *Suspicion*—Employees may not trust management.[19]

VISIT THE NET

Gives reasons why some organizations avoid strategic planning. (www.mindtools.com/plfailpl.html)

Pitfalls in Strategic Planning

Strategic planning is an involved, intricate, and complex process that takes an organization into uncharted territory. It does not provide a ready-to-use prescription for success; instead, it takes the organization through a journey and offers a framework for addressing questions and solving problems. Being aware of potential pitfalls and being prepared to address them is essential to success.

Some pitfalls to watch for and avoid in strategic planning are these:

- Using strategic planning to gain control over decisions and resources
- Doing strategic planning only to satisfy accreditation or regulatory requirements
- Too hastily moving from mission development to strategy formulation
- Failing to communicate the plan to employees, who continue working in the dark
- Top managers making many intuitive decisions that conflict with the formal plan
- Top managers not actively supporting the strategic-planning process
- Failing to use plans as a standard for measuring performance
- Delegating planning to a "planner" rather than involving all managers
- Failing to involve key employees in all phases of planning

VISIT THE NET

Provides nice discussion of the limitations of strategic planning process within an organization. (www.des.calstate.edu/limitations.html)

- Failing to create a collaborative climate supportive of change
- Viewing planning as unnecessary or unimportant
- Becoming so engrossed in current problems that insufficient or no planning is done
- Being so formal in planning that flexibility and creativity are stifled.[20]

Guidelines for Effective Strategic Management

Failing to follow certain guidelines in conducting strategic management can foster criticisms of the process and create problems for the organization. An integral part of strategy evaluation must be to evaluate the quality of the strategic-management process. Issues such as "Is strategic management in our firm a people process or a paper process?" should be addressed.

Even the most technically perfect strategic plan will serve little purpose if it is not implemented. Many organizations tend to spend an inordinate amount of time, money, and effort on developing the strategic plan, treating the means and circumstances under which it will be implemented as afterthoughts! Change comes through implementation and evaluation, not through the plan. A technically imperfect plan that is implemented well will achieve more than the perfect plan that never gets off the paper on which it is typed.[21]

Strategic management must not become a self-perpetuating bureaucratic mechanism. Rather, it must be a self-reflective learning process that familiarizes managers and employees in the organization with key strategic issues and feasible alternatives for resolving those issues. Strategic management must not become ritualistic, stilted, orchestrated, or too formal, predictable, and rigid. Words supported by numbers, rather than numbers supported by words, should represent the medium for explaining strategic issues and organizational responses. A key role of strategists is to facilitate continuous organizational learning and change.

R. T. Lenz offered some important guidelines for effective strategic management:

Keep the strategic-management process as simple and nonroutine as possible. Eliminate jargon and arcane planning language. Remember, strategic management is a process for fostering learning and action, not merely a formal system for control. To avoid routinized behavior, vary assignments, team membership, meeting formats, and the planning calendar. The process should not be totally predictable, and settings must be changed to stimulate creativity. Emphasize word-oriented plans with numbers as back-up material. If managers cannot express their strategy in a paragraph or so, they either do not have one or do not understand it. Stimulate thinking and action that challenge the assumptions underlying current corporate strategy. Welcome bad news. If strategy is not working, managers desperately need to know it. Further, no pertinent information should be classified as inadmissible merely because it cannot be quantified. Build a corporate culture in which the role of strategic management and its essential purposes are understood. Do not permit "technicians" to co-opt the process. It is ultimately a process for learning and action. Speak of it in these terms. Attend to psychological, social, and political dimensions, as well as the information infrastructure and administrative procedures supporting it.[22]

An important guideline for effective strategic management is open-mindedness. A willingness and eagerness to consider new information, new viewpoints, new ideas, and new possibilities is essential; all organizational members must share a spirit of inquiry and learning. Strategists such as chief executive officers, presidents, owners of small businesses, and heads of government agencies must commit themselves to listen to and understand managers' positions well enough to be able to restate those positions to the managers' satisfaction. In addition, managers and employees throughout the firm should be able to describe the strategists' positions to the satisfaction of the strategists. This degree of discipline will promote understanding and learning.

No organization has unlimited resources. No firm can take on an unlimited amount of debt or issue an unlimited amount of stock to raise capital. Therefore, no organization can pursue all the strategies that potentially could benefit the firm. Strategic decisions thus always have to be made to eliminate some courses of action and to allocate organizational resources among others. Most organizations can afford to pursue only a few corporate-level strategies at any given time. It is a critical mistake for managers to pursue too many strategies at the same time, thereby spreading the firm's resources so thin that all strategies are jeopardized. Joseph Charyk, CEO of the Communication Satellite Corporation (Comsat), said, "We have to face the cold fact that Comsat may not be able to do all it wants. We must make hard choices on which ventures to keep and which to fold."

Strategic decisions require trade-offs such as long-range versus short-range considerations or maximizing profits versus increasing shareholders' wealth. There are ethics issues too. Strategy trade-offs require subjective judgments and preferences. In many cases, a lack of objectivity in formulating strategy results in a loss of competitive posture and profitability. Most organizations today recognize that strategic-management concepts and techniques can enhance the effectiveness of decisions. Subjective factors such as attitudes toward risk, concern for social responsibility, and organizational culture will always affect strategy-formulation decisions, but organizations need to be as objective as possible in considering qualitative factors.

Business Ethics and Strategic Management

Business ethics can be defined as principles of conduct within organizations that guide decision making and behavior. Good business ethics is a prerequisite for good strategic management; good ethics is just good business!

A rising tide of consciousness about the importance of business ethics is sweeping the world. Strategists are the individuals primarily responsible for ensuring that high ethical principles are espoused and practiced in an organization. All strategy formulation, implementation, and evaluation decisions have ethical ramifications.

Newspapers and business magazines daily report legal and moral breaches of ethical conduct by both public and private organizations. The biggest payouts for class-action legal fraud suits ever were against Enron ($7.16 billion), WorldCom ($6.16 billion), Cendant ($3.53 billion), Tyco ($2.98 billion), AOL Time Warner ($2.5 billion), Nortel Networks ($2.47 billion), and Royal Ahold ($1.09 billion).

Managers and employees of firms must be careful not to become scapegoats blamed for company environmental wrongdoings. Harming the natural environment is unethical, illegal, and costly. When organizations today face criminal charges for polluting the environment, firms increasingly are turning on their managers and employees to win leniency for themselves. Employee firings and demotions are becoming common in pollution-related legal suits. Managers being fired at Darling International, Inc., and Niagara Mohawk Power Corporation for being indirectly responsible for their firms polluting water exemplifies this corporate trend. Therefore, managers and employees today must be careful not to ignore, conceal, or disregard a pollution problem, or they may find themselves personally liable. In this regard, more and more companies are becoming ISO 14001 certified, as indicated in the "Natural Environment Perspective" on pages 52–53.

A new wave of ethics issues related to product safety, employee health, sexual harassment, AIDS in the workplace, smoking, acid rain, affirmative action, waste disposal, foreign business practices, cover-ups, takeover tactics, conflicts of interest, employee privacy, inappropriate gifts, security of company records, and layoffs has accentuated the need for strategists to develop a clear code of business ethics. United Technologies Corporation has issued a twenty-one-page code of ethics and named a new vice president of business ethics. Baxter Travenol Laboratories, IBM, Caterpillar Tractor, Chemical Bank, ExxonMobil, Dow Corning, and Celanese are firms that have formal codes of business ethics. A *code of business ethics* can provide a basis on which policies can be devised to guide daily behavior and decisions at the work site.

VISIT THE NET

Describes "Why Have a Code of Ethics" and gives "Guidelines on Writing a Code of Ethics." (www. ethicsweb.ca/codes)

VISIT THE NET

An excellent Web site to obtain additional information regarding business ethics is (www.ethicsweb.ca/codes); it describes "Why Have a Code of Ethics" and gives "Guidelines on Writing a Code of Ethics."

VISIT THE NET

Professor Hansen at Stetson University provides a strategic management slide show for this entire text. (www.stetson.edu/~rhansen/strategy)

Merely having a code of ethics, however, is not sufficient to ensure ethical business behavior. A code of ethics can be viewed as a public relations gimmick, a set of platitudes, or window dressing. To ensure that the code is read, understood, believed, and remembered, organizations need to conduct periodic ethics workshops to sensitize people to workplace circumstances in which ethics issues may arise.[23] If employees see examples of punishment for violating the code and rewards for upholding the code, this helps reinforce the importance of a firm's code of ethics.

An ethics "culture" needs to permeate organizations! To help create an ethics culture, Citicorp developed a business ethics board game that is played by forty thousand employees in forty-five countries. Called "The Word Ethic," this game asks players business ethics questions, such as how do you deal with a customer who offers you football tickets in exchange for a new, backdated retirement savings account? Diana Robertson at the Wharton School of Business believes the game is effective because it is interactive. Many organizations, such as Prime Computer and Kmart, have developed a code-of-conduct manual outlining ethical expectations and giving examples of situations that commonly arise in their businesses. Harris Corporation's managers and employees are warned that failing to report an ethical violation by others could bring discharge.

One reason strategists' salaries are high compared to those of other individuals in an organization is that strategists must take the moral risks of the firm. Strategists are responsible for developing, communicating, and enforcing the code of business ethics for their organizations. Although primary responsibility for ensuring ethical behavior rests with a firm's strategists, an integral part of the responsibility of all managers is to provide ethics leadership by constant example and demonstration. Managers hold positions that enable them to influence and educate many people. This makes managers responsible for developing and implementing ethical decision making. Gellerman and Drucker, respectively, offer some good advice for managers:

> All managers risk giving too much because of what their companies demand from them. But the same superiors, who keep pressing you to do more, or to do it better, or faster, or less expensively, will turn on you should you cross that fuzzy line between right and wrong. They will blame you for exceeding instructions or for ignoring their warnings. The smartest managers already know that the best answer to the question "How far is too far?" is don't try to find out.[24]

NATURAL ENVIRONMENT PERSPECTIVE
Using ISO 14000 Certification to Gain Strategic Advantage

Based in Geneva, Switzerland, the ISO (International Organization for Standardization) is a network of the national standards institutes of 147 countries, one member per country. ISO is the world's largest developer of standards. Widely accepted all over the world, ISO standards are voluntary because the organization has no legal authority to enforce their implementation. ISO itself does not regulate or legislate. Governmental agencies in various countries, such as the Environmental Protection Agency in the United States, have adopted ISO standards as part of their regulatory framework, and the standards are the basis of much legislation. Adoptions are sovereign decisions by the regulatory authorities, governments, and/or companies concerned.

What Are ISO 14000 and ISO 14001?

ISO 14000 refers to a series of voluntary standards in the environmental field. The ISO 14000 family of standards concerns the extent to which a firm minimizes harmful effects on the environment caused by its activities and continually monitors and improves its own environmental performance. Included in the ISO 14000 series are the ISO 14001 standards in fields such as environmental auditing, environmental performance evaluation, environmental labeling, and life-cycle assessment. ISO 14001 is a set of standards adopted by thousands of firms worldwide to certify to their constituencies that they are conducting business in an environmentally friendly manner. ISO 14001 standards offer a universal technical standard for environmental compliance that more and more firms are requiring not only of themselves but also of their suppliers and distributors.

Requirements for ISO 14001 Certification

The ISO 14001 standard requires that a community or organization put in place and implement a series of practices and procedures that, when taken together, result in an environmental management system. ISO 14001 is not a technical standard and as such does not in any way replace technical requirements embodied in statutes or regulations. It also does not set prescribed standards of performance for organizations. The major requirements of an EMS under ISO 14001 include the following:

- Establish an EMS that includes commitments to prevention of pollution, continual improvement in overall environmental performance, and compliance with all applicable statutory and regulatory requirements.
- Identify all aspects of the organization's activities, products, and services that could have a significant impact on the environment, including those that are not regulated.
- Set performance objectives and targets for the management system that link back to three policies: (1) prevention of pollution, (2) continual improvement, and (3) compliance.
- Implement an EMS to meet environmental objectives that include training employees, establishing work instructions and practices, and establishing the actual metrics by which the objectives and targets will be measured.
- Audit the operation of the EMS.
- Take corrective actions when deviations from the EMS occur.

Conclusion

ISO 14001 standards on air, water, and soil quality, and on emissions of gases and radiation, contribute to preserving the environment in which we all live and work. The U.S.

United States, Yellowstone National Park, Mammoth Hot Springs. *Source:* Andy Holligan (c) Dorling Kindersley

Environmental Protection Agency (EPA) now offers a guide entitled "Environmental Management Systems (EMS): An Implementation Guide for Small and Medium Sized Organizations." The publication offers a plain-English, commonsense guide to becoming ISO 14001 certified. Not being ISO 14001 certified can be a strategic disadvantage for towns, counties, and companies as people today expect organizations to minimize or, even better, to eliminate environmental harm they cause.

Source: Adapted from the www.iso14000.com Web site and the www.epa.gov Web site.

A man (or woman) might know too little, perform poorly, lack judgment and ability, and yet not do too much damage as a manager. But if that person lacks character and integrity—no matter how knowledgeable, how brilliant, how successful— he destroys. He destroys people, the most valuable resource of the enterprise. He destroys spirit. And he destroys performance. This is particularly true of the people at the head of an enterprise. For the spirit of an organization is created from the top. If an organization is great in spirit, it is because the spirit of its top people is great. If it decays, it does so because the top rots. As the proverb has it, "Trees die from the top." No one should ever become a strategist unless he or she is willing to have his or her character serve as the model for subordinates.[25]

No society anywhere in the world can compete very long or successfully with people stealing from one another or not trusting one another, with every bit of information requiring notarized confirmation, with every disagreement ending up in litigation, or with government having to regulate businesses to keep them honest. Being unethical is a recipe for headaches, inefficiency, and waste. History has proven that the greater the trust and confidence of people in the ethics of an institution or society, the greater its economic strength. Business relationships are built mostly on mutual trust and reputation. Short-term decisions based on greed and questionable ethics will preclude the necessary self-respect to gain the trust of others. More and more firms believe that ethics training and an ethics culture create strategic advantage.

Some business actions considered to be unethical include misleading advertising or labeling, causing environmental harm, poor product or service safety, padding expense accounts, insider trading, dumping banned or flawed products in foreign markets, lack of equal opportunities for women and minorities, overpricing, hostile takeovers, moving jobs overseas, and using nonunion labor in a union shop.[26]

Internet fraud, including hacking into company computers and spreading viruses, has become a major unethical activity that plagues every sector of online commerce from banking to shopping sites. More than three hundred Web sites now show individuals how to hack into computers; this problem has become endemic nationwide and around the world.

Ethics training programs should include messages from the CEO emphasizing ethical business practices, the development and discussion of codes of ethics, and procedures for discussing and reporting unethical behavior. Firms can align ethical and strategic decision making by incorporating ethical considerations into long-term planning, by integrating ethical decision making into the performance appraisal process, by encouraging whistle-blowing or the reporting of unethical practices, and by monitoring departmental and corporate performance regarding ethical issues.

In a final analysis, ethical standards come out of history and heritage. Our predecessors have left us with an ethical foundation to build upon. Even the legendary football coach Vince Lombardi, who coached the U.S. Green Bay Packers, knew that some things were worth more than winning, and he required his players to have three kinds of loyalty: to God, to their families, and to the Green Bay Packers, "in that order."

Comparing Business and Military Strategy

A strong military heritage underlies the study of strategic management. Terms such as *objectives, mission, strengths,* and *weaknesses* first were formulated to address problems on the battlefield. According to *Webster's New World Dictionary,* strategy is "the science of planning and directing large-scale military operations, of maneuvering forces into the most advantageous position prior to actual engagement with the enemy." The word *strategy* comes from the Greek *strategos,* which refers to a military general and combines *stratos* (the army) and *ago* (to lead). The history of strategic planning began in the military. A key aim of both business and military strategy is "to gain competitive advantage." In many respects, business strategy is like military strategy, and military strategists have learned much over the centuries that can benefit business strategists today. Both business and military organizations try to use their own strengths to exploit competitors' weaknesses. If an organization's overall strategy is wrong (ineffective), then all the efficiency in the world may not be enough to allow success. Business or military success is generally not the happy result of accidental strategies. Rather, success is the product of both continuous attention to changing external and internal conditions and the formulation and implementation of insightful adaptations to those conditions. The element of surprise provides great competitive advantages in both military and business strategy; information systems that provide data on opponents' or competitors' strategies and resources are also vitally important.

Of course, a fundamental difference between military and business strategy is that business strategy is formulated, implemented, and evaluated with an assumption of *competition,* whereas military strategy is based on an assumption of *conflict.* Nonetheless, military conflict and business competition are so similar that many strategic-management techniques apply equally to both. Business strategists have access to valuable insights that military thinkers have refined over time. Superior strategy formulation and implementation can overcome an opponent's superiority in numbers and resources.

Both business and military organizations must adapt to change and constantly improve to be successful. Too often, firms do not change their strategies when their environment and competitive conditions dictate the need to change. Gluck offered a classic military example of this:

> When Napoleon won, it was because his opponents were committed to the strategy, tactics, and organization of earlier wars. When he lost—against Wellington, the Russians, and the Spaniards—it was because he, in turn, used tried-and-true strategies against enemies who thought afresh, who were developing the strategies not of the last war but of the next.[27]

Similarities can be construed from Sun Tzu's writings to the practice of formulating and implementing strategies among businesses today. Table 1-2 provides narrative excerpts from *The Art of War.* As you read through Table 1-2, consider which of the principles of war apply to business strategy as companies today compete aggressively to survive and grow.

The Nature of Global Competition

For centuries before Columbus discovered America and surely for centuries to come, businesses have searched and will continue to search for new opportunities beyond their national boundaries. There has never been a more internationalized and economically competitive society than today's. Some U.S. industries, such as textiles, steel, and consumer electronics, are in complete disarray as a result of the international challenge.

Organizations that conduct business operations across national borders are called *international firms* or *multinational corporations.* The term *parent company* refers to a firm investing in international operations, while *host country* is the country where that business is conducted. The strategic-management process is conceptually the same for multinational firms as for purely domestic firms; however, the process is more complex for international firms because of the presence of more variables and relationships. The social, cultural, demographic, environmental, political, governmental, legal, technological, and competitive opportunities and threats that face a multinational corporation are almost limitless, and the number and complexity of these factors increase dramatically with the number of products produced and the number of geographic areas served.

More time and effort are required to identify and evaluate external trends and events in multinational corporations than in domestic corporations. Geographical distance, cultural and national differences, and variations in business practices often make communication between domestic headquarters and overseas operations difficult. Strategy implementation can be more difficult because different cultures have different norms, values, and work ethics.

Advancements in telecommunications are drawing countries, cultures, and organizations worldwide closer together. Foreign revenue as a percent of total company revenues already exceeds 50 percent in hundreds of U.S. firms, including ExxonMobil, Gillette, Dow Chemical, Citicorp, Colgate-Palmolive, and Texaco. Unilever had $10 billion and $21.3 billion in domestic and foreign revenues, respectively, in 2006. A primary reason why most domestic firms are engaging in global operations is that growth in demand for goods and services outside the United States is considerably higher than inside. For example, the domestic food industry is growing just 3 percent per year, so Kraft Foods, the second largest food company in the world behind Nestle, is focusing on foreign acquisitions. Shareholders and investors expect sustained growth in revenues from firms; satisfactory

TABLE 1-2 **Excerpts from Sun Tzu's *The Art of War* Writings**

- War is a matter of vital importance to the state: a matter of life or death, the road either to survival or ruin. Hence, it is imperative that it be studied thoroughly.
- Warfare is based on deception. When near the enemy, make it seem that you are far away; when far away, make it seem that you are near. Hold out baits to lure the enemy. Strike the enemy when he is in disorder. Avoid the enemy when he is stronger. If your opponent is of choleric temper, try to irritate him. If he is arrogant, try to encourage his egotism. If enemy troops are well prepared after reorganization, try to wear them down. If they are united, try to sow dissension among them. Attack the enemy where he is unprepared, and appear where you are not expected. These are the keys to victory for a strategist. It is not possible to formulate them in detail beforehand.
- A speedy victory is the main object in war. If this is long in coming, weapons are blunted and morale depressed. When the army engages in protracted campaigns, the resources of the state will fall short. Thus, while we have heard of stupid haste in war, we have not yet seen a clever operation that was prolonged.
- Generally, in war the best policy is to take a state intact; to ruin it is inferior to this. To capture the enemy's entire army is better than to destroy it; to take intact a regiment, a company, or a squad is better than to destroy it. For to win one hundred victories in one hundred battles is not the acme of skill. To subdue the enemy without fighting is the supreme excellence. Those skilled in war subdue the enemy's army without battle.
- The art of using troops is this: When ten to the enemy's one, surround him. When five times his strength, attack him. If double his strength, divide him. If equally matched, you may engage him with some good plan. If weaker, be capable of withdrawing. And if in all respects unequal, be capable of eluding him.
- Know your enemy and know yourself, and in a hundred battles you will never be defeated. When you are ignorant of the enemy but know yourself, your chances of winning or losing are equal. If ignorant both of your enemy and of yourself, you are sure to be defeated in every battle.
- He who occupies the field of battle first and awaits his enemy is at ease, and he who comes later to the scene and rushes into the fight is weary. And therefore, those skilled in war bring the enemy to the field of battle and are not brought there by him. Thus, when the enemy is at ease, be able to tire him; when well fed, be able to starve him; when at rest, be able to make him move.
- Analyze the enemy's plans so that you will know his shortcomings as well as his strong points. Agitate him to ascertain the pattern of his movement. Lure him out to reveal his dispositions and to ascertain his position. Launch a probing attack to learn where his strength is abundant and where deficient. It is according to the situation that plans are laid for victory, but the multitude does not comprehend this.
- An army may be likened to water, for just as flowing water avoids the heights and hastens to the lowlands, so an army should avoid strength and strike weakness. And as water shapes its flow in accordance with the ground, so an army manages its victory in accordance with the situation of the enemy. And as water has no constant form, there are in warfare no constant conditions. Thus, one able to win the victory by modifying his tactics in accordance with the enemy situation may be said to be divine.
- If you decide to go into battle, do not anounce your intentions or plans. Project "business as usual."
- Unskilled leaders work out their conflicts in courtrooms and battlefields. Brilliant strategists rarely go to battle or to court; they generally achieve their objectives through tactical positioning well in advance of any confrontation.
- When you do decide to challenge another company (or army), much calculating, estimating, analyzing, and positioning bring triumph. Little computation brings defeat.
- Skillful leaders do not let a strategy inhibit creative counter-movement. Nor should commands from those at a distance interfere with spontaneous maneuvering in the immediate situation.
- When a decisive advantage is gained over a rival, skillful leaders do not press on. They hold their position and give their rivals the opportunity to surrender or merge. They do not allow their forces to be damaged by those who have nothing to lose.
- Brillant strategists forge ahead with illusion, obscuring the area(s) of major confrontation, so that opponents divide their forces in an attempt to defend many areas. Create the appearance of confusion, fear, or vulnerability so the opponent is helplessly drawn toward this illusion of advantage.

(Note: Substitute the words *strategy* or *strategic planning* for *war* or *warfare*)

Source: Adapted from *The Art of War* and from the Web site www.ccs.neu.edu/home/thigpen/html/art_of_war.html.

growth for many firms can only be achieved by capitalizing on demand outside their domestic countries. Computer shipments grew 21 percent in China in 2006, so Dell has greatly expanded its operations in China. Joint ventures and partnerships between domestic and foreign firms are becoming the rule rather than the exception!

The lineup of competitors in virtually all industries today is global. Global competition is more than a management fad. General Motors, Ford, and Chrysler compete with Toyota and Hyundai. General Electric and Westinghouse battle Siemens and Mitsubishi. Caterpillar and John Deere compete with Komatsu. Goodyear battles Michelin, Bridgestone/Firestone, and Pirelli. Boeing competes with Airbus. Only a few

U.S. industries—such as furniture, printing, retailing, consumer packaged goods, and retail banking—are not yet greatly challenged by foreign competitors. But many products and components in these industries too are now manufactured in foreign countries.

International operations can be as simple as exporting a product to a single foreign country or as complex as operating manufacturing, distribution, and marketing facilities in many countries. Firms are acquiring foreign companies and forming joint ventures with them and vice versa. This trend is accelerating dramatically. International expansion is no guarantee of success, however.

Advantages and Disadvantages of International Operations

Firms have numerous reasons for formulating and implementing strategies that initiate, continue, or expand involvement in business operations across national borders. Perhaps the greatest advantage is that firms can gain new customers for their products and services, thus increasing revenues. Growth in revenues and profits is a common organizational objective and often an expectation of shareholders because it is a measure of organizational success.

In addition to seeking growth, firms have the following potentially advantageous reasons to initiate, continue, and expand international operations:

1. Foreign operations can absorb excess capacity, reduce unit costs, and spread economic risks over a wider number of markets.
2. Foreign operations can allow firms to establish low-cost production facilities in locations close to raw materials and/or cheap labor.
3. Competitors in foreign markets may not exist, or competition may be less intense than in domestic markets.
4. Foreign operations may result in reduced tariffs, lower taxes, and favorable political treatment in other countries.
5. Joint ventures can enable firms to learn the technology, culture, and business practices of other people and to make contacts with potential customers, suppliers, creditors, and distributors in foreign countries.
6. Many foreign governments and countries offer varied incentives to encourage foreign investment in specific locations.
7. Economies of scale can be achieved from operation in global rather than solely domestic markets. Larger-scale production and better efficiencies allow higher sales volumes and lower-price offerings.

A firm's power and prestige in domestic markets may be significantly enhanced with various stakeholder groups if the firm competes globally. Enhanced prestige can translate into improved negotiating power among creditors, suppliers, distributors, and other important groups.

There are also numerous potential disadvantages of initiating, continuing, or expanding business across national borders. One risk is that foreign operations could be seized by nationalistic factions. Other disadvantages include the following:

1. Firms confront different and often little-understood social, cultural, demographic, environmental, political, governmental, legal, technological, economic, and competitive forces when internationally doing business. These forces can make communication difficult between the parent firm and subsidiaries.
2. Weaknesses of competitors in foreign lands are often overestimated, and strengths are often underestimated. Keeping informed about the number and nature of competitors is more difficult when internationally doing business.
3. Language, culture, and value systems differ among countries, and this can create barriers to communication and problems managing people.
4. Gaining an understanding of regional organizations such as the European Economic Community, the Latin American Free Trade Area, the International Bank for Reconstruction and Development, and the International Finance Corporation is difficult but is often required in internationally doing business.

5. Dealing with two or more monetary systems can complicate international business operations.

6. The availability, depth, and reliability of economic and marketing information in different countries vary extensively, as do industrial structures, business practices, and the number and nature of regional organizations.

Conclusion

All firms have a strategy, even if it is informal, unstructured, and sporadic. All organizations are heading somewhere, but unfortunately some organizations do not know where they are going. The old saying "If you do not know where you are going, then any road will lead you there!" accents the need for organizations to use strategic-management concepts and techniques. The strategic-management process is becoming more widely used by small firms, large companies, nonprofit institutions, governmental organizations, and multinational conglomerates alike. The process of empowering managers and employees has almost limitless benefits.

Organizations should take a proactive rather than a reactive approach in their industry, and they should strive to influence, anticipate, and initiate rather than just respond to events. The strategic-management process embodies this approach to decision making. It represents a logical, systematic, and objective approach for determining an enterprise's future direction. The stakes are generally too high for strategists to use intuition alone in choosing among alternative courses of action. Successful strategists take the time to think about their businesses, where they are with their businesses, and what they want to be as organizations—and then they implement programs and policies to get from where they are to where they want to be in a reasonable period of time.

It is a known and accepted fact that people and organizations that plan ahead are much more likely to become what they want to become than those that do not plan at all. A good strategist plans and controls his or her plans, while a bad strategist never plans and then tries to control people! This textbook is devoted to providing you with the tools necessary to be a good strategist.

Success in business increasingly depends upon offering products and services that are competitive on a world basis, not just on a local basis. If the price and quality of a firm's products and services are not competitive with those available elsewhere in the world, the firm may soon face extinction. Global markets have become a reality in all but the most remote areas of the world. Certainly throughout the United States, even in small towns, firms feel the pressure of world competitors. Nearly half of all the automobiles sold in the United States, for example, are made in Japan and Germany.

We invite you to visit the David page on the Prentice Hall Companion Web site at www.prenhall.com/david for this chapter's review quiz.

Key Terms and Concepts

Annual Objectives (p. 45)
Business Ethics (p. 51)
Code of Business Ethics (p. 51)
Competitive Advantage (p. 39)
Empowerment (p. 47)
Environmental Scanning (p. 43)
External Opportunities (p. 43)
External Threats (p. 43)
Host Country (p. 55)
Internal Strengths (p. 44)
Internal Weaknesses (p. 44)
International Firms (p. 55)
Intuition (p. 38)
ISO 14000 (p. 52)

ISO 14001 (p. 52)
Long-Range Planning (p. 36)
Long-Term Objectives (p. 44)
Mission Statements (p. 43)
Multinational Corporations (p. 55)
Parent Company (p. 55)
Policies (p. 45)
Strategic Management (p. 36)
Strategic-Management Model (p. 46)
Strategic-Management Process (p. 37)
Strategic Planning (p. 36)
Strategies (p. 44)
Strategists (p. 42)
Strategy Evaluation (p. 37)
Strategy Formulation (p. 37)
Strategy Implementation (p. 37)
Sustained Competitive Advantage (p. 41)
Vision Statement (p. 43)

Issues for Review and Discussion

1. Explain why the strategic management class is often called a "capstone course."
2. What aspect of strategy formulation do you think requires the most time? Why?
3. Why is strategy implementation often considered the most difficult stage in the strategic-management process?
4. Why is it so important to integrate intuition and analysis in strategic management?
5. Explain the importance of a vision and a mission statement.
6. Discuss relationships among objectives, strategies, and policies.
7. Why do you think some chief executive officers fail to use a strategic-management approach to decision making?
8. Discuss the importance of feedback in the strategic-management model.
9. How can strategists best ensure that strategies will be effectively implemented?
10. Give an example of a recent political development that changed the overall strategy of an organization.
11. Who are the major competitors of your college or university? What are their strengths and weaknesses? What are their strategies? How sucessful are these institutions compared to your college?
12. If you owned a small business, would you develop a code of business conduct? If yes, what variables would you include? If no, how would you ensure that ethical business standards were being followed by your employees?
13. Would strategic-management concepts and techniques benefit foreign businesses as much as domestic firms? Justify your answer.
14. What do you believe are some potential pitfalls or risks in using a strategic-management approach to decision making?
15. In your opinion, what is the single major benefit of using a strategic-management approach to decision making? Justify your answer.
16. Compare business strategy and military strategy.
17. What do you feel is the relationship between personal ethics and business ethics? Are they— or should they be—the same?
18. Why is it important for all business majors to study strategic management since most students will never become a chief executive officer nor even a top manager in a large company?
19. Explain why consumption patterns are becoming similar worldwide. What are the strategic implications of this trend?
20. What are the advantages and disadvantages of beginning export operations in a foreign country?
21. Describe the content available on the SMCO Web site at www.strategyclub.com.
22. List four financial and four nonfinancial benefits of a firm engaging in strategic planning.
23. Why is it that a firm can normally sustain a competitive advantage for only a limited period of time?
24. Why it is not adequate to simply obtain competitive advantage?
25. How can a firm best achieve sustained competitive advantage?
26. Compare and contrast ISO 14000 and 14001.

Notes

1. Peter Drucker, *Management: Tasks, Responsibilities, and Practices* (New York: Harper & Row, 1974): 611.
2. Alfred Sloan, Jr., *Adventures of the White Collar Man* (New York: Doubleday, 1941): 104.
3. Quoted in Eugene Raudsepp, "Can You Trust Your Hunches?" *Management Review* 49, no. 4 (April 1960): 7.
4. Stephen Harper, "Intuition: What Separates Executives from Managers," *Business Horizons* 31, no. 5 (September–October 1988): 16.
5. Ron Nelson, "How to Be a Manager," *Success* (July–August 1985): 69.
6. Bruce Henderson, *Henderson on Corporate Strategy* (Boston: Abt Books, 1979): 6.
7. Robert Waterman, Jr., *The Renewal Factor: How the Best Get and Keep the Competitive Edge* (New York: Bantam, 1987). See also *BusinessWeek* (September 14, 1987): 100. Also, see *Academy of Management Executive* 3, no. 2 (May 1989): 115.
8. Ethan Smith, "How Old Media Can Survive in a New World," *Wall Street Journal* (May 23, 2005): R4.
9. Gian Fulgoni, "Web Can Pay Off for Traditional Retailers," *Wall Street Journal* (December 23, 2006): A7.
10. Jayne O'Donnell, "Computers Bumped from Top of Online Sales," *USA Today* (May 14, 2007): 1B.
11. Daniel Delmar, "The Rise of the CSO," *Organization Design* (March–April 2003): 8–10.
12. John Pearce II and Fred David, "The Bottom Line on Corporate Mission Statements," *Academy of Management Executive* 1, no. 2 (May 1987): 109.
13. Fred R. David, "How Companies Define Their Mission," *Long Range Planning* 22, no. 1 (February 1989): 91.
14. Jack Pearce and Richard Robinson, *Strategic Management,* 7th ed. (New York: McGraw-Hill, 2000): 8.
15. Ann Langley, "The Roles of Formal Strategic Planning," *Long Range Planning* 21, no. 3 (June 1988): 40.
16. Bernard Reimann, "Getting Value from Strategic Planning," *Planning Review* 16, no. 3 (May–June 1988): 42.
17. G. L. Schwenk and K. Schrader, "Effects of Formal Strategic Planning in Financial Performance in Small Firms: A Meta-Analysis," *Entrepreneurship and Practice* 3, no. 17 (1993): 53–64. Also, C. C. Miller and L. B. Cardinal, "Strategic Planning and Firm Performance: A Synthesis of More Than Two Decades of Research," *Academy of Management Journal* 6, no. 27 (1994): 1649–1665; Michael Peel and John Bridge, "How Planning and Capital Budgeting Improve SME Performance," *Long Range Planning* 31, no. 6 (October 1998): 848–856; Julia Smith, "Strategies for Start-Ups," *Long Range Planning* 31, no. 6 (October 1998): 857–872.
18. Gordon Greenley, "Does Strategic Planning Improve Company Performance?" *Long Range Planning* 19, no. 2 (April 1986): 106.
19. Adapted from: www.mindtools.com/plreschn.html.
20. Adapted from the Web sites: www.des.calstate.edu/limitations.html and www.entarga.com/stratplan/purposes.html.
21. Dale McConkey, "Planning in a Changing Environment," *Business Horizons* (September–October 1988): 66.
22. R. T. Lenz, "Managing the Evolution of the Strategic Planning Process," *Business Horizons* 30, no. 1 (January–February 1987): 39.
23. Joann Greco, "Privacy—Whose Right Is It Anyhow?" *Journal of Business Strategy* (January–February 2001): 32.
24. Saul Gellerman, "Why 'Good' Managers Make Bad Ethical Choices," *Harvard Business Review* 64, no. 4 (July–August 1986): 88.
25. Drucker, 462, 463.

26. Gene Laczniak, Marvin Berkowitz, Russell Brooker, and James Hale, "The Ethics of Business: Improving or Deteriorating?" *Business Horizons* 38, no. 1 (January–February 1995): 43.

27. Frederick Gluck, "Taking the Mystique out of Planning," *Across the Board* (July–August 1985): 59.

Current Readings

Adner, R., and P. Zemsky. "A Demand-Based Perspective on Sustainable Competitive Advantage." *Strategic Management Journal* 27, no. 3 (March 2006): 215.

Bigley, Gregory A., Will Felps, and Thomas M. Jones. "Ethical Theory and Stakeholder-Related Decisions: The Role of Stakeholder Culture." *The Academy of Management Review* 32, no. 1 (January 2007): 137.

Boiral, Olivier. "Global Warming: Should Companies Adopt a Proactive Strategy?" *Long Range Planning* 39, no. 3 (June 2006): 315.

Bower, Joseph L., and Clark G. Gilbert. "How Managers' Everyday Decisions Create—or Destroy—Your Company's Strategy." *Harvard Business Review* (February 2007): 72.

Cardy, Robert L., and T. T. Selvarajan. "Competencies: Alternative Frameworks for Competitive Advantage." *Business Horizons* 49, no. 3 (May–June 2006): 235.

Certo, S. Trevis, and Matthen Semadeni. "Strategy Research and Panel Data: Evidence and Implication." *Journal of Management* 32, no. 3 (June 2006): 449.

Certo, Samuel C., S. Trevis Certo, and Christopher R. Reutzel. "Spotlight on Entrepreneurship." *Business Horizons* 49, no. 4 (July-August 2006): 265.

Clement, Ronald W. "Just How Unethical Is American Business?" *Business Horizons* 49, no. 4 (July–August 2006): 313.

Dane, Erik, and Michael G. Pratt. "Exploring Intuition and Its Role in Managerial Decision Making." *The Academy of Management Review* 32, no. 1 (January 2007): 33.

Dew, N., S. Read, S. D. Saravathy, and R. Wiltbank. "What to Do Next? The Case for Non-Predictive Strategy." *Strategic Management Journal* 27, no. 10 (October 2006): 981.

Etzion, Dror. "Research on Organizations and the Natural Environment, 1922-Present: A Review." *Journal of Management* 33, no. 4 (August 2007): 637.

Harrison, Ann E., and Margaret S. McMillan. "Dispelling Some Myths About Offshoring." *The Academy of Management Perspectives* 20, no. 4 (November 2006): 6.

Heine, K., and N. Stieglitz. "Innovations and the Role of Complementarities in a Strategic Theory of the Firm." *Strategic Management Journal* 28, no. 1 (January 2007): 1.

Hill, Linda A. "The Tests of a Leader: Becoming the Boss." *Harvard Business Review* (January 2007): 48.

Hill, Linda A. "The Tests of a Leader: Perspectives Moments of Truth." *Harvard Business Review* (January 2007): 15.

Hitt, Michael A. "Spotlight on Strategic Management." *Business Horizons* 49, no. 5 (September–October 2006): 349.

Hutzchenreuter, Thomas, and Ingo Kleindienst. "Strategy Process Research: What Have We Learned and What Is Still to Be Explored." *Journal of Management* 32, no. 5 (October 2006): 673.

Pangarkar, Nitin, and Jie Wu. "Rising to the Global Challenge: Strategies for Firms in Emerging Markets." *Long Range Planning* 39, no. 3 (June 2006): 295.

Pudelko, Markus. "Some Good Recipes for Globalization—But Quite a Few Ingredients Are Missing." *The Academy of Management Perspectives* 20, no. 2 (May 2006): 78.

Sonenshein, Scott. "The Role of Construction, Institution, and Justification, in Responding to Ethical Issues at Work: The Sensemaking-Institution Model." *The Academy of Management Review* 32, no. 4 (October 2007): 1022.

Walfisz, Martin, Timothy L. Wilson, and Peter Zackariasson. "Real-Time Strategy: Evolutionary Game Development." *Business Horizons* 49, no. 6 (November–December 2006): 487.

COHESION CASE 2008

Walt Disney Company—2007

Dr. Mernoush Banton

Florida International University

www.disney.com

NYSE: DIS

Headquartered in Burbank, California, Walt Disney Company for eighty years has captured the attention of millions of people around the world, offering family entertainment at theme parks, resorts, recreations, movies, TV shows, radio programming, and memorabilia. Under new CEO Bob Iger who replaced Michael Eisner in 2005, Disney's net income soared 38 percent in 2007 to $4.68 billion, while revenues climbed 5.2 percent to $35.5 billion. Disney had two box-office smash hits in 2006: (1) *Cars* and (2) *Pirates of the Caribbean: Dead Man's Chest*. Then in 2007, Disney's *Pirates of the Caribbean Two* movie as well as *Meet the Robinsons* and also *Ratatouille,* a movie from Disney's Pixar division, were hits. CEO Iger is trying, however, to resuscitate the Disneyland theme parks in Paris and Hong Kong. He has put Disney movies and ABC shows on Apple's iPod, which too has greatly benefited Disney. He plans to spend $1.1 billion in 2008–2011 to revitalize the Disney California Adventure in Anaheim, California, which has not been doing well.

History

Mr. Walt Disney and his brother Roy arrived in California in the summer of 1923 to sell his cartoon called *Alice's Wonderland*. A distributor named M. J. Winkler contracted to distribute the *Alice Comedies* on October 16, 1923, and the Disney Brothers Cartoon Studio was founded. Over the years, the company produced many cartoons, from *Oswald the Lucky Rabbit* (1927) to *Silly Symphonies* (1932), *Snow White and the Seven Dwarfs* (1937), and *Pinocchio* and *Fantasia* (1940). The name of the company was changed to Walt Disney Studio in 1925.

Do the same for gap inc.

Mickey Mouse balloons.
Source: Lourens Smak/Alamy Images

Mickey Mouse emerged in 1928 with the first cartoon in sound. In 1950, Disney completed its first live-action film, *Treasure Island,* and in 1954, the company began television with Disneyland anthology series. In 1955, Disney's most successful series, *The Mickey Mouse Club*, began. Also in 1955, the new Disneyland Park in California was opened.

Disney created a series of releases from the 1950s through the 1970s, including *The Shaggy Dog, Zorro, Mary Poppins,* and *The Love Bug*. Mr. Walt Disney died in 1966. In 1969, the Disney studio started its educational films and materials. Another important time of Disney's history was opening the Walt Disney World project in Orlando, Florida in 1971. In 1982, the Epcot Center opened as part of Walt Disney World. In 1983, Tokyo Disneyland opened.

After leaving the network television in 1983, the company created a popular cable network, The Disney Channel. In 1985, Disney's Touchstone division began the successful *Golden Girls* and *Disney Sunday Movie*. In 1988, Disney opened Grand Floridian Beach and Caribbean Beach Resorts at Walt Disney World along with three new gated attractions: the Disney/MGM Studios Theme Park, Pleasure Island, and Typhoon Lagoon. At the same time, filmmaking hit new heights as Disney for the first time led Hollywood studios in box-office gross. Some of the successful films were: *Who Framed Roger Rabbit, Good Morning Vietnam, Three Men and a Baby*, and later, *Honey, I Shrunk the Kids; Dick Tracy; Pretty Woman;* and *Sister Act*. Disney moved into new areas by starting Hollywood Pictures and acquiring the Wrather Corp. (owner of the Disneyland Hotel) and television station KHJ (Los Angeles), which was renamed KCAL. In merchandising, Disney purchased Childcraft and opened numerous highly successful and profitable Disney Stores.

By 1992, Disney's animation began reaching even greater audiences with *The Little Mermaid, The Beauty and the Beast,* and *Aladdin*. Hollywood Records was formed to offer a wide selection of recordings ranging from rap to movie soundtracks. New television shows, such as *Live with Regis and Kathy Lee, Empty Nest, Dinosaurs,* and *Home Improvement*, expanded Disney's television base. For the first time, Disney moved into publishing, forming Hyperion Books, Hyperion Books for Children, and Disney Press, which released books on Disney and non-Disney subjects. In 1991, Disney purchased *Discover* magazine, the leading consumer science monthly. As a totally new venture, Disney was awarded, in 1993, the franchise for a National Hockey League team, the Mighty Ducks of Anaheim.

In 1992, Disneyland Paris opened in France. Disney successfully completed many projects throughout the 1990s by venturing into Broadway shows, opening up 725 Disney Stores, acquiring the California Angels baseball team, opening Disney's Wide World of Sports in Walt Disney World, and acquiring Capital Cities/ABC.

From 2000 to 2007, Disney created new attractions in its theme parks, produced many successful films, opened new hotels, and built Hong Kong Disneyland. For eight decades, Walt Disney Company has successfully established itself as a pioneer in the field of family entertainment.

Internal Issues

Corporate Structure and Mission

As indicated in Exhibit 1-1, Walt Disney Company operates using a strategic business unit (SBU) type organizational structure consisting of four SBUs (1) Disney Consumer Products, (2) Studio Entertainment, (3) Parks and Resorts, and (4) Media Networks and Broadcasting. Note all the well-known large divisions that are part of the Disney umbrella of companies, ranging from ESPN Inc. to Buena Vista Records to ABC Television and more. This is a huge, well-known and well-managed, diversified corporation. Disney is financially strong as indicated in Exhibits 1-2 and 1-3.

Disney does not have a stated vision statement.

The company's mission statement is as follows:

> The mission of Walt Disney Company is to be one of the world's leading producers and providers of entertainment and information. Using our portfolio of brands to differentiate our content, services and consumer products, we seek to develop the most creative, innovative and profitable entertainment experiences and related products in the world.

Financials By Segment

Exhibit 1-4 reveals Disney's revenue and operating income by each business segment. Note that the Disney Media Networks segment brings in the most revenues and operating income. This segment, as well as the Parks & Resorts segment, is growing. However, the company's Studio Entertainment segment and their Consumer Products segment have experienced declining revenues in the last three years. These are problem areas for the company.

EXHIBIT 1-1 **Disney's Corporate Structure**

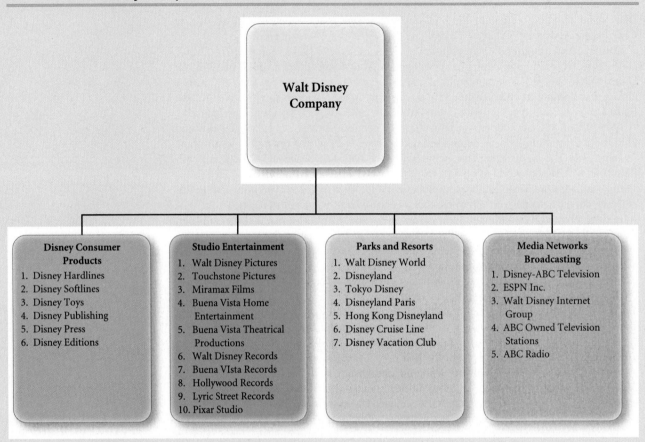

EXHIBIT 1-2 **Consolidated Income Statement**

(In Millions, Except Per Share Data)	2007	2006	2005	2004
Revenues	$ 35,510	$ 34,285	$ 31,944	$ 30,752
Costs and expenses	(28,729)	(28,807)	(27,837)	(26,704)
Gains on sale of equity investment and businesses	1,052	70	26	—
Restructuring and impairment (charges) and other credits, net	—	18	(32)	(64)
Net interest expense	(593)	(592)	(597)	(617)
Equity in the income of investees	485	473	483	372
Income before income taxes, minority interests and the cumulative effect of accounting change	7,725	5,447	3,987	3,739
Income taxes	(2,874)	(1,890)	(1,241)	(1,197)
Minority interests	(177)	(183)	(177)	(197)
Income before the cumulative effect of accounting change	4,674	3,374	2,569	2,345
Cumulative effect of accounting change	13	—	(36)	—
Net income	$ 4,687	$ 3,374	$ 2,533	$ 2,345
Earnings per share before the cumulative effect of accounting change:				
Diluted	$ 2.25	$ 1.64	$ 1.24	$ 1.12
Basic	$ 2.34	$ 1.68	$ 1.27	$ 1.14

(continued)

EXHIBIT 1-2 Consolidated Income Statement—continued

Cumulative effect of accounting change per share	$	—	$	—	$	(0.02)	$	—
Earnings per share:							
Diluted	$	2.25	$	1.64	$	1.22	$	1.12
Basic	$	2.34	$	1.68	$	1.25	$	1.14
Average number of common and common equivalent shares outstanding:							
Diluted		2,092		2,076		2,089		2,106
Basic		2,004		2,005		2,028		2,049

Source: Walt Disney Company—*Form 10K* 2006 and 2007.

EXHIBIT 1-3 Consolidated Balance Sheet

(In Millions, Except Per Share Data)	2007	2006	2005
Assets			
Current assets			
Cash and cash equivalents	$ 3,670	$ 2,411	$ 1,723
Receivables	5,032	4,707	4,585
Inventories	641	694	626
Television costs	559	415	510
Deferred income taxes	862	592	749
Other current assets	550	743	652
Total current assets	11,314	9,562	8,845
Film and television costs	5,123	5,235	5,427
Investments	995	1,315	1,226
Parks, resorts and other property, at cost			
Attractions buildings and equipment	30,260	28,843	27,570
Accumulated depreciation	(15,145)	(13,781)	(12,605)
	15,115	15,062	14,965
Projects in progress	1,147	913	874
Land	1,171	1,192	1,129
Total Fixed Assets	17,433	17,167	16,968
Intangible assets, net	2,494	2,907	2,731
Goodwill	22,085	22,505	16,974
Other assets	1,484	1,307	987
Total Assets	$60,928	$59,998	$53,158
Liabilities and Shareholders' Equity			
Current liabilities			
Accounts payable and other accrued liabilities	$ 5,949	$ 5,917	$ 5,339
Current portion of borrowings	3,280	2,682	2,310
Unearned royalties and other advances	2,162	1,611	1,519
Total current liabilities	11,391	10,210	9,168
Borrowings	11,892	10,843	10,157
Deferred income taxes	2,573	2,651	2,430
Other long-term liabilities	3,024	3,131	3,945
Minority interests	1,295	1,343	1,248
Total Liabilites	30,175	28,178	26,948

(*continued*)

EXHIBIT 1-3 Consolidated Balance Sheet—continued

Shareholders' equity
 Preferred stock $.01 per value
  Authorized—100 million shares, Issued—none
 Common stock, $.01 per value
  Authorized—3.6 billion shares.

Issued—2.6 billion shares at September 29, 2007 and 2.5 billion at October 1, 2006	24,207	22,377	13,288
Retained earnings	24,805	20,630	17,775
Accumulated other comprehensive loss	(157)	(8)	(572)
	48,855	42,999	30,491
Treasury stock, at cost 436.0 million shares at September 30, 2006 and 192.8 million shares at October 1, 2005	(18,102)	(11,179)	(4,281)
Total Shareholders' Equity	30,753	31,820	26,210
Total Liabilities and Shareholders' Equity	$60,928	$59,998	$53,158

Source: Walt Disney Company—*Annual Report* 2006 and 2007.

Exhibit 1-5 provides Disney's revenue and operating income by geographic region. Note that Disney derives 77 percent of its revenue and 76 percent of its operating income from operations in the United States and Canada. The company's revenues and income are both growing in all regions of the world, with Europe being second behind the United States/Canada in both revenues and income.

EXHIBIT 1-4 Revenue and Operating Income by Segment

(In Millions)	2007	2006	2005	2004
Revenue				
Media Networks	$15,046	$14,638	$13,207	$11,778
Parks & Resorts	10,626	9,925	9,023	7,750
Studio Entertainment				
Third parties		7,410	7,499	8,637
Intersegment		119	88	76
	7,491	7,529	7,587	8,713
Consumer Products				
Third parties		2,312	2,215	2,587
Intersegment		(119)	(88)	(76)
	2,347	2,193	2,127	2,511
Total Consolidated Revenues	$35,510	$34,285	$31,944	$30,752
Segment operating income				
Media Networks	$ 4,285	$ 3,610	$ 3,209	$ 2,574
Parks & Resorts	1,710	1,534	1,178	1,077
Studio Entertainment	1,210	729	207	662
Consumer Products	631	618	543	547
Total segment operating income	$ 7,827	$ 6,491	$ 5,137	$ 4,860

Source: Walt Disney Company—*Annual Report* 2006 and 2007.

EXHIBIT 1-5   Revenue and Operating Income by Region

(In Millions)	2007	2006	2005	2004
Revenue				
United States and Canada	$27,286	$26,565	$24,806	$24,012
Europe	5,898	5,266	5,207	4,721
Asia/Pacific	1,732	1,917	1,451	1,547
Latin America and Other	594	537	480	472
	$35,510	$34,285	$31,944	$30,752
Segment operating income				
United States and Canada	$ 6,042	$ 4,938	$ 3,963	$ 3,307
Europe	1,192	918	738	868
Asia/Pacific	437	542	386	582
Latin America and Other	156	93	50	103
	$ 7,827	$ 6,491	$ 5,137	$ 4,860

Source: Walt Disney Company—*Annual Report* 2006 and 2007.

Business Segments

In percentage terms, Disney revenues by segment in 2006 were derived from Media Networks (43 percent), Parks & Resorts (29 percent), Studio Entertainment (22 percent), and Consumer Products (6 percent). Operating income was derived from Media Networks (55 percent), Parks & Resorts (24 percent), Studio Entertainment (11 percent), and Consumer Products (10 percent). The Studio Entertainment segment thus created 22 percent of revenues but only 11 percent of operating income in 2006, somewhat of a problem.

Media Networks/Broadcasting

Disney owns ABC Television Network, which includes ABC Entertainment, ABC Daytime, ABC News, ABC Sports, ABC Kids, Touchstone Television, and ABC Radio. Also included in this segment, Disney owns ESPN, Disney Channel, ABC Family, Toon Disney, SOAPnet, and Buena Vista Television. Disney has equity interest in Lifetime Entertainment Services, A&E Television Networks, E! Entertainment, ESPN, History Channel, The Biography Channel, Hyperion Books, and Disney Mobile.

The increase in revenue in this segment was primarily due to growth from cable and satellite operators, which are generally derived from fees charged on a per-subscriber basis, contractual rate increases, and higher adverting rates at ESPN. The increase in broadcasting revenue was due to growth at the ABC Television Network and increased sales of Touchstone Television series. The growth at the ABC Television Network was primarily due to an increase in prime-time advertising revenues resulting from higher rates and advertising revenues from the Super Bowl. Increase in sales from Touchstone Television series was as a result of higher international syndication and DVD sales of hit dramas such as *Lost, Grey's Anatomy,* and *Desperate Housewives,* as well as higher third-party license fees led by *Scrubs,* which completed its fifth season of network television.

In February 2006, Disney and Citadel Broadcasting Corporation (Citadel) announced an agreement to merge the ABC Radio business, which consists of 22 of Disney's company-owned radio stations and the ABC Radio Network, with Citadel. The ESPN Radio and Radio Disney networks and station businesses are not included in the transaction.

Two major TV networks of Walt Disney Company (ABC and ESPN) recently struck a deal with cable operator Cox Communication whereby these companies now offer hit shows and football games on demand. While advertising in the network is a source of additional revenue for the broadcasters, it requires selectivity for charging for each episode. Video-on-demand is a major industry and growing rapidly, expected to be a 3.9 billion-dollar industry by 2010.

Recently, Disney unveiled Disney Xtreme Digital, a networking site aimed at children less than 14 years of age. This service competes against MySpace (owned by News Corporation). Walt Disney just reported an increase in fiscal 2007 second-quarter net income mostly as a result of strong gains at cable network ESPN and surprise movie hits such as *Wild Hogs*. Major

EXHIBIT 1-6 **Media Network Segment: Revenue and Operating Income**

(In Millions)	2007	2006	2005	2004	CHANGE 2007 vs. 2006	2006 vs. 2005	2005 vs. 2004
Revenue							
Cable Networks	$ 9,167	$ 8,001	$ 7,262	$ 8,001	12%	10%	13%
Broadcasting	5,879	6,637	5,945	6,637	(1)%	12%	11%
Total	$15,046	$14,638	$13,207	$14,638	7%	11%	12%
Segment operating income							
Cable Networks	$ 3,582	$ 3,004	$ 2,745	$ 2,329	19%	9%	18%
Broadcasting	703	606	464	245	48%	31%	89%
Total	$ 4.285	$ 3,610	$ 3,209	$ 2,574	23%	12%	25%

Source: Walt Disney Company, *Annual Report* 2006 and 2007.

investments have been placed in new releases and sequences to be released in the second and third quarter of 2007. The Media Networks division generated the highest profit of any Disney segment during the second quarter of 2007.

In November 2006, Disney sold its 39.5 percent interest in E! Entertainment Television (E!) to Comcast (which owned the remainder of the interests in E!) for $1.2 billion. This resulted in an after-tax income of $0.5 billion, which was recorded in the first quarter of fiscal year 2007. Specific financial information for the Media Networks segment is provided in Exhibit 1-6. Disney's domestic broadcast television stations are listed in Exhibit 1-7 while its international media network operations are listed in Exhibit 1-8. Analysts expect Disney's revenues derived from Internet operations to rise 40 percent in 2007 and another 30 percent in 2008 (*Standard & Poor's Stock Report*—April 28, 2007).

Parks and Resorts

Disney owns and operates Walt Disney World Resort and Cruise Lines in Florida, Disneyland Resort in California, ESPN Zone facilities in many states, 17 hotels at the Walt Disney World Resort, Disney's Fort Wilderness Camping and Recreation, Downtown Disney, Disney's Wide World of Sports, Disney Cruise Line, 7 Disney Vacation Club Resorts, Adventures by Disney, and 5 resort locations with 11 theme parks on 3 continents. With theme parks, Disney has 51 percent ownership in Disneyland Resort Paris, 43 percent ownership in Hong Kong Disneyland,

EXHIBIT 1-7 **Disney's Domestic Broadcast Television Stations (2007)**

MARKET	TV STATION	ANALOG CHANNEL	TELEVISION MARKET RANKING
New York, NY	WABC-TV	7	1
Los Angeles, CA	KABC-TV	7	2
Chicago, IL	WLS-TV	7	3
Philadelphia, PA	WPVI-TV	6	4
San Francisco, CA	KGO-TV	7	5
Houston, TX	KTRK-TV	13	10
Raleigh-Durham, NC	WTVD-TV	11	29
Fresno, CA	KFSN-TV	30	55
Flint, MI	WJRT-TV	12	66
Toledo, OH	WTVG-TV	13	71

Source: Walt Disney Company, *Form 10K* (2007).

EXHIBIT 1-8 **Disney's International Cable Satellite Networks and Broadcast Operations**

PROPERTY	ESTIMATED SUBSCRIBERS (In Millions)	OWNERSHIP %
ESPN(1)	92	80.0
ESPN2(1)	91	80.0
ESPN Classic(1)	62	80.0
ESPNEWS(1)	51	80.0
Disney Channel(1)	89	100.0
International Disney Channels(2)	54	100.0
Toon Disney(1)	57	100.0
Lifetime Television(1)	92	50.0
A&E(1)	92	37.5
ABC Family(1)	91	100.0
The History Channel(1)	91	37.5
E! Entertainment Television(1)	89	39.6
A&E International(2)	75	37.5
Lifetime Movie Network(1)	51	50.0
Lifetime Real Women(2)	16	50.0
Jetix Europe(2)	46	73.7
Jetix Latin America(2)	15	100.0
SOAPnet(1)	53	100.0
Style(1)	44	39.6
The Biography Channel(1)	39	37.5
History International(1)	39	37.5

(1) Estimated U.S. subscriber counts according to Nielsen Media Research as of September 30, 2006.

(2) Not rated by Nielsen. Subscriber count represents number of subscribers receiving the service based on internal management reports.

Source: Walt Disney Company, *Form 10K* (2006).

100 percent ownership in Tokyo Disney Resort as well as Disneyland in both California and Florida. Exhibit 1-9 summarizes Disney's parks and resort holdings.

Disney revenues at its Parks and Resorts division increased 10 percent in 2006 to $9.9 billion due to increases of $647 million and $255 million at its domestic and international resorts, respectively. Higher guest spending was due to a higher average daily hotel room rate, higher average ticket prices, and greater merchandise spending at both resorts.

Disney's 50th anniversary celebration at its parks and resorts increased attendance and hotel occupancy. International revenue growth reflected the first full year of theme park operations at Hong Kong Disneyland Resort as compared to the prior year when the park opened in mid-September 2005. Disneyland Resort Paris also experienced increased revenues. Some of the increase in revenue was offset by the unfavorable impact of foreign currency translation as a result of the strengthening of the U.S. dollar against the Euro. Operating income from the Parks and Resorts segment increased 30 percent, or $356 million, to $1.5 billion. Exhibit 1-10 presents Disney's attendance, per capita theme park guest spending, and hotel statistics for its domestic

EXHIBIT 1-9   **Disney's Offerings under Parks and Resorts**

WALT DISNEY WORLD RESORTS	DISNEYLAND RESORT	DISNEYLAND RESORT PARIS	HONG KONG DISNEYLAND RESORT	TOKYO DISNEY RESORT	DISNEY CRUISE LINE	ESPN ZONE	WALT DISNEY IMAGINEERING
Epcot	Disneyland	Disneyland Park	Hong Kong Disneyland	Tokyo Disneyland			
Disney-MGM Studios	Disneyland's California Adventure	Walt Disney Studios Park	Resort Facilities	Tokyo DisneySea			
Magic Kingdom	Resort Facilities						
Disney's Animal Kingdom							
Resort Facilities							

Source: Walt Disney Company, *Form 10K* (2006).

EXHIBIT 1-10   **Disney Parks and Resorts Data (2006 versus 2005)**

	EAST COAST RESORTS		WEST COST RESORTS		TOTAL DOMESTIC RESORTS	
	FY 2006	FY 2005	FY 2006	FY 2005	FY 2006	FY 2005
Increase in attendance	5%	5%	6%	4%	5%	5%
Increase in per capital guest spending	1%	2%	8%	14%	3%	5%
Occupancy	86%	83%	93%	90%	87%	83%
Available room nights (in thousands)	8,834	8,777	810	810	9,644	9,587
Per room guest spending	$211	$199	$287	$272	$218	$206

Source: Walt Disney Company—*Annual Report* (2006).

properties. Exhibit 1-11 provides 2006 attendance figures for Disney theme parks. These parks accounted for almost 30 percent of Disney's 2006 revenues, and reported a 30 percent increase in operating income.

The company also has been hosting VIP tours (additional fees apply), offering added-value services such as number of attractions being covered along with personal guided tours, preferred seating, and front-of-line access to rides. The company also offers package deals for major corporations and schools.

Disney has plans to change its concept of the theme parks from the masses to a more concentrated perspective. This strategy would allow Disney to offer more stand-alone theme parks and resorts in cities and beaches, as well as Disney-branded retail and dining districts, and smaller and more sophisticated parks. Disney is also planning to build time-share vacation homes in places like the Caribbean. Two of the challenges with this strategy would be (1) tailoring the niche attractions to the local markets while keeping the Disney brand reputation, and (2) avoiding cannibalization of existing parks and attractions.

Studio Entertainment

Disney produces live-action and animated motion pictures, direct-to-video programming, musical recordings, and live-stage plays. Disney motion pictures are distributed under the names Walt Disney Pictures and Television, Touchstone Pictures, Hollywood Pictures, Miramax Films, and Buena Vista Home Entertainment International that includes Walt Disney Records, Buena Vista Records, Hollywood Records, Lyric Street Records, and Disney Music Publishing. In May 2006, Disney acquired Pixar, a computer animation leader. As of September 2006,

EXHIBIT 1-11 **Disney Theme Park Attendance in 2006 (In Millions)**

PARK	ATTENDANCE (IN MILLIONS)
Magic Kingdom (Florida)	16.64
Disneyland (California)	14.73
Tokyo Disneyland	12.90
Tokyo Disney Sea	12.10
Disneyland Paris	10.60
Epcot (Florida)	10.46
Disney-MGM Studios (Florida)	9.10
Animal Kingdom (Florida)	8.91
California Adventure	5.95
Hong Kong Disneyland	5.20
Walt Disney Studios Paris	2.20

Source: Adapted from Merissa Marr, "Disney's $1 Billion Adventure," *Wall Street Journal* (October 17, 2007): p. B1 and B4.

Disney had released 894 full-length movies, 77 full-length animated features, and 542 cartoon shorts. Product offerings include Pay-per-View, Pay Television, Free Television, Pay Television 2, and International Television.

Disney revenues from its Studio Entertainment segment decreased 1 percent, or $58 million, to $7.5 billion primarily due to lower worldwide home entertainment. The increase in worldwide theatrical motion picture distribution revenues was primarily due to the strong box-office performance of selected movies. Operating income from this segment increased $522 million to $729 million.

In August 2005, Disney entered into a film financing arrangement with a group of investors who funded $500 million or about 40 percent of the production and marketing costs of a slate of up to thirty-two live-action films, excluding certain titles such as *The Chronicles of Narnia: The Lion, The Witch and The Wardrobe* and, in general, sequels to previous films, in return for approximately 40 percent of the future net cash flows generated by these films. By entering into minority-owned business transactions, Disney is reducing the risks as well as rewards from the performance of live-action firm production and distribution.

Consumer Products

Disney's Consumer Products segment includes partners with licenses, manufacturers, publishers, and retailers worldwide who design, promote, and sell a wide variety of products based on new and existing Disney characters. The product offerings are: Character Merchandise and Publications Licensing, Books and Magazines, Buena Vista Games, DisneyShopping.com, and The Disney Store. Products include books, interactive games, food and beverages, fine art, apparel, toys, and even home décor.

Disney's 2006 revenues from this segment increased 3 percent to $2.2 billion. Sales growth at Buena Vista Games was due to the release of self-published titles based on *The Chronicles of Narnia: The Lion, The Witch and The Wardrobe, Chicken Little,* and *Pirates of the Caribbean.* Sales growth at Merchandise Licensing was driven by higher earned royalties across multiple product categories, led by the strong performance of *Cars, Disney Princess*, and *Pirates of the Caribbean* merchandise.

Operating income of this segment increased 14 percent to $618 million, mostly due to growth at Merchandise Licensing. The decrease at Buena Vista Games was driven by increased product development spending on future self-published titles. In 2006, Disney sold 365 of its stores to the Children's Place under a franchising agreement.

Competition

For an organization as large and diversified as Walt Disney Company, competitors differ in each segment of business. Time Warner is a major competitor to Disney and is composed of five divisions: AOL, Cable, Filmed Entertainment, Networks, and Publishing. Time Warner

EXHIBIT 1-12 **Disney versus the Industry — Comparative Data**

DIRECT COMPETITOR COMPARISON

	DIS	TWX	INDUSTRY
Market Cap	$ 71.40B	81.43B	2.24B
Employees	133,000	92,700	1.69K
Quarterly Rev Growth	0.60%	9.20%	7.30%
Revenue	$ 35.20B	45.17B	946.15M
Gross Margin	19.33%	42.45%	34.61%
EBITDA	$ 8.74B	12.08B	135.44M
Operating Margins	18.12%	17.95%	16.55%
Net Income	$ 4.54B	5.12B	9.58M
EPS	$ 2.123	1.549	0.08
P/E	$ 16.97	13.89	19.35
PEG (5 yr expected)	1.37	1.54	1.54
P/S	2.02	1.79	2.37

DIS = Walt Disney Company

TWX = Time Warner Inc.

Industry = Entertainment - Diversified

Source: Adapted from finance.yahoo.com (May, 2007).

owns Time Inc., AOL, Warner Brothers, and TBS Networks. Walt Disney generally is classified as Entertainment-Diversified, which directly competes with Time Warner, Inc. (as shown in Exhibit 1-12). Note that Disney's EPS and P/E ratios are below the industry average but above Time Warner Inc.

CBS Corporation and News Corporation directly compete with the Walt Disney Company in the Media Network segment, but are not rivals in the Consumer Products and Parks and Resorts segments. CBS Corporation was a part of Viacom, Inc. but now operates independently under CBS Corp. News Corporation is a diversified international media and entertainment company that operates in eight segments: Filmed Entertainment, Television, Cable Network Programming, Direct Broadcast Satellite Television, Magazines and Inserts, Newspapers, Book Publishing, and Other. Due to recent corporate restructuring for both CBS Corporation and News Corp., there are no industry data available for comparison purposes. Competition for each segment of Walt Disney is discussed below.

Competition — Media Networks/Broadcasting

Global media is a $1 trillion industry that includes advertising, cable firms, newspapers, radio, and television. This industry is dominated by conglomerates Walt Disney, Time Warner Inc., New York Times, News Corp., and CBS Corporation. Typically, these companies prosper during election years due to heavy advertising revenue invested by the politicians. Special events such as the Olympics also generates additional advertising revenue for such companies.

Walt Disney competes for viewers primarily with other television networks, independent television stations, and other video media such as cable and satellite television programming services, DVD, video games, and the Internet. Radio networks compete with other radio network stations and programming services. Advertising dollars, a major source of income for Walt Disney, also competes with other advertising media such as newspapers, magazines, billboards, and the Internet. According to Research Alert (25 [7]: 3, April 06, 2007), an overwhelming majority of consumers (92.5 percent) regularly or occasionally research products online before buying them in person. Men (43.7 percent) are significantly more likely than women (26.7 percent) to regularly research products online before buying. As a trend, younger consumers are more likely than older consumers to research products online; 25–34-year-olds (95 percent) are more likely than all other age groups to do so.

41

EXHIBIT 1-13 **Disney Rival Firms in Media Networks/Broadcasting — Percent**

INDICATES ATTRACTIVENESS OF THAT OUTLET TO CONSUMERS AGE 18–24

Discovery Networks	72%
Disney/ESPN Media Networks	68%
MTV Networks	52%
Turner Entertainment Networks	48%
Scripps Networks	43%
NBC Universal Cable	39%
Comcast Cable Networks	34%
Fox Cable Networks	31%

Source: Adapted from *Multichannel News*, 28 (10): 30, March 05, 2007.

Consumers 18–24 are more likely than other age groups to share information about products they've searched for online using a variety of media, such as text messaging and instant messaging. Men, more likely than women, use new technologies such as blogs and online communities to share their opinions. Exhibits 1-12 and 1-13 reveal some major competitors to Disney in this segment of business, as well as percentages that indicate attractiveness of that venue to consumers age 18–24.

CBS Corporation is comprised of the following segments: Television, Radio, Outdoor, and Publishing. CBS Television is comprised of CBS Network and its own television stations, television production and syndication, Showtime, and CSTV Networks. In 2006, the CBS Television segment of this corporation contributed 66 percent of total revenue (approximately $9.4 billion). The Radio segment of CBS Corp. owns radio stations in most of the large U.S. markets and the revenue primarily is generated from advertising sales. In 2006, the Radio segment of CBS Corp. generated 14 percent of the company's total revenue (approximately $2.0 billion).

News Corp., with $25.3 billion in revenue, operates in eight industry segments: Filmed Entertainment, Television, Cable Network Programming, Direct Broadcast Satellite Television, Magazines and Inserts, Newspapers, Book Publishing, and Other. For the fiscal year of 2006, the Filmed Entertainment, Television, Cable Network Programming, and Direct Broadcast Satellite Television contributed 68.8 percent or $17.4 billion to the company's total revenue. The company has been moving aggressively toward digital technologies such as broadband, mobility, storage, and wireless. In 2005, News Corp. acquired MySpace.com, the Internet's most popular social networking site, and IGN.com (a gaming and entertainment site). The company has reported an increase in traffic at most of their preexisting sites such as newspaper, cable networks, and local TV stations.

In June 2007, Fox TV, owned by News Corp., had the most popular shows on television with an average audience of 6.7 million every night, followed by CBS with 7.6 million viewers during each prime time, Walt Disney Company's ABC with 5.4 million viewers per night, and finally NBC (owned by General Electric Company) with 4.8 million viewers during each prime-time period.

Disney also has to compete with satellite providers such as DirecTV in the media network and broadcasting segment. It has been reported that DirecTV has had steady sales growth for the past four quarters from 8 percent to 16 percent with earnings growth jumping from 222 percent to 667 percent over the same period.

Time Warner's media and entertainment segments own AOL, Cable, Filmed Entertainment, Networks, and Publishing. The Cable segment services primarily analog and digital video services, and advanced services such as VOD and HDTV with set-top boxed equipped with digital video recorders. To improve this segment of their business, Time Warner just acquired Adelphia for $8.9 billion in cash. Its Film Entertainment segment produces and distributes theatrical motion pictures and television shows. The Network segment consists of HBO and Cinemax pay television programming services. The Publishing segment publishes magazines and Web sites in a variety of areas and has a strategic alliance with Google, Inc. Exhibit 1-14 provides Time Warner's revenue by segment.

EXHIBIT 1-14 **Time Warner Inc. Revenue (In Millions) by Segment (2006)**

SEGMENT	REVENUE
Cable	11,767
AOL	7,866
Filmed Entertainment	10,625
Networks	10,273
Publishing	5,278

Source: Time Warner Inc., *Form 10K* (2006).

Competition — Parks and Resorts

Disney's theme parks and resorts compete with all other forms of entertainment, lodging, tourism, and recreational activities. Many uncontrollable factors impact this Disney segment, including business cycle and exchange rate fluctuations, travel industry trends, amount of available leisure time, oil and transportation prices, and weather patterns. Seasonality is another concern for this segment as all of the theme parks and the associated resort facilities are operated on a year-round basis. Historically, the theme parks and resort business experiences fluctuations in theme park attendance and resort occupancy resulting from the seasonal nature of vacation travel and local entertainment excursions. Peak attendance and resort occupancy generally occur during the summer months when school vacations take place and during early-winter and spring-holiday periods. Disney's three largest theme parks, Magic Kingdom in Orlando, Tokyo Disneyland, and Disneyland Paris, had in 2005 16.2, 13.0, and 10.2 million visitors.

According to a survey conducted by the International Association of Amusement Parks and Attractions, in 2005, 335 million people visited over 600 amusement parks in the United States, generating $11.2 billion in revenue. The attendance in amusement parks has continued to increase and is projected to continue in a steady growth. In 2004, 28 percent of Americans claimed they had visited an amusement park and one half had plans to do so in 2006.

The second largest amusement park after Disney is Six Flags, Inc., based in Oklahoma City, Oklahoma, with 32 parks, with more than $1 billion in revenue (2005). Due to demographic changes and increase in aging population, Viacom Inc. has started opening adult playgrounds offering virtual reality games.

Hong Kong's oldest amusement park, Ocean Park, has been doing much better than Disney's Hong Kong Disneyland. *USA Today* (June 15, 2007, p. 9A) reported that Hong Kong Disneyland has been struggling and based on the company's report to the Securities and Exchange Commission (SEC), the company might have to persuade lenders to refinance the debt. Ocean Park has been having the advantage of understanding the local market since they have been around for more than 30 years. It also seems that Hong Kong residents are not very impressed with the small version of Disneyland built there since many have visited Disneyland in Tokyo or Anaheim, California. Comprising over 215 acres, Ocean Park's annual attendance in 2004, 2005, and 2006 has been 3.7 million, 4.0 million, and 4.4 million with profits growing also to an annual high of $20.1 million in 2006. At 310 acres, Hong Kong Disneyland is the smallest Disney theme park.

Competition — Studio Entertainment

The success of Studio Entertainment operations fluctuate due to the timing and performance of releases in the theatrical, home entertainment, and television markets. Release dates are determined by several factors, including competition and the timing of vacation and holiday periods. This segment of Disney competes with all forms of entertainment. A significant number of companies produce and/or distribute theatrical and television films, exploit products in the home entertainment market, provide pay television programming services, and sponsor live theater. The company also competes to obtain creative and performing talents, story properties, advertiser support, broadcast rights, and market share.

For years, movies have been a reasonably priced entertainment for many individuals, couples, and families. A geographic breakdown of movie revenues are United States (49.8 percent), Europe (33 percent), and Asia and developed countries (14 percent). A few companies dominate the industry and control the production and distribution of most movies. Some key competitors in this segment along with their 2007 forecast (% of industry revenue) are: Warner Brothers (17.10 percent), Walt Disney (11.70 percent), Twentieth Century Fox (10.3 percent), Viacom (6.3 percent), and other (54.6 percent).

Competition — Consumer Products

The leading competitors to Disney in this segment are Warner Brothers, Fox, Sony, Marvel, and Nickelodeon. Disney competes in its character merchandising and other licensing, publishing, interactive, and retail activities with other licensors, publishers, and retailers of character, brand, and celebrity names. Disney is perhaps the largest worldwide licensor of character-based merchandise and producer/distributor of children's film-related products based on retail sales. Operating results for the licensing and retail distribution business are influenced by seasonal consumer purchasing behavior and by the timing and performance of animated theatrical releases.

Conclusion

As a content-oriented company, Walt Disney's strategy for many years has been to match creativity and innovation with international expansion and leveraging of new technologies. Disney continuously has to adapt to demographic changes in order to deliver products and services that match changing consumer preferences across countries. Although Disney under CEO Iger has had positive growth in both revenue and earnings, there are still strong competitors and substantial risks in the entertainment industry. Competitors are consolidating and spending aggressively to promote new hit movies and TV shows.

It is difficult to manage a firm as diversified as Disney. CEO Iger has delegated accountability and responsibility much more so, however, than former CEO Eisner and this is good for the company. The Internet, however, is a threat to Disney as consumers of all ages use the Internet more and more for entertainment. Consumer preferences are shifting to more on-demand movies and shows. There is a growing risk of copyright infringements and unauthorized sharing of movies, DVDs, and other digital products. Companies such as Walt Disney spend millions of dollars to protect their intellectual property worldwide in order to maintain their competitive edge.

Increases in unemployment, interest rates, and fuel costs limit consumers' disposable income for entertainment expenses. These threats vary across continents and countries where Disney operates and oftentimes force consumers to other low-cost entertainment activities. Disney is performing well, but analysts are concerned about its level of goodwill, long-term debt, and its weak performance in the Studio Entertainment segment.

Prepare a three-year strategic plan with supporting analyses and recommendations for CEO Iger to present to his board of directors.

References

Datamonitor Industry Market Research

finance.yahoo.com

Investor's Business Daily

Multichannel News — www.multichannel.com

News Corporation — www.newscorp.com

Wall Street Journal — www.wsj.com

The Walt Disney Company — www.disney.com

TheStreet.com — www.thestreet.com

Time Warner Company — www.timewarner.com

Standard & Poor's — www.standardandpoors.com

USAtoday.com — www.usatoday.com

• EXPERIENTIAL EXERCISES

Experiential Exercise 1A

Getting Familiar with Strategy Terms

Purpose

The purpose of this exercise is to get you familiar with strategy terms introduced and defined in Chapter 1. Let's apply these terms to Walt Disney Company (stock symbol = DIS).

Instructions

Step 1   Go to http://www.disney.go.com/home/html/index.html, which is Walt Disney Company's Web site. Click on Corporate Info, then click on Investor Relations, and then click on *Form 10K*. Print a copy of the 2007 *Form 10K*. (Note: The *Form 10K* may be 100 pages so you may want to print this in your college library, but this Disney document will be used throughout this course. The *Form 10K* contains excellent information for developing a list of internal strengths and weaknesses of DIS. The 2007 *Form 10K* was not available when the case was written so it can also be used to update the case.

Step 2   Go to your college library and make a copy of Standard & Poor's Industry Surveys for two industries: (1) Broadcasting and Cable Industry and (2) Movies and Home Entertainment. These two documents will contain excellent information for developing a list of external opportunities and threats facing DIS.

Step 3   Using the Walt Disney Company Cohesion Case, the 2007 *Form 10K*, and the Industry Survey documents, on a separate sheet of paper list what you consider to be DIS's three major strengths, three major weaknesses, three major opportunities, and three major threats. Each factor listed for this exercise must include a %, #, $, or ratio to reveal some quantified fact or trend. These factors provide the underlying basis for a strategic plan because a firm strives to take advantage of strengths, improve weaknesses, avoid threats, and capitalize on opportunities.

Step 4   Through class discussion, compare your lists of external and internal factors to those developed by other students and add to your lists of factors. Keep this information for use in later exercises at the end of other chapters.

Experiential Exercise 1B

Evaluating Codes of Business Ethics

Purpose

This exercise aims to familiarize you with corporate codes of business ethics. Called Standards of Business Conduct both in the Walt Disney Company and its leading competitor, News Corporation, the business ethics statements for these two firms are provided at http://corporate.disney.go.com/corporate/conduct_standards3.html and www.newscorp.com/corp_gov/sobc.html, respectively. Headquartered in Washington, DC, News Corporation is a $27 billion global media giant that owns Fox Studios, 20th Century Fox, HarperCollins book publishing company, DirecTV, and many other segments that compete with Walt Disney. Both firms strive to operate in an ethical manner.

Instructions

Step 1   Go to the two Web sites listed above and print the Standards of Business Conduct for (1) Walt Disney Company and (2) News Corporation. Read the two statements.

Step 2   On a separate sheet of paper, list three aspects that you like most and three aspects that you like least about (1) the Walt Disney statement and (2) the News Corporation statement. In other words, compare the two Standards of Business Conduct statements. Conclude by indicating which statement of conduct you like best. Why do you think it is best?

Step 3   Explain why having a code of business ethics is not sufficient for ensuring ethical behavior in an organization. What other means are necessary to help ensure ethical behavior? Give the class an example of a breach of ethical conduct that you recall in your work experience.

Experiential Exercise 1C

The Ethics of Spying on Competitors

Purpose

This exercise gives you an opportunity to discuss in class ethical and legal issues related to methods being used by many companies to spy on competing firms. Gathering and using information about competitors is an area of strategic management that Japanese firms do more proficiently than American firms.

Instructions

On a separate sheet of paper, number from 1 to 18. For the eighteen spying activities listed as follows, indicate whether or not you believe the activity is ethical or unethical and legal or illegal. Place either an *E* for ethical or *U* for unethical, and either an *L* for legal or an *I* for illegal for each activity. Compare your answers to those of your classmates and discuss any differences.

1. Buying competitors' garbage
2. Dissecting competitors' products
3. Taking competitors' plant tours anonymously
4. Counting tractor-trailer trucks leaving competitors' loading bays
5. Studying aerial photographs of competitors' facilities
6. Analyzing competitors' labor contracts
7. Analyzing competitors' help-wanted ads
8. Quizzing customers and buyers about the sales of competitors' products
9. Infiltrating customers' and competitors' business operations
10. Quizzing suppliers about competitors' level of manufacturing
11. Using customers to buy out phony bids
12. Encouraging key customers to reveal competitive information
13. Quizzing competitors' former employees
14. Interviewing consultants who may have worked with competitors
15. Hiring key managers away from competitors
16. Conducting phony job interviews to get competitors' employees to reveal information
17. Sending engineers to trade meetings to quiz competitors' technical employees
18. Quizzing potential employees who worked for or with competitors

Experiential Exercise 1D

Strategic Planning for My University

Purpose

External and internal factors are the underlying bases of strategies formulated and implemented by organizations. Your college or university faces numerous external opportunities/threats and has many internal strengths/weaknesses. The purpose of this exercise is to illustrate the process of identifying critical external and internal factors.

External influences include trends in the following areas: economic, social, cultural, demographic, environmental, technological, political, legal, governmental, and competitive. External factors could include declining numbers of high school graduates; population shifts; community relations; increased competitiveness among colleges and universities; rising numbers of adults returning to college; decreased support from local, state, and federal agencies; increasing numbers of foreign students attending U.S. colleges; and a rising number of Internet courses.

Internal factors of a college or university include faculty, students, staff, alumni, athletic programs, physical plant, grounds and maintenance, student housing, administration, fund-raising, academic programs, food services, parking, placement, clubs, fraternities, sororities, and public relations.

Instructions

Step 1   On a separate sheet of paper, write four headings: External Opportunities, External Threats, Internal Strengths, and Internal Weaknesses.

Step 2   As related to your college or university, list five factors under each of the four headings.

Step 3   Discuss the factors as a class. Write the factors on the board.

Step 4   What new things did you learn about your university from the class discussion? How could this type of discussion benefit an organization?

Experiential Exercise 1E

Strategic Planning at a Local Company

Purpose

This activity is aimed at giving you practical knowledge about how organizations in your city or town are doing strategic planning. This exercise also will give you experience interacting on a professional basis with local business leaders.

Instructions

Step 1   Use the telephone to contact business owners or top managers. Find an organization that does strategic planning. Make an appointment to visit with the strategist (president, chief executive officer, or owner) of that business.

Step 2   Seek answers to the following questions during the interview:
- How does your firm formally conduct strategic planning? Who is involved in the process?
- Does your firm have a written mission statement? How was the statement developed? When was the statement last changed?
- What are the benefits of engaging in strategic planning?
- What are the major costs or problems in doing strategic planning in your business?
- Do you anticipate making any changes in the strategic planning process at your company? If yes, please explain.

Step 3   Report your findings to the class.

Experiential Exercise 1F

Does My University Recruit in Foreign Countries?

Purpose

A competitive climate is emerging among colleges and universities around the world. Colleges and universities in Europe and Japan are increasingly recruiting U.S. students to offset declining enrollments. Foreign students already make up more than one-third of the student body at many U.S. universities. The purpose of this exercise is to identify particular colleges and universities in foreign countries that represent a competitive threat to U.S. institutions of higher learning.

Instructions

Step 1   Select a foreign country. Conduct research to determine the number and nature of colleges and universities in that country. What are the major educational institutions in that country? What programs are those institutions recognized for offering? What percentage of undergraduate and graduate students attending those institutions are U.S. citizens? Do these institutions actively recruit U.S. students?

Step 2   Prepare a report for the class that summarizes your research findings. Present your report to the class.

47

Experiential Exercise 1G

Getting Familiar with SMCO

Purpose

This exercise is designed to get you familiar with the Strategic Management Club Online (SMCO), which offers many benefits for the strategy student. The SMCO site also offers templates for doing case analyses in this course.

Instructions

Step 1 Go to the www.strategyclub.com Web site. Review the various sections of this site.

Step 2 Select a section of the SMCO site that you feel will be most useful to you in this class. Write a one-page summary of that section and describe why you feel it will benefit you most.

Part 2 • Strategy Formulation

2 | The Business Vision and Mission

University Case Competition Gala: *Source:* Bruce Williams

chapter objectives

After studying this chapter, you should be able to do the following:

1. Describe the nature and role of vision and mission statements in strategic management.

2. Discuss why the process of developing a mission statement is as important as the resulting document.

3. Identify the components of mission statements.

4. Discuss how clear vision and mission statements can benefit other strategic-management activities.

5. Evaluate mission statements of different organizations.

6. Write good vision and mission statements.

This chapter focuses on the concepts and tools needed to evaluate and write business vision and mission statements. A practical framework for developing mission statements is provided. Actual mission statements from large and small organizations and for-profit and nonprofit enterprises are presented and critically examined. The process of creating a vision and mission statement is discussed.

We can perhaps best understand vision and mission by focusing on a business when it is first started. In the beginning, a new business is simply a collection of ideas. Starting a new business rests on a set of beliefs that the new organization can offer some product or service to some customers, in some geographic area, using some type of technology, at a profitable price. A new business owner typically believes that the management philosophy of the new enterprise will result in a favorable public image and that this concept of the business can be communicated to, and will be adopted by, important constituencies. When the set of beliefs about a business at its inception is put into writing, the resulting document mirrors the same basic ideas that underlie the vision and mission statements. As a business grows, owners or managers find it necessary to revise the founding set of beliefs, but those original ideas usually are reflected in the revised statements of vision and mission.

Vision and mission statements often can be found in the front of annual reports. They often are displayed throughout a firm's premises and are distributed with company information sent to constituencies. The statements are part of numerous internal reports, such as loan requests, supplier agreements, labor relations contracts, business plans, and customer service agreements. In a recent study, researchers concluded that 90 percent of all companies have used a mission statement sometime in the previous five years.[1]

VISIT THE NET

Gives an introduction to the vision concept. (www.csuchico.edu/mgmt/ strategy/module1/sld007.htm)

What Do We Want to Become?

It is especially important for managers and executives in any organization to agree upon the basic vision that the firm strives to achieve in the long term. A vision statement should answer the basic question, "What do we want to become?" A clear vision provides the foundation for developing a comprehensive mission statement. Many organizations have both a vision and mission statement, but the vision statement should be established first and foremost. The vision statement should be short, preferably one sentence, and as many managers as possible should have input into developing the statement.

Several example vision statements are provided in Table 2-1.

TABLE 2-1   Vision Statement Examples

Tyson Foods' vision is to be the world's first choice for protein solutions while maximizing shareholder value. *(Author comment: Good statement, unless Tyson provides nonprotein products)*

General Motors' vision is to be the world leader in transportation products and related services. *(Author comment: Good statement)*

PepsiCo's responsibility is to continually improve all aspects of the world in which we operate—environment, social, economic— creating a better tomorrow than today. *(Author comment: Statement is too vague; it should reveal beverage and food business)*

Dell's vision is to create a company culture where environmental excellence is second nature. *(Author comment: Statement is too vague; it should reveal computer business in some manner; the word environmental is generally used to refer to natural environment so is unclear in its use here)*

The vision of First Reliance Bank is to be recognized as the largest and most profitable bank in South Carolina. *(Author comment: This is a very small, new bank headquartered in Florence, South Carolina, so this goal is not achievable in five years; the statement is too futuristic)*

Samsonite's vision is to provide innovative solutions for the traveling world. *(Author comment: Statement needs to be more specific, perhaps mention luggage; statement as is could refer to air carriers or cruise lines, which is not good)*

Royal Caribbean's vision is to empower and enable our employees to deliver the best vacation experience for our guests, thereby generating superior returns for our shareholders and enhancing the well-being of our communities. *(Author comment: Statement is good, but could end after the word "guests")*

Procter & Gamble's vision is to be, and be recognized as, the best consumer products company in the world. *(Author comment: Statement is too vague and readability is not that good)*

What Is Our Business?

Current thought on mission statements is based largely on guidelines set forth in the mid-1970s by Peter Drucker, who is often called "the father of modern management" for his pioneering studies at General Motors Corporation and for his 22 books and hundreds of articles. Drucker has been called "the preeminent management thinker of our time."

Drucker says that asking the question "What is our business?" is synonymous with asking the question "What is our mission?" An enduring statement of purpose that distinguishes one organization from other similar enterprises, the *mission statement* is a declaration of an organization's "reason for being." It answers the pivotal question "What is our business?" A clear mission statement is essential for effectively establishing objectives and formulating strategies.

Sometimes called a *creed statement,* a statement of purpose, a statement of philosophy, a statement of beliefs, a statement of business principles, or a statement "defining our business," a mission statement reveals what an organization wants to be and whom it wants to serve. All organizations have a reason for being, even if strategists have not consciously transformed this reason into writing. As illustrated in Figure 2-1, carefully prepared statements of vision and mission are widely recognized by both practitioners and academicians as the first step in strategic management.

Some example mission statements are provided in Table 2-2.

VISIT THE NET

Gives an introduction to the mission concept. (www.csuchico.edu/mgmt/strategy/module1/sld008.htm)

TABLE 2-2   Example Mission Statements

Fleetwood Enterprises will lead the recreational vehicle and manufactured housing industries (2, 7) in providing quality products, with a passion for customer-driven innovation (1). We will emphasize training, embrace diversity and provide growth opportunities for our associates and our dealers (9). We will lead our industries in the application of appropriate technologies (4). We will operate at the highest levels of ethics and compliance with a focus on exemplary corporate governance (6). We will deliver value to our shareholders, positive operating results and industry-leading earnings (5). *(Author comment: Statement lacks two components: Markets and Concern for Public Image)*

We aspire to make PepsiCo the world's (3) premier consumer products company, focused on convenient foods and beverages (2). We seek to produce healthy financial rewards for investors (5) as we provide opportunities for growth and enrichment to our employees (9), our business partners and the communities (8) in which we operate. And in everything we do, we strive to act with honesty, openness, fairness and integrity (6). *(Author comment: Statement lacks three components: Customers, Technology, and Self-Concept)*

We are loyal to Royal Caribbean and Celebrity and strive for continuous improvement in everything we do. We always provide service with a friendly greeting and a smile (7). We anticipate the needs of our customers and make all efforts to exceed our customers' expectations (1). We take ownership of any problem that is brought to our attention. We engage in conduct that enhances our corporate reputation and employee morale (9). We are committed to act in the highest ethical manner and respect the rights and dignity of others (6). *(Author comment: Statement lacks five components: Products/Services, Markets, Technology, Concern for Survival/Growth/Profits, Concern for Public Image)*

Dell's mission is to be the most successful computer company (2) in the world (3) at delivering the best customer experience in markets we serve (1). In doing so, Dell will meet customer expectations of highest quality; leading technology (4); competitive pricing; individual and company accountability (6); best-in-class service and support (7); flexible customization capability (7); superior corporate citizenship (8); financial stability (5). *(Author comment: Statement lacks only one component: Concern for Employees)*

Procter & Gamble will provide branded products and services of superior quality and value (7) that improve the lives of the world's (3) consumers. As a result, consumers (1) will reward us with industry leadership in sales, profit (5), and value creation, allowing our people (9), our shareholders, and the communities (8) in which we live and work to prosper. *(Author comment: Statement lacks three components: Products/Services, Technology, and Philosophy)*

At L'Oreal, we believe that lasting business success is built upon ethical (6) standards which guide growth and on a genuine sense of responsibility to our employees (9), our consumers, our environment and to the communities in which we operate (8). *(Author comment: Statement lacks six components: Customers, Products/Services, Markets, Technology, Concern for Survival/Growth/Profits, Concern for Public Image)*

Note: The numbers in parentheses correspond to the nine components listed on page 93; author comment also refers to those components.

FIGURE 2-1

A Comprehensive Strategic-Management Model

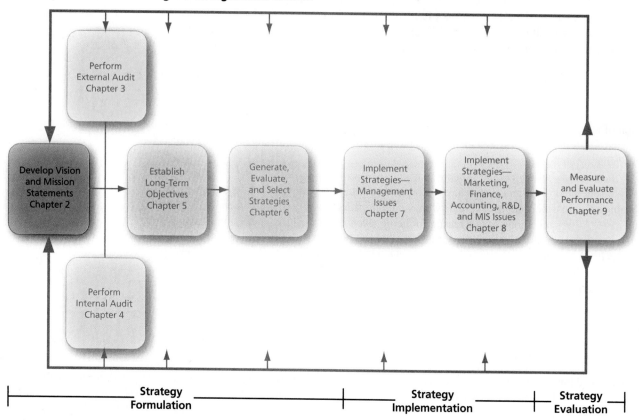

Source: Fred R. David, "How Companies Define Their Mission," *Long Range Planning* 22, no. 3 (June 1988): 40.

A business mission is the foundation for priorities, strategies, plans, and work assignments. It is the starting point for the design of managerial jobs and, above all, for the design of managerial structures. Nothing may seem simpler or more obvious than to know what a company's business is. A steel mill makes steel, a railroad runs trains to carry freight and passengers, an insurance company underwrites fire risks, and a bank lends money. Actually, "What is our business?" is almost always a difficult question and the right answer is usually anything but obvious. The answer to this question is the first responsibility of strategists. Only strategists can make sure that this question receives the attention it deserves and that the answer makes sense and enables the business to plot its course and set its objectives.[2]

Some strategists spend almost every moment of every day on administrative and tactical concerns, and strategists who rush quickly to establish objectives and implement strategies often overlook the development of a vision and mission statement. This problem is widespread even among large organizations. Many corporations in America have not yet developed a formal vision or mission statement.[3] An increasing number of organizations are developing these statements.

Some companies develop mission statements simply because they feel it is fashionable, rather than out of any real commitment. However, as will be described in this chapter, firms that develop and systematically revisit their vision and mission statements, treat them as living documents, and consider them to be an integral part of the firm's culture realize great benefits. Johnson & Johnson (J&J), the maker of medical-related products, is an example firm. J&J managers meet regularly with employees to review, reword, and reaffirm the firm's vision and mission. The entire J&J workforce recognizes the value that top management places on this exercise, and these employees respond accordingly.

Vision versus Mission

Many organizations develop both a mission statement and a vision statement. Whereas the mission statement answers the question "What is our business," the *vision statement* answers the question "What do we want to become?" Many organizations have both a mission and vision statement.

It can be argued that profit, not mission or vision, is the primary corporate motivator. But profit alone is not enough to motivate people.[4] Profit is perceived negatively by some employees in companies. Employees may see profit as something that they earn and management then uses and even gives away to shareholders. Although this perception is undesired and disturbing to management, it clearly indicates that both profit and vision are needed to effectively motivate a workforce.

When employees and managers together shape or fashion the vision and mission statements for a firm, the resultant documents can reflect the personal visions that managers and employees have in their hearts and minds about their own futures. Shared vision creates a commonality of interests that can lift workers out of the monotony of daily work and put them into a new world of opportunity and challenge.

The Process of Developing Vision and Mission Statements

As indicated in the strategic-management model, clear vision and mission statements are needed before alternative strategies can be formulated and implemented. It is important to involve as many managers as possible in the process of developing these statements, because through involvement, people become committed to an organization.

A widely used approach to developing a vision and mission statement is first to select several articles about these statements and ask all managers to read these as background information. Then ask managers themselves to prepare a vision and mission statement for the organization. A facilitator, or committee of top managers, should then merge these statements into a single document and distribute the draft statements to all managers. A request for modifications, additions, and deletions is needed next, along with a meeting to revise the document. To the extent that all managers have input into and support the final documents, organizations can more easily obtain managers' support for other strategy formulation, implementation, and evaluation activities. Thus, the process of developing a vision and mission statement represents a great opportunity for strategists to obtain needed support from all managers in the firm.

During the process of developing vision and mission statements, some organizations use discussion groups of managers to develop and modify existing statements. Some organizations hire an outside consultant or facilitator to manage the process and help draft the language. Sometimes an outside person with expertise in developing such statements, who has unbiased views, can manage the process more effectively than an internal group or committee of managers. Decisions on how best to communicate the vision and mission to all managers, employees, and external constituencies of an organization are needed when the documents are in final form. Some organizations even develop a videotape to explain the statements, and how they were developed.

An article by Campbell and Yeung emphasizes that the process of developing a mission statement should create an "emotional bond" and "sense of mission" between the organization and its employees.[5] Commitment to a company's strategy and intellectual agreement on the strategies to be pursued do not necessarily translate into an emotional bond; hence, strategies that have been formulated may not be implemented. These researchers stress that an emotional bond comes when an individual personally identifies with the underlying values and behavior of a firm, thus turning intellectual agreement and commitment to strategy into a sense of mission. Campbell and Yeung also differentiate between the terms *vision* and *mission,* saying that vision is "a possible and desirable future state of an organization" that includes specific goals, whereas mission is more associated with behavior and the present.

VISIT THE NET

Gives questions that help form an effective vision and mission statement. (www.csuchico.edu/mgmt/strategy/module1/sld009.htm)

Importance (Benefits) of Vision and Mission Statements

The importance (benefits) of vision and mission statements to effective strategic management is well documented in the literature, although research results are mixed. Rarick and Vitton found that firms with a formalized mission statement have twice the average return on shareholders' equity than those firms without a formalized mission statement have; Bart and Baetz found a positive relationship between mission statements and organizational performance; *BusinessWeek* magazine reports that firms using mission statements have a 30 percent higher return on certain financial measures than those without such statements; however, some studies have found that having a mission statement does not directly contribute positively to financial performance.[6] The extent of manager and employee involvement in developing vision and mission statements can make a difference in business success. This chapter provides guidelines for developing these important documents. In actual practice, wide variations exist in the nature, composition, and use of both vision and mission statements. King and Cleland recommend that organizations carefully develop a written mission statement in order to keep the following benefits:

VISIT THE NET

(http://sbinformation.about.com/cs/businessplans/a/mission.htm)

1. To ensure unanimity of purpose within the organization
2. To provide a basis, or standard, for allocating organizational resources
3. To establish a general tone or organizational climate
4. To serve as a focal point for individuals to identify with the organization's purpose and direction, and to deter those who cannot from participating further in the organization's activities
5. To facilitate the translation of objectives into a work structure involving the assignment of tasks to responsible elements within the organization
6. To specify organizational purposes and then to translate these purposes into objectives in such a way that cost, time, and performance parameters can be assessed and controlled.[7]

Reuben Mark, former CEO of Colgate, maintains that a clear mission increasingly must make sense internationally. Mark's thoughts on vision are as follows:

> When it comes to rallying everyone to the corporate banner, it's essential to push one vision globally rather than trying to drive home different messages in different cultures. The trick is to keep the vision simple but elevated: "We make the world's fastest computers" or "Telephone service for everyone." You're never going to get anyone to charge the machine guns only for financial objectives. It's got to be something that makes people feel better, feel a part of something.[8]

A Resolution of Divergent Views

Another benefit of developing a comprehensive mission statement is that divergent views among managers can be revealed and resolved through the process. The question "What is our business?" can create controversy. Raising the question often reveals differences among strategists in the organization. Individuals who have worked together for a long time and who think they know each other suddenly may realize that they are in fundamental disagreement. For example, in a college or university, divergent views regarding the relative importance of teaching, research, and service often are expressed during the mission statement development process. Negotiation, compromise, and eventual agreement on important issues are needed before people can focus on more specific strategy formulation activities.

> "What is our mission?" is a genuine decision; and a genuine decision must be based on divergent views to have a chance to be a right and effective decision. Developing a business mission is always a choice between alternatives, each of which rests on different assumptions regarding the reality of the business and its environment. It is always a high-risk decision. A change in mission always leads to

changes in objectives, strategies, organization, and behavior. The mission decision is far too important to be made by acclamation. Developing a business mission is a big step toward management effectiveness. Hidden or half-understood disagreements on the definition of a business mission underlie many of the personality problems, communication problems, and irritations that tend to divide a top-management group. Establishing a mission should never be made on plausibility alone, should never be made fast, and should never be made painlessly.[9]

Considerable disagreement among an organization's strategists over vision and mission statements can cause trouble if not resolved. For example, unresolved disagreement over the business mission was one of the reasons for W. T. Grant's bankruptcy and eventual liquidation. As one executive reported:

> There was a lot of dissension within the company whether we should go the Kmart route or go after the Montgomery Ward and JCPenney position. Ed Staley and Lou Lustenberger (two top executives) were at loggerheads over the issue, with the upshot being we took a position between the two and that consequently stood for nothing.[10]

Too often, strategists develop vision and business mission statements only when the organization is in trouble. Of course, it is needed then. Developing and communicating a clear mission during troubled times indeed may have spectacular results and even may reverse decline. However, to wait until an organization is in trouble to develop a vision and mission statement is a gamble that characterizes irresponsible management. According to Drucker, the most important time to ask seriously, "What do we want to become?" and "What is our business?" is when a company has been successful:

> Success always obsoletes the very behavior that achieved it, always creates new realities, and always creates new and different problems. Only the fairy tale story ends, "They lived happily ever after." It is never popular to argue with success or to rock the boat. The ancient Greeks knew that the penalty of success can be severe. The management that does not ask "What is our mission?" when the company is successful is, in effect, smug, lazy, and arrogant. It will not be long before success will turn into failure. Sooner or later, even the most successful answer to the question "What is our business?" becomes obsolete.[11]

In multidivisional organizations, strategists should ensure that divisional units perform strategic-management tasks, including the development of a statement of vision and mission. Each division should involve its own managers and employees in developing a vision and mission statement that is consistent with and supportive of the corporate mission.

An organization that fails to develop a vision statement as well as a comprehensive and inspiring mission statement loses the opportunity to present itself favorably to existing and potential stakeholders. All organizations need customers, employees, and managers, and most firms need creditors, suppliers, and distributors. The vision and mission statements are effective vehicles for communicating with important internal and external stakeholders. The principal benefit of these statements as tools of strategic management is derived from their specification of the ultimate aims of a firm:

> They provide managers with a unity of direction that transcends individual, parochial, and transitory needs. They promote a sense of shared expectations among all levels and generations of employees. They consolidate values over time and across individuals and interest groups. They project a sense of worth and intent that can be identified and assimilated by company outsiders. Finally, they affirm the company's commitment to responsible action, which is symbiotic with its need to preserve and protect the essential claims of insiders for sustained survival, growth, and profitability of the firm.[12]

Characteristics of a Mission Statement

A Declaration of Attitude

A mission statement is more than a statement of specific details; it is a declaration of attitude and outlook. It usually is broad in scope for at least two major reasons. First, a good mission statement allows for the generation and consideration of a range of feasible alternative objectives and strategies without unduly stifling management creativity. Excess specificity would limit the potential of creative growth for the organization. On the other hand, an overly general statement that does not exclude any strategy alternatives could be dysfunctional. Lenovo Computer's mission statement, for example, should not open the possibility for diversification into pesticides—or Volkswagen's into food processing.

Second, a mission statement needs to be broad to effectively reconcile differences among, and appeal to, an organization's diverse *stakeholders,* the individuals and groups of individuals who have a special stake or claim on the company. Stakeholders include employees, managers, stockholders, boards of directors, customers, suppliers, distributors, creditors, governments (local, state, federal, and foreign), unions, competitors, environmental groups, and the general public. Stakeholders affect and are affected by an organization's strategies, yet the claims and concerns of diverse constituencies vary and often conflict. For example, the general public is especially interested in social responsibility, whereas stockholders are more interested in profitability. Claims on any business literally may number in the thousands, and they often include clean air, jobs, taxes, investment opportunities, career opportunities, equal employment opportunities, employee benefits, salaries, wages, clean water, and community services. All stakeholders' claims on an organization cannot be pursued with equal emphasis. A good mission statement indicates the relative attention that an organization will devote to meeting the claims of various stakeholders. Many firms are environmentally proactive in response to the concerns of stakeholders, as indicated in the "Natural Environment Perspective" box.

The fine balance between specificity and generality is difficult to achieve, but it is well worth the effort. George Steiner offers the following insight on the need for a mission statement to be broad in scope:

> Most business statements of mission are expressed at high levels of abstraction. Vagueness nevertheless has its virtues. Mission statements are not designed to express concrete ends, but rather to provide motivation, general direction, an image, a tone, and a philosophy to guide the enterprise. An excess of detail could prove counterproductive since concrete specification could be the base for rallying opposition. Precision might stifle creativity in the formulation of an acceptable mission or purpose. Once an aim is cast in concrete, it creates a rigidity in an organization and resists change. Vagueness leaves room for other managers to fill in the details, perhaps even to modify general patterns. Vagueness permits more flexibility in adapting to changing environments and internal operations. It facilitates flexibility in implementation.[13]

In addition to being broad in scope, an effective mission statement should not be too lengthy; recommended length is less than 250 words. An effective mission statement should arouse positive feelings and emotions about an organization; it should be inspiring in the sense that it motivates readers to action. A mission statement should be enduring. All of the above are desired characteristics of a statement. An effective mission statement generates the impression that a firm is successful, has direction, and is worthy of time, support, and investment—from all socioeconomic groups of people.

It reflects judgments about future growth directions and strategies that are based upon forward-looking external and internal analyses. A business mission should provide useful criteria for selecting among alternative strategies. A clear mission statement provides a basis for generating and screening strategic options. The statement of mission should be dynamic in orientation, allowing judgments about the most promising growth directions and those considered less promising.

51

NATURAL ENVIRONMENT PERSPECTIVE
Is Your Firm Environmentally Proactive?

Conducting business in a way that preserves the natural environment is more than just good public relations; it is good business. Preserving the environment is a permanent part of doing business for the following reasons:

1. Consumer demand for environmentally safe products and packages is high.
2. Public opinion demanding that firms conduct business in ways that preserve the natural environment is strong.
3. Environmental advocacy groups now have over 20 million Americans as members.
4. Government environmental regulations are changing rapidly and becoming more complex.
5. More lenders are examining the environmental liabilities of businesses seeking loans.
6. Many consumers, suppliers, distributors, and investors shun doing business with environmentally weak firms.
7. Liability suits and fines against firms having environmental problems are on the rise.

More firms are becoming environmentally proactive, which means they are taking the initiative to develop and implement strategies that preserve the environment while enhancing their efficiency and effectiveness. The old undesirable alternative is to be environmentally reactive—waiting until environmental pressures are thrust upon a firm by law or consumer pressure. A reactive environmental policy often leads to high cleanup costs, numerous liability suits, loss in market share, reduced customer loyalty, and higher medical costs. In contrast, a proactive policy views environmental pressures as opportunities and includes such actions as developing green products and packages, conserving energy, reducing waste, recycling, and creating a corporate culture that is environmentally sensitive.

A proactive policy forces a company to innovate and upgrade processes; this leads to reduced waste, improved efficiency, better quality, and greater profits. Successful firms today assess "the profit in preserving the environment" in decisions ranging from developing a mission statement to determining plant location, manufacturing technology, design, products, packaging, and consumer relations. A proactive environmental policy is simply good business.

For example, more than 373,000 big-rig trucks were produced in North America in 2006, a record, but new U.S. regulations on big truck emissions have dropped that number to about 220,000 in 2007. New required diesel technology has reduced emissions by up to 98 percent in all new big trucks, at an average cost increase of $12,000 per truck. "Clean air is not free," says Rich Moskowitz, who handles regulatory affairs for the American Trucking Association, which supports the transition.

Sources: Adapted from "The Profit in Preserving America," *Forbes* (November 11, 1991): 181–189; Forest Beinhardt, "Bringing the Environment Down to Earth," *Harvard Business Review* (July–August 1999): 149–158; Christine Rosen; "Environmental Strategy and Competitive Advantage," *California Management Review* 43, 3 (Spring 2001): 8–15; and Chris Woodyard, "Cleaner Diesel Engine Rules Take Effect," *USA Today* (December 29, 2006): 1B.

Mount Everest along the border between China and Nepal.
Source: Getty Images

A Customer Orientation

A good mission statement describes an organization's purpose, customers, products or services, markets, philosophy, and basic technology. According to Vern McGinnis, a mission statement should (1) define what the organization is and what the organization aspires to be, (2) be limited enough to exclude some ventures and broad enough to allow for creative growth, (3) distinguish a given organization from all others, (4) serve as a framework for evaluating both current and prospective activities, and (5) be stated in terms sufficiently clear to be widely understood throughout the organization.[14]

A good mission statement reflects the anticipations of customers. Rather than developing a product and then trying to find a market, the operating philosophy of organizations should be to identify customers' needs and then provide a product or service to fulfill those needs.

Good mission statements identify the utility of a firm's products to its customers. This is why AT&T's mission statement focuses on communication rather than on its telephones; it is why ExxonMobil's mission statement focuses on energy rather than on the oil and gas it produces; it is why the railroad Union Pacific's mission statement focuses on transportation rather than on railroads; it is why Universal Studio's mission statement focuses on entertainment rather than on movies. The following utility statements are relevant in developing a mission statement:

Do not offer me things.

Do not offer me clothes. Offer me attractive looks.

Do not offer me shoes. Offer me comfort for my feet and the pleasure of walking.

Do not offer me a house. Offer me security, comfort, and a place that is clean and happy.

Do not offer me books. Offer me hours of pleasure and the benefit of knowledge.

Do not offer me records. Offer me leisure and the sound of music.

Do not offer me tools. Offer me the benefits and the pleasure that come from making beautiful things.

Do not offer me furniture. Offer me comfort and the quietness of a cozy place.

Do not offer me things. Offer me ideas, emotions, ambience, feelings, and benefits.

Please, do not offer me *things*.

A major reason for developing a business mission statement is to attract customers who give meaning to an organization. Hotel customers today want to use the Internet, so more and more hotels are providing Internet service. A classic description of the purpose of a business reveals the relative importance of customers in a statement of mission:

It is the customer who determines what a business is. It is the customer alone whose willingness to pay for a good or service converts economic resources into wealth and things into goods. What a business thinks it produces is not of first importance, especially not to the future of the business and to its success. What the customer thinks he/she is buying, what he/she considers value, is decisive—it determines what a business is, what it produces, and whether it will prosper. And what the customer buys and considers value is never a product. It is always utility, meaning what a product or service does for him or her. The customer is the foundation of a business and keeps it in existence.[15]

A Declaration of Social Policy

As indicated in Table 2-3, another characteristic of mission statements is that they shoud reveal that the firm is socially responsible. The term *social policy* embraces managerial philosophy and thinking at the highest levels of an organization. For this reason, social policy affects the development of a business mission statement. Social issues mandate that strategists consider not only what the organization owes its various stakeholders but also what responsibilities the firm has to consumers, environmentalists, minorities, communities, and other groups. After decades of debate on the topic of social responsibility, many firms still struggle to determine appropriate social policies.

The issue of social responsibility arises when a company establishes its business mission. The impact of society on business and vice versa is becoming more pronounced each year. Social policies directly affect a firm's customers, products and services, markets, technology, profitability, self-concept, and public image. An organization's social policy should be integrated into all strategic-management activities, including the development of a mission statement. Corporate social policy should be designed and articulated during strategy formulation, set and administered during strategy implementation, and reaffirmed or changed during strategy evaluation.[16] The emerging view of social responsibility holds that social issues should be attended to both directly and indirectly in determining strategies. In 2007, the most admired U.S. companies for social responsibility were as follows:

1. CHS
2. United Parcel Service
3. Whole Foods Market
4. McDonald's
5. Alcan
6. YRC Worldwide
7. Starbucks
8. International Paper
9. Vulcan Materials
10. Walt Disney

From a social responsibility perspective, the least admired U.S. companies in 2007 were:

1. Visteon
2. Dana
3. CA
4. Delphi
5. Federal-Mogul
6. ArvinMeritor
7. Huntsman
8. Navistar International
9. Lyondell Chemical
10. Toys "R" Us [17]

Firms should strive to engage in social activities that have economic benefits. For example, Merck & Co. recently developed the drug ivermectin for treating river blindness, a disease caused by a fly-borne parasitic worm endemic in poor, tropical areas of Africa, the Middle East, and Latin America. In an unprecedented gesture that reflected its corporate commitment to social responsibility, Merck then made ivermectin available at no cost to medical personnel throughout the world. Merck's action highlights the dilemma of orphan drugs, which offer pharmaceutical companies no economic incentive for development and distribution.

Despite differences in approaches, most U.S. companies try to ensure outsiders that they conduct their businesses in socially responsible ways. As indicated in the Global Perspective, an increasing number of Japanese firms are embracing the notion of equal employment opportunity for women. The mission statement is an effective instrument for conveying this message.

Some strategists agree with U.S. consumer advocate Ralph Nader, who proclaims that organizations have tremendous social obligations. Others agree with economics Nobel Prize winner Milton Friedman, the economist, who maintains that organizations have no obligation to do any more for society than is legally required. Most strategists agree that the first social responsibility of any business must be to make enough profit to cover the costs of the future, because if this is not achieved, no other social responsibility can be met. Strategists should examine social problems in terms of potential costs and benefits to the firm, and they should address social issues that could benefit the firm most.

VISIT THE NET

Provides example mission and vision statements that can be critiqued. (www.csuchico.edu/mgmt/strategy/module1/sld015.htm; www.csuchico.edu/mgmt/strategy/module1/sld014.htm; www.csuchico.edu/mgmt/strategy/module1/sld017.htm)

GLOBAL PERSPECTIVE
Social Policies on Retirement: Japan Versus the World

Some countries around the world are facing severe workforce shortages associated with their aging populations. The percentage of persons age 65 or older reached 20 percent in 2006 in both Japan and Italy, and will reach 20 percent in 2036 in China and the United States. Persons age 65 and older will reach 20 percent of the population in Germany and France in 2009 and 2018 respectively. Unlike the United States, Japan is reluctant to rely on large-scale immigration to bolster its workforce. Instead, Japan is providing incentives for its elderly to work until ages 65 to 75. Western European countries are doing the opposite, providing incentives for its elderly to retire at ages 55 to 60. The International Labor Organization says 71 percent of Japanese men ages 60 to 64 work, compared to 57 percent of American men and just 17 percent of French men in the same age group.

Mr. Sachiko Ichioka, a typical 67-year-old man in Japan, says, "I want to work as long as I'm healthy. The extra money means I can go on trips, and I'm not a burden on my children." Better diet and health care have raised Japan's life expectancy now to 82, the highest in the world. Japanese women are having on average only 1.28 children compared to 2.04 in the United States. Keeping the elderly at work, coupled with reversing the old-fashioned trend of keeping women at home, are

Japan's two key remedies for sustaining its workforce in factories and businesses. This prescription for dealing with problems associated with an aging society should be considered by many countries around the world. The Japanese government is phasing in a shift from ages 60 to 65 as the date when a person may begin receiving a pension, and premiums paid by Japanese employees are rising while payouts are falling. Unlike the United States, Japan has no law against discrimination based on age.

Japan's huge national debt, 175 percent of GDP compared to 65 percent for the United States, is difficult to lower with a falling population because Japan has fewer taxpaying workers. Worker productivity increases in Japan are not able to offset declines in number of workers, thus resulting in a decline in overall economic production. Like many countries, Japan does not view immigration as a good means to solve this problem. A leading Japanese economist and high government official, Ms. Hiroko Ota, says, "I would like to bring about a labor big bang. We need women to work while bringing up children. I want to make Japan an open country that grows along with the rest of Asia."

Japan's shrinking workforce has become such a concern that the government has just recently allowed an unspecified number of Indonesian and Filipino nurses

Indian wedding participants in Rajpipla, Gujarat wearing traditional clothing. *Source:* Christopher and Sally Gable (c) Dorling Kindersley

and caregivers to work in Japan for two years. The number of working-age Japanese—those between ages 15 and 64—is projected to shrink to 70 million by 2030, from 83 million in 2007. For many years, Japan has been known for its resistance to mass immigration, but the country is now starting to use more foreigners—known as *gaikokujin roudousha* in Japanese. Foreign workers, especially Filipinos, are being hired now to work in agriculture and factories throughout Japan.

From 1639 to 1854, Japan banned nearly all foreigners from entering the country. The percentage of foreign workers to the total population is 20 percent in the United States, nearly 10 percent in Germany, 5 percent in the United Kingdom, and less than 1 percent in Japan. But most Japanese now acknowledge that this percentage must move upward and perhaps quickly for their nation's economy to prosper.

Source: Adapted from Sebastian Moffett, "Fat-Aging Japan Keeps Its Elders on the Job Longer," *Wall Street Journal* (June 15, 2005): A1, A8; Sebastian Moffett, "Japan Seeks More Efficiency as Population Drops," *Wall Street Journal* (December 12, 2006): A2; Yuka Hayashi, "Japan Turns to Foreign Workers Amid Labor Crunch," *Wall Street Journal* (November 30, 2006): A10; and Yuka Hayashi and Sebastian Moffett, "Cautiously, an Aging Japan Warms to Foreign Workers," *Wall Street Journal* (May 25, 2007): A1, A12.

Mission Statement Components

Mission statements can and do vary in length, content, format, and specificity. Most practitioners and academicians of strategic management feel that an effective statement exhibits nine characteristics or components. Because a mission statement is often the most visible and public part of the strategic-management process, it is important that it includes all of these essential components:

1. ***Customers***—Who are the firm's customers?
2. ***Products or services***—What are the firm's major products or services?
3. ***Markets***—Geographically, where does the firm compete?
4. ***Technology***—Is the firm technologically current?
5. ***Concern for survival, growth, and profitability***—Is the firm committed to growth and financial soundness?
6. ***Philosophy***—What are the basic beliefs, values, aspirations, and ethical priorities of the firm?
7. ***Self-concept***—What is the firm's distinctive competence or major competitive advantage?
8. ***Concern for public image***—Is the firm responsive to social, community, and environmental concerns?
9. ***Concern for employees***—Are employees a valuable asset of the firm?

Excerpts from the mission statements of different organizations are provided in Table 2-4 to exemplify the nine essential *mission statement components*.

TABLE 2-3   **Characteristics of a Mission Statement**

- Broad in scope
- Less than 250 words in length
- Inspiring
- Identify the utility of a firm's products
- Reveal that the firm is socially responsible
- Reveal that the firm is environmentally responsible
- Include nine components
       customers, products or services, markets, technology, concern for survival/growth/
       profits, philosophy, self-concept, concern for public image, concern for employees
- Enduring

TABLE 2-4   Examples of the Nine Essential Components of a Mission Statement

1. Customers

We believe our first responsibility is to the doctors, nurses, patients, mothers, and all others who use our products and services. (Johnson & Johnson)

To earn our customers' loyalty, we listen to them, anticipate their needs, and act to create value in their eyes. (Lexmark International)

2. Products or Services

AMAX's principal products are molybdenum, coal, iron ore, copper, lead, zinc, petroleum and natural gas, potash, phosphates, nickel, tungsten, silver, gold, and magnesium. (AMAX Engineering Company)

Standard Oil Company is in business to find and produce crude oil, natural gas, and natural gas liquids; to manufacture high-quality products useful to society from these raw materials; and to distribute and market those products and to provide dependable related services to the consuming public at reasonable prices. (Standard Oil Company)

3. Markets

We are dedicated to the total success of Corning Glass Works as a worldwide competitor. (Corning Glass Works)

Our emphasis is on North American markets, although global opportunities will be explored. (Blockway)

4. Technology

Control Data is in the business of applying micro-electronics and computer technology in two general areas: computer-related hardware; and computing-enhancing services, which include computation, information, education, and finance. (Control Data)

We will continually strive to meet the preferences of adult smokers by developing technologies that have the potential to reduce the health risks associated with smoking. (RJ Reynolds)

5. Concern for Survival, Growth, and Profitability

In this respect, the company will conduct its operations prudently and will provide the profits and growth which will assure Hoover's ultimate success. (Hoover Universal)

To serve the worldwide need for knowledge at a fair profit by adhering, evaluating, producing, and distributing valuable information in a way that benefits our customers, employees, other investors, and our society. (McGraw-Hill)

6. Philosophy

Our world-class leadership is dedicated to a management philosophy that holds people above profits. (Kellogg)

It's all part of the Mary Kay philosophy—a philosophy based on the golden rule. A spirit of sharing and caring where people give cheerfully of their time, knowledge, and experience. (Mary Kay Cosmetics)

7. Self-Concept

Crown Zellerbach is committed to leapfrogging ongoing competition within 1,000 days by unleashing the constructive and creative abilities and energies of each of its employees. (Crown Zellerbach)

8. Concern for Public Image

To share the world's obligation for the protection of the environment. (Dow Chemical)

To contribute to the economic strength of society and function as a good corporate citizen on a local, state, and national basis in all countries in which we do business. (Pfizer)

9. Concern for Employees

To recruit, develop, motivate, reward, and retain personnel of exceptional ability, character, and dedication by providing good working conditions, superior leadership, compensation on the basis of performance, an attractive benefit program, opportunity for growth, and a high degree of employment security. (The Wachovia Corporation)

To compensate its employees with remuneration and fringe benefits competitive with other employment opportunities in its geographical area and commensurate with their contributions toward efficient corporate operations. (Public Service Electric & Gas Company)

VISIT THE NET

Provides mission statement information on nonprofit firms. (http://www.nonprofits.org/npofaq/03/21.html)

Writing and Evaluating Mission Statements

Perhaps the best way to develop a skill for writing and evaluating mission statements is to study actual company missions. Therefore, the mission statements presented on page 83 are evaluated based on the nine desired components.

There is no one best mission statement for a particular organization, so good judgment is required in evaluating mission statements. Note earlier in Table 2-2 on page 83 that numbers provided in each statement reveal what components are included in the respective documents. Among the statements in Table 2-2, note that the Dell mission statement is the best because it lacks only one component, whereas the L'Oreal statement is the worst, lacking six of the nine recommended components. Realize that some individuals are more demanding than others in assessing mission statements in this manner. For example, if a statement merely includes the word "customers" without specifying who the customers are, is that satisfactory? Ideally a statement would provide more than simply inclusion of a single word such as "products" or "employees" regarding a respective component. Why? Because the statement should be informative, inspiring, enduring, and serve to motivate stakeholders to action. Evaluation of a mission statement regarding inclusion of the nine components is just the beginning of the process to assess a statement's overall effectiveness.

Conclusion

Every organization has a unique purpose and reason for being. This uniqueness should be reflected in vision and mission statements. The nature of a business vision and mission can represent either a competitive advantage or disadvantage for the firm. An organization achieves a heightened sense of purpose when strategists, managers, and employees develop and communicate a clear business vision and mission. Drucker says that developing a clear business vision and mission is the "first responsibility of strategists."

A good mission statement reveals an organization's customers; products or services; markets; technology; concern for survival, growth, and profitability; philosophy; self-concept; concern for public image; and concern for employees. These nine basic components serve as a practical framework for evaluating and writing mission statements. As the first step in strategic management, the vision and mission statements provide direction for all planning activities.

Well-designed vision and mission statements are essential for formulating, implementing, and evaluating strategy. Developing and communicating a clear business vision and mission are the most commonly overlooked tasks in strategic management. Without clear statements of vision and mission, a firm's short-term actions can be counterproductive to long-term interests. Vision and mission statements always should be subject to revision, but, if carefully prepared, they will require infrequent major changes. Organizations usually reexamine their vision and mission statements annually. Effective mission statements stand the test of time.

Vision and mission statements are essential tools for strategists, a fact illustrated in a short story told by Porsche former CEO Peter Schultz:

> Three people were at work on a construction site. All were doing the same job, but when each was asked what his job was, the answers varied: "Breaking rocks," the first replied; "Earning a living," responded the second; "Helping to build a cathedral," said the third. Few of us can build cathedrals. But to the extent we can see the cathedral in whatever cause we are following, the job seems more worthwhile. Good strategists and a clear mission help us find those cathedrals in what otherwise could be dismal issues and empty causes.[18]

We invite you to visit the David page on the Prentice Hall Companion Web site at www.prenhall.com/david for this chapter's review quiz.

Key Terms and Concepts

Concern for Employees (p. 93)
Concern for Public Image (p. 93)
Concern for Survival, Growth, and Profitability (p. 93)
Creed Statement (p. 83)
Customers (p. 93)
Markets (p. 93)
Mission Statement (p. 83)

Issues for Review and Discussion

1.   Compare and contrast vision statements with mission statements in terms of composition and importance.
2.   Do local service stations need to have written vision and mission statements? Why or why not?
3.   Why do you think organizations that have a comprehensive mission tend to be high performers? Does having a comprehensive mission cause high performance?
4.   Explain why a mission statement should not include strategies and objectives.
5.   What is your college or university's self-concept? How would you state that in a mission statement?
6.   Explain the principal value of a vision and a mission statement.
7.   Why is it important for a mission statement to be reconciliatory?
8.   In your opinion, what are the three most important components that should be included when writing a mission statement? Why?
9.   How would the mission statements of a for-profit and a nonprofit organization differ?
10.   Write a vision and mission statement for an organization of your choice.
11.   Conduct a search on the Internet with the keywords *vision statement* and *mission statement*. Find various company vision and mission statements, and evaluate the documents. Write a one-page single-spaced report on your findings.
12.   Who are the major stakeholders of the bank that you locally do business with? What are the major claims of those stakeholders?
13.   How could a strategist's attitude toward social responsibility affect a firm's strategy? What is your attitude toward social responsibility?
14.   List seven characteristics of a mission statement.
15.   List eight benefits of a having a clear mission statement.
16.   How often do you think a firm's vision and mission statements should be changed?

Notes

1.   Barbara Bartkus, Myron Glassman, and Bruce McAfee, "Mission Statements: Are They Smoke and Mirrors?" *Business Horizons* (November–December 2000): 23.
2.   Peter Drucker, *Management: Tasks, Responsibilities, and Practices* (New York: Harper & Row, 1974): 61.
3.   Fred David, "How Companies Define Their Mission," *Long Range Planning* 22, no. 1 (February 1989): 90–92; John Pearce II and Fred David, "Corporate Mission Statements: The Bottom Line," *Academy of Management Executive* 1, no. 2 (May 1987): 110.
4.   Joseph Quigley, "Vision: How Leaders Develop It, Share It and Sustain It," *Business Horizons* (September–October 1994): 39.
5.   Andrew Campbell and Sally Yeung, "Creating a Sense of Mission," *Long Range Planning* 24, no. 4 (August 1991): 17.
6.   Charles Rarick and John Vitton, "Mission Statements Make Cents," *Journal of Business Strategy* 16 (1995): 11. Also, Christopher Bart and Mark Baetz, "The Relationship Between Mission Statements and Firm Performance: An Exploratory Study," *Journal of Management Studies* 35 (1998): 823; "Mission Possible," *BusinessWeek* (August 1999): F12.
7.   W. R. King and D. I. Cleland, *Strategic Planning and Policy* (New York: Van Nostrand Reinhold, 1979): 124.
8.   Brian Dumaine, "What the Leaders of Tomorrow See," *Fortune* (July 3, 1989): 50.
9.   Drucker, 78, 79.
10.   "How W. T. Grant Lost $175 Million Last Year," *BusinessWeek* (February 25, 1975): 75.
11.   Drucker, 88.
12.   John Pearce II, "The Company Mission as a Strategic Tool," *Sloan Management Review* 23, no. 3 (Spring 1982): 74.

13.   George Steiner, *Strategic Planning: What Every Manager Must Know* (New York: The Free Press, 1979): 160.

14.   Vern McGinnis, "The Mission Statement: A Key Step in Strategic Planning," *Business* 31, no. 6 (November–December 1981): 41.

15.   Drucker, 61.

16.   Archie Carroll and Frank Hoy, "Integrating Corporate Social Policy into Strategic Management," *Journal of Business Strategy* 4, no. 3 (Winter 1984): 57.

17.   http://money.cnn.com/magazines/fortune/mostadmired/2007/best_worst/best4.html.

18.   Robert Waterman, Jr., *The Renewal Factor: How the Best Get and Keep the Competitive Edge* (New York: Bantam, 1987); *BusinessWeek* (September 14, 1987): 120.

Current Readings

Aguilera,, Ruth V., Deborah E. Rupp, Cynthia A. Williams, and Ganapathi. "Corporate Social Responsibility and Firm Performance: Investor Preferences and Corporate Strategies." *The Academy of Management Review* 32, no. 3 (July 2007): 836.

Baetz, Mark C., and Christopher K. Bart. "Developing Mission Statements Which Work." *Long Range Planning* 29, no. 4 (August 1996): 526–533.

Barnett, M. L., and R. M. Salomon. "Beyond Dichotomy: The Curvilinear Relationship Between Social Responsibility and Financial Performance." *Strategic Management Journal* 27, no. 11 (November 2006): 1101.

Bartkus, Barbara, Myron Glassman, and R. Bruce McAfee. "Mission Statements: Are They Smoke and Mirrors?" *Business Horizons* 43, no. 6 (November–December 2000): 23.

Bloom, M., P. David, and A. J. Hillman. "Investor Activism, Managerial Responsiveness, and Corporate Social Performance." *Strategic Management Journal* 28, no. 1 (January 2007): 91.

Brabet, Julienne, and Mary Klemm. "Sharing the Vision: Company Mission Statements in Britain and France." *Long Range Planning* (February 1994): 84–94.

Collins, James C., and Jerry I. Porras. "Building a Visionary Company." *California Management Review* 37, no. 2 (Winter 1995): 80–100.

Collins, James C., and Jerry I. Porras. "Building Your Company's Vision." *Harvard Business Review* (September–October 1996): 65–78.

Cummings, Stephen, and John Davies. "Brief Case—Mission, Vision, Fusion." *Long Range Planning* 27, no. 6 (December 1994): 147–150.

Dalton, Catherine M. "When Organizational Values Are Mere Rhetoric." *Business Horizons* 49, no. 5 (September–October 2006): 345.

Davies, Stuart W., and Keith W. Glaister. "Business School Mission Statements—The Bland Leading the Bland?" *Long Range Planning* 30, no. 4 (August 1997): 594–604.

Day, George S., and Paul Schoemaker, "Peripheral Vision: Sensing and Acting on Weak Signals." *Long Range Planning* 37, no. 2 (April 2004): 117.

Dowling, Grahame R. "Corporate Reputations: Should You Compete on Yours?" *California Management Review* 46, no. 3 (Spring 2004): 19.

Gietzmann, Miles. "Disclosure of Timely and Forward-Looking Statements and Strategic Management of Major Institutional Ownership." *Long Range Planning* 39, no. 4 (August 2006): 409.

Gratton, Lynda. "Implementing a Strategic Vision—Key Factors for Success." *Long Range Planning* 29, no. 3 (June 1996): 290–303.

Greenfield, W. M. "In the Name of Corporate Social Responsibility." *Business Horizons* 47, no. 1 (January–February 2004): 19.

Hollender, Jeffery. "What Matters Most: Corporate Values and Social Responsibility." *California Management Review* 46, no. 4 (Summer 2004): 111.

Larwood, Laurie, Cecilia M. Falbe, Mark P. Kriger, and Paul Miesing. "Structure and Meaning of Organizational Vision." *Academy of Management Journal* 38, no. 3 (June 1995): 740–769.

Lissak, Michael, and Johan Roos. "Be Coherent, Not Visionary." *Long Range Planning* 34, no. 1 (February 2001): 53.

Mackey, Alison, Tyson B. Mackey, and Jay Barney. "Corporate Social Responsibility and Firm Performance: Investor Preferences and Corporate Strategies." *The Academy of Management Review* 32, no. 3 (July 2007): 817.

McTavish, Ron. "One More Time: What Business Are You In?" *Long Range Planning* 28, no. 2 (April 1995): 49–60.

Perrini, Francesco. "Corporate Social Responsibility: Doing the Most Good for Your Company and Your Cause." *The Academy of Management Perspectives* 20, no. 2 (May 2006): 90.

• EXPERIENTIAL EXERCISES

• EXPERIENTIAL EXERCISES

Experiential Exercise 2A

Evaluating Mission Statements

Purpose

A business mission statement is an integral part of strategic management. It provides direction for formulating, implementing, and evaluating strategic activities. This exercise will give you practice evaluating mission statements, a skill that is a prerequisite to writing a good mission statement.

Instructions

Step 1   On a clean sheet of paper, prepare a 9 × 3 matrix. Place the nine mission statement components down the left column and the following three companies across the top of your paper.

Step 2   Write *Yes* or *No* in each cell of your matrix to indicate whether you feel the particular mission statement has included the respective component.

Step 3   Turn your paper in to your instructor for a classwork grade.

Mission Statements

General Motors

Our mission is to be the world leader in transportation products and related services. We aim to maintain this position through enlightened customer enthusiasm and continuous improvement driven by the integrity, teamwork, innovation and individual respect and responsibility of our employees.

North Carolina Zoo

Our mission is to encourage understanding of and commitment to the conservation of the world's wildlife and wild places through recognition of the interdependence of people and

Epcot at Disney World in the U.S. state of Florida. *Source:* Ted Poweski

nature. We will do this by creating a sense of enjoyment, wonder and discovery throughout the Park and in our outreach programs.

Samsonite

Our mission is to be the leader in the travel industry. Samsonite's ambition is to provide unparalleled durability, security and dependability in all of its products, through leading edge functionality, features, innovation, technology, contemporary aesthetics and design. In order to fill every niche in the travel market, Samsonite will seek to create strategic alliances, combining our strengths with other partners in our brands.

Experiential Exercise 2B

Evaluating Walt Disney's Vision and Mission Statement

Purpose

There is always room for improvement in regard to an existing vision and mission statement. Currently the Walt Disney Company does not have a vision statement, so this exercise will ask you to develop one. The company does have a mission statement, but analysts feel that the statement could be improved.

The mission of the Walt Disney Company is to be one of the world's leading producers and providers of entertainment and information. Using our portfolio of brands to differentiate our content, services and consumer products, we seek to develop the most creative, innovative and profitable entertainment experiences and related products in the world.

Instructions

Step 1	Refer back to page 63 the Cohesion Case for Walt Disney's mission statement.
Step 2	On a clean sheet of paper, write a one-sentence vision statement for the Walt Disney Company.
Step 3	On that same sheet of paper, evaluate Walt Disney's mission statement. Which of the nine recommended components are lacking in the company's current statement?
Step 4	Write an improved mission statement for Walt Disney that meets the eight characteristics summarized in Table 2-3.

Experiential Exercise 2C

Writing a Vision and Mission Statement for My University

Purpose

Most universities have a vision and mission statement. The purpose of this exercise is to give you practice writing a vision and mission statement for a nonprofit organization such as your own university.

Instructions

Step 1	Write a vision statement and a mission statement for your university. Your mission statement should meet the eight characteristics summarized in Table 2-3.
Step 2	Read your vision and mission statement to the class.
Step 3	Determine whether your institution has a vision and/or mission statement. Look in the front of the college handbook. If your institution has a written statement, contact an appropriate administrator of the institution to inquire as to how and when the statement was prepared. Share this information with the class. Analyze your college's vision and mission statement in light of the concepts presented in this chapter.

Experiential Exercise 2D

Conducting Mission Statement Research

Purpose

This exercise gives you the opportunity to study the nature and role of vision and mission statements in strategic management.

Instructions

Step 1   Call various organizations in your city or county to identify firms that have developed a formal vision and/or mission statement. Contact nonprofit organizations and government agencies in addition to small and large businesses. Ask to speak with the director, owner, or chief executive officer of each organization. Explain that you are studying vision and mission statements in class and are conducting research as part of a class activity.

Step 2   Ask several executives the following four questions, and record their answers.
1.   When did your organization first develop its vision and/or mission statement? Who was primarily responsible for its development?
2.   How long have your current statements existed? When were they last modified? Why were they modified at that time?
3.   By what process are your firm's vision and mission statements altered?
4.   How are your vision and mission statements used in the firm?

Step 3   Provide an overview of your findings to the class.

3 The External Assessment

A Retreat for Strategic Planning on the Adriatic Sea. *Source:* Forest David

chapter objectives

After studying this chapter, you should be able to do the following:

1. Describe how to conduct an external strategic-management audit.

2. Discuss 10 major external forces that affect organizations: economic, social, cultural, demographic, environmental, political, governmental, legal, technological, and competitive.

3. Identify key sources of external information, including the Internet.

4. Discuss important forecasting tools used in strategic management.

5. Discuss the importance of monitoring external trends and events.

6. Explain how to develop an EFE Matrix.

7. Explain how to develop a Competitive Profile Matrix.

8. Discuss the importance of gathering competitive intelligence.

9. Describe the trend toward cooperation among competitors.

10. Discuss the economic environment in Russia.

11. Discuss the global challenge facing American firms.

12. Discuss market commonality and resource similarity in relation to competitive analysis.

Experiential Exercises

Experiential Exercise 3A
Developing an EFE Matrix for Walt Disney Company

Experiential Exercise 3B
The External Assessment

Experiential Exercise 3C
Developing an EFE Matrix for My University

Experiential Exercise 3D
Developing a Competitive Profile Matrix for Walt Disney Company

Experiential Exercise 3E
Developing a Competitive Profile Matrix for My University

This chapter examines the tools and concepts needed to conduct an external strategic management audit (sometimes called *environmental scanning* or *industry analysis*). An *external audit* focuses on identifying and evaluating trends and events beyond the control of a single firm, such as increased foreign competition, population shifts to the Sunbelt, an aging society, consumer fear of traveling, and stock market volatility. An external audit reveals key opportunities and threats confronting an organization so that managers can formulate strategies to take advantage of the opportunities and avoid or reduce the impact of threats. This chapter presents a practical framework for gathering, assimilating, and analyzing external information. The Industrial Organization (I/O) view of strategic management is introduced.

The Nature of an External Audit

VISIT THE NET

Reveals how strategic planning evolved from long-range planning and environmental scanning (external audit or assessment). (horizon.unc.edu/projects/seminars/futuresresearch/strategic. asp#planning)

The purpose of an *external audit* is to develop a finite list of opportunities that could benefit a firm and threats that should be avoided. As the term *finite* suggests, the external audit is not aimed at developing an exhaustive list of every possible factor that could influence the business; rather, it is aimed at identifying key variables that offer actionable responses. Firms should be able to respond either offensively or defensively to the factors by formulating strategies that take advantage of external opportunities or that minimize the impact of potential threats. Figure 3-1 illustrates how the external audit fits into the strategic-management process.

Key External Forces

External forces can be divided into five broad categories: (1) economic forces; (2) social, cultural, demographic, and environmental forces; (3) political, governmental, and legal forces; (4) technological forces; and (5) competitive forces. Relationships among these

FIGURE 3-1

A Comprehensive Strategic-Management Model

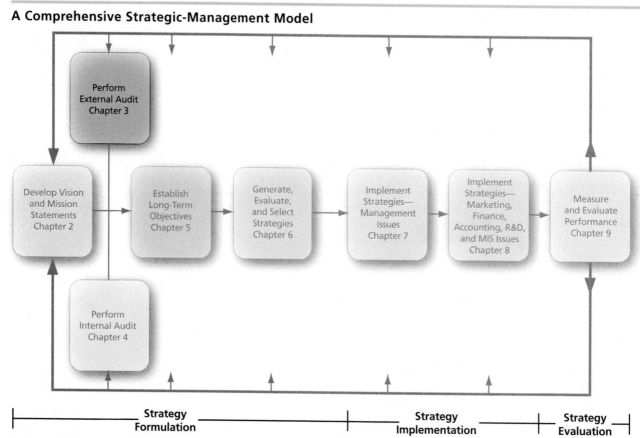

Source: Fred R. David, "How Companies Define Their Mission," *Long Range Planning* 22, no. 3 (June 1988): 40.

FIGURE 3-2

Relationships Between Key External Forces and an Organization

Pay Attention to this chart

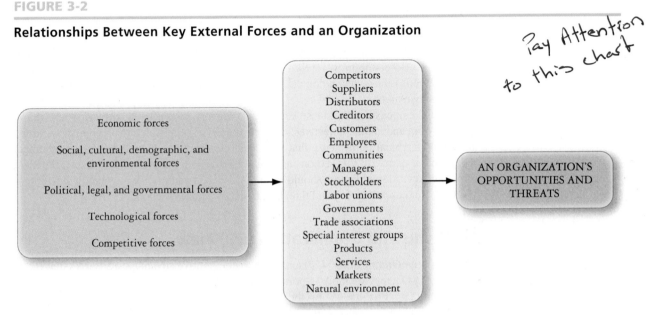

forces and an organization are depicted in Figure 3-2. External trends and events significantly affect all products, services, markets, and organizations in the world.

Changes in external forces translate into changes in consumer demand for both industrial and consumer products and services. External forces affect the types of products developed, the nature of positioning and market segmentation strategies, the type of services offered, and the choice of businesses to acquire or sell. External forces directly affect both suppliers and distributors. Identifying and evaluating external opportunities and threats enables organizations to develop a clear mission, to design strategies to achieve long-term objectives, and to develop policies to achieve annual objectives.

The increasing complexity of business today is evidenced by more countries developing the capacity and will to compete aggressively in world markets. Foreign businesses and countries are willing to learn, adapt, innovate, and invent to compete successfully in the marketplace. There are more competitive new technologies in Europe and Asia today than ever before. U.S. businesses can no longer beat foreign competitors with ease.

The Process of Performing an External Audit

The process of performing an external audit must involve as many managers and employees as possible. As emphasized in earlier chapters, involvement in the strategic-management process can lead to understanding and commitment from organizational members. Individuals appreciate having the opportunity to contribute ideas and to gain a better understanding of their firms' industry, competitors, and markets.

To perform an external audit, a company first must gather competitive intelligence and information about economic, social, cultural, demographic, environmental, political, governmental, legal, and technological trends. Individuals can be asked to monitor various sources of information, such as key magazines, trade journals, and newspapers. These persons can submit periodic scanning reports to a committee of managers charged with performing the external audit. This approach provides a continuous stream of timely strategic information and involves many individuals in the external-audit process. The Internet provides another source for gathering strategic information, as do corporate, university, and public libraries. Suppliers, distributors, salespersons, customers, and competitors represent other sources of vital information.

Once information is gathered, it should be assimilated and evaluated. A meeting or series of meetings of managers is needed to collectively identify the most important opportunities and threats facing the firm. These key external factors should be listed on flip charts or a chalkboard. A prioritized list of these factors could be obtained by requesting that all managers rank the factors identified, from 1 for the most important opportunity/threat to 20 for the least important opportunity/threat. These key external factors can vary over time and by industry. Relationships with suppliers or distributors are often a critical success factor. Other variables commonly used include market share, breadth of competing products, world economies, foreign affiliates, proprietary and key account advantages, price competitiveness, technological advancements, population shifts, interest rates, and pollution abatement.

Freund emphasized that these key external factors should be (1) important to achieving long-term and annual objectives, (2) measurable, (3) applicable to all competing firms, and (4) hierarchical in the sense that some will pertain to the overall company and others will be more narrowly focused on functional or divisional areas.[1] A final list of the most important key external factors should be communicated and distributed widely in the organization. Both opportunities and threats can be key external factors.

The Industrial Organization (I/O) View

The *Industrial Organization (I/O)* approach to competitive advantage advocates that external (industry) factors are more important than internal factors in a firm achieving competitive advantage. Proponents of the I/O view, such as Michael Porter, contend that organizational performance will be primarily determined by industry forces. Porter's Five-Forces Model, presented later in this chapter, is an example of the I/O perspective, which focuses upon analyzing external forces and industry variables as a basis for getting and keeping competitive advantage. Competitive advantage is determined largely by competitive positioning within an industry, according to I/O advocates. Managing strategically from the I/O perspective entails firms striving to compete in attractive industries, avoiding weak or faltering industries, and gaining a full understanding of key external factor relationships within that attractive industry. I/O research was mainly conducted from the 1960s to the 1980s and provided important contributions to our understanding of how to gain competitive advantage.

I/O theorists contend that the industry in which a firm chooses to compete has a stronger influence on the firm's performance than do the internal functional decisions managers make in marketing, finance, and the like. Firm performance, they contend, is primarily based more on industry properties, such as economies of scale, barriers to market entry, product differentiation, and level of competitiveness than on internal resources, capabilities, structure, and operations. Research findings suggest that approximately 20 percent of a firm's profitability can be explained by the industry, whereas 36 percent of the variance in profitability is attributed to the firm's internal factors (see the RBV discussion in the next chapter).[2]

The I/O view has enhanced our understanding of strategic management. However, it is not a question of whether external or internal factors are more important in gaining and maintaining competitive advantage. Effective integration and understanding of *both* external and internal factors is the key to securing and keeping a competitive advantage. In fact, as will be discussed in Chapter 6, matching key external opportunities/threats with key internal strengths/weaknesses provides the basis for successful strategy formulation.

Economic Forces

Increasing numbers of two-income households is an economic trend in the United States. Individuals place a premium on time. Improved customer service, immediate availability, trouble-free operation of products, and dependable maintenance and repair services are becoming more important. People today are more willing than ever to pay for good service if it limits inconvenience.

Economic factors have a direct impact on the potential attractiveness of various strategies. For example, when interest rates rise, funds needed for capital expansion become more costly or unavailable. Also, when interest rates rise, discretionary income declines, and the demand for discretionary goods falls. When stock prices increase, the desirability of equity as a source of capital for market development increases. Also, when the market rises, consumer and business wealth expands. A summary of economic variables that often represent opportunities and threats for organizations is provided in Table 3-1.

Trends in the U.S. dollar's value have significant and unequal effects on companies in different industries and in different locations. For example, the pharmaceutical, tourism, entertainment, motor vehicle, aerospace, and forest products industries benefit greatly when the dollar falls against the yen and euro. Agricultural and petroleum industries are hurt by the dollar's rise against the currencies of Mexico, Brazil, Venezuela, and Australia. Generally, a strong or high dollar makes U.S. goods more expensive in overseas markets. This worsens the U.S. trade deficit. When the value of the dollar falls, tourism-oriented firms benefit because Americans do not travel abroad as much when the value of the dollar is low; rather, foreigners visit and vacation more in the United States.

A low value of the dollar means lower imports and higher exports; it helps U.S. companies' competitiveness in world markets. The dollar has fallen to record lows against the euro and yen, which makes U.S. goods cheaper to foreign consumers and combats deflation by pushing up prices of imports. However, European firms such as Volkswagen AG, Nokia Corp., and Michelin complain that the strong euro hurts their financial performance. The low value of the dollar benefits the U.S. economy in many ways. First, it helps to stave off the risks of deflation in the United States and also reduces the U.S. trade deficit. In addition, the low value of the dollar raises the foreign sales and profits of domestic firms, thanks to dollar-induced gains, and encourages foreign countries to lower interest rates and loosen fiscal policy, which stimulates worldwide economic expansion. Some sectors, such as consumer staples, energy, materials, technology, and health care, especially benefit from a low value of the dollar. Manufacturers in many domestic industries in fact benefit because of a weak dollar, which forces foreign rivals to raise prices and extinguish discounts. Domestic firms with big overseas sales, such as McDonald's, greatly benefit from a weak dollar.

The country of Slovenia, just east of Italy, adopted the euro in 2007, in what Prime Minister Janez Jansa called the "biggest national achievement" since the country joined the European Union in 2004. Adoption of the common currency is expected to bring macroeconomic stability to the country, increase its exports, and yield productivity gains. A downside, however, is that adoption of the euro means a country such as Slovenia gives up its ability to fix its own interest rates, which could increase inflation and prices within the country.

TABLE 3-1 Key U.S. Economic Variables to Be Monitored

Shift to a service economy in the United States	Import/export factors
Availability of credit	Demand shifts for different categories of goods and services
Level of disposable income	Income differences by region and consumer groups
Propensity of people to spend	Price fluctuations
Interest rates	Export of labor and capital from the United States
Inflation rates	
Money market rates	Monetary policies
Federal government budget deficits	Fiscal policies
Gross domestic product trend	Tax rates
Consumption patterns	European Economic Community (EEC) policies
Unemployment trends	
Worker productivity levels	Organization of Petroleum Exporting Countries (OPEC) policies
Value of the dollar in world markets	
Stock market trends	Coalitions of Lesser Developed Countries (LDC) policies
Foreign countries' economic conditions	

Social, Cultural, Demographic, and Environmental Forces

Social, cultural, demographic, and environmental changes have a major impact upon virtually all products, services, markets, and customers. Small, large, for-profit and nonprofit organizations in all industries are being staggered and challenged by the opportunities and threats arising from changes in social, cultural, demographic, and environmental variables. In every way, the world is much different today than it was yesterday, and tomorrow promises even greater changes.

The United States, for example, is getting older and less Caucasian. The oldest members of America's 76 million baby boomers plan to retire in 2011, and this has lawmakers and younger taxpayers deeply concerned about who will pay their Social Security, Medicare, and Medicaid retirement benefits. Individuals age 65 and older in the United States as a percent of the population will rise to 18.5 percent by 2025.

By the year 2075, the United States will have no racial or ethnic majority. This forecast is aggravating tensions over issues such as immigration and affirmative action. The U.S. states of Hawaii, California, and New Mexico already have no majority race or ethnic group.

The seven states with the highest percentage of minorities (African -Americans, Native Americans, Asians, Hispanics, Native Hawaiians) are: Nevada (25 percent), Arizona (20 percent), Georgia (14 percent), Florida (13 percent), Idaho (13 percent), North Carolina (10 percent), and Colorado (10 percent).[3]

The population of the world surpassed 6.8 billion in 2008. Remaining solely domestic is an increasingly risky strategy, especially as the world population continues to grow to an estimated 8 billion in 2028 and 9 billion in 2054.

Social, cultural, demographic, and environmental trends are shaping the way people live, work, produce, and consume. New trends are creating a different type of consumer and, consequently, a need for different products, different services, and different strategies. For example, there are now more American households with people living alone or with unrelated people than there are households consisting of married couples with children. American households are also making more and more purchases online. Beer consumption in the United States is growing at only 0.5 percent per year, whereas wine consumption is growing 3.5 percent and distilled spirits consumption is growing at 2.0 percent.[4] Beer is still the most popular alcoholic beverage in the United States, but its market share has dropped from 59.5 percent in its peak year of 1995 to 56.7 percent today. For a wine company such as Gallo, this trend is an opportunity whereas for a firm such as Adolph Coors Brewing, this trend is an external threat.

The trend toward an older populace is good news for restaurants, hotels, airlines, cruise lines, tours, resorts, theme parks, luxury products and services, recreational vehicles, home builders, furniture producers, computer manufacturers, travel services, pharmaceutical

Senior citizens tossing frisbee on the beach. *Source:* Stock Connection

firms, automakers, and funeral homes. Older Americans, for example, are especially interested in health care, financial services, travel, crime prevention, and leisure. The world's longest-living people are the Japanese, with Japanese women living to 86.3 years and men living to 80.1 years on average. By 2050, the Census Bureau projects that the number of Americans age 100 and older will increase to over 834,000 from just under 100,000 centenarians in the United States in 2000. Americans age 65 and over will increase from 12.6 percent of the U.S. population in 2000 to 20.0 percent by the year 2050.

The aging of the population affects the strategic orientation of nearly all organizations. Apartment complexes for the elderly, with one meal a day, transportation, and utilities included in the rent, have increased. Called *lifecare facilities,* these complexes now exceed 2 million. Some well-known companies building these facilities include Avon, Marriott, and Hyatt. Individuals age 65 and older in the United States comprise 13 percent of the total population; Japan's elderly population ratio is 17 percent, and Germany's is 19 percent.

Americans are on the move in a population shift to the South and West (Sunbelt) and away from the Northeast and Midwest (Frostbelt). The U.S. Internal Revenue Service provides the U.S. Census Bureau with massive computer files of demographic data. By comparing individual address changes from year to year, the Census Bureau publishes extensive information about population shifts across the country. All of these facts represent major opportunities and threats for some companies. For example, the four fastest growing U.S. states in rank order are Arizona, Nevada, Idaho, Georgia, and Texas, whereas four states (Louisiana, Rhode Island, New York, Michigan) and Washington, D.C. lost residents in 2006. In the Northeast, the states of New York, New Jersey, and Massachusetts continue to lose large numbers of people to other states. In the Midwest, the big losers of residents annually are Illinois, Michigan, and Ohio. The fastest growing large metropolitan areas in the United States are Dallas–Fort Worth, Houston, Atlanta, Phoenix, Las Vegas, and Riverside, California.[5] Hard number data related to this information can represent key opportunities for many firms and thus can be essential for successful strategy formulation, including where to locate new plants and distribution centers and where to focus marketing efforts.

Except for terrorism, no greater threat to business and society exists than the voracious, continuous decimation and degradation of our natural environment. The U.S. Clean Air Act went into effect in 1994. The U.S. Clean Water Act went into effect in 1984. A summary of important social, cultural, demographic, and environmental variables that represent opportunities or threats for virtually all organizations is given in Table 3-2.

Political, Governmental, and Legal Forces

National, state, and local governments are major regulators, deregulators, subsidizers, employers, and customers of organizations. Political, governmental, and legal factors, therefore, can represent key opportunities or threats for both small and large organizations.

For industries and firms that depend heavily on government contracts or subsidies, political forecasts can be the most important part of an external audit. Changes in patent laws, antitrust legislation, tax rates, and lobbying activities can affect firms significantly. The U.S. Justice Department offers excellent information at its Web site (www.usdoj.gov) on such topics.

In the world of biopolitics, Americans are still deeply divided over issues such as assisted suicide, genetic testing, genetic engineering, cloning, stem-cell research, and abortion.

As indicated in the Natural Environment Perspective, American business leaders are also divided on their support for the Kyoto Protocol to cap emissions from industrialized nations. The Kyoto Protocol expires in 2012.

The increasing global interdependence among economies, markets, governments, and organizations makes it imperative that firms consider the possible impact of political variables on the formulation and implementation of competitive strategies.

In Europe, many large multinational firms such as John Deere, Polo Ralph Lauren, Gillette, Cargill, and General Mills are moving their headquarters from France,

TABLE 3-2   Key Social, Cultural, Demographic, and Environmental Variables

Childbearing rates	Attitudes toward retirement
Number of special-interest groups	Attitudes toward leisure time
Number of marriages	Attitudes toward product quality
Number of divorces	Attitudes toward customer service
Number of births	Pollution control
Number of deaths	Attitudes toward foreign peoples
Immigration and emigration rates	Energy conservation
Social Security programs	Social programs
Life expectancy rates	Number of churches
Per capita income	Number of church members
Location of retailing, manufacturing, and service businesses	Social responsibility
Attitudes toward business	Attitudes toward careers
Lifestyles	Population changes by race, age, sex, and level of affluence
Traffic congestion	Attitudes toward authority
Inner-city environments	Population changes by city, county, state, region, and country
Average disposable income	Value placed on leisure time
Trust in government	Regional changes in tastes and preferences
Attitudes toward government	Number of women and minority workers
Attitudes toward work	Number of high school and college graduates by geographic area
Buying habits	Recycling
Ethical concerns	Waste management
Attitudes toward saving	Air pollution
Sex roles	Water pollution
Attitudes toward investing	Ozone depletion
Racial equality	Endangered species
Use of birth control	
Average level of education	
Government regulation	

Netherlands, and Germany to Switzerland and Ireland to avoid costs associated with *tax harmonization*—a term that refers to the EU's effort to end competitive tax breaks among member countries. Although the EU strives to standardize tax breaks, member countries vigorously defend their right to politically and legally set their own tax rates. Behind Switzerland as the most attractive European location for corporations, Ireland keeps its corporate tax rates low, which is why Ingersoll-Rand recently moved much of its operations there.

The European Union celebrated its 51st anniversary in 2008, but the 27 member countries have agreed not to allow any other countries to join until 2010. The Union desires to get all member countries on board with signing of its constitution and also desires more trade between member countries. A recent report by Bruegel, a think tank in Brussels, reveals that member EU countries still spend 86 percent of their income on goods and services made at home and just 10 percent on those from other EU countries. France wants Europe's social welfare model included in the EU constitution, others do not. Poland wants Christianity mentioned, others such as France do not. Britain says the word "constitution" cannot be used, others disagree. And Italy was voted into the EU with a public debt of more than 120 percent of gross domestic product, twice the ratio allowed under EU rules. Some countries that have petitioned to be admitted to the EU include Ukraine, Georgia, Croatia, Turkey, and Macedonia.

NATURAL ENVIRONMENT PERSPECTIVE
American Business Leaders Pushing for Legislation on Climate Change

General Electric's CEO Jeffrey Immelt, Dupont's Chad Holliday, and Duke Energy's Jim Rogers are driving forces in Washington, D.C. behind a group of ten CEOs who are pressuring Congress, the Business Roundtable, and the government to cap greenhouse-gas emissions. Emission caps are already in place in Europe and California. American business leaders have generally come about-face and now support legislation to curb emissions and global warming, even though the coal industry, oil industry, and a few politicians still oppose such efforts. GE says it has a $20 billion backlog of orders for its "ecomagination" products, which include fuel-efficient jet engines and locomotives, wind turbines, and compact fluorescent light bulbs. Alcoa, Caterpillar, and Toyota also are companies making excellent progress on natural environment issues and lobbying other firms to do likewise.

Carbon dioxide, the main greenhouse gas, is produced when fossil fuels such as coal, oil, and natural gas are burned. However, even the Electric Power Supply Association, which represents about one-third of U.S. power generation, now lobbies legislators to enact legislation to cap emissions. Business leaders desire a single national emissions cap to take precedence over different state emission caps that are emerging. Even Exxon Mobil, a long-time opponent of government curbs on global-warming emissions, has ceased verbal and monetary opposition and now is trying to influence the nature of such curbs. Still, both Exxon and the U.S. government oppose the Kyoto Protocol, the global-warming treaty that caps emissions from industrialized nations.

Even the airline industry, including both airports and air carriers, is feeling pressure to reduce pollution. Every year the industry discards more than 6,000 tons of aluminum cans, 9,000 tons of plastic, and enough newspapers and magazines to fill a football field to a depth of 230 feet. Airport and air carrier recycling programs are generally underdeveloped because both ports and carriers are preoccupied with security and finances. Airliners emit carbon dioxide and nitrogen oxides high in the atmosphere and both gases contribute to global warming.

Among U.S. states, California leads the way in pushing for high environmental standards. New California laws mandate that 20 percent of the state's energy supply is to come from renewable resources, such as wind and solar power, by 2010. Unfortunately, however, California

The Purcell Mountains in Alberta, Canada.
Source: Peter Wilson (c) Dorling Kindersley

state law still prohibits construction of more nuclear plants even though they emit no greenhouse gases.

Among companies, the top five buyers of green power, purchased by total kilowatt hours and as a percentage of their total purchased electricity use, are PepsiCo, Wells Fargo, Whole Foods, U.S. Air Force, and Johnson & Johnson. Both PepsiCo and organic grocer Whole Foods get 100 percent of their power from green sources such as wind, solar, hydroelectric, and nuclear.

Sources: Adapted from Alan Murray, "Why Key Executives Are Warming to Legislation on Climate Change," *Wall Street Journal* (February 7, 2007): A10; Jeffrey Ball, "Electric Industry to Call for Cap on Emissions," *Wall Street Journal* (February 7, 2007): A4; Susan Carey, "Airlines Feel Pressure as Pollution Fight Takes Off," *Wall Street Journal* (December 12, 2006): A6; Rebecca Smith, "California Kindles Green Energy," *Wall Street Journal* (December 26, 2006): A2; John Fialka and Kathryn Kranhold, "GE Fights EPA's Tougher Smog Proposals," *Wall Street Journal* (February 13, 2007): A2; and Bruce Horovitz, "PepsiCo Takes Top Spot in Global Warming Battle," *USA Today* (April 30, 2007): B1.

TABLE 3-3 Some Political, Governmental, and Legal Variables

Government regulations or deregulations	Sino-American relationships
Changes in tax laws	Russian-American relationships
Special tariffs	European-American relationships
Political action committees	African-American relationships
Voter participation rates	Import–export regulations
Number, severity, and location of government protests	Government fiscal and monetary policy changes
Number of patents	Political conditions in foreign countries
Changes in patent laws	Special local, state, and federal laws
Environmental protection laws	Lobbying activities
Level of defense expenditures	Size of government budgets
Legislation on equal employment	World oil, currency, and labor markets
Level of government subsidies	Location and severity of terrorist activities
Antitrust legislation	Local, state, and national elections

Political relations between Japan and China have thawed considerably in recent years, which is good for the world economy because China's low-cost manufactured goods have become essential for the functioning of most industrialized nations. China's Premier Wen Jiabao addressed the Japanese parliament in April 2007, something no Chinese leader has done for more than twenty years, and Japanese Prime Minister Shinzo Abe has visited Beijing. Japan's largest trading partner is China, and China's third-largest trading partner is Japan—after the European Union, number one, and the United States, number two.

A world market has emerged from what previously was a multitude of distinct national markets, and the climate for international business today is much more favorable than yesterday. Mass communication and high technology are creating similar patterns of consumption in diverse cultures worldwide. This means that many companies may find it difficult to survive by relying solely on domestic markets.

It is no exaggeration that in an industry that is, or is rapidly becoming, global, the riskiest possible posture is to remain a domestic competitor. The domestic competitor will watch as more aggressive companies use this growth to capture economies of scale and learning. The domestic competitor will then be faced with an attack on domestic markets using different (and possibly superior) technology, product design, manufacturing, marketing approaches, and economies of scale. A few examples suggest how extensive the phenomenon of world markets has already become. Hewlett-Packard's manufacturing chain reaches halfway around the globe, from well-paid, skilled engineers in California to low-wage assembly workers in Malaysia. General Electric has survived as a manufacturer of inexpensive audio products by centralizing its world production in Singapore.[6]

Laws, regulatory agencies, and special-interest groups can have a major impact on the strategies of small, large, for-profit, and nonprofit organizations. Many companies have altered or abandoned strategies in the past because of political or governmental actions. A summary of political, governmental, and legal variables that can represent key opportunities or threats to organizations is provided in Table 3-3.

Technological Forces

Revolutionary technological changes and discoveries are having a dramatic impact on organizations. Superconductivity advancements alone, which increase the power of electrical products by lowering resistance to current, are revolutionizing business operations, especially in the transportation, utility, health care, electrical, and computer industries.

The *Internet* is acting as a national and global economic engine that is spurring productivity, a critical factor in a country's ability to improve living standards; and it is saving companies billions of dollars in distribution and transaction costs from direct sales to self-service systems.

The Internet is changing the very nature of opportunities and threats by altering the life cycles of products, increasing the speed of distribution, creating new products and services, erasing limitations of traditional geographic markets, and changing the historical trade-off between production standardization and flexibility. The Internet is altering economies of scale, changing entry barriers, and redefining the relationship between industries and various suppliers, creditors, customers, and competitors.

To effectively capitalize on e-commerce, a number of organizations are establishing two new positions in their firms: *chief information officer (CIO)* and *chief technology officer (CTO)*. This trend reflects the growing importance of *information technology (IT)* in strategic management. A CIO and CTO work together to ensure that information needed to formulate, implement, and evaluate strategies is available where and when it is needed. These individuals are responsible for developing, maintaining, and updating a company's information database. The CIO is more a manager, managing the overall external-audit process; the CTO is more a technician, focusing on technical issues such as data acquisition, data processing, decision-support systems, and software and hardware acquisition.

Technological forces represent major opportunities and threats that must be considered in formulating strategies. Technological advancements can dramatically affect organizations' products, services, markets, suppliers, distributors, competitors, customers, manufacturing processes, marketing practices, and competitive position. Technological advancements can create new markets, result in a proliferation of new and improved products, change the relative competitive cost positions in an industry, and render existing products and services obsolete. Technological changes can reduce or eliminate cost barriers between businesses, create shorter production runs, create shortages in technical skills, and result in changing values and expectations of employees, managers, and customers. Technological advancements can create new competitive advantages that are more powerful than existing advantages. No company or industry today is insulated against emerging technological developments. In high-tech industries, identification and evaluation of key technological opportunities and threats can be the most important part of the external strategic-management audit.

Organizations that traditionally have limited technology expenditures to what they can fund after meeting marketing and financial requirements urgently need a reversal in thinking. The pace of technological change is increasing and literally wiping out businesses every day. An emerging consensus holds that technology management is one of the key responsibilities of strategists. Firms should pursue strategies that take advantage of technological opportunities to achieve sustainable, competitive advantages in the marketplace.

> Technology-based issues will underlie nearly every important decision that strategists make. Crucial to those decisions will be the ability to approach technology planning analytically and strategically. . . . technology can be planned and managed using formal techniques similar to those used in business and capital investment planning. An effective technology strategy is built on a penetrating analysis of technology opportunities and threats, and an assessment of the relative importance of these factors to overall corporate strategy.[7]

In practice, critical decisions about technology too often are delegated to lower organizational levels or are made without an understanding of their strategic implications. Many strategists spend countless hours determining market share, positioning products in terms of features and price, forecasting sales and market size, and monitoring distributors; yet too often, technology does not receive the same respect.

Not all sectors of the economy are affected equally by technological developments. The communications, electronics, aeronautics, and pharmaceutical industries are much more volatile than the textile, forestry, and metals industries. For strategists in industries affected by rapid technological change, identifying and evaluating technological opportunities and threats can represent the most important part of an external audit.

For example, in the office supply industry, business customers find that purchasing supplies over the Internet is more convenient than shopping in a store. Office Depot was the first office supply company to establish a Web site for this purpose and remains the largest Internet office supply retailer, with close to $1 billion in sales. Staples, Inc., has recently also entered the Internet office supply business with its staples.com Web site, but it has yet to make a profit on these operations, although revenue from the site is growing dramatically.

Competitive Forces

VISIT THE NET

Provides information regarding the importance of gathering information about competitors. This Web site offers audio answers to key questions about intelligence systems. (www.fuld.com)

The top five U.S. competitors in four different industries are identified in Table 3-4. An important part of an external audit is identifying rival firms and determining their strengths, weaknesses, capabilities, opportunities, threats, objectives, and strategies.

Collecting and evaluating information on competitors is essential for successful strategy formulation. Identifying major competitors is not always easy because many firms have divisions that compete in different industries. Many multidivisional firms generally do not provide sales and profit information on a divisional basis for competitive reasons. Also, privately held firms do not publish any financial or marketing information. Addressing questions about competitors such as those presented in Table 3-5 is important in performing an external audit.

Competition in virtually all industries can be described as intense—and sometimes as cutthroat. For example, when Circuit City falters its major competitor, Best Buy, cuts prices, adds stores, and increases advertising aimed to further its rival's demise. Best Buy is opening 130 new stores in 2007, many near Circuit City stores, while Circuit City is closing underperforming stores, considering a sale of its 510-store chain in Canada, and

TABLE 3-4   The Top U.S. Five Competitors in Four Different Industries in 2006

	2006 Sales (In Millions)	% Change from 2005	2006 Profits (In Millions)	% Change from 2005
		Beverages		
Coca-Cola	24,088	+4	5,080	+4
Pepsi Bottling	12,730	+7	522	+12
Coca-Cola Enterprises	19,804	+6	(1,143)	−322
Anheuser-Busch	15,717	+5	1,965	+7
Molson Coors Brewing	5,903	+3	361	+168
		Pharmaceuticals		
Johnson & Johnson	53,324	+6	11,053	+6
Pfizer	52,415	+2	19,337	+139
Merck	22,636	+3	4,434	−4
Abbott Laboratories	22,476	+1	1,717	−49
Wyeth	20,351	+9	4,197	+15
		Industrial and Farm Equipment		
Caterpillar	41,517	+14	3,537	+24
Deere	22,769	+4	1,694	+17
Illinois Tool Works	14,055	+9	1,718	+15
Eaton	12,370	+11	950	+18
Cummins	11,362	+15	715	+30
		Computers		
Hewlett-Packard	91,658	+6	6,198	+158
IBM	91,424	+0	9,492	+20
Dell	57,095	+2	2,614	−27
Xerox	15,895	+1	1,210	+24
Apple Computer	19,315	+9	2,614	+50

Source: Adapted from *Fortune*, April 30, 2007, F50–F73.

TABLE 3-5 Key Questions About Competitors

1. What are the major competitors' strengths?
2. What are the major competitors' weaknesses?
3. What are the major competitors' objectives and strategies?
4. How will the major competitors most likely respond to current economic, social, cultural, demographic, environmental, political, governmental, legal, technological, and competitive trends affecting our industry?
5. How vulnerable are the major competitors to our alternative company strategies?
6. How vulnerable are our alternative strategies to successful counterattack by our major competitors?
7. How are our products or services positioned relative to major competitors?
8. To what extent are new firms entering and old firms leaving this industry?
9. What key factors have resulted in our present competitive position in this industry?
10. How have the sales and profit rankings of major competitors in the industry changed over recent years? Why have these rankings changed that way?
11. What is the nature of supplier and distributor relationships in this industry?
12. To what extent could substitute products or services be a threat to competitors in this industry?

laying off another 3,400 employees in fiscal 2007. Best Buy's first-quarter 2007 profits were up 18 percent, while Circuit City again lost money.

As Dollar General, based in the U.S. state of Tennessee, falters its major competitor, Family Dollar Stores, based in the U.S. state of North Carolina, intensifies its efforts to cripple Dollar General. With 6,300 stores and $6.4 billion in annual sales, the smaller Family Dollar Stores is rapidly gaining on Dollar General, an 8,260-store chain with $9.2 billion in annual sales. Whereas Dollar General is closing stores, revamping inventory strategy, and laying off employees, Family Dollar is growing and practicing "zone pricing"—raising or lowering prices on given items at given stores to capitalize on competitive pressure. Dollar General uses "uniform pricing," which refers to consistent prices from store to store. Weakened, Dollar General was bought out by Kohlberg Kravis Roberts in 2007. If a firm detects weakness in a competitor, no mercy at all is shown in capitalizing on its problems.

Seven characteristics describe the most competitive companies:

1. Market share matters; the 90th share point isn't as important as the 91st, and nothing is more dangerous than falling to 89.
2. Understand and remember precisely what business you are in.
3. Whether it's broke or not, fix it—make it better; not just products, but the whole company, if necessary.
4. Innovate or evaporate; particularly in technology-driven businesses, nothing quite recedes like success.
5. Acquisition is essential to growth; the most successful purchases are in niches that add a technology or a related market.
6. People make a difference; tired of hearing it? Too bad.
7. There is no substitute for quality and no greater threat than failing to be cost-competitive on a global basis.

These are complementary concepts, not mutually exclusive ones.[8]

Competitive Intelligence Programs

What is competitive intelligence? *Competitive intelligence (CI)*, as formally defined by the Society of Competitive Intelligence Professionals (SCIP), is a systematic and ethical process for gathering and analyzing information about the competition's activities and general business trends to further a business's own goals (SCIP Web site).

Good competitive intelligence in business, as in the military, is one of the keys to success. The more information and knowledge a firm can obtain about its competitors, the more likely it is that it can formulate and implement effective strategies. Major competitors' weaknesses can represent external opportunities; major competitors' strengths may represent key threats.

According to *BusinessWeek* magazine, there are more than 5,000 corporate spies now actively engaged in intelligence activities, and 9 out of 10 large companies have employees dedicated solely to gathering competitive intelligence.[9] The article contends that many large U.S. companies spend more than $1 million annually tracking their competitors. Evidence suggests that the benefits of corporate spying include increased revenues, lower costs, and better decision making.

Unfortunately, the majority of U.S. executives grew up in times when U.S. firms dominated foreign competitors so much that gathering competitive intelligence did not seem worth the effort. Too many of these executives still cling to these attitudes—to the detriment of their organizations today. Even most MBA programs do not offer a course in competitive and business intelligence, thus reinforcing this attitude. As a consequence, three strong misperceptions about business intelligence prevail among U.S. executives today:

1. Running an intelligence program requires lots of people, computers, and other resources.
2. Collecting intelligence about competitors violates antitrust laws; business intelligence equals espionage.
3. Intelligence gathering is an unethical business practice.[10]

All three of these perceptions are totally misguided. Any discussions with a competitor about price, market, or geography intentions could violate antitrust statutes, but this fact must not lure a firm into underestimating the need for and benefits of systematically collecting information about competitors for the purpose of enhancing a firm's effectiveness. The Internet has become an excellent medium for gathering competitive intelligence. Information gathering from employees, managers, suppliers, distributors, customers, creditors, and consultants also can make the difference between having superior or just average intelligence and overall competitiveness.

VISIT THE NET

Describes the nature and role of strategic planning in a firm. (www. nonprofits.org/npofaq/03/22.html)

Firms need an effective competitive intelligence (CI) program. The three basic missions of a CI program are (1) to provide a general understanding of an industry and its competitors, (2) to identify areas in which competitors are vulnerable and to assess the impact strategic actions would have on competitors, and (3) to identify potential moves that a competitor might make that would endanger a firm's position in the market.[11] Competitive information is equally applicable for strategy formulation, implementation, and evaluation decisions. An effective CI program allows all areas of a firm to access consistent and verifiable information in making decisions. All members of an organization—from the chief executive officer to custodians—are valuable intelligence agents and should feel themselves to be a part of the CI process. Special characteristics of a successful CI program include flexibility, usefulness, timeliness, and cross-functional cooperation.

The increasing emphasis on *competitive analysis* in the United States is evidenced by corporations putting this function on their organizational charts under job titles such as Director of Competitive Analysis, Competitive Strategy Manager, Director of Information Services, or Associate Director of Competitive Assessment. The responsibilities of a *director of competitive analysis* include planning, collecting data, analyzing data, facilitating the process of gathering and analyzing data, disseminating intelligence on a timely basis, researching special issues, and recognizing what information is important and who needs to know. Competitive intelligence is not corporate espionage because 95 percent of the information a company needs to make strategic decisions is available and accessible to the public. Sources of competitive information include trade journals, want ads, newspaper articles, and government filings, as well as customers, suppliers, distributors, competitors themselves, and the Internet.

Unethical tactics such as bribery, wiretapping, and computer break-ins should never be used to obtain information. Marriott and Motorola—two U.S. companies that do a particularly good job of gathering competitive intelligence—agree that all the information you could wish for can be collected without resorting to unethical tactics. They keep their intelligence staffs small, usually under five people, and spend less than $200,000 per year on gathering competitive intelligence.

Unilever sued Procter & Gamble (P&G) over that company's corporate-espionage activities to obtain the secrets of its Unilever hair-care business. After spending $3 million

85

to establish a team to find out about competitors in the domestic hair-care industry, P&G allegedly took roughly 80 documents from garbage bins outside Unilever's Chicago offices. P&G produces Pantene and Head & Shoulders shampoos, while Unilever has hair-care brands such as ThermaSilk, Suave, Salon Selectives, and Finesse. Similarly, Oracle Corp. recently admitted that detectives it hired paid janitors to go through Microsoft Corp.'s garbage, looking for evidence to use in court.

An interesting aspect of any competitive analysis discussion is whether strategies themselves should be secret or open within firms. The Chinese warrior Sun Tzu and military leaders today strive to keep strategies secret, as war is based on deception. However, for a business organization, secrecy may not be best. Keeping strategies secret from employees and stakeholders at large could severely inhibit employee and stakeholder communication, understanding, and commitment and also forgo valuable input that these persons could have regarding formulation and/or implementation of that strategy. Thus strategists in a particular firm must decide for themselves whether the risk of rival firms easily knowing and exploiting a firm's strategies is worth the benefit of improved employee and stakeholder motivation and input. Most executives agree that some strategic information should remain confidential to top managers, and that steps should be taken to ensure that such information is not disseminated beyond the inner circle. For a firm that you may own or manage, would you advocate openness or secrecy in regard to strategies being formulated and implemented?

Cooperation Among Competitors

VISIT THE NET

Gives 30+ pages of excellent detail on "Developing a Business Strategy." (www.planware.org/strategy.htm)

Strategies that stress cooperation among competitors are being used more. For example, Lockheed teamed up with British Aerospace PLC to compete against Boeing Company to develop the next-generation U.S. fighter jet. Lockheed's cooperative strategy with a profitable partner in the Airbus Industrie consortium encourages broader Lockheed–European collaboration as Europe's defense industry consolidates. The British firm offers Lockheed special expertise in the areas of short takeoff and vertical landing technologies, systems integration, and low-cost design and manufacturing.

Cooperative agreements between competitors are even becoming popular. For collaboration between competitors to succeed, both firms must contribute something distinctive, such as technology, distribution, basic research, or manufacturing capacity. But a major risk is that unintended transfers of important skills or technology may occur at organizational levels below where the deal was signed.[12] Information not covered in the formal agreement often gets traded in the day-to-day interactions and dealings of engineers, marketers, and product developers. Firms often give away too much information to rival firms when operating under cooperative agreements! Tighter formal agreements are needed.

Perhaps the best example of rival firms in an industry forming alliances to compete against each other is the airline industry. Today there are three major alliances. The Star Alliance has 16 airlines such as Air Canada, Mexicana, Spanair, United, and Varig; the OneWorld Alliance has 8 airlines such as American, British Air, and LanChile; and finally, SkyTeam Alliance has 6 airlines such as Air France, Delta, and Korean Air. KLM is set to join SkyTeam soon, Swiss International is scheduled to join OneWorld, and USAirways is scheduled to join Star Alliance. Firms are moving to compete as groups within alliances more and more as it becomes increasingly difficult to survive alone in some industries.

The idea of joining forces with a competitor is not easily accepted by Americans, who often view cooperation and partnerships with skepticism and suspicion. Indeed, joint ventures and cooperative arrangements among competitors demand a certain amount of trust if companies are to combat paranoia about whether one firm will injure the other. However, multinational firms are becoming more globally cooperative, and increasing numbers of domestic firms are joining forces with competitive foreign firms to reap mutual benefits. Kathryn Harrigan at Columbia University says, "Within a decade, most companies will be members of teams that compete against each other." Northrop Grumman is planning to partner with Airbus parent EADS in Europe to battle Boeing for a Pentagon contract for aerial-refueling planes. These talks are ongoing at this time. EADS is a French/German company but is perceived widely as French because Airbus planes are assembled in France. Northrop is based in Los Angeles.

U.S. companies often enter alliances primarily to avoid investments, being more interested in reducing the costs and risks of entering new businesses or markets than in acquiring new skills. In contrast, *learning from the partner* is a major reason why Asian and European firms enter into cooperative agreements. U.S. firms, too, should place learning high on the list of reasons to be cooperative with competitors. U.S. companies often form alliances with Asian firms to gain an understanding of their manufacturing excellence, but Asian competence in this area is not easily transferable. Manufacturing excellence is a complex system that includes employee training and involvement, integration with suppliers, statistical process controls, value engineering, and design. In contrast, U.S. know-how in technology and related areas can be imitated more easily. U.S. firms thus need to be careful not to give away more intelligence than they receive in cooperative agreements with rival Asian firms.

Market Commonality and Resource Similarity

By definition, competitors are firms that offer similar products and services in the same market. Markets can be geographic or product areas or segments. For example, in the insurance industry the markets are broken down into commercial/consumer, health/life, and Europe/Asia. Researchers use the terms *market commonality* and *resource similarity* to study rivalry among competitors. *Market commonality* can be defined as the number and significance of markets that a firm competes in with rivals.[13] *Resource similarity* is the extent to which the type and amount of a firm's internal resources are comparable to a rival.[14] One way to analyze competitiveness between two or among several firms is to investigate market commonality and resource similarity issues while looking for areas of potential competitive advantage along each firm's value chain.

Competitive Analysis: Porter's Five-Forces Model

As illustrated in Figure 3-3, *Porter's Five-Forces Model* of competitive analysis is a widely used approach for developing strategies in many industries. The intensity of competition among firms varies widely across industries. Table 3-6 reveals the average profit margin and return on investment for firms in different industries. Note the substantial variation among industries. For example, the range in profit margin goes from 0 to 18 for food production to computer software, respectively. Intensity of competition is highest in lower-return industries. The collective impact of competitive forces is so brutal in some industries that the market is clearly "unattractive" from a profit-making standpoint. Rivalry among existing firms is severe, new rivals can enter the industry with relative

FIGURE 3-3

The Five-Forces Model of Competition

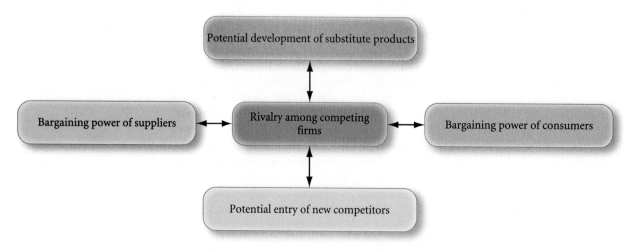

TABLE 3-6 Intensity of Competition among Firms in Different Industries (A through H industries only)

Industry	Profit Margin	Return on Investment
Aerospace and Defense	6	6
Airlines	2	2
Apparel	5	8
Automotive Retailing	1	3
Beverages	7	4
Building Materials, Glass	14	14
Chemicals	5	5
Commercial Banks	16	1.3
Computer Peripherals	8	7
Computer Software	18	8
Computers, Office Equipment	6	7
Diversified Financials	12	1
Diversified Outsourcing Services	4	5
Electronics, Electrical Equipment	7	8
Energy	3	3
Engineering, Construction	2	4
Entertainment	10	4
Financial Data Services	10	6
Food and Drug Stores	2	5
Food Consumer Products	5	6
Food Production	0	1
Food Services	4	7
Forest and Paper Products	3	4
Furniture	5	7
General Merchandisers	3	5
Health Care: Insurance	5	8
Health Care: Medical Facilities	4	4
Health Care: Pharmacy	3	9
Home Equipment/Furnishings	4	6
Homebuilders	6	6
Hotels, Casinos, Resorts	7	3

Source: Adapted from John Moore, "Ranked Within Industries," *Fortune* (April 30, 2007): F-50 to F-75.

ease, and both suppliers and customers can exercise considerable bargaining leverage. According to Porter, the nature of competitiveness in a given industry can be viewed as a composite of five forces:

1. Rivalry among competing firms
2. Potential entry of new competitors
3. Potential development of substitute products
4. Bargaining power of suppliers
5. Bargaining power of consumers

The following three steps for using Porter's Five-Forces Model can reveal whether competition in a given industry is such that the firm can make an acceptable profit:

1. Identify key aspects or elements of each competitive force that impact the firm.
2. Evaluate how strong and important each element is for the firm.
3. Decide whether the collective strength of the elements is worth the firm entering or staying in the industry.

VISIT THE NET

Gives good information about why employees may resist change. (http://www.mindtools.com/)

Rivalry Among Competing Firms

Rivalry among competing firms is usually the most powerful of the five competitive forces. The strategies pursued by one firm can be successful only to the extent that they provide competitive advantage over the strategies pursued by rival firms. Changes in strategy by one firm may be met with retaliatory countermoves, such as lowering prices, enhancing quality, adding features, providing services, extending warranties, and increasing advertising.

Free-flowing information on the Internet is driving down prices and inflation worldwide. The Internet, coupled with the common currency in Europe, enables consumers to make price comparisons easily across countries. Just for a moment, consider the implications for car dealers who used to know everything about a new car's pricing, while you, the consumer, knew very little. You could bargain, but being in the dark, you rarely could win. Now you can go to Web sites such as CarPoint.com or Edmunds.com and learn more about new car prices than the car salesperson, and you can even shop online in a few hours at every dealership within 500 kilometers to find the best price and terms. So you, the consumer, can win. This is true in many, if not most, business-to-consumer and business-to-business sales transactions today.

The intensity of rivalry among competing firms tends to increase as the number of competitors increases, as competitors become more equal in size and capability, as demand for the industry's products declines, and as price cutting becomes common. Rivalry also increases when consumers can switch brands easily; when barriers to leaving the market are high; when fixed costs are high; when the product is perishable; when consumer demand is growing slowly or declines such that rivals have excess capacity and/or inventory; when the products being sold are commodities (not easily differentiated such as gasoline); when rival firms are diverse in strategies, origins, and culture; and when mergers and acquisitions are common in the industry. As rivalry among competing firms intensifies, industry profits decline, in some cases to the point where an industry becomes inherently unattractive.

Rivalry in the automobile industry is fierce. As Ford and General Motors' market shares steadily decline, Toyota and Honda have stepped up their marketing and production efforts in the United States. Toyota is currently building its eighth North American assembly plant, in the southeast United States. Toyota's new plant starts production in 2009 and has a capacity of 200,000 vehicles annually. Ford and GM are both losing money in their North American auto operations. When rival firms sense weakness, typically they will intensify both marketing and production efforts to capitalize on the "opportunity."

Potential Entry of New Competitors

Whenever new firms can easily enter a particular industry, the intensity of competitiveness among firms increases. Barriers to entry, however, can include the need to gain economies of scale quickly, the need to gain technology and specialized know-how, the lack of experience, strong customer loyalty, strong brand preferences, large capital requirements, lack of adequate distribution channels, government regulatory policies, tariffs, lack of access to raw materials, possession of patents, undesirable locations, counterattack by entrenched firms, and potential saturation of the market.

Despite numerous barriers to entry, new firms sometimes enter industries with higher-quality products, lower prices, and substantial marketing resources. The strategist's job, therefore, is to identify potential new firms entering the market, to monitor the new rival firms' strategies, to counterattack as needed, and to capitalize on existing strengths and opportunities. When the threat of new firms entering the market is strong, incumbent firms generally fortify their positions and take actions to deter new entrants, such as lowering prices, extending warranties, adding features, or offering financing specials.

Potential Development of Substitute Products

In many industries, firms are in close competition with producers of substitute products in other industries. Examples are plastic container producers competing with glass, paper-board, and aluminum can producers, and acetaminophen manufacturers competing with other manufacturers of pain and headache remedies. The presence of substitute products puts a ceiling on the price that can be charged before consumers will switch to the substitute product. Price ceilings equate to profit ceilings and more intense competition among rivals. Producers of eyeglasses and contact lenses, for example, face increasing competitive pressures from laser eye surgery. Producers of sugar face similar pressures from artificial sweeteners. Newspapers and magazines face substitute-product competitive pressures from the Internet and 24-hour cable television. The magnitude of competitive pressure derived from development of substitute products is generally evidenced by rivals' plans for expanding production capacity, as well as by their sales and profit growth numbers.

Competitive pressures arising from substitute products increase as the relative price of substitute products declines and as consumers' switching costs decrease. The competitive strength of substitute products is best measured by the inroads into the market share those products obtain, as well as those firms' plans for increased capacity and market penetration.

Bargaining Power of Suppliers

The bargaining power of suppliers affects the intensity of competition in an industry, especially when there is a large number of suppliers, when there are only a few good substitute raw materials, or when the cost of switching raw materials is especially costly. It is often in the best interest of both suppliers and producers to assist each other with reasonable prices, improved quality, development of new services, just-in-time deliveries, and reduced inventory costs, thus enhancing long-term profitability for all concerned.

Firms may pursue a backward integration strategy to gain control or ownership of suppliers. This strategy is especially effective when suppliers are unreliable, too costly, or not capable of meeting a firm's needs on a consistent basis. Firms generally can negotiate more favorable terms with suppliers when backward integration is a commonly used strategy among rival firms in an industry.

However, in many industries it is more economical to use outside suppliers of component parts than to self-manufacture the items. This is true, for example, in the outdoor power equipment industry where producers of lawn mowers, rotary tillers, leaf blowers, and edgers such as Murray generally obtain their small engines from outside manufacturers such as Briggs & Stratton who specialize in such engines and have huge economies of scale.

In more and more industries, sellers are forging strategic partnerships with select suppliers in efforts to (1) reduce inventory and logistics costs (e.g., through just-in-time deliveries); (2) speed the availability of next-generation components; (3) enhance the quality of the parts and components being supplied and reduce defect rates; and (4) squeeze out important cost savings for both themselves and their suppliers.[15]

Bargaining Power of Consumers

When customers are concentrated or large or buy in volume, their bargaining power represents a major force affecting the intensity of competition in an industry. Rival firms may offer extended warranties or special services to gain customer loyalty whenever the bargaining power of consumers is substantial. Bargaining power of consumers also is higher when the products being purchased are standard or undifferentiated. When this is the case, consumers often can negotiate selling price, warranty coverage, and accessory packages to a greater extent.

The bargaining power of consumers can be the most important force affecting competitive advantage. Consumers gain increasing bargaining power under the following circumstances:

1. If they can inexpensively switch to competing brands or substitutes
2. If they are particularly important to the seller
3. If sellers are struggling in the face of falling consumer demand
4. If they are informed about sellers' products, prices, and costs
5. If they have discretion in whether and when they purchase the product[16]

Sources of External Information

A wealth of strategic information is available to organizations from both published and unpublished sources. Unpublished sources include customer surveys, market research, speeches at professional and shareholders' meetings, television programs, interviews, and conversations with stakeholders. Published sources of strategic information include periodicals, journals, reports, government documents, abstracts, books, directories, newspapers, and manuals. The Internet has made it easier for firms to gather, assimilate, and evaluate information.

The Internet offers consumers and businesses a widening range of services and information resources from all over the world. Interactive services offer users not only access to information worldwide but also the ability to communicate with the person or company that created the information. Historical barriers to personal and business success—time zones and diverse cultures—are being eliminated. The Internet has become as important to our society as television and newspapers.

VISIT THE NET

Gives an extensive slide show presentation about strategic management, from beginning to the end of the process. (www.csuchico.edu/mgmt/strategy/)

Forecasting Tools and Techniques

Forecasts are educated assumptions about future trends and events. Forecasting is a complex activity because of factors such as technological innovation, cultural changes, new products, improved services, stronger competitors, shifts in government priorities, changing social values, unstable economic conditions, and unforeseen events. Managers often must rely upon published forecasts to effectively identify key external opportunities and threats.

A sense of the future permeates all action and underlies every decision a person makes. People eat expecting to be satisfied and nourished—in the future. People sleep assuming that in the future they will feel rested. They invest energy, money, and time because they believe their efforts will be rewarded in the future. They build highways assuming that automobiles and trucks will need them in the future. Parents educate children on the basis of forecasts that they will need certain skills, attitudes, and knowledge when they grow up. The truth is we all make implicit forecasts throughout our daily lives. The question, therefore, is not whether we should forecast but rather how we can best forecast to enable us to move beyond our ordinarily unarticulated assumptions about the future. Can we obtain information and then make educated assumptions (forecasts) to better guide our current decisions to achieve a more desirable future state of affairs? We should go into the future with our eyes and our minds open, rather than stumble into the future with our eyes closed.[17]

Many publications and sources on the Internet forecast external variables. Several published examples include *Industry Week*'s "Trends and Forecasts," *BusinessWeek*'s "Investment Outlook," and Standard & Poor's *Industry Survey*. The reputation and continued success of these publications depend partly on accurate forecasts, so published sources of information can offer excellent projections. An especially good Web site for industry forecasts is finance.yahoo.com. Just insert a firm's stock symbol and go from there.

Sometimes organizations must develop their own projections. Most organizations forecast (project) their own revenues and profits annually. Organizations sometimes forecast market share or customer loyalty in local areas. Because forecasting is so important in strategic management and because the ability to forecast (in contrast to the ability to use a forecast) is essential, selected forecasting tools are examined further here.

Forecasting tools can be broadly categorized into two groups: quantitative techniques and qualitative techniques. Quantitative forecasts are most appropriate when historical data are available and when the relationships among key variables are expected to remain the same in the future. *Linear regression,* for example, is based on the assumption that the future will be just like the past—which, of course, it never is. As historical relationships become less stable, quantitative forecasts become less accurate.

No forecast is perfect, and some forecasts are even wildly inaccurate. This fact accents the need for strategists to devote sufficient time and effort to study the underlying bases for published forecasts and to develop internal forecasts of their own. Key external opportunities and threats can be effectively identified only through good forecasts. Accurate forecasts can provide major competitive advantages for organizations. Forecasts are vital to the strategic-management process and to the success of organizations.

Making Assumptions

Planning would be impossible without assumptions. McConkey defines assumptions as the "best present estimates of the impact of major external factors, over which the manager has little if any control, but which may exert a significant impact on performance or the ability to achieve desired results."[18] Strategists are faced with countless variables and imponderables that can be neither controlled nor predicted with 100 percent accuracy. Wild guesses should never be made in formulating strategies, but reasonable assumptions based on available information must always be made.

By identifying future occurrences that could have a major effect on the firm and by making reasonable assumptions about those factors, strategists can carry the strategic-management process forward. Assumptions are needed only for future trends and events that are most likely to have a significant effect on the company's business. Based on the best information at the time, assumptions serve as checkpoints on the validity of strategies. If future occurrences deviate significantly from assumptions, strategists know that corrective actions may be needed. Without reasonable assumptions, the strategy-formulation process could not proceed effectively. Firms that have the best information generally make the most accurate assumptions, which can lead to major competitive advantages.

The Global Challenge

Foreign competitors are battering firms in many industries. In its simplest sense, the international challenge faced by firms is twofold: (1) how to gain and maintain exports to other nations and (2) how to defend domestic markets against imported goods. Few companies can afford to ignore the presence of international competition. Firms that seem insulated and comfortable today may be vulnerable tomorrow; banks have been an example, but this too is changing.

A world economy and monetary system are emerging. Corporations in every corner of the globe are taking advantage of the opportunity to share in the benefits of worldwide economic development. Markets are shifting rapidly and in many cases converging in tastes, trends, and prices. Innovative transport systems are accelerating the transfer of technology. Shifts in the nature and location of production systems, especially to China and India, are reducing the response time to changing market conditions.

More and more countries around the world are welcoming foreign investment and capital. As a result, labor markets have steadily become more international. East Asian countries have become market leaders in labor-intensive industries, Brazil offers abundant natural resources and rapidly developing markets, and Germany offers skilled labor and technology. The drive to improve the efficiency of global business operations is leading to greater functional specialization. This is not limited to a search for the familiar low-cost labor in Latin America or Asia. Other considerations include the cost of energy, availability of resources, inflation rates, existing tax rates, and the nature of trade regulations.

When it joined the World Trade Organization in 2001, China agreed to respect copyright protections and liberalize restrictions on the import and distribution of foreign-made goods. However, in 2008 Chinese counterfeiters still can be criminally prosecuted for commercial piracy only when caught in possession of at least 500 counterfeit items.[19] Chanel, LVMH, Prada, Burberry, and Pinault-Printemps-Redoute Gucci successfully sued a market stallholder in Beijing for copyright infringement on a full range of counterfeit goods. And China still has substantial barriers to sales of authentic copyrighted products. U.S. Trade Representative Susan Schwab says, "This is more than a handbag here or a logo item there; it is often theft on a grand scale." China's counterfeit trade practices contribute to an annual bilateral trade deficit of about $250 billion with the United States. Chinese pirating of products is an external threat facing many firms around the world.

Multinational Corporations

Multinational corporations (MNCs) face unique and diverse risks, such as expropriation of assets, currency losses through exchange rate fluctuations, unfavorable foreign court interpretations of contracts and agreements, social/political disturbances, import/export restrictions, tariffs, and trade barriers. Strategists in MNCs are often confronted with the need to be globally competitive and nationally responsive at the same time. With the rise in world commerce, government and regulatory bodies are more closely monitoring foreign business practices. The United States Foreign Corrupt Practices Act, for example, defines corrupt practices in many areas of business. A sensitive issue is that some MNCs sometimes violate legal and ethical standards of the home country, but not of the host country.

Before entering international markets, firms should scan relevant journals and patent reports, seek the advice of academic and research organizations, participate in international trade fairs, form partnerships, and conduct extensive research to broaden their contacts and diminish the risk of doing business in new markets. Firms can also reduce the risks of doing business internationally by obtaining insurance from the U.S. government's Overseas Private Investment Corporation (OPIC). Note in the "Global Perspective" section that General Motors and Ford, large American MNCs, are now being challenged not only by German and Japanese auto firms but also by Chinese auto firms.

GLOBAL PERSPECTIVE
China's Automobile Producers Heading to the United States in 2008

China's auto exports doubled in 2006 from the previous year to a record 340,000 units. Vice Minister of Commerce Wei Jianguo says, "China is aiming to lift the value of its vehicle and auto parts exports to $120 billion, or 10 percent of the world's total vehicle trading volume in the next ten years." China's seven million automobiles produced in 2006 catapulted the country ahead of Germany to become the world's number three automobile producer behind the United States and Japan. Chrysler has agreed to sell China's Chery Automobile Company subcompact cars in the United States in 2008.

A Chinese automaker, Changfeng Group, displayed five new vehicles at the 2007 Detroit Auto Show, marking the first Chinese autos on show in the United States. China has more than 100 automakers and the government in Beijing desires to see these firms consolidate and expand globally. The majority owner of Changfeng, Anhui Changfeng Yangzi Motor Manufacturing, is especially interested in promoting its Liebao brand in North America. Other Chinese automakers with plans to market cars in the United States for the first time next year include Great Wall Motor Company and Geely Automobile Company.

Source: Adapted from "China Auto Exports Doubled During 2006," *Wall Street Journal* (January 2, 2007): A16; and Norihiko Shirouzu, "Obscure Chinese Car Maker Seeks U.S. Presence," *Wall Street Journal* (January 3, 2007): B1.

A steelworker operates equipment at a car-part manufacturing plant outside of Beijing. *Source:* National Geographic Image Collection

93

Globalization

Globalization is a process of worldwide integration of strategy formulation, implementation, and evaluation activities. Strategic decisions are made based on their impact upon global profitability of the firm, rather than on just domestic or other individual country considerations. A global strategy seeks to meet the needs of customers worldwide, with the highest value at the lowest cost. This may mean locating production in countries with the lowest labor costs or abundant natural resources, locating research and complex engineering centers where skilled scientists and engineers can be found, and locating marketing activities close to the markets to be served. A global strategy includes designing, producing, and marketing products with global needs in mind, instead of considering individual countries alone. A global strategy integrates actions against competitors into a worldwide plan.

Globalization of industries is occurring for many reasons, including a worldwide trend toward similar consumption patterns, the emergence of global buyers and sellers, and e-commerce and the instant transmission of money and information across continents. The Olympics, the World Bank, world trade centers, the Red Cross, the Internet, environmental conferences, telecommunications, and economic summits all contribute to global interdependencies and the emerging global marketplace.

It is clear that different industries become global for different reasons. The need to amortize massive R&D investments over many markets is a major reason why the aircraft manufacturing industry became global. Monitoring globalization in one's industry is an important strategic-management activity. Knowing how to use that information for one's competitive advantage is even more important. For example, firms may look around the world for the best technology and select one that has the most promise for the largest number of markets. When firms design a product, they design it to be marketable in as many countries as possible. When firms manufacture a product, they select the lowest-cost source, which may be Japan for semiconductors, Sri Lanka for textiles, Malaysia for simple electronics, and Europe for precision machinery. MNCs design manufacturing systems to accommodate world markets. One of the riskiest strategies for a domestic firm is to remain solely a domestic firm in an industry that is rapidly becoming global.

Industry Analysis: The External Factor Evaluation (EFE) Matrix

An *External Factor Evaluation (EFE) Matrix* allows strategists to summarize and evaluate economic, social, cultural, demographic, environmental, political, governmental, legal, technological, and competitive information. Illustrated in Table 3-7, the EFE Matrix can be developed in five steps:

1. List key external factors as identified in the external-audit process. Include a total of 10 to 20 factors, including both opportunities and threats, that affect the firm and its industry. List the opportunities first and then the threats. Be as specific as possible, using percentages, ratios, and comparative numbers whenever possible.
2. Assign to each factor a weight that ranges from 0.0 (not important) to 1.0 (very important). The weight indicates the relative importance of that factor to being successful in the firm's industry. Opportunities often receive higher weights than threats, but threats can receive high weights if they are especially severe or threatening. Appropriate weights can be determined by comparing successful with unsuccessful competitors or by discussing the factor and reaching a group consensus. The sum of all weights assigned to the factors must equal 1.0.
3. Assign a rating between 1 and 4 to each key external factor to indicate how effectively the firm's current strategies respond to the factor, where 4 = *the response is superior*, 3 = *the response is above average*, 2 = *the response is average*, and 1 = *the response is poor*. Ratings are based on effectiveness of the firm's strategies. Ratings are thus company-based, whereas the weights in Step 2 are industry-based. It is important to note that both threats and opportunities can receive a 1, 2, 3, or 4.

4. Multiply each factor's weight by its rating to determine a weighted score.
5. Sum the weighted scores for each variable to determine the total weighted score for the organization.

Regardless of the number of key opportunities and threats included in an EFE Matrix, the highest possible total weighted score for an organization is 4.0 and the lowest possible total weighted score is 1.0. The average total weighted score is 2.5. A total weighted score of 4.0 indicates that an organization is responding in an outstanding way to existing opportunities and threats in its industry. In other words, the firm's strategies effectively take advantage of existing opportunities and minimize the potential adverse effects of external threats. A total score of 1.0 indicates that the firm's strategies are not capitalizing on opportunities or avoiding external threats.

An example of an EFE Matrix is provided in Table 3-7 for a local ten-theatre cinema complex. Note that the most important factor to being successful in this business is "Trend toward healthy eating eroding concession sales" as indicated by the 0.12 weight. Also note that the local cinema is doing excellent in regard to handling two factors, "TDB University is expanding 6 percent annually" and "Trend toward healthy eating eroding concession sales." Perhaps the cinema is placing flyers on campus and also adding yogurt and healthy drinks to its concession menu. Note that you may have a 1, 2, 3, or 4 anywhere down the Rating column. Note also that the factors are stated in quantitative terms to the extent possible, rather than being stated in vague terms. Quantify the factors as much as possible in constructing an EFE Matrix. Finally, note that the total weighted score of 2.58 is above the average (midpoint) of 2.5, so this cinema business is doing pretty well, taking advantage of the external opportunities and avoiding the threats facing the firm. There is definitely room for improvement, though, because the highest total weighted score would be 4.0. As indicated by ratings of 1, this business needs to capitalize more on the "two new neighborhoods nearby" opportunity and the "movies rented from Time Warner" threat.

TABLE 3-7 EFE Matrix for a Local Ten-Theatre Cinema Complex

Key External Factors	Weight	Rating	Weighted Score
Opportunities			
1. Rowan Province is growing 8% annually in population	0.05	3	0.15
2. TDB University is expanding 6% annually	0.08	4	0.32
3. Major competitor across town recently ceased operations	0.08	3	0.24
4. Demand for going to cinema growing 10% annually	0.07	2	0.14
5. Two new neighborhoods being developed within 3 miles	0.09	1	0.09
6. Disposable income among citizens grew 5% in prior year	0.06	3	0.18
7. Unemployment rate in county declined to 3.1%	0.03	2	0.06
Threats			
8. Trend toward healthy eating eroding concession sales	0.12	4	0.48
9. Demand for online movies and DVDs growing 10% annually	0.06	2	0.12
10. Commercial property adjacent to cinemas for sale	0.06	3	0.18
11. TDB University installing an on-campus movie theatre	0.04	3	0.12
12. County and city property taxes increasing 25% this year	0.08	2	0.16
13. Local religious groups object to movies being shown	0.04	3	0.12
14. Movies rented from local Blockbuster store up 12%	0.08	2	0.16
15. Movies rented last quarter from Time Warner up 15%	0.06	1	0.06
Total	**1.00**		**2.58**

95

Note also that there are many percentage-based factors among the group. Be quantitative to the extent possible! Note also that the ratings range from 1 to 4 on both the opportunities and threats.

The Competitive Profile Matrix (CPM)

The *Competitive Profile Matrix (CPM)* identifies a firm's major competitors and its particular strengths and weaknesses in relation to a sample firm's strategic position. The weights and total weighted scores in both a CPM and an EFE have the same meaning. However, *critical success* factors in a CPM include both internal and external issues; therefore, the ratings refer to strengths and weaknesses, where 4 = major strength, 3 = minor strength, 2 = minor weakness, and 1 = major weakness. There are some important differences between the EFE and CPM. First of all, the critical success factors in a CPM are broader, they do not include specific or factual data, and they even may focus on internal issues. The critical success factors in a CPM also are not grouped into opportunities and threats as they are in an EFE. In a CPM, the ratings and total weighted scores for rival firms can be compared to the sample firm. This comparative analysis provides important internal strategic information.

A sample Competitive Profile Matrix is provided in Table 3-8. In this example, the two most important factors to being successful in the industry are "advertising" and "global expansion," as indicated by weights of 0.20. If there were no weight column in this analysis, note that each factor then would be equally important. Thus, having a weight column makes for a more robust analysis, because it enables the analyst to assign higher and lower numbers to capture perceived or actual levels of importance. Note in Table 3-8 that Company 1 is strongest on "product quality," as indicated by a rating of 4, whereas Company 2 is strongest on "advertising." Overall, Company 1 is strongest, as indicated by the total weighted score of 3.15.

Other than the critical success factors listed in the example CPM, factors often included in this analysis include breadth of product line, effectiveness of sales distribution, proprietary or patent advantages, location of facilities, production capacity and efficiency, experience, union relations, technological advantages, and e-commerce expertise.

A word on interpretation: Just because one firm receives a 3.2 rating and another receives a 2.80 rating in a Competitive Profile Matrix, it does not follow that the first firm is 20 percent better than the second. Numbers reveal the relative strengths of firms, but their implied precision is an illusion. Numbers are not magic. The aim is not to arrive at a single number, but rather to assimilate and evaluate information in a meaningful way that aids in decision making.

TABLE 3-8 An Example Competitive Profile Matrix

Critical Success Factors	Weight	Company 1 Rating	Company 1 Score	Company 2 Rating	Company 2 Score	Company 3 Rating	Company 3 Score
Advertising	0.20	1	0.20	4	0.80	3	0.60
Product Quality	0.10	4	0.40	3	0.30	2	0.20
Price Competitiveness	0.10	3	0.30	2	0.20	4	0.40
Management	0.10	4	0.40	3	0.20	3	0.30
Financial Position	0.15	4	0.60	2	0.30	3	0.45
Customer Loyalty	0.10	4	0.40	3	0.30	2	0.20
Global Expansion	0.20	4	0.80	1	0.20	2	0.40
Market Share	0.05	1	0.05	4	0.20	3	0.15
Total	**1.00**		**3.15**		**2.50**		**2.70**

Note: (1) The ratings values are as follows: 1 = major weakness, 2 = minor weakness, 3 = minor strength, 4 = major strength. (2) As indicated by the total weighted score of 2.50, Competitor 2 is weakest. (3) Only eight critical success factors are included for simplicity; this is too few in actuality.

TABLE 3-9   Another Example of a Competitive Profile Matrix

Critical Success Factors	Weight	Company 1		Company 2		Company 3	
		Rating	Weighted Score	Rating	Weighted Score	Rating	Weighted Score
Market share	0.15	3	0.45	2	0.30	4	0.60
Inventory system	0.08	2	0.16	2	0.16	4	0.32
Financial position	0.10	2	0.20	3	0.30	4	0.40
Product quality	0.08	3	0.24	4	0.32	3	0.24
Consumer loyalty	0.02	3	0.06	3	0.06	4	0.08
Sales distribution	0.10	3	0.30	2	0.20	3	0.30
Global expansion	0.15	3	0.45	2	0.30	4	0.60
Organization structure	0.05	3	0.15	4	0.20	2	0.10
Production capacity	0.04	3	0.12	2	0.08	4	0.16
E-commerce	0.10	3	0.30	1	0.10	4	0.40
Customer service	0.10	3	0.30	2	0.20	4	0.40
Price competitive	0.02	4	0.08	1	0.02	3	0.06
Management experience	0.01	2	0.02	4	0.04	2	0.02
Total	**1.00**		**2.83**		**2.28**		**3.68**

Another Competitive Profile Matrix is provided in Table 3-9. Note that Company 2 has the best product quality and management experience; Company 3 has the best market share and inventory system; and Company 1 has the best price as indicated by the ratings.

Conclusion

Increasing turbulence in markets and industries around the world means the external audit has become an explicit and vital part of the strategic-management process. This chapter provides a framework for collecting and evaluating economic, social, cultural, demographic, environmental, political, governmental, legal, technological, and competitive information. Firms that do not mobilize and empower their managers and employees to identify, monitor, forecast, and evaluate key external forces may fail to anticipate emerging opportunities and threats and, consequently, may pursue ineffective strategies, miss opportunities, and invite organizational demise. Firms not taking advantage of the Internet are technologically falling behind.

A major responsibility of strategists is to ensure development of an effective external-audit system. This includes using information technology to devise a competitive intelligence system that works. The external-audit approach described in this chapter can be used effectively by any size or type of organization. Typically, the external-audit process is more informal in small firms, but the need to understand key trends and events is no less important for these firms. The EFE Matrix and Porter's Five-Forces Model can help strategists evaluate the market and industry, but these tools must be accompanied by good intuitive judgment. Multinational firms especially need a systematic and effective external-audit system because external forces among foreign countries vary so greatly.

We invite you to visit the David page on the Prentice Hall Companion Web site at www.prenhall.com/david for this chapter's review quiz.

Key Terms and Concepts

Chief Information Officer (CIO) (p. 113)
Chief Technology Officer (CTO) (p. 113)
Competitive Analysis (p. 116)
Competitive Intelligence (CI) (p. 115)

Issues for Review and Discussion

1. Explain how to conduct an external strategic-management audit.
2. Identify a recent economic, social, political, or technological trend that significantly affects financial institutions.
3. Discuss the following statement: Major opportunities and threats usually result from an interaction among key environmental trends rather than from a single external event or factor.
4. Identify two industries experiencing rapid technological changes and three industries that are experiencing little technological change. How does the need for technological forecasting differ in these industries? Why?
5. Use Porter's Five-Forces Model to evaluate competitiveness within the U.S. banking industry.
6. What major forecasting techniques would you use to identify (1) economic opportunities and threats and (2) demographic opportunities and threats? Why are these techniques most appropriate?
7. How does the external audit affect other components of the strategic-management process?
8. As the owner of a small business, explain how you would organize a strategic-information scanning system. How would you organize such a system in a large organization?
9. Construct an EFE Matrix for an organization of your choice.
10. Make an appointment with a librarian at your university to learn how to use online databases. Report your findings in class.
11. Give some advantages and disadvantages of cooperative versus competitive strategies.
12. As strategist for a local bank, explain when you would use qualitative versus quantitative forecasts.
13. What is your forecast for interest rates and the stock market in the next several months? As the stock market moves up, do interest rates always move down? Why? What are the strategic implications of these trends?
14. Explain how information technology affects strategies of the organization where you worked most recently.
15. Let's say your boss develops an EFE Matrix that includes 62 factors. How would you suggest reducing the number of factors to 20?
16. Discuss the ethics of gathering competitive intelligence.
17. Discuss the ethics of cooperating with rival firms.
18. Visit the SEC Web site at www.sec.gov, and discuss the benefits of using information provided there.
19. What are the major differences between U.S. and multinational operations that affect strategic management?
20. Why is globalization of industries a common factor today?
21. Do you agree with I/O theorists that external factors are more important than internal factors to a firm's achieving competitive advantage? Explain both your and their position.
22. Define, compare, and contrast the weights versus ratings in an EFE versus IFE Matrix.
23. Develop a Competitive Profile Matrix for your university. Include six factors.
24. List the 10 external areas that give rise to opportunities and threats.

Notes

1. York Freund, "Critical Success Factors," *Planning Review* 16, no. 4 (July–August 1988): 20.
2. A. M. McGahan, "Competition, Strategy and Business Performance," *California Management Review* 41, no. 3 (1999): 74–101; A. McGahan and M. Porter, "How Much Does Industry Matter Really?," *Strategic Management Journal* 18, no. 8 (1997): 15–30.
3. Ken Jackson, "State Population Changes by Race, Ethnicity," *USA Today* (May 17, 2007): 2A.
4. S&P Industry Surveys, Beverage Industry, 2005.
5. Ken Thurston, "Population Change in States' Top Urban Areas," *USA Today* (April 5, 2007): 13A.
6. Frederick Gluck, "Global Competition in the 1990s," *Journal of Business Strategy* (Spring 1983): 22–24.
7. John Harris, Robert Shaw, Jr., and William Sommers, "The Strategic Management of Technology," *Planning Review* 11, no. 11 (January–February 1983): 28, 35.
8. Bill Saporito, "Companies That Compete Best," *Fortune* (May 22, 1989): 36.
9. Louis Lavelle, "The Case of the Corporate Spy," *BusinessWeek* (November 26, 2001): 56–57.
10. Kenneth Sawka, "Demystifying Business Intelligence," *Management Review* (October 1996): 49.
11. John Prescott and Daniel Smith, "The Largest Survey of 'Leading-Edge' Competitor Intelligence Managers," *Planning Review* 17, no. 3 (May–June 1989): 6–13.
12. Gary Hamel, Yves Doz, and C. K. Prahalad, "Collaborate with Your Competitors—and Win," *Harvard Business Review* 67, no. 1 (January–February 1989): 133.
13. M.J. Chen. "Competitor Analysis and Interfirm Rivalry: Toward a Theoretical Integration," *Academy of Management Review* 21 (1996): 106.
14. S. Jayachandran, J. Gimeno, and P. R. Varadarajan, "Theory of Multimarket Competition: A Synthesis and Implications for Marketing Strategy," *Journal of Marketing* 63, 3 (1999): 59; and M. J. Chen. "Competitor Analysis and Interfirm Rivalry: Toward a Theoretical Integration," *Academy of Management Review* 21 (1996): 107–108.
15. Arthur Thompson, Jr., A. J. Strickland III, and John Gamble, *Crafting and Executing Strategy: Text and Readings* (New York: McGraw-Hill/Irwin, 2005): 63.
16. Michael E. Porter, *Competitive Strategy: Techniques for Analyzing Industries and Competitors* (New York: Free Press, 1980): 24–27.
17. horizon.unc.edu/projects/seminars/futuresresearch/rationale.asp.
18. Dale McConkey, "Planning in a Changing Environment," *Business Horizons* 31, no. 5 (September–October 1988): 67.
19. David Lynch, "U.S. Complains to WTO on China," *USA Today* (April 10, 2007): B1.

Current Readings

Baron, Robert A. "Opportunity Recognition as Pattern Recognition: How Entrepreneurs 'Connect the Dots' to Identify New Business Opportunities." *The Academy of Management Perspectives* 20, no. 1 (February 2006): 104.

Brews, Peter and Devararat Purohit. "Strategic Planning in Unstable Environments." *Long Range Planning* 40, no. 1 (February 2007): 64.

Gottschlag, Oliver and Maurizo Zollo. "Interest Alignment and Competitive Advantage." *The Academy of Management Review* 32, no. 2 (April 2007): 418.

Hambrick, Donald C. "Upper Echelons Theory: An Update" *The Academy of Management Review* 32, no. 2 (April 2007): 334.

Hult, G. T. M., D. J. Ketchen Jr., and T. B. Palmer. "Firm, Strategic Group, and Industry Influences on Performance." *Strategic Management Journal* 28, no. 2 (February 2007): 147.

King, Andrew. "Cooperation Between Corporations and Environmental Groups: A Transaction Cost Perspective." *The Academy of Management Perspectives* 32, no. 3 (July 2007): 889.

Rousseau, Denise M. and Rosemary Blatt. "Global Competition's Perfect Storm: Why Business and Labor Cannot Solve Their Problems Alone." *The Academy of Management Perspectives* 21, no. 2 (May 2007): 16.

Slone, Reuben E., John T. Mentzer, and Paul J. Dittmann "Are You the Weakest Link in Company's Supply Chain?" *Harvard Business Review* (September): 116.

• EXPERIENTIAL EXERCISES

DISNEY

Experiential Exercises 3A

Developing an EFE Matrix for Walt Disney Company

Purpose

This exercise will give you practice developing an EFE Matrix. An EFE Matrix summarizes the results of an external audit. This is an important tool widely used by strategists.

Instructions

Step 1   Join with two other students in class, and jointly prepare an EFE Matrix for Walt Disney Company. Refer back to the Cohesion Case and to Experiential Exercise 1A, if necessary, to identify external opportunities and threats. Use the information in the S&P Industry Surveys that you copied as part of Experiential Exercise 1A. Be sure not to include strategies as opportunities, but do include as many $'s, %'s, #'s, and ratios as possible.

Step 2   All three-person teams participating in this exercise should record their EFE total weighted scores on the board. Put your initials after your score to identify it as your team's.

Step 3   Compare the total weighted scores. Which team's score came closest to the instructor's answer? Discuss reasons for variation in the scores reported on the board.

Experiential Exercise 3B

The External Assessment

Purpose

This exercise will help you become familiar with important sources of external information available in your college library. A key part of preparing an external audit is searching the Internet and examining published sources of information for relevant economic, social,

A pair of Mickey and Minnie Mouse painted cast phenolic napkin rings. *Source:* (c) Judith Miller / Dorling Kindersley / Wallis and Wallis

cultural, demographic, environmental, political, governmental, legal, technological, and competitive trends and events. External opportunities and threats must be identified and evaluated before strategies can be formulated effectively.

Instructions

Step 1	Select a company or business where you currently or previously have worked. Conduct an external audit for this company. Find opportunities and threats in recent issues of newspapers and magazines. Search for information using the Internet. Use the following four Web sites: http://marketwatch.multexinvestor.com http://moneycentral.msn.com http://financeyahoo.com www.clearstation.com https://us.etrade.com/e/t/invest/markets.
Step 2	On a separate sheet of paper, list 10 opportunities and 10 threats that face this company. Be specific in stating each factor.
Step 3	Include a bibliography to reveal where you found the information.
Step 4	Write a three-page summary of your findings, and submit it to your instructor.

Experiential Exercise 3C

Developing an EFE Matrix for My University

Purpose

More colleges and universities are embarking upon the strategic-management process. Institutions are consciously and systematically identifying and evaluating external opportunities and threats facing higher education in your state, the nation, and the world.

Instructions

Step 1	Join with two other individuals in class and jointly prepare an EFE Matrix for your institution.
Step 2	Go to the board and record your total weighted score in a column that includes the scores of all three-person teams participating. Put your initials after your score to identify it as your team's.
Step 3	Which team viewed your college's strategies most positively? Which team viewed your college's strategies most negatively? Discuss the nature of the differences.

Experiential Exercise 3D

Developing a Competitive Profile Matrix for Walt Disney Company

Purpose

Monitoring competitors' performance and strategies is a key aspect of an external audit. This exercise is designed to give you practice evaluating the competitive position of organizations in a given industry and assimilating that information in the form of a Competitive Profile Matrix.

Instructions

Step 1	Turn back to the Cohesion Case and review the section on competitors (pages 71–75).
Step 2	On a separate sheet of paper, prepare a Competitive Profile Matrix that includes Walt Disney, Time Warner, and News Corporation.
Step 3	Turn in your Competitive Profile Matrix for a classwork grade.

Experiential Exercise 3E

Developing a Competitive Profile Matrix for My University

Purpose

Your college or university competes with all other educational institutions in the world, especially those in your own state. State funds, students, faculty, staff, endowments, gifts, and federal funds are areas of competitiveness. Other areas include athletic programs, dorm life, academic reputation, location, and career services. The purpose of this exercise is to give you practice thinking competitively about the business of education in your state.

Instructions

Step 1 Identify two colleges or universities in your state that compete directly with your institution for students. Interview several persons, perhaps classmates, who are aware of particular strengths and weaknesses of those universities. Record information about the two competing universities.

Step 2 Prepare a Competitive Profile Matrix that includes your institution and the two competing institutions. Include at least the following ten factors in your analysis:

1. Tuition costs
2. Quality of faculty
3. Academic reputation
4. Average class size
5. Campus landscaping
6. Athletic programs
7. Quality of students
8. Graduate programs
9. Location of campus
10. Campus culture

Step 3 Submit your Competitive Profile Matrix to your instructor for evaluation.

4 The Internal Assessment

The New York Stock Exchange. *Source:* EMGEducation Management Group

chapter objectives

After studying this chapter, you should be able to do the following:

1. Describe how to perform an internal strategic-management audit.

2. Discuss the Resource-Based View (RBV) in strategic management.

3. Discuss key interrelationships among the functional areas of business.

4. Compare and contrast culture in the United States with other countries.

5. Identify the basic functions or activities that make up management, marketing, finance/accounting, production/operations, research and development, and management information systems.

6. Explain how to determine and prioritize a firm's internal strengths and weaknesses.

7. Explain the importance of financial ratio analysis.

8. Discuss the nature and role of management information systems in strategic management.

9. Develop an Internal Factor Evaluation (IFE) Matrix.

10. Explain benchmarking as a strategic management tool.

experiential exercises

Experiential Exercise 4A
Performing a Financial Ratio Analysis for Walt Disney (DIS)

Experiential Exercise 4B
Constructing an IFE Matrix for Walt Disney (DIS)

Experiential Exercise 4C
Constructing an IFE Matrix for My University

This chapter focuses on identifying and evaluating a firm's strengths and weaknesses in the functional areas of business, including management, marketing, finance/accounting, production/operations, research and development, and management information systems. Relationships among these areas of business are examined. Strategic implications of important functional area concepts are examined. The process of performing an internal audit is described. The Resource-Based View (RBV) of strategic management is introduced as is the Value Chain Analysis (VCA) concept.

The Nature of an Internal Audit

VISIT THE NET

Excellent strategic planning quotes. (www.planware.org/quotes.htm#3)

All organizations have strengths and weaknesses in the functional areas of business. No enterprise is equally strong or weak in all areas. LG Electronics, for example, is known for excellent appliance production and product design, whereas Procter & Gamble is known for superb marketing. Internal strengths/weaknesses, coupled with external opportunities/threats and a clear statement of mission, provide the basis for establishing objectives and strategies. Objectives and strategies are established with the intention of capitalizing upon internal strengths and overcoming weaknesses. The internal-audit part of the strategic-management process is illustrated in Figure 4-1.

Key Internal Forces

It is not possible in a business policy text to review in depth all the material presented in courses such as marketing, finance, accounting, management, management information systems, and production/operations; there are many subareas within these functions, such as customer service, warranties, advertising, packaging, and pricing under marketing.

For different types of organizations, such as hospitals, universities, and government agencies, the functional business areas, of course, differ. In a hospital, for example,

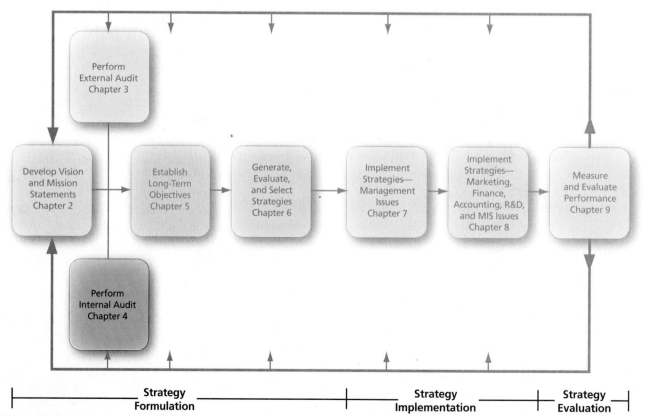

functional areas may include cardiology, hematology, nursing, maintenance, physician support, and receivables. Functional areas of a university can include athletic programs, placement services, housing, fundraising, academic research, counseling, and intramural programs. Within large organizations, each division has certain strengths and weaknesses.

A firm's strengths that cannot be easily matched or imitated by competitors are called *distinctive competencies.* Building competitive advantages involves taking advantage of distinctive competencies. For example, Siemens exploits its distinctive competence in research and development by producing a wide range of innovative products. Strategies are designed in part to improve on a firm's weaknesses, turning them into strengths—and maybe even into distinctive competencies.

Some researchers emphasize the importance of the internal audit part of the strategic-management process by comparing it to the external audit. Robert Grant concluded that the internal audit is more important, saying:

> In a world where customer preferences are volatile, the identity of customers is changing, and the technologies for serving customer requirements are continually evolving; an externally focused orientation does not provide a secure foundation for formulating long-term strategy. When the external environment is in a state of flux, the firm's own resources and capabilities may be a much more stable basis on which to define its identity. Hence, a definition of a business in terms of what it is capable of doing may offer a more durable basis for strategy than a definition based upon the needs which the business seeks to satisfy.[1]

The Process of Performing an Internal Audit

The process of performing an *internal audit* closely parallels the process of performing an external audit. Representative managers and employees from throughout the firm need to be involved in determining a firm's strengths and weaknesses. The internal audit requires gathering and assimilating information about the firm's management, marketing, finance/accounting, production/operations, research and development (R&D), and management information systems operations. Key factors should be prioritized as described in Chapter 3 so that the firm's most important strengths and weaknesses can be determined collectively.

Compared to the external audit, the process of performing an internal audit provides more opportunity for participants to understand how their jobs, departments, and divisions fit into the whole organization. This is a great benefit because managers and employees perform better when they understand how their work affects other areas and activities of the firm. For example, when marketing and manufacturing managers jointly discuss issues related to internal strengths and weaknesses, they gain a better appreciation of the issues, problems, concerns, and needs of all the functional areas. In organizations that do not use strategic management, marketing, finance, and manufacturing managers often do not interact with each other in significant ways. Performing an internal audit thus is an excellent vehicle or forum for improving the process of communication in the organization. *Communication* may be the most important word in management.

Performing an internal audit requires gathering, assimilating, and evaluating information about the firm's operations. Critical success factors, consisting of both strengths and weaknesses, can be identified and prioritized in the manner discussed in Chapter 3. According to William King, a task force of managers from different units of the organization, supported by staff, should be charged with determining the 10 to 20 most important strengths and weaknesses that should influence the future of the organization. He says:

> The development of conclusions on the 10 to 20 most important organizational strengths and weaknesses can be, as any experienced manager knows, a difficult task, when it involves managers representing various organizational interests and points of view. Developing a 20-page list of strengths and weaknesses could be accomplished relatively easily, but a list of the 10 to 15 most important ones involves significant analysis and negotiation. This is true because of the judgments that are required and the impact which such a list will inevitably have as it is used in the formulation, implementation, and evaluation of strategies.[2]

VISIT THE NET

Provides the complete strategic plan for the Wyoming Insurance Department Agency in the United States, including its list of strengths and weaknesses. (www.state.wy.us/state/strategy/insurance.html)

Strategic management is a highly interactive process that requires effective coordination among management, marketing, finance/accounting, production/operations, R&D, and management information systems managers. Although the strategic-management process is overseen by strategists, success requires that managers and employees from all functional areas work together to provide ideas and information. Financial managers, for example, may need to restrict the number of feasible options available to operations managers, or R&D managers may develop products for which marketing managers need to set higher objectives. A key to organizational success is effective coordination and understanding among managers from all functional business areas. Through involvement in performing an internal strategic-management audit, managers from different departments and divisions of the firm come to understand the nature and effect of decisions in other functional business areas in their firm. Knowledge of these relationships is critical for effectively establishing objectives and strategies.

A failure to recognize and understand relationships among the functional areas of business can be detrimental to strategic management, and the number of those relationships that must be managed increases dramatically with a firm's size, diversity, geographic dispersion, and the number of products or services offered. Governmental and nonprofit enterprises traditionally have not placed sufficient emphasis on relationships among the business functions. Some firms place too great an emphasis on one function at the expense of others. Ansoff explained:

> During the first fifty years, successful firms focused their energies on optimizing the performance of one of the principal functions: production/operations, R&D, or marketing. Today, due to the growing complexity and dynamism of the environment, success increasingly depends on a judicious combination of several functional influences. This transition from a single function focus to a multifunction focus is essential for successful strategic management.[3]

Financial ratio analysis exemplifies the complexity of relationships among the functional areas of business. A declining return on investment or profit margin ratio could be the result of ineffective marketing, poor management policies, research and development errors, or a weak management information system. The effectiveness of strategy formulation, implementation, and evaluation activities hinges upon a clear understanding of how major business functions affect one another. For strategies to succeed, a coordinated effort among all the functional areas of business is needed. In the case of planning, George wrote:

> We may conceptually separate planning for the purpose of theoretical discussion and analysis, but in practice, neither is it a distinct entity nor is it capable of being separated. The planning function is mixed with all other business functions and, like ink once mixed with water, it cannot be set apart. It is spread throughout and is a part of the whole of managing an organization.[4]

The Resource-Based View (RBV)

Gaining in popularity in the 1990s and continuing today, the *Resource-Based View (RBV)* approach to competitive advantage contends that internal resources are more important for a firm than external factors in achieving and sustaining competitive advantage. In contrast to the I/O theory presented in the previous chapter, proponents of the RBV view contend that organizational performance will primarily be determined by internal resources that can be grouped into three all-encompassing categories: physical resources, human resources, and organizational resources.[5] Physical resources include all plant and equipment, location, technology, raw materials, machines; human resources include all employees, training, experience, intelligence, knowledge, skills, abilities; and organizational resources include firm structure, planning processes, information systems, patents, trademarks, copyrights, databases, and so on. RBV theory asserts that resources are actually what helps a firm exploit opportunities and neutralize threats.

The basic premise of the RBV is that the mix, type, amount, and nature of a firm's internal resources should be considered first and foremost in devising strategies that can lead to sustainable competitive advantage. Managing strategically according to the RBV involves developing and exploiting a firm's unique resources and capabilities, and continually maintaining and strengthening those resources. The theory asserts that it is advantageous for a firm to pursue a strategy that is not currently being implemented by any competing firm. When other firms are unable to duplicate a particular strategy, then the focal firm has a sustainable competitive advantage, according to RBV theorists. For a resource to be valuable, however, it must be either (1) rare, (2) hard to imitate, or (3) not easily substitutable. Often called *empirical indicators,* these three characteristics of resources enable a firm to implement strategies that improve its efficiency and effectiveness and lead to a sustainable competitive advantage. The more a resource(s) is rare, nonimitable, and nonsubstitutable, the stronger a firm's competitive advantage will be and the longer it will last.

Rare resources are resources that other competing firms do not possess. If many firms have the same resource, then those firms will likely implement similar strategies, thus giving no one firm a sustainable competitive advantage. This is not to say that resources that are common are not valuable; they do indeed aid the firm in its chance for economic prosperity. However, to sustain a competitive advantage, it is more advantageous if the resource(s) is also rare.

It is also important that these same resources be difficult to imitate. If firms cannot easily gain the resources, say RBV theorists, then those resources will lead to a competitive advantage more so than resources easily imitable. Even if a firm employs resources that are rare, a sustainable competitive advantage may be achieved only if other firms cannot easily obtain these resources.

The third empirical indicator that can make resources a source of competitive advantage is substitutability. Borrowing from Porter's Five-Forces Model, to the degree that there are no viable substitutes, a firm will be able to sustain its competitive advantage. However, even if a competing firm cannot perfectly imitate a firm's resource, it can still obtain a sustainable competitive advantage of its own by obtaining resource substitutes.

The RBV has continued to grow in popularity and continues to seek a better understanding of the relationship between resources and sustained competitive advantage in strategic management. However, as alluded to in Chapter 3, one cannot say with any degree of certainty that either external or internal factors will always or even consistently be more important in seeking competitive advantage. Understanding both external and internal factors, and more importantly, understanding the relationships among them, will be the key to effective strategy formulation (discussed in Chapter 6). Since both external and internal factors continually change, strategists seek to identify and take advantage of positive changes and buffer against negative changes in a continuing effort to gain and sustain a firm's competitive advantage. This is the essence and challenge of strategic management, and oftentimes survival of the firm hinges on this work.

Integrating Strategy and Culture

Relationships among a firm's functional business activities perhaps can be exemplified best by focusing on organizational culture, an internal phenomenon that permeates all departments and divisions of an organization. *Organizational culture* can be defined as "a pattern of behavior that has been developed by an organization as it learns to cope with its problem of external adaptation and internal integration, and that has worked well enough to be considered valid and to be taught to new members as the correct way to perceive, think, and feel."[6] This definition emphasizes the importance of matching external with internal factors in making strategic decisions.

Organizational culture captures the subtle, elusive, and largely unconscious forces that shape a workplace. Remarkably resistant to change, culture can represent a major strength or weakness for the firm. It can be an underlying reason for strengths or weaknesses in any of the major business functions.

Defined in Table 4-1, *cultural products* include values, beliefs, rites, rituals, ceremonies, myths, stories, legends, sagas, language, metaphors, symbols, heroes, and heroines. These products or dimensions are levers that strategists can use to influence and direct strategy formulation, implementation, and evaluation activities. An organization's culture compares to an individual's personality in the sense that no two organizations have the same culture and no two individuals have the same personality. Both culture and personality are fairly enduring and can be warm, aggressive, friendly, open, innovative, conservative, liberal, harsh, or likable.

Dimensions of organizational culture permeate all the functional areas of business. It is something of an art to uncover the basic values and beliefs that are deeply buried in an organization's rich collection of stories, language, heroes, and rituals, but cultural products can represent both important strengths and weaknesses. Culture is an aspect of an organization that can no longer be taken for granted in performing an internal strategic-management audit because culture and strategy must work together.

The strategic-management process takes place largely within a particular organization's culture. Lorsch found that executives in successful companies are emotionally committed to the firm's culture, but he concluded that culture can inhibit strategic management in two basic ways. First, managers frequently miss the significance of changing external conditions because they are blinded by strongly held beliefs. Second, when a particular culture has been effective in the past, the natural response is to stick with it in the future, even during times of major strategic change.[7] An organization's culture must support the collective commitment of its people to a common purpose. It must foster competence and enthusiasm among managers and employees.

Organizational culture significantly affects business decisions and thus must be evaluated during an internal strategic-management audit. If strategies can capitalize on cultural strengths, such as a strong work ethic or highly ethical beliefs, then management often can swiftly and easily implement changes. However, if the firm's culture is not supportive, strategic changes may be ineffective or even counterproductive. A firm's culture can become antagonistic to new strategies, with the result being confusion and disorientation.

TABLE 4-1   Cultural Products and Associated Definitions

Rites	Relatively elaborate, dramatic, planned sets of activities that consolidate various forms of cultural expressions into one event, carried out through social interactions, usually for the benefit of an audience
Ceremonial	A system of several rites connected with a single occasion or event
Ritual	A standardized, detailed set of techniques and behaviors that manage anxieties but seldom produce intended, technical consequences of practical importance
Myth	A dramatic narrative of imagined events, usually used to explain origins or transformations of something; also, an unquestioned belief about the practical benefits of certain techniques and behaviors that is not supported by facts
Saga	A historical narrative describing the unique accomplishments of a group and its leaders, usually in heroic terms
Legend	A handed-down narrative of some wonderful event that is based on history but has been embellished with fictional details
Story	A narrative based on true events, sometimes a combination of truth and fiction
Folktale	A completely fictional narrative
Symbol	Any object, act, event, quality, or relation that serves as a vehicle for conveying meaning, usually by representing another thing
Language	A particular form or manner in which members of a group use sounds and written signs to convey meanings to each other
Metaphors	Shorthand of words used to capture a vision or to reinforce old or new values
Values	Life-directing attitudes that serve as behavioral guidelines
Belief	An understanding of a particular phenomenon
Heroes/Heroine	Individuals whom the organization has legitimized to model behavior for others

Source: Adapted from H. M. Trice and J. M. Beyer, "Studying Organizational Cultures through Rites and Ceremonials," *Academy of Management Review* 9, no. 4 (October 1984): 655.

An organization's culture should infuse individuals with enthusiasm for implementing strategies. Allarie and Firsirotu emphasized the need to understand culture:

Culture provides an explanation for the insuperable difficulties a firm encounters when it attempts to shift its strategic direction. Not only has the "right" culture become the essence and foundation of corporate excellence, it is also claimed that success or failure of reforms hinges on management's sagacity and ability to change the firm's driving culture in time and in time with required changes in strategies.[8]

The potential value of organizational culture has not been realized fully in the study of strategic management. Ignoring the effect that culture can have on relationships among the functional areas of business can result in barriers to communication, lack of coordination, and an inability to adapt to changing conditions. Some tension between culture and a firm's strategy is inevitable, but the tension should be monitored so that it does not reach a point at which relationships are severed and the culture becomes antagonistic. The resulting disarray among members of the organization would disrupt strategy formulation, implementation, and evaluation. On the other hand, a supportive organizational culture can make managing much easier.

Internal strengths and weaknesses associated with a firm's culture sometimes are overlooked because of the interfunctional nature of this phenomenon. It is important, therefore, for strategists to understand their firm as a sociocultural system. Success is often determined by linkages between a firm's culture and strategies. The challenge of strategic management today is to bring about the changes in organizational culture and individual mind-sets that are needed to support the formulation, implementation, and evaluation of strategies.

Domestic versus Foreign Cultures

To successfully compete in world markets, managers must obtain a better knowledge of historical, cultural, and religious forces that motivate and drive people in other countries. In Japan, for example, business relations operate within the context of *Wa,* which stresses group harmony and social cohesion. In China, business behavior revolves around *guanxi,* or personal relations. In Korea, activities involve concern for *inhwa,* or harmony based on respect of hierarchical relationships, including obedience to authority.[9]

In Europe, it is generally true that the farther north on the continent, the more participatory the management style. Most European workers are unionized and enjoy more frequent vacations and holidays than U.S. workers. A 90-minute lunch break plus 20-minute morning and afternoon breaks are common in European firms. Guaranteed permanent employment is commonly a part of employment contracts in Europe. In socialist countries such as France, Belgium, and the United Kingdom, the only ground for immediate dismissal from work is a criminal offense. A six-month trial period at the beginning of employment is usually part of the contract with a European firm. Many Europeans resent pay-for-performance, commission salaries, and objective measurement and reward systems. This is true especially of workers in southern Europe. Many Europeans also find the notion of team spirit difficult to grasp because the unionized environment has dichotomized worker–management relations throughout Europe.

A weakness that U.S. firms have in competing with Pacific Rim firms is a lack of understanding of Asian cultures, including how Asians think and behave. Spoken Chinese, for example, has more in common with spoken English than with spoken Japanese or Korean. Managers around the world face the responsibility of having to exert authority while at the same time trying to be liked by subordinates. U.S. managers consistently put more weight on being friendly and liked, whereas Asian and European managers exercise authority often without this concern. Americans tend to use first names instantly in business dealings with foreigners, but foreigners find this presumptuous. In Japan, for example, first names are used only among family members and intimate friends; even longtime business associates and coworkers shy away from the use of first names. Other cultural differences or pitfalls that managers need to know about are given in Table 4-2.

U.S. managers have a low tolerance for silence, whereas Asian managers view extended periods of silence as important for organizing and evaluating one's thoughts. U.S. managers are much more action-oriented than their counterparts around the world; they rush to appointments, conferences, and meetings—and then feel the day has been productive. But for foreign managers, resting, listening, meditating, and thinking is considered productive. Sitting through a conference without talking is unproductive in the United States, but it is viewed as positive in Japan if one's silence helps preserve unity.

U.S. managers also put greater emphasis on short-term results than foreign managers do. In marketing, for example, Japanese managers strive to achieve "everlasting customers," whereas many Americans strive to make a one-time sale. Marketing managers in Japan see making a sale as the beginning, not the end, of the selling process. This is an important distinction. Japanese managers often criticize U.S. managers for worrying more about shareholders, whom they do not know, than employees, whom they do know. Americans refer to "hourly employees," whereas many Japanese companies still refer to "lifetime employees."

Rose Knotts recently summarized some important cultural differences between U.S. and foreign managers:[10]

1.   Americans place an exceptionally high priority on time, viewing time as an asset. Many foreigners place more worth on relationships. This difference results in foreign managers often viewing U.S. managers as "more interested in business than people."
2.   Personal touching and distance norms differ around the world. Americans generally stand about three feet from each other when carrying on business conversations, but Arabs and Africans stand about one foot apart. Touching another person with the left hand in business dealings is taboo in some countries. American managers need to learn the personal-space rules of foreign managers with whom they interact in business.
3.   People in some cultures do not place the same significance on material wealth as American managers often do. Lists of the "largest corporations" and "highest-paid" executives abound in the United States. "More is better" and "bigger is better" in the United States, but not everywhere. This can be a consideration in trying to motivate individuals in other countries.
4.   Family roles and relationships vary in different countries. For example, males are valued more than females in some cultures, and peer pressure, work situations, and business interactions reinforce this phenomenon.

TABLE 4-2   Cultural Pitfalls That You Need to Know

- Waving is a serious insult in Greece and Nigeria, particularly if the hand is near someone's face.
- Making a "good-bye" wave in Europe can mean "No," but it means "Come here" in Peru.
- In China, last names are written first.
- A man named Carlos Lopez-Garcia should be addressed as Mr. Lopez in Latin America, but as Mr. Garcia in Brazil.
- Breakfast meetings are considered uncivilized in most foreign countries.
- Latin Americans are on average 20 minutes late to business appointments.
- Direct eye contact is impolite in Japan.
- Don't cross your legs in any Arab or many Asian countries—it's rude to show the sole of your shoe.
- In Brazil, touching your thumb and first finger—an American "Okay" sign—is the equivalent of raising your middle finger.
- Nodding or tossing your head back in southern Italy, Malta, Greece, and Tunisia means "No." In India, this body motion means "Yes."
- Snapping your fingers is vulgar in France and Belgium.
- Folding your arms across your chest is a sign of annoyance in Finland.
- In China, leave some food on your plate to show that your host was so generous that you couldn't finish.
- Do not eat with your left hand when dining with clients from Malaysia or India.
- One form of communication works the same worldwide. It's the smile—so take that along wherever you go.

5. Language differs dramatically across countries, even in countries where people speak the same language. Words and expressions commonly used in one country may be disrespectful in another.

6. Business and daily life in some societies are governed by religious factors. Prayer times, holidays, daily events, and dietary restrictions, for example, need to be respected by foreign managers not familiar with these practices in some countries.

7. Time spent with the family and the quality of relationships are more important in some cultures than the personal achievement and accomplishments espoused by the traditional U.S. manager. For example, where a person stands in the hierarchy of a firm's organizational structure, how large the firm is, and where the firm is located are much more important factors to U.S. managers than to many foreign managers.

8. Many cultures around the world value modesty, team spirit, collectivity, and patience much more than the competitiveness and individualism that are so important in the United States.

9. Punctuality is a valued personal trait when conducting business in the United States, but it is not revered in many of the world's societies. Eating habits also differ dramatically across cultures. For example, belching is acceptable in many countries as evidence of satisfaction with the food that has been prepared. Chinese culture considers it good manners to sample a portion of each food served.

10. To prevent social blunders when meeting with managers from other lands, one must learn and respect the rules of etiquette of others. Sitting on a toilet seat is viewed as unsanitary in most countries, but not in the United States. Leaving food or drink after dining is considered impolite in some countries, but not in China. Bowing instead of shaking hands is customary in many countries. Many cultures view Americans as unsanitary for locating toilet and bathing facilities in the same area, whereas Americans view people of some cultures as unsanitary for not taking a bath or shower every day.

11. Americans often do business with individuals they do not know, but this practice is not accepted in many other cultures. In Mexico and Japan, for example, an amicable relationship is often mandatory before conducting business.

In many countries, effective managers are those who are best at negotiating with government bureaucrats rather than those who inspire workers. Many U.S. managers are uncomfortable with nepotism and bribery, which are common in many countries. In almost every country except the United States, bribery is tax deductible.

The United States has gained a reputation for defending women from sexual harassment and minorities from discrimination, but not all countries embrace the same values.

American managers in China have to be careful about how they arrange office furniture because Chinese workers believe in *feng shui*, the practice of harnessing natural forces. U.S. managers in Japan have to be careful about *nemaswashio*, whereby Japanese workers expect supervisors to alert them privately of changes rather than informing them in a meeting. Japanese managers have little appreciation for versatility, expecting all managers to be the same. In Japan, "If a nail sticks out, you hit it into the wall," says Brad Lashbrook, an international consultant for Wilson Learning.

Probably the biggest obstacle to the effectiveness of managers from any country working in another is the fact that it is almost impossible to change the attitude of a foreign workforce. "The system drives you; you cannot fight the system or culture," says Bill Parker, president of Phillips Petroleum in Norway.

Management

The *functions of management* consist of five basic activities: planning, organizing, motivating, staffing, and controlling. An overview of these activities is provided in Table 4-3.

Planning

The only thing certain about the future of any organization is change, and *planning* is the essential bridge between the present and the future that increases the likelihood of achieving desired results. Planning is the process by which one determines whether to attempt a

TABLE 4-3   **The Basic Functions of Management**

Function	Description	Stage of Strategic-Management Process When Most Important
Planning	Planning consists of all those managerial activities related to preparing for the future. Specific tasks include forecasting, establishing objectives, devising strategies, developing policies, and setting goals.	Strategy Formulation
Organizing	Organizing includes all those managerial activities that result in a structure of task and authority relationships. Specific areas include organizational design, job specialization, job descriptions, job specifications, span of control, unity of command, coordination, job design, and job analysis.	Strategy Implementation
Motivating	Motivating involves efforts directed toward shaping human behavior. Specific topics include leadership, communication, work groups, behavior modification, delegation of authority, job enrichment, job satisfaction, needs fulfillment, organizational change, employee morale, and managerial morale.	Strategy Implementation
Staffing	Staffing activities are centered on personnel or human resource management. Included are wage and salary administration, employee benefits, interviewing, hiring, firing, training, management development, employee safety, affirmative action, equal employment opportunity, union relations, career development, personnel research, discipline policies, grievance procedures, and public relations.	Strategy Implementation
Controlling	Controlling refers to all those managerial activities directed toward ensuring that actual results are consistent with planned results. Key areas of concern include quality control, financial control, sales control, inventory control, expense control, analysis of variances, rewards, and sanctions.	Strategy Evaluation

task, works out the most effective way of reaching desired objectives, and prepares to overcome unexpected difficulties with adequate resources. Planning is the start of the process by which an individual or business may turn empty dreams into achievements. Planning enables one to avoid the trap of working extremely hard but achieving little.

Planning is an up-front investment in success. Planning helps a firm achieve maximum effect from a given effort. Planning enables a firm to take into account relevant factors and focus on the critical ones. Planning helps ensure that the firm can be prepared for all reasonable eventualities and for all changes that will be needed. Planning enables a firm to gather the resources needed and carry out tasks in the most efficient way possible. Planning enables a firm to conserve its own resources, avoid wasting ecological resources, make a fair profit, and be seen as an effective, useful firm. Planning enables a firm to identify precisely what is to be achieved and to detail precisely the who, what, when, where, why, and how needed to achieve desired objectives. Planning enables a firm to assess whether the effort, costs, and implications associated with achieving desired objectives are warranted.[11] Planning is the cornerstone of effective strategy formulation. But even though it is considered the foundation of management, it is commonly the task that managers neglect most. Planning is essential for successful strategy implementation and strategy evaluation, largely because organizing, motivating, staffing, and controlling activities depend upon good planning.

The process of planning must involve managers and employees throughout an organization. The time horizon for planning decreases from two to five years for top-level to less than six months for lower-level managers. The important point is that all managers do planning and should involve subordinates in the process to facilitate employee understanding and commitment.

Planning can have a positive impact on organizational and individual performance. Planning allows an organization to identify and take advantage of external opportunities as well as minimize the impact of external threats. Planning is more than extrapolating from the past and present into the future. It also includes developing a mission, forecasting future events and trends, establishing objectives, and choosing strategies to pursue.

An organization can develop synergy through planning. *Synergy* exists when everyone pulls together as a team that knows what it wants to achieve; synergy is the 2 + 2 = 5 effect. By establishing and communicating clear objectives, employees and managers can work together toward desired results. Synergy can result in powerful competitive advantages. The strategic-management process itself is aimed at creating synergy in an organization.

Planning allows a firm to adapt to changing markets and thus to shape its own destiny. Strategic management can be viewed as a formal planning process that allows an organization to pursue proactive rather than reactive strategies. Successful organizations strive to control their own futures rather than merely react to external forces and events as they occur. Historically, organisms and organizations that have not adapted to changing conditions have become extinct. Swift adaptation is needed today more than ever because changes in markets, economies, and competitors worldwide are accelerating.

Organizing

The purpose of *organizing* is to achieve coordinated effort by defining task and authority relationships. Organizing means determining who does what and who reports to whom. There are countless examples in history of well-organized enterprises successfully competing against—and in some cases defeating—much stronger but less-organized firms. A well-organized firm generally has motivated managers and employees who are committed to seeing the organization succeed. Resources are allocated more effectively and used more efficiently in a well-organized firm than in a disorganized firm.

The organizing function of management can be viewed as consisting of three sequential activities: breaking down tasks into jobs (work specialization), combining jobs to form departments (departmentalization), and delegating authority. Breaking down tasks into jobs requires the development of job descriptions and job specifications. These tools clarify for both managers and employees what particular jobs entail. In *The Wealth of Nations,* published in 1776, Adam Smith, who is considered today to be the "father" of economics, cited the advantages of work specialization in the manufacture of pins:

> One man draws the wire, another straightens it, a third cuts it, a fourth points it, a fifth grinds it at the top for receiving the head. Ten men working in this manner can produce 48,000 pins in a single day, but if they had all wrought separately and independently, each might at best produce twenty pins in a day.[12]

Combining jobs to form departments results in an organizational structure, span of control, and a chain of command. Changes in strategy often require changes in structure because positions may be created, deleted, or merged. Organizational structure dictates how resources are allocated and how objectives are established in a firm. Allocating resources and establishing objectives geographically, for example, is much different from doing so by product or customer.

The most common forms of departmentalization are functional, divisional, strategic business unit, and matrix. These types of structure are discussed further in Chapter 7.

Delegating authority is an important organizing activity, as evidenced in the old saying "You can tell how good a manager is by observing how his or her department functions when he or she isn't there." Employees today are more educated and more capable of participating in organizational decision making than ever before. In most cases, they expect to be delegated authority and responsibility and to be held accountable for results. Delegation of authority is embedded in the strategic-management process.

Motivating

Motivating can be defined as the process of influencing people to accomplish specific objectives.[13] Motivation explains why some people work hard and others do not. Objectives, strategies, and policies have little chance of succeeding if employees and managers are not motivated to implement strategies once they are formulated. The motivating function of management includes at least four major components: leadership, group dynamics, communication, and organizational change.

When managers and employees of a firm strive to achieve high levels of productivity, this indicates that the firm's strategists are good leaders. Good leaders establish rapport with subordinates, empathize with their needs and concerns, set a good example, and are trustworthy and fair. Leadership includes developing a vision of the firm's future and inspiring people to work hard to achieve that vision. Kirkpatrick and Locke reported that certain traits also characterize effective leaders: knowledge of the business, cognitive ability, self-confidence, honesty, integrity, and drive.[14]

Research suggests that democratic behavior on the part of leaders results in more positive attitudes toward change and higher productivity than does autocratic behavior. Drucker said:

> Leadership is not a magnetic personality. That can just as well be demagoguery. It is not "making friends and influencing people." That is flattery. Leadership is the lifting of a person's vision to higher sights, the raising of a person's performance to a higher standard, the building of a person's personality beyond its normal limitations.[15]

Group dynamics play a major role in employee morale and satisfaction. Informal groups or coalitions form in every organization. The norms of coalitions can range from being very positive to very negative toward management. It is important, therefore, that strategists identify the composition and nature of informal groups in an organization to facilitate strategy formulation, implementation, and evaluation. Leaders of informal groups are especially important in formulating and implementing strategy changes.

Communication, perhaps the most important word in management, is a major component in motivation. An organization's system of communication determines whether strategies can be implemented successfully. Good two-way communication is vital for gaining support for departmental and divisional objectives and policies. Top-down communication can encourage bottom-up communication. The strategic-management process becomes a lot easier when subordinates are encouraged to discuss their concerns, reveal their problems, provide recommendations, and give suggestions. A primary reason for instituting strategic management is to build and support effective communication networks throughout the firm.

> The manager of tomorrow must be able to get his people to commit themselves to the business, whether they are machine operators or junior vice-presidents. Ah, you say, participative management. Have a cigar. But just because most managers tug a forelock at the P word doesn't mean they know how to make it work. Today, throwing together a few quality circles won't suffice. The key issue will be empowerment, a term whose strength suggests the need to get beyond merely sharing a little information and a bit of decision making.[16]

Staffing

The management function of *staffing*, also called *personnel management* or *human resource management,* includes activities such as recruiting, interviewing, testing, selecting, orienting, training, developing, caring for, evaluating, rewarding, disciplining, promoting, transferring, demoting, and dismissing employees, as well as managing union relations.

Staffing activities play a major role in strategy-implementation efforts, and for this reason, human resource managers are becoming more actively involved in the strategic-management process. It is important to identify strengths and weaknesses in the staffing area.

The complexity and importance of human resource activities have increased to such a degree that all but the smallest organizations now need a full-time human resource manager. Numerous court cases that directly affect staffing activities are decided each day. Organizations and individuals can be penalized severely for not following federal, state, and local laws and guidelines related to staffing. Line managers simply cannot stay abreast of all the legal developments and requirements regarding staffing. The human resources department coordinates staffing decisions in the firm so that an organization as a whole meets legal requirements. This department also provides needed consistency in administering company rules, wages, and policies.

Human resource management is particularly challenging for international companies. For example, the inability of spouses and children to adapt to new surroundings has become a major staffing problem in overseas transfers. The problems include premature returns, job performance slumps, resignations, discharges, low morale, marital discord, and general discontent. Some firms have begun screening and interviewing spouses and children before assigning persons to overseas positions. The 3M Corporation introduces children to peers in the target country and offers spouses educational benefits.

Strategists are becoming increasingly aware of how important human resources are to effective strategic management. Human resource managers are becoming more involved and more proactive in formulating and implementing strategies. They provide leadership for organizations that are restructuring, or they allow employees to work at home.

Controlling

The *controlling* function of management includes all of those activities undertaken to ensure that actual operations conform to planned operations. All managers in an organization have controlling responsibilities, such as conducting performance evaluations and taking necessary action to minimize inefficiencies. The controlling function of management is particularly important for effective strategy evaluation. Controlling consists of four basic steps:

1. Establishing performance standards
2. Measuring individual and organizational performance
3. Comparing actual performance to planned performance standards
4. Taking corrective actions

Measuring individual performance is often conducted ineffectively or not at all in organizations. Some reasons for this shortcoming are that evaluations can create confrontations that most managers prefer to avoid, can take more time than most managers are willing to give, and can require skills that many managers lack. No single approach to measuring individual performance is without limitations. For this reason, an organization should examine various methods, such as the graphic rating scale, the behaviorally anchored rating scale, and the critical incident method, and then develop or select a performance-appraisal approach that best suits the firm's needs. Increasingly, firms are striving to link organizational performance with managers' and employees' pay. This topic is discussed further in Chapter 7.

Management Audit Checklist of Questions

The following checklist of questions can help determine specific strengths and weaknesses in the functional area of business. An answer of *no* to any question could indicate a potential weakness, although the strategic significance and implications of negative answers, of course, will vary by organization, industry, and severity of the weakness. Positive or yes answers to the checklist questions suggest potential areas of strength.

1. Does the firm use strategic-management concepts?
2. Are company objectives and goals measurable and well communicated?
3. Do managers at all hierarchical levels plan effectively?
4. Do managers delegate authority well?
5. Is the organization's structure appropriate?
6. Are job descriptions and job specifications clear?
7. Is employee morale high?
8. Are employee turnover and absenteeism low?
9. Are organizational reward and control mechanisms effective?

Marketing

Marketing can be described as the process of defining, anticipating, creating, and fulfilling customers' needs and wants for products and services. There are seven basic *functions of marketing:* (1) customer analysis, (2) selling products/services, (3) product and service planning, (4) pricing, (5) distribution, (6) marketing research, and (7) opportunity analysis.[17] Understanding these functions helps strategists identify and evaluate marketing strengths and weaknesses.

Customer Analysis

Customer analysis—the examination and evaluation of consumer needs, desires, and wants—involves administering customer surveys, analyzing consumer information, evaluating market positioning strategies, developing customer profiles, and determining optimal market segmentation strategies. The information generated by customer analysis can be essential in developing an effective mission statement. Customer profiles can reveal the demographic characteristics of an organization's customers. Buyers, sellers, distributors, salespeople, managers, wholesalers, retailers, suppliers, and creditors can all participate in gathering information to successfully identify customers' needs and wants. Successful organizations continually monitor present and potential customers' buying patterns.

Selling Products/Services

Successful strategy implementation generally rests upon the ability of an organization to sell some product or service. *Selling* includes many marketing activities, such as advertising, sales promotion, publicity, personal selling, sales force management, customer relations, and dealer relations. These activities are especially critical when a firm pursues a market penetration strategy. The effectiveness of various selling tools for consumer and industrial products varies. Personal selling is most important for industrial goods companies, and advertising is most important for consumer goods companies. During the CBS TV network's telecast of Super Bowl XXXVIX on February 4, 2007, a 30-second advertisement cost $2.6 million, up 4 percent from the prior year when the network ABC broadcast the game. But the Super Bowl continues to be among the few television events that draw a huge audience, about 100 million each year, according to Nielsen Media Research. Anheuser-Busch was again the biggest advertiser, with 10 advertising slots in the game.

Internet advertising is growing rapidly in many parts of the world. *Source:* PhotoEdit, Inc.

Advertising on television is declining dramatically while Internet advertising is growing rapidly. Newspaper advertising declined 2.4 percent in 2006 while magazine advertising rose 3.8 percent.[18]

Retailer JCPenney Co. recently unveiled a new marketing campaign centered around the slogan "Every Day Matters," after abandoning its prior slogan, "It's All Inside." Penney's hopes the slogan will become as powerful as Nike's "Just Do It." Penney's new slogan aims to create an emotional connection between the store and its customers, rather than emphasize its broad selection of merchandise. Determining organizational strengths and weaknesses in the selling function of marketing is an important part of performing an internal strategic-management audit.

With regard to advertising products and services on the Internet, a new trend is to base advertising rates exclusively on sales rates. This new accountability contrasts sharply with traditional broadcast and print advertising, which bases rates on the number of persons expected to see a given advertisement. The new cost-per-sale online advertising rates are possible because any Web site can monitor which user clicks on which advertisement and then can record whether that consumer actually buys the product. If there are no sales, then the advertisement is free.

In a major strategic shift, pharmaceutical companies are significantly reducing the number of their salespersons who call on primary-care doctors such as internists and general practitioners. For example, drug maker Wyeth is reducing by 30 percent its sales force to less than 5,000 persons. The strategic shift among drug firms is to drastically reduce multiple salespeople calling on identical doctors. This common but costly strategy, called *mirroring*, has alienated physicians. Pfizer, which has the world's largest drug sales force, is cutting its sales force dramatically.

Product and Service Planning

Product and service planning includes activities such as test marketing; product and brand positioning; devising warranties; packaging; determining product options, product features, product style, and product quality; deleting old products; and providing for customer service. Product and service planning is particularly important when a company is pursuing product development or diversification.

One of the most effective product and service planning techniques is *test marketing*. Test markets allow an organization to test alternative marketing plans and to forecast future sales of new products. In conducting a test market project, an organization must decide how many cities to include, which cities to include, how long to run the test, what information to collect during the test, and what action to take after the test has been completed. Test marketing is used more frequently by consumer goods companies than by industrial goods companies. Test marketing can allow an organization to avoid substantial losses by revealing weak products and ineffective marketing approaches before large-scale production begins.

Pricing

Five major stakeholders affect *pricing* decisions: consumers, governments, suppliers, distributors, and competitors. Sometimes an organization will pursue a forward integration strategy primarily to gain better control over prices charged to consumers. Governments can impose constraints on price fixing, price discrimination, minimum prices, unit pricing, price advertising, and price controls. For example, the U.S. Robinson-Patman Act, prohibits manufacturers and wholesalers from discriminating in price among channel member purchasers (suppliers and distributors) if competition is injured.

Competing organizations must be careful not to coordinate discounts, credit terms, or condition of sale; not to discuss prices, markups, and costs at trade association meetings; and not to arrange to issue new price lists on the same date, to rotate low bids on contracts, or to uniformly restrict production to maintain high prices. Strategists should view price from both a short-run and a long-run perspective, because competitors can copy price changes with relative ease. Often a dominant firm will aggressively match all price cuts by competitors.

With regard to pricing, as the value of the euro increases, European multinational companies have a choice. They can raise prices in the local currency of a foreign country or risk losing sales and market share. Alternatively, multinational firms can keep prices steady and face reduced profit when their export revenue is reported in their home countries.

Intense price competition coupled with Internet price-comparative shopping in most industries has reduced profit margins to bare minimum levels for most companies. For example, airline tickets, rental car prices, and even computer prices are lower today than they have been in many years.

Distribution

Distribution includes warehousing, distribution channels, distribution coverage, retail site locations, sales territories, inventory levels and location, transportation carriers, wholesaling, and retailing. Most producers today do not sell their goods directly to consumers. Various marketing entities act as intermediaries; they bear a variety of names such as wholesalers, retailers, brokers, facilitators, agents, vendors—or simply distributors.

Distribution becomes especially important when a firm is striving to implement a market development or forward integration strategy. Some of the most complex and challenging decisions facing a firm concern product distribution. Intermediaries flourish in our economy because many producers lack the financial resources and expertise to carry out direct marketing. Manufacturers who could afford to sell directly to the public often can gain greater returns by expanding and improving their manufacturing operations. Even General Motors would find it very difficult to buy out its more than 18,000 independent dealers.

Successful organizations identify and evaluate alternative ways to reach their ultimate market. Possible approaches vary from direct selling to using just one or many wholesalers and retailers. Strengths and weaknesses of each channel alternative should be determined according to economic, control, and adaptive criteria. Organizations should consider the costs and benefits of various wholesaling and retailing options. They must consider the need to motivate and control channel members and the need to adapt to changes in the future. Once a marketing channel is chosen, an organization usually must adhere to it for an extended period of time.

Marketing Research

Marketing research is the systematic gathering, recording, and analyzing of data about problems relating to the marketing of goods and services. Marketing research can uncover critical strengths and weaknesses, and marketing researchers employ numerous scales, instruments, procedures, concepts, and techniques to gather information. Marketing research activities support all of the major business functions of an organization. Organizations that possess excellent marketing research skills have a definite strength in pursuing generic strategies.

The President of PepsiCo said, "Looking at the competition is the company's best form of market research. The majority of our strategic successes are ideas that we borrow from the marketplace, usually from a small regional or local competitor. In each case, we spot a promising new idea, improve on it, and then out-execute our competitor."[19]

Opportunity Analysis

The seventh function of marketing is *opportunity analysis,* which involves assessing the costs, benefits, and risks associated with marketing decisions. Three steps are required to perform a *cost/benefit analysis:* (1) compute the total costs associated with a decision, (2) estimate the total benefits from the decision, and (3) compare the total costs with the total benefits. When expected benefits exceed total costs, an opportunity becomes more attractive. Sometimes the variables included in a cost/benefit analysis cannot be quantified or even measured, but usually reasonable estimates can be made to

119

allow the analysis to be performed. One key factor to be considered is risk. Cost/benefit analysis should also be performed when a company is evaluating alternative ways to be socially responsible.

Marketing Audit Checklist of Questions

The following questions about marketing, much like the earlier questions for management, are pertinent:

1. Are markets segmented effectively?
2. Is the organization positioned well among competitors?
3. Has the firm's market share been increasing?
4. Are present channels of distribution reliable and cost-effective?
5. Does the firm have an effective sales organization?
6. Does the firm conduct market research?
7. Are product quality and customer service good?
8. Are the firm's products and services priced appropriately?
9. Does the firm have an effective promotion, advertising, and publicity strategy?
10. Are marketing, planning, and budgeting effective?
11. Do the firm's marketing managers have adequate experience and training?

Finance/Accounting

Financial condition is often considered the single best measure of a firm's competitive position and overall attractiveness to investors. Determining an organization's financial strengths and weaknesses is essential to effectively formulating strategies. A firm's liquidity, leverage, working capital, profitability, asset utilization, cash flow, and equity can eliminate some strategies as being feasible alternatives. Financial factors often alter existing strategies and change implementation plans.

An especially good Web site from which to obtain financial information about a company is https://us.etrade.com/e/t/invest/markets, which provides excellent financial ratio, stock, and valuation information on all U.S. publicly held companies. Simply insert the company's stock symbol when the screen first loads and a wealth of information follows. Another nice site for obtaining financial information is www.forbes.com. Be sure to access the Manufacturing and Service section of www.strategyclub.com for excellent financial-related Web sites.

Finance/Accounting Functions

According to James Van Horne, the *functions of finance/accounting* comprise three decisions: the investment decision, the financing decision, and the dividend decision.[20] Financial ratio analysis is the most widely used method for determining an organization's strengths and weaknesses in the investment, financing, and dividend areas. Because the functional areas of business are so closely related, financial ratios can signal strengths or weaknesses in management, marketing, production, research and development, and management information systems activities. It is important to note here that financial ratios are equally applicable in for-profit and nonprofit organizations. Even though nonprofit organizations obviously would not have return-on-investment or earnings-per-share ratios, they would routinely monitor many other special ratios. For example, a church would monitor the ratio of dollar contributions to number of members, while a zoo would monitor dollar food sales to number of visitors. A university would monitor number of students divided by number of professors. Therefore, be creative when performing ratio analysis for nonprofit organizations because they strive to be financially sound just as for-profit firms do.

The *investment decision,* also called *capital budgeting,* is the allocation and reallocation of capital and resources to projects, products, assets, and divisions of an organization. Once strategies are formulated, capital budgeting decisions are required to successfully implement strategies. The *financing decision* determines the best capital structure for the firm and includes examining various methods by which the firm can raise capital (for example, by issuing stock, increasing debt, selling assets, or using a combination of these approaches). The financing decision must consider both short-term and long-term needs for working capital. Two key financial ratios that indicate whether a firm's financing decisions have been effective are the debt-to-equity ratio and the debt-to-total-assets ratio.

Dividend decisions concern issues such as the percentage of earnings paid to stockholders, the stability of dividends paid over time, and the repurchase or issuance of stock. Dividend decisions determine the amount of funds that are retained in a firm compared to the amount paid out to stockholders. Three financial ratios that are helpful in evaluating a firm's dividend decisions are the earnings-per-share ratio, the dividends-per-share ratio, and the price-earnings ratio. The benefits of paying dividends to investors must be balanced against the benefits of internally retaining funds, and there is no set formula on how to balance this trade-off. For the reasons listed here, dividends are sometimes paid out even when funds could be better reinvested in the business or when the firm has to obtain outside sources of capital:

1. Paying cash dividends is customary. Failure to do so could be thought of as a stigma. A dividend change is considered a signal about the future.
2. Dividends represent a sales point for investment bankers. Some institutional investors can buy only dividend-paying stocks.
3. Shareholders often demand dividends, even in companies with great opportunities for reinvesting all available funds.
4. A myth exists that paying dividends will result in a higher stock price.

Among Standard & Poors (S&P) 500 companies in the United States, for example, only 295 raised their dividend payout in 2006, down from 306 in 2005. Only six S&P 500 companies began paying dividends in 2006 for the first time, down from 10 in both 2005 and 2004. Dividend-paying companies in the S&P 500 outperformed non-dividend-paying companies by 3.7 percent in 2006, but paying dividends is becoming less common than buying back one's stock (Treasury stock) as a use for net income.[21] Alcoa is in the process of buying back 10 percent of its shares outstanding, and also just approved a 13 percent increase in its dividend payout.

The largest pharmaceutical company in the world, Pfizer, in 2007 raised its dividend 21 percent to 29 cents per share on the heels of a 26 percent increased in its dividend payout the prior year. Analysts say Pfizer did this to appease investors who were restless over its sliding stock price and who no longer viewed Pfizer as a growth stock. Pfizer in 2007 is also eliminating 10,000 jobs and closing some plants and research sites.

Wal-Mart Stores approved a 31 percent increase in the company's annual dividend, in a move to return $3.6 billion to shareholders in its 2008 fiscal year. The world's largest retailer said its annual dividend for the year ending January 31, 2008 would rise to 88 cents per share from 67 cents previously.

Maytag cut its dividend payout from 18 cents per share, which had been in place since 1998, to 9 cents per share following an 80 percent collapse in first-quarter 2005 company earnings. Maytag has been slow to move its manufacturing outside the United States to capitalize on lower labor costs. Only 12 percent of Maytag products are made outside the United States, although it just closed a refrigerator factory in the state of Illinois, and reopened that factory in Reynosa, Mexico.

Basic Types of Financial Ratios

Financial ratios are computed from an organization's income statement and balance sheet. Computing financial ratios is like taking a picture because the results reflect a situation at just one point in time. Comparing ratios over time and to industry averages is more likely to result in meaningful statistics that can be used to identify and evaluate strengths and weaknesses. Trend analysis, illustrated in Figure 4-2, is a useful technique that incorporates both the time and industry average dimensions of financial ratios. Note that the dotted lines reveal projected ratios. Some Web sites, such as those provided in Table 4-4 calculate financial ratios and provide data with charts. Four major sources of industry-average financial ratios follow:

1. Dun & Bradstreet's *Industry Norms and Key Business Ratios*—Fourteen different ratios are calculated in an industry-average format for 800 different types of

VISIT THE NET

Enter your stock symbol and then access the up-to-date financial news about the company. (http://finance.yahoo.com)

FIGURE 4-2

A Financial Ratio Trend Analysis

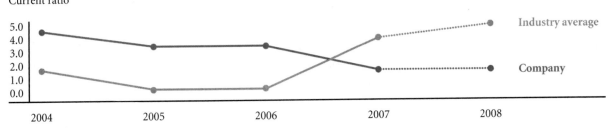

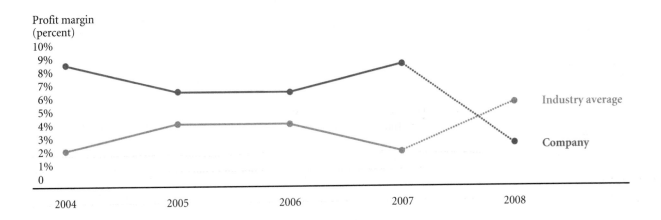

TABLE 4-4 **Excellent Web Sites to Obtain Information on Companies, Including Financial Ratios**

http://marketwatch.multexinvestor.com
http://moneycentral.msn.com
http://finance.yahoo.com
www.clearstation.com
https://us.etrade.com/e/t/invest/markets

businesses. The ratios are presented by Standard Industrial Classification (SIC) number and are grouped by annual sales into three size categories.

2. Robert Morris Associates' *Annual Statement Studies*—Sixteen different ratios are calculated in an industry-average format. Industries are referenced by SIC numbers published by the Bureau of the Census. The ratios are presented in four size categories by annual sales for all firms in the industry.

3. *Almanac of Business & Industrial Financial Ratios*—Twenty-two financial ratios and percentages are provided in an industry-average format for all major industries. The ratios and percentages are given for 12 different company-size categories for all firms in a given industry.

4. *U.S. Federal Trade Commission Reports*—The FTC publishes quarterly financial data, including ratios on manufacturing companies. FTC reports include analyses by industry group and asset size.

Table 4-5 provides a summary of key financial ratios showing how each ratio is calculated and what each ratio measures. However, all the ratios are not significant for all industries and companies. For example, accounts receivable turnover and average collection

TABLE 4-5   **A Summary of Key Financial Ratios**

Ratio	How Calculated	What It Measures
Liquidity Ratios		
Current Ratio	$$\frac{\text{Current assets}}{\text{Current liabilities}}$$	The extent to which a firm can meet its short-term obligations
Quick Ratio	$$\frac{\text{Current assets minus inventory}}{\text{Current liabilities}}$$	The extent to which a firm can meet its short-term obligations without relying upon the sale of its inventories
Leverage Ratios		
Debt-to-Total-Assets Ratio	$$\frac{\text{Total debt}}{\text{Total assets}}$$	The percentage of total funds that are provided by creditors
Debt-to-Equity Ratio	$$\frac{\text{Total debt}}{\text{Total stockholders' equity}}$$	The percentage of total funds provided by creditors versus by owners
Long-Term Debt-to-Equity Ratio	$$\frac{\text{Long-term debt}}{\text{Total stockholders' equity}}$$	The balance between debt and equity in a firm's long-term capital structure
Times-Interest-Earned Ratio	$$\frac{\text{Profits before interest and taxes}}{\text{Total interest charges}}$$	The extent to which earnings can decline without the firm becoming unable to meet its annual interest costs
Activity Ratios		
Inventory Turnover	$$\frac{\text{Sales}}{\text{Inventory of finished goods}}$$	Whether a firm holds excessive stocks of inventories and whether a firm is slowly selling its inventories compared to the industry average
Fixed Assets Turnover	$$\frac{\text{Sales}}{\text{Fixed assets}}$$	Sales productivity and plant and equipment utilization
Total Assets Turnover	$$\frac{\text{Sales}}{\text{Total assets}}$$	Whether a firm is generating a sufficient volume of business for the size of its asset investment
Accounts Receivable Turnover	$$\frac{\text{Annual credit sales}}{\text{Accounts receivable}}$$	The average length of time it takes a firm to collect credit sales (in percentage terms)
Average Collection Period	$$\frac{\text{Accounts receivable}}{\text{Total credit sales}/365 \text{ days}}$$	The average length of time it takes a firm to collect on credit sales (in days)
Profitability Ratios		
Gross Profit Margin	$$\frac{\text{Sales minus cost of goods sold}}{\text{Sales}}$$	The total margin available to cover operating expenses and yield a profit
Operating Profit Margin	$$\frac{\text{Earnings before interest and taxes (EBIT)}}{\text{Sales}}$$	Profitability without concern for taxes and interest
Net Profit Margin	$$\frac{\text{Net income}}{\text{Sales}}$$	After-tax profits per euro of sales

TABLE 4-5   A Summary of Key Financial Ratios—continued

Ratio	How Calculated	What It Measures
Profitability Ratios		
Return on Total Assets (ROA)	$\dfrac{\text{Net income}}{\text{Total assets}}$	After-tax profits per dollar of assets; this ratio is also called return on investment (ROI)
Return on Stockholders' Equity (ROE)	$\dfrac{\text{Net income}}{\text{Total stockholders' equity}}$	After-tax profits per dollar of stockholders' investment in the firm
Earnings Per Share (EPS)	$\dfrac{\text{Net income}}{\text{Number of shares of common stock outstanding}}$	Earnings available to the owners of common stock
Price-Earnings Ratio	$\dfrac{\text{Market price per share}}{\text{Earnings per share}}$	Attractiveness of firm on equity markets
Growth Ratios		
Sales	Annual percentage growth in total sales	Firm's growth rate in sales
Net Income	Annual percentage growth in profits	Firm's growth rate in profits
Earnings Per Share	Annual percentage growth in EPS	Firm's growth rate in EPS
Dividends Per Share	Annual percentage growth in dividends per share	Firm's growth rate in dividends per share

period are not very meaningful to a company that primarily does a cash receipts business. Key financial ratios can be classified into the following five types:

1. *Liquidity ratios* measure a firm's ability to meet maturing short-term obligations.
   Current ratio
   Quick (or acid-test) ratio

2. *Leverage ratios* measure the extent to which a firm has been financed by debt.
   Debt-to-total-assets ratio
   Debt-to-equity ratio
   Long-term debt-to-equity ratio
   Times-interest-earned (or coverage) ratio

3. *Activity ratios* measure how effectively a firm is using its resources.
   Inventory turnover
   Fixed assets turnover
   Total assets turnover
   Accounts receivable turnover
   Average collection period

4. *Profitability ratios* measure management's overall effectiveness as shown by the returns generated on sales and investment.
   Gross profit margin
   Operating profit margin
   Net profit margin
   Return on total assets (ROA)

Return on stockholders' equity (ROE)
Earnings per share (EPS)
Price-earnings ratio

5. *Growth ratios* measure the firm's ability to maintain its economic position in the growth of the economy and industry.
Sales
Net income
Earnings per share
Dividends per share

Financial ratio analysis must go beyond the actual calculation and interpretation of ratios. The analysis should be conducted on three separate fronts:

1. *How has each ratio changed over time?* This information provides a means of evaluating historical trends. It is important to note whether each ratio has been historically increasing, decreasing, or nearly constant. For example, a 10 percent profit margin could be bad if the trend has been down 20 percent each of the last three years. But a 10 percent profit margin could be excellent if the trend has been up, up, up. Therefore, calculate the percentage change in each ratio from one year to the next to assess historical financial performance on that dimension. Identify and examine large percent changes in a financial ratio from one year to the next.

2. *How does each ratio compare to industry norms?* A firm's inventory turnover ratio may appear impressive at first glance but may pale when compared to industry standards or norms. Industries can differ dramatically on certain ratios. For example grocery companies, such as Royal Ahold, have a high inventory turnover whereas automobile dealerships have a lower turnover. Therefore, comparison of a firm's ratios within its particular industry can be essential in determining strength/weakness.

3. *How does each ratio compare with key competitors?* Oftentimes competition is more intense between several competitors in a given industry or location than across all rival firms in the industry. When this is true, financial ratio analysis should include comparison to those key competitors. For example, if a firm's profitability ratio is trending up over time and compares favorably to the industry average, but it is trending down relative to its leading competitor, there may be reason for concern.

Financial ratio analysis is not without some limitations. First of all, financial ratios are based on accounting data, and firms differ in their treatment of such items as depreciation, inventory valuation, research and development expenditures, pension plan costs, mergers, and taxes. Also, seasonal factors can influence comparative ratios. Therefore, conformity to industry composite ratios does not establish with certainty that a firm is performing normally or that it is well managed. Likewise, departures from industry averages do not always indicate that a firm is doing especially well or badly. For example, a high inventory turnover ratio could indicate efficient inventory management and a strong working capital position, but it also could indicate a serious inventory shortage and a weak working capital position.

It is important to recognize that a firm's financial condition depends not only on the functions of finance, but also on many other factors that include (1) management, marketing, management production/operations, research and development, and management information systems decisions; (2) actions by competitors, suppliers, distributors, creditors, customers, and shareholders; and (3) economic, social, cultural, demographic, environmental, political, governmental, legal, and technological trends. Even natural environment liabilities can affect financial ratios, as indicated in the "Natural Environment Perspective." So financial ratio analysis, like all other analytical tools, should be used wisely.

NATURAL ENVIRONMENT PERSPECTIVE
European Union Countries Impose Strict Curbs on Use of Chemicals Among Manufacturers

The European Union in 2007 greatly expanded its campaign against industrial pollutants by imposing sweeping restrictions on manufacturers regarding their use of chemicals in producing products. Tough new laws to start in 2008 require all EU firms to document how some 30,000 chemicals are used in products from cleaning liquids and plastics to furniture and electronics. Europe has been a leader for a decade in requiring electronics companies, automakers, and others to clean up their acts. The new EU laws require manufacturers to cease using 1,500 of the most dangerous chemicals known or suspected to cause cancer, birth defects, and other serious illnesses. Also, the new laws require EU countries to cut their emissions in the 2008–2012 period by a collective 7 percent from the 2005 level.

Many other global manufacturers hope to be considered so-called downstream users of such chemicals as opposed to manufacturers or importers, and thus avoid the new laws. Whereas Europe relies on government regulation, the United States relies more on lawsuits to provide a strong incentive for manufacturers to avoid endangering human health and the environment. But increasingly the corporate world in the United States is pushing federal and state governments to regulate carbon-dioxide emissions.

Source: Adapted from Mary Jacoby, "Companies Brace for EU Chemical Curbs," *Wall Street Journal* (December 13, 2006): A4.

Water Polo Match In Dubrovnik. *Source:* Fred David

Finance/Accounting Audit Checklist

The following finance/accounting questions, like the similar questions about marketing and management earlier, should be examined:

1. Where is the firm financially strong and weak as indicated by financial ratio analyses?
2. Can the firm raise needed short-term capital?
3. Can the firm raise needed long-term capital through debt and/or equity?
4. Does the firm have sufficient working capital?
5. Are capital budgeting procedures effective?

6. Are dividend payout policies reasonable?
7. Does the firm have good relations with its investors and stockholders?
8. Are the firm's financial managers experienced and well trained?

Production/Operations

The *production/operations function* of a business consists of all those activities that transform inputs into goods and services. Production/operations management deals with inputs, transformations, and outputs that vary across industries and markets. A manufacturing operation transforms or converts inputs such as raw materials, labor, capital, machines, and facilities into finished goods and services. As indicated in Table 4-6, Roger Schroeder suggested that production/operations management comprises five functions or decision areas: process, capacity, inventory, workforce, and quality.

Most automakers require a 30-day notice to build vehicles, but Toyota Motor fills a buyer's new car order in just 5 days. Honda Motor was considered the industry's fastest producer, filling orders in 15 days. Automakers have for years operated under just-in-time inventory systems, but Toyota's 360 suppliers are linked to the company via computers on a virtual assembly line. The new Toyota production system was developed in the company's Ontario, Canada, plant and now applies to its Solara, Camry, Corolla, and Tacoma vehicles.

Production/operations activities often represent the largest part of an organization's human and capital assets. In most industries, the major costs of producing a product or service are incurred within operations, so production/operations can have great value as a competitive weapon in a company's overall strategy. Strengths and weaknesses in the five functions of production can mean the success or failure of an enterprise. For example, the average hourly pay of employees can significantly affect total production costs—and as evidenced in the "Global Perspective," there is great variation in average employee pay among countries.

Many production/operations managers are finding that cross-training of employees can help their firms respond faster to changing markets. Cross-training of workers can increase efficiency, quality, productivity, and job satisfaction. For example, at General Motors' gear and axle plant, costs related to product defects were reduced 400 percent in two years as a result of cross-training workers. A shortage of qualified labor in the United States is another reason cross-training is becoming a common management practice.

Singapore rivals Hong Kong as an attractive site for locating production facilities in Southeast Asia. Singapore is a city-state near Malaysia. An island nation of about 4 million, Singapore is changing from an economy built on trade and services to one built on information technology. A large-scale program in computer education for older (over age 26)

TABLE 4-6 The Basic Functions of Production Management

Function	Description
1. Process	Process decisions concern the design of the physical production system. Specific decisions include choice of technology, facility layout, process flow analysis, facility location, line balancing, process control, and transportation analysis.
2. Capacity	Capacity decisions concern determination of optimal output levels for the organization—not too much and not too little. Specific decisions include forecasting, facilities planning, aggregate planning, scheduling, capacity planning, and queuing analysis.
3. Inventory	Inventory decisions involve managing the level of raw materials, work-in-process, and finished goods. Specific decisions include what to order, when to order, how much to order, and materials handling.
4. Workforce	Workforce decisions are concerned with managing the skilled, unskilled, clerical, and managerial employees. Specific decisions include job design, work measurement, job enrichment, work standards, and motivation techniques.
5. Quality	Quality decisions are aimed at ensuring that high-quality goods and services are produced. Specific decisions include quality control, sampling, testing, quality assurance, and cost control.

Source: Adapted from R. Schroeder, *Operations Management* (New York: McGraw-Hill, 1981): 12.

GLOBAL PERSPECTIVE
Automobile Industry Work Week and Hourly Pay Variation Across Countries

Employees at the giant Volkswagen plant in Wolfsburg, Germany, enjoyed the shortest work week in the global auto industry, 28.8 hours, until early 2007 when the firm bumped this number up to 33 hours at the company's German plants. Still, 33 is low compared to General Motors' 40-hour norm and even less than the 35-hour standard at other German car makers. Germany is home to the world's highest-paid auto workers, with Volkswagen paying $69 an hour, compared with the national average of $44 in Germany. The average hourly pay for auto workers in other countries is:

Germany	$44.05
United States	33.95

Canada	29.17
Japan	27.38
France	26.34
South Korea	15.82
Mexico	3.50

With unemployment running about 10 percent in Germany, companies have more leverage to demand concessions from unions and employees. Volkswagen plans to shed up to 20,000 jobs—mostly in Germany—between 2007 and 2009.

Source: Adapted from Stephen Power, "VW's 28-Hour Workweek Goes Kaputt in Wolfsburg," *Wall Street Journal* (January 5, 2007): B1.

Volkswagon Employees in Germany. *Source:* Photographer Peter Frischmuth / argus. Courtesy Peter Arnold, Inc.

residents is very popular. Singapore children receive outstanding computer training in schools. All government services are computerized nicely. Singapore lures multinational businesses with great tax breaks, world-class infrastructure, excellent courts that efficiently handle business disputes, exceptionally low tariffs, large land giveaways, impressive industrial parks, excellent port facilities, and a government very receptive to and cooperative with foreign businesses. Foreign firms now account for 70 percent of manufacturing output in Singapore.

In terms of ship container traffic processed annually, Singapore has the largest and busiest seaport in the world, followed by Hong Kong, Shanghai, Los Angeles, Busan (South Korea), Rotterdam, Hamburg, New York, and Tokyo. The Singapore seaport is five times the size of the New York City seaport.[22]

TABLE 4-7   Implications of Various Strategies on the Production/Operations Function

Various Strategies	Implications
1. Compete as low-cost provider of goods or services	Creates high barriers to entry
	Creates larger market
	Requires longer production runs and fewer product changes
	Requires special-purpose equipment and facilities
2. Compete as high-quality provider	Offers more total profit from a smaller volume of sales
	Requires more quality-assurance effort and higher operating cost
	Requires more precise equipment, which is more expensive
	Requires highly skilled workers, necessitating higher wages and greater training efforts
3. Stress customer service	Requires more service people, service parts, and equipment
	Requires rapid response to customer needs or changes in customer tastes
	Requires a higher inventory investment
4. Provide rapid and frequent introduction of new products	Requires versatile equipment and people
	Has higher research and development costs
	Has high retraining and tooling costs
	Provides lower volumes for each product and fewer opportunities for improvements due to the learning curve
5. Vertical integration	Enables company to control more of the process
	May require entry into unfamilar business areas
	May require high capital investment as well as technology and skills beyond those currently available
6. Consolidate processing (centralize)	Can result in economies of scale
	Can locate near one major customer or supplier
	Vulnerability: one strike, fire, or flood can halt the entire operation
7. Disperse processing of service (decentralize)	Can be near more customers and resources
	Requires more complex coordination and duplication of some personnel and equipment at each location
	If each location produces one product in the line, then other products still must be transported to be available at all locations
	If each location specializes in a type of component for all products, the company is vulnerable to strike, fire, flood, and so on
	If each location provides total product line, then economies of scale may not be realized
8. Stress the use of mmmechanization, automation, robots	Requires high capital investment
	Reduces flexibility
	May affect labor relations
	Makes maintenance more crucial
9. Stress stability of employment	Serves the security needs of employees and may develop employee loyalty
	Helps to attract and retain highly skilled employees
	May require revisions of make-or-buy decisions, use of idle time, inventory, and subcontractors as demand fluctuates

Source: Adapted from J. Dilworth, *Production and Operations Management: Manufacturing and Nonmanufacturing,* 2nd ed. Copyright © 1983 by Random House, Inc. Reprinted by permission of Random House, Inc.

There is much reason for concern that many organizations have not taken sufficient account of the capabilities and limitations of the production/operations function in formulating strategies. Scholars contend that this neglect has had unfavorable consequences on corporate performance in America. As shown in Table 4-7, James Dilworth outlined several types of strategic decisions that a company might make with the production/operations implications of those decisions. Production capabilities and policies can also greatly affect strategies.

Production/Operations Audit Checklist

Questions such as the following should be examined:

1. Are supplies of raw materials, parts, and subassemblies reliable and reasonable?
2. Are facilities, equipment, machinery, and offices in good condition?
3. Are inventory-control policies and procedures effective?
4. Are quality-control policies and procedures effective?
5. Are facilities, resources, and markets strategically located?
6. Does the firm have technological competencies?

Research and Development

The fifth major area of internal operations that should be examined for specific strengths and weaknesses is *research and development (R&D)*. Many firms today conduct no R&D, and yet many other companies depend on successful R&D activities for survival. Firms pursuing a product development strategy especially need to have a strong R&D orientation.

Organizations invest in R&D because they believe that such an investment will lead to a superior product or service and will give them competitive advantages. Research and development expenditures are directed at developing new products before competitors do, at improving product quality, or at improving manufacturing processes to reduce costs.

Effective management of the R&D function requires a strategic and operational partnership between R&D and the other vital business functions. A spirit of partnership and mutual trust between general and R&D managers is evident in the best-managed firms today. Managers in these firms jointly explore; assess; and decide the what, when, where, why, and how much of R&D. Priorities, costs, benefits, risks, and rewards associated with R&D activities are discussed openly and shared. The overall mission of R&D thus has become broad-based, including supporting existing businesses, helping launch new businesses, developing new products, improving product quality, improving manufacturing efficiency, and deepening or broadening the company's technological capabilities.[23]

The best-managed firms today seek to organize R&D activities in a way that breaks the isolation of R&D from the rest of the company and promotes a spirit of partnership between R&D managers and other managers in the firm. R&D decisions and plans must be integrated and coordinated across departments and divisions by having the departments share experiences and information. The strategic-management process facilitates this cross-functional approach to managing the R&D function.

Internal and External R&D

Cost distributions among R&D activities vary by company and industry, but total R&D costs generally do not exceed manufacturing and marketing start-up costs. Four approaches to determining R&D budget allocations commonly are used: (1) financing as many project proposals as possible, (2) using a percentage-of-sales method, (3) budgeting about the same amount that competitors spend for R&D, or (4) deciding how many successful new products are needed and working backward to estimate the required R&D investment.

R&D in organizations can take two basic forms: (1) internal R&D, in which an organization operates its own R&D department, and/or (2) contract R&D, in which a firm hires independent researchers or independent agencies to develop specific products. Many companies use both approaches to develop new products. A widely used approach for obtaining outside R&D assistance is to pursue a joint venture with another firm. R&D strengths (capabilities) and weaknesses (limitations) play a major role in strategy formulation and strategy implementation.

Most firms have no choice but to continually develop new and improved products because of changing consumer needs and tastes, new technologies, shortened product life cycles, and increased domestic and foreign competition. A shortage of ideas for new products, increased global competition, increased market segmentation, strong special-interest groups, and increased government regulations are several factors making the successful development of new products more and more difficult, costly, and risky. In the pharmaceutical industry, for example, only one out of every few thousand drugs created in the laboratory ends up on pharmacists' shelves. Scarpello, Boulton, and Hofer emphasized that different strategies require different R&D capabilities:

> The focus of R&D efforts can vary greatly depending on a firm's competitive strategy. Some corporations attempt to be market leaders and innovators of new products, while others are satisfied to be market followers and developers of currently available products. The basic skills required to support these strategies will vary, depending on whether R&D becomes the driving force behind competitive strategy. In cases where new product introduction is the driving force for strategy, R&D activities must be extensive. The R&D unit must then be able to advance scientific and technological knowledge, exploit that knowledge, and manage the risks associated with ideas, products, services, and production requirements.[24]

Companies in the United States are expected to spend about $219 billion on R&D in 2007, a 3.4 percent increase over 2006.[25] Analysts expect annual increases of about 3 to 4 percent in R&D spending among U.S. companies through 2010. U.S. firms on average and collectively spend more on R&D than any other country in the world, although China's R&D spending is increasing at an annual rate of about 17 percent. U.S. corporate spending alone on R&D is 64 percent more than all R&D spending in China, including corporate, government, and academia combined.

Research and Development Audit

Questions such as the following should be asked in performing an R&D audit:

1.   Does the firm have R&D facilities? Are they adequate?
2.   If outside R&D firms are used, are they cost-effective?
3.   Are the organization's R&D personnel well qualified?
4.   Are R&D resources allocated effectively?
5.   Are management information and computer systems adequate?
6.   Is communication between R&D and other organizational units effective?
7.   Are present products technologically competitive?

Management Information Systems

Information ties all business functions together and provides the basis for all managerial decisions. It is the cornerstone of all organizations. Information represents a major source of competitive management advantage or disadvantage. Assessing a firm's internal strengths and weaknesses in information systems is a critical dimension of performing an internal audit. The company motto of Mitsui, a large Japanese trading company, is "Information is the lifeblood of the company." A satellite network connects Mitsui's 200 worldwide offices.

A management information system's purpose is to improve the performance of an enterprise by improving the quality of managerial decisions. An effective information system thus collects, codes, stores, synthesizes, and presents information in such a manner that it answers important operating and strategic questions. The heart of an information system is a database containing the kinds of records and data important to managers.

A *management information system* receives raw material from both the external and internal evaluation of an organization. It gathers data about marketing, finance, production, and personnel matters internally, and social, cultural, demographic, environmental, economic, political, governmental, legal, technological, and competitive factors externally. Data are integrated in ways needed to support managerial decision making.

There is a logical flow of material in a computer information system, whereby data are input to the system and transformed into output. Outputs include computer printouts, written reports, tables, charts, graphs, checks, purchase orders, invoices, inventory records, payroll accounts, and a variety of other documents. Payoffs from alternative strategies can be calculated and estimated. *Data* become *information* only when they are evaluated, filtered, condensed, analyzed, and organized for a specific purpose, problem, individual, or time.

An effective management information system utilizes computer hardware, software, models for analysis, and a database. Some people equate information systems with the advent of the computer, but historians have traced recordkeeping and non-computer data processing to Babylonian merchants living in 3500 B.C. Benefits of an effective information system include an improved understanding of business functions, improved communications, more informed decision making, a better analysis of problems, and improved control.

Because organizations are becoming more complex, decentralized, and globally dispersed, the function of information systems is growing in importance. Spurring this advance is the falling cost and increasing power of computers. There are costs and benefits associated with obtaining and evaluating information, just as with equipment and land. Like equipment, information can become obsolete and may need to be purged from the system. An effective information system is like a library, collecting, categorizing, and filing data for use by managers throughout the organization. Information systems are a major strategic resource, monitoring internal and external issues and trends, identifying competitive threats, and assisting in the implementation, evaluation, and control of strategy.

We are truly in an information age. Firms whose information-system skills are weak are at a competitive disadvantage. On the other hand, strengths in information systems allow firms to establish distinctive competencies in other areas. Low-cost manufacturing and good customer service, for example, can depend on a good information system.

Strategic-Planning Software

Some strategic decision support systems, however, are too sophisticated, expensive, or restrictive to be used easily by managers in a firm. This is unfortunate because the strategic-management process must be a people process to be successful. People make the difference! Strategic-planning software should thus be simple and unsophisticated. Simplicity allows wide participation among managers in a firm and participation is essential for effective strategy implementation.

One strategic-planning software product that parallels this text and offers managers and executives a simple yet effective approach for developing organizational strategies is CheckMATE. This personal computer software performs planning analyses and generates strategies a firm could pursue. CheckMATE incorporates the most modern strategic-planning techniques. No previous experience with computers or knowledge of strategic planning is required of the user. CheckMATE thus promotes communication, understanding, creativity, and forward thinking among users.

CheckMATE is not a spreadsheet program or database; it is an expert system that carries a firm through strategy formulation and implementation. A major strength of CheckMATE strategic-planning software is its simplicity and participative approach. The user is asked appropriate questions, responses are recorded, information is assimilated, and results are printed. Individuals can independently work through the software, and then the program will develop joint recommendations for the firm.

Specific analytical procedures included in the CheckMATE program are Strategic Position and Action Evaluation (SPACE) analysis, Strengths-Weaknesses-Opportunities-Threats (SWOT) analysis, Internal-External (IE) analysis, and Grand Strategy Matrix analysis. These widely used strategic-planning analyses are described in Chapter 6.

An individual license for CheckMATE costs $295. More information about CheckMATE can be obtained at www.checkmateplan.com.

Management Information Systems Audit

Questions such as the following should be asked when conducting this audit:

1. Do all managers in the firm use the information system to make decisions?
2. Is there a chief information officer or director of information systems position in the firm?

3. Are data in the information system updated regularly?
4. Do managers from all functional areas of the firm contribute input to the information system?
5. Are there effective passwords for entry into the firm's information system?
6. Are strategists of the firm familiar with the information systems of rival firms?
7. Is the information system user-friendly?
8. Do all users of the information system understand the competitive advantages that information can provide firms?
9. Are computer training workshops provided for users of the information system?
10. Is the firm's information system continually being improved in content and user-friendliness?

Value Chain Analysis (VCA)

According to Porter, the business of a firm can best be described as a *value chain,* in which total revenues minus total costs of all activities undertaken to develop and market a product or service yields value. All firms in a given industry have a similar value chain, which includes activities such as obtaining raw materials, designing products, building manufacturing facilities, developing cooperative agreements, and providing customer service. A firm will be profitable as long as total revenues exceed the total costs incurred in creating and delivering the product or service. Firms should strive to understand not only their own value chain operations but also their competitors', suppliers', and distributors' value chains.

Value chain analysis (VCA) refers to the process whereby a firm determines the costs associated with organizational activities from purchasing raw materials to manufacturing product(s) to marketing those products. VCA aims to identify where low-cost advantages or disadvantages exist anywhere along the value chain from raw material to customer service activities. VCA can enable a firm to better identify its own strengths and weaknesses, especially as compared to competitors' value chain analyses and their own data examined over time.

Substantial judgment may be required in performing a VCA because different items along the value chain may impact other items positively or negatively, so there exist complex interrelationships. For example, exceptional customer service may be especially expensive yet may reduce the costs of returns and increase revenues. Cost and price differences among rival firms can have their origins in activities performed by suppliers, distributors, creditors, or even shareholders. Despite the complexity of VCA, the initial step in implementing this procedure is to divide a firm's operations into specific activities or business processes. Then the analyst attempts to attach a cost to each discrete activity, and the costs could be in terms of both time and money. Finally, the analyst converts the cost data into information by looking for competitive cost strengths and weaknesses that may yield competitive advantage or disadvantage. Conducting a VCA is supportive of the RBV's examination of a firm's assets and capabilities as sources of distinctive competence.

When a major competitor or new market entrant offers products or services at very low prices, this may be because that firm has substantially lower value chain costs or perhaps the rival firm is just waging a desperate attempt to gain sales or market share. Thus value chain analysis can be critically important for a firm in monitoring whether its prices and costs are competitive. An example value chain is illustrated in Figure 4-3. There can be more than a hundred particular value-creating activities associated with the business of producing and marketing a product or service, and each one of the activities can represent a competitive advantage or disadvantage for the firm. The combined costs of all the various activities in a company's value chain define the firm's cost of doing business. Firms should determine where cost advantages and disadvantages in their value chain occur *relative to the value chain of rival firms.*

Value chains differ immensely across industries and firms. Whereas a paper products company, such as Stone Container, would include on its value chain timber farming, logging, pulp mills, and papermaking, a computer company such as Hewlett-Packard would

133

FIGURE 4-3

An Example Value Chain for a Typical Manufacturing Firm

Supplier Costs ———
      Raw materials ———
      Fuel ———
      Energy ———
      Transportation ———
      Truck drivers ———
      Truck maintenance ———
      Component parts ———
      Inspection ———
      Storing ———
      Warehouse ———

Production Costs ———
      Inventory system ———
      Receiving ———
      Plant layout ———
      Maintenance ———
      Plant location ———
      Computer ———
      R&D ———
      Cost accounting ———

Distribution Costs ———
      Loading ———
      Shipping ———
      Budgeting ———
      Personnel ———
      Internet ———
      Trucking ———
      Railroads ———
      Fuel ———
      Maintenance ———

Sales and Marketing Costs ———
      Salespersons ———
      Web site ———
      Internet ———
      Publicity ———
      Promotion ———
      Advertising ———
      Transportation ———
      Food and lodging ———

Customer Service Costs ———
      Postage ———
      Phone ———
      Internet ———
      Warranty ———

Management Costs ———
      Human resources ———
      Administration ———
      Employee benefits ———
      Labor relations ———
      Managers ———
      Employees ———
      Finance and legal ———

FIGURE 4-4

Translating Company Performance of Value Chain Activities into Competitive Advantage

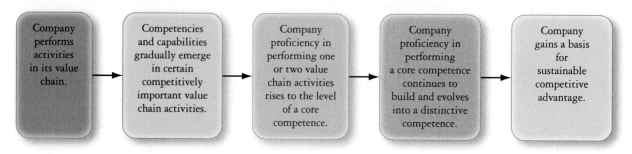

Source: Arthur Thompson, Jr., A. J. Strickland III, and John Gamble. *Crafting and Executing Strategy: Text and Readings* (New York: McGraw-Hill/Irwin, 2005): 108. Used by permission of McGraw-Hill.

include programming, peripherals, software, hardware, and laptops. A motel would include food, housekeeping, check-in and check-out operations, Web site, reservations system, and so on. However all firms should use value chain analysis to develop and nurture a core competence and convert this competence into a distinctive competence. A *core competence* is a value chain activity that a firm performs especially well. When a core competence evolves into a major competitive advantage, then it is called a *distinctive competence.* Figure 4-4 illustrates this process.

More and more companies are using VCA to gain and sustain competitive advantage by being especially efficient and effective along various parts of the value chain. For example, Wal-Mart has built powerful value advantages by focusing on exceptionally tight inventory control, volume purchasing of products, and offering exemplary customer service. Computer companies in contrast compete aggressively along the distribution end of the value chain. Of course, price competitiveness is a key component of effectiveness among both mass retailers and computer firms.

Benchmarking

Benchmarking is an analytical tool used to determine whether a firm's value chain activities are competitive compared to rivals and thus conducive to winning in the marketplace. Benchmarking entails measuring costs of value chain activities across an industry to determine "best practices" among competing firms for the purpose of duplicating or improving upon those best practices. Benchmarking enables a firm to take action to improve its competitiveness by identifying (and improving upon) value chain activities where rival firms have comparative advantages in cost, service, reputation, or operation.

The hardest part of benchmarking can be gaining access to other firms' value chain activities with associated costs. Typical sources of benchmarking information, however, include published reports, trade publications, suppliers, distributors, customers, partners, creditors, shareholders, lobbyists, and willing rival firms. Some rival firms share benchmarking data. However, the International Benchmarking Clearinghouse provides guidelines to help ensure that restraint of trade, price fixing, bid rigging, bribery, and other improper business conduct do not arise between participating firms.

Due to the popularity of benchmarking today, numerous consulting firms such as Accenture, AT Kearney, Best Practices Benchmarking & Consulting, as well as the Strategic Planning Institute's Council on Benchmarking, gather benchmarking data, conduct benchmarking studies, and distribute benchmark information without identifying the sources.

The Internal Factor Evaluation (IFE) Matrix

A summary step in conducting an internal strategic-management audit is to construct an *Internal Factor Evaluation (IFE) Matrix.* This strategy-formulation tool summarizes and evaluates the major strengths and weaknesses in the functional areas of a business, and it also provides a basis for identifying and evaluating relationships among those areas. Intuitive judgments are required in developing an IFE Matrix, so the appearance of a scientific approach should not be interpreted to mean this is an all-powerful technique. A thorough understanding of the factors included is more important than the actual numbers. Similar to the EFE Matrix and Competitive Profile Matrix described in Chapter 3, an IFE Matrix can be developed in five steps:

1. List key internal factors as identified in the internal-audit process. Use a total of from 10 to 20 internal factors, including both strengths and weaknesses. List strengths first and then weaknesses. Be as specific as possible, using percentages, ratios, and comparative numbers.
2. Assign a weight that ranges from 0.0 (not important) to 1.0 (all-important) to each factor. The weight assigned to a given factor indicates the relative importance of the factor to being successful in the firm's industry. Regardless of whether a key factor is an internal strength or weakness, factors considered to have the greatest effect on organizational performance should be assigned the highest weights. The sum of all weights must equal 1.0.
3. Assign a 1-to-4 rating to each factor to indicate whether that factor represents a major weakness (rating = 1), a minor weakness (rating = 2), a minor strength (rating = 3), or a major strength (rating = 4). Note that strengths must receive a 3 or 4 rating and weaknesses must receive a 1 or 2 rating. Ratings are thus company-based, whereas the weights in step 2 are industry-based.
4. Multiply each factor's weight by its rating to determine a weighted score for each variable.
5. Sum the weighted scores for each variable to determine the total weighted score for the organization.

Regardless of how many factors are included in an IFE Matrix, the total weighted score can range from a low of 1.0 to a high of 4.0, with the average score being 2.5. Total weighted scores well below 2.5 characterize organizations that are weak internally, whereas scores significantly above 2.5 indicate a strong internal position. Like the EFE Matrix, an IFE Matrix should include from 10 to 20 key factors. The number of factors has no effect upon the range of total weighted scores because the weights always sum to 1.0.

When a key internal factor is both a strength and a weakness, the factor should be included twice in the IFE Matrix, and a weight and rating should be assigned to each statement. For example, the Playboy logo both helps and hurts Playboy Enterprises; the logo attracts customers to *Playboy* magazine, but it keeps the Playboy cable channel out of many markets. Be as quantitative as possible when stating factors. Use $'s, %'s, #'s, and ratios to the extent possible.

An example of an IFE Matrix is provided in Table 4-8 for a retail computer store. Note that the two most important factors to be successful in the retail computer store business are "revenues from repair/service in the store" and "location of the store." Also note that the store is doing best on "average customer purchase amount" and "in-store technical support." The store is having major problems with its carpet, bathroom, paint, and checkout procedures. Note also that the matrix contains substantial quantitative data rather than vague statements; this is excellent. Overall, this store receives a 2.5 total weighted score, which on a 1-to-4 scale is exactly average/halfway, indicating there is definitely room for improvement in store operations, strategies, policies, and procedures.

The IFE Matrix provides important information for strategy formulation. For example, this retail computer store might want to hire another checkout person and repair its carpet, paint, and bathroom problems. Also, the store may want to increase advertising for its repair/services, because that is a really important (weight 0.15) factor to being successful in this business.

In multidivisional firms, each autonomous division or strategic business unit should construct an IFE Matrix. Divisional matrices then can be integrated to develop an overall corporate IFE Matrix.

TABLE 4-8   **A Sample Internal Factor Evaluation Matrix for a Retail Computer Store**

Key Internal Factors	Weight	Rating	Weighted Score
Strengths			
1. Inventory turnover increased from 5.8 to 6.7	0.05	3	0.15
2. Average customer purchase increased from $97 to $128	0.07	4	0.28
3. Employee morale is excellent	0.10	3	0.30
4. In-store promotions resulted in 20 percent increase in sales	0.05	3	0.15
5. Newspaper advertising expenditures increased 10 percent	0.02	3	0.06
6. Revenues from repair/service segment of store up 16 percent	0.15	3	0.45
7. In-store technical support personnel have MIS college degrees	0.05	4	0.20
8. Store's debt-to-total assets ratio declined to 34 percent	0.03	3	0.09
9. Revenues per employee up 19 percent	0.02	3	0.06
Weaknesses			
1. Revenues from software segment of store down 12 percent	0.10	2	0.20
2. Location of store negatively impacted by new Highway 34	0.15	2	0.30
3. Carpet and paint in store somewhat in disrepair	0.02	1	0.02
4. Bathroom in store needs refurbishing	0.02	1	0.02
5. Revenues from businesses down 8 percent	0.04	1	0.04
6. Store has no Web site	0.05	2	0.10
7. Supplier on-time delivery increased to 2.4 days	0.03	1	0.03
8. Often customers have to wait to check out	0.05	1	0.05
Total	**1.00**		**2.50**

Conclusion

Management, marketing, finance/accounting, production/operations, research and development, and management information systems represent the core operations of most businesses. A strategic-management audit of a firm's internal operations is vital to organizational health. Many companies still prefer to be judged solely on their bottom-line performance. However, an increasing number of successful organizations are using the internal audit to gain competitive advantages over rival firms.

Systematic methodologies for performing strength-weakness assessments are not well developed in the strategic-management literature, but it is clear that strategists must identify and evaluate internal strengths and weaknesses in order to effectively formulate and choose among alternative strategies. The EFE Matrix, Competitive Profile Matrix, IFE Matrix, and clear statements of vision and mission provide the basic information needed to successfully formulate competitive strategies. The process of performing an internal audit represents an opportunity for managers and employees throughout the organization to participate in determining the future of the firm. Involvement in the process can energize and mobilize managers and employees.

We invite you to visit the David page on the Prentice Hall Companion Web site at www.prenhall.com/david for this chapter's review quiz.

Key Terms and Concepts

Activity Ratios (p. 155)
Benchmarking (p. 166)
Capital Budgeting (p. 151)
Communication (p. 137)
Controlling (p. 147)

Issues for Review and Discussion

1. Explain why prioritizing the relative importance of strengths and weaknesses in an IFE Matrix is an important strategic-management activity.
2. How can delegation of authority contribute to effective strategic management?
3. Diagram a formal organizational chart that reflects the following positions: a president, 2 executive officers, 4 middle managers, and 18 lower-level managers. Now, diagram three overlapping and hypothetical informal group structures. How can this information be helpful to a strategist in formulating and implementing strategy?
4. Which of the three basic functions of finance/accounting do you feel is most important in a small electronics manufacturing concern? Justify your position.
5. Do you think aggregate R&D expenditures for U.S. firms will increase or decrease next year? Why?
6. Explain how you would motivate managers and employees to implement a major new strategy.
7. Why do you think production/operations managers often are not directly involved in strategy-formulation activities? Why can this be a major organizational weakness?
8. Give two examples of staffing strengths and two examples of staffing weaknesses of an organization with which you are familiar.

9. Would you ever pay out dividends when your firm's annual net profit is negative? Why? What effect could this have on a firm's strategies?

10. If a firm has zero debt in its capital structure, is that always an organizational strength? Why or why not?

11. Describe the production/operations system in a police department.

12. After conducting an internal audit, a firm discovers a total of 100 strengths and 100 weaknesses. What procedures then could be used to determine the most important of these? Why is it important to reduce the total number of key factors?

13. Why do you believe cultural products affect all the functions of business?

14. Do you think cultural products affect strategy formulation, implementation, or evaluation the most? Why?

15. Identify cultural products at your college or university. Do these products, viewed collectively or separately, represent a strength or weakness for the organization?

16. Describe the management information system at your college or university.

17. Explain the difference between data and information in terms of each being useful to strategists.

18. What are the most important characteristics of an effective management information system?

19. Compare and contrast U.S. versus foreign cultures in terms of doing business.

20. Do you agree or disagree with the RBV theorists that internal resources are more important for a firm than external factors in achieving and sustaining competitive advantage? Explain your and their position.

21. Define and discuss "empirical indicators."

22. Define and discuss the "spam" problem in the United States.

23. Define and explain value chain analysis (VCA).

24. List five financial ratios that may be used by your university to monitor operations.

25. Explain benchmarking.

Notes

1. Robert Grant, "The Resource-Based Theory of Competitive Advantage: Implications for Strategy Formulation," *California Management Review* (Spring 1991): 116.

2. Reprinted by permission of the publisher from "Integrating Strength–Weakness Analysis into Strategic Planning," by William King, *Journal of Business Research* 2, no. 4: p. 481. Copyright 1983 by Elsevier Science Publishing Co., Inc.

3. Igor Ansoff, "Strategic Management of Technology" *Journal of Business Strategy* 7, no. 3 (Winter 1987): 38.

4. Claude George, Jr., *The History of Management Thought*, 2nd ed. (Upper Saddle River, N.J.: Prentice-Hall, 1972): 174.

5. J. B. Barney, "Firm Resources and Sustained Competitive Advantage," *Journal of Management* 17 (1991): 99–120; J.B. Barney, "The Resource-Based Theory of the Firm," *Organizational Science* 7 (1996): 469; J.B. Barney, "Is the Resource-Based 'View' a Useful Perspective for Strategic Management Research? Yes." *Academy of Management Review* 26, no. 1 (2001): 41–56.

6. Edgar Schein, *Organizational Culture and Leadership* (San Francisco: Jossey-Bass, 1985): 9.

7. John Lorsch, "Managing Culture: The Invisible Barrier to Strategic Change," *California Management Review* 28, no. 2 (1986): 95–109.

8. Y. Allarie and M. Firsirotu, "How to Implement Radical Strategies in Large Organizations," *Sloan Management Review* (Spring 1985): 19.

9. Jon Alston, "Wa, Guanxi, and Inhwa: Managerial Principles in Japan, China and Korea," *Business Horizons* 32, no. 2 (March–April 1989): 26.

10. Rose Knotts, "Cross-Cultural Management: Transformations and Adaptations," *Business Horizons* (January–February 1989): 29–33.

11. www.mindtools.com/plfailpl.html.

12. Adam Smith, *The Wealth of Nations* (New York: Modern Library, 1937): 3–4.

13. Richard Daft, *Management*, 3rd ed. (Orlando, FL: Dryden Press, 1993): 512.

139

14. Shelley Kirkpatrick and Edwin Locke, "Leadership: Do Traits Matter?" *Academy of Management Executive* 5, no. 2 (May 1991): 48.

15. Peter Drucker, *Management Tasks, Responsibilities, and Practice* (New York: Harper & Row, 1973): 463.

16. Brian Dumaine, "What the Leaders of Tomorrow See," *Fortune* (July 3, 1989): 51.

17. J. Evans and B. Bergman, *Marketing* (New York: Macmillan, 1982): 17.

18. Emily Steel, "Ad Cutbacks Likely Signal Budget Shift," *Wall Street Journal* (March 14, 2007): B3.

19. Quoted in Robert Waterman, Jr., "The Renewal Factor," *BusinessWeek* (September 14, 1987): 108.

20. J. Van Horne, *Financial Management and Policy* (Upper Saddle River, N.J.: Prentice-Hall, 1974): 10.

21. Matt Krantz, "Dividend Payouts Grow Less Richly," *USA Today* (December 27, 2006): B1.

22. Kevin Klowden, "The Quiet Revolution in Transportation," *Wall Street Journal* (April 24, 2007): A14.

23. Philip Rousebl, Kamal Saad, and Tamara Erickson, "The Evolution of Third Generation R&D,"*Planning Review* 19, no. 2 (March–April 1991): 18–26.

24. Vida Scarpello, William Boulton, and Charles Hofer, "Reintegrating R&D into Business Strategy," *Journal of Business Strategy* 6, no. 4 (Spring 1986): 50–51.

25. Gautam Naik, "U.S. Companies Are Poised to Ramp Up R&D Spending," *Wall Street Journal* (January 25, 2007):A14.

Current Readings

Acedo, F. J., C. Barroso, and J. L. Galan. "The Resource-Based Theory: Dissemination and Main Trends." *Strategic Management Journal* 27, no. 7 (July 2006): 621.

Campbell, John L., "Why Would Corporation Behave in Socially Responsible Ways?" *The Academy of Management Perspective* 32, no. 3 (July 2007): 946.

Fang, Y., M. Wade, A. Delios, and P.W. Beamish, "International Diversification, Subsidiary Performance, and the Mobility of Knowledge Resources." *Strategic Management Journal* 28, no. 10 (October 2007): 1053.

Hitt, Michael A., and Jamie D. Collins, "Business Ethics, Strategic Decision Making, and Firm Performance." *Business Horizon* 50, no. 5 (September–October 2007): 353.

Lepak, David P., Ken G. Smith, and M. Susan Taylor. "Value Creation and Value Capture: A Multilevel Perspective." *Academy of Management Review* 32, no. 1 (January 2007): 180.

Ling Yan, Hao Zhao and Robert A. Baron. "Influence of Founder-CEO's Personal Values on Firm Performance: Moderating Effects of Firm Age and Size." *Journal of Management* 33, no. 5 (October 2007): 673.

Jiang, Bin and Patrick J. Murphy. "Do Business School Professors Make Good Executive Managers." *The Academy of Management Perspective* 21, no. 3 (August 2007): 29.

Newbert, S. L. "Empirical Research on the Resource-Based View of the Firm: An Assessment and Suggestions for Future Research." *Strategic Management Journal* 28, no. 2 (February 2007): 121.

Ployhart, Robert E. "Staffing in the 21st Century: New Challenges and Strategic Opportunities." *Journal of Management* 32, no. 6 (December 2006): 868.

Priem, Richard L. "A Consumer Perspective on Value Creation." *Academy of Management Review* 32, no. 1 (January 2007): 219.

Schreyogg, G., and M. Kliesh–Eberl. "How Dynamic Can Organizational Capabilities Be? Towards a Dual-Process Model of Capability Dynamization." *Strategic Management Journal* 28, no. 9 (September 2007): 913.

Sidle, Stuart D. "The Danger of Do Nothing Leaders." *The Academy of Management Perspective* 21, no. 2 (May 2007): 75.

• EXPERIENTIAL EXERCISES

Experiential Exercise 4A

Performing a Financial Ratio Analysis for Walt Disney Company (DIS)

Purpose

Financial ratio analysis is one of the best techniques for identifying and evaluating internal strengths and weaknesses. Potential investors and current shareholders look closely at firms' financial ratios, making detailed comparisons to industry averages and to previous periods of time. Financial ratio analyses provide vital input information for developing an IFE Matrix.

Instructions

Step 1	On a separate sheet of paper, number from 1 to 20. Referring to Walt Disney's income statement and balance sheet (pp. 64–65), calculate 20 financial ratios for 2007 for the company. Use Table 4-5 as a reference.
Step 2	In a second column, indicate whether you consider each ratio to be a strength, a weakness, or a neutral factor for Walt Disney.
Step 3	Go to the Web sites in Table 4-4 that calculate Disney's financial ratios, without your having to pay a subscription (fee) for the service. Make a copy of the ratio information provided and record the source. Report this research to your classmates and your professor.

A 1970s painted bisque Walt Disney Productions Donald Duck figurine.
Source: (c) Judith Miller / Dorling Kindersley / Three Sisters

Experiential Exercise 4B

Constructing an IFE Matrix for Walt Disney Company

Purpose

This exercise will give you experience in developing an IFE Matrix. Identifying and prioritizing factors to include in an IFE Matrix fosters communication among functional and divisional managers. Preparing an IFE Matrix allows human resource, marketing, production/operations, finance/accounting, R&D, and management information systems managers to articulate their concerns and thoughts regarding the business condition of the firm. This results in an improved collective understanding of the business.

Instructions

Step 1 Join with two other individuals to form a three-person team. Develop a team IFE Matrix for Walt Disney.

Step 2 Compare your team's IFE Matrix to other teams' IFE Matrices. Discuss any major differences.

Step 3 What strategies do you think would allow Walt Disney to capitalize on its major strengths? What strategies would allow Walt Disney to improve upon its major weaknesses?

Experiential Exercise 4C

Constructing an IFE Matrix for My University

Purpose

This exercise gives you the opportunity to evaluate your university's major strengths and weaknesses. As will become clearer in the next chapter, an organization's strategies are largely based upon striving to take advantage of strengths and improving upon weaknesses.

Instructions

Step 1 Join with two other individuals to form a three-person team. Develop a team IFE Matrix for your university. You may use the strengths/weaknesses determined in Experimental Exercise 1D.

Step 2 Go to the board and diagram your team's IFE Matrix.

Step 3 Compare your team's IFE Matrix to other teams' IFE Matrices. Discuss any major differences.

Step 4 What strategies do you think would allow your university to capitalize on its major strengths? What strategies would allow your university to improve upon its major weaknesses?

5 Strategies in Action

Japanese students in class. *Source:* AP World Wide Photos

chapter objectives

After studying this chapter, you should be able to do the following:

1. Discuss the value of establishing long-term objectives.

2. Identify 16 types of business strategies.

3. Identify numerous examples of organizations pursuing different types of strategies.

4. Discuss guidelines when particular strategies are most appropriate to pursue.

5. Discuss Porter's five generic strategies.

6. Describe strategic management in nonprofit, governmental, and small organizations.

7. Discuss joint ventures as a way to enter the Russian market.

8. Discuss the Balanced Scorecard.

9. Compare and contrast financial with strategic objectives.

10. Discuss the levels of strategies in large versus small firms.

11. Explain the First Mover Advantages concept.

12. Discuss recent trends in outsourcing.

13. Discuss strategies for competing in turbulent, high-velocity markets.

Hundreds of companies today, including Toyota, IBM, Searle, and Nestlé, have embraced strategic planning fully in their quest for higher revenues and profits. Kent Nelson, former chair of UPS, explains why his company has created a new strategic-planning department: "Because we're making bigger bets on investments in technology, we can't afford to spend a whole lot of money in one direction and then find out five years later it was the wrong direction."[1]

This chapter brings strategic management to life with many contemporary examples. Sixteen types of strategies are defined and exemplified, including Michael Porter's generic strategies: cost leadership, differentiation, and focus. Guidelines are presented for determining when it is most appropriate to pursue different types of strategies. An overview of strategic management in nonprofit organizations, governmental agencies, and small firms is provided.

Long-Term Objectives

Long-term objectives represent the results expected from pursuing certain strategies. Strategies represent the actions to be taken to accomplish long-term objectives. The time frame for objectives and strategies should be consistent, usually from two to five years.

The Nature of Long-Term Objectives

Objectives should be quantitative, measurable, realistic, understandable, challenging, hierarchical, obtainable, and congruent among organizational units. Each objective should also be associated with a timeline. Objectives are commonly stated in terms such as growth in assets, growth in sales, profitability, market share, degree and nature of diversification, degree and nature of vertical integration, earnings per share, and social responsibility. Clearly established objectives offer many benefits. They provide direction, allow synergy, aid in evaluation, establish priorities, reduce uncertainty, minimize conflicts, stimulate exertion, and aid in both the allocation of resources and the design of jobs.

Long-term objectives are needed at the corporate, divisional, and functional levels of an organization. They are an important measure of managerial performance. Many practitioners and academicians attribute a significant part of U.S. industry's competitive decline to the short-term, rather than long-term, strategy orientation of managers in the United States. Arthur D. Little argues that bonuses or merit pay for managers today must be based to a greater extent on long-term objectives and strategies. A general framework for relating objectives to performance evaluation is provided in Table 5-1. A particular organization could tailor these guidelines to meet its own needs, but incentives should be attached to both long-term and annual objectives.

Clearly stated and communicated objectives are vital to success for many reasons. First, objectives help stakeholders understand their role in an organization's future. They also provide a basis for consistent decision making by managers whose values and attitudes differ. By reaching a consensus on objectives during strategy-formulation activities, an organization can minimize potential conflicts later during implementation. Objectives set forth organizational priorities and stimulate exertion and accomplishment. They serve as standards by which individuals, groups, departments, divisions, and entire organizations can be evaluated. Objectives provide the basis for designing jobs and organizing activities

TABLE 5-1 **Varying Performance Measures by Organizational Level**

Organizational Level	Basis for Annual Bonus or Merit Pay
Corporate	75% based on long-term objectives
	25% based on annual objectives
Division	50% based on long-term objectives
	50% based on annual objectives
Function	25% based on long-term objectives
	75% based on annual objectives

to be performed in an organization. They also provide direction and allow for organizational synergy.

Without long-term objectives, an organization would drift aimlessly toward some unknown end. It is hard to imagine an organization or individual being successful without clear objectives. Success only rarely occurs by accident; rather, it is the result of hard work directed toward achieving certain objectives.

Financial versus Strategic Objectives

Income statement

Two types of objectives are especially common in organizations: financial and strategic objectives. Financial objectives include those associated with growth in revenues, growth in earnings, higher dividends, larger profit margins, greater return on investment, higher earnings per share, a rising stock price, improved cash flow, and so on; while strategic objectives include things such as a larger market share, quicker on-time delivery than rivals, shorter design-to-market times than rivals, lower costs than rivals, higher product quality than rivals, wider geographic coverage than rivals, achieving ISO 14001 certification, achieving technological leadership, consistently getting new or improved products to market ahead of rivals, and so on.

Although financial objectives are especially important in firms, oftentimes there is a trade-off between financial and strategic objectives such that crucial decisions have to be made. For example, a firm can do certain things to maximize short-term financial objectives that would harm long-term strategic objectives. To improve financial position in the short run through higher prices may, for example, jeopardize long-term market share. The dangers associated with trading off long-term strategic objectives with near-term bottom-line performance are especially severe if competitors relentlessly pursue increased market share at the expense of short-term profitability. And there are other trade-offs between financial and strategic objectives, related to riskiness of actions, concern for business ethics, need to preserve the natural environment, and social responsibility issues. Both financial and strategic objectives should include both annual and long-term performance targets. Ultimately, the best way to sustain competitive advantage over the long run is to relentlessly pursue strategic objectives that strengthen a firm's business position over rivals. Financial objectives can best be met by focusing first and foremost on achievement of strategic objectives that improve a firm's competitiveness and market strength.

Not Managing by Objectives

An unknown educator once said, "If you think education is expensive, try ignorance." The idea behind this saying also applies to establishing objectives. Strategists should avoid the following alternative ways to "not managing by objectives."

VISIT THE NET

Provides a short essay about the resurgence of strategic planning in companies. (www.businessweek. com/1996/35/b34901.htm)

- *Managing by Extrapolation*—adheres to the principle "If it ain't broke, don't fix it." The idea is to keep on doing about the same things in the same ways because things are going well.
- *Managing by Crisis*—based on the belief that the true measure of a really good strategist is the ability to solve problems. Because there are plenty of crises and problems to go around for every person and every organization, strategists ought to bring their time and creative energy to bear on solving the most pressing problems of the day. Managing by crisis is actually a form of reacting rather than acting and of letting events dictate the what and when of management decisions.
- *Managing by Subjectives*—built on the idea that there is no general plan for which way to go and what to do; just do the best you can to accomplish what you think should be done. In short, "Do your own thing, the best way you know how" (sometimes referred to as *the mystery approach to decision making* because subordinates are left to figure out what is happening and why).
- *Managing by Hope*—based on the fact that the future is laden with great uncertainty and that if we try and do not succeed, then we hope our second (or third) attempt will succeed. Decisions are predicted on the hope that they will work and the good times are just around the corner, especially if luck and good fortune are on our side![2]

The Balanced Scorecard

Developed in 1993 by Harvard Business School professors Robert Kaplan and David Norton, and refined continually through today, the Balanced Scorecard is a strategy evaluation and control technique.[3] Balanced Scorecard derives its name from the perceived need of firms to "balance" financial measures that are oftentimes used exclusively in strategy evaluation and control with nonfinancial measures such as product quality and customer service. An effective Balanced Scorecard contains a carefully chosen combination of strategic and financial objectives tailored to the company's business. As a tool to manage and evaluate strategy, the Balanced Scorecard is currently in use at Infosys Technologies, United Parcel Service, 3M Corporation, Sharp Corporation, and hundreds of other firms. For example, 3M Corporation has a financial objective to achieve annual growth in earnings per share of 10 percent or better, as well as a strategic objective to have at least 30 percent of sales come from products introduced in the past four years. The overall aim of the Balanced Scorecard is to "balance" shareholder objectives with customer and operational objectives. Obviously, these sets of objectives interrelate and many even conflict. For example, customers want low price and high service, which may conflict with shareholders' desire for a high return on their investment. The Balanced Scorecard concept is consistent with the notions of continuous improvement in management (CIM) and total quality management (TQM).

Although the Balanced Scorecard concept will be covered in more detail in Chapter 9 as it relates to evaluating strategies, it should be noted here that firms should establish objectives and evaluate strategies on items other than financial measures. This is the basic tenet of the Balanced Scorecard. Financial measures and ratios are vitally important. However, of equal importance are factors such as customer service, employee morale, product quality, pollution abatement, business ethics, social responsibility, community involvement, and other such items. In conjunction with financial measures, these "softer" factors comprise an integral part of both the objective-setting process and the strategy-evaluation process. These factors can vary by organization, but such items, along with financial measures, comprise the essence of a Balanced Scorecard. A Balanced Scorecard for a firm is simply a listing of all key objectives to work toward, along with an associated time dimension of when each objective is to be accomplished, as well as a primary responsibility or contact person, department, or division for each objective.

Types of Strategies

The model illustrated in Figure 5-1 provides a conceptual basis for applying strategic management. Defined and exemplified in Table 5-2, alternative strategies that an enterprise could pursue can be categorized into 11 actions—forward integration, backward integration, horizontal integration, market penetration, market development, product development, related diversification, unrelated diversification, retrenchment, divestiture, and liquidation. Each alternative strategy has countless variations. For example, market penetration can include adding salespersons, increasing advertising expenditures, couponing, and using similar actions to increase market share in a given geographic area.

Many, if not most, organizations simultaneously pursue a combination of two or more strategies, but a *combination strategy* can be exceptionally risky if carried too far. No organization can afford to pursue all the strategies that might benefit the firm. Difficult decisions must be made. Priority must be established. Organizations, like individuals, have limited resources. Both organizations and individuals must choose among alternative strategies and avoid excessive indebtedness.

Hansen and Smith explain that strategic planning involves "choices that risk resources" and "trade-offs that sacrifice opportunity." In other words, if you have a strategy to go north, then you must buy snowshoes and warm jackets (spend resources) and forgo the opportunity of "faster population growth in southern states." You cannot have a strategy to go north and then take a step east, south, or west "just to be on the safe side." Firms spend resources and focus on a finite number of opportunities in pursuing strategies to achieve an uncertain outcome in the future. Strategic planning is much more than a roll of the dice; it is a wager based on predictions and hypotheses that are continually tested and refined by knowledge, research, experience, and learning. Survival of the firm itself may hinge on your strategic plan.[4]

FIGURE 5-1

A Comprehensive Strategic-Management Model

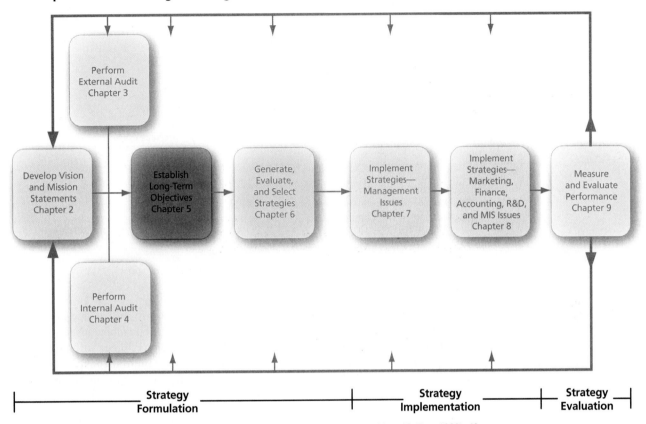

Source: Fred R. David, "How Companies Define Their Mission," *Long Range Planning* 22, no. 3 (June 1988): 40.

TABLE 5-2 **Alternative Strategies Defined and Exemplified**

Strategy	Definition	2007 Examples
Forward Integration	Gaining ownership or increased control over distributors or retailers	Southwest Airlines just began selling tickets through Galileo
Backward Integration	Seeking ownership or increased control of a firm's suppliers	Hilton Hotels could acquire a large furniture manufacturer
Horizontal Integration	Seeking ownership or increased control over competitors	Huntington Bancshares and Sky Financial Group in Ohio merged
Market Penetration	Seeking increased market share for present products or services in present markets through greater marketing efforts	McDonald's is spending millions on its "Shrek the Third" promotions aimed at convincing consumers it offers healthy items
Market Development	Introducing present products or services into new geographic area	Burger King opened its first restaurant in Japan
Product Development	Seeking increased sales by improving present products or services or developing new ones	Google introduced "Google Presents" to compete with Microsoft's PowerPoint
Related Diversification	Adding new but related products or services	MGM Mirage is opening its first noncasino luxury hotel
Unrelated Diversification	Adding new, unrelated products or services	Ford Motor Company entered the industrial bank business
Retrenchment	Regrouping through cost and asset reduction to reverse declining sales and profit	Discovery Channel closed its 103 mall-based and stand-alone stores to focus on the Internet—and laid off 25% of its workforce
Divestiture	Selling a division or part of an organization	Whirlpool sold its struggling Hoover floor-care business to Techtronic Industries
Liquidation	Selling all of a company's assets, in parts, for their tangible worth	Follow Me Charters sold all of its assets and ceased doing business

FIGURE 5-2

Levels of Strategies with Persons Most Responsible

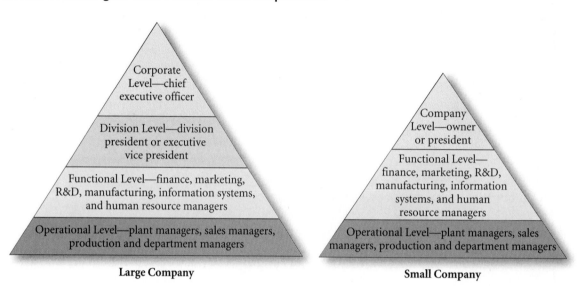

Organizations cannot do too many things well because resources and talents get spread thin and competitors gain advantage. In large diversified companies, a combination strategy is commonly employed when different divisions pursue different strategies. Also, organizations struggling to survive may simultaneously employ a combination of several defensive strategies, such as divestiture, liquidation, and retrenchment.

Levels of Strategies

Strategy making is not just a task for top executives. As discussed in Chapter 1, middle- and lower-level managers too must be involved in the strategic-planning process to the extent possible. In large firms, there are actually four levels of strategies: corporate, divisional, functional, and operational—as illustrated in Figure 5-2. However, in small firms, there are actually three levels of strategies: company, functional, and operational.

In large firms, the persons primarily responsible for having effective strategies at the various levels include the CEO at the corporate level; the president or executive vice president at the divisional level; the respective chief finance officer (CFO), chief information officer (CIO), human resource manager (HRM), chief marketing officer (CMO), and so on, at the functional level; and the plant manager, regional sales manager, and so on, at the operational level. In small firms, the persons primarily responsible for having effective strategies at the various levels include the business owner or president at the company level and then the same range of persons at the lower two levels, as with a large firm.

It is important to note that all persons responsible for strategic planning at the various levels ideally participate and understand the strategies at the other organizational levels to help ensure coordination, facilitation, and commitment while avoiding inconsistency, inefficiency, and miscommunication. Plant managers, for example, need to understand and be supportive of the overall corporate strategic plan (game plan) while the president and the CEO need to be knowledgeable of strategies being employed in various sales territories and manufacturing plants.

Integration Strategies

Forward integration, backward integration, and horizontal integration are sometimes collectively referred to as *vertical integration* strategies. Vertical integration strategies allow a firm to gain control over distributors, suppliers, and/or competitors.

Forward Integration

Forward integration involves gaining ownership or increased control over distributors or retailers. Increasing numbers of manufacturers (suppliers) today are pursuing a forward integration strategy by establishing Web sites to directly sell products to consumers. This strategy is causing turmoil in some industries. For example, Dell Computer recently began pursuing forward integration by establishing its own stores-within-a-store in Sears. This strategy supplements Dell's mall-based kiosks, which enable customers to see and try Dell computers before they purchase one. Neither the Dell kiosks nor the Dell stores-within-a-store stock computers. Customers still will order Dells exclusively by phone or over the Internet, which historically differentiated Dell from other computer firms.

An effective means of implementing forward integration is *franchising.* Businesses use franchising to distribute their products or services. They can expand rapidly by franchising because costs and opportunities are spread among many individuals. Total sales by franchises in the United States alone are annually about $1 trillion.

However, a growing trend is for franchisees, who for example may operate 10 franchised restaurants, stores, or whatever, to buy out their part of the business from their franchiser (corporate owner). There is a growing rift between franchisees and franchisers as the segment often outperforms the parent. For example, McDonald's today owns less than 23 percent of its 32,000 restaurants, down from 26 percent in 2006. Restaurant chains are increasingly being pressured to own fewer of their locations. McDonald's recently sold 1,600 of its Latin America and Caribbean restaurants to Woods Staton, a former McDonald's executive. Companies such as McDonald's are using proceeds from the sale of company stores/restaurants to franchisees to buy back company stock, pay higher dividends, and make other investments to benefit shareholders.

The huge forest products firm Boise Cascade, which owns 2.3 million acres of timberlands and more than two dozen paper and building-products mills, continues to pursue forward integration, as evidenced by its recent acquisition of OfficeMax, the third-largest retail-office-products company after Staples and Office Depot. OfficeMax has more than 1,000 superstores and has lately focused on boosting domestic sales and on remodeling stores, rather than expanding internationally. A risk to Boise Cascade in making this acquisition is that Staples and Office Depot could drop the Boise Cascade line of products, viewing the company now to be more a competitor than a supplier.

Amway and Mary Kay in 2007 were granted licenses to sell products in China, ending years of waiting by the two U.S. companies and a relaxation of curbs on direct sales that Beijing began as part of its obligations in joining the World Trade Organization. Other direct sales firms, including Nu Skin Enterprises and Avon Products, also were granted approval. These firms almost all have stores in China but only in 2007 were finally given permission to use the door-to-door sales techniques. Many direct sales firms have jumped on this opportunity by extending their forward integration strategy of adding distributorships and salespersons in China.

Six guidelines for when forward integration may be an especially effective strategy are:[5]

- When an organization's present distributors are especially expensive, or unreliable, or incapable of meeting the firm's distribution needs.
- When the availability of quality distributors is so limited as to offer a competitive advantage to those firms that integrate forward.
- When an organization competes in an industry that is growing and is expected to continue to grow markedly; this is a factor because forward integration reduces an organization's ability to diversify if its basic industry falters.
- When an organization has both the capital and human resources needed to manage the new business of distributing its own products.
- When the advantages of stable production are particularly high; this is a consideration because an organization can increase the predictability of the demand for its output through forward integration.
- When present distributors or retailers have high profit margins; this situation suggests that a company profitably could distribute its own products and price them more competitively by integrating forward.

Backward Integration

Both manufacturers and retailers purchase needed materials from suppliers. *Backward integration* is a strategy of seeking ownership or increased control of a firm's suppliers. This strategy can be especially appropriate when a firm's current suppliers are unreliable, too costly, or cannot meet the firm's needs.

When you buy a box of Pampers diapers at Wal-Mart, a scanner at the store's checkout counter instantly zaps an order for more diapers to Procter & Gamble Company. In contrast, in most hospitals, reordering supplies is a logistical nightmare. Inefficiency caused by lack of control of suppliers in the health care industry is, however, rapidly changing as many giant health care purchasers, such as the U.S. Defense Department and Columbia/HCA Healthcare Corporation, move to require electronic bar codes on every supply item purchased. This allows instant tracking and recording without invoices and paperwork. Of the estimated $83 billion spent annually on hospital supplies, industry reports indicate that $11 billion can be eliminated through more effective backward integration.

Some industries in the United States, such as the automotive and aluminum industries, are reducing their historical pursuit of backward integration. Instead of owning their suppliers, companies negotiate with several outside suppliers. Ford buys over half of its component parts from outside suppliers such as TRW, Eaton, General Electric, and Johnson Controls. *De-integration* makes sense in industries that have global sources of supply. Companies today shop around, play one seller against another, and go with the best deal. Global competition is also spurring firms to reduce their number of suppliers and to demand higher levels of service and quality from those they keep. Although traditionally relying on many suppliers to ensure uninterrupted supplies and low prices, American firms now are following the lead of Japanese firms, which have far fewer suppliers and closer, long-term relationships with those few. "Keeping track of so many suppliers is onerous," says Mark Shimelonis, formerly of Xerox.

Seven guidelines for when backward integration may be an especially effective strategy are:[6]

- When an organization's present suppliers are especially expensive, or unreliable, or incapable of meeting the firm's needs for parts, components, assemblies, or raw materials.
- When the number of suppliers is small and the number of competitors is large.
- When an organization competes in an industry that is growing rapidly; this is a factor because integrative-type strategies (forward, backward, and horizontal) reduce an organization's ability to diversify in a declining industry.
- When an organization has both capital and human resources to manage the new business of supplying its own raw materials.
- When the advantages of stable prices are particularly important; this is a factor because an organization can stabilize the cost of its raw materials and the associated price of its product(s) through backward integration.
- When present supplies have high profit margins, which suggests that the business of supplying products or services in the given industry is a worthwhile venture.
- When an organization needs to quickly acquire a needed resource.

Horizontal Integration

Horizontal integration refers to a strategy of seeking ownership of or increased control over a firm's competitors. One of the most significant trends in strategic management today is the increased use of horizontal integration as a growth strategy. Mergers, acquisitions, and takeovers among competitors allow for increased economies of scale and enhanced transfer of resources and competencies. Kenneth Davidson makes the following observation about horizontal integration:

The trend towards horizontal integration seems to reflect strategists' misgivings about their ability to operate many unrelated businesses. Mergers between direct competitors are more likely to create efficiencies than mergers between unrelated businesses, both because there is a greater potential for eliminating duplicate facilities and

VISIT THE NET

Provides Dr. Hansen's course syllabus, which includes excellent links. (www.stetson.edu/rhansen/stratsyl.html)

because the management of the acquiring firm is more likely to understand the business of the target.[7]

The Chicago Mercantile Exchange (CME) acquired the CBOT Holdings exchange in mid-2007 for about $8 billion, creating the world's largest derivatives exchange, with dominant positions in several futures markets from soybeans to eurodollars. There is rapid consolidation among exchanges worldwide. For example, the New York Stock Exchange recently acquired the pan-European exchange Euronext NV.

Five guidelines for when horizontal integration may be an especially effective strategy are:[8]

- When an organization can gain monopolistic characteristics in a particular area or region without being challenged by the federal government for "tending substantially" to reduce competition.
- When an organization competes in a growing industry.
- When increased economies of scale provide major competitive advantages.
- When an organization has both the capital and human talent needed to successfully manage an expanded organization.
- When competitors are faltering due to a lack of managerial expertise or a need for particular resources that an organization possesses; note that horizontal integration would not be appropriate if competitors are doing poorly, because in that case overall industry sales are declining.

Intensive Strategies

Market penetration, market development, and product development are sometimes referred to as *intensive strategies* because they require intensive efforts if a firm's competitive position with existing products is to improve.

Market Penetration

A *market penetration* strategy seeks to increase market share for present products or services in present markets through greater marketing efforts. This strategy is widely used alone and in combination with other strategies. Market penetration includes increasing the number of salespersons, increasing advertising expenditures, offering extensive sales promotion items, or increasing publicity efforts.

Five guidelines for when market penetration may be an especially effective strategy are:[9]

- When current markets are not saturated with a particular product or service.
- When the usage rate of present customers could be increased significantly.
- When the market shares of major competitors have been declining while total industry sales have been increasing.
- When the correlation between euro sales and euro marketing expenditures historically has been high.
- When increased economies of scale provide major competitive advantages.

Market Development

Market development involves introducing present products or services into new geographic areas. For example, Chicago-based United Airlines in 2007 won a four-way contest to provide new service to China. Air service between the United States and China is restricted to a negotiated number of flights and through 2007, United rather than American, Continental, or Northwest will be providing this service. The world's largest trans-Pacific passenger carrier, United has served China for 20 years and is adding new nonstop flights from the United States to both Beijing and Shanghai.

Likewise, for example, General Motors sold more cars outside the United States in both 2005 and 2006 than inside the United States. Ford Motor and many other domestic firms have greater revenue and profits from business outside the United States than here at home. Dunkin' Donuts has more than 1,700 restaurants outside the United States in 30 countries and opened its first store in Taiwan in 2007. Starbucks plans to eventually have thousands of stores in China, making that country the chain's largest market outside the United States. Best Buy Company opened its first store in China in 2007.

Wal-Mart plans to open its first stores in Russia and India in 2007. Wal-Mart's international division is growing faster than the firm's flagship U.S. business. Four non-Chinese banks began operations in China in 2007: Citigroup Inc., HSBC Holdings PLC, Standard Chartered Bank PLC, and Bank of East Asia Ltd.

Polo Ralph Lauren recently expanded its presence in Japan by acquiring Impact 21 Company, a licensee for men's and women's jeans, apparel, and accessories. Japan is now Ralph Lauren's second largest market at 10 percent of revenues. Ralph Lauren paid 2,600 yen ($21.82) per share for Impact 21.

Toyota announced in mid-2007 that its five-year strategy to build manufacturing plants in the United States (market development) was misguided and is being replaced now by "build plants in Japan and export to the USA." This new strategy reveals a rare misstep for Toyota, which has surpassed General Motors as the largest auto firm by anticipating the desires of U.S. car buyers better than its Detroit competitors.

Six guidelines for when market development may be an especially effective strategy are:[10]

- When new channels of distribution are available that are reliable, inexpensive, and of good quality.
- When an organization is very successful at what it does.
- When new untapped or unsaturated markets exist.
- When an organization has the needed capital and human resources to manage expanded operations.
- When an organization has excess production capacity.
- When an organization's basic industry is becoming rapidly global in scope.

Product Development

Product development is a strategy that seeks increased sales by improving or modifying present products or services. Product development usually entails large research and development expenditures. For example, Apple Computer in 2007 introduced the media-playing cell phone, called the iPhone, after working with Cingular Wireless for over a year to develop the phone, which is being sold in both Apple and Cingular stores. The iPhone is the latest example of how lines between the entertainment and telecom industries are becoming blurred, with cable companies developing phone products and phone companies developing cable products. Examples of such competing products that were recently released are SonyEricsson's Walkman phone, Motorola's RAZR handset, Research in Motion's BlackBerry Pearl, and Palm Inc.'s Treo 750.

Five guidelines for when product development may be an especially effective strategy to pursue are:[11]

- When an organization has successful products that are in the maturity stage of the product life cycle; the idea here is to attract satisfied customers to try new (improved) products as a result of their positive experience with the organization's present products or services.
- When an organization competes in an industry that is characterized by rapid technological developments.
- When major competitors offer better-quality products at comparable prices.
- When an organization competes in a high-growth industry.
- When an organization has especially strong research and development capabilities.

Diversification Strategies

There are two general types of *diversification strategies*: related and unrelated. Businesses are said to be *related* when their value chains posses competitively valuable cross-business strategic fits; businesses are said to be *unrelated* when their value chains are so dissimilar that no competitively valuable cross-business relationships exist.[12] Most companies favor related diversification strategies in order to capitalize on synergies as follows:

- Transferring competitively valuable expertise, technological know-how, or other capabilities from one business to another.
- Combining the related activities of separate businesses into a single operation to achieve lower costs.
- Exploiting common use of a well-known brand name.
- Cross-business collaboration to create competitively valuable resource strengths and capabilities[13].

Diversification strategies are becoming less popular as organizations are finding it more difficult to manage diverse business activities. In the 1960s and 1970s, the trend was to diversify so as not to be dependent on any single industry, but the 1980s saw a general reversal of that thinking. Diversification is now on the retreat. Michael Porter, of the Harvard Business School, says, "Management found it couldn't manage the beast." Hence, businesses are selling, or closing, less profitable divisions in order to focus on core businesses.

The greatest risk of being in a single industry is having all of the firm's eggs in one basket. Although many firms are successful operating in a single industry, new technologies, new products, or fast-shifting buyer preferences can decimate a particular business. For example, digital cameras are decimating the film and film processing industry, and cell phones have permanently altered the long-distance telephone calling industry.

Diversification must do more than simply spread business risk across different industries, however, because shareholders could accomplish this by simply purchasing equity in different firms across different industries or by investing in mutual funds. Diversification makes sense only to the extent the strategy adds more to shareholder value than what shareholders could accomplish acting individually. Thus, the chosen industry for diversification must be attractive enough to yield consistently high returns on investment and offer potential across the operating divisions for synergies greater than those entities could achieve alone.

A few companies today, however, pride themselves on being conglomerates, from small firms such as Pentair Inc., and Blount International to huge companies such as Textron, Allied Signal, Emerson Electric, General Electric, Viacom, and Samsung. Samsung, for example, now has global market share leadership in many diverse areas, including cell phones (10 percent), big-screen televisions (32 percent), MP3 players (13 percent), DVD players (11 percent), and microwave ovens (25 percent).[14] Similarly, Textron, through numerous diverse acquisitions, now produces and sells Cessna airplanes, Bell helicopters, Jacobsen lawn mowers, golf products, transmissions, consumer loans, and telescopic machinery. Conglomerates prove that focus and diversity are not always mutually exclusive.

Many strategists contend that firms should "stick to the knitting" and not stray too far from the firm's basic areas of competence. However, diversification is still sometimes an appropriate strategy, especially when the company is competing in an unattractive industry. For example, United Technologies is diversifying away from its core aviation business due to the slumping airline industry. Most recently, United Technologies acquired British electronic-security company Chubb PLC, which follows up its acquisition of Otis Elevator Company and Carrier air conditioning to reduce its dependence on the volatile airline industry. Hamish Maxwell, Philip Morris's former CEO, says, "We want to become a consumer-products company." Diversification makes sense for Philip Morris because cigarette consumption is declining, product liability suits are a risk, and some investors reject tobacco stocks on principle.

Related Diversification

An example of related diversification is the AT&T acquisition of BellSouth in 2007, which was the largest telecommunications acquisition ever approved in the United States and represented AT&T's entry (diversification) into Internet video service. AT&T and Verizon Communications, its major competitor, are adding television to the roster of services they offer consumers so they can better compete with cable companies that already offer bundles of television, phone, and Internet service.

Google's stated strategy is to organize all the world's information into searchable form, diversifying the firm beyond its roots as a Web search engine that sells advertising. The Google acquisition of the Web site YouTube was an example of a related diversification strategy because YouTube contains so many video clips from television shows and commercials. Google wants to diversify further into the television and cablevision business. Google plans to scan millions of books from university and public libraries into a database. Google's acquisition of DoubleClick, also in 2007, was further diversification into the business of placing, or "serving," the electronic advertisements that dot Web sites.

Seagate Technology pursued related diversification recently when it acquired EVault because this moved the company from disk drives to data-storage services. Now Seagate is a major provider of data backup and archival services for small and mid-size businesses. Similarly, Cisco Systems recently diversified with its acquisition of Web Ex Communications because it moved Cisco from manufacturing computer routers, switches, and network gear into online conferencing services.

When diversifying away from familiar products/services, firms must be careful to enter new areas mindful of environmental concerns. The "Natural Environment Perspective" reveals two animal species at risk because of weak corporate environmental policies/operations.

Six guidelines for when related diversification may be an effective strategy are as follows.[15]

- When an organization competes in a no-growth or a slow-growth industry.
- When adding new, but related, products would significantly enhance the sales of current products.
- When new, but related, products could be offered at highly competitive prices.
- When new, but related, products have seasonal sales levels that counterbalance an organization's existing peaks and valleys.
- When an organization's products are currently in the declining stage of the product's life cycle.
- When an organization has a strong management team.

NATURAL ENVIRONMENT PERSPECTIVE
Songbirds and Coral Reefs in Trouble

Songbirds

Bluebirds are one of 76 songbird species in the United States that have dramatically declined in numbers in the last two decades. Not all birds are considered songbirds, and why birds sing is not clear. Some scientists say they sing when calling for mates or warning of danger, but many scientists now contend that birds sing for sheer pleasure. Songbirds include chickadees, orioles, swallows, mockingbirds, warblers, sparrows, vireos, and the wood thrush. "These birds are telling us there's a problem, something's out of balance in our environment," says Jeff Wells, bird conservation director for the National Audubon Society. Songbirds may be telling us that their air or water is too dirty or that we are destroying too much of their habitat. People collect Picasso paintings and save historic buildings. "Songbirds are part of our natural heritage. Why

should we be willing to watch songbirds destroyed any more than allowing a great work of art to be destroyed?" asks Wells. Whatever message songbirds are singing to us today about their natural environment, the message is becoming less and less heard nationwide. Listen when you go outside today. Each of us as individuals, companies, states, and countries should do what we reasonably can to help improve the natural environment for songbirds.

Coral Reefs

The ocean covers more than 71 percent of the Earth. The destructive effect of commercial fishing on ocean habitats coupled with increasing pollution runoff into the ocean and global warming of the ocean have decimated fisheries, marine life, and coral reefs around the world. The unfortunate consequence of fishing over the last century has been *overfishing*—with the principal reasons being politics and greed. Trawl fishing with nets destroys coral reefs and has been compared to catching squirrels by cutting down forests, because bottom nets scour and destroy vast areas of the ocean. The great proportion of marine life caught in a trawl is "by-catch" juvenile fish and other life that are killed and discarded. Warming of the ocean due to CO_2 emissions also kills thousands of acres of coral reefs annually. The total area of fully protected marine habitats in the United States is only about 50 square miles, compared to some 93 million acres of national wildlife refuges and national parks on the nation's land. A healthy ocean is vital to the economic and social future of the nation—and, indeed, all countries of the world. Everything we do on land ends up in the ocean, so we all must become better stewards of this last frontier on Earth in order to sustain human survival and the quality of life.

Sources: Adapted from Tom Brook, "Declining Numbers Mute Many Birds' Songs," *USA Today* (September 11, 2001): 4A. Also adapted from John Ogden, "Maintaining Diversity in the Oceans," *Environment* (April 2001): 29–36.

Sailing Over a Coral Reef. *Source:* Fred David

Unrelated Diversification

An unrelated diversification strategy favors capitalizing upon a portfolio of businesses that are capable of delivering excellent financial performance in their respective industries, rather than striving to capitalize on value chain strategic fits among the businesses. Firms that employ unrelated diversification continually search across different industries for companies that can be acquired for a deal and yet have potential to provide a high return on investment. Pursuing unrelated diversification entails being on the hunt to acquire companies whose assets are undervalued, or companies that are financially distressed, or companies that have high growth prospects but are short on investment capital. An obvious drawback of unrelated diversification is that the parent firm must have an excellent top management team that plans, organizes, motivates, delegates, and controls effectively. It is much more difficult to manage businesses in many industries than in a single industry. However, some firms are successful pursuing unrelated diversification, such as Walt Disney, which owns the ABC network; Viacom, which owns the CBS network; and General Electric, which owns the NBC network. Thus the three major television networks are all owned by diversified firms.

Many more firms have failed at unrelated diversification than have succeeded due to immense management challenges. However, unrelated diversification can be good, as it is for Cendant Corp., which owns the real-estate firm Century 21, the car-rental agency Avis, the travel-booking sites Orbitz and Flairview Travel, and the hotel brands Days Inn and

Howard Johnson. The brokerage firm Morgan Stanley is pursuing unrelated diversification by building a $1 billion casino in Atlantic City in the U.S. state of New Jersey. In addition, Morgan Stanley recently obtained an 18 percent stake in Trump Entertainment Resorts. Also in 2007, Morgan Stanley acquired 13 luxury hotels in Japan for $2.4 billion from All Nippon Airways, further diversifying the firm into hotel management.

Best known for its thermostats and aircraft engines, Honeywell International in 2007 began producing flat-panel television sets. This was Honeywell's first foray into consumer electronics. There is speculation that Honeywell will soon diversify further and enter the computer monitor and display business. Regarding consumer electronics, the largest such retailer, Best Buy, in 2007 paid $97 million to buy a Seattle-based company called Speakeasy, which provides broadband Internet and Internet-based phone services to small businesses. This was an unrelated diversification move by Best Buy.

Wal-Mart recently renegotiated the terms of leases with a number of banks operating in its stores, giving the company itself the explicit right to offer mortgages, home-equity lines of credit, and consumer loans. In some locations, Wal-Mart also may offer debit cards and investment and insurance products either directly or through a third-party vendor. Wal-Mart's desire to enter the banking business has drawn fierce opposition from the banking industry, some members of Congress, and activist groups. There are currently 300 different banks with 1,200 branches inside Wal-Mart stores across the United States, and Wal-Mart plans to add 200 more by 2009. Fifteen commercial firms already own banks, including the motorcycle maker Harley-Davidson and the retailer Target Corp.[16]

An increasing number of hospitals are creating miniature malls by offering banks, bookstores, coffee shops, restaurants, drugstores, and other retail stores within their buildings. Many hospitals previously had only cafeterias, gift shops, and maybe a pharmacy, but the movement into malls and retail stores is aimed at improving the ambiance for patients and their visitors. The new University Pointe Hospital in the U.S. state of Ohio has 75,000 square feet of retail space. The CEO says, "Unless we diversify our revenue, we won't be able to fulfill our mission of providing health care. We want our hospital to be a place that people want to go to."[17]

Another example of unrelated diversification strategy would be the recent General Electric (GE) acquisition of Vivendi Universal Entertainment (VUE). VUE is a television and theme park empire, while GE is a highly diversified conglomerate. VUE owns and operates Universal Studios theme parks. GE owns National Broadcasting Corporation (NBC) and also produces home appliances and scores of other products. General Electric is a classic firm that is highly diversified. GE makes locomotives, lightbulbs, power plants, and refrigerators; GE manages more credit cards than American Express; GE owns more commercial aircraft than American Airlines.

Ten guidelines for when unrelated diversification may be an especially effective strategy are:[18]

- When revenues derived from an organization's current products or services would increase significantly by adding the new, unrelated products.
- When an organization competes in a highly competitive and/or a no-growth industry, as indicated by low industry profit margins and returns.
- When an organization's present channels of distribution can be used to market the new products to current customers.
- When the new products have countercyclical sales patterns compared to an organization's present products.
- When an organization's basic industry is experiencing declining annual sales and profits.
- When an organization has the capital and managerial talent needed to compete successfully in a new industry.
- When an organization has the opportunity to purchase an unrelated business that is an attractive investment opportunity.
- When there exists financial synergy between the acquired and acquiring firm. (Note that a key difference between related and unrelated diversification is that the former should be based on some commonality in markets, products, or technology, whereas the latter should be based more on profit considerations.)

- When existing markets for an organization's present products are saturated.
- When antitrust action could be charged against an organization that historically has concentrated on a single industry.

Defensive Strategies

In addition to integrative, intensive, and diversification strategies, organizations also could pursue retrenchment, divestiture, or liquidation.

Retrenchment

Retrenchment occurs when an organization regroups through cost and asset reduction to reverse declining sales and profits. Sometimes called a *turnaround* or *reorganizational strategy,* retrenchment is designed to fortify an organization's basic distinctive competence. During retrenchment, strategists work with limited resources and face pressure from shareholders, employees, and the media. Retrenchment can entail selling off land and buildings to raise needed cash, pruning product lines, closing marginal businesses, closing obsolete factories, automating processes, reducing the number of employees, and instituting expense control systems.

The telecommunications equipment vendor, Nortel, cut another 2,900 jobs in 2007, bringing its workforce to about 31,000, down from 95,000 in 2001. The retrenchment strategy is part of CEO Mike Zafirovski's strategy to stay only in businesses in which Nortel has a 20 percent global market share. Chief Strategy Officer George Riedel of Nortel says, "In the past, we were trying to be all things to all people. Now we're focused on doing a few things that matter."

The electronics retailer Circuit City is closing 62 stores in Canada in 2007 and 7 stores in the U.S. as the firm continues to struggle against fierce rival Best Buy. Circuit City also is laying off employees and shuffling its top manager team in restructuring moves aimed to reverse declining sales and margins.

Eastman Kodak completed a three-year retrenchment strategy in 2007 during which the firm laid off 30,000 employees and incurred $3.8 billion in restructuring costs. Kodak's workforce declined to about 28,000 at year-end 2007, down from 40,000 at the end of 2006, and down from its peak of 145,000 in 1984. Kodak rolled out a new inkjet printer in 2007 and does well in motion-picture film for movies, but continues to struggle in consumer film and disposable cameras. Kodak's new inkjet printers scan and copy documents, Web pages, and photos using cartridges priced far less than those of its competitors.

DaimlerChrysler AG cut 10,000 jobs and closing factories in Newark, Delaware, and St. Louis as part of a retrenchment strategy that also includes turning away from big pickups and sport-utility vehicles. Chrysler's goal now is not to get bigger but rather to make money.

The furniture maker La-Z-Boy in 2007 is closing three plants, consolidating three others into one facility, and eliminating 500 jobs, or 4.4 percent of its overall workforce of 11,300 employees. The company expects to save $11 million annually by doing so.

Citigroup is in the midst of a major retrenchment/restructuring whereby the firm is laying off 15,000 employees or 5 percent of the bank's global workforce of 327,000. An additional 10,000 or more U.S. jobs are moving to cheaper overseas locations such as India. Citigroup is the world's largest bank.

In some cases, *bankruptcy* can be an effective type of retrenchment strategy. Bankruptcy can allow a firm to avoid major debt obligations and to void union contracts. There are five major types of U.S. bankruptcies allowable by law: Chapter 7, Chapter 9, Chapter 11, Chapter 12, and Chapter 13.

Chapter 7 bankruptcy is a liquidation procedure used only when a corporation sees no hope of being able to operate successfully or to obtain the necessary creditor agreement. All the organization's assets are sold in parts for their tangible worth.

Chapter 9 bankruptcy applies to municipalities. A municipality that successfully declared bankruptcy is Camden, New Jersey, the fifth-poorest city in the United States. A crime-ridden city of 87,000, Camden received $62.5 million in state aid and has withdrawn its bankruptcy petition. Between 1980 and 2000, only 18 U.S. cities declared bankruptcy. Some U.S. states do not allow municipalities to declare bankruptcy.

Chapter 11 bankruptcy allows organizations to reorganize and come back after filing a petition for protection. Business bankruptcy filings dropped to a 10-year-low in fiscal 2006, reflecting the easy access to capital that troubled companies had enjoyed. Chapter 11 filings dropped by 20 percent to 27, 333 in the 12 months ending September 30, according to the Administrative Office of the U.S. Courts. However, analysts expect a surge in bankruptcy filings in 2007–2008 due to tightening credit markets and greater price competitiveness among firms.

New Century Financial, a large subprime mortgage lender, filed for Chapter 11 bankruptcy in April 2007 and laid off more than one half of its workforce. The company at the same time divested its mortgage-servicing assets to Carrington Capital Management, which provided $150 million to New Century to allow the firm to stay in business during bankruptcy reorganization.

Northwest Airlines emerged from bankruptcy in mid-2007 after two years of regrouping under that protection. Northwest is stronger on exit than entry, but the air carrier still has to contend with rising and high fuel costs, unhappy employees, intense competition, and slowing domestic demand. Other airlines still operating under Chapter 11 bankruptcy are UAL Corp, Delta Air Lines, and US Airways.

Startup wireless carrier Amp'dMobile filed for Chaper 11 bankruptcy in June 2007 after it ran out of cash. The company has assets of less than $100 million but is more than that amount in debt.

Chapter 12 bankruptcy was created by the U.S. Family Farmer Bankruptcy Act of 1986. This law became effective in 1987 and provides special relief to family farmers with debt equal to or less than $1.5 million.

Chapter 13 bankruptcy is a reorganization plan similar to Chapter 11, but it is available only to U.S. small businesses owned by individuals with unsecured debts of less than $100,000 and secured debts of less than $350,000. The Chapter 13 debtor is allowed to operate the business while a plan is being developed to provide for the successful operation of the business in the future.

Five guidelines for when retrenchment may be an especially effective strategy to pursue are as follows:[19]

- When an organization has a clearly distinctive competence but has failed consistently to meet its objectives and goals over time.
- When an organization is one of the weaker competitors in a given industry.
- When an organization is plagued by inefficiency, low profitability, poor employee morale, and pressure from stockholders to improve performance.
- When an organization has failed to capitalize on external opportunities, minimize external threats, take advantage of internal strengths, and overcome internal weaknesses over time; that is, when the organization's strategic managers have failed (and possibly will be replaced by more competent individuals).
- When an organization has grown so large so quickly that major internal reorganization is needed.

Divestiture

Selling a division or part of an organization is called *divestiture*. Divestiture often is used to raise capital for further strategic acquisitions or investments. Divestiture can be part of an overall retrenchment strategy to rid an organization of businesses that are unprofitable, that require too much capital, or that do not fit well with the firm's other activities. Divestiture has also become a popular strategy for firms to focus on their core businesses and become less diversified. For example, Germany's Merck KGaA is selling its generic-drug division in order to focus on branded drugs and chemicals. Merck also is trying to sell its consumer health care business for the same reason. Akzo Nobel NV of the Netherlands is trying to sell its pharmaceuticals division, Organon BioSciences, in order to focus on its chemicals and paint operations. Switzerland's Norvartis AG recently sold its medical-nutrition division to focus on drugs and vaccines. Siemens AG has been divesting its telecommunications businesses to focus on medical diagnostics.

International Paper is selling its beverage-packaging and chemical operations so it can focus on uncoated paper and packaging. Morgan Stanley plans to jettison its Discover credit-card business to focus on its brokerage business. Even Time Warner recently divested the Atlanta Braves baseball team to Liberty Media Corp. for $460 million. Ford Motor Company recently divested Aston Martin, the British brand of car most famous for its association with the James Bond films.

Headquartered in Birmingham, Alabama, HealthSouth Corporation sold its surgery division to private-investment partnership TPG Inc. in 2007. Formerly Texas Pacific Group, TPG now manages more than $30 billion in assets. HealthSouth also divested its outpatient rehabilitation centers in 35 states as the firm strives to refocus on its inpatient-rehabilitation business. Refocusing by divesting has thus become a very common strategy being employed by firms in many industries in 2006–2008. Table 5-3 provides a list of some recent divestitures.

Six guidelines for when divestiture may be an especially effective strategy to pursue follows:[20]

- When an organization has pursued a retrenchment strategy and failed to accomplish needed improvements.
- When a division needs more resources to be competitive than the company can provide.
- When a division is responsible for an organization's overall poor performance.
- When a division is a misfit with the rest of an organization; this can result from radically different markets, customers, managers, employees, values, or needs.

TABLE 5-3 **Recent Divestitures**

Parent Company	Part Being Divested	Acquiring Company
San Miguel Corp.	Soft drink bottling	Coca-Cola Co.
CBS	Seven TV stations	Cerberus Capital Mgt.
Lacofinance SA	Svedka Vodka	Constellation Brands
Polish Government	PZL Mielec	Sikorsky Aircraft
Delphi Corp.	Vehicle interiors	Renco Group Inc.
International Paper	Beverage packing	Carter Holt Harvey Ltd.
International Paper	Chemical operations	Rhone Capital LLC
American Skiing Co.	Steamboat Ski & Resort	Intrawest Corp.
Novartis AG	Medical nutrition	Nestle SA
Genworth Financial	Life and health insurance	Sun Life Financial
Ingersoll-Rand Co.	Road development	Volvo AB
Lyondell Chemical	Inorganic chemicals	National Industrialization
Colgate-Palmolive	Latin American bleach	Clorox
Lafarge SA	Roofing unit	PAI Partners
Ford Motor Company	Climate control	Valeo SA
Ahold NV	Polish grocery stores	Carrefour SA
Mirant Corp.	Mirant Asia Pacific	Marubeni Corp.
Dubai Ports World	U.S. assets	AIG Global Investment
Polaris Financial Group	Bank of Overseas China	Citigroup Inc.
Raytheon Co.	Aircraft manufacturing	Hawker Beechcraft
McClatchy Company	Minneapolis Star Tribune	Avista Capital Partners
Alliant Energy	Interstate Power & Light	ITC Holdings
Kraft Foods	Hot cereals	B&G Foods
Kraft Foods	Minute Rice	Ebro Puleva
Gordon Gaming Corp.	Sahara Hotel & Casino	SBE Entertainment
Accor SA	30 hotels	Land Securities Group PLC

- When a large amount of cash is needed quickly and cannot be obtained reasonably from other sources.
- When government antitrust action threatens an organization.

Liquidation

Selling all of a company's assets, in parts, for their tangible worth is called *liquidation*. Liquidation is a recognition of defeat and consequently can be an emotionally difficult strategy. However, it may be better to cease operating than to continue losing large sums of money. For example, Canadian discount airline, Jetsgo, in 2005, halted operations, filed for bankruptcy, and then liquidated. Canada's third-largest airline, Jetsgo was launched three years earlier from Montreal. Jetsgo competed against WestJet, based in Calgary, Alberta, and Air Canada, based in Montreal. Analysts had long predicted that Jetsgo would fail, given the company's rock-bottom ticket prices and aggressive expansion.

Thousands of small businesses in the United States liquidate annually without ever making the news. It is tough to start and successfully operate a small business. In China and Russia, thousands of government-owned businesses liquidate annually as those countries try to privatize and consolidate industries.

Three guidelines for when liquidation may be an especially effective strategy to pursue are:[21]

- When an organization has pursued both a retrenchment strategy and a divestiture strategy, and neither has been successful.
- When an organization's only alternative is bankruptcy. Liquidation represents an orderly and planned means of obtaining the greatest possible cash for an organization's assets. A company can legally declare bankruptcy first and then liquidate various divisions to raise needed capital.
- When the stockholders of a firm can minimize their losses by selling the organization's assets.

Michael Porter's Five Generic Strategies

Probably the three most widely read books on competitive analysis in the 1980s were Michael Porter's *Competitive Strategy* (Free Press, 1980), *Competitive Advantage* (Free Press, 1985), and *Competitive Advantage of Nations* (Free Press, 1989). According to Porter, strategies allow organizations to gain competitive advantage from three different bases: cost leadership, differentiation, and focus. Porter calls these bases *generic strategies*. *Cost leadership* emphasizes producing standardized products at a very low per-unit cost for consumers who are price-sensitive. Two alternative types of cost leadership strategies can be defined. Type 1 is a *low-cost* strategy that offers products or services to a wide range of customers at the lowest price available on the market. Type 2 is a *best-value* strategy that offers products or services to a wide range of customers at the best price-value available on the market; the best-value strategy aims to offer customers a range of products or services at the lowest price available compared to a rival's products with similar attributes. Both Type 1 and Type 2 strategies target a large market.

Porter's Type 3 generic strategy is *differentiation*. *Differentiation* is a strategy aimed at producing products and services considered unique industrywide and directed at consumers who are relatively price-insensitive.

Focus means producing products and services that fulfill the needs of small groups of consumers. Two alternative types of focus strategies are Type 4 and Type 5. Type 4 is a *low-cost focus* strategy that offers products or services to a small range (niche group) of customers at the lowest price available on the market. Examples of firms that use the Type 4 strategy include Jiffy Lube International and Pizza Hut, as well as local used car dealers and hot dog restaurants. Type 5 is a *best-value focus* strategy that offers products or services to a small range of customers at the best price-value available on the market. Sometimes called "focused differentiation," the best-value focus strategy aims to offer a niche group of customers products or services that meet their tastes and requirements better than rivals' products do. Both

Type 4 and Type 5 focus strategies target a small market. However, the difference is that Type 4 strategies offer products services to a niche group at the lowest price, whereas Type 5 offers products/services to a niche group at higher prices but loaded with features so the offerings are perceived as the best value. Examples of firms that use the Type 5 strategy include Cannondale (top-of-the-line mountain bikes), Maytag (washing machines), and Lone Star Restaurants (steak house), as well as bed-and-breakfast inns and local retail boutiques.

Porter's five strategies imply different organizational arrangements, control procedures, and incentive systems. Larger firms with greater access to resources typically compete on a cost leadership and/or differentiation basis, whereas smaller firms often compete on a focus basis. Porter's five generic strategies are illustrated in Figure 5-3. Note that a differentiation strategy (Type 3) can be pursued with either a small target market or a large target market. However, it is not effective to pursue a cost leadership strategy in a small market because profits margins are generally too small. Likewise, it is not effective to pursue a focus strategy in a large market because economies of scale would generally favor a low-cost or best-value cost leaderships strategy to gain and/or sustain competitive advantage.

Porter stresses the need for strategists to perform cost-benefit analyses to evaluate "sharing opportunities" among a firm's existing and potential business units. Sharing activities and resources enhances competitive advantage by lowering costs or increasing differentiation. In addition to prompting sharing, Porter stresses the need for firms to effectively "transfer" skills and expertise among autonomous business units in order to gain competitive advantage. Depending upon factors such as type of industry, size of firm, and nature of competition, various strategies could yield advantages in cost leadership, differentiation, and focus.

Cost Leadership Strategies (Type 1 and Type 2)

A primary reason for pursuing forward, backward, and horizontal integration strategies is to gain low-cost or best-value cost leadership benefits. But cost leadership generally must be pursued in conjunction with differentiation. A number of cost elements affect the relative attractiveness of generic strategies, including economies or diseconomies of scale achieved, learning and experience curve effects, the percentage of capacity utilization achieved, and linkages with suppliers and distributors. Other cost elements to consider in choosing among alternative strategies include the potential for sharing costs and knowledge

FIGURE 5-3

Porter's Five Generic Strategies

Type 1: Cost Leadership—Low Cost
Type 2: Cost Leadership—Best Value
Type 3: Differentiation
Type 4: Focus—Low Cost
Type 5: Focus—Best Value

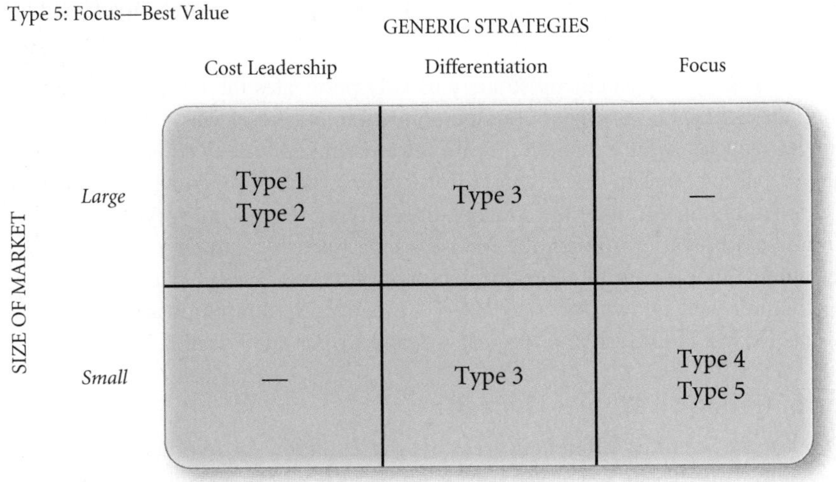

Source: Adapted from Michael E. Porter, *Competitive Strategy: Techniques for Analyzing Industries and Competitors* (New York: Free Press, 1980): 35–40.

within the organization, R&D costs associated with new product development or modification of existing products, labor costs, tax rates, energy costs, and shipping costs.

Striving to be the low-cost producer in an industry can be especially effective when the market is composed of many price-sensitive buyers, when there are few ways to achieve product differentiation, when buyers do not care much about differences from brand to brand, or when there are a large number of buyers with significant bargaining power. The basic idea is to underprice competitors and thereby gain market share and sales, entirely driving some competitors out of the market. Companies employing a low-cost (Type 1) or best-value (Type 2) cost leadership strategy must achieve their competitive advantage in ways that are difficult for competitors to copy or match. If rivals find it relatively easy or inexpensive to imitate the leader's cost leadership methods, the leaders' advantage will not last long enough to yield a valuable edge in the marketplace. Recall that for a resource to be valuable, it must be either rare, hard to imitate, or not easily substitutable. To successfully employ a cost leadership strategy, a firm must ensure that its total costs across its overall value chain are lower than competitors' total costs. There are two ways to accomplish this:[22]

1. Perform value chain activities more efficiently than rivals and control the factors that drive the costs of value chain activities. Such activities could include altering the plant layout, mastering newly introduced technologies, using common parts or components in different products, simplifying product design, finding ways to operate close to full capacity year-round, and so on.
2. Revamp the firm's overall value chain to eliminate or bypass some cost-producing activities. Such activities could include securing new suppliers or distributors, selling products online, relocating manufacturing facilities, avoiding the use of union labor, and so on.

When employing a cost leadership strategy, a firm must be careful not to use such aggressive price cuts that their own profits are low or nonexistent. Constantly be mindful of cost-saving technological breakthroughs or any other value chain advancements that could erode or destroy the firm's competitive advantage. A Type 1 or Type 2 cost leadership strategy can be especially effective under the following conditions:[23]

1. When price competition among rival sellers is especially vigorous.
2. When the products of rival sellers are essentially identical and supplies are readily available from any of several eager sellers.
3. When there are few ways to achieve product differentiation that have value to buyers.
4. When most buyers use the product in the same ways.
5. When buyers incur low costs in switching their purchases from one seller to another.
6. When buyers are large and have significant power to bargain down prices.
7. When industry newcomers use introductory low prices to attract buyers and build a customer base.

A successful cost leadership strategy usually permeates the entire firm, as evidenced by high efficiency, low overhead, limited perks, intolerance of waste, intensive screening of budget requests, wide spans of control, rewards linked to cost containment, and broad employee participation in cost control efforts. Some risks of pursuing cost leadership are that competitors may imitate the strategy, thus driving overall industry profits down; that technological breakthroughs in the industry may make the strategy ineffective; or that buyer interest may swing to other differentiating features besides price. Several example firms that are well known for their low-cost leadership strategies are Wal-Mart, BIC, McDonald's, METRO Cash & Carry, Makro, and Briggs and Stratton.

Differentiation Strategies (Type 3)

Different strategies offer different degrees of differentiation. Differentiation does not guarantee competitive advantage, especially if standard products sufficiently meet customer needs or if rapid imitation by competitors is possible. Durable products protected by barriers to quick copying by competitors are best. Successful differentiation can mean greater product flexibility, greater compatibility, lower costs, improved service, less maintenance, greater convenience, or more features. Product development is an example of a strategy that offers the advantages of differentiation.

A differentiation strategy should be pursued only after a careful study of buyers' needs and preferences to determine the feasibility of incorporating one or more differentiating features into a unique product that features the desired attributes. A successful differentiation strategy allows a firm to charge a higher price for its product and to gain customer loyalty because consumers may become strongly attached to the differentiation features. Special features that differentiate one's product can include superior service, spare parts availability, engineering design, product performance, useful life, gas mileage, or ease of use.

A risk of pursuing a differentiation strategy is that the unique product may not be valued highly enough by customers to justify the higher price. When this happens, a cost leadership strategy easily will defeat a differentiation strategy. Another risk of pursuing a differentiation strategy is that competitors may quickly develop ways to copy the differentiating features. Firms thus must find durable sources of uniqueness that cannot be imitated quickly or cheaply by rival firms.

Common organizational requirements for a successful differentiation strategy include strong coordination among the R&D and marketing functions and substantial amenities to attract scientists and creative people. Firms can pursue a differentiation (Type 3) strategy based on many different competitive aspects. For example, Mountain Dew and root beer have a unique taste; Lowe's, B&Q, and Wal-Mart offer wide selection and one-stop shopping; Dell Computer and FedEx offer superior service; BMW and Porsche offer engineering design and performance; Siemens AG and Hewlett-Packard offer a wide range of products; and E*Trade and Ameritrade offer Internet convenience. Differentiation opportunities exist or can potentially be developed anywhere along the firm's value chain, including supply chain activities, product R&D activities, production and technological activities, manufacturing activities, human resource management activities, distribution activities, or marketing activities.

The most effective differentiation bases are those that are hard or expensive for rivals to duplicate. Competitors are continually trying to imitate, duplicate, and outperform rivals along any differentiation variable that has yielded competitive advantage. For example, when Nippon Airways cut its prices, JAL quickly followed suit. When Caterpillar instituted its quick-delivery-of-spare-parts policy, John Deere soon followed suit. To the extent that differentiating attributes are tough for rivals to copy, a differentiation strategy will be especially effective, but the sources of uniqueness must be time-consuming, cost prohibitive, and simply too burdensome for rivals to match. A firm, therefore, must be careful when employing a differentiation (Type 3) strategy. Buyers will not pay the higher differentiation price unless their perceived value exceeds the price they are paying.[24] Based upon such matters as attractive packaging, extensive advertising, quality of sales presentations, quality of Web site, list of customers, professionalism, size of the firm, and/or profitability of the company, perceived value may be more important to customers than actual value.

A Type 3 differentiation strategy can be especially effective under the following conditions:[25]

1. When there are many ways to differentiate the product or service and many buyers perceive these differences as having value.
2. When buyer needs and uses are diverse.
3. When few rival firms are following a similar differentiation approach.
4. When technological change is fast paced and competition revolves around rapidly evolving product features.

Focus Strategies (Type 4 and Type 5)

A successful focus strategy depends on an industry segment that is of sufficient size, has good growth potential, and is not crucial to the success of other major competitors. Strategies such as market penetration and market development offer substantial focusing advantages. Midsize and large firms can effectively pursue focus-based strategies only in conjunction with differentiation or cost leadership–based strategies. All firms in essence follow a differentiated strategy. Because only one firm can differentiate itself with the lowest cost, the remaining firms in the industry must find other ways to differentiate their products.

Focus strategies are most effective when consumers have distinctive preferences or requirements and when rival firms are not attempting to specialize in the same target segment. Starbucks is pursuing a focus strategy as it recently acquired Seattle Coffee's U.S. and Canadian operations for $72 million. Based in Seattle, Starbucks now owns Seattle's 150 coffee shops and its wholesale contracts with about 12,000 grocery stores and food service stores that distribute Seattle coffee beans.

In the insurance industry, Safeco recently divested its life insurance and investment management divisions to focus exclusively on property casualty insurance operations. The Seattle-based company's strategy is just one of many examples of consolidation in the insurance industry where firms strive to focus on one type of insurance rather than many types.

Japan's second-largest airline by revenue, All Nippon Airways, has a stated strategy to focus on core passenger and cargo flight operations, so the firm is divesting all other assets. This strategy led to All Nippon selling its 13 luxury hotels in 2007 to Morgan Stanley.

Risks of pursuing a focus strategy include the possibility that numerous competitors will recognize the successful focus strategy and copy it or that consumer preferences will drift toward the product attributes desired by the market as a whole. An organization using a focus strategy may concentrate on a particular group of customers, geographic markets, or on particular product-line segments to serve a well-defined but narrow market better than competitors who serve a broader market.

A low-cost (Type 4) or best-value (Type 5) focus strategy can be especially attractive under the following conditions:[26]

1. When the target market niche is large, profitable, and growing.
2. When industry leaders do not consider the niche to be crucial to their own success.
3. When industry leaders consider it too costly or difficult to meet the specialized needs of the target market niche while taking care of their mainstream customers.
4. When the industry has many different niches and segments, thereby allowing a focuser to pick a competitively attractive niche suited to its own resources.
5. When few, if any, other rivals are attempting to specialize in the same target segment.

Strategies for Competing in Turbulent, High-Velocity Markets

The world is changing more and more rapidly, and consequently industries and firms themselves are changing faster than ever. Some industries are changing so fast that researchers call them *turbulent, high-velocity markets,* such as telecommunications, medical, biotechnology, pharmaceuticals, computer hardware, software, and virtually all Internet-based industries. High-velocity change is clearly becoming more and more the rule rather than the exception, even in such industries as toys, phones, banking, defense, publishing, and communication.

As illustrated in Figure 5-4, meeting the challenge of high-velocity change presents the firm with a choice of whether to react, anticipate, or lead the market in terms of its own strategies. To primarily react to changes in the industry would be a defensive strategy used to counter, for example, unexpected shifts in buyer tastes and technological breakthroughs. The react-to-change strategy would not be as effective as the anticipate-change strategy, which would entail devising and following through with plans for dealing with the expected changes. However, firms ideally strive to be in a position to lead the changes in high-velocity markets, whereby they pioneer new and better technologies and products and set industry standards. As illustrated, being the leader or pioneer of change in a high-velocity market is an aggressive, offensive strategy that includes rushing next-generation products to market ahead of rivals and being continually proactive in shaping the market to one's own benefit. Although a lead-change strategy is best whenever the firm has the resources to pursue this

165

FIGURE 5-4

Meeting the Challenge of High-Velocity Change

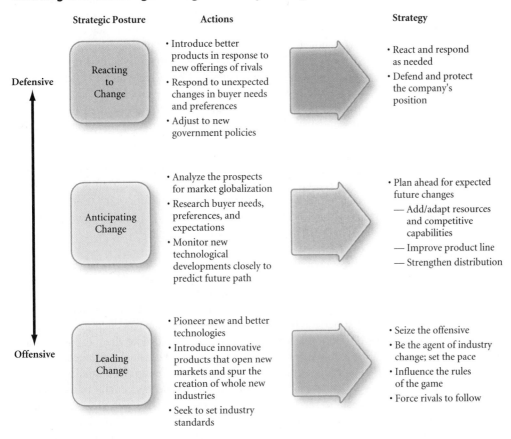

approach, on occasion even the strongest firms in turbulent industries have to employ the react-to-the-market strategy and the anticipate-the-market strategy.

Means for Achieving Strategies

Joint Venture/Partnering

Joint venture is a popular strategy that occurs when two or more companies form a temporary partnership or consortium for the purpose of capitalizing on some opportunity. Often, the two or more sponsoring firms form a separate organization and have shared equity ownership in the new entity. Other types of *cooperative arrangements* include research and development partnerships, cross-distribution agreements, cross-licensing agreements, cross-manufacturing agreements, and joint-bidding consortia. Burger King recently formed a "conceptual agreement" with its fierce rival, Hungry Jacks, in Australia, whereby the two firms will join forces against market leader McDonald's. All Burger Kings in Australia are being renamed Hungry Jacks, but Burger King retains ownership under the unusual agreement. With this agreement, Australia becomes Burger King's fourth-largest country market, tied with Spain.

U.S. regional airline operator Mesa Air Group, based in the U.S. state of Arizona, recently formed a joint venture with Chinese carrier Shenzhen Airlines, based in Shenzhen, China, to create China's first commuter airline. The first joint venture ever between U.S. and Chinese passenger airlines, Bejing Airlines now links Beijing with many poorly or nonserved cities in China and Southeast Asia. One of China's largest privately owned carriers, Shenzhen Airlines aims to expand its fleet to 80 planes by 2008 and 160 planes by 2015.

Joint ventures and cooperative arrangements are being used increasingly because they allow companies to improve communications and networking, to globalize operations, and to minimize risk. Joint ventures and partnerships are often used to pursue an opportunity that is too complex, uneconomical, or risky for a single firm to pursue alone. Such business creations also are used when achieving and sustaining competitive advantage when an industry requires a broader range of competencies and know-how than any one firm can marshal. Armani's joint venture is with Emaar Hotels & Resorts LLC to create, among others, the tallest building in the world in 2008: a 2,000-foot-tall hotel in Dubai's Burj Dubai. Kathryn Rudie Harrigan, professor of strategic management at Columbia University, summarizes the trend toward increased joint venturing:

> In today's global business environment of scarce resources, rapid rates of technological change, and rising capital requirements, the important question is no longer "Shall we form a joint venture?" Now the question is "Which joint ventures and cooperative arrangements are most appropriate for our needs and expectations?" followed by "How do we manage these ventures most effectively?"[27]

In a global market tied together by the Internet, joint ventures, and partnerships, alliances are proving to be a more effective way to enhance corporate growth than mergers and acquisitions.[28] Strategic partnering takes many forms, including outsourcing, information sharing, joint marketing, and joint research and development. Many companies, such as Eli Lilly, now host partnership training classes for their managers and partners. There are today more than 10,000 joint ventures formed annually, more than all mergers and acquisitions. There are countless examples of successful strategic alliances, such as Starbucks' recent joint venture with China's President Coffee to open hundreds of new Starbuck coffee shops in China. For 4,500 years, China has been a country of tea drinkers, but Seattle-based Starbucks is having success building Chinese taste for coffee. Microsoft's online-services division recently formed a joint venture with Shanghai Alliance Investment to launch MSN China throughout China. The new company, Shanghai MSN Network Communications Technology, serves China's online consumers: 100 million (and growing) at that time. As evidence of Microsoft's determination to enter the telecom market, the firm has formed a partnership with France Telecom SA, one of the world's largest telecommunications operators. Since people increasingly interact with the Internet using either a cell phone or television, Microsoft is using the alliance to push its voice-over-Internet protocol (VOIP), which is a handheld device that combines cell phone usage with Internet coverage.

A major reason why firms are using partnering as a means to achieve strategies is globalization. Wal-Mart's successful joint venture with Mexico's Cifra is indicative of how a domestic firm can benefit immensely by partnering with a foreign company to gain substantial presence in that new country. Technology also is a major reason behind the need to form strategic alliances, with the Internet linking widely dispersed partners. The Internet paved the way and legitimized the need for alliances to serve as the primary means for corporate growth.

Evidence is mounting that firms should use partnering as a means for achieving strategies. However, the sad fact is that most U.S. firms in many industries—such as financial services, forest products, metals, and retailing—still operate in a merger or acquire mode to obtain growth. Partnering is not yet taught at most business schools and is often viewed within companies as a financial issue rather than a strategic issue. However, partnering has become a core competency, a strategic issue of such importance that top management involvement initially and throughout the life of an alliance is vital.[29]

Joint ventures among once rival firms are commonly being used to pursue strategies ranging from retrenchment to market development.

Although ventures and partnerships are preferred over mergers as a means for achieving strategies, certainly they are not all successful. The good news is that joint ventures and partnerships are less risky for companies than mergers, but the bad news is that many alliances fail. *Forbes* has reported that about 30 percent of all joint ventures and partnership alliances are outright failures, while another 17 percent have limited success and then dissipate due to problems.[30] There are countless examples of failed joint ventures. A few common problems that cause joint ventures to fail are as follows:

1. Managers who must collaborate daily in operating the venture are not involved in forming or shaping the venture.
2. The venture may benefit the partnering companies but may not benefit customers, who then complain about poorer service or criticize the companies in other ways.
3. The venture may not be supported equally by both partners. If supported unequally, problems arise.
4. The venture may begin to compete more with one of the partners than the other.[31]

Six guidelines for when a joint venture may be an especially effective strategy to pursue are:[32]

- When a privately-owned organization is forming a joint venture with a publicly owned organization; there are some advantages to being privately held, such as closed ownership; there are some advantages of being publicly held, such as access to stock issuances as a source of capital. Sometimes, the unique advantages of being privately and publicly held can be synergistically combined in a joint venture.
- When a domestic organization is forming a joint venture with a foreign company; a joint venture can provide a domestic company with the opportunity for obtaining local management in a foreign country, thereby reducing risks such as expropriation and harassment by host country officials.
- When the distinct competencies of two or more firms complement each other especially well.
- When some project is potentially very profitable but requires overwhelming resources and risks; the Alaskan pipeline is an example.
- When two or more smaller firms have trouble competing with a large firm.
- When there exists a need to quickly introduce a new technology.

Merger/Acquisition

Merger and acquisition are two commonly used ways to pursue strategies. A *merger* occurs when two organizations of about equal size unite to form one enterprise. An *acquisition* occurs when a large organization purchases (acquires) a smaller firm, or vice versa. When a merger or acquisition is not desired by both parties, it can be called a *takeover* or *hostile takeover*. In contrast, if the acquisition is desired by both firms, it is termed a *friendly merger*. Most mergers are friendly.

There were numerous examples in 2007 of hostile takeover attempts. For example, in the United States, AirTran Airways launched a $345 million tender offer to acquire Midwest Airlines' shares directly from shareholders in hopes of forcing the Midwest board to sell the firm. AirTran has even offered to keep serving free chocolate chip cookies on all Midwest flights if the board will sell. Even though Oji Paper's $1.4 billion bid for Hokuetsu Paper Mills made sense for an industry hammered by costs and competition, it failed. "We have a spirit of independence in our corporate culture," Hokuetsu's president Masaaki Miwa said. "Over the past 100 years of our history we faced a critical earthquake and survived it with perseverance and endurance."

There are numerous and powerful forces driving once-fierce rivals to merge around the world, however. Some of these forces are deregulation, technological change, excess capacity, inability to boost profits through price increases, a depressed stock market, and the need to gain economies of scale. Other forces spurring acquisitions include increased market power, reduced entry barriers, reduced cost of new product development, increased speed of products to market, lowered risk compared to developing new products, increased diversification, avoidance of excessive competition, and opportunity to learn and develop new capabilities.

The year 2006 witnessed more mergers than ever worldwide, and analysts predict that the 2007 dollar volume of transactions will exceed $4 trillion for the first time ever.

Merger mania is being fueled by robust stock markets, cheap and available debt, and firms desiring to expand globally. The total of $3.79 trillion in merger transactions worldwide in 2006 beat the previous record of $3.4 trillion in 2000, and was a whopping 38 percent higher than in 2005. There were 55 merger transactions in 2006 valued at more than $10 billion apiece with the AT&T acquisition of BellSouth topping the list at $72.7 billion. Across the globe, $1.1 trillion of companies traded hands in the first quarter of 2007, 27 percent higher than the same period in 2006. The 2007 figures were more startling in the United States, where the volume of deals surged 32 percent from 2006 to $439 billion.[33]

Private-equity firms played a bigger-than-ever role in the merger frenzy, with a hand in 20 percent of the world's acquisitions.[34] Mergers in Europe rose 39 percent in 2006 to $1.43 trillion, compared with a 36 percent increase to $1.56 trillion in the United States. The world's five largest merger advisor/transaction firms are Goldman Sachs, Citigroup, Morgan Stanley, J.P. Morgan, and Merrill Lynch.

In China, there were 2,263 acquisitions in 2006, up from 1,786 in 2005.[35] The 2006 dollar total of acquisitions reached $103.8 billion, up 68 percent from 2005. Through mergers, the Chinese central government wants to reduce the number of state-owned companies from 161 in 2007 to 80 in 2010. Stephen Green, an economist with Standard Chartered, commented regarding the surge in acquisitions in China: "It should make things more efficient. You're looking for economies of scale, horizontal and vertical integration, improving quality of management, and also the ability to wipe out your competitors and gain pricing power." This comment reveals the motivation for most acquisitions in Europe and the United States.

In Japan, companies in 2006–2008 start acquiring other firms worldwide after a lull in this activity in 2000–2005. Japanese firms bought more than 300 foreign companies for a total exceeding $20 billion in 2006, double the figure in 2004. For example, Japan's largest tobacco company, Japan Tobacco Inc., is acquiring Gallaher Group PLC of Britain in the largest Japanese deal ever for a foreign company. Unheard of prior to 2006 in Japan, hostile takeovers are also being tried. As we mentioned, Oji Paper launched an unsolicited $1.4 billion bid for rival Hokuetsu Paper Mills. This was the first hostile takeover battle between two Japanese blue-chip companies.

In Japan, new guidelines in 2007 make it much easier and actually encourage Japanese firms to merge. The value of merger/acquisition deals among Japanese companies has steadily risen over the past five years, hitting 15 trillion yen ($124 billion) in 2006. There were 2,775 deals in 2006, up 1.8 percent from 2005 and much higher than the 1,752 in 2002.

Sirius and XM Satellite Radio, two fierce rival firms in the satellite radio business, merged in 2007, creating a company valued at more than $13 billion. Neither company had a made a profit prior to the merger, and each firm's satellite radios were designed for it and cannot receive the other's signal. General Motors, Toyota, and Honda were big XM subscribers, while Ford, DaimlerChrylser, and VW/Audi were exclusive Sirius customers. The combined company is developing radio receivers that receive input from both XM and Sirius satellites.

Private-Equity Acquisitions

Private-equity firms such as Kohlberg Kravis Roberts (KKR) have made many if not most of the acquisitions in recent years. The pace and number of private-equity acquisitions was a key new trend in 2006–2007 in the merger world. Cheap and plentiful debt has propelled private-equity firms to be the most active acquirer's in today's business marketplace. These firms acquire companies and then sell them at premium prices. That is the intent of virtually all private-equity acquisitions—buy low and sell high later—which is arguably just good business.

Two private-equity firms, Apollo Management and Texas Pacific, recently paid $16.7 billion to acquire Harrah's Entertainment, the world's largest casino company. Another private-equity group, Colony Capital LLC, recently acquired Station Casinos Inc. Another,

Apax Partners, just acquired Chicago insurance brokerage Hub International. Perseus LLC recently acquired Avalon Publishing Group and Consortium Book Sales & Distribution. The recent $32 billion purchase of the largest electric company in Texas, TXU, was by two private-equity firms, KKR and Texas Pacific Group. Goodyear Tire & Rubber just divested its engineered-products division to a private-equity firm Carlyle Partners for $1.48 billion. Home-services operator ServiceMaster Company was recently acquired by private-equity firm Clayton, Dubilier & Rice for $4.8 billion.

The proliferation of private-equity deals has resulted in union leaders worldwide lobbying governments to impose restrictions on this activity. Union leaders argue that such deals suppress the bargaining power of unions and also promote widening income disparity between corporate executives and workers, despite growth in profits and productivity. Hundreds of private-equity investors such as Darby Overseas Investments Ltd., Cerberus Capital Management LP, and Blackstone Group are acquiring small firms in Asia, capitalizing on rapid growth there.

A recent article reveals that in 2006 private-equity firms launched 14 hostile or unsolicited takeover bids in Europe and this continued in 2007.[36] Three private-equity firms recently made an unsolicited bid for J Sainsbury PLC, a British grocery chain, in what would be Europe's largest private-equity deal. Countrywide PLC was recently acquired by private-equity company 3i Group PLC for 551 pence a share, which was a premium of 90 pence to the 461 pence that Countrywide PLC's shares were trading.

Blackstone Group, which had acquired Celanese, Vanguard Health, Nielsen, SunGard, TRW Automotive, Travelport, and Naico in recent years, is trying to go public, which could alter the private-equity business model. Generally these firms avoid SEC disclosure rules regarding executive pay and other matters by staying private. Going public would require Blackstone to reveal some of its secrets for wresting huge profits from the companies it acquires and thus expose the firm to criticism.

Not all mergers are effective and successful. Pricewaterhouse Coopers LLP recently researched mergers and found that the average acquirer's stock was 3.7 percent lower than its industry peer group a year later. *BusinessWeek* magazine and the *Wall Street Journal* studied mergers and concluded that about half produced negative returns to shareholders. Investor Warren Buffett once said in a speech that "too-high purchase price for the stock of an excellent company can undo the effects of a subsequent decade of favorable business developments." Research suggests that perhaps 20 percent of all mergers and acquisitions are successful, approximately 60 percent produce disappointing results, and the last 20 percent are clear failures.[37] So a merger between two firms can yield great benefits, but the price and reasoning must be right.

Some key reasons why many mergers and acquisitions fail are:

- Integration difficulties
- Inadequate evaluation of target
- Large or extraordinary debt
- Inability to achieve synergy
- Too much diversification
- Managers overly focused on acquisitions
- Too large an acquisition
- Difficult to integrate different organizational cultures
- Reduced employee morale due to layoffs and relocations

Among mergers, acquisitions, and takeovers in recent years, same-industry combinations have predominated. A general market consolidation is occurring in many industries, especially banking, insurance, defense, and health care, but also in pharmaceuticals, food, airlines, accounting, publishing, computers, retailing, financial services, and biotechnology. For example, SXR Uranium One Inc. recently purchased rival uranium miner UrAsia Energy Ltd, creating the world's second-largest uranium company after Cameco Corp. Similarly, Tenaris SA, based in Luxembourg and the world's biggest maker of steel tubes used in oil exploration and production, recently acquired rival Hydril Company, based in the United States.

Table 5-4 shows some mergers and acquisitions completed in 2007. There are many reasons for mergers and acquisitions, including the following:

- To provide improved capacity utilization
- To make better use of the existing sales force
- To reduce managerial staff
- To gain economies of scale
- To smooth out seasonal trends in sales
- To gain access to new suppliers, distributors, customers, products, and creditors
- To gain new technology
- To reduce tax obligations

TABLE 5-4   The Largest Mergers Completed Globally in 2007

Acquiring Firm	Acquired Firm	Price (In Billions)
AT&T (U.S.)	BellSouth Corp. (U.S.)	72.7
E.On (Germany)	Endesa (Spain)	46.9
Suez (France)	Gaz de France (France)	39.5
Banca Intesa (Italy)	SanPaolo IMI (Italy)	37.6
Porsche (Germany)	Volkswagen (Germany)	36.8
Mittal Steel (Netherlands)	Arcelor (Luxembourg)	33.8
Investor Group (U.S.)	TXU (U.S.)	32.1
Statoil (Norway)	Norsk Hydro (Norway)	30.8
America Movil (Mexico)	America Telecom (Mexico)	30.5
Freeport-McMoran (U.S.)	Phelps Dodge (U.S.)	25.8
Wachovia (U.S.)	Golden West Financial (U.S.)	25.5
CVS (U.S.)	Caremark Rx (U.S.)	23.0
Iberdrola (Spain)	Scottish Power (U.K.)	22.2
Airport Develop (Spain)	BAA (U.K.)	21.8
Investor Group (U.S.)	HCA (U.S.)	21.2
Bayer (Germany)	Schering (Germany)	20.6
Investor Group (U.S.)	Clear Channel Communications (U.S.)	18.7
Cia Vale do Rio Doce (Brazil)	Inco (Canada)	18.0
Blackstone Group (U.S.)	Equity Office Properties (U.S.)	18.0
Firestone Holdings (U.S.)	Freescale Semiconductor (U.S)	17.7
Xstrata (Switzerland)	Falconbridge (Canada)	17.4
Investor Group (U.S.)	Harrah's Entertainment (U.S.)	17.2
Investor Group (U.S.)	Alliance Boots (U.K.)	16.8
Johnson & Johnson (U.S.)	Pfizer Consumer Healthcare (U.S.)	16.6
Penn National Gaming (U.S.)	Harrah's Entertainment (U.S.)	16.5
Vodafone (U.K.)	Hutchison Essar (India)	16.5
Anadarko Petroleum (U.S.)	Kerr-McGee (U.S.)	16.1
Bank of New York (U.S.)	Mellon Financial (U.S.)	15.7
Imperial Tobacco (U.K.)	Altadis (Spain)	15.4
Capital One Financial (U.S.)	North Fork Bancorp (U.S.)	15.1
JTI Management (U.K.)	Gallaher Group (U.K.)	14.7
Investor Group (U.S.)	Kinder Morgan (U.S.)	14.6
Schering-Plough (U.S)	Organon Biosci (Netherlands)	14.4
BB Mobile (Japan)	Vodafone KK (Japan)	14.3
Linde (Germany)	BOC Group (U.K.)	14.1

Source: Adapted from Dennis Berman, "Can M&A's 'Best of Times' Get Better?" *Wall Street Journal* (January 2, 2007): R5; and Dennis Berman, "Mergers Hit Record, with Few Stop Signs," *Wall Street Journal* (April 2, 2007): C11.

The volume of mergers completed annually worldwide is growing dramatically and exceeds $1 trillion. There are annually more than 10,000 mergers in the United States alone that total more than $700 billion. The proliferation of mergers is fueled by companies' drive for market share, efficiency, and pricing power, as well as by globalization, the need for greater economies of scale, reduced regulation and antitrust concerns, the Internet, and e-commerce.

A *leveraged buyout* (LBO) occurs when a corporation's shareholders are bought (hence *buyout*) by the company's management and other private investors using borrowed funds (hence *leverage*).[38] Besides trying to avoid a hostile takeover, other reasons for initiating an LBO are senior management decisions that particular divisions do not fit into an overall corporate strategy or must be sold to raise cash, or receipt of an attractive offering price. An LBO takes a corporation private.

First Mover Advantages

First mover advantages refer to the benefits a firm may achieve by entering a new market or developing a new product or service prior to rival firms.[39] Some advantages of being a first mover include securing access to rare resources, gaining new knowledge of key factors and issues, and carving out market share and a position that is easy to defend and costly for rival firms to overtake. First mover advantages are analogous to taking the high ground first, which puts one in an excellent strategic position to launch aggressive campaigns and to defend territory. Being the first mover can be especially wise when such actions (1) build a firm's image and reputation with buyers, (2) produce cost advantages over rivals in terms of new technologies, new components, new distribution channels, and so on, (3) create strongly loyal customers, and (4) make imitation or duplication by a rival hard or unlikely.[40] To sustain the competitive advantage gained by being the first mover, such a firm also needs to be a fast learner. There would, however, be risks associated with being the first mover, such as unexpected and unanticipated problems and costs that occur from being the first firm doing business in the new market. Therefore, being a slow mover (also called *fast follower* or *late mover*) can be effective when a firm can easily copy or imitate the lead firm's products or services. If technology is advancing rapidly, slow movers can often leapfrog a first mover's products with improved second-generation products. However, slow movers often are relegated to relying on the first mover being a slow mover and making strategic and tactical mistakes. This situation does not occur often, so first mover advantages clearly offset the first mover disadvantages most of the time.

Strategic-management research indicates that first mover advantages tend to be greatest when competitors are roughly the same size and possess similar resources. If competitors are not similar in size, then larger competitors can wait while others make initial investments and mistakes, and then respond with greater effectiveness and resources.

Verizon, along with five Asian partner firms, expects to complete in 2008 the first high-speed optical cable directly linking China and the United States. Existing cables between the two countries go through Japan, slowing down service. China has 449 million cell phone users, making it the largest cellular market in the world. Verizon says this "first mover" cable will be able to support up to 62 million phone calls simultaneously, and the firm expects to see a positive return on its investment in the first year.

Not being the first mover can sometimes result in failure. For example, eBay expanded into Japan in 1999 but was five months behind rival Yahoo, which launched its own auction site that year in partnership with Japan's Softbank Corp. eBay never caught up with Yahoo. It exited Japan in 2002 and has not returned. Similarly, eBay was second getting into China behind YaoBao of Alibaba.com Corp. eBay is now struggling in China, and Yahoo has obtained a 40 percent stake in Alibaba. Martin Wu, chief executive of eBay's Chinese division, recently resigned abruptly.

Outsourcing

Business-process outsourcing (BPO) is a rapidly growing new business that involves companies taking over the functional operations, such as human resources, information systems, payroll, accounting, customer service, and even marketing of other firms.

Companies are choosing to outsource their functional operations more and more for several reasons: (1) it is less expensive, (2) it allows the firm to focus on its core businesses, and (3) it enables the firm to provide better services. Other advantages of outsourcing are that the strategy (1) allows the firm to align itself with "best-in-world" suppliers who focus on performing the special task, (2) provides the firm flexibility should customer needs shift unexpectedly, and (3) allows the firm to concentrate on other internal value chain activities critical to sustaining competitive advantage. BPO is a means for achieving strategies that are similar to partnering and joint venturing. The worldwide BPO market exceeded $173 billion in 2007.

Many firms, such as Visteon Corp. and J. P. Morgan Chase & Co., outsource their computer operations to IBM, which competes with firms such as Electronic Data Systems and Computer Sciences Corp., in the computer outsourcing business. 3M Corp. is outsourcing all of its manufacturing operations to Flextronics International Ltd. of Singapore or Jabil Circuit in the United States. 3M is also outsourcing all design and manufacturing of low-end standardized volume products by building a new design center in Taiwan.

European and U.S. companies for more than a decade have been outsourcing their manufacturing, tech support, and back-office work, but most insisted on keeping research and development activities in-house. However, an ever-growing number of firms today are outsourcing their product design to Asian developers. China and India are becoming increasingly important suppliers of intellectual property. For companies that include Hewlett-Packard, PalmOne, Dell, Sony, Apple, Kodak, Motorola, Nokia, Ericsson, Lucent, Cisco, and Nortel, the design of personal computers and cameras is mostly outsourced to China and India.

Companies in 2007 paid about $68 billion in outsourcing operations to other firms, but the details of what work to outsource, to whom, where, and for how much can challenge even the biggest, most sophisticated companies.[41] And some outsourcing deals do not work out, such as the J.P. Morgan Chase deal with IBM and Dow Chemical's deal with Electronic Data Systems. Both outsourcing deals were abandoned after several years. Lehman Brothers Holdings and Dell Inc. both recently reversed decisions to move customer call centers to India after a customer rebellion. As indicated in the "Global Perspective," India has become a booming place for outsourcing. According to Michael Corbett, chairman of the International Association of Outsourcing Professionals, India commands 45 percent of all back-office outsourcing, 29 percent of all call centers, 48 percent of all information technology outsourcing, 29 percent of all procurement outsourcing, and 45 percent of all product development outsourcing.[42]

GLOBAL PERSPECTIVE
Joint Ventures Mandatory for All Foreign Firms in India

India's economy (gross domestic product/GDP) expanded 9.2 percent in fiscal year ending March 31, 2007, up from 9 percent a year earlier. This is the fastest annual expansion India has seen in 18 years, and ranks India slightly below China's world-leading annual economic growth rate of 10.7 percent. This rapid growth is transforming the lives of many of India's one billion people. India's manufacturing sector grew 11.3 percent this fiscal year, up from 9.1 percent a year earlier. India's rapid growth has greatly increased wages, stocks, land prices, and interest rates.

Amid fast growth has come a 6.6 percent inflation rate, which is hurting the poor, especially in urban areas, as prices of food and staples have skyrocketed. Millions of people in India live on the margins of subsistence, so even small price increases on food and staples are painful. The government of India is highly in debt, 80 percent of GDP, and is cutting expenses to curtail spending, so the gap between rich and poor is widening further. (The U.S. federal debt is about 65 percent of GDP) But India's middle class is growing, so foreign firms continue to invest. Nissan Motor is building a factory in

Chennai in conjunction with Mahindra & Mahindra Ltd., India's largest maker of jeeps and tractors. The factory will start operating in 2009. And General Motors is expected to launch its compact Chevrolet Spark in India in 2008.

Joint ventures remain mandatory for foreign companies doing business in India. Verizon Business India, a joint venture between Verizon and Videocon Group of Mumbai, is rapidly expanding its phone and Internet services in India to compete more fiercely with AT&T and other telecom companies. Almost 20 million new cell phone customers are added in India every quarter, about the same rate of increase as in China—compared with only about 2.8 million new cell phone customers added in the United States quarterly. India's Reliance Communications Ltd. is in a battle with Britain's Vodafone Group PLC for control of India's fourth-largest cellular service, Hutchison Essar. But Vodafone must find a local partner because Indian law restricts foreign firms to 74 percent ownership of any India-based firm.

Most joint ventures among firms in India and foreign firms fail. Of 25 major joint ventures between foreign and Indian companies between 1993 and 2003, only three survive today. The Indian government has eased the joint venture restriction in the investment-banking

industry, but not in other areas. Even Wal-Mart has an Indian partner, Bharti Enterprises Ltd. Heavy friction exists in virtually all joint ventures in India. John Band, president of Zoom Cortex in Mumbai, says, "Anyone that gets into a joint venture in India should assume it will fail and should be comfortable with the terms of what happens when it does fail."

Due to tourism growing 12 percent annually, hotel chains are scrambling to get established in India. Hilton Hotels just established a joint venture with New Delhi–based DLF Ltd. to develop 75 hotels in India in 2007–2010. Marriott, Four Seasons, and Carlson Companies are also establishing joint ventures in India and building hotels rapidly.

Source: Adapted from Eric Bellman and P. R. Venkat, "India's Growth Raises Fears Rates May Rise," *Wall Street Journal* (February 8, 2007): A6; Dionne Searcey, "Verizon Targets Business in India," *Wall Street Journal* (February 6, 2007): A7; Peter Wonacott, "India Faces Dark Side of Its Boom," *Wall Street Journal* (February 27, 2007): A10; Amy Chozick, "Nissan Enters Venture to Build Indian Plant," *Wall Street Journal* (February 27, 2007): A4; Cassell Bryan and Eric Bellman, "Vodafone, Reliance Gear Up for Battle in India," *Wall Street Journal* (December 22, 2006): B4; Peter Wonacott and Eric Bellman, "Foreign Firms Find Rough Passage to India," *Wall Street Journal* (February 1, 2007): A6; and Binny Sabharwal, "Hilton Expands in India as Market Demand Soars," *Wall Street Journal* (May 10, 2007): D6.

Downtown traffic in India. *Source:* Andy Crawford (c) Dorling Kindersley

Strategic Management in Nonprofit and Governmental Organizations

The strategic-management process is being used effectively by countless nonprofit and governmental organizations, such as the Red Cross, chambers of commerce, educational institutions, medical institutions, public utilities, libraries, government agencies, and churches. The nonprofit sector, surprisingly, is by far America's largest employer. Many nonprofit and governmental organizations outperform private firms and corporations on innovativeness, motivation, productivity, and strategic management. For many nonprofit examples of strategic planning in practice, click on Strategic Planning Links found at the www.strategyclub.com Web site.

Compared to for-profit firms, nonprofit and governmental organizations may be totally dependent on outside financing. Especially for these organizations, strategic management provides an excellent vehicle for developing and justifying requests for needed financial support.

Educational Institutions

Educational institutions are more frequently using strategic-management techniques and concepts. Richard Cyert, former president of Carnegie Mellon University said "I believe we do a far better job of strategic management than any company I know." Population shifts in the United States are but one factor causing trauma for educational institutions that have not planned for changing enrollments. Schools in the Northeast are recruiting more heavily in the Southeast and West. This trend represents a significant change in the competitive climate for attracting the best high school graduates each year.

Online college degrees are becoming common and represent a threat to traditional colleges and universities. "You can put the kids to bed and go to law school," says Andrew Rosen, chief operating officer of Kaplan Education Centers, a subsidiary of the Washington Post Company.

For a list of college strategic plans, click on Strategic Planning Links found at the www.strategyclub.com Web site, and scroll down through the academic sites.

Medical Organizations

The $200 billion U.S. hospital industry, for example, is experiencing declining margins, excess capacity, bureaucratic overburdening, poorly planned and executed diversification strategies, soaring health care costs, reduced federal support, and high administrator turnover. The seriousness of this problem is accented by a 20 percent annual decline in use by inpatients nationwide. Declining occupancy rates, deregulation, and accelerating growth of health maintenance organizations, preferred provider organizations, urgent care centers, outpatient surgery centers, diagnostic centers, specialized clinics, and group practices are other major threats facing hospitals today. Many private and state-supported medical institutions are in financial trouble as a result of traditionally taking a reactive rather than a proactive approach in dealing with their industry.

Hospitals—originally intended to be warehouses for people dying of tuberculosis, smallpox, cancer, pneumonia, and infectious diseases—are creating new strategies today as advances in the diagnosis and treatment of chronic diseases are undercutting that earlier mission. Hospitals are beginning to bring services to the patient as much as bringing the patient to the hospital; health care is more and more being concentrated in the home and in the residential community, not on the hospital campus. Chronic care will require day-treatment facilities, electronic monitoring at home, user-friendly ambulatory services, decentralized service networks, and laboratory testing. A successful hospital strategy for the future will require renewed and deepened collaboration with physicians, who are central to hospitals' well-being, and a reallocation of resources from acute to chronic care in home and community settings.

Current strategies being pursued by many hospitals include creating home health services, establishing nursing homes, and forming rehabilitation centers. Backward integration

Issues for Review and Discussion

1. How does strategy formulation differ for a small versus a large organization? How does it differ for a for-profit versus a nonprofit organization?
2. Give recent examples of market penetration, market development, and product development.
3. Give recent examples of forward integration, backward integration, and horizontal integration.
4. Give recent examples of related and unrelated diversification.
5. Give recent examples of joint venture, retrenchment, divestiture, and liquidation.
6. Do you think hostile takeovers are unethical? Why or why not?
7. What are the major advantages and disadvantages of diversification?
8. What are the major advantages and disadvantages of an integrative strategy?
9. How does strategic management differ in for-profit and nonprofit organizations?
10. Why is it not advisable to pursue too many strategies at once?
11. Consumers can purchase tennis shoes, food, cars, boats, and insurance on the Internet. Are there any products today than cannot be purchased online? What is the implication for traditional retailers?
12. What are the pros and cons of a firm merging with a rival firm?
13. Visit the CheckMATE strategic-planning software Web site at www.checkmateplan.com, and discuss the benefits offered.
14. Compare and contrast financial objectives with strategic objectives. Which type is more important in your opinion? Why?
15. Diagram a two-division organizational chart that includes a CEO, COO, CIO, CSO, CFO, CMO, HRM, R&D, and two division presidents. *Hint:* Division presidents report to the COO.
16. How do the levels of strategy differ in a large firm versus a small firm?
17. List 11 types of strategies. Give a hypothetical example of each strategy listed.
18. Discuss the nature of as well as the pros and cons of a "friendly merger" versus "hostile takeover" in acquiring another firm. Give an example of each.
19. Define and explain "first mover advantages."
20. Define and explain "outsourcing."
21. Discuss the business of offering a BBA or MBA degree online.
22. What strategies are best for turbulent, high-velocity markets?

Notes

1. John Byrne, "Strategic Planning—It's Back," *BusinessWeek* (August 26, 1996): 46.
2. Steven C. Brandt, *Strategic Planning in Emerging Companies* (Reading, MA: Addison-Wesley, 1981). Reprinted with permission of the publisher.
3. R. Kaplan and D. Norton, "Putting the Balanced Scorecard to Work," *Harvard Business Review* (September–October, 1993): 147.

4. F. Hansen and M. Smith, "Crisis in Corporate America: The Role of Strategy," *Business Horizons* (January–February 2003): 9.

5. Adapted from F. R. David, "How Do We Choose Among Alternative Growth Strategies?" *Managerial Planning* 33, no. 4 (January–February 1985): 14–17, 22.

6. Ibid.

7. Kenneth Davidson, "Do Megamergers Make Sense?" *Journal of Business Strategy* 7, no. 3 (Winter 1987): 45.

8. Op. cit., David.

9. Ibid.

10. Op. cit., David.

11. Ibid.

12. Arthur Thompson, Jr., A. J. Strickland III, and John Gamble. *Crafting and Executing Strategy: Text and Readings* (New York: McGraw-Hill/Irwin, 2005): 241.

13. Michael E. Porter, *Competitive Strategy: Techniques for Analyzing Industries and Competitors* (New York: Free Press, 1980): 53–57, 318–319.

14. "The Samsung Way," *BusinessWeek* (June 16, 2003): 56–60.

15. Sheila Muto, "Seeing a Boost, Hospitals Turn to Retail Stores," *Wall Street Journal* (November 7, 2001): B1, B8.

16. Damian Paletta, "Wal-Mart, in New Leases, Frees Itself for Banking Push," *Wall Street Journal* (March 15, 2007): A2.

17. Op. cit., David.

18. Op. cit., David.

19. Op. cit., David.

20. Ibid.

21. Ibid.

22. Michael Porter, *Competitive Advantage* (New York: Free Press, 1985): 97. Also, Arthur Thompson, Jr., A. J. Strickland III, and John Gamble, *Crafting and Executing Strategy: Text and Readings* (New York: McGraw-Hill/Irwin, 2005): 117.

23. Arthur Thompson, Jr., A. J. Strickland III, and John Gamble, *Crafting and Executing Strategy: Text and Readings* (New York: McGraw-Hill/Irwin, 2005): 125–126.

24. Porter, *Competitive Advantage,* pp. 160–162.

25. Thompson, Strickland, and Gamble: 129–130.

26. Ibid., 134.

27. Kathryn Rudie Harrigan, "Joint Ventures: Linking for a Leap Forward," *Planning Review* 14, no. 4 (July–August 1986): 10.

28. Matthew Schifrin, "Partner or Perish," *Forbes* (May 21, 2001): 26.

29. Ibid., p. 28.

30. Nikhil Hutheesing, "Marital Blisters," *Forbes* (May 21, 2001): 32.

31. Ibid., p. 32.

32. Steven Rattner, "Mergers: Windfalls or Pitfalls?" *Wall Street Journal* (October 11, 1999): A22; Nikhil Deogun, "Merger Wave Spurs More Stock Wipeouts," *Wall Street Journal* (November 29, 1999): C1.

33. Dennis Berman, "Mergers Hit Record, with Few Stop Signs," *Wall Street Journal* (April 2, 2007): C11.

34. Dennis Berman, "Can M&A's 'Best of Times' Get Better?" *Wall Street Journal* (January 2, 2007): R5.

35. Andrew Batson, "Merger Mania Strikes China," *Wall Street Journal* (January 12, 2007): C5.

36. Henny Sender, "New Predator in Takeovers," *Wall Street Journal* (February 26, 2007): C1.

37. J. A. Schmidt, "Business Perspective on Mergers and Acquisitions," in J. A. Schmidt, ed., *Making Mergers Work,* Alexandria, VA: Society for Human Resource Management, (2002): 23–46.

38. Joel Millman, "Mexican Mergers/Acquisitions Triple from 2001," *Wall Street Journal* (December 27, 2002): A2.

39. Robert Davis, "Net Empowering Patients," *USA Today* (July 14, 1999): 1A.

40. M. J. Gannon, K. G. Smith, and C. Grimm, "An Organizational Information-Processing Profile of First Movers," *Journal of Business Research* 25 (1992): 231–241; M. B. Lieberman and D. B. Montgomery, "First Mover Advantages," *Strategic Management Journal* 9 (Summer 1988): 41–58.

41. Scott Thurm, "Behind Outsourcing: Promise and Pitfalls," *Wall Street Journal* (February 26, 2007): B3.

42. www.fortune.com/sections.

43. Some articles are Keith D. Brouthers, Floris Andriessen, and Igor Nicolaes, "Driving Blind: Strategic Decision-Making in Small Companies," *Long Range Planning* 31 (1998): 130–138; Javad Kargar, "Strategic Planning System Characteristics and Planning Effectiveness in Small Mature Firms," *Mid-Atlantic Journal of Business* 32, no. 1 (1996): 19–35; Michael J. Peel and John Bridge, "How Planning and Capital Budgeting Improve SME Performance," *Long Range Planning* 31, no. 6 (1998): 848–856; Larry R. Smeltzer, Gail L. Fann, and V. Neal Nikolaisen, "Environmental Scanning Practices in Small Business," *Journal of Small Business Management* 26, no. 3 (1988): 55–63; and Michael P. Steiner and Olaf Solem, "Factors for Success in Small Manufacturing Firms," *Journal of Small Business Management* 26, no. 1 (1988): 51–57.

44. Anne Carey and Grant Jerding, "Internet's Reach on Campus," *USA Today* (August 26, 1999): A1; Bill Meyers, "It's a Small-Business World," *USA Today* (July 30, 1999): B1–2.

Current Readings

Barney, Jay B., Seung-Hyun Lee, and Mike W. Peng. "Bankruptcy Law and Entrepreneurship Development: A Real Options Perspective." *The Academy of Management Review* 32, no. 1 (January 2007): 257.

Brauer, Matthias. "What Have We Acquired and What Should We Acquire in Divestiture Research? A Review and Research Agenda." *Journal of Management* 32, no. 6 (December 2006): 751.

Bucerius, M., and C. Homburg. "Is Speed of Integration Really a Success Factor of Mergers and Acquisitions? An Analysis of the Role of Internal and External Relatedness." *Strategic Management Journal* 27, no. 4 (April 2006): 347.

Chakrabarti, A., I. Mahmood, and K. Singh. "Diversification and Performance: Evidence from East Asian Firms." *Strategic Management Journal* 28, no. 2 (February 2007): 101.

Connelly, Brian, Michael A. Hitt, and Laszlo Tihanyi. "International Diversification: Antecedents, Outcomes, and Moderators." *Journal of Management* 32, no. 6 (December 2006): 831.

Dacin, M. T., C. Oliver, and J. P. Roy. "The Legitimacy of Strategic Alliances: An Institutional Perspective." *Strategic Management Journal* 28, no. 2 (February 2007): 169.

Deutsch, Yuval, Thomas Keil, and Tomi Laamanen. "Decision Making in Acquisitions: The Effect of Outside Directors' Compensation on Acquisition Patterns." *Journal of Management* 33, no. 1 (February 2007): 30.

Frynas, J. G., K. Mellahi, and G. A. Pigman. "First Mover Advantages in International Business and Firm-Specific Political Resources." *Strategic Management Journal* 27, no. 4 (April 2006): 321.

Fuentelsaz, L., and J. Gómez. "Multipoint Competition, Strategic Similarity and Entry to Geographic Markets." *Strategic Management Journal* 27, no. 5 (May 2006): 477.

Hipkin, Ian, and Pete Naudé, "Developing Effective Alliance Partnerships." *Long Range Planning* 39, no. 1 (February 2006): 51.

Hitt, M. A., L. A. Jobe, and F. T. Rothaermel. "Balancing Vertical Integration and Strategic Outsourcing: Effects on Product Portfolio, Product Success, and Firm Performance." *Strategic Management Journal* 27, no. 11 (November 2006): 1033.

Hyland, MaryAnne, and Monica Yang. "Who Do Firms Imitate? A Multilevel Approach to Examining Sources of Imitation in the Choice of Mergers and Acquisitions." *Journal of Management* 32, no. 3 (June 2006): 381.

Iverson, Roderick D., and Christopher D. Zatzick. "High Involvement Management and Workforce Reduction: Competitive Advantage or Disadvantage?" *Academy of Management Journal* 49, no. 5 (October 2006): 999.

Krishnan, Rekha, Xavier Martin, and Niels G. Noorderhaven. "When Does Trust Matter to Alliance Performance?" *Academy of Management Journal* 49, no. 5 (October 2006): 894.

Lavie, Dovev, and Lori Rosenkopf. "Balancing Exploration and Exploitation in Alliance Formation." *Academy of Management Journal* 49, no. 4 (August 2006): 797.

Luo, Y. "Are Joint Venture Partners More Opportunistic in a More Volatile Environment?" *Strategic Management Journal* 28, no. 1 (January 2007): 39.

Meyer, Klaus E., and Yen Thi Thu Tran. "Market Penetration and Acquisition Strategies for Emerging Economics." *Long Range Planning* 39, no. 2 (April 2006): 177.

Michael, Steven C., and John A. Pearce II. "Strategies to Prevent Economic Recessions from Causing Business Failure." *Business Horizons* 49, no. 3 (May–June 2006): 201.

Miller, D. J. "Technological Diversity, Related Diversification, and Firm Performance." *Strategic Management Journal* 27, no. 7 (July 2006): 601.

Pehrsson, A. "Business Relatedness and Performance: A Study of Managerial Perceptions." *Strategic Management Journal* 27, no. 3 (March 2006): 265.

Suarez, Fernando F. and Gianvito Lanzolla. "The Role of Environmental Dynamics in Building a First Mover Advantage Theory." *The Academy of Management Review* 32, no. 2 (April 2007): 377.

Wirtz, Bernd W., Alexander Mathieu, and Oliver Schilke. "Strategy in High-Velocity Environments." *Long Range Planning* 40, no. 3 (June 2007): 295.

• EXPERIENTIAL EXERCISES

Experiential Exercise 5A

What Strategies Should Walt Disney Pursue in 2008–2009?

Purpose

In performing business policy case analysis, you can find information about the respective company's actual and planned strategies. Comparing what is planned versus *what you recommend* is an important part of case analysis. Do not recommend what the firm actually plans, unless in-depth analysis of the situation reveals those strategies to be best among all feasible alternatives. This exercise gives you experience conducting library and Internet research to determine what Walt Disney should do in 2008.

Instructions

Step 1   Look up Walt Disney and News Corporation using the Web sites provided in Table 4-4. Find some recent articles about firms in this industry. Scan Moody's, Dun & Bradstreet, and Standard & Poor's publications for information.

Step 2   Summarize your findings in a three-page report entitled "Strategies Being Pursued by Walt Disney in 2008."

Source: (c) Judith Miller / Dorling Kindersley / Three Sisters

Experiential Exercise 5B

Examining Strategy Articles

Purpose

Strategy articles can be found weekly in journals, magazines, and newspapers. By reading and studying strategy articles, you can gain a better understanding of the strategic-management process. Several of the best journals in which to find corporate strategy articles are *Advanced Management Journal, Business Horizons, Long Range Planning, Journal of Business Strategy*, and *Strategic Management Journal*. These journals are devoted to reporting the results of empirical research in management. They apply strategic-management concepts to specific organizations and industries. They introduce new strategic-management techniques and provide short case studies on selected firms.

Other good journals in which to find strategic-management articles are *Harvard Business Review, Sloan Management Review, California Management Review, Academy of Management Review, Academy of Management Journal, Academy of Management Executive, Journal of Management*, and *Journal of Small Business Management*.

In addition to journals, many magazines regularly publish articles that focus on business strategies. Several of the best magazines in which to find applied strategy articles are *Dun's Business Month, Fortune, Forbes, BusinessWeek, Inc.*, and *Industry Week*. Newspapers such as *USA Today, Wall Street Journal, New York Times,* and *Barrons* cover strategy events when they occur—for example, a joint venture announcement, a bankruptcy declaration, a new advertising campaign start, acquisition of a company, divestiture of a division, a chief executive officer's hiring or firing, or a hostile takeover attempt.

In combination, journal, magazine, and newspaper articles can make the strategic-management course more exciting. They allow current strategies of for-profit and non-profit organizations to be identified and studied.

Instructions

Step 1   Go to your college library and find a recent journal article that focuses on a strategic-management topic. Select your article from one of the journals listed previously, not from a magazine. Copy the article and bring it to class.

Step 2   Give a 3-minute oral report summarizing the most important information in your article. Include comments giving your personal reaction to the article. Pass your article around in class.

Experiential Exercise 5C

Classifying Some Year 2007 Strategies

Purpose

This exercise can improve your understanding of various strategies by giving you experience classifying strategies. This skill will help you use the strategy-formulation tools presented later. Consider the following 12 (actual or possible) year-2007 strategies by various firms:

1. Dunkin' Donuts is increasing the number of its U.S. stores from 5,500 to 15,000.
2. Brown-Forman Corp. sold its Hartmann luggage and leather-goods business.
3. Motorola, which makes TVs, acquired Terayon Communication, a supplier of TV equipment.
4. Macy's department stores is adding bistros and Starbucks coffee shops at many of its stores.
5. Dell just allowed Wal-Mart to begin selling its computers. This was its first move away from direct mail order selling of computers.
6. Motorola cut 7,500 additional jobs in 2007–2008.
7. Hilton Hotels is building 55 new properties in Russia, the United Kingdom, and Central America in 2007–2008.
8. Video-sharing Web site YouTube in mid-2007 launched its services into nine new countries.
9. Cadbury Schweppes PLC is slashing 7,500 jobs, shedding product variations, and closing factories globally to cut costs in 2007–2008.

10.   General Electric sold its plastics division for $11.6 million to Saudi Basic Industries Corp. of Saudi Arabia.
11.   Cadbury Schweppes PLC, the maker of Trident gum, just bought Turkish gum maker Intergum.
12.   Limited Brands is selling its Express and Limited divisions to focus on its Victoria's Secret and Bath & Body Works divisions.

Instructions

Step 1	On a separate sheet of paper, number from 1 to 12. These numbers correspond to the strategies described.
Step 2	What type of strategy best describes the 12 actions cited? Indicate your answers.
Step 3	Exchange papers with a classmate, and grade each other's paper as your instructor gives the right answers.

Experiential Exercise 5D

How Risky Are Various Alternative Strategies?

Purpose

This exercise focuses on how risky various alternative strategies are for organizations to pursue. Different degrees of risk are based largely on varying degrees of *externality,* defined as movement away from present business into new markets and products. In general, the greater the degree of externality, the greater the probability of loss resulting from unexpected events. High-risk strategies generally are less attractive than low-risk strategies.

Instructions

Step 1	On a separate sheet of paper, number vertically from 1 to 10. Think of 1 as "most risky," 2 as "next most risky," and so forth to 10, "least risky."
Step 2	Write the following strategies beside the appropriate number to indicate how risky you believe the strategy is to pursue: horizontal integration, related diversification, liquidation, forward integration, backward integration, product development, market development, market penetration, retrenchment, and unrelated diversification.
Step 3	Grade your paper as your teacher gives you the right answers and supporting rationale. Each correct answer is worth 10 points.

Experiential Exercise 5E

Developing Alternative Strategies for My University

Purpose

It is important for representatives from all areas of a college or university to identify and discuss alternative strategies that could benefit faculty, students, alumni, staff, and other constituencies. As you complete this exercise, notice the learning and understanding that occurs as people express differences of opinion. Recall that *the process of planning is more important than the document.*

Instructions

Step 1	Recall or locate the external opportunity/threat and internal strength/weakness factors that you identified as part of Experiential Exercise 1D. If you did not do that exercise, discuss now as a class important external and internal factors facing your college or university.
Step 2	Identify and put on the chalkboard alternative strategies that you feel could benefit your college or university. Your proposed actions should allow the institution to capitalize on particular strengths, improve upon certain weaknesses, avoid external threats, and/or take advantage of particular external opportunities. List 12 possible strategies on the board. Number the strategies as they are written on the board.

Step 3   On a separate sheet of paper, number from 1 to 12. Everyone in class individually should rate the strategies identified, using a 1 to 3 scale, where 1 = *I do not support implementation*, 2 = *I am neutral about implementation*, and 3 = *I strongly support implementation*. In rating the strategies, recognize that your institution cannot do everything desired or potentially beneficial.

Step 4   Go to the board and record your ratings in a row beside the respective strategies. Everyone in class should do this, going to the board perhaps by rows in the class.

Step 5   Sum the ratings for each strategy so that a prioritized list of recommended strategies is obtained. This prioritized list reflects the collective wisdom of your class. Strategies with the highest score are deemed best.

Step 6   Discuss how this process could enable organizations to achieve understanding and commitment from individuals.

Step 7   Share your class results with a university administrator, and ask for comments regarding the process and top strategies recommended.

Experiential Exercise 5F

Lessons in Doing Business Globally

Purpose

The purpose of this exercise is to discover some important lessons learned by local businesses that do business internationally.

Instructions

Contact several local business leaders by phone. Find at least three firms that engage in international or export operations. Visit the owner or manager of each business in person. Ask the businessperson to give you several important lessons that his or her firm has learned in globally doing business. Record the lessons on paper, and report your findings to the class.

6

Strategy Analysis and Choice

College Student Athlete. *Source:* David Cannon (c) Dorling Kindersley

chapter objectives

After studying this chapter, you should be able to do the following:

1. Describe a three-stage framework for choosing among alternative strategies.

2. Explain how to develop a SWOT Matrix, SPACE Matrix, BCG Matrix, IE Matrix, and QSPM.

3. Identify important behavioral, political, ethical, and social responsibility considerations in strategy analysis and choice.

4. Discuss the role of intuition in strategic analysis and choice.

5. Discuss the role of organizational culture in strategic analysis and choice.

6. Discuss the role of a board of directors in choosing among alternative strategies.

experiential exercises

Experiential Exercise 6A
Developing a SWOT Matrix for Walt Disney

Experiential Exercise 6B
Developing a SPACE Matrix for Walt Disney

Experiential Exercise 6C
Developing a BCG Matrix for Walt Disney

Experiential Exercise 6D
Developing a QSPM for Walt Disney

Experiential Exercise 6E
Formulating Individual Strategies

Experiential Exercise 6F
The Mach Test

Experiential Exercise 6G
Developing a BCG Matrix for My University

Experiential Exercise 6H
The Role of Boards of Directors

Experiential Exercise 6I
Locating Companies in a Grand Strategy Matrix

Strategy analysis and choice largely involve making subjective decisions based on objective information. This chapter introduces important concepts that can help strategists generate feasible alternatives, evaluate those alternatives, and choose a specific course of action. Behavioral aspects of strategy formulation are described, including politics, culture, ethics, and social responsibility considerations. Modern tools for formulating strategies are described, and the appropriate role of a board of directors is discussed.

The Nature of Strategy Analysis and Choice

As indicated by Figure 6-1, this chapter focuses on generating and evaluating alternative strategies, as well as selecting strategies to pursue. Strategy analysis and choice seek to determine alternative courses of action that could best enable the firm to achieve its mission and objectives. The firm's present strategies, objectives, and mission, coupled with the external and internal audit information, provide a basis for generating and evaluating feasible alternative strategies.

Unless a desperate situation confronts the firm, alternative strategies will likely represent incremental steps that move the firm from its present position to a desired future position. Alternative strategies do not come out of the wild blue yonder; they are derived from the firm's vision, mission, objectives, external audit, and internal audit; they are consistent with, or build on, past strategies that have worked well. Note from the "Natural Environment Perspective" box that the strategies of both companies and countries are increasingly scrutinized and evaluated from a natural environment perspective. Companies such as Wal-Mart now monitor not only the price its vendors offer for products, but also how those products are made in terms of environmental practices. A growing number of business schools offer separate courses and even a concentration in environmental management or *sustainability,* the idea that a business can meet its financial goals without hurting the environment.

FIGURE 6-1

A Comprehensive Strategic-Management Model

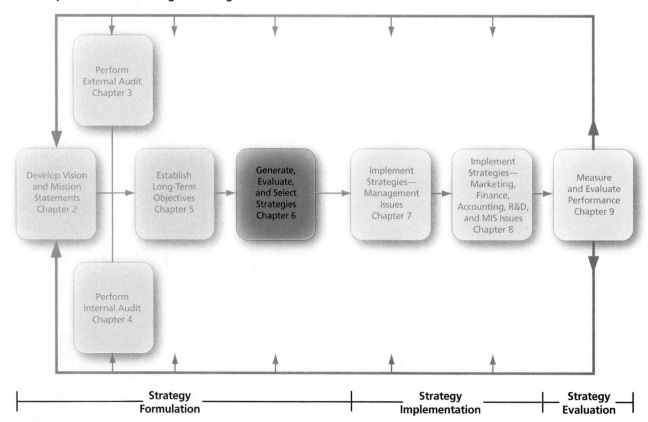

Source: Fred R. David, "How Companies Define Their Mission," *Long Range Planning* 22, no. 3 (June 1988): 40.

NATURAL ENVIRONMENT PERSPECTIVE
What Is a Sustainability Report?

No business wants a reputation as being a big polluter; that could hurt it in the marketplace, jeopardize its standing in the community, and invite scrutiny by regulators, investors, and environmentalists. Accordingly, governments increasingly encourage businesses to behave responsibly. Various governments mandate that businesses publicly report the pollutants and wastes their facilities produce.

Wal-Mart Stores is one among many companies today that annually provide a report on the firm's social-responsibility practices. Called "sustainability" or "corporate social-responsibility" reports, these documents disclose to shareholders information about the firm's labor practices, product sourcing, energy efficiency, environmental impact, and business ethics practices. It is just good business today for a business to provide a Sustainability Report annually to the public. With 60,000 suppliers and $350 billion in annual sales, Wal-Mart "works with its suppliers to take nonrenewable energy off our shelves and out of the lives of our customers," says Wal-Mart CEO Lee Scott. Many firms use the Wal-Mart Sustainability Report as a benchmark, guideline, and model to follow in preparing their own report.

The Global Reporting Initiative has issued a set of detailed reporting guidelines specifying what information should go into sustainability reports. Wal-Mart now monitors not only prices its vendors offer for products, but also how those products are made and the vendor's social-responsibility and environmental practices. The proxy advisory firm Institutional Shareholder Services reports that an

increasing number of shareholder groups are pushing firms to provide sustainability information annually. Wal-Mart also now encourages and expects its 1.35 million U.S. employees to adopt what it calls Personal Sustainability Projects, which include such measures as organizing weight-loss or smoking-cessation support groups, biking to work, or starting recycling programs.

Wal-Mart is installing solar panels in its stores in California and Hawaii, providing as much as 30 percent of the power in some stores. Wal-Mart may go national with solar power if this test works well. Also moving to solar energy is department-store chain Kohl's Corp., which is converting 64 of its 80 California stores to using solar power. There are big subsidies for solar installations in some states.

The world's second largest retailer behind Wal-Mart, Home Depot, recently more than doubled its offering of environmentally friendly products such as all-natural insect repellent. Home Depot has made it much easier for consumers to find its organic products by using special labels similar to Timberland's (the outdoor company) Green Index tags. Another huge retailer, Target, now offers more than 500 choices of organic certified food and has 18 buildings in the U.S. state of California alone powered only by solar energy.

Source: Antonie Boessenkool, "Activists Push More Firms on Social Responsibility," *Wall Street Journal* (January 31, 207): B13; Kris Hudson, "Wal-Mart Wants Supplies, Workers to Join Green Effort," *Wall Street Journal* (February 2, 2007): A14; and Jayne O'Donnell and Christine Dugas, "More Retailers Go for Green—The Eco Kind," *USA Today* (April 18, 2007): 3B.

Some Organic Certified Food. *Source:* Ian O'Leary (c) Dorling Kindersley

The Process of Generating and Selecting Strategies

VISIT THE NET

Cautions that planners must not usurp the responsibility of line managers in strategic planning. (www.csuchico.edu/mgmt/ strategy/module1/sld050.htm)

Strategists never consider all feasible alternatives that could benefit the firm because there are an infinite number of possible actions and an infinite number of ways to implement those actions. Therefore, a manageable set of the most attractive alternative strategies must be developed. The advantages, disadvantages, trade-offs, costs, and benefits of these strategies should be determined. This section discusses the process that many firms use to determine an appropriate set of alternative strategies.

Identifying and evaluating alternative strategies should involve many of the managers and employees who earlier assembled the organizational vision and mission statements, performed the external audit, and conducted the internal audit. Representatives from each department and division of the firm should be included in this process, as was the case in previous strategy-formulation activities. Recall that involvement provides the best opportunity for managers and employees to gain an understanding of what the firm is doing and why and to become committed to helping the firm accomplish its objectives.

All participants in the strategy analysis and choice activity should have the firm's external and internal audit information by their sides. This information, coupled with the firm's mission statement, will help participants crystallize in their own minds particular strategies that they believe could benefit the firm most. Creativity should be encouraged in this thought process.

Alternative strategies proposed by participants should be considered and discussed in a meeting or series of meetings. Proposed strategies should be listed in writing. When all feasible strategies identified by participants are given and understood, the strategies should be ranked in order of attractiveness by all participants, with 1 = should not be implemented, 2 = possibly should be implemented, 3 = probably should be implemented, and 4 = definitely should be implemented. This process will result in a prioritized list of best strategies that reflects the collective wisdom of the group.

A Comprehensive Strategy-Formulation Framework

Important strategy-formulation techniques can be integrated into a three-stage decision-making framework, as shown in Figure 6-2. The tools presented in this framework are applicable to all sizes and types of organizations and can help strategists identify, evaluate, and select strategies.

Stage 1 of the formulation framework consists of the EFE Matrix, the IFE Matrix, and the Competitive Profile Matrix (CPM). Called the *Input Stage*, Stage 1 summarizes the basic input information needed to formulate strategies. Stage 2, called the *Matching Stage*, focuses upon generating feasible alternative strategies by aligning key external and internal

FIGURE 6-2

The Strategy-Formulation Analytical Framework

STAGE 1: THE INPUT STAGE		
External Factor Evaluation (EFE) Matrix	Competitive Profile Matrix (CPM)	Internal Factor Evaluation (IFE) Matrix

STAGE 2: THE MATCHING STAGE				
Strengths-Weaknesses-Opportunities-Threats (SWOT) Matrix	Strategic Position and Action Evaluation (SPACE) Matrix	Boston Consulting Group (BCG) Matrix	Internal-External (IE) Matrix	Grand Strategy Matrix

STAGE 3: THE DECISION STAGE
Quantitative Strategic Planning Matrix (QSPM)

factors. Stage 2 techniques include the Strengths-Weaknesses-Opportunities-Threats (SWOT) Matrix, the Strategic Position and Action Evaluation (SPACE) Matrix, the Boston Consulting Group (BCG) Matrix, the Internal-External (IE) Matrix, and the Grand Strategy Matrix. Stage 3, called the *Decision Stage*, involves a single technique, the Quantitative Strategic Planning Matrix (QSPM). A QSPM uses input information from Stage 1 to objectively evaluate feasible alternative strategies identified in Stage 2. A QSPM reveals the relative attractiveness of alternative strategies and thus provides objective basis for selecting specific strategies.

All nine techniques included in the *strategy-formulation framework* require the integration of intuition and analysis. Autonomous divisions in an organization commonly use strategy-formulation techniques to develop strategies and objectives. Divisional analyses provide a basis for identifying, evaluating, and selecting among alternative corporate-level strategies.

Strategists themselves, not analytic tools, are always responsible and accountable for strategic decisions. Lenz emphasized that the shift from a words-oriented to a numbers-oriented planning process can give rise to a false sense of certainty; it can reduce dialogue, discussion, and argument as a means for exploring understandings, testing assumptions, and fostering organizational learning.[1] Strategists, therefore, must be wary of this possibility and use analytical tools to facilitate, rather than to diminish, communication. Without objective information and analysis, personal biases, politics, emotions, personalities, and *halo error* (the tendency to put too much weight on a single factor) unfortunately may play a dominant role in the strategy-formulation process.

The Input Stage

Procedures for developing an EFE Matrix, an IFE Matrix, and a CPM were presented in Chapters 3 and 4. The information derived from these three matrices provides basic input information for the matching and decision stage matrices described later in this chapter.

The input tools require strategists to quantify subjectivity during early stages of the strategy-formulation process. Making small decisions in the input matrices regarding the relative importance of external and internal factors allows strategists to more effectively generate and evaluate alternative strategies. Good intuitive judgment is always needed in determining appropriate weights and ratings.

The Matching Stage

Strategy is sometimes defined as the match an organization makes between its internal resources and skills and the opportunities and risks created by its external factors.[2] The matching stage of the strategy-formulation framework consists of five techniques that can be used in any sequence: the SWOT Matrix, the SPACE Matrix, the BCG Matrix, the IE Matrix, and the Grand Strategy Matrix. These tools rely upon information derived from the input stage to match external opportunities and threats with internal strengths and weaknesses. *Matching* external and internal critical success factors is the key to effectively generating feasible alternative strategies. For example, a firm with excess working capital (an internal strength) could take advantage of the cell phone industry's 20 percent annual growth rate (an external opportunity) by acquiring Cellfone, Inc., a firm in the cell phone industry. This example portrays simple one-to-one matching. In most situations, external and internal relationships are more complex, and the matching requires multiple alignments for each strategy generated. The basic concept of matching is illustrated in Table 6-1.

Any organization, whether military, product-oriented, service-oriented, governmental, or even athletic, must develop and execute good strategies to win. A good offense without a good defense, or vice versa, usually leads to defeat. Developing strategies that use strengths to capitalize on opportunities could be considered an offense, whereas strategies designed to improve upon weaknesses while avoiding threats could be termed defensive. Every organization has some external opportunities and threats and internal strengths and weaknesses that can be aligned to formulate feasible alternative strategies.

VISIT THE NET

Gives purpose and characteristics of objectives. (www.csuchico.edu/ mgmt/strategy/module1/sld022. htm)

VISIT THE NET

Gives example objectives. (www.csuchico.edu/mgmt/ strategy/module1/sld024.htm)

TABLE 6-1 Matching Key External and Internal Factors to Formulate Alternative Strategies

Key Internal Factor		Key External Factor		Resultant Strategy
Excess working capacity (an internal strength)	+	20 percent annual growth in the cell phone industry (an external opportunity)	=	Acquire Cellfone, Inc.
Insufficient capacity (an internal weakness)	+	Exit of two major foreign competitors from the industry (an external opportunity)	=	Pursue horizontal integration by buying competitors' facilities
Strong R&D expertise (an internal strength)	+	Decreasing numbers of younger adults (an external threat)	=	Develop new products for older adults
Poor employee morale (an internal weakness)	+	Strong union activity (an external threat)	=	Develop a new employee benefits package

VISIT THE NET

Gives a nice sample strategic plan, including the bases for developing a SWOT Matrix. (www.planware. org/strategicsample.htm) and (http://sbinformation.about.com/cs/bestpractices/a/swot.htm)

The Strengths-Weaknesses-Opportunities-Threats (SWOT) Matrix

The *Strengths-Weaknesses-Opportunities-Threats (SWOT) Matrix* is an important matching tool that helps managers develop four types of strategies: SO (strengths-opportunities) Strategies, WO (weaknesses-opportunities) Strategies, ST (strengths-threats) Strategies, and WT (weaknesses-threats) Strategies.[3] Matching key external and internal factors is the most difficult part of developing a SWOT Matrix and requires good judgment—and there is no one best set of matches. Note in Table 6-1 that the first, second, third, and fourth strategies are SO, WO, ST, and WT strategies, respectively.

SO Strategies use a firm's internal strengths to take advantage of external opportunities. All managers would like their organizations to be in a position in which internal strengths can be used to take advantage of external trends and events. Organizations generally will pursue WO, ST, or WT strategies to get into a situation in which they can apply SO Strategies. When a firm has major weaknesses, it will strive to overcome them and make them strengths. When an organization faces major threats, it will seek to avoid them to concentrate on opportunities.

WO Strategies aim at improving internal weaknesses by taking advantage of external opportunities. Sometimes key external opportunities exist, but a firm has internal weaknesses that prevent it from exploiting those opportunities. For example, there may be a high demand for electronic devices to control the amount and timing of fuel injection in automobile engines (opportunity), but a certain auto parts manufacturer may lack the technology required for producing these devices (weakness). One possible WO Strategy would be to acquire this technology by forming a joint venture with a firm having competency in this area. An alternative WO Strategy would be to hire and train people with the required technical capabilities.

ST Strategies use a firm's strengths to avoid or reduce the impact of external threats. This does not mean that a strong organization should always meet threats in the external environment head-on. An example of ST Strategy occurred when Texas Instruments used an excellent legal department (a strength) to collect nearly $700 million in damages and royalties from nine Japanese and Korean firms that infringed on patents for semiconductor memory chips (threat). Rival firms that copy ideas, innovations, and patented products are a major threat in many industries. This is still a major problem for firms selling products in China.

WT Strategies are defensive tactics directed at reducing internal weakness and avoiding external threats. An organization faced with numerous external threats and internal weaknesses may indeed be in a precarious position. In fact, such a firm may have to fight for its survival, merge, retrench, declare bankruptcy, or choose liquidation.

A schematic representation of the SWOT Matrix is provided in Figure 6-3. Note that a SWOT Matrix is composed of nine cells. As shown, there are four key factor cells, four strategy cells, and one cell that is always left blank (the upper-left cell). The four strategy cells, labeled *SO, WO, ST*, and *WT*, are developed after completing four key factor cells, labeled *S, W, O*, and *T*. There are eight steps involved in constructing a SWOT Matrix:

1. List the firm's key external opportunities.
2. List the firm's key external threats.
3. List the firm's key internal strengths.
4. List the firm's key internal weaknesses.

FIGURE 6-3

A SWOT Matrix for a Retail Computer Store

	Strengths	Weaknesses
	1. Inventory turnover up 5.8 to 6.7	1. Software revenues in store down 12%
	2. Average customer purchase up $97 to $128	2. Location of store hurt by new Hwy 34
	3. Employee morale is excellent	3. Carpet and paint in store in disrepair
	4. In-store promotions = 20% increase in sales	4. Bathroom in store needs refurbishing
	5. Newspaper advertising expenditures down 10%	5. Total store revenues down 8%
	6. Revenues from repair/service in-store up 16%	6. Store has no Web site
	7. In-store technical support persons have MIS degrees	7. Supplier on-time-delivery up to 2.4 days
	8. Store's debt-to-total assets ratio down 34%	8. Customer checkout process too slow
		9. Revenues per employee up 19%
Opportunities	**SO Strategies**	**WO Strategies**
1. Population of city growing 10%	1. Add 4 new in-store promotions monthly (S4,O3)	1. Purchase land to build new store (W2, O2)
2. Rival computer store opening 1 kilometer away		
3. Vehicle traffic passing store up 12%	2. Add 2 new repair/service persons (S6, O5)	2. Install new carpet/paint/bath (W3, W4, O1)
4. Vendors average six new products/yr	3. Send flyer to all seniors over age 55 (S5, O5)	3. Up Web site services by 50% (W6, O7, O8)
5. Senior citizen use of computers up 8%		
6. Small business growth in area up 10%		4. Launch mailout to to all Realtors in city (W5, O7)
7. Desire for Web sites up 18% by Realtors		
8. Desire for Web sites up 12% by small firms		
Threats	**ST Strategies**	**WT Strategies**
1. Best Buy opening new store in 1yr nearby	1. Hire two more repair persons and market these new services (S6, S7, T1)	1. Hire 2 new cashiers (W8, T1, T4)
2. Local university offers computer repair		2. Install new carpet/paint/bath (W3, W4, T1)
3. New bypass Hwy 34 in 1 yr will divert traffic	2. Purchase land to build new store (S8, T3)	
4. New mall being built nearby		
5. Gas prices up 14%	3. Raise out-of-store service calls from $60 to $80 (S6, T5)	
6. Vendors raising prices 8%		

5. Match internal strengths with external opportunities, and record the resultant SO Strategies in the appropriate cell.
6. Match internal weaknesses with external opportunities, and record the resultant WO Strategies.
7. Match internal strengths with external threats, and record the resultant ST Strategies.
8. Match internal weaknesses with external threats, and record the resultant WT Strategies.

There are some important aspects of a SWOT Matrix evidenced in Figure 6-3. For example, note that both the internal/external factors and the SO/ST/WO/WT Strategies are stated in quantitative terms to the extent possible. This is important. For example, regarding the second SO #2 and ST #1 strategies, if the analyst just said "Add new repair/service persons" the reader might think that 20 new repair/service persons are needed. Actually only two are needed. Always *be specific* to the extent possible in stating factors and strategies.

It is also important to include the "S1, O2" type notation after each strategy in a SWOT Matrix. This notation reveals the rationale for each alternative strategy. Strategies do not rise out of the blue. Note in Figure 6-3 how this notation reveals the internal/external factors that were matched to formulate desirable strategies. For example, note that this retail computer store business may need to "purchase land to build new store" because a new Highway 34 will make its location less desirable. The notation (W2, O2) and (S8, T3) in Figure 6-3 exemplifies this matching process.

The purpose of each Stage 2 matching tool is to generate feasible alternative strategies, not to select or determine which strategies are best. Not all of the strategies developed in the SWOT Matrix, therefore, will be selected for implementation.

The strategy-formulation guidelines provided in Chapter 5 can enhance the process of matching key external and internal factors. For example, when an organization has both the capital and human resources needed to distribute its own products (internal strength) and distributors are unreliable, costly, or incapable of meeting the firm's needs (external threat), forward integration can be an attractive ST Strategy. When a firm has excess production capacity (internal weakness) and its basic industry is experiencing declining annual sales and profits (external threat), related diversification can be an effective WT Strategy.

Although the SWOT matrix is widely used in strategic planning, the analysis does have some limitations.[4] First, SWOT does not show how to achieve a competitive advantage, so it must not be an end in itself. The matrix should be the starting point for a discussion on how proposed strategies could be implemented as well as cost-benefit considerations that ultimately could lead to competitive advantage. Second, SWOT is a static assessment (or snapshot) in time. A SWOT matrix can be like studying a single frame of a motion picture where you see the lead characters and the setting but have no clue as to the plot. As circumstances, capabilities, threats, and strategies change, the dynamics of a competitive environment may not be revealed in a single matrix. Third, SWOT analysis may lead the firm to overemphasize a single internal or external factor in formulating strategies. There are interrelationships among the key internal and external factors that SWOT does not reveal that may be important in devising strategies.

VISIT THE NET

Gives excellent information about the need for planning. (http://www.mindtools.com/)

The Strategic Position and Action Evaluation (SPACE) Matrix

The *Strategic Position and Action Evaluation (SPACE) Matrix*, another important Stage 2 matching tool, is illustrated in Figure 6-4. Its four-quadrant framework indicates whether aggressive, conservative, defensive, or competitive strategies are most appropriate for a given organization. The axes of the SPACE Matrix represent two internal dimensions (*financial strength [FS]* and *competitive advantage [CA]*) and two external dimensions (*environmental stability [ES]* and *industry strength [IS]*). These four factors are perhaps the most important determinants of an organization's overall strategic position.[5]

Depending upon the type of organization, numerous variables could make up each of the dimensions represented on the axes of the SPACE Matrix. Factors that were included earlier in the firm's EFE and IFE Matrices should be considered in developing a SPACE Matrix. Other variables commonly included are given in Table 6-2. For example, return on investment, leverage, liquidity, working capital, and cash flow are commonly considered to be determining factors of an organization's financial strength. Like the SWOT Matrix, the SPACE Matrix should be both tailored to the particular organization being studied and based on factual information as much as possible.

The steps required to develop a SPACE Matrix are as follows:

1. Select a set of variables to define financial strength (FS), competitive advantage (CA), environmental stability (ES), and industry strength (IS).
2. Assign a numerical value ranging from +1 (worst) to +6 (best) to each of the variables that make up the FS and IS dimensions. Assign a numerical value ranging from –1 (best) to –6 (worst) to each of the variables that make up the ES and CA

FIGURE 6-4

The SPACE Matrix

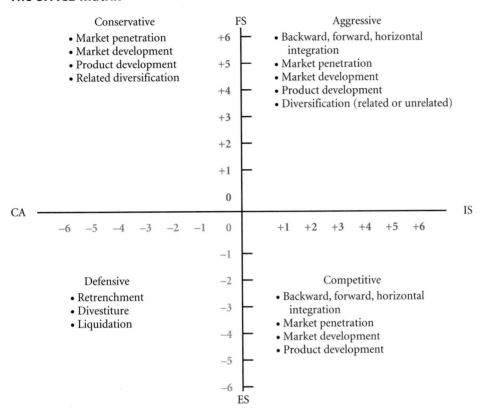

Source: H. Rowe, R. Mason, and K. Dickel, *Strategic Management and Business Policy: A Methodological Approach* (Reading, MA: Addison-Wesley Publishing Co. Inc., © 1982): 155. Reprinted with permission of the publisher.

TABLE 6-2   Example Factors That Make Up the SPACE Matrix Axes

Internal Strategic Position	External Strategic Position
Financial Strength (FS)	*Environmental Stability (ES)*
Return on investment	Technological changes
Leverage	Rate of inflation
Liquidity	Demand variability
Working capital	Price range of competing products
Cash flow	Barriers to entry into market
Inventory turnover	Competitive pressure
Earnings per share	Ease of exit from market
Price earnings ratio	Price elasticity of demand
	Risk involved in business
Competitive Advantage (CA)	*Industry Strength (IS)*
Market share	Growth potential
Product quality	Profit potential
Product life cycle	Financial stability
Customer loyalty	Technological know-how
Competition's capacity utilization	Resource utilization
Technological know-how	Ease of entry into market
Control over suppliers and distributors	Productivity, capacity utilization

Source: H. Rowe, R. Mason, and K. Dickel, *Strategic Management and Business Policy: A Methodological Approach* (Reading, MA: Addison-Wesley Publishing Co. Inc., © 1982): 155–156. Reprinted with permission of the publisher.

FIGURE 6-5

Example Strategy Profiles

Aggressive Profiles

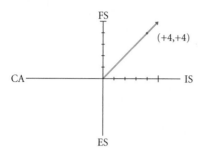

A financially strong firm that has achieved major competitive advantages in a growing and stable industry

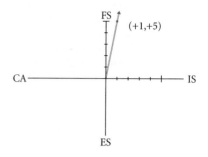

A firm whose financial strength is a dominating factor in the industry

Conservative Profiles

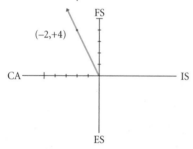

A firm that has achieved financial strength in a stable industry that is not growing; the firm has few competitive advantages

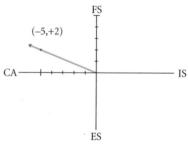

A firm that suffers from major competitive disadvantages in an industry that is technologically stable but declining in sales

Competitive Profiles

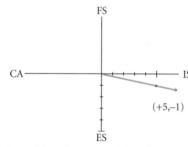

A firm with major competitive advantages in a high-growth industry

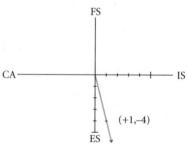

An organization that is competing fairly well in an unstable industry

Defensive Profiles

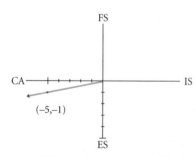

A firm that has a very weak competitive position in a negative growth, stable industry

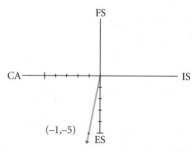

A financially troubled firm in a very unstable industry

Source: H. Rowe, R. Mason, and K. Dickel, *Strategic Management and Business Policy: A Methodological Approach* (Reading, MA: Addison-Wesley Publishing Co. Inc., © 1982): 155. Reprinted with permission of the publisher.

dimensions. On the FS and CA axes, make comparison to competitors. On the IS and ES axes, make comparison to other industries.

3. Compute an average score for FS, CA, IS, and ES by summing the values given to the variables of each dimension and then by dividing by the number of variables included in the respective dimension.

4. Plot the average scores for FS, IS, ES, and CA on the appropriate axis in the SPACE Matrix.

5. Add the two scores on the x-axis and plot the resultant point on X. Add the two scores on the y-axis and plot the resultant point on Y. Plot the intersection of the new xy point.

6. Draw a *directional vector* from the origin of the SPACE Matrix through the new intersection point. This vector reveals the type of strategies recommended for the organization: aggressive, competitive, defensive, or conservative.

Some examples of strategy profiles that can emerge from a SPACE analysis are shown in Figure 6-5. The directional vector associated with each profile suggests the type of strategies to pursue: aggressive, conservative, defensive, or competitive. When a firm's directional vector is located in the *aggressive quadrant* (upper-right quadrant) of the SPACE Matrix, an organization is in an excellent position to use its internal strengths to (1) take advantage of external opportunities, (2) overcome internal weaknesses, and (3) avoid external threats. Therefore, market penetration, market development, product development, backward integration, forward integration, horizontal integration, diversification, or a combination strategy all can be feasible, depending on the specific circumstances that face the firm.

The directional vector may appear in the *conservative quadrant* (upper-left quadrant) of the SPACE Matrix, which implies staying close to the firm's basic competencies and not taking excessive risks. Conservative strategies most often include market penetration, market development, product development, and related diversification. The directional vector may be located in the lower-left or *defensive quadrant* of the SPACE Matrix, which suggests that the firm should focus on rectifying internal weaknesses and avoiding external threats. Defensive strategies include retrenchment, divestiture, liquidation, and related diversification. Finally, the directional vector may be located in the lower-right or *competitive quadrant* of the SPACE Matrix, indicating competitive strategies. Competitive strategies include backward, forward, and horizontal integration; market penetration; market development and product development.

A SPACE Matrix analysis for a hypothetical bank is provided in Table 6-3. Note that competitive type strategies are recommended.

The Boston Consulting Group (BCG) Matrix

Autonomous divisions (or profit centers) of an organization make up what is called a *business portfolio*. When a firm's divisions compete in different industries, a separate strategy often must be developed for each business. The *Boston Consulting Group (BCG) Matrix* and the *Internal-External (IE) Matrix* are designed specifically to enhance a multidivisional firm's efforts to formulate strategies. (BCG is a private management consulting firm based in Boston. BCG employs about 1,400 consultants worldwide.)

The BCG Matrix graphically portrays differences among divisions in terms of relative market share position and industry growth rate. The BCG Matrix allows a multidivisional organization to manage its portfolio of businesses by examining the relative market share position and the industry growth rate of each division relative to all other divisions in the organization. *Relative market share position* is defined as the ratio of a division's own market share (or revenues) in a particular industry to the market share (or revenues) held by the largest rival firm in that industry. Note in Table 6-4 that Budget Rent-a-Car's relative market share position in the U.S. market is 6.9 divided by 49.6 = 19.1 percent, which along the x-axis of a BCG Matrix would be pretty close to the right-hand side. Be mindful that relative market share position could also be determined by dividing Budget's revenues by the leader Enterprise's revenues.

TABLE 6-3 A SPACE Matrix for a Bank

Financial Strength	Ratings
The bank's primary capital ratio is 7.23 percent, which is 1.23 percentage points over the generally required ratio of 6 percent.	1.0
The bank's return on assets is negative 0.77, compared to a bank industry average ratio of positive 0.70.	1.0
The bank's net income was $183 million, down 9 percent from a year earlier.	3.0
The bank's revenues increased 7 percent to $3.46 billion.	<u>4.0</u>
	9.0

Industry Strength	
Deregulation provides geographic and product freedom.	4.0
Deregulation increases competition in the banking industry.	2.0
A new law allows the bank to acquire other banks in other provinces.	<u>4.0</u>
	10.0

Environmental Stability	
Less-developed countries are experiencing high inflation and political instability.	−4.0
Headquartered in Qingdao, the bank historically has been heavily dependent on the steel, oil, and gas industries.	−5.0
Banking deregulation has created instability throughout the industry.	<u>−4.0</u>
	−13.0

Competitive Advantage	
The bank provides data processing services for more than 450 institutions in 15 provinces.	−2.0
Superregional banks, international banks, and nonbanks are becoming increasingly competitive.	−5.0
The bank has a large customer base.	<u>−2.0</u>
	−9.0

Conclusion

ES Average is −13.0 ÷ 3 = −4.33   IS Average is + 10.0 ÷ 3 = 3.33

CA Average is −9.0 ÷ 3 = −3.00   FS Average is + 9.0 ÷ 4 = 2.25

Directional Vector Coordinates: x-axis: −3.00 + (+3.33) = +0.33

$\qquad\qquad\qquad\qquad\quad$ y-axis: −4.33 + (+2.25) = -2.08

The bank should pursue Competitive Strategies.

Relative market share position is given on the x-axis of the BCG Matrix. The midpoint on the x-axis usually is set at .50, corresponding to a division that has half the market share of the leading firm in the industry. The y-axis represents the industry growth rate in sales, measured in percentage terms. The growth rate percentages on the y-axis could range from −20 to +20 percent, with 0.0 being the midpoint. The average annual increase in revenues for several leading firms in the industry would be a good estimate of the value. Also, various sources such as the S&P Industry Survey would provide this value. These numerical ranges on the x- and y-axes are often used, but other numerical values could be established as deemed appropriate for particular organizations.

An example of a BCG Matrix appears in Figure 6-6. Each circle represents a separate division. The size of the circle corresponds to the proportion of corporate **revenue** generated by that business unit, and the pie slice indicates the proportion of corporate **profits** generated by that division. Divisions located in Quadrant I of the BCG Matrix are called "Question Marks," those located in Quadrant II are called "Stars," those located in Quadrant III are called "Cash Cows," and those divisions located in Quadrant IV are called "Dogs."

TABLE 6-4   Market Share Data for Selected Industries in 2007

U.S. Car Market Share (2007)

General Motors	24.6%
Nissan	6.2%
DaimlerChrysler	14.4%
Ford	17.5%
Honda	9.2%
Toyota	15.4%

U.S. Top Banks by Domestic Deposits Market Share (2007)

Bank of America	9.0%
J.P. Morgan Chase	6.9%
Wachovia/Golden West Financial	5.8%
Wells Fargo	4.6%
Citigroup	3.5%

U.S. Top Airlines Market Share (2007)

American	15.7%
United	12.1%
Delta	11.8%
Southwest	11.5%
Continental	7.5%
Northwest	7.0%
U.S. Airways	4.7%
America West	3.9%

U.S. Top Rental Car Companies (2007)

Enterprise	49.6%
Hertz	23.7%
Avis	9.9%
Budget	6.9%
Alamo National	5.2%
Dollar	4.7%

Market Share of Top Selling Vodkas Worldwide

Smirnoff	21.4%
Absolut	9.2%
Stolichnaya	2.4%
Skyy	2.4%
Grey Goose	2.3%
Finlandia	2.1%
Ketel One	1.7%

Source: Adapted from Neal Boudette, "Big Dealer to Detroit: Fix How You Make Cars," *Wall Street Journal* (February 9, 2007): A8; Charles Fried, "Bank of America Quietly Targets a Barrier to Growth," *Wall Street Journal* (January 16, 2007): A19; Susan Carey, Melanie Trottman, and Dennis Berman, "UAL, Continental Discuss Merger as Airman Presses Bid for Midwest," *Wall Street Journal* (December 13, 2006): A1; Gary Stoller, "Enterprise Muscles Its Way onto Airport Scene," *USA Today* (December 22, 2006): B1, B2; and Deborah Ball, "As Vodka Sales Skyrocket, Many Newcomers Pour In," *Wall Street Journal* (January 26, 2007): B1.

- ***Question Marks***—Divisions in Quadrant I have a low relative market share position, yet they compete in a high-growth industry. Generally these firms' cash needs are high and their cash generation is low. These businesses are called *Question Marks* because the organization must decide whether to strengthen them by pursuing an intensive strategy (market penetration, market development, or product development) or to sell them.

FIGURE 6-6

The BCG Matrix

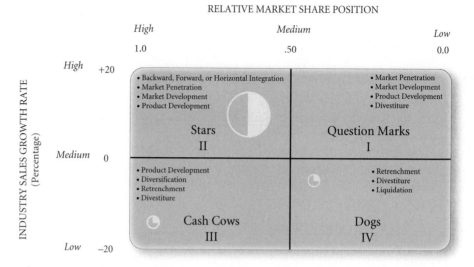

Source: Adapted from Boston Consulting Group, *Perspectives on Experience* (Boston: The Boston Consulting Group, 1974).

- *Stars*—Quadrant II businesses (*Stars*) represent the organization's best long-run opportunities for growth and profitability. Divisions with a high relative market share and a high industry growth rate should receive substantial investment to maintain or strengthen their dominant positions. Forward, backward, and horizontal integration; market penetration; market development; and product development are appropriate strategies for these divisions to consider.
- *Cash Cows*—Divisions positioned in Quadrant III have a high relative market share position but compete in a low-growth industry. Called *Cash Cows* because they generate cash in excess of their needs, they are often milked. Many of today's Cash Cows were yesterday's Stars. Cash Cow divisions should be managed to maintain their strong position for as long as possible. Product development or diversification may be attractive strategies for strong Cash Cows. However, as a Cash Cow division becomes weak, retrenchment or divestiture can become more appropriate.
- *Dogs*—Quadrant IV divisions of the organization have a low relative market share position and compete in a slow- or no-market-growth industry; they are *Dogs* in the firm's portfolio. Because of their weak internal and external position, these businesses are often liquidated, divested, or trimmed down through retrenchment. When a division first becomes a Dog, retrenchment can be the best strategy to pursue because many Dogs have bounced back, after strenuous asset and cost reduction, to become viable, profitable divisions.

The major benefit of the BCG Matrix is that it draws attention to the cash flow, investment characteristics, and needs of an organization's various divisions. The divisions of many firms evolve over time: Dogs become Question Marks, Question Marks become Stars, Stars become Cash Cows, and Cash Cows become Dogs in an ongoing counterclockwise motion. Less frequently, Stars become Question Marks, Question Marks become Dogs, Dogs become Cash Cows, and Cash Cows become Stars (in a clockwise motion). In some organizations, no cyclical motion is apparent. Over time, organizations should strive to achieve a portfolio of divisions that are Stars.

One example of a BCG Matrix is provided in Figure 6-7, which illustrates an organization composed of five divisions with annual sales ranging from $5,000 to $60,000. Division 1 has the greatest sales volume, so the circle representing that division is the largest one in the matrix. The circle corresponding to Division 5 is the smallest because its sales volume ($5,000) is least among all the divisions. The pie slices within the circles

FIGURE 6-7

An Example BCG Matrix

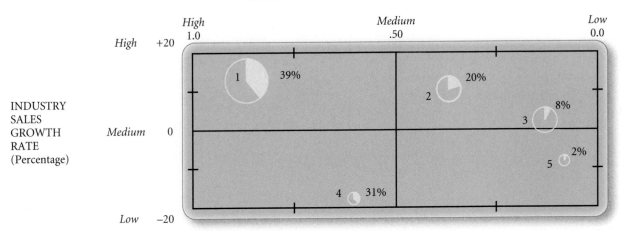

Division	Revenues	Percent Revenues	Profits	Percent Profits	Percent Market Share	Percent Growth Rate
1	$60,000	37	$10,000	39	80	+15
2	40,000	24	5,000	20	40	+10
3	40,000	24	2,000	8	10	+1
4	20,000	12	8,000	31	60	−20
5	5,000	3	500	2	5	−10
Total	**$165,000**	**100**	**$25,500**	**100**	—	—

reveal the percent of corporate profits contributed by each division. As shown, Division 1 contributes the highest profit percentage, 39 percent. Notice in the diagram that Division 1 is considered a Star, Division 2 is a Question Mark, Division 3 is also a Question Mark, Division 4 is a Cash Cow, and Division 5 is a Dog.

The BCG Matrix, like all analytical techniques, has some limitations. For example, viewing every business as either a Star, Cash Cow, Dog, or Question Mark is an oversimplification; many businesses fall right in the middle of the BCG Matrix and thus are not easily classified. Furthermore, the BCG Matrix does not reflect whether or not various divisions or their industries are growing over time; that is, the matrix has no temporal qualities, but rather it is a snapshot of an organization at a given point in time. Finally, other variables besides relative market share position and industry growth rate in sales, such as size of the market and competitive advantages, are important in making strategic decisions about various divisions.

An example BCG Matrix for Limited Brands, Inc., is provided in Figure 6-8. Headquartered in Columbus, Ohio, Limited Brands has five divisions, led by Victoria's Secret Stores, which generate nearly one-half of company profits. Also note in Figure 6-8 that the Henri Bendel division had an operating loss of $188 million. Take note how the % profit column is calculated because oftentimes a firm will have a division that incurs a loss for a year. In terms of the pie slice in circle 5 of the diagram, note that it is a *different color* from the positive profit segments in the other circles. (Note: Limited Brands' sales are 2006 actual but profits are 2006 estimate.)

The Internal-External (IE) Matrix

The *Internal-External (IE) Matrix* positions an organization's various divisions in a nine-cell display, illustrated in Figure 6-9. The IE Matrix is similar to the BCG Matrix in that both tools involve plotting organization divisions in a schematic diagram; this is why they are both called "portfolio matrices." Also, the size of each circle represents the percentage sales contribution of each division, and pie slices reveal the percentage profit contribution of each division in both the BCG and IE Matrix.

FIGURE 6-8

An Example BCG Matrix for The Limited (2006 year-end)

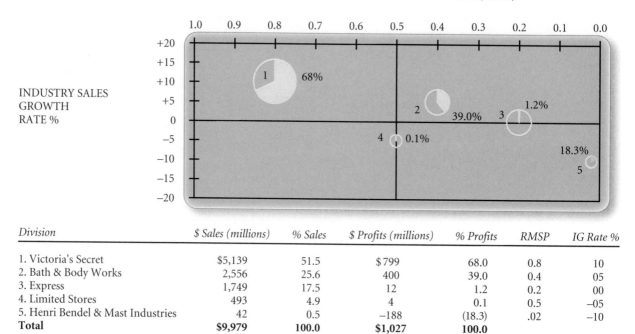

Division	$ Sales (millions)	% Sales	$ Profits (millions)	% Profits	RMSP	IG Rate %
1. Victoria's Secret	$5,139	51.5	$799	68.0	0.8	10
2. Bath & Body Works	2,556	25.6	400	39.0	0.4	05
3. Express	1,749	17.5	12	1.2	0.2	00
4. Limited Stores	493	4.9	4	0.1	0.5	−05
5. Henri Bendel & Mast Industries	42	0.5	−188	(18.3)	.02	−10
Total	**$9,979**	**100.0**	**$1,027**	**100.0**		

FIGURE 6-9

The Internal–External (IE) Matrix

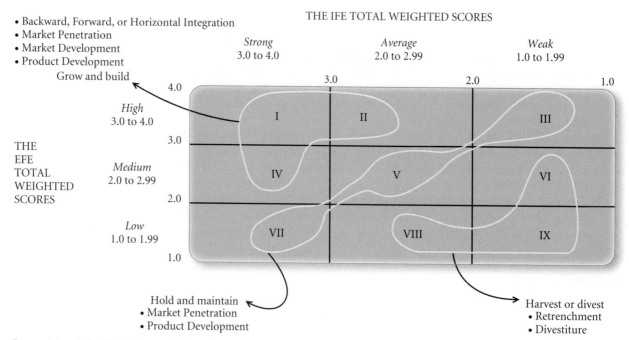

Source: Adapted. The IE Matrix was developed from the General Electric (GE) Business Screen Matrix. For a description of the GE Matrix see Michael Allen, "Diagramming GE's Planning for What's WATT," in R. Allio and M. Pennington, eds., *Corporate Planning: Techniques and Applications* (New York: AMACOM, 1979).

But there are some important differences between the BCG Matrix and the IE Matrix. First, the axes are different. Also, the IE Matrix requires more information about the divisions than the BCG Matrix. Furthermore, the strategic implications of each matrix are different. For these reasons, strategists in multidivisional firms often develop both the BCG Matrix and the IE Matrix in formulating alternative strategies. A common practice is to develop a BCG Matrix and an IE Matrix for the present and then develop projected matrices to reflect expectations of the future. This before-and-after analysis forecasts the expected effect of strategic decisions on an organization's portfolio of divisions.

The IE Matrix is based on two key dimensions: the IFE total weighted scores on the *x*-axis and the EFE total weighted scores on the *y*-axis. Recall that each division of an organization should construct an IFE Matrix and an EFE Matrix for its part of the organization. The total weighted scores derived from the divisions allow construction of the corporate-level IE Matrix. On the *x*-axis of the IE Matrix, an IFE total weighted score of 1.0 to 1.99 represents a weak internal position; a score of 2.0 to 2.99 is considered average; and a score of 3.0 to 4.0 is strong. Similarly, on the *y*-axis, an EFE total weighted score of 1.0 to 1.99 is considered low; a score of 2.0 to 2.99 is medium; and a score of 3.0 to 4.0 is high.

The IE Matrix can be divided into three major regions that have different strategy implications. First, the prescription for divisions that fall into cells I, II, or IV can be described as *grow and build*. Intensive (market penetration, market development, and product development) or integrative (backward integration, forward integration, and horizontal integration) strategies can be most appropriate for these divisions. Second, divisions that fall into cells III, V, or VII can be managed best with *hold and maintain* strategies; market penetration and product development are two commonly employed strategies for these types of divisions. Third, a common prescription for divisions that fall into cells VI, VIII, or IX is *harvest or divest*. Successful organizations are able to achieve a portfolio of businesses positioned in or around cell I in the IE Matrix.

An example of a completed IE Matrix is given in Figure 6-10, which depicts an organization composed of four divisions. As indicated by the positioning of the circles, *grow*

FIGURE 6-10

An Example IE Matrix

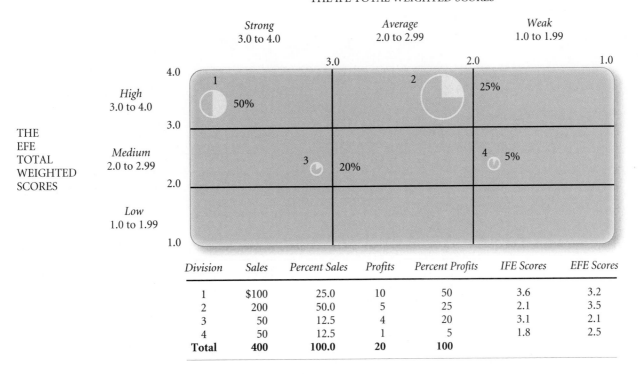

THE IFE TOTAL WEIGHTED SCORES

Division	Sales	Percent Sales	Profits	Percent Profits	IFE Scores	EFE Scores
1	$100	25.0	10	50	3.6	3.2
2	200	50.0	5	25	2.1	3.5
3	50	12.5	4	20	3.1	2.1
4	50	12.5	1	5	1.8	2.5
Total	**400**	**100.0**	**20**	**100**		

and build strategies are appropriate for Division 1, Division 2, and Division 3. Division 4 is a candidate for *harvest or divest.* Division 2 contributes the greatest percentage of company sales and thus is represented by the largest circle. Division 1 contributes the greatest proportion of total profits; it has the largest-percentage pie slice.

As indicated in Figure 6-11, Harrah's recently constructed an IE Matrix for its five product segments. Note that its Casino Division has the largest revenues (as indicated by the largest circle) and the largest profits (as indicated by the largest pie slice) in the matrix. Harrah's could also develop a Land-Based versus Riverboat versus Indian Gaming IE Matrix with three circles. It is common for organizations to develop both geographic and product-based IE Matrices to more effectively formulate strategies and allocate resources among divisions. In addition, firms often prepare an IE (or BCG) Matrix for competitors. Furthermore, firms will often prepare "before and after" IE (or BCG) Matrices to reveal the situation at present versus the expected situation after one year. This latter idea minimizes the limitation of these matrices being a "snapshot in time." In performing case analysis, feel free to estimate the IFE and EFE scores for the various divisions based upon your research into the company and industry—rather than preparing a separate IE Matrix for each division.

The Grand Strategy Matrix

In addition to the SWOT Matrix, SPACE Matrix, BCG Matrix, and IE Matrix, the *Grand Strategy Matrix* has become a popular tool for formulating alternative strategies. All organizations can be positioned in one of the Grand Strategy Matrix's four strategy quadrants. A firm's divisions likewise could be positioned. As illustrated in Figure 6-12, the Grand Strategy Matrix is based on two evaluative dimensions: competitive position and market (industry) growth. Any industry whose annual growth in sales exceeds 5 percent could be

FIGURE 6-11

The IE Matrix for Harrah's

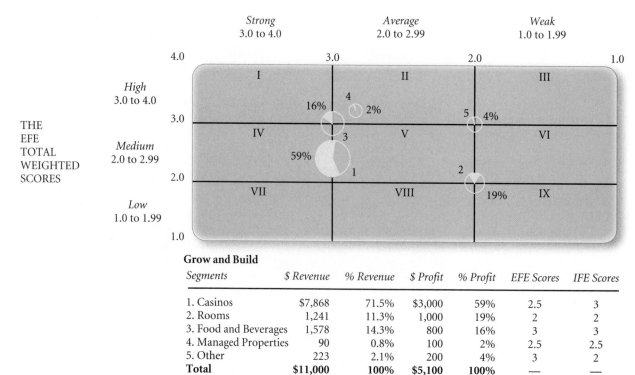

Grow and Build						
Segments	*$ Revenue*	*% Revenue*	*$ Profit*	*% Profit*	*EFE Scores*	*IFE Scores*
1. Casinos	$7,868	71.5%	$3,000	59%	2.5	3
2. Rooms	1,241	11.3%	1,000	19%	2	2
3. Food and Beverages	1,578	14.3%	800	16%	3	3
4. Managed Properties	90	0.8%	100	2%	2.5	2.5
5. Other	223	2.1%	200	4%	3	2
Total	**$11,000**	**100%**	**$5,100**	**100%**	—	—

FIGURE 6-12

The Grand Strategy Matrix

Source: Adapted from Roland Christensen, Norman Berg, and Malcolm Salter, *Policy Formulation and Administration* (Homewood, IL: Richard D. Irwin, 1976): 16–18.

considered to have rapid growth. Appropriate strategies for an organization to consider are listed in sequential order of attractiveness in each quadrant of the matrix.

Firms located in Quadrant I of the Grand Strategy Matrix are in an excellent strategic position. For these firms, continued concentration on current markets (market penetration and market development) and products (product development) is an appropriate strategy. It is unwise for a Quadrant I firm to shift notably from its established competitive advantages. When a Quadrant I organization has excessive resources, then backward, forward, or horizontal integration may be effective strategies. When a Quadrant I firm is too heavily committed to a single product, then related diversification may reduce the risks associated with a narrow product line. Quadrant I firms can afford to take advantage of external opportunities in several areas. They can take risks aggressively when necessary.

Firms positioned in Quadrant II need to evaluate their present approach to the marketplace seriously. Although their industry is growing, they are unable to compete effectively, and they need to determine why the firm's current approach is ineffective and how the company can best change to improve its competitiveness. Because Quadrant II firms are in a rapid-market-growth industry, an intensive strategy (as opposed to integrative or diversification) is usually the first option that should be considered. However, if the firm is lacking a distinctive competence or competitive advantage, then horizontal integration is often a desirable alternative. As a last resort, divestiture or liquidation should be considered. Divestiture can provide funds needed to acquire other businesses or buy back shares of stock.

Quadrant III organizations compete in slow-growth industries and have weak competitive positions. These firms must make some drastic changes quickly to avoid further decline and possible liquidation. Extensive cost and asset reduction (retrenchment) should be pursued first. An alternative strategy is to shift resources away from the current business into different areas (diversify). If all else fails, the final options for Quadrant III businesses are divestiture or liquidation.

Finally, Quadrant IV businesses have a strong competitive position but are in a slow-growth industry. These firms have the strength to launch diversified programs into more promising growth areas: Quadrant IV firms have characteristically high cash-flow levels and limited internal growth needs and often can pursue related or unrelated diversification successfully. Quadrant IV firms also may pursue joint ventures.

The Decision Stage

Analysis and intuition provide a basis for making strategy-formulation decisions. The matching techniques just discussed reveal feasible alternative strategies. Many of these strategies will likely have been proposed by managers and employees participating in the strategy analysis and choice activity. Any additional strategies resulting from the matching analyses could be discussed and added to the list of feasible alternative options. As indicated earlier in this chapter, participants could rate these strategies on a 1 to 4 scale so that a prioritized list of the best strategies could be achieved.

The Quantitative Strategic Planning Matrix (QSPM)

Other than ranking strategies to achieve the prioritized list, there is only one analytical technique in the literature designed to determine the relative attractiveness of feasible alternative actions. This technique is the *Quantitative Strategic Planning Matrix (QSPM)*, which comprises Stage 3 of the strategy-formulation analytical framework.[6] This technique objectively indicates which alternative strategies are best. The QSPM uses input from Stage 1 analyses and matching results from Stage 2 analyses to decide objectively among alternative strategies. That is, the EFE Matrix, IFE Matrix, and Competitive Profile Matrix that make up Stage 1, coupled with the SWOT Matrix, SPACE Matrix, BCG Matrix, IE Matrix, and Grand Strategy Matrix that make up Stage 2, provide the needed information for setting up the QSPM (Stage 3). The QSPM is a tool that allows strategists to evaluate alternative strategies objectively, based on previously identified external and internal critical success factors. Like other strategy-formulation analytical tools, the QSPM requires good intuitive judgment.

The basic format of the QSPM is illustrated in Table 6-5. Note that the left column of a QSPM consists of key external and internal factors (from Stage 1), and the top row consists of feasible alternative strategies (from Stage 2). Specifically, the left column of a

TABLE 6-5 **The Quantitative Strategic Planning Matrix—QSPM**

Key Factors	Weight	Strategic Alternatives		
		Strategy 1	Strategy 2	Strategy 3
Key External Factors				
Economy				
Political/Legal/Governmental				
Social/Cultural/Demographic/Environmental				
Technological				
Competitive				
Key Internal Factors				
Management				
Marketing				
Finance/Accounting				
Production/Operations				
Research and Development				
Management Information Systems				

QSPM consists of information obtained directly from the EFE Matrix and IFE Matrix. In a column adjacent to the critical success factors, the respective weights received by each factor in the EFE Matrix and the IFE Matrix are recorded.

The top row of a QSPM consists of alternative strategies derived from the SWOT Matrix, SPACE Matrix, BCG Matrix, IE Matrix, and Grand Strategy Matrix. These matching tools usually generate similar feasible alternatives. However, not every strategy suggested by the matching techniques has to be evaluated in a QSPM. Strategists should use good intuitive judgment in selecting strategies to include in a QSPM.

Conceptually, the QSPM determines the relative attractiveness of various strategies based on the extent to which key external and internal critical success factors are capitalized upon or improved. The relative attractiveness of each strategy within a set of alternatives is computed by determining the cumulative impact of each external and internal critical success factor. Any number of sets of alternative strategies can be included in the QSPM, and any number of strategies can make up a given set, but only strategies within a given set are evaluated relative to each other. For example, one set of strategies may include diversification, whereas another set may include issuing stock and selling a division to raise needed capital. These two sets of strategies are totally different, and the QSPM evaluates strategies only within sets. Note in Table 6-5 that three strategies are included, and they make up just one set.

A QSPM for a retail computer store is provided in Table 6-6. This example illustrates all the components of the QSPM: Strategic Alternatives, Key Factors, Weights, Attractiveness Scores (AS), Total Attractiveness Scores (TAS), and the Sum Total Attractiveness Score. The three new terms just introduced—(1) Attractiveness Scores, (2) Total Attractiveness Scores, and (3) the Sum Total Attractiveness Score—are defined and explained as the six steps required to develop a QSPM are discussed:

Step 1 *Make a list of the firm's key external opportunities/threats and internal strengths/weaknesses in the left column of the QSPM.* This information should be taken directly from the EFE Matrix and IFE Matrix. A minimum of 10 external key success factors and 10 internal key success factors should be included in the QSPM.

Step 2 *Assign weights to each key external and internal factor.* These weights are identical to those in the EFE Matrix and the IFE Matrix. The weights are presented in a straight column just to the right of the external and internal critical success factors.

Step 3 *Examine the Stage 2 (matching) matrices, and identify alternative strategies that the organization should consider implementing.* Record these strategies in the top row of the QSPM. Group the strategies into mutually exclusive sets if possible.

Step 4 *Determine the Attractiveness Scores (AS)* defined as numerical values that indicate the relative attractiveness of each strategy in a given set of alternatives. *Attractiveness Scores (AS)* are determined by examining each key external or internal factor, one at a time, and asking the question "Does this factor affect the choice of strategies being made?" If the answer to this question is *yes*, then the strategies should be compared relative to that key factor. Specifically, Attractiveness Scores should be assigned to each strategy to indicate the relative attractiveness of one strategy over others, considering the particular factor. The range for Attractiveness Scores is 1 = not attractive, 2 = somewhat attractive, 3 = reasonably attractive, and 4 = highly attractive. Work row by row in developing a QSPM. If the answer to the previous question is *no,* indicating that the respective key factor has no effect upon the specific choice being made, then do not assign Attractiveness Scores to the strategies in that set. Use a dash to indicate that the key factor does not affect the choice being made. *Note:* If you assign an AS score to one strategy, then assign AS score(s) to the other. In other words, if one strategy receives a dash, then all others must receive a dash in a given row.

Step 5 *Compute the Total Attractiveness Scores. Total Attractiveness Scores (TAS)* are defined as the product of multiplying the weights (Step 2) by the Attractiveness

TABLE 6-6 **A QSPM for a Retail Computer Store**

		STRATEGIC ALTERNATIVES			
		1		2	
		Buy New Land and Build New Larger Store		Fully Renovate Existing Store	
Key Factors	Weight	AS	TAS	AS	TAS
Opportunities					
1. Population of city growing 10%	0.10	4	0.40	2	0.20
2. Rival computer store opening 1 kilometer away	0.10	2	0.20	4	0.40
3. Vehicle traffic passing store up 12%	0.08	1	0.80	4	0.32
4. Vendors average six new products/year	0.05	—		—	
5. Senior citizen use of computers up 8%	0.05	—		—	
6. Small business growth in area up 10%	0.10	—		—	
7. Desire for Web sites up 18% by realtors	0.06	—		—	
8. Desire for Web sites up 12% by small firms	0.06	—		—	
Threats					
1. Rival is opening new store nearby in 1 year	0.15	4	0.60	3	0.45
2. Local university offers computer repair	0.08	—		—	
3. New bypass for Hwy 34 in 1 year will divert traffic	0.12	4		1	
4. New mall being built nearby	0.08	2		4	
5. Gas prices up 14%	0.04	—		—	
6. Vendors raising prices 8%	0.03	—		—	
	1.00				
Strengths					
1. Inventory turnover increased from 5.8 to 6.7	0.05	—		—	
2. Average customer purchase increased from $97 to $128	0.07	2	0.14	4	0.28
3. Employee morale is excellent	0.10	—		—	
4. In-store promotions resulted in 20% increase in sales	0.05	—		—	
5. Newspaper advertising expenditures increased 10%	0.02	—		—	
6. Revenues from repair/service segment of store up 16%	0.15	4	0.60	3	0.45
7. In-store technical support personnel have MIS college degrees	0.05	—		—	
8. Store's debt-to-total assets ratio declined to 34%	0.03	4	0.12	2	0.06
9. Revenues per employee up 19%	0.02	—		—	
Weaknesses					
1. Revenues from software segment of store down 12%	0.10	—		—	
2. Location of store negatively impacted by new Highway 34	0.15	4	0.60	1	0.15
3. Carpet and paint in store somewhat in disrepair	0.02	1	0.02	4	0.08
4. Bathroom in store needs refurbishing	0.02	1	0.02	4	0.08
5. Revenues from businesses down 8%	0.04	3	0.12	4	0.16
6. Store has no Web site	0.05	—		—	
7. Supplier on-time delivery increased to 2.4 days	0.03	—		—	
8. Often customers have to wait to check out	0.05	2	0.10	4	0.20
Total	1.00		3.72		2.83

Scores (Step 4) in each row. The Total Attractiveness Scores indicate the relative attractiveness of each alternative strategy, considering only the impact of the adjacent external or internal critical success factor. The higher the Total Attractiveness Score, the more attractive the strategic alternative (considering only the adjacent critical success factor).

Step 6 *Compute the Sum Total Attractiveness Score.* Add Total Attractiveness Scores in each strategy column of the QSPM. The *Sum Total Attractiveness Scores (STAS)* reveal which strategy is most attractive in each set of alternatives. Higher scores indicate more attractive strategies, considering all the relevant external and internal factors that could affect the strategic decisions. The magnitude of the difference between the Sum Total Attractiveness Scores in a given set of strategic alternatives indicates the relative desirability of one strategy over another.

In Table 6-6, two alternative strategies—(1) buy new land and build new larger store and (2) fully renovate existing store—are being considered by a computer retail store. Note by sum total attractiveness scores of 3.72 versus 2.83 that the analysis indicates the business should buy new land and build a new larger store. Note the use of dashes to indicate which factors do not affect the strategy choice being considered. If a particular factor affects one strategy but not the other, it affects the choice being made, so attractiveness scores should be recorded for both strategies. Never rate one strategy and not the other. Note also in Table 6-6 that there are no double 1's, 2's, 3's, or 4's in a row. Never duplicate scores in a row. Never work column by column; always prepare a QSPM working row by row. If you have more than one strategy in the QSPM, then let the AS scores range from 1 to "the number of strategies being evaluated." This will enable you to have a different AS score for each strategy. These are all important guidelines to follow in developing a QSPM. In actual practice, the store did purchase the new land and build a new store; the business also did some minor refurbishing until the new store was operational.

There should be a rationale for each AS score assigned. Note in Table 6-6 in the first row that the "city population growing 10 percent annually" opportunity could be capitalized on best by strategy 1, "building the new, larger store," so an AS score of 4 was assigned to Strategy 1. AS scores, therefore, are not mere guesses; they should be rational, defensible, and reasonable.

Avoid giving each strategy the same AS score. Note in Table 6-6 that dashes are inserted all the way across the row when used. Also note that double 4's, or double 3's, or double 2's, or double 1's are never in a given row. Again work row by row, not column by column. These are important guidelines to follow in constructing a QSPM.

Positive Features and Limitations of the QSPM

A positive feature of the QSPM is that sets of strategies can be examined sequentially or simultaneously. For example, corporate-level strategies could be evaluated first, followed by division-level strategies, and then function-level strategies. There is no limit to the number of strategies that can be evaluated or the number of sets of strategies that can be examined at once using the QSPM.

Another positive feature of the QSPM is that it requires strategists to integrate pertinent external and internal factors into the decision process. Developing a QSPM makes it less likely that key factors will be overlooked or weighted inappropriately. A QSPM draws attention to important relationships that affect strategy decisions. Although developing a QSPM requires a number of subjective decisions, making small decisions along the way enhances the probability that the final strategic decisions will be best for the organization. A QSPM can be adapted for use by small and large for-profit and nonprofit organizations so can be applied to virtually any type of organization. A QSPM can especially enhance strategic choice in multinational firms because many key factors and strategies can be considered at once. It also has been applied successfully by a number of small businesses.[7]

The QSPM is not without some limitations. First, it always requires intuitive judgments and educated assumptions. The ratings and attractiveness scores require judgmental decisions, even though they should be based on objective information. Discussion among strategists, managers, and employees throughout the strategy-formulation process, including development of a QSPM, is constructive and improves strategic decisions. Constructive discussion during strategy analysis and choice may arise because of genuine differences of interpretation of information and varying opinions. Another limitation of the QSPM is that it can be only as good as the prerequisite information and matching analyses upon which it is based.

Cultural Aspects of Strategy Choice

All organizations have a culture. *Culture* includes the set of shared values, beliefs, attitudes, customs, norms, personalities, heroes, and heroines that describe a firm. Culture is the unique way an organization does business. It is the human dimension that creates solidarity and meaning, and it inspires commitment and productivity in an organization when strategy changes are made. All human beings have a basic need to make sense of the world, to feel in control, and to make meaning. When events threaten meaning, individuals react defensively. Managers and employees may even sabotage new strategies in an effort to recapture the status quo.

It is beneficial to view strategic management from a cultural perspective because success often rests upon the degree of support that strategies receive from a firm's culture. If a firm's strategies are supported by cultural products such as values, beliefs, rites, rituals, ceremonies, stories, symbols, language, heroes, and heroines, then managers often can implement changes swiftly and easily. However, if a supportive culture does not exist and is not cultivated, then strategy changes may be ineffective or even counterproductive. A firm's culture can become antagonistic to new strategies, and the result of that antagonism may be confusion and disarray.

Strategies that require fewer cultural changes may be more attractive because extensive changes can take considerable time and effort. Whenever two firms merge, it becomes especially important to evaluate and consider culture-strategy linkages.

Culture provides an explanation for the difficulties a firm encounters when it attempts to shift its strategic direction, as the following statement explains:

> Not only has the "right" corporate culture become the essence and foundation of corporate excellence, but success or failure of needed corporate reforms hinges on management's sagacity and ability to change the firm's driving culture in time and in tune with required changes in strategies.[8]

The Politics of Strategy Choice

All organizations are political. Unless managed, political maneuvering consumes valuable time, subverts organizational objectives, diverts human energy, and results in the loss of some valuable employees. Sometimes political biases and personal preferences get unduly embedded in strategy choice decisions. Internal politics affect the choice of strategies in all organizations. The hierarchy of command in an organization, combined with the career aspirations of different people and the need to allocate scarce resources, guarantees the formation of coalitions of individuals who strive to take care of themselves first and the organization second, third, or fourth. Coalitions of individuals often form around key strategy issues that face an enterprise. A major responsibility of strategists is to guide the development of coalitions, to nurture an overall team concept, and to gain the support of key individuals and groups of individuals.

In the absence of objective analyses, strategy decisions too often are based on the politics of the moment. With development of improved strategy-formation tools, political factors become less important in making strategic decisions. In the absence of objectivity, political factors sometimes dictate strategies, and this is unfortunate. Managing political relationships is an integral part of building enthusiasm and esprit de corps in an organization.

A classic study of strategic management in nine large corporations examined the political tactics of successful and unsuccessful strategists.[9] Successful strategists were found to let weakly supported ideas and proposals die through inaction and to establish additional hurdles or tests for strongly supported ideas considered unacceptable but not openly opposed. Successful strategists kept a low political profile on unacceptable proposals and strived to let most negative decisions come from subordinates or a group consensus, thereby reserving their personal vetoes for big issues and crucial moments. Successful strategists did a lot of chatting and informal questioning to stay abreast of how things were progressing and to know when to intervene. They led strategy but did not dictate it. They gave few orders, announced few decisions, depended heavily on informal questioning, and sought to probe and clarify until a consensus emerged.

Successful strategists generously and visibly rewarded key thrusts that succeeded. They assigned responsibility for major new thrusts to *champions,* the individuals most strongly identified with the idea or product and whose futures were linked to its success. They stayed alert to the symbolic impact of their own actions and statements so as not to send false signals that could stimulate movements in unwanted directions.

Successful strategists ensured that all major power bases within an organization were represented in, or had access to, top management. They interjected new faces and new views into considerations of major changes. This is important because new employees and managers generally have more enthusiasm and drive than employees who have been with the firm a long time. New employees do not see the world the same old way; nor do they act as screens against changes. Successful strategists minimized their own political exposure on highly controversial issues and in circumstances in which major opposition from key power centers was likely. In combination, these findings provide a basis for managing political relationships in an organization.

Because strategies must be effective in the marketplace and capable of gaining internal commitment, the following tactics used by politicians for centuries can aid strategists:

- *Equifinality*—It is often possible to achieve similar results using different means or paths. Strategists should recognize that achieving a successful outcome is more important than imposing the method of achieving it. It may be possible to generate new alternatives that give equal results but with far greater potential for gaining commitment.
- *Satisfying*—Achieving satisfactory results with an acceptable strategy is far better than failing to achieve optimal results with an unpopular strategy.
- *Generalization*—Shifting focus from specific issues to more general ones may increase strategists' options for gaining organizational commitment.
- *Focus on Higher-Order Issues*—By raising an issue to a higher level, many short-term interests can be postponed in favor of long-term interests. For instance, by focusing on issues of survival, the airline and automotive industries were able to persuade unions to make concessions on wage increases.
- *Provide Political Access on Important Issues*—Strategy and policy decisions with significant negative consequences for middle managers will motivate intervention behavior from them. If middle managers do not have an opportunity to take a position on such decisions in appropriate political forums, they are capable of successfully resisting the decisions after they are made. Providing such political access provides strategists with information that otherwise might not be available and that could be useful in managing intervention behavior.[10]

Governance Issues

A "director," according to Webster's Dictionary, is "one of a group of persons entrusted with the overall direction of a corporate enterprise." A *board of directors* is a group of individuals who are elected by the ownership of a corporation to have oversight and guidance over management and who look out for shareholders' interests. The act of oversight and direction is referred to as *governance*. The National Association of Corporate Directors defines governance as "the characteristic of ensuring that long-term strategic objectives and plans are established and that the proper management structure is in place to achieve those objectives, while at the same time making sure that the structure functions to maintain the corporation's integrity, reputation, and responsibility to its various constituencies." This broad scope of responsibility for the board shows how boards are being held accountable for the entire performance of the firm. In the Worldcom, Tyco, and Enron bankruptcies and scandals, the firms' boards of directors were sued by shareholders for mismanaging their interests. New accounting rules in the United States and Europe now enhance corporate-governance codes and require much more extensive financial disclosure among publicly held firms. The roles and duties of a board of directors can be divided into four broad categories, as indicated in Table 6-7.

Until recently, boards of directors did most of their work sitting around polished wooden tables. However, Hewlett-Packard's directors, among many others, now log on to

TABLE 6-7 Board of Director Duties and Responsibilities

1. CONTROL AND OVERSIGHT OVER MANAGEMENT
   a. Select the Chief Executive Officer (CEO).
   b. Sanction the CEO's team.
   c. Provide the CEO with a forum.
   d. Ensure managerial competency.
   e. Evaluate management's performance.
   f. Set management's salary levels, including fringe benefits.
   g. Guarantee managerial integrity through continuous auditing.
   h. Chart the corporate course.
   i. Devise and revise policies to be implemented by management.

2. ADHERENCE TO LEGAL PRESCRIPTIONS
   a. Keep abreast of new laws.
   b. Ensure the entire organization fulfills legal prescriptions.
   c. Pass bylaws and related resolutions.
   d. Select new directors.
   e. Approve capital budgets.
   f. Authorize borrowing, new stock issues, bonds, and so on.

3. CONSIDERATION OF STAKEHOLDERS' INTERESTS
   a. Monitor product quality.
   b. Facilitate upward progression in employee quality of work life.
   c. Review labor policies and practices.
   d. Improve the customer climate.
   e. Keep community relations at the highest level.
   f. Use influence to better governmental, professional association, and educational contacts.
   g. Maintain good public image.

4. ADVANCEMENT OF STOCKHOLDERS' RIGHTS
   a. Preserve stockholders' equity.
   b. Stimulate corporate growth so that the firm will survive and flourish.
   c. Guard against equity dilution.
   d. Ensure equitable stockholder representation.
   e. Inform stockholders through letters, reports, and meetings.
   f. Declare proper dividends.
   g. Guarantee corporate survival.

their own special board Web site twice a week and conduct business based on extensive confidential briefing information posted there by the firm's top management team. Then the board members meet face to face and fully informed every two months to discuss the biggest issues facing the firm. Even the decision of whether to locate operations in countries with low corporate tax rates would be reviewed by a board of directors—as indicated in the "Global Perspective."

GLOBAL PERSPECTIVE
Corporate Tax Rates Worldwide—Europe Is Lowest and Getting Lower

The lowest corporate tax rates among developed countries reside in Europe and European countries are lowering tax rates further to attract investment. The average corporate tax rate among European Union countries is 26 percent, compared with 30 percent in the Asia-Pacific region and nearly 40 percent in the United States and Japan. Ireland and the former Soviet-bloc nations of Eastern Europe recently slashed corporate tax rates to nearly zero, attracting substantial investment. Germany cut its corporate tax rate from 39 percent in 2007 to just under 30 percent in 2008. Great Britain cut its corporate tax rate to 28 percent from 30 percent. France plans to cut its rate from 34 percent to 27 percent in 2008.

Other factors besides the corporate tax rate obviously affect companies' decisions to locate plants and facilities. For example, the large and affluent market and efficient infrastructure in Germany and Britain attract companies, but the high labor costs and strict labor laws keep other companies away.

Ralph Gomory, president of the Alfred P. Sloan Foundation and a former top executive at IBM, warns of a growing divergence between the interests of U.S. corporations and the interests of the United States. Specifically, he says U.S. trade liberalization/globalization policies for the last two decades have encouraged corporations to seek the lowest-cost locations for their operations. The new 1,200-worker Intel semiconductor plant in Vietnam is just one example among thousands. Gomory says the United States must use the corporate income tax to greatly *reward* companies that invest in jobs here, especially high-tech jobs, and must greatly *penalize* companies that move facilities overseas. We must make it in the self-interest of companies to invest in America, Gomory says. Otherwise, living standards here will inevitably decline and America will severely weaken economically.

Source: Adapted from Marcus Walker, "Europe Competes for Investment with Lower Corporate Tax Rates," *Wall Street Journal* (April 17, 207): A12.

Source: John Heseltine (c) Dorling Kindersley

Today, boards of directors are composed mostly of outsiders who are becoming more involved in organizations' strategic management. The trend in the United States, for example, is toward much greater board member accountability with smaller boards, now averaging 12 members rather than 18 as they did a few years ago. *BusinessWeek* magazine recently evaluated the boards of most large U.S. companies and provided the following "principles of good governance":

1. No more than two directors are current or former company executives.
2. No directors do business with the company or accept consulting or legal fees from the firm.
3. The audit, compensation, and nominating committees are made up solely of outside directors.
4. Each director owns a large equity stake in the company, excluding stock options.
5. At least one outside director has extensive experience in the company's core business and at least one has been CEO of an equivalent-size company.
6. Fully employed directors sit on no more than four boards and retirees sit on no more than seven.
7. Each director attends at least 75 percent of all meetings.
8. The board meets regularly without management present and evaluates its own performance annually.
9. The audit committee meets at least four times a year.
10. The board is frugal on executive pay, diligent in CEO succession oversight responsibilities, and prompt to act when trouble arises.
11. The CEO is not also the chairperson of the board.
12. Shareholders have considerable power and information to choose and replace directors.
13. Stock options are considered a corporate expense.
14. There are no interlocking directorships (where a director or CEO sits on another director's board).[11]

BusinessWeek identified some of the "worst" U.S. boards as those at Apple, Conseco, Gap, Kmart, Qwest, Tyson Foods, and Xerox. The "best" boards were those at 3M, Apria Healthcare, Colgate-Palmolive, General Electric, Home Depot, Intel, Johnson & Johnson, Medtronic, Pfizer, and Texas Instruments. Being a member of a board of directors today requires much more time, is much more difficult, and requires much more technical knowledge and financial commitment than in the past. Jeff Sonnerfeld, associate dean of the Yale School of Management, says, "Boards of directors are now rolling up their sleeves and becoming much more closely involved with management decision making." Since the Enron and Worldcom scandals, company CEOs and boards are required to personally certify financial statements; company loans to company executives and directors are illegal; and there is faster reporting of insider stock transactions.

Just as directors are beginning to place more emphasis on staying informed about an organization's health and operations, they are also taking a more active role in ensuring that publicly issued documents are accurate representations of a firm's status. It is becoming widely recognized that a board of directors has legal responsibilities to stockholders and society for all company activities, for corporate performance, and for ensuring that a firm has an effective strategy. Failure to accept responsibility for auditing or evaluating a firm's strategy is considered a serious breach of a director's duties. Stockholders, government agencies, and customers are filing legal suits against directors for fraud, omissions, inaccurate disclosures, lack of due diligence, and culpable ignorance about a firm's operations with increasing frequency. Liability insurance for directors has become exceptionally expensive and has caused numerous directors to resign.

More than 50 percent of outside directors at Fortune 500 firms have quit in recent years.[12] The 12 former Worldcom directors paid $25 million out of pocket to settle shareholder claims, and this has set a precedent for director liability. Among the Fortune 1,000 firms, board member average pay increased 32 percent since U.S. Sarbanes-Oxley Act was enacted in 2002 to $57,000 annually. This is commensurate with members' increased responsibility and liability under the act. In the last 10 years, the percentage of those boards that include at least one woman rose from 63 to 82 percent; the percentage of those boards that have a least one member of an ethnic minority rose from 44 to 76 percent.

The Sarbanes-Oxley Act resulted in scores of boardroom overhauls among publicly traded companies. The jobs of chief executive and chairman are now held by separate persons, and board audit committees must now have at least one financial expert as a member. Board audit committees now meet 10 or more times per year, rather than 3 or 4 times as they did prior to the act. The act put an end to the "country club" atmosphere of most boards and has shifted power from CEOs to directors. Although aimed at public companies, the act has also had a similar impact on privately owned companies.[13]

In Sweden, a new law has recently been passed requiring 25 percent female representation in boardrooms. The Norwegian government has passed a similar law that requires 40 percent of corporate director seats to go to women. In the United States, women currently hold about 13 percent of board seats at S&P 500 firms and 10 percent at S&P 1,500 firms. The Investor Responsibility Research Center in Washington, D.C. reports that minorities hold just 8.8 percent of board seats of S&P 1,500 companies. Progressive firms realize that women and minorities ask different questions and make different suggestions in boardrooms than white men, which is helpful because women and minorities comprise much of the consumer base everywhere.

A direct response of increased pressure on directors to stay informed and execute their responsibilities is that audit committees are becoming commonplace. A board of directors should conduct an annual strategy audit in much the same fashion that it reviews the annual financial audit. In performing such an audit, a board could work jointly with operating management and/or seek outside counsel. Boards should play a role beyond that of performing a strategic audit. They should provide greater input and advice in the strategy-formulation process to ensure that strategists are providing for the long-term needs of the firm. This is being done through the formation of three particular board committees: nominating committees to propose candidates for the board and senior officers of the firm; compensation committees to evaluate the performance of top executives and determine the terms and conditions of their employment; and audit committees to give board-level attention to company accounting and financial policies and performance.

Conclusion

The essence of strategy formulation is an assessment of whether an organization is doing the right things and how it can be more effective in what it does. Every organization should be wary of becoming a prisoner of its own strategy, because even the best strategies become obsolete sooner or later. Regular reappraisal of strategy helps management avoid complacency. Objectives and strategies should be consciously developed and coordinated and should not merely evolve out of day-to-day operating decisions.

An organization with no sense of direction and no coherent strategy precipitates its own demise. When an organization does not know where it wants to go, it usually ends up some place it does not want to be. Every organization needs to consciously establish and communicate clear objectives and strategies.

Modern strategy-formulation tools and concepts are described in this chapter and integrated into a practical three-stage framework. Tools such as the SWOT Matrix, SPACE Matrix, BCG Matrix, IE Matrix, and QSPM can significantly enhance the quality of strategic decisions, but they should never be used to dictate the choice of strategies. Behavioral, cultural, and political aspects of strategy generation and selection are always important to consider and manage. Because of increased legal pressure from outside groups, boards of directors are assuming a more active role in strategy analysis and choice. This is a positive trend for organizations.

We invite you to visit the David page on the Prentice Hall Companion Web site at www.prenhall.com/david for this chapter's review quiz.

VISIT THE NET

Provides answers to "Frequently Asked Questions About Strategic Planning." (www.allianceonline. org/faqs.html)

Key Terms and Concepts

Aggressive Quadrant (p. 229)
Attractiveness Scores (AS) (p. 239)
Board of Directors (p. 243)
Boston Consulting Group (BCG) Matrix (p. 229)
Business Portfolio (p. 229)
Cash Cows (p. 232)
Champions (p. 243)
Competitive Advantage (CA) (p. 226)
Competitive Quadrant (p. 229)
Conservative Quadrant (p. 229)
Culture (p. 242)
Decision Stage (p. 223)
Defensive Quadrant (p. 229)
Directional Vector (p. 229)
Dogs (p. 232)
Environmental Stability (ES) (p. 226)
Financial Strength (FS) (p. 226)
Governance (p. 244)
Grand Strategy Matrix (p. 236)
Halo Error (p. 223)
Industry Strength (IS) (p. 226)
Input Stage (p. 222)
Internal-External (IE) Matrix (p. 229)
Matching (p. 223)
Matching Stage (p. 222)
Quantitative Strategic Planning Matrix (QSPM) (p. 238)
Question Marks (p. 231)
Relative Market Share Position (p. 229)
SO Strategies (p. 224)
Stars (p. 232)
Strategic Position and Action Evaluation (SPACE) Matrix (p. 226)
Strategy-Formulation Framework (p. 223)
Strengths-Weaknesses Opportunities-Threats (SWOT) Matrix (p. 224)
ST Strategies (p. 224)
Sum Total Attractiveness Scores (STAS) (p. 241)
Sustainability (p. 220)
Total Attractiveness Scores (TAS) (p. 239)
WO Strategies (p. 224)
WT Strategies (p. 224)

Issues for Review and Discussion

1. How would application of the strategy-formulation framework differ from a small to a large organization?
2. What types of strategies would you recommend for an organization that achieves total weighted scores of 3.6 on the IFE and 1.2 on the EFE Matrix?
3. Given the following information, develop a SPACE Matrix for the XYZ Corporation: FS = +2; ES = −6; CA = −2; IS = +4.
4. Given the information in the following table, develop a BCG Matrix and an IE Matrix:

Divisions	1	2	3
Profits	$10	$15	$25
Sales	$100	$50	$100
Relative Market Share	0.2	0.5	0.8
Industry Growth Rate	+.20	+.10	−.10
IFE Total Weighted Scores	1.6	3.1	2.2
EFE Total Weighted Scores	2.5	1.8	3.3

5.   Explain the steps involved in developing a QSPM.
6.   How would you develop a set of objectives for your school or business?
7.   What do you think is the appropriate role of a board of directors in strategic management? Why?
8.   Discuss the limitations of various strategy-formulation analytical techniques.
9.   Explain why cultural factors should be an important consideration in analyzing and choosing among alternative strategies.
10. How are the SWOT Matrix, SPACE Matrix, BCG Matrix, IE Matrix, and Grand Strategy Matrix similar? How are they different?
11. How would for-profit and nonprofit organizations differ in their applications of the strategy-formulation framework?
12. Develop a SPACE Matrix for a company that is weak financially and is a weak competitor. The industry for this company is pretty stable, but the industry's projected growth in revenues and profits is not good. Label all axes and quadrants.
13. List four limitations of a BCG Matrix.
14. Make up an example to show clearly and completely that you can develop an IE Matrix for a three-division company, where each division has $10, $20, and $40 in revenues and $2, $4, and $1 in profits. State other assumptions needed. Label axes and quadrants.
15. What procedures could be necessary if the SPACE vector falls right on the axis between the Competitive and Defensive quadrants?
16. In a BCG Matrix or the Grand Strategy Matrix, what would you consider to be a rapid market (or industry) growth rate?
17. What are the pros and cons of a company (and country) participating in a Sustainability Report?
18. How does the Sarbanes-Oxley Act of 2002 impact boards of directors?
19. Rank *BusinessWeek*'s "principles of good governance" from 1 to 14 (1 being most important and 14 least important) to reveal your assessment of these new rules.
20. Why is it important to work row by row instead of column by column in preparing a QSPM?
21. Why should one avoid putting double 4's in a row in preparing a QSPM?
22. Envision a QSPM with no weight column. Would that still be a useful analysis? Why or why not? What do you lose by deleting the weight column?
23. Prepare a BCG Matrix for a two-division firm with sales of $5 and $8 versus profits of $3 and $1, respectively? State assumptions for the RMSP and IGR axes to enable you to construct the diagram.
24. Consider developing a before-and-after BCG or IE Matrix to reveal the expected results of your proposed strategies. What limitation of the analysis would this procedure overcome somewhat?
25. If a firm has the leading market share in its industry, where on the BCG Matrix would the circle lie?
26. If a firm competes in a very unstable industry, such as telecommunications, where on the ES axis of the SPACE Matrix would you plot the appropriate point?
27. Why do you think the SWOT Matrix is the most widely used of all strategy matrices?
28. The strategy templates described at the www.strategyclub.com Web site have templates for all of the Chapter 6 matrices. How could those templates be useful in preparing an example BCG or IE Matrix?

Notes

1.   R. T. Lenz, "Managing the Evolution of the Strategic Planning Process," *Business Horizons* 30, no. 1 (January–February 1987): 37.
2.   Robert Grant, "The Resource-Based Theory of Competitive Advantage: Implications for Strategy Formulation," *California Management Review* (Spring 1991): 114.
3.   Heinz Weihrich, "The TOWS Matrix: A Tool for Situational Analysis," *Long Range Planning* 15, no. 2 (April 1982): 61. Note: Although Dr. Weihrich first modified SWOT analysis to form the TOWS matrix, the acronym SWOT is much more widely used than TOWS in practice, so this edition reflects a change to SWOT from the use of TOWS in previous editions.
4.   Greg, Dess, G. T. Lumpkin and Alan Eisner, *Strategic Management: Text and Cases* (New York: McGraw-Hill/Irwin, 2006): 72.

5. H. Rowe, R. Mason, and K. Dickel, *Strategic Management and Business Policy: A Methodological Approach* (Reading, MA: Addison-Wesley, 1982): 155–156. Reprinted with permission of the publisher.

6. Fred David, "The Strategic Planning Matrix—A Quantitative Approach," *Long Range Planning* 19, no. 5 (October 1986): 102; Andre Gib and Robert Margulies, "Making Competitive Intelligence Relevant to the User," *Planning Review* 19, no. 3 (May–June 1991): 21.

7. Fred David, "Computer-Assisted Strategic Planning in Small Businesses," *Journal of Systems Management* 36, no. 7 (July 1985): 24–34.

8. Y. Allarie and M. Firsirotu, "How to Implement Radical Strategies in Large Organizations," *Sloan Management Review* 26, no. 3 (Spring 1985): 19. Another excellent article is P. Shrivastava, "Integrating Strategy Formulation with Organizational Culture," *Journal of Business Strategy* 5, no. 3 (Winter 1985): 103–111.

9. James Brian Quinn, *Strategies for Changes: Logical Incrementalism* (Homewood, IL: Richard D. Irwin, 1980): 128–145. These political tactics are listed in A. Thompson and A. Strickland, *Strategic Management: Concepts and Cases* (Plano, TX: Business Publications, 1984): 261.

10. William Guth and Ian MacMillan, "Strategy Implementation Versus Middle Management Self-Interest," *Strategic Management Journal* 7, no. 4 (July–August 1986): 321.

11. Louis Lavelle, "The Best and Worst Boards," *BusinessWeek* (October 7, 2002): 104–110.

12. Anne Fisher, "Board Seats Are Going Begging," *Fortune* (May 16, 2005): 204.

13. Matt Murray, "Private Companies Also Feel Pressure to Clean Up Acts," *Wall Street Journal* (July 22, 2003): B1.

Current Readings

Benz, Matthias, and Bruno S. Frey. "Corporate Governance: What Can We Learn from Public Governance?" *The Academy of Management Review* 32, no. 1 (January 2007): 92.

Dalton, Catherine M., and Dan R. Dalton "Spotlight on Corporate Governance." *Business Horizons* 49, no. 2 (March–April 2006): 91.

Drew, Stephen A., Patricia C. Kelley, and Terry Kendrick. "Class: Five Elements of Corporate Governance to Manage Strategic Risk." *Business Horizons* 49, no. 2 (March–April 2006): 127.

Gillis, William E. "How Much Is Too Much? Board of Director Responses to Shareholder Concerns About CEO Stock Options." *The Academy of Management Perspectives* 20, no. 2 (May 2006): 70.

Hillman, Amy J., Christine Shropshire, and Albert A. Cannella Jr. "Organizational Predictors of Women on Corporate Boards." *The Academy of Management Journal* 50, no. 4 (August 2007): 941.

Hoffman, W.H. "Strategies for Managing a Portfolio of Alliances." *Strategic Management Journal* 28, no. 8 (August 2007): 827.

Kor, Y. Y. "Direct and Interaction Effects of Top Management Team and Board Compositions on R&D Investment Strategy." *Strategic Management Journal* 27, no. 11 (November 2006): 1081.

Rehbein, Kathleen. "Explaining CEO Compensation: How Do Talent, Governance, and Markets Fit In?" *The Academy of Management Perspective* 21, no. 1 (February 2007): 75.

• EXPERIENTIAL EXERCISES

Experiential Exercise 6A

Developing a SWOT Matrix for Walt Disney

Purpose

The most widely used strategy-formulation technique among U.S. firms is the SWOT Matrix. This exercise requires the development of a SWOT Matrix for Walt Disney. Matching key external and internal factors in a SWOT Matrix requires good intuitive and conceptual skills. You will improve with practice in developing a SWOT Matrix.

Instructions

Recall from Experiential Exercise 1A that you already may have determined Walt Disney's external opportunites/threats and internal strengths/weaknesses. This information could be used to complete this exercise. Follow the steps outlined as follows:

Step 1	On a separate sheet of paper, construct a large nine-cell diagram that will represent your SWOT Matrix. Appropriately label the cells.
Step 2	Appropriately record Walt Disney's opportunities/threats and strengths/weaknesses in your diagram.
Step 3	Match external and internal factors to generate feasible alternative strategies for Walt Disney. Record SO, WO, ST, and WT strategies in the appropriate cells of the SWOT Matrix. Use the proper notation to indicate the rationale for the strategies. You do not necessarily have to have strategies in all four strategy cells.
Step 4	Compare your SWOT Matrix to another student's SWOT Matrix. Discuss any major differences.

Experiential Exercise 6B

Developing a SPACE Matrix for Walt Disney

Purpose

Should Walt Disney pursue aggressive, conservative, competitive, or defensive strategies? Develop a SPACE Matrix for Walt Disney to answer this question. Elaborate on the strategic implications of your directional vector. Be specific in terms of strategies that could benefit Walt Disney.

Instructions

Step 1	Join with two other people in class and develop a joint SPACE Matrix for Walt Disney.
Step 2	Diagram your SPACE Matrix on the board. Compare your matrix with other team's matrices.
Step 3	Discuss the implications of your SPACE Matrix.

Experiential Exercise 6C

Developing a BCG Matrix for Walt Disney

Purpose

Portfolio matrices are widely used by multidivisional organizations to help identify and select strategies to pursue. A BCG analysis identifies particular divisions that should

A 1970s Walt Disney's "Goofy" Pez dispenser.
Source: (c) Judith Miller / Dorling Kindersley / Atomic Age

receive fewer resources than others. It may identify some divisions that need to be divested. This exercise can give you practice developing a BCG Matrix.

Instructions

Step 1   Place the following five column headings at the top of a separate sheet of paper: Divisions, Revenues, Profits, Relative Market Share Position, Industry Growth Rate. Down the far left of your page, list Disney's four divisions, which are (1) Studio Entertainment, (2) Parks and Resorts, (3) Media Networks, and (4) Consumer Products. Now turn back to the Cohesion Case and find information to fill in all the cells in your 4 × 5 data table.

Step 2   Complete a BCG Matrix for Walt Disney.

Step 3   Compare your BCG Matrix to other students' matrices. Discuss any major differences.

Experiential Exercise 6D

Developing a QSPM for Walt Disney

Purpose

This exercise can give you practice developing a Quantitative Strategic Planning Matrix to determine the relative attractiveness of various strategic alternatives.

Instructions

Step 1   Join with two other students in class to develop a joint QSPM for Walt Disney.

Step 2   Go to the blackboard and record your strategies and their Sum Total Attractiveness Score. Compare your team's strategies and Sum Total Attractiveness Score to those of other teams. Be sure not to assign the same AS score in a given row. Recall that dashes should be inserted all the way across a given row when used.

Step 3   Discuss any major differences.

Experiential Exercise 6E

Formulating Individual Strategies

Purpose

Individuals and organizations are alike in many ways. Each has competitors, and each should plan for the future. Every individual and organization faces some external opportunities and threats and has some internal strengths and weaknesses. Both individuals and organizations establish objectives and allocate resources. These and other similarities make it possible for individuals to use many strategic-management concepts and tools. This exercise is designed to demonstrate how the SWOT Matrix can be used by individuals to plan their futures. As one nears completion of a college degree and begins interviewing for jobs, planning can be particularly important.

Instructions

On a separate sheet of paper, construct a SWOT Matrix. Include what you consider to be your major external opportunities, your major external threats, your major strengths, and your major weaknesses. An internal weakness may be a low grade point average. An external opportunity may be that your university offers a graduate program that interests you. Match key external and internal factors by recording in the appropriate cell of the matrix alternative strategies or actions that would allow you to capitalize upon your strengths, overcome your weaknesses, take advantage of your external opportunities, and minimize the impact of external threats. Be sure to use the appropriate matching notation in the strategy cells of the matrix. Because every individual (and organization) is unique, there is no one right answer to this exercise.

Experiential Exercise 6F

The Mach Test

Purpose

The purpose of this exercise is to enhance your understanding and awareness of the impact that behavioral and political factors can have on strategy analysis and choice.

Instructions

Step 1   On a separate sheet of paper, number from 1 to 10. For each of the 10 statements given as follows, record a *1, 2, 3, 4,* or *5* to indicate your attitude, where

> 1 = I disagree a lot.
> 2 = I disagree a little.
> 3 = My attitude is neutral.
> 4 = I agree a little.
> 5 = I agree a lot.

1. The best way to handle people is to tell them what they want to hear.
2. When you ask someone to do something for you, it is best to give the real reason for wanting it, rather than a reason that might carry more weight.
3. Anyone who completely trusts anyone else is asking for trouble.
4. It is hard to get ahead without cutting corners here and there.
5. It is safest to assume that all people have a vicious streak, and it will come out when they are given a chance.
6. One should take action only when it is morally right.
7. Most people are basically good and kind.
8. There is no excuse for lying to someone else.
9. Most people forget more easily the death of their father than the loss of their property.
10. Generally speaking, people won't work hard unless they're forced to do so.

Step 2   Add up the numbers you recorded beside statements 1, 3, 4, 5, 9, and 10. This sum is Subtotal One. For the other four statements, reverse the numbers you recorded, so a *5* becomes a *1, 4* becomes *2, 2* becomes *4, 1* becomes *5,* and *3* remains *3.* Then add those four numbers to get Subtotal Two. Finally, add Subtotal One and Subtotal Two to get your Final Score.

Your Final Score

Your Final Score is your Machiavellian Score. Machiavellian principles are defined in a dictionary as "manipulative, dishonest, deceiving, and favoring political expediency over morality." These tactics are not desirable, are not ethical, and are not recommended in the strategic-management process! You may, however, encounter some highly Machiavellian individuals in your career, so beware. It is important for strategists not to manipulate others in the pursuit of organizational objectives. Individuals today recognize and resent manipulative tactics more than ever before. J. R. Ewing (on *Dallas,* a television show in the 1980s) was a good example of someone who was a high Mach (score over 30). The National Opinion Research Center used this short quiz in a random sample of U.S. adults and found the national average Final Score to be 25.[1] The higher your score, the more Machiavellian (manipulative) you tend to be. The following scale is descriptive of individual scores on this test:

- Below 16: Never uses manipulation as a tool.
- 16 to 20: Rarely uses manipulation as a tool.
- 21 to 25: Sometimes uses manipulation as a tool.
- 26 to 30: Often uses manipulation as a tool.
- Over 30: Always uses manipulation as a tool.

Test Development

The Mach (Machiavellian) test was developed by Dr. Richard Christie, whose research suggests the following tendencies:

1. Men generally are more Machiavellian than women.
2. There is no significant difference between high Machs and low Machs on measures of intelligence or ability.
3. Although high Machs are detached from others, they are detached in a pathological sense.
4. Machiavellian scores are not statistically related to authoritarian values.
5. High Machs tend to be in professions that emphasize the control and manipulation of individuals—for example, law, psychiatry, and behavioral science.
6. Machiavellianism is not significantly related to major demographic characteristics such as educational level or marital status.
7. High Machs tend to come from a city or have urban backgrounds.
8. Older adults tend to have lower Mach scores than younger adults.[2]

A classic book on power relationships, *The Prince,* was written by Niccolo Machiavelli. Several excerpts from *The Prince* follow:

Men must either be cajoled or crushed, for they will revenge themselves for slight wrongs, while for grave ones they cannot. The injury therefore that you do to a man should be such that you need not fear his revenge.

We must bear in mind . . . that there is nothing more difficult and dangerous, or more doubtful of success, than an attempt to introduce a new order of things in any state. The innovator has for enemies all those who derived advantages from the old order of things, while those who expect to be benefitted by the new institution will be but lukewarm defenders.

A wise prince, therefore, will steadily pursue such a course that the citizens of his state will always and under all circumstances feel the need for his authority, and will therefore always prove faithful to him.

A prince should seem to be merciful, faithful, humane, religious, and upright, and should even be so in reality, but he should have his mind so trained that, when occasion requires it, he may know how to change to the opposite.[3]

Notes

1. Richard Christie and Florence Geis, *Studies in Machiavellianism* (Orlando, FL: Academic Press, 1970). Material in this exercise adapted with permission of the authors and the Academic Press.
2. Ibid., 82–83.
3. Niccolo Machiavelli, *The Prince* (New York: The Washington Press, 1963).

Experiential Exercise 6G

Developing a BCG Matrix for My University

Purpose

Developing a BCG Matrix for many nonprofit organizations, including colleges and universities, is a useful exercise. Of course, there are no profits for each division or department—and in some cases no revenues. However, you can be creative in performing a BCG Matrix. For example, the pie slice in the circles can represent the number of majors receiving jobs upon graduation, the number of faculty teaching in that area, or some other variable that you believe is important to consider. The size of the circles can represent the number of students majoring in particular departments or areas.

Instructions

Step 1	On a separate sheet of paper, develop a BCG Matrix for your university. Include all academic schools, departments, or colleges.
Step 2	Diagram your BCG Matrix on the blackboard.
Step 3	Discuss differences among the BCG Matrices on the board.

Experiential Exercise 6H

The Role of Boards of Directors

Purpose

This exercise will give you a better understanding of the role of boards of directors in formulating, implementing, and evaluating strategies.

Instructions

Identify a person in your community who serves on a board of directors. Make an appointment to interview that person, and seek answers to the following questions. Summarize your findings in a five-minute oral report to the class.

- On what board are you a member?
- How often does the board meet?
- How long have you served on the board?
- What role does the board play in this company?
- How has the role of the board changed in recent years?
- What changes would you like to see in the role of the board?
- To what extent do you prepare for the board meeting?
- To what extent are you involved in strategic management of the firm?

Experiential Exercise 6I

Locating Companies in a Grand Strategy Matrix

Purpose

The Grand Strategy Matrix is a popular tool for formulating alternative strategies. All organizations can be positioned in one of the Grand Strategy Matrix's four strategy quadrants. The divisions of a firm likewise could be positioned. The Grand Strategy Matrix is based on two evaluative dimensions: competitive position and market growth. Appropriate strategies for an organization to consider are listed in sequential order of attractiveness in each quadrant of the matrix. This exercise gives you experience using a Grand Strategy Matrix.

Instructions

Using the year-end 2006 financial information provided, prepare a Grand Strategy Matrix on a separate sheet of paper. Write the respective company names in the appropriate quadrant of the matrix. Based on this analysis, what strategies are recommended for each company?

Company	Company Sales/ Profit Growth (%)	Industry	Industry Sales/ Profit Growth (%)
Ford Motor	−10% / −723%	Motor vehicles	+3% / −14%
Oshkosh Truck	+16% / +28%	Motor vehicles	+3% / −14%
International Paper	−6% / −5%	Forest/paper products	−2% / −10%
Weyerhaeuser	−3% / −38%	Forest/paper products	−2% / −10%
La-Z-Boy	−6% / −108%	Furniture	+8% / +8%
Herman Miller	+15% / +46%	Furniture	+8% / +8%
MGM Mirage	+17% / +46%	Hotels/casinos	+23% / +51%
Marriott International	+5% / −9%	Hotels/casinos	+23% / +51%

Part 3 • Strategy Implementation

7

Implementing Strategies: Management and Operations Issues

Loggers at work. *Source:* Peter Buckley

The strategic-management process does not end when the firm decides what strategy or strategies to pursue. There must be a translation of strategic thought into strategic action. This translation is much easier if managers and employees of the firm understand the business, feel a part of the company, and through involvement in strategy-formulation activities have become committed to helping the organization succeed. Without understanding and commitment, strategy-implementation efforts face major problems.

Implementing strategy affects an organization from top to bottom; it affects all the functional and divisional areas of a business. It is beyond the purpose and scope of this text to examine all of the business administration concepts and tools important in strategy implementation. This chapter focuses on management issues most central to implementing strategies in the year 2007, and Chapter 8 focuses on marketing, finance/accounting, R&D, and management information systems issues.

> Even the most technically perfect strategic plan will serve little purpose if it is not implemented. Many organizations tend to spend an inordinate amount of time, money, and effort on developing the strategic plan, treating the means and circumstances under which it will be implemented as afterthoughts! Change comes through implementation and evaluation, not through the plan. A technically imperfect plan that is implemented well will achieve more than the perfect plan that never gets off the paper on which it is typed.[1]

The Nature of Strategy Implementation

The strategy-implementation stage of strategic management is revealed in Figure 7-1. Successful strategy formulation does not guarantee successful strategy implementation. It is always more difficult to do something (strategy implementation) than to say you are going to do it (strategy formulation)! Although inextricably linked, strategy implementation is

VISIT THE NET

Gives a good definition of strategy implementation. (www. csuchico.edu/mgmt/strategy/ module/sld044.htm)

FIGURE 7-1

Comprehensive Strategic-Management Model

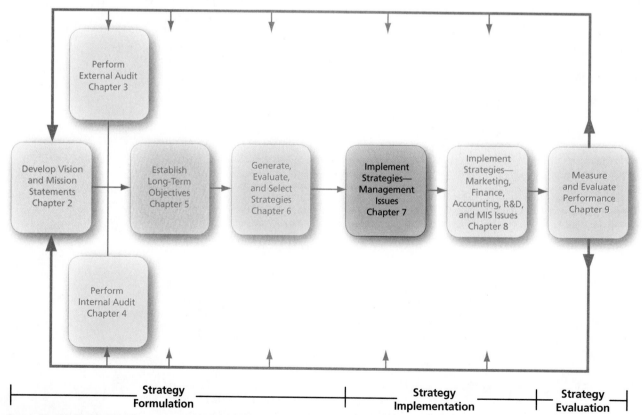

Source: Fred R. David, "How Companies Define Their Mission," *Long Range Planning* 22, no. 3 (June 1988): 40.

fundamentally different from strategy formulation. Strategy formulation and implementation can be contrasted in the following ways:

- Strategy formulation is positioning forces before the action.
- Strategy implementation is managing forces during the action.
- Strategy formulation focuses on effectiveness.
- Strategy implementation focuses on efficiency.
- Strategy formulation is primarily an intellectual process.
- Strategy implementation is primarily an operational process.
- Strategy formulation requires good intuitive and analytical skills.
- Strategy implementation requires special motivation and leadership skills.
- Strategy formulation requires coordination among a few individuals.
- Strategy implementation requires coordination among many individuals.

Strategy-formulation concepts and tools do not differ greatly for small, large, for-profit, or nonprofit organizations. However, strategy implementation varies substantially among different types and sizes of organizations. Implementing strategies requires such actions as altering sales territories, adding new departments, closing facilities, hiring new employees, changing an organization's pricing strategy, developing financial budgets, developing new employee benefits, establishing cost-control procedures, changing advertising strategies, building new facilities, training new employees, transferring managers among divisions, and building a better management information system. These types of activities obviously differ greatly between manufacturing, service, and governmental organizations.

Management Perspectives

In all but the smallest organizations, the transition from strategy formulation to strategy implementation requires a shift in responsibility from strategists to divisional and functional managers. Implementation problems can arise because of this shift in responsibility, especially if strategy-formulation decisions come as a surprise to middle- and lower-level managers. Managers and employees are motivated more by perceived self-interests than by organizational interests, unless the two coincide. Therefore, it is essential that divisional and functional managers be involved as much as possible in strategy-formulation activities. Of equal importance, strategists should be involved as much as possible in strategy-implementation activities.

Management issues central to strategy implementation include establishing annual objectives, devising policies, allocating resources, altering an existing organizational structure, restructuring and reengineering, revising reward and incentive plans, minimizing resistance to change, matching managers with strategy, developing a strategy-supportive culture, adapting production/operations processes, developing an effective human resources function, and, if necessary, downsizing. Management changes are necessarily more extensive when strategies to be implemented move a firm in a major new direction.

Managers and employees throughout an organization should participate early and directly in strategy-implementation decisions. Their role in strategy implementation should build upon prior involvement in strategy-formulation activities. Strategists' genuine personal commitment to implementation is a necessary and powerful motivational force for managers and employees. Too often, strategists are too busy to actively support strategy-implementation efforts, and their lack of interest can be detrimental to organizational success. The rationale for objectives and strategies should be understood and clearly communicated throughout an organization. Major competitors' accomplishments, products, plans, actions, and performance should be apparent to all organizational members. Major external opportunities and threats should be clear, and managers' and employees' questions should be answered. Top-down flow of communication is essential for developing bottom-up support.

Firms need to develop a competitor focus at all hierarchical levels by gathering and widely distributing competitive intelligence; every employee should be able to benchmark her or his efforts against best-in-class competitors so that the challenge becomes personal.

This is a challenge for strategists of the firm. Firms should provide training for both managers and employees to ensure that they have and maintain the skills necessary to be world-class performers.

Annual Objectives

Establishing annual objectives is a decentralized activity that directly involves all managers in an organization. Active participation in establishing annual objectives can lead to acceptance and commitment. *Annual objectives* are essential for strategy implementation because they (1) represent the basis for allocating resources; (2) are a primary mechanism

FIGURE 7-2

The Stamus Company's Hierarchy of Aims

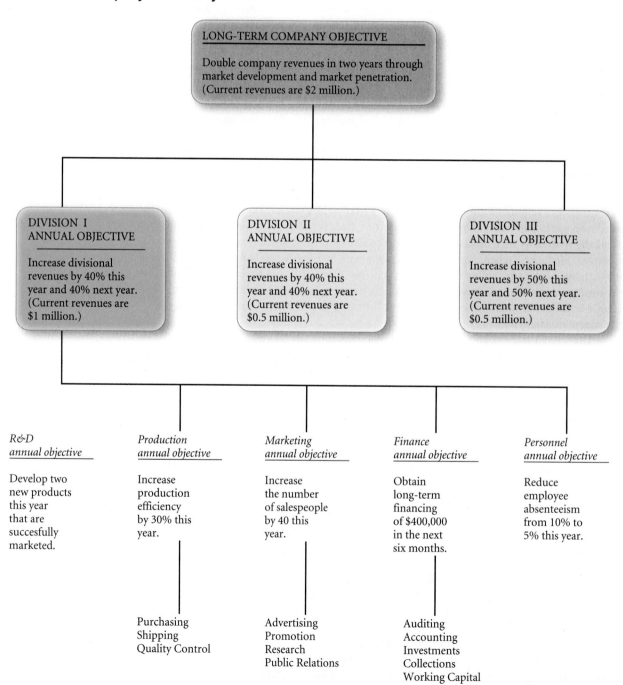

LONG-TERM COMPANY OBJECTIVE

Double company revenues in two years through market development and market penetration. (Current revenues are $2 million.)

DIVISION I ANNUAL OBJECTIVE

Increase divisional revenues by 40% this year and 40% next year. (Current revenues are $1 million.)

DIVISION II ANNUAL OBJECTIVE

Increase divisional revenues by 40% this year and 40% next year. (Current revenues are $0.5 million.)

DIVISION III ANNUAL OBJECTIVE

Increase divisional revenues by 50% this year and 50% next year. (Current revenues are $0.5 million.)

R&D annual objective

Develop two new products this year that are succesfully marketed.

Production annual objective

Increase production efficiency by 30% this year.

Marketing annual objective

Increase the number of salespeople by 40 this year.

Finance annual objective

Obtain long-term financing of $400,000 in the next six months.

Personnel annual objective

Reduce employee absenteeism from 10% to 5% this year.

Purchasing
Shipping
Quality Control

Advertising
Promotion
Research
Public Relations

Auditing
Accounting
Investments
Collections
Working Capital

for evaluating managers; (3) are the major instrument for monitoring progress toward achieving long-term objectives; and (4) establish organizational, divisional, and departmental priorities. Considerable time and effort should be devoted to ensuring that annual objectives are well conceived, consistent with long-term objectives, and supportive of strategies to be implemented. Approving, revising, or rejecting annual objectives is much more than a rubber-stamp activity. The purpose of annual objectives can be summarized as follows:

> Annual objectives serve as guidelines for action, directing and channeling efforts and activities of organization members. They provide a source of legitimacy in an enterprise by justifying activities to stakeholders. They serve as standards of performance. They serve as an important source of employee motivation and identification. They give incentives for managers and employees to perform. They provide a basis for organizational design.[2]

Clearly stated and communicated objectives are critical to success in all types and sizes of firms. Annual objectives, stated in terms of profitability, growth, and market share by business segment, geographic area, customer groups, and product, are common in organizations. Figure 7-2 illustrates how the Stamus Company could establish annual objectives based on long-term objectives. Table 7-1 reveals associated revenue figures that correspond to the objectives outlined in Figure 7-2. Note that, according to plan, the Stamus Company will slightly exceed its long-term objective of doubling company revenues between 2008 and 2009.

Figure 7-2 also reflects how a hierarchy of annual objectives can be established based on an organization's structure. Objectives should be consistent across hierarchical levels and form a network of supportive aims. *Horizontal consistency of objectives* is as important as *vertical consistency of objectives*. For instance, it would not be effective for manufacturing to achieve more than its annual objective of units produced if marketing could not sell the additional units.

Annual objectives should be measurable, consistent, reasonable, challenging, clear, communicated throughout the organization, characterized by an appropriate time dimension, and accompanied by commensurate rewards and sanctions. Too often, objectives are stated in generalities, with little operational usefulness. Annual objectives, such as "to improve communication" or "to improve performance," are not clear, specific, or measurable. Objectives should state quantity, quality, cost, and time—and also be verifiable. Terms and phrases such as *maximize, minimize, as soon as possible,* and *adequate* should be avoided.

Annual objectives should be compatible with employees' and managers' values and should be supported by clearly stated policies. More of something is not always better. Improved quality or reduced cost may, for example, be more important than quantity. It is important to tie rewards and sanctions to annual objectives so that employees and managers understand that achieving objectives is critical to successful strategy implementation. Clear annual objectives do not guarantee successful strategy implementation, but they do increase the likelihood that personal and organizational aims can be accomplished. Overemphasis on achieving objectives can result in undesirable conduct, such as faking the numbers, distorting the records, and letting objectives become ends in themselves. Managers must be alert to these potential problems.

TABLE 7-1 The Stamus Company's Revenue Expectations (In $Euros)

	2008	2009	2010
Division I Revenues	1.0	1.400	1.960
Division II Revenues	0.5	0.700	0.980
Division III Revenues	0.5	0.750	1.125
Total Company Revenues	**2.0**	**2.850**	**4.065**

Policies

Changes in a firm's strategic direction do not occur automatically. On a day-to-day basis, policies are needed to make a strategy work. Policies facilitate solving recurring problems and guide the implementation of strategy. Broadly defined, *policy* refers to specific guidelines, methods, procedures, rules, forms, and administrative practices established to support and encourage work toward stated goals. Policies are instruments for strategy implementation. Policies set boundaries, constraints, and limits on the kinds of administrative actions that can be taken to reward and sanction behavior; they clarify what can and cannot be done in pursuit of an organization's objectives. For example, Carnival's *Paradise* cruise ship has a no smoking policy anywhere, anytime aboard ship. It is the first cruise ship to comprehensively ban smoking. Another example of corporate policy relates to surfing the Web while at work. About 40 percent of companies today do not have a formal policy preventing employees from surfing the Internet, but software is being marketed now that allows firms to monitor how, when, where, and how long various employees use the Internet at work.

Policies let both employees and managers know what is expected of them, thereby increasing the likelihood that strategies will be implemented successfully. They provide a basis for management control, allow coordination across organizational units, and reduce the amount of time managers spend making decisions. Policies also clarify what work is to be done and by whom. They promote delegation of decision making to appropriate managerial levels where various problems usually arise. Many organizations have a policy manual that serves to guide and direct behavior. Wal-Mart has a policy that it calls the "10 Foot" Rule, whereby customers can find assistance within 10 feet of anywhere in the store. This is a welcomed policy in Japan where Wal-Mart is trying to gain a foothold; 58 percent of all retailers in Japan are mom-and-pop stores and consumers historically have had to pay "top yen" rather than "discounted prices" for merchandise.

Policies can apply to all divisions and departments (for example, "We are an equal opportunity employer"). Some policies apply to a single department ("Employees in this department must take at least one training and development course each year"). Whatever their scope and form, policies serve as a mechanism for implementing strategies and obtaining objectives. Policies should be stated in writing whenever possible. They represent the means for carrying out strategic decisions. Examples of policies that support a company strategy, a divisional objective, and a departmental objective are given in Table 7-2.

Some example issues that may require a management policy are as follows:

- To offer extensive or limited management development workshops and seminars
- To centralize or decentralize employee-training activities
- To recruit through employment agencies, college campuses, and/or newspapers
- To promote from within or to hire from the outside
- To promote on the basis of merit or on the basis of seniority
- To tie executive compensation to long-term and/or annual objectives
- To offer numerous or few employee benefits
- To negotiate directly or indirectly with labor unions
- To delegate authority for large expenditures or to centrally retain this authority
- To allow much, some, or no overtime work
- To establish a high- or low-safety stock of inventory
- To use one or more suppliers
- To buy, lease, or rent new production equipment
- To greatly or somewhat stress quality control
- To establish many or only a few production standards
- To operate one, two, or three shifts
- To discourage using insider information for personal gain
- To discourage sexual harassment
- To discourage smoking at work
- To discourage insider trading
- To discourage moonlighting

TABLE 7-2   A Hierarchy of Policies

Company Strategy

Acquire a chain of retail stores to meet our sales growth and profitability objectives.

Supporting Policies

1. "All stores will be open from 8 A.M. to 8 P.M. Monday through Saturday." (This policy could increase retail sales if stores currently are open only 40 hours a week.)

2. "All stores must submit a Monthly Control Data Report." (This policy could reduce expense-to-sales ratios.)

3. "All stores must support company advertising by contributing 5 percent of their total monthly revenues for this purpose." (This policy could allow the company to establish a national reputation.)

4. "All stores must adhere to the uniform pricing guidelines set forth in the Company Handbook." (This policy could help assure customers that the company offers a consistent product in terms of price and quality in all its stores.)

Divisional Objective

Increase the division's revenues from €10 million in 2007 to €15 million in 2008.

Supporting Policies

1. "Beginning in January 2008, each one of this division's salespersons must file a weekly activity report that includes the number of calls made, the number of miles traveled, the number of units sold, the euro volume sold, and the number of new accounts opened." (This policy could ensure that salespersons do not place too great an emphasis in certain areas.)

2. "Beginning in January 2008, this division will return to its employees 5 percent of its gross revenues in the form of a holiday bonus." (This policy could increase employee productivity.)

3. "Beginning in January 2008, inventory levels carried in warehouses will be decreased by 30 percent in accordance with a just-in-time (JIT) manufacturing approach." (This policy could reduce production expenses and thus free funds for increased marketing efforts.)

Production Department Objective

Increase production from 20,000 units in 2007 to 30,000 units in 2008.

Supporting Policies

1. "Beginning in January 2008, employees will have the option of working up to 20 hours of overtime per week." (This policy could minimize the need to hire additional employees.)

2. "Beginning in January 2008, perfect attendance awards in the amount of $100 will be given to all employees who do not miss a workday in a given year." (This policy could decrease absenteeism and increase productivity.)

3. "Beginning in January 2008, new equipment must be leased rather than purchased." (This policy could reduce tax liabilities and thus allow more funds to be invested in modernizing production processes.)

Resource Allocation

Resource allocation is a central management activity that allows for strategy execution. In organizations that do not use a strategic-management approach to decision making, resource allocation is often based on political or personal factors. Strategic management enables resources to be allocated according to priorities established by annual objectives.

Nothing could be more detrimental to strategic management and to organizational success than for resources to be allocated in ways not consistent with priorities indicated by approved annual objectives.

All organizations have at least four types of resources that can be used to achieve desired objectives: financial resources, physical resources, human resources, and technological resources. Allocating resources to particular divisions and departments does not mean that strategies will be successfully implemented. A number of factors commonly prohibit effective resource allocation, including an overprotection of resources, too great an emphasis on short-run financial criteria, organizational politics, vague strategy targets, a reluctance to take risks, and a lack of sufficient knowledge.

Below the corporate level, there often exists an absence of systematic thinking about resources allocated and strategies of the firm. Yavitz and Newman explain why:

> Managers normally have many more tasks than they can do. Managers must allocate time and resources among these tasks. Pressure builds up. Expenses are too high. The CEO wants a good financial report for the third quarter. Strategy formulation

and implementation activities often get deferred. Today's problems soak up available energies and resources. Scrambled accounts and budgets fail to reveal the shift in allocation away from strategic needs to currently squeaking wheels.[3]

The real value of any resource allocation program lies in the resulting accomplishment of an organization's objectives. Effective resource allocation does not guarantee successful strategy implementation because programs, personnel, controls, and commitment must breathe life into the resources provided. Strategic management itself is sometimes referred to as a "resource allocation process."

Managing Conflict

Interdependency of objectives and competition for limited resources often leads to conflict. *Conflict* can be defined as a disagreement between two or more parties on one or more issues. Establishing annual objectives can lead to conflict because individuals have different expectations and perceptions, schedules create pressure, personalities are incompatible, and misunderstandings between line managers (such as production supervisors) and staff managers (such as human resource specialists) occur. For example, a collection manager's objective of reducing bad debts by 50 percent in a given year may conflict with a divisional objective to increase sales by 20 percent.

Establishing objectives can lead to conflict because managers and strategists must make trade-offs, such as whether to emphasize short-term profits or long-term growth, profit margin or market share, market penetration or market development, growth or stability, high risk or low risk, and social responsiveness or profit maximization. Conflict is unavoidable in organizations, so it is important that conflict be managed and resolved before dysfunctional consequences affect organizational performance. Conflict is not always bad. An absence of conflict can signal indifference and apathy. Conflict can serve to energize opposing groups into action and may help managers identify problems.

Various approaches for managing and resolving conflict can be classified into three categories: avoidance, defusion, and confrontation. *Avoidance* includes such actions as ignoring the problem in hopes that the conflict will resolve itself or physically separating the conflicting individuals (or groups). *Defusion* can include playing down differences between conflicting parties while accentuating similarities and common interests, compromising so that there is neither a clear winner nor loser, resorting to majority rule, appealing to a higher authority, or redesigning present positions. *Confrontation* is exemplified by exchanging members of conflicting parties so that each can gain an appreciation of the other's point of view or holding a meeting at which conflicting parties present their views and work through their differences.

Matching Structure with Strategy

VISIT THE NET

Provides software to easily draw organizational charts. You may download the SmartDraw software and use it free for 30 days. (www. smartdraw.com)

Changes in strategy often require changes in the way an organization is structured for two major reasons. First, structure largely dictates how objectives and policies will be established. For example, objectives and policies established under a geographic organizational structure are couched in geographic terms. Objectives and policies are stated largely in terms of products in an organization whose structure is based on product groups. The structural format for developing objectives and policies can significantly impact all other strategy-implementation activities.

The second major reason why changes in strategy often require changes in structure is that structure dictates how resources will be allocated. If an organization's structure is based on customer groups, then resources will be allocated in that manner. Similarly, if an organization's structure is set up along functional business lines, then resources are allocated by functional areas. Unless new or revised strategies place emphasis in the same areas as old strategies, structural reorientation commonly becomes a part of strategy implementation.

Changes in strategy lead to changes in organizational structure. Structure should be designed to facilitate the strategic pursuit of a firm and, therefore, follow strategy. Without a strategy or reasons for being (mission), companies find it difficult to design an effective structure. Chandler found a particular structure sequence to be repeated often as organizations grow and change strategy over time; this sequence is depicted in Figure 7-3.

There is no one optimal organizational design or structure for a given strategy or type of organization. What is appropriate for one organization may not be appropriate for a similar firm, although successful firms in a given industry do tend to organize themselves in a similar way. For example, consumer goods companies tend to emulate the divisional structure-by-product form of organization. Small firms tend to be functionally structured (centralized). Medium-sized firms tend to be divisionally structured (decentralized). Large firms tend to use a strategic business unit (SBU) or matrix structure. As organizations grow, their structures generally change from simple to complex as a result of concatenation, or the linking together of several basic strategies.

Numerous external and internal forces affect an organization; no firm could change its structure in response to every one of these forces, because to do so would lead to chaos. However, when a firm changes its strategy, the existing organizational structure may become ineffective. Symptoms of an ineffective organizational structure include too many levels of management, too many meetings attended by too many people, too much attention being directed toward solving interdepartmental conflicts, too large a span of control, and too many unachieved objectives. Changes in structure can facilitate strategy-implementation efforts, but changes in structure should not be expected to make a bad strategy good, to make bad managers good, or to make bad products sell.

Structure undeniably can and does influence strategy. Strategies formulated must be workable, so if a certain new strategy required massive structural changes it would not be an attractive choice. In this way, structure can shape the choice of strategies. But a more important concern is determining what types of structural changes are needed to implement new strategies and how these changes can best be accomplished. We examine this issue by focusing on seven basic types of organizational structure: functional, divisional by geographic area, divisional by product, divisional by customer, divisional process, strategic business unit (SBU), and matrix.

The Functional Structure

The most widely used structure is the functional or centralized type because this structure is the simplest and least expensive of the seven alternatives. A *functional structure* groups tasks and activities by business function, such as production/operations, marketing, finance/accounting, research and development, and management information systems. A university may structure its activities by major functions that include academic affairs, student services, alumni relations, athletics, maintenance, and accounting. Besides being

VISIT THE NET

Lists some items that strategy implementation must include. (www.csuchico.edu/mgmt/ strategy/module1/sld045.htm)

FIGURE 7-3

Chandler's Strategy-Structure Relationship

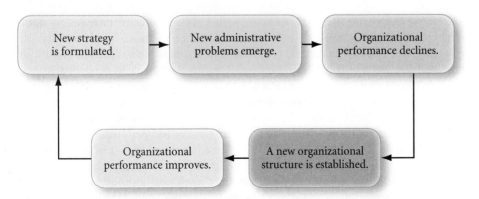

Source: Adapted from Alfred Chandler, *Strategy and Structure* (Cambridge, MA: MIT Press, 1962).

simple and inexpensive, a functional structure also promotes specialization of labor, encourages efficient use of managerial and technical talent, minimizes the need for an elaborate control system, and allows rapid decision making.

Some disadvantages of a functional structure are that it forces accountability to the top, minimizes career development opportunities, and is sometimes characterized by low employee morale, line/staff conflicts, poor delegation of authority, and inadequate planning for products and markets.

A functional structure often leads to short-term and narrow thinking that may undermine what is best for the firm as a whole. For example, the research and development department may strive to overdesign products and components to achieve technical elegance, while manufacturing may argue for low-frills products that can be mass produced more easily. Thus, communication is often not as good in a functional structure. Schein gives an example of a communication problem in a functional structure:

> The word "marketing" will mean product development to the engineer, studying customers through market research to the product manager, merchandising to the salesperson, and constant change in design to the manufacturing manager. Then when these managers try to work together, they often attribute disagreements to personalities and fail to notice the deeper, shared assumptions that vary and dictate how each function thinks.[4]

Most large companies have abandoned the functional structure in favor of decentralization and improved accountability. However, two large firms that still successfully use a functional structure are Nucor Steel and Sharp, the $17 billion consumer electronics firm.

The Divisional Structure

The *divisional* or *decentralized structure* is the second most common type used by U.S. businesses. As a small organization grows, it has more difficulty managing different products and services in different markets. Some form of divisional structure generally becomes necessary to motivate employees, control operations, and compete successfully in diverse locations. The divisional structure can be organized in one of four ways: *by geographic area*, *by product* or *service*, *by customer*, or *by process*. With a divisional structure, functional activities are performed both centrally and in each separate division.

Cisco Systems recently discarded its divisional structure by customer and reorganized into a functional structure. CEO John Chambers replaced the three-customer structure based on big businesses, small businesses, and telecoms, and now the company has centralized its engineering and marketing units so that they focus on technologies such as wireless networks. Chambers says the goal was to eliminate duplication, but the change should not be viewed as a shift in strategy. Chambers's span of control in the new structure is reduced from 15 to 12 managers reporting directly to him. He continues to operate Cisco without a chief operating officer or a number-two executive.

Sun Microsystems recently reduced the number of its business units from seven to four. Kodak recently reduced its number of business units from seven by-customer divisions to five by-product divisions. As consumption patterns become increasingly similar worldwide, a by-product structure is becoming more effective than a by-customer or a by-geographic type divisional structure. In the restructuring, Kodak eliminated its global operations division and distributed those responsibilities across the new by-product divisions.

A divisional structure has some clear advantages. First and perhaps foremost, accountability is clear. That is, divisional managers can be held responsible for sales and profit levels. Because a divisional structure is based on extensive delegation of authority, managers and employees can easily see the results of their good or bad performances. As a result, employee morale is generally higher in a divisional structure than it is in a centralized structure. Other advantages of the divisional design are that it creates career development opportunities for managers, allows local control of situations, leads to a competitive climate within an organization, and allows new businesses and products to be added easily.

The divisional design is not without some limitations, however. Perhaps the most important limitation is that a divisional structure is costly, for a number of reasons. First, each division requires functional specialists who must be paid. Second, there exists some duplication of staff services, facilities, and personnel; for instance, functional specialists are also needed centrally (at headquarters) to coordinate divisional activities. Third, managers must be well qualified because the divisional design forces delegation of authority; better-qualified individuals require higher salaries. A divisional structure can also be costly because it requires an elaborate, headquarters-driven control system. Fourth, competition between divisions may become so intense that it is dysfunctional and leads to limited sharing of ideas and resources for the common good of the firm. Ghoshal and Bartlett, two leading scholars in strategic management, note the following:

> As their label clearly warns, divisions divide. The divisional model fragments companies' resources; it creates vertical communication channels that insulate business units and prevents them from sharing their strengths with one another. Consequently, the whole of the corporation is often less than the sum of its parts. A final limitation of the divisional design is that certain regions, products, or customers may sometimes receive special treatment, and it may be difficult to maintain consistent, companywide practices. Nonetheless, for most large organizations and many small firms, the advantages of a divisional structure more than offset the potential limitations.[5]

A *divisional structure by geographic area* is appropriate for organizations whose strategies need to be tailored to fit the particular needs and characteristics of customers in different geographic areas. This type of structure can be most appropriate for organizations that have similar branch facilities located in widely dispersed areas. A divisional structure by geographic area allows local participation in decision making and improved coordination within a region. Hershey Foods is an example of a company organized using the divisional by geographic region type of structure. Hershey's divisions are United States, Canada, Mexico, Brazil, and Other. Analysts contend that this type of structure may not be best for Hershey because consumption patterns for candy are quite similar worldwide. An alternative—and perhaps better—type of structure for Hershey would be divisional by product because the company produces and sells three types of products worldwide: (1) chocolate, (2) nonchocolate, and (3) grocery.

The *divisional structure by product (or services)* is most effective for implementing strategies when specific products or services need special emphasis. Also, this type of structure is widely used when an organization offers only a few products or services or when an organization's products or services differ substantially. The divisional structure allows strict control over and attention to product lines, but it may also require a more skilled management force and reduced top management control. General Motors, DuPont, and Procter & Gamble use a divisional structure by product to implement strategies. Huffy, the largest bicycle company in the world, is another firm that is highly decentralized based on a divisional-by-product structure. Huffy's divisions are the Bicycle division, the Gerry Baby Products division, the Huffy Sports division, YLC Enterprises, and Washington Inventory Service. Harry Shaw, Huffy's chairman, believes decentralization is one of the keys to Huffy's success.

Eastman Chemical established a new by-product divisional organizational structure. The company's two new divisions, Eastman Company and Voridian Company, focus on chemicals and polymers, respectively. The Eastman division focuses on coatings, adhesives, inks, and plastics, whereas the Voridian division focuses on fibers, polyethylene, and other polymers. Microsoft recently reorganized the whole corporation into three large divisions-by-product. Headed by a president, the new divisions are (1) platform products and services, (2) business, and (3) entertainment and devices. The Swiss electrical-engineering company ABB Ltd. recently scrapped its two core divisions, (1) power technologies and (2) automation technologies, and replaced them with five new divisions: (1) power products, (2) power systems, (3) automation products, (4) process automation, and (5) robotics.

When a few major customers are of paramount importance and many different services are provided to these customers, then a *divisional structure by customer* can be the most effective way to implement strategies. This structure allows an organization to cater effectively to the requirements of clearly defined customer groups. For example, book publishing companies often organize their activities around customer groups, such as colleges, secondary schools, and private commercial schools. Some airline companies have two major customer divisions: passengers and freight or cargo services. Merrill Lynch is organized into separate divisions that cater to different groups of customers, including wealthy individuals, institutional investors, and small corporations. Motorola's semiconductor chip division is also organized divisionally by customer, having three separate segments that sell to (1) the automotive and industrial market, (2) the mobile phone market, and (3) the data-networking market. The automotive and industrial segment is doing well, but the other two segments are faltering, which is a reason why Motorola is trying to divest its semiconductor operations.

A *divisional structure by process* is similar to a functional structure, because activities are organized according to the way work is actually performed. However, a key difference between these two designs is that functional departments are not accountable for profits or revenues, whereas divisional process departments are evaluated on these criteria. An example of a divisional structure by process is a manufacturing business organized into six divisions: electrical work, glass cutting, welding, grinding, painting, and foundry work. In this case, all operations related to these specific processes would be grouped under the separate divisions. Each process (division) would be responsible for generating revenues and profits. The divisional structure by process can be particularly effective in achieving objectives when distinct production processes represent the thrust of competitiveness in an industry.

The Strategic Business Unit (SBU) Structure

As the number, size, and diversity of divisions in an organization increase, controlling and evaluating divisional operations become increasingly difficult for strategists. Increases in sales often are not accompanied by similar increases in profitability. The span of control becomes too large at top levels of the firm. For example, in a large conglomerate organization composed of 90 divisions, such as ConAgra, the chief executive officer could have difficulty even remembering the first names of divisional presidents. In multidivisional organizations, an SBU structure can greatly facilitate strategy-implementation efforts. ConAgra has put its many divisions into three primary SBUs: (1) food service (restaurants), (2) retail (grocery stores), and (3) agricultural products.

The SBU structure groups similar divisions into strategic business units and delegates authority and responsibility for each unit to a senior executive who reports directly to the chief executive officer. This change in structure can facilitate strategy implementation by improving coordination between similar divisions and channeling accountability to distinct business units. In a 100-division conglomerate, the divisions could perhaps be regrouped into 10 SBUs according to certain common characteristics, such as competing in the same industry, being located in the same area, or having the same customers.

Two disadvantages of an SBU structure are that it requires an additional layer of management, which increases salary expenses. Also, the role of the group vice president is often ambiguous. However, these limitations often do not outweigh the advantages of improved coordination and accountability. Another advantage of the SBU structure is that it makes the tasks of planning and control by the corporate office more manageable.

Honeywell International reorganized its aerospace division in 2005 from a products-based structure based on engines, electronics, wheels, brakes, and so on to three strategic business units: (1) air transport and regional transport, (2) business and general aviation, and (3) defense and space. Honeywell is not shedding any businesses in this reorganization. The firm wants to simplify its interactions with customers by reducing the number of layers in its organization. Atlantic Richfield and Fairchild Industries are examples of firms that successfully use an SBU-type structure.

As illustrated in Figure 7-4, Sonoco Products Corporation, which operates petroleum and crude oil pipelines and refines and markets gasoline, motor oils, lubricants, and petrochemicals, utilizes an SBU organizational structure. Note that Sonoco's SBUs—Industrial Products and Consumer Products—each have four autonomous divisions that have their own sales, manufacturing, R&D, finance, HRM, and MIS functions.

The Matrix Structure

A *matrix structure* is the most complex of all designs because it depends upon both vertical and horizontal flows of authority and communication (hence the term *matrix*). In contrast, functional and divisional structures depend primarily on vertical flows of authority and communication. A matrix structure can result in higher overhead because it creates more management positions. Other disadvantages of a matrix structure that contribute to overall complexity include dual lines of budget authority (a violation of the unity-of-command principle), dual sources of reward and punishment, shared authority, dual reporting channels, and a need for an extensive and effective communication system.

Despite its complexity, the matrix structure is widely used in many industries, including construction, health care, research, and defense. Some advantages of a matrix structure are that project objectives are clear, there are many channels of communication, workers can see the visible results of their work, and shutting down a project can be accomplished relatively easily. Another advantage of a matrix structure is that it facilitates the use of specialized personnel, equipment, and facilities. Functional resources are shared in a matrix structure, rather than duplicated as in a divisional structure. Individuals with a high degree of expertise can divide their time as needed among projects, and they in turn develop their own skills and competencies more than in other structures. Walt Disney Corp. relies on a matrix structure.

A typical matrix structure is illustrated in Figure 7-5. Note that the letters (A through Z[4]) refer to managers. For example, if you were manager A, you would be responsible for financial aspects of Project 1, and you would have two bosses: the Project 1 Manager on site and the CFO off site.

For a matrix structure to be effective, organizations need participative planning, training, clear mutual understanding of roles and responsibilities, excellent internal communication, and mutual trust and confidence. The matrix structure is being used more frequently by U.S. businesses because firms are pursuing strategies that add new products, customer groups, and technology to their range of activities. Out of these changes are coming

FIGURE 7-4

Sonoco Products' SBU Organizational Chart

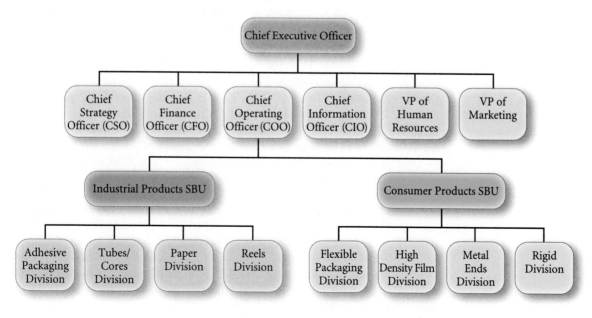

FIGURE 7-5

An Example Matrix Structure

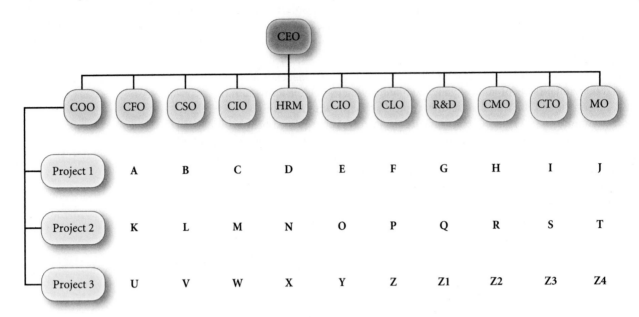

Notes: Titles spelled out as follows.

Chief Executive Officer (CEO)
Chief Finance Officer (CFO)
Chief Strategy Officer (CSO)
Chief Information Officer (CIO)
Human Resources Manager (HRM)
Chief Operating Officer (COO)
Chief Legal Officer (CLO)
Research & Development Officer (R&D)
Chief Marketing Officer (CMO)
Chief Technology Officer (CTO)
Competitive Intelligence Officer (CIO)
Maintenance Officer (MO)

product managers, functional managers, and geographic-area managers, all of whom have important strategic responsibilities. When several variables, such as product, customer, technology, geography, functional area, and line of business, have roughly equal strategic priorities, a matrix organization can be an effective structural form.

Some Do's and Don'ts in Developing Organizational Charts

Students analyzing strategic management cases are often asked to revise and develop a firm's organizational structure. This section provides some basic guidelines for this endeavor. There are some basic do's and don'ts in regard to devising or constructing organizational charts, especially for midsize to large firms. First of all, reserve the title CEO for the top executive of the firm. Don't use the title "president" for the top person; use it for the division top managers if there are divisions within the firm. Also, do not use the title "president" for functional business executives. They should have the title "chief," or "vice president," or "manager," or "officer," such as "Chief Information Officer," or "VP of Human Resources." Further, do not recommend a dual title (such as "CEO and president") for just one executive. The chairman of the board and CEO of Bristol-Myers Squibb, Peter Dolan, recently gave up his title as chairman. However, Pfizer's CEO, Jeffrey Kindler, recently added chairman of the board to his title when he succeeded Hank McKinnell as chairman of Pfizer's board. And Comverse Technology recently named Andre Dahan as its president, chief executive officer, and board director. Actually, "chairperson" is much better than "chairman" for this title.

Directly below the CEO, it is best to have a COO (chief operating officer) with any division presidents reporting directly to the COO. On the same level as the COO and also reporting to the CEO, draw in your functional business executives, such as a CFO (chief financial officer), VP of human resources, a CSO (chief strategy officer), a CIO (chief information officer), a CMO (chief marketing Officer), a VP of R&D, a VP of legal affairs, an investment relations officer, maintenance officer, and so on. Note in Figure 7-6 that these positions are labeled and placed appropriately. Note that a controller and/or treasurer would normally report to the CFO.

In developing an organizational chart, avoid having a particular person reporting to more than one person above in the chain of command. This would violate the unity-of-command principle of management that "every employee should have just one boss." Also, do not have the CFO, CIO, CSO, human resource officer, or other functional positions report to the COO. All these positions report directly to the CEO.

A key consideration in devising an organizational structure concerns the divisions. Note whether the divisions (if any) of a firm presently are established based upon geography, customer, product, or process. If the firm's organizational chart is not available, you often can devise a chart based on the titles of executives. An important case analysis activity is for you to decide how the divisions of a firm should be organized for maximum effectiveness. Even if the firm presently has no divisions, determine whether the firm would operate better with divisions. In other words, which type of divisional breakdown do you (or your group or team) feel would be best for the firm in allocating resources, establishing objectives, and devising compensation incentives? This important strategic decision faces many midsize and large firms (and teams of students analyzing a strategic-management case). As consumption patterns become more and more similar worldwide, the divisional-by-product form of structure is increasingly the most effective. Be mindful that all firms

FIGURE 7-6

Typical Top Managers of a Large Firm

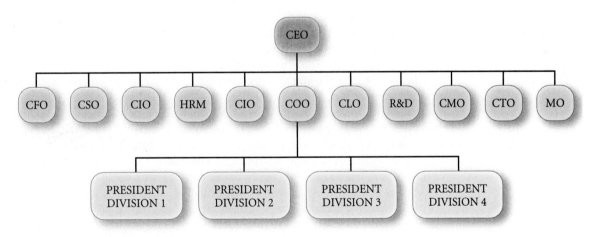

Notes: Titles spelled out as follows.

Chief Executive Officer (CEO)
Chief Finance Officer (CFO)
Chief Strategy Officer (CSO)
Chief Information Officer (CIO)
Human Resources Manager (HRM)
Chief Operating Officer (COO)
Chief Legal Officer (CLO)
Research & Development Officer (R&D)
Chief Marketing Officer (CMO)
Chief Technology Officer (CTO)
Competitive Intelligence Officer (CIO)
Maintenance Officer (MO)

have functional staff below their top executive and often readily provide this information, so be wary of concluding prematurely that a particular firm utilizes a functional structure. If you see the word "president" in the titles of executives, coupled with financial-reporting segments, such as by product or geographic region, then the firm is divisionally structured.

If the firm is large with numerous divisions, decide whether an SBU type of structure would be more appropriate to reduce the span of control reporting to the COO. Note in Figure 7-4 that the Sonoco Products' strategic business units (SBUs) are based on product groupings. An alternative SBU structure would have been to base the division groupings on location. One never knows for sure if a proposed or actual structure is indeed most effective for a particular firm. Note from Chandler's strategy-structure relationship illustrated previously in this chapter that declining financial performance signals a need for altering the structure.

Restructuring, Reengineering, and E-Engineering

Restructuring and reengineering are becoming commonplace on the corporate landscape across the United States and Europe. *Restructuring*—also called *downsizing*, *rightsizing*, or *delayering*—involves reducing the size of the firm in terms of number of employees, number of divisions or units, and number of hierarchical levels in the firm's organizational structure. This reduction in size is intended to improve both efficiency and effectiveness. Restructuring is concerned primarily with shareholder well-being rather than employee well-being.

Recessionary economic conditions have forced many European companies to downsize, laying off managers and employees. This was almost unheard of prior to the mid-1990s because European labor unions and laws required lengthy negotiations or huge severance checks before workers could be terminated. In contrast to the United States, labor union executives of large European firms sit on most boards of directors.

Job security in European companies is slowly moving toward a U.S. scenario, in which firms lay off almost at will. From banks in Milan to factories in Mannheim, European employers are starting to show people the door in an effort to streamline operations, increase efficiency, and compete against already slim and trim U.S. firms. Massive U.S.-style layoffs are still rare in Europe, but unemployment rates throughout the continent are rising quite rapidly. European firms still prefer to downsize by attrition and retirement rather than by blanket layoffs because of culture, laws, and unions.

In contrast, *reengineering* is concerned more with employee and customer well-being than shareholder well-being. Reengineering—also called process management, process innovation, or process redesign—involves reconfiguring or redesigning work, jobs, and processes for the purpose of improving cost, quality, service, and speed. Reengineering does not usually affect the organizational structure or chart, nor does it imply job loss or employee layoffs. Whereas restructuring is concerned with eliminating or establishing, shrinking or enlarging, and moving organizational departments and divisions, the focus of reengineering is changing the way work is actually carried out.

Reengineering is characterized by many tactical (short-term, business-function-specific) decisions, whereas restructuring is characterized by strategic (long-term, affecting all business functions) decisions. Developed by Motorola in 1986 and made famous by CEO Jack Welch at General Electric and more recently by Robert Nardelli, former CEO of Home Depot, *Six Sigma* is a quality-boosting process improvement technique that entails training several key persons in the firm in the techniques to monitor, measure, and improve processes and eliminate defects. Six Sigma has been widely applied across industries from retailing to financial services. CEO Dave Cote at Honeywell and CEO Jeff Immelt at General Electric spurred acceptance of Six Sigma, which aims to improve work processes and eliminate waste by training "select" employees who are given judo titles such as Master Black Belts, Black Belts, and Green Belts.

Six Sigma has been criticized in a recent *Wall Street Journal* article that cited many example firms whose stock price fell for a number of years after adoption of Six Sigma. The technique's reliance on the special group of trained employees is problematic and its use within retail firms such as Home Depot has not been as successful as in manufacturing firms.[6]

The Internet is ushering in a new wave of business transformation. No longer is it enough for companies to put up simple Web sites for customers and employees. To take full advantage of the Internet, companies must change the way they distribute goods, deal with suppliers, attract customers, and serve customers. The Internet eliminates the geographic protection/monopoly of local businesses. Basically, companies must reinvent the way they do business to take full advantage of the Internet. This whole process is being called e-engineering.[7] Dow Corning Corporation and many others have recently appointed an e-commerce top executive.

Restructuring

Firms often employ restructuring when various ratios appear out of line with competitors as determined through benchmarking exercises. Recall that *benchmarking* simply involves comparing a firm against the best firms in the industry on a wide variety of performance-related criteria. Some benchmarking ratios commonly used in rationalizing the need for restructuring are headcount-to-sales-volume, or corporate-staff-to-operating-employees, or span-of-control figures.

The primary benefit sought from restructuring is cost reduction. For some highly bureaucratic firms, restructuring can actually rescue the firm from global competition and demise. But the downside of restructuring can be reduced employee commitment, creativity, and innovation that accompanies the uncertainty and trauma associated with pending and actual employee layoffs. During 2007, Hershey Company, headquartered in Hershey, Pennsylvania, announced a three-year restructuring plan that includes 1,500 job cuts, closing certain production lines, outsourcing more activities, and building a production plant in Mexico. Hershey's financial performance of late has failed to meet Wall Street expectations.

Parent company European Aeronautic Defence & Space Company in Paris has approved a restructuring plan named Power8 for the beleaguered Airbus aircraft company. Airbus in 2007 continued to struggle to compete against rival Boeing and as part of its restructuring is cutting jobs and closing factories. But France and Germany are arguing on the best way to restructure because both countries are key underwriters of Airbus.

Another downside of restructuring is that many people today do not aspire to become managers, and many present-day managers are trying to get off the management track.[8] Sentiment against joining management ranks is higher today than ever. About 80 percent of employees say they want nothing to do with management, a major shift from just a decade ago when 60 to 70 percent hoped to become managers. Managing others historically led to enhanced career mobility, financial rewards, and executive perks; but in today's global, more competitive, restructured arena, managerial jobs demand more hours and headaches with fewer financial rewards. Managers today manage more people spread over different locations, travel more, manage diverse functions, and are change agents even when they have nothing to do with the creation of the plan or disagree with its approach. Employers today are looking for people who can do things, not for people who make other people do things. Restructuring in many firms has made a manager's job an invisible, thankless role. More workers today are self-managed, entrepreneurs, interpreneurs, or team-managed. Managers today need to be counselors, motivators, financial advisors, and psychologists. They also run the risk of becoming technologically behind in their areas of expertise. "Dilbert" cartoons commonly portray managers as enemies or as morons.

It is interesting to note that laying off employees in France is almost impossible due to labor laws that require lengthy negotiations and expensive severance packages for any individuals who are laid off. French CEOs feel that the strict layoff policies are crippling France's economy and companies. This is true because other European countries, such as Germany, have recently made it much easier for companies to lay off employees to stay competitive—and indeed to survive. Moulinex is an example of a French company that recently tried to lay off 670 employees but was denied this option, so the firm fell into bankruptcy and possible liquidation.

Reengineering

The argument for a firm engaging in reengineering usually goes as follows: Many companies historically have been organized vertically by business function. This arrangement has led over time to managers' and employees' mind-sets being defined by their particular functions rather than by overall customer service, product quality, or corporate performance. The logic is that all firms tend to bureaucratize over time. As routines become entrenched, turf becomes delineated and defended, and politics takes precedence over performance. Walls that exist in the physical workplace can be reflections of "mental" walls.

In reengineering, a firm uses information technology to break down functional barriers and create a work system based on business processes, products, or outputs rather than on functions or inputs. Cornerstones of reengineering are decentralization, reciprocal interdependence, and information sharing. A firm that exemplifies complete information sharing is Springfield Remanufacturing Corporation, which provides to all employees a weekly income statement of the firm, as well as extensive information on other companies' performances.

The *Wall Street Journal* noted that reengineering today must go beyond knocking down internal walls that keep parts of a company from cooperating effectively; it must also knock down the external walls that prohibit or discourage cooperation with other firms— even rival firms.[9] A maker of disposable diapers echoes this need differently when it says that to be successful "cooperation at the firm must stretch from stump to rump."

Hewlett-Packard is a good example of a company that has knocked down the external barriers to cooperation and practices modern reengineering. The HP of today shares its forecasts with all of its supply-chain partners and shares other critical information with its distributors and other stakeholders. HP does all the buying of resin for its many manufacturers, giving it a volume discount of up to 5 percent. HP has established many alliances and cooperative agreements of the kind discussed in Chapter 5.

A benefit of reengineering is that it offers employees the opportunity to see more clearly how their particular jobs affect the final product or service being marketed by the firm. However, reengineering can also raise manager and employee anxiety, which, unless calmed, can lead to corporate trauma.

Linking Performance and Pay to Strategies

Most companies today are practicing some form of pay-for-performance for employees and managers other than top executives. New research suggests that companies gave annual pay raises for 2007 of 3.7 percent, but performance-based pay raises and incentive bonuses are rapidly gaining in popularity.[10] About 80 percent of all companies now offer some type of bonus plan, which provides companies the flexibility to rein in costs during tight years but to share profits during abundant years. Companies are also increasingly segmenting employees based on their performance rather than job function as firms seek to attract and keep the best employees.

Staff control of pay systems often prevents line managers from using financial compensation as a strategic tool. Flexibility regarding managerial and employee compensation is needed to allow short-term shifts in compensation that can stimulate efforts to achieve long-term objectives.

How can an organization's reward system be more closely linked to strategic performance? How can decisions on salary increases, promotions, merit pay, and bonuses be more closely aligned to support the long-term strategic objectives of the organization? There are no widely accepted answers to these questions, but a dual bonus system based on both annual objectives and long-term objectives is becoming common. The percentage of a manager's annual bonus attributable to short-term versus long-term results should vary by hierarchical level in the organization. A chief executive officer's annual bonus could, for example, be determined on a 75 percent short-term and 25 percent long-term basis. It is important that bonuses not be based solely on short-term results because such a system ignores long-term company strategies and objectives.

Wal-Mart Stores in 2007 revamped its bonus program for hourly employees as the firm began paying bonuses based on sales, profit, and inventory performance at individual stores on a quarterly, rather than annual, basis. The average full-time employee at Wal-Mart in the United States is paid $10.51 per hour, but this is significantly below the $17.46 average paid to rival Costco Wholesale Corp.'s employees.[11]

Aflac, Inc. in early 2007 became the first company to give investors a nonbinding vote on executive pay starting in 2009. Shareholders at numerous other companies including Verizon, Bank of New York, and Morgan Stanley are demanding a say-so in regard to executive pay. The U.S. House of Representatives recently passed a bill to formalize this shareholder tactic, which is gaining steam across the country as a means to combat exorbitant executive pay. For example, Verizon's CEO Ivan Seidenberg's total compensation in 2006 was $21.3 million.

In an effort to cut costs and increase productivity, more and more Japanese companies are switching from seniority-based pay to performance-based approaches. Toyota has switched to a full merit system for 20,000 of its 70,000 white-collar workers. Fujitsu, Sony, Matsushita Electric Industrial, and Kao also have switched to merit pay systems. This switching is hurting morale at some Japanese companies, which have trained workers for decades to cooperate rather than to compete and to work in groups rather than individually.

Richard Brown, CEO of Electronic Data Systems (EDS), recently removed the bottom 20 percent of EDS's sales force and said,

> You have to start with an appraisal system that gives genuine feedback and differentiates performance. Some call it ranking people. That seems a little harsh. But you can't have a manager checking a box that says you're either stupendous, magnificent, very good, good, or average. Concise, constructive feedback is the fuel workers use to get better. A company that doesn't differentiate performance risks losing its best people.[12]

Profit sharing is another widely used form of incentive compensation. More than 30 percent of U.S. companies have profit sharing plans, but critics emphasize that too many factors affect profits for this to be a good criterion. Taxes, pricing, or an acquisition would wipe out profits, for example. Also, firms try to minimize profits in a sense to reduce taxes.

Still another criterion widely used to link performance and pay to strategies is gain sharing. *Gain sharing* requires employees or departments to establish performance targets; if actual results exceed objectives, all members get bonuses. More than 26 percent of U.S. companies use some form of gain sharing; about 75 percent of gain sharing plans have been adopted since 1980. Carrier, a subsidiary of United Technologies, has had excellent success with gain sharing in its six plants in New York; Firestone's tire plant in the U.S. state of North Carolina has experienced similar success with gain sharing.

Criteria such as sales, profit, production efficiency, quality, and safety could also serve as bases for an effective *bonus system.* If an organization meets certain understood, agreed-upon profit objectives, every member of the enterprise should share in the harvest. A bonus system can be an effective tool for motivating individuals to support strategy-implementation efforts. BankAmerica, for example, recently overhauled its incentive system to link pay to sales of the bank's most profitable products and services. Branch managers receive a base salary plus a bonus based both on the number of new customers and on sales of bank products. Every employee in each branch is also eligible for a bonus if the branch exceeds its goals. Thomas Peterson, a top BankAmerica executive, says, "We want to make people responsible for meeting their goals, so we pay incentives on sales, not on controlling costs or on being sure the parking lot is swept."

Five tests are often used to determine whether a performance-pay plan will benefit an organization:

1. ***Does the plan capture attention?*** Are people talking more about their activities and taking pride in early successes under the plan?
2. ***Do employees understand the plan?*** Can participants explain how it works and what they need to do to earn the incentive?

3. *Is the plan improving communication?* Do employees know more than they used to about the company's mission, plans, and objectives?
4. *Does the plan pay out when it should?* Are incentives being paid for desired results—and being withheld when objectives are not met?
5. *Is the company or unit performing better?* Are profits up? Has market share grown? Have gains resulted in part from the incentives?[13]

In addition to a dual bonus system, a combination of reward strategy incentives, such as salary raises, stock options, fringe benefits, promotions, praise, recognition, criticism, fear, increased job autonomy, and awards, can be used to encourage managers and employees to push hard for successful strategic implementation. The range of options for getting people, departments, and divisions to actively support strategy-implementation activities in a particular organization is almost limitless. Merck, for example, recently gave each of its 37,000 employees a 10-year option to buy 100 shares of Merck stock at a set price of $127. Steven Darien, Merck's vice president of human resources, says, "We needed to find ways to get everyone in the workforce on board in terms of our goals and objectives. Company executives will begin meeting with all Merck workers to explore ways in which employees can contribute more."

Increasing criticism aimed at chief executive officers for their high pay has resulted in executive compensation being linked more closely than ever before to performance of their firms. Although the linkage between CEO pay and corporate performance is getting closer, CEO pay still can be astronomical. However, CEO Gerald Grinstein of Delta Airlines in 2007 agreed to accept no stock or cash bonus when his firm emerged from bankruptcy to be the second-largest U.S. airline in stock-market value, behind Southwest Airlines. In contrast among large U.S. banks, CEO Kenneth Lewis of Bank of America received pay of $27.9 million in 2006, CEO Charles Prince of Citigroup received $26 million, and CEO Kennedy Thompson of Wachovia received $23.8 million. But Yahoo's CEO Terry Semel made $71.7 million in 2006 and was the highest paid CEO, followed by XTO Energy CEO Bob Simpson, who made $59.5 million, and Occidental Petroleum CEO Ray Irani, who made $52.8 million.

Managing Resistance to Change

No organization or individual can escape change. But the thought of change raises anxieties because people fear economic loss, inconvenience, uncertainty, and a break in normal social patterns. Almost any change in structure, technology, people, or strategies has the potential to disrupt comfortable interaction patterns. For this reason, people resist change. The strategic-management process itself can impose major changes on individuals and processes. Reorienting an organization to get people to think and act strategically is not an easy task.

Resistance to change can be considered the single greatest threat to successful strategy implementation. Resistance regularly occurs in organizations in the form of sabotaging production machines, absenteeism, filing unfounded grievances, and an unwillingness to cooperate. People often resist strategy implementation because they do not understand what is happening or why changes are taking place. In that case, employees may simply need accurate information. Successful strategy implementation hinges upon managers' ability to develop an organizational climate conducive to change. Change must be viewed as an opportunity rather than as a threat by managers and employees.

Resistance to change can emerge at any stage or level of the strategy-implementation process. Although there are various approaches for implementing changes, three commonly used strategies are a force change strategy, an educative change strategy, and a rational or self-interest change strategy. A *force change strategy* involves giving orders and enforcing those orders; this strategy has the advantage of being fast, but it is plagued by low commitment and high resistance. The *educative change strategy* is one that presents information to convince people of the need for change; the disadvantage of an educative change strategy is that implementation becomes slow and difficult. However, this type of strategy evokes greater commitment and less resistance than does the force change strategy.

Finally, a *rational* or *self-interest change strategy* is one that attempts to convince individuals that the change is to their personal advantage. When this appeal is successful, strategy implementation can be relatively easy. However, implementation changes are seldom to everyone's advantage.

The rational change strategy is the most desirable, so this approach is examined a bit further. Managers can improve the likelihood of successfully implementing change by carefully designing change efforts. Jack Duncan described a rational or self-interest change strategy as consisting of four steps. First, employees are invited to participate in the process of change and in the details of transition; participation allows everyone to give opinions, to feel a part of the change process, and to identify their own self-interests regarding the recommended change. Second, some motivation or incentive to change is required; self-interest can be the most important motivator. Third, communication is needed so that people can understand the purpose for the changes. Giving and receiving feedback is the fourth step: everyone enjoys knowing how things are going and how much progress is being made.[14]

Igor Ansoff summarized the need for strategists to manage resistance to change as follows:

> Observation of the historical transitions from one orientation to another shows that, if left unmanaged, the process becomes conflict-laden, prolonged, and costly in both human and financial terms. Management of resistance involves anticipating the focus of resistance and its intensity. Second, it involves eliminating unnecessary resistance caused by misperceptions and insecurities. Third, it involves mustering the power base necessary to assure support for the change. Fourth, it involves planning the process of change. Finally, it involves monitoring and controlling resistance during the process of change.[15]

Because of diverse external and internal forces, change is a fact of life in organizations. The rate, speed, magnitude, and direction of changes vary over time by industry and organization. Strategists should strive to create a work environment in which change is recognized as necessary and beneficial so that individuals can more easily adapt to change. Adopting a strategic-management approach to decision making can itself require major changes in the philosophy and operations of a firm.

Strategists can take a number of positive actions to minimize managers' and employees' resistance to change. For example, individuals who will be affected by a change should be involved in the decision to make the change and in decisions about how to implement the change. Strategists should anticipate changes and develop and offer training and development workshops so that managers and employees can adapt to those changes. They also need to effectively communicate the need for changes. The strategic-management process can be described as a process of managing change. Robert Waterman describes how successful organizations involve individuals to facilitate change:

> Implementation starts with, not after, the decision. When Ford Motor Company embarked on the program to build the highly successful Taurus, management gave up the usual, sequential design process. Instead it showed the tentative design to the workforce and asked its help in devising a car that would be easy to build. Team Taurus came up with no less than 1,401 items suggested by Ford employees. What a contrast from the secrecy that characterized the industry before. When people are treated as the main engine rather than interchangeable parts, motivation, creativity, quality, and commitment to implementation go up.[16]

Organizational change should be viewed today as a continuous process rather than as a project or event. The most successful organizations today continuously adapt to changes in the competitive environment, which themselves continue to change at an accelerating rate. It is not sufficient today to simply react to change. Managers need to anticipate change and ideally be the creator of change. Viewing change as a continuous process is in stark contrast to an old management doctrine regarding change, which was to unfreeze behavior, change the behavior, and then refreeze the new behavior. The new "continuous organizational change" philosophy should mirror the popular "continuous quality improvement philosophy."

Managing the Natural Environment

All business functions are affected by natural environment considerations or by striving to make a profit. However, both employees and consumers are especially resentful of firms that take from more than give to the natural environment; likewise, people today are especially appreciative of firms that conduct operations in a way that mend rather than harm the environment. But a rapidly increasing number of companies are implementing tougher environmental regulation because it makes economic sense. General Electric, for example, plans to achieve $20 billion in sales by 2010 in eco-friendly technologies that include cleaner coal-fired power plants, a diesel-and-electric hybrid locomotive, and agricultural silicon that cuts the amount of water and pesticide used in spraying fields. This is double GE's sales today in "green" products.[17] GE has a goal to improve its energy efficiency by 30 percent between 2005 and 2012.

Earth itself has become a stakeholder for all business firms. Consumer interest in businesses preserving nature's ecological balance and fostering a clean, healthy environment is high. As indicated in the "Natural Environment Perspective," an increasing number of businesses today are considering the amount of formal training in environmental matters that prospective managers have received.

The ecological challenge facing all organizations requires managers to formulate strategies that preserve and conserve natural resources and control pollution. Special natural environment issues include ozone depletion, global warming, depletion of rain forests, destruction of animal habitats, protecting endangered species, developing biodegradable products and packages, waste management, clean air, clean water, erosion, destruction of natural resources, and pollution control. Firms increasingly are developing green product lines that are biodegradable and/or are made from recycled products. Green products sell well.

The U.S. Environmental Protection Agency recently reported that U.S. citizens and organizations annually spend more than about $200 billion on pollution abatement. Environmental concerns touch all aspects of a business's operations, including workplace risk exposures, packaging, waste reduction, energy use, alternative fuels, environmental cost accounting, and recycling practices.

Managing as if Earth matters requires an understanding of how international trade, competitiveness, and global resources are connected. Managing environmental affairs can no longer be simply a technical function performed by specialists in a firm; more emphasis must be placed on developing an environmental perspective among all employees and managers of the firm. Many companies are moving environmental affairs from the staff side of the organization to the line side, thus making the corporate environmental group report directly to the chief operating officer.

Societies have been plagued by environmental disasters to such an extent recently that firms failing to recognize the importance of environmental issues and challenges could suffer severe consequences. Managing environmental affairs can no longer be an incidental or secondary function of company operations. Product design, manufacturing, and ultimate disposal should not merely reflect environmental considerations, but also be driven by them. Firms that manage environmental affairs will enhance relations with consumers, regulators, vendors, and other industry players—substantially improving their prospects of success.

Firms should formulate and implement strategies from an environmental perspective. Environmental strategies could include developing or acquiring green businesses, divesting or altering environment-damaging businesses, striving to become a low-cost producer through waste minimization and energy conservation, and pursuing a differentiation strategy through green-product features. In addition to creating strategies, firms could include an environmental representative on the board of directors, conduct regular envrionmental audits, implement bonuses for favorable environmental results, become involved in environmental issues and programs, incorporate environmental values in mission statements, establish environmentally oriented objectives, acquire environmental skills, and provide environmental training programs for company employees and managers.

NATURAL ENVIRONMENT PERSPECTIVE
In Hiring, Do Companies Consider Environmental Training of Students?

The *Wall Street Journal* reports that companies actively consider environmental training in employees they hire. A recent study reported that 77 percent of corporate recruiters said "it is important to hire students with an awareness of social and environmental responsibility." According to Ford Motor Company's director of corporate governance, "We want students who will help us find solutions to societal challenges and we have trouble hiring students with such skills" (Alsop, 2001). The Aspen Institute contends that most business schools currently do not, but should, incorporate environmental training in all facets of their core curriculum, not just in special elective courses. The Institute reports that in the United States, the University of Texas, the University of North Carolina, and the University of Michigan, among others, are at the cutting edge in providing environmental coverage at their respective MBA levels. Companies today do consider business schools with the best environmental programs to prepare students more

effectively for the business world; companies favor hiring graduates from these universities.

Findings from research suggest that business schools at the undergraduate level are doing a poor job of educating students on environmental issues. Because business students with limited knowledge on environmental issues may make poor decisions, business schools should address environmental issues more in their curricula. Failure to do so could result in graduates making inappropriate business decisions in regard to the natural environment. Failing to provide adequate coverage of natural environment issues and decisions in their training could make those students less attractive to employers than graduates from other universities.

Sources: Adapted from R. Alsop, "Corporations Still Put Profits First, But Social Concerns Gain Ground," *Wall Street Journal* (2001): B14, Jane Kim, "Business Schools Take a Page from Kinder, Gentler Textbook," *Wall Street Journal* (October 22, 2003): B2C; and Beth Gardner, "Business Schools Going Green," *Wall Street Journal* (June 6, 2007): B5A.

Source: Tom Watson

Creating a Strategy-Supportive Culture

Strategists should strive to preserve, emphasize, and build upon aspects of an existing *culture* that support proposed new strategies. Aspects of an existing culture that are antagonistic to a proposed strategy should be identified and changed. Substantial research indicates that new strategies are often market-driven and dictated by competitive forces. For this reason, changing a firm's culture to fit a new strategy is usually more effective than changing a strategy to fit an existing culture. Numerous techniques are available to alter an organization's culture, including recruitment, training, transfer, promotion, restructure of an organization's design, role modeling, and positive reinforcement.

Jack Duncan described *triangulation* as an effective, multi-method technique for studying and altering a firm's culture.[18] Triangulation includes the combined use of obtrusive observation, self-administered questionnaires, and personal interviews to determine the nature of a firm's culture. The process of triangulation reveals changes that need to be made to a firm's culture to benefit strategy.

Schein indicated that the following elements are most useful in linking culture to strategy:

1. Formal statements of organizational philosophy, charters, creeds, materials used for recruitment and selection, and socialization
2. Designing of physical spaces, facades, buildings
3. Deliberate role modeling, teaching, and coaching by leaders
4. Explicit reward and status system, promotion criteria
5. Stories, legends, myths, and parables about key people and events
6. What leaders pay attention to, measure, and control
7. Leader reactions to critical incidents and organizational crises
8. How the organization is designed and structured
9. Organizational systems and procedures
10. Criteria used for recruitment, selection, promotion, leveling off, retirement, and "excommunication" of people[19]

In the personal and religious side of life, the impact of loss and change is easy to see.[20] Memories of loss and change often haunt individuals and organizations for years. Ibsen wrote, "Rob the average man of his life illusion and you rob him of his happiness at the same stroke."[21] When attachments to a culture are severed in an organization's attempt to change direction, employees and managers often experience deep feelings of grief. This phenomenon commonly occurs when external conditions dictate the need for a new strategy. Managers and employees often struggle to find meaning in a situation that changed many years before. Some people find comfort in memories; others find solace in the present. Weak linkages between strategic management and organizational culture can jeopardize performance and success. Deal and Kennedy emphasized that making strategic changes in an organization always threatens a culture:

> People form strong attachments to heroes, legends, the rituals of daily life, the hoopla of extravaganza and ceremonies, and all the symbols of the workplace. Change strips relationships and leaves employees confused, insecure, and often angry. Unless something can be done to provide support for transitions from old to new, the force of a culture can neutralize and emasculate strategy changes.[22]

The Mexican Culture

VISIT THE NET

Provides nice information on "What Is Culture" and also provides additional excellent links to other culture sites. (http://www.managementhelp.org/org_thry/culture/culture.htm)

Mexico always has been and still is an authoritarian society in terms of schools, churches, businesses, and families. Employers seek workers who are agreeable, respectful, and obedient, rather than innovative, creative, and independent. Mexican workers tend to be activity oriented rather than problem solvers. When visitors walk into a Mexican business, they are impressed by the cordial, friendly atmosphere. This is almost always true because Mexicans desire harmony rather than conflict; desire for harmony is part of the social fabric in worker–manager relations. There is a much lower tolerance for adversarial relations or friction at work in Mexico as compared to the United States.

Mexican employers are paternalistic, providing workers with more than a paycheck, but in return they expect allegiance. Weekly food baskets, free meals, free bus service, and free day care are often part of compensation. The ideal working condition for a Mexican worker is the family model, with people all working together, doing their share, according to their designated roles. Mexican workers do not expect or desire a work environment in which self-expression and initiative are encouraged. Whereas U.S. business embodies individualism, achievement, competition, curiosity, pragmatism, informality, spontaneity, and doing more than expected on the job, Mexican businesses stress collectivism, continuity, cooperation, belongingness, formality, and doing exactly what you're told.

In Mexico, business associates rarely entertain each other at their homes, which are places reserved exclusively for close friends and family. Business meetings and entertaining are nearly always done at a restaurant. Preserving one's honor, saving face, and looking important are also exceptionally important in Mexico. This is why Mexicans do not accept criticism and change easily; many find it humiliating to acknowledge having made a mistake. A meeting among employees and managers in a business located in Mexico is a forum for giving orders and directions rather than for discussing problems or participating in decision making. Mexican workers want to be closely supervised, cared for, and corrected in a civil manner. Opinions expressed by employees are often regarded as back talk in Mexico. Mexican supervisors are viewed as weak if they explain the rationale for their orders to workers.

Mexicans do not feel compelled to follow rules that are not associated with a particular person in authority they work for or know well. Thus, signs to wear earplugs or safety glasses, or attendance or seniority policies, and even one-way street signs are often ignored. Whereas Americans follow the rules, Mexicans often do not.

Life is slower in Mexico than in the United States. The first priority is often assigned to the last request, rather than to the first. Telephone systems break down. Banks may suddenly not have pesos. Phone repair can take months. Electricity for an entire plant or town can be down for hours or even days. Business and government offices open and close at different hours. Buses and taxis may be hours off schedule. Meeting times for appointments are not rigid. Tardiness is common everywhere. Effectively doing business in Mexico requires knowledge of the Mexican way of life, culture, beliefs, and customs.

The Japanese Culture

The Japanese place great importance upon group loyalty and consensus, a concept called *Wa*. Nearly all corporate activities in Japan encourage *Wa* among managers and employees. *Wa* requires that all members of a group agree and cooperate; this results in constant discussion and compromise. Japanese managers evaluate the potential attractiveness of alternative business decisions in terms of the long-term effect on the group's *Wa*. This is why silence, used for pondering alternatives, can be a plus in a formal Japanese meeting. Discussions potentially disruptive to *Wa* are generally conducted in very informal settings, such as at a bar, so as to minimize harm to the group's *Wa*. Entertaining is an important business activity in Japan because it strengthens *Wa*. Formal meetings are often conducted in informal settings. When confronted with disturbing questions or opinions, Japanese managers tend to remain silent, whereta tend to respond directly, defending themselves through explanation and argument.

Note in the "Global Perspective" that when negotiating orally with Japanese executives, one must periodically allow for a time of silence and must not ask, "How was your weekend?" which could be viewed as intrusive.

Most Japanese managers are reserved, quiet, distant, introspective, and other oriented, whereas most U.S. managers are talkative, insensitive, impulsive, direct, and individual oriented. Americans often perceive Japanese managers as wasting time and carrying on pointless conversations, whereas U.S. managers often use blunt criticism, ask prying questions, and make quick decisions. These kinds of cultural differences have disrupted many potentially productive Japanese–American business endeavors. Viewing the Japanese communication style as a prototype for all Asian cultures is a stereotype that must be avoided.

GLOBAL PERSPECTIVE
American versus Foreign Communication Differences

As Americans increasingly interact with managers in other countries, it is important to be sensitive to foreign business cultures. Americans too often come across as intrusive, manipulative, and garrulous, and this impression reduces their effectiveness in communication. *Forbes* magazine recently provided the following cultural hints from Charis Intercultural Training:

1. Italians, Germans, and French generally do not soften up executives with praise before they criticize. Americans do soften up folks, and this practice seems manipulative to Europeans.
2. Israelis are accustomed to fast-paced meetings and have little patience for American informality and small talk.
3. British executives often complain that American executives chatter too much. Informality, egalitarianism, and spontaneity from Americans in business settings jolt many foreigners.

4. Europeans feel they are being treated like children when asked to wear name tags by Americans.
5. Executives in India are used to interrupting one another. Thus, when American executives listen without asking for clarification or posing questions, they are viewed by Indians as not paying attention.
6. When negotiating orally with Malaysian or Japanese executives, it is appropriate to periodically allow for a time of silence. However, no pause is needed when negotiating in Israel.

Refrain from asking foreign managers questions such as "How was your weekend?" That is intrusive to foreigners, who tend to regard their business and private lives as totally separate.

Source: Adapted from Lalita Khosla, "You Say Tomato," *Forbes* (May 21, 2001): 36.

Outside the Glass Factory In Murano/Venice, Italy.
Source: Donald A Hoffend

Americans have more freedom to control their own fates than do the Japanese. Life in the United States and life in Japan are very different; the United States offers more upward mobility to its people. This is a great strength of the United States. Sherman explained:

America is not like Japan and can never be. America's strength is the opposite: It opens its doors and brings the world's disorder in. It tolerates social change that would tear most other societies apart. This openness encourages Americans to adapt as individuals rather than as a group. Americans go west to California to get a new start; they move east to Manhattan to try to make the big time; they move to Vermont or to a farm to get close to the soil. They break away from their parents' religions or values or class; they rediscover their ethnicity. They go to night school; they change their names.[23]

Production/Operations Concerns When Implementing Strategies

Production/operations capabilities, limitations, and policies can significantly enhance or inhibit the attainment of objectives. Production processes typically constitute more than 70 percent of a firm's total assets. A major part of the strategy-implementation process takes place at the production site. Production-related decisions on plant size, plant location, product design, choice of equipment, kind of tooling, size of inventory, inventory control, quality control, cost control, use of standards, job specialization, employee training, equipment and resource utilization, shipping and packaging, and technological innovation can have a dramatic impact on the success or failure of strategy-implementation efforts.

Examples of adjustments in production systems that could be required to implement various strategies are provided in Table 7-3 for both for-profit and nonprofit organizations. For instance, note that when a bank formulates and selects a strategy to add 10 new branches, a production-related implementation concern is site location. The largest bicycle company in the United States, Huffy, recently ended its own production of bikes and now contracts out those services to Asian and Mexican manufacturers. Huffy focuses instead on the design, marketing, and distribution of bikes, but it no longer produces bikes itself. The company closed its plants in the U.S. states of Ohio, Missouri, and Mississippi.

Just-in-time (JIT) production approaches have withstood the test of time. JIT significantly reduces the costs of implementing strategies. With JIT, parts and materials are delivered to a production site just as they are needed, rather than being stockpiled as a hedge against later deliveries. Harley-Davidson reports that at one plant alone, JIT freed $22 million previously tied up in inventory and greatly reduced reorder lead time.

Factors that should be studied before locating production facilities include the availability of major resources, the prevailing wage rates in the area, transportation costs related to shipping and receiving, the location of major markets, political risks in the area or country, and the availability of trainable employees.

For high-technology companies, production costs may not be as important as production flexibility because major product changes can be needed often. Industries such as biogenetics and plastics rely on production systems that must be flexible enough to allow frequent changes and the rapid introduction of new products. An article in the *Harvard Business Review* explained why some organizations get into trouble:

> They too slowly realize that a change in product strategy alters the tasks of a production system. These tasks, which can be stated in terms of requirements for cost, product flexibility, volume flexibility, product performance, and product consistency,

TABLE 7-3 Production Management and Strategy Implementation

Type of Organization	Strategy Being Implemented	Production System Adjustments
Hospital	Adding a cancer center (Product Development)	Purchase specialized equipment and add specialized people.
Bank	Adding 10 new branches (Market Development)	Perform site location analysis.
Beer brewery	Purchasing a barley farm operation (Backward Integration)	Revise the inventory control system.
Steel manufacturer	Acquiring a fast-food chain (Unrelated Diversification)	Improve the quality control system.
Computer company	Purchasing a retail distribution chain (Forward Integration)	Alter the shipping, packaging, and transportation systems.

determine which manufacturing policies are appropriate. As strategies shift over time, so must production policies covering the location and scale of manufacturing facilities, the choice of manufacturing process, the degree of vertical integration of each manufacturing facility, the use of R&D units, the control of the production system, and the licensing of technology.[24]

A common management practice, cross-training of employees, can facilitate strategy implementation and can yield many benefits. Employees gain a better understanding of the whole business and can contribute better ideas in planning sessions. Production/operations managers need to realize, however, that cross-training employees can create problems related to the following issues:

1. It can thrust managers into roles that emphasize counseling and coaching over directing and enforcing.
2. It can necessitate substantial investments in training and incentives.
3. It can be very time-consuming.
4. Skilled workers may resent unskilled workers who learn their jobs.
5. Older employees may not want to learn new skills.

Human Resource Concerns When Implementing Strategies

The job of human resource manager is changing rapidly as companies continue to downsize and reorganize. Strategic responsibilities of the human resource manager include assessing the staffing needs and costs for alternative strategies proposed during strategy formulation and developing a staffing plan for effectively implementing strategies. This plan must consider how best to manage spiraling health care insurance costs. Employers' health coverage expenses consume an average 26 percent of firms' net profits, even though most companies now require employees to pay part of their health insurance premiums. The plan must also include how to motivate employees and managers during a time when layoffs are common and workloads are high.

The human resource department must develop performance incentives that clearly link performance and pay to strategies. The process of empowering managers and employees through their involvement in strategic-management activities yields the greatest benefits when all organizational members understand clearly how they will benefit personally if the firm does well. Linking company and personal benefits is a major new strategic responsibility of human resource managers. Other new responsibilities for human resource managers may include establishing and administering an *employee stock ownership plan (ESOP)*, instituting an effective child-care policy, and providing leadership for managers and employees in a way that allows them to balance work and family.

A well-designed strategic-management system can fail if insufficient attention is given to the human resource dimension. Human resource problems that arise when businesses implement strategies can usually be traced to one of three causes: (1) disruption of social and political structures, (2) failure to match individuals' aptitudes with implementation tasks, and (3) inadequate top management support for implementation activities.[25]

Strategy implementation poses a threat to many managers and employees in an organization. New power and status relationships are anticipated and realized. New formal and informal groups' values, beliefs, and priorities may be largely unknown. Managers and employees may become engaged in resistance behavior as their roles, prerogatives, and power in the firm change. Disruption of social and political structures that accompany strategy execution must be anticipated and considered during strategy formulation and managed during strategy implementation.

A concern in matching managers with strategy is that jobs have specific and relatively static responsibilities, although people are dynamic in their personal development. Commonly used methods that match managers with strategies to be implemented include transferring managers, developing leadership workshops, offering career development activities, promotions, job enlargement, and job enrichment.

A number of other guidelines can help ensure that human relationships facilitate rather than disrupt strategy-implementation efforts. Specifically, managers should do a lot of chatting and informal questioning to stay abreast of how things are progressing and to know when to intervene. Managers can build support for strategy-implementation efforts by giving few orders, announcing few decisions, depending heavily on informal questioning, and seeking to probe and clarify until a consensus emerges. Key thrusts that succeed should be rewarded generously and visibly.

It is surprising that so often during strategy formulation, individual values, skills, and abilities needed for successful strategy implementation are not considered. It is rare that a firm selecting new strategies or significantly altering existing strategies possesses the right line and staff personnel in the right positions for successful strategy implementation. The need to match individual aptitudes with strategy-implementation tasks should be considered in strategy choice.

Inadequate support from strategists for implementation activities often undermines organizational success. Chief executive officers, small business owners, and government agency heads must be personally committed to strategy implementation and express this commitment in highly visible ways. Strategists' formal statements about the importance of strategic management must be consistent with actual support and rewards given for activities completed and objectives reached. Otherwise, stress created by inconsistency can cause uncertainty among managers and employees at all levels.

Perhaps the best method for preventing and overcoming human resource problems in strategic management is to actively involve as many managers and employees as possible in the process. Although time-consuming, this approach builds understanding, trust, commitment, and ownership and reduces resentment and hostility. The true potential of strategy formulation and implementation resides in people.

Employee Stock Ownership Plans (ESOPs)

An *ESOP* is a tax-qualified, defined-contribution, employee-benefit plan whereby employees purchase stock of the company through borrowed money or cash contributions. ESOPs empower employees to work as owners; this is a primary reason why the number of ESOPs have grown dramatically to more than 10,000 firms covering more than 10 million employees. ESOPs now control more than $600 billion in corporate stock in the United States.

Besides reducing worker alienation and stimulating productivity, ESOPs allow firms other benefits, such as substantial tax savings. Principal, interest, and dividend payments on ESOP-funded debt are tax deductible. Banks lend money to ESOPs at interest rates below prime. This money can be repaid in pretax dollars, lowering the debt service as much as 30 percent in some cases. "The ownership culture really makes a difference, when management is a facilitator, not a dictator," says Corey Rosen, executive director of the U.S. National Center for Employee Ownership. The eight largest 100 percent employee-owned U.S. companies are listed in Table 7-4.

TABLE 7-4 The Eight Largest ESOP Firms in the USA in 2007

Firm	Headquarters Location	Industry	Number of Employees
Publix Supermarkets	Lakeland, FL	Supermarkets	136,000
Science Applications	San Diego, CA	R&D and computers	43,000
Price Chopper	Schenectady, NY	Supermarkets	22,000
Lifetouch	Minneapolis, MN	Photography	18,000
Nypro	Clinton, MA	Plastics mfg.	13,000
Parsons	Pasadena, CA	Engineering	10,000
Houchens Industries	Bowling Green, KY	Supermarkets	9,300
Amsted Industries	Chicago, IL	Industrial mfg.	9,100

Source: Adapted from Edward Iwata, "ESOPs Can Offer Both Upsides, Drawbacks," *USA Today* (April 3, 2007): 2B.

If an ESOP owns more than 50 percent of the firm, those who lend money to the ESOP are taxed on only 50 percent of the income received on the loans. ESOPs are not for every firm, however, because the initial legal, accounting, actuarial, and appraisal fees to set up an ESOP are about $50,000 for a small or midsized firm, with annual administration expenses of about $15,000. Analysts say ESOPs also do not work well in firms that have fluctuating payrolls and profits. Human resource managers in many firms conduct preliminary research to determine the desirability of an ESOP, and then they facilitate its establishment and administration if benefits outweigh the costs.

Wyatt Cafeterias, a southwestern United States operator of 120 cafeterias, also adopted the ESOP concept to prevent a hostile takeover. Employee productivity at Wyatt greatly increased since the ESOP began, as illustrated in the following quote:

> The key employee in our entire organization is the person serving the customer on the cafeteria line. In the past, because of high employee turnover and entry-level wages for many line jobs, these employees received far less attention and recognition than managers. We now tell the tea cart server, "You own the place. Don't wait for the manager to tell you how to do your job better or how to provide better service. You take care of it." Sure, we're looking for productivity increases, but since we began pushing decisions down to the level of people who deal directly with customers, we've discovered an awesome side effect—suddenly the work crews have this "happy to be here" attitude that the customers really love.[26]

Balancing Work Life and Home Life

Work/family strategies have become so popular among companies today that the strategies now represent a competitive advantage for those firms that offer such benefits as elder care assistance, flexible scheduling, job sharing, adoption benefits, an on-site summer camp, employee help lines, pet care, and even lawn service referrals. New corporate titles such as work/life coordinator and director of diversity are becoming common.

Working Mother magazine (www.workingmother.com) annually published its listing of "The 100 Best Companies for Working Mothers" in the United States. Three especially important variables used in the ranking were availability of flextime, advancement opportunities, and equitable distribution of benefits among companies. Other important criteria are compressed weeks, telecommuting, job sharing, childcare facilities, maternity leave for both parents, mentoring, career development, and promotion for women. *Working Mother's* top 10 best companies for working women in 2007 are provided in Table 7-5. *Working Mother* also conducts extensive research to determine the best U.S. firms for women of color.

Human resource managers need to foster a more effective balancing of professional and private lives because more people today are now part of two-career families. A corporate objective to become more lean and mean must today include consideration for the fact that a good home life contributes immensely to a good work life.

TABLE 7-5 **The 10 Best U.S. Firms for Women to Work for in 2007**

1.	Abbott
2.	Bon Secours Richmond Health System
3.	Ernst & Young
4.	HSBC—North America
5.	IBM
6.	JPMorgan Chase
7.	Patagonia
8.	PricewaterhouseCoopers
9.	Principal Financial Group
10.	S. C. Johnson & Son

Source: Adapted from www.workingmother.com (2007).

The work/family issue is no longer just a women's issue. Some specific measures that firms are taking to address this issue are providing spouse relocation assistance as an employee benefit; providing company resources for family recreational and educational use; establishing employee country clubs, such as those at IBM and Bethlehem Steel; and creating family/work interaction opportunities. A study by Joseph Pleck of Wheaton College found that in companies that do not offer paternity leave for fathers as a benefit, most men take short, informal paternity leaves anyway by combining vacation time and sick days.

Some organizations have developed family days, when family members are invited into the workplace, taken on plant or office tours, dined by management, and given a chance to see exactly what other family members do each day. Family days are inexpensive and increase the employee's pride in working for the organization. Flexible working hours during the week are another human resource response to the need for individuals to balance work life and home life. The work/family topic is being made part of the agenda at meetings and thus is being discussed in many organizations.

There are now nine Fortune 500 companies with female CEOs, and four of the nine outperformed the S&P Index in 2006. Two very large firms, Archer Daniels Midland and PepsiCo, in 2006 promoted women to the position of CEO, Patricia Woertz and Indra Nooyi, respectively. eBay in 2006 became a Fortune 500 firm and its CEO, Meg Whitman, has for many years led that firm to excellence. Patricia Russ, CEO of Lucent Technologies, was selected to be CEO of Alcatel-Lucent, headquartered in Paris. Unfortunately, 48 percent of Fortune 1,000 companies still have no women in their top ranks. But firms that do promote women appear to be making it a top priority, placing women on a faster track to top management than men.[27]

Overall, women CEOs are doing very well in the United States. For example, Mary Sammons, CEO of Rite Aid, increased the firm's stock 61 percent in 2006 versus a 13.5 percent average for all S&P 500 firms. CEO Susan Ivey of Reynolds American raised that firm's stock 37 percent. CEO Andrea Jung of Avon Products raised that firm's stock 17 percent, as did CEO Anne Mulcahy of Xerox. CEO Paula Reynolds of Safeco raised that firm's stock 12 percent. CEO Brenda Barnes of Sara Lee is leading that firm in a restructuring process.

There is great room for improvement in removing the *glass ceiling* domestically, especially considering that women make up 47 percent of the U.S. labor force. *Glass ceiling* refers to the invisible barrier in many firms that bars women and minorities from top-level management positions. Nonetheless, the United States leads the world in promoting women and minorities into mid- and top-level managerial positions in business.

Boeing's firing of CEO Harry Stonecipher for having an extramarital affair raised public awareness of office romance. However, just 12 percent of 391 companies surveyed by the American Management Association have written guidelines on office dating.[28] The fact of the matter is that most employers in the United States turn a blind eye to marital cheating. Some employers, such as Southwest Airlines, which employs more than 1,000 married couples, explicitly allow consensual office relationships. Research suggests that more men than women engage in extramarital affairs at work, roughly 22 percent to 15 percent; however, the percentage of women having extramarital affairs is increasing steadily, whereas the percentage of men having affairs with co-workers is holding steady.[29] If an affair is disrupting your work, then "the first step is to go to the offending person privately and try to resolve the matter. If that fails, then go to the human-resources manager seeking assistance."[30] Filing a discrimination lawsuit based on the affair is recommended only as a last resort because courts generally rule that co-workers' injuries are not pervasive enough to warrant any damages.

Benefits of a Diverse Workforce

Toyota has committed almost $8 billion over 10 years to diversify its workforce and to use more minority suppliers. Hundreds of other firms are also striving to become more diversified in their workforces. TJX Companies, the parent of 1,500 T. J. Maxx and Marshall's stores, has reaped great benefits and is an exemplary company in terms of diversity. A recent *Wall Street Journal* article listed, in order of importance, the following major benefits of having a diverse workforce:[31]

1. Improves corporate culture
2. Improves employee morale
3. Leads to higher retention of employees
4. Leads to easier recruitment of new employees
5. Decreases complaints and litigation
6. Increases creativity
7. Decreases interpersonal conflict between employees
8. Enables the organization to move into emerging markets
9. Improves client relations
10. Increases productivity
11. Improves the bottom line
12. Maximizes brand identity
13. Reduces training costs

An organization can perhaps be most effective when its workforce mirrors the diversity of its customers. For global companies, this goal can be optimistic, but it is a worthwhile goal.

Conclusion

Successful strategy formulation does not at all guarantee successful strategy implementation. Although inextricably interdependent, strategy formulation and strategy implementation are characteristically different. In a single word, strategy implementation means *change*. It is widely agreed that "the real work begins after strategies are formulated." Successful strategy implementation requires the support of, as well as discipline and hard work from, motivated managers and employees. It is sometimes frightening to think that a single individual can irreparably sabotage strategy-implementation efforts.

Formulating the right strategies is not enough, because managers and employees must be motivated to implement those strategies. Management issues considered central to strategy implementation include matching organizational structure with strategy, linking performance and pay to strategies, creating an organizational climate conducive to change, managing political relationships, creating a strategy-supportive culture, adapting production/operations processes, and managing human resources. Establishing annual objectives, devising policies, and allocating resources are central strategy-implementation activities common to all organizations. Depending on the size and type of the organization, other management issues could be equally important to successful strategy implementation.

We invite you to visit the David page on the Prentice Hall Companion Web site at www.prenhall.com/david for this chapter's review quiz.

Key Terms and Concepts

Annual Objectives (p. 262)
Avoidance (p. 266)
Benchmarking (p. 275)
Bonus System (p. 277)
Conflict (p. 266)
Confrontation (p. 266)
Culture (p. 282)
Decentralized Structure (p. 268)
Defusion (p. 266)
Delayering (p. 274)
Divisional Structure by Geographic Area, Product, Customer, or Process (p. 268)

Issues for Review and Discussion

1. Allocating resources can be a political and an ad hoc activity in firms that do not use strategic management. Why is this true? Does adopting strategic management ensure easy resource allocation? Why?

2. Compare strategy formulation with strategy implementation in terms of each being an art or a science.

3. Describe the relationship between annual objectives and policies.

4. Identify a long-term objective and two supporting annual objectives for a familiar organization.

5. Identify and discuss three policies that apply to your present business policy class.

6. Explain the following statement: Horizontal consistency of goals is as important as vertical consistency.

7. Describe several reasons why conflict may occur during objective-setting activities.

8. In your opinion, what approaches to conflict resolution would be best for resolving a disagreement between a personnel manager and a sales manager over the firing of a particular salesperson? Why?

9. Describe the organizational culture of your college or university.

10. Explain why organizational structure is so important in strategy implementation.

11. In your opinion, how many separate divisions could an organization reasonably have without using an SBU-type organizational structure? Why?

12. Would you recommend a divisional structure by geographic area, product, customer, or process for a medium-sized bank in your local area? Why?

13. What are the advantages and disadvantages of decentralizing the wage and salary functions of an organization? How could this be accomplished?

14. Consider a college organization with which you are familiar. How did management issues affect strategy implementation in that organization?

15. As production manager of a local newspaper, what problems would you anticipate in implementing a strategy to increase the average number of pages in the paper by 40 percent?

16. Do you believe expenditures for child care or fitness facilities are warranted from a cost-benefit perspective? Why or why not?

17. Explain why successful strategy implementation often hinges on whether the strategy-formulation process empowers managers and employees.

18. Compare and contrast the cultures in Mexico and Japan.

19. Discuss the glass ceiling in the United States, giving your ideas and suggestions.
20. Discuss three ways discussed in this book for linking performance and pay to strategies.
21. List the different types of organizational structure. Diagram what you think is the most complex of these structures and label your chart clearly.
22. List the advantages and disadvantages of a functional versus a divisional organizational structure.
23. Compare and contrast the U.S. business culture with the Mexican business culture.
24. Discuss recent trends in women and minorities becoming top executives in the United States.
25. Discuss recent trends in firms downsizing family-friendly programs.
26. Research the latest developments in the class-action lawsuit involving women managers versus Wal-Mart Stores and report your findings to the class.
27. List seven guidelines to follow in developing an organizational chart.

Notes

1. Dale McConkey, "Planning in a Changing Environment," *Business Horizons* (September–October 1988): 66.
2. A. G. Bedeian and W. F. Glueck, *Management*, 3rd ed. (Chicago: The Dryden Press, 1983): 212.
3. Boris Yavitz and William Newman, *Strategy in Action: The Execution, Politics, and Payoff of Business Planning* (New York: The Free Press, 1982): 195.
4. Schein, E. H. "Three Cultures of Management: The Key to Organizational Learning," *Sloan Management Review* 38, 1 (1996): 9–20.
5. S. Ghoshal, and C. A. Bartlett, "Changing the Role of Management: Beyond Structure to Processes." *Harvard Business Review* 73, 1 (1995): 88.
6. Karen Richardson, "The 'Six Sigma' Factor for Home Depot," *Wall Street Journal* (January 4, 2007): C3.
7. Steve Hamm and Marcia Stepanek, "From Reengineering to E-engineering," *BusinessWeek* (March 22, 1999): EB15.
8. "Want to Be a Manager? Many People Say No, Calling Job Miserable," *Wall Street Journal* (April 4, 1997): 1; Stephanie Armour, "Management Loses Its Allure," *USA Today* (October 10, 1997): 1B.
9. Paul Carroll, "No More Business as Usual, Please. Time to Try Something Different," *Wall Street Journal* (October 23, 2001): A24.
10. Jeff Opdyke, "Companies Strive to Find True Stars for Raises, Bonus," *Wall Street Journal* (December 20, 2006): D3.
11. Kris Maher and Kris Hudson, "Wal-Mart to Sweeten Bonus Plans for Staff," *Wall Street Journal* (March 22, 2007): A11.
12. Richard Brown, "Outsider CEO: Inspiring Change with Force and Grace," *USA Today* (July 19, 1999): 3B.
13. Yavitz and Newman, 58.
14. Jack Duncan, *Management* (New York: Random House, 1983): 381–390.
15. H. Igor Ansoff, "Strategic Management of Technology," *Journal of Business Strategy* 7, no. 3 (Winter 1987): 38.
16. Robert Waterman, Jr., "How the Best Get Better," *BusinessWeek* (September 14, 1987): 104.
17. Katherine Kranhold and Jeffrey Ball, "GE to Spend More on Projects Tied to Climate Change," *Wall Street Journal* (May 9, 2005): A2.
18. Jack Duncan, "Organizational Culture: Getting a Fix on an Elusive Concept," *Academy of Management Executive* 3, no. 3 (August 1989): 229.
19. E. H. Schein, "The Role of the Founder in Creating Organizational Culture," *Organizational Dynamics* (Summer 1983): 13–28.
20. T. Deal and A. Kennedy, "Culture: A New Look Through Old Lenses," *Journal of Applied Behavioral Science* 19, no. 4 (1983): 498–504.
21. H. Ibsen, "The Wild Duck," in O. G. Brochett and L. Brochett (eds.), *Plays for the Theater* (New York: Holt, Rinehart & Winston, 1967); R. Pascale, "The Paradox of 'Corporate

Culture': Reconciling Ourselves to Socialization," *California Management Review* 28, no. 2 (1985): 26, 37–40.

22. T. Deal and A. Kennedy, *Corporate Cultures: The Rites and Rituals of Corporate Life* (Reading, MA: Addison-Wesley, 1982): 256.

23. Stratford Sherman, "How to Beat the Japanese," *Fortune* (April 10, 1989): 145.

24. Robert Stobaugh and Piero Telesio, "Match Manufacturing Policies and Product Strategy," *Harvard Business Review* 61, no. 2 (March–April 1983): 113.

25. R. T. Lenz and Marjorie Lyles, "Managing Human Resource Problems in Strategy Planning Systems," *Journal of Business Strategy* 60, no. 4 (Spring 1986): 58.

26. J. Warren Henry, "ESOPs with Productivity Payoffs," *Journal of Business Strategy* (July–August 1989): 33.

27. Del Jones, "Women-Led Firms Lift Stock Standing," *USA Today* (December 27, 2006): 3B.

28. Sue Shellenbarger, "Employers Often Ignore Office Affairs, Leaving Co-workers in Difficult Spot," *Wall Street Journal* (March 10, 2005): D1.

29. Ibid.

30. Ibid.

31. Julie Bennett, "Corporate Downsizing Doesn't Deter Search for Diversity," *Wall Street Journal* (October 23, 2001): B18.

Current Readings

Bartol, Kathryn M., Edwin A. Locke, and Abhishek Srivastava. "Empowering Leadership in Management Teams: Effects on Knowledge Sharing, Efficacy, and Performance." *Academy of Management Journal* 49, no. 6 (December 2006): 1239.

Bebchuk, Lucian A., and Jesse M. Fried. "Pay Without Performance: Overview of the Issues." *The Academy of Management Perspectives* 20, no. 1 (February 2006): 5.

Becker, Brian E., and Mark A. Huselid. "Strategic Human Resources Management: Where Do We Go from Here?" *Journal of Management* 32, no. 6 (December 2006): 898.

Bower, Joseph L., and Clark G. Gilbert. "How Managers' Everyday Decisions Create or Destroy Your Company's Strategy." *Harvard Business Review* (February 2007): 72.

Breene, Timothy R.S., Paul F. Nunes, and Walter E. Shill. "The Chief Strategy Officer." *Harvard Business Review* (October 2007) 84.

Colella, Adrienne, Ramona L. Paetzold, Michael J. Wesson, and Asghar Zardkoohi. "Exposing Pay Secrecy." *The Academy of Management Review* 32, no. 1 (January 2007): 55.

Conyon, Martin J. "Executive Compensation and Incentives." *The Academy of Management Perspectives* 20, no. 1 (February 2006): 25.

Deckop, John R., Shruti Gupta, and Kimberly K. Merriman. "The Effects of CEO Pay Structure on Coporate Social Performance." *Journal of Management* 32, no. 3 (June 2006): 329.

Harris, Dawn, Constance E. Helfat, and Paul J. Wolfson. "The Pipeline to the Top: Women and Men in the Top Executive Ranks of U.S. Corporations." *The Academy of Management Perspectives* 20, no. 4 (November 2006): 42.

Karim, S. "Modularity in Organizational Structure: The Reconfiguration of Internally Developed and Acquired Business Units." *Strategic Management Journal* 27, no. 9 (September 2006): 799.

Marler, J. H., and Y. Yanadori. "Compensation Strategy: Does Business Strategy Influence Compensation in High-Technology Firms?" *Strategic Management Journal* 27, no. 6 (June 2006): 559.

Wasserman, Noam. "Stewards, Agents, and the Founder Discount: Executive Compensation in New Ventures." *Academy of Management Journal* 49, no. 5 (October 2006): 960.

Wimbush, James C. "Spotlight on Human Resource Management." *Business Horizons* 49, no. 6 (November–December 2006): 433.

Zhang, Y. "The Presence of a Separate COO/President and Its Impact on Strategic Change and CEO Dismissal." *Strategic Management Journal* 27, no. 3 (March 2006): 283.

• EXPERIENTIAL EXERCISES

Three 1980s Disney themed "Viewmaster 3-D" reels, comprising Peter Pan, Cinderella, and The Little Mermaid. *Source:* (c) Judith Miller / Dorling Kindersley / Three Sisters.

Experiential Exercise 7A

Revising Walt Disney's Organizational Chart

Purpose

Developing and altering organizational charts is an important skill for strategists to possess. This exercise can improve your skill in altering an organization's hierarchical structure in response to new strategies being formulated.

Instructions

Step 1   Turn to the Walt Disney Cohesion Case (p. 62) and review the organizational chart. On a separate sheet of paper, answer the following questions:

1. What type of organizational chart is illustrated for Disney?

2. What improvements could you recommend for the Disney organizational chart? Give your reasoning for each suggestion.

3. What aspects of Disney's chart do you especially like?

4. What type of organizational chart do you believe would best suit Disney? Why?

5. What would be alternative (better) words for Disney's segment names?

6. Suppose Disney asked you to develop a different SBU-type structure for the company. Illustrate that here.

Experiential Exercise 7B

Do Organizations Really Establish Objectives?

Purpose

Objectives provide direction, allow synergy, aid in evaluation, establish priorities, reduce uncertainty, minimize conflicts, stimulate exertion, and aid in both the allocation of

263

resources and the design of jobs. This exercise will enhance your understanding of how organizations use or misuse objectives.

Instructions

Step 1   Join with one other person in class to form a two-person team.

Step 2   Contact by telephone the owner or manager of an organization in your city or town. Request a 30-minute personal interview or meeting with that person for the purpose of discussing "business objectives." During your meeting, seek answers to the following questions:

1. Do you believe it is important for a business to establish and clearly communicate long-term and annual objectives? Why or why not?

2. Does your organization establish objectives? If yes, what type and how many? How are the objectives communicated to individuals? Are your firm's objectives in written form or simply communicated orally?

3. To what extent are managers and employees involved in the process of establishing objectives?

4. How often are your business objectives revised and by what process?

Step 3   Take good notes during the interview. Let one person be the note taker and one person do most of the talking. Have your notes typed up and ready to turn in to your professor.

Step 4   Prepare a 5-minute oral presentation for the class, reporting the results of your interview. Turn in your typed report.

Experiential Exercise 7C

Understanding My University's Culture

Purpose

It is something of an art to uncover the basic values and beliefs that are buried deeply in an organization's rich collection of stories, language, heroes, heroines, and rituals, yet culture can be the most important factor in implementing strategies.

Instructions

Step 1   On a separate sheet of paper, list the following terms: hero/heroine, belief, metaphor, language, value, symbol, story, legend, saga, folktale, myth, ceremony, rite, and ritual.

Step 2   For your college or university, give examples of each term. If necessary, speak with faculty, staff, alumni, administration, or fellow students of the institution to identify examples of each term.

Step 3   Report your findings to the class. Tell the class how you feel regarding cultural products being consciously used to help implement strategies.

8

Implementing Strategies: Marketing, Finance/Accounting, R&D, and MIS Issues

"notable quotes"

The greatest strategy is doomed if it's implemented badly.

BERNARD REIMANN

There is no "perfect" strategic decision. One always has to pay a price. One always has to balance conflicting objectives, conflicting opinions, and conflicting priorities. The best strategic decision is only an approximation—and a risk.

PETER DRUCKER

The real question isn't how well you're doing today against your own history, but how you're doing against your competitors.

DONALD KRESS

As market windows open and close more quickly, it is important that R&D be tied more closely to corporate strategy.

WILLIAM SPENSER

Most of the time, strategists should not be formulating strategy at all; they should be getting on with implementing strategies they already have.

HENRY MINTZBERG

It is human nature to make decisions based on emotion, rather than on fact. But nothing could be more illogical.

TOSHIBA CORPORATION

No business can do everything. Even if it has the money, it will never have enough good people. It has to set priorities. The worst thing to do is a little bit of everything. This makes sure that nothing is being accomplished. It is better to pick the wrong priority than none at all.

PETER DRUCKER

Weisloch, Germany: Parents of College Students. *Source:* Florian Fritsch

chapter objectives

After studying this chapter, you should be able to do the following:

1. Explain market segmentation and product positioning as strategy-implementation tools.

2. Discuss procedures for determining the worth of a business.

3. Explain why projected financial statement analysis is a central strategy-implementation tool.

4. Explain how to evaluate the attractiveness of debt versus stock as a source of capital to implement strategies.

5. Discuss the nature and role of research and development in strategy implementation.

6. Explain how management information systems can determine the success of strategy-implementation efforts.

Strategies have no chance of being implemented successfully in organizations that do not market goods and services well, in firms that cannot raise needed working capital, in firms that produce technologically inferior products, or in firms that have a weak information system. This chapter examines marketing, finance/accounting, R&D, and management information systems (MIS) issues that are central to effective strategy implementation. Special topics include market segmentation, market positioning, evaluating the worth of a business, determining to what extent debt and/or stock should be used as a source of capital, developing projected financial statements, contracting R&D outside the firm, and creating an information support system. Manager and employee involvement and participation are essential for success in marketing, finance/accounting, R&D, and MIS activities.

The Nature of Strategy Implementation

The quarterback can call the best play possible in the huddle, but that does not mean the play will go for a touchdown. The team may even lose yardage unless the play is executed (implemented) well. Less than 10 percent of strategies formulated are successfully implemented! There are many reasons for this low success rate, including failing to appropriately segment markets, paying too much for a new acquisition, and falling behind competitors in R&D.

Strategy implementation directly affects the lives of plant managers, division managers, department managers, sales managers, product managers, project managers, personnel managers, staff managers, supervisors, and all employees. In some situations, individuals may not have participated in the strategy-formulation process at all and may not appreciate, understand, or even accept the work and thought that went into strategy formulation. There may even be foot dragging or resistance on their part. Managers and employees who do not understand the business and are not committed to the business may attempt to sabotage strategy-implementation efforts in hopes that the organization will return to its old ways. The strategy-implementation stage of the strategic-management process is highlighted in Figure 8-1.

Marketing Issues

Countless marketing variables affect the success or failure of strategy implementation, and the scope of this text does not allow us to address all those issues. Some examples of marketing decisions that may require policies are as follows:

1. To use exclusive dealerships or multiple channels of distribution
2. To use heavy, light, or no TV advertising
3. To limit (or not) the share of business done with a single customer
4. To be a price leader or a price follower
5. To offer a complete or limited warranty
6. To reward salespeople based on straight salary, straight commission, or a combination salary/commission
7. To advertise online or not

A marketing issue of increasing concern to consumers today is the extent to which companies can track individuals' movements on the Internet—and even be able to identify an individual by name and e-mail address. Individuals' wanderings on the Internet are no longer anonymous, as many persons still believe. Marketing companies such as Doubleclick, Flycast, AdKnowledge, AdForce, and Real Media have sophisticated methods to identify who you are and your particular interests.[1] If you are especially concerned about being tracked, visit the www.networkadvertising.org Web site that gives details about how marketers today are identifying you and your buying habits.

FIGURE 8-1

A Comprehensive Strategic-Management Model

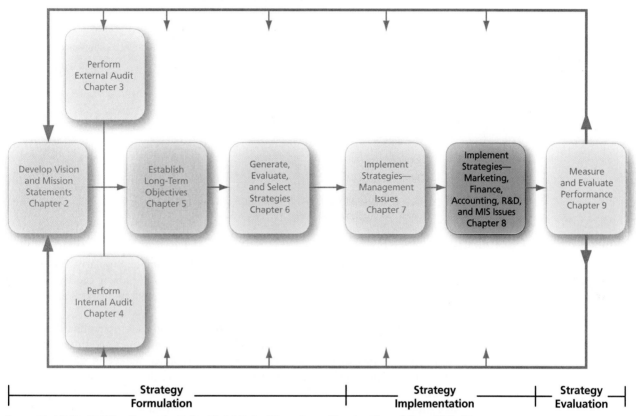

Source: Fred R. David, "How Companies Define Their Mission," *Long Range Planning* 22, no. 3 (June 1988): 40.

Two variables are of central importance to strategy implementation: *market segmentation* and *product positioning.* Market segmentation and product positioning rank as marketing's most important contributions to strategic management.

Market Segmentation

Market segmentation is widely used in implementing strategies, especially for small and specialized firms. Market segmentation can be defined as the subdividing of a market into distinct subsets of customers according to needs and buying habits.

Market segmentation is an important variable in strategy implementation for at least three major reasons. First, strategies such as market development, product development, market penetration, and diversification require increased sales through new markets and products. To successfully implement these strategies, new or improved market-segmentation approaches are required. Second, market segmentation allows a firm to operate with limited resources because mass production, mass distribution, and mass advertising are not required. Market segmentation enables a small firm to compete successfully with a large firm by maximizing per-unit profits and per-segment sales. Finally, market segmentation decisions directly affect *marketing mix variables:* product, place, promotion, and price, as indicated in Table 8-1. For example, SnackWells, a pioneer in reduced-fat snacks, has shifted its advertising emphasis from low-fat to great taste as part of its new market-segmentation strategy.

Perhaps the most dramatic new market-segmentation strategy is the targeting of regional tastes. Firms from McDonald's to Samsung are increasingly modifying their products to meet different regional preferences. Campbell's has a spicier version of its

VISIT THE NET

Provides CheckMATE, the industry leader in strategic planning software worldwide. This is easy-to-use software that is Windows-based. (www.checkmateplan.com)

TABLE 8–1   The Marketing Mix Component Variables

Product	Place	Promotion	Price
Quality	Distribution channels	Advertising	Level
Features and	Distribution coverage	Personal selling	Discounts and
options	Outlet location	Sales promotion	allowances
Style	Sales territories	Publicity	Payment terms
Brand name	Inventory levels		
Packaging	and locations		
Product line	Transportation		
Warranty	carriers		
Service level			
Other services			

Source: E. Jerome McCarthy, *Basic Marketing: A Managerial Approach,* 9th ed.
(Homewood, IL: Richard D. Irwin, Inc., 1987): 37–44.

nacho cheese soup for the Southwest United States, for example. Similarly, Burger King offers breakfast burritos in the U.S. state of New Mexico but not in the U.S. state of South Carolina. Geographic and demographic bases for segmenting markets are the most commonly employed, as illustrated in Table 8-2.

Evaluating potential market segments requires strategists to determine the characteristics and needs of consumers, to analyze consumer similarities and differences, and to develop consumer group profiles. Segmenting consumer markets is generally much simpler and easier than segmenting industrial markets, because industrial products, such as electronic circuits and forklifts, have multiple applications and appeal to diverse customer groups. Note in Figure 8-2 that customer age is used to segment automobile car purchases. Note that some older buyers especially like Cadillacs and Buicks.

Segmentation is a key to matching supply and demand, which is one of the thorniest problems in customer service. Segmentation often reveals that large, random fluctuations in demand actually consist of several small, predictable, and manageable patterns.

FIGURE 8-2

Average Age of Automobile Buyers, by Brand

Plymouth	38	Pontiac	42	Infiniti	45
Mitsubishi	38	Acura	42	Subaru	45
Volkswagen	38	Hyundai	42	Oldsmobile	46
Honda	41	Suzuki	42	Saturn	46
Isuzu	41	Audi	42	Chrysler	47
Kia	41	Daewoo	43	Lexus	47
Land Rover	41	Chevrolet	43	Jaguar	49
Mazda	41	Porsche	43	Mercury	50
Nissan	41	Saab	43	Lincoln	51
BMW	42	GMC	44	Cadillac	53
Dodge	42	Toyota	44	Buick	57
Jeep	42	Volvo	44		
Ford	42	Mercedes-Benz	45		

Source: Adapted from Norihiko Shirouzu, "This Is Not Your Father's Toyota," *Wall Street Journal* (March 26, 2002): B1.

TABLE 8–2 Alternative Bases for Market Segmentation

Variable	Typical Breakdowns
Geographic	
Region	Pacific, Mountain, West North Central, West South Central, East North Central, East South Central, South Atlantic, Middle Atlantic, New England
Province Size	A, B, C, D
City Size	Under 5,000; 5,000–20,000; 20,001–50,000; 50,001–100,000; 100,001–250,000; 250,001–500,000; 500,001–1,000,000; 1,000,001–4,000,000; 4,000,001 or over
Density	Urban, suburban, rural
Climate	Northern, southern
Demographic	
Age	Under 6, 6–11, 12–19, 20–34, 35–49, 50–64, 65+
Gender	Male, female
Family Size	1–2, 3–4, 5+
Family Life Cycle	Young, single; young, married, no children; young, married, youngest child under 6; young, married, youngest child 6 or over; older, married, with children; older, married, no children under 18; older, single; other
Income	Under €10,000; €10,001–€15,000; €15,001–€20,000; €20,001–€30,000; €30,001–€50,000; €50,001–€70,000; €70,001–€100,000; over €100,000
Occupation	Professional and technical; managers, officials, and proprietors; clerical and sales; craftspeople; foremen; operatives; farmers; retirees; students; housewives; unemployed
Education	Primary school or less; some secondary school; secondary school graduate; some college; college graduate
Religion	Islamic, Hindu, Buddhist, Catholic, Protestant, Jewish, other
Race	Asian, Hispanic, White, African American
Nationality	British, Indian, Chinese, French, German, Scandinavian, Italian, Latin American, Middle Eastern, Japanese
Psychographic	
Social Class	Lower lowers, upper lowers, lower middles, upper middles, lower uppers, upper uppers
Personality	Compulsive, gregarious, authoritarian, ambitious
Behavioral	
Use Occasion	Regular occasion, special occasion
Benefits Sought	Quality, service, economy
User Status	Nonuser, ex-user, potential user, first-time user, regular user
Usage Rate	Light user, medium user, heavy user
Loyalty Status	None, medium, strong, absolute
Readiness Stage	Unaware, aware, informed, interested, desirous, intending to buy
Attitude Toward Product	Enthusiastic, positive, indifferent, negative, hostile

Source: Adapted from Philip Kotler, *Marketing Management: Analysis, Planning and Control,* © 1984: 256. Adapted by permission of Prentice-Hall, Inc., Upper Saddle River, New Jersey.

Matching supply and demand allows factories to produce desirable levels without extra shifts, overtime, and subcontracting. Matching supply and demand also minimizes the number and severity of stock-outs. The demand for hotel rooms, for example, can be dependent on foreign tourists, businesspersons, and vacationers. Focusing separately on these three market segments, however, can allow hotel firms to more effectively predict overall supply and demand.

Banks now are segmenting markets to increase effectiveness. "You're dead in the water if you aren't segmenting the market," says Anne Moore, president of a bank consulting firm. The Internet makes market segmentation easier today because consumers naturally form "communities" on the Web.

Does the Internet Make Market Segmentation Easier?

Yes. The segments of people whom marketers want to reach online are much more precisely defined than the segments of people reached through traditional forms of media, such as television, radio, and magazines. For example, Quepasa.com is widely visited by Hispanics. Marketers aiming to reach college students, who are notoriously difficult to reach via traditional media, focus on sites such as collegeclub.com and studentadvantage.com. The gay and lesbian population has always been difficult to reach via traditional media but now can be focused on at sites such as gay.com. Marketers can reach persons interested in specific topics, such as travel or fishing, by placing banners on related Web sites.

People all over the world are congregating into virtual communities on the Web by becoming members/customers/visitors of Web sites that focus on an endless range of topics. People in essence segment themselves by nature of the Web sites that comprise their "favorite places," and many of these Web sites sell information regarding their "visitors." Businesses and groups of individuals all over the world pool their purchasing power in Web sites to get volume discounts.

Product Positioning

After markets have been segmented so that the firm can target particular customer groups, the next step is to find out what customers want and expect. This takes analysis and research. A severe mistake is to assume the firm knows what customers want and expect. Countless research studies reveal large differences between how customers define service and rank the importance of different service activities and how producers view services. Many firms have become successful by filling the gap between what customers and producers see as good service. What the customer believes is good service is paramount, not what the producer believes service should be.

Identifying target customers upon whom to focus marketing efforts sets the stage for deciding how to meet the needs and wants of particular consumer groups. Product positioning is widely used for this purpose. Positioning entails developing schematic representations that reflect how your products or services compare to competitors' on dimensions most important to success in the industry. The following steps are required in product positioning:

1. Select key criteria that effectively differentiate products or services in the industry.
2. Diagram a two-dimensional product-positioning map with specified criteria on each axis.
3. Plot major competitors' products or services in the resultant four-quadrant matrix.
4. Identify areas in the positioning map where the company's products or services could be most competitive in the given target market. Look for vacant areas (niches).
5. Develop a marketing plan to position the company's products or services appropriately.

Because just two criteria can be examined on a single product-positioning map, multiple maps are often developed to assess various approaches to strategy implementation. Multidimensional scaling could be used to examine three or more criteria simultaneously, but this technique requires computer assistance and is beyond the scope of this text. Some examples of product-positioning maps are illustrated in Figure 8-3.

Some rules for using product positioning as a strategy-implementation tool are the following:

1. Look for the hole or *vacant niche*. The best strategic opportunity might be an unserved segment.
2. Don't squat between segments. Any advantage from squatting (such as a larger target market) is offset by a failure to satisfy one segment. In decision-theory terms, the intent here is to avoid suboptimization by trying to serve more than one objective function.

VISIT THE NET

Provides the 2007–2017 Strategic Plan of the U.S. National Archives and Records Administration, including Annual Performance Plans. (www.archives.gov/about_us/ strategic_planning_and_reporting/ 2003_strategic_plan.html)

271

FIGURE 8-3

Examples of Product-Positioning Maps

A. A PRODUCT-POSITIONING MAP
   FOR BANKS

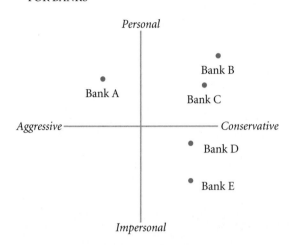

B. A PRODUCT-POSITIONING MAP
   FOR PERSONAL COMPUTERS

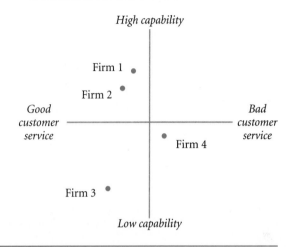

C. A PRODUCT-POSITIONING MAP FOR
   MENSWEAR RETAIL STORES

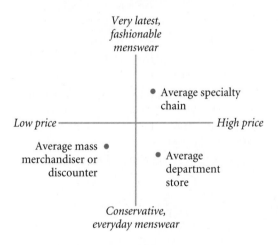

D. A PRODUCT-POSITIONING MAP
   FOR THE RENTAL CAR MARKET

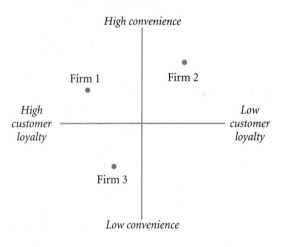

3. Don't serve two segments with the same strategy. Usually, a strategy successful with one segment cannot be directly transferred to another segment.

4. Don't position yourself in the middle of the map. The middle usually means a strategy that is not clearly perceived to have any distinguishing characteristics. This rule can vary with the number of competitors. For example, when there are only two competitors, the middle becomes the preferred strategic position.[2]

An effective product-positioning strategy meets two criteria: (1) it uniquely distinguishes a company from the competition, and (2) it leads customers to expect slightly less service than a company can deliver. Firms should not create expectations that exceed the service the firm can or will deliver. Network Equipment Technology is an example of a company that keeps customer expectations slightly below perceived performance. This is a constant challenge for marketers. Firms need to inform customers about what to expect and then exceed the promise. Underpromise and then overdeliver is the key!

Finance/Accounting Issues

In this section, we examine several finance/accounting concepts considered to be central to strategy implementation: acquiring needed capital, developing projected financial statements, preparing financial budgets, and evaluating the worth of a business. Some examples of decisions that may require finance/accounting policies are these:

1. To raise capital with short-term debt, long-term debt, preferred stock, or common stock
2. To lease or buy fixed assets
3. To determine an appropriate dividend payout ratio
4. To use LIFO (Last-in, First-out), FIFO (First-in, First-out), or a market-value accounting approach
5. To extend the time of accounts receivable
6. To establish a certain percentage discount on accounts within a specified period of time
7. To determine the amount of cash that should be kept on hand

NATURAL ENVIRONMENT PERSPECTIVE
Strategic Management of Your Health

The *BusinessWeek* cover story article on February 26, 2007 details how firms are striving to lower accelerating costs of employees' health care insurance premiums. Many firms such as Scotts Miracle-Gro Company, which makes gardening products; IBM; and Microsoft, are implementing wellness programs, requiring employees to get healthier or pay higher insurance premiums. Employees that do get healthier win bonuses, free trips, and pay lower premiums, while nonconforming employees pay higher premiums and receive no "healthy" benefits. Wellness of employees has become a strategic issue for many firms. Most firms require a health examination as a part of an employment application, and healthiness is more and more becoming a hiring factor. Michael Porter, co-author of *Redefining Health Care*, says: "We have this notion that you can gorge on hot dogs, be in a pie-eating contest, and drink every day, and society will take care of you. We can't afford to let individuals drive up company costs because they're not willing to address their own health problems."

Wellness programs such as the one at Scotts provide counseling to employees and seek lifestyle changes to achieve healthier living. For example, trans fats are a major cause of heart disease. Near elimination of trans fats in one's diet will reduce one's risk for heart attack by as much as 19 percent, according to a recent article. New York City now requires restaurants to inform customers about levels of trans fat being served in prepared foods. Chicago is considering a similar ban on trans fats. Denmark in 2003 became the first country to strictly regulate trans fats.

Restaurant chains are only slowly reducing trans fat levels in served foods because (1) trans fat oils make fried foods crispier, (2) trans fats give baked goods a longer shelf life, (3) trans fat oils can be used multiple times compared to other cooking oils, and (4) trans fat oils taste better. Three U.S. restaurant chains have switched to trans fat–free oils—Chili's, Ruby Tuesday, and Wendy's—but many U.S. chains still use trans fat oils, including Kentucky Fried Chicken, McDonald's, Dunkin' Donuts, Taco Bell, and Burger King. Marriott International in February 2007 eliminated trans fats from the food it serves at its 2,300 North American hotels, becoming the first big hotel chain to do so, although the 18-hotel Lowes luxury chain is close behind. Marriott's change includes its Renaissance, Courtyard, and Residence Inn brands.

Saturated fats are also bad, so one should avoid eating too much red meat and dairy products, which are high in saturated fats. The following seven lifestyle habits may significantly improve one's health and longevity:

1. Eat nutritiously—eat a variety of fruits and vegetables daily because they have ingredients that the body uses to repair and strengthen itself.

2. Stay hydrated—drink plenty of water to aid the body in eliminating toxins and to enable body organs to function efficiently; the body is mostly water.

3. Get plenty of rest—the body repairs itself during rest, so get at least seven hours of sleep nightly.

4. Get plenty of exercise—exercise vigorously at least 30 minutes daily so the body can release toxins and strengthen vital organs.

5. Reduce stress—the body's immune system is weakened when one is under stress, making the body vulnerable to many ailments, so keep stress to a minimum.

6. Do not smoke—smoking kills, no doubt about it.

7. Take vitamin supplements—consult your physician, but because it is difficult for diet alone to supply all the nutrients and vitamins needed, supplements can be helpful in achieving good health and longevity.

Source: Adapted from Michelle Conlin, "Get Healthy—or Else," *BusinessWeek* (February 26, 2007): 58–69; Lauren Etter, "Trans Fats: Will They Get Shelved?" *Wall Street Journal* (December 8, 2006): A6; and Joel Fuhrman, MD, *Eat to Live* (Boston: Little Brown, 2003).

Eating Healthy Is a Key to Success in Life. *Source:* Andy Crawford (c) Dorling Kindersley

As indicated in the "Natural Environment Perspective," employees' health is increasingly being viewed as an important financial management issue in firms. Employee wellness has become a strategic issue. As medical doctor and book author Joel Fuhrman says, we all should "Eat to Live" rather than "Live to Eat."

Acquiring Capital to Implement Strategies

Successful strategy implementation often requires additional capital. Besides net profit from operations and the sale of assets, two basic sources of capital for an organization are debt and equity. Determining an appropriate mix of debt and equity in a firm's capital structure can be vital to successful strategy implementation. An *Earnings Per Share/Earnings Before Interest and Taxes (EPS/EBIT) analysis* is the most widely used technique for determining whether debt, stock, or a combination of debt and stock is the best alternative for raising capital to implement strategies. This technique involves an examination of the impact that debt versus stock financing has on earnings per share under various assumptions as to EBIT.

Theoretically, an enterprise should have enough debt in its capital structure to boost its return on investment by applying debt to products and projects earning more than the cost of the debt. In low earning periods, too much debt in the capital structure of an organization can endanger stockholders' returns and jeopardize company survival. Fixed debt obligations generally must be met, regardless of circumstances. This does not mean that stock issuances are always better than debt for raising capital. Some special concerns with stock issuances are dilution of ownership, effect on stock price, and the need to share future earnings with all new shareholders.

Without going into detail on other institutional and legal issues related to the debt versus stock decision, EPS/EBIT may be best explained by working through an example. Let's say the Brown Company needs to raise €1 million to finance implementation of a market-development strategy. The company's common stock currently sells for €50 per share, and 100,000 shares are outstanding. The prime interest rate is 10 percent, and the company's tax rate is 50 percent. The company's earnings before interest and taxes next year are expected to be €2 million if a recession occurs, €4 million if the economy stays as is, and €8 million if the economy significantly improves. EPS/EBIT analysis can be used to determine if all stock, all debt, or some combination of stock and debt is the best capital financing alternative. The EPS/EBIT analysis for this example is provided in Table 8-3.

As indicated by the EPS values of 9.5, 19.50, and 39.50 in Table 8-3, debt is the best financing alternative for the Brown Company if a recession, boom, or normal year is expected. An EPS/EBIT chart can be constructed to determine the break-even point, where one financing alternative becomes more attractive than another. Figure 8-4 indicates that issuing common stock is the least attractive financing alternative for the Brown Company.

EPS/EBIT analysis is a valuable tool for making the capital financing decisions needed to implement strategies, but several considerations should be made whenever using this technique. First, profit levels may be higher for stock or debt alternatives when EPS levels are lower. For example, looking only at the earnings after taxes (EAT) values in Table 8-3, you can see that the common stock option is the best alternative, regardless of economic conditions. If the Brown Company's mission includes strict profit maximization, as opposed to the maximization of stockholders' wealth or some other criterion, then stock rather than debt is the best choice of financing.

Another consideration when using EPS/EBIT analysis is flexibility. As an organization's capital structure changes, so does its flexibility for considering future capital needs. Using all debt or all stock to raise capital in the present may impose fixed obligations, restrictive covenants, or other constraints that could severely reduce a firm's ability to raise additional capital in the future. Control is also a concern. When additional stock is issued to finance strategy implementation, ownership and control of the enterprise are diluted. This

TABLE 8-3   EPS/EBIT Analysis for the Brown Company (In Millions)

	Common Stock Financing			Debt Financing			Combination Financing		
	Recession	Normal	Boom	Recession	Normal	Boom	Recession	Normal	Boom
EBIT	€ 2.0	€ 4.0	€ 8.0	€ 2.0	€ 4.0	€ 8.0	€ 2.0	€ 4.0	€ 8.0
Interest[a]	0	0	0	.10	.10	.10	.05	.05	.05
EBT	2.0	4.0	8.0	1.9	3.9	7.9	1.95	3.95	7.95
Taxes	1.0	2.0	4.0	.95	1.95	3.95	.975	1.975	3.975
EAT	1.0	2.0	4.0	.95	1.95	3.95	.975	1.975	3.975
#Shares[b]	.12	.12	.12	.10	.10	.10	.11	.11	.11
EPS[c]	8.33	16.66	33.33	9.5	19.50	39.50	8.86	17.95	36.14

[a]The annual interest charge on €1 million at 10% is €100,000 and on €0.5 million is €50,000. This row is in €, not %.

[b]To raise all of the needed €1 million with stock, 20,000 new shares must be issued, raising the total to 120,000 shares outstanding. To raise one-half of the needed €1 million with stock, 10,000 new shares must be issued, raising the total to 110,000 shares outstanding.

[c]EPS = Earnings After Taxes (EAT) divided by shares (number of shares outstanding).

FIGURE 8-4

An EPS/EBIT Chart for the Brown Company

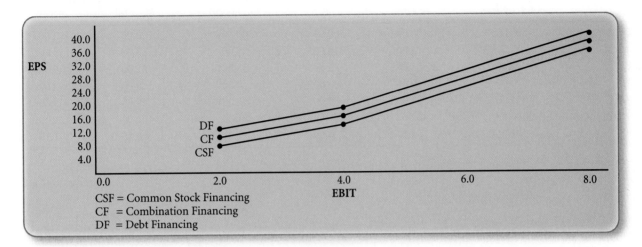

CSF = Common Stock Financing
CF = Combination Financing
DF = Debt Financing

can be a serious concern in today's business environment of hostile takeovers, mergers, and acquisitions.

Dilution of ownership can be an overriding concern in closely held corporations in which stock issuances affect the decision-making power of majority stockholders. For example, the Smucker family owns 30 percent of the stock in Smucker's, a well-known jam and jelly company. When Smucker's acquired Dickson Family, Inc., the company used mostly debt rather than stock in order not to dilute the family ownership.

When using EPS/EBIT analysis, timing in relation to movements of stock prices, interest rates, and bond prices becomes important. In times of depressed stock prices, debt may prove to be the most suitable alternative from both a cost and a demand standpoint. However, when cost of capital (interest rates) is high, stock issuances become more attractive.

Tables 8-4 and 8-5 provide EPS/EBIT analyses for two companies—Gateway and Boeing. Notice in those analyses that the combination stock/debt options vary from 30/70 to 70/30. Any number of combinations could be explored. However, sometimes in preparing the EPS/EBIT graphs, the lines will intersect, thus revealing break-even points

TABLE 8-4 **EPS/EBIT Analysis for Gateway (M = In Millions)**

Amount Needed: $1,000 M

EBIT Range: − $500 M to + $100 M to + $500 M

Interest Rate: 5%

Tax Rate: 0% (because the firm has been incurring a loss annually)

Stock Price: $6.00

# of Shares Outstanding: 371 M

	Common Stock Financing			Debt Financing		
	Recession	*Normal*	*Boom*	*Recession*	*Normal*	*Boom*
EBIT	(500.00)	100.00	500.00	(500.00)	100.00	500.00
Interest	0.00	0.00	0.00	50.00	50.00	50.00
EBT	(500.00)	100.00	500.00	(550.00)	50.00	450.00
Taxes	0.00	0.00	0.00	0.00	0.00	0.00
EAT	(500.00)	100.00	500.00	(550.00)	50.00	450.00
#Shares	537.67	537.67	537.67	371.00	371.00	371.00
EPS	**(0.93)**	**0.19**	**0.93**	**(1.48)**	**0.13**	**1.21**

(continued)

TABLE 8-4 EPS/EBIT Analysis for Gateway (M = In Millions)—continued

	70 Percent Stock—30 Percent Debt			70 Percent Debt—30 Percent Stock		
	Recession	*Normal*	*Boom*	*Recession*	*Normal*	*Boom*
EBIT	(500.00)	100.00	500.00	(500.00)	100.00	500.00
Interest	15.00	15.00	15.00	35.00	35.00	35.00
EBT	(515.00)	85.00	485.00	(535.00)	65.00	465.00
Taxes	0.00	0.00	0.00	0.00	0.00	0.00
EAT	(515.00)	85.00	485.00	(535.00)	65.00	465.00
#Shares	487.67	487.67	487.67	421.00	421.00	421.00
EPS	**(1.06)**	**0.17**	**0.99**	**(1.27)**	**0.15**	**1.10**

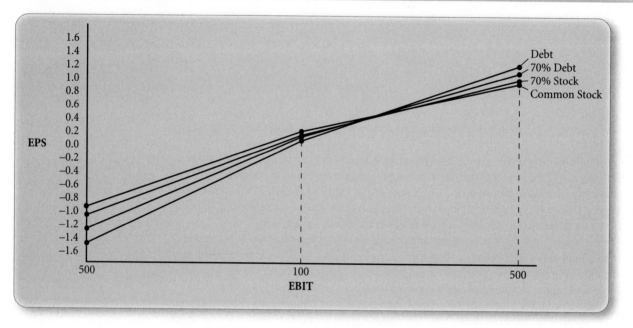

Conclusion: Gateway should use common stock to raise capital in recession or normal economic conditions but should use debt financing under boom conditions. Note that stock is the best alternative under all three conditions according to EAT (profit maximization), but EPS (maximize shareholders' wealth) is the better ratio to make this decision.

TABLE 8-5 EPS/EBIT Analysis for Boeing (M = In Millions)

Amount Needed: $10,000 M

Interest Rate: 5%

Tax Rate: 7%

Stock Price: $53.00

# of Shares Outstanding: 826 M

	Common Stock Financing			Debt Financing		
	Recession	*Normal*	*Boom*	*Recession*	*Normal*	*Boom*
EBIT	1,000.00	2,500.00	5,000.00	1,000.00	2,500.00	5,000.00
Interest	0.00	0.00	0.00	500.00	500.00	500.00
EBT	1,000.00	2,500.00	5,000.00	500.00	2,000.00	4,500.00
Taxes	70.00	175.00	350.00	35.00	140.00	315.00
EAT	930.00	2,325.00	4,650.00	465.00	1,860.00	4,185.00
# Shares	1,014.68	1,014.68	1,014.68	826.00	826.00	826.00
EPS	**0.92**	**2.29**	**4.58**	**0.56**	**2.25**	**5.07**

(*continued*)

277

TABLE 8-5 EPS/EBIT Analysis for Boeing (M = In Millions)—continued

	70% Stock—30% Debt			70% Debt—30% Stock		
	Recession	Normal	Boom	Recession	Normal	Boom
EBIT	1,000.00	2,500.00	5,000.00	1,000.00	2,500.00	5,000.00
Interest	150.00	150.00	150.00	350.00	350.00	350.00
EBT	850.00	2,350.00	4,850.00	650.00	2,150.00	4,650.00
Taxes	59.50	164.50	339.50	45.50	150.50	325.50
EAT	790.50	2,185.50	4,510.50	604.50	1,999.50	4,324.50
# Shares	958.08	958.08	958.08	882.60	882.60	882.60
EPS	**0.83**	**2.28**	**4.71**	**0.68**	**2.27**	**4.90**

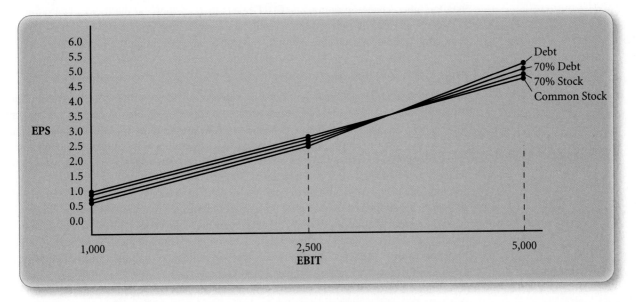

Conclusion: Boeing should use common stock to raise capital in recession (see 0.92) or normal (see 2.29) economic conditions but should use debt financing under boom conditions (see 5.07). Note that a dividends row is absent from this analysis. The more shares outstanding, the more dividends to be paid (if the firm pays dividends), which would lower the common stock EPS values.

at which one financing alternative becomes more or less attractive than another. The slope of these lines will be determined by a combination of factors including stock price, interest rate, number of shares, and amount of capital needed. Also, it should be noted here that the best financing alternatives are indicated by the highest EPS values. In Tables 8-4 and 8-5, note that the tax rates for the companies vary considerably and should be computed from the respective income statements by dividing taxes paid by income before taxes.

In Table 8-4, the higher EPS values indicate that Gateway should use stock to raise capital in recession or normal economic conditions but should use debt financing under boom conditions. Stock is the best alternative for Gateway under all three conditions if EAT (profit maximization) were the decision criteria, but EPS (maximize shareholders' wealth) is the better ratio to make this decision. Firms can do many things in the short run to maximize profits, so investors and creditors consider maximizing shareholders' wealth to be the better criteria for making financing decisions.

In Table 8-5, note that Boeing should use stock to raise capital in recession (see 0.92) or normal (see 2.29) economic conditions but should use debt financing under boom conditions (see 5.07). Let's calculate here the number of shares figure of 1014.68 given under Boeing's stock alternative. Divide $10,000 M funds needed by the stock price of $53 = 188.68 M new shares to be issued + the 826 M shares outstanding already = 1014.68 M shares under the stock scenario. Along the final row, EPS is the number of shares outstanding divided by EAT in all columns.

Note in Table 8-4 and Table 8-5 that a dividends row is absent from both the Gateway and Boeing analyses. The more shares outstanding, the more dividends to be paid (if the firm indeed pays dividends). Paying dividends lowers EAT, which lowers the stock EPS values whenever this aspect is included. To consider dividends in an EPS/EBIT analysis, simply insert another row for "Dividends" right below the "EAT" row and then insert an "Earnings After Taxes and Dividends" row. Considering dividends would make the analysis more robust.

Note in both the Gateway and Boeing graphs, there is a break-even point between the normal and boom range of EBIT where the debt option overtakes the 70% Debt/30% Stock option as the best financing alternative. A break-even point is where two lines cross each other. A break-even point is the EBIT level where various financing alternative represented by lines crossing are equally attractive in terms of EPS. Both the Gateway and Boeing graphs indicate that EPS values are highest for the 100 percent debt option at high EBIT levels. The two graphs also reveal that the EPS values for 100 percent debt increase faster than the other financing options as EBIT levels increase beyond the break-even point. At low levels of EBIT however, both the Gateway and Boeing graphs indicate that 100 percent stock is the best financing alternative because the EPS values are highest.

Projected Financial Statements

Projected financial statement analysis is a central strategy-implementation technique because it allows an organization to examine the expected results of various actions and approaches. This type of analysis can be used to forecast the impact of various implementation decisions (for example, to increase promotion expenditures by 50 percent to support a market-development strategy, to increase salaries by 25 percent to support a market-penetration strategy, to increase research and development expenditures by 70 percent to support product development, or to sell $1 million of common stock to raise capital for diversification). Nearly all financial institutions require at least three years of projected financial statements whenever a business seeks capital. A projected income statement and balance sheet allow an organization to compute projected financial ratios under various strategy-implementation scenarios. When compared to prior years and to industry averages, financial ratios provide valuable insights into the feasibility of various strategy-implementation approaches.

Primarily as a result of the Enron collapse and accounting scandal and the ensuing U.S. Sarbanes-Oxley Act, companies today are being much more diligent in preparing projected financial statements to "reasonably rather than too optimistically" project future expenses and earnings. There is much more care not to mislead shareholders and other constituencies.[3]

A 2008 projected income statement and a balance sheet for the Litten Company are provided in Table 8-6. The projected statements for Litten are based on five assumptions: (1) The company needs to raise $45 million to finance expansion into foreign markets; (2) $30 million of this total will be raised through increased debt and $15 million through common stock; (3) sales are expected to increase 50 percent; (4) three new facilities, costing a total of $30 million, will be constructed in foreign markets; and (5) land for the new facilities is already owned by the company. Note in Table 8-6 that Litten's strategies and their implementation are expected to result in a sales increase from $100 million to $150 million and in a net increase in income from $6 million to $9.75 million in the forecasted year.

There are six steps in performing projected financial analysis:

1. Prepare the projected income statement before the balance sheet. Start by forecasting sales as accurately as possible. Be careful not to blindly push historical percentages into the future with regard to revenue (sales) increases. Be mindful of what the firm did to achieve those past sales increases, which may not be appropriate for the future unless the firm takes similar or analogous actions (such as opening a similar number of stores, for example). If dealing with a manufacturing firm, also be mindful that if the firm is operating at 100 percent capacity running three eight-hour shifts per day, then probably new manufacturing facilities (land, plant, and equipment) will be needed to increase sales further.

2. Use the percentage-of-sales method to project cost of goods sold (CGS) and the expense items in the income statement. For example, if CGS is 70 percent of sales

TABLE 8-6 A Projected Income Statement and Balance Sheet for the Litten Company (In Millions)

	Prior Year 2007	Projected Year 2008	Remarks
PROJECTED INCOME STATEMENT			
Sales	$100	$150.00	50% increase
Cost of Goods Sold	70	105.00	70% of sales
Gross Margin	30	45.00	
Selling Expense	10	15.00	10% of sales
Administrative Expense	5	7.50	5% of sales
Earnings Before Interest and Taxes	15	22.50	
Interest	3	3.00	
Earnings Before Taxes	12	19.50	
Taxes	6	9.75	50% rate
Net Income	**6**	**9.75**	
Dividends	2	5.00	
Retained Earnings	4	4.75	
PROJECTED BALANCE SHEET			
Assets			
Cash	5	7.75	Plug figure
Accounts Receivable	2	4.00	100% increase
Inventory	20	45.00	
Total Current Assets	27	56.75	
Land	15	15.00	
Plant and Equipment	50	80.00	Add three new plants at $10 million each
Less Depreciation	10	20.00	
Net Plant and Equipment	40	60.00	
Total Fixed Assets	55	75.00	
Total Assets	**82**	**131.75**	
Liabilities			
Accounts Payable	10	10.00	
Notes Payable	10	10.00	
Total Current Liabilities	20	20.00	
Long-term Debt	40	70.00	Borrowed $30 million
Additional Paid-in-Capital	20	35.00	Issued 100,000 shares at $150 each
Retained Earnings	2	6.75	$2 + $4.75
Total Liabilities and Net Worth	**82**	**131.75**	

in the prior year (as it is in Table 8-6), then use that same percentage to calculate CGS in the future year—unless there is a reason to use a different percentage. Items such as interest, dividends, and taxes must be treated independently and cannot be forecasted using the percentage-of-sales method.

3. Calculate the projected net income.
4. Subtract from the net income any dividends to be paid for that year. This remaining net income is retained earnings (RE). Bring this retained earnings amount for that year (NI − DIV = RE) over to the balance sheet by adding it to the prior year's RE shown on the balance sheet. In other words, every year a firm adds its RE for that particular year (from the income statement) to its historical RE total on the balance sheet. Therefore, the RE amount on the balance sheet is a cumulative number rather than money available for strategy implementation! Note that RE is the **first** projected balance sheet item to be entered. Due to this accounting procedure in developing projected financial statements, the RE amount on the balance sheet is usually a large number. However, it also can be a low or even negative number if the firm has been

incurring losses. The only way for RE to decrease from one year to the next on the balance sheet is (1) if the firm incurred an earnings loss that year or (2) the firm had positive net income for the year but paid out dividends more than the net income. Be mindful that RE is the key link between a projected income statement and balance sheet, so be careful to make this calculation correctly.

5. Project the balance sheet items, beginning with retained earnings and then forecasting stockholders' equity, long-term liabilities, current liabilities, total liabilities, total assets, fixed assets, and current assets (in that order). Use the cash account as the plug figure—that is, use the cash account to make the assets total the liabilities and net worth. Then make appropriate adjustments. For example, if the cash needed to balance the statements is too small (or too large), make appropriate changes to borrow more (or less) money than planned.

6. List comments (remarks) on the projected statements. Any time a significant change is made in an item from a prior year to the projected year, an explanation (remark) should be provided. Remarks are essential because otherwise pro formas are meaningless.

Projected Financial Statement Analysis for Mattel, Inc.

Since so many strategic management students have limited experience developing projected financial statements, let's apply the steps outlined on the previous pages to Mattel, the huge toy company headquartered in El Segundo, California. Mattel designs, manufactures, and markets toy products from fashion dolls to children's books. The company Web site is www.mattel.com. Mattel's recent income statements and balance sheets are provided in Table 8-7 and Table 8-8 respectively.

TABLE 8-7   Mattel's Actual Income Statements (In Thousands)

	2006	2005	2004
Total Revenue	$5,650,156	5,179,016	5,102,786
Cost of Revenue	3,038,363	2,806,148	2,692,061
Gross Profit	2,611,793	2,372,868	2,410,725
Operating Expenses			
Research Development	-	-	-
Selling General and Administrative	1,882,975	1,708,339	1,679,908
Non-Recurring	-	-	-
Others	-	-	-
Total Operating Expenses	-	-	-
Operating Income or Loss	728,818	664,529	730,817
Income from Continuing Operations			
Total Other Income/Expenses Net	34,791	64,010	43,201
Earnings Before Interest and Taxes	763,609	728,539	774,018
Interest Expense	79,853	76,490	77,764
Income Before Tax	683,756	652,049	696,254
Income Tax Expense	90,829	235,030	123,531
Minority Interest	-	-	-
Net Income from Continuing Ops	592,927	417,019	572,723
Non-Recurring Events			
Discontinued Operations	-	-	-
Extraordinary Items	-	-	-
Effect of Accounting Changes	-	-	-
Other Items	-	-	-
Net Income	592,927	417,019	572,723
Preferred Stock and Other Adjustments	-	-	-
Net Income Applicable to Common Shares	$592,927	$417,019	$572,723

TABLE 8-8 Mattel's Actual Balance Sheets (In Thousands)

	2006	2005	2004
Assets			
Current Assets			
Cash and Cash Equivalents	$1,205,552	997,734	1,156,835
Short-Term Investments	-	-	-
Net Receivables	943,813	760,643	759,033
Inventory	383,149	376,897	418,633
Other Current Assets	317,624	277,226	302,649
Total Current Assets	2,850,138	2,412,500	2,637,150
Long-Term Investments	-	-	-
Property, Plant, and Equipment	536,749	547,104	586,526
Goodwill	845,324	718,069	735,680
Intangible Assets	70,593	20,422	22,926
Accumulated Amortization	-	-	-
Other Assets	149,912	178,304	201,836
Deferred Long-Term Asset Charges	503,168	495,914	572,374
Total Assets	$4,955,884	4,372,313	4,756,492
Liabilities			
Current Liabilities			
Accounts Payable	$1,518,234	1,245,191	1,303,822
Short/Current Long-Term Debt	64,286	217,994	423,349
Other Current Liabilities	-	-	-
Total Current Liabilities	1,582,520	1,463,185	1,727,171
Long-Term Debt	635,714	525,000	400,000
Other Liabilities	304,676	282,395	243,509
Deferred Long-Term Liability Charges	-	-	-
Minority Interest	-	-	-
Negative Goodwill	-	-	-
Total Liabilities	2,522,910	2,270,580	2,370,680
Stockholders' Equity			
Misc. Stocks, Options, Warrants	-	-	-
Redeemable Preferred Stock	-	-	-
Preferred Stock	-	-	-
Common Stock	441,369	441,369	441,369
Retained Earnings	1,652,140	1,314,068	1,093,288
Treasury Stock	(996,981)	(935,711)	(473,349)
Capital Surplus	1,613,307	1,589,281	1,594,332
Other Stockholders' Equity	(276,861)	(307,274)	(269,828)
Total Stockholders' Equity	2,432,974	2,101,733	2,385,812
Total Liabilities and SE	$4,955,884	4,372,313	4,756,492

159,101 difference

In Tables 8-9 and 8-10, Mattel's projected income statements and balance sheets respectively for 2007, 2008, and 2009 are provided based on the following hypothetical strategies:

1. The company desires to build 20 Mattel stores annually at a cost of $1 million each.
2. The company plans to develop new toy products at an annual cost of $10 million.
3. The company plans to increase its advertising/promotion expenditures 30 percent over three years, at a cost of $30 million ($10 million per year).
4. The company plans to buy back $100 million of its own stock (called Treasury stock) annually for the next three years.

TABLE 8-9 Mattel's Projected Income Statements (In Thousands)

	2009	2008	2007	Author Comment
Total Revenue	$7,520,357	6,836,688	6,215,171	up 10% annually
Cost of Revenue	4,060,992	3,691,811	3,356,192	remains 54%
Gross Profit	3,459,365	3,144,877	2,858,979	subtraction
Operating Expenses				
Research Development	10,000	10,000	10,000	total $30M new
Selling General and Administrative	2,491,717	2,256,107	2,051,006	remains 33% + $10 M annually
Non-Recurring	-	-	-	
Others	-	-	-	
Total Operating Expenses	-	-	-	
Operating Income or Loss	957,648	878,770	797,973	subtraction
Income from Continuing Operations				
Total Other Income/Expenses Net	34,791	34,791	34,791	keep it the same
Earnings Before Interest and Taxes	992,439	913,561	832,764	addition
Interest Expense	97,823	91,423	85,442	up 7%; LTD up 7%
Income Before Tax	894,616	822,138	737,322	
Income Tax Expense	90,829	90,829	90,829	keep it the same
Minority Interest	-	-	-	
Net Income from Continuing Ops	803,787	731,309	646,493	subtraction
Discontinued Operations	-	-	-	
Extraordinary Items	-	-	-	
Effect of Accounting Changes	-	-	-	
Other Items	-	-	-	
Net Income	803,787	731,309	646,493	
Preferred Stock and Other Adjustments	-	-	-	
Net Income Applicable to Common Shares	$803,787	731,309	646,493	

5. The company expects revenues to increase 10 percent annually with the above strategies. Mattel can handle this increase with existing production facilities.
6. Dividend payout will be increased from 57 percent of net income to 60 percent.
7. To finance the $380 million total cost for the above strategies, Mattel plans to use long-term debt for $150 million ($50 million per year for three years) and $230 million by issuing stock ($77 million per year for three years).

The Mattel projected financial statements were prepared using the six steps outlined on prior pages and the above seven strategy statements. Note the cash account is used as the plug figure, and it is too high, so Mattel could reduce this number and concurrently reduce a liability and/or equity account the same amount to keep the statement in balance. Rarely is the cash account perfect on the first pass through, so adjustments are needed and made. However, these adjustments are *not* made on the projected statements given in Tables 8-9 and 8-10, so that the seven strategy statements above can be more readily seen on respective rows. Note the author's comments on Tables 8-9 and 8-10 that help explain changes in the numbers.

The U.S. Securities and Exchange Commission (SEC) conducts fraud investigations if projected numbers are misleading or if they omit information that's important to investors. Projected statements must conform with generally accepted accounting principles (GAAP) in the United States and must not be designed to hide poor expected results. The Sarbanes-Oxley Act requires U.S. CEOs and CFOs of corporations to personally sign their firms' financial statements attesting to their accuracy. These executives could thus be held personally liable for misleading or inaccurate statements. The collapse of the Arthur Andersen accounting firm, along with its client Enron, fostered a "zero tolerance" policy among auditors and shareholders with regard to a firm's financial statements. But plenty of firms still "inflate" their financial projections and call them "pro formas," so investors, shareholders, and other stakeholders must still be wary of different companies' financial projections.[4]

TABLE 8-10   Mattel's Projected Balance Sheets (In Thousands)

	2009	2008	2007	Author Comment
Assets				
Current Assets				
Cash and Cash Equivalents	$3,232,406	2,972,664	2,570,635	too high, could reduce this and pay off some LTD to keep balance
Short-Term Investments	-	-	-	
Net Receivables	943,813	760,643	759,033	
Inventory	509,969	463,609	421,463	up 10% annually
Other Current Assets	317,624	317,624	317,624	keep it the same
Total Current Assets				
Long-Term Investments	-	-	-	
Property, Plant, and Equipment	596,749	576,749	556,749	up $20M annually
Goodwill	845,324	845,324	845,324	keep it the same
Intangible Assets	70,593	70,593	70,593	keep it the same
Accumulated Amortization	-	-	-	
Other Assets	149,912	149,912	149,912	keep it the same
Deferred Long-Term Asset Charges	503,168	503,168	503,168	keep it the same
Total Assets	7,169,558	6,660,286	6,194,501	
Liabilities				
Current Liabilities				
Accounts Payable	1,518,234	1,518,234	1,518,234	keep it the same
Short/Current Long-Term Debt	64,286	64,286	64,286	keep it the same
Other Current Liabilities	-	-	-	
Total Current Liabilities	1,582,520	1,582,520	1,582,520	
Long-Term Debt	785,714	735,714	685,714	up $50M annually
Other Liabilities	304,676	304,676	304,676	keep it the same
Deferred Long-Term Liability Charges	-	-	-	
Minority Interest	-	-	-	
Negative Goodwill	-	-	-	
Total Liabilities	2,672,910	2,622,910	2,572,910	
Stockholders' Equity				
Misc. Stocks, Options, Warrants	-	-	-	
Redeemable Preferred Stock	-	-	-	
Preferred Stock	-	-	-	
Common Stock	441,369	441,369	441,369	keep it the same
Retained Earnings	2,961,092	2,478,820	2,040,035	60% of NI = div
Treasury Stock	(1,296,981)	(1,196,981)	(1,096,981)	up $100M annually
Capital Surplus	2,114,307	2,037,307	1,960,307	up $77M annually
Other Stockholders' Equity	(276,861)	(276,861)	(276,861)	keep it the same
Total Stockholders' Equity	4,496,648	4,037,376	3,621,591	addition
Total Liabilities and SE	$7,169,558	6,660,286	6,194,501	addition

Financial Budgets

A *financial budget* is a document that details how funds will be obtained and spent for a specified period of time. Annual budgets are most common, although the period of time for a budget can range from one day to more than 10 years. Fundamentally, financial budgeting is a method for specifying what must be done to complete strategy implementation successfully. Financial budgeting should not be thought of as a tool for limiting expenditures but rather as a method for obtaining the most productive and profitable use of an organization's resources. Financial budgets can be viewed as the planned allocation of a firm's resources based on forecasts of the future.

There are almost as many different types of financial budgets as there are types of organizations. Some common types of budgets include cash budgets, operating budgets, sales budgets, profit budgets, factory budgets, capital budgets, expense budgets, divisional budgets, variable budgets, flexible budgets, and fixed budgets. When an organization is experiencing financial difficulties, budgets are especially important in guiding strategy implementation.

Perhaps the most common type of financial budget is the *cash budget*. The U.S. Financial Accounting Standards Board (FASB) has mandated that every publicly held company in the United States must issue an annual cash-flow statement in addition to the usual financial reports. The statement includes all receipts and disbursements of cash in operations, investments, and financing. It supplements the Statement on Changes in Financial Position formerly included in the annual reports of all publicly held companies. A cash budget for the year 2009 for the Toddler Toy Company is provided in Table 8-11. Note that Toddler is not expecting to have surplus cash until November 2009.

Financial budgets have some limitations. First, budgetary programs can become so detailed that they are cumbersome and overly expensive. Overbudgeting or underbudgeting can cause problems. Second, financial budgets can become a substitute for objectives. A budget is a tool and not an end in itself. Third, budgets can hide inefficiencies if based solely on precedent rather than on periodic evaluation of circumstances and standards. Finally, budgets are sometimes used as instruments of tyranny that result in frustration, resentment, absenteeism, and high turnover. To minimize the effect of this last concern, managers should increase the participation of subordinates in preparing budgets.

Evaluating the Worth of a Business

Evaluating the worth of a business is central to strategy implementation because integrative, intensive, and diversification strategies are often implemented by acquiring other firms. Other strategies, such as retrenchment and divestiture, may result in the sale of a division of an organization or of the firm itself. Thousands of transactions occur each year in which businesses are bought or sold in the United States. In all these cases, it is necessary to establish the financial worth or cash value of a business to successfully implement strategies.

All the various methods for determining a business's worth can be grouped into three main approaches: what a firm owns, what a firm earns, or what a firm will bring in the

TABLE 8-11 **Six-Month Cash Budget for the Toddler Toy Company in 2009**

Cash Budget (In Thousands)	July	Aug.	Sept.	Oct.	Nov.	Dec.	Jan.
Receipts							
Collections	$12,000	$21,000	$31,000	$35,000	$22,000	$18,000	$11,000
Payments							
Purchases	14,000	21,000	28,000	14,000	14,000	7,000	
Wages and Salaries	1,500	2,000	2,500	1,500	1,500	1,000	
Rent	500	500	500	500	500	500	
Other Expenses	200	300	400	200	—	100	
Taxes	—	8,000	—	—	—	—	
Payment on Machine	—	—	10,000	—	—	—	
Total Payments	$16,200	$31,800	$41,400	$16,200	$16,000	$8,600	
Net Cash Gain (Loss) During Month	−4,200	−10,800	−10,400	18,800	6,000	9,400	
Cash at Start of Month if No Borrowing Is Done	6,000	1,800	−9,000	−19,400	−600	5,400	
Cumulative Cash (Cash at start plus gains or minus losses)	1,800	−9,000	−19,400	−600	5,400	14,800	
Less Desired Level of Cash	−5,000	−5,000	−5,000	−5,000	−5,000	−5,000	
Total Loans Outstanding to Maintain $5,000 Cash Balance	$3,200	$14,000	$24,400	$5,600	—	—	
Surplus Cash	—	—	—	—	400	9,800	

market. But it is important to realize that valuation is not an exact science. The valuation of a firm's worth is based on financial facts, but common sense and intuitive judgment must enter into the process. It is difficult to assign a monetary value to some factors—such as a loyal customer base, a history of growth, legal suits pending, dedicated employees, a favorable lease, a bad credit rating, or good patents—that may not be reflected in a firm's financial statements. Also, different valuation methods will yield different totals for a firm's worth, and no prescribed approach is best for a certain situation. Evaluating the worth of a business truly requires both qualitative and quantitative skills.

The first approach in evaluating the worth of a business is determining its net worth or stockholders' equity. Net worth represents the sum of common stock, additional paid-in capital, and retained earnings. After calculating net worth, add or subtract an appropriate amount for goodwill, overvalued or undervalued assets, and intangibles. Whereas intangibles include copyrights, patents, and trademarks, goodwill arises only if a firm acquires another firm and pays more than the book value for that firm. For example, in late 2007 when M&F Worldwide acquired the much larger check-printing and software firm John H. Harland Company for $1.7 billion, that equated to $52.75 per share, even though John Harland's stock price was only $44.47. So M&F paid a 19 percent premium over the book value (number of shares outstanding times stock price) for John Harland's stock. M&F now carries this on its balance sheet as goodwill. Paying over book value happens quite often. Cisco Systems in late 2007 paid a 23 percent premium in their acquisition of WebEx Communications.

Phillips Electronics NV recently bought U.S.-based Color Kinetics for $794 million to expand its lighting business. This equated to $34 a share, or a 14 percent premium over Color Kinetics' closing share price that day of $29.79. This total provides a reasonable estimate of a firm's monetary value. If a firm has goodwill, it will be listed on the balance sheet, perhaps as "intangibles." It should be noted that Financial Accounting Standard Board (FASB) Rule 142 requires companies to admit once a year if the premiums they paid for acquisitions, called goodwill, were a waste of money. Goodwill is not a good thing to have on a balance sheet. Note in Table 8-12 that Mattel's goodwill of $845 million as a percent of its total assets ($4,955 million) is 17.1 percent, which is extremely high compared to Nordstrom's goodwill of $51 million as a percentage of its total assets ($4,821 million), 1.1 percent. Pfizer's goodwill to total assets percentage also is high at 18.7 percent. As noted in the "Global Perspective" box, accounting standards worldwide are converging, which is good.

The second approach to measuring the value of a firm grows out of the belief that the worth of any business should be based largely on the future benefits its owners may derive through net profits. A conservative rule of thumb is to establish a business's worth as five times the firm's current annual profit. A five-year average profit level could also be used. When using the approach, remember that firms normally suppress earnings in their financial statements to minimize taxes.

The third approach, letting the market determine a business's worth, involves three methods. First, base the firm's worth on the selling price of a similar company. A potential problem, however, is that sometimes comparable figures are not easy to locate, even though substantial information on firms that buy or sell to other firms is available in major libraries. The second approach is called the *price-earnings ratio method.* To use this method, divide the market price of the firm's common stock by the annual earnings per share and multiply this number by the firm's average net income for the past five years. The third method can be called the *outstanding shares method.* To use this method, simply multiply the number of shares outstanding by the market price per share and add a premium. The premium is simply a per-share dollar amount that a person or firm is willing to pay to control (acquire) the other company.

Business evaluations are becoming routine in many situations. Businesses have many strategy-implementation reasons for determining their worth in addition to preparing to be sold or to buy other companies. Employee plans, taxes, retirement packages, mergers, acquisitions, expansion plans, banking relationships, death of a principal, divorce, partnership agreements, and tax audits are other reasons for a periodic valuation. It is just good business to have a reasonable understanding of what your firm is worth. This knowledge protects the interests of all parties involved.

TABLE 8-12 **Company Worth Analysis for Mattel, Nordstrom, and Pfizer (year-end 2006, in $millions, except stock price and EPS)**

Input Data	Mattel	Nordstrom	Pfizer
Shareholders' Equity	$2,432	$2,168	$71,358
Net Income (NI)	592	677	19,337
Stock Price	25	55	25
EPS	1.48	2.55	2.58
# of Shares Outstanding	393	257	7,090
Goodwill	845	51	20,876
Total Assets	4,955	4,821	114,837
Company Worth Analyses			
1. Shareholders' Equity plus Goodwill	$3,277	$2,219	$92,244
2. Net Income × 5	2,960	3,385	96,685
3. (Stock Price/EPS) × NI	10,000	14,601	187,374
4. # of Shares Out × Stock Price	9,825	14,135	177,250
5. Enterprise Value according to http://finance.yahoo.com	10,840	14,480	168,990
6. Five Method Average	7,380	9,764	144,508
$Goodwill/$Total Assets	17.1%	1.1%	18.7%

GLOBAL PERSPECTIVE
Globally Standardizing Accounting Standards

The Financial Accounting Standards Board (FASB) in the U.S. and its counterpart, the International Accounting Standards Board (IASB), are each modifying its "rules" in an effort to globally converge accounting standards. It is unusual for the FASB to change simply to meet the IASB, but there is more and more movement from both sides toward convergence. Standard setters in both the United States and other countries mutually desire that the financial statements of a company—say in France—one day will be comparable to those in any other country. Accounting standards convergence would greatly simplify cross-border investment, interaction, and trade.

The FASB and the IASB began meeting twice yearly in 2002. The European Union of countries has agreed to adopt the IASB's standards by 2005. About 91 countries worldwide will require their companies to comply with IASB standards by 2005. However, there still exist many differences between FASB and IASB standards. For example, the FASB does not allow for upward reevaluation of property, plant, and equipment, whereas the IASB permits periodic reevaluation up or down of assets. Thus, property, plant, and equipment on the statements of U.S. firms is often worth a lot more than reflected on the books. For another example, the IASB wants to remove net income from the income statement, but the

FASB has not reached a decision on this issue. There are also differences between the FASB and IASB in accounting for acquisitions as well as differences about when revenue should be booked.

The United States and the European Union signed a new agreement in May 2007 that paves the way for a single trans-Atlantic accounting standard by 2009. The agreement allows many public U.S. companies to drop American generally accepted accounting principles (GAAP) in favor of more flexible international financial reporting standards (IFRS). The U.S. Securities and Exchange Commission (SEC) voted unanimously on June 20, 2007 to allow companies based outside the United States to file financial results using IFRS, without reconciling the figures to GAAP. Later in 2007, the SEC votes on whether to allow U.S. companies to choose whether to file financial statements either under GAAP or IFRS. Part of the motivation for approving such actions is that U.S. stock exchanges are losing market share to London and Hong Kong. The SEC wants more stock listings in the United States. Some analysts believe GAAP will soon be eliminated entirely for everyone.

South Korean companies must adopt international financial reporting standards starting in 2011. This requirement is aimed at building investor confidence through increased transparency. The new regulations are spurring growth in Korea. The perception of weak accounting and disclosure standards in South Korea has been a problem for years for that economy. All publicly held European Union companies must file results using IFRS.

The statutory authority to set accounting standards for public companies in the United States rests with the SEC, although GAAP is overseen by the Financial Accounting Standards Board (FASB), a 24-year-old private-sector group based in Norwalk, Connecticut.

One day decades in the future, there may be one currency worldwide. Certainly, convergence between accounting systems among countries worldwide would be a step in that direction. Establishment of the euro was a big step, too. Convergence of accounting systems simply makes doing business worldwide much easier.

Source: Adapted from Cassell Bryan-Low, "Accounting's Global Rule Book," *Wall Street Journal* (November 28, 2003): C1; John McKinnon, "U.S., EU to Streamline Accounting," *Wall Street Journal* (May 1, 2007): A8; and Kara Scannell and David Reilly, "Foreign Afffair: Is End Near for 'U.S. Only' Accounting?" *Wall Street Journal* (June 21, 2007): C1.

China, Yunnan, Xishuangbanna, Jinghong, Dai women selling vegetables at busy street market. *Source:* Nigel Hicks (c) Dorling Kindersley

Table 8-12 provides the cash value analyses for three companies—Mattel, Nordstrom, and Pfizer—for year-end 2006. Notice that there is significant variation among the four methods used to determine cash value. For example, the worth of the toy company Mattel ranged from $2.29 billion to $10.84 billion. Obviously, if you were selling your company, you would seek the larger values, while if purchasing a company you would seek the lower values. In practice, substantial negotiation takes place in reaching a final compromise (or averaged) amount. Also recognize that if a firm's net income is negative, theoretically the approaches involving that figure would result in a negative number, implying that the firm would pay you to acquire them. Of course, you obtain all of the firm's debt and liabilities in an acquisition, so theoretically this would be possible.

At year-end 2006, Mattel, Nordstrom, and Pfizer had $845 million, $51 million, and $20.876 billion in goodwill respectively on their balance sheets. Most creditors and investors feel that goodwill indeed should be added to the stockholders' equity in calculating worth of a business, but some feel it should be subtracted, and still others feel it should not be included at all. Perhaps whether you are buying or selling the business may determine whether you negotiate to add or subtract goodwill in the analysis. Goodwill is sometimes listed as intangibles on the balance sheet, but technically intangibles refers to patents, trademarks, and copyrights, rather than the value a firm paid over book value for an acquisition, which is goodwill. If a firm paid less than book value for an acquisition, that could be called negative goodwill—which is a line item on Mattel's balance sheets.

Deciding Whether to Go Public

Going public means selling off a percentage of your company to others in order to raise capital in a stock market; consequently, it dilutes the owners' control of the firm. Going public is not recommended for companies with less than $10 million in sales because the initial costs can be too high for the firm to generate sufficient cash flow to make going public worthwhile. One dollar in four is the average total cost paid to lawyers, accountants, and underwriters when an initial stock issuance is under $1 million; 1 dollar in 20 will go to cover these costs for issuances over $20 million.

In addition to initial costs involved with a stock offering, there are costs and obligations associated with reporting and management in a publicly held firm. For firms with more than $10 million in sales, going public can provide major advantages: It can allow the firm to raise capital to develop new products, build plants, expand, grow, and market products and services more effectively.

Research and Development (R&D) Issues

Research and development (R&D) personnel can play an integral part in strategy implementation. These individuals are generally charged with developing new products and improving old products in a way that will allow effective strategy implementation. R&D employees and managers perform tasks that include transferring complex technology, adjusting processes to local raw materials, adapting processes to local markets, and altering products to particular tastes and specifications. Strategies such as product development, market penetration, and related diversification require that new products be successfully developed and that old products be significantly improved. But the level of management support for R&D is often constrained by resource availability.

Technological improvements that affect consumer and industrial products and services shorten product life cycles. Companies in virtually every industry are relying on the development of new products and services to fuel profitability and growth.[5] Surveys suggest that the most successful organizations use an R&D strategy that ties external opportunities to internal strengths and is linked with objectives. Well-formulated R&D policies match market opportunities with internal capabilities. R&D policies can enhance strategy implementation efforts to:

1. Emphasize product or process improvements.
2. Stress basic or applied research.
3. Be leaders or followers in R&D.
4. Develop robotics or manual-type processes.
5. Spend a high, average, or low amount of money on R&D.
6. Perform R&D within the firm or to contract R&D to outside firms.
7. Use university researchers or private-sector researchers.

There must be effective interactions between R&D departments and other functional departments in implementing different types of generic business strategies. Conflicts between marketing, finance/accounting, R&D, and information systems departments can be minimized with clear policies and objectives. Table 8-13 gives some examples of R&D activities that could be required for successful implementation of various strategies. Many utility, energy, and automotive companies are employing their research and development departments to determine how the firm can effectively reduce its gas emissions.

TABLE 8–13 Research and Development Involvement in Selected Strategy-Implementation Situations

Type of Organization	Strategy Being Implemented	R&D Activity
Pharmaceutical company	Product development	Test the effects of a new drug on different subgroups.
Boat manufacturer	Related diversification	Test the performance of various keel designs under various conditions.
Plastic container manufacturer	Market penetration	Develop a biodegradable container.
Electronics company	Market development	Develop a telecommunications system in a foreign country.

Many firms wrestle with the decision to acquire R&D expertise from external firms or to develop R&D expertise internally. The following guidelines can be used to help make this decision:

1. If the rate of technical progress is slow, the rate of market growth is moderate, and there are significant barriers to possible new entrants, then in-house R&D is the preferred solution. The reason is that R&D, if successful, will result in a temporary product or process monopoly that the company can exploit.

2. If technology is changing rapidly and the market is growing slowly, then a major effort in R&D may be very risky, because it may lead to the development of an ultimately obsolete technology or one for which there is no market.

3. If technology is changing slowly but the market is growing quickly, there generally is not enough time for in-house development. The prescribed approach is to obtain R&D expertise on an exclusive or nonexclusive basis from an outside firm.

4. If both technical progress and market growth are fast, R&D expertise should be obtained through acquisition of a well-established firm in the industry.[6]

There are at least three major R&D approaches for implementing strategies. The first strategy is to be the first firm to market new technological products. This is a glamorous and exciting strategy but also a dangerous one. Firms such as Sony and 3M have been successful with this approach, but many other pioneering firms have fallen, with rival firms seizing the initiative.

A second R&D approach is to be an innovative imitator of successful products, thus minimizing the risks and costs of start-up. This approach entails allowing a pioneer firm to develop the first version of the new product and to demonstrate that a market exists. Then, laggard firms develop a similar product. This strategy requires excellent R&D personnel and an excellent marketing department.

A third R&D strategy is to be a low-cost producer by mass-producing products similar to but less expensive than products recently introduced. As a new product is accepted by customers, price becomes increasingly important in the buying decision. Also, mass marketing replaces personal selling as the dominant selling strategy. This R&D strategy, requires substantial investment in plant and equipment but fewer expenditures in R&D than the two approaches described previously.

R&D activities among firms need to be more closely aligned to business objectives. There needs to be expanded communication between R&D managers and strategists. Corporations are experimenting with various methods to achieve this improved communication climate, including different roles and reporting arrangements for managers and new methods to reduce the time it takes research ideas to become reality.

Perhaps the most current trend in R&D management has been lifting the veil of secrecy whereby firms, even major competitors, are joining forces to develop new products. Collaboration is on the rise due to new competitive pressures, rising research costs, increasing regulatory issues, and accelerated product development schedules. Companies not only are working more closely with each other on R&D, but they are also turning to consortia at universities for their R&D needs. More than 600 research consortia are now in operation in the United States alone, for example. Lifting of R&D secrecy among many firms through collaboration has allowed the marketing of new technologies and products even before they are available for sale. For example, some firms are collaborating on the efficient design of solar panels to power homes and businesses.

Management Information Systems (MIS) Issues

Firms that gather, assimilate, and evaluate external and internal information most effectively are gaining competitive advantages over other firms. Recognizing the importance of having an effective *management information system (MIS)* will not be an option in the future; it will be a requirement. Information is the basis for understanding in a firm. In many industries, information is becoming the most important factor in differentiating successful from unsuccessful firms. The process of strategic management is facilitated immensely in firms that have an effective information system. Many companies are establishing a new approach to information systems, one that blends the technical knowledge of the computer experts with the vision of senior management.

Information collection, retrieval, and storage can be used to create competitive advantages in ways such as cross-selling to customers, monitoring suppliers, keeping managers and employees informed, coordinating activities among divisions, and managing funds. Like inventory and human resources, information is now recognized as a valuable organizational asset that can be controlled and managed. Firms that implement strategies using the best information will reap competitive advantages in the twenty-first century.

A good information system can allow a firm to reduce costs. For example, online orders from salespersons to production facilities can shorten materials ordering time and reduce inventory costs. Direct communications between suppliers, manufacturers, marketers, and customers can link together elements of the value chain as though they were one organization. Improved quality and service often result from an improved information system.

Firms must increasingly be concerned about computer hackers and take specific measures to secure and safeguard corporate communications, files, orders, and business conducted over the Internet. Thousands of companies today are plagued by computer hackers who include disgruntled employees, competitors, bored teens, sociopaths, thieves, spies, and hired agents. Computer vulnerability is a giant, expensive headache.

The credit-reporting firm Dun & Bradstreet is an example of a company that has an excellent information system. Every D&B customer and client in the world has a separate nine-digit number. The database of information associated with each number has become so widely used that it is like a business Social Security number. D&B reaps great competitive advantages from its information system.

In many firms, information technology is doing away with the workplace and allowing employees to work at home or anywhere, anytime. The mobile concept of work allows employees to work the traditional 9-to-5 workday across any of the 24 time zones around the globe. Affordable desktop videoconferencing software developed by AT&T, Lotus, or Vivo Software allows employees to "beam in" whenever needed. Any manager or employee who travels a lot away from the office is a good candidate for working at home rather than in an office provided by the firm. Salespersons or consultants are good examples, but any person whose job largely involves talking to others or handling information could easily operate at home with the proper computer system and software.

Many people see the officeless office trend as leading to a resurgence of family togetherness in some societies. Even the design of homes may change from having large open areas to having more private small areas conducive to getting work done.[7]

Conclusion

Successful strategy implementation depends on cooperation among all functional and divisional managers in an organization. Marketing departments are commonly charged with implementing strategies that require significant increases in sales revenues in new areas and with new or improved products. Finance and accounting managers must devise effective strategy-implementation approaches at low cost and minimum risk to that firm. R&D managers have to transfer complex technologies or develop new technologies to successfully implement strategies. Information systems managers are being called upon more and more to provide leadership and training for all individuals in the firm. The nature and role of marketing, finance/accounting, R&D, and management information systems activities, coupled with the management activities described in Chapter 7, largely determine organizational success.

We invite you to visit the David page on the Prentice Hall Companion Web site at www.prenhall.com/david for this chapter's review quiz.

Key Terms and Concepts

Cash Budget (p. 316)
EPS/EBIT Analysis (p. 305)
Financial Budget (p. 315)
Management Information System (MIS) (p. 322)
Market Segmentation (p. 299)
Marketing Mix Variables (p. 299)
Outstanding Shares Method (p. 317)
Price-Earnings Ratio Method (p. 317)
Product Positioning (p. 299)
Projected Financial Statement Analysis (p. 310)
Research and Development (R&D) (p. 320)
Vacant Niche (p. 302)

Issues For Review and Discussion

1. Suppose your company has just acquired a firm that produces battery-operated lawn mowers, and strategists want to implement a market-penetration strategy. How would you segment the market for this product? Justify your answer.
2. Explain how you would estimate the total worth of a business.
3. Diagram and label clearly a product-positioning map that includes six fast-food restaurant chains.
4. Explain why EPS/EBIT analysis is a central strategy-implementation technique.
5. How would the R&D role in strategy implementation differ in small versus large organizations?
6. Discuss the limitations of EPS/EBIT analysis.
7. Explain how marketing, finance/accounting, R&D, and management information systems managers' involvement in strategy formulation can enhance strategy implementation.
8. Consider the following statement: "Retained earnings on the balance sheet are not monies available to finance strategy implementation." Is it true or false? Explain.
9. Explain why projected financial statement analysis is considered both a strategy-formulation and a strategy-implementation tool.
10. Describe some marketing, finance/accounting, R&D, and management information systems activities that a small restaurant chain might undertake to expand into a neighboring state.
11. Discuss the management information system at your college or university.
12. What effect is e-commerce having on firms' efforts to segment markets?
13. How has the Sarbanes-Oxley Act of 2002 changed CEOs' and CFOs' handling of financial statements?
14. To what extent have you been exposed to natural environment issues in your business courses? Which course has provided the most coverage? What percentage of your business courses provided no coverage? Comment.
15. Complete the following EPS/EBIT analysis for a company whose stock price is $20, interest rate on funds is 5 percent, tax rate is 20 percent, number of shares outstanding is 500 million, and EBIT range is $100 million to $300 million. The firm needs to raise $200 million in capital. Use the table accompanying to complete the work.
16. Under what conditions would retained earnings on the balance sheet decrease from one year to the next?
17. In your own words, list all the steps in developing projected financial statements.
18. Based on the financial statements provided for Walt Disney (pp 64–65), how much dividends in dollars did Walt Disney pay in 2006? In 2007?
19. Based on the financial statements provided in this chapter for the Litten Company, calculate the value of this company if you know that its stock price is $20 and it has 1 million shares outstanding. Calculate four different ways and average.
20. Why should you be careful not to use historical percentages blindly in developing projected financial statements?

21. In developing projected financial statements, what should you do if the $ amount you must put in the cash account (to make the statement balance) is far more (or less) than desired?
22. Why is it both important and necessary to segment markets and target groups of customers, rather than market to all possible consumers?
23. In full detail, explain the following EPS/EBIT chart.

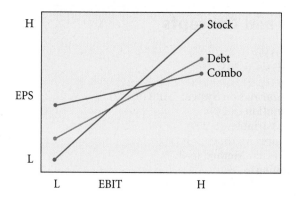

100% Common Stock	100% Debt Financing	20%Debt–80%Stock
EBIT		
Interest		
EBT		
Taxes		
EAT		
# Shares		
EPS		

Notes

1. Leslie Miller and Elizabeth Weise, "E-Privacy—FTC Studies 'Profiling' by Web Sites," *USA Today* (November 8, 1999): 1A, 2A.
2. Ralph Biggadike, "The Contributions of Marketing to Strategic Management," *Academy of Management Review* 6, no. 4 (October 1981): 627.
3. Phyllis Plitch, "Companies in Many Sectors Give Earnings a Pro Forma Makeover, Survey Finds," *Wall Street Journal* (January 22, 2002): A4.
4. Michael Rapoport, "Pro Forma Is a Hard Habit to Break," *Wall Street Journal* (September 18, 2003): B3A.
5. Amy Merrick, "U.S. Research Spending to Rise Only 3.2 Percent," *Wall Street Journal* (December 28, 2001): A2.
6. Pier Abetti, "Technology: A Key Strategic Resource," *Management Review* 78, no. 2 (February 1989): 38.
7. Adapted from Edward Baig, "Welcome to the Officeless Office," *BusinessWeek* (June 26, 1995).

Current Readings

Dean, Alison and Martin Kretschmer. "Can Ideas Be Capital? Factors of Production in the Postindustrial Economy: A Review and Critique." *The Academy of Management Review* 32, no. 2 (April 2007): 573).

Fine, Leslie M. "Selling and sales management." *Business Horizon* 50, no. 3 (May-June 2007): 185.

Fine, Leslie M. "Spotlight on Marketing." *Business Horizons* 49, no. 3 (May–June 2006): 179.

Herremans, Irene, John K. Ryans, Jr., and Linda C. Ueltschy. "Marketing: Who's Really Minding the Store Globally?" *Business Horizons* 49, no. 2 (March–April 2006): 139.

Katsikeas, C. S., S. Samiee, and M. Theodosiou. "Strategy Fit and Performance Consequences of International Marketing." *Strategic Management Journal* 27, no. 9 (September 2006): 867.

Mani, S., K.D. Anita, and A. Rindfleisch. "Entry Mode and Equity Level: A Multilevel Examination of Foreign Direct Investment Ownership Structure." *Strategic Management Journal* 28, no. 8 (August 2007): 857–867.

• EXPERIENTIAL EXERCISES

Experiential Exercise 8A

Developing a Product-Positioning Map for Walt Disney

Purpose

Organizations continually monitor how their products and services are positioned relative to competitors. This information is especially useful for marketing managers but is also used by other managers and strategists.

Instructions

Step 1   On a separate sheet of paper, develop a product-positioning map for Walt Disney. Include Time Warner, and News Corporation in your diagram.

Step 2   At the chalkboard, diagram your product-positioning map.

Step 3   Compare your product-positioning map with those diagrammed by other students. Discuss any major differences.

A Mickey Mouse Disneyland promotional badge. *Source:* (c) Judith Miller / Dorling Kindersley / Cad Van Swankster at The Girl Can't Help It

Experiential Exercise 8B

Performing an EPS/EBIT Analysis for Walt Disney

Purpose

An EPS/EBIT analysis is one of the most widely used techniques for determining the extent that debt and/or stock should be used to finance strategies to be implemented. This exercise can give you practice performing EPS/EBIT analysis.

Instructions (1-1-08 Data)

Let's say Walt Disney needs to raise $1 billion to revamp its California Adventure theme park. Determine whether Walt Disney should have used all debt, all stock, or a 50-50 combination of debt and stock to finance this market-development strategy. Assume a 38 percent tax rate, 5 percent interest rate, Walt Disney stock price of $30 per share, and an annual dividend of $0.30 per share of common stock. The EBIT range for 2008 is between $7.725 billion and $10 billion. A total of 2 billion shares of common stock are outstanding. Develop an EPS/EBIT chart to reflect your analysis.

Experiential Exercise 8C

Preparing Projected Financial Statements for Walt Disney

Purpose

This exercise is designed to give you experience preparing projected financial statements. Pro forma analysis is a central strategy-implementation technique because it allows managers to anticipate and evaluate the expected results of various strategy-implementation approaches.

Instructions

Step 1   Work with a classmate. Develop a 2008 projected income statement and balance sheet for Walt Disney. Assume that Walt Disney plans to raise $900 million in 2008 to begin serving new countries and plans to obtain 50 percent financing from a bank and 50 percent financing from a stock issuance. Make other assumptions as needed, and state them clearly in written form.

Step 2   Compute Walt Disney current ratio, debt-to-equity ratio, and return-on-investment ratio for 2006 and 2007. How do your 2008 projected ratios compare to the 2006 and 2007 ratios? Why is it important to make this comparison? Use http://finance.yahoo.com to obtain 2007 financial statements.

Step 3   Bring your projected statements to class, and discuss any problems or questions you encountered.

Step 4   Compare your projected statements to the statements of other students. What major differences exist between your analysis and the work of other students?

Experiential Exercise 8D

Determining the Cash Value of Walt Disney

Purpose

It is simply good business practice to periodically determine the financial worth or cash value of your company. This exercise gives you practice determining the total worth of a company using several methods. Use year-end 2007 data as given in the Cohesion Case on pp. 64–65.

Instructions

Step 1   Calculate the financial worth of Walt Disney based on four methods: (1) the net worth or stockholders' equity, (2) the future value of Walt Disney earnings, (3) the price-earnings ratio, and (4) the outstanding shares method.

Step 2   In a dollar amount, how much is Walt Disney worth?

Step 3   Compare your analyses and conclusions with those of other students.

Experiential Exercise 8E

Developing a Product-Positioning Map for My University

Purpose

The purpose of this exercise is to give you practice developing product-positioning maps. Nonprofit organizations, such as universities, are increasingly using product-positioning maps to determine effective ways to implement strategies.

Instructions

Step 1   Join with two other people in class to form a group of three.

Step 2   Jointly prepare a product-positioning map that includes your institution and four other colleges or universities in your state.

Step 3   At the chalkboard, diagram your product-positioning map.

Step 4   Discuss differences among the maps diagrammed on the board.

Experiential Exercise 8F

Do Banks Require Projected Financial Statements?

Purpose

The purpose of this exercise is to explore the practical importance and use of projected financial statements in the banking business.

Instructions

Contact two local bankers by phone and seek answers to the questions that follow. Record the answers you receive, and report your findings to the class.

1. Does your bank require projected financial statements as part of a business loan application?
2. How does your bank use projected financial statements when they are part of a business loan application?
3. What special advice do you give potential business borrowers in preparing projected financial statements?

Part 4 • Strategy Evaluation

9 Strategy Review, Evaluation, and Control

"notable quotes"

Complicated controls do not work. They confuse. They misdirect attention from what is to be controlled to the mechanics and methodology of the control.

SEYMOUR TILLES

Although Plan A may be selected as the most realistic ... the other major alternatives should not be forgotten. They may well serve as contingency plans.

DALE MCCONKEY

Organizations are most vulnerable when they are at the peak of their success.

R. T. LENZ

Strategy evaluation must make it as easy as possible for managers to revise their plans and reach quick agreement on the changes.

DALE MCCONKEY

While strategy is a word that is usually associated with the future, its link to the past is no less central. Life is lived forward but understood backward. Managers may live strategy in the future, but they understand it through the past.

HENRY MINTZBERG

Unless strategy evaluation is performed seriously and systematically, and unless strategists are willing to act on the results, energy will be used up defending yesterday. No one will have the time, resources, or will to work on exploiting today, let alone to work on making tomorrow.

PETER DRUCKER

Executives, consultants, and B-school professors all agree that strategic planning is now the single most important management issue and will remain so for the next five years. Strategy has become a part of the main agenda at lots of organizations today. Strategic planning is back with a vengeance.

JOHN BYRNE

Planners should not plan, but serve as facilitators, catalysts, inquirers, educators, and synthesizers to guide the planning process effectively.

A. HAX AND N. MAJLUF

Time to Receive Diplomas. *Source:* Bryan David

chapter objectives

After studying this chapter, you should be able to do the following:

1. Describe a practical framework for evaluating strategies.

2. Explain why strategy evaluation is complex, sensitive, and yet essential for organizational success.

3. Discuss the importance of contingency planning in strategy evaluation.

4. Discuss the role of auditing in strategy evaluation.

5. Explain how computers can aid in evaluating strategies.

6. Discuss the Balanced Scorecard.

7. Discuss three twenty-first-century challenges in strategic management.

The best-formulated and best-implemented strategies become obsolete as a firm's external and internal environments change. It is essential, therefore, that strategists systematically review, evaluate, and control the execution of strategies. This chapter presents a framework that can guide managers' efforts to evaluate strategic-management activities, to make sure they are working, and to make timely changes. Management information systems being used to evaluate strategies are discussed. Guidelines are presented for formulating, implementing, and evaluating strategies.

The Nature of Strategy Evaluation

VISIT THE NET

Gives excellent additional information about evaluating strategies, including some analytical tools. (www.mindtools. com/plevplan.html)

The strategic-management process results in decisions that can have significant, long-lasting consequences. Erroneous strategic decisions can inflict severe penalties and can be exceedingly difficult, if not impossible, to reverse. Most strategists agree, therefore, that strategy evaluation is vital to an organization's well-being; timely evaluations can alert management to problems or potential problems before a situation becomes critical. Strategy evaluation includes three basic activities: (1) examining the underlying bases of a firm's strategy, (2) comparing expected results with actual results, and (3) taking corrective actions to ensure that performance conforms to plans. The strategy-evaluation stage of the strategic-management process is illustrated in Figure 9-1.

Adequate and timely feedback is the cornerstone of effective strategy evaluation. Strategy evaluation can be no better than the information on which it is based. Too much pressure from top managers may result in lower managers contriving numbers they think will be satisfactory.

Strategy evaluation can be a complex and sensitive undertaking. Too much emphasis on evaluating strategies may be expensive and counterproductive. No one likes to be evaluated too closely! The more managers attempt to evaluate the behavior of others, the less control they have. Yet too little or no evaluation can create even worse problems. Strategy evaluation is essential to ensure that stated objectives are being achieved.

FIGURE 9-1

A Comprehensive Strategic-Management Model

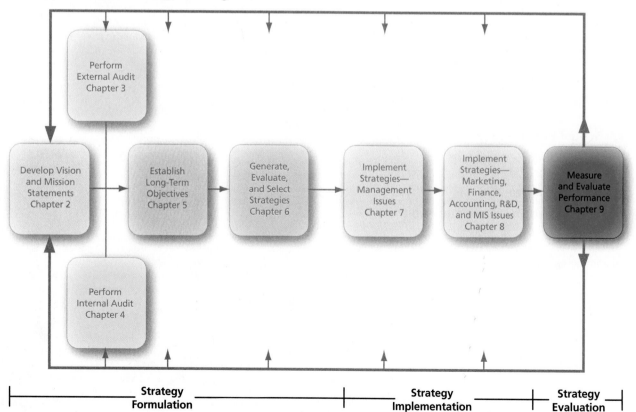

Source: Fred R. David, "How Companies Define Their Mission," *Long Range Planning* 22, no. 3 (June 1988): 40.

In many organizations, strategy evaluation is simply an appraisal of how well an organization has performed. Have the firm's assets increased? Has there been an increase in profitability? Have sales increased? Have productivity levels increased? Have profit margin, return on investment, and earnings-per-share ratios increased? Some firms argue that their strategy must have been correct if the answers to these types of questions are affirmative. Well, the strategy or strategies may have been correct, but this type of reasoning can be misleading because strategy evaluation must have both a long-run and short-run focus. Strategies often do not affect short-term operating results until it is too late to make needed changes.

It is impossible to demonstrate conclusively that a particular strategy is optimal or even to guarantee that it will work. One can, however, evaluate it for critical flaws. Richard Rumelt offered four criteria that could be used to evaluate a strategy: consistency, consonance, feasibility, and advantage. Described in Table 9-1, *consonance* and *advantage* are mostly based on a firm's external assessment, whereas *consistency* and *feasibility* are largely based on an internal assessment.

TABLE 9-1   Rumelt's Criteria for Evaluating Strategies

consistency

A strategy should not present inconsistent goals and policies. Organizational conflict and interdepartmental bickering are often symptoms of managerial disorder, but these problems may also be a sign of strategic inconsistency. Three guidelines help determine if organizational problems are due to inconsistencies in strategy:

- If managerial problems continue despite changes in personnel and if they tend to be issue-based rather than people-based, then strategies may be inconsistent.
- If success for one organizational department means, or is interpreted to mean, failure for another department, then strategies may be inconsistent.
- If policy problems and issues continue to be brought to the top for resolution, then strategies may be inconsistent.

consonance

Consonance refers to the need for strategists to examine *sets of trends*, as well as individual trends, in evaluating strategies. A strategy must represent an adaptive response to the external environment and to the critical changes occurring within it. One difficulty in matching a firm's key internal and external factors in the formulation of strategy is that most trends are the result of interactions among other trends. For example, the day-care explosion came about as a combined result of many trends that included a rise in the average level of education, increased inflation, and an increase in women in the workforce. Although single economic or demographic trends might appear steady for many years, there are waves of change going on at the interaction level.

feasibility

A strategy must neither overtax available resources nor create unsolvable subproblems. The final broad test of strategy is its feasibility; that is, can the strategy be attempted within the physical, human, and financial resources of the enterprise? The financial resources of a business are the easiest to quantify and are normally the first limitation against which strategy is evaluated. It is sometimes forgotten, however, that innovative approaches to financing are often possible. Devices, such as captive subsidiaries, sale-lease-back arrangements, and tying plant mortgages to long-term contracts, have all been used effectively to help win key positions in suddenly expanding industries. A less quantifiable, but actually more rigid, limitation on strategic choice is that imposed by individual and organizational capabilities. In evaluating a strategy, it is important to examine whether an organization has demonstrated in the past that it possesses the abilities, competencies, skills, and talents needed to carry out a given strategy.

advantage

A strategy must provide for the creation and/or maintenance of a competitive advantage in a selected area of activity. Competitive advantages normally are the result of superiority in one of three areas: (1) resources, (2) skills, or (3) position. The idea that the positioning of one's resources can enhance their combined effectiveness is familiar to military theorists, chess players, and diplomats. Position can also play a crucial role in an organization's strategy. Once gained, a good position is defensible—meaning that it is so costly to capture that rivals are deterred from full-scale attacks. Positional advantage tends to be self-sustaining as long as the key internal and environmental factors that underlie it remain stable. This is why entrenched firms can be almost impossible to unseat, even if their raw skill levels are only average. Although not all positional advantages are associated with size, it is true that larger organizations tend to operate in markets and use procedures that turn their size into advantage, while smaller firms seek product/market positions that exploit other types of advantage. The principal characteristic of good position is that it permits the firm to obtain advantage from policies that would not similarly benefit rivals without the same position. Therefore, in evaluating strategy, organizations should examine the nature of positional advantages associated with a given strategy.

Source: Adapted from Richard Rumelt, "The Evaluation of Business Strategy," in W. F. Glueck (ed.), *Business Policy and Strategic Management* (New York: McGraw-Hill, 1980): 359–367.

VISIT THE NET

Describes the how and why of strategy evaluation. (www. csuchico.edu/mgmt/strategy/ module1/sld046.htm)

Strategy evaluation is important because organizations face dynamic environments in which key external and internal factors often change quickly and dramatically. Success today is no guarantee of success tomorrow! An organization should never be lulled into complacency with success. Countless firms have thrived one year only to struggle for survival the following year. Organizational trouble can come swiftly, as further evidenced by the examples described in Table 9-2.

Strategy evaluation is becoming increasingly difficult with the passage of time, for many reasons. Domestic and world economies were more stable in years past, product life cycles were longer, product development cycles were longer, technological advancement was slower, change occurred less frequently, there were fewer competitors, foreign companies were weak, and there were more regulated industries. Other reasons why strategy evaluation is more difficult today include the following trends:

1. A dramatic increase in the environment's complexity
2. The increasing difficulty of predicting the future with accuracy
3. The increasing number of variables
4. The rapid rate of obsolescence of even the best plans
5. The increase in the number of both domestic and world events affecting organizations
6. The decreasing time span for which planning can be done with any degree of certainty[1]

A fundamental problem facing managers today is how to effectively control employees in light of modern organizational demands for greater flexibility, innovation, creativity, and initiative from employees.[2] How can managers today ensure that empowered employees acting in an entrepreneurial manner do not put the well-being of the business at risk? A bribery scandal at Siemens cost the company a €201 million fine and reduced its price per share by an estimated €2 to €3. Sears, Roebuck and Company took a $60 million charge against earnings after admitting that its automobile service businesses were performing unnecessary repairs. The costs to companies such as these in terms of damaged reputations, fines, missed opportunities, and diversion of management's attention are enormous.

TABLE 9-2 **Examples of Organizational Demise**

A. Some Large Companies That Experienced a Large Drop in Revenues in 2006 vs. 2005		B. Some Large Companies That Experienced a Large Drop in Profits in 2006 vs. 2005	
Avis Budget Group	−71%	Avis Budget Group	−249%
American Express	−10%	Coca-Cola Enterprises	−322%
Brinks	−44%	Mosaic	−173%
Dynegy	−69%	Dynegy	−423%
First Data	−33%	Sungard Data Systems	−201%
Louisiana-Pacific	−18%	Centene	−178%
Saks	−40%	WCI Communities	−95%
Spectrum Brands	−434%	Spectrum Brands	−1,027%
Visteon	−33%	Clorox	−15%
OGE Energy	−33%	SAIC	−95%
Laidlaw International	−15%	Boston Scientific	−670%
Duke Energy	−16%	New York Times	−309%
Aquila	−14%	R.H. Donnelley	−452%

When empowered employees are held accountable for and pressured to achieve specific goals and are given wide latitude in their actions to achieve them, there can be dysfunctional behavior. For example, Nordstrom, the upscale fashion retailer known for outstanding customer service, was subjected to lawsuits and fines when employees underreported hours worked in order to increase their sales per hour—the company's primary performance criterion. Nordstrom's customer service and earnings were enhanced until the misconduct was reported, at which time severe penalties were levied against the firm.

The Process of Evaluating Strategies

Strategy evaluation is necessary for all sizes and kinds of organizations. Strategy evaluation should initiate managerial questioning of expectations and assumptions, should trigger a review of objectives and values, and should stimulate creativity in generating alternatives and formulating criteria of evaluation.[3] Regardless of the size of the organization, a certain amount of *management by wandering around* at all levels is essential to effective strategy evaluation. Strategy-evaluation activities should be performed on a continuing basis, rather than at the end of specified periods of time or just after problems occur. Waiting until the end of the year, for example, could result in a firm closing the barn door after the horses have already escaped.

VISIT THE NET

Elaborates on the "taking corrective actions" phase of strategy evaluation. (www. csuchico.edu/mgmt/strategy/ module1/sld047.htm)

Evaluating strategies on a continuous rather than on a periodic basis allows benchmarks of progress to be established and more effectively monitored. Some strategies take years to implement; consequently, associated results may not become apparent for years. Successful strategies combine patience with a willingness to promptly take corrective actions when necessary. There always comes a time when corrective actions are needed in an organization! Centuries ago, a writer (perhaps Solomon) made the following observations about change:

There is a time for everything,
A time to be born and a time to die,
A time to plant and a time to uproot,
A time to kill and a time to heal,
A time to tear down and a time to build,
A time to weep and a time to laugh,
A time to mourn and a time to dance,
A time to scatter stones and a time to gather them,
A time to embrace and a time to refrain,
A time to search and a time to give up,
A time to keep and a time to throw away,
A time to tear and a time to mend,
A time to be silent and a time to speak,
A time to love and a time to hate,
A time for war and a time for peace.[4]

Managers and employees of the firm should be continually aware of progress being made toward achieving the firm's objectives. As critical success factors change, organizational members should be involved in determining appropriate corrective actions. If assumptions and expectations deviate significantly from forecasts, then the firm should renew strategy-formulation activities, perhaps sooner than planned. In strategy evaluation, like strategy formulation and strategy implementation, people make the difference. Through involvement in the process of evaluating strategies, managers and employees become committed to keeping the firm moving steadily toward achieving objectives.

A Strategy-Evaluation Framework

Table 9-3 summarizes strategy-evaluation activities in terms of key questions that should be addressed, alternative answers to those questions, and appropriate actions for an organization to take. Notice that corrective actions are almost always needed except when (1) external and internal factors have not significantly changed and (2) the firm is progressing

TABLE 9-3   A Strategy-Evaluation Assessment Matrix

Have Major Changes Occurred in the Firm Internal Strategic Position?	Have Major Changes Occurred in the Firm External Strategic Position?	Has the Firm Progressed Satisfactorily Toward Achieving Its Stated Objectives?	Result
No	No	No	Take corrective actions
Yes	Yes	Yes	Take corrective actions
Yes	Yes	No	Take corrective actions
Yes	No	Yes	Take corrective actions
Yes	No	No	Take corrective actions
No	Yes	Yes	Take corrective actions
No	Yes	No	Take corrective actions
No	No	Yes	Continue present strategic course

satisfactorily toward achieving stated objectives. Relationships among strategy-evaluation activities are illustrated in Figure 9-2.

Reviewing Bases of Strategy

As shown in Figure 9-2, *reviewing the underlying bases of an organization's strategy* could be approached by developing a revised EFE Matrix and IFE Matrix. A *revised IFE Matrix* should focus on changes in the organization's management, marketing, finance/accounting, production/operations, R&D, and management information systems strengths and weaknesses. A *revised EFE Matrix* should indicate how effective a firm's strategies have been in response to key opportunities and threats. This analysis could also address such questions as the following:

1. How have competitors reacted to our strategies?
2. How have competitors' strategies changed?
3. Have major competitors' strengths and weaknesses changed?
4. Why are competitors making certain strategic changes?
5. Why are some competitors' strategies more successful than others?
6. How satisfied are our competitors with their present market positions and profitability?
7. How far can our major competitors be pushed before retaliating?
8. How could we more effectively cooperate with our competitors?

Numerous external and internal factors can prevent firms from achieving long-term and annual objectives. Externally, actions by competitors, changes in demand, changes in technology, economic changes, demographic shifts, and governmental actions may prevent objectives from being accomplished. Internally, ineffective strategies may have been chosen or implementation activities may have been poor. Objectives may have been too optimistic. Thus, failure to achieve objectives may not be the result of unsatisfactory work by managers and employees. All organizational members need to know this to encourage their support for strategy-evaluation activities. Organizations desperately need to know as soon as possible when their strategies are not effective. Sometimes managers and employees on the front lines discover this well before strategists.

External opportunities and threats and internal strengths and weaknesses that represent the bases of current strategies should continually be monitored for change. It is not really a question of whether these factors will change but rather when they will change and in what ways. Some key questions to address in evaluating strategies follow:

1. Are our internal strengths still strengths?
2. Have we added other internal strengths? If so, what are they?
3. Are our internal weaknesses still weaknesses?

VISIT THE NET

The U.S. Small Business Administration Web site provides a 40-page Business Plan Outline. (www.sba.gov/starting_/business/ planning/basic.html)

303

FIGURE 9-2

A Strategy-Evaluation Framework

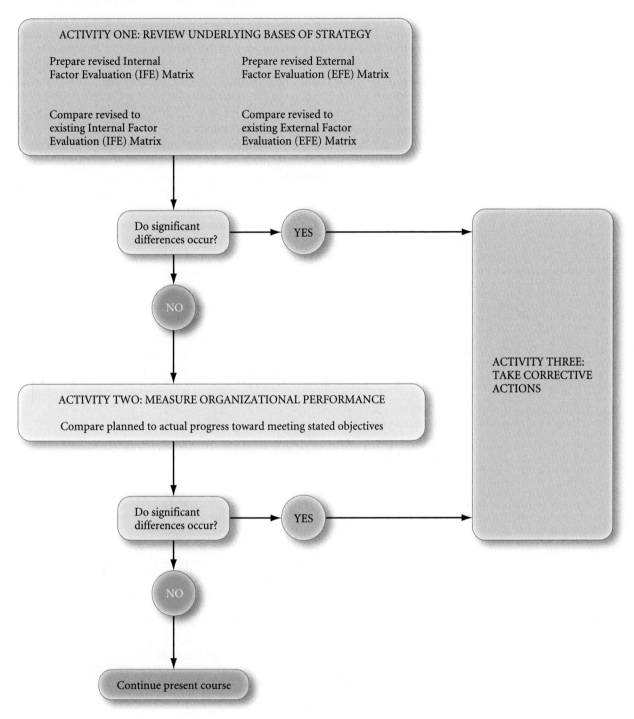

4. Do we now have other internal weaknesses? If so, what are they?
5. Are our external opportunities still opportunities?
6. Are there now other external opportunities? If so, what are they?
7. Are our external threats still threats?
8. Are there now other external threats? If so, what are they?
9. Are we vulnerable to a hostile takeover?

Measuring Organizational Performance

Another important strategy-evaluation activity is *measuring organizational performance*. This activity includes comparing expected results to actual results, investigating deviations from plans, evaluating individual performance, and examining progress being made toward meeting stated objectives. Both long-term and annual objectives are commonly used in this process. Criteria for evaluating strategies should be measurable and easily verifiable. Criteria that predict results may be more important than those that reveal what already has happened. For example, rather than simply being informed that sales in the last quarter were 20 percent under what was expected, strategists need to know that sales in the next quarter may be 20 percent below standard unless some action is taken to counter the trend. Really effective control requires accurate forecasting.

Failure to make satisfactory progress toward accomplishing long-term or annual objectives signals a need for corrective actions. Many factors, such as unreasonable policies, unexpected turns in the economy, unreliable suppliers or distributors, or ineffective strategies, can result in unsatisfactory progress toward meeting objectives. Problems can result from ineffectiveness (not doing the right things) or inefficiency (poorly doing the right things).

Determining which objectives are most important in the evaluation of strategies can be difficult. Strategy evaluation is based on both quantitative and qualitative criteria. Selecting the exact set of criteria for evaluating strategies depends on a particular organization's size, industry, strategies, and management philosophy. An organization pursuing a retrenchment strategy, for example, could have an entirely different set of evaluative criteria from an organization pursuing a market-development strategy. Quantitative criteria commonly used to evaluate strategies are financial ratios, which strategists use to make three critical comparisons: (1) comparing the firm's performance over different time periods, (2) comparing the firm's performance to competitors', and (3) comparing the firm's performance to industry averages. Some key financial ratios that are particularly useful as criteria for strategy evaluation are as follows:

1. Return on investment (ROI)
2. Return on equity (ROE)
3. Profit margin
4. Market share
5. Debt to equity
6. Earnings per share
7. Sales growth
8. Asset growth

But there are some potential problems associated with using quantitative criteria for evaluating strategies. First, most quantitative criteria are geared to annual objectives rather than long-term objectives. Also, different accounting methods can provide different results on many quantitative criteria. Third, intuitive judgments are almost always involved in deriving quantitative criteria. For these and other reasons, qualitative criteria are also important in evaluating strategies. Human factors such as high absenteeism and turnover rates, poor production quality and quantity rates, or low employee satisfaction can be underlying causes of declining performance. Marketing, finance/accounting, R&D, or management information systems factors can also cause financial problems. Seymour Tilles identified six qualitative questions that are useful in evaluating strategies:

1. Is the strategy internally consistent?
2. Is the strategy consistent with the environment?
3. Is the strategy appropriate in view of available resources?
4. Does the strategy involve an acceptable degree of risk?
5. Does the strategy have an appropriate time framework?
6. Is the strategy workable?[5]

Some additional key questions that reveal the need for qualitative or intuitive judgments in strategy evaluation are as follows:

1. How good is the firm's balance of investments between high-risk and low-risk projects?

2.   How good is the firm's balance of investments between long-term and short-term projects?
3.   How good is the firm's balance of investments between slow-growing markets and fast-growing markets?
4.   How good is the firm's balance of investments among different divisions?
5.   To what extent are the firm's alternative strategies socially responsible?
6.   What are the relationships among the firm's key internal and external strategic factors?
7.   How are major competitors likely to respond to particular strategies?

Taking Corrective Actions

The final strategy-evaluation activity, *taking corrective actions*, requires making changes to competitively reposition a firm for the future. Examples of changes that may be needed are altering an organization's structure, replacing one or more key individuals, selling a division, or revising a business mission. Other changes could include establishing or revising objectives, devising new policies, issuing stock to raise capital, adding additional salespersons, differently allocating resources, or developing new performance incentives. Taking corrective actions does not necessarily mean that existing strategies will be abandoned or even that new strategies must be formulated.

> The probabilities and possibilities for incorrect or inappropriate actions increase geometrically with an arithmetic increase in personnel. Any person directing an overall undertaking must check on the actions of the participants as well as the results that they have achieved. If either the actions or results do not comply with preconceived or planned achievements, then corrective actions are needed.[6]

No organization can survive as an island; no organization can escape change. Taking corrective actions is necessary to keep an organization on track toward achieving stated objectives. In his thought-provoking books *Future Shock* and *The Third Wave,* Alvin Toffler argued that business environments are becoming so dynamic and complex that they threaten people and organizations with *future shock*, which occurs when the nature, types, and speed of changes overpower an individual's or organization's ability and capacity to adapt. Strategy evaluation enhances an organization's ability to adapt successfully to changing circumstances. Brown and Agnew referred to this notion as *corporate agility.*[7]

Taking corrective actions raises employees' and managers' anxieties. Research suggests that participation in strategy-evaluation activities is one of the best ways to overcome individuals' resistance to change. According to Erez and Kanfer, individuals accept change best when they have a cognitive understanding of the changes, a sense of control over the situation, and an awareness that necessary actions are going to be taken to implement the changes.[8]

Strategy evaluation can lead to strategy-formulation changes, strategy-implementation changes, both formulation and implementation changes, or no changes at all. Strategists cannot escape having to revise strategies and implementation approaches sooner or later. Hussey and Langham offered the following insight on taking corrective actions:

> Resistance to change is often emotionally based and not easily overcome by rational argument. Resistance may be based on such feelings as loss of status, implied criticism of present competence, fear of failure in the new situation, annoyance at not being consulted, lack of understanding of the need for change, or insecurity in changing from well-known and fixed methods. It is necessary, therefore, to overcome such resistance by creating situations of participation and full explanation when changes are envisaged.[9]

Corrective actions should place an organization in a better position to capitalize upon internal strengths; to take advantage of key external opportunities; to avoid, reduce, or mitigate external threats; and to improve internal weaknesses. Corrective actions should have a proper time horizon and an appropriate amount of risk. They should be internally consistent and socially responsible. Perhaps most important, corrective actions strengthen an organization's competitive position in its basic industry. Continuous strategy evaluation keeps strategists close to the pulse of an organization and provides information needed for an effective strategic-management system. Carter Bayles described the benefits of strategy evaluation as follows:

> Evaluation activities may renew confidence in the current business strategy or point to the need for actions to correct some weaknesses, such as erosion of product superiority or technological edge. In many cases, the benefits of strategy evaluation are much more far-reaching, for the outcome of the process may be a fundamentally new strategy that will lead, even in a business that is already turning a respectable profit, to substantially increased earnings. It is this possibility that justifies strategy evaluation, for the payoff can be very large.[10]

The Balanced Scorecard

Introduced earlier in the Chapter 5 discussion of objectives, the Balanced Scorecard is an important strategy-evaluation tool. It is a process that allows firms to evaluate strategies from four perspectives: financial performance, customer knowledge, internal business processes, and learning and growth. The *Balanced Scorecard* analysis requires that firms seek answers to the following questions and utilize that information, in conjunction with financial measures, to adequately and more effectively evaluate strategies being implemented:

1. How well is the firm continually improving and creating value along measures such as innovation, technological leadership, product quality, operational process efficiencies, and so on?
2. How well is the firm sustaining and even improving upon its core competencies and competitive advantages?
3. How satisfied are the firm's customers?

A sample Balanced Scorecard is provided in Table 9-4. Notice that the firm examines six key issues in evaluating its strategies: (1) Customers, (2) Managers/Employees, (3) Operations/Processes, (4) Community/Social Responsibility, (5) Business Ethics/Natural Environment, and (6) Financial. The basic form of a Balanced Scorecard may differ for different organizations. The Balanced Scorecard approach to strategy evaluation aims to balance long-term with short-term concerns, to balance financial with nonfinancial concerns, and to balance internal with external concerns. It can be an excellent management tool, and it is used successfully today by Moscow Bank, Exxon/Mobil Corporation, Sharp Corporation, SAS Institute, and numerous other firms. For example, Unilever has a financial objective to grow revenues by 5 percent to 6 percent annually. The company also has a strategic objective to reduce its 1,200 food, household, and personal care products to 400 core brands within three years. The Balanced Scorecard would be constructed differently, that is, adapted, to particular firms in various industries with the underlying theme or thrust being the same, which is to evaluate the firm's strategies based upon both key quantitative and qualitative measures.

Published Sources of Strategy-Evaluation Information

A number of publications are helpful in evaluating a firm's strategies. For example, *Fortune* annually identifies and evaluates the Fortune 1,000 (the largest manufacturers) and the Fortune 50 (the largest retailers, transportation companies, utilities, banks, insurance companies, and diversified financial corporations in the United States). *Fortune* ranks the best and worst performers on various factors, such as return on investment, sales volume, and profitability. In its March issue each year, *Fortune* publishes its strategy-evaluation research in an article entitled "America's Most Admired Companies." Eight key attributes serve as evaluative criteria: people management; innovativeness; quality of products or services; financial soundness; social responsibility; use of corporate assets;

TABLE 9-4   An Example Balanced Scorecard

Area of Objectives	Measure or Target	Time Expectation	Primary Responsibility
Customers			
1.			
2.			
3.			
4.			
Managers/Employees			
1.			
2.			
3.			
4.			
Operations/Processes			
1.			
2.			
3.			
4.			
Community/Social Responsibility			
1.			
2.			
3.			
4.			
Business Ethics/Natural Environment			
1.			
2.			
3.			
4.			
Financial			
1.			
2.			
3.			
4.			

long-term investment; and quality of management. In October of each year, *Fortune* publishes additional strategy-evaluation research in an article entitled "The World's Most Admired Companies." *Fortune's* 2007 evaluation in Table 9-5 reveals the firms most admired (best managed) in their industry. The most admired company in the world in 2007 was General Electric, followed by Toyota Motor, Procter & Gamble, Johnson & Johnson and Apple.[11]

Forbes, *BusinessWeek*, *Industry Week*, and *Dun's Business Month* also periodically publish detailed evaluations of businesses and industries. Although published sources of strategy-evaluation information focus primarily on large, publicly held businesses, the comparative ratios and related information are widely used to evaluate small businesses and privately owned firms as well.

Characteristics of an Effective Evaluation System

Strategy evaluation must meet several basic requirements to be effective. First, strategy-evaluation activities must be economical; too much information can be just as bad as too

TABLE 9-5 **The Most Admired Companies in Various Industries (2007)**

Industry	The Most Admired Company
Financial data services	Dun & Bradstreet
Insurance: Life and health	Northwestern Mutual
Insurance: Property and casualty	Berkshire Hathaway
Megabanks, credit card companies	American Express
Mortgage services	LandAmerica Financial Group
Securities	Lehman Brothers Holdings
Apparel	Nike #1, Polo Ralph Lauren #2
Beverages	Anheuser-Busch #1, Coca-Cola #3
Consumer food products	Nestle #1, PepsiCo #2
Food production	Bunge #1, Pilgrim's Pride #2
Household and personal products	P & G #1, Estee Lauder #2
Food services	Starbucks #1, McDonald's #2
General merchandisers	Nordstrom
Specialty retailers	Costco Wholesale
Furniture	Herman Miller
Homebuilders	Centex #1, Toll Brothers #4

Source: Adapted from: Eugenia Levenson, "America's Most Admired Companies," *Fortune* (March 19, 2007): 90–100.

little information; and too many controls can do more harm than good. Strategy-evaluation activities also should be meaningful; they should specifically relate to a firm's objectives. They should provide managers with useful information about tasks over which they have control and influence. Strategy-evaluation activities should provide timely information; on occasion and in some areas, managers may daily need information. For example, when a firm has diversified by acquiring another firm, evaluative information may be needed frequently. However, in an R&D department, daily or even weekly evaluative information could be dysfunctional. Approximate information that is timely is generally more desirable as a basis for strategy evaluation than accurate information that does not depict the present. Frequent measurement and rapid reporting may frustrate control rather than give better control. The time dimension of control must coincide with the time span of the event being measured.

Strategy evaluation should be designed to provide a true picture of what is happening. For example, in a severe economic downturn, productivity and profitability ratios may drop alarmingly, although employees and managers are actually working harder. Strategy evaluations should fairly portray this type of situation. Information derived from the strategy-evaluation process should facilitate action and should be directed to those individuals in the organization who need to take action based on it. Managers commonly ignore evaluative reports that are provided only for informational purposes; not all managers need to receive all reports. Controls need to be action-oriented rather than information-oriented.

The strategy-evaluation process should not dominate decisions; it should foster mutual understanding, trust, and common sense. No department should fail to cooperate with another in evaluating strategies. Strategy evaluations should be simple, not too cumbersome, and not too restrictive. Complex strategy-evaluation systems often confuse people and accomplish little. The test of an effective evaluation system is its usefulness, not its complexity.

Large organizations require a more elaborate and detailed strategy-evaluation system because it is more difficult to coordinate efforts among different divisions and functional areas. Managers in small companies often communicate daily with each other and their employees and do not need extensive evaluative reporting systems. Familiarity with local environments usually makes gathering and evaluating information much easier for small organizations than for large businesses. But the key to an effective strategy-evaluation system may be the ability to convince participants that failure to accomplish certain objectives within a prescribed time is not necessarily a reflection of their performance.

There is no one ideal strategy-evaluation system. The unique characteristics of an organization, including its size, management style, purpose, problems, and strengths, can determine a strategy-evaluation and control system's final design. Robert Waterman offered the following observation about successful organizations' strategy-evaluation and control systems:

> Successful companies treat facts as friends and controls as liberating. Morgan Guaranty and Wells Fargo not only survive but thrive in the troubled waters of bank deregulation, because their strategy evaluation and control systems are sound, their risk is contained, and they know themselves and the competitive situation so well. Successful companies have a voracious hunger for facts. They see information where others see only data. They love comparisons, rankings, anything that removes decision making from the realm of mere opinion. Successful companies maintain tight, accurate financial controls. Their people don't regard controls as an imposition of autocracy but as the benign checks and balances that allow them to be creative and free.[12]

Contingency Planning

A basic premise of good strategic management is that firms plan ways to deal with unfavorable and favorable events before they occur. Too many organizations prepare contingency plans just for unfavorable events; this is a mistake, because both minimizing threats and capitalizing on opportunities can improve a firm's competitive position.

Regardless of how carefully strategies are formulated, implemented, and evaluated, unforeseen events, such as strikes, boycotts, natural disasters, arrival of foreign competitors, and government actions, can make a strategy obsolete. To minimize the impact of potential threats, organizations should develop contingency plans as part of their strategy-evaluation process. *Contingency plans* can be defined as alternative plans that can be put into effect if certain key events do not occur as expected. Only high-priority areas require the insurance of contingency plans. Strategists cannot and should not try to cover all bases by planning for all possible contingencies. But in any case, contingency plans should be as simple as possible.

Some contingency plans commonly established by firms include the following:

1. If a major competitor withdraws from particular markets as intelligence reports indicate, what actions should our firm take?
2. If our sales objectives are not reached, what actions should our firm take to avoid profit losses?
3. If demand for our new product exceeds plans, what actions should our firm take to meet the higher demand?
4. If certain disasters occur—such as loss of computer capabilities; a hostile takeover attempt; loss of patent protection; or destruction of manufacturing facilities because of earthquakes, tornados, or hurricanes—what actions should our firm take?
5. If a new technological advancement makes our new product obsolete sooner than expected, what actions should our firm take?

Too many organizations discard alternative strategies not selected for implementation although the work devoted to analyzing these options would render valuable information. Alternative strategies not selected for implementation can serve as contingency plans in case the strategy or strategies selected do not work. Companies and governments are increasingly considering nuclear-generated electricity as the most efficient means of power generation. Many contingency plans certainly call for nuclear power rather than for coal- and gas-derived electricity. As indicated in the "Global Perspective," the United States is well below many countries in the world in the percentage of power derived from nuclear power plants. See the "Global Perspective" for states in the country that lead in nuclear power generation.

The United States and Western Europe continue to waver on the use of atomic energy, while Eastern European countries build new-generation nuclear power stations to meet rising demand. Note in the following list that the United States is well behind almost all European countries on the use of nuclear fuel for electricity generation.

Country	Percent of Electricity Derived from Nuclear Power
France	78.1%
Lithuania	72.1
Slovakia	55.2
Belgium	55.1
Sweden	51.8
Bulgaria	41.6
Switzerland	40.0
Slovenia	38.8
Hungary	33.8
Germany	32.1
Czech Republic	31.2
Finland	26.6
Spain	22.9
United States	19.9
United Kingdom	13.4

Although coal and natural gas power plants may be safer (and that is debatable), the nuclear option surely is cleaner and more powerful. East European countries are thus building new nuclear plants to meet growing demand, while the United States and Western Europe have this option only in their contingency plans. New nuclear plants today are being built in France, the Czech Republic, Slovakia, Romania, Finland, and Bulgaria, while Germany, England, and the United States discuss closing some of their plants. Germany, in fact, is committed to being a nuclear-free state by 2021, which means closing 19 nuclear plants that today account for 30 percent of that country's power-generating capacity.

TXU Corporation, NRG Energy, Exelon Corporation, and Amarillo Power are firms in the United States that plan to build nuclear power plants in the state of Texas in the next decade. Two reasons for the spur in nuclear power in Texas are: (1) Utilities in Texas no longer have monopolistic territories, and (2) environmental groups in Texas are reversing their negative view of nuclear power, having concluded that global warming is so severe and the time for action is so short that nuclear power is a far better option than coal-fired plants.

Finland is building the first nuclear generating plant in Western Europe since 1991. The plant will open in 2010. Switzerland just lifted its moratorium on new nuclear plants. Belarus starts construction of a nuclear plant in 2008 that will begin generating power in 2014. In addition to nuclear energy, countries are also scrambling to install solar photovoltaic power to avoid CO_2 emissions and obtain carbon credits from the government. A recent *USA*

France, River Seine, view of nuclear plants.
Source: Christopher and Sally Gable (c) Dorling Kindersley

Today article reports that 1,744 megawatts of solar photovoltaic power were installed worldwide in 2006. The following countries reveal where those solar stations were built in terms of percentage of the 1,744 megawatts:

Germany	55 percent
Rest of Europe	11 percent
Japan	17 percent
United States and Other	9 percent

Source: Adapted from Nina Sovich, "Europe's New Nuclear Standoff: Eastern States Embrace Atomic Energy, as Western Neighbors Waver," *Wall Street Journal* (June 29, 2005): A13; Rebecca Smith, "TXU Sheds Coal Plan, Charts Nuclear Path," *Wall Street Journal* (April 10, 2007): A2; Jeffrey Ball, "Cows, Climate Change and Carbon Credits," *USA Today* (June 14, 2007): B1, B2; and Jeffrey Stinson, "Europe Warms to Nuclear Energy," *USA Today* (June 4, 2007): A1.

When strategy-evaluation activities reveal the need for a major change quickly, an appropriate contingency plan can be executed in a timely way. Contingency plans can promote a strategist's ability to respond quickly to key changes in the internal and external bases of an organization's current strategy. For example, if underlying assumptions about the economy turn out to be wrong and contingency plans are ready, then managers can make appropriate changes promptly.

In some cases, external or internal conditions present unexpected opportunities. When such opportunities occur, contingency plans could allow an organization to quickly capitalize on them. Linneman and Chandran reported that contingency planning gave users, such as DuPont, Dow Chemical, Consolidated Foods, and Emerson Electric, three major benefits: (1) It permitted quick response to change, (2) it prevented panic in crisis situations, and (3) it made managers more adaptable by encouraging them to appreciate just how variable the future can be. They suggested that effective contingency planning involves a seven-step process:

1. Identify both beneficial and unfavorable events that could possibly derail the strategy or strategies.
2. Specify trigger points. Calculate about when contingent events are likely to occur.
3. Assess the impact of each contingent event. Estimate the potential benefit or harm of each contingent event.
4. Develop contingency plans. Be sure that contingency plans are compatible with current strategy and are economically feasible.
5. Assess the counterimpact of each contingency plan. That is, estimate how much each contingency plan will capitalize on or cancel out its associated contingent event. Doing this will quantify the potential value of each contingency plan.
6. Determine early warning signals for key contingent events. Monitor the early warning signals.
7. For contingent events with reliable early warning signals, develop advance action plans to take advantage of the available lead time.[13]

Auditing

A frequently used tool in strategy evaluation is the audit. *Auditing* has been defined as "a systematic process of objectively obtaining and evaluating evidence regarding assertions about economic actions and events to ascertain the degree of correspondence between these assertions and established criteria, and communicating the results to interested users."[14] Since the Enron, Worldcom, and Johnson & Johnson scandals, auditing has taken on greater emphasis and care in companies. Independent auditors basically are certified public accountants (CPAs) who provide their services to organizations for a fee; they examine the financial statements of an organization to determine whether they have been prepared according to the standards set by the International

Auditing and Assurance Standards Board (IAASB) and whether they fairly represent the activities of the firm. Public accounting firms often have a consulting arm that provides strategy-evaluation services.

Government auditors are responsible for making sure that organizations comply with a nation's laws, statutes, and policies. The third group of auditors consists of employees within an organization who are responsible for safeguarding company assets, for assessing the efficiency of company operations, and for ensuring that generally accepted business procedures are practiced.

The Environmental Audit

For an increasing number of firms, overseeing environmental affairs is no longer a technical function performed by specialists; rather, it has become an important strategic-management concern. Product design, manufacturing, transportation, customer use, packaging, product disposal, and corporate rewards and sanctions should reflect environmental considerations. Firms that effectively manage environmental affairs are benefiting from constructive relations with employees, consumers, suppliers, and distributors. As indicated in the "Natural Environment Perspective," China is home to 16 of the world's 20 most polluted cities.

Shimell emphasized the need for organizations to conduct environmental audits of their operations and to develop a Corporate Environmental Policy (CEP).[15] Shimell contended that an environmental audit should be as rigorous as a financial audit and should include training workshops in which staff can help design and implement the policy. The CEP should be budgeted, and requisite funds should be allocated to ensure that it is not a public relations facade. A Statement of Environmental Policy should be published periodically to inform shareholders and the public of environmental actions taken by the firm.

Instituting an environmental audit can include moving environmental affairs from the staff side of the organization to the line side. Some firms are also introducing environmental criteria and objectives in their performance appraisal instruments and systems. Conoco, for example, ties compensation of all its top managers to environmental action plans. Occidental Chemical includes environmental responsibilities in all its job descriptions for positions.

Twenty-First-Century Challenges in Strategic Management

Three particular challenges or decisions that face all strategists today are (1) deciding whether the process should be more an art or a science, (2) deciding whether strategies should be visible or hidden from stakeholders, and (3) deciding whether the process should be more top-down or bottom-up in their firm.[16]

The Art or Science Issue

This textbook is consistent with most of the strategy literature in advocating that strategic management be viewed more as a science than an art. This perspective contends that firms need to systematically assess their external and internal environments, conduct research, carefully evaluate the pros and cons of various alternatives, perform analyses, and then decide upon a particular course of action. In contrast, Mintzberg's notion of "crafting" strategies embodies the artistic model, which suggests that strategic decision making be based primarily on holistic thinking, intuition, creativity, and imagination.[17] Mintzberg and his followers reject strategies that result from objective analysis, preferring instead subjective imagination. "Strategy scientists" reject strategies that emerge from emotion, hunch, creativity, and politics. Proponents of the artistic view often consider strategic planning exercises to be time poorly spent. The Mintzberg philosophy insists on informality,

NATURAL ENVIRONMENT PERSPECTIVE
China Vastly Polluted

China has compressed a normal century of economic development into one generation and ravaged its air, soil, and water in the process. China is today home to 16 of the world's 20 most polluted cities, and it battles soil erosion, spreading deserts, polluted water, and smog everywhere. About 40 percent of Chinese cities lack sewage treatment facilities. All of China's major rivers are dangerously polluted, and two-thirds of the country's rivers and lakes are severely polluted. Data indicate that 340 million of the 1.3 billion Chinese (26 percent) lack access to clean drinking water, and 10 percent of China's farmland is polluted.

Research shows that deposits of mercury accumulating in the western United States originated from coal-burning power plants in China. These plants produce 70 to 90 percent of China's energy, but the surging Chinese economy is demanding more and more energy. The deputy director for China's State Environmental Protection Administration (EPA) recently told state media that environmental issues have "become a key bottleneck" for the economy. China's own Modernization Report issued in January 2007 acknowledged that the country has made no progress in protecting the environment over the past three years. Although China signed the Kyoto Protocol, it has been exempted from the treaty's greenhouse-gas limits.

The good news is that China's central government recognizes pollution to be a strategic problem for the country and is taking steps to improve the situation, but it may be too little, too late as global warming and climate issues ravage the country. China's State Environmental Protection Administration recently published a list of 82 large projects, valued at a total of $14.4 billion, that it said had failed to comply with environmental regulations, mostly in the steel, chemical, and metallurgy industries. Chinese officials estimate that one-fifth of the power plants in China are illegal, generating enough power to light up all of Britain.

In 2006, China had 161 serious environmental accidents, the most ever, according to Pan Yue, deputy director of China's EPA. Mr. Pan also says "the year 2006 was the most grim year ever for China's environmental situation." Rising sea levels now threaten the deltas of the Yellow, Yangtze, and Pearl rivers—home to the bulk of China's manufacturing and export business. China will thus soon become concerned about global warming.

China overtook the United States by 7.5 percent as the world's top producer of carbon dioxide emissions in 2006. China's emissions per capita are of course less than those of the United States, but in volume and quantity it now leads all countries of the world in air pollutants.

Source: Adapted from Calurn MacLeod, "China Envisions Environmentally Friendly 'Eco-City,'" *USA Today* (February 16, 2007): 9A; Shai Oster, "China Cracks Down on Power Companies in Tough Antipollution Campaign," *Wall Street Journal* (January 12, 2007): A9; Shai Oster, "China Tilts Green," *Wall Street Journal* (February 13, 2007): A4; and "China Passes U.S. on CO_2 output," *Wall Street Journal* (June 22, 2007): A4.

School for the Arts-Children's Palace, Shanghai. *Source:* Mrs. Feldheim

whereas strategy scientists (and this text) insist on more formality. Mintzberg refers to strategic planning as an "emergent" process whereas strategy scientists use the term "deliberate" process.[18]

The answer to the art versus science question is one that strategists must decide for themselves, and certainly the two approaches are not mutually exclusive. In deciding which approach is more effective, however, consider that the business world today has become increasingly complex and more intensely competitive. There is less room for error in strategic planning. Recall that Chapter 1 discussed the importance of intuition and experience and subjectivity in strategic planning, and even the weights and ratings discussed in Chapters 3, 4, and 6 certainly require good judgment. But the idea of deciding upon strategies for any firm without thorough research and analysis, at least in the mind of this writer, is unwise. Certainly, in smaller firms there can be more informality in the process compared to larger firms, but even for smaller firms, a wealth of competitive information is available on the Internet and elsewhere and should be collected, assimilated, and evaluated before deciding on a course of action upon which survival of the firm may hinge. The livelihood of countless employees and shareholders may hinge on the effectiveness of strategies selected. Too much is at stake to be less than thorough in formulating strategies. It is not wise for a strategist to rely too heavily on gut feeling and opinion instead of research data, competitive intelligence, and analysis in formulating strategies.

The Visible or Hidden Issue

There are certainly good reasons to keep the strategy process and strategies themselves visible and open rather than hidden and secret. There are also good reasons to keep strategies hidden from all but top-level executives. Strategists must decide for themselves what is best for their firms. This text comes down largely on the side of being visible and open, but certainly this may not be best for all strategists and all firms. As pointed out in Chapter 1, Sun Tzu argued that all war is based on deception and that the best maneuvers are those not easily predicted by rivals. Business is analogous to war.

Some reasons to be completely open with the strategy process and resultant decisions are these:

1. Managers, employees, and other stakeholders can readily contribute to the process. They often have excellent ideas. Secrecy would forgo many excellent ideas.
2. Investors, creditors, and other stakeholders have greater basis for supporting a firm when they know what the firm is doing and where the firm is going.
3. Visibility promotes democracy, whereas secrecy promotes autocracy. Most firms prefer democracy over autocracy as a management style.
4. Participation and openness enhance understanding, commitment, and communication within the firm.

Reasons why some firms prefer to conduct strategic planning in secret and keep strategies hidden from all but the highest-level executives are as follows:

1. Free dissemination of a firm's strategies may easily translate into competitive intelligence for rival firms who could exploit the firm given that information.
2. Secrecy limits criticism, second guessing, and hindsight.
3. Participants in a visible strategy process become more attractive to rival firms who may lure them away.
4. Secrecy limits rival firms from imitating or duplicating the firm's strategies and undermining the firm.

The obvious benefits of the visible versus hidden extremes suggest that a working balance must be sought between the apparent contradictions. Parnell says that in a perfect world all key individuals both inside and outside the firm should be involved in strategic planning, but in practice particularly sensitive and confidential information should always remain strictly confidential to top managers.[19] This balancing azct is difficult but essential for survival of the firm.

The Top-Down or Bottom-Up Approach

Proponents of the top-down approach contend that top executives are the only persons in the firm with the collective experience, acumen, and fiduciary responsibility to make key strategy decisions. In contrast, bottom-up advocates argue that lower- and middle-level managers and employees who will be implementing the strategies need to be actively involved in the process of formulating the strategies to ensure their support and commitment. Recent strategy research and this textbook emphasize the bottom-up approach, but earlier work by Schendel and Hofer stressed the need for firms to rely on perceptions of their top managers in strategic planning.[20] Strategists must reach a working balance of the two approaches in a manner deemed best for their firms at a particular time, while cognizant of the fact that current research supports the bottom-up approach, at least among U.S. firms. Increased education and diversity of the workforce at all levels are reasons why middle- and lower-level managers—and even nonmanagers—should be invited to participate in the firm's strategic planning process, at least to the extent that they are willing and able to contribute.

Conclusion

This chapter presents a strategy-evaluation framework that can facilitate accomplishment of annual and long-term objectives. Effective strategy evaluation allows an organization to capitalize on internal strengths as they develop, to exploit external opportunities as they emerge, to recognize and defend against threats, and to mitigate internal weaknesses before they become detrimental.

Strategists in successful organizations take the time to formulate, implement, and then evaluate strategies deliberately and systematically. Good strategists move their organization forward with purpose and direction, continually evaluating and improving the firm's external and internal strategic positions. Strategy evaluation allows an organization to shape its own future rather than allowing it to be constantly shaped by remote forces that have little or no vested interest in the well-being of the enterprise.

Although not a guarantee for success, strategic management allows organizations to make effective long-term decisions, to execute those decisions efficiently, and to take corrective actions as needed to ensure success. Computer networks and the Internet help to coordinate strategic-management activities and to ensure that decisions are based on good information. The Checkmate Strategic Planning Software is especially good in this regard (www.checkmateplan.com). A key to effective strategy evaluation and to successful strategic management is an integration of intuition and analysis:

> A potentially fatal problem is the tendency for analytical and intuitive issues to polarize. This polarization leads to strategy evaluation that is dominated by either analysis or intuition, or to strategy evaluation that is discontinuous, with a lack of coordination among analytical and intuitive issues.[21]

Strategists in successful organizations realize that strategic management is first and foremost a people process. It is an excellent vehicle for fostering organizational communication. People are what make the difference in organizations.

> The real key to effective strategic management is to accept the premise that the planning process is more important than the written plan, that the manager is continuously planning and does not stop planning when the written plan is finished. The written plan is only a snapshot as of the moment it is approved. If the manager is not planning on a continuous basis—planning, measuring, and revising—the written plan can become obsolete the day it is finished. This obsolescence becomes more of a certainty as the increasingly rapid rate of change makes the business environment more uncertain.[22]

We invite you to visit the David page on the Prentice Hall Companion Web site at www.prenhall.com/david for this chapter's review quiz.

Key Terms and Concepts

Advantage (p. 331)
Auditing (p. 343)
Balanced Scorecard (p. 338)
Consistency (p. 331)
Consonance (p. 331)
Contingency Plans (p. 341)
Corporate Agility (p. 337)
Feasibility (p. 331)
Future Shock (p. 337)
Management by Wandering Around (p. 333)
Measuring Organizational Performance (p. 336)
Reviewing the Underlying Bases of an Organization's Strategy (p. 334)
Revised EFE Matrix (p. 334)
Revised IFE Matrix (p. 334)
Taking Corrective Actions (p. 337)

Issues for Review and Discussion

1. Why has strategy evaluation become so important in business today?
2. BellSouth Services is considering putting divisional EFE and IFE matrices online for continual updating. How would this affect strategy evaluation?
3. What types of quantitative and qualitative criteria do you think Meg Whitman, CEO of eBay, uses to evaluate the company's strategy?
4. As owner of a local, independent supermarket, explain how you would evaluate the firm's strategy.
5. Under what conditions are corrective actions not required in the strategy-evaluation process?
6. Identify types of organizations that may need to more frequently evaluate strategy than others. Justify your choices.
7. As executive director of the state forestry commission, in what way and how frequently would you evaluate the organization's strategies?
8. Identify some key financial ratios that would be important in evaluating a bank's strategy.
9. As owner of a chain of hardware stores, describe how you would approach contingency planning.
10. Strategy evaluation allows an organization to take a proactive stance toward shaping its own future. Discuss the meaning of this statement.
11. Explain and discuss the Balanced Scorecard.
12. Why is the Balanced Scorecard an important topic both in devising objectives and in evaluating strategies?
13. Develop a Balanced Scorecard for a local fast-food restaurant.
14. Do you believe strategic management should be more visible or hidden as a process in a firm? Explain.
15. Do you feel strategic management should be more a top-down or bottom-up process in a firm? Explain.
16. Do you believe strategic management is more an art or a science? Explain.

Notes

1. Dale McConkey, "Planning in a Changing Environment," *Business Horizons* (September–October 1988): 64.
2. Robert Simons, "Control in an Age of Empowerment," *Harvard Business Review* (March–April 1995): 80.
3. Dale Zand, "Reviewing the Policy Process," *California Management Review* 21, no. 1 (Fall 1978): 37.

4. Eccles. 3: 1–8.
5. Seymour Tilles, "How to Evaluate Corporate Strategy," *Harvard Business Review* 41 (July–August 1963): 111–121.
6. Claude George, Jr., *The History of Management Thought* (Upper Saddle River, New Jersey: Prentice Hall, 1968): 165–166.
7. John Brown and Neil Agnew, "Corporate Agility," *Business Horizons* 25, no. 2 (March–April 1982): 29.
8. M. Erez and F. Kanfer, "The Role of Goal Acceptance in Goal Setting and Task Performance," *Academy of Management Review* 8, no. 3 (July 1983): 457.
9. D. Hussey and M. Langham, *Corporate Planning: The Human Factor* (Oxford, England: Pergamon Press, 1979): 138.
10. Carter Bayles, "Strategic Control: The President's Paradox," *Business Horizons* 20, no. 4 (August 1977): 18.
11. Eugenia Levenson, "America's Most Admired Companies," *Fortune* (March 19, 2007): 92.
12. Robert Waterman, Jr., "How the Best Get Better," *BusinessWeek* (September 14, 1987): 105.
13. Robert Linneman and Rajan Chandran, "Contingency Planning: A Key to Swift Managerial Action in the Uncertain Tomorrow," *Managerial Planning* 29, no. 4 (January–February 1981): 23–27.
14. American Accounting Association, *Report of Committee on Basic Auditing Concepts* (1971): 15–74.
15. Pamela Shimell, "Corporate Environmental Policy in Practice," *Long Range Planning* 24, no. 3 (June 1991): 10.
16. John Parnell, "Five Critical Challenges in Strategy Making," *SAM Advanced Management Journal* 68, no. 2 (Spring 2003): 15–22.
17. Henry Mintzberg, "Crafting Strategy," *Harvard Business Review* (July–August, 1987): 66–75.
18. Henry Mintzberg and J. Waters, "Of Strategies, Deliberate and Emergent," *Strategic Management Journal* 6, no. 2: 257–272.
19. Parnell, 15–22.
20. D. E. Schendel and C. W. Hofer (Eds.), *Strategic Management* (Boston: Little, Brown, 1979).
21. Michael McGinnis, "The Key to Strategic Planning: Integrating Analysis and Intuition," *Sloan Management Review* 26, no. 1 (Fall 1984): 49.
22. McConkey, 72.

Current Readings

Barsade, Sigal G. and Donald E. Gibson. "Why Does Affect Matter in Organizations." *The Academy of Management Perspective* 21, no. 1 (February 2007): 36.
Berry, Leonard L. "The best companies are generous companies." *Business Horizon* 50, no. 4 (July-August 2007): 263.
Burlingham, Bo. "Small Giants: Companies That Choose to Be Great Instead of Big." *Business Horizons* 50, no. 3 (May-June 2007): 185.
Nag, R., D.C. Hambrick, and M.J. Chen. "What is Strategic Management, Really? Inductive Derivation of a Consensus Definition of the Field." *Strategic Management Journal* 935, no. 28 (September 2007): 935.
Seo, Myeong-Gu. "Being Emotional during Decision Making—Good or Bad? An Empirical Investigation." *The Academy of Management Journal* 50, no. 4 (August 2007): 923.
Stadler, Christian. "The Four Principles of Enduring Success." *Harvard Business Review* (July-August 2007) 62.

• EXPERIENTIAL EXERCISES

Experiential Exercise 9A

Preparing a Strategy-Evaluation Report for Walt Disney

Purpose

This exercise can give you experience locating strategy-evaluation information. Use of the Internet coupled with published sources of information can significantly enhance the strategy-evaluation process. Performance information on competitors, for example, can help put into perspective a firm's own performance.

Instructions

Step 1   Visit http://marketwatch.multexinvestor.com, http://moneycentral.msn.com, http://finance.yahoo.com, www.clearstation.com to locate strategy-evaluation information on competitors. Read 5 to 10 articles written in the last six months that discuss the family entertainment industry.

Step 2   Summarize your research findings by preparing a strategy-evaluation report for your instructor. Include in your report a summary of Walt Disney's strategies and performance in 2007 and a summary of your conclusions regarding the effectiveness of Walt Disney's strategies.

Step 3   Based on your analysis, do you feel that Walt Disney is pursuing effective strategies? What recommendations would you offer to Walt Disney's chief executive officer?

Mickey Mouse balloons.
Source: Lourens Smak/Almay Images

Experiential Exercise 9B

Evaluating My University's Strategies

Purpose

An important part of evaluating strategies is determining the nature and extent of changes in an organization's external opportunities/threats and internal strengths/weaknesses. Changes in these underlying critical success factors can indicate a need to change or modify the firm's strategies.

Instructions

As a class, discuss positive and negative changes in your university's external and internal factors during your college career. Begin by listing on the board new or emerging opportunities and threats. Then identify strengths and weaknesses that have changed significantly during your college career. In light of the external and internal changes that were identified, discuss whether your university's strategies need modifying. Are there any new strategies that you would recommend? Make a list to recommend to your department chair, dean, president, or chancellor.

Experiential Exercise 9C

Who Prepares an Environmental Audit?

Purpose

The purpose of this activity is to determine the nature and prevalence of environmental audits among companies in your state.

Instructions

Contact by phone at least five different plant managers or owners of large businesses in your area. Seek answers to the following questions. Present your findings in a written report to your instructor.

1. Does your company conduct an environmental audit? If yes, please describe the nature and scope of the audit.
2. Are environmental criteria included in the performance evaluation of managers? If yes, please specify the criteria.
3. Are environmental affairs more a technical function or a management function in your company?
4. Does your firm offer any environmental workshops for employees? If yes, please describe them.

Part 5 • Strategic Management Case Analysis

How to Prepare and Present a Case Analysis

chapter objectives

After studying this chapter, you should be able to do the following:

1. Describe the case method for learning strategic-management concepts.

2. Identify the steps in preparing a comprehensive written case analysis.

3. Describe how to give an effective oral case analysis presentation.

4. Discuss special tips for doing case analysis.

steps in presenting an oral case analysis

Oral Presentation—Step 1
Introduction (2 minutes)

Oral Presentation—Step 2
Mission/Vision (4 minutes)

Oral Presentation—Step 3
Internal Assessment (8 minutes)

Oral Presentation—Step 4
External Assessment (8 minutes)

Oral Presentation—Step 5
Strategy Formulation (14 minutes)

Oral Presentation—Step 6
Strategy Implementation (8 minutes)

Oral Presentation—Step 7
Strategy Evaluation (2 minutes)

Oral Presentation—Step 8
Conclusion (4 minutes)

The purpose of this section is to help you analyze strategic-management cases. Guidelines for preparing written and oral case analyses are given, and suggestions for preparing cases for class discussion are presented. Steps to follow in preparing case analyses are provided. Guidelines for making an oral presentation are described.

What Is a Strategic-Management Case?

A *strategic-management* (or *business policy) case* describes an organization's external and internal conditions and raises issues concerning the firm's mission, strategies, objectives, and policies. Most of the information in a business policy case is established fact, but some information may be opinions, judgments, and beliefs. Strategic-management cases are more comprehensive than those you may have studied in other courses. They generally include a description of related management, marketing, finance/accounting, production/operations, R&D, computer information systems, and natural environment issues. A strategic-management case puts the reader on the scene of the action by describing a firm's situation at some point in time. Strategic-management cases are written to give you practice applying strategic-management concepts. The case method for studying strategic management is often called *learning by doing*.

Guidelines for Preparing Case Analyses

The Need for Practicality

There is no such thing as a complete case, and no case ever gives you all the information you need to conduct analyses and make recommendations. Likewise, in the business world, strategists never have all the information they need to make decisions: information may be unavailable or too costly to obtain, or it may take too much time to obtain. So in preparing strategic-management cases, do what strategists do every day—make reasonable assumptions about unknowns, clearly state assumptions, perform appropriate analyses, and make decisions. *Be practical*. For example, in performing a projected financial analysis, make reasonable assumptions, appropriately state them, and proceed to show what impact your recommendations are expected to have on the organization's financial position. Avoid saying "I don't have enough information." You can always supplement the information provided in a case with Internet and library research.

The Need for Justification

The most important part of analyzing cases is not what strategies you recommend but rather how you support your decisions and how you propose that they be implemented. There is no single best solution or one right answer to a case, so give ample justification for your recommendations. This is important. In the business world, strategists usually do not know if their decisions are right until resources have been allocated and consumed. Then it is often too late to reverse a decision. This cold fact accents the need for careful integration of intuition and analysis in preparing business policy case analyses.

The Need for Realism

Avoid recommending a course of action beyond an organization's means. *Be realistic*. No organization can possibly pursue all the strategies that could potentially benefit the firm. Estimate how much capital will be required to implement what you recommended. Determine whether debt, stock, or a combination of debt and stock could be used to obtain the capital. Make sure your recommendations are feasible. Do not prepare a case analysis that omits all arguments and information not supportive of your recommendations. Rather, present the major advantages and disadvantages of several feasible alternatives. Try not to exaggerate, stereotype, prejudge, or overdramatize. Strive to demonstrate that your interpretation of the evidence is reasonable and objective.

The Need for Specificity

Do not make broad generalizations such as "The company should pursue a market penetration strategy." Be specific by telling *what, why, when, how, where*, and *who*. Failure to use specifics is the single major shortcoming of most oral and written case analyses. For example, in an internal audit say, "The firm's current ratio fell from 2.2 in 2007 to 1.3 in 2008, and this is considered to be a major weakness," instead of "The firm's financial condition is bad." Rather than concluding from a Strategic Position and Action Evaluation (SPACE) Matrix that a firm should be defensive, be more specific, saying "The firm should consider closing three plants, laying off 280 employees, and divesting itself of its chemical division, for a net savings of $20.2 million in 2008." Use ratios, percentages, numbers, and dollar estimates. Businesspeople dislike generalities and vagueness.

The Need for Originality

Do not necessarily recommend the course of action that the firm plans to take or actually undertook, even if those actions resulted in improved revenues and earnings. The aim of case analysis is for you to consider all the facts and information relevant to the organization at the time, to generate feasible alternative strategies, to choose among those alternatives, and to defend your recommendations. Put yourself back in time to the point when strategic decisions were being made by the firm's strategists. Based on the information available then, what would you have done? Support your position with charts, graphs, ratios, analyses, and the like—not a revelation from the library. You can become a good strategist by thinking through situations, making management assessments, and proposing plans yourself. *Be original.* Compare and contrast what you recommend versus what the company plans to do or did.

The Need to Contribute

Strategy formulation, implementation, and evaluation decisions are commonly made by a group of individuals rather than by a single person. Therefore, your professor may divide the class into three- or four-person teams and ask you to prepare written or oral case analyses. Members of a strategic-management team, in class or in the business world, differ on their aversion to risk, their concern for short-run versus long-run benefits, their attitudes toward social responsibility, and their views concerning globalization. There are no perfect people, so there are no perfect strategies. Be open-minded to others' views. *Be a good listener and a good contributor.*

Preparing a Case for Class Discussion

Your professor may ask you to prepare a case for class discussion. Preparing a case for class discussion means that you need to read the case before class, make notes regarding the organization's external opportunities/threats and internal strengths/weaknesses, perform appropriate analyses, and come to class prepared to offer and defend some specific recommendations.

The Case Method versus Lecture Approach

The case method of teaching is radically different from the traditional lecture approach, in which little or no preparation is needed by students before class. The *case method* involves a classroom situation in which students do most of the talking; your professor facilitates discussion by asking questions and encouraging student interaction regarding ideas, analyses, and recommendations. Be prepared for a discussion along the lines of "What would you do, why would you do it, when would you do it, and how would you do it?" Prepare answers to the following types of questions:

- What are the firm's most important external opportunities and threats?
- What are the organization's major strengths and weaknesses?
- How would you describe the organization's financial condition?
- What are the firm's existing strategies and objectives?
- Who are the firm's competitors, and what are their strategies?

- What objectives and strategies do you recommend for this organization? Explain your reasoning. How does what you recommend compare to what the company plans?
- How could the organization best implement what you recommend? What implementation problems do you envision? How could the firm avoid or solve those problems?

The Cross-Examination

Do not hesitate to take a stand on the issues and to support your position with objective analyses and outside research. Strive to apply strategic-management concepts and tools in preparing your case for class discussion. Seek defensible arguments and positions. Support opinions and judgments with facts, reasons, and evidence. Crunch the numbers before class! Be willing to describe your recommendations to the class without fear of disapproval. Respect the ideas of others, but be willing to go against the majority opinion when you can justify a better position.

Business policy case analysis gives you the opportunity to learn more about yourself, your colleagues, strategic management, and the decision-making process in organizations. The rewards of this experience will depend on the effort you put forth, so do a good job. Discussing business policy cases in class is exciting and challenging. Expect views counter to those you present. Different students will place emphasis on different aspects of an organization's situation and submit different recommendations for scrutiny and rebuttal. Cross-examination discussions commonly arise, just as they occur in a real business organization. Avoid being a silent observer.

Preparing a Written Case Analysis

In addition to asking you to prepare a case for class discussion, your professor may ask you to prepare a written case analysis. Preparing a written case analysis is similar to preparing a case for class discussion, except written reports are generally more structured and more detailed. There is no ironclad procedure for preparing a written case analysis because cases differ in focus; the type, size, and complexity of the organizations being analyzed also vary.

When writing a strategic-management report or case analysis, avoid using jargon, vague or redundant words, acronyms, abbreviations, sexist language, and ethnic or racial slurs. And watch your spelling! Use short sentences and paragraphs and simple words and phrases. Use quite a few subheadings. Arrange issues and ideas from the most important to the least important. Arrange recommendations from the least controversial to the most controversial. Use the active voice rather than the passive voice for all verbs; for example, say "Our team recommends that the company diversify" rather than "It is recommended by our team to diversify." Use many examples to add specificity and clarity. Tables, figures, pie charts, bar charts, timelines, and other kinds of exhibits help communicate important points and ideas. Sometimes a picture *is* worth a thousand words.

The Executive Summary

Your professor may ask you to focus the written case analysis on a particular aspect of the strategic-management process, such as (1) to identify and evaluate the organization's existing mission, objectives, and strategies; or (2) to propose and defend specific recommendations for the company; or (3) to develop an industry analysis by describing the competitors, products, selling techniques, and market conditions in a given industry. These types of written reports are sometimes called *executive summaries*. An executive summary usually ranges from three to five pages of text in length, plus exhibits.

The Comprehensive Written Analysis

Your professor may ask you to prepare a *comprehensive written analysis*. This assignment requires you to apply the entire strategic-management process to the particular organization. When preparing a comprehensive written analysis, picture yourself as a consultant who has been asked by a company to conduct a study of its external and internal environment and to make specific recommendations for its future. Prepare exhibits to support your recommendations. Highlight exhibits with some discussion in the paper. Comprehensive written analyses are usually about 10 pages in length, plus exhibits.

Steps in Preparing a Comprehensive Written Analysis

In preparing a **written** case analysis, you could follow the steps outlined here, which correlate to the stages in the strategic-management process and the chapters in this text. (Note—The steps in presenting an **oral** case analysis are given on p. 362, are more detailed, and could be used here).

Step 1   Identify the firm's existing vision, mission, objectives, and strategies.

Step 2   Develop vision and mission statements for the organization.

Step 3   Identify the organization's external opportunities and threats.

Step 4   Construct a Competitive Profile Matrix (CPM).

Step 5   Construct an External Factor Evaluation (EFE) Matrix.

Step 6   Identify the organization's internal strengths and weaknesses.

Step 7   Construct an Internal Factor Evaluation (IFE) Matrix.

Step 8   Prepare a Strengths-Weaknesses-Opportunities-Threats (SWOT) Matrix, Strategic Position and Action Evaluation (SPACE) Matrix, Boston Consulting Group (BCG) Matrix, Internal-External (IE) Matrix, Grand Strategy Matrix, and Quantitative Strategic Planning Matrix (QSPM) as appropriate. Give advantages and disadvantages of alternative strategies.

Step 9   Recommend specific strategies and long-term objectives. Show how much your recommendations will cost. Clearly itemize these costs for each projected year. Compare your recommendations to actual strategies planned by the company.

Step 10   Specify how your recommendations can be implemented and what results you can expect. Prepare forecasted ratios and projected financial statements. Present a timetable or agenda for action.

Step 11   Recommend specific annual objectives and policies.

Step 12   Recommend procedures for strategy review and evaluation.

Making an Oral Presentation

Your professor may ask you to prepare a strategic-management case analysis, individually or as a group, and present your analysis to the class. Oral presentations are usually graded on two parts: content and delivery. *Content* refers to the quality, quantity, correctness, and appropriateness of analyses presented, including such dimensions as logical flow through the presentation, coverage of major issues, use of specifics, avoidance of generalities, absence of mistakes, and feasibility of recommendations. *Delivery* includes such dimensions as audience attentiveness, clarity of visual aids, appropriate dress, persuasiveness of arguments, tone of voice, eye contact, and posture. Great ideas are of no value unless others can be convinced of their merit through clear communication. The guidelines presented here can help you make an effective oral presentation.

Organizing the Presentation

Begin your presentation by introducing yourself and giving a clear outline of topics to be covered. If a team is presenting, specify the sequence of speakers and the areas each person will address. At the beginning of an oral presentation, try to capture your audience's interest and attention. You could do this by displaying some products made by the company, telling an interesting short story about the company, or sharing an experience you had that is related to the company, its products, or its services. You could develop or obtain a video to show at the beginning of class; you could visit a local distributor of the firm's products and tape a personal interview with the business owner or manager. A light or humorous introduction can be effective at the beginning of a presentation.

Be sure the setting of your presentation is well organized, with seats for attendees, flip charts, a transparency projector, and whatever else you plan to use. Arrive at the classroom at least 15 minutes early to organize the setting, and be sure your materials are ready to go. Make sure everyone can see your visual aids well.

Controlling Your Voice

An effective rate of speaking ranges from 100 to 125 words per minute. Practice your presentation aloud to determine if you are going too fast. Individuals commonly speak too fast when nervous. Breathe deeply before and during the presentation to help yourself slow down. Have a cup of water available; pausing to take a drink will wet your throat, give you time to collect your thoughts, control your nervousness, slow you down, and signal to the audience a change in topic.

Avoid a monotone by placing emphasis on different words or sentences. Speak loudly and clearly, but don't shout. Silence can be used effectively to break a monotone voice. Stop at the end of each sentence, rather than running sentences together with *and* or *uh*.

Managing Body Language

Be sure not to fold your arms, lean on the podium, put your hands in your pockets, or put your hands behind you. Keep a straight posture, with one foot slightly in front of the other. Do not turn your back to the audience; doing so is not only rude, but it also prevents your voice from projecting well. Avoid using too many hand gestures. On occasion, leave the podium or table and walk toward your audience, but do not walk around too much. Never block the audience's view of your visual aids.

Maintain good eye contact throughout the presentation. This is the best way to persuade your audience. There is nothing more reassuring to a speaker than to see members of the audience nod in agreement or smile. Try to look everyone in the eye at least once during your presentation, but focus more on individuals who look interested than on those who seem bored. To stay in touch with your audience, use humor and smiles as appropriate throughout your presentation. A presentation should never be dull!

Speaking from Notes

Be sure not to read to your audience because reading puts people to sleep. Perhaps worse than reading is merely reciting what you have memorized. Do not try to memorize anything. Rather, practice unobtrusively using notes. Make sure your notes are written clearly so you will not flounder when trying to read your own writing. Include only main ideas on your note cards. Keep note cards on a podium or table if possible so that you won't drop them or get them out of order; walking with note cards tends to be distracting.

Constructing Visual Aids

Make sure your visual aids are legible to individuals in the back of the room. Use color to highlight special items. Avoid putting complete sentences on visual aids; rather, use short phrases and then orally elaborate on issues as you make your presentation. Generally, there should be no more than four to six lines of text on each visual aid. Use clear headings and subheadings. Be careful about spelling and grammar; use a consistent style of lettering. Use masking tape or an easel for posters—do not hold posters in your hand. Transparencies and handouts are excellent aids; however, be careful not to use too many handouts or your audience may concentrate on them instead of you during the presentation.

Answering Questions

It is best to field questions at the end of your presentation, rather than during the presentation itself. Encourage questions, and take your time to respond to each one. Answering questions can be persuasive because it involves you with the audience. If a team is giving the presentation, the audience should direct questions to a specific person. During the question-and-answer period, be polite, confident, and courteous. Avoid verbose responses. Do not get defensive with your answers, even if a hostile or confrontational question is asked. Staying calm during potentially disruptive situations, such as a cross-examination, reflects self-confidence, maturity, poise, and command of the particular company and its industry. Stand up throughout the question-and-answer period.

Tips for Success in Case Analysis

Strategic-management students who have used this text over 10 editions offer you the following tips for success in doing case analysis. The tips are grouped into two basic sections: (1) Content Tips and (2) Process Tips. Content tips relate especially to the content of your case analysis, whereas the Process tips relate mostly to the process that you and your group mates undergo in preparing and delivering your case analysis/presentation.

Content Tips

1. Use the www.strategyclub.com Web site resources. The software described there is especially useful.
2. In preparing your external assessment, use the Industry survey material in your college library.
3. Go to www.euronext.com, http://www.nni.nikkei.co.jp, http://finance.yahoo.com, or http://moneycentral.msn/investor/home.asp and enter your company's stock symbol.
4. View your case analysis and presentation as a product that must have some competitive factor to favorably differentiate it from the case analyses of other students.
5. Develop a mind-set of *why*, continually questioning your own and others' assumptions and assertions.
6. Because business policy is a capstone course, seek the help of professors in other specialty areas when necessary.
7. Read your case frequently as work progresses so you don't overlook details.
8. At the end of each group session, assign each member of the group a task to be completed for the next meeting.
9. Become friends with the library and the Internet.
10. Be creative and innovative throughout the case analysis process.
11. A goal of case analysis is to improve your ability to think clearly in ambiguous and confusing situations; do not get frustrated that there is no single best answer.
12. Do not confuse symptoms with causes; do not develop conclusions and solutions prematurely; recognize that information may be misleading, conflicting, or wrong.
13. Work hard to develop the ability to formulate reasonable, consistent, and creative plans; put yourself in the strategist's position.
14. Develop confidence in using quantitative tools for analysis. They are not inherently difficult, it is just practice and familiarity you need.
15. Strive for excellence in writing and in the technical preparation of your case. Prepare nice charts, tables, diagrams, and graphs. Use color and unique pictures. No messy exhibits! Use PowerPoint.
16. Do not forget that the objective is to learn; explore areas with which you are not familiar.
17. Pay attention to detail.
18. Think through alternative implications fully and realistically. The consequences of decisions are not always apparent. They often affect many different aspects of a firm's operations.
19. Provide answers to such fundamental questions as *what, when, where, why, who,* and *how*.
20. Do not merely recite ratios or present figures. Rather, develop ideas and conclusions concerning the possible trends. Show the importance of these figures to the corporation.
21. Support reasoning and judgment with factual data whenever possible.
22. Your analysis should be as detailed and specific as possible.
23. A picture speaks a thousand words, and a creative picture gets you an A in many classes.

24. Emphasize the Recommendations and Strategy Implementation sections. A common mistake is to spend too much time on the external or internal analysis parts of your paper. Always remember that the recommendations and implementation sections are the most important part of the paper or presentation.

Process Tips

1. When working as a team, encourage most of the work to be done individually. Use team meetings mostly to assimilate work. This approach is most efficient.
2. If allowed to do so, invite questions throughout your presentation.
3. During the presentation, keep good posture, eye contact, voice tone, and project confidence. Do not get defensive under any conditions or with any questions.
4. Prepare your case analysis in advance of the due date to allow time for reflection and practice. Do not procrastinate.
5. Maintain a positive attitude about the class, working *with* problems rather than against them.
6. Keep in tune with your professor, and understand his or her values and expectations.
7. Other students will have strengths in functional areas that will complement your weaknesses, so develop a cooperative spirit that moderates competitiveness in group work.
8. When preparing a case analysis as a group, divide into separate teams to work on the external analysis and internal analysis.
9. Have a good sense of humor.
10. Capitalize on the strengths of each member of the group; volunteer your services in your areas of strength.
11. Set goals for yourself and your team; budget your time to attain them.
12. Foster attitudes that encourage group participation and interaction. Do not be hasty to judge group members.
13. Be prepared to work. There will be times when you will have to do more than your share. Accept it, and do what you have to do to move the team forward.
14. Think of your case analysis as if it were really happening; do not reduce case analysis to a mechanical process.
15. To uncover flaws in your analysis and to prepare the group for questions during an oral presentation, assign one person in the group to actively play the devil's advocate.
16. Do not schedule excessively long group meetings; two-hour sessions are about right.
17. Push your ideas hard enough to get them listened to, but then let up; listen to others and try to follow their lines of thinking; follow the flow of group discussion, recognizing when you need to get back on track; do not repeat yourself or others unless clarity or progress demands repetition.
18. Develop a case-presentation style that is direct, assertive, and convincing; be concise, precise, fluent, and correct.
19. Have fun when at all possible. Preparing a case is frustrating at times, but enjoy it while you can; it may be several years before you are playing CEO again.
20. In group cases, do not allow personality differences to interfere. When they occur, they must be understood for what they are—and then put aside.
21. Get things written down (drafts) as soon as possible.
22. Read everything that other group members write, and comment on it in writing. This allows group input into all aspects of case preparation.
23. Adaptation and flexibility are keys to success; be creative and innovative.
24. Neatness is a real plus; your case analysis should look professional.
25. Let someone else read and critique your presentation several days before you present it.
26. Make special efforts to get to know your group members. This leads to more openness in the group and allows for more interchange of ideas. Put in the time and effort necessary to develop these relationships.

27. Be constructively critical of your group members' work. Do not dominate group discussions. Be a good listener and contributor.
28. Learn from past mistakes and deficiencies. Improve upon weak aspects of other case presentations.
29. Learn from the positive approaches and accomplishments of classmates.

Sample Case Analysis Outline

There are musicians who play wonderfully without notes and there are chefs who cook wonderfully without recipes, but most of us prefer a more orderly cookbook approach, at least in the first attempt at doing something new. Therefore the following eight steps may serve as a basic outline for you in presenting a strategic plan for your firm's future. This outline is not the only approach used in business and industry for communicating a strategic plan, but this approach is time-tested, it does work, and it does cover all of the basics. You may amend the content, tools, and concepts given to suit your own company, audience, assignment, and circumstances, but it helps to know and understand the rules before you start breaking them.

Depending upon whether your class is 50 minutes or 75 minutes and how much time your professor allows for your case presentation, the following outlines what generally needs to be covered. A recommended time (in minutes) as part of the presentation is given for an overall 50-minute event. Of course, all cases are different, some being about for-profit and some about not-for-profit organizations, for example, so the scope and content of your analysis may vary. Even if you do not have time to cover all areas in your oral presentation, you may be asked to prepare these areas and give them to your professor as a "written case analysis." Be sure in an oral presentation to manage time knowing that your recommendations and associated costs are the most important part. You should go to www.strategyclub.com and utilize that information and software in preparing your case analysis. Good luck.

• STEPS IN PRESENTING AN ORAL CASE ANALYSIS

Oral Presentation—Step 1

Introduction (2 minutes)

a. Introduce yourselves by name and major. Establish the time setting of your case and analysis. Prepare your strategic plan for the three years 2008–2011.
b. Introduce your company and its products/services; capture interest.
c. Show the outline of your presentation and tell who is doing what parts.

Oral Presentation—Step 2

Mission/Vision (4 minutes)

a. Show existing mission and vision statements if available from the firm's Web site, or annual report, or elsewhere.
b. Show your "improved" mission and vision and tell why it is improved.
c. Compare your mission and vision to a leading competitor's statements.
d. Comment on your vision and mission in terms of how they support the strategies you envision for your firm.

Oral Presentation—Step 3

Internal Assessment (8 minutes)

a. Give your financial ratio analysis. Highlight especially good and bad ratios. Do not give definitions of the ratios and do not highlight all the ratios.
b. Show the firm's organizational chart found or "created based on executive titles." Identify the type of chart as well as good and bad aspects. Unless all white males comprise the chart, peoples' names are generally not important because positions reveal structure as people come and go.
c. Present your improved/recommended organizational chart. Tell why you feel it is improved over the existing chart.
d. Show a market positioning map with firm and competitors. Discuss the map in light of strategies you envision for firm versus competitors' strategies.
e. Identify the marketing strategy of the firm in terms of good and bad points versus competitors and in light of strategies you envision for the firm.
f. Show a map locating the firm's operations. Discuss in light of strategies you envision. Also, perhaps show a Value Chain Analysis chart.
g. Discuss (and perhaps show) the firm's Web site and e-commerce efforts/abilities in terms of good and bad points.
h. Show your "value of the firm" analysis.
i. List up to 20 of the firm's strengths and weaknesses. Go over each one listed without "reading" them verbatim.
j. Show and explain your Internal Factor Evaluation (IFE) Matrix.

Oral Presentation—Step 4

External Assessment (8 minutes)

a. Identify and discuss major competitors. Use pie charts, maps, tables, and/or figures to show the intensity of competition in the industry.
b. Show your Competitive Profile Matrix. Include at least 12 factors and two competitors.
c. Summarize key industry trends citing Standard & Poor's *Industry Survey* or Chamber of Commerce statistics, etc. Highlight key external trends as they impact the firm, in areas such as the economic, social, cultural, demographic, geographic, technological, political, legal, governmental, and natural environment.

d. List up to 20 of the firm's opportunities and threats. Make sure your opportunities are not stated as strategies. Go over each one listed without "reading" them verbatim.

e. Show and explain your External Factor Evaluation (EFE) Matrix.

Oral Presentation—Step 5

Strategy Formulation (14 minutes)

a. Show and explain your SWOT Matrix, highlighting each of your strategies listed.

b. Show and explain your SPACE Matrix, using half of your "space time" on calculations and the other half on implications of those numbers. Strategy implications must be specific rather than generic. In other words, use of a term such as "market penetration" is not satisfactory alone as a strategy implication.

c. Show your Boston Consulting Group (BCG) Matrix. Again focus on both the numbers and the strategy implications. Do multiple BCG Matrices if possible, including domestic versus global, or another geographic breakdown. Develop a product BCG if at all possible. Comment on changes to this matrix as per strategies you envision. Develop this matrix even if you do not know the profits per division and even if you have to estimate the axes information. However, make no wild guesses on axes or revenue/profit information.

d. Show your Internal-External (IE) Matrix. Because this analysis is similar to the BCG, see the preceding comments.

e. Show your Grand Strategy Matrix. Again focus on implications after giving the quadrant selection. Reminder: Use of a term such as "market penetration" is not satisfactory alone as a strategy implication. Be more specific. Elaborate.

f. Show your Quantitative Strategic Planning Matrix (QSPM). Be sure to explain your strategies to start with here. Do not go back over the internal and external factors. Avoid having more than one 4, 3, 2, or 1 in a row. If you rate one strategy, you need to rate the other because, that particular factor is affecting the choice. Work row by row rather than column by column on preparing the QSPM.

g. Present your Recommendations Page. This is the most important page in your presentation. Be specific in terms of both strategies and estimated costs of those strategies. *Total your estimated costs.* You should have six or more strategies. Divide your strategies into two groups: (1) Existing Strategies to Be Continued, and (2) New Strategies to Be Started.

Oral Presentation—Step 6

Strategy Implementation (8 minutes)

a. Show and explain your EPS/EBIT analysis to reveal whether stock, debt, or a combination is best to finance your recommendations. Graph the analysis. Decide which approach to use if there are any given limitations of the analysis.

b. Show your projected income statement. Relate changes in the items to your recommendations rather than blindly going with historical percentage changes.

c. Show your projected balance sheet. Relate changes in your items to your recommendations. Be sure to show the retained earnings calculation and the results of your EPS/EBIT decision.

d. Show your projected financial ratios and highlight several key ratios to show the benefits of your strategic plan.

Oral Presentation—Step 7

Strategy Evaluation (2 minutes)

a. Prepare a Balanced Scorecard to show your expected financial and nonfinancial objectives recommended for the firm.

Oral Presentation—Step 8

Conclusion (4 minutes)

a. Compare and contrast your strategic plan versus the company's own plans for the future.

b. Thank audience members for their attention. Seek and answer questions.

INDEX

Strategic Management

• CASES

Estée Lauder Companies, Inc. — 2008

Sharynn Tomlin
Angelo State University

EL

www.ELCompanies.com

Based in New York City, Estée Lauder is a manufacturer and marketer of four cosmetic product lines: 1) skin care, 2) makeup, 3) fragrances, and 4) hair care products. These products are sold in over 130 countries and territories under brand names that include Estée Lauder, Aramis, Clinique, Prescriptives, Lab Series, Origins, MAC, Bobbi Brown, La Mer, Aveda, Jo Malone, Bumble and Bumble, Darphin, Rodan + Fields, American Beauty, Flirt!, Good Skin and Grassroots. Estée Lauder also has global licenses for fragrances and cosmetics sold under brand names that include Tommy Hilfiger, Donna Karan, Michael Kors, Donald Trump, Sean John, Missoni, and Daisy Fuentes. Estée Lauder announced in June 2007 that it might acquire skin care company Murad Inc., based in El Segundo, California. Murad sells skin care products and dietary supplements on the Internet and via infomercials, and also in spas and stores such as Sephora and Bath and Body Works. Estée Lauder's final 2007 sales increased 7 percent to $7.037 billion.

Estée Lauder sells its products mainly through upscale department stores, specialty retailers, upscale perfumeries and pharmacies, and prestige salons and spas. In addition, its products are sold in freestanding company-owned stores and spas as well as its own and other authorized retailers' Web sites. You can also find Estée Lauder products for sale at stores on cruise ships, on television direct marketing channels, and at in-flight and duty-free shops.

Estée Lauder's range of skincare products for women and men include moisturizers, creams, lotions, cleansers, sunscreens, and self-tanning products, a number of which are developed for use on particular areas of the body, such as the face, the hands, or around the eyes. Skincare products account for about 37 percent of net sales as compared to makeup products that account for about 39 percent of sales.

The company's makeup products include lipsticks, lip glosses, mascaras, foundations, eye shadows, nail polishes, and powders, as well as related items such as compacts, brushes, and other makeup tools. Fragrances for women and men comprise about 19 percent of sales. Fragrances are sold in perfume sprays and colognes, as well as lotions, powders, creams, and soaps.

Finally, Estée Lauder sells hair care products in salons and freestanding retail stores. These products include hair color and styling products, shampoos, conditioners, and finishing sprays. In fiscal 2006, hair care products accounted for about 5 percent of sales. Each of the company's brands has a single global image that is promoted with consistent logos, packaging, and advertising designed to differentiate it from other brands.

History

Beauty, youth, and being forever young are common themes in the personal products industry. A young entrepreneur named Estée Lauder felt that she could provide a product that espoused those qualities. Estée Lauder Company was founded in 1946 by Estée Lauder and her husband Joseph Lauder. Estée was always interested in beauty and began her business selling the skin care products her chemist uncle, John Schotz, developed. Her first products were sold to beauty salons and hotels.

In the early years, Estée was unable to convince Madison Avenue to carry her products. Facing this rejection, she began to market her products directly to customers. With that success, the Lauders began targeting high-class customers by selling products exclusively through boutiques and department stores. In 1948, Estée Lauder established their first department store account with Saks Fifth Avenue in New York. During the next 15 years, the products were selectively distributed in other stores in the United States. In 1960 the company globalized their operations with the introduction of Estée Lauder products at Harrods in London, with the Hong Kong market opening the following year.

The first Estée Lauder products sold were Super Rich All Purpose Creme, Creme Pack, Cleansing Oil, and Skin Lotion. Additional brands such as Aramis, a line of prestige fragrance and grooming products for men was launched in 1964, and Clinique, the first dermatologist-guided, allergy-tested, fragrance-free cosmetics brand was launched in 1968. Prescriptives and Origins Natural Resources were early brands too. Estée Lauder acquired more brand licensing of names such as Tommy Hilfiger, MAC, Bobbi Brown, La Mer, Kiton fragrances, Donna Karan, and Aveda.

Mrs. Estée Lauder was named one of ten Outstanding Women in Business in the United States by business and financial editors in 1967. A year later she received the Spirit of Achievement Award from Albert Einstein College of Medicine at Yeshiva University. This was the same year that the company expanded again by opening Clinique Laboratories, Inc. In 1983, their products were introduced in the Soviet Union.

In 1998, Estée Lauder began selling a variety of products over the Internet and was one of the first major cosmetics firms to offer online shopping. A new division called ELC Online was created to manage all online strategies and activities for all of its brands. During this same time frame other acquisitions included Jo Malone, Stila Cosmetics, and Gloss.com. New York-based Bumble and Bumble LLC was acquired. In 2003, Darphin and Rodan + Fields were acquired and a license with Michael Kors was signed shortly afterward. In 2004, the company's teen-oriented Jane business was sold and Estée Lauder launched Beauty, Flirt, and Good Skin through its BeautyBank division, followed by Grassroots in 2005 and Daisy Fuentes in 2006.

The year 2006 also saw license agreements with Sean John, Missoni, and Donald Trump, and the Stila brand was sold. Today Estée Lauder Companies has 26 brands, sells products in over 130 countries and territories, and employs over 22,000 people worldwide. Although Mrs. Estée Lauder passed away in April 2004, she witnessed the growth of a small home operation into a worldwide corporation with annual revenues of more than $5 billion. She was very proud that her company went public in 1995 and today is led by Estée and Joseph's children and grandchildren.

Mission Statement

In a short, succinct statement, Estée Lauder Companies, Inc. states that their vision is "bringing the best to everyone we touch."[1] Furthermore, the company is committed to uncompromised ethics and integrity. For all employees domestically and globally, and the board of directors, the highest standard of ethics is a condition of employment. The company's official home page elaborates by stating the following:

> We are a family company committed to working together with uncompromising ethics and integrity. We strive to always:
>
> 1. Provide customers with innovative cosmetic products of the highest quality.
> 2. Deliver outstanding service by treating each individual as we ourselves would like to be treated.
> 3. Create an environment that fosters personal growth and well being.
> 4. Build partnerships with our suppliers, retailers and colleagues based on fairness and trust.
> 5. Enhance our reputation of image, style and prestige.
> 6. Pursue profit, but never at the expense of quality, service or reputation.

7. Eliminate waste and reduce inefficiencies in order to provide maximum value to our customers.
8. Be responsible citizens in every community we serve.[2]

Organizational Structure

As illustrated in Exhibit 1, it is not clear whether Estée Lauder uses a traditional functional structure or some type of divisional structure. It is managed primarily by Lauder family members as both the chief executive officer (CEO) and chairman of the board are Lauders. There are

EXHIBIT 1   Organizational Chart

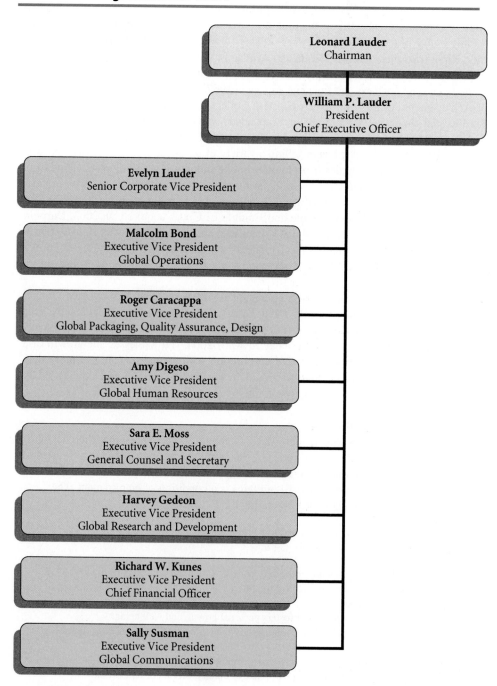

Source: Adapted from http://www.elcompanies.com

EXHIBIT 2   Firm's Facilities

Facility	Location
Manufacturing 15 focused factories	United States, Belgium, Switzerland, United Kingdom and Canada
Research and Development 400 scientists	Melville, New York; Oevel, Belgium; Tokyo, Japan; Markham, Ontario; Blaine, Minnesota; Shanghai, China; Kobe, Japan
Business Offices 43 worldwide	North America, South America, Central America, Asia, Europe, Middle East, Australia, New Zealand, Africa

Source: http://www.elcompanies.com

four group presidents who report to the CEO, but it is not clear whether these four persons have authority over the four product lines or four geographic areas of the world. The management systems at all Estée Lauder manufacturing operations conform to the ISO 14001 standards. Estée Lauder has offices, stores, and facilities all over the world as indicated in Exhibit 2.

Financial Position

As indicated in Exhibit 3, Estée Lauder's 2006 sales increased 3 percent to $6,463.8 million due to growth in their makeup, skin care, and hair care product categories, which was partially offset by lower sales in the fragrance product category. The net increase reflects

EXHIBIT 3   Consolidated Statements of Earnings

Year Ended June 30 (In millions, except per share data)	2007	2006	2005	2004
Net Sales	$ 7,037.5	6,463.8	6,280.0	5,741.5
Cost of sales	1,774.8	1,686.6	1,602.8	1,464.3
Gross Profit	5,262.7	4,777.2	4,677.2	4,277.2
Operating expenses:				
Selling, general and administrative	4,511.7	4,065.5	3,950.4	3,609.5
Special charges related to cost savings initiative	1.1	92.1	–	–
Related party royalties	–	–	–	18.8
	–	4,157.6	3,950.4	3,628.3
Operating Income	749.9	619.6	726.8	648.9
Interest expense, net	38.9	23.8	13.9	27.1
Earnings before Income Taxes, Minority Interest and Discontinued Operations	711.0	595.8	712.9	621.8
Provision for income taxes	255.2	259.7	293.7	234.4
Minority interest, net of tax	(7.1)	(11.6)	(9.3)	(8.9)
Net Earnings from Continuing Operations	448.7	324.5	409.9	378.5
Discontinued operations, net of tax	.5	(80.3)	(3.8)	(36.4)
Net Earnings	$ 449.2	244.2	406.1	342.1
Basic net earnings per common share:				
Net earnings from continuing operations		1.51	1.82	1.66
Discontinued operations, net of tax		(.37)	(.02)	(.16)
Net earnings		1.14	1.80	1.50
Diluted net earnings per common share:				
Net earnings from continuing operations		1.49	1.80	1.64

continued

EXHIBIT 3 **Consolidated Statements of Earnings—continued**

Year Ended June 30
(In millions, except per share data)

	2007	2006	2005	2004
Discontinued operations, net of tax		(.37)	(.02)	(.16)
Net earnings		1.12	1.78	1.48
Weighted average common shares outstanding:				
Basic		215.0	225.3	228.2
Diluted		217.4	228.6	231.6
Cash dividends declared per share		.40	.40	.30

Source: http://www.elcompanies.com

sales growth in all geographic regions. Note that cost of sales as a percentage of total sales increased to 26.1 percent as compared with 25.5 percent in the prior year. Operating income decreased 15 percent to $619.6 million, and the operating margin was 9.6 percent of sales in fiscal 2006 as compared with 11.6 percent in the prior year. Note in Exhibit 4 that Estée Lauder's long-term debt decreased 4.6 percent to $431 million in 2006.

EXHIBIT 4 **Consolidated Balance Sheets**

All Amounts in Millions Except Share Data (Year Ended June 30)

	2007	2006	2005
ASSETS			
Current Assets			
Cash and cash equivalents	$ 253.7	368.6	553.3
Accounts receivables, net	860.5	771.2	776.6
Inventory and promotional merchandise	855.8	766.3	768.3
Prepaid expenses and other current assets	269.4	270.8	204.4
Total Current Assets	2,239.4	2,176.9	2,302.6
Property, Plant, and Equipment, net	880.8	758.0	694.2
Other Assets			
Investments, at cost or market value	22.2	13.4	12.3
Goodwill	651.3	635.8	720.6
Other intangible assets, net	113.4	77.0	71.8
Other assets, net	218.6	123.0	84.3
Total Other Assets	1,005.5	849.2	889.0
Total Assets	$ 4,125.7	3,784.1	3,885.8
LIABILITIES AND STOCKHOLDERS' EQUITY			
Current Liabilities			
Short-term debt	60.4	89.7	263.6
Accounts payable	1,440.3	264.5	249.4
Accrued income taxes	–	135.5	109.9
Other accrued liabilities	–	948.5	874.8
Total Current Liabilities	1,500.7	1,438.2	1,497.7
Noncurrent Liabilities			
Long-term debt	1,028.1	431.8	451.1
Other noncurrent liabilities	376.6	266.4	228.4
Total Noncurrent Liabilities	$ 1,404.7	698.2	679.5

continued

EXHIBIT 4   Consolidated Balance Sheets—continued

All Amounts in Millions Except Share Data (Year Ended June 30)		
	2007	2006	2005
Commitments and Contingencies			
Minority Interest	21.3	25.4	15.8
Total Liabilities	2,926.7		
Stockholders' Equity			
Common stock, $.01 par value; 650,000,000 shares			
Class A authorized; shares issued: 164,837,563 at June 30,			
2006 and 159,837,545 at June 30, 2005; 240,000,000			
shares			
Class B authorized; shares issued and outstanding:			
85,305,915 at June 30, 2006 and 87,640,901 at June 30,			
2005	2.6	2.5	2.5
Paid-in capital (capital surplus)	801.7	581.0	465.2
Retained earnings	2,731.5	2,361.9	2,203.2
Accumulated other comprehensive income	54.7	64.7	9.4
	3,590.5	3,010.1	2,680.3
Less: Treasury stock, at cost; 38,382,458 Class A shares at			
June 30, 2006 and 27,174,160 Class A shares at June 30,			
2005	(2,391.5)	(1,387.8)	(987.5)
Total Stockholders' Equity	1,199.0	1,622.3	1,692.8
Total Liabilities and Stockholders' Equity	$4,125.7	3,784.1	3,885.8

Source: http://www.elcompanies.com

Finances by Product

As indicated in Exhibit 5, the company's sales of skin care products increased 2 percent or $48.7 million to $2,400.8 million primarily due to new product launches. Makeup net sales increased 6 percent or $137.4 million to $2,504.2 million, reflecting growth from the makeup artist brands of approximately $179 million. Net sales of fragrance products decreased 4 percent or $47.3 million to $1,213.3 million as the company continue to struggle in this product category, particularly in the Americas region. Hair care net sales increased 16 percent or $44.8 million to $318.7 million, primarily due to sales growth from Bumble and Bumble and Aveda products.

Finances by Geographic Region

Exhibit 5 also reveals that Estée Lauder's sales in the Americas increased 3 percent to $3,446.4 million, led by growth in the United States of about $190 million, primarily attributable to makeup artist and hair care brands, Internet distribution, and the introduction of new fragrances. Net sales growth in Canada, Latin America, and Mexico contributed an additional $48 million to the increase.

In Europe, the Middle East, and Africa, net sales increased 2 percent to $2,147.7 million. Markets in Russia and the United Kingdom benefited from the success of the DKNY Be Delicious franchise and the sale of MAC products. These increases were partially offset by decreases of approximately $26 million in Spain and Italy. Spain's and Italy's sales were adversely affected by changes in the distribution policy and a difficult retail environment. Net sales in Europe, the Middle East, and Africa increased 5 percent.

The company's 2006 sales in the Asia/Pacific region increased 6 percent to $869.7 million. Strategic growth in China combined with positive results in Korea and Hong Kong, contributed about $57 million to sales growth of this region. These increases were partially offset by decreases in Japan and Australia of about $18 million. Japan's results were negatively impacted due to the strengthening of the U.S. dollar against the Japanese yen. The decrease in Australia reflected a slower and difficult retail environment, particularly in the fragrance category. Net sales in Asia/Pacific increased 7 percent.

EXHIBIT 5 Financial Data per Segment for 2004–2007 (In Thousands)

Revenues				
	2007	2006	2005	2004
Skin Care	$2,601,000	$2,400,800	$2,352,100	$2,140,100
Makeup	2,712,700	2,504,200	2,423,100	2,148,300
Fragrance	1,308,600	1,213,300	1,260,600	1,221,100
Hair Care	377,100	318,700	273,900	249,400
Other	38,100	26,800	26,600	31,500
Total	**$7,037,500**	**$6,463,800**	**$6,336,300**	**$5,790,400**

Operating Income				
	2007	2006	2005	2004
Skin Care	$341,500	$346,400	$365,800	$336,300
Makeup	339,300	329,400	294,900	257,700
Fragrance	28,100	7,700	35,800	24,800
Hair Care	42,500	26,500	22,800	23,600
Other	(1,500)	1,700	1,300	1,600
Total	**$749,900**	**$711,700**	**$720,600**	**$644,000**

Geographic Revenues Analysis				
	2007	2006	2005	2004
Asia/Pacific	$ 983,200	$ 869,700	$ 835,500	$ 771,400
Europe/Middle East/Africa	2,493,400	2,147,700	2,118,600	1,870,200
Americas	3,560,900	3,446,400	3,382,200	3,148,800
Total	**$7,037,500**	**$6,463,800**	**$6,336,300**	**$5,790,400**

Source: Mergentonline.com

Marketing

Product

Estée Lauder markets more than 9,000 quality products under its portfolio of brands. Exhibit 6 summarizes the various products and dates of product launch or acquisition. Estée Lauder was the first major prestige cosmetics firm to offer shopping via the Internet. Department stores remain the best venue for high service and great brands since $7.6 billion in beauty sales were generated in U.S. department stores in 2006, representing 18 percent of the total beauty market in the United States. Dan Brestle, COO of Estée Lauder, stated that distribution channels in North America, sales on TV, and sales in doctors' offices are growing. However, the major shift has been in mall-based specialty stores. In Europe, the skincare business continues to migrate to pharmacies. While there is growth in perfumeries in Asia, the Asian department store continues to dominate that channel.[3]

Promotion

Estée Lauder was the first cosmetics company to offer free samples and gift-with-purchase and continues this strategy today. The company was also the first in the industry to introduce consistent brand imagery around the world. For this purpose, the company uses celebrities as endorsers in testimonial advertising for commercials on TV, as well as in magazines. Elizabeth Hurley, Carolyn Murphy, Liya Kebede, Gwyneth Paltrow, and Anja Rubik have been signed by the company, as well as Hilary Rhoda, who was named the new face of Estée Lauder in January 2007.

EXHIBIT 6   Estée Lauder Brands

Brand Name Acquired	Year
Estée Lauder	1946
Aramis	1964
Clinique	1968
Prescriptives	1979
Lab Series Skin Care for Men	1987
Origins	1990
MAC	1994
La Mer	1995
Bobbi Brown	1995
Tommy Hilfiger	1993
Kiton	1995
Donna Karan	1997
Aveda	1997
Jo Malone	1999
Bumble and Bumble	2000
Michael Kors	2003
Darphin	2003
Rodan + Fields	2003
American Beauty	2004
good skin™	2004
Flirt!	2004
Donald Trump, The Fragrance	2004
grassroots™	2005
Sean John Fragrances	2005
MISSONI	2005
Daisy Fuentes	2006

Source: http://www.elcompanies.com

Price

Estée Lauder prices vary from product to product and from brand to brand, but tend to be in the mid-high to high range of the industry. Prestige pricing appears to be an effective strategy given their target markets.

Industry Factors

Much of the expected growth in the personal products industry will be fueled by the rising demand from emerging and developing markets. Estimates have shown that in "the next 20 years . . . 70 million people across the globe [will] reach an income level that allows purchasing of cosmetic products."[4] The U.S. Census Bureau predicts that by the year 2030, Americans over the age of 65 will represent one-fifth of the population, which is expected to devote a substantial part of their discretionary income to anti-aging products. Younger consumers, age 20–30 years old, are choosing to invest their purchasing dollars in preventive cosmetics to battle the effects of aging, and even teens are spending money on these types of products.

The world's aging population will multiple by 2.5 times in the next 40 years, representing over 33 percent of the total population. All geographic regions will be impacted by this increase, including high growth countries such as China and India. Additionally, the life expectancy of the aging population will continue to improve, with the difference between men and women gradually diminishing.

Companies will continue to devote substantial sums to research and development of new and appealing products. However, given the competitive pricing at megastores such as Wal-Mart, companies may be challenged to continue their patterns of innovative research. Additionally, there have been consumer complaints and inquiries into the use of animal testing for new products and many personal care product companies are dropping this form of product testing for more humane and creative testing techniques.

Though the federal Food and Drug Administration does not require testing of cosmetics, the agency has notified manufacturers that it would start to enforce labeling that included the statement "Warning—the safety of this product has not been determined."[5] However, these issues are not new, having affected the industry for more than 100 years.

Concerns about the use of aerosols and fluorocarbons which first emerged in the mid-1960s still remains an issue, especially as the need for decreasing damaging environmental pollutants continues to be debated by governments, companies, and consumers. Recent restrictions on products that can be carried in-flight have created uncertainty in the outlook for the travel retail business. In fiscal 2006, the travel retail business comprised approximately 7 percent of total net sales, and accounted for approximately 20 percent of operating income.

Competitors

Top competitors in the cosmetics business are diversified with many brand names and a wide range of products. A summary of key financial data on Estée Lauder and competitors is shown in Exhibit 7.

L'Oreal

L'Oreal is one of the worldwide leaders in cosmetics and distributes products in 130 countries with 19 global brands and offices in 58 countries. In 2006, the company statements reflected €15.7 billion in consolidated sales, operating profits of €2.5 billion, and a commitment of 3.4 percent of the annual sales to research and development.

Procter & Gamble

Procter & Gamble has consistently pursued globalization with over 135,000 employees working in over 80 countries and distribution of consumer products in 140 countries. The P&G brand portfolio includes Pampers, Tide, Ariel, Always, Pantene, Bounty, Folgers, Pringles, Charmin, Downy, Iams, Crest, Actonel, and Olay. While probably the most diversified, with a greater depth of product lines, Procter & Gamble continues to show strong growth and profitability. For the 2006 fiscal year, the company saw their fifth consecutive

EXHIBIT 7   Info on Competitors (2006) (in millions; amounts in US$ unless denoted otherwise)

Company	Revenues	EBITDA	Net Income	Total Assets	Total Liabilities	PE Ratio
Alberto-Culver	$ 3,772	378.9	205.3	2,582.5	823.6	20.80
Avon Products	8,763.9	477.6	917.0	5,238.2	4,447.8	28.91
Colgate-Palmolive	12,237.7	2,489.2	1,353.4	9,138	7,727	22.98
Estée Lauder	6,463.8	818	244.2	3,784.1	2,136.4	23.25
L'Oreal (euros)	15,729.3	3,157.4	2,062.1	24,783	10,158.8	NA
Procter & Gamble	68,222	16,159	8,684	135,695	72,787	20.11
Revlon	1,331.4	60.5	−251.3	931.9	2,161.7	−2.62
Unilever (euros)	39,642	4,687	5,015	37,072	25,400	NA

Source: Mergentonline.com

year of sales growth and free cash flow productivity. P&G reported $68.2 billion of revenues with a net income of $8.6 billion in 2006.

Unilever

Unilever, the Anglo-Dutch food and personal products group, has 400 brands that span over 14 categories of home, personal care, and food products. Examples of their brands include Sunsilk, Suave, Dove, Lipton, and Hellman's. With a sales growth of 3.8 percent, increased operating margins, and net profits increasing 10 percent (€5.4 million) since 2005, the company remains a strong competitive player. The growing financial health of the company enabled Unilever to return €750 million to shareholders as a one-off dividend. The personal care products division continues to represent an impressive share of their growth, showing an increase of 6.3 percent in 2006.

The percentage of Unilever's U.S. research conducted online has more than doubled to 80 percent in five years. While the U.S. is its most advanced market, Unilever envisages similar trends in countries where Internet access is widely available, such as the United Kingdom and Japan. The shift to Internet projects by Unilever, which spends an estimated €400 million a year (2006) on research, reflects the Web's accelerating impact on the global market research industry.

Colgate-Palmolive

Colgate-Palmolive, who marks their 200th year in 2006, markets a variety of products in the oral, personal, and home care segments. The company had industry-leading revenues of $11.3 billion in 2006 with a gross margin of 54.4 percent and a price earnings ratio of 26.77. The company reported a net income of $1,351,400,000 in 2006. Colgate-Palmolive also has a strong and supportive relationship with professional and trade groups that has increased with the introduction of new dental products.

Avon

Avon Products Incorporated sells beauty and related products consisting of cosmetics, fragrances, skin care, and toiletries. Their principal offices are located in New York City near Estée Lauder. As the world's largest direct seller of personal products (primarily cosmetics), Avon markets their products in over 100 countries through over 5 million independent sales representatives. Avon's product line includes beauty products, fashion jewelry, and apparel. Their top-selling products include brand names such as Avon Color, Anew, Skin-So-Soft, Avon Solutions, Advance Techniques, Avon Naturals, Mark, and Avon Wellness. Despite 2006, considered a transition year in the company's restructuring efforts, Avon Products had total revenues of $8.7 billion, with a gross margin of 60.80, a price earning ratio of 34.07, and net income of $477,600,000. Committed to their restructuring efforts, advertising increases by 83 percent, new market development such as China, and product and brand innovation, Avon continues to be a formidable competitor. Avon now has more than 700,000 saleswomen in China alone.

Alberto-Culver

Alberto-Culver Company operates a beauty supply distribution network and develops, manufactures, and sells consumer beauty products with a strong presence in the professional salon market. The company is led by Carol L. Bernick as chairman and V. James Marino as chief executive officer and president with headquarters in Melrose Park, Illinois. Alberto-Culver Company had $3.5 billion worth of revenues in 2006 with a gross margin of 50.22 percent, a price earnings ratio of 10.27, and a net income of $210,901,000.

Revlon

Revlon Worldwide Corporation offers a variety of cosmetic and beauty products under multiple brands. Revlon is one of the best known brand names in the world and the company excels at mass marketing. The company is led by Wade H. Nichols, III as senior vice president and general counsel and Howard Gittis as chairman, with principal offices in New York, New York. Revlon Worldwide Corporation had $2.1 billion in total revenues in 2006 with a gross margin of 66.51 percent. The company's net income was $94,600,000 for 2006. International markets showed an increase in the first quarter of 2007 of 6.4 percent to $135.3 million, compared with net sales of $127.2 million in the first quarter of 2006.

Conclusion

At a recent meeting of the Estée Lauder stockholders, William Lauder stated about the company's future plans that "we expect to enhance our leadership in prestige beauty around the world. We will continue to deliver innovative, cutting-edge products and build strong global brands. We will target and reach diverse consumers by leveraging numerous distribution channels in key markets all over the world. Our goal is to optimize, diversify, and grow the business over the long term."[6] With these goals in mind, Estée Lauder has developed a long-term strategy based on five imperatives:

- Optimization of brand portfolio
- Strengthening of product categories
- Strengthening and expansion of global markets
- Diversification and strengthening of channels of distribution
- Operational and cost excellence.[7]

Acknowledgments: Joshua Colyar, Anna Flores, Pauline Gullett, Logan Mueller, Daniel Nichols, and Jasmine Reimann for their valued input.

Endnotes

1. http://www.elcompanies.com
2. http://www.elcompanies.com
3. www.lexisnexis.com/EsteeLauder
4. http://www.researchandmarkets.com/reports
5. "Toiletries and Cosmetics." *Encyclopedia of Global Industries.* Online Edition, Thomson Gale, 2006.
6. www.lexisnexis.com/esteelauder
7. www.elcompanies/el2006-10K

2 Revlon, Inc. — 2007

M. Jill Austin
Middle Tennessee State University

REV

www.revlon.com

Revlon, Inc. has a 75-year history of providing high-quality products at affordable prices to women. According to the company's Web site,

> Revlon is a world leader in cosmetics, skin care, fragrance and personal care and is a leading mass-market cosmetics brand. Our vision is to provide glamour, excitement and innovation through quality products at affordable prices.

Led by David Kennedy, president and CEO, Revlon recently consolidated some sales and marketing functions to reduce operational costs. The company also eliminated some senior positions and reduced staffing by about 8 percent of their U.S. workforce to save approximately $33 million a year. Net sales for 2006 decreased by $1 million to $1,331 billion (compared to $1,332 billion in 2005), and net losses in 2006 were $251 million following a loss of $84 million in 2005. The company has posted losses for eight consecutive years and has struggled with debt since Ron Perelman purchased a majority stake in the company in 1985. Revlon is a company in trouble.

Revlon products are sold in more than 100 countries around the world with sales outside the United States comprising 43 percent of sales in 2006. A map of worldwide operations of Revlon, Inc. is shown in Exhibit 1.

EXHIBIT 1   Map of Worldwide Operations of Revlon, Inc.

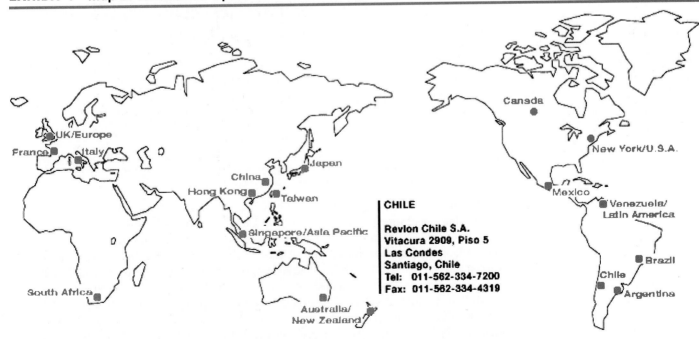

EXHIBIT 2 Revlon, Inc. Principal Brands and Selected Products

Cosmetics	Hair	Beauty Tools	Fragrance	Antiperspirants/Deodorants	Skin Care
Revlon	Color Silk	Revlon	Charlie	Mitchum	Gatineau
Almay*	Colorist	Expert Effect	Jean Naté	Almay	Almay
	Frost & Glow				Ultima II
	Flex				
	Bozzano				

Source: Revlon, Inc. 2006, *Form 10-K*, p. 5.

Revlon's product categories include skin care, cosmetics, personal care, fragrance, and professional products. Some of the company's most recognized brand names are Revlon, Ultima II, ColorStay, Almay, Charlie, Flex, Mitchum, Jean Naté, and ColorSilk. The company continues to introduce new products. Almay Intense Eye Color (package that combines eyeliner, mascara, and eye shadow) was successfully introduced in 2005, and Almay Smart Shade (colorless foundation that changes to correct color when applied) and ColorStay Smooth Lip Color were introduced in 2006. Exhibit 2 shows Revlon's products in each business category.

The company's long-term mission is to emerge as the dominant cosmetics and personal care firm in the twenty-first century by appealing to young/trendy women, health-conscious women (skin care), and older women with its variety of brands.

Revlon's sales in the first six months of 2007 increased 4.8 percent to $677.8 million, compared to net sales of $646.6 million in the first six months of 2006. In the United States, sales in the first six months of 2007 increased 5.1 percent to $397.5 million, compared with sales of $378.3 million in the first six months of 2006. Revlon's international sales in the first six months of 2007 increased 4.5 percent to $280.3 million, compared with net sales of $268.3 million in the first six months of 2006, while international net sales in the first six months of 2007 advanced 2.6 percent versus sales in 2006.

The company's U.S. market share for the second quarter of 2007 for the Revlon, Almay, and Vital Radiance (which was discontinued in September 2006) color cosmetics brands, and for women's hair color, antiperspirants and deodorants, and beauty tools are summarized in the following table:

Revlon's Market Share Percent

	Q2 of 2007	Q2 of 2006	Change
Color Cosmetics	19.5%	22.0%	−2.5
Revlon brand	13.4	14.3	−0.9
Almay brand	6.1	6.4	−0.3
Vital Radiance brand	0.0	1.4	−1.4
Women's Hair Color	11.2	9.0	2.2
Antiperspirants/Deodorants	5.9	6.4	−0.5
Revlon Beauty Tools	24.3	27.0	−2.7

History

Revlon, Inc. was formed in 1932 by brothers Charles and Joseph Revson and Charles Lachmann with a $300 investment. Charles Lachmann was a nail polish supplier who is most notably remembered for his contribution of the "L" in the Revlon name. Charles Revson was the primary force behind the success of Revlon until his death in 1968. In the early years, Revson developed a near monopoly on beauty parlor sales by selling his nail polish door-to-door at salons. He expanded into the lipstick market with the slogan "Matching Lips and Fingertips." Revson was a hard taskmaster, expecting the same whole life devotion of his workers that he gave to Revlon. He would hold meetings until two in the morning, call employees at home to discuss business, curse employees, and pretend to fall asleep during some presentations.

The company started with only one product—nail enamel. Revlon nail enamel was manufactured with pigments instead of the dyes typically used in nail enamel manufacturing. This approach allowed Revlon to market a large number of color options to consumers relatively quickly. It took the three company founders just six years to transform their small nail enamel company into a multimillion-dollar organization. This successful collaboration launched one of the most recognizable brands and companies in the world.

Originally Revlon offered its nail enamels through a limited distribution system in which professional salons carried the products. However, as the 1930s progressed, the products were distributed widely in select drug stores and department stores. As the world entered WWII, Revlon contributed to the war effort by providing first aid kits and dye markers for the U.S. Navy. After the war, Revlon expanded its product lines with the introduction of manicure and pedicure instruments (a natural complement to the nail enamel products). Revlon management recognized global demand potential and began offering company products in a number of new markets. Stock was first offered in the company in 1955. The 1960s were associated with the "American Look" campaign designed to introduce the All-American girl to the world cosmetics market via well-known U.S. models. Further identifying with the changing role of women, the Charlie fragrance line was introduced in the early 1970s. Sales for this extremely popular line surpassed $1 billion by 1977.

After the death of Charles Revson, Michel Bergerac took control of the company. He built up the pharmaceutical side of the business. By 1985, two-thirds of Revlon's sales were health care products such as Tums and Oxy acne medications, and the company was losing ground in cosmetics. Millionaire Ronald Perelman made five offers to purchase Revlon and eventually took over the company for $1.8 billion in a leveraged buyout. Perelman returned the company to its roots and sold off the health care products. He refocused the company to become an internationally known manufacturer and seller of cosmetics and fragrances. Perelman took the company private in 1987 by buying the stock of all public shareholders. A subsidiary of MacAndrews & Forbes stills holds 83 percent of the outstanding shares of Revlon, and Perelman is chairman and chief executive officer of MacAndrews & Forbes Holdings, Inc. The company was taken public in 1996 and is traded on the New York Stock Exchange (NYSE).

In September 1996, Revlon was given approval to manufacture, distribute, and market Revlon products in China, and the first manufactured goods rolled off the production line in December 1996. The company acquired Bionature S.A., a South American manufacturer of hair and personal care products in 1997. The completion of acquisitions in South America increased distribution and manufacturing capabilities in these markets. In an effort to reduce expenses, the company's worldwide professional products line was sold for $315 million in March 2000 and two months later, the Argentina brand Plusbelle was sold for $46 million. In November 2000, the company closed three manufacturing plants and reduced their workforce by 1,115 employees (14 percent of the workforce) in an effort to improve efficiency. Additional cost reductions were made in 2001 when warehouse and manufacturing space was reduced by 55 percent. The company closed its in-house advertising division the same year. The Colorama brand of cosmetics was sold in 2001 for $50 million to L'Oreal. Managers reviewed the strengths and weaknesses of Revlon in 2002 in an attempt to evaluate the company's businesses so improvements could be planned.

Despite financial struggles, Revlon continued to launch or reintroduce new product lines. The 33-year-old Ultima II brand was reintroduced in 2001, and Charlie perfume was reintroduced in 2002. Revlon and Pacific World Corporation agreed in October 2002 to jointly manufacture a line of nail and nail care products. Moisturous Lipcolor (24 shades of hydrating lipstick) was sold beginning in 2002 and the Moonlit Mauve color collection and Almay Bright Eyes products were introduced in fall 2003. In February 2003, the company received cash in the amount of $150 million from MacAndrews & Forbes Holdings, Inc. to implement some of its growth and stabilization plans.

Present Conditions

Revlon has struggled in recent years and has amassed debt of almost $2.3 billion. After two years of research and development, Revlon launched Vital Radiance, a cosmetic line for older women, in January 2006. With 100 products, it was the largest launch since ColorStay in 1994. The Vital Radiance line offered special color palette products, subdued eye shadows, and hydrating formula products designed to appeal to older women and baby boomers. The products were priced from $12 to $19 each. However, the new brand was not well received by the market. Other companies already provide competing products, and the prices for the Vital Radiance line were more expensive than products typically sold by the major retailers such as Wal-Mart and Walgreens that sell other Revlon products. Revlon discontinued the Vital Radiance brand in September 2006. Expectations are that the negative impact of the Vital Radiance brand on Revlon, Inc. will be approximately $110 million.

Revlon planned to launch a new prestige fragrance called Flair in 2006, but delayed the launch until debt could be restructured. The company issued $185 million in stock in 2006 to raise money to reduce debt. MacAndrews & Forbes Holdings agreed to purchase a portion of the stock and to purchase any stock not purchased by current stockholders after the offering. MacAndrews also extended a line of credit of $87 million to Revlon. These dollars should help Revlon recover from losses due to the Vital Radiance line. Net sales for U.S. and international operations by product category are shown in Exhibit 3.

Demographic and Social Trends

The cosmetics and personal care industry is impacted by two major changes in the demographic composition of the United States: the aging population and the change in proportions of racial and ethnic populations. Aging baby boomers make up a significant proportion of the adult U.S. population. The 75 million Americans born between 1946 and 1964 are a significant market for the cosmetics/personal care industry. The aging of the population has been coupled with a mini baby boom. Many baby boomers have high levels of disposable income and are brand-loyal consumers. In addition, it appears that baby boomers' consumption patterns and rates have not necessarily changed as they have aged. The number of people in the mature market (55 and older) also continues to increase in number. Many of these consumers are wealthier and more willing to spend than ever

EXHIBIT 3 Sales by Geographic Area and Product Category (In $ Millions)

| | Year Ended December 31 | | | | | |
	2006		2005		2004	
Geographic area:						
Net sales:		%		%		%
United States	$ 764.9	57	$ 788.3	59	$ 792.7	61
International	566.5	43	544.0	41	504.5	39
	$ 1,331.4		$ 1,332.3		$ 1,297.2	

| | Year Ended December 31 | | | | | |
	2006		2005		2004	
Classes of similar products:						
Net sales:						
Cosmetics, skin care, and fragrances	$ 832.0	62	$ 904.3	68	$ 874.7	67
Personal care	499.4	38	428.0	32	422.5	33
	$ 1,331.4		$ 1,332.3		$ 1,297.2	

Source: Revlon, Inc. 2006, *Form 10-K*, p. F-54.

before. Also, women in the mature age group remain active in the workforce for longer periods of time than in the past.

Another market segment of interest to cosmetics companies is the U.S. teen market (ages 12–19) since females in this age group will number almost 20 million by 2010. The ethnic/racial makeup of the American population is shifting. While African Americans represent the largest minority segment, the Hispanic American segment is the fastest growing and is projected to be the largest minority segment in the United States by the year 2010 with approximately 40.5 million individuals. The result is that the non-Hispanic white share of the U.S. population is expected to decline to 68 percent by the year 2010. The Asian American population is also growing rapidly. International sales of cosmetics/skin care products are also impacted by ethnic/racial issues. There are significant opportunities for companies in Asian countries, which house 60 percent of world's population. The youthful, increasingly affluent Latin American countries also represent a growth opportunity. Since the majority of personal care products are currently sold in the United States, Japan, Canada, and European countries (less than 20 percent of the world's population), the potential for sales of personal care products around the world is excellent.

Other social and demographic issues that may impact the industry include consumers' concerns about product safety and the use of animal testing by cosmetics companies. Increasingly, cosmetics/personal care is not an industry for women only; men purchase personal care products such as skin creams and hair care products/dyes, and many men are trying cosmetics in an effort to improve their appearance. The market for hair coloring has expanded, with teenagers and adults wanting more vibrant coloring options.

Older people tend to spend less on cosmetics, and this is a growing problem for the industry. Gas prices are high and rising leaving most Americans with less disposable income for purchasing cosmetics. In March 2006, many major retailers, including Wal-Mart, reduced inventory levels, leaving cosmetic companies with fewer opportunities to stock additional products on retail store shelves. The value of the dollar has dropped to historic lows, which benefits cosmetics firms that do considerable global business, such as Avon. Women in China, India, and the Middle East are rapidly growing interested in purchasing more cosmetics and fragrances.

Competition

Competition is intense in the cosmetics/skin care industry. The industry is a $200 billion business worldwide. Today large numbers of women prefer purchasing these items at drugstores, supermarkets, and mass volume retailers such as K-Mart and Wal-Mart; from door-to-door sellers such as Avon; and on the Internet. Revlon's major competitors include Procter & Gamble, Avon Products, Estée Lauder Companies, L'Oreal, and Unilever. Other competitors include small companies such as Urban Decay; specialty stores such as Bath and Body Works, Body Shop, and Sephora; and retailers selling their own brands such as Gap, Banana Republic, and Victoria's Secret. Competition for the African-American market is also increasing with brands such as Fashion Fair and cosmetics lines launched by Iman and Patti LaBelle.

Procter and Gamble

Procter & Gamble (P&G) is a multinational company offering products in a wide range of categories including personal care, cosmetics, fragrances, hair care, and skin care. Some of the P&G products outside the cosmetics/skin care industry include diapers, baking mixes, bleach, dish care products, juice, laundry products, oral care products, and peanut butter. The company operates in more than 70 countries.

Revlon faces competition from P&G in a number of product categories. P&G offers hair care products through its Pantene, Head & Shoulders, and Herbal Essences brands. P&G skin care lines include Olay, Noxzema, and Gillette. P&G acquired Gillette for $57 billion in 2005. Fragrance lines sold by P&G include Giorgio, Hugo Boss, Old Spice, and Lacoste. The P&G cosmetics line includes Cover Girl and Max Factor. In 2006, beauty care products contributed $21.1 billion to sales and $3.1 billion

EXHIBIT 4 **Financial Information for Procter & Gamble (In $ Millions)**

	2004	2005	2006
Net Sales	$51,407	56,741	68,222
Operating Income	9,382	10,469	13,249
Net Earnings	6,156	6,923	8,684
Long-Term Debt	12,554	12,887	35,976
Shareholders' Equity	$18,190	18,475	62,908

Source: http://www.pg.com

to profit for P&G. P&G offers a line of cosmetics for baby boomers called Cover Girl Advanced Radiance. Currently, Drew Barrymore, Jennifer O'Neill, Queen Latifah, and Dominique Dawes promote Cover Girl products, and Carmen Electra and Denise Richards promote Max Factor products. Selected financial information for Procter & Gamble is shown in Exhibit 4.

L'Oreal

L'Oreal is the world's largest cosmetics firm. L'Oreal acquired Maybelline, one of its leading competitors, in 1996 for $758 million. This move was an attempt to strengthen its position in the U.S. market. L'Oreal previously held only a 7.5 percent share of the market, but the acquisition of Maybelline made L'Oreal the number two cosmetics firm in the United States. L'Oreal competes with Revlon in the area of cosmetics (L'Oreal, Maybelline, and Garnier), hair care (L'Oreal, Matrix, and Redken), and fragrances (Giorgio Armani and Ralph Lauren perfumes). Some advertising spokespersons for L'Oreal are Béyonc Knowles and Katharine McPhee (American Idol). Financial information for L'Oreal is shown in Exhibit 5.

Unilever

Unilever is an Anglo-Dutch firm that until recently has been noted as a manufacturer of soap/detergent products and food products. The company also manufacturers personal care products and cosmetics, which makes up 26 percent of their business. Some of the Unilever brands include mass skin care products (Dove, Ponds, Vaseline) and hair care products (Dove and Sunsilk). Unilever sold its prestige fragrance line (Calvin Klein, Chloe, Obsession, Eternity, and Escape) to Coty for $800 million in 2005. The company produced controversial ads in 2005 for Dove called "Love Yourself" and "You Go Girl" for an anticellulite firming cream featuring noncelebrity models. The Campaign for Real Beauty launched in 2006 used noncelebrities to promote Dove brand soap; the company thought a celebrity would be counterproductive to the campaign theme. The company leads the hair care market in Africa, the Middle East, Latin America, and Asia/Pacific. Their skin care products lead the market in North America, Africa, Latin

EXHIBIT 5 **L'Oreal Financial Information (Euros in Millions)**

	2004	2005	2006
Sales	€13,641	14,533	15,790
Operating Profit	2,089	2,266	2,541
Non-Current Assets	15,734	18,686	19,155
Current Assets	4,075	4,537	4,847
Loans and Debt	1,568	2,217	3,329
Shareholders' Equity	11,825	14,657	14,624

Source: http://www.loreal.com

EXHIBIT 6   Financial Information for Unilever (Euros in Millions)

	2004	2005	2006
Net Profit	€2,941	3,975	5,015
Total Non-Current Assets	27,571	28,358	27,571
Total Assets Less Current Liabilities	23,188	24,106	23,188
Total Non-Current Liabilities	11,516	15,341	11,516
Shareholders' Equity	11,230	8,361	23,188

Source: http://www.unilever.com

America, Asia/Pacific, and the Middle East. Financial results for Unilever are shown in Exhibit 6.

Avon Products, Inc.

Avon is the number one direct seller of cosmetics and beauty products in the world. Their direct sales force numbers five million people in 114 countries. Some brand names for Avon products include Avon Color, Avon Skin Care Solutions, Anew, Skin-So-Soft, and Mark. Jennifer Hudson and Salma Hayek are celebrity spokespersons for Avon. Avon sells vitamins and nutritional supplements as well as jewelry, gift items, lingerie, and a skin care line for older women. The company reduced its number of management levels from fifteen to eight in 2005 with expectations that it would save $100 million in 2006 and $200 million in 2007. Avon managers also began two other cost-cutting measures in 2006: a strategic sourcing initiative designed to centralize purchasing and a product line simplification plan that will reduce the number of items offered by 25 to 40 percent.

Avon products can be purchased at http://www.avon.com. However, 98 percent of Avon revenue is generated by sales representatives. To address sales representatives' concerns that Internet sales would reduce their sales, Avon is allowing sales representatives to have their own Web sites. Avon posted sales of nearly $8.6 billion dollars in 2006. Selected financial information is provided in Exhibit 7.

Estée Lauder

The Estée Lauder Companies, Inc. manufactures and markets cosmetics, fragrances, skin care products, and hair care products for sale in 103 countries and territories. Some of the company's cosmetics/skin care brands include Estée Lauder and Clinique. Estée Lauder holds the worldwide license for fragrances and cosmetics with the brand names Tommy Hilfiger and Donna Karan (DKNY). In 2005, Estée Lauder and celebrity designer Tom Ford partnered to launch a collection. Other Estée Lauder brands include Bobbi Brown Essentials, Prescriptives, MAC, Bobbi Brown, La Mer, Donna Karan, Aveda, Jo Malone, Bumble and Bumble, Darphin, Michael Kors, American Beauty, Flirt!, Good Skin, and Grassroots. Some of the advertising spokespersons for the company

EXHIBIT 7   Financial Information for Avon Products (In $ Millions)

	2004	2005	2006
Total Revenue	$7,747.8	8,149.6	8,763.9
Operating Profit	1,229	1,149	761.4
Net Income	846.1	847.6	477.6
Total Assets	4,148.1	4,761.4	5,238.2
Long-Term Debt	866.3	766.5	1,170.7
Stockholders' Equity	$750.2	794.2	790.4

Source: http://www.avon.com

EXHIBIT 8   Financial Information for Estée Lauder Companies, Inc. (In $ Millions)

	2004	2005	2006
Net Sales	$5,742	6,280	6,464
Operating Income	649	727	620
Net Earnings	342	406	244
Total Assets	3,708.1	3,885.5	3,784.1
Long-Term Debt	461.5	679.5	698.2
Stockholders' Equity	$1,733.5	1,692.8	1,622.3

Source: http://www.elcompanies.com

are models Liya Kebede and Carolyn Murphy, and actresses Elizabeth Hurley and Gwyneth Paltrow.

Selected financial information for Estée Lauder is shown in Exhibit 8.

Internal Factors

Social Responsibility

Revlon and its employees are active in supporting women's health programs and other community efforts. In the last decade, Revlon spent more than $25 million on services and research that help women. Singer Sheryl Crow serves on an advisory board for Revlon/UCLA Women's Cancer Research Programs National Clinical Network of Oncologists. Crow helps the organization identify communities around the United States that are underserved for women's breast cancer treatment. Crow is also an ambassador for the National Breast Cancer Coalition that is supported by Revlon. As part of her work for Revlon and breast cancer awareness, Crow participates in the Revlon Walk/Run in New York City and Los Angeles. Revlon has a partnership with the National Council of Negro Women to help support wellness programs for African American women. The company also supports New York Women in Film.

Organization/Management

David Kennedy was selected as Chairman and CEO in 2006, the third CEO since 2000. A former Coca-Cola executive, he served Revlon as chief financial officer before being promoted to CEO. Kennedy began cost cutting in February 2006 with an announcement that 164 jobs would be cut. During 2006 and 2007, Kennedy planned to cut a total of 250 jobs (8 percent of the workforce). The company is also being restructured to consolidate marketing/creative functions and international divisions. Two vice president positions were eliminated and the marketing leadership reports directly to Kennedy. Executives leading the international divisions also now report directly to Kennedy instead of to a division vice president. The company believes that restructuring will cost $29 million, but will save the company $34 million a year in reduced expenses. Revlon's major management positions are shown in Exhibit 9.

Marketing

The primary customers for Revlon products are large mass merchandisers and chain drug stores such as Walgreens, Wal-Mart, Target, K-Mart, CVS, Eckerd, and Rite Aid. Revlon provides point-of-sale displays and samples for these stores. Wal-Mart sales were 23 percent of Revlon sales in 2006. Revlon's products are also sold through its Web sites http://www.revlon.com and http://www.almay.com. New product development continues to be a primary objective of Revlon even in bad financial times. Revlon spent $24.4 million on research and development efforts in 2006 and employed 170 people in this effort.

EXHIBIT 9   Organization Chart for Revlon, Inc.

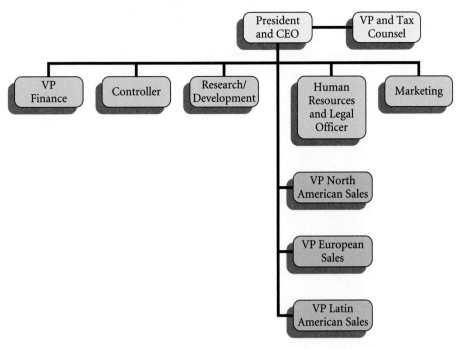

Source: Based on Revlon, Inc. 2006, *Form 10-K* and "Revlon Accelerates Cost Reduction and Margin Improvement," *PR Newswire*, September 25, 2006.

Advertising continues to be one of the primary areas of promotion spending by Revlon, which spent approximately $120 million on U.S. advertising in 2006. Current Revlon spokespersons include Halle Berry, Susan Sarandon, Julianne Moore, Kate Bosworth, Janice King, Sheryl Crow, and Eva Mendes. Sheryl Crow was hired in 2007 to promote Revlon Colorist (a fade resistant hair color) with a debut of the ad on the Super Bowl telecast. The ads with Crow featured her singing the Buddy Holly hit "Not Fade Away."

Manufacturing/Distribution

Globalization of the company's manufacturing and distribution efforts has enabled the consolidation of production facilities and provided increased operating efficiency and better use of capital assets. The number of Revlon production facilities has been reduced and centralized to cover core regions. Currently, the company has production facilities in Oxford, North Carolina and Irvington, New Jersey as well as in Mexico, Venezuela, South Africa, China, and France. Several of the company's plants have ISO-9000 certification signifying their commitment to quality manufacturing standards. The Revlon Phoenix Site Distribution Center handles components and raw materials as well as finished stocks of cosmetics and personal care products.

Financial Conditions

Long-term debt at the end of 2006 was nearly $2.3 billion. For this reason, the company continues its restructuring program. The company's restructuring costs for 2002 through 2006 are shown in Exhibit 10.

Note in Exhibit 11 (statement of operations) that sales decreased in 2004, 2005, and again in 2006. Revlon's net losses in 2006 were $50.2 million. According to balance sheet information in Exhibit 12, current assets and total assets decreased while current liabilities and total liabilities increased from 2005 to 2006.

EXHIBIT 10   Restructuring Costs as of December 31, 2006 (In $ Millions)

	Balance Beginning of	Expenses, Net	Utilized, Net		Balance
			Cash	Noncash	
2006					
Employee severance and other personnel benefits:					
2003 programs	$ 1.2	$ (0.3)	$ (0.8)	$ -	$ 0.1
2004 programs	2.4	-	(2.3)	-	0.1
February 2006 program	-	10.1	(6.7)	-	3.4
September 2006 program	-	17.5	(3.7)	-	13.8
Other 2006 programs[a]	-	0.3	(0.2)	-	0.1
	3.6	27.6	(13.7)	-	17.5
Leases and equipment write-offs	0.6	(0.2)	0.2	(0.2)	0.4
	$ 4.2	$ 27.4	$ (13.5)	$ (0.2)	$ 17.9
2005					
Employee severance and other personnel benefits:					
2003 programs	$ 3.1	$ -	$ (1.7)	$ (0.2)	$ 1.2
2004 programs	5.1	1.5	(3.9)	(0.3)	2.4
	8.2	1.5	(5.6)	(0.5)	3.6
Leases and equipment write-offs	2.9	-	(2.0)	(0.3)	0.6
	$ 11.1	$ 1.5	$ (7.6)	$ (0.8)	$ 4.2
2004					
Employee severance and other personnel benefits:					
2000 program	$ 1.8	$ -	$ (1.8)	$ -	$ -
2003 program	5.0	0.1	(2.4)	0.4	3.1
2004 program	-	5.9	(0.8)	-	5.1
	6.8	6.0	(5.0)	0.4	8.2
Leases and equipment write-offs	2.2	(0.2)	0.6	0.3	2.9
	$ 9.0	$ 5.8	$ (4.4)	$ 0.7	$ 11.1

Source: Revlon, Inc. 2006, *Form 10-K*, p. F-16.

Future Outlook

Rumors have it that Revlon in China is adopting Avon's door-to-door sales tactics. Do you think that is a good strategy or not, and why? If yes, to what extent should this new forward integration strategy be pursued? If China, why not put salespersons on the ground in other countries such as India and even the United States? CEO Kennedy and the Revlon management team need a clear strategic plan and seek your advice. As Revlon deals with its debt problems and tries to continue its strategy of innovation, product development, and globalization, several issues must be considered:

1. Should Revlon concentrate its efforts on international markets, given the low value of the dollar and competitive pressures? What countries should Revlon focus on?
2. Should Revlon diversify its operations or develop joint ventures with other cosmetics companies? Would jewelry be a good industry to enter given the aging society?

**EXHIBIT 11   Revlon, Inc. Consolidated Statement of Operations
(In $ Millions, except per share data)**

	Year Ended December 31		
	2006	2005	2004
Net sales	$ 1,331.4	$ 1,332.3	$ 1,297.2
Cost of sales	545.5	508.1	485.3
Gross profit	785.9	824.2	811.9
Selling, general and administrative expenses	808.7	757.8	717.6
Restructuring costs and other, net	27.4	1.5	5.8
Operating (loss) income	(50.2)	64.9	88.5
Other expenses (income):			
Interest expense	148.8	130.0	130.8
Interest income	(1.1)	(5.8)	(4.8)
Amortization of debt issuance costs	7.5	6.9	8.2
Foreign currency (gains) losses, net	(1.5)	0.5	(5.2)
Loss on early extinguishment of debt	23.5	9.0	90.7
Miscellaneous, net	3.8	(0.5)	2.0
Other expenses, net	181.0	140.1	221.7
Loss before income taxes	(231.2)	(75.2)	(133.2)
Provision for income taxes	20.1	8.5	9.3
Net loss	$ (251.3)	$ (83.7)	$ (142.5)
Basic and diluted loss per common share	$ (0.62)	$ (0.22)	$ (0.47)
Weighted average number of common shares outstanding:			
Basic and diluted	404,542,722	374,060,951	303,428,981

Source: Revlon, Inc. 2006, *Form 10-K*, p. F-5.

3. Does Revlon have too many brands? Should the company keep brands such as ColorStay and get rid of brands such as Mitchum?
4. Should Revlon agree to sell itself to Perlman or to a rival firm? What is Revlon worth on the market?

References

Atlas, Riva. "Revlon Running Near Empty," http://www.NYTimes.com (August 28, 2003).

Brookman, Faye. "Revlon's Exec Shuffle Raises Questions," *Women's Wear Daily*, September 22, 2006.

Davis, Riccardo. "Revlon to Shut Plant, Ax 900 Jobs in Valley," *The Arizona Republic* (November 2, 2000), p. A1.

D'Innocenzio, Anne. "Revlon Targets Older Women to Perk up Sales," *Associated Press Financial Wire*, April 10, 2006.

Maynard, Jill. "Rethinking Revlon," *International Cosmetics News*, October 1, 2006.

"Revlon Accelerates Cost Reduction and Margin Improvement," *PR Newswire US*, September 2006.

Revlon, Inc. 2006 *Annual Report.*

"Sheryl Crow Launches New Revlon Colorist," *PR Newswire US*, January 31, 2007.

Spears, John. "Revlon to Shed 120 Jobs in Shift to U.S.," *The Toronto Star* (October 25, 2000).

"Stahl Resigns as Revlon President, CEO," AFX.COM, September 18, 2006.

EXHIBIT 12   Revlon, Inc. Consolidated Balance Sheets ($ in millions, except per share data)

	December 31, 2006	December 31, 2005
ASSETS		
Current assets:		
Cash and cash equivalents	$ 35.4	$ 32.5
Trade receivables, less allowances of $17.7 and $18.9 as of December 31, 2006 and 2005, respectively	207.8	282.2
Inventories	186.5	220.6
Prepaid expenses and other	58.3	56.7
Total current assets	488.0	592.0
Property, plant and equipment, net	115.3	119.7
Other assets	142.4	146.0
Goodwill, net	186.2	186.0
Total assets	$ 931.9	$ 1,043.7
LIABILITIES AND STOCKHOLDERS' DEFICIENCY		
Current liabilities:		
Short-term borrowings	$ 9.6	$ 9.0
Current portion of long-term debt	-	-
Accounts payable	95.1	133.1
Accrued expenses and other	272.5	328.4
Total current liabilities	377.2	470.5
Long-term debt	1,501.8	1,413.4
Long-term pension and other post-retirement plan liabilities	175.7	162.4
Other long-term liabilities	107.0	93.3
Stockholders' deficiency:		
Class B Common Stock, par value $0.01 per share; 200,000,000 shares authorized, 31,250,000 issued and outstanding as of December 31, 2006 and 2005, respectively	0.3	0.3
Class A Common Stock, par value $0.01 per share; 900,000,000 shares authorized and 390,001,154 and 344,472,735 shares issued as of December 31, 2006 and 2005, respectively	3.8	3.4
Additional paid-in capital	884.9	764.8
Treasury stock, at cost; 429,666 and 236,315 shares of Class A Common Stock as of December 31, 2006 and 2005, respectively	(1.4)	(0.8)
Accumulated deficit	(1,993.2)	(1,741.9)
Accumulated other comprehensive loss	(124.2)	(121.7)
Total stockholders' deficiency	(1,229.8)	(1,095.9)
Total liabilities and stockholders' deficiency	$ 931.9	$ 1,043.7

Source: Revlon, Inc. 2006, *Form 10-K*, p. F-4.

http://www.avon.com
http://www.elcompanies.com
http://www.loreal.com
http://www.pg.com
http://www.revlon.com
http://www.unilever.com

3 Krispy Kreme Doughnuts — 2008

Forest R. David
Francis Marion University

Mario Musa
University of Mostar (in Bosnia)

KKD

www.krispykreme.com

Krispy Kreme Doughnuts (KKD) produces approximately 5.5 million doughnuts a day consisting of over 20 varieties. When KKD's trademark doughnut, the Original Glazed, is hot off the glazing process and still warm, they proudly turn on their neon light to encourage customers into the store. KKD serves customers in 395 stores operating in 40 states in the United States, and in 10 foreign countries including Australia, Canada, Hong Kong, Indonesia, Japan, Kuwait, Mexico, the Philippines, South Korea, and the United Kingdom. Of the 395 stores, 282 are owned by franchisees and the balance of 113 are owned by the corporation. Over 50 stores are located ouside of the United State, Canada, and Mexico.

KKD's fiscal 2008 year began on January 29, 2007. The company's systemwide second quarter fiscal 2008 sales decreased approximately 0.5 percent from the second quarter of fiscal 2007. KKD's total average weekly sales per store decreased approximately 2.8 percent to approximately $37,500. Company stores' average weekly sales per store increased 1.6 percent to approximately $51,800. Revenues for the second quarter of fiscal 2008 decreased 7.5 percent to $104.1 million compared to $112.5 million in the second quarter of the prior year. Company stores' revenues decreased 4.7 percent to $75.3 million. Franchise revenues were flat at $5.1 million, and KK Supply Chain revenues decreased 16.8 percent to $23.7 million.

KKD's net loss for the second quarter of fiscal 2008 was $27.0 million, compared to a net loss of $4.6 million in the comparable period of fiscal 2007. "After several quarters of progress on our turnaround, second quarter results did not meet our expectations," said Daryl Brewster, the company's president and chief executive officer. "We are taking steps to transform KKD and improve its performance." KKD is trying to increase the percentage of stores operated by franchisees.

During the second quarter of fiscal 2008, 19 new Krispy Kreme stores, comprised of 3 factory stores and 16 satellites, were opened systemwide, and 12 Krispy Kreme stores, comprised of 5 factory stores and 7 satellites, were closed systemwide. This brought the total number of stores systemwide at the end of the second quarter of fiscal 2008 to 411, consisting of 299 factory stores and 112 satellites. The net increase of 7 stores in the quarter reflects a net increase of 13 international stores and a net decrease of 6 domestic stores. Franchisees closed 13 stores in the first six months of fiscal 2008, and KKD anticipated closure of a significant number of additional franchise stores during the balance of the fiscal year.

Krispy Kreme doughnuts and snacks are also sold at thousands of supermarkets, convenience stores, and other retail outlets throughout the United States. As of January 28, 2007, KKD had 4,759 employees, down from 6,982 employees only two years earlier. It is interesting to note that during this period of reducing its labor force, the company entered all the foreign countries listed above (except for Australia and Canada, where they were already operating) accounting for the bulk of the international stores.

History

KKD was founded in 1937 and became a publicly-traded company in April 2000. Vernon Rudolph opened a doughnut company, Krispy Kreme, on July 13, 1937, in Winston-Salem, North Carolina. The company started out by selling doughnuts to local grocery stores. People walking in front of the bakery soon began stopping by to ask if they could purchase the doughnuts hot. Rudolph decided to cut a hole in the wall of the bakery so that his Hot Original Glazed doughnuts could be sold directly to the customer, marking the introduction of Krispy Kreme's retail service.

During the 1950s, the doughnut-making process was mechanized with the new Krispy Kreme automatic doughnut cutter. Hand-cut doughnuts became a thing of the past. All processes in the bakery became entirely automatic. This was the initial version of Krispy Kreme's continuous yeast doughnut-making equipment.

KKD stock opened around $10 a share and by 2003 was trading in the $50 range, more than a 400 percent increase in only two years. Times soon turned sour for KKD, however, as the stock price fell amid serious accounting irregularities in 2005. CEO Scott Livengood was outsted, and KKD became the target of a federal criminal inquiry in New York and a Securities and Exchange Commission probe into financial irregularities. In addition, KKD also faced several lawsuits, including one alleging that workers lost millions of dollars in retirement savings because KKD executives hid evidence of declining sales and profits. Another lawsuit claimed KKD had systematically inflated its prices and engaged in deceptive business practices.

Most of these issues were settled outside of court. After the stock price hit a low of just under $4 a share in the fourth quarter 2005, the stock rebounded to over $8 a share in the second quarter of 2007. The company continued to report negative net income. However, these concerns were tempered somewhat by the company's massive cost-cutting practices, which reduced negative net income from $198 million in January 2005 to $42 million in January 2007. KKD became up-to-date on all their SEC filings in January of 2007.

Company Stores

Krispy Kreme is a vertically integrated company with three reportable segments: (1) company store operations, (2) franchise operations, and (3) KK Supply Chain operations. Exhibit 1 provides a segmented account of revenues and expenses for Krispy Kreme. The largest segment of total revenue and total operating expenses is derived from company store operations, followed by KK Supply Chain. Franchise operations make up only 4.6 percent of total revenue. Note that total KKD revenues fell 23 percent in fiscal 2006 to $416 million.

Exhibit 2 provides a detailed listing of KKD stores so that one may see trends both domestically and globally, in openings and closings. KKD company stores, owned by the KKD Company, are consolidated joint ventures; there are 113 units in this division.

EXHIBIT 1   KKD's Revenues and Expenses by Segment

	Year End (Dollars in thousands)	
	January 28, 2007	January 29, 2006
Revenues By Business Segment		
Company Stores	$326,199	$398,450
Franchise	21,075	18,394
KK Supply Chain	113,921	126,517
Total Revenues	**$416,195**	**$543,361**
Percentage of Total Revenues		
Company Stores	70.7%	73.3%
Franchise	4.6	3.4
KK Supply Chain	24.7	23.3
Total Revenues	**100%**	**100%**

continued

EXHIBIT 1   KKD's Revenues and Expenses by Segment—continued

	Year End (Dollars in thousands)	
	January 28, 2007	January 29, 2006
Direct Operating Expenses		
Company Stores	$290,097	$361,265
Franchise	4,602	5,017
KK Supply Chain	94,680	108,309
Total Operating Expenses	**$389,379**	**$474,591**
Percentage of Direct Operating Expenses		
Company Stores	88.9%	90.7%
Franchise	21.8%	27.3%
KK Supply Chain	83.1%	85.6%
Total Direct Operating Expenses	**84.4%**	**87.3%**

Source: www.krispykreme.com

Both company-owned stores and franchise stores make and sell doughnuts and complementary products through on-premises and off-premises sales channels. On-premise KKD sales include direct in-store sales to customers visiting inside or coming through the drive-through window. Discounted sales for community organization fundraising purposes are also included in on-premises sales. Off-premises sales include fresh-doughnut distributions of branded, unbranded, and/or private-label doughnuts to grocery and convenience stores. These doughnuts are sold packaged or unpackaged from a retailer's display case.

Company stores' revenues decreased 18 percent to $326 million in fiscal 2007 from $398 million in fiscal 2006. The decreased in revenue is mostly attributed to a 26 percent decrease in store operating weeks which was partially offset by a 11 percent increase in average weekly sales per store. The decrease in operating weeks reflects the number of factory stores sold since 2005. The 11 percent increase in average weekly sales per store reflects closing the poorer performing stores, consolidating production into a smaller number of factory stores, specific price increases, and improved sales volume through convenience stores and grocery stores. However, as a result of the restructuring, direct operating expenses as a percentage of company stores' revenues decreased 3 percent in fiscal 2007 from fiscal 2006.

Domestic Stores

As of January 28, 2007, KKD operated 272 domestic stores, of which 239 were factory stores and 33 were satellite stores. These store numbers reflect the opening in fiscal 2007 of 9 domestic stores and the closing of 71 domestic stores. Of the 9 stores opened in fiscal 2007, 1 was a company store. Of the 71 stores closed in fiscal 2007, 11 were company stores, including 3 operated by Glazed Investments, a former consolidated franchisee.

KKD does not expect to open many if any domestic factory stores in the near future. Currently, KKD does not have an updated registered Uniform Franchise Offering Circular ("UFOC"), which prevents it from offering franchises to new domestic franchisees.

International Stores

As of January 28, 2007, there were a total of 123 Krispy Kreme stores (including 66 satellites) operated internationally, located in Australia, Canada, Hong Kong, Indonesia, Japan, Kuwait, Mexico, the Philippines, South Korea and the United Kingdom. In fiscal 2007, 60 new international stores were opened, and 5 international stores were closed. KKD is concentrated on development efforts primarily in Asia and the Middle East. These two geographic areas offer KKD favorable population demographics, relatively high levels of consumer sweet goods consumption and the popularity of Western brands in these markets.

EXHIBIT 2   KKD Number of Stores Data

	At January 28, 2007	At January 29, 2006	At January 30, 2005
By Owner:			
Company Stores			
Company	113	118	131
Consolidated Franchisees	—	15	54
Total Company Stores	113	133	185
Franchise Stores			
Associates	52	57	59
Area Developers	230	212	189
Total Franchise Stores	282	269	248
Total Systemwide	395	402	433
By Type:			
Factory Stores			
Company	108	113	124
Consolidated Franchisees	—	15	51
Associates	43	47	54
Area Developers	145	148	167
Total Factory Stores	296	323	396
Satellites			
Company	5	5	7
Consolidated Franchisees	—	—	3
Associates	9	10	5
Area Developers	85	64	22
Total Satellites	99	79	37
Total Systemwide	395	402	433
By Location:			
Domestic Stores			
Company	107	112	131
Consolidated Franchisees	—	15	41
Associates	52	57	59
Area Developers	113	150	165
Total Domestic Stores	272	334	396
International Stores:			
Company	6	6	—
Consolidated Franchisees	—	—	13
Associates	—	—	—
Area Developers	117	62	24
Total International Stores	123	68	37
Total Systemwide	395	402	433

Source: www.krispykreme.com

During fiscal 2007, KKD awarded development rights in the Middle East, Hong Kong, Macau, Tokyo, the Philippines, and Indonesia. The development and franchise agreements for these territories provide for the development of approximately 200 stores, including both factory stores and satellites, over the next five years. As of January 28, 2007, 17 stores were opened under these new agreements.

Competition

KKD competes in the quick-service restaurant (QSR) industry. Stock share prices in this industry have begun to rebound from a recent drop caused by aggressive price discounts by industry leaders McDonald's and Burger King. Stable same-store sales growth and positive operating conditions have also contributed to the surge in casual-dining industry stocks.

The casual-dining sector continues to gain share from fast-food chains, as an older, wealthier population favors dining in full-service restaurants. This trend is expected to continue. Food product price inflation has been increasing since 2004 so major companies are lowering development costs of new restaurants and slowing expansion in the overstored U.S. fast-food market. Reducing the cost of new units should enhance companies' returns on investment and improve entry into smaller markets. Some fast-food companies are looking to international expansion for growth, while others are investigating new formulas to find ways to grow. There is a new trend toward providing "healthy" choices.

During the past two decades, an ever-increasing precentage of U.S. food dollars has gone to eating out. With a greater percentage of Americans working, there has been less time available for at-home food preparation. Krispy Kreme believes this trend along with growth in two-income households will increase snack-food consumption and further growth of doughnut sales.

Dunkin' Donuts

The number-one competitor of Krispy Kreme is Dunkin' Donuts. Founded in 1950 and owned by Allied Domecq PLC, Dunkin' Donuts is an international company whose core businesses are in spirits and wine, and quick-service restaurants. Dunkin' Donuts has over 7,000 stores in 2007, up from 5,438 stores two years earlier. There are 1,900 stores in over 30 countries outside the United States and over 5,300 stores located in the United States, up from 3,836 two years earlier. Bill Rosenberg founded Dunkin' Donuts in Quincy, Massachusetts.

Sizing up the competition, one glazed doughnut from Dunkin' Donuts has 180 calories, while one Hot Original Glazed doughnut from Krispy Kreme has 200 calories. Dunkin' Donuts carries 25 varieties of doughnuts as well as beverages, bagels, and breakfast sandwiches. Krispy Kreme sells espresso coffee, frozen blends, plain or flavored milk, and has over 20 varieties of doughnuts; in addition it has special flavors such as the Pumpkin Spice doughnut offered during the fall months.

Starbucks Corporation

Since KKD sells drip coffee, espresso, frozen beverages, and plain or flavored milk, Starbucks also is a KKD competitor. Starbucks purchases and roasts high-quality whole bean coffees, which it sells, together with fresh, rich-brewed coffees, primarily through approximately 12,000 retail stores located in the United States, Asia-Pacific, Europe, the Middle East, Africa, and Latin America, up from 6,800 two years earlier. Starbucks offers a wide selection of pastries and confections in addition to coffee and coffee-making equipment and accessories.

Tim Hortons

Tim Hortons is Canada's largest restaurant chain, which started operating in 1964 as a coffee and doughnut place. The company quickly grew in size and expanded its menu with pastries and home-style lunches. Tim Hortons merged with Wendy's in 1995, and this opened many opportunities for an expansion into the United States. The company operates standard restaurants, nonstandard restaurants, and combination restaurants, but its strongest brand remains Tim Hortons coffee. Because of the similarity in history and presence in Canada and the United States, Tim Hortons is a strong competitor to KKD.

As of December 31, 2006, Tim Hortons and its franchisees operated 2,711 restaurants in Canada and 336 restaurants in the United States under the name Tim Hortons. Tim Hortons is based in Oakville, Canada and has regional offices in Lachine, Canada; Brighton, Michigan; Williamsville, New York; and West Greenwich, Rhode Island.

Internal Factors

Franchise Operations

There are 282 franchise KKD stores that are owned by either area developers or associates. This is up from 188 just two years earlier as the company is trying to increasingly find franchisees rather than self-own KKD stores. Franchise stores pay royalties to Krispy Kreme that amount to 3 percent of onsite sales and 1 percent of other sales, i.e. for use of the Krispy Kreme name and expertise. Two franchise programs are offered. First, in the Associate Program, which is the original program, franchisees pay royalties of 3 percent of on-premises sales and 1 percent of all other sales with the exception of private labels. Second, the Area Developer Program was developed in the mid-1990s, in which royalties of 4.5 to 6 percent of all sales are paid along with franchise fees ranging from $20,000 to $50,000 per store. Almost all area developers and associates contribute 1 percent and 0.25 percent respectively of all sales to the national advertising and brand development fund. Krispy Kreme offers franchises in the U.S. market as well as the global market.

Franchise revenues, consisting mostly of franchise fees and royalties, increased over 14 percent to $21 million in fiscal 2007 from $18 million one year earlier. Krispy Kreme's total revenues from franchise fees rose $2.3 million in fiscal 2007.

KK Supply Chain

Both franchise stores and company stores are required to purchase all supplies from KK Supply Chain which provides all supplies including foodstuffs, equipment, signage, and uniforms. The KK Supply Chain unit buys and processes all ingredients used in the doughnut mixes and manufactures the doughnut-making equipment that all stores are required to purchase. KK Supply Chain also includes the coffee roasting operations and also ships all food ingredients, juices, display cases, uniforms, and other items to Krispy Kreme locations on a weekly basis by common carrier.

Sales to franchise stores decreased 10 percent to $114 million in fiscal 2007. The division attributes much of this decline to lower sales by franchisees which resulted in a 13 percent decrease in doughnut ingredients and coffee. Also, this drop in sales can be explained by the large increase in the international presence of KKD. Most internationally located stores purchase their ingredients from local merchants rather than KK Supply Chain. The sales of mixes and other supplies were partly offset by a 26 percent increase in equipment, furniture, fixtures, and similar items.

Finance

KKD has experienced falling revenues annually for several years and negative net incomes, but note in Exhibit 3 that the negative profit levels are improving. Exhibit 3 provides the company's consolidated Income Statement and Exhibit 4 provides the recent Balance Sheets.

Marketing

On-premises KKD sales include counter sales and drive-through window sales. Krispy Kreme is involved in community organization fundraiser events in which it offers doughnuts at a discounted price for community fundraising projects. Off-premise sales include branded, unbranded, and private-label sales to grocery stores and convenience stores. Krispy Kreme entices customers with its doughnut-making "theaters," which are stores that have glass viewing areas that allow customers to watch the actual doughnut-making process. Generations of loyal customers have grown to love the one-of-a-kind taste of Krispy Kreme doughnuts.

Production

Each Krispy Kreme Doughnut store is a doughnut factory that has the capacity to produce from 4,000 dozen to over 10,000 dozen doughnuts daily. KK Supply Chain manufactures the doughnut-making equipment and produces the doughnut mixes that all stores are required to purchase. KKD relocated the Chicago-based Digital Java to its hometown—Winston-Salem, North Carolina. The full beverage program was implemented

EXHIBIT 3   KKD's Income Statement (000 omitted)

Income Statement

PERIOD ENDING	Jan. 28, 2007	Jan. 29, 2006	Jan. 30, 2005
Total Revenue	$ **461,195**	**543,361**	**707,766**
Cost of Revenue	389,379	474,591	597,110
Gross Profit	**71,816**	**68,770**	**110,656**
Operating Expenses			
Research Development	—	—	—
Selling General and Administrative	48,860	67,727	56,472
Non-Recurring	28,491	90,895	161,847
Others	21,046	28,920	31,934
Total Operating Expenses	—	—	—
Operating Income or Loss	**(26,581)**	**(118,772)**	**(139,597)**
Income from Continuing Operations			
Total Other Income/Expenses Net	6,732	2,603	(7,157)
Earnings Before Interest and Taxes	(20,691)	(116,325)	(146,754)
Interest Expense	20,334	20,211	6,875
Income Before Tax	(41,025)	(136,536)	(153,629)
Income Tax Expense	1,211	(776)	9,674
Minority Interest	—	4,181	6,249
Net Income from Continuing Ops	(42,236)	(135,760)	(157,054)
Non-Recurring Events			
Discontinued Operations	—	—	(40,054)
Extraordinary Items	—	—	—
Effect of Accounting Changes	—	—	(1,231)
Other Items	—	—	—
Net Income	$ **(42,236)**	**(135,760)**	**(198,339)**
Preferred Stock and Other Adjustments	—	—	—
Net Income Applicable to Common Shares	**($42,236)**	**($135,760)**	**($198,339)**

Source: www.krispykreme.com

in approximately 70 KKD locations. It is anticipated that the remaining stores will receive the new beverage program, primarily espresso and frozen beverages, in the next 12 to 18 months.

Management

KKD's upper management structure is comprised of four executive officers, including the president and chief executive officer, and six senior vice presidents. Exhibit 5 provides a list and a graphic representation of the company's management structure.

Global Issues

Doughnuts are a traditional favorite pastry of Europeans although they tend to be more loyal to their local brands of doughnuts, and almost every country has its own name for a doughnut. In Italy, a doughnut is called *fritole,* in France it is *beignol,* while Germans enjoy their *krapfen.* Every major European country has its own way of making, distributing, and selling doughnuts. Three most promising markets are the United Kingdom, Germany, and Spain. Doughnuts are offered in small bakery shops, supermarkets, and department stores.

All major European and American doughnut chains are rolling into Asia, especially China, Taiwan, Japan, and South Korea. Asia is known for its love for the sweets and

EXHIBIT 4   **KKD's Balance Sheets (000 omitted)**

PERIOD ENDING	Jan. 28, 2007	Jan. 29, 2006	Jan. 30, 2005
Assets			
Current Assets			
Cash and Cash Equivalents	$ 36,242	16,980	27,686
Short-Term Investments	—	—	—
Net Receivables	64,227	83,546	49,621
Inventory	26,162	41,985	28,591
Other Current Assets	5,187	4,514	13,465
Total Current Assets	**131,818**	**147,025**	**119,363**
Long Term Investments	4,261	14,734	9,618
Property Plant and Equipment	168,654	205,579	309,214
Goodwill	28,094	29,181	32,692
Intangible Assets	1,900	2,925	4,211
Accumulated Amortization	—	—	—
Other Assets	9,226	3,584	4,034
Deferred Long Term Asset Charges	5,539	7,827	1,146
Total Assets	**349,492**	**410,855**	**480,278**
Liabilities			
Current Liabilities			
Accounts Payable	133,140	149,373	61,058
Short/Current Long-Term Debt	1,730	4,486	48,097
Other Current Liabilities	—	60	8,480
Total Current Liabilities	**134,870**	**153,919**	**117,635**
Long-Term Debt	105,966	147,417	117,397
Other Liabilities	25,656	—	—
Deferred Long-Term Liability Charges	4,038	848	3,913
Minority Interest	—	—	390
Negative Goodwill	—	—	—
Total Liabilities	**270,530**	**302,184**	**239,335**
Stockholders' Equity			
Misc Stocks Options Warrants	—	—	—
Redeemable Preferred Stock	—	—	—
Preferred Stock	—	—	—
Common Stock	310,942	298,255	295,611
Retained Earnings	(233,246)	(191,010)	(55,250)
Treasury Stock	—	—	—
Capital Surplus	—	—	—
Other Stockholders' Equity	1,266	1,426	582
Total Stockholders' Equity	**78,962**	**108,671**	**240,943**
Total Liabilities and SE	**$349,492**	**410,855**	**480,278**

Source: www.krispykreme.com

openness to foreign foods, and doughnut stores are filling a growing demand for the sweet treats that can also be used as gifts.

Krispy Kreme has teamed up with Harrod's department store in London as the place to debut doughnuts in Britain. Americans and the British differ in eating habits and office

EXHIBIT 5   KKD's Top Management

1. Daryl G. Brewster, *President and Chief Executive Officer*
2. Jeffrey L. Jervik, *Executive Vice President of U.S. Operations*
3. Sandra K. Michel, *Executive Vice President and General Counsel*
4. Douglas R. Muir, *Executive Vice President and Chief Financial Officer*
5. Kenneth J. Hudson, *Senior Vice President of Human Resources and Organizational Development*
6. Steven A. Lineberger, *Senior Vice President of Strategic Growth Initiatives*
7. Thomas C. McNeil, *Senior Vice President of Safety and Risk Management*
8. Stanley L. Parker, *Senior Vice President of Strategic Marketing*
9. M. Bradley Wall, *Senior Vice President of Supply Chain*
10. Jeffrey B. Welch, *Senior Vice President of International and Development*

Source: www.krispykreme.com

etiquette. The British are accustomed to their traditional English breakfast of eggs, bacon, and milk. KKD plans to convince the British to replace the biscuit, which is a cookie, with a doughnut for their snack food, and to buy doughnuts by the dozen to take to the office. Many people in Britain do not have cars; therefore they cannot stop by the drive-through on their way to work. Office etiquette also is more formal in Britain and a dozen Krispy Kreme Hot Glazed Original doughnuts would cost about five British pounds, which is about $10.00. Krispy Kreme will also offer the tea-drinking British its own custom brews of coffee.

KKD's largest competitor, Dunkin' Donuts, can be found throughout the world. Dunkin' Donuts currently has locations in Aruba, the Bahamas, Brazil, Brunei, Bulgaria, Canada, Chile, Colombia, the Dominican Republic, Ecuador, Germany, Greece, Guam, Guatemala, Indonesia, Korea, Lebanon, Malaysia, Mexico, New Zealand, Pakistan, Peru, the Philippines, Puerto Rico, Qatar, Saudi Arabia, Spain, Thailand, Turkey, the United States, and the UAE.

Future Outlook

Exhibit 6 and Exhibit 7 detail KKD's income by store type as well as the company's recent store openings and closings. Krispy Kreme plans to continue to open stores internationally in Japan and Spain and increase their presence in countries where they currently operate. But will other cultures love the same sweet, calorie-laden snacks that Americans enjoy? One way for Krispy Kreme to balance its sweet bakery offerings is to consider developing healthier snack-food alternatives. According to experts at the Centers for Disease Control and Prevention based in Atlanta, one out of three adult Americans is overweight. Fast food is considered to be a major contributor to obesity and can be found anywhere, even in hospitals. For example, Krispy Kreme has a dough-

EXHIBIT 6   KKD Domestic versus Global Income (In Thousands)

	Jan. 28, 2007	Jan. 29, 2006	Jan. 30, 2005
	(Loss) from continuing operations:		
Domestic	$ (45,705)	$ (130,411)	$ (131,061)
Foreign	4,680	(6,125)	(16,319)
	$ (41,025)	$ (136,536)	(147,380)
(Loss) from discontinued operations (all domestic)	—	—	(37,847)
Total (loss) before inc. taxes	$ (41,025)	$ (136,536)	$ (185,227)

Source: www.krispykreme.com

EXHIBIT 7   KKD—Number of Factory Stores

	COMPANY	FRANCHISE	TOTAL
FEBRUARY 1, 2004	141	216	357
Opened	24	36	60
Closed	(14)	(7)	(21)
Transferred	24	(24)	—
JANUARY 30, 2005	175	221	396
Opened	3	13	16
Closed	(47)	(42)	(89)
Transferred	(3)	3	—
JANUARY 29, 2006	128	195	323
Opened	—	30	30
Closed	(9)	(48)	(57)
Transferred	(11)	11	—
JANUARY 28, 2007	108	188	296

Source: www.krispykreme.com

nut counter located inside Atlanta's St. Joseph's Hospital. Most fast-food restaurants are revising their menus to include "healthier" choices. Krispy Kreme continues to look for ways to integrate a complete range of products and services; perhaps it should develop a new "low-calorie" doughnut selection. KKD also needs to find new ways to eliminate trans fats in their products.

Determine whether you think KKD should continue to expand globally, and if so, where and how fast, or should the firm be expanding further domestically? Develop a three-year strategic plan for KKD which is trying to recover from several years of weak performance, especially as compared to rival Dunkin' Donuts.

Pilgrim's Pride Corporation — 2007

4

James L. Harbin
Texas A&M University–Texarkana

PPC

www.pilgrimspride.com
With the late December 2006 acquisition of Gold Kist, Pilgrim's Pride had finally leapfrogged Tyson Foods to become the world's leading chicken company in terms of production and the fourth-largest U.S. meat protein company by revenues. Not bad considering that in the dark days of the late 1980s, Bo Pilgrim had offered to sell the company to Tyson. After initially agreeing to terms, Tyson had backed out of the deal. However for the first year ever, Pilgrim's 2006 revenues had decreased and the company's net income was negative $34 million. For the third quarter ended June 30, 2007, Pilgrim's Pride revenues rose 40 percent to $5.45 billion, but their net loss totaled $13.8 million versus a loss of $26.7 million the prior year. Revenue increases reflected higher sales from chicken and turkey products in the United States. However, Pilgrim's Pride is struggling to assimilate its recent Gold Kist acquisition and lowered both its earnings and stock price estimates in October 2007. The company needs a clear strategic plan for the future.

Headquartered in Pittsburg, Texas, Pilgrim's Pride is engaged in the production, processing, and marketing of fresh chicken and further processed and prepared chicken products. It is the largest chicken company in the United States and Puerto Rico and the second-largest in Mexico. With sales of over $5 billion in 2006, Pilgrim's Pride employs approximately 56,500 people and operates 37 processing and 12 prepared-food facilities. Total exports for 2006 were 8 percent of net sales.

Pilgrim's remarkable growth, from one feed store operation 60 years ago to estimated sales of $8 billion in 2007, took place in a largely commodity industry in which, every year for the past 50 years, economists have been predicting doom and gloom. Some of the big issues facing Pilgrim's today are the questionable future growth of chicken consumption, the amount of consolidation the industry has undergone, cost pressures of feed, avian influenza, and many more in an extremely low-profit industry.

Bo Pilgrim's Background and Philosophy
Lonnie "Bo" Pilgrim's pose with a broad-brimmed black pilgrim's hat (and often holding his stuffed chicken, Henrietta) has developed into an established icon; maybe not in the same category as Mickey Mouse, but definitely on par with Colonel Sanders. His story is one of deprivation and determination and then success. Born in northwest Texas in 1928, he was the fourth of seven children. His father died when Bo was nine, and he left home at twelve to live with his grandmother.

Bo has always had an entrepreneurial spirit, from hawking sodas to local factory workers, peddling newspapers, hauling gravel, and sacking groceries—all before he was eighteen—to showing up unannounced in some CEO's office to sell his chicken products today. Bo has always been the ultimate salesperson for him and his company.

Mr. Pilgrim, at 78, still plays a major role in overseeing the direction of the company as its chairman. The Pilgrim family controls approximately 62 percent of the company's voting power. None of Bo's children (two sons and one daughter) have expressed any interest in becoming the company CEO.

When asked about his secret of success, Bo responded, "Take your abilities, season them with experience on the job, and combine that with drive and motivation, and you will be successful. The way to make a difference in your life is to make that *mind-boggling decision not to be average.*"

Visitors to corporate headquarters get parking spaces marked with a picture of a chicken and the words "Pullet in here." The first-floor lobby walls are festooned with more than 300 samples of memorabilia of Pilgrim and his company—wooden thank-you plaques, framed newspaper clippings, and photographs of him with prominent politicians (including President George Bush). In the second-floor executive office suite, representations of chickens are everywhere—there are ceramic chickens, oil paintings of chickens, photographs of chickens, and stuffed chickens. There is a two-story bust of Bo atop the entrance of another office building.

Bo shares three business lessons learned from his experiences in his 2005 book *One Pilgrim's Progress*. First, you have to seize the good opportunities as they come your way, regardless of your strategic plans. Two, you have to coordinate your enterprises as you expand. Each expansion has to fit in the big picture. And three, you have to trust God with orchestrating your master plan. He is a deeply religious man; on any given Sunday, you are apt to find him teaching a Sunday school class, just as he has for the last 50 years.

Vision and Mission

In the original brainstorming session to develop a vision and mission statement for the company, many felt that they might end up with a mission statement rather than a mission. The difference, according to Monty Henderson, then president and CEO, was "that a mission statement becomes very wordy and usually winds up as a long paragraph or two that no one—not even the authors—can remember and usually winds up in a file somewhere. A mission, by contrast, is known by everyone, practiced daily by everyone, and becomes a way of life."

After much discussion about the business, the customers, and the competition, the group came to a consensus that Pilgrim's vision is "to achieve and maintain leadership in each product and service that we provide." To achieve this goal, the group felt that its mission was summed up as follows: "Our job is outstanding customer satisfaction . . . every day." Because of the increased emphasis on the international market, Pilgrim's later amended its vision: "To be a world-class chicken company—better than the best."

Bo Pilgrim's personal vision for the company stretches beyond the continental United States. "The mission behind Pilgrim's is to help save rural America in the United States and the people of Mexico by providing jobs in the production of chickens. They must be versatile, economical, and wholesome chickens to feed the rest of the world. We'll use the best affordable technology and science to improve our systems. That's broader than just making money out of chickens."

Company Growth

Pilgrim's has grown from one livestock feed store in East Texas to what is now the largest chicken producer in America. In 2007, Pilgrim's was named to *Fortune's* "List of America's Most Admired Companies" for the fifth consecutive year. Wal-Mart also honored the company as the 2006 supplier of the year in the food product industry.

Following several small acquisitions in the 1950s and 1960s, Pilgrim's purchased WLR Foods, Inc. in 2001 for $300 million. This expanded their operations from coast to coast, made them the second-largest chicken company and put them back in the turkey business as the fourth-largest turkey company. One analyst described the WLR deal as pricy (Pilgrim's paid about twice per share what WLR stock was trading at when the deal was announced). Another described WLR as a company "going nowhere fast" that would benefit from being absorbed by a bigger and more competitive player.

With the $600 million purchase of ConAgra in 2003, Pilgrim's doubled their size and became the second-largest poultry processor. ConAgra was the largest acquisition in the industry at that time. With the acquisition, Pilgrim's had 15 percent of the market and was twice the size of the number three player. President O. B. Goolsby of Pilgrim's believed that the increased scale would lead to increased prowess to compete more effectively in a consolidating marketplace and that the importance of a wide footprint cannot be overestimated. Some analysts, however, described the acquisition as a dice roll for both companies because of the cyclical nature and the traditional excess capacity of the industry.

Then in 2006 came the Gold Kist takeover. At that time, Gold Kist was the third-largest poultry processor in America. This was a hostile take over involving a four-month proxy battle. Although Gold Kist's management was opposed, the stockholders weren't. Pilgrim's Pride paid a 62 percent premium for Gold Kist over the price of stock on the date of the initial bid. Pilgrim's said that buying Gold Kist would create a bigger company (increasing market share from approximately 16 percent to roughly 25 percent) that could better serve large customers such as Wal-Mart, with more plants in different parts of the country. It also allowed Pilgrim's to enter the big Florida market and be more competitive with foreign poultry producers. After the $1 billion in cash and assumption of $144 million in debt payment for Gold Kist, Moody's Investor Services downgraded Pilgrim's credit rating. Their rationale was "that in addition to the increased debt and leverage, the company will have a difficult time integrating Gold Kist into its own." Peter Abdill, Moody's vice president, stated, "While the acquisition makes strategic sense and is a good addition to Pilgrim's portfolio, the transaction will add a significant amount of leverage to the company at a time when Pilgrim's earnings have been under a lot of pressure." An additional downside of the deal, according to another financial analyst, "was that domestic organic growth prospects would be limited for the combined company."

While mergers and acquisitions can strengthen a company's pricing power, increase distribution capabilities, and ease entry into new markets, many studies show that most—some estimates are 70 percent or more—fail to deliver their intended benefits and destroy economic value in the process. Mergers and acquisitions in the meat industry may be more about economic power than economic efficiency says one industry critic. Often the only people who profit from mergers and acquisitions are key executives and investment bankers. Yet they continue to flourish—in 2007 Chrysler had a number of suitors willing to pay about a tenth of the $40 billion Daimler paid for it not long ago.

Mexico

The company first expanded into Mexico in 1987. In the last ten years, sales to Mexico have doubled. In 2006, Mexican sales were $$419 million or 9 percent of net sales. Prior to the ConAgra acquisition, Mexican sales represented approximately 16 percent of net sales.

In Mexico, where product differentiation has traditionally been limited, product quality, service, and price have been the most critical competitive factors. However, the Mexican market is maturing at an accelerating rate and customers are increasingly selecting value-added products. Although the North American Free Trade Agreement went into effect in 1994, reduced tariffs were to be phrased in on poultry products. On January 1, 2008, the tariff will be zero.

Pilgrim's has the largest U.S. production and distribution capacities near the Mexican border, giving them a strategic advantage. Their distribution network in Mexico serves 29 of the 32 Mexican states, encompassing almost 94 percent of the total population of Mexico.

Competition

While there are other competitors, Pilgrim's number one competitor has been, and continues to be, Tyson Foods. Together they control 50 percent of the U.S. chicken market. Tyson's 2006 net sales were $25.6 billion, of which $8 billion was in chickens. 2006 was a bad year for the whole industry because Hurricane Katrina damaged operations in the South and also because of concerns about bird flu overseas. These issues contributed to a $196 million net income loss for Tyson that year. In part, as a result of that loss, Tyson implemented an aggressive cost-cutting program involving various plant closings, workforce reductions and overhead cuts.

After several "go, no-go" decisions on extending their expertise to other meats, Tyson acquired IBP Inc., the world's largest producer of fresh beef and pork, in an approximate $3 billion-plus deal in 2001. Today, beef accounts for almost half of Tyson's sales, while chicken accounts for one third. Tyson's goal is to become a one-stop shop for protein. The belief is that its customers will be drawn to the ease of buying from one single supplier. Bo Pilgrim, on the other hand, has been quoted as saying, "We won't get far from the chicken."

Broiler Industry

The chicken industry in the United States may be one of the most successful sectors in agriculture. They traditionally operated in cycles of about three years, going from an undersupply to a glutted market and back to an undersupply. This was referred to as the "sell it or smell it" trap.

Industry leaders recognized early on that if they owned the chicken throughout the production cycle—from farm to grocery case—they could reduce manufacturing costs, streamline production, improve quality, and therefore, increase profit margins. Efficiency in chicken production has increase from 1935 when it took 112 days and 4.4 pounds of feed to grow a 2.85-pound chicken, to today's figures of 47 days and 1.95 pounds of feed to grow a 5.0-pound chicken.

This "vertical integration" model of poultry production is used by nearly every major poultry company today. Vertical integration in the poultry industry was listed as one of the top ten events having the greatest impact on the meat industry during the twentieth century. Other top ten events pertinent to the poultry industry were the passage of the Federal Meat Inspection Act (1906), the development of refrigerated rail cars and trucks and the national interstate highway system, the growth of fast-food chains, and the passage of both the Humane Slaughter Act (1958) and the Poultry Products Act (1957).

The growing, slaughtering, and processing of chickens continues to present environmental challenges. Meeting this challenge in a low-profit industry is difficult. According to the CDC, there are an estimated 76 million cases of food-borne illnesses each year in the United States, the vast majority of which are mild and cause symptoms that last a day or two. Some are more serious, leading to 325,000 hospitalizations and 5000 deaths annually. Although disputed by the industry and the U.S. Agriculture Department, a late 2006 report of a survey conducted by *Consumer Reports* stated that 83 percent of chicken sold in the U.S. grocery stores may contain bacteria that cause food-borne illnesses.

Shortly after the dog-food scare of 2006, it was announced that chickens in 38 farms in Indiana had been fed with a similar chemical. That same week, a former Federal Health official, testifying before a Congressional committee, said, "Our food safety security system is broken."

Profitability

Industry profitability is primarily a function of the consumption of chicken and competing meats and the costs of feed grains. The chicken companies have spent much of their energy trying to escape the commodity cycle through marketing, branding, and further processing. Frank Perdue, with his classic commercials, was the first to demonstrate that a company could charge a premium price for a brand-name bird. Today, the biggest producers all play the brand-loyalty game. This leaves the chicken producers in an odd situation; they are commodity concerns trying to behave like consumer-products companies. As Prudential-Bache's John McMillin foretold in the 1980s, "The chicken industry will become better capitalized, more competitive—and less profitable."

Profitability in this industry can be significantly influenced by feed costs, which are affected by a number of factors unrelated to the broiler industry, including legislation that provides discretion to the federal government to set price and income supports for grain. Historically, feed costs have averaged approximately 50 percent of total production costs of nonvalued products and have fluctuated substantially with the price of corn, milo, and soybean meal. By comparison, feed costs typically average approximately 25 percent of total production costs of further processed and prepared chicken products such as nuggets, fillets, and deli products; as a result, increased emphasis on sales of such products by chicken producers reduces the sensitivity of earnings to feed cost movements.

Although feed costs may vary dramatically, the production costs of chicken are not as severely affected by changing feed ingredient prices as are the production costs of beef and pork. Chickens require approximately two pounds of dry feed to produce one pound of meat, compared to cattle and hogs, which require approximately seven and three pounds, respectively, of feed.

Industry Problems

The poultry industry is one beset with multiple common problems. These range from labor recruitment/retention, working conditions, growers who are dissatisfied with their income and contracts, pollution and waste generated throughout the various stages of operations, meat that arrives at the marketplace contaminated with salmonella or listeriosis, and various animal rights groups attempting to impose their views on the meat industry, just to name a few. Taken individually or collectively, these problems result in bad public relations and negative impacts on the bottom line for an industry whose margins are already razor thin.

The industry struggles to find enough cheap, unskilled labor to staff its processing plants. Turnover is extremely high and often runs to 100 percent annually. Alleged use of illegal immigrants in the industry did little to help positive public relations. Solutions are automation and higher wages. Labor makes up only about 10 percent of the total cost of production, meaning that raising wages would result in only minor cost increases to the consumer. But in an industry where two cents a pound can make a difference, no company seems willing to make the first move.

Conditions on the production line can be tough. Injury statistics from the Occupational Safety and Health Administration for 2000 reveal that one out of every seven poultry workers was injured on the job, more than double the average for all private industries. Poultry workers are also 14 times more likely to suffer debilitating injuries from repetitive trauma.

The industry's biggest worry may be microscopic in physical size. The growing and processing of chickens encourages the growth of bacteria such as salmonella and listeriosis. Partly to hold down the price of poultry, the industry has put little effort into producing cleaner chickens, relying instead on consumers to cook the meat thoroughly. In October of 2002, Pilgrim's recalled 27 million pounds of chicken and turkey meat processed at its recently acquired WLR Foods facilities that might have been contaminated with listeria monocytogenes. At that time, it was the largest meat recall in USDA history.

Consolidation in the industry has resulted in the country being carved up into regional monopolies, and these processors can then dictate terms to the growers. The vast majority of growers receive only short-term contracts from the processors; this puts the farmers at a distinct disadvantage when negotiating contract terms. In some cases, growers have received as little as $579 in annual income per 20,000-bird-capacity chicken house.

Changing Supply and Demand

Chicken has grown from a poor man's food to the preferred meat of the world. Few Americans before the 1950s ate much chicken. Per capita poultry consumption was approximately 9 pounds in the early 1950s. U.S. per capita consumption of chicken is now slightly over 100 pounds per person, and we are paying less per pound today than 50 years ago.

Before 1970, most poultry bought by consumers was whole chickens and turkeys, and the export business was almost nonexistent. It would have been difficult to find a restaurant or fast-food outlet selling chicken sandwiches or nuggets. Deboned chicken breasts did not exist. By the early 1980s, consumers preferred cut-up and further-processed chickens to the traditional whole bird. By 2001, chicken exports to foreign markets accounted for approximately 20 percent of total American production with more than $2 billion in sales. It is estimated that U.S. companies own 38 percent of global market share.

Chicken consumption surpassed beef consumption in 1992. Chicken had already surpassed pork consumption in 1985. The USDA estimates that chicken

EXHIBIT 1 **Per Capita Consumption of Poultry and Livestock**

Year	Beef	Pork	Chicken
1970	84.6	55.8	40.3
1975	88.2	42.9	39.0
1980	76.6	57.3	48.0
1982	77.0	49.1	49.6
1985	79.2	51.9	53.1
1990	67.8	49.7	61.5
1992	66.2	52.8	67.5
1995	66.6	51.8	69.5
2000	67.7	51.2	78.0
2005	65.5	50.0	87.0
2008 Est.	64.0	49.5	86.2

Source: Adapted from National Chicken Council, Statistics & Research.

consumption will increase at a 3 percent compounded annual growth rate into the future. Consumption of chicken in Mexico has accelerated from less than 30 pounds in 1989 to almost 50 pounds in 2002. The United States' chicken sales were close to $40 billion in 2007.

The major factors influencing this growth in consumption are consumer awareness of the health and nutritional characteristics of chicken, the price advantage of chicken relative to red meat, and the convenience of further processed and prepared chicken products. This growth has been enhanced by new product forms and packaging that increase convenience and product versatility. A larger, more affluent, mobile population has created a demand for more convenient foods. People are willing to trade dollars for time, and the industry has cashed in by providing value-added products.

While the domestic chicken and other proteins market is relatively mature and likely to grow modestly, the global market is poised for rapid growth. In China, India, and many other nations, as disposable income increases, the U.S. agribusiness industry is well positioned to take advantage of future increases in worldwide food demand. Another thing that bodes well for the American processors is the fact that many global markets prefer dark-meat thighs and drumsticks, while many Americans are willing to pay much higher prices for white breast meat. American processors have also learned—and benefited—from the fact that overseas countries provide a market for low value parts (chicken feet, tails, wingtips, gizzards) at a higher price than Americans are willing to pay. "Upgrading dark-meat sales options is the biggest opportunity for our industry and this company over the next ten years," says O. B. Goolsby, appointed as Pilgrim's president in November of 2003. "We are currently deboning a huge percentage of our white-meat production, leaving us somewhat dependent on what is happening in the dark-meat commodity export markets around the world."

On the downside of doing business overseas in this industry are many problems. Problems like costs of shipping, refrigeration (there are only 1,500 refrigerated trucks in all of India), import duties and taxes all make investment risky overseas.

The Future for Pilgrim's and the Industry

In the next 25 years there will be another 1.5 billion people on the planet and as standards of living improve, people will buy more protein. Per capita consumption of protein is predicted to grow 25 percent in 25 years. In the not too distant future, per capita consumption of chicken could more than double throughout the world. Americans, alone, spent over a billion dollars a day eating out in 2000. With 70 percent of mothers working outside the home and 40 percent not knowing what they will eat as late as four o'clock in the afternoon, meal planning and preparation take a back seat to convenience and eating out. This trend will no doubt be repeated progressively throughout the world.

In America, it could be that the demand for chicken relative to other meats has peaked. Future growth could be limited to population growth and increased demand for value-added items. Both the beef and pork industry have stepped up their ads of "eat more beef" and "the other white meat." It is probably safe to project that the yearly growth in America for chicken will fall to a more modest 4–6 percent range.

Few industries are as vulnerable to events beyond their control as the meat and poultry industry. In addition to the avian flu and the Hurricane Katrina disaster, chicken operators came under intense pressure from costs associated with grain—primarily corn in late 2006 and 2007. Although there are more than 3,500 uses for corn, 60 percent of U.S. corn is used for livestock feed. The price of corn, the main feed for livestock, drove the cost of feeding chickens up 40 percent. As the price of petroleum drives the demand for alternative fuels up, more and more corn is diverted to the production of ethanol. This has created a fuel versus food debate. Dick Bond, CEO of Tyson. says, "We must carefully consider the negative and unintended consequences of overusing grains." According to Bo Pilgrim, "There is no question that the *ill-advised* public policy encouraging corn-based ethanol production has had a significant detrimental effect on our industry, as well as on other meat protein producers that rely on corn as their primary animal feed."

There may be a silver lining of sorts with the rising cost of fuel and feed for meat producers. Animal fat—the stuff that doesn't even get into hot dogs—can be converted into bio-diesel fuel, which can be used in most diesel engines. In mid-2007, Tyson, the largest producer of animal fat, announced a joint project with Conoco Phillips to produce and market diesel fuel for U.S. vehicles using beef, pork, and poultry fat. Companies like Smithfield Foods and Pilgrim's Pride might also benefit from a jump into the fuel industry.

In January of 2007, Pilgrim's announced a 5 percent production cutback to try to strike a better balance between supply and demand. Pilgrim's expects to save $100 million with the Gold Kist acquisition, primarily from optimization of production and distribution facilities as well as other cost savings.

A lot has changed in the chicken industry over the years. At one time there were over 1000 chicken companies in the United States. Today there are just a handful of major producers and a few dozen smaller players. The survivors will continue to be those that are able to respond quickly and decisively to the ever-changing tastes of customers while having the resources necessary to invest in new technology, enhanced food-safety systems, and other processes.

At the end of the day says another analyst, "this is a commodity-based industry and investors have to expect swings." Bo's take is, "Raising chickens is unpredictable, financially speaking."

Prepare a three-year strategic plan for Pilgrim's. Among the many issues facing the company would be questions like the following: Where should they concentrate their efforts now? Should they continue to acquire in order to gain even more clout in the chicken industry? If so, whom might they purchase? Whom could they afford at this time? Or does Pilgrim's need to concentrate, at least in the short run, on maximizing the savings and advantages the Gold Kist acquisition brings them? Should they reconsider entering other meat industries as Tyson has done? How can they best position themselves in the future to regain profitability?

EXHIBIT 2   Key People in Pilgrim's Pride

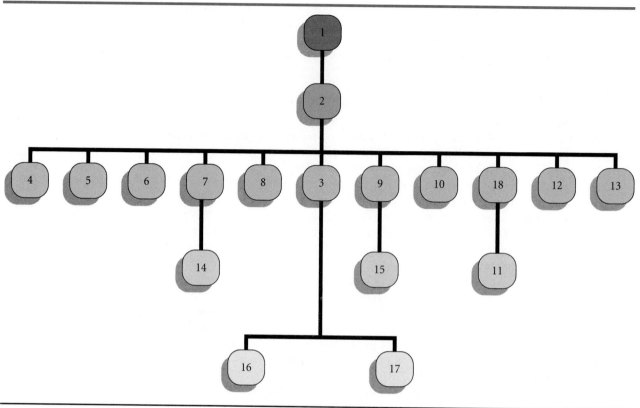

1. Chairman	Lonnie (Bo) Pilgrim
2. CEO, President, and Director	O. B. Goolsby, Jr.
3. COO	J. Clinton Rivers
4. EVP, CFO, Sec. Tres., and Dir.	Richard A. Cogdill
5. EVP, Human Resources	Jane T. Brookshire
6. EVP, Cage Ready and Supply Operations	Robert L. Hendrix
7. EVP, Prepared Foods	Walter F. Shafer III
8. EVP, Fresh Foodservice	Joseph Moran
9. EVP, Sales & Marketing	Robert A. Wright
10. VP, Government Affairs	A. Wayne Lord
11. VP, Corporate Communications	Gary L Rhodes
12. VP, Investor Relations	Kathy M. Costner
13. VP, Research and Development	Ted Davis
14. VP, Quality Assurance, Prepared Foods	John Southerland
15. VP, Marketing	Dan Emery
16. President, Mexico Operations	Alejandro M. Mann
17. President, Puerto Rico Operations	Hector L. Mattei-Calvo
18. Director, Corporate Communications	Ray Atkinson

EXHIBIT 3

Consolidated Statements of Income (Loss)
Pilgrim's Pride Corporation

(In thousands except per share date)	Three Years Ended September 30		
	2006	2005	2004
Net Sales	$ 5,235,565	$ 5,666,275	$ 5,363,723
Cost and Expenses:			
Cost of sales	4,937,965	4,921,076	4,794,415
Cost of sales-restructuring		–	64,160
Non-recurring recoveries	–	–	(23,891)
	4,937,965	4,921,076	4,834,684
Gross Profit	297,600	745,199	529,039
Selling, general and administrative	294,598	309,387	255,802
Other restructuring charges	–	–	7,923
	294,598	309,387	263,725
Operating Income	3,002	435,812	265,314
Other Expense (Income):			
Interest expense	50,601	49,585	54,436
Interest income	(10,048)	(5,653)	(2,307)
Foreign exchange (gain) loss	144	(474)	205
Miscellaneous, net	(1,378)	(11,169)	(4,445)
	39,349	32,289	56,779
Income (Loss) Before Income Taxes	(36,317)	403,523	208,535
Income Tax Expense (Benefit)	(2,085)	138,544	80,195
Net Income (Loss)	$ (34,232)	$ 264,979	$ 128,340
Net Income (Loss) Per Common Share-Basic and Diluted	$ (0.51)	$ 3.98	$ 2.05

See Notes to Consolidated Financial statements

EXHIBIT 4 Pilgrim's Pride Balance Sheets (In Thousands)

PERIOD ENDING	September 30, 2006	October 1, 2005	October 2, 2004
Assets			
Current Assets			
Cash and Cash Equivalents	$ 156,404	132,567	38,165
Short-Term Investments	21,246	–	–
Net Receivables	309,604	313,635	330,764
Inventory	585,940	527,329	609,997
Other Current Assets	32,480	25,884	38,302
Total Current Assets	1,105,674	999,415	1,017,228
Long-Term Investments	115,375	304,593	–
Property, Plant and Equipment	1,154,994	1,154,097	1,178,675
Goodwill	–	–	–
Intangible Assets	–	–	–
Accumulated Amortization	–	–	–
Other Assets	50,825	53,798	50,086
Deferred Long-Term Asset Charges	–	–	–
Total Assets	$ 2,426,868	2,511,903	2,245,989

continued

EXHIBIT 4 Pilgrim's Pride Balance Sheets (In Thousands)—continued

PERIOD ENDING	September 30, 2006	October 1, 2005	October 2, 2004
Liabilities			
Current Liabilities			
Accounts Payable	$ 566,515	586,211	625,074
Short/Current Long-Term Debt	10,322	8,603	8,428
Other Current Liabilities	–	–	–
Total Current Liabilities	576,837	594,814	633,502
Long-Term Debt	554,876	518,863	535,866
Other Liabilities	–	–	–
Deferred Long-Term Liability Charges	175,869	173,232	152,455
Minority Interest	1,958	1,396	1,210
Negative Goodwill	–	–	–
Total Liabilities	**1,309,540**	**1,288,305**	**1,323,033**
Stockholders' Equity			
Misc Stocks Options Warrants	–	–	–
Redeemable Preferred Stock	–	–	–
Preferred Stock	–	–	–
Common Stock	665	668	668
Retained Earnings	646,750	753,527	492,542
Treasury Stock	–	(1,568)	(1,568)
Capital Surplus	469,779	471,344	431,662
Other Stockholders' Equity	134	(373)	(348)
Total Stockholders' Equity	1,117,328	1,223,598	922,956
Total Liab and SE	$ 2,426,868	2,511,903	2,245,989
Net Tangible Assets	$ 1,117,328	$ 1,223,598	$ 922,956

Source: Adapted from http://finance.yahoo.com.

EXHIBIT 5 Pilgrim Pride's Sales by Segments (In Thousands)

	September 30, 2006	October 1, 2005	October 2, 2004
Net Sales to Customers:			
Chicken:			
United States	$ 4,098,403	$ 4,411,269	$ 4,091,706
Mexico	418,745	403,353	362,442
Subtotal	$ 4,517,148	$ 4,814,622	$ 4,454,148
Turkey	130,901	204,838	286,252
Other Products:			
United States	570,510	626,056	600,091
Mexico	17,006	20,759	23,232
Subtotal	587,516	646,815	623,323
Total	$ 5,235,565	$ 5,666,275	$ 5,363,723
Operating Income (Loss)			
Chicken:			
United States	$ 28,619	$ 405,662	$ 329,694

continued

EXHIBIT 5   Pilgrim Pride's Sales by Segments (In Thousands)—continued

	September 30, 2006	October 1, 2005	October 2, 2004
Mexico	(17,960)	39,809	(7,619)
Subtotal	10,659	445,471	322,075
Turkey	(15,511)	(22,539)	(96,839)
Other Products:			
United States	6,216	8,250	35,969
Mexico	1,638	4,630	4,033
Subtotal	7,854	12,880	40,002
Non-recurring recoveries:	–	–	76
Total	3,002	435,812	265,314

	September 30, 2006	October 2, 2005	October 2, 2004
U.S. Chicken Sales:			
Prepared Foods:			
Foodservice	$1,567,297	$1,622,901	$1,647,904
Retail	308,486	283,392	213,775
Total Prepared Foods	1,875,783	1,906,293	1,861,679
Fresh Chicken:			
Foodservice	1,388,451	1,509,189	1,328,883
Retail	496,560	612,081	653,798
Total Fresh Chicken	1,885,011	2,121,270	1,982,681
Export and Other:			
Export:			
Prepared Foods	64,338	59,473	34,735
Chicken	257,823	303,150	212,611
Total Export	322,823	362,623	247,346
Other Chicken By-Products	15,448	21,083	-
Total Export and Other	337,609	383,706	247,346
Total U.S. Chicken	4,098,403	4,411,269	4,091,706
Mexico Chicken Sales:	418,745	403,353	362,442
Total Chicken Sales	4,517,148	4,814,622	4,454,148
U.S. Turkey Sales:			
Foodservice	30,269	73,908	120,676
Retail	96,968	125,741	154,289
	127,237	199,649	274,965
Export and Other	3,664	5,189	11,287
Total U.S. Turkey Sales	130,901	204,838	286,252
Other Products:			
United States	570,510	626,056	600,091
Mexico	17,006	20,759	23,232
Total Other Products	587,516	646,815	623,323
Total Net Sales	$5,235,565	$5,666,275	$5,363,723

Source: Pilgrim's Pride, *2006 Annual Report*, pp. 12, 100.

5 Coca-Cola Company — 2007

Alen Badal
The Union Institute

KO

www.coca-cola.com

Employing about 71,000 people worldwide in over 200 countries, Coca-Cola Company (Coke) is the world's largest beverage company with products that include Coca-Cola, Diet Coke, Sprite, and Fanta. Coke produces about 400 brands consisting of over 2,600 beverage products, such as water, juice and juice drinks, sports drinks, energy drinks, teas, and coffees. Coke products are distributed through restaurants, grocery markets, street vendors, and others, all of which sell to the end users: consumers, who consume in excess of 1.4 billion servings daily. In the summer of 2007, Coke acquired Energy Brands, Inc., which produces Glaceau—a vitamin water ranked second behind PepsiCo's Propel in the fitness market—for $4.1 billion. Coke is concerned that the trend toward more healthy eating and drinking will hurt sales of their traditional sugar and sugar-substitute–based drinks.

Headquartered in Atlanta, Georgia and founded in 1886, Coke posted revenues of $24 billion in 2006, up 4.2 percent from 2005. Net income was $5.08 billion, also up 4.2 percent from 2005. Coca-Cola Enterprises reported third quarter 2007 earnings in line with estimates, as price increases driven by rising aluminum and sweetener costs cut into demand in North America. Coke's net income rose 25.8 percent for its largest bottler, but earnings from operations fell as shipment volume weakened in both North America and Europe. Coke posted net income of $268 million, or 55 cents per share, for the third quarter, compared with $213 million, or 44 cents per share, a year earlier. Net operating revenue rose 3.6 percent to $5.41 billion. The company shipped 2.5 percent fewer cases during the quarter, compared with a year earlier, while costs rose 6 percent and price per case rose 4 percent, excluding the impact of the weaker dollar.

The company's income statements and balance sheets are provided in Exhibits 1 and 2.

EXHIBIT 1 **Coca-Cola Company Income Statements (In Thousands)**

Period Ending	Dec. 31, 2006	Dec. 31, 2005	Dec. 31, 2004
Total Revenue	$24,088,000	23,104,000	21,962,000
Cost of Revenue	8,164,000	8,195,000	7,638,000
Gross profit	**15,924,000**	**14,909,000**	**14,324,000**
Operating Expenses	—	—	—
Research & Development	—	—	—
Selling, Gen & Admin	9,616,000	8,824,000	8,626,000
Non-Recurring	—	—	—
Others	—	—	—
Total Operating Exp	—	—	—

continued

EXHIBIT 1 Coca-Cola Company Income Statements (In Thousands)— continued

Period Ending	Dec. 31, 2006	Dec. 31, 2005	Dec. 31, 2004
Operating Income or Loss	**6,308,000**	**6,085,000**	**5,698,000**
Income from Cont Oper	—	—	—
Total Other Inc/Exp Net	388,000	845,000	720,000
EBIT	6,798,000	6,930,000	6,418,000
Interest Expense	220,000	240,000	196,000
Income Before Tax	6,578,000	6,690,000	6,222,000
Income Tax Expense	1,498,000	1,818,000	1,375,000
Minority Interest	—	—	—
Net Inc. from Cont. Ops	5,080,000	4,872,000	4,847,000
Non-Recurring Events	—	—	—
Discont. Oper	—	—	—
Extraordinary Items	—	—	—
Effect of Acct Changes	—	—	—
Other Items	—	—	—
Net Income	**$5,080,000**	**4,872,000**	**4,847,000**

Source: www.finance.yahoo.com

Divisions

The Coca-Cola Company's (Coke's) operating segments include (1) Africa, (2) East and South East Asia and Pacific Rim, (3) European Union, (4) Latin America, (5) North America, 6) North Asia, Eurasia, and the Middle East, and 7) bottling investments. Not all soft drink products/flavors of the company are available in all the operating groups.

Africa

Africa's largest private-sector employer with 55,000 employees, Coke receives annual awards as the favorite drink in South Africa. Headquartered in Johannesburg, South

EXHIBIT 2 Coca-Cola Company Balance Sheets (In Thousands)

Period Ending	Dec. 31, 2006	Dec. 31, 2005	Dec. 31, 2004
Assets			
Current Assets			
Cash & Cash Equiv	$2,440,000	4,701,000	6,707,000
Short-Term Invest	150,000	66,000	61,000
Net Receivables	2,704,000	2,281,000	2,171,000
Inventory	1,641,000	1,424,000	1,420,000
Other Current Assets	1,506,000	1,778,000	1,735,000
Total Current Assets	**8,441,000**	**10,250,000**	**12,094,000**
Long-Term Investments	6,783,000	6,922,000	6,252,000
Property, Plant & Equip	6,903,000	5,786,000	6,091,000
Goodwill	1,403,000	1,047,000	1,097,000
Intangible Assets	3,732,000	2,774,000	2,739,000
Accumulated Amortization	—	—	—
Other Assets	2,533,000	2,648,000	3,054,000
Def Long-Term Asset Charges	168,000	—	—
Total Assets	**29,963,000**	**29,427,000**	**31,327,000**

continued

EXHIBIT 2   Coca-Cola Company Balance Sheets (In Thousands)—continued

Period Ending	Dec. 31, 2006	Dec. 31, 2005	Dec. 31, 2004
Liabilities			
Current Liabilities			
Accounts Payable	5,622,000	5,290,000	4,751,000
Short/Current	3,268,000	4,546,000	6,021,000
Long-Term Debt			
Other Current Liabilities	—	—	199,000
Total Current Liabilities	**8,890,000**	**9,836,000**	**10,971,000**
Long-Term Debt	1,314,000	1,154,000	1,157,000
Other Liabilities	1,873,000	1,730,000	2,814,000
Deferred Long-Term	608,000	352,000	450,000
Liability Charges			
Minority Interest	358,000	—	—
Negative Goodwill	—	—	—
Total Liabilities	**13,043,000**	**13,072,000**	**15,392,000**
Stockholders' Equity			
Misc Stock Opt Warrants			
Redeemable Pref Stock			
Preferred Stock			
Common Stock	878,000	877,000	875,000
Retained Earnings	33,468,000	31,299,000	29,105,000
Treasury Stock	(22,118,000)	(19,644,000)	(17,625,000)
Capital Surplus	5,983,000	5,492,000	4,928,000
Other Stockholders' Equity	(1,291,000)	(1,669,000)	(1,348,000)
Total Stockholders' Equity	$16,920,000	16,355,000	15,935,000
Total Liabilities and SE	**$29,963,000**	**$29,427,000**	**$31,327,000**

Source: www.finance.yahoo.com

Africa, this Coke segment also has a large office in Cairo, Egypt. As indicated in Exhibit 3, Coke's operating revenues in percentage terms dropped from 4.8 percent to 4.6 percent in 2006—from the Africa division.

East and South Asia and Pacific Rim

Coke experienced a 5 percent unit case volume decrease in 2006 in their East and South Asia and Pacific Rim division, as indicated in Exhibit 4. Declining Coke sales in India and the Philippines were a problem in 2006. Affordability and availability of Coke products is what hurt the business in the Philippines. Coke recently acquired Coca-Cola Bottlers Philippines, Inc. to address the challenge. This division benefited from the successful 2006 launch of Coca-Cola Zero in Australia and Thailand.

European Union

The 2006 FIFA (Fédération Internationale de Football Association) World Cup in Germany was a success for Coke with the "It's Your Heimspiel—Make It Real!" campaign. This division had a 6 percent unit case volume growth in 2006 versus 2005. Success factors of the region have been a combination of new products, innovative packaging, and collaborating with customers. A few of Coke's powerful brands in Europe include, Aquarius, Nestea, and Powerade. Coke recently acquired mineral water company Apollinaris (Germany) and Traficante (Italy) to add to its existing five water-brand lineup of Ciel, Valser, Toppur, Kropla Beskidu, and Dasani, which is available in four flavors.

EXHIBIT 3   Coca-Cola Company Net Operating Revenues by Segment

Year Ended December 31	2006	2005	2004
Africa	4.6%	4.8%	4.4%
East, South Asia & Pacific Rim	3.3	3.1	3.2
European Union	14.6	17.8	18.0
Latin America	10.3	8.9	8.2
North America	29.1	28.9	29.5
North Asia, Eurasia & Middle East	16.5	17.7	17.9
Bottling Investments	21.2	18.4	18.3
Corporate	0.4	0.4	0.5

Note: The operating segment is as a percentage of the company net operating revenues as of the date/years above.
Source: www.thecoca-colacompany.com

In collaboration with Apple iTunes, Coke is involved in a digital program that focuses on youth. Sensitivity marketing, such as the company's commitment not to advertise to target audiences under the age of 12 has gained the respect of the European Commission.

Latin America

Coke's top three markets include, one, the United States; two, Mexico; and three, Brazil. The beverage portfolio gained 7 percentage points in 2006 with the company looking to expand its product lines. Coke's focus on Latin America is on adding more water, juice, and juice/sports drinks. The company recently acquired Jugos del Valle, S.A.B de C.V. to strengthen their presence in this region with more juice beverages.

Coke of late has focused on more nutritional offerings, such as Minute Maid Forte in Mexico, flavored water in Colombia, and 100% Cepita Juice in Argentina. Coke is relying on its digital marketing platform in Latin America to build and strengthen its relationship with consumers, which has registered more than 5 million visitors in Mexico and Brazil.

North America

The company has been successful in its implementation of "MyCokeRewards," which involved about 3.5 million participating subjects and where greater than 1.5 million rewards were claimed. The program was bilingual and Internet-based. Coke expanded this program in 2007. According to *Le Monde*, Coke products comprise 70 percent of the sodas drunk in Mexico!

EXHIBIT 4   Coca-Cola Company Volume Operating Segments

	Percentage Change			
	2006 vs. 2005 Unit Cases/Gallons		2005 vs. 2004 Unit Cases/Gallons	
Year Ended December 31				
Worldwide	4%	4%	4%	4%
International	6	5	5	4
Africa	4	3	—	7
East, South Asia & Pacific Rim	(5)	(4)	(4)	(6)
European Union	6	4	—	—
Latin America	7	7	6	6
North America	—	—	2	1
North Asia, Eurasia & Middle East	11	7	15	10
Bottling Investments	16	N/A	6	N/A

Note: Bottling Investments segment data reflects unit case volume growth for consolidated bottlers only. Geographic segment data reflects unit case volume growth for all bottlers in the applicable geographic areas, both consolidated and unconsolidated.
Source: www.thecoca-colacompany.com

Coke is test marketing coffee/tea—dispensing technology via the Far Coast Brand, which is a concept store that first opened in Toronto, Canada in 2006. They launched a calorie-burning beverage called Enviga and nationally launched Vault in 2006, which is an energy soda. Coke has a strong leadership team headed by CEO Isadell as featured in Exhibit 5.

North Asia, Eurasia, and the Middle East

This division in 2006 produced an 11 percent unit case volume increase for Coke. There are approximately 10,000 Coke employees in Russia, which is one of the country's largest foreign-based firms. The Russian market performed strongly for Coke in 2006 and the company acquired the Multon juice operation to expand their Russian beverage portfolio. Coke is the top seller of nonalcoholic beverages in Russia with a 22 percent unit case volume growth in 2006.

China is a huge Coke customer as well and yielded a 15 percent unit case volume growth in 2006. Coke recently purchased Kerry Beverages Limited, which was one of the largest bottlers in China. The Turkish market was also strong for Coke in 2006, which more than doubled in unit case volume over the last 10 years. Coke sales in Japan did not meet company expectations in 2006.

Bottling Investments

Coke is increasing investment in its bottling investments, front-end capability, equipment, and people/training. This segment has performed well for Coke in recent years. Coke recently became the number one German bottler. Coke has focused on route-to-market design and optimization of the infrastructure in its bottling operations in India. Coke recently acquired Kerry Beverages Limited and Apollinaris GmbH.

EXHIBIT 5 Coca-Cola Company Executive Officers

Organizational chart based on info below

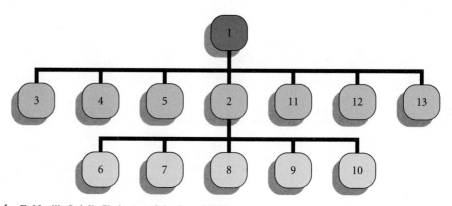

1. E. Neville Isdell, Chairman of the Board/CEO
2. Muhtar Kent, President & COO
3. Irial Finan, EVP & President Bottling Invest/Supply Chain
4. Gary P. Fayard, CFO and EVP
5. Mary E. Minnick, EVP & President MKT Strategy/Innovation
6. Ahmet Bozer, President of the Eurasia Group
7. Dominique Reiniche, President European Union Market
8. Alexander B. Cummings, President of the African Group
9. Jose Octavio Reyes, President Latin America Group
10. Glenn G. Jordan, President of the Pacific Group
11. Geoffrey J. Kelly, SVP & General Counsel
12. Cynthia P. McCaque, SVP & Director of Human Resources
13. Thomas G. Mattin, SVP & Director Public Affairs/Communication
14. Danny L. Strickland, SVP Consumer Innovation/R&D Officer
15. J. Alexander M. Douglas Jr. SVP & President N. America Group

Coke's long-term bottling strategy is to reduce ownership interests in bottlers and/or sell the company's interests to investee bottlers. Prime investees where Coke has no controlling ownership interest at year-end 2006 include:

1. Coca-Cola Enterprises Inc. (CCE)—Coke owns approximately 35 percent of this company which is the world's largest bottler of Coke beverages. In 2006, sales of syrups, concentrates, and finished products by the company to CCE were approximately $5.4 billion. In 2006, CCE produced approximately 60 percent of the unit case volume for Coca-Cola.
2. Coca-Cola Hellenic Bottling Company S.A. (Coca-Cola HBC)—Coke owns approximately 23 percent of this company, which bottles Coke products in Armenia, Austria, Bulgaria, Nigeria, Poland, and other countries. In 2006, 44 percent of the business was conducted for Coca-Cola Company.
3. Coca-Cola FEMSA, S.A.B. de C.V. (Coca-Cola FEMSA)—Coke owns approximately 32 percent of this company; 62 percent of the business was conducted for Coke. A sample of the countries served include, Colombia, Mexico, Argentina, and Brazil.
4. Coca-Cola Amatil Limited (Coca-Cola Amatil)—Coke owns approximately 32 percent of this company; 50 percent of the business is for Coke. Some countries served by this division include, New Zealand, South Korea, and Australia.
5. Other Interests include ready-to-drink tea and coffee businesses with Nestle. Products of this division are sold not only in the United States but also 63 other countries, except Japan. As a result of the proposed break-off between Coca-Cola and Nestle around the tea business, Coca-Cola could now enter Japan and other countries with the tea business.

Coke recently purchased Odwalla at a price that is considered a bargain: $186 million. Coke also just purchased Fuze for $250 million, which supported their non-carbonated portfolio. International revenues are critical for the company as its North America revenues amount to only 28 percent of total revenues. Exhibits 3 and 4 list the company's volume operating changes in its segments and the net operating revenues by segments.

Competitors

The Coca-Cola Company has two major rivals: PepsiCo and Cadbury Schweppes PLC. It's interesting to note that PepsiCo has more than double the employees as Coca-Cola, as listed in Exhibit 6. Groupe Danone competes to a lesser degree with Coke. The number three soft drink producer, Cadbury Schweppes PLC (behind Coca-Cola and PepsiCo Inc.), is a diversified company that produces and markets beverages, chocolate, and chewing gum. Cadbury plans to divest its beverage division in 2007. Hershey Foods has expressed interest as well as various private-equity firms.

PepsiCo

PepsiCo (www.pepsico.com) is a fierce competitor in the beverage industry's two fastest growing categories: water and sports drinks. The company's portfolio contains the number one water brand, Aquafina, and the leading sports drink brand Gatorade. PepsiCo leads in the bottled tea market with Brisk, co-marketed with Lipton. PepsiCo has its own coffee product, Frappuccino, marketed in a joint-venture with Starbucks. PepsiCo doubled its Gatorade sales in the past five years.

PepsiCo obtains 60 percent of its revenues from its snack division. The division has succeeded in these health-conscious times with a campaign called Smart Spot that emphasizes "better for you" products. These products meet the Food and Drug Administration and the National Academy of Sciences nutritional criteria.

PepsiCo has tailored brands that have been very successful in different countries, such as crab and duck flavored chips available in China and lentil-based snacks available in India. Perhaps the creative marketing strategies stem from the company's home-grown managers. Emerging markets, such as Mexico, China, Russia, and Brazil, are targeted by the company to provide affordable snacks financially.

PepsiCo recently ranked #19 among America's most admired companies, while ranking #10 as the world's most admired company. PepsiCo consists of approximately

EXHIBIT 6 Direct Competitor Comparison

	KO	CSG	PEP	Industry
Market Cap	$111.18B	26.33B	103.10B	2.21B
Employees	71,000	70,000	168,000	1.40K
Qtrly Rev Growth	6.90%	7.80%	2.80%	6.60%
Revenue	$24.09B	14.57B	35.14B	1.43B
Gross Margin	66.12%	14.00%	55.14%	40.48%
EBITDA	$7.86B	2.43B	8.46B	152.55M
Oper Margins	26.97%	13.24%	18.33%	5.26%
Net Income	$5.08B	1.03B	5.63B	23.24M
EPS	$2.162	4.39	3.344	0.63
P/E	$22.21	11.56	18.82	23.01
PEG (5 yr expected)	2.34	2.48	1.75	2.34
P/S	4.63	1.82	2.98	1.27

CSG= Cadbury Schweppes PLC

PEP= PepsiCo, Inc.

Industry= Beverages-Soft Drinks

Source: finance.yahoo.com

168,000 employees and had 2006 revenues of more than $35 billion. PepsiCo is comprised of Frito-Lay North America, PepsiCo Beverages North America, PepsiCo International, and Quaker Foods North America. The company's brands are available in about 200 markets, which generate sales of about $92 billion. While PepsiCo brands have existed for more than 100 years, the corporation was founded in 1965 by way of a merger of Pepsi-Cola and Frito-Lay. Tropicana was added in 1998, when PepsiCo merged with the Quaker Oats Company. Gatorade is also an important product in the company's portfolio.

PepsiCo conducts its business in North America, Latin America, Europe, the Middle East, Africa, and Asia Pacific. Even though sales have declined for PepsiCo domestically, overseas revenues have been strong particularly in the Middle East, Argentina, China, and Brazil. Frito-Lay is the largest profit source of late for the company. The international market has served the snack division well with operating profit rising 26 percent and snack volume up 9 percent in 2006. Mexico and Russia were two strong contributing markets for PepsiCo.

PepsiCo's beverage volume increased 7 percent in the Middle East, Argentina, China, and Brazil in 2006. The company's Frito-Lay North American operation yielded an increase of 8 percent profit with snack volume rising 3 percent attributed to new products and improved Doritos brand sales.

Cadbury Schweppes PLC

Cadbury Schweppes PLC (www.cadburyschweppes.com) is the world's largest confectionery company and has a strong regional beverage presence in the Americas and Australia. The company dates back over 200 years with brands such as Cadbury, Schweppes, Halls, Trident, Dr Pepper, Snapple, Trebor, Dentyne, 7Up, Bubblicious, and Bassett, employing approximately 60,000 associates. The company's brand icons include Mott's, Canada Dry, Halls, Trident, Dentyne, Bubblicious, Trebor, Bassett, Dr Pepper, 7Up, and Snapple. The company was the winner of Britain's most admired award company in 2004.

Groupe Danone

Groupe Danone (www.danone.com) in 2005 shared first place worldwide in bottled water (volume) selling nearly 20 billion liters and 70 percent of its sales were in emerging markets. Danone's primary brand in bottled water is Evian. Danone sells flavored waters and focuses on health-conscious consumers. One brand is Levite, which is a big success in

Mexico. The company continues to add new drinks in different markets, such as Taillefine Fiz in France, which is a zero-calorie soda that has achieved a number two ranking in the French low-calorie segment.

Soft Drink Industry

The soft drink industry primarily consists of PepsiCo, Coca Cola Company, and Cadbury Schweppes PLC. Federal regulations may prohibit PepsiCo and Coke from bidding for Cadbury's carbonated soft drink business. Analysts however believe the brand Snapple, which Cadbury sells, would be a good fit for Coke. PepsiCo would likely benefit most from acquiring Cadbury's Mexican assets with such strong brands as Squirt, Crush, and Canada Dry.

Since Coke and Nestle are parting ways on selling tea in the United States, this may open doors for PepsiCo. Bottled tea is one of the fastest growing drinks in the industry. The 50-50 joint venture between Nestle and Coca-Cola was established in 2001 known as the Beverage Partners Worldwide, but now is proposed to come to an end. Coke's North America segment revenues have been increased from 2004–2006, as indicated in Exhibit 7.

The rising cost of raw materials such as corn, oranges, and fuel/electricity has hurt the beverage industry. The price of corn increased 57 percent from December 2005 to December 2006 as a result of the growing demand for ethanol and other pressures. The price of orange juice increased by more than 60 percent in 2006 on the New York Board of Trade due to hurricane damage in the state of Florida.

Water is the main substance in the manufacturing of soft drinks. The limitation of water in some parts of the world causes systems to purify water to be utilized, resulting in an increase in manufacturing costs per unit. The United States is a leader among countries experiencing problems with obesity. Many states now ban the selling of some soft drink brands in public schools due to obesity issues among youth. Moreover, the use of some ingredients in Coke products may be hazardous to one's health and regulations may soon require warning labels. The low value of the dollar is also problematic in a global environment. Coke derives approximately 72 percent of their revenues from outside the United States. Exhibit 8 displays Coke's International versus United States net operating revenues. A majority of Coke's revenues come from its international division.

The Future

The two words Pepsi and Coke are often used interchangeably by many consumers expressing their interest in a soft drink. There is no doubt that both soft drink manufacturers are pleased their brand is used to communicate the need and/or want of a soft drink by name. However, which company's level of consumer loyalty outweighs the other?

Marketing snacks and soft drinks is where Coke may find itself at a disadvantage considering the subsidiary divisions that PepsiCo owns. Should Coke strive to enter the snack business from which its rival PepsiCo derives so much revenue? Develop a three-year strategic plan to assess two identified strategies for COO Kent to consider implementing.

EXHIBIT 7   Coca-Cola Company Operating Segment Total Net Revenues (In $ Millions)

Segment	Africa	East, South Asia, and Pacific Rim	European Union	Latin America	North America	North Asia, Eurasia, and Middle East	Bottling Investment	Corporate	Eliminations	Consolidated
2006	$1,140	$872	$4,364	$2,616	$7,029	$4,123	$5,198	$93	$(1,347)	$24,088
2005	$1,120	$779	$4,911	$2,158	$6,676	$4,219	$4,262	$83	$(1,104)	$23,104
2004	$971	$815	$4,686	$1,847	$6,423	$3,981	$3,975	$101	$(1,057)	$21,742

Source: www.thecoca-colacompany.com *(Form 10K)*

EXHIBIT 8   Coca-Cola Company Geographic Data (In $ Millions)

Year Ended December 31	2006	2005	2004
Net operating revenues:			
United States	$6,662	$6,299	$6,084
International	$17,426	$16,805	$15,658
Net operating revenues	$24,088	$23,104	$21,742
Property, plant and equipment—net:			
United States	$2,607	$2,309	$2,371
International	$4,296	$3,522	$3,720
Property, plant and equipment—net	$6,903	$5,831	$6,091

Source: www.thecoca-colacompany.com *(Form 10K)*

References

www.thecoca-colacompany.com
The *Wall Street Journal*–Europe, March 31–April 1, 2007
The *Wall Street Journal*, February 9, 2007
Le Monde Journal (French), January 29, 2006
Fortune magazine, March 19, 2007
http://biz.yahoo.com, March 27, 2007
http://yahoo.reuters.com, March 27, 2007
http://articles.moneycentral.msn.com/Investing/CompanyFocus/
    PepsiPopsWithASnackFoodEmpire.aspx
http://articles.moneycentral.msn.com/Investing/StreetPatrol/
    CocaColaSharesTheRealThing.aspx
http://in.ibtimes.com/articles/20070428/coke-eyes-energy-brands-glaceau-for-3-billion-
    tatas-to-gain.htm

Anheuser-Busch Companies, Inc. — 2007

6

Alen Badal
The Union Institute

BUD

www.anheuser-busch.com

In an era when obesity is on the rise (beer bellies) and drinking trends have gone from beer to wine, Anheuser-Busch Companies, Inc. (ABI) finds itself needing to change in order to ensure "This bud's for you!" The Budweiser brand was first introduced in 1876, but it did not sell well in 2006. Neither did the company's Michelob brand. But ABI's imported brands such as Bass and Stella are doing very well. Total ABI revenues in 2006 were $15.7 billion, nearly the same as the prior year, and shareholders are not pleased. ABI's net income is down 12.7 percent from two years prior, as indicated in Exhibit 1.

ABI recently tested Jekyll & Hyde, a distilled spirit that can be served as a layered shot. This product has provided the company with a better understanding of the distribution process of a liquor-based product. The company has also recently invested in Spykes, a flavored shot beverage, but soon after (May 2007) stopped producing the product because of its appeal to underage drinkers and its weak performance (sales). Most of the pressure to cease production of Spykes came from advocacy groups and state attorneys who accused ABI of targeting underage drinkers. ABI also collaborates with Hansen Natural Corporation to distribute energy drinks.

ABI's long-term debt exceeds $7.6 billion as seen in Exhibit 2. This number, coupled with a Goodwill number of over $1.3 billion on the balance sheet concerns top management.

EXHIBIT 1 Anheuser-Busch Income Statement (In Thousands)

Period Ending	Dec. 31, 06	Dec. 31, 05	Dec. 31, 04
Total Revenue	$15,717,100	15,035,700	14,934,200
Cost of Revenue	10,165,000	9,579,500	8,982,500
Gross Profit	5,552,100	5,456,200	5,951,700
SG&I	2,832,500	2,730,200	2,590,700
Non-Recurring	–	105,000	–
Operating Inc. or Loss	2,719,600	2,621,000	3,361,000
Income from Cont-Operations	(9,000)	5,100	43,400
EBIT	2,710,600	2,626,100	3,404,400
Interest Expense	433,700	434,600	405,000
Income Before Tax	2,276,900	2,191,500	2,999,400
Income Tax Exp	900,500	850,400	1,163,200
Minority Interest	588,000	–	–
Net Inc. from Cont. Ops.	1,965,200	1,839,200	2,240,300
Net Income	$1,965,200	$1,839,200	$2,240,300

Source: www.finance.yahoo.com

EXHIBIT 2   **Anheuser-Busch Balance Sheet**

Period Ending	December 31, 06	December 31, 05	December 31, 04
Assets			
Current Assets			
Cash & Cash Equiv.	$219,200	225,800	228,100
Short-Term Invest.	–	–	–
Net Receivables	720,200	681,400	696,100
Inventory	694,900	654,500	690,300
Other Current Assets	195,200	197,000	203,900
Total Current Assets	1,829,500	1,758,700	1,818,400
Long-Term Investments	3,680,300	3,448,200	3,150,200
Property, Plant & Equip.	8,916,100	9,041,600	8,847,400
Goodwill	1,317,500	1,011,800	984,100
Intangible Assets	229,700	220,800	207,800
Accumulated Amortiz.	–	–	–
Other Assets	584,100	1,073,900	1,165,500
Deferred Long-Term Asset Charges	–	–	–
Total Assets	16,377,200	16,555,000	16,173,400
Liabilities			
Current Liabilities			
Accounts Payable	2,027,200	1,780,800	1,764,300
Short/Current Long-Term Debt	–	–	–
Other Current Liabilities	218,900	201,800	204,700
Total Current Liabilities	2,246,100	1,982,600	1,969,000
Long-Term Debt	7,653,500	7,972,100	8,278,600
Other Liabilities	1,344,400	1,574,600	1,530,500
Deferred Long-Term Liability Charges	1,194,500	1,682,400	1,727,200
Total Liabilities	12,438,500	13,211,700	13,505,300
Shareholders' Equity			
Common Stock	1,473,700	1,468,600	1,463,000
Retained Earnings	16,741,000	16,445,600	15,407,200
Treasury Stock	(16,007,700)	(15,258,900)	(14,638,500)
Capital Surplus	2,962,500	1,601,800	1,425,300
Other Stockholders' Equity	(1,230,800)	(913,800)	(988,900)
Total Stockholders' Equity	3,938,700	3,343,300	2,668,100
Net Tangible Assets	$2,571,500	$2,110,700	$1,476,200
Total Liabilities and Shareholders' Equity	$16,377,200	$16,555,000	$16,173,400

Source: www.finance.yahoo.com

Exhibit 3 reveals ABI's organizational structure to be a divisional by product/geographic region hybrid. Analysts question whether a straight division by product structure would be better for the company.

EXHIBIT 3   Corporate Officers of Anheuser-Busch Companies, Inc.

1. August A. Busch IV, President & CEO
2. Thomas W. Santel, President & CEO, ABI
3. Michael S. Harding, CEO & President, ABI Packing Group
4. Keith M. Kasen, Board Chairman and President, Busch Entertainment
5. Stephen J. Burrows, President & CEO, Asia-Pacific Operations, ABI
6. Douglas J. Muhleman, Group VP, Brewing and Technology
7. Mark T. Bobak, Group VP and Chief Legal Officer
8. Robert C. Lackhy, EVP, Global Industry Development, ABI
9. Francine I. Katz, VP, Communication and Consumer Affairs
10. W. Randolf Baker, VP and CFO
11. Joseph P. Castellano, VP and CIO
12. Michael J. Owens, VP Sales and Marketing, ABI
13. Anthony T. Ponturo, VP Global Media & Sports Marketing
14. John F. Kelly, VP & Controller
15. Marlene V. Coulis, VP Brand Management, ABI
16. David A. Peacock, VP Business Operations, ABI
17. John T. Farrell, VP Corporate Human Resources

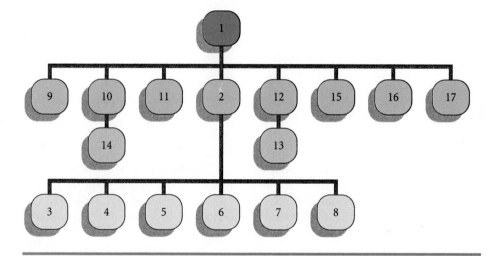

Divisions

Led by CEO August A. Busch IV, ABI operates in four segments or divisions: domestic beer, international beer, entertainment, and packaging.

Domestic Beer

In the United States, beer represents 57 percent of all alcoholic beverages sold, and ABI has 48.4 percent of the market in 2006, down from 48.8 percent the prior year. ABI's Budweiser and Budweiser Light are the top-selling premium beers in the world. Other company brands include Michelob, Busch, and the Natural families. Bud Light produced revenue gains of 4.2 percent in 2006 while Michelob Ultra Amber also had impressive gains. However, rival Coors beer is doing especially well with its marketing message of "refreshment as cold as the Rockies" and its focus on brands such as Coors Light, Blue Moon, and Keystone Light.

EXHIBIT 4   Gross Sales/Income Comparisons of Anheuser-Busch Companies, Inc.

	Beer Segment (In $ Millions)					
Segment:	Domestic Beer			International Beer		
Year:	2006	2005	2004*	2006	2005	2004*
Income Statement Information						
Gross Sales:	$13,394	$13,067	$13,388	$1,235.6	$1,165.5	$1,015.1
Net Sales-Intersegment	$2.8	$2.7	$2.8	–	–	–
Net Sales-External	$11,388.2	$11,079.8	$11,365.9	$998.2	$932.8	$809.9
Depreciation & Amortization	$715.1	$706.6	$680.5	$51.2	$52.1	$35.0
Income before Income Tax	$2,758.5	$2,675.6	$3,279.0	$76.7	$86.5	$130.9
Equity Income, Net of Tax	$3.4	–	–	$585.4	$498.1	$404.1
Net Income	$1,713.7	$1,658.9	$2,033.0	$633.0	$551.7	$485.3
Balance Sheet Information						
Total Assets	$7,988.3	$8,019.0	$7,857.9	$5,350.6	$5,049.2	$4,683.9
Equity Method Investments	$67.8	–	–	$3,604.6	$3,373.1	$2,686.2
Goodwill	$21.2	$21.2	$21.2	$1,283.0	$1,261.1	$1,177.8
Foreign-Located Fixed Assets	–	–	–	$517.7	$510.3	$451.5
Capital Expenditures	$516.7	$851.7	$800.0	$36.9	$72.8	$56.5

Source: Anheuser-Busch 2006 Annual Report [modified version] (www.anheuser-busch.com)

Note*: In 2005 the company began reporting its transportation business in Domestic Beer and its real estate business in Corporate. These businesses formerly comprised the Other segment. Results for 2004 have been updated to conform to this convention.

In a joint venture with Constellation Brands, ABI owns 50 percent of Grupo Modelo, which has 40 percent of the import beer market share in the United States with the Corona beer brand. ABI recently acquired Rolling Rock, a leading brand of beer in the craft and specialty segment. The company shipped 102.3 million barrels of beer in 2006, which was more than twice its closest competitor!

ABI's sales from domestic beer operations have remained steady at just over $13 billion for the last three years, as seen in Exhibit 4. Net income from domestic beer sales grew 3.3 percent in 2006.

International Beer

International beer sales represent 32 percent of ABI's net income. ABI products are popular in China. Russia is the fifth largest market for ABI. Anheuser-Busch's Bud Light sales were up 38 percent in Canada in 2006. The company is doing well in Latin America, Mexico, Chile, Brazil, Argentina, Colombia, and Honduras. ABI's international division operates 15 breweries with 14 located in China and one in the United Kingdom. China's beer consumption levels have accounted for 45 percent of the growth in the global beer volume. ABI owns Harbin, a leading brewer in China, and plans to expand Harbin brands to the domestic premium beer segment.

Tsingtao, China's leading brand of beer, has 13 percent of the market in that country. ABI has a 27 percent equity ownership in Tsingtao, which is available in more than 50 countries. Mexico is the largest export market for ABI, but company exports to Canada increased 38 percent in 2006.

Packaging Operations

ABI's packaging group consists of can production, recycling, label-making, and glass operations. In 2006, the demand for cans and lids exceeded company expectations and resulted in a pretax profit of $145 million, a 2.5 percent increase over the prior year. ABI

EXHIBIT 5   Gross Sales/Income of Anheuser-Busch Companies, Inc.

	Packaging & Entertainment Segment (In $ Millions)					
Segment:	Packaging			Entertainment		
Year:	2006	2005	2004*	2006	2005	2004*
Income Statement Information						
Gross Sales:	$2,562.3	$2,383.6	$2,276.8	$1,178.5	$1,084.8	$989.3
Net Sales-Intersegment	$896.4	$871.1	$2,275.8	–	–	–
Net Sales-External	$1,665.9	$1,512.5	$880.1	$1,178.5	$1,048.8	$989.3
Depreciation & Amortization	$76.9	$83.3	$1,396.7	$99.0	$93.9	$91.8
Income before Income Tax	$145.0	$141.5	83.9	$232.8	$205.9	$172.7
Equity Income, Net of Tax	–	–	–	–	–	–
Net Income	$89.9	$87.7	$101.6	$144.3	$127.7	$107.1
Balance Sheet Information						
Total Assets	$781.5	$764.4	$808.8	$1,479.1	$1,400.8	$1,378.9
Equity Method Investments	–	–	–	–	–	–
Goodwill	$21.9	$21.9	$21.9	$288.3	$288.3	$288.3
Foreign-Located Fixed Assets	–	–	–	–	–	–
Capital Expenditures	$55.9	$55.0	$56.3	$157.6	$104.2	$131.9

Source: Anheuser-Busch 2006 Annual Report [modified version] (www.anheuser-busch.com)

Note*: In 2005 the company began reporting its transportation business in Domestic Beer and its real estate business in Corporate. These businesses formerly comprised the Other segment. Results for 2004 have been updated to conform to this convention.

produces cans for Hansen Natural Corporation. Metal Container Corporation, however, supplies approximately 60 percent of ABI's domestic beer cans and 75 percent of the domestic lids.

Anheuser-Busch Recycling Corporation is one the world's largest recyclers of aluminum cans. As indicated in Exhibit 5, ABI revenues from its packaging division increased 7.5 percent to just over $2.5 billion in 2006. Net income from packaging operations increased 2.5 percent. ABI's precision printing and packaging operations produce more than 20 billion labels for Anheuser-Busch annually. The division also provides labels to other food/beverage manufacturers. ABI's Longhorn Glass Corporation produces longneck bottles for Anheuser-Busch's Houston brewery.

Entertainment Segment

ABI owns theme parks in Orlando, Florida; San Diego, California; and San Antonio, Texas; Busch Gardens Africa in Tampa, Florida; Busch Gardens Europe in Williamsburg, Virginia; Discovery Cove in Orlando, Florida; Sesame Place near Philadelphia, Pennsylvania; Water Country USA in Williamsburg, Virginia; and Adventure Island in Tampa, Florida. Busch Gardens Europe, which opened the world's tallest roller coaster, was voted the "World's Best Theme Park" in 2006, and was named the "World's Most Beautiful Park" for the sixteenth consecutive year by the National Amusement Park Historical Association. ABI's Aquatic theme park is under construction and scheduled to open in Orlando, Florida in 2008.

The pretax profit for the entertainment segment was $233 million in 2006, up 13 percent from 2005. This segment has achieved consistent profits for the last seven years. The increase is attributed to higher park-entry fees, increased consumer spending at the park, and increased attendance rates. More than 22 million guests visited ABI parks in 2006. Revenues for 2006 were $1.178 billion from entertainment operations, up 8.6 percent.

Industry Trends

Sales of higher-end import and craft beers increased 11 percent in 2006. Over the past 5 years, total alcohol servings (spirits) increased 1.7 percent annually, which is a growth rate faster than for beer alone. China's is currently the world's largest beer market. Worldwide beer consumption is expected to grow by 2 to 3 percent annually through the end of this decade. However in developed markets, such as Western Europe, the United States, Australia, and Japan, the overall growth rate is forecasted to be close to zero. Any growth at all in these markets is expected to be by way of premium/import and specialty segments, which is expected to increase approximately 4 percent while the standard beer market declines. The international premium beer segment is expected to grow over 6 percent annually.

In less developed areas of the world such as Central and Eastern Europe, Latin America, Asia, and Africa, beer consumption is increasing at a rate of 3 to 4 percent annually. This is attributed to a growing population, increases in personal income, and a shift from the consumption of traditional (hard) liquors toward beer. Higher priced lagers have achieved higher sales increases; however, more stability is evident from mainstream/basic brewed beers. Anheuser-Busch achieved an international net income of $633.0 million in 2006 as compared to $551.7 million in 2005.

In the United States, the sale of alcoholic beverages generated revenues of $148 billion in 2006, up 1.5 percent over 2005. ABI achieved increasing international beer sales over the last 3 years, but only flat domestic beer sales, which is a concern for the company. Sales of beer, cider and flavored alcoholic beverages account for 53 percent of the U.S. beverage market. Spirits (hard alcohol) and wine account for 30 percent and 17 percent of the market respectively. Consumers prefer wine and spirits more than beer in the United States.

Competitors

Anheuser-Busch, SABMiller, and Molson Coors products account for two-thirds of the total alcohol sales in the United States. Light and low-carbohydrate brew sales have also increased as a result of greater consumer awareness for healthier lifestyles. As seen in Exhibit 6, ABI's 2006 earnings per share (EPS) was only 2.558 whereas Molson Coors' EPS was 4.521. Note in Exhibit 6, however, that the average size of company in the brewing business has 480 employees compared to ABI's 30,183, so mostly these are small breweries. Also note that the average EPS for all firms in the brewing industry is only 1.82, well below ABI's 4.521 EPS, so many of these small firms are not performing well. Many of

EXHIBIT 6   Direct Competitor Comparison

	ABI	Coors	Industry
Market Cap	$38.10B	8.20B	2.36B
Employees	30,183	9,550	480
Qtrly Rev Growth	2.70%	6.50%	14.80%
Revenue	15.82B	5.92B	1.17B
Gross Margin	35.39%	40.46%	40.44%
EBITDA	4.33B	1.12B	477.20M
Operating Margins	17.16%	11.52%	9.87%
Net Income	1.98B	411.36M	116.08M
EPS	2.558	4.521	1.82
P/E	19.60	20.47	22.43
PEG (5 yr expected)	1.97	1.78	1.83
P/S	2.40	1.40	1.76

Source: www.finance.yahoo.com

these small firms may be ripe for acquisition, and rival firms to ABI are reported to be engaging in such discussion with these small firms.

Molson Coors Brewing Company

Coors and Coors Light brands were named top beer brand in a national customer loyalty study for the third consecutive year (www.coors.com). Coors has been able to engage and create loyal customers. Molson Coors is one of the world's largest brewers with net sales of more than $5.6 billion. Molson Coors is a leading brewer in Canada by way of Molson Canada and in the United Kingdom by Coors Brewers Ltd. In the United States, the company is known as Coors Brewing Company. The Molson Coors Brewing Company employs over 11,000 worldwide. The company has 10 breweries located in 3 different countries brewing over 40 brands, including Molson Canadian, Grolsch, Coors Fine Light, Coors Light, and Carling.

On May 18, 2007, Coors announced the introduction of a cold-activated bottle. The bottle contains mountains on the label in thermochromatic ink that turns blue when the Coors Light has been chilled to the perfect temperature designated by the company. The cold-activated bottle is available on all 12-ounce Coors and Coors Light bottles.

SABMiller PLC

SABMiller (sabmiller.com) brews beer on five continents (over 60 countries) with over 200 brands and had a 19 percent revenue increase in 2006. The company's brands include Peroni Nastro Azzurro, Pilsner Urquell, Miller Genuine Draft, Castle Lager, Miller Lite, Aguila, Tyskie, and Snow. The company acquired Miller Brewing Company in 2002.

SABMiller has noted that premium brands of beer are the fastest growing in the global market; the company's Peroni Nastro brand achieved an increase of 45 percent in 2006. The company continues to introduce ingredients aimed at different consumers (women), such as a lighter apple-based beer in Poland. SABMiller continues to emphasize to customers that its products include fewer carbohydrates, have more color, and taste better! Miller products often win at the company-sponsored point-of-sale taste tests known as the Miller Light Taste Challenge.

SABMiller has collaborated with a distribution partner to build a Greenfield brewery in Vietnam, which is one of the fastest growing beer markets in the world. The project is due to be completed by the end of 2007. In Europe, SABMiller is focusing on increasing business in Germany, Turkey, Scandinavia, and Spain.

Heineken NV

Heineken NV (www.heinekeninternational.com) brews two international beers: Heineken and Amstel. Heineken also owns a portfolio of more than 170 beer brands, such as Cruz Campo, Tiger, Zywiec, Birra Moretti, Ochota, Murphy's, and Star. The company brews lagers, specialty beers, light beers (low-calorie beers), and alcohol-free beers and even soft drinks in some markets. Heineken owns 115 breweries in more than 65 countries representing six geographical areas: Western Europe, Central and Eastern Europe, the Americas, Africa, the Middle East, and Asia-Pacific. Heineken employs approximately 65,648 employees worldwide.

The Future

Domestic sales of traditional beer does not have that bright of a future due to intense price competition among brands and consumer preferences shifting more to wine over beer. Since ABI derives most of its revenues from domestic sales of traditional beer, the company has a problem. Perhaps ABI needs to acquire some European brewers or form joint ventures with foreign brewers.

Anheuser-Busch's third quarter 2007 net sales increased 7.9 percent over the prior year's third quarter. For the first nine months of 2007, net sales increased 5.7 percent. "We are pleased with our earnings performance this quarter, with all of our operating segments reporting higher sales and profits," said August A. Busch IV, president and chief executive officer of the company.

Consistent with the pattern in recent years, Anheuser-Busch plans to implement price increases on the majority of its U.S. beer volume in early 2008, with increases in several states in the fourth quarter 2007.

The company's reported beer volume for the third quarter and nine months of 2007 is summarized here (in millions of barrels) for the period ended September 30, 2007.

	Third Quarter 2007 versus 2006			Nine Months 2007 versus 2006		
	2007	# Barrels	%	2007	# Barrels	%
United States	28.0	Up 0.6	Up 2.0%	81.3	Up 1.3	Up 1.7%
International	7.1	Up 0.5	Up 8.2%	18.2	Up 1.1	Up 6.1%
Worldwide	35.1	Up 1.1	Up 3.2%	99.5	Up 2.4	Up 2.4%
Equity Partners	9.9	Up 0.7	Up 7.6%	25.6	Up 1.5	Up 6.4%
Total Brand	45.0	Up 1.8	Up 4.1%	125.1	Up 3.9	Up 3.2%

Anheuser's U.S. beer market share for the nine months of 2007 was 48.8 percent compared to the prior year market share of 48.7 percent. Market share is based on estimated U.S. beer industry shipment volume using information provided by the Beer Institute and the U.S. Department of Commerce.

Prepare a three-year strategic plan for CEO August Busch who leads a 17-person, male-dominated executive team in the process of deciding what direction the firm should take in the future. Both Molson Coors and SABMiller seem to adapt more readily to changes in the beer brewery industry and both are more profitable than ABI. Maybe theme parks and entertainment is where ABI should concentrate their efforts. But then again, ABI is the leader in beer and likely will never abandon that business.

References

www.biz.yahoo.com/bw ("Coors and Coors Light Named Top Beer in National Customer Loyalty Study for Third Consecutive Year")

http://www.anheuserbusch.com

http://www.coors.com

https://www.molsoncoors.com

http://www.millerbrewing.com

http://www.investor.reuters.com

http://biz.yahoo.com/ap/070518/market_spotlight_bud_woes.html?.v=1

7 Hewlett Packard Corporation — 2007

Mernoush Banton
Florida International University

HPQ

www.hp.com

Hewlett-Packard (HP) had $91.7 billion in annual revenue in 2006 compared to $91.4 billion for IBM, making HP for the first time ever the world's largest technology vendor in terms of sales. HP also now is the largest company in worldwide personal computer (PC) sales, surpassing rival Dell, market research firms Gartner and IDC reported in October 2006. The gap between HP and Dell widened substantially at the end of 2006, with HP taking a near 3.5 percent market share lead. For the nine months ended July 31, 2007, Hewlett-Packard's revenues rose 13 percent to $75.99 billion. Net income rose 13 percent to $5.1 billion. Revenues reflect increased income from HP's Personal Systems Group and Imaging & Printing Group and higher income from its Enterprise Storage & Servers segment. Net income reflects decreased research and development expenses and the presence of gain on pension curtailments and pension settlements. In September 2007, HP completed the acquisition of Opsware Inc. and a month later HP completed the acquisition of Neoware Inc.

HP's remarkable turnaround since 2005 has been headed by Todd Bradley. who refocused HP on retail distribution of computers rather than trying to defeat Dell in the Internet and phone PC business. Now trying to regroup and recover, Dell in May 2007 began for the first time to sell PCs through retailers—Wal-Mart stores and Sam's Club stores. Dell is a fierce competitor with limited brick-and-mortar facilities and employees compared to HP and fewer middleman expenses. HP vs Dell is a classic corporate battle although there are many other rival firms such as IBM, Apple, and Canon, as well as foreign rival firms such as Lenovo.

According to NPD Group, 61 percent of PCs sold to consumers in the first quarter of 2007 were bought in a store, up from nearly 54 percent in 2005. HP increased its share of that market worldwide to 12.3 percent in 2007, up from 9.2 percent in 2006, while Dell's share dipped to 43.6 percent from 47.8 percent. (Christopher Lawton, "How HP Reclaimed Its PC Lead Over Dell," *Wall Street Journal,* June 4, 2007: A1-A10.)

HP's Asian-Pacific region, comprised mainly of China and India but also including Russia and Japan, accounted for $4.5 billion of HP's total revenue of $25.5 billion for the three months ended April 30, 2007. That was a 16 percent increase over the year-earlier period and was the fastest growing geographical area for HP. By 2011, India's technology industry will exceed $110 billion in annual revenue, up from $48.5 billion in 2006. HP currently has a 21 percent market share in India's personal computer market, well ahead of India's HCL Technologies Ltd., which has 14 percent and China's Lenovo Group Ltd., which has 10 percent. HP has 29,000 employees in India, second behind the United States in HP work force numbers. HP has a huge technology research lab in Bangalore, India.

History

As indicated in Exhibit 1, HP has historically been known for introducing numerous innovative products. The company provides technology solutions to consumers, businesses and institutions globally and is headquartered in Palo Alto, California with approximately 156,000 employees. HP is considered one of the world's largest information technology

EXHIBIT 1   HP Timeline

Year	Event
1938	Bill Hewlett and Dave Packard started part-time in a garage with $538 in working capital. The new product was HP200A, an electronic instrument used to test sound equipment.
1939	The partnership is formalized and they decided the company's name with a coin toss.
1940s	As HP grew, the partners created a management style of open corporate culture. The "Open Door Policy" empowered employees with decisions and provided a direct link to management where they could voice concerns and/or issues. By creating this policy, open cubicles were set up for employees to work in and managers worked in offices that had no doors. By 1949, the company's revenue was $2.2 million with 166 employees.
1950s	During this era, HP grew by maturing its processes in technology of electronics. The company went public in 1957 and established its corporate headquarters in Palo Alto, California. HP also started its path to globalization by establishing manufacturing and marketing operations in Europe. By the end of 1959, HP's revenue reached $48 million with 2,378 employees.
1960s	HP continues its growth by expanding into medical electronics and analytical instrumentation. It developed its first computer, HP2116A. The company continued its expansion overseas by forming subsidiaries in Asia. By the end of 1969, HP's revenue reached $326 million with 15,840 employees.
1970s	With significant growth, HP's revenue reached $2.4 billion with over 50,000 employees.
1980s	HP entered into printer market. Celebrating their 50th anniversary, HP's sales grew to $11.9 billion with 95,000 employees.
1990s	At the end of this era, HP spins off its measurement and component businesses to form a new company, Agilent Technologies. The new CEO, Carly Fiorina focuses on reinventing the company's growth by planning the acquisition of Compaq Computers Corporation. HP's revenue now is at $42 billion with 84,400 employees.
2000s	In 2002, HP completes its merger with Compaq Computers Corporation and further its products to an array of IT solutions. By the end of 2006, HP's revenue was over $91.6 billion with 156,000 employees.

Source: www.hp.com

firms with recorded revenues of $91,658 million during the fiscal year ended October 2006, an increase of 5.7 percent over 2005. The operating profit of the company was $6,809 million during fiscal year 2006, as compared to the net profit of $2,298 million in 2005. HP is doing great, largely at Dell's expense.

Products / Services

HP is a leading global company, offering products, technologies, software, solutions, and services to consumers, small and medium-size businesses, and large organizations (public and education sectors). The company does business in seven different segments, as illustrated in Exhibit 2.

EXHIBIT 2   HP's Organizational Structure by Business Segment

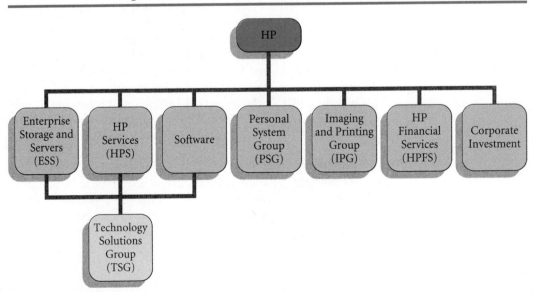

EXHIBIT 3   Overview of Net Revenue and Earnings per Business Segment (2006) (In Millions)

	HP Consolidated	ESS	HPS	Software	IPG	PSG	HPFS
Net Revenue	$91,658	$17,308	$15,617	$ 1,301	$26,786	$29,166	$ 2,078
Earnings from Operations	$ 6,560	$ 1,446	$ 1,507	$ 85	$ 3,978	$ 1,152	$ 147

Source: HP, *Form 10K* (2006)

For up-selling and cross-selling opportunities, Enterprise Storage and Servers (ESS), HP Services (HPS), and Software are structured through the Technology Solutions Group (TSG). Exhibit 3 provides an overview of the company's performance and earnings for each business segment.

Technology Solutions Group (TSG)

This segment offers information technology services to enterprise and mid-market business customers. Within this segment, Enterprise Storage and Servers (ESS) offer industry-standard server platforms to small and medium-sized businesses (SMB). ESS provides products in a number of categories such as Industry Standard Servers (ProLiant and HP BladeSystem), Business Critical Systems (Itanium® based Integrity services, Superdome, Integrity NonStop, HP 9000, HP AlphaServers, OpenVMS, and MIPs-based NonStop servers), and Storage (StorageWorks).

HP Services (HPS) provides information technology services (stand-alone product support to a more complex business environment), consulting and integration (from architect, design and implement technology, and industry-specific solutions), and managed services (outsourcing, transformational infrastructure services, client computing management services, managed Web services, application services and business process outsourcing).

Software provides management software solutions including support for organizations to manage their IT infrastructure, operations, applications, and business processes. This segment also delivers a collection of comprehensive, carrier-grade software platforms for developing and deploying next-generation voice, data, and converged services.

Personal Systems Group (PSG)

This segment provides commercial and consumer PCs (HP Compaq Tablet PC, HP Medial Center PCs, HP Pavilion, Compaq Presario series), workstations (computer animation and engineering design), handheld computing devices (Hp iPAQ Pocket PC), digital entertainment systems (HD DVD and RW drives and DVD writers, and LCD flat-panel televisions), calculators, and other related accessories, software and services for commercial and consumer markets. In recent years, there has been a shift from typical desktop PCs to a more mobile product line such as notebooks.

Imaging and Printing Group (IPG)

This segment of the business provides consumer and commercial printer hardware, printing supplies, printing media, and scanning devices. This segment also is moving toward more commercial and industrial printing solutions such as outdoor signage and graphic arts business. For performance reporting purposes, the company groups inkjet printers, digital photography, and entertainment products and services into consumer hardware. The commercial market includes LaserJet printers, graphics and imaging products. The printer supplies are categorized separately.

HP Financial Services

This segment of HP supports and enhances HP's global product and service solutions by offering a broad range of financial management services to its customers. This segment of the business allows customers to acquire and finance complete IT solutions including hardware, software, and other IT-related services. This service adds value to HP's product

EXHIBIT 4 Consolidated Income Statement, Fiscal Year Ended October 31, 2006

	For the fiscal years ended October 31		
	2006	2005	2004
	In millions, except per share amounts		
Net revenue:			
Products	$73,557	$68,945	$64,046
Services	17,773	17,380	15,470
Financing income	328	371	389
Total net revenue	91,658	86,696	79,905
Costs and expenses:			
Cost of products	55,248	52,550	48,659
Cost of services	13,930	13,674	11,962
Financing interest	249	216	190
Research and development	3,591	3,490	3,563
Selling, general and administrative	11,266	11,184	10,496
Amortization of purchased intangible assets	604	622	603
Restructuring charges	158	1,684	114
In-process research and development charges	52	2	37
Pension curtailment	—	(199)	—
Acquisition-related charges	—	—	54
Total operating expenses	85,098	83,223	75,678
Earnings from operations	6,560	3,473	4,227
Interest and other, net	606	189	35
Gains (losses) on investments	25	(13)	4
Dispute settlement	—	(106)	(70)
Earnings before taxes	7,191	3,543	4,196
Provision for taxes	993	1,145	699
Net earnings	$ 6,198	$ 2,398	$ 3,497
Net earnings per share:			
Basic	$ 2.23	$ 0.83	$ 1.16
Diluted	$ 2.18	$ 0.82	$ 1.15
Weighted average shares used to compute net earnings per share:			
Basic	2,782	2,879	3,024
Diluted	2,852	2,909	3,055

Source: HP, Form 10K (2006).

packaging, allowing their customers alternative financing solutions thus improving the customer's cash flow, technology, and capacity needs.

Corporate Investments

This segment of the business is managed by the Office of Strategy and Technology which includes HP Laboratories. The revenue from this segment of the business is based on the sale of certain network infrastructure products such as Ethernet switch products and licensing specific HP technology to third parties.

Finance

As shown in the HP income statement in Exhibit 4, the last three years has witnessed continuous growth in sales, net earnings, and earnings per share. The balance sheet in Exhibit 5 shows the company's consolidated balance sheet.

EXHIBIT 5   Consolidated Balance Sheet (2006)

	October 31	
	2006	2005
	In millions, except par value	
ASSETS		
Current assets:		
Cash and cash equivalents	$16,400	$13,911
Short-term investments	22	18
Accounts receivable	10,873	9,903
Financing receivables	2,440	2,551
Inventory	7,750	6,877
Other current assets	10,779	10,074
Total current assets	48,264	43,334
Property, plant and equipment	6,863	6,451
Long-term financing receivables and other assets	6,649	7,502
Goodwill	16,853	16,441
Purchased intangible assets	3,352	3,589
Total assets	$81,981	$77,317
LIABILITIES AND STOCKHOLDERS' EQUITY		
Current liabilities:		
Notes payable and short-term borrowings	$ 2,705	$ 1,831
Accounts payable	12,102	10,223
Employee compensation and benefits	3,148	2,343
Taxes on earnings	1,905	2,367
Deferred revenue	4,309	3,815
Accrued restructuring	547	1,119
Other accrued liabilities	11,134	9,762
Total current liabilities	35,850	31,460
Long-term debt	2,490	3,392
Other liabilities	5,497	5,289
Commitments and contingencies		
Stockholders' equity:		
Preferred stock, $0.01 par value (300 shares authorized; none issued)	—	—
Common stock, $0.01 par value (9,600 shares authorized; 2,732 and 2,837 shares issued and outstanding, respectively)	27	28
Additional paid-in capital	17,966	20,490
Prepaid stock repurchase	(596)	—
Retained earnings	20,729	16,679
Accumulated other comprehensive income (loss)	18	(21)
Total stockholders' equity	38,144	37,176
Total liabilities and stockholders' equity	$81,981	$77,317

Source: HP, *Form 10K* (2006).

Marketing

HP promotes its products directly to consumers, businesses, and through a variety of business partners. Exhibit 6 provides a summary of the company's distribution channel.

HP's goal has been selling and marketing its products and services through programs designed to improve profit margins. The key to their overall efforts in delivering superior

EXHIBIT 6 HP's Distribution Channel

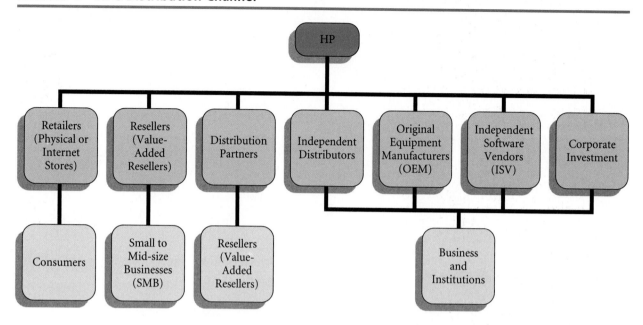

products is to actively invest in research and development, patent their new products, and manage their procurement and labor expenses. In 2007, the company started a new branding effort with its channel partners by borrowing from Dell's direct-sales marketing. The campaign highlights some benefits channel partners can bring. They also focus on direct sales campaigns, a strategy that made Dell Inc. very successful. HP's annual budget for business to business marketing is approximately $208 million.

HP offers a variety of choices to manage aging and unwanted computers in order to minimize the impact on the environment:

1. Trade-in: This services offers the opportunity to capture the fair market value of aging technology and upgrade to a new HP product.
2. Return for Cash: Financial Services (HPFS) pays companies for qualified computer equipment that no longer is needed or wanted.
3. Recycle: HP offers easy to recycle unwanted computer hardware and printing supplies.
4. Donate: The partnership with the National Cristina Foundation (NCF) enables the company to make it easy for computer users to donate their used computer equipment. (Source: www.hp.com.)

Industry/Competition

In the first quarter of 2007, worldwide unit sales of PCs rose 10.9 percent, better than the three previous quarters. However, the sales in the United States only increased by 3.6 percent. In the first quarter in 2006, HP had a 28 percent increase in unit sales worldwide and a 26 percent gain in the United States, whereas Dell Inc. had a decline of 6.9 percent worldwide and 14 percent in the United States. Meanwhile, other companies had unit sales increases: Lenovo (17.4 percent), Acer (41.4 percent), and Toshiba (12.7 percent).

In general, technology products have a short product life cycle. Consumers are aggressively shopping for new products and are demanding new features. Consumers also are becoming more savvy in understanding technology and use the Internet as a primary source for research before making a technology-related purchase.

Apple Computer

Sales of Apple computers (Macs) have kept pace with significant growth in overall PC shipments during the first quarter of 2007. In regard to computer sales in the United States, Apple is one of the fastest growing computer manufacturers. While Microsoft's Windows Vista helped drive PC sales in the first quarter of 2007, Apple was able to match the market with stronger portable sales and an increase in units moved through retail channels (see Exhibit 7).

EXHIBIT 7 Preliminary U.S. PC Vendor Unit Shipment Estimates for 1Q 07 (Thousands of Units)

Company	1Q 07 Shipments	1Q 07 Market Share (%)	1Q 06 Shipments	1Q 06 Market Share (%)	1Q 07–1Q 06 Growth (%)
Dell Inc.	4,126	27.9	4,881	33.9	–15.5
HP	3,807	25.7	3,027	21.0	25.8
Gateway	1,147	7.7	1,225	8.5	–6.3
Toshiba	805	5.4	635	4.4	26.8
Apple Computer	741	5.0	570	4.0	30.0
Others	4,185	28.3	4,057	28.2	3.1
Total	14,811	100.0	14,395	100.0	2.9

Source: Adapted from Gartner, http://www.macnn.com/articles/07/04/18/apple.share.grows.by.30

In the laptop market, Lenovo (now maker of ThinkPads), Acer, Apple, HP, and Dell are aggressively seeking the business customer since laptops are priced about 10 percent higher than the industry average. In the laptop market, Lenovo controls about 12 percent of the global corporate market, Dell Inc. controls 19 percent, and HP has 16 percent of the market. Other companies have also started branding their durability to business customers. For example, Panasonic Corp., which makes high-priced, ultra-rugged computers for the military and law enforcement, has developed a line of Toughbook products aimed at business users, but they are generally costlier than most ThinkPads.

In the printing supply market, HP competes with companies such Eastman Kodak, Canon, and other generic brands (private labels such as Staples, Office Depot, and Office Max). The substitute products such as "remanufactured" or "refilled" ink cartridges have been gaining market share. To complete in this competitive market, HP and other brand name companies are reducing the selling price of their ink cartridges (to around $15); however, they contain less ink which causes the cost of printing per page to be higher for consumers. To persuade customer to buy brand-name ink cartridges, the companies are reducing the cost of the printers but making up the loss by selling the ink cartridges at a higher price.

In the United States, HP's direct competitors are Canon Inc., Dell Inc., and IBM, all considered to be part of the diversified computer systems industry (see Exhibit 8).

EXHIBIT 8 Direct Competitor Comparison (July 2007)

	HP	CANON	DELL	IBM	Industry
Market Cap	$ 119.45B	77.16B	64.96B	161.06B	359.21M
Employees	156,000	118,499	65,200	366,486	1.74K
Qtrly Rev Growth	13.20%	12.60%	2.90%	6.60%	5.70%
Revenue	97.06B	34.63B	N/A	92.79B	456.28M
Gross Margin	24.46%	49.74%	N/A	42.33%	36.03%
EBITDA	10.72B	8.29B	N/A	19.20B	17.29M
Oper Margins	7.85%	17.42%	N/A	14.40%	–0.31%
Net Income	6.39B	3.88B	N/A	9.55B	–218.03K
EPS	2.295	2.92	N/A	6.262	N/A
P/E	19.87	19.99	N/A	17.32	20.04
PEG (5 yr expected)	1.18	2.27	1.87	1.48	1.48
P/S	1.24	2.23	N/A	1.74	1.24

Industry = Diversified Computer Systems

Source: http://finance.yahoo.com

EXHIBIT 9 Computer Hardware (U.S.) Ranked by Sales (July 2007)

Company	Symbol	Price	Change	Market Cap	P/E
International Business Machines Corp.	IBM	$ 108.47	–0.51%	161.06B	$ 17.32
Hewlett-Packard Co.	HPQ	45.61	–0.80%	119.45B	19.87
Dell Inc.	DELL	29.08	0.24%	64.96B	N/A
Cisco Systems, Inc.	CSCO	28.42	–0.18%	172.55B	25.51
Xerox Corp.	XRX	18.94	–1.04%	17.75B	14.97
Sun Microsystems Inc.	SUNW	5.43	0.93%	19.39B	N/A
Seagate Technology	STX	23.49	–0.34%	12.77B	36.36
Apple Inc.	AAPL	130.61	–1.28%	112.97B	41.32
NCR Corp.	NCR	54.00	0.39%	9.71B	26.24
EMC Corporation	EMC	18.73	0.38%	39.30B	32.86

Source: http://finance.yahoo.com

In the computer hardware segment only, HP's direct competitors are listed in Exhibit 9 and Exhibit 10 for the U.S. market and non-U.S. market, respectively.

International

About 20 percent of the PCs sold in 2006 in China cost between $300 and $400. China is one of the world's fastest-growing computer markets. In 2006, computer shipments worldwide grew by 10 percent, where as in China the growth was 21 percent, reaching $14 billion, making China the second-largest computer market after the United States. Recently, Dell Inc. announced that they are aggressively improving their global strategy by introducing a new computer (EC280) with a price starting at about $335 which will be available first in China and then other countries such as India and Brazil.

In respect to market share in China, the market leaders are Lenovo, Founder Technology Group Corporation, and then Dell. Lenovo dominates the Chinese consumer PC market and has teamed up with Microsoft Corporation by offering "pay as you go" computer model that puts a PC in a consumer's hands for an upfront price of about $150. Because China is a lucrative market in consumer PCs, Lenovo Group Ltd., Dell Inc., Acer Inc., and HP are aggressively pushing their brands into Asia. In 2006, HP reported that over 60 percent of its overall net revenue was generated from outside the United States.

Hewlett-Packard's Home Products Division (HPD) had been selling its Pavilion line of personal computers in Europe since around 1995. During this period, HPD had entered and exited Germany, struggled in France and the United Kingdom, and restructured its European operations twice.

EXHIBIT 10 Computer Hardware (Non-U.S.) Ranked by Sales (July 2007)

Company	Symbol	Price	Change	Market Cap	P/E
Toshiba Corporation	TOSBF.PK	8.60	0.00%	N/A	N/A
Canon Inc.	CAJ	58.369	–0.16%	77.16B	19.99
NEC Corp.	NIPNY	5.12	0.39%	10.37B	170.67
	FJTSY.PK	35.10	0.00%	N/A	N/A
Hitachi Ltd.	HIT	71.01	–0.18%	23.61B	N/A
	RICOY.OB	116.85	0.73%	N/A	N/A
Seiko Epson Corporation	Private				
Fujitsu Siemens Computers (Holding) BV	Private				
Oki Electric Industry Company, Limited	Private				
Acer Inc.	Private				

Source: http://finance.yahoo.com

EXHIBIT 11   HP's Recent Acquisitions

- OuterBay: February 2006, HP acquired OuterBay, a leading provider of archiving software for enterprise applications and databases. OuterBay is headquartered in Cupertino, California, with offices in the U.S., U.K., and India.
- Silverwire: June 2006, HP acquired Silverwire Holding AG, a commercial digital photography solutions and software provider with a strong presence in the retail photo market. Silverwire is headquartered in Zug, Switzerland.
- VoodooPC: September 2006, HP acquired VoodooPC, a maker of high-performance gaming, luxury, and entertainment PCs based in Calgary, Alberta, Canada. This acquisition closed early in November 2006.
- Mercury Interactive: November 2006, HP acquired Mercury Interactive (MERQ.PK), a company that provides business technology optimization software (i.e., software that helps a company govern, develop, and maintain its technology stack.
- Knightsbridge Solutions: December 2006, HP acquired Knightsbridge Solutions, a Business Intelligence / Data Warehousing consultancy based out of Chicago.
- Bitfone: December 2006, HP acquired Bitfone Corp., a privately held global software and services company that develops software solutions for mobile device management for the wireless industry.
- Bristol Technology: February 2007, HP acquired Bristol Technology Inc., a leading provider of technologies that monitor business transactions. Bristol is a private company based in Danbury, Connecticut.
- Polyserve: February 2007, HP acquired PolyServe, Inc., a leading provider of storage software for application and file serving utilities. Founded in 1999, PolyServe is headquartered in Beaverton, Ore., has 117 employees, and serves more than 500 customers in a variety of industries including finance, energy, and technology. Financial terms of the transaction were not disclosed. HP had an existing relationship with the company, OEMing some of their products as the HP StorageWorks Enterprise File Services Clustered Gateway.
- Tabblo: March 2007, HP acquired Tabblo Inc., a privately-held developer of Web-based software located in Cambridge, Mass. HP plans to leverage Tabblo's technologies to make printing from the Web easier and more convenient than it is today. Tabblo's technology allows people to simply and efficiently arrange and print text, graphics, and photos from the Web. This is made possible by Tabblo's custom template engine, using an AJAX-enriched interface. HP plans to make this simple-to-use Web-printing experience broadly available to people by working with other companies to integrate the technology into their Web sites. Together, HP and its partner companies will provide customers with a vastly improved Web-based printing experience to meet the ever-growing need for simplified Internet-based printing.
- Arteis: April 2007, HP acquired Arteis, a company that operates Logoworks, a leading distributed web-based graphic design service provider. Arteis is a private company based in Lindon, Utah.
- SPI Dynamics: June 2007, HP acquired SPI Dynamics, a provider of Web application security assessment software and services. The new business would be integrated into the Software Unit of TSG.

Source: Adapted from www.wikipedia.com.

Conclusion

As indicated at the beginning of the case, HP and Dell are embroiled in a dogfight with HP having just overtaken Dell in total revenues, market share, and financial condition. But Dell still has by far the dominant position in Internet and phone sales of PCs. Dell computers are now available in Wal-Mart stores and Sam's Clubs in a break from their historical absence in retail stores.

Where do you feel HP should concentrate globally to continue its recent good fortune? What product lines do you feel HP should focus on to best compete in the technology industry? Note in Exhibit 11 that HP has been on the acquisition trail extensively and desires to continue this growth strategy. Identify three acquisition candidates that you would recommend HP acquire. Prepare a three-year strategic plan for HP.

References
finance.yahoo.com
hardware.seekingalpha.com/
www.about.com
www.answers.com
www.channelinsider.com
www.crn.com
www.hp.com
www.investor.reuters.com
www.money.cnn.com
www.wsj.com

International Business Machines — 2007

Vijaya Narapareddy
University of Denver

IBM

www.ibm.com

In July 2007, International Business Machines (IBM) signed an $84.4 million deal with Spanish utility Iberdrola, one of the world's largest producers of renewable energy, to open an Innovation Center at Iberdrola in Salamanca, Spain to develop new information technologies and provide services for the utility. Also that month, IBM announced that it is creating a Global Center of Excellence for Nuclear Power in France to develop software and consulting services for the design, construction, and operation of nuclear power plants. IBM is capitalizing on the global warming-triggered revival of interest in nuclear power as an alternative to coal-fired plants. France obtains 80 percent of electricity from nuclear power. "Nuclear power plant license extensions and new plant construction are driving the need for sophisticated risk modeling and information tools," said Guido Bartels, general Manager for IBM Global Energy and Utilities Industry, in a statement.

IBM's organizational structure is provided in Exhibit 1. Note that CEO/President Samuel Palmisano, Executive VP Nicholas Donofrio, fourteen Senior VPs and three other VPs are repositioning IBM from a computer company to an information technology services company through a series of acquisitions and divestitures as shown in Exhibit 2. In 2006, 13 acquisitions of approximately $4.8 billion were completed, enabling IBM to expand its software and services business.

For the nine months ending September 30, 2007, IBM's revenue's increased 7 percent to $69.92 billion. Net income from continuing operations increased 9 percent to $6.46 billion. Revenues reflect an increase in income from the company's Global Technology Services segment and higher sales from both its Software segment and Global Business services segment. Net income also reflects higher gross margin and higher intellectual property income.

In July 2007, IBM acquired Watchfire Corporation. A privately held security and compliance testing software company based in Waltham, Massachusetts. In August 2007, IBM acquired WebDialogs, Inc., and then a month later completed the acquisition of DataMirror.Corp.

Company History

Based in Armonk, New York, IBM was founded in 1888 as "Herman Hollerith and the Tabulating Machine Company." It was incorporated in 1911 as "Computing-Tabulating-Recording Co." The company later changed its name to International Business Machines (IBM) Corporation in 1924 after becoming a Fortune 500 company. Also known as "Big Blue," IBM has won several accolades. It is known to have more patents than any other American technology company. In addition to being ranked among the "Worldwide Top 20 Semiconductor Sales Leaders," to date, IBM boasts of its employees' achievements in the field of science and technology three Nobel Prizes, four Turing Awards, five National Medals of Technology, and five National Medals of Science.

IBM is well-known for its sales-centered business culture as it continues to hire its executives and managers from its sales force. Its current CEO/President, Samuel Palmisano, started his career as a salesman with the company. The company's traditional culture of wearing a dark suit, white shirt, and tie changed in the 1990s under the leadership of then CEO Lou Gerstner.

IBM began to chart a new course in 2003 using a very unique approach. It engaged 50,000 employees in an online intranet discussion over a period of three days using its Jam

EXHIBIT 1 IBM's Organizational Structure

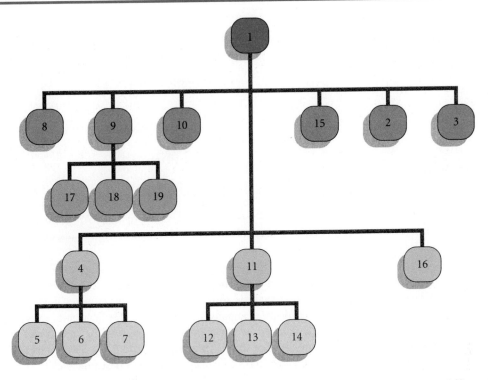

	Age	Officer since
1. Samuel J. Palmisano, Chairman of the Board, President and CEO	55	1997
2. Nicholas M. Donofrio, Innovation and Technology, Executive VP	61	1995

Senior Vice Presidents:

3. Michael E. Daniels, Global Technology Services	52	2005
4. Douglas T. Elix, Group Executive, Sales and Distribution	58	1999
5. J. Bruce Harreld, Marketing and Strategy	56	1995
6. Paul M. Horn, Research	60	1996
7. Jon C. Iwata, Communications	44	2002
8. John E. Kelly, III, Technology and Intellectual Property	53	2000
9. Mark Loughridge, Chief Financial Officer	53	1998
10. J. Randall MacDonald, Human Resources	58	2000
11. Steven A. Mills, Group Executive, Software Group	55	2000
12. Robert W. Moffat, Jr., Integrated Operations	50	2002
13. Virginia M. Rometty, Global Business Services	49	2005
14. Linda S. Sanford, Enterprise On Demand Transformation	54	2000
15. Robert C. Weber, Legal and Regulatory Affairs, and General Counsel	56	2006
16. William M. Zeitler, Group Executive, Systems and Technology Group	59	2000

Vice Presidents:

17. Jesse J. Greene, Jr., Treasurer	61	2002
18. Daniel E. O'Donnell, Secretary	59	1998
19. Timothy S. Shaughnessy, Controller	49	2004

Source: http://www.sec.gov/Archives/edgar/data/51143/000104746907001434/0001047469-07-001434-index.htm, p. 9.

EXHIBIT 2 Recent IBM Acquisitions and Divestitures

IT INDUSTRY LANDSCAPE		PRE 2004	2004	2005	2006
Business Value		PwCC	Daksh Maersk IT	Corio Equalent	Viacore
Infrastructure Value *Hardware* *Software* *Services*	Acquisitions	Lotus Tivoli Rational Informix Sector7 Access360	Logical Networks Cyanea Candle Trigo Tech Venetica Schiumberger	Healthlink SRD Ascential DWL DataPower Isogon Collation Melosys	Micromuse FileNet MRO CIMS Labs Language Analysis System Unicorn REMBO BuildForge Webify ISS
Component Value	Divestitures	Network HDD DRAM Displays	EDI Services 4xx Power PC	PCs	

Source: www.ibm.com; 2006 *Annual Report*, p. 16.

technology. The content generated during those discussions was then analyzed using eClassifier, a sophisticated text analysis software. Three themes emerged during this 2003 Jam, which form the basis for the company's core values, "Dedication to every Client's success," "Innovation that matters for our company and the world," and "Trust and personal responsibility in all relationships." Subsequently, a 2004 Jam enabled 52,000 employees over a period of three days to discuss and select best practices to support the three values adopted earlier. The InnovationJam, launched in June and September of 2006, engaged 150,000 employees residing in 104 countries, their families, partners, customers, and universities in two brainstorming sessions spanning 72 hours each, resulting in the compilation of over 46,000 ideas. In November 2006, IBM announced that it will commit $100 million to the ten best ideas generated during the InnovationJams. This is how IBM does strategic planning, transforming itself to a innovation-centric globally integrated corporation that focuses on new high-profit high-value-added businesses and services.

   IBM reports results of its operations in eight industry sectors as listed in Exhibit 3. Note that the $290 million growth in revenues generated by continuing operations in 2006 is mainly fueled by approximately 18 percent growth in the Original Equipment Manufacturers (OEM) segment. This segment, in turn, is driven by rising demand for

EXHIBIT 3 IBM Revenues by Industry Sector (In $ Millions)

FOR THE YEAR ENDED DECEMBER 31	2006	2005*	YR. TO YR. PERCENT CHANGE	YR. TO YR. PERCENT CHANGE CONSTANT CURRENCY
Industry Sector:				
Financial Services	$ 25,181	$ 24,186	4.1 %	3.8 %
Public	13,401	14,064	(4.7)	(5.3)
Industrial	11,535	11,699	(1.4)	(1.6)
Distribution	9,034	8,959	0.8	0.3
Communications	8,679	8,601	0.9	0.6
Small & Medium Business	16,981	17,597	(3.5)	(3.8)
Original Equip Manufacturers (OEM)	3,856	3,271	17.9	17.9
Other	2,756	2,757	(0.1)	0.0
Total	**$ 91,424**	$ 91,134	0.3 %	(0.0)%

* Reclassified to conform with 2006 presentation.

Source: http://www.sec.gov/Archives/edgar/data/51143/000104746907001434/0001047469-07-001434-index.htm., Exhibit 13, p. 22.

game processors in the microelectronics business. Note in Exhibit 3 that IBM's sales/revenues declined in 2006 in three of the industry sectors: (1) public, (2) industrial, and (3) small/medium business.

Global Operations

IBM operates in 170 countries, with about 60 percent of its revenues being generated outside the United States. About 30 percent of IBM's employees are in Asia Pacific, 45 percent are in the United States., and 35 percent are in other countries IBM's R&D system employs over 20,000 software developers in 61 labs located in 15 countries, and 3,000 scientists and technologists work at its Research Centers operating in China, India, Israel, Japan, Switzerland, and the United States.

In addition to industry segments, IBM provides results of its operations in four geographic segments: (1) Americas, (2) Europe/Middle East/Africa, (3) Asia Pacific, and (4) OEM. IBM's subsidiaries worldwide are listed in Exhibit 4 with Revenues by

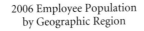

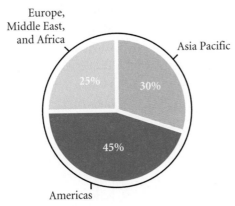

Source: www.ibm.com/2006_ibm_annual.pdf

EXHIBIT 4   IBM's Global Subsidiaries

Company Name	State or country of incorporation or organization
IBM Credit LLC	USA (Delaware)
IBM International Foundation	USA (Delaware)
IBM International Services Corporation	USA (Delaware)
IBM Business Transformation Center, S.r.l	Costa Rica
Tivoli Systems, Inc	USA (Delaware)
IBM World Trade Corporation	USA (Delaware)
IBM Bahamas Limited	Bahamas
WTC Insurance Corporation, Ltd	Bermuda
IBM Canada Limited—IBM Canada Limitee	Canada
IBM Argentina Sociedad Anonima	Argentina
IBM Canada Credit Services Company	Canada
IBM Canada Holding Company, Limited Partnership	Canada
IBM Americas Holding Limited	Bermuda
IBM Brasil—Industria, Maquinas e Servicos Limitada	Brazil
IBM de Bolivia, S.A	Bolivia
IBM de Chile, S.A.C	Chile
IBM del Ecuador, C.A	Ecuador

continued

EXHIBIT 4 **IBM's Global Subsidiaries—continued**

Company Name	State or country of incorporation or organization
Grupo IBM Mexico, S.A. de C.V	Mexico
IBM de Mexico, S.A	Mexico
IBM del Uruguay, S.A	Uruguay
IBM de Venezuela, S.A	Venezuela
IBM A/NZ Holdings Pty. Limited	Australia
IBM Australia Limited	Australia
IBM New Zealand Limited	New Zealand
IBM India Private Ltd	India
PT IBM Indonesia	Indonesia
IBM World Trade Asia Holdings LLC	USA (Delaware)
YK IBM AP Holdings	Japan
IBM Japan, Ltd	Japan
IBM Korea, Inc	Korea (South)
IBM Malaysia Sdn. Bhd	Malaysia
IBM Philippines, Incorporated	Philippines
IBM Thailand Company Limited	Thailand
IBM Vietnam Company	Vietnam
IBM Bulgaria Ltd	Bulgaria
IBM Croatia Ltd./IBM Hrvatska d.o.o	Croatia
IBM Egypt Business Support Services	Egypt
IBM Eesti Osauhing (IBM Estonia Ou)	Estonia
IBM Italia S.p.A	Italy
Companhia IBM Portuguesa, S.A	Portugal
IBM Hellas Information Handling Systems S.A	Greece
IBM Israel Limited	Israel
IBM (International Business Machines) Turk Limited Sirketi	Turkey
IBM South Africa Group Ltd	South Africa
IBM South Africa (Pty) Ltd	South Africa
IBM East Africa Limited	Kenya
Sabiedriba ar irobezotu atbildibu IBM Latvija	Latvia
IBM Lietuva	Lithuania
IBM Holdings B.V	Netherlands
IBM Global Holdings B.V	Netherlands
IBM Central Holding GmbH	Germany
IBM Deutschland GmbH	Germany
IBM Oesterreich Internationale Bueromaschinen Gesellschaft m.b.H	Austria
IBM (Schweiz)-IBM (Suisse)-IBM (Svizzera)-IBM (Switzerland)	Switzerland
IBM Central and Eastern Europe B.V	Netherlands
IBM Ceska Republika spol. s.r.o	Czech Republic

continued

EXHIBIT 4   IBM's Global Subsidiaries—continued

Company Name	State or country of incorporation or organization
IBM East Europe/Asia Ltd	Russia
IBM—International Business Machines d.o.o., Belgrade	Serbia and Montenegro
IBM Polska Sp.z.o.o	Poland
IBM Romania Srl	Romania
IBM Slovensko spol s.r.o	Slovak Republic
IBM Ukraine	Ukraine
IBM International Holdings B.V	Netherlands
IBM China Holdings B.V	Netherlands
IBM China Company Limited	P.R.C.
IBM China/Hong Kong Limited	Hong Kong
IBM Ireland Limited	Ireland
IBM Singapore Pte. Ltd	Singapore
International Business Machines Corporation Magyarorszagi Kft	Hungary
Lefern Limited	Ireland
IBM International Treasury Services Company	Ireland
IBM North Region Holdings	United Kingdom
IBM Nederland N.V	Netherlands
IBM United Kingdom Holdings Limited	United Kingdom
IBM United Kingdom Limited	United Kingdom
IBM International B.V	Netherlands
IBM de Colombia, S.A	Colombia
IBM del Peru, S.A	Peru
IBM Europe Holdings B.V	Netherlands
Compagnie IBM France, S.A.S	France
IBM Maroc	Morocco
IBM Tunisie	Tunisia
IBM Taiwan Holdings B.V	Netherlands
IBM Taiwan Corporation	Taiwan
International Business Machines of Belgium S.A	Belgium
International Business Machines West Africa Limited	Nigeria
IBM Slovenija d.o.o	Slovenia
International Business Machines, S.A	Spain
IBM Nordic Aktiebolag	Sweden
IBM Danmark A/S	Denmark
International Business Machines A/S	Norway
Oy International Business Machines AB	Finland
International Business Machines Svenska A.B	Sweden
IBM Middle East FZ-LLC	United Arab Emirates

(A) Minor percentage held by other IBM shareholders subject to repurchase option.
(B) Remaining percentage owned by other wholly-owned IBM company(s).

Source: www.sec.gov; EX-21 4 a2175501zex-21.htm

EXHIBIT 5   IBM Revenues by Geographic Area (In $ Millions)

For the Year Ended December 31	2006		2005		Yr. to Yr. Percent Change
Geographies:	%	$	%	$	
Americas	**43.2**	**39,511**	42.6	38,817	1.8%
Europe/Middle East/Africa	**33.4**	**30,491**	33.4	30,428	0.2
Asia Pacific	**19.2**	**17,566**	20.4	18,618	(5.7)
OEM	**4.2**	**3,856**	3.6	3,271	17.9
Total	**100**	**91,424**	100	91,134	0.3 %

Source: http://www.sec.gov/Archives/edgar/data/51143/000104746907001434/0001047469-07-001434-index.htm, Exhibit 13, p. 22.

Geographic segment shown in Exhibit 5. Note that the Americas represent over 40 percent of the company's revenues. This segment grew 1.6 percent from 2005 to 2006 while revenues in the other regions declined. In contrast, the OEM segment, which is the smallest at less than 5 percent of total revenues, experienced the largest growth of approximately 18 percent.

Revenue growth from 2005 to 2006 is the highest in India (38 percent), followed by Russia (21 percent), Brazil (19 percent), and China (16 percent). Excluding the PC business, these four markets alone grew 21 percent in 2006. By 2010, the IT markets in these four countries are expected to grow twice as fast as in the rest of the world. This growth is expected to be equal to over $150 billion in IT services.

Business Segments

Several years ago, IBM divested its personal computers and hard disk drives businesses as they were becoming mature and commodity-like businesses. IBM has since then concentrated on becoming stronger in high-value-added businesses like service-oriented architecture (SOA), information on demand, business process services, and open modular systems for businesses of all sizes. IBM concentrates on the development and manufacture of the advanced information technologies, including computer systems, software, storage systems, and microelectronics. The company reports results in both geographic terms and by product.

As presented in Exhibit 6, IBM is structurally organized in three segments or divisions: (1) systems and financing, (2) software, and (3) services. The systems and financing segment offers servers; data storage products, including disk, tape, optical, and storage area networks; microprocessors and integrated circuits; system and component design services, and technology and manufacturing consulting services; printing systems, including production and on-demand print solutions, enterprise print technologies, and related software; and point-of-sale retail systems. This segment also offers short-term inventory and accounts receivable financing; lease and loan financing; and sells and leases used equipment.

IBM's software segment provides information management software for database, content management, and information integration; lotus software for collaboration, messaging, and social networking; rational software, a process automation tool; Tivoli software for infrastructure management, including security and storage management; Websphere software for Web-enabled applications; product life-cycle management software; and operating system software.

IBM's services segment offers business process outsourcing, consulting and systems integration, strategic outsourcing services, integrated technology services, IT infrastructure maintenance services, application management services for packaged software and custom and legacy applications, and applications on demand services. IBM serves banking, insur-

EXHIBIT 6   IBM's Three Core Business Segments

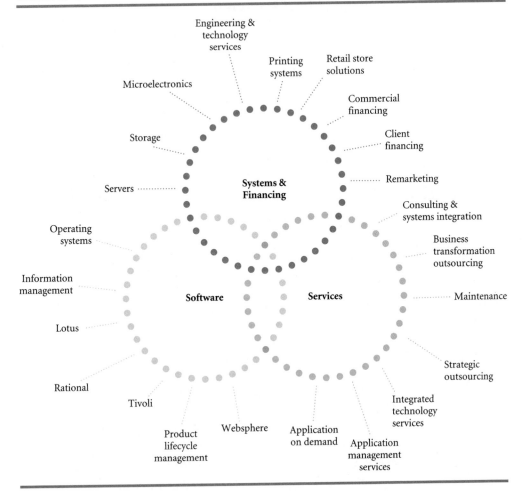

Source: www.ibm.com; 2006 *Annual Report*, p. 17.

EXHIBIT 7   IBM's Revenue by Product (In $ Millions)

For the Year Ended December 31	2006	Annual Change	2005	Annual Change
Statement of Earnings Revenue Presentation:	$	%	$	%
Global Technology Services	48,247	1.8	47,407	1.7
Hardware	22,499	(7.6)	24,343	(8.3)
Software	18,204	8.2	16,830	7.5
Global Financing	2,379	(1.1)	2,407	(1.6)
Other	94	(36.4)	147	(33.4)
Total	**91,424**	0.3	91,134	(0.0)

Source: http://www.sec.gov/Archives/edgar/data/51143/000104746907001434/0001047469-07-001434-index.htm., Exhibit 13, p. 22.

ance, education, government, healthcare, life sciences, aerospace and defense, automotive, chemical and petroleum, electronics, distribution, and communication markets.

The company's revenues by segment are displayed in Exhibit 7 and reveal that global services account for more than half of the company's revenues, followed by the hardware and software segments, respectively. Note that in 2006, while IBM had minimal revenue growth, the software business was the only segment experiencing signifi-

EXHIBIT 8 **Revenues, Gross Profit, and Pretax Income by Product (as a Percentage of Total Revenues)**

Revenues for the Year Ended December 31	2006	2005
Global Technology Services	**35.6%**	36.0%
Global Business Services	**17.6**	18.2
Total Global Services	**53.2**	54.1
Hardware	**24.2**	23.9
Global Financing	**2.6**	2.7
Total Hardware/Financing	**26.8**	26.7
Software	**20.0**	19.2
Total	**100.0%**	100.0%

Source: http://www.sec.gov/Archives/edgar/data/51143/000104746907001434/0001047469-07-001434-index.htm., Exhibit 13, p. 23.

Gross Profit

For the Year Ended December 31	2006	2005	Yr. to Yr. Change
Consolidated Gross			
Profit Margins:			
Global Services	**27.5%**	26.0%	1.5 pts.
Hardware	**37.0**	35.1	1.9
Software	**85.2**	84.9	0.3
Global Financing	**50.3**	54.7	(4.4)
Other	**(13.2)**	45.2	(58.4)
Total	**41.9%**	40.1%	1.8 pts.

Source: http://www.sec.gov/Archives/edgar/data/51143/000104746907001434/0001047469-07-001434-index.htm., Exhibit 13, p. 25.

Pretax Income by Business Segment

2006 Segment Pretax
Income Mix

Source: www.ibm.com; 2006 *Annual Report*, p. 6

cant growth (8.2 percent), followed by global services (1.8 percent). The remaining three business segments experienced declines in revenues.

Data presented in Exhibit 8 reveal similar trends. Revenues from the global technology sevices, global business services, and global financing as a percentage of total revenues all declined in 2006 while the hardware and software segments showed modest gains. About 40 percent of IBM's pretax income in 2006 is contributed by software, 37 percent by services, and the remaining 23 percent by systems and financing.

EXHIBIT 9   Direct Competitor Comparison

	IBM	EDS	HP	MS	Industry
Market Cap	$156.28B	14.11B	116.85B	281.93B	353.77M
Employees	366,486	131,000	156,000	71,000	1.74K
Qtrly Rev Growth	6.60%	2.90%	13.20%	32.10%	5.70%
Revenue	92.79B	21.41B	97.06B	49.56B	456.28M
Gross Margin	42.33%	13.59%	24.46%	80.66%	36.03%
EBITDA	19.20B	2.28B	10.72B	20.91B	17.29M
Operating Margin	14.40%	4.75%	7.85%	39.10%	-3.71%
Net Income	9.55B	631.00M	6.39B	13.86B	-218.03K
EPS	6.262	1.156	2.295	1.382	N/A
P/E Ratio	16.81	23.99	19.44	21.32	19.44
PEG (5 yr expected):	1.43	0.83	1.15	1.62	1.43
	1.70	0.66	1.20	5.76	1.13

EDS = Electronic Data Systems
HP = Hewlett-Packard
MS = Microsoft
Industry = Diversified Computer Systems

Source: Adapted from http://finance.yahoo.com

Competition

IBM is a key player in the hypercompetitive Diversified Computer Systems industry proliferated by global giants ranked in the Fortune 50 companies as well as small yet fast-growing specialized organizations around the world. It ranks second in market capitalization, net income, and long-term growth behind Microsoft in the Diversified Computer Systems industry, but leads the industry in sales ($92.79 billion) and number of employees (366,486). Key competitor data is given in Exhibit 9. Note that IBM's key competitors in the industry are Microsoft, Hewlett Packard, and Electronic Data Systems.

Microsoft (MSFT)

Founded by Bill Gates and Paul Allen in 1975 in Albuquerque, New Mexico, MSF is a formidable competitor in the industry. Headquartered in Redmond, Washington, MSF is a leading provider of operating systems and software. Its Microsoft Windows operating system and Microsoft Office software dominate the marketplace.

With a market cap of nearly $282 billion, MSF is a market leader in gross margins (80.7 percent), operating margins (39.1 percent), and quarterly revenue growth of 32.1 percent. With 71,000 employees (less than 20 percent of IBM's employees) worldwide (in 102 countries), MSF is a nimble and aggressive organization. The company is diversified through its holdings of the MSNBC cable television network, the MSN Internet Portal, and the Microsoft Encarta. In addition, it sells computer hardware products (e.g., Microsoft Mouse), and popular home entertainment products, such as the X-box, Zune, and MSN TV.

In January 2007, the Harris Interactive/The Wall Street Journal Reputation Quotient survey concluded that MSFT has the world's best corporate reputation based on its strong financial performance, visionary leadership, workplace environment rankings, and the charitable deeds of the Bill and Melinda Gates Foundation throughout the world. MSF views its major competitor, however, to be Google rather than IBM.

Hewlett-Packard (HPQ)

HPQ, also known as HP, is the largest company in the industry in sales ($97.1 billion). Headquartered in Palo Alto, California, HP is well known worldwide for its printers, personal computers, and related services. Founded in 1939 by William Hewlett and David Packard, HP currently ranks number one in personal computer sales, ahead of Dell. Based on its estimates for 2007, HP has the strong potential to be the first IT company to surpass the $100 billion mark. After its merger with Compaq in 2002, HP has grown to offer a full range of services to architect, implement, and support IT infrastructure in addition to its existing hardware and software businesses. With 157,000 employees and a market cap of $117 billion, HP is a strong competitor to IBM.

Electronic Data Systems (EDS)

Headquartered in Plano, Texas and established in 1962 by Ross Perot, EDS has 131,000 employees. Approximately 80 percent of EDS stock is held by institutional investors and mutual fund owners. It offers a host of information technology and business process outsourcing services worldwide. About 60 percent of its revenues come from the Americas, 30 percent from Europe, Middle East, and Africa, and 5 percent from Asia Pacific. In 2006, it divested its subsidiary, A.T. Kearney, a management consulting company, and acquired two leading companies from Bangalore, India. These acquisitions allow the company to offer onshore and offshore testing and quality assurance services. EDS's clients include large companies in the manufacturing, financial services, healthcare, communications, energy, transportation, and consumer and retail industries, and governments around the world. With a market cap of $14.1 billion and revenues of $21.4 billion, it trails behind the big three in the industry.

Finance

Exhibit 10 reveals IBM's income statement and shows a dramatic decline of over $5.1 billion in revenues between 2004 and 2005, followed by a growth of $290 million from 2005 to 2006.

EXHIBIT 10 **IBM's Income Statement (In Thousands)**

PERIOD ENDING	Dec. 31, 2006	Dec. 31, 2005	Dec. 31, 2004
Total Revenue	$91,424,000	91,134,000	96,293,000
Cost of Revenue	53,129,000	54,602,000	60,261,000
Gross Profit	38,295,000	36,532,000	36,032,000
Operating Expenses			
Research Development	6,107,000	5,842,000	5,673,000
Selling, General and Administrative	20,259,000	21,314,000	19,384,000
Non-Recurring	(900,000)	–	(1,169,000)
Others	–	–	–
Total Operating Expenses	–	–	–
Operating Income or Loss	12,829,000	9,376,000	12,144,000
Income from Continuing Operations			
Total Other Income/Expenses Net	766,000	3,070,000	23,000
Earnings Before Interest and Taxes	13,595,000	12,446,000	12,167,000
Interest Expense	278,000	220,000	139,000
Income Before Tax	13,317,000	12,226,000	12,028,000
Income Tax Expense	3,901,000	4,232,000	3,580,000
Minority Interest	–	–	–
Net Income From Continuing Ops	9,416,000	7,994,000	8,448,000
Non-Recurring Events			
Discontinued Operations	76,000	(24,000)	(18,000)
Extraordinary Items	–	–	–
Effect of Accounting Changes	–	(36,000)	–
Other Items	–	–	–
Net Income	9,492,000	7,934,000	8,430,000
Preferred Stock and Other Adjustments	–	–	–
Net Income Applicable to Common Shares	$9,492,000	$7,934,000	$8,430,000

Source: Adapted from http://finance.yahoo.com

EXHIBIT 11   IBM's Balance Sheet (In Thousands)

Balance Sheet

PERIOD ENDING	Dec. 31, 2006	Dec. 31, 2005	Dec. 31, 2004
ASSETS			
Current Assets			
Cash and Cash Equivalents	$8,022,000	12,568,000	10,053,000
Short-Term Investments	2,634,000	1,118,000	517,000
Net Receivables	28,655,000	26,193,000	30,365,000
Inventory	2,810,000	2,841,000	3,316,000
Other Current Assets	2,539,000	2,941,000	2,719,000
Total Current Assets	44,660,000	45,661,000	46,970,000
Long-Term Investments	18,449,000	14,602,000	16,418,000
Property, Plant and Equipment	14,439,000	13,756,000	15,175,000
Goodwill	12,854,000	9,441,000	8,437,000
Intangible Assets	2,202,000	1,663,000	1,789,000
Accumulated Amortization	–	–	–
Other Assets	10,629,000	20,625,000	20,394,000
Deferred Long-Term Asset Charges	–	–	–
Total Assets	103,233,000	105,748,000	109,183,000
LIABILITIES			
Current Liabilities			
Accounts Payable	18,006,000	17,292,000	24,524,000
Short/Current Long-Term Debt	8,902,000	7,216,000	8,099,000
Other Current Liabilities	13,182,000	10,644,000	7,175,000
Total Current Liabilities	40,090,000	35,152,000	39,798,000
Long-Term Debt	13,780,000	15,425,000	14,828,000
Other Liabilities	17,690,000	22,073,000	24,810,000
Deferred Long-Term Liability Charges	3,167,000	–	–
Minority Interest	–	–	–
Negative Goodwill	–	–	–
Total Liabilities	74,727,000	72,650,000	79,436,000
Stockholders' Equity			
Misc Stocks Options Warrants	–	–	–
Redeemable Preferred Stock	–	–	–
Preferred Stock	–	–	–
Common Stock	31,271,000	28,926,000	18,355,000
Retained Earnings	52,432,000	44,734,000	42,464,000
Treasury Stock	(46,296,000)	(38,546,000)	(31,072,000)
Capital Surplus	–	–	–
Other Stockholders' Equity	(8,901,000)	(2,016,000)	–
Total Stockholders' Equity	28,506,000	33,098,000	29,747,000
Total Liabilities and SE	$103,223,000	105,748,000	109,183,000

Source: Adapted from http://finance.yahoo.com

Even though this recent growth pales in comparison to prior years, IBM's net income has increased by $1.6 billion or 20 percent from 2005. A major portion of the gains come from a $1.06 billion (5 percent) decrease in SGA (selling general and administrative) expenses during this period. This decrease can mainly be attributed to the restructuring charges in 2005.

Exhibit 11 presents the IBM balance sheets from 2004 through 2006 and shows some interesting trends. The company's current ratio declines from 1.18 in 2004 to 1.11 in 2006. Note that IBM's goodwill on its balance sheet is up 36 percent in 2006 to a staggering $12.8 billion. This is not good. The company's long-term debt declines 10.6 percent to $13.7 billion.

Conclusion

IBM has come a long way in its efforts to transform itself into an innovation-driven integrated global company as it seeks to pursue value-added businesses and services that will generate high value for its customers and high profits for its shareholders. Whether it is on the right path to accomplishing its goals or not can be seen through key trends in its performance. Exhibit 12 displays trends in the company's pretax income and gross margins. This exhibit depicts a favorable trend in both the gross margins and pretax net income in 2002 through 2006.

EXHIBIT 12 Trends in IBM's Pretax Income and Gross Margins, 2002–2006

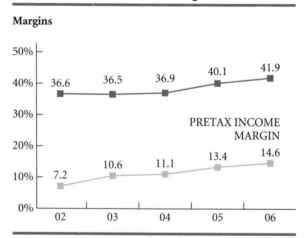

Source: www.ibm.com; 2006 *Annual Report*, p. 7

EXHIBIT 13 Trends in IBM's Earnings per Share

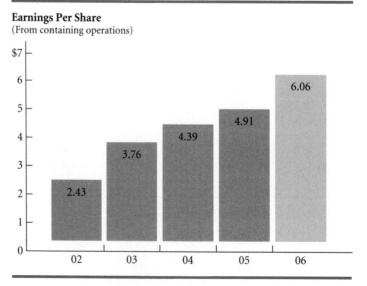

Source: www.ibm.com; 2006 *Annual Report*, p.7

EXHIBIT 14   IBM's Selling, General and Administrative Expenses (In Millions)

For the Year Ended December 31	2006	2005*	Yr. to Yr. Change
Selling, general and administrative expense:			
Selling, general and administrative—base	**$ 17,459**	$ 16,620	5.0%
Advertising and promotional expense	**1,195**	1,284	(6.9)
Workforce reductions—ongoing	**289**	289	0.4
Restructuring	**(7)**	1,482	NM
Amortization expense—acquired intangibles	**208**	218	(4.5)
Retirement-related expense	**587**	846	(30.6)
Stock-based compensation	**541**	606	(10.7)
Bad debt expense	**(13)**	(31)	(57.2)
Total	**$ 20,259**	$ 21,314	(4.9%)

Reclassified to conform with 2006 presentation.
NM—*Not meaningful*

Source: http://www.sec.gov/Archives/edgar/data/51143/000104746907001434/0001047469-07-001434-index.htm, p. 26.

Exhibit 13 shows trends in IBM's earnings per share. In 2002, earnings from continuing operations were $2.43 per share, rising steadily to $6.06 in 2006. This constitutes a 149 percent gain over a period of four years, averaging an annual gain of 0.37 percent or approximately 91 cents. This is impressive as compared to other domestic competitors in its strategic group presented in Exhibit 8. In 2006, the top performer in this metric is IBM while the next-best performer is HP at $2.30 EPS.

Details of the SGA expenses shown in Exhibit 14 demonstrate that IBM's advertising and promotion expenses decrease 7 percent, from about $1.3 billion in 2005 to $1.2 billion in 2006. Its research and development expenses shown in its income statement (Exihibit 9), when expressed as a percentage of sales, rise meekly from 5.9 percent in 2004 to 6.4 percent in 2005, and 6.7 percent in 2006.

Is IBM compromising its efforts to be the customer- and innovation-driven company it seeks to be in this globally competitive environment? Evaluate its new strategic plan and present your recommendations.

References

www.eds.com
www.finance.yahoo.com
www.hp.com
www.ibm.com
www.microsoft.com
www.sec.gov
www.en.wikipedia.org

Ford Motor Company — 2007

Alen Badal
The Union Institute

FORD

www.ford.com

An American icon for over a century, Ford Motor Company (Ford) is experiencing difficult times. The company's net income was negative $1.6 billion in 2006 as revenues declined 9 percent.

For the six months ended June 30, 2007, Ford's revenues increased 6 percent to $87.26 billion. Net income totaled $434 million versus a loss of $1.75 billion the prior year. Ford's revenues reflect an increase in automotive sales and higher financial services revenues. Despite these increases, before year-end 2007, Toyota Motor was expected to replace Ford as the number 2 automaker after GM in the United States. Edmunds.com chief economist Jesse Toprak predicted Ford's sales would drop 16 percent in October 2007, while Toyota's sales would rise.

Ford wants to reduce its sales to rental-car agencies because they hurt brand image and resale values. In September 2006, for example, Ford sold nearly 23,000 of its old Taurus models to fleets. In 2007, Ford is no longer selling the old Taurus, and its new Taurus cannot make up the lost volume. Ford sold 4,230 new Taurus sedans in September 2007, according to Autodata.

Back in 1903, Mr. Henry Ford and eleven associates started the company. The Mustang, F-150, Thunderbird, Lincoln, and Jaguar are just a few Ford vehicles that roam the highways worldwide. But both Ford and General Motors are losing market share daily to Toyota and other foreign automakers. Gas prices are skyrocketing and neither Ford nor GM have vehicles on dealer lots that consumers desire as much as those of Toyota, BMW, Volkswagen, and Honda.

Headquartered in Dearborn, Michigan, Ford has a 17.5 percent market share of the auto manufacturing industry. Ford manufactures and distributes vehicles across six continents with a team of about 300,000 employees, operating about 108 plants globally. Other Ford products include Aston Martin, Land Rover, Lincoln, Mazda, Mercury, and Volvo. Ford also operates two service businesses: (1) Ford Motor Credit Company and (2) Genuine Parts and Motorcraft.

Ford strives to create business value without harming the environment. The company produces hybrid energy vehicles and has joined forces with British Petroleum (BP) to develop hydrogen power. Ford's Rouge Center in Dearborn, Michigan has the world's largest living roof, which covers the Dearborn Truck Plant's final assembly building.

Ford has announced that by 2008 it will "idle" nine North American manufacturing facilities. The company officers/managers will hold each other accountable in a team-oriented fashion. Weekly, half-day sessions will take place to discuss challenges and strategies developed as a team. The focus of the company is to fix its North American operation. The new CEO, Alan Mulally, is leading this effort. Exhibit 1 features the top management of Ford.

EXHIBIT 1   Ford Motor Company Corporate Officers (Senior and Group Executives Listed Only)

William Clay Ford, Jr., Executive Chairman
Alan Mulally, President & CEO
Donat R. Leclair, Executive V.P. & CFO
Lewis W. K. Booth, Exec. V.P. Ford of Europe/P.A.G.
Mark Fields, Executive V.P. & President, The Americas
Mark A. Schulz, Executive V.P.
Michael E. Bannister, Group V.P./Chair-CEO Ford Credit
Francisco N. Codina, Group V.P. Marketing/Sales/Service
John Fleming, Group V.P. President/CEO Ford of Europe
Joe W. Laymon, Group V.P. Corporate HR & Labor Affairs
John G. Parker, Group V.P. Asia Pacific & Africa
Derrick M. Kuzak, Group V.P. Global Product Development
J.C. Mays, Group V.P. Design & Chief Creative Officer
Richard Parry-Jones, Group V.P., Chief Technical officer
Ziad S. Ojakli Group V.P. Corporate Affairs

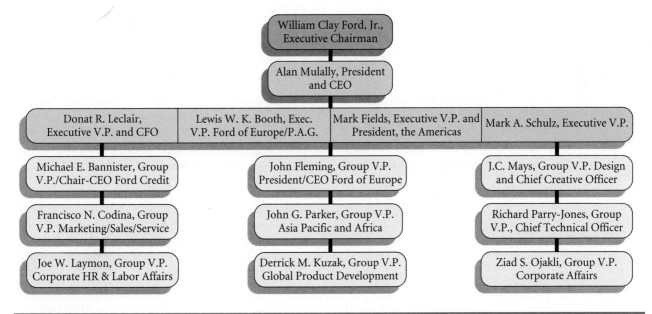

Source: www.ford.com

Ford Divisions

Ford is generally perceived as being an affordable brand name catering to a wide variety of consumer needs and wants. Ford's cars, trucks, and sport utility vehicles (SUVs) range from the Mustang and F-150 truck in America to the Mondeo in Europe and the EcoSport in South America and Asia. According to Auto Data Inc., the big three manufacturers (GM, Ford, and Chrysler) own 91 percent of the full-size truck segment compared to 5.5 percent for Toyota.

Lincoln/Mercury

Ford's Lincoln (www.lincoln.com) vehicles are perceived as a luxury line and include five models such as the popular Navigator and Town Car. Ford's Mercury (mercuryvehicles.com) line offers seven different models, such as the Monterey and the Montego.

Mazda

A Japanese line named after the ancient god of wisdom, Mazda (www.mazda.com), started in 1931. Now owned by Ford, Mazda offers 11 different models in 54 countries, plus the Mazda Verisa that is available only in Japan. The company posted record earnings in fiscal

EXHIBIT 2   Mazda Financial Data

Fiscal Year	FY139	FY140
Year Ended	March 31, 2005	March 31, 2006
Revenue (¥mil)	2,695,564	2,919,823
Operating profit / (loss) (¥mil)	82,947	123,435
Ordinary profit / (loss) (¥mil)	73,056	101,470
Net profit / (loss) (¥mil)	45,772	66,711
Net assets (¥mil)	267,815	398,024
Total assets (¥mil)	1,767,846	1,788,659
Net assets per share (¥)	220.22	284.28
Net profit / (loss) per share (¥)	37.63	51.53
Net profit per share, diluted (¥)	32.41	47.25

Source: Adapted from www.mazda.com

2006 with $2,919 million. Mazda is headquartered in Japan. Exhibit 2 contains the revenues in previous years for Mazda. Mazda is the sole manufacturer in the world of gasoline, diesel, and rotary internal combustion engines.

Volvo

Volvo (www.volvocars.com), a brand name that created the first 3-point seat belt, has built strong brand recognition as a safe vehicle. Formed in 1927 in Sweden, Volvo began exporting cars to the United States in 1955. Ford acquired Volvo in 1999 and the brand has been successful. Volvo markets in some 58 countries. Still based in Sweden, this division of Ford employs more than 83,000 employees. Volvo achieved net sales of SEK 248,135 million in 2006.

Jaguar and Land Rover

Jaguar's (www.jaguar.com) car manufacturing operations started in 1945 and was acquired by Ford in 1989. Jaguar markets models worldwide.

Land Rover (www.landrover.com) currently offers four types of SUVs that are sold around the world in over 140 countries. A British original since 1948, Land Rover manufactures all-wheel-drive vehicles.

Aston Martin

Established in 1914, Aston Marin (www.astonmartin.com) offers three different models. Ford sold this British brand in March of 2007 to a consortium of investors, but retains a $77 million stake in the company. According to CEO Mulally, the sale benefited Ford by cutting factory capacity and enabling the company to produce vehicles at a faster rate. Ford continues to support the consortium of investors with safety, emissions, and other technological needs.

Ford Motor Credit

Founded in 1923, Ford Motor Credit Company (www.fordcredit.com) offers financing to consumers and dealerships nationwide and is the world's largest finance company. Ford Motor Credit offers innovative products and competitive financing rates with flexible terms applied toward leasing and/or financing vehicle purchases. This division also assists dealerships with funding for such purposes as improving sites and acquiring real estate. Ford's credit division achieved $16.5 billion in 2006 as compared to $15.9 billion in 2005 as noted in Exhibit 3. That was a 3.7 percent increase. The Hertz operation achieved sales of $7.4 billion in 2005, but was divested in 2006.

Genuine Parts & Service

Introduced in 1991, Genuine Parts & Service (www.genuineflmservice.com) offers the know-how about parts, repairs, and maintenance to owners of Ford, Lincoln, and Mercury vehicles.

EXHIBIT 3   Ford Financial Services Sector Revenues (In $ Billions)

Divisions	2006	2005
Ford Credit	$16.5	$15.9
Other Financial Services	$0.3	$0.1
Hertz Operating Results	*	$7.4
Total	$16.8	$23.4

*Hertz was sold during the 4th quarter of 2005.

Source: Adapted from www.ford.com

Motorcraft

Ford purchased Electric Autolite Company in 1961, but later changed the name to Motorcraft (www.motorcraft.com). This division makes parts for Mercury, Lincoln, and Ford vehicles. The Web site www.ford.com enables consumers to search for (and obtain) parts by vehicle make, model, year, and identification number.

Global Operations

Ford's S-Max was the "car of the year in Europe—2006." Ford recently opened a research and engineering center in China. The Ford Mazda automobile in 2007 will produce in excess of 410,000 units, with plans to establish some 200-plus dealerships in China.

In Australia, Ford is designing and engineering a global light commercial vehicle that will eventually be sold in some 80 countries. Ford is developing the Falcon and the Territory model for Australia and other markets. The Falcon has been successful in New Zealand and the Territory model is a success in South Africa and Thailand.

Ford's Premier Automotive Group European business (PAG Division) is expected to be profitable in 2007, but Ford does not expect to turn a profit in its North America division until 2009. Exhibits 4 and 5 provide Ford's geographic segment net income and total revenue data respectively for 2006 versus 2005. Exhibit 6 provides market share data by geographic area. Note that the PAG division increased profits to $8.6 billion in 2006, up from $8 billion in 2005. Ford's South America and Europe divisions also increased profits in 2006 as compared to 2005. Ford experienced a decline in the U.S. market share in 2006, as featured in Exhibit 6. The share of the market in Europe and Asia Pacific/Africa remained the same for Ford in 2006 versus 2005.

Note in Exhibit 5. that Ford's revenues from North America decreased by more than $10 million in 2006. Ford's PAG group's revenues remained about the same in 2006. Fluctuating currency exchange rates and an increase in raw materials costs hurt profit margins. The British pound (£) reached a 2:1 ratio in early 2007 while the euro (€) and Japanese Yen (¥) currencies have also been rising quickly against the U.S. dollar ($).

Exhibits 7 and 8 reveal Ford's financial figures over a span of 3 years. Note that Ford's negative $12.6 billion really has the firm in a bind.

The Japanese automakers, Honda, Toyota, and Nissan, have been slow to enter China. However, all these firms are now rapidly boosting efforts in China by building manufacturing

EXHIBIT 4   2005 versus 2006 Ford Net Income Data

	2005	2006
Ford South America: $1.3 billion		$1.7 billion
Ford Europe: $7.9 billion		$8.8 billion
Ford's Premier Automotive Group (P.A.G); $8.0 billion		$8.6 billion

Source: Adapted from www.ford.com

EXHIBIT 5   Full Year Automotive Revenue Summary

	Revenue	
	2005(Mil)	2006(Mil)
North America	$80,662	$69,425
South America	4,366	5,697
Total Americas	$85,028	$75,122
Europe	$29,918	$30,408
P.A.G.	30,283	30,028
Total Europe/P.A.G.	$60,201	$60,436
Asia Pacific & Africa	$7,684	$6,539
Mazda & Assoc. Oper.	561	1,224
Total AP & Africa/Mazda	$8,245	$7,763
Other Automotive	—	—
Total Automotive	$153,474	$143,321

Source: www.ford.com

plants and introducing new models. As indicated in Exhibit 9, Volkswagen's market share was 16 percent in 2006 and GM had a 10.7 percent share of the same market. Ford has a 5.7 percent share of the China market followed by Honda with 5.0 percent. Honda was the first to enter the China market in 1999 and sold 320,000 vehicles in 2006. Toyota entered China in 2002 and has since announced projected sales of 400,000 vehicles in 2007.

China's market is two-tier; demands exist at both the high- and low-end price ranges and models. Toyota first discovered this by testing the market with a lesser known brand—Vios, which failed. Consumers expressed interest in known brands. As a result, Toyota plans to offer the Corolla sedan and the Lexus LS460L. GM entered in the 1990s with Buick and Cadillac models. Volkswagen offers its Audi line and compact models: Gold and Polo, in China.

Competition

DaimlerChrysler AG, General Motors Corporation, and Toyota Motor Corporation are three of Ford's major competitors. In the first quarter of 2007, Toyota outsold GM and all other auto producers to become the largest automaker. Toyota's production plans suggest the company could hold the leading position for the entire year. One reason for the slip into second place for GM is the company's reduced sales to rental car fleets as well as perceived lower quality and fuel efficiency.

EXHIBIT 6   Ford Motor Company Automotive Sector Market Share

	Market Share	
Markets	2006	2005
USA	16%	17%
South America	11.5%	12%
Europe	8.5%	8.5%
P.A.G.(USA/Europe)	1.1/2.1%	1.2/2.2%
Asia Pacific/Africa	2.4%	2.4%

Source: Adapted from www.ford.com

EXHIBIT 7   Ford Motor Company—Income Statement (In Thousands)

Period Ending	Dec. 31, 2006	Dec. 31, 2005	Dec. 31, 2004
Total Revenue	$ 160,123,000	176,896,000	171,652,000
Cost of Revenue	148,869,000	144,924,000	135,856,000
Gross Profit	11,254,000	31,972,000	35,796,000
Operating Expense	—	—	—
Research Development	—	—	—
Selling, Gen & Admin	19,180,000	18,768,000	23,903,000
Non-Recurring	—	—	—
Others	241,000	6,337,000	2,212,000
Total Operating Expenses			
Operating Income or Loss	**(8,167,000)**	**(7,962,000)**	**(10,681,000)**
Income from Continuing Oper	—	—	—
Total Other Income/Exp. Net	1,899,000	1,249,000	1,243,000
EBIT	(6,268,000)	9,496,000	11,924,000
Interest Expense	8,783,000	8,417,000	7,071,000
Minority Interest	(210,000)	(280,000)	(282,000)
Net Income from Cont. Ops	(12,615,000)	1,644,000	3,634,000
Non-Recurring Events	—	—	—
Discontinued Operations	2,000	47,000	(147,000)
Extraordinary Items	—	—	—
Effect of Acct. Changes	—	(251,000)	—
Other Items	—	—	—
Net Income	**($12,613,000)**	**1,440,000**	**3,487,000**
Preferred Stock and Other Adjustments	—	—	—
Net Income Applicable to Common Shares	**($12,613,000)**	**$1,440,000**	**$3,478,000**

Source: finance.yahoo.com

Auto manufacturers face high expectations from consumers to offer more options, more makes, and more models of vehicles. Exhibit 10 provides a direct competitor comparison of auto firms' financial performances. Note that GM revenues annually exceed $200 billion and Toyota has the highest gross margins at 27.49 percent. Exhibit 11 reports 2006 market share figures for the U.S. automotive market, which notes Ford ranking number 2 behind GM. GM also had the highest inventory with more than one million vehicles.

DiamlerChrysler AG

Founded in 1883, DaimlerChrysler AG is headquartered in Stuttgart, Germany (www.daimlerchrysler.com). The company holds 14.4 percent of the U.S. market share. AG's product/service lines include Mercedes Car Group; Chrysler Group; Commercial Vehicles; and Financial Services. AG's product lines include both Jeep and Dodge. The company sells parts and vehicle accessories under a MOPAR brand name. The company's commercial vehicle lines include Orion and Thomas Built Buses.

AG offers a financial/credit services business and had annual revenues of $200.1 billion in 2006. The company has about 382,724 employees. DaimlerChrysler AG divested 80 percent of its Chrysler Group division in May of 2007 for $7.4 billion to Cerberus, a private-equity firm. The company will hold onto their other divisions, such as the profitable Mercedes-Benz segment.

EXHIBIT 8 Ford Motor Company—Balance Sheet

Period Ending	Dec. 31, 2006	Dec. 31, 2005	Dec. 31, 2004
Assets			
Current Assets			
Cash and Cash Equiv	$ 28.894.000	28,410,000	23,511,000
Short-Term Investments		10,321,000	
Not Receivables	8,772,000	5,744,000	15,137,000
Inventory	11,578,000	10,271,000	10,766,000
Other Current Assets		8,177,000	
Total Current Assets	**49,244,000**	**62,923,000**	**49,414,000**
Long-Term Investments	136,378,000	139,955,000	155,912,000
Property, Plant and Equip	38,505,000	40,349,000	44,551,000
Goodwill	5,839,000	5,125,000	6,104,000
Intangible Assets	30,932,000	820,000	1,167,000
Accumulated Amortization			
Other Assets	12,706,000	15,765,000	30,676,000
Deferred Long-Term Charges	4,950,000	10,999,000	4,830,000
Total Assets	**278,554,000**	**275,936,000**	**292,654,000**
Liabilities			
Current Liabilities			
Accounts Payable	24,416,000	48,404,000	52,676,000
Short/Current Long-Term Debt		978,000	
Other Current Liabilities	28,128,000	4,222,000	
Total Current Liabilities	**52,544,000**	**53,604,000**	**52,676,000**
Long-Term Debt	172,049,000	152,300,000	172,973,000
Other Liabilities	51,477,000	44,135,000	43,912,000
Deferred Long-Term Liability Charges	4,790,000	11,333,000	6,171,000
Minority Interest	1,159,000	1,122,000	877,000
Negative Goodwill	—	—	—
Total Liabilities	**282,019,000**	**262,494,000**	**276,609,000**
Stockholders' Equity	—	—	—
Misc Stocks Options Warrants	—	—	—
Redeemable Preferred Stock	—	—	—
Preferred Stock	—	—	—
Common Stock	19,000	19,000	19,000
Retained Earnings	(17,000)	(13,064,000)	11,175,000
Treasury Stock	(183,000)	(833,000)	(1,728,000)
Capital Surplus	4,562,000	4,872,000	5,321,000
Other Stockholders' Equity	(7,846,000)	(3,680,000)	1,258,000
Total Stockholders' Equity	**(3,465,000)**	**13,442,000**	**16,045,000**
Net Tangible Assets	**($40,236,000)**	**$7,497,000**	**$8,774,000**
Total Liabilities and Stockholders' Equity	**278,554,000**	**275,936,000**	**292,654,000**

Source: finance.yahoo.com

EXHIBIT 9 **Automakers' 2006 Market Share in China**

Volkswagen	16.4%
GM	10.7%
Hyundai	9.8%
Honda	7.7%
Chevy	7.2%
Toyota	6.6%
Ford	5.7%
Nissan	5.0%
FAW	4.9%
Geely	4.9%

Source: Wall Street Journal, May 16, 2007.

GM

Headquartered in Detroit, Michigan, GM (www.gm.com) employs 335,000 and reported annual revenues of $207 billion in 2006 as compared to $192 in 2005. The company operates globally and has approximately 7,350 dealerships in the United States, 750 in Canada, and 300 in Mexico along with 15,600 distribution outlets overseas. The company also operates a financing and insurance operation. Saab, Pontiac, and Cadillac are among the many GM models. GM held an industry leading 24.6 percent of the U.S. market share in 2006.

GM sold more than 9 million cars in 2006 and achieved growth in sales in the Asia/Pacific region. GM's Saab experienced record sales, but global GM sales were down about 1 percent in 2006 compared to 2005. The company witnessed sales growth, however, of up to 17 percent in the Africa, Middle East, and Latin America regions in 2006.

EXHIBIT 10 **Direct Competitor Comparison**

Company Symbol:	F	DCX	GM	TM	Industry
Market Cap	$ 16.49B	65.55B	20.37B	238.37B	140.65B
Employees	300,000	382,724	335,000	285,977	144.79K
Quarterly Rev Growth	−8.40%	−7.80%	3.60%	15.20%	3.70%
Revenue	166.13B	198.67B	206.71B	193.05B	187.84B
Gross Margin	4.48%	17.67%	0.54%	27.49%	17.67%
EBITDA	8.67B	20.72B	4.09B	31.31B	20.63B
Oper margins	−3.04%	1.62%	−5.74%	9.65%	3.16%
Net Income	−6.82B	4.73B	−9.58B	13.28B	6.32M
EPS	−3.723	4.599	−17.124	8.26	1.14
P/E	N/A	13.94	N/A	15.99	16.35
PEG (5 yr. expected)	N/A	N/A	1.25	N/A	1.81
P/S	0.10	.32	0.09	1.24	1.14

DCX = DaimlerChrysler AG
GM = General Motors
TM = Toyota Motor Corp.
Industry = Auto Manufacturers-Major
Source: finance.yahoo.com

EXHIBIT 11   U.S. Automotive Market Share/Inventory in 2006

	U.S. Market Share	Inventory
GM	24.6%	1,028,783
Nissan	6.2%	242,187
DaimlerChrysler	14.4%	538,438
Ford	17.5%	624,754
Honda	9.1%	225,293
Toyota	15.4%	320,282

Source: Wall Street Journal, February 9, 2007, p. A8.

Toyota Motor Corporation

Headquartered in Toyota City, Japan, Toyota (www.toyota.co.jp) reported annual revenues of $179 billion in 2006. Toyota currently holds 15.4 percent of the U.S. market share. The company has 285,977 employees and was founded in 1933. It was recently ranked by *Fortune* as the overall #3 most admired company, and is America's best automaker. The company has five production plants in the United States making Toyota engines, vehicles, and car components.

Toyota operates in three segments: Automotive Operations, Financial Service Operations, and Other Operations. Toyota models produced include the Corolla and RAV4. Its financial services division helps consumers financially purchase vehicles and provides inventory financing to dealers.

Toyota operates an e-commerce marketplace known as Gazoo.com and sells vehicles in Japan, North America, Europe, and Asia. Toyota has been making a strong push in the French market with an increase of 11 percent of registrations, yielding a market share of 4.9 percent in 2006. Toyota plans to open a manufacturing plant in Mississippi by 2010 to build Highlanders. Toyota sales in Japan have decreased of late, but exports continue to be a big success for the company.

Industry Analysis

The auto manufacturing industry has been affected by such factors as rising fuel costs and interest rates. According to a *Wall Street Journal* article (February 9, 2007), auto dealers are pushing for change among manufacturers. Auto makers have faced rising costs of health care and pensions. The big three hope to gain concessions from the United Auto Workers regarding labor costs expected to take place in 2007. The mass production of vehicles has resulted in manufacturers pressuring dealers to increase their inventory and then they offer incentives to assist dealers to sell stock.

According to an automotive research firm, CSM Worldwide, auto makers have excess capacity estimated at 16 percent and 14 percent respectively in North America and Europe. The weak U.S. dollar benefits manufacturers such as Toyota.

Production raw material costs for steel and resins are rising. Gasoline and energy costs continue to rise, affecting production and sales of vehicles. Even the decline of home construction in the United States has affected the demand for truck sales. CO_2 emission standards for light and heavy vehicles have become stricter in the United States, increasing auto manufacturers' costs to produce engines. Strict regulations took effect on January 1, 2007.

Decreasing the number of days a vehicle sits on the car lot is a priority. This has been the result of dealerships, "speaking up" regarding the amount of unsold stock they have and the lack of desired options/make/models they have in stock. Dealers want manufacturers to refrain from the business model of being production-driven and instead focus more on consumer wants. Some manufacturers have placed blame on limited supplier inventory as the reason for lower sales; however, the responsibility ultimately lies with the manufacturers to provide dealers with what they want in order for the dealers to finalize the sales.

Industry manufacturers are downsizing, laying employees off, and/or restructuring. This has led to a decrease in the overall organizational morale within the industry. Some manufacturers are closing out certain models and then bringing one or more back on the production lines, such as Ford bringing the Taurus model to production.

In recent years, Americans have experienced financial hardships due to increasing mortgage rates. With foreclosures on the rise, automobile manufacturers are encountering challenges financing cars. Manufacturers have begun offering financial incentives to dealers in the quest of selling particular brands. Toyota is offering incentives of $2,000 to purchase the base model B-cab Tundra pickup, which was redesigned to better compete with Detroit's Big Three truck manufacturers. GM and Chrysler are offering similar incentives to entice consumers. GM is offering such incentives as up to $1,000 off some full-size pickups. Chrysler is offering free Hemi engine upgrades and cash incentives of up to $5,000 on select Dodge Ram pickups.

The Future

Ford must adapt better to an increasingly competitive environment in the auto industry. Japanese and German auto firms now have the upper hand on Ford. And there are new Chinese auto firms gaining strength and soon to enter the U.S. market. Gas prices continue to rise in the United States as customers desire hybrid and fuel-efficient vehicles. The value of the dollar is so low now it gives other firms a competitive advantage over Ford. American consumers are generally strapped for cash and leveraged up as much as they can go.

Develop a strategic plan of action for Ford Motor Company. Provide a detailed strategic analysis for CEO Alan Mulally. Include the methodology and costs associated with implementation of your recommended strategies for the next three years.

References

http://finance.yahoo.com
Wall Street Journal, February 9, 2007
Wall Street Journal, March 6, 2007
Wall Street Journal-Europe, April 3, 2007
Wall Street Journal-Europe, April 5-9, 2007
Wall Street Journal, May 16, 2007
Fortune magazine, March 19, 2007
www.aol.com(money & finance)
www.ford.com
www.lincoln.com
www.mazda.com
www.volvocars.com
www.jaguar.com
www.landrover.com
www.astonmartin.com
www.fordcredit.com
www.genuineflmservice.com
www.motorcraft.com
www.gm.com
www.toyota.co.jp
moneycentral.msn.com
www.daimlerchrysler.com
www.washingtonpost.com
biz.yahoo.com
www.media.ford.com
USA Today, April 25, 2007
http://www.msnbc.msn.com/id/18645179/

Winnebago Industries — 2008

Eugene M. Bland
Texas A&M University–Corpus Christi

John G. Marcis
Coastal Carolina University

WGO

www.winnebagoind.com

At the Winnebago's Dealer Days event held May 14–16, 2007 at the Mirage in Las Vegas, this Forest City, Iowa–based company unveiled its exciting, new 2008 motor homes. With a theme of "Dialed In," Winnebago introduced a lineup featuring 25 model lines and 93 floorplans, 49 percent of which were new or redesigned for 2008. Winnebago currently has 290 dealers located throughout the United States and Canada. Most of these are not exclusive Winnebago dealers, meaning that many are also automobile dealerships and the like. Winnebago's financial results in 2006 and the prior year were not good. Revenues for fiscal year ended August 25, 2007 increased only $5.7 million, or 0.7 percent. This slight increase was due to an average price increase of 4.9 percent because Winnebago's number of units sold in fiscal 2007 actually decreased 3.8 percent. The company's net income decreased 7.1 percent in fiscal 2007.

Saving money is nice, but it is not the real reason that people travel in a motor home. Motor homing is just plain fun. Motor homers are an adventurous lot—they like to go, see, and do. Recreational vehicle (RV) owners say that they not only save money when camping but can avoid the bother of having to stop for restaurants and bathrooms. Florida residents have replaced Californians as the most active motor home campers. New Yorkers are third on the "most on the go" list.

Motor home traveling is purported to be much less expensive than traveling by car or plane and staying in a motel. Motor homers often spend summers where it is cool and winters where it is warm. In fact, industry advertisements tout the RV lifestyle with the slogan "Wherever you go, you're always at home."

Early Motor Homing

The first motor home was built in 1915 to take people from the Atlantic Coast to San Francisco. It had wooden wheels and hard rubber tires. It was promoted as having all the comforts of an ocean cruiser. By the 1920s, the house car had become a fixture in the United States and a symbol of freedom. All kinds of house cars could be seen traveling across America's dirt roads. They ranged from what looked like large moving cigars to two-story houses, with porches, on wheels. But these house cars featured poor weight distribution, poor insulation, and poor fuel economy. From the 1930s to the 1950s they gave way in popularity to the trailer.

In the mid-1950s, motor homes were called motorized trailers. Although these motorized trailers were overweight, underpowered, and poorly insulated, they were a vast improvement over the house cars of the 1920s. In the 1960s, motor homing became much more popular, largely as a result of the innovations of Winnebago. From Forest City, Iowa, where the company was founded in 1958, Winnebago set the pace for new development of motor homes. The Winnebago name became a household word. Buyers of motor homes were asked, "When will your Winnebago be delivered?"

Overview

Winnebago is a leading manufacturer of motor homes. The company uses state-of-the-art computer-aided design and manufacturing systems on automotive-style assembly lines. Although Winnebago Industries competes with four other RV producers, the name *Winnebago* is considered synonymous with the term *motor home*. Winnebago's home page can be accessed at http://www.winnebagoind.com and corporate press releases are available at two sites: http://www.prnewswire.com and http://investor.stockpoint.com/.

Winnebago Industries is financially stable: The firm owns its land, buildings, and equipment, and has no long-term debt. The firm had an enviable cash and marketable securities balance of $24,934,000 at the end of their August 2006 fiscal year. This provides the company with the opportunity for future long-term growth. In 1998, the board of directors approved a general plan to repurchase outstanding shares of the firm's stock. The repurchase initiatives in 1998 and 1999 resulted in 13.1 percent of the outstanding shares of Winnebago's stock being repurchased by the firm. Following the 2003 death of Luise Hanson, the widow of company founder John Hanson, Winnebago industries repurchased 1,450,000 shares (8 percent of the total shares outstanding) from the estate. The company authorized the repurchase of an additional 1,006,546 shares in 2005 for an aggregate price of approximately $30 million. In 2006, the board announced a new $50 million share repurchase authorization. Chairman and CEO Bruce Hertzke announced "We continue to believe that the repurchase of Winnebago stock is a good means to enhance shareholder value." In summary, between 1997 and 2006, the company has repurchased over 22.8 million shares of stock for a total of $308 million. Further, the board authorized the doubling of the cash dividend for fiscal 2004. Winnebago Industries will now pay a $.10 per share quarterly dividend, instead of a semiannual dividend.

Winnebago's revenues for the fiscal year ended August 26, 2006, decreased to $864.4 million (52 weeks) from $992 million in 2005 (53 weeks). Motor home shipments (Class A and C) during the fifty-two-week fiscal 2006 were 9,843 units, a decrease of 794 units from the fifty-three-week fiscal 2005 shipment of 10,637. These are not trends the company wants to see continue. High gas prices in the United States worry Winnebago managers and dealers.

Ethics does not take a back seat to profits at Winnebago Industries. The company has a 13-point code of ethics. This code addresses the firm's belief that its employees should, among other things, comply with the law, avoid conflicts of interest, protect and properly use company assets, and report any illegal or unethical behavior. The board of directors has adopted an additional five point code of conduct applicable specifically to the CEO and senior financial officers. The Winnebago Code of Ethics and the Code of Ethics for the CEO and senior financial officers are available at http://209.213.122.67/framesets/investors.php.

Internal Issues

Mission and Vision Statement

Winnebago does not have a vision statement. Their motto however is "Quality is a Journey—Not a Destination." From the beginning, the company recognized the critical roles played by employees, customers, and dealers in the total quality process. Winnebago does have a Mission Statement, a Statement of Values, and a Statement of Guiding Principles. The company's mission statement is as follows:

> Winnebago Industries is a leading United States manufacturer of motor homes and related products and services. Our mission is to continually improve our products and services to meet or exceed the expectations of our customers. We emphasize employee teamwork and involvement in identifying and implementing programs to save time and lower production costs while maintaining the highest quality of products. These strategies have allowed us to prosper as a business with a high degree of integrity and to provide a reasonable return for our shareholders, the owners of our business.

Production Facilities

Winnebago has major production facilities in Forest City, Iowa. Over 20 buildings at this location comprise over two million square feet (approximately 60 acres under roof) and contain the company's manufacturing, maintenance, and service operations. There are also satellite-manufacturing facilities at both Hampton and Lorimor in Iowa. These two facilities add another 700,000 square feet of manufacturing space. All corporate facilities in Forest City are located on approximately 784 acres of land owned by Winnebago. In March 2003, the newest production facility in Charles City, Iowa, began operation. This 204,000 square foot facility increased the manufacturing capacity of the firm by nearly 30 percent. The purpose of this expansion was to increase production of Class C motor homes in Charles City and allow the Forest City plant to specialize in the production of Class A motor homes.

Winnebago has three 900-foot assembly lines for final assembly of motor homes. Statistical process control is practiced at Winnebago and has enhanced the quality of its van products. As a motor home progresses through the assembly line, quality control is carefully monitored. Units are taken randomly from the line for a thorough examination. The performance of every RV is tested before it is delivered to a dealer's lot. Some of the tests routinely performed include lamination strength, appliance performance, chip resistance, vibration, drop, salt spray, and crash tests. In November 2006, Winnebago received its eleventh consecutive Recreation Vehicle Dealer's Association Quality Circle Award, the only company to receive the award all 11 years. On receiving the award Chairman and CEO Bruce Hertzke stated, "We view the DSI survey as a vital measurement tool for the quality of our products, our sales and service programs and our manufacturing process. We believe the survey provides us with important benchmark information that shows how our dealer partners perceive the quality of Winnebago Industries products and services."

Research and Development

Winnebago uses a state-of-the-art, computer-aided design/computer-aided manufacturing (CAD/CAM) system in producing low-cost sheet metal parts, new paint lines for steel and aluminum parts, and modifications of assembly equipment. One of Winnebago's product-testing facilities at Forest City houses some of the most sophisticated technology being used in the RV industry. Included in the process are a high- and low-temperature chamber for subjecting parts to extreme temperatures and high stress, and a computerized road simulator that can imitate years of road wear in a few days.

Product Line

Winnebago Industries offers over 85 different floor plans. Roughly one-third of these models were either new or redesigned for the 2007 model year. Winnebago manufactures two principal types of recreational vehicles as indicated in Exhibit 1. Class A motor homes and Class C motor homes. Class A motor homes are constructed on a chassis that already

---

EXHIBIT 1 Motor Home Product Classification

Class A Motor Homes

These are conventional motor homes constructed directly on medium-duty truck chassis which include the engine and drive train components. The living area of the driver's compartment is designed and produced by Winnebago Industries.

Class B Van Campers

These are panel-type trucks to which sleeping, kitchen, and toilet facilities are added. These models also have a top extension to provide headroom.

Class C Motor Homes

These are motor homes built on a van-type chassis on which Winnebago Industries constructs a living area with access to the driver's compartment.

Source: Winnebago Industries, *2001 Annual Report*, p. 16.

EXHIBIT 2   Winnebago Industries, Inc., Unit Sales of Recreation Vehicles

Year Ended	August 2007	August 2006	August 2005	August 2004	August 2003	August 2002
Class A	5,031	4,455	6,674	8,108	6,705	6,725
Class C	4,438	5,388	3,963	4,408	4,021	4,329
Total	9,469	9,843	10,637	12,516	10,726	11,054

Source: 2006 *10-K Report.*

has the engine and drive components and are available in either gas or diesel engines. They range in length from 33 to 37 feet and can sell for over a quarter million dollars.

Since 1998, Winnebago has maintained the number one position in retail sales of Class C motor homes. In fact, with an expanded product line, Winnebago's market share for the first eight months of 2006 increased from 19.3 percent to 25.1 percent from the same period of the previous year. Class C motor homes are constructed on a van chassis with the driver's compartment accessible to the living area. These motor homes are compact, easy to drive, and available in both gasoline and diesel models. They range from 22 to 31 feet in length and have six popular floor plans. Typical options of a Class C vehicle include six feet of headroom, shower, stove, sink, refrigerator, and two double beds. Winnebago introduced two fuel-efficient models (the Winnebago View and the Itasca Navion) in 2006. In addition, new floor plans and full-body paint options were introduced in the 2007 Class C product line.

Motor home shipments (Class A and C) during the fifty-two-week fiscal 2006 were 9,843 and 9,469 in 2007 units as indicated in Exhibit 2. This was a decrease of 794 units from the fifty-three-week fiscal 2005 shipment of 10,637 and a decrease of 374 in 2007. As reported in respective 10-K reports, market share increased from 17.5 percent in 2005 to 19 percent in 2006. Exhibit 3 provides a breakdown of the annual unit sales. As of August 26, 2006, backorders for Class A and Class C motor homes were 1,696 units (compared to 2,059 in August of 2005).

Winnebago's partnership with Volkswagen to produce Class B motor homes ended in August 2002. Winnebago did not produce significantly more than 2,500 Class B units annually. Technically, they did not produce Class B units, rather they converted panel-type trucks to campers by adding a top extension for additional headroom, a kitchen, and sleeping and toilet facilities.

Marketing

Consumer research reveals that demographics for motor home buyers are undergoing change. Traditionally, buyers have been "woofies" (representing "well-off older folks" and defined as people over 50 years of age with discretionary income available) with time to enjoy leisure travel and outdoor recreation. According to research, an individual in the United States is turning 50 every 7.5 seconds, contributing an additional 350,000 people per *month* to that prime target market. Available demographic information indicates that this trend augurs well for sales growth through 2012. Population forecasts show that the motor home industry's target population, people between 55 and 64 years of age, will increase about 45 percent over the next decade, compared to the 8 percent growth in the general population. Additionally, a 2001 University of Michigan "RV Consumer Demographic Study" found that the age of interested consumers has been expanding to include younger buyers, as well as older buyers.

The peak selling season for RVs has historically been spring and summer. Winnebago markets Class A and Class C motor homes under the Winnebago and Itasca brand names, through a network of approximately 290 unique dealers in 2007 in the United States and, to a limited extent, Canada. At Winnebago, the trend is toward a smaller number of dealers who have larger market areas. These fewer, but larger, dealers are expected to offer more services to customers and should be better able to provide customer support after the sale.

Winnebago Industries believes it has the most comprehensive service program in the RV industry. With the purchase of any new Class A or Class C motor home, Winnebago offers a comprehensive 12-month/15,000-mile warranty, a 3-year/36,000 mile warranty on sidewalls and slideout room assemblies, and a 10-year fiberglass roof warranty. Winnebago also instituted a "toll-free hotline" where experienced service advisors respond to inquiries from prospective customers and expedite and resolve warranty issues. Every owner of a new Winnebago motor home receives free roadside assistance for 12 months.

Winnebago products are not inexpensive. RV sales are influenced by several external forces. Clearly, the favorable demographic trend has helped to increase the demand for the company's wares. However, prices for fuel, both gasoline and diesel, influence product demand. Relatively low and stable interest rates are also important for the company's sales outlook. As interest rates rise, so does the cost of financing a customer's purchase as well as the consumer's opportunity cost of funds.

Organizational Structure

Winnebago's organizational chart is provided in Exhibit 3. Note that the company operates using a functional organizational structure rather than a divisional structure. There is only one woman among the top management team, Sarah Nielsen, the chief financial

EXHIBIT 3   Winnebago's Organizational Chart

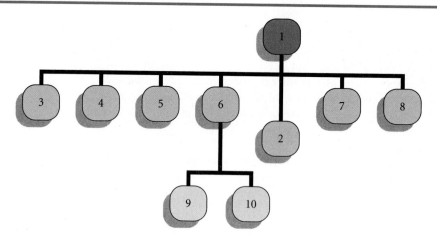

Executive Officers of Winnebago Industries

Name	Office (Year First Elected an Officer)	Age
1. Bruce D. Hertzke +	Chairman of the Board and Chief Executive Officer (1989)	55
2. Robert J. Olson	President (1996)	55
3. Raymond M. Beebe	Vice President, General Counsel and Secretary (1974)	64
4. Robert L. Gossett	Vice President, Administration (1998)	55
5. Roger W. Martin	Vice President, Sales and Marketing (2003)	46
6. Sarah N. Nielsen	Vice President, Chief Financial Officer (2005)	33
7. William J. O'Leary	Vice President, Product Development (2001)	57
8. Randy J. Potts	Vice President, Manufacturing (2006)	47
9. Brian J. Hrubes	Controller (1996)	55
10. Joseph L. Soczek, Jr.	Treasurer (1996)	63

Note: + Director

Source: 2006 *10-K Report* (Amended to reflect the May 2007 retirement of Edwin Barker, president, who was replaced by Senior Vice President of Operations Robert Olson.)

EXHIBIT 4 **Winnebago Industries, Inc. Consolidated Statements of Income**

	Year Ended		
(In thousands, except per share data)	August 25, 2007	August 26, 2006	August 27, 2005
Net revenues	$ 870,152	$ 864,403	$ 991,975
Cost of goods sold	770,955	759,502	854,997
Gross profit	99,197	104,901	136,978
Operating expenses:			
Selling	19,865	19,619	19,936
General and administrative	24,446	22,184	18,787
Tótal operating expenses	44,311	41,803	38,723
Operating income	54,886	63,098	98,255
Financial income	6,523	5,097	2,635
Income before taxes	61,409	68,195	100,890
Provision for taxes	19,845	23,451	35,817
Net income	$ 41,564	$ 44,744	$ 65,073
Income per common share:			
Basic	$ 1.33	$ 1.39	$ 1.95
Diluted	$ 1.32	$ 1.37	$ 1.92
Weighted average common shares outstanding:			
Basic	31,162	32,265	33,382
Diluted	31,415	32,550	33,812

Source: http://finance.yahoo.com

officer. Most large firms such as Winnebago operate from some type of divisional or strategic business unit type structure in order to delegate accountability and responsibility more effectively.

Finance

As indicated in Exhibit 4, Winnebago's banner 2004 year has been followed by both revenue and net income steadily falling. Revenues reached $864.40 million for the 2006 fiscal year (compared with $991.98 million for the 2005 fiscal year). Income from operations for the year dropped to $63 million from $98.26 million. Production for the fifty-two-week 2006 period was down 824 units from the fifty-three-week 2005 period. Management attributed this sales decrease to the record high fuel prices experienced in the 2006 selling season and to interest rates rebounding from 45-year lows. Management also noted the market had shifted from Class A motor homes toward the smaller Class C motor homes. While Statistical Surveys, Inc. reported industry RV sales down 13.1 percent, Winnebago management reported a sales decrease of only 7.5 percent. Further, even though revenues declined nearly $128 million in 2006, cash flow from operations reached $113.26 million, nearly 44 percent higher than the $78.8 million in 2005.

As indicated in Exhibit 5, Winnebago has no long-term debt. While this financial structure all but eliminates the company's default risk, it also means the firm is foregoing the benefit that the tax deductibility of interest payments provides. The absence of long-term debt and resulting reliance on equity financing raises the company's weighted average cost of capital. Many other industrial firms have used this low interest rate period to refinance existing debt and even to issue new debt.

External Issues

Winnebago's motor homes can attract a low-frills buyer desiring the most stripped-down RV, the person with expensive tastes desiring the ultimate in RV luxury, and everyone in between. RVs can be purchased or rented. Many families unable to buy an RV often can

EXHIBIT 5 Winnebago Industries, Inc. Consolidated Balance Sheets

(In thousands, except per share data)	August 25, 2007	August 26, 2006
Assets		
Current assets:		
Cash and cash equivalents	$ 6,889	$ 24,934
Short-term investments	102,650	129,950
Receivables, less allowance for doubtful accounts ($133 and $164, respectively)	30,285	20,859
Inventories	101,208	77,081
Prepaid expenses and other assets	3,981	5,269
Deferred income taxes	12,687	9,067
Total current assets	257,700	267,160
Property and equipment, at cost:		
Land	934	946
Buildings	59,525	59,378
Machinery and equipment	98,026	99,839
Transportation equipment	9,593	9,561
Total property and equipment, at cost	168,078	169,724
Accumulated depreciation	(116,689)	(112,817)
Total property and equipment, net	51,389	56,907
Investment in life insurance	20,015	20,814
Deferred income taxes	19,856	25,002
Other assets	17,550	14,832
Total assets	$ 366,510	$ 384,715
Liabilities and Stockholders' Equity		
Current liabilities:		
Accounts payable	$ 35,286	$ 27,923
Income taxes payable	4,252	7,876
Accrued expenses:		
Accrued compensation	16,946	12,498
Product warranties	11,259	9,523
Self-insurance	7,919	7,842
Promotional	3,793	5,253
Accrued dividends	3,546	3,109
Other	5,836	6,098
Total current liabilities	88,837	80,122
Postretirement health care and deferred compensation benefits, net or current portion	69,319	86,271
Contingent liabilities and commitments		
Stockholders' equity:		
Capital stock common, par value $ 0.50, authorized 60,000 shares, issued 51,776 shares	25,888	25,888
Additional paid-in capital	28,646	22,268
Retained earnings	509,056	480,446
Accumulated other comprehensive income	11,090	–
Treasury stock, at cost (22,223 and 20,633 shares, respectively)	(366,326)	(310,280)
Total stockholders' equity	208,354	218,322
Total liabilities and stockholders' equity	$ 366,510	$ 384,715

Source: http://finance.yahoo.com

rent one to take on vacation. As the baby boomers age and approach retirement (it is estimated that 350,000 people will turn 50 every month), many of them will consider selling their primary residence, purchasing and moving into a motor home, and traveling to any point they desire in North America.

In April 2007, *Hotel and Motel Management* magazine reported, "Since 2003, demand for hotel rooms has increased by 10.2 percent, while the net change in supply has been almost flat, which in turn has placed pricing power firmly in the hands of hotel managers. According to Smith Travel Research (STR), the average cost of renting a hotel room in the top 50 U.S. cities has increased by 23.0 percent during this time" (http://www.hotelmotel.com/hotelmotel/article/articleDetail.jsp?id=418695).

Compared to the cost of owning/renting and operating an RV, the costs of staying in a motor home versus a motel are about the same. Motor home sales historically increase whenever travel, tourism, and vacationing gain in popularity. The converse is also true.

There are about 122,000 campsites in U.S. state parks, including 4,500 maintained by the U.S. Forest Service and 100 in the National Parks System. In addition, there are more than 15,000 private campgrounds and over 1,620 county parks in the United States. Winnebagos can access nearly all of these sites. However, the economic uncertainty introduced since the terrorist attacks of September 11, 2001, and the continued "War on Terror" have served to cloud the fiscal picture of leisure-related activities like RVing.

High gas prices are a major threat to motor home manufacturers, as are rising interest rates and declines in consumers' disposable income. The aging American society and retirement of baby boomers are positive trends affecting firms in this industry. Florida, California, and New York, heavy RV customer states, are a long way from Iowa, so Winnebago incurs significant distribution expenses.

Competitors

As listed below, Winnebago faces four large, formidable competitors that strive to take market share away from the big Iowa-based company. Several of these competitors, especially Fleetwood, gain significant economies of scale on Winnebago by manufacturing both motor homes and mobile homes. Many of the parts and design of motor and mobile homes are similar as is the production process, but to date Winnebago has never manufactured mobile homes.

Company (Stock Symbol)	Headquarters Location
1. Coachman Industries, Inc. (COA)	Elkhart, IN
2. Fleetwood Enterprises, Inc. (FLE)	Riverside, CA
3. Monaco Coach Corp. (MNC)	Junction City, OR
4. Thor Industries Inc (THO)	Jackson, OH

http://www.coachmen.com/

http://www.fleetwood.com/

http://www.monaco-online.com/

http://www.thorindustries.com/

Winnebago is a "pure play" in the RV industry. Ninety-five percent of their revenues come from the production and sale of recreational vehicles and parts and the other 5 percent comes from manufactured products. In addition to RVs, Winnebago's competitors also produce manufactured housing (mobile homes) and buses. All these product lines are exposed to interest rate risk. The recent "meltdown" of the subprime mortgage market is likely to adversely impact these competitors more than Winnebago Industries. It is very likely that mortgage underwriters are going to raise the minimum credit score and return to the more traditional mortgage terms and away from interest only, adjustable rate, and balloon loans. This will not harm Winnebago as much as it harms Winnebago's competitors because RV purchasers are not as likely as manufactured home purchasers to apply for these types of loans.

EXHIBIT 6   Winnebago versus Rival Firms

	WGO	COA	FLE	THO	Industry
Market Cap	$925.70M	158.21M	572.64M	2.42B	465.52M
Employees	3,150	2,655	11,500	9,363	6,667
Qtrly Rev Growth	–3.60%	–19.90%	–24.10%	–4.40%	–13.0%
Revenue	826.50M	532.07M	2.10B	3.03B	782.43M
Gross Margin	11.35%	8.35%	14.50%	14.11%	14.50%
EBITDA	61.98M	–26.74M	–10.97M	259.37M	26.40M
Oper Margins	6.13%	–6.27%	–1.75%	8.04%	2.34%
Net Income	37.94M	–44.07M	–45.92M	161.70M	–118.44K
EPS	1.193	–2.884	–0.768	2.855	N/A
P/E	24.56	N/A	N/A	15.24	16.58

Note:
COA = Coachmen Industries Inc.
FLE = Fleetwood Enterprises Inc.
THO = Thor Industries Inc.
Industry = Recreational Vehicles
Source: Adapted from http://finance.yahoo.com.

Coachman Industries produces both RVs and modular housing. RV sales generate over 70 percent of their revenues and modular homes sales generate the remainder. Fleetwood Enterprises produces motor homes, travel trailers, as well as manufactured housing. In terms of sales, Fleetwood continues to be the largest firm in the RV industry. Historically, Monaco Coach Corporation specialized in the production of premium RVs, producing bus-sized, diesel-fueled RVs ranging in price from $100,000 to over $1 million. However, in 2000-2001, Monaco started to diversify into the smaller Class C motor home market. As a result, Monaco had a substantial jump in revenues ($937.1 million to $1,222.7 million) from 2001 to 2002 but have held relatively stable from 2002 to 2006. Thor Industries emerged in 2002–2003 as a major firm in the RV industry. Thor manufactures both RVs and buses. However, due to an investigation at a subsidiary, Thor recently had to restate its financial statements for the years 2004 through 2006, inclusive. As of this writing, the restatements have not been released. Thor, like Winnebago, has no long-term debt, and that is not likely to change as a result of the restatement.

As indicated in Exhibit 6 developed in mid-2007, all firms in the motor home industry have experienced negative growth in recent quarters. Note also that Winnebago's gross margin is below Fleetwood, Thor, and the industry average.

Industry Outlook

Calendar years 2003 and 2004 were good years for the RV industry. Gas prices were generally falling and interest rates were near-record lows. Housing prices across the country were rising, giving some people reason to take out second mortgages to "cash out the equity" of their homes. However, the 2005 and 2006 period showed that interest rates can rise, that home values do not always grow at 10 percent a year, and that oil prices can breach and stay above $60 a barrel. Rising oil prices generally result in higher fuel prices and when fuel prices rise, the prices for a wide variety of consumer goods and services will often rise. As prices in general rise, consumers feel their purchasing power decline and reduce their purchases of "big-ticket" items.

Regarding the long-term prospects for the RV industry, the size of the 55-to-64 age group is expected to increase by approximately 45 percent over the next decade (as compared with an overall population growth rate of about 8 percent) and this portends increased sales growth of RVs into the next decade. This age group is usually at the peak of their earning power. They are likely to have sent the children through college and are now able to enjoy the "empty nest." Industry sales should also be positively influenced by the factors that increase the wealth and incomes of this group. Continued low financing rates, low fuel prices, tax cuts on capital gains and dividends, health care reform, the growth of the national economy, and the return on the stock market positively impact the wealth and disposable incomes of this group. Conversely, sustained higher interest rates and fuel prices will be detrimental to the market.

Conclusion

Assume you recently accepted a management position with Winnebago Industries and your first assignment is to prepare a three-year strategic plan for Winnebago Industries. Complete this assignment for the company. Include in your analysis a detailed internal and external assessment of the company. Determine whether you believe Winnebago should expand, diversify, make acquisitions, retrench, backward integrate, or establish more dealers to reverse the negative financial results of recent months and years. Would manufactured housing (mobile homes) be an area that Winnebago should expand into now?

11 Skoda Auto — 2007

Marlene Reed
Baylor University

Rochelle R. Brunson
Alvin College

www.skoda-auto.com/global

A favorite subject of jokes in the Czech Republic (formerly Czechoslovakia) has historically been the Skoda—the first car ever produced in Eastern Europe. Before Volkswagen took over the company in 1999, people would often ask, "Have you heard the one about . . ."

"How do you double the value of a Skoda? Fill it with gasoline."

"What do you call a Skoda convertible? A dumpster."

"Why does the Skoda have a heated rear window? To keep your hands warm when you are pushing it."

Despite a bad reputation throughout the twentieth century, Skoda produced 556,347 vehicles in 2006, the most ever in a single year for them and up 12.6 percent over 2005. Skoda introduced two new vehicles in 2006, the Skoda Roomster and the Skoda Fabia hatchback. Also in 2006, Skoda won numerous awards for producing a quality automobile. Skoda is the largest employer in the Czech Republic with 22,554 full-time employees—an increase of 7 percent over a year earlier. Headquartered in Milada Boleslav in the Czech Republic, Skoda's manufacturing plant there is an impressive structure of glass and steel, which was designed by the famous architect Dr. Gunter Henn and based on the concept presented in Professor Hans-Joachim Warnecke's 1990 work, *The Fractal Factory*.

As indicated in Exhibit 1, Skoda's 2006 revenues and net income were 203 billion and 11 billion Czech crowns, up 8.7 percent and 40.1 percent respectively from 2005. (The 2006 exchange rate was 22 Czech crowns to $1.00.). Skoda's recent balance sheets are provided in Exhibit 2.

Skoda is not without problems. The global automobile industry has become intensely competitive with Toyota, Nissan, and Honda attacking worldwide, General Motors and Ford Motor regrouping, Chinese auto firms expanding globally, and Skoda's parent, Volkswagen, having financial troubles. Skoda also has problems with their assembly plants in some countries. Skoda's management wonders whether they should continue building assembly plants outside of the Czech Republic and whether Skoda automobiles should be exported to the United States.

History

The small business that eventually became Skoda Automobile Company was formed in 1895 when Vaclav Laurin, a mechanic, and Vaclav Klement, a bookseller, joined together to manufacture the Slavia bicycle in the town of Mlada Boleslav, Czechoslovakia, about 40 miles northeast of Prague. Four years later, the company began producing motorcycles and had a total workforce of 68 people. In 1901, the company began using its motorcycle parts in the production of motor vehicles with four wheels and a 2-cylinder engine.

EXHIBIT 1 Skoda Income Statement for the Year Ended
December 31, 2006 (in Millions of Czech Crowns)

Item	2006	2005	2004
Sales	**203,659**	**187,382**	**155,396**
Cost of goods sold	175,636	162,738	140,996
Gross profit	**28,023**	**23,644**	**14,400**
Distribution expenses	11,903	10,611	6,137
Administrative expenses	3,587	3,686	3,157
Other operating income	4,747	4,027	3,147
Other operating expenses	2,678	2,525	2,964
Operating profit	**14,602**	**10,860**	**5,289**
Financial income	644	482	360
Financial expenses	1,048	1,269	1,225
Financial result	**(404)**	**(564)**	**(865)**
Profit before income tax	**14,198**	**10,073**	**4,424**
Income tax expense/(income)	3,136	2,180	1,291
- current	3,638	2,320	1,475
- deferred	(502)	(140)	(184)
Profit for the year	**11,062**	**7,893**	**3,133**

When the Nazis marched into Czechoslovakia in 1939, Hitler grabbed Skoda Auto and made it an armaments factory that was a part of the Hermann-Goering-Werke. He also ordered Skoda to move the steering wheel of its autos to the left side, where it has remained ever since.

As soon as World War II was over, the company was nationalized by the Soviets, who had taken over the country, and renamed it AZNP Skoda. Under the Soviets, Skoda gained a monopoly status as the only Czech passenger car manufacturer, and this is when the jokes really began as the quality of the automobile began to slide. After 1960, Skoda began producing cars for the mass market that had little style and often looked like a metal box. As poor as their quality was, the Skoda was still ahead of its Eastern European counterparts such as Trabant, Wartburg, and Lada.

Interestingly, the name "Skoda" in the Czech language means "a shame," and the company in the 40 years of the Soviet regime certainly lived up to its name. It was unfortunate that the oldest car company in Central Europe fell greatly in both quality and prestige. Because of a lack of innovation, its models became outdated, its factories became inefficient, and its workers were not well trained.

When consumers were forced to purchase automobiles from Soviet companies and were prevented from purchasing goods outside the region, there was no real incentive to produce a competitive automobile. Likewise, workers who were guaranteed "lifetime employment" by the government were not motivated to produce quality products in order to keep their jobs.

On November 17, 1989, a student rally for freedom began at Wenceslas Square in Prague, and within two weeks the Communist government had relinquished power to the government in what would later be referred to as a "Velvet Revolution." In 1993, Czechoslovakia split into two parts—the Czech Republic and Slovakia. The Czech Republic began to put into place laws to encourage privatization of national assets and the development of new entrepreneurial enterprises. The privatization of national companies took place by three means: A sale of the assets to outside owners (often companies from other countries); a management-employee buyout; and voucher privatization in which citizens were given vouchers for a minimal price that they could use to purchase the stock of national companies that were being privatized.

EXHIBIT 2   **Skoda Balance Sheet for the Year Ended December 31, 2006 (in Millions of Czech Crowns)**

ASSETS	2006	2005	2004
Intangible assets	13,351	13,210	12,602
Property, plant and equipment	39,809	41,466	42,236
Investments in associates	187	–	608
Other receivables and financial assets	387	374	346
Non-current assets	**54,070**	**55,023**	**55,792**
Inventories	12,248	12,270	9,232
Trade receivables	5,497	6,624	7,048
Current tax receivables	449	231	-
Other receivables and financial assets	28,436	14,430	11,600
Cash	4,512	1,176	4,534
Current assets	**51,142**	**34,331**	**32,414**
TOTAL ASSETS	**105,212**	**89,755**	**88,206**

EQUITY			
Share capital	16,709	16,709	16,709
Share premium	1,578	1,578	1,578
Reserves	39,961	28,395	25,860
TOTAL EQUITY	**58,321**	**46,757**	**44,147**

LIABILITIES			
Non-current financial liabilities	1,995	4,990	4,986
Other non-current liabilities	834	631	–
Deferred tax liabilities	2,528	2,837	2,982
Non-current tax payables	398	268	–
Non-current provisions	4,997	4,111	3,368
TOTAL NON-CURRENT LIABILITIES	**12,277**	**12,837**	**11,336**
Current financial liabilities	5,331	2,475	7,734
Trade payables	19,168	18,855	19,904
Other current liabilities	3,153	2,328	1,138
Current tax payables	1,945	1,056	849
Current provisions	4,997	5,447	3,098
TOTAL CURRENT LIABILITIES	**34,594**	**30,161**	**32,723**
TOTAL EQUITY AND LIABILITIES	**105,212**	**89,755**	**88,206**

After the Velvet Revolution in Czechoslovakia in 1989, a Republic was formed, and Vaclav Havel was elected president. The government immediately began to seek a buyer for Skoda as a part of its privatization of national assets. That buyer was found, and on April 16, 1991, Skoda became the fourth brand of the Volkswagen Group after VW, Audi, and Seat (the Spanish subsidiary). Volkswagen bought a 70 percent interest in the company, and the Czech government retained a 30 percent interest. In 2000, Volkswagen bought out the remaining 30 percent interest from the Czech government.

The new infusion of capital and emphasis on research and development from Volkswagen brought forth such popular models as the smaller Felicia, the larger middle-class model Octavia, and the latest products—the Superb sedan and the roomy Roomster. These models began to take market share from other car manufacturers in the Western European small car market. Exhibit 3 provides a picture of the Skoda Superb.

Skoda progressed so well improving the efficiency and attractiveness of its cars that in 2006, Skoda brand vehicles received the following honors: 1st place "Car of the Year" for Skoda Roomster in Estonia, Finland, and Bulgaria; 1st place "Auto Trophy" in the Minivan category for Skoda Roomster; 1st place "Family Car of the Year" for Skoda Roomster in Sweden and Belgium; and "Red Dot" design award for Skoda Octavia Combi.

Volkswagen: The Parent Company

Volkswagen (VW) is Europe's largest carmaker, annually producing approximately 5 million cars, trucks, and vans such as the Passat, Jetta, Rabbit, New Beetle, Golf, and Fox. Volkswagen also produces a full line of luxury cars such as Audi, Lamborghini, Bentley, and Bugatti. Volkswagen operates plants in Africa, the Americas, the Asia/Pacific region, and Europe. Volkswagen also owns 34 percent of the voting rights in Swedish truck maker Scania.

In 2007, Volkswagen however has high production costs, products with inflated sticker prices, and deteriorating quality. In order to turn the company around, VW is planning to save $8.4 billion from operations by 2010. Their plan also calls for introducing as many as 10 new, low-price models. VW's global markets are also suffering. Sales of VW products in the United States are falling, and its new models are experiencing sluggish sales in Europe. The once-dominant position VW held in China is now being threatened by General Motors. VW realizes that exports out of Europe are a key to its survival, and competitors like Nissan and Toyota are extending market share at a rapid pace. The company's losses in 2005 in the United States alone were more than $1 billion, a greater loss per car even than General Motors.

Strategic plans at Volkswagen call for wage costs, trimming the number of jobs, and cutting back on its current overcapacity of 30 percent. They are also considering the sale of some operations. VW has already sold their car rental business, Europcar, to European investment firm Eurazeo. They are now considering selling Gedas AG, an automotive technology consulting firm. Early in 2006, VW announced that it planned to cut 20,000 jobs over the next three years.[1]

Skoda Today

Mission Statement

Skoda developed the following mission statement:

> Three basic values of the Skoda brand are:
>
> **Intelligence**—We continuously seek innovative technical solutions and new ways in which to care for and approach the customers that are most important for us. Our conduct toward the customers is aboveboard, and we respect their desires and needs.
>
> **Attractiveness**—We develop automobiles that are aesthetically and technically of high standard and always constitute an attractive offer for our customers not only in terms of design or technical parameters but also the wide range of offered services.
>
> **Dedication**—We are following the steps of founders our company Messrs. Laurin and Klement. We are enthusiastically working on the further development of our vehicles; we identify ourselves with our products.

Top Management

Skoda follows a German model for its corporate governance, which utilizes members of the board of directors as members of senior management of the company. In accordance with its articles of association, the general meeting (the sole shareholder—Volkswagen) elects and recalls members of the board of directors and decides how they will be compensated for their work. The board of directors, in turn, elects and recalls its chairman. As Skoda's statutory body, the board of directors runs all company's operations and acts in its name. The board has six members, each with a term of office of three years, and multiple terms are possible. Each of the six members of the board of directors runs one of Skoda's six departments. Skoda's board members are listed in Exhibit 3.

Central Europe Operations

Despite flat markets in Central Europe in 2006, Skoda maintained its position as the number one carmaker in this region. In Poland, the brand's second largest market in this region, 28,783 vehicles were sold (up 4.1 percent from 2005). This corresponds to a market share of 12.0 percent, making Skoda the market leader in Poland. In Slovakia, the sales of Skoda vehicles grew by 3.0 percent and remained the market leader by a wide margin.

In the Czech Republic, the overall passenger car market contracted in comparison with 2005—confirming an ongoing declining trend. This decline was offset by rapid expansion of the overall market for light commercial vehicles. Skoda did maintain its vehicles sales volume in 2006 and retained its position of domestic market leader in both the passenger car and light commercial vehicle segments.

Compared to 2006, demand for new passenger cars in markets in Central Europe is expected to remain flat. Positive movement can be anticipated in the Polish (year-on-year growth of 2.0 percent) market, while the Hungarian market is forecasted to decline substantially (–9.0 percent).

Eastern Europe Operations

The highest growth in 2006 sales was achieved by Skoda in Eastern Europe. A total of 70,986 vehicles were delivered in this region, an increase of 52.0 percent over 2005. One of the key markets in the region is Russia, where sales of Skoda doubled in 2006. In Romania, sales of Skoda vehicles were up 37.8 percent over the last year. Likewise, sales of Skoda in Ukraine were up 64.2 percent over the previous year.

The forecast for the overall markets for new passenger cars in Eastern Europe was one of growth in 2007, the most dynamic market being Russia (+11.0 percent).

EXHIBIT 3 Skoda Board of Directors/Senior Management

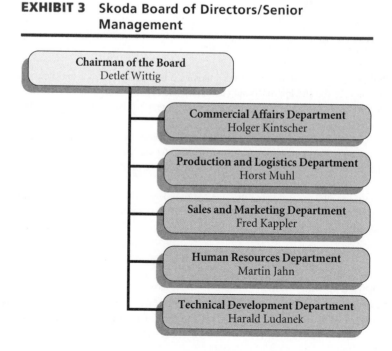

Western Europe Operations

Skoda grew its Western Europe market share to 2.1 percent in 2006. (The 2005 market share was 1.9 percent.) A total of 301,343 vehicles were delivered to customers in the region (+9.1 percent year-on-year). Over 10 percent sales growth was recorded in the following Western European countries: Germany, Spain, Belgium, Greece, Switzerland, Finland, and Luxembourg. The most vehicles were sold in Germany—103,931 vehicles total which was up 15.3 percent over 2005.

In 2007, overall demand for new passenger cars in Western Europe was forecast as likely to fall slightly (–1.0 percent) compared to 2006, primarily as a result of anticipated declines in the German (–2.6 percent) and British (–1.5 percent) markets. The French market was expected to improve (+4.5 percent).

Asia

Skoda's deliveries in Asia in 2006 totaled 36,541 vehicles, up 21.1 percent over the previous year. India, again the largest market, saw 12,105 vehicles delivered to customers for a year-on-year increase of 35.2 percent. Other important markets were Turkey (5,725 vehicles compared to 7,261 in 2005), Egypt (3,683 vehicles compared to 2,328 in 2005), and Israel (3,518 vehicles compared to 2,900 in 2005).

By 2006, Skoda had developed its production facilities even further in other countries. In May of 2006, an agreement was signed for a joint manufacturing plant for the Volkswagen and Skoda Auto brands in Kaluga, Russia. The first vehicle bound for the Russian market to leave the gates of the joint plant will be a Skoda Octavia, and this event was to take place as early as autumn of 2007.

In June of 2006, a licensing agreement was signed to allow production of the Skoda Fabia and Skoda Superb model lines in China. In the run-up to its Chinese market launch in 2007, Skoda presented the new Skoda Octavia model at the Beijing Motor Show in November 2006.

Skoda produces finished vehicles as well as vehicle kits in various stages of assembly. The vehicle kits are shipped from the production plants and assembled in their assembly plants. The company also manufactures engines, gearboxes, engine and gearbox components, and genuine parts and accessories.

Skoda's 2006 revenues broken down by product category are provided in Exhibit 4.

Skoda assembly plants were recently opened in Kazakhstan, Ukraine, Bosnia and Herzegovina, and India. Exhibit 5 identifies the countries to which Skoda automobiles were shipped from 2000 to 2006. Note the decreasing trend in the Czech Republic and Central Europe while Eastern and Western Europe and Asia are growing. In total, Skoda operated in nearly 90 countries all over the globe. Exhibit 6 illustrates the Skoda Auto Group Structure around the world.

Marketing

In addition to a growing number of vehicle deliveries worldwide, Skoda has developed a network of authorized sales and service partners (up 5.5 percent from 2005). To assure that its customers receive service standards compliance and improved service quality, Skoda

EXHIBIT 4   Skoda Sales Revenues by Product Lines in 2006

Product	Percent of Revenues
Vehicles	88.7%
Parts & accessories	7.3
Supplies to other VW companies	2.9
Other goods & services	1.1
Total	100.0%

EXHIBIT 5 **Skoda Vehicle Deliveries by Region from 2000 to 2006**

Country	2000	2001	2002	2003	2004	2005	2006
Czech Republic	80,882	82,405	74,466	71,522	64,676	65,166	65,171
Central Europe (excluding CR)	89,517	92,766	82,549	93,474	87,139	73,855	75,626
Eastern Europe	13,116	24,167	27,224	26,652	31,564	46,692	70,986
Western Europe	229,109	244,099	238,323	235,861	240,672	276,216	301,343
Overseas & Asia	22,779	16,815	22,963	22,249	27,624	30,182	36,541

has trained over 4,400 service employees in the Czech Republic and abroad. The construction of 100 new Skoda dealerships also illustrates strong growth of the brand's distribution network.

A new type of marketing communication was developed for the Skoda Roomster aimed at a new target audience. The company envisions that the Roomster is not just a means of transportation for this customer segment, but it is also a way to express their personal style. The comprehensive campaign developed for the launch of this new model is

EXHIBIT 6 **Skoda Auto Group Structure**

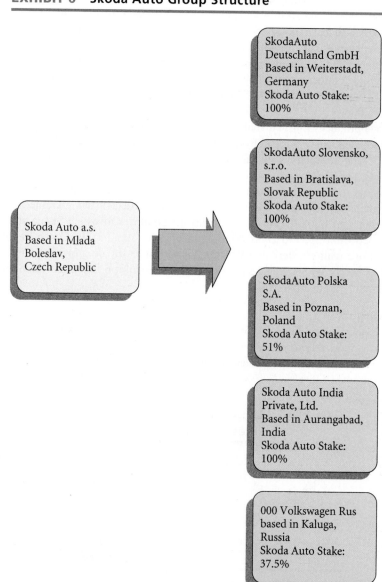

based on the claim, "Find your own room," which emphasizes the principal features of the car which are styling, roominess, and perspective.

Education

Skoda established the Skoda Auto School of Economics in 2000 as the first company-operated university in the Czech Republic. Skoda decided to hire highly proficient university professors to teach in the school, and the university was subsequently fully accredited for awarding degrees. In the several years since its inception, the number of applicants for the school has grown to the point that demand has outstripped supply. The three-and-a-half year bachelor program allows students to work in the plant to earn credit for their studies in management, and the first students enrolled in the school graduated in 2004.

Beginning in 2006, the university began offering a master's degree in management. A total of 585 students were enrolled in the school in 2006, and 157 graduates were awarded bachelor's degrees. Approximately, one-half of the graduates found jobs working for the company or its suppliers. Another one-third elected to continue their studies in the master's degree program.

Suppliers

One of the key components of Skoda's strategy is quality. Suppliers are selected in a systematic and controlled process which involves the technical development and production functions. The most important activity of the purchasing department in 2006 was to secure everything needed for the series production of the new model line, the Skoda Roomster.

In 2006, production-related purchasing was CZK 208.8 billion in comparison to CZK 105.2 billion in 2005. The share by domestic suppliers was 62.6 percent, and in 2005 it was 63.9 percent. Suppliers from Central and Eastern Europe who satisfy the strict eligibility conditions are winning contracts within the Volkswagen Group.

The selection of suppliers is powered by modern information and communications technology. One of the most important applications in Skoda's Internet B28 platform is online negotiations. A total of 403 online negotiations took place in 2006 as compared to 220 such negotiations in 2005.

Quality

A key part of the integrated management system at Skoda is the quality management system. The company is subjected to audit for compliance with the international ISO 9001:2000 standard. In the autumn of 2006, TUV NORD carried out the second audit of this system. The result was a renewal of the certificate which was granted in 2004. This certificate documents that Skoda has introduced and uses a quality management system in the areas of development, production, sales, and service and that the system used complies with the ISO standard.

Health Management

In October of 2006, Skoda launched the "Healthy Company" program which focuses on improving employee health and fighting diseases. Individual measures taken in the program focus on support for healthy diets, bolstering the immune system, the cessation of smoking, and improving conditions in the workplace. Skoda also put into operation a central first-aid clinic in accordance with the newly revamped Integrated Rescue System.

The company places a great deal of emphasis on improving work conditions based on the results of measurements of employees' physical duress and ergonomic analyses of individual work areas. A number of ergonomic measures were implemented in the body shop and the vehicle assembly area (e.g. strategically placed special palettes and stands to ease parts handling, utilizing robots on selected work procedures, optimizing tool and jig placement, etc.).

In addition, a Pandemic Plan was drawn up to address the potential danger of bird flu. At Skoda's expense, a total of 5,074 employees were vaccinated against the seasonal flu. Treatment and reconditioning spa trips were utilized by a total of 1,364 employees. The average work attendance in 2006 was 96.6 percent.

The success of Skoda has reverberated throughout Europe. The French automobile manufacturer Renault decided to invest in Automobile Dacia of Romania to produce a car that would sell for about $5,000 for the emerging markets of Eastern Europe. Likewise, General Motors invested $100 million in a partnership with Auto Vaz of Russia to produce an inexpensive mini-SUV for sale in that country and eventually be exported elsewhere. Skoda itself decided to produce 50 prototypes of the new mid-size Bentley in the Czech Republic in a move that shocked the United Kingdom automotive industry.

Trends in the World Automobile Industry

Such substitute products as bicycles are being replaced by automobiles in many countries. Until the beginning of the 21st century, cars were out of the reach of most Chinese—even the middle class. But as incomes increased and tariffs on imported cars began to fall after Beijing's accession to the World Trade Organization and imported models began to flood the market, domestic producers were forced to cut their prices.

A price war is heating up with sticker prices on Chinese cars falling by as much as 15 percent. In the first years of the 21st century, 100 state-owned car companies still existed in China, and most were losing money. The government was encouraging the merger of many of these firms to achieve economies of scale. Industry projections suggested that the strongest potential growth in automobile sales would be in the developing countries of Asia, South America, Eastern Europe, and Africa rather than the mature economies of Western Europe, North America, and Japan.

Mergers of automobile companies are being considered in China, and there was a strong movement worldwide to an amalgamation of automobile companies located in different countries. In February of 2007, DaimlerChrysler AG acknowledged that it might have to find a partner or spin off its ailing U.S. arm (Chrysler) due to the depth of the crisis facing Detroit's automakers. The list of potential partners included Renault SA and Nissan Motor Company. Nissan had hinted earlier that it was interested in a North American partner.

Ford Motor Company CEO Alan Mulally also expressed interest in assessing whether Ford could rely on other companies for some manufacturing or other tasks. Toyota had suggested in 2006 that it was interested in further conversations with Ford. Ford also was searching for a buyer for its Range Rover and Jaguar divisions, which were showing a lack of profitability.

In 2006, General Motors considered an alliance with Renault and Nissan before deciding to remain as they are. However, GM executives have made it clear that they anticipate their company's future growth will come largely from outside the United States—partly by making use of existing low-cost partners such as South Korea's GM Daewoo Auto & Technology Company and China's Shanghai Automotive Industries Corporation.

Unfortunately, many of the cross-border mergers and joint ventures in the industry in the past had a difficult time surviving. For instance, the joint venture between General Motors and Saab cost General Motors $2 billion, which would be difficult to recoup. In addition, Ford bought Jaguar in the early 1990s and invested approximately $5 billion in that model; but by 2007 Ford was considering finding a buyer for it. Other global ventures that did not have positive outcomes were Ford-ACE, Chrysler-Lamborghini, Chrysler-Rootes, Renault-Volvo, BMW-Rover, and Volkswagen-Rolls. For the high cost of acquisition, the automobile companies might have more easily created their own new models.[2]

In making plant location decisions, companies normally consider the following factors: labor costs, energy costs, access to a workforce that has the right skills, access to the necessary infrastructure (roads, railroads, favorable political climate), and closeness to important global markets. The Skoda plant in the Czech Republic had been a good selection for Volkswagen for those reasons. There was also a tendency to move to just-in-time inventory systems at automobile manufacturers around the world, which caused suppliers to move their operations closer to auto plants. This movement was occurring around the Skoda plant at Milada Boleslav.

Another haunting problem is the ever-escalating price of nonrenewable energy sources and the higher petroleum prices that resulted. Even as newer forms of renewable energy sources were being developed, automobile manufacturers were rushing to their drawing boards in an attempt to be among the first in the market to design and manufacture automobiles operating on those newer forms of energy. Toyota had led the way with this movement; and after taking a decade to sell its first 1 million gasoline-electric hybrid vehicles worldwide, the company stated in 2007 that it plans to sell 1 million a year by 2010.

The Future

The automobile industry has gone from primarily a national to a regional and finally a global marketplace. Skoda has to decide whether to continue the movement of assembly plants abroad when the Czech Republic had such inexpensive labor. Prepare a three-year strategic plan for the Skoda board of directors who manage the company.

References

1. Hoovers, a D&B Company. http://premium.hoovers.com/subscribe/co/profile.xhtml? ID=ffffcrxhyyrhfrjtsh
2. Flint, Jerry (January 1999). Global math. *Ward's Auto World*, Volume 35, Issue 1, p. 15.

12 S/W Printing Company

Joseph Aniello
Francis Marion University

Brianna Zhang
Francis Marion University

www.swprinting.com

In this era of large corporations and one-stop, big box superstores like Wal-Mart and Office Depot, the idea of a family-owned, family-run business sounds nostalgic. Motivated by the idea of becoming a family enterprise, the Powers family purchased a 70-year-old business named S/W Printing in Florence, South Carolina in 2001. The Powers were walking blind into a business in which they had no applicable experience.

Fast forward to 2007, S/W Printing has become the premier commercial printer in Florence, with an expanding capacity and ability to produce high-quality small and large projects at affordable prices. Together with their determination and keen sense of relationship building, S/W Printing is increasingly building a legacy for future generations as it continues to grow.

Background and History

In 1932, Strickland Printing opened in downtown Florence, South Carolina. It was a thriving family-operated business until 1988 when Joe Strickland, the patriarch, died. The company struggled until 1990 when the remaining family members were unable to continue the success and were forced to sell the business to two couples from Ohio.

The purchase of the business brought about an immediate change in the name Rich and Phyllis Snyder became the "S" and Jim and Berta Wilde became the "W" in the newly named S/W Printing Company. As time passed, the Snyders and the Wildes liked the small business lifestyle but were slow in response to the ever-changing printing industry. S/W Printing Company was just marking time as their lack of investments for capital equipment improvements and little effort to grow sales and profits had created a large gap for competition to come. In fact, a partner of the old Strickland Printing owners took over another existing Florence print shop, Patillos, and provided formidable competition just around the corner.

After about 10 years, the owners of S/W Printing Company decided that they had enough of the printing business and sold the entire operation to Steve and Susan Powers in 2001. S/W Printing Company became a wholly owned subsidiary of Pee Dee Printing, Inc. as run by the corporate officers of Steve Powers, president and Susan Powers, vice president. Their motivation for the purchase was twofold: to provide a potential source of income for the family until Steve and Susan retired and to leave a viable career path for their only child, son Jason Powers.

EXHIBIT 1 Product Sales Data (Product and Services Section)

Type of Income	2006 Invoices	2005 Invoices
*Signs/Banners	$ 6,208.56	$ 0.00
HIGH-SPEED RISO DIGITAL	442.82	0.00
WIDE FORMAT	2,102.47	0.00
COLOR PRINTS	26,364.65	8,591.47
BLACK & WHITE COPYING	34,153.11	29,040.77
FULL COLOR PRINTING	42,746.75	594.50
Blank stock	12,462.48	7,939.36
SPECIAL ORDER	168,179.65	133,842.85
Bindery	56,026.49	30,873.80
BUSINESS CARDS	30,703.50	38,309.00
Printing	336,835.32	306,721.45
Pre-press	30.00	259.00
Ink Charges	9,020.00	7,683.52
Extra Charges	2,640.70	1,518.25
*Discounts Given	(8,381.51)	(3,543.20)
Subtotal	$719,434.99	$561,830.77

Products and Services

The mission statement of S/W Printing is to provide customers with high-quality profes-sional printing services at affordable prices. As a medium-size commercial printer, S/W Printing has the ability to produce brochures, business cards, business forms, copies, letter-head/envelopes, promotional items, invitations, and graphic design services at fairly rea-sonable rates. The on-site printing press allows for a faster turnaround on orders along with the available delivery service. The on-site set up is state-of-the-art with an offset lithogra-phy along with full-color digital printing units.

Prior to 2006, S/W Printing did not carry signs and banners. After many requests, an investigation was conducted to determine the cost associated to offer the service. The results were favorable and were added to the current services. A listing of the products and services provided by S/W Printing is provided in Exhibit 1. Note the outstanding growth in color printing but the negative growth in business cards.

S/W Printing understands that customers need timely service and has tried to create an effective start-to-finish process. The customer can receive a quote for services via phone, e-mail, or the Web site. Currently, the Printers Plus® software is used to generate quotes and record sales for each customer.

After receiving approval from the customer, the order is placed on the schedule for completion. The turnover time depends on the quantity and the overall production sched-ule. Throughout the process, the customer is welcome to call or review the status of the project through the Web site using their given user name and password. An additional ser-vice is delivery, which is offered only to customers within a 30-mile radius.

Organizational Structure

An organizational chart for S/W Printing is provided in Exhibit 2. Obviously this is a small family-run business with just a few employees.

**EXHIBIT 2   S/W Printing's Organization Chart
(Organization Structure Section)**

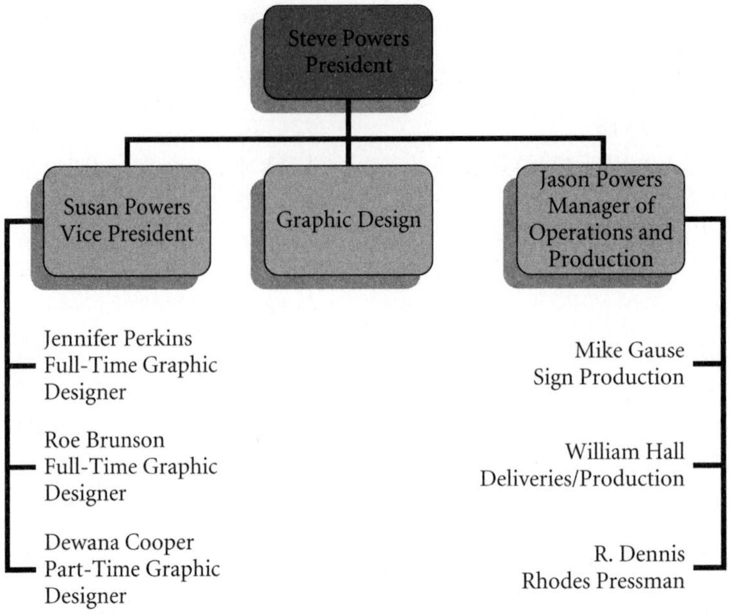

President

Steve Powers is primarily responsible for sales and marketing, along with general management. The dramatic 20 percent increase each year since the purchase of S/W Printing in 2001 can arguably be attributed to the personal selling strength of Steve Powers. In his former career, he rose through the ranks to become a vice president of sales and marketing at a well-known coin machine and amusement company. He continues to use the same drive to distinguish S/W Printing from other printers in the area.

Vice President

Susan Powers began working for S/W Printing in 2004 and is primarily responsible for the financial and administrative areas. She prides herself on S/W Printing's ability and decision to pay all bills early while demonstrating patience with their customers' individual payment situations. Susan has strong management skills with over 30 years of retail management experience.

Manager of Production and Operations

Jason Powers is responsible for production and distribution. He excels in the mechanical aspects of print production as he manages all aspects of production. Jason graduated in 2004 from Francis Marion University with a degree in political science. During his time at S/W Printing, Jason is learning about the different aspects of the business as he is being groomed to take over the family business.

Marketing

Through his charismatic personal selling and ambitious networking program, Steve Powers's greatest business asset is developing relationships with people in the community. He has made a conscious effort to join such organizations as the Rotary and the United Way. Another voluntary organization that is particularly helpful to his physical establishment and business is the Florence Downtown Development Corporation, which is responsible for such activities as local festivals, merchant associations, and revitalization efforts. Steve Powers has been able to turn many trial jobs into regular customers. Many of the accounts have grown as the clients' businesses have grown, in no small part to Steve's personal attention.

Since the acquisition in 2001, S/W Printing has used other marketing and advertising methods to further strengthen the brand image. Newspaper ads in the *Morning News* and *News Journal* are purchased for the special tabloid sections approximately 3 times a year at an average rate of $300 per ad. S/W Printing has also purchased an ad in *Images*, a local economic development magazine. A television ad was produced several years ago and like radio commercials the air time was acquired using trade and barter agreements. In early 2007, S/W Printing began looking at the possibility of purchasing billboard space at a rate of $9,000 for a three-location, six-month contract. While the move to billboard has not been decided, there are prime billboard locations near both main competitors, M&M Document Center and Office Depot.

S/W Printing uses the conventional marketing collateral such as business cards and brochures. In early 2007, S/W Printing created a new Web site to better showcase their services. The Web site provides an informational overview of the services available and an avenue for current customers to reorder, review, and find out the job status without having to contact S/W Printing through traditional methods. However, S/W Printing is finding that most customers have yet to embrace the electronic method, which creates a considerable amount of administrative time to complete orders. Furthermore, payments are not accepted and automatic quotes cannot be generated through the Web site.

City of Florence and Surrounding Area

Florence is strategically centered at the crossroads of Interstates 20 and 95 as well as the center of an eight-county region known as the Pee Dee. The largest town in the Pee Dee, Florence draws a large number of consumers from smaller towns and communities around the area. Between 1980 to 2000, the population of Florence County grew 14 percent from 110,163 to 125,761. It is expected that the county will grow to approximately 167,720 by 2008. The county seat, Florence had a recorded population of 31,388 in 2005 with an anticipated growth of 6 percent each year.

In 2006, Florence made commitments to create their own economic impact plans through the redevelopment of the downtown area. From the growing redevelopment of downtown, S/W Printing is very well positioned geographically, as well as professionally, for the economic expansions of the cultural, historic, and commercial districts as outlined by the urban redevelopment firm.

With two large regional hospitals, Carolinas Hospital System and McLeod Regional Medical Center, the city is a major source of economic focus of the Pee Dee region of South Carolina. Florence is not just a one-dimensional economy based on the hospitals and all ancillary products and services. Additionally, it has major manufacturing facilities for such global producers as Honda, General Electric, and Roche. A study by Pollina Corporate Real Estate has ranked South Carolina as the top pro-business state in 2005 and 2006 after reviewing 29 factors.

However, the majority of businesses within Florence and surrounding areas are classified as small businesses. In fact, the zip code of S/W Printing (29501) has by far the largest concentration of business than the five other zip codes of Florence. These factors make for numerous opportunities going forward into the near and mid-future for S/W Printing and other small/mid-size establishments.

Competition

Competition is intense within the printing industry as it is known for its associated price elasticity. As a matter of fact, three printing businesses have already gone out of business since the purchase of S/W by the Powers family in 2001. The established firms of Patillo Printing in 2002, WC Printing in 2003, and Staples in 2005 have all closed. The closing of these businesses would seemingly open the door for S/W Printing to gain more market share. However, there are still two main competitors that S/W Printing needs to remain aware of within a 5-mile radius: M&M Document Center and Office Depot. Exhibit 3 reveals the location of S/W, M&M, and Office Depot.

EXHIBIT 3 **Map of S/W Printing Location versus Rival Firms**

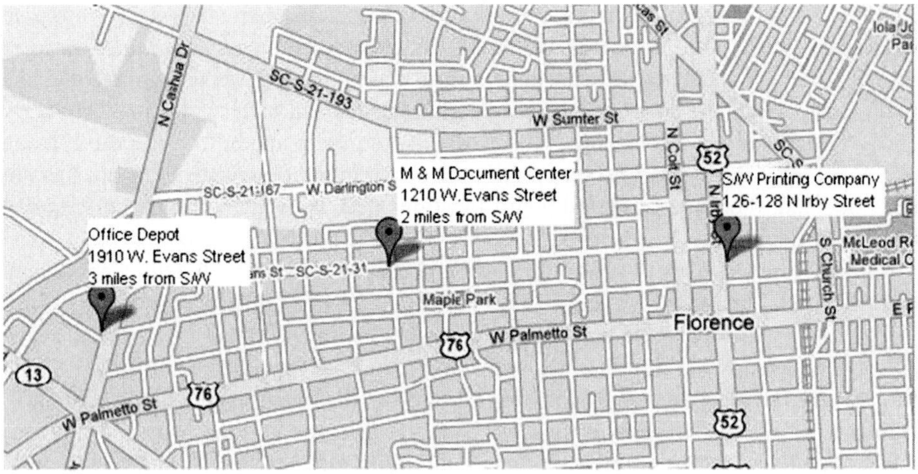

M&M Document Center

www.mmdocumentcenter.com

M&M Document Center has been in operation in the Pee Dee Region for almost 30 years. Located near downtown Florence, M&M Document Center offers services that are similar to S/W Printing from copying to design to finishing without the on-site press operation. M&M Document Center is known as a digital copy shop and jobs outtasks that can not be completed by in-house equipment. Aside from the traditional printing options, M&M Document Center can produce vinyl and electrical signs, along with trade show displays. As a locally owned business as well, M&M Document Center has the ability to develop relationships with customers. Also, their advertising and marketing efforts include, but are not limited to, a larger font listing in the yellow pages, radio, and local vendor shows. In 2006, M&M Document Center was sold and is in the process of reorganization. S/W Printing feels that M&M Document Center leads them in the copy jobs because S/W Printing offers the services but does not promote copies.

Office Depot

www.officedepot.com/dps

The large chain store that provides office supplies nationwide has a store located in Florence. Since the closing of the Florence Staples in 2005, Office Depot is the only large office supply chain. The Florence store has expanded to include a design, print, and ship department to give consumers another outlet for quality design and print work at a lower price whether in the store or at home or work without a minimum printing allowance. Much like M&M Document Center, Office Depot also favors more of a digital copy shop. As a large corporate chain, the ability to create a personal relationship with customers is seemingly difficult.

In-House

Another competitor is actually the in-house print operations of both small and large businesses as well as government and educational institutions. With technology becoming more affordable, many consumers and businesses have embraced the do-it-yourself mentality to lessen cost and time for smaller or even larger jobs. All in all, the cost of each service for the consumer or business is often calculated to determine which is most cost effective to outsource. Furthermore, an increasing number of government agencies and corporations within Florence have an in-house printing facility to complete the majority of their projects such as ESAB, McLeod Health, Florence School District One, and Francis Marion University.

EXHIBIT 4   **S/W Printing's Income Statements**

	2006	2005
Revenues	$762,792	$595,860
Cost of Goods Sold	343,257	269,140
General Expenses	398,564	341,639
Other Income (loss)	633	(361)
Net Income (loss)	**21,604**	**(15,280)**

Financial Issues

As seen from their financials, S/W Printing's professional and timely image has translated quite well in the revenue with a 28 percent increase from 2005 to 2006. While 2005 was not a bad year with an increase in sales of 25 percent from 2004, the cost of good sold and the expenses left the year-end in the negative. S/W Printing's recent income statements and balance sheets are provided in Exhibits 4 and 5 respectively. Note that total revenues and net income are up nicely in 2006 while total assets decreased that year from 2005.

As indicated in Exhibit 1, the sales data from 2005 to 2006 show some definite areas of growth and decline in one year. The two noticeable areas of increase are full color printing with 7090 percent and bindery with 81 percent. Business cards decreased by 20 percent over the one-year period. It would appear that signs/banners, high-speed riso digital, and wide format printing were added in 2006. With the new

EXHIBIT 5   **S/W Printing's Balance Sheets**

Current Assets	2006	2005
Cash and Cash Equivalents	$47,031	$58,109
Accounts Receivable	54,000	48,525
Inventory	17,636	17,500
Other Current Assets	62,468	62,320
Property & Equipment		
Total Property and Equipment	114,934	117,331
Total Assets	**296,069**	**363,785**
Current Liabilities		
Accounts Payable	14,268	14,753
Payroll Liabilities	6,511	4,611
Sales Taxes Payable	161	2,125
Current Maturity of LTD	18,500	18,500
Long-Term Liabilities		
Total LT Liabilities	284,101	336,432
Shareholders' Equity		
Common Stock	1,000	1,000
Additional Paid-in-Capital	3,000	0
Accumulated Adjustments	1,644	1,644
Current Earnings	6,324	(15,280)
Total Equity	**11,968**	**(12,636)**
Total L & SE	**$296,069**	**$363,785**

additions in the last fiscal year, it is unclear if the added areas will be noted as value-added product lines.

In 2005 and 2006, the City of Florence was the largest customer with 6.5 percent of the revenue generated from the contracted account. One area of weakness is that S/W Printing only has one contracted account, which is the City of Florence. The majority of the sales are open sales by repeat customers or walk-ins. In the absence of contract work, S/W Printing can only hope repeat customers and walk-ins will continue to be available to generate sales.

S/W Printing has opted to purchase the printing equipment instead of renting due to the overall savings. Most of the equipment would be classified as a capital expense and is generally over $100,000. Due to the large expense in equipment, S/W Printing has a significantly larger overhead than M&M Document and those in-house printing shops. The only equipment that is leased are the copy machines that charge a "click rate" per month.

While Susan Powers maintains the record keeping, a new accountant was hired at the end of 2005 because the previous accountant did not provide a satisfactory service. Steve and Susan are currently receiving a minimal paycheck because they want to reinvest as much as possible into the business to foster the future growth.

Looking Forward

The future for S/W Printing is certainly positive as the growth of services continues. As S/W Printing looks to the future, the following milestones will assist in furthering the growth:

- Expanding the products and services to potentially include document storage and imaging, along with vinyl vehicle wraps
- Acquiring more large-volume contracts with local businesses
- Establish a cross-training strategy to create more efficiency within the business
- Partner with large government and private in-house printing facilities to secure spillover or unequipped jobs
- Promote and utilize the Web site function to cut down the administrative time to process orders
- Develop more contract printing to ensure a known amount of revenue

13 Waterford Wedgwood PLC — 2008

Brandan L. Still
Harvard Law School

Lisa D. McNary
North Carolina State University

Clare Burns
Lamar University

WATFF (on London Exchange)

www.waterfordwedgwood.com

Over the past two centuries, Waterford Crystal has grown to be one of the world's best known and valued crystal brands. In addition to gracing the tables of royalty, fine establishments, and families, Waterford crystal adorns the New Year's Eve Ball in Times Square, trophies for championships in almost every major sport, and the chandeliers in the Kennedy Center, Windsor Castle, and Westminster Abbey.

The beauty and refinement of the Waterford crystal reflect the creativity and skill of its artisans and craftsmen. The designs reveal a uniquely Irish influence coupled with the finest in modern design. Waterford pieces become family heirlooms cherished for generations and in style for lifetimes. Waterford has recently diversified into other areas of household luxury products and entered into a number of collaborative and cooperative relationships with famous designers including Versace, Bulgari, Jasper Conrad, and John Roche, as well as internationally known chefs.

However, Waterford has come upon hard times of late. The company's net income for 2007 was negative 270.8 million euros, preceded by negative 183.9 million euros in 2006. Waterford needs a clear strategic plan for the future.

History

Glass has been regarded with significant respect in civilizations since the dawning of the Iron Age. Evidence of glassmaking has been found by archaeologists in Ireland dating as far back as the 13th century. Waterford Crystal was founded over 225 years ago on the quays of the Irish port of Waterford by two prominent developers and businessmen, brothers William and George Penrose. They employed a number of local artisans who produced a crystal of brilliance and clarity unmatched by any in the British Isles. In short order, merchant ships with cargoes of the fine crystal were bound for ports throughout Europe and across the Atlantic in North America. The crystal produced in Waterford City developed an unequalled reputation in a relatively short period of time. However, the company ceased operating for more than a hundred years after falling on hard times.

Following World War II, in an era of increasing Irish independence and enterprise, glassmaking once again commenced in Waterford and a small factory was set up only

$1^1/_2$ miles from the original factory on Merchant's Quay. Since that time, Waterford has opened additional factories in Ireland and around the world, but its principal production site remains just outside of Waterford.

In 1967, Waterford became a listed company on the London Stock Exchange. The present Waterford Crystal maintains strong ties with its predecessor—namely, a dedication to purity of color, design, and quality in their crystal. However, the company today comprises far more than just crystal. Waterford Wedgwood, plc, the modern holding company created by a merger between Waterford Crystal and the English ceramics company, Wedgwood, in 1986, contains divisions producing products ranging from the traditional crystal to linens and homewares as well as writing instruments and ceramic flatwares. The combined company (the Group) is listed on the Irish and London Stock Exchanges under the stock symbol WATFF. The Group's organizational chart is presented in Exhibit 1.

Mission/Vision/Value Statements

Waterford Wedgwood has no vision statement. However, the company's mission statement states its desire to be "the world's leading portfolio of luxury lifestyle brands with particular emphasis on tabletop, gifting and the home." The company's Code of Corporate Conduct includes detailed statements of values in relation to different stakeholders including shareholders, customers, and employees. For example, the value statement on business integrity states, "The Group trusts and respects all of its Directors and employees and aims to conduct business through people who will apply uncompromising integrity, by strictly adhering to standards of personal honesty in their dealings with others to earn their trust." The entire Code of Corporate Conduct is available at www.waterfordwedgwood.com/investor.asp.

EXHIBIT 1 Organizational Chart

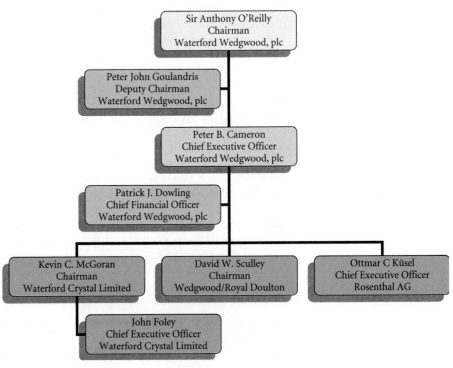

Source: Waterford Wedgewood Investor Relations, http://www.waterfordwedgwood.com/investor_directors_info_5.asp.

EXHIBIT 2   Waterford Brand Structure

Waterford Wedgwood, PLC		
Ceramics Group	Waterford Crystal	W-C Designs/Spring
• Wedgwood • Rosenthal • Royal Doulton • Hutschenreuther • Coalport • Mason's • Johnson Brothers • Royal Albert • Minton	• Waterford Crystal • Marquis by Waterford • Stuart Crystal • Cash's Mail Order	• W-C Designs • Spring

Business Organization

Waterford Wedgwood holds a "portfolio of brands" and divides these brands among three operating groups: (1) Waterford Crystal, (2) Ceramics Group, and (3) W-C Designs and Spring. These groups comprise 26.9 percent, 67.6 percent, and 5.5 percent of revenue, respectively, for the fiscal year ending March 2007. The three groups are the result of a recent consolidation from five operating groups to three and the sale of All-Clad, an American cookware company. The brand structure of the groups is shown in Exhibit 2. Waterford sells products in North America, Europe (excluding the United Kingdom), the United Kingdom, and the Far East, which accounted for 41.1 percent, 26.3 percent, 16.6 percent, and 10.0 percent respectively of the company's total revenue in the fiscal year ended March 31, 2007.

Waterford Crystal

Four main brands reside within the Waterford Crystal operating group: (1) Waterford Crystal, (2) Marquis by Waterford, (3) Stuart Crystal, and (4) Cash's Mail Order. Waterford Crystal is a hand-blown, hand-cut crystal primarily made at the company's facilities in Ireland; however, some production for smaller and midrange-priced pieces has been shifted to continental European production facilities.

The production process is based on an artisan process. Craftsmen are apprenticed for a number of years into one of three crafts: blowing, cutting, or engraving. After a period of approximately ten years, these craftsmen become master craftsmen and enter the normal workforce at the factory. From that point on, they are paid on a piece-rate basis for the pieces they work that pass inspection after their step of the process. For example, a blower blows a glass vase and it is inspected after blowing; if passed, the blower is paid and the piece will go to a cutter, whose work is subsequently inspected. No manufacturer's seconds are sold; any piece not passing inspection at any point is broken and recycled.

Waterford Crystal is one of the company's flagship brands and undoubtedly has one of the highest profiles. Long considered traditional and elegant, this brand has entered into cooperative branding and design arrangements with modern designers, resulting in a number of sub-lines of the traditional Waterford Crystal brand including the Jasper Conrad and John Roche lines. Once Waterford Crystal introduces a stemware design, the design is never retired, allowing for the completion of settings over time and replacement of any broken pieces. The company acquired Cash's Mail Order in 2002 and sells both the Group's and other licensed products via catalogue, primarily to the United States. Marquis by Waterford is a machine-cut crystal crafted in continental Europe. The same blend of ingredients is used as in Waterford Crystal, but the crystal is not hand-crafted. These pieces contain a range of design styles and a wide range of product variety. Marquis does not command the same prices as true Waterford Crystal; it is considered an entry-level crystal product that could promote trading-up by consumers. Stuart Crystal, a British crystal company with a strong presence in the United Kingdom market, was acquired in 1995 and is manufactured primarily in continental Europe.

Ceramics Group

The Ceramics operating group consists primarily of Wedgwood, Royal Doulton, Rosenthal, and Hutschenreuther. Wedgwood is a manufacturer of ceramic tableware and giftware; the Wedgwood brand umbrella includes fine china, earthenware, and other brands acquired through acquisitions including Coalport and Johnson Brothers. Royal Doulton, acquired in 2005, is a large producer of chinaware under the Royal Doulton, Minton, and Royal Albert brands. Rosenthal, a German manufacturer of ceramic and porcelain tableware, was acquired in 1997–1998. Hutschenreuther, a German brand of porcelain tableware and giftware, was acquired in 2002. Production in the ceramics group is divided between the United Kingdom, Indonesia, and Germany.

W-C Designs and Spring

The W-C Designs and Spring operating group comprises a much smaller portion of the business and reflects relatively new additions to the brand portfolio. Ashling Corporation, owner of the W-C Designs brand, was acquired in 2001, and Spring, a small premium cookware manufacturer, was acquired in 2002. These brands have led to the introduction of flatware, linens, and other household products under the W-C Designs brand and the Spring brand. As mentioned above, these products only generate 5 percent of the total revenue of the Group but they are gradually working into co-promotion opportunities with more traditional Waterford Wedgwood products in department and specialty stores as well as penetrating new retail outlets and broadening access to Waterford Wedgwood products. Overall, approximately a third of the production of the Group is outsourced to manufacturers in Germany, other European countries, and Asia.

Internal Issues

Finance

Wedgwood is not doing well financially. The Group's consolidated financial statements for the year ended March 31, 2007 were prepared in accordance with International Financial Reporting Standards (IFRS). The financial statements for the year ended March 31, 2007 were previously prepared in accordance with Irish Generally Accepted Accounting Principles and were restated on a consistent basis, except where otherwise required or permitted by IFRS 1, "First Time Adoption of International Accounting Standards."

The company is in a state of balance sheet insolvency. When the company restated their 2007 financial statements, they recognized a deficit pertaining to the defined benefit pension schemes in non-current liabilities, and this resulted in a deficit in their equity account. The deficit has increased due to losses experienced by the company in 2006 and 2007.

The company has struggled to maintain sales, which have declined every year since 2000, with the exception of 2003 in which sales remained flat at constant exchange rates. The increase in sales in 2006 was solely due to the acquisition of Royal Doulton in January of 2005. Revenues declined in fiscal 2007 from 772.6 million euro to 741.5 million euro. The company has faced significant problems with debt management but has recently concluded a restructuring that is expected to result in significant cost savings. The company has sold some businesses, including All-Clad, consolidated some of its operating groups, and completed a series of financial transactions, including an open offer of shares, in order to fund operating losses, regain financial footing, and more effectively manage debt.

The Group's income statements for 2007 and 2006 and recent balance sheets are provided in Exhibits 3 and 4. Interim financial information for 2007 and 2006 is also included in Exhibit 4, so a more thorough analysis of the company's results of operations can be performed. Segment information has been included in Exhibit 5 for the purpose of analyzing the individual financial results of the three operating divisions.

Marketing and Distribution

Waterford Wedgwood distributes its products through a multi-channel distribution network (including wholesalers and arrangements with select retail and department chains), direct

EXHIBIT 3   Waterford Wedgwood Consolidated Income Statement

(Amounts stated in millions of euros except per share data)
Year Ended March 31

	2007	2006	2005
Revenue	**€ 741.5**	**€ 772.6**	**€ 699.7**
Cost of sales	(387.5)	(452.6)	(423.2)
Gross profit/(loss)	354.0	320.0	276.5
Operating loss before exceptional items	**(14.9)**	**(68.2)**	**(73.0)**
Exceptional items	(2.2)	(62.6)	(105.6)
Operating loss	**(17.1)**	**(130.8)**	**(178.6)**
Finance income and costs:			
Interest receivable and similar income	0.2	0.5	0.3
Interest payable and similar charges before exceptional items	(53.9)	(49.8)	(47.4)
Exceptional finance costs	–	(9.3)	(19.1)
Loss before income tax	(70.8)	(189.4)	(244.8)
Income tax income/(expense)	(0.4)	0.5	(1.3)
Exceptional income tax expense	–	–	(12.0)
Loss for the year — continuing operations	**(71.2)**	**(188.9)**	**(258.1)**
Profit for the year from discontinued operations	–	–	106.8
Loss for the year	**(71.2)**	**(188.9)**	**(151.3)**
(Loss) profit attributable to:			
- Equity holders of the company	(71.3)	(190.8)	(149.2)
- Minority interests	0.1	1.9	(2.1)
	(71.2)	(188.9)	(151.3)
Loss per share — continuing operations			
- Basic and diluted (cents)		**(4.96)**	**(16.87)**
Earnings per share — discontinued operations			
- Basic and diluted (cents)			**7.04**
Loss per share - continuing and discontinued operations			
- Basic and diluted (cents)		**(4.96)**	**(9.83)**

Sources: Waterford Wedgwood 2007 *Annual Report* and Accounts, Waterford Wedgwood 2007 *Annual Report* and Accounts, http://www.waterfordwedgwood.com/investor_financialReports.asp.

retail from company-owned establishments (including the Waterford Crystal Gallery at the Waterford, Ireland factory), mail order, and via regional Internet retail Web sites.

Department store displays, word of mouth, and the Web sites are the primary marketing tools utilized by the company, but these are also supplemented by more traditional advertising efforts. The iconic status of a number of the company's brands allows the company to maintain its image without relying heavily on advertising. In addition to these efforts, the company continues to be involved with the creation of trophies for major sporting events and with special projects such as the Times Square New Year's Eve Ball.

The company also introduces special pieces to commemorate special events. For example, the company introduced a Waterford Crystal football helmet and football to commemorate the University of Florida's collegiate football championship in 2007. These products enhance the image of the company and may increase the customer base beyond traditional crystal buyers.

EXHIBIT 4 Waterford Wedgwood Consolidated Balance Sheet

(Amounts stated in millions of euros)

As of	31 Mar 2007	31-Mar 2006	31-Mar 2005	1-Apr2004*
ASSETS				
Non-current assets				
Property, plant and equipment	€ 154.5	€ 174.1	€ 214.3	€ 221.6
Intangible assets	124.7	124.6	128.9	105.2
Financial assets	3.4	3.6	3.4	12.7
Trade and other receivables	1.2	0.6	2.1	0
Deferred income tax assets	1.2	1.3	1.0	13.3
Total non-current assets	**285.0**	**304.2**	**349.7**	**352.8**
Current assets				
Inventories	249.4	233.7	222.1	295.5
Trade and other receivables	115.2	117.0	105.7	120.4
Derivative financial instruments	3.3	1.0		
Cash and cash equivalents	17.8	25.8	20.0	51.6
Total current assets	**385.7**	**377.5**	**347.8**	**467.5**
TOTAL ASSETS	**670.7**	**681.7**	**697.5**	**820.3**
LIABILITIES				
Finance lease obligations	24.0	22.7	24.1	18.4
Retirement benefit obligations	147.8	234.6	283.7	161.9
Deferred income tax liabilities	11.0	10.6	12.0	
Provisions for other liabilities & charges	11.7	15.0	4.8	
Borrowings	402.0	371.8	299.4	422.9
Trade and other payables	6.1	7.0	3.7	9.8
Total non-current liabilities	**602.6**	**661.7**	**627.7**	**613.0**
Current liabilities				
Trade and other payables	156.1	148.6	163.2	174.5
Finance lease obligations	3.0	3.1	1.7	1.1
Current income tax liabilities	5.3	6.0	6.8	5.8
Deferred income tax liabiltiies	1.0	0.7		
Provisions for other liabilities & charges	11.0	29.0	15.2	11.6
Total current liabilities	**176.4**	**187.4**	**186.9**	**193.0**
TOTAL LIABILITIES	**779.0**	**849.1**	**814.6**	**806.0**
TOTAL ASSETS LESS TOTAL LIABILITIES		**(167.4)**	**(117.1)**	**14.3**
EQUITY				
Capital and reserves attributable to the				
Company's equity holders				
Equity share capital	399.0	324.1	197.1	73.5
Share premium account	201.9	203.7	208.5	213.7
Retained losses	715.6	(698.8)	(522.6)	(278.2)

continued

EXHIBIT 4 **Waterford Wedgwood Consolidated Balance Sheet—continued**

Cash flow hedging reserve	3.3	1.0		
Other reserves	0.8	0.3	(0.4)	2.8
	(110.6)	(169.7)	(117.4)	11.8
Minority interests	2.3	2.3	0.3	2.5
TOTAL EQUITY	**(108.3)**	**(167.4)**	**(117.1)**	**14.3**
Total Equaity and Liabil	670.7	681.7	697.9	820.3

Note: *Transition date from Irish GAAP to IFRS

Sources: Waterford Wedgwood 2006 *Annual Report* and Accounts, Waterford Wedgwood 2005 *Annual Report* and Accounts, Waterford Wedgwood 2004 *Annual Report* and Accounts, http://www.waterfordwedgwood.com/investor_financialReports.asp.

Inheritance is a problem for Waterford in that many of the types of products sold by the company are considered "heirloom" items that are handed down from one generation to the next, reducing sales. This practice also encourages a brand perception of Waterford Wedgwood as old or associated with prior generations.

The Group's various brands are generally not marketed together as complementary products; each brand tends to be marketed individually. The company also faces questions regarding the allocation of marketing resources to newer product lines. Whatever the company is doing, its financial performance is not positive.

In the prior fiscal year ending March 2006, 44.5 percent of the Group's sales came from Europe, 38.9 percent from North America, 10.1 percent from Asia (primarily Japan), and 5.5 percent from the rest of the world (primarily Australia). This dispersion of sales causes the company to be very sensitive to exchange rates and other economic fluctuations in each of its markets. The company's primarily centralized production for each of its products results in significant transportation costs for the products to reach their markets.

EXHIBIT 5 **Financial Data By Segment**

	Fiscal year ended March 31	
	2006	2007
	(euro in millions)	
Revenue by segment:		
Waterford Crystal	206.5	199.4
Ceramics Group	527.8	501.5
W-C Designs & Spring	38.3	40.6
Revenue	772.6	741.5
Operating profit/(loss) by segment:		
Waterford Crystal	(18.1)	11.2
Ceramics Group	(99.1)	(19.1)
W-C Designs & Spring	(1.0)	(1.2)
Unallocated costs	(12.6)	(8.0)
Operating profit/(loss)	(130.8)	(17.1)
Net Operating expenses by segment:		
Waterford Crystal	224.6	188.2
Ceramics Group	626.9	520.6
W-C Designs & Spring	39.3	41.8
Unallocated costs	12.6	8.0
Total operating expenses	903.4	758.6

Source: Company *Annual Report,* 2007, p. 8

As the statistics show, a significant amount of the Group's sales come from North America and from Europe with Asian sales a distant third. Opportunity exists for growth in the Asian region, especially among brand-conscious Japanese consumers.

Competition

The market for luxury homewares has traditionally been segmented with different producers producing significantly different products. However, as Waterford Wedgwood has expanded their product lines, they have entered into the strategic areas of other rival manufacturers. One example of this can be found in their Waterford Crystal brand where the number of pieces containing colored crystal has increased in recent years. This type of piece has traditionally been the preserve of other European crystal manufacturers. In addition to existing manufacturers, the Group faces the potential for competition from new manufacturers in lower-cost countries in eastern Europe.

While the Group itself has taken advantage of the ability to manufacture at lower costs in Asia, these areas present the potential for competition as well. The lower labor costs, less stringent regulation, and a more limited view of intellectual property present in some Asian countries all present significant challenges to competing companies from outside Asia.

Two of the Group's established competitors include Steuben and Baccarat. Steuben is a division of Corning Incorporated (known as Corning Glass Works until 1989) based in Corning, NY. Steuben offers a full line of luxury glass products including barware, stemware, vases, and decorative pieces. These items are crafted almost exclusively out of clear glass. In 2003, Steuben added several product lines including barware, stemware, and tableware produced in Germany to its portfolio. However, most of Steuben's glassware is designed and produced at the company's Corning headquarters. The company distributes its products through its Web site and specialty retailers. Steuben makes up a relatively small portion of Corning's sales. The division, aggregated with several other small divisions, comprises approximately 8 percent of Corning's total sales or approximately $400 million.

Baccarat is a French crystal company based in Levallois Perret, France, with a wide range of luxury glass items including jewelry, tableware, stemware, lighting, and decorative crystal. Baccarat is well known for its vividly colored glassware and contemporary designs. In addition to glassware the company offers fashion accessories crafted from gold, silver, and precious stones. Baccarat distributes its products through high-end retailers throughout the world. Baccarat had sales of $187 million in 2006 and net income of $10.9 million.

The Future

Waterford Wedgwood is attempting to more effectively manage its labor costs, as well as continue to introduce new and contemporary product lines to complement its existing offerings. High labor costs (much related to hand-crafting) have been a continuing problem, and the company's recent closing of its plant in Dungarvan, Ireland, resulted in the layoff of several hundred employees.

The company continues to introduce additional product lines to follow trends while maintaining quality and tradition. The possibility of the dilution of the brand is always present, and the company seeks to strike a close balance between flexibility in new product offerings and the maintenance of the iconic status of its brands.

In addition to the simple addition of product lines, the company plans to increase the number of distribution channels through which their products are sold. This includes a desire to place their products in additional retailers such as Bed Bath & Beyond in the United States as well as in wine shops through a collaborative branding arrangement with Robert Mondavi, an American winemaker. Alliances such as these are considered a method to achieve both an increase in product lines as well as possible increases in distribution channels.

Tradition and quality have always been the foundation of Waterford Wedgwood's success. Is it possible for the company to maintain its tradition while introducing contemporary products attractive to customers? Can the company expand into additional markets while maintaining quality and managing costs? Can the company maintain quality and effectively manage costs? Based on the interim, annual, and segment financial data presented, does it appear the restructuring will be successful and a turnaround is beginning to occur?

Prepare a three-year strategic plan for Waterford Wedgwood. Address opportunities for sales growth both in product design and in newer markets, such as Japan, and threats presented by competition both in Europe and Asia. Evaluate the strength of the public's ongoing positive perception of the Waterford Wedgwood brands and the ongoing weakness in sales and dependence on the United States market. Imagine that you are the CEO of Waterford Wedgwood as you evaluate the factors that will influence the company's direction over the next three years. What type of strategy should be pursued? How should any changes be financed? Develop projected financial statements for the first year of implementation to assess the impact of any changes that you will make.

EXHIBIT 6   Segment Operating Analysis

	Fiscal year ended March 31, 2006	% Margin[1]	Fiscal year ended March 31, 2007	% Margin[1]
	(euro in millions, except percentages)			
Operating profit/(loss) by segment as reported:				
Waterford Crystal	(18.1)	(8.8%)	11.2	5.6%
Ceramics Group	(99.1)	(18.8%)	(19.1)	(3.8%)
W-C Designs & Spring	(1.0)	(2.6%)	(1.2)	(0.3%)
Unallocated costs	(12.6)	n/a	(8.0)	n/a
Operating profit/(loss) as reported	(130.8)	(16.9%)	(17.1)	(2.3%)
Exceptional items by segment:				
Waterford Crystal	(5.8)	(2.8%)	(1.1)	(0.6%)
Ceramics Group	(56.8)	(10.8%)	(1.1)	(0.2%)
W-C Designs & Spring	–	n/a	–	n/a
Unallocated costs	–	n/a	–	n/a
Exceptional items	(62.6)	(8.1%)	(2.2)	(0.3%)
Operating profit/(loss) by segment before exceptional items:				
Waterford Crystal	(12.3)	(6.0%)	12.3	6.2%
Ceramics Group	(42.3)	(8.0%)	(18.0)	(3.6%)
W-C Designs & Spring	(1.0)	(2.6%)	(1.2)	(3.0%)
Unallocated costs	(12.6)	n/a	(8.0)	n/a
Operating profit/(loss) before exceptional items	(68.2)	(8.8%)	(14.9)	(2.0%)

[1] Margin is calculated for each of the periods presented by dividing operating profit/(loss) and exceptional changes for each segment by the applicable segment revenue figure.

Source: Company *Annual Report,* 2007, p. 10.

References

Waterford Wedgwood 2006 *Annual Report* and Accounts, available from http://www.waterfordwedgwood.com/investor_financialReports.asp, last accessed 04/28/2007.

Waterford Wedgwood 2007 *Annual Report* and Accounts, available from http://www.waterfordwedgwood.com/investor_financialReports.asp, last accessed 04/28/2007.

"Waterford Wedgwood Corporate Profile," available from http://www.waterfordwedgwood.com/investor_corpProfile1.asp, last accessed 04/28/2007.

Waterford Wedgwood Investor Relations, available from http://www.waterfordwedgwood.com/investor.asp, last accessed 04/28/2007.

Waterford Wedgwood, plc, available from http://www.answers.com/topic/waterford-wedgwood-plc, last accessed 04/28/2007.

Acknowledgments

The authors would like to thank Lamar University (of the Texas State University system), especially Provost and Executive Vice President Dr. Stephen Doblin, for the funding that allowed Brandan L. Still to conduct onsite research in Ireland in March 2006 for the preparation of this case.

http://www.waterfordwedgwood.com/pdf/waterfordwedgwood_Annual_Report_2006.pdf
http://www.waterfordwedgwood.com/investor.asp
http://www.waterford.com
http://finance.google.com/finance?cid=15501976
http://www.answers.com/topic/waterford-wedgwood-plc
http://steuben.com/index.cfm
http://www.baccarat.fr/en/index.htm

Toll Brothers, Inc. — 2007

Randy Harris
California State University, Stanislaus

TOL

www.tollbrothers.com

"There are too many soft markets at this stage of the selling season to call a general upturn in the new-home market," said Robert Toll. "Demand varies greatly from week to week in individual markets."[1] Toll, chairman and chief executive officer of Toll Brothers, Inc., a leading U.S. builder of luxury homes, had just announced a 67 percent drop in its fiscal first quarter 2007 net income. Total revenue was also down, dropping 19 percent from $1.34 billion in the first quarter of fiscal 2006 to $1.09 billion. Toll Brothers had also seen a steep drop in net contracts for new home construction. First-quarter fiscal 2007 net signed contracts for new home construction came in at $748.7 million, versus $1.14 billion for first quarter 2006. This drop in new home contracts represented a 34 percent decline. Cancellations of housing contracts, which had historically run about 7 percent for Toll Brothers, were now running at a rate of 29.8 percent. Nevertheless, Robert Toll remained upbeat in his outlook. "We believe that pent-up demand is building in many markets as potential buyers bide their time until they are confident that prices have firmed," he said.[2] Toll Brothers' net income for the second quarter of 2007 declined 27.8 percent to $26.4 million. The company needs a clear strategic plan.

Company History

Toll Brothers, with headquarters in Horsham, Pennsylvania, was founded in 1967. Originally, the company built houses predominantly in the suburbs of Philadelphia, Delaware, and southern New Jersey. Toll Brothers became a publicly traded company in 1986. Expansion came soon after, with Toll expanding in 1988 into the Boston, MA and Baltimore, MD markets. By 1991, the company had expanded operations to include the suburbs of New York City, Connecticut, and areas surrounding Washington, DC.

Nationwide expansion for Toll Brothers began in the 1990s. In 1994, at the end of a nationwide housing slump, Toll purchased several distressed properties in the greater Los Angeles metro area. Following closely behind the Los Angeles acquisitions, Toll expanded into North Carolina, Florida, Texas, and the San Francisco Bay Area of northern California. In 1995, Toll Brothers purchased a home builder, Geoffrey H. Edmunds, which was based in the Scottsdale/Phoenix markets of Arizona. Several national acquisitions soon followed. By 1997, Toll Brothers had entered the active adult community market, and had also become heavily involved with the development of nearly a dozen new golf communities. Golf course designers for Toll Brothers' exclusive golf communities included Arnold Palmer, Greg Norman, and Peter Dye.

Historically, Toll had focused predominantly on building single-family detached homes, often on land plots significantly larger than those of other builders. By 2003, however, Toll had expanded into the high-rise construction market with the acquisition of the Manhattan Building Company in 2003. After this acquisition, Toll acquired other high and mid-rise builders in Jacksonville, Orlando, Phoenix, and Philadelphia. By 2004, Toll Brothers had launched a major urban initiative with the construction of an 800-unit luxury condominium project in Hoboken, New Jersey, as well as other projects throughout the greater New York City metropolitan area.

EXHIBIT 1   Toll Brothers Home Data 2001–2006

	2001	2002	2003	2004	2005	2006
Number of homes closed	4,358	4,430	4,911	6,627	8,769	8,601
Sales value of homes closed (in $000's)	2,180,469	2,279,261	2,731,044	3,839,451	5,759,301	5,945,169
Number of homes contracted	4,314	5,070	6,132	8,684	10,372	6,164
Sales value of homes contracted (in $000's)	2,158,536	2,734,457	3,475,992	5,641,454	7,152,463	4,460,734
Number of homes in backlog	2,702	3,342	4,652	6,709	8,805	6,533
Sales value of homes in backlog (in $000's)	1,403,588	1,858,784	2,631,900	4,433,905	6,014,648	4,488,400
Number of selling communities	155	170	200	230	230	300
Homes sites						
Owned	25,081	25,822	29,081	29,804	35,838	41,808
Optioned	13,165	15,022	18,977	30,385	47,288	31,960
Total	39,146	40,844	48,058	60,189	83,126	73,768

Source: Toll Brothers *Annual Reports.*

Company Operations

The company conducts its national operations from its corporate offices in Horsham, a suburb just north of Philadelphia. Toll operates four large manufacturing facilities located in (1) Morrisville, PA, (2) Emporia, VA, (3) Knox, IN, and (4) Fairless Hills, PA. The facility in Fairless Hills is leased, while the other three are company owned. At these four facilities, Toll manufactures open wall panels, roof and floor trusses, interior and exterior millwork, and other construction materials in bulk for Toll operations.

As of October 31 of the 2006 fiscal year-end for Toll, the company was selling homes in 398 communities, representing approximately 31,910 home sites. They also owned or controlled through options approximately 41,858 home sites in 300 proposed communities. Toll Brothers expected to be selling homes in approximately 340 communities at the end of fiscal 2007. In the company's core business, single-family detached homes, Toll operates from 207 communities at prices that generally ranged from $280,000 to $2.1 million. The average sale price of a Toll home was approximately $688,000. Toll employs 5,542 persons full-time—245 in executive positions, 524 engaged in sales, 547 project managers, 2,252 administrative or clerical, 1,159 construction workers, 350 golf course operators, and 235 persons in manufacturing and distribution.

New home sales for Toll Brothers had peaked in April of 2005, followed by a significant drop-off in sales. Closings on houses sold peaked two quarters later, in October of 2005, and also experienced sharp declines thereafter. Contract cancellations for new homes, which had seriously affected fiscal 2006 revenues and profits, did appear to be leveling off somewhat, and inventory levels also showed some signs of dropping. "The cancellation level has dropped to 16 percent in the last five weeks from a high of 36 percent," said Robert Toll. However, he said, "the market is still beset with speculation . . . it may take longer in some areas to pare the number of unsold properties."[3]

Company Segments

Toll Brothers manufactures luxury single and multi-family housing in four geographic markets: North, Mid-Atlantic, South, and West. The North segment consisted of operations in the states of Connecticut, Illinois, Massachusetts, Michigan, Minnesota, New Hampshire, New Jersey, New York, Ohio, and Rhode Island. In fiscal 2006, the North segment had delivered 1,983 homes, versus 1,870 homes in fiscal 2005. Revenues were commensurately higher, at $1.4 billion, representing sales growth of 27 percent in fiscal 2006. The value of new contracts signed in fiscal 2006 for the North region dropped, however, by 22 percent to $1.18 billion from the previous year's $1.52 billion. This drop in new contracts signed was attributed to a general slowdown in the housing market, and signaled that sales and profits in the North segment would also drop in the year ahead.

The Mid-Atlantic segment of Toll Brothers consisted of operations in the states of Delaware, Maryland, Pennsylvania, Virginia, and West Virginia. Revenues from operations in the Mid-Atlantic region dropped by 14 percent, down from $2.0 billion in fiscal 2005 to $1.78 billion in fiscal 2006. Units delivered also dropped from 3,290 homes in fiscal 2005 to 2,697 homes in fiscal 2006. Net new contracts signed in the Mid-Atlantic region dropped sharply in fiscal 2006, down 43 percent from fiscal 2005. Toll Brothers cited a significantly higher number of contract cancellations in the Mid-Atlantic region, as well as weak demand.

The South region of Toll Brothers consisted of operations in the states of Florida, North Carolina, South Carolina, Tennessee, and Texas. Revenues for the South region increased sharply from $721 million in fiscal 2005 to $1.2 billion in fiscal 2006, an increase of 65 percent. Units delivered rose from 1,312 to 2,017, and income from South region operations doubled from $81 million to $161.8 million in fiscal 2006. Strong growth, particularly in Florida and Texas, accounted for much of the region's standout performance. Unfortunately, net new contracts signed in fiscal 2006 were down 39 percent from fiscal 2005 to $800 million. Florida was singled out as the reason for the decline of the South region's new contracts. While Toll Brothers had opened several new home communities in Florida, market conditions were weak there, and contract cancellations had been significantly higher than anticipated.

The West region of Toll Brothers was composed of operations in the states of Arizona, California, Colorado, and Nevada. Sales in the West declined 9 percent from $1.8 million to $1.7 million in fiscal 2006. Units sold also declined from 2,297 to 1,904, and income before taxes also dropped $112.3 million to $338.5 million. Toll attributed the drop in the West primarily to California, which also had a significantly higher number of contract cancellations.

Toll Brothers' Price Points and Customers

While the average price for a Toll Brothers house is $688,000, the company sells houses at a number of price points. The largest segment, homes priced between $300,000 and $749,999, comprised 64 percent of Toll sales in fiscal 2006. The next largest segment was only a third of the previous segment. Homes priced between $750,000 and $999,999 were 21 percent of sales. The Estate segment, homes priced from $1 million and up, were 12 percent of Toll sales. Homes priced below $300,000 made up only 3 percent of the Toll sales portfolio. Fully 67 percent of Toll Brothers' sales were priced under $750,000.

These home prices, however, only represented the base price for a Toll home. Optional features, such as additional garages, guest suites, extra fireplaces, and larger lot sizes, were typically added on by home buyers to customize their homes. The number of "extras" and optional features typically requested by a Toll customer increased as the size and base price of the home under consideration got larger. On average, extras and optional features added 21 percent, or $121,000, to the base price of a Toll Brothers home.

Toll Brothers regards the typical customer for a Toll home as an "upscale" luxury home buyer, and considers that there are four main types of buyer groups for their home. The first, the "move-up" market, is typically baby boomers. The largest group of baby boomers, Americans born between the years 1954 and 1964, are in their prime income earning years, typically the peak for moving up and buying a larger, more expensive home. Toll worked to capture the market for these boomers that sought to sell their earlier, often first, home and "move up" to a Toll Brothers luxury offering in an exclusive community.

The "empty-nester" market is the second target demographic for Toll homes. "Empty-nesters" are Americans 50 years old or older whose children, now college age or older, had left home. The leading edge of the baby boomers, those born between 1945 and 1964, are now in their late 50s and early 60s and are now part of the "empty-nester" market. Toll Brothers seeks to provide homes and communities that cater to this affluent niche, offering home designs with features such as one-story living and first-floor master bedroom suites, and building communities with extra features such as golf courses, country clubs, and recreation centers.

Active adults, families where at least one member is 55 years or older, represent the third main target group for Toll. Active adults want communities that typically restrict the presence of small children and young adults. Toll sells homes in 18 different communities where age is a qualifying factor. Toll Brothers considers active-adult communities to be a significant growth area, and plans to open additional such communities during the next few years.

The final group for Toll is the second-home market. Second homes for affluent families typically are purchased in locations that offer some type of scenic location or favorable weather conditions. Toll sell many homes in this market in states such as Arizona, California, Florida, and Nevada.

A growing market for Toll Brothers that cross all of the above four customer types and price points is the urban luxury market. Toll identified a growing market of move-up families, empty-nesters, and young professionals that wanted to live in or near to major urban areas. Toll has recently begun to offer high-, mid-, and low-rise luxury communities that cater to individuals seeking access to these urban areas. These communities, typically high-density projects such as a high-rise development in New Jersey, or condominiums and townhomes in Dublin, California, offer luxury and quick access via public transit into urban areas such as New York City or the San Francisco Bay Area.

Competition

Toll Brothers considers its primary competition to be small, private builders. While other homebuilders build or sell homes on a national level, Toll Brothers primarily sell, luxury homes at much higher price points than the average national homebuilder. For example, while the average home price on a home sold by Toll is approximately $692,000, other national homebuilders have average sales prices in the $300,000 range or less. Toll Brothers believes that they compete primarily on the basis of price, location, design, quality, service, and reputation.

Management Team

Three executives constitute the core management team for Toll Brothers: Robert Toll, Zvi Barzilay, and Joel Rassman. Robert I. Toll is the chairman and chief executive officer (CEO) of Toll Brothers, Inc. Mr. Toll had been chairman and CEO of Toll Brothers since its founding in 1967. Mr. Toll received a bachelor of arts degree from Cornell University in 1963, and graduated cum laude with an LLB degree from the University of Pennsylvania law school in 1966. Mr. Toll was named Entrepreneur of the Year by Cornell University in 2005. Mr. Toll and his wife live in Bucks County, PA, north of Philadelphia. They have five children and nine grandchildren. Robert Toll's brother, Bruce Toll, is vice chairman of the board for Toll Brothers and the president of BET Investments, an office and commercial real estate company.

Zvi Barzilay is the president and chief operating officer for Toll Brothers. Mr. Barzilay is responsible for all aspects of company operations, including homebuilding, land purchases, architecture, golf course operations, and product development. Mr. Barzilay was also instrumental to the growth of Toll Integrated Systems, the company's manufacturing subsidiary. Mr. Barzilay holds a bachelor in architecture degree from the University of Maryland and a master's in urban design/real estate development from Harvard University. Mr. Barzilay joined Toll Brothers in 1980. Prior to joining Toll Brothers, Mr. Barzilay was, among other things, the chief center city planner for the Philadelphia City Planning Commission.

Joel H. Rassman is the executive vice president, treasurer, and chief financial officer for Toll Brothers. Mr. Rassman's primary area of responsibility is the financial operations of Toll Brothers, including mortgage banking, accounting, internal auditing, and tax operations. Mr. Rassman was a 1967 graduate of Bernard Baruch College in accounting, and was instrumental in the efforts by Toll Brothers to prepare for the initial public offering of Toll Brothers stock in 1986. M. Rassman is a member of both the New York State Society of Certified Public Accountants and the American Institute of Certified Public Accountants.

Financial Status

From the firm's initial public offering, Toll Brothers had been an excellent investment for shareholders. From 1986 to 2006, the firm had delivered better than a 20 percent compound average annual growth rate in total revenues, net income, and earnings per share. Their profit margins were among the highest among homebuilders, and Toll enjoyed an investment-grade corporate credit rating from Standard & Poor's, Moody's, and Fitch. Total revenues, which stood at $124.6 million in 1986, had grown to approximately $6 billion by the end of 2006.

Net income, however, had peaked in fiscal 2005. While the company had net income of $806 million in 2005, it had dropped to $687 million in fiscal 2006. First quarter 2007 sales and net income had also slumped, as noted previously. The weakness in sales was persistent throughout all four regions for Toll Brothers. One notable exception to this overall trend was the New York and New Jersey area, particularly developments in or around New York City.

Concurrent with the sharp slowdown in 2006 and early 2007, Toll Brothers had experienced a notable increase in inventories. Inventories for the company had increased from $3.8 billion in fiscal 2004 to $5.0 billion in fiscal 2005. The company added another billion in fiscal 2006, with fully $6 billion dollars in inventory on the company's balance sheets. While this was problematic, Mr. Toll had noted some signs of improvement. "We're now running at half the pace of inventory that we had three or four months ago," he said. "So I would guess, and that's all it is, that it'll be another four or five months before you finally burn off inventory in most of the markets." On the other hand, Toll noted, "The market is still beset by speculation, and it may take longer in some areas to pare the number of unsold properties."[4]

EXHIBIT 2 Toll Brothers Consolidated Statements of Income 2001–2006 (Amounts in thousands of U.S. dollars, except per share data)

	2001	2002	2003	2004	2005	2006
Revenues						
Home sales	$2,180,469	2,279,261	2,731,044	3,839,451	5,759,301	5,945,169
Land sales	27,530	36,183	27,399	22,491	34,124	8,173
Equity earnings from unconsolidated entities	6,756	1,870	981	15,731	27,744	48,361
Interest and other	14,850	11,658	15,817	15,420	41,197	52,664
Percentage of completion						170,111
Total Revenues	2,229,605	2,328,972	2,775,241	3,893,093	5,862,366	6,224,478
Costs and Expenses						
Home sales	1,602,276	1,655,331	1,977,439	2,747,274	3,902,697	4,263,200
Land sales	21,464	25,671	17,875	15,775	24,416	6,997
Selling, general administrative	209,729	236,123	288,337	381,080	482,786	573,404
Interest	58,247	64,529	73,245	93,303	125,283	121,993
Early debt retirement expense			7,192	8,229	4,056	
Percentage of completion						132,268
Total Costs	1,891,716	1,981,654	2,364,088	3,245,661	4,539,238	5,097,862
Income before taxes	337,889	347,318	411,153	647,432	1,323,128	1,126,616
Income taxes	124,216	127,431	151,333	238,321	517,018	439,403
Net Income	213,673	219,887	259,820	409,111	806,110	687,213
Earnings per share						
Basic	$ 2.98	$3.12	$3.68	$5.50	$5.23	$4.45
Diluted	$ 2.76	$2.91	$3.44	$5.04	$4.78	$4.17

Note: Toll Brothers stock had a two-for-one stock split on July 8, 2005.

Source: Toll Brothers Annual Reports.

EXHIBIT 3 Toll Brothers Consolidated Balance Sheets 2001–2006 (Amounts in thousands of U.S. dollars)

	2001	2002	2003	2004	2005	2006
Assets						
Cash and equivalents	$ 182,840	102,337	425,251	465,834	689,219	632,524
Marketable securities				115,029		
Inventory	2,183,541	2,551,061	3,080,349	3,878,260	5,068,624	6,095,702
Property, construction and office equipment, net	33,095	38,496	43,711	52,429	79,524	99,089
Receivables, prepaid expenses and other assets	74,481	95,065	113,633	146,212	185,620	160,446
Contracts receivable						170,111
Mortgage loans receivable	26,758	63,949	57,500	99,914	99,858	130,326
Customer deposits held in escrow	17,303	23,019	31,547	53,929	68,601	49,676
Investments in unconsolidated entities	14,182	21,438	35,400	93,971	152,394	245,667
Total Assets	2,532,200	2,895,365	3,787,391	4,905,578	6,343,840	7,583,541
Liabilities						
Loans payable	362,712	253,194	281,697	340,380	250,552	736,934
Senior notes			546,669	845,665	1,140,028	1,141,167
Subordinated notes	669,581	819,663	620,000	450,000	350,000	350,000
Mortgage company warehouse loan	24,754	48,996	49,939	92,053	89,674	119,705
Customer deposits	101,778	134,707	176,710	291,424	415,602	360,147
Accounts payable	132,970	126,391	151,730	181,972	256,557	292,171
Accrued expenses	229,671	281,275	346,944	574,202	791,769	825,288
Income taxes payable	98,151	101,630	137,074	209,895	282,147	334,500
Total Liabilities	1,619,617	1,765,856	2,310,763	2,985,591	3,576,329	4,159,912
Minority Interest					3,940	7,703
Stockholders' Equity						
Common stock, par	369	740	770	770	1,563	1,563
Additional paid-in capital	107,014	102,600	190,596	200,938	242,546	220,783
Retained earnings	882,281	1,101,799	1,361,619	1,770,730	2,576,061	3,263,274
Treasury stock, at cost	(77,081)	(75,630)	(76,357)	(52,451)	(56,599)	(69,694)
Total Stockholders' Equity	912,583	1,129,506	1,476,628	1,919,987	2,763,571	3,415,926
Total Liabilities and Stockholders' Equity	$2,532,200	2,895,365	3,787,391	4,905,578	6,343,840	7,583,541

Source: Toll Brothers *Annual Reports.*

Liabilities for Toll Brothers had also begun to slowly creep up. By year-end fiscal 2006, the company had $736 million in notes payable on its books, up sharply from $250 million in fiscal 2005. Senior notes had also expanded, and now topped $1.1 billion, up from $845 million in fiscal 2004. The company had recently secured a $1.8 billion bank credit facility, and had extended the terms of the arrangement through March 2011. Toll believed that this new bank credit facility was a major plus for the company, and positioned Toll Brothers well for possible acquisitions. Toll said, ". . . with this credit line, $600 million in cash on hand, and no major corporate debt maturities until 2011, we believe we are ready to take advantage of opportunities that may arise in this market."[5]

Stock Performance

Toll Brothers stock (NYSE: TOL) had been through a bumpy ride in the last several years. The stock price peaked in July 2005 at $58.67 per share. From there the stock had fallen sharply, bottoming out at $22.22 per share in July of 2006. The stock recovered gradually into early 2007, only to come under more selling pressure in late February and early

March. As of late March 2007, the stock traded in a broad range of between $28 and $32 per share. Robert Toll said, "Insiders own 30 percent of our stock. We are keenly focused on the fact that today's stock price, although up 45 percent from its recent low . . . is still down 45 percent from its peak."[6]

U.S. Homebuilding Industry

There were approximately 1.38 million new homes sold in the United States in 2005, according to the Standard and Poor's Industry Surveys. From 1995 to 2005, sales of new single-family homes grew from about 667,000 homes per year to 1.38 million, representing an average annual growth rate over this time period of 7.5 percent per year.

The homebuilding industry is large and highly fragmented, and only a relatively few builders actually compete on a nationwide basis. Most homebuilders are small, independent, "mom and pop" style operations, with many being privately held small businesses. In 2005, the 100 largest homebuilders in the United States sold 504,670 new homes. This represented only 36.5 percent of the total number of new homes sold in the United States. The nation's largest homebuilder, D.R. Horton, had home sales that accounted for less than 4 percent of the industry's total sales.

While the U.S. market remained fragmented, the large U.S. homebuilders were increasingly consolidating the U.S. homebuilding industry. For example, the ten largest homebuilders in the United States now account for 21 percent of all U.S. new home sales. Growth of large U.S. builders has been rapid. In the mid-1990s, the ten largest builders accounted for less than 9 percent of total industry sales. The compound average growth rate of the ten largest builders, at 13.8 percent over the last decade, has far outpaced the growth of the homebuilding industry as a whole. Many large homebuilders entered new markets in the United States through acquisitions, often acquiring smaller builders when market conditions were favorable.

Competition

Competition in the U.S. homebuilding industry is intense, and homebuilders utilize a number of different marketing channels to make sales. Homebuilders typically employ their own in-house sales brokers, but are also increasingly utilizing independent real estate brokers to make sales as well. Prospective customers are contacted through a variety of marketing channels, including newspaper and magazine advertising, billboards, direct mail, and personal contacts. The World Wide Web has also begun to play an increasingly prominent role in the marketing of new homes. Almost all of the large builders use Web sites to generate sales, and many builders are increasingly using Web technologies to allow customers to select features on their new home purchases and to design custom options. Homebuilders also typically build model homes at the entrance to

EXHIBIT 4 Top Ten U.S. Single-Family Homebuilders, 2005

Company	Total U.S. Home Closings	Home Building Revenues ($Mil)	Net Income ($Mil)	Return on Equity (%)	Earnings Per Share ($)
D. R. Horton	51,383	14,246	1,470.5	31.6	4.71
Pulte Homes	45,630	14,694	1,436.9	27.4	5.62
Lennar Corp.	42,359	13,867	1,344.4	28.9	8.65
Centex Corp.	37,022	14,673	1,221.0	26.3	9.62
KB Home	31,009	9,442	842.4	34.3	10.29
Beazer Homes USA	18,401	5,189	262.5	19.2	6.49
Hovnanian Enterprises	17,783	5,879	471.8	31.4	7.51
The Ryland Group	16,673	4,818	447.1	36.8	9.52
MDC Holdings	15,307	4,880	505.7	30.0	11.48
NVR Inc.	13,787	5,262	697.6	92.3	110.36

Source: Standard & Poor's *Industry Surveys: Homebuilding,* 2006.

their developments, allowing prospective customers to enter and actually see a finished model of the developer's homes.

The number one homebuilder in the United States, based on the number of new homes sold, is D. R. Horton. In 2005, Horton had closed on 51,383 homes. Pulte Homes is a close second on home closings, at 45,630 home sold, but actually edged out Horton in terms of total revenues. Earnings for all of the top homebuilders were extremely strong during the years 2002 to 2005. One homebuilder, NVR Inc., reported a return on equity of 92.3 percent in 2005, according to Standard and Poor's.

Results for almost all of the homebuilders has deteriorated sharply of late. D. R. Horton's first quarter 2007 earnings missed analysts forecasts, and the company predicted sharply lower revenues and earnings for the remainder of 2007. Lennar Corp. posted a 73 percent drop in profits for its 2007 fiscal first quarter, KB Homes had reported an 84 percent decrease in profits for first quarter fiscal 2007, Pulte Homes missed analysts' estimates, and Hovnanian Enterprises reported a fiscal 2007 first quarter loss.

During a press conference in March 2007, Lennar's CEO, Stuart Miller, warned that he couldn't forecast when the housing market would stabilize, and revoked the company's prior financial guidance to analysts for fiscal 2007. "The typically stronger spring selling season has not yet materialized," he said.[7] Miller emphasized that the strategy for Lennar going forward would be to create a firm foundation for the company as market conditions continue to deteriorate. "Our overriding strategy is defined by our focus on our balance sheet," he said. "Our company has intensified the focus on generating strong cash flow at the expense of maintaining margins."[8]

New Home Sales

New home sales had peaked in 2005. From February of 2005, when new home sales hit a seasonally adjusted annual rate of 1,324,000 homes, sales had begun a steep descent. By February of 2007, new home sales were reported at a seasonally adjusted annual rate of 848,000 homes, down almost 36 percent from February of 2005. Adding to the downturn, the seasonally adjusted estimate of new houses for sale at the end of February 2007 was 546,000 homes, which represented a total U.S. supply of 8.1 months of inventory at the current rate of sales.

The rate of new home sales was the lowest since June of 2000, when new home sales had slumped to a seasonally adjusted annual rate of 793,000 homes. Further, the inventory of new homes was growing. "There is an enormous backlog of unsold new homes that have to be worked off," said Ray Stone, chief economist for Stone & McCarthy Research.[9]

EXHIBIT 5 New U.S. One-Family Houses Sold January 2005 – February 2007 (Units in Thousands)

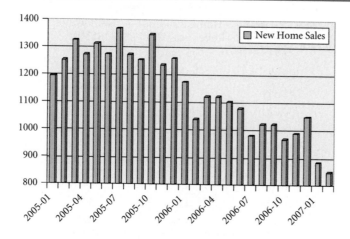

Source: U.S. Department of Housing and Urban Development.

Conclusion

Toll Brothers' current mission statement is as follows:

> We design, build, market, and arrange financing for single-family detached and attached homes in luxury residential communities. We are also involved, directly and through joint ventures, in projects where we are building, or converting existing rental apartment buildings into, high-, mid-, and low-rise luxury homes. We cater to move-up, empty nesters, active-adult, age-qualified and second-home buyers in 21 states of the United States.

There are several options that Toll could pursue moving forward. The first option is to expand operations through selective acquisitions. Smaller builders, increasingly under pressure, now make appealing acquisition candidates for Toll during the downturn. Toll could acquire some of these smaller homebuilders to increase the future scope of Toll operations. Likewise, other companies and builders could potentially be willing to sell distressed assets such as land. Toll could potentially acquire such assets at a significantly reduced cost. Obviously, the quicker the housing market recovery, the faster that such distressed assets could be effectively utilized. In the event of a prolonged housing downturn, such distressed companies or assets could jeopardize profitability and cash flows for Toll Brothers.

A second option would be to maintain or grow Toll Brothers' market share through aggressive price discounting, sales incentives, and other marketing promotions. Increasing the price discounting at various Toll communities could potentially stem the tide of rising cancellations and the downturn in sales, as well as further reduce Toll's inventory of unsold houses. Increasingly aggressive price promotions could also potentially pressure Toll competitors in these markets. A potential drawback to this approach, however, would be further deterioration in margins for the company.

Finally, Toll could begin aggressively reducing costs and overhead throughout its corporate operations. While it would not be possible to reduce costs on houses and communities currently completed, Toll could potentially reduce corporate expenses by canceling further land acquisitions, pressuring subcontractors for price cuts, downsizing employees, and closing selected Toll operations in underperforming markets. This option was not without its drawbacks, however. While these actions could reduce costs for Toll in the short-term, engaging in such drastic and aggressive cost-cutting could also potentially endanger the longer-term profitability and growth of the company.

Prepare a three-year strategic plan for CEO Robert Toll.

Endnotes

1. Lam, J. & Corkery, M. (February 23, 2007). "Toll Brothers Net Falls 67%; Outlook Is Cut." *Wall Street Journal.*
2. Seeking Alpha. (February 22, 2007). "Toll Brothers F1Q07 (Qtr End 1/31/07) Earnings Call Transcript." Retrieved at www.seekingalpha.com.
3. Louis, B. & Crenson. (March 7, 2007). "Toll Cancellations Drop; Horton to Miss Projections." *Bloomberg News.* Retrieved at www.bloomberg.com.
4. Ibid.
5. Toll Brothers *Annual Report*, 2006. Retrieved at www.tollbrothers.com.
6. Ibid.
7. Sechler, B. (March 27, 2007). "Lennar's Net Income Drops 73% Amid Deteriorating Housing Market." *Wall Street Journal.* Retrieved at online.wsj.com.
8. Miller, S. (March 27, 2007). "Lennar CEO: Worst Not Over." *Calculated Risk.* Transcript of Lennar CEO comments retrieved at www.calculatedrisk.blogspot.com.
9. Nutting, R. (March 26, 2007). "New Home Sales Fall to Seven-Year Low." *MarketWatch.* Retrieved at www.marketwatch.com.

15 Cellox — 2007

A. Gregory Stone

Timothy A. O. Redmer
Regent University

www.cellox.com

www.celblox.com

"Houses are blowing away in hurricanes and I have the product to literally change the land-scape," lamented David Pace, owner of Cellox, LLC. "The third pig of the three little pigs had good reason to build his house out of brick and mortar as opposed to his brothers, who made their houses of sticks and straw." David owns a patented insulated concrete form (ICF) product for the home construction market. It is notably superior to his competitors', products, but it is difficult to persuade builders to change from stick construction to his concrete-based product.

"Practical pig knew he would face the wind of the Big Bad Wolf some day, so he wanted to build things right!" Then the Big Bad Wolves—hurricanes Katrina, Rita, and Wilma—assailed the Gulf Coast states and blew the stick homes down. David was right, but Cellox is headquartered in and manufacturing ICFs in Reedsburg, Wisconsin—over 1,000 miles away from the hurricane-stricken South. Cellox's current vision statement is: "Cellox is Committed to the ideals of Quality, Service, People, and the Utilization of technology dedicated to 'Making it Happen.' "

Cellox produces the highest quality product with top-of-the-line components in an industry with 40-plus competitors. David Pace believes his small company can dom-inate the market for insulated concrete forms (ICFs). However, as indicated in Exhibit 1,

EXHIBIT 1 Cellox Financial Information

	Cellox Inc. Income Statement (Numbers are in $1,000s)		
	Dec. 31, 2006	Dec. 31, 2005	Dec. 31, 2004
Sales	$3,469.6	1,707.4	2,105.4
Cost of Goods Sold	2,167.1	961.7	1,140.5
Gross Margin	1,302.5	745.7	964.9
Production Expenses	485.0	239.5	412.0
Facility Expenses	156.0	239.9	497.0
Depreciation Expense	219.2	60.2	103.0
Operating Income	442.3	206.1	−47.0
Sales Expenses	318.5	110.3	180.4
Administration Expenses	354.5	137.6	153.7
Income Before Interest & Taxes	−230.7	−41.8	−381.0
Interest Expense	142.5	79.5	37.5
Income Before Tax	−373.1	−121.3	−418.6
Tax	−134.3	−43.3	−149.4
Net Income/Loss =	**−238.8**	**−78.0**	**−269.2**

Cellox had a net income of negative $238,000 in 2006 following similar losses in both 2005 and 2004. The balance sheets in Exhibit 2 reveal that Cellox currently has more than $2 million in long-term debt on its balance.

When David purchased Cellox in 2003, the business was near bankruptcy, being plagued by poor leadership, weak customer service, and lax production controls, often manufacturing more units than they could sell in a given amount of time, thereby creating the need for warehousing. In spite of a critical cash flow issue, he increased sales by expanding the production and warehouse capacity.

In order for Cellox to survive, David must cultivate customer demand in two target customer populations—(1) construction contractors, especially home builders, and (2) individuals wanting to build a house. Reaching these two customer populations is critical. David needs a clear strategic plan for the future, including a vision statement and mission statement. Most of all Cellox needs customers.

EXHIBIT 2   Cellox Inc.

Balance Sheet
(Numbers are in $1,000s)

	Dec. 31, 2006	Dec. 31, 2005	Dec. 31, 2004
Assets			
Current Assets			
Cash and Equivalents	$59.2	115.5	10.1
Accounts Receivable	434.8	184.4	178.2
Inventory	451.3	390.7	274.5
Other Current Assets	29.3	30.9	24.3
Total Current Assets	974.6	721.5	487.1
Long-Term Assets			
Property, Plant & Equipment (net)	1,685.3	1,685.2	1,227.1
Total Assets	2,659.9	2,406.7	1,714.1
Liabilities			
Current Liabilities			
Accounts Payable	598.4	375.4	321.5
Short-Term Notes Payable	12.5	133.2	138.9
Interest Payable	48.3	16.2	8.3
Other Current Liabilities	97.6	66.0	38.8
Total Current Liabilities	756.8	590.8	507.5
Long-Term Notes Payable	2,024.0	1,698.0	1,010.7
Total Liabilities	2,780.8	2,288.8	1,518.2
Owners Equity			
Capital	132.0	132.0	132.0
Retained Earnings	–252.9	–14.1	63.9
Total Owners' Equity	–120.9	117.9	195.9
Total Liabilities & Owners' Equity	**2,659.9**	**2,406.7**	**1,714.1**

History

Founded in 1961 in Reedsburg, located 65 miles northwest of Madison, Wisconsin, Cellox manufactures three types of polystyrene[1] products, which comprise three divisions of the business as follows:

1. Protective packing material (PPM) used to ship products
2. Point-of-purchase (PoP) products
3. Insulated concrete forms (ICFs)

David Pace, a 62-year-old successful entrepreneur, took pride in identifying companies that were candidates for a turnaround—companies that could be purchased at a favorable price and made profitable. He had built Pace Industries, the largest manufacturer of extruded plastic sheeting, into a multimillion-dollar company known worldwide for its high-quality products, customer service, and innovative human resource programs. Leaving Pace Industries gave David the opportunity to apply his leadership and business skills in new venues. He was especially satisfied when he found Cellox for sale—a floundering company that needed to improve production, improve operations, improve employee compensation and benefits, increase corporate morale, reestablish the customer base, and regain the stakeholders' confidence.

David's professional management expertise was developed in plastic injection molding[2] and plastic sheet extrusion.[3] He had worked in various plastic mediums ranging from polystyrene to resins. Although Cellox appeared to be in operational disarray, David saw past this to the significant possibilities it had for the marketplace—building homes that could withstand hurricane and tornado-force winds.

Cellox possessed a committed and hard-working staff dedicated to seeing the company succeed. It also had products that, with the right production and marketing strategy, could increase profit margins, dominate market share, and drive industry standards. David believed his experience would be just what the company needed and envisioned a successful turnaround within two years. In December 2003, David purchased Cellox.

Divisions

Exhibit 3. shows the relative size of the various divisions of Cellox.

EXHIBIT 3   Cellox Percent of Revenues by Division from 2004–2006

Division	FY 2006	FY 2005	FY 2004
Point-of-Purchase (PoP)	0.308	0.339	0.373
Protective Packing Material (PPM)	0.360	0.361	0.406
Insulated Concrete Forms (ICFs)	0.230	0.283	0.216
Total =	**0.898**	**0.983**	**0.995**

Protective Packing Material (PPM)

Protective packing material used in shipping fragile electronic components is comprised of standard polystyrene forms such as the three-sided corner pieces that surround a product in its carton, along with other rectangular forms of various thicknesses used in packing for protected shipping. Hundreds of companies with the same manufacturing capability produce PPM. Margins are extremely low and any pricing advantage is usually found through ancillary charges related to shipping and handling. Customer service, especially rapid-order turnaround and on-time or early delivery, is critically important in securing consistent customer orders. Cellox's primary customer base is located within a 300-mile radius of Reedsburg, which includes such metropolitan areas as Green Bay, Duluth, Minneapolis, St. Paul, Chicago, and Milwaukee.

The packing material production division is the least critical component of Cellox. However, it uses the idle capacity of equipment and employees to consistently help defray overhead costs. With this philosophy, pricing can cover only marginal costs with a suitable profit margin versus trying to cover full costs plus generate a normally adequate profit margin. Cellox's ability to quote a potentially lower price also helps generate additional sales volume. At the same time, management carefully monitors this division and the price of petroleum so that they do not underquote, thereby losing money—a big challenge with fluctuating petroleum costs, which significantly impact manufacturing costs in this industry.

Point-of-Purchase (PoP)

The point-of-purchase (PoP) division consists of special-order and standard in-stock three-dimensional polystyrene forms, in which Cellox has distinguished its products through custom finishing. These items are typically used in promotion and advertising. Examples include a three-foot Jolly Green Giant figure; various-sized Pillsbury Dough Boys; basketballs, baseballs, and golf balls with various logos and designs; custom-decorated surfboards; coolers and bait buckets; and simulated fireplaces and trees used as backdrops in photo shoots. Cellox usually makes the product and the customer retains rights to the mold. Sometimes Cellox is asked to design and develop a mold for production or use a standard mold they already own. Depending on its size and complexity, a mold costs between $25,000 to over $40,000 to create. Cellox makes minor modifications to existing tools, if required, or contracts with a tool-and-die company to manufacture molds.

The total cost of the mold, or a portion of it if Cellox retains partial ownership, is incorporated into the customer's order. Consequently, customers are encouraged to request a significant volume of product to justify the up-front mold development cost.

For its 20 years of existence, the PoP division has been the primary revenue-producer for Cellox. The company is especially proud of the custom-finishing work they do, as many pieces are hand-painted and must meet a high standard of quality. The company is innovative in its creative development of coatings, providing a finished product look that appears to be "real" until its light weight gives its actual composition away. These three-dimensional figures are popular and attract customers when used effectively in marketing displays at retail outlets. They are light and easy to handle and ship. Their one drawback— they are not especially durable. Polystyrene cracks, chips, and breaks easily if mishandled, driving a segment of the customer market to the more traditional and less costly form of two-dimensional advertising.

In 2001, the PoP division began suffering a decrease in units sold. A decline in customer service, along with rising raw material prices, caused several large customers to seek other suppliers or stop using polystyrene forms in their promotion and advertising. Cellox staff became discouraged and idle production capacity increased; it became harder for the company to cover its fixed costs. When David Pace purchased the company in December 2003, the company was on the brink of collapse. By late 2004, David Pace added sales staff to the PoP division to regain previous customers and look for new customers. By mid-2005, PoP slowly started growing sales again with brighter prospects for the future.

Insulated Concrete Forms

The third Cellox division represents a relatively new product to the construction industry. The costs of wood, steel, and other traditional construction materials have all increased in recent years. This has refocused consumer attention on the insulated concrete form (ICF), and its popularity has been increasing. David Pace believes ICF has incredible potential for long-term market success. He patented the Cellox ICF product and named it CELBLOX.

It is an energy-efficient building material used in constructing exterior walls for residential and commercial buildings. A CELBLOX ICF is a form comprised of two identical panels of foam insulation called expanded polystyrene (EPS). Embedded in each foam panel are plastic studs[4] called webs. The foam panels are linked with plastic ties[5] that connect to the panels' webs. The CELBLOX products are preformed interlocking blocks that a builder sets in place like building blocks. The contractor then pours a slurry[6] of concrete into the ICF blocks. ICF walls can be built by anyone with carpentry and concrete experience and specific training, which is provided through a Cellox factory seminar.

As the concrete sets, the ICFs actually stay in place, and the result is a durable, long-lasting wall with significant structural integrity and additional insulation and sound barrier benefits. Any of the typical exterior building materials (e.g., brick, stone, stucco, vinyl, etc.) can be attached outside, and drywall can be attached inside.

ICF Construction Costs

The cost of ICF walls is the same or slightly higher than that of typical frame construction. ICF homes increase construction costs 1 percent to 4 percent over traditional wood frame houses of the same design. A typical new U.S. home costs between $60 to $100 per square foot. Building the walls of ICFs adds $1 to $4 to this square-foot figure. Since ICF houses are more energy-efficient, however, the heating and cooling equipment installed can be far smaller than in a traditional wood-frame house. This can cut the cost of the final house by an estimated $0.75 per square foot. Consequently, the net extra cost is more realistically about $0.25 to $3.25 per square foot.

There are over 40 ICF manufacturers nationwide and just as many or more methods of manufacturing ICFs. CELBLOX can withstand winds of 180 miles per hour, making this form of construction especially desirable in hurricane-prone regions of the United States such as in the south and southeast. Currently, Cellox can produce 800 CELBLOX per day using two 8-hour shifts, 5 days a week. Given that it takes around 1,000 blocks to make a relatively small three-bedroom home, their potential capacity, if working 24 hours per day, 7 days per week, is about 350 homes per year. With the right marketing, demand for the product could increase significantly. Even if there are over 40 manufacturers of ICFs, the CELBLOX product has enough distinguishing features and benefits that it could capture an ever-growing share of an emerging ICF market.

According to ICF industry reports, only about 4 percent of the construction market currently uses these materials. Consequently, within the residential construction industry, there is significant room for growth, especially in light of ICFs' energy efficiency, their ability to withstand extreme weather, and their resistance to wood-destroying insects. David Pace sees the future as long-term and large when he states, "A hundredfold increase in the next 10 years is possible, and we can do it!"

Contractors, however, generally resist ICFs because they prefer to work with materials they are familiar with, and they avoid new materials they do not know about or for which they have no technical support. Shipping costs can also add significantly to the overall cost. The shipping cost alone dictates that ICF producers have to consider a regional distribution system to remain competitive with wood and metal construction to and gain a competitive advantage over other ICF manufacturers not locally based. Consequently, Cellox is forced to concentrate on its primary geographic market located within a 300-mile radius unless it manufactures and distributes the product through other regional distribution networks.

David Pace is aggressively tackling all of these issues through product quality, a decentralized product distribution system, and construction crew franchising to install ICFs, and he is targeting storm-ravaged areas for marketing the improved method for rebuilding. David sees the greatest need for CELBLOX in places such as Florida and the Gulf Coast of the United States, which have suffered catastrophic damage from hurricanes in recent years. These areas also have significant problems with insects, mold, mildew, and high energy costs for air conditioning. As David attracts support from the insurance and mortgage industries, CELBLOX has all the ingredients for success by being in the right place at the right time with the right product.

Finding CELBLOX Customers

After purchasing Cellox, David initiated an aggressive campaign to encourage former PoP customers to work with Cellox again. However, finding construction industry contractors and educating people who intend to build their homes has been far more challenging than anticipated.

Construction workers prefer to work with materials with which they are familiar, even if they cost more, use more labor, and are less energy efficient. Homeowners who are not that familiar with construction techniques generally assume that 2×4 framing ("stick-built"[7]) is the only way to build the exterior walls of a home. And contractors are used to working primarily with wood or steel 2×4s, because construction mistakes are relatively easy and inexpensive to correct. With concrete, however, once it has hardened, it is difficult to change. (See http://www.icfhomes.com, http://www.toolbase.org/Technology-Inventory/walls/Insulating-Concrete-Forms, and http://www.forms.org.)

There is no easy way to communicate directly with people "thinking" about building a home. Those who happen to discover and desire the ICF technology are often actually discouraged by local contractors who are unfamiliar with and untrained in using the ICF construction technique. They then direct the homeowner to the more traditional construction methods. The vast majority of the population is not even familiar with this construction process, so for David, it is almost like starting at "square one."

Increasing Production to Meet Future Sales

David Pace has prepared Cellox to meet the anticipated CELBLOX production demand. He has installed molding machines capable of producing different quantities of the CELBLOX product. For example, it takes about 150 to 180 seconds for one operator to insert the vinyl plastic studs and a total of around 240 seconds to complete the molding process for six ICF blocks, which equals 90 panels (or 45 blocks an hour).

New molding machines can produce 8 panels—a 33 percent increase in panels per cycle—every 120–135 seconds, and they take only 20–90 seconds to load. This new machinery almost doubles the parts-per-hour production. Consequently, capacity can stay ahead of demand as each new machine can produce 120 blocks per hour, or enough for one house approximately every 8 hours.

Marketing is critical to sell CELBLOX. To date, market research at Cellox tends to be any information the sales force happens to glean from the field. Product literature consists of brochures and one-sheet user guides that have been developed over the last several years. Cellox has a Web site and attends an occasional convention or show for contractors and/or homeowners. CELBLOX sales to contractors are considered a key success factor and the future lifeblood of Cellox.

Customer service is also critical for sales. Employees consistently tout the new outstanding customer service, which is displayed in various ways: a quick return call on a telephone query; being nice to people visiting the home office; assisting a contractor through a difficult construction site dilemma; and so forth. ICF users sometimes need more communication and someone to "walk them through" a technical construction challenge. A botched job on the construction site can mean a tarnished image for both the contractor and CELBLOX, regardless of who was at fault. Providing technical expertise is critical.

David passionately wants to make CELBLOX available to churches "at cost," enabling them to build stronger and higher-quality buildings. Not only will they be able to reap the benefits of lower energy operating costs, but he believes this will make them better stewards of their resources in the process.

Human Resources

Along with his many company leadership responsibilities, David is actively involved with marketing and sales. He is a firm believer in the numerous superior qualities and benefits of CELBLOX. While he has many ideas on how to get the product to the customers, he does not have the time to do the job alone.

When David bought the company, he reduced the employee population from 40 to 14 (a large portion of the cuts were salaried employees) and reduced wages across the board for those who remained due to a critical cash flow shortage.

Some Cellox managers believe PoP does not have high growth potential, but does have a good profit margin. CELBLOX, on the other hand, has high growth potential, but competition keeps the margin far lower than for PoP. In late 2005, David hired an MBA

EXHIBIT 4   Organization Chart for Cellox

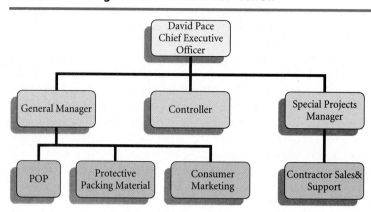

graduate with a specialization in marketing to help develop the marketing and sales initiatives. Uncomfortable with cold calling potential customers, that individual submitted his resignation nine months later. David is looking for qualified candidates to fill some critical positions in the company.

Summary

As David enters his fourth year leading Cellox, he knows the company's survival and financial success is dependent on CELBLOX. Despite David's positive attitude and entrepreneurial success, however, Cellox cannot continue operating at a loss. Creditors may soon come calling if profitability is not restored soon. Cellox needs to develop a clear strategic plan for the future.

Endnotes

1. **Styrene**, a petroleum by-product, is the primary raw material from which polystyrene is made. A naturally occurring substance, styrene is present in many foods and beverages, including wheat, beef, strawberries, peanuts, and coffee beans. Polystyrene foam products are 95% air and only 5% polystyrene. The most recognizable forms of polystyrene packaging are expanded and extruded foams (sometimes incorrectly called Styrofoam®, a Dow Chemical Co. trademarked form of polystyrene foam insulation). Foamed polystyrene is used to make cups, bowls, plates, trays, clamshell containers, meat trays, and egg cartons, as well as protective packaging for shipping electronics and other fragile items.

2. **Injection molding** involves taking plastic in the form of pellets or granules and heating it until a melt is obtained. The melt is then forced into a split-die chamber/mold where it is allowed to cool into the desired shape. The mold is opened and the part is ejected, at which time the cycle is repeated.

3. **Plastic sheet extrusion** is the process of converting plastic pellets or powder into cut sheets or rolls of plastic. This sheet can be further processed into parts via thermoforming. The sheet extrusion process can yield sheet products with thicknesses ranging from less than 0.010 in. (film) up to and exceeding 2.0 inch, with widths as great as 30 ft.

4. These are equivalent to furring strips, which are used to form a level surface to which a surface product (drywall, brick, stucco, etc.) can be attached.

5. Two plastic hinged pieces that "lock" in place when opened to form a specific width between the panels.

6. A **slurry** is a suspension formed when a quantity of powder is mixed into a liquid in which the solid is only slightly soluble (or not soluble). Slurries usually contain large amounts of solid and are more viscous and generally of higher density than the liquid from which they are formed. Concrete (specifically, Portland cement concrete) is created using a concrete mix of Portland cement, gravel, and sand. The material is

applied or poured as a freshly mixed slurry and worked mechanically to compact the interior and force some of the thinner cement slurry to the surface to produce a smoother, denser surface free from honeycombing.

7. A home that is "**stick-built**" is constructed on the building site, piece by piece. Manufactured and modular homes are not classified as stick-built because they are made mostly in the factory and transported to the site. A custom home and a home made according to stock building plans may both be stick-built, provided that they are constructed on the land where they will remain.

16 E*Trade Financial, Inc. — 2007

Amit J. Shah
Frostburg State University

ETFC

www.etrade.com

If someone asks you if you are "online," your answer probably is "of course." According to a recent *Newsweek* article, "Hi-Tech's New Day," "75 percent of Americans use the Internet and spend an average of three hours a day online." Today almost everything is or can be done on a personal computer. From banking to investing, E*Trade is capitalizing on the computer and Internet revolution. However, for the second quarter of 2007, E*Trade's net income declined 6 percent to $159.1 million.

E*Trade Financial Inc. is an online brokerage firm that allows you to trade equities, keep your portfolio updated, and obtain market information around the clock. E*Trade receives a commission from each trade and receives interest on the short positions of its clients. Its more than 4.5 million account holders can trade stocks in person, by phone, or by using the Internet. E*Trade launched its global trading platform in six international markets: Canada, Hong Kong, U.K., France, Germany, and Japan. The company is positioning itself to be much more than simply a brokerage firm. Slowly but surely, E*Trade is becoming a complete financial support and execution portal for individuals, offering everything you need to do in your financial life.

History

Founded as a service bureau in 1982 by Bill Porter, a physicist and inventor, the early E*Trade provided online quote and trading services to Fidelity, Charles Schwab, and Quick & Reilly. Seeing the opportunity to capitalize on a potentially huge discount brokerage, Bill came up with an idea that would allow individuals to use their personal computers to invest, paying far less than the traditional brokerage fees. It would take several years for the world to catch up with Bill's vision. In 1992, E*Trade Securities, Inc. was born and began to offer online investing services through America Online and CompuServe. With the launch of www.etrade.com in 1996, the demand for E*Trade's services exploded.

E*Trade went public in August 1996 and completed another stock offering one year later when Bill handed the reins over to Christos Cotsakos, who came to E*Trade with over 20 years of senior management experience at Federal Express and A.C. Nielsen. Under Christos' leadership, E*Trade became a global leader in online personal financial services with branded Web sites around the world. The company introduced E*Trade Bank in 2000 with the purchase of Telebanc Financial (now E*Trade Financial), an online bank with more than 100,000 depositors. E*Trade also bought Card Capture Services (now E*Trade Access), an operator of more than 9,000 ATMs across the United States. Continuing to expand its global reach, E*Trade acquired Canadian firm Versus Technologies, a provider of electronic trading services, and teamed up with UBS Warburg to allow non-U.S. investors to buy U.S. securities without needing to trade in dollars. Later its E*Trade

International Capital announced plans to offer an initial public offering (IPO) to European investors.

In 2001, E*Trade entered consumer lending when it acquired online mortgage originator LoansDirect (now E*Trade Mortgage). E*Trade sold substantially all of its assets and liabilities of E*Trade Access in 2004. In an attempt to further its dominance in the financial industry in 2005, E*Trade acquired Harris Direct, formerly a discount brokerage service of Bank of Montreal, and BrownCo, formerly a discount brokerage service of J.P. Morgan.

Headquartered in New York City, E*Trade had 4,705 employees at year-end 2006. In late 2006, Retirement Advisors of America, Inc. (RAA), a Dallas, Texas–based investment advisory company, was acquired. RAA manages more than $1 billion in assets, which "is expected to provide a predictable and recurring revenue stream with a scalable business platform that can manage additional client assets with minimal incremental expense," E*Trade said. In 2006, E*Trade's revenue rose to $2.4 billion and net income rose to $629 million.

External Factors

Despite the best effort of companies in the electronic investment services industry to reduce cyclicality, their business is still closely tied to the economy, corporate earnings, technology, and the stock market. The U.S. economy was on the verge of slipping into a recession in 2007 according to a prediction from the former U.S. Federal Reserve chairman, Alan Greenspan. On February 27, 2007, the U.S. stock market suffered the worst one-day point loss since 2001 when China fueled concerns about global economic growth. Along with the global events, the U.S. budget deficit remains a concern as well, despite the fact it fell to the lowest level in four years. The value of the dollar has fallen to historic lows.

Although U.S. real gross domestic product (GDP) grew 3.2 percent in 2005, the recovery has remained tentative. The Federal Reserve has left the federal funds rate unchanged since June 29, 2006, however, inflation risks are still lingering. Amid the threat of another global slowdown, geopolitical fears, and numerous corporate scandals, stock markets have remained turbulent. Year-to-date through November 2006, the S&P 500 Composite Stock Index rose 0.87 percent, while the NASDAQ Composite rose 0.88 percent. Overseas markets have been slightly better.

A flood of corporate accounting and other scandals have weighed on stock prices and led to a crisis of confidence among investors. Industry regulators are working to promote increased integrity and transparency among corporations and investment business, but it may take some time to restore investors' confidence. Until then, conditions in the brokerage industry will remain challenging. Although Standard & Poor's expected the aggregate pretax profits of corporate America to improve in 2007, the increases would be driven largely by lower operating costs. Net revenue growth was expected on average to be weak. Investment industry is regulated by the U.S. federal and state regulatory agencies and securities exchanges and by several non-U.S. governmental agencies and regulatory bodies. E*Trade faces both banking and securities extensive rules and regulations.

The brokerage industry revenue rose 39 percent in 2006, year to year, to $287.6 billion. In 2007, revenue was expected to rise 13 percent to $325 billion, which indicates the earnings momentum of the industry has slowed. This stunt in earnings can be attributed to the subprime mortgage market crisis that affected the industry throughout the year.

Since 2001, online brokers have slashed costs in order to increase productivity and shore up profitability. That year, E*Trade incurred more than $227 million in charges to restructure its operations. The company consolidated several centers, reduced headcount, and exited several foreign markets. At the same time, E*Trade expanded into new businesses, such as market-making and mortgage lending, that would complement its core businesses.

The electronic investment industry relies heavily on technology, specifically, computers and Internet. It is vulnerable to disruptions from natural disasters, spam and virus attacks, and security breaches by hackers. Investment companies as well as their customers both face these technological risks.

Competitors

The market for electronic financial services over the Internet and other alternative channels continues to quickly grow and is extremely competitive. As E*Trade continues to diversify and expand its services beyond online domestic retail brokerage offerings to include banking, global cross-border trading, mutual fund offerings, market-making, consumer lending, institutional investing, financial advice, and insurance, the number of competitors in these varied marketplaces is also increasing. E*Trade faces direct competition from full-commission brokerage firms, discount brokerage firms, online brokerage firms, pure-play Internet banks, traditional "brick and mortar" commercial banks, and savings banks. These competitors provide touch-tone telephone, voice response, online banking services, electronic bill payment services, and a host of other financial products. In addition, E*Trade competes with mutual fund companies, which provide money market funds and cash management accounts.

Some mutual fund firms, such as Putnam, have been accused recently of ethical wrongdoings. In 2005, the Securities and Exchange Committee charged Putnam a $40 million penalty related to their "shelf space" arrangements with broker-dealers. Putnam failed to adequately disclose conflicts of interest from arrangements for increased visibility within the broker-dealers' distribution systems to the board of trustees and their shareholders. Recently, there has been a far-reaching probe into the mutual fund industry about widespread wrongdoing and market manipulation.

Firms in the mutual fund industry have been accused of using two illegal practices: (1) late-day trading and (2) market timing. In late-day trading, a firm illegally buys shares after the market closes in order to take advantage of early evening news that will pump up the stock price by morning, allowing it to sell the next day at a profit. In market timing, firms quickly trade large blocks of shares, hoping to reap big profits by small fluctuations in share price. While the practice is not illegal, mutual funds were allowing powerful investors to make the risky trades at the expense of small-time, long-term investors, who are barred from the practice. As a result of these wrongdoings, more and more customers are moving away from mutual fund firms, such as Putnam, and turning toward investing companies such as E*Trade.

E*Trade's main competitors are Fidelity Investments, Charles Schwab (SCHW), TD Ameritrade (AMTD), and Financial Institutions (FISI). Fidelity Investments is a group of privately held companies that is currently the largest broker in the industry with almost $13 billion in revenue. Schwab is the second largest broker in the industry with revenues totaling almost $4.7 billion at year-end 2006. E*Trade ranked third with $2.4 billion in revenues. TD Ameritrade has about $1.8 billion in revenues, and finally, the Warsaw, New York–based firm, Financial Institutions, has approximately $88 million in revenues. Exhibit 1 presents selected financial information on E*Trade's key competitors.

Based in Omaha, Nebraska, TD Ameritrade provides online brokerage services, an Internet-based personal financial management service, touch-tone telephone and market data, and research tools. Ameritrade's services are very similar to those of E*Trade. The company was founded in 1971. It was formerly known as Ameritrade Holding Corporation and changed its name to TD Ameritrade Holding Corporation in January 2006. In 2006, TD Ameritrade reported revenues of $1.8 billion, which was up from $977 million from the previous year.

EXHIBIT 1 **Competitors' Selected Financial Information**
Year Ended December 31, 2006
(in millions, except per share data)

	Charles Schwab	Ameritrade
Statements of Operations Data:		
Operating revenues	$4,309	$1,804
Operating expenses:		
Compensation and benefits	1,619	350
Professional services	285	88
Occupancy and equipment	260	75
Advertising and market development	189	164
Communications	180	65
Depreciation and amortization	157	21
Other operating expenses	143	45
Total operating expenses	2,833	1,028
Income before income taxes	1,476	776
Income tax expense	585	331
Net income	1,227	527
Earnings per common share:		
Basic	0.97	0.97
Diluted	0.95	0.95
Balance Sheet Data:		
Cash and cash equivalents	$4,507	$364
Total Property, Plant and Equipment	602	57
Total Assets	48,992	16,558
Total Liabilities	43,984	14,828
Total stockholders' equity	5,008	1,730

Source: Company 10-K Reports

Internal Factors

E*Trade's Vision Statement
E*Trade's vision is "to empower self-directed investors to make informed investment decisions and take control of their financial future with anytime, anywhere access to the world's major investment markets."

E*Trade's Mission Statement

> To create long-term shareholder value through superior financial performance driven by the delivery of a diversified range of innovative, customer-focused financial products and services and supported by an operating culture based on the highest levels of teamwork, efficiency and integrity.

Organizational Structure
In attempts to cut costs and streamline the organization as a whole, E*Trade has reduced the amount of people needed to maintain the firm. Currently it employs about 4,100 employees. Exhibit 2 shows E*Trade's organization chart. Note that the firm does not have

EXHIBIT 2   E*Trade's Organizational Chart

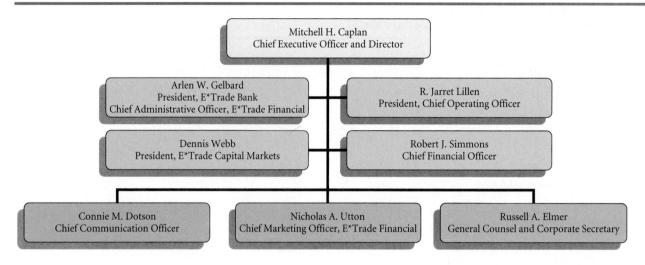

Source: Adapted based on 2007 Officer Team.

a chief operating officer. There are basically two divisions: E*Trade Banking and E*Trade Capital Markets. However, the most significant subsidiaries of the company include E*Trade Bank, E*Trade Capital Markets, E*Trade Clearing, and E*Trade Securities. E*Trade offers, either alone or with its partners, branded retail Web sites in the United States, Canada, Denmark, Finland, France, Germany, Hong Kong, Iceland, Italy, Sweden, the UAE, and the United Kingdom. E*Trade has also licensed its name to companies that operate in Australia, Japan, and Korea.

E*Trade's primary retail products and services consist of (1) investing and trading, (2) banking, and (3) lending. E*Trade's total net revenue increased 42 percent in 2006 to $2.4 billion. Its retail and institutional commission revenue increased 36 percent to $625.3 million in 2006 compared to 2005. The retail segment revenues increased 52 percent to $695.2 million and the institutional segment income increased 60 percent to $305.5 million in 2006 compared to 2005. E*Trade reported a net income of $629 million in fiscal 2006. Exhibit 3 and Exhibit 4 present E*Trade's consolidated financial statements. Exhibits 5 and 6 present E*Trade's retail and institutional segment information.

EXHIBIT 3   E*Trade Financial, Inc. and Subsidiaries Consolidated Statement of Income (in thousands, except per share amounts)

Revenue:	Year Ended December 31, 2006	Year Ended December 31, 2005	Year Ended December 31, 2004
Operating interest income	$ 2,774,679	$ 1,650,264	$ 1,145,597
Operating interest expense	(1,374,647)	(779,164)	(510,455)
Net operating interest income	1,400,032	871,000	635,142
Provision for loan losses	(44,970)	(54,016)	(38,121)
Net operating interest after provision for loan losses	1,355,062	817,084	597,021
Commission	625,265	458,834	431,638
Service charges and fees	137,441	135,314	97,575
Principal transactions	110,235	99,336	126,893
Gain on sales of loans and securities, net	55,986	98,588	140,718
Other revenue	136,332	94,419	89,077

continued

EXHIBIT 3 E*Trade Financial, Inc. and Subsidiaries Consolidated Statement of Income
(in thousands, except per share amounts)—Continued

Revenue:	Year Ended December 31, 2006	Year Ended December 31, 2005	Year Ended December 31, 2004
Total non-interest income	$1,065,259	886,761	885,901
Total net revenue	2,420,321	1,703,845	1,482,922
Expense excluding interest:			
Compensation and benefits	469,202	380,803	350,440
Clearing and servicing	253,040	189,736	162,354
Advertising and market development	119,782	105,935	62,155
Communication	110,346	82,485	69,674
Professional services	96,947	77,416	69,014
Depreciation and amortization	73,845	74,981	77,892
Occupancy and equipment	85,568	69,089	69,572
Amortization of other intangibles	46,220	43,765	19,443
Facility restructuring and other exit activities	28,537	(30,017)	15,688
Other	136,042	59,860	90,891
Total expense excluding interest	1,419,529	1,054,053	987,123
Income before other income (expense), income taxes, minority interest, discontinued operations, and cumulative effect of accounting change	1,000,792	649,792	495,799
Other income (expense):			
Corporate interest revenue	8,433	11,043	6,692
Corporate interest expense	(152,496)	(73,965)	(47,525)
Gain on sales and impairment of investments	70,796	83,144	128,111
Loss on early extinguishment of debt	(1,179)	—	(22,972)
Equity in income of investments and venture funds	2,451	6,103	4,382
Total other income (expense)	(71,995)	26,334	68,688
Income before other income (expense), income taxes, minority interest, discontinued operations and cumulative effect of accounting change	928,797	676,126	564,487
Income tax expense	301,983	229,823	181,764
Minority interest in subsidiaries	—	65	893
Net income from continuing operations	626,814	446,238	381,830
Discontinued operations, net of tax:			
Loss from discontinued operations	(721)	(21,495)	(32,755)
Gain on disposal of discontinued operations	2,766	4,023	31,408
Gain (loss) from discontinued operations, net of tax	2,045	(17,472)	(1,347)
Cumulative effect of accounting change, net of tax	—	1,646	—
Net income	**$ 628,859**	**$ 430,412**	**$ 380,483**
Basic earnings per share from continuing operations	$ 1.49	$ 1.20	$ 1.04

Source: E*Trade Group Inc., *Form 10K* (2006).

EXHIBIT 4   E*Trade Financial, Inc. and Subsidiaries Consolidated Balance Sheet (in thousands, except share amounts)

ASSETS	2006	2005
Cash and Equivalents	$ 1,212,234	$ 844,188
Cash and investments required to be segregated under federal or other regulations	281,622	610,174
Trading securities	178,600	146,657
Available-for-sales, mortgage-backed, and investment securities (includes securities pledged to creditors with the right to sell or repledge of $11,087,961 and $11,792,684 at December 31, 2006 and 2005, respectively)	13,921,983	12,763,438
Loans held-for-sale	283,496	87,371
Brokerage receivables, net	7,636,352	7,174,175
Loans receivable, net (net of allowance for loan losses $67,628 and $63,286 at December 31, 2006 and 2005, respectively	26,372,697	19,424,895
Property and equipment, net	318,389	299,256
Goodwill	2,072,920	2,003,456
Other intangibles, net	471,933	532,108
Other assets	989,077	681,968
Total Assets	**$ 53,739,303**	**$ 44,567,686**

LIABILITIES AND STOCKHOLDERS' EQUITY		
Liabilities:		
Deposits	$ 24,071,012	$ 15,948,015
Securities sold under agreements to repurchase	9,792,422	11,101,542
Brokerage payables	7,824,704	7,342,208
Other borrowings	5,323,962	4,206,996
Senior notes	1,401,592	1,401,947
Mandatory convertible notes	440,557	435,589
Convertible subordinated notes	—	185,165
Accounts payable, accrued, and other liabilities	688,664	546,664
Total Liabilities	49,542,933	41,168,126
Stockholders' Equity:		
Common stock, $0.01 per value, shares authorized: 600,000,000; shares issued and out-standing: 426,304,136 and 416,582,164 at December 31, 2006 and 2005, respectively	4,263	4,166
Additional paid-in capital ("APIC")	3,184,290	2,990,676
Retained earnings	1,209,289	580,430
Accumulated other comprehensive loss	(201,472)	(175,712)
Total shareholders' equity	**4,196,370**	**3,399,560**
Total liabilities and stockholders' equity	**$ 53,739,303**	**$ 44,567,686**

Source: E*Trade Group Inc., *Form 10K* (2006).

E*Trade is trying to regain investor confidence after the former CEO, Christos Cotsakos, received a 2001 pay package valued at $80 million even as the company's share price plummeted. Although Mr. Cotsakos repaid $20 million, the company was still in desperate need of new leadership. Mitchell Caplan replaced Mr. Cotsakos in January 2003 and has been restructuring the organization further and cutting more unnecessary expenditures, like the $14,000 a month concierge service for 200 or so employees in Rancho Cordova, California.

EXHIBIT 5   Retail Segment Income

	Year Ended December 31			Variance 2006 vs. 2005	
	2006	2005	2004	Amount	%
Retail segment income:					
Net operating interest income after provision for loan losses	$ 883,563	$ 445,124	$322,278	$438,439	98%
Commission	479,876	339,654	328,889	140,222	41%
Service charges and fees	115,672	116,102	84,445	(430)	(0)%
Gain on sales of loans and securities, net	36,698	63,705	93,694	(27,007)	(42)%
Other revenue	138,316	112,836	106,457	25,480	23%
Net segment revenue	1,654,125	1,077,421	935,763	576,704	54%
Total segment expense	958,882	618,664	628,146	340,218	55%
Total retail segment income	$ 695,243	$ 458,757	$307,617	$236,486	52%

EXHIBIT 6   Institutional Segment Income

	Year Ended December 31			Variance 2006 vs. 2005	
	2006	2005	2004	Amount	%
Institutional segment income:					
Net operating interest income after provision for loan losses	471,499	372,122	274,743	99,377	27%
Commission	145,389	119,180	102,749	26,209	22%
Service charges and fees	21,769	19,212	13,130	2,557	13%
Principal transactions	110,235	99,175	126,893	11,060	11%
Gain on sales of loans and securities, net	19,288	35,153	47,024	(15,865)	(45)%
Other revenue	9,269	10,383	16,684	(1,114)	(11)%
Net segment revenue	777,449	655,225	581,223	122,224	19%
Total segment expense	471,900	464,190	393,041	7,710	2%
Total institutional segment income	$305,549	$191,035	$188,182	$114,514	60%

Marketing

E*Trade increased its advertising and marketing development expenditures by 13 percent in 2006 to $119.8 million as compared to 2005. E*Trade discontinued advertising in the Super Bowl in 2001. E*Trade uses co-branding to market its services at a discounted price. For example, E*Trade and Hilton HHonors Worldwide have a marketing relationship that provides Hilton HHonors members with HHonors bonus points when they open an account with E*Trade. The agreement offers HHonors members the opportunity to earn 5,000 HHonors points when they open a new E*Trade account, and enables E*Trade to reach a large and highly attractive group of consumers with an expressed allegiance to one of the world's leading frequent-traveler programs.

Conclusion

Opportunities are endless for E*Trade. To sustain and grow its competitive advantage, what strategies should E*Trade pursue? Under the leadership of CEO Mitchell Caplan, E*Trade may want to expand its global trading platform to give customers access to over 42 international exchanges and related currencies. It could also offer customers certificates of deposit in foreign currencies to give investors new opportunities to diversify their portfolios. E*Trade could try to acquire TD Ameritrade or another online brokerage firm to gain economies of scale and market share.

17 Amazon.com — 2007

M. Jill Austin
Middle Tennessee State University

AMZN

http://www.amazon.com

Based in Seattle, Washington, Amazon.com sells approximately five million different book titles, but the company also sells hundreds of other products ranging from musical instruments and electronics to pet supplies. The company's forty-one product categories are shown in Exhibit 1. For the third quarter of 2007, Amazon's net income increased 2.5 percent to $80 million, while revenues increased 13 percent to $3.2 billion.

In addition to selling products, Amazon.com offers services to Web developers, independent film and music producers, and also offers third-party seller transactions on its Web site to customers such as Target, Office Depot, and to small businesses. Amazon also contracts with other businesses to offer distribution and warehouse storage services. The mission of Amazon.com is:

> to be the Earth's most customer-centric company, where customers can find and discover anything they might want to buy online, and endeavors to offer customers the lowest possible prices.

The company's third-party seller businesses account for 28 percent of units sold. International business is approximately 45 percent of sales, while nonmedia represent 34 percent of sales. Exhibit 2 provides information for sales by geographic division and by product type.

EXHIBIT 1 Amazon.com Product Categories

Books, Music & Movies	Consumer Electronics	Food & Household	Clothing & Jewelry
	Audio & Video	Gourmet Food	Apparel &
Books	Camera & Photo	Grocery	Accessories
DVD	Cell Phones & Service	Pet Supplies	Jewelry & Watches
Music	Musical Instruments	**Home & Garden**	Shoes
Magazines &	All Electronics	Bed & Bath	Health & Beauty
Newspapers	**Computer & Office**	Fresh Flowers and	Beauty
Amazon Shorts	Computers & Add-Ons	Plants	Health & Personal
Textbooks	Office Products	Furniture & Décor	Care
Unbox Video	Software	Home Improvement	Kids & Baby
Downloads	**Tools & Automotive**	Kitchen & Housewares	Apparel (Kids &
VHS	Automotive	Outdoor Living	Baby)
Toys & Video Games	Industrial & Scientific	All Home & Garden	Baby
Toys & Games	Lawn & Garden		Sports & Fitness
Video Games	Equipment		Exercise & Fitness
	Tools & Hardware		Sports & Outdoors

Source: http://www.amazon.com.

EXHIBIT 2   Net Sales by Geographic Area and Product Type

	Year Ended December 31		
	2006	2005	2004
	(in millions)		
Net Sales:			
North America	$ 5,869	$ 4,711	$ 3,847
International	4,842	3,779	3,074
Consolidated	$ 10,711	$ 8,490	$ 6,921
Net Sales:			
North America			
Media	$ 3,582	$ 3,046	$ 2,589
Electronics and other general merchandise	2,024	1,443	1,128
Other (1)	263	222	130
Total North America	$ 5,869	$ 4,711	$ 3,847
International			
Media	$ 3,485	$ 2,885	$ 2,513
Electronics and other general merchandise	1,337	886	559
Other (1)	20	8	2
Total International	$ 4,842	$ 3,779	$ 3,074
Consolidated			
Media	$ 7,067	$ 5,931	$ 5,102
Electronics and other general merchandise	3,361	2,329	1,687
Other (1)	283	230	132
Total consolidated	$ 10,711	$ 8,490	$ 6,921

Source: Amazon.com 2006 *Form 10-K*, pp. 31–32.

Consumer products are sold through the following Web sites: http://www.amazon.com (United States), http://www.amazon.co.uk (United Kingdom), http://www.amazon.de (Germany), http://www.amazon.co.jp (Japan), http://www.amazon.fr (France), http://www.amazon.ca (Canada), and http://joyo.com (China). Products sold on these Web sites are shown in Exhibit 3.

Industry experts list customer trust as critical to Amazon.com's success. The company has a history of providing secure transactions, being reliable and efficient in the fulfillment of orders, and emphasizing price discounts. Amazon managers work continually to improve the shopping experience for customers through development of intuitive and simple Web site navigation. The Amazon.com Web site provides the kind of shopping experience customers relied on years ago when business owners knew their customers because Amazon has the ability to offer unique recommendations to individuals and uses blogs for customers' book reviews that create a community.

Amazon continues to develop new services, new product offerings, and partnerships while continuing to establish existing services. According to founder and CEO Jeff Bezos, the company plans to continue this strategy.

Our established businesses are well-rooted young trees. They are growing, enjoy high returns on capital, and operate in very large market segments. These characteristics set a high bar for any new business we would start. Before we invest our shareholders' money in a new business, we must convince ourselves that the new opportunity can generate the returns on capital our investors expected when they invested in Amazon. And we must convince ourselves that the new business can grow to a scale where it can be significant in the context of our overall company.

EXHIBIT 3   Products Sold in International Environments

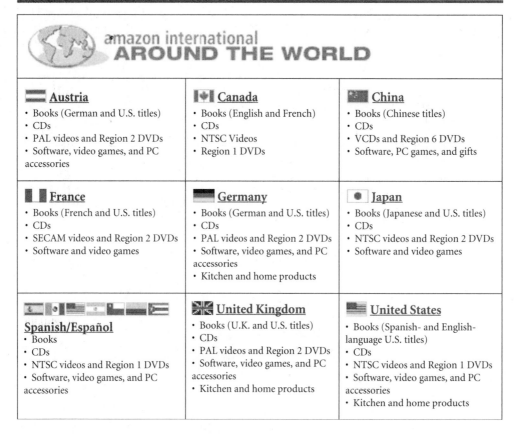

Source: http://www.amazon.com.

History

While Jeff Bezos worked for Shaw & Co. from 1990 to 1994, he was asked to investigate Internet business opportunities for the company. Bezos recommended that Shaw & Co. get into the business of selling books online, but his idea was rejected by company management. Bezos decided to resign from the company and pursue the idea on his own under the company name of Cadabra, Inc. (quickly renamed Amazon). In November 1994, Bezos and two associates set up their business in a converted garage. Amazon.com opened for business on July 16, 1995 and went public in May of 1997 with an initial public offering of three million shares ($18 each). In 1996, the company first exceeded $10 million in book sales. However, Amazon did not make a profit until 2003. The first decade of operations did not always run smoothly and industry critics predicted several times that Amazon would fail, especially during the dot-com industry collapse in the early 1990s.

The Year 2006

Amazon opened its Emergency Preparedness Store (within the Tools & Hardware Store) in June 2006. This store offers checklists for both preparation and recovery from natural disasters such as hurricanes, tornados, floods, and earthquakes and one-stop shopping for tools, first aid supplies, communication devices, and safety equipment. Customers can also find resources from the National Weather Service, National Hurricane Center, Federal Emergency Management Agency, and American Red Cross on the store site. Amazon launched its Grocery Store as a market test in May 2006 and officially launched the business in July 2006. The store offers more than 1,200 brands (Kashi, Nestle, Kellogg, Kraft,

Procter & Gamble) of non-perishable items. About half of the current product selection is natural and organic products such as Wild Oats, Newman's Own, and Nature's Gate.

Amazon's new Toy and Baby Store opened in July 2006. Types of products offered include toys, clothing (children from birth to 2 years), blankets and other baby room supplies, furniture, and educational games. A Baby registry is available for customers to register so friends can purchase the perfect gifts for babies. The products offered at this store are available from companies such as Target, eToys, Discovery Channel Store, and Babystyle. Amazon's grand opening of the Automotive Parts and Accessories Store was held in October 2006. The Automotive Store offers more than a million parts from 250 leading parts and accessories retailers such as Auto Barn, HorsepowerFreaks, and Summit Racing Equipment. Some of the brands offered through the site include Fram, Holley, Lund, Raybestos, and Schumacher. A service called Part Finder allows customers to find the correct parts to fit their vehicles (for approximately 10,000 different American cars or trucks).

Some of the new services recently offered to consumers include video and audio downloading. In September 2006, Amazon launched Amazon Unbox, a video download service. Customers can download movies, videos, and television shows to their personal computers. Technology allows these downloads to be purchased from one computer (such as at the office or public library) and downloaded on another computer (such as a home computer). CustomFlix Labs, Inc. (a wholly owned subsidiary of Amazon.com) introduced CD on demand in September 2006. This service offers music content owners such as independent musicians and labels the opportunity to offer CDs through Amazon with no inventory required. Amazon produces the CDs as they are ordered by Amazon customers. Amazon also offers a similar on-demand service for DVDs. A fee-based membership program called Amazon Prime was introduced in October 2006. This program costs $79.00 per year and allows members to receive express two-day shipping for free and requires no minimum purchase requirement for the express shipping.

Amazon provides several e-commerce services to other businesses. Some of these include Merchants@, Amazon Enterprise Solutions, Web site by Amazon, and Fulfillment by Amazon. The company also has contracts and strategic alliances to provide technology, fulfillment and other services, and to power third-party Web sites, and to enable third parties to offer products or services through the Amazon.com Web site. Amazon Web Services is offered to software developers. Amazon currently has a community of over 240,000 registered developers to provide storage and compute capacity.

Amazon launched two new services for businesses in 2006: Fulfillment by Amazon and Webstores by Amazon. Fulfillment by Amazon allows Amazon customers to receive free shipping when buying from Amazon partners, and the program also provides an opportunity for businesses to use Amazon's order fulfillment service and post-purchase customer service. Businesses pay 50 cents per item plus 40 cents per pound and a storage fee of 45 cents per cubic foot per month for the service that frees businesses from the time and money required for distribution services for products they sell online. Webstores by Amazon allows businesses to create their own e-commerce sites by selecting from a variety of layout options. One example of a company using this service is Seattle Gift Shop. The company created a Webstore at www.seattlegifts.com using layout options offered by Amazon. The company pays Amazon a commission of 7 percent and a monthly fee of $59.95. In addition to providing layouts for Web sites, Amazon covers credit card processing fees and fraud protection for online orders.

Demographic and Social Trends

The Internet has changed the way consumers purchase products and the way consumers receive information about products. The United States has more than half of the world's Internet users. Estimates are that 71 percent of U.S. households had Internet access by the end of 2005. Projections are that the number of U.S. households with Internet access will increase to 79 percent by 2010. Standard and Poor's experts project that Internet retail sales will increase by 29 percent in 2006 and by 19 percent in 2007.

Internet technology allows consumer businesses to target large groups of customers without having to set up brick-and-mortar stores and creates opportunities for traditional retailers to attract potential customers and to keep current customers. The Internet also provides power for customers, who may research product features and pricing and make comparisons among competitors selling similar products. In addition to offering information to consumers, the convenience of shopping on the Internet is an attraction to busy consumers.

The 75 million Americans born between 1946 and 1964 are a significant market for online shopping. Many of these baby boomers have significant levels of disposable income and are brand-loyal customers. While they are not as computer savvy as many of their children and grandchildren, baby boomers lead busy lives and are likely to be drawn to online shopping because of its convenience. Another market segment of interest to online consumer companies is the U.S. teen market (ages 12–19). These consumers are Internet savvy and are likely to embrace Internet purchasing as they become adults. They are already proficient in downloading Internet materials to MP3 players and will embrace technology that allows the purchase of music, DVDs, and television shows. People in their twenties are likely also an important segment for online consumer companies. While this group does not yet have high levels of disposable income, these consumers do embrace technology and expect consumer companies to market to them through the Internet.

Another social trend that may impact online consumer companies is the popularity of social networks. Networks such as MySpace and Facebook are popular among high school students, college students, and young adults. These networks connect people with one another through virtual worlds and offer opportunities for making friends, dating, and establishing business contacts. This group of consumers will likely expect social networks to be part of the Web sites of online consumer companies.

Economic Issues

Consumer confidence and consumer debt impact consumer online purchases. As consumer confidence improves, consumers purchase more online, and when consumers have less confidence in the economy, they purchase fewer consumer items. Gas prices, prices of consumer goods, the continuing wars in Iraq and Afghanistan, and the price of housing are major contributors to levels of consumer confidence in the United States. Credit card debt could negatively impact consumer spending if consumers begin to feel their debt levels are too high. A good economy also contributes to more people purchasing computers and to higher levels of consumer Internet access.

International economies provide unique challenges for Internet consumer companies. Many emerging economies in Asia and eastern Europe are eager to have mass marketers enter operations in their countries, but operating situations are generally uncertain. Countries such as Brazil and Mexico have experienced hyperinflation for several years. The economies in Japan, Latin America, and many European countries have also slowed in recent years. High inflation, the strength of the dollar in international markets, and the fluctuation of foreign currency exchange rates all pose difficulties for companies operating in international markets. There are also possible risks associated with the fluctuation of foreign currencies. A strong U.S. dollar will hurt the value of international currencies while a weak dollar will help the value of international currencies. Both Amazon.com and eBay benefited from a historically weak U.S. dollar in 2006–2007.

The economies of other countries and consumers' ability to purchase Internet products and services are impacted by government regulation and political instability. The value-added tax imposed by the European Union on U.S. providers of certain online products and services (such as software, auctions, and music downloads) could impact sales of U.S.-based online companies. China has also recently increased Internet-related regulation that could impact the ability of U.S. online companies to sell their products in China.

Competition

Direct competitors for Amazon.com include physical-world retailers; online e-commerce Web sites (including sites that sell or distribute digital content); book publishers; and distributors, manufacturers, and producers of products sold by Amazon. Major physical-world retailers include stores such as Best Buy, Wal-Mart, Target, Sears, and Office Depot. The primary competitive factors in the retail market segment are price, availability, selection, convenience, brand recognition, customer service, and ability to adapt to changing conditions.

Amazon also has a number of indirect competitors including companies that provide e-commerce services such as Web site development, third-party fulfillment companies, and customer-service companies that provide infrastructure Web services. Other indirect competitors are media companies, comparison shopping Web sites, and Web search engines. Some example e-commerce competitors include eBay.com, toysrus.com, and target.com. Download service competitors include Apple Computer, Google.com, and other DVD rental services such as Netflix and Blockbuster that provide video downloading.

The major competitors in the book sales market that was revolutionized by Amazon.com include Barnes & Noble, Borders, and Books-A-Million. Information about these companies is provided in the following sections.

Barnes & Noble

Barnes & Noble opened its retail stores in 1974, acquired B. Dalton (bookseller) in 1986, and went public in 1993. Barnes & Noble pioneered the concept of the bookseller superstore in 1990 by selling a large inventory of books along with music, DVDs, and magazines. The company acquired Sterling Publishing, a leading publisher of how-to, home design, health, and reference books, in 1993. Sterling currently has 5,000 active book titles. Barnes & Noble Classics (company book publishing imprint) sold more than 500,000 units in its first year of publication. Since the mid-1990s, Barnes & Noble has won several contracts to operate bookstores at colleges and universities. The company attracts millions of online visitors each month (http://www.bn.com and http://www.barnes&noble.com) and serves online customers in more than 200 countries.

In February 2007, Barnes & Noble was the nation's largest brick-and-mortar bookseller with 793 stores operating in 50 states. The typical Barnes & Noble store offers a large inventory of books, a large children's department and newsstand area, and a music listening system that allows customers to listen to music before purchasing. Wi-Fi service is available for a fee and a membership program that provides customers with discounted books is provided to interested customers. Financial information for Barnes & Noble is shown in Exhibit 4.

Borders Group

The Borders Group operates more than 1,200 Borders and Waldenbooks stores in the United States and in countries such as Singapore, New Zealand, and Australia. Borders Group is planning to sell its 71 United Kingdom stores and concentrate its retail store

EXHIBIT 4 Financial Information for Barnes & Noble (In $ Thousands)

	2005	2006
Net Sales	$ 5,103,004	$ 5,261,254
Operating Income	251,824	253,384
Net Earnings	146,681	150,507
Total Assets	3,156,250	3,196,798
Long-Term Debt	435,623	534,935
Stockholders' Equity	1,115,841	1,164,865

Source: Barnes & Noble 2006 *Form 10-K*, pp. F-20, F-21.

EXHIBIT 5 **Financial Information for Borders Group (In $ Millions)**

	2005	2006
Net Sales	$ 4,079.2	$ 4,113.5
Operating Income	173.4	(136.8)
Net Earnings	101.0	(151.3)
Total Assets	2,572.2	2,613.4
Long-Term Debt	5.4	5.2
Stockholders' Equity	927.8	642.0

Source: Borders Group 2006 *Form 10-K*, pp. 43, 44.

business on the U.S. market. The company has struggled financially in recent years, in part due to competitors' sale of music downloads that has cut Borders' sales of CDs significantly. Borders initially launched its Web site in 1998 and then partnered with Amazon.com from 2001 to 2007. The company planned to launch its own Web site as early as 2008, ending the seven-year partnership with Amazon. As part of its cost-cutting plan, Borders will close about half of its Waldenbooks stores and will likely sell off or franchise most of its international business. By the end of 2008, Borders expects to have about 300 Waldenbooks stores instead of the 564 it had at the end of 2006. Financial information for Borders Group is shown in Exhibit 5.

Books-A-Million

Founded in 1917 as a street-corner newsstand in Florence, Alabama, Books-A-Million is currently the third largest book retailing chain in the United States. Books-A-Million is the premier book retailing chain in the southeastern United States with more than 200 stores in nineteen states and Washington, D.C. The company offers three retail store formats: Books-A-Million superstores with over 20,000 square feet, Bookland stores with 3,500 to 4,000 square feet (operates in malls), and Joe Muggs Newsstands with 3,000 square feet. Books-A-Million also has a wholesale and distribution division, an e-commerce division, and an Internet development and services company called Net Central that is located in Nashville, Tennessee. Financial information for Books-A-Million is shown in Exhibit 6.

Internal Issues

Marketing

Amazon's marketing strategy is designed to increase customer traffic on the company's Web sites, to promote repeat purchases, to build awareness of products and services available, and to strengthen the Amazon.com brand name. Amazon.com uses e-mail campaigns, portal advertising, and sponsored search as their primary means of advertising. Special promotions are also used, such as the Xbox 360 game console promotion that was

EXHIBIT 6 **Financial Information for Books-A-Million (In $ Thousands)**

	2007	2006	2005
Net Sales	$520,416	$503,751	$474,099
Operating Income	$30,099	$23,037	$18,092
Net Earnings	$18,887	$13,067	$10,199
Total Assets	$304,037	$311,659	$300,812
Long-Term Debt	$7,100	$7,200	$7,500
Stockholders Equity	$157,034	$145,009	$134,859

Source: 2007 *Annual Report*, http://www.booksamillion.com.

held in December 2006. During this promotion, the company sold 1,000 units in twenty-nine seconds for two-thirds off the regular price. A total of four million orders were placed on the Amazon.com Web site during that same day. Amazon also markets its products through their Associates Program where they contract with other Web sites to direct customers to Amazon Web sites to purchase products. Amazon pays commissions to participants in the program for customer referrals that result in sales. Target, Office Depot, Shutterfly, Fidelity Investments, Tire Track, Weight Watchers, and many small retailers have stores on the Amazon.com Web site.

Excellent customer service is an essential marketing strategy. Company managers focus on continuous innovation to provide convenience for customers. Specifically, the management team wants to ensure fast and reliable fulfillment, efficient customer service, easy-to-use functionality, and a trusted online transaction environment. Conveniences such as "1 Click" purchases, "Look Inside the Book" features, and "Search Inside the Book" features provide an information-rich environment. Amazon also offers customer reviews, gift guides, Web pages tailored to individual customer preferences, wish lists, buying guides, and wedding and baby registries. One example of information provided by Amazon to assist customers is the "Best of 2006 List" that includes the company's most wished for, favorite gift products, best selling, and most positively reviewed products of 2006.

Distribution Issues

Amazon.com leases corporate headquarters offices in Seattle, Washington. Other facilities such as fulfillment and warehouse centers and customer service offices are located throughout the United States, primarily in California, Delaware, Florida, Kansas, Kentucky, Nevada, North Dakota, Pennsylvania, South Carolina, Texas, Virginia, Washington, West Virginia, and Wisconsin. The company leases a corporate office, fulfillment and warehouse operations, customer service, and other facilities outside of the United States. The international offices are primarily located in China, France, Germany, India, Ireland, Japan, Luxembourg, and the United Kingdom. Amazon entered into an agreement with BNSF Logistics in 2006 to assist Amazon in managing the U.S. inbound flow of goods to optimize availability on the items customers want to order. Fulfillment capacity was expanded in 2005 and 2006 to twelve million square feet.

E-commerce Technology

Amazon.com has been a pioneer in its Web site design, testing, and optimization and has excelled in use of technology to personalize the customers' shopping experiences. Amazon has its own proprietary technology and licenses technology from other companies. The

---

EXHIBIT 7   Recent Amazon.com Partnerships

Points International Ltd. (www.points.com)—The world's leading reward management portal and Amazon.com agreement allows customers to swap their miles or points for Amazon.com gift certificates (2005 agreement).

Coinstar, Inc.—Customers can exchange coins at Coinstar Centers with no transaction fees and receive Amazon.com gift certificates (2005 agreement).

Fidelity Investments, Weight Watchers, Shutterfly (digital photography co.), and SideStep (travel search engine) opened online stores on Amazon.com (2005 agreement).

Comcast opened an online store on Amazon.com. Customers can purchase high-speed Internet and related services (2006 agreement).

TiVo, Inc.—Amazon Unibox on TiVo is a service to provide TiVo subscribers movies and TV shows from leading studios and networks (2007 agreement).

Sources: "Cash Goes In, Gift Certificate Comes Out," *Business Wire,* September 13, 2005. "Comcast to Offer Its High-Speed Internet Service on Amazon.com," *PR Newswire US,* November 20, 2006. "Points.com Teams Up with Amazon.com to Provide Greater Reward Options," *Canada Newswire,* September 28, 2005. "TiVo, Inc. and Amazon.com Announce New Service Enabling Amazon Unibox Video Downloads to TiVo," *Business Wire,* February 7, 2007.

company's current strategy is to focus its development efforts on innovation by creating and enhancing its proprietary software and by licensing or acquiring commercially developed technology for other applications when it is needed. Amazon invests in several areas of technology, including digital initiatives, seller platforms, and Web services. These computer applications are needed for such activities as fulfillment, customer service operations, order tracking, managing inventory, ensuring proper shipment of orders, and facilitating payment transactions.

Management and Organization

Amazon has historically hired the best executives available from Wal-Mart, Microsoft, Barnes & Noble, and Symantec to work in areas such as marketing, software development, financing, and distribution. The company employed approximately 13,900 people (includes both full-time and part-time employees) at the end of 2006. The company hires independent contractors and temporary workers to supplement their workforce, particularly during the holiday season. None of the company's employees are represented by unions. Amazon depends on quality personnel to maintain and improve its technology systems and to handle customer service issues. Jeff Bezos has been CEO since the company was founded in 1995. An organization chart for the company is shown in Exhibit 8.

Financial Conditions

As shown in Exhibit 9, the statement of operations indicates an increase in Amazon's sales from 2005 to 2006 ($8.5 billion to $10.7 billion) and a decrease of net income during the same time of almost $169 million (net income of $190 million in 2006 and $359 million in 2005). Also note in Exhibit 9 that the company had increases in expenses for fulfillment, marketing, and technology from 2005 to 2006. As provided in Exhibit 10, the Amazon.com balance sheet shows increases in total assets from 2005 to 2006 ($3.7 billion to $4.4 billion), but increases in current liabilities of about $600 million during this same time ($1.9 billion in 2005 to $2.5 billion in 2006). The accumulated deficit for Amazon in 2006 was $1.837 billion while the total stockholders' equity was $431 million.

In August 2006, Amazon announced it would repurchase up to $500 million of Amazon common stock through 2008 if the company determines that its shares are undervalued.

EXHIBIT 8　Organization Chart for Amazon.com

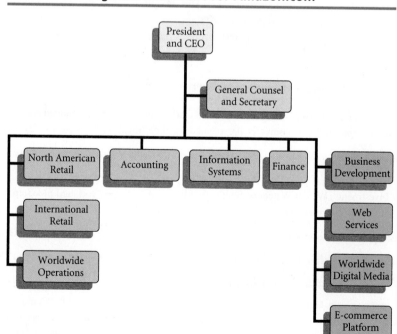

Source: Adapted from Amazon.com 2007 *Form 10-K*, p. 7.

EXHIBIT 9   Amazon.com, Inc. Consolidated Statements of Operations (in Millions, Except Per Share Data)

	Year Ended December 31		
	2006	2005	2004
Net sales	$10,711	$ 8,490	$ 6,921
Cost of sales	8,255	6,451	5,319
Gross profit	2,456	2,039	1,602
Operating expenses (1):			
Fulfillment	937	745	601
Marketing	263	198	162
Technology and content	662	451	283
General and administrative	195	166	124
Other operating expense (income)	10	47	(8)
Total operating expenses	2,067	1,607	1,162
Income from operations	389	432	440
Interest income	59	44	28
Interest expense	(78)	(92)	(107)
Other income (expense), net	(4)	2	(5)
Remeasurements and other	11	42	(1)
Total non-operating expense	(12)	(4)	(85)
Income before income taxes	377	428	355
Provision (benefit) for income taxes	187	95	(233)
Income before cumulative effect of change in accounting principle	190	333	588
Cumulative effect of change in accounting principle	—	26	—
Net income	$ 190	$ 359	$ 588
Basic earnings per share:			
Prior to cumulative effect of change in accounting principle	$ 0.46	$ 0.81	$ 1.45
Cumulative effect of change in accounting principle	—	0.06	—
	$ 0.46	$ 0.87	$ 1.45
Diluted earnings per share:			
Prior to cumulative effect of change in accounting principle	$ 0.45	$ 0.78	$ 1.39
Cumulative effect of change in accounting principle	—	0.06	—
	$ 0.45	$ 0.84	$ 1.39
Weighted average shares used in computation of earnings per share:			
Basic	416	412	406
Diluted	424	426	425
(1) Includes stock-based compensation as follows:			
Fulfillment	$ 24	$ 16	$ 10
Marketing	4	6	4
Technology and content	54	45	32
General and administrative	19	20	12

Source: Amazon.com 2006 *Form 10-K*, p. 47.

EXHIBIT 10 **Amazon.com, Inc. Consolidated Balance Sheets (in Millions, Except Per Share Data)**

	December 31	
	2006	2005
ASSETS		
Current assets:		
Cash and cash equivalents	$ 1,022	$ 1,013
Marketable securities	997	987
Inventories	877	566
Accounts receivable, net and other	399	274
Deferred tax assets	78	89
Total current assets	3,373	2,929
Fixed assets, net	457	348
Deferred tax assets	199	223
Goodwill	195	159
Other assets	139	37
Total assets	$ 4,363	$ 3,696
LIABILITIES AND STOCKHOLDERS' EQUITY		
Current liabilities:		
Accounts payable	$ 1,816	$ 1,366
Accrued expenses and other	716	533
Total current liabilities	2,532	1,899
Long-term debt	1,247	1,480
Other long-term liabilities	153	71
Commitments and contingencies		
Stockholders' equity:		
Preferred stock, $0.01 par value:		
Authorized shares—500		
Issued and outstanding shares—none	—	—
Common stock, $0.01 par value:		
Authorized shares—5,000		
Issued and outstanding shares—414 and 416	4	4
Treasury stock, at cost	(252)	—
Additional paid-in capital	2,517	2,263
Accumulated other comprehensive income (loss)	(1)	6
Accumulated deficit	(1,837)	(2,027)
Total stockholders' equity	431	246
Total liabilities and stockholders' equity	$ 4,363	$ 3,696

Source: Amazon.com 2006 *Form 10-K*, p. 48.

Future Outlook

Amazon.com has five challenges for the future:

- Competition in both the retail and e-commerce market is increasing.
- Expansion into new countries and into new product segments creates risks as Amazon must adapt its technology and business practices to diverse international environments.

- Expenses for free shipping and the Amazon membership plan expenses must be monitored to be sure these strategies are generating their intended business results of higher sales levels.
- Technology infrastructure must be monitored and updated to ensure that customers can be served without interruption.
- Lawsuits that challenge the company's use of technologies that personalize the shopping experience and make the shopping experience more efficient must be defended.

As Amazon.com deals with these challenges and tries to continue its strategies of developing new services, product offerings, and partnerships while continuing to establish existing services, several issues must be considered:

1. What portion of the business should be focused on sales of products, sales of services to consumers, business partnerships for sales, and partnerships for order fulfillment/Web services? Is it possible for the company to become too diversified or to get too far away from its initial business of selling books?
2. Who are the likely competitors of Amazon.com in the future? How can the company ensure that it can compete effectively in its diverse businesses?
3. How should the company decide on opportunities for entering new international markets? How much emphasis should be placed on this strategy?
4. Should Amazon continue to offer "super saver shipping," free shipping plans, and membership plans that offer free express shipping, or do these services cost too much to be a useful strategy?
5. How can the company keep up with technology developments? Should they consider acquiring companies that have proprietary technology that might be useful to the company in offering its services? Or are partnerships through contract an adequate means of gaining the necessary emerging technologies for company operations?
6. How much of an issue are the lawsuits filed against the company? Are these lawsuits likely to impact the day-to-day operations of the company?
7. Should the increases in fulfillment, marketing, and technology costs in 2006 concern company managers? Or are these temporary issues that will result in additional profits in the future?

References

"Amazon.com Announces the Launch of Its Grocery Store," *Business Wire*, July 17, 2007.
"Amazon Launches New Automotive Parts and Accessories Store with over 1 Million Automotive Products Available," *PR Newswire US*, October 26, 2007.
"Amazon Launches New Services to Help Small and Medium-Sized Businesses Enhance Their Customer Offerings by Accessing Amazon's Order Fulfillment, Customer Service, and Website Functionality," *Business Wire*, September 19, 2006.
"Borders Books a Big Loss," *Business Week Online*, March 23, 2007.
"CustomFlix and Amazon.com Launch CD On Demand Service," *Business Wire*, September 19, 2006.
http://www.amazon.com
http://www.bn.com
http://www.booksamillion.com
http://www.borders.com
Kirsch, Adam. "The New Amazonians," *The New York Sun*, July 11, 2005.
Perez, Juan Carlos. "Amazon.com Turns 10," *InfoWorld Daily News*, July 15, 2005.
"Stanford Graduate School of Business and Amazon.com Announce Winner of the Amazon.com Nonprofit Innovation Award," *Business Wire*, October, 15, 2005.
"Three Lucky Libraries to Get the Gift of Literature through Amazon.com's 'Wish for Lit' Program," *Business Wire*, January 18, 2007.

18 Zale Corporation — 2008

Sharynn Tomlin
Angelo State University

ZLC

www.zalecorp.com

Zale Corporation is the largest chain of specialty retail jewelry stores in the United States. It currently operates 2,349 stores in the United States, Puerto Rico, and Canada, employs approximately 16,900 employees, operates in various segments serving different customer demands. Zale Corporation has been profitable throughout most of its history. However, Zale has recently encountered setbacks including unprofitable margins, unstable leadership, declining market share, and a 50 percent drop in 2006 net income to $53.6 million. Zale's revenues in 2007 declined slightly from 2006 to $2.4 billion.

Zale is now going back to its roots with a new strategy that focuses on Middle America, wide merchandise assortments, competitive pricing, great value, and a new CEO to execute this strategy, Mary Burton. Ms. Burton's first full year as Zale's new CEO was 2007.

History

Morris B. Zale opened his first jewelry store in Wichita Falls, Texas, in 1924. From its inception, Zale stores offered credit, with payments typically spread out over 12 months. Despite the great depression of the 1930s Zale continued to expand, growing to 12 stores by 1941 with revenues over $2.73 million. Zale avoided debt during these periods and most earnings were reinvested in the company.

By the mid-1960s, Zale operated the world's largest retail jewelry chain. The company again made a major acquisition in 1962 by acquiring Bailey Banks & Biddle. By 1974, in addition to its retail jewelry stores, Zale had grown to include 351 shoe stores, 83 drug stores, 146 clothing stores, 25 sporting goods stores, and 13 tobacco/newsstand concessions.

By the early 1980s, Zale began selling off its non-jewelry retail operations. During the 1980s, jewelry sales bottomed out, due in most part to the recession of the 80's. Moreover, the value of gold and diamonds, which generally appreciates, began to fluctuate. Profits slipped from $33 million in 1981 to a loss of $6 million in 1982. By 1986, the company suffered a loss of $60 million. Due to the lack of profits, Zale disposed of its European retail operations. In 1988, the Zale Company was sold to Peoples Jewelers and the Austrian Swarovski Company, each with 50 percent ownership, and they took Zale private. In 1990, Zale posted a $64 million loss and then a loss of $106 million in the first six months of 1991, followed by filing for bankruptcy in 1992.

Zale emerged from bankruptcy in 1993 with 700 fewer stores. In 1994, Robert DiNicola, ex-CEO of Macy's, was hired, ushering in a new era of recovery for the debt-plagued company. By 1998, Zale appeared completely recovered from bankruptcy, with revenues exceeding $1.43 billion. DiNicola retired in 2002, and Mary Forte was named CEO. Ms. Forte resigned in 2006 and Betsy Burton replaced her. Zale of late has lost market share to Signet LLC and has even considered merging with Signet Group LLC, but CEO Burton has rejected the idea. On December 20, 2007 Neil Goldberg took the position of presidency.

Zale's current organizational structure is shown in Exhibit 1.

EXHIBIT 1   Organizational Structure

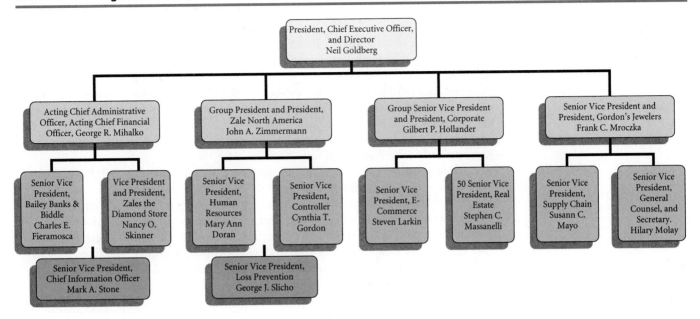

External Issues

The jewelry industry was expected to grow to $61.8 billion in 2007. Brand recognition is paramount in gaining and sustaining market share, and there was growing international competition. The retail fine jewelry industry is segmented into two types: chain stores and independents, with chain stores holding the largest share of the market.

Jewelry stores employment exceeded 155,000 people in the mid-2000s, with most of the 30,000 stores located in California, Texas, New York, and Florida. The majority of jewelry sales occur in New York, Chicago, Los Angeles, Boston, and Washington, D.C. A strong economy and low unemployment boosts the sale of luxury goods, including jewelry. As consumer discretionary expenditures decrease, jewelry retailers are often the first affected by cooling economic conditions.

According to *Jewelers' Circular Keystone*, as well as the U.S. Census Bureau, about 25 percent of the specialty retail purchases traditionally occur in December with diamond jewelry accounting for nearly 50 percent of the specialty retailer sales. However, in the last few years consumers have shown an increased interest in designer jewelry. According to statistics offered by Claritas Inc., "Chicago will lead with jewelry and watch sales totaling about $2.5 billion into 2007 . . . the average consumer will spend about $500 per year on fine jewelry . . . Jewelry sales were expected to rise to $61.8 billion by 2007."[1] Although Wal-Mart generates the highest jewelry sales, Zale remains the dominant specialty retailer.

Due in part to the technological advancement of communications in the early part of the past decade, mass merchants, such as home shopping channels, mail-order firms, and other discounters, quickly emerged as a competitive force. This trend was followed by the explosive growth of Internet sales. As of 2006, online jewelry sales was the fastest growing category and accounts for 3.6 percent of sales, a 20 percent increase from 2005 and generating online sales in excess of $2 billion. Specialty retailers have also included the distribution of store catalogs in order to generate sales.

Introduction of synthetic diamonds at a fraction of the cost of natural diamonds may also become a major competitive factor in the near future. Apollo Diamond Inc., located in Boston, Massachusetts, and Gemesis Corp. of Sarasota, Florida, who have manufactured synthetic diamonds, have been overwhelmed with the positive response from consumers.

An online poll conducted by *CNBC* revealed that about "71 percent of consumers would also be willing to purchase the synthetic diamond rather than the natural diamond."[2]

Environmental and Social Responsibility

Nearly 80 percent of newly mined gold is used in jewelry, so jewelers like Zale and others play a significant role in saving and sustaining the environment. Eight leading jewelers, including Zale Corporation, Cartier, and Tiffany & Co., are supporting organizations that oppose the mining of so-called "dirty gold." With this influential backing, the pressure on the gold mining industry is rising. To resolve growing concern about how gold is produced, Jewelers of America and other jewelry and mining groups created the Council for Responsible Jewelry Practices in May 2005.

Nongovernmental organizations such as Oxfam America and Earthworks launched the "No Dirty Gold" campaign in 2004, speaking in the name of communities whose livelihoods and environments are threatened by irresponsible gold mining. The "No Dirty Gold" campaign promotes a system to determine where and under what circumstances gold is mined. Similar to the campaign to eliminate conflict diamonds, the "No Dirty Gold" campaign is based on the Golden Rules that represent human rights and environmental reform standards for the mining industry. Zale, Cartier, Tiffany & Co., and others are among the twelve leading jewelers that have endorsed the Golden Rules.

Competition

In 2005, 24,741 jewelry retailers operated in the United States. Leading the pack were Zale Corporation and Tiffany & Co., both generating revenues in excess of $2 billion annually. Traditional jewelry retailers offer customers upscale merchandise, preferential treatment, and product savvy personnel, attributes not common among the discounters and Internet retailers. Diamonds continue to dominate overall sales with bridal seasons and holidays remaining the optimum buying periods.

Zale faces a variety of competitors who are not exclusively operating in the jewelry industry, such as department stores like JCPenney, discounters like Wal-Mart, online retailers, and television home shopping programs such as QVC. Even though Wal-Mart has the largest market share in the industry, it is not considered a direct Zale competitor. However, the following competitors target the exact same markets as does Zale.

Signet (www.signetgroupplc.com)

Signet Group PLC originated as a single jewelry shop in Richmond, Surrey, England in 1949. Now Signet is the world's largest specialty retail jeweler. Today, Signet Group conducts operations in both the United States. and the United Kingdom. In the United States, Signet operates (2006) 1,221 stores in 50 states with sales making up a market share of 3.9 percent of the total U.S. jewelry market. Nationwide, its mall stores are known as Kay Jewelers and regionally under several other different brand names. Jared, The Galleria of Jewelry, is the trade name of their U.S. superstores.

Signet operated 591 stores in the United Kingdom as of 2006 under the names H. Samuel, Ernest Jones, and Leslie Davis. Its U.K. sales made up 17 percent of the total U.K. jewelry market. Kay Jewelers also conducts worldwide e-commerce at its Web site, www. kay.com. In 2006, Signet reported an 8.5 percent revenue growth, which averaged to a 4.8 percent revenue growth over the past five years.

Tiffany & Co. (www.tiffany.com)

Tiffany & Co. was founded in 1837 and is now a jeweler and specialty retailer, whose merchandise offerings include an extensive selection of jewelry (82 percent of net sales in fiscal 2005), as well as timepieces, sterling silverware, china, crystal, stationery, fragrances, and accessories. In 2005 Tiffany & Co. accumulated net sales of $2.395 billion, which demonstrates growth in net sales compared to 2004 of about 8.6 percent. Today, more than

150 Tiffany & Co. stores and boutiques serve customers in the U.S. and international markets. There were 8,120 employees around the world as of January 31, 2006.

Tiffany uses several channels of distribution. More than 50 percent of U.S. retail of 2005 covered store retail and non-Internet business-to-business sales; 38 percent consisted of international retail and wholesale, as well as a limited amount of business-to-business and Internet sales. About 6 percent of sales were attributable to direct marketing such as direct mail catalog, and so on, and 5 percent from other channels. For 2005, the United States represented approximately 60 percent of Tiffany's net sales. Japan represented 20 percent, other Asia-Pacific at 8 percent, Europe 6 percent, and the remainder in other markets.

Odimo Inc. (www.diamond.com)

Odimo Inc. competes directly with Zale in online sales. Odimo sells fine jewelry, luxury goods, and brand-name watches. Since its formation in 1998, Odimo has not achieved a net profit in a single year and has accumulated a $67 million deficit in nine years of operation. However, the company continues to remain solvent and keeps on making acquisitions and expanding its product lines. Since the 2000 and 2002 acquisitions of www.worldofwatches.com and www.ashford.com, "the company's sales and revenues have continued to take monumental steps forward, but they have still never been able to climb out of the red."[3]

Blue Nile Inc. (www.bluenile.com)

Blue Nile Inc. is another online diamond dealer in direct competition with Zale. Blue Nile is experiencing explosive growth and amazing profits and does not maintain any significant product inventories. When a customer orders a diamond from Blue Nile, the company places an order for the product from one of twelve wholesale suppliers that it uses. The wholesaler then ships the diamond to Blue Nile, and the stone is set, polished, and shipped. All of this is done for a mere 23 percent markup in an industry where 50 percent has always been the norm.

Since going public in May of 2006, Blue Nile's stock has increased by 32 percent. What started out as a "small Internet venture has become a giant in the industry that now sells as many engagement rings in the United States as Tiffany & Co."[4] Exhibit 2 summarizes the sales and other financial data for Zale's major competitors.

Internal Issues

Zale, at fiscal year-end 2006 (July 31), operated 1,456 specialty retail jewelry stores, 817 kiosks, and 76 carts located mainly throughout shopping malls in the United States, Canada, and Puerto Rico, employing approximately 16,900 employees. A listing of the U.S. facilities by state is shown in Exhibit 3. Its headquarters is approximately 430,000

EXHIBIT 2   Competitors—Retail Jewelry Industry

Competitors Retail (Specialty) Industry	Revenue (M)	Profit Margin (12 mos)	Employees	Market Cap (M)
Signet	$3,403.50	11.20%	15,652	$3,917.00
Zale	$2,439.00	3.40%	16,900	$1,234.60
Tiffany	$2,395.20	15.20%	8,120	$5,780.70
Blue Nile	$251.60	7.90%	133	$616.80
Odimo	$51.80	−47.90%	113	$1.50
USN	$27.30	−70.80%	74	$0.60
Elegant Illusions	$9.30	2.10%	124	$1.90
Promotora Valle Hermoso	$0.20	−1740.20%	32	$9.20

Source: http://www.investor.reuters.com/business/BusCompanyCompetitorsPeers.aspx?ticker=SIG&symbol=SIG&target=%2fbusiness%2fbuscompany%2fbuscompcpfake%2fbuscompc_p

square feet and is located in Irving, Texas. In Toronto, Canada, Zale has a center for distribution and production operations of 26,280 square feet as well as a 20,000-square-foot distribution and warehousing facility in Irving, Texas.

Accounting

From an accounting standpoint, 2006 was at best a marginal year for the Zale Company. Debt increased, earnings per share decreased sharply, cost of sales was higher, and liquidity was down. The American Jobs Creation Act or AJCA created a $6.8 million tax break

EXHIBIT 3 Firm's Facilities

States	Zales	Gordon's
Alabama	11	2
Alaska	6	0
Arizona	10	9
Arkansas	9	6
California	58	1
Colorado	13	9
Connecticut	10	0
Delaware	2	4
Florida	51	33
Georgia	22	6
Hawaii	6	0
Idaho	4	0
Illinois	26	4
Indiana	14	5
Iowa	10	1
Kansas	10	6
Kentucky	8	0
Louisiana	15	11
Maine	2	0
Maryland	21	10
Massachusetts	18	5
Michigan	28	1
Minnesota	9	13
Mississippi	7	2
Missouri	15	7
Montana	2	0
Nebraska	4	1
Nevada	5	4
New Hampshire	5	0
New Jersey	20	4
New Mexico	12	5
New York	36	1
North Carolina	20	1
North Dakota	4	0
Ohio	31	0
Oklahoma	12	9
Oregon	5	2

continued

EXHIBIT 3   **Firm's Facilities—continued**

States	Zales	Gordon's
Pennsylvania	31	26
Rhode Island	3	1
South Carolina	11	1
South Dakota	3	0
Tennessee	17	9
Texas	74	62
Utah	6	0
Vermont	2	0
Virginia	25	8
Washington	16	8
West Virginia	5	1
Wisconsin	12	0
Total U.S.	**746**	**27**

for the Zale Company in 2006. The act allows companies to exclude up to 85 percent of foreign earned income as long as the company repatriates the funds in the United States. Zale incurred a $21.2 million loss on the closing of 32 Bailey Banks and Biddle stores.

Finance

Financial performance in 2006 and 2007 were lackluster. However, in addressing shareholders, CEO Burton stated that Zale had a strong balance sheet. Total assets for fiscal year end July 31, 2007, increased 10.4 percent compared to fiscal year 2006. The increase in assets was attributed in large part to inventory. Zale attributed some of its inventory woes to the closing of 32 Bailey Banks and Biddle stores. Zale also maintained that it invests in inventory in order to have a dominant assortment in both diamond solitaires and diamond fashions for the Zale brand. Analysts suggested that sluggish Zale sales also contributed to inventory problems.

Zale's long-term debt increased significantly from $129 million (FY2005) to $227 million (2007) as shown in Exhibit 4, the consolidated balance sheet.

Zale states that its substantial long-term debt is the primary reason it has not paid dividends since 1993 and does not anticipate dividend payments in the foreseeable future. However, Zale did make an effort to reward its shareholders by returning $100 million in the form of share buybacks for fiscal year 2006.

Zale's consolidated statement of operations is shown in Exhibit 5.

Zale Divisions

Zale divides its finances between three major segments: fine jewelry, kiosk jewelry, and all other. Of these three, fine jewelry and kiosk jewelry account for all but less than 1 percent of the numbers, with most of the information in "all other" being insurance proceeds, loose ends, and unallocated funds and liabilities.

Fine Jewelry

The fine jewelry segment of Zale is made up of (1) Zale North America (Zale Jewelers, Peoples Jewelers, and Mappins Jewelers), (2) Zales Outlet, (3) Gordon's Jewelers, and (4) Bailey Banks and Biddle Fine Jewelers. Zale North America accounted for well over half of the company's 2006 revenue. Zales Jewelers contributed nearly 44 percent of the overall revenues with Peoples and Mappins combining for anther 9 percent. Zales Outlet made up about 7 percent of the firm's 2006 revenues with average sales of $398 per transaction. Gordon's Jewelers accounted for 14 percent of the sales for the entire company and averaged $416 per transaction in 2006. The Bailey Banks and Biddle brand name contributed 13 percent of the company's gross sales, and averaged $1,610 per transaction, but the

EXHIBIT 4 Zale Corporation's Balance Sheets

	All numbers in thousands		
Period Ending	Jul. 31, 2007	Jul. 31, 2006	Jul. 31, 2005
Assets			
Current Assets			
Cash and Cash Equivalents	37,643	42,594	55,446
Short-Term Investments	–	–	–
Net Receivables	–	–	–
Inventory	1,021,164	903,294	853,580
Other Current Assets	113,511	103,356	64,042
Total Current Assets	**1,172,318**	**1,049,244**	**973,068**
Long-Term Investments	-	21,948	23,640
Property, Plant and Equipment	304,396	283,721	282,033
Goodwill	100,740	96,339	90,774
Intangible Assets	–	–	–
Accumulated Amortization	–	–	–
Other Assets	35,187	11,316	11,385
Deferred Long-Term Asset Charges	1,305	–	–
Total Assets	**1,613,946**	**1,462,568**	**1,380,900**
Liabilities			
Current Liabilities			
Accounts Payable	344,957	403,129	382,337
Short/Current Long-Term Debt	–	–	–
Other Current Liabilities	29,501	–	–
Total Current Liabilities	**374,458**	**403,129**	**382,337**
Long-Term Debt	227,306	202,813	129,800
Other Liabilities	40,118	55,377	51,175
Deferred Long-Term Liability Charges	69,491	–	–
Minority Interest	–	–	–
Negative Goodwill	–	–	–
Total Liabilities	**711,373**	**661,319**	**563,312**
Stockholders' Equity			
Misc Stocks Options Warrants	–	–	–
Redeemable Preferred Stock	–	–	–
Preferred Stock	–	–	–
Common Stock	487	482	531
Retained Earnings	868,111	808,859	755,237
Treasury Stock	(150,000)	(150,000)	(50,000)
Capital Surplus	138,036	110,105	88,970
Other Stockholders Equity	45,939	31,803	22,850
Total Stockholders Equity	**902,573**	**801,249**	**817,588**
Total Liabilities and SE	**$ 1,613,946**	**$ 1,462,568**	**$ 1,380,900**

Source: http://finance.yahoo.com/q/bs?s=ZLC&annual

EXHIBIT 5 Zale Corporation's Income Statement

Period Ending	All numbers in thousands		
	Jul. 31, 2007	Jul. 31, 2006	Jul. 31, 2005
Total Revenue	**$ 2,437,075**	**2,438,977**	**2,383,066**
Cost of Revenue	1,194,399	1,215,636	1,157,226
Gross Profit	**1,242,676**	**1,223,341**	**1,225,840**
Operating Expenses			
Research Development	–	–	–
Selling General and Administrative	1,070,478	1,080,754	988,197
Non Recurring	–	–	–
Others	69,071	61,452	59,840
Total Operating Expenses	–	–	–
Operating Income or Loss	**103,127**	**81,135**	**177,803**
Income from Continuing Operations			
Total Other Income/Expenses Net	–	–	–
Earnings Before Interest And Taxes	103,127	81,135	177,803
Interest Expense	18,969	11,185	7,725
Income Before Tax	84,158	69,950	170,078
Income Tax Expense	24,906	16,328	63,303
Minority Interest	–	–	–
Net Income From Continuing Ops	59,252	53,622	106,775
Non-recurring Events			
Discontinued Operations	–	–	–
Extraordinary Items	–	–	–
Effect Of Accounting Changes	–	–	–
Other Items	–	–	–
Net Income	**59,252**	**53,622**	**106,775**
Preferred Stock And Other Adjustments	–	–	–
Net Income Applicable To Common Shares	**$ 59,252**	**$ 53,622**	**$ 106,775**

Source: http://finance.yahoo.com/q/is?s=ZLC&annual

reports also state that these figures do not include the 32 stores in this line that were closed in 2006. Exclusion of that fact may lead these numbers to be exaggerated.

Kiosk Jewelry

This segment of Zale operates under the brand names Piercing Pagoda, Plumb Gold, Silver and Gold Connections, and Peoples II. These locations are small and sell lower priced products. The group as a whole contributed about 22 percent of the company's revenues and averaged $38 per transaction in 2006.

All Other

This segment is made up of Zale Indemnity Company, Zale Life Insurance Company, and Jewel Re-Insurance Company. These companies market insurance to Zales credit card holders and issue insurance policies on jewelry and stones. This segment accounted for less than 1 percent of the company's 2006 revenues. Sales data by brand is shown in Exhibit 6 and by segments in Exhibit 7.

EXHIBIT 6   Operations by Brand 2004–2006

	Year Ended July 31		
	2006	2005	2004
Total Revenues (in thousands)			
Zales (including ZLC Direct)	$ 1,092,625	$ 1,079,230	$ 1,070,576
Zales Outlet	177,736	166,000	137,613
Gordon's	339,510	324,854	313,881
Bailey Banks & Biddle (a)	309,311	320,869	326,086
Peoples (b)	229,574	198,308	174,058
Piercing Pagoda	268,936	274,296	269,660
Peoples II	7,683	6,601	–
Insurance Revenues/Other	13,602	12,908	12,566
	$ 2,438,977	$ 2,383,066	$ 2,304,440
Average Sales Per Location (c)			
Zales	$ 1,383,000	$ 1,366,000	$ 1,390,000
Zales Outlet	1,360,000	1,249,000	1,287,000
Gordon's	1,200,000	1,112,000	1,101,000
Bailey Banks & Biddle	3,738,000	3,474,000	2,848,000
Peoples	1,397,000	1,140,000	1,041,000
Piercing Pagoda	332,000	343,000	339,000
Peoples II	82,000	100,000	–

Source: Zale Corporation, *2006 Annual Report,* p. 7.

Marketing and Strategy

Zale is primarily pursuing a direct sales strategy, offering products throughout all segments from basic to fine jewelry. This strategy is characterized by a typical business-to-customer (B2C) relationship. However, channels differ depending upon the type of store and design. Online shopping is available at some stores, thus approaching the customer through a different direct channel. The most typical direct marketing tool that Zale utilizes is direct retailing. Direct mail and online shopping make up only a fraction of the total sales.

Zale uses all its different store types to serve the variety of needs of its customers. Kiosks primarily offer moderately priced jewelry to a broad range of customers. Zale Outlets target slightly higher-income females. Gordon's Jewelers is a regional jeweler focusing primarily on customer-driven assortments, whereas Bailey Banks & Biddle Fine Jewelers offer luxury and designer jewelry and prestige watches to attract the more affluent customers. The Zale strategy is composed of three components: "(1) Regain Market Share, (2) Improve Gross Margin, and (3) Invest in People."[5]

Regain Market Share

Since the 2006 holiday strategy failed to be profitable, Zale has refocused to emphasize "diamond fashion such as solitaire engagement rings, dominant assortments across bridal and diamond fashion and consistent assortments of moderately priced merchandise across all stores."[6] For the next holiday season, a return to "Zales, the Diamond Store" is planned with an emphasis on the breadth and depth of assortments and additional investment and training in personnel, in an attempt to stimulate store revenues and regain market leadership. Zale believes that it is essential for an industry leader to set new milestones and benchmarks in delivering innovative and creatively designed products. To regain market share, Zale uses economies of scale in purchasing, leasing, advertising, and administrative costs, which is accomplished by utilizing their widely spread network of retailers and distributions centers throughout all 50 states in the United States, and Puerto Rico and Canada.

EXHIBIT 7   Segment Data

Selected Financial Data by Segment	Year Ended July 31				
	2006	2005	2004	2003	2002
	(amounts in thousands, except per share amounts)				
Revenues					
Fine Jewelry	$ 2,149,217	$ 2,089,261	$ 2,022,214	$ 1,939,454	$ 1,900,177
Kiosk	276,619	280,897	269,660	256,665	273,225
All Other	13,141	12,908	12,566	16,122	18,325
Total Revenues	$ 2,438,977	$ 2,383,066	$ 2,304,440	$ 2,212,241	$ 2,191,727
Depreciation & Amortization Expense					
Fine Jewelry	$ 43,273	$ 44,410	$ 41,757	$ 40,915	$ 40,453
Kiosk	5,571	4,708	4,199	4,653	5,618
All Other	–	–	–	–	–
Unallocated	10,927	10,722	10,425	10,122	12,269
Total Depreciation & Amortization Expense	$ 59,771	$ 59,840	$ 56,381	$ 55,690	$ 58,340
Operating Earnings (Loss)					
Fine Jewelry	$ 108,082	$ 147,414	$ 153,739	$ 151,650	$ 145,816
Kiosk	20,402	29,030	25,951	(125,629)	20,335
All Other	6,443	6,824	6,603	7,894	9,705
Unallocated	(53,792)	(5,465)	(9,939)	(6,991)	(6,205)
Total Operating Earnings	$ 81,135	$ 177,803	$ 176,354	$ 26,924	$ 169,651
Assets					
Fine Jewelry	$ 1,119,679	$ 1,103,142	$ 1,055,755	$ 1,036,080	$ 1,022,790
Kiosk	124,415	117,125	111,238	96,485	238,048
All Other	39,261	35,670	37,737	38,217	38,788
Unallocated	$ 179,213	$ 124,963	$ 137,354	$ 123,324	$ 189,639
Total Assets	$ 1,462,568	$ 1,380,900	$ 1,342,084	$ 1,294,106	$ 1,489,265
Capital Expenditures					
Fine Jewelry	$ 54,942	$ 59,587	$ 42,535	$ 27,064	$ 41,602
Kiosk	7,750	8,650	6,038	6,383	3,644
All Other	–	–	–	–	–
Unallocated	20,026	14,887	12,215	10,132	8,913
Total Capital	$ 82,718	$ 83,124	$ 60,788	$ 43,579	$ 54,159

Source: Zale Corporation, *2006 Annual Report,* p. 7.

In addition, 32 stores of Bailey Banks & Biddle have been closed due to long-term positioning strategy and profitability issues, as well as three repair stores that were tested as a concept. However, in 2007, opening of 58 stores and 10 kiosks was planned as well as refurbishing or relocating approximately 170 stores and kiosks. These actions were expected to improve the company's market share.

Information Systems

In 2005 Zale Corporation began "updating its point-of-sale system in an initiative to provide more efficient checkouts for customers."[7] Zale continued this upgrade into 2006 with the implementation of a planning, merchandising, and allocation system in hopes of achieving supply chain benefits. The new modular system, expected to be fully implemented by 2009, is a different direction from their previously enterprise-wide system.

Zale has outsourced management of its LAN operations and desktop support, WAN management, enterprise server processing operations, client-server systems, and e-business hosting, to Affiliated Computer Services since 1996. ACS is a Fortune 1000 company specializing in business processing and information technology services in 47 countries. Zale renewed its contract with them in 2002.

The information collected by Zale Corporation's information systems allows management to monitor, review, and control operations for each store down to each individual transaction. Information such as store activity, transaction amounts, and merchandise sales by employee are available to senior management. For site selection, Zale implemented a software package in 2005 designed to aid in real estate decisions.

E-Commerce

As of May 25, 2005, Zale's e-commerce systems are outsourced to GSI Commerce Inc. "GSI assembles and manages e-commerce Web sites as well as customer service and order fulfillment services. The services provided by GSI cover all Zale brands and include Web hosting, site infrastructure development, site administration, order management, and the Web commerce engine."[8] The systems were previously operated by an in-house staff of 20 to 30 employees who now focus on the Internet marketing aspects of the site, rather than day-to-day site operations. However, currently only zales.com and baileybanksandbiddle.com allow purchase transactions over the Web. Although zales.com accounted for only 1 percent of total revenues in 2006, both it and baileybanksandbiddle.com experienced 30 percent growth from 2005.

The Web site for Zales Jewelers, zales.com, is designed as a merchant e-commerce model. This B2C Web site has purchasing features such as an online shopping basket and checkout. Customers can pay for orders with their credit card, Zales card, or Zales gift card. Purchases made on the site are protected by VeriSign Secured services that protect credit card and other confidential information through industry standard secure encryption technology. Customers are also protected by a "Secure Shopping Guarantee" which states that Zale will cover liability up to $50 for fraudulent charges not covered by their bank if the unauthorized credit card use occurred through no fault of their own. One feature lacking from the usual click-and-mortar e-business model is the option for in-store pickup. The site only allows for shoppers to have items delivered directly to the mailing address that the customer specifies.

Personalized shopping features included on the site are a "Design Your Own" section, allowing shoppers to create their own style of ring; a "Personalized" section, giving customers the ability to specify engravings on select products; and a "Wedding" section, focusing on wedding-related products. The site also features a store locator, a "Jewelry 101" buyer's guide, and a quick search for locating specific items by keyword or item number.

The Bailey Banks & Biddle Web site, offers functional content almost identical to zales.com. The difference between the two sites is mainly the product catalog and the site layout and graphics. The Gordon's Jewelers Web site (www.gordonsjewelers.com), the Zales Outlet Web site (www.zalesoutlet.com), the Peoples Jewelers Web site (www.peoplesjewellers.com), the Mappins Jewelers Web site (www.mappinsjewellers.com), and the Piercing Pagoda Web site (www.pagoda.com) don't allow online shopping; they provide strictly information. These sites each provide basic features such as a store locator, buyer guide, mailing list, and employment information. One problem that can be found on each of these sites is an unavailable, non-interactive product catalog. The Zale Corporation Web site (www.zalecorp.com) provides company information and shareholder information such as its annual reports.

Research and Development

Research and development is limited in scope in the jewelry industry. However, since the early part of the last decade, sales of watches and related products have continued to increase. While the increase of watch sales are partly attributable to the influence of fashion designers who have made watches a status symbol, technology will also play a role in increasing sales with the introduction of watches that have the capability to connect to the Internet. Research and development will play a role in the jewelry industry as consumers demand more technologically advanced products.

Conclusion

Zale desires to regain its once stellar performance in the jewelry retailing industry. Competition from retail giants and other specialty jewelry competitors have made it difficult for Zale to recover from its below average performance of the past six years. The lack of consistent leadership, unfocused strategy, and uncertain economy have also contributed to this burden. However, Zale has a new CEO and a new strategy with the goal of improving performance by repositioning the Zale brand, clearing out old inventory, strengthening profitability, and gaining market share. Zale is confident that if its strategy succeeds, it will once again be considered the king of the retail jewelry industry.

Acknowledgments

The author would like to acknowledge the contributions of Ross Hood, Philipp Kordes, Lonnie Lovell, Philip Mischke, Frank Morphis, Shea Owens, Fred Reyes, and Ana Salcido.

References

1. http://www.zalecorp.com/corporate/corporate.aspx?pid
2. Ibid.
3. Ibid.
4. Ibid.
5. Zale Corporation, *2006 Annual Report*, p. 4.
6. Zale Corporation, *2006 Annual Report*, p. 5.
7. Power, D., "Zale Dips Toe in New Pos.," *WWD*, 0149-5380, p. 14, Dec. 14, 2005.
8. http://www.gsicommerce.com/news/newsDetail.jsp?rpt=rpt_press_release_detail.jsp?newsId=21822038

19 Gap Inc. — 2007

Sharynn Tomlin
Angelo State University

GPS

www.gap.com

Headquartered in San Francisco, California and owner of Gap, Old Navy, GapBody, GapKids, BabyGap, and Banana Republic stores and brands, Gap, Inc. is a struggling specialty retailing company operating about 3,000 stores primarily in the United States. Retail and outlet stores sell company brands of casual apparel, accessories, and personal care products for men, women, and children. The company provides a wide range of family clothing products, including denim, khakis, and T-shirts, fashion apparel, shoes, accessories, intimate apparel, and personal care products. The company offers products through gap.com, bananarepublic.com, and oldnavy.com Web sites in the United States.

Gap operates stores in the United States, Canada, the United Kingdom, France, and Japan. All Gap clothing is private-label merchandise made specifically for the company. From the design board to store displays, Gap controls all aspects of its trademark casual look. In July 2007, Gap Inc. introduced a credit card that consumers can use outside its own stores and still earn rewards at its stores. Rival firms such as Nordstrom, Lowe's, and Saks also have introduced similar cards and Gap is trying to catch up to these and other competitors that have adapted more quickly to changing customer tastes over recent years. Gap is struggling to reverse consecutive years of declining sales and profits. Its net income for the first quarter of 2007 fell another 26 percent to negative $45 million, and the company closed its Forth & Towne chain. Gap Inc. is looking for a new CEO to replace interim CEO Robert Fisher.

History

In 1969, Doris and Don Fisher entered the clothing retail business with the vision of creating a unique shopping experience. The idea behind the first Gap store, founded in San Francisco, was to provide fresh, casual, American style. By 1970, sales reached $2 million and the Fishers opened their second store in San Jose, California. In 1980, Gap Inc. dropped Levis and other brands and began focusing on its own private label. In 1983, Gap acquired Banana Republic and a year later entered the international market by opening a store in London, England and Vancouver, British Columbia, and annual sales reached $1 billion.

In 1990, Gap opened BabyGap and debuted the GapKids store in San Francisco. Two years later, Gap became the second largest selling apparel brand in the world. In 1993, Gap continued its global expansion by entering the French marketplace. The following year Gap introduced Old Navy with the first store opening in Colma, California, and in

Canada. The company opened its 20,000-square-foot Gap stores in Tokyo in 1996. In 1998, Gap launched its first store in Alaska to complete its presence in all 50 states.

In 2005, the company revamped its online stores, offering more convenience and interactive shopping. That same year, Gap introduced Forth & Towne in Chicago and New York. The store caters to baby-boomer women, offering stylish, age-appropriate clothing that is especially appealing to their femininity and individuality. The following year, Gap added PiperLime to its online brands.

Disappointing performance and negative press relating to labor practices led the company to further undergo major changes. Cyclical and season sales prompted the company to seek new means of balancing their holiday products with more traditional gift-giving products. Gap international store sales were negatively impacted by weak markets in Europe and Japan. In 2004, Gap sold all of its German operations to H&M, its major competitor in Europe. However, the decline carried into 2005 with 2 percent decrease in net sales and with the closing of more than 100 underperforming stores.

The years 2006 and 2007 were disappointing with falling sales and profits. Then on January 22, 2007, Gap CEO Paul Pressler resigned and Robert Fisher became interim CEO. In February 2007, Marka Hasen replaced Cynthia Harris to lead the Gap division, and the company discontinued its Forth & Towne stores and brands.

Mission Statement

Gap, Inc. strives to be a leader in the specialty family clothing industry and has strongly espoused the importance of their customers and employees. Their mission statement exemplifies this philosophy:

> Gap, Inc. is a brand-builder. We create emotional connections with customers around the world through inspiring product design, unique store experiences and compelling marketing. Our purpose? Simply, to make it easy for you to express your personal style throughout your life. We have more than 150,000 passionate, talented people around the world who help bring this purpose to life for our customers. Across our company and embedded in our culture are key values that guide our success: integrity, respect, open-mindedness, quality and balance. Everyday, we honor these values and exemplify our belief in doing business in a socially responsible way.

Source: www.gap.com

Code of Business Ethics

Gap, Inc. has also recognized that strong business ethics is one of the most important company issues and has a well-established code of ethics, translated in 65 different languages that addresses the different aspects and guidelines about its purpose, responsibilities, laws, reporting code violations, retaliation, policy changes and waivers. The code proposes a responsible and ethical work environment for all Gap, Inc. employees and directors and addresses the following most common ethical problems: conflict of interest, discrimination or harassment, workplace violence, complaints to government agencies, international trade regulations, bribes and improper payments, antitrust laws and selling practices, product integrity, commerical transactions, brand protection, and political contributions and activities.

Organizational Structure

Recent organizational changes have challenged the company to seek the most efficient management for the growing Gap organization. A copy of the current organizational structure is shown in Exhibit 1. A current listing of company stores is shown in Exhibit 2.

EXHIBIT 1 Organizational Structure

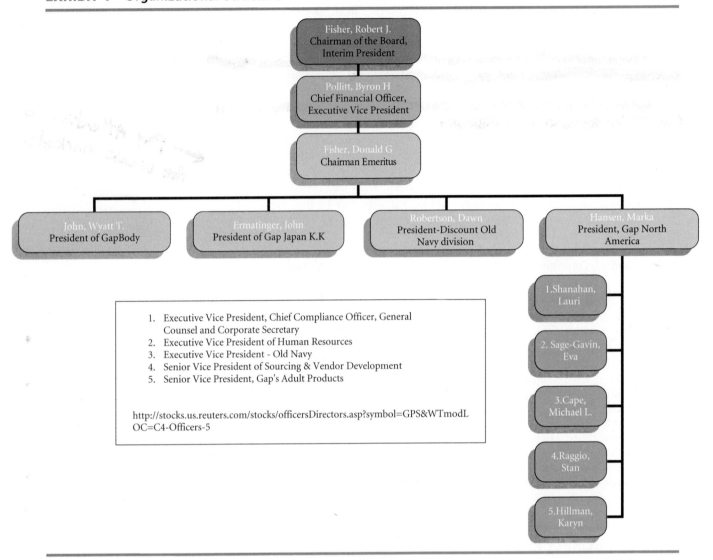

1. Executive Vice President, Chief Compliance Officer, General Counsel and Corporate Secretary
2. Executive Vice President of Human Resources
3. Executive Vice President - Old Navy
4. Senior Vice President of Sourcing & Vendor Development
5. Senior Vice President, Gap's Adult Products

http://stocks.us.reuters.com/stocks/officersDirectors.asp?symbol=GPS&WTmodLOC=C4-Officers-5

Source: www.gap.com

EXHIBIT 2 Gap Inc. Facilities

Q4
GAP INC. STORE COUNT, AS OF FEBRUARY 3, 2007
(Updated Quarterly)

TOTAL STORES

GAP	
UNITED STATES	1,199
CANADA	94
BANANA REPUBLIC	
UNITED STATES	495
CANADA	26
OLD NAVY	
UNITED STATES	949
CANADA	63

continued

EXHIBIT 2   Gap Inc. Facilities—continued

FORTH & TOWNE	
UNITED STATES	19
INTERNATIONAL	
UNITED KINGDOM	135
FRANCE	33
JAPAN	118
TOTAL	3,131

Source: www.gap.com

Industry Issues

Edward P. Lazear, Chairman of the Council of Economic Advisers, has stated that "Unemployment remains remarkably low, business inventories are lean compared with sales, and now industrial production is on the rise. The economy has experienced over five years of uninterrupted growth, averaging 2.9 percent per year since the expansion began in 2001 and real GDP is projected to grow at about the historic average in 2008 and for the remaining decade."[1] Overall inflation, as measured by the Consumer Price Index (CPI), has been relatively higher than originally expected, and recent forecasts have emphasized that the core CPI (excluding volatile energy and food prices) has remained moderate. Furthermore, economic data have shown that consumer purchasing has seen a gain of 6.9 percent which is the highest since 2000.[2] A significant portion of all apparel acquisitions are with credit cards. However, consumer perceptions of the credit markets fell sharply in March, 2007 according to the Personal Credit Index, which fell "15 points from 105 in January and 105 in February to 90 in March. This is the lowest level for the Personal Credit Index since November, 2006."[3]

Most industry trends affecting the apparel industry are driven by changing demographics, consumer preferences and spending patterns. According to census data, the U.S. population is expected to grow to over 310 million in 2015. This trend is also observable in other countries. Demographically, while much of the boom in retail sales is attributable to the 77 million baby boomers, there has been a shift in their purchasing priorities to children's educational costs, retirement, elder care, health care, housing, and leisure activities. However, while this group spends less disposable income on clothing, they still remain the biggest per capita consumers of apparel.

Globally, the United States faces strong competition mainly from Asian countries with low labor costs as shown in recent (2007) trade statistics. The United States is currently experiencing an industry trade deficit of approximately $103,171,126,000, an export growth of 5.8 percent and an import growth of 6.5 percent as compared to countries such as China and Vietnam with export growth rates in excess of 20 percent and strong trade surpluses. The elimination of trade quotas in 2005 has created a dramatic shift in the apparel industry. Outsourcing and new distribution channels have opened new doors for those in the industry willing to take advantage of the opportunities and risk. Companies that will gain most of this development are those that are able to shorten their production without sacrificing their quality and value. Companies specializing in "high-end products and capable of outsourcing production or managing the design and marketing aspects of their business"[4] are major competitiors exhibiting solid performance and market share.

In the apparel industry, low labor cost in manufacturing is not enough to be successful for companies involved in fashion. Companies must have "sufficient product differentiation and global branding in order to demand a higher price. They must also take into consideration how much of their product to supply, since economies of scale make it less costly and more profitable to produce a greater amount; however, by producing less they can create a sense of exclusivity and additional value."[5] Given these conditions, companies such as Nike, Inc., VF Corporation, and Levi Strauss appear to be fairing better than the average.

Consumers are obsessed with promotional pricing. For many apparel products, the consumer is willing to wait for price reductions before purchasing. Vendors, consequently, have to lower the prices at introduction and finally need even larger end-of-season mark-downs, when they try to move inventory out of the stores to make way for new assortments. According to a study by the U.S. Department of Commerce, the expenditures for apparel and footwear recently declined from about 7.5 percent of total consumption expenditures to about 4 percent. Furthermore, there is an increasing amount of discounters and outlets that penetrate the market and offer low prices.[6]

In the past, retailers would stock merchandise well in advance of the season in which they would be worn. Today, consumers tend to purchase as the need arises, with little consideration of advance purchases, requiring companies to be more informed about changing attitudes and preferences. Furthermore, while the benefits of offshore production have been more cost efficient, the increase lead time for production has made it more difficult for manufacturers to respond to immediate customer needs. Therefore, domestic production is required to fill these more immediate changes, small orders, and seasonal or special items.

Distribution

Distribution is a key factor for an apparel manufacturer. Customers demand immediate availability of apparel products and when that availability is not present, the customer will often not delay the purchase but look for other substitute products. This immediacy or quick response time translates to maintaining higher levels of inventory. However, companies realize that lean inventories result in cost efficiencies that can be passed on to the customer. Accordingly, companies are developing new point-of-sale technologies that enable better tracking of inventory and communication between the retailer and vendor to supply inventory as needed. Other new technologies in the planning stage include improvements for custom production, mass customization, and Internet-based communications networks linking manufacturers to suppliers, allowing retailers to better tailors their products to the needs of the shopper.

In general, women's apparel is usually sold in department stores and men's apparel in discount stores. However, as Internet applications continue to grow, it is forecast that sales through traditional channels will decrease. The biggest issue with Internet purchases is still that are intangible: Consumers cannot see, touch, and try on products they are considering buying.

Competition

The Gap, Inc. faces strong competition from Abercrombie & Fitch Co., American Eagle, Nordstrom's, and TJX Companies (Marshalls and TK Maxx).

Abercrombie & Fitch Co.

Founded in 1892 and is headquartered in New Albany, Ohio. Abercrombie & Fitch Co., through its subsidiaries, operates as a specialty retailer in the United States and Canada. Its stores sell casual apparel, such as knit shirts, graphic T-shirts, jeans, woven shirts, and shorts; and personal care and other accessories for men, women, and kids under the Abercrombie & Fitch, Abercrombie, Hollister, and RUEHL brands. In addition, the company's stores offer films, photos, postcards, desktop images, and screen savers. The company operates 850 stores in 49 states, the District of Columbia, and Canada.

American Eagle

American Eagle was once a provider of outdoor gear, but now the mall-based retailer sells casual apparel and accessories (shirts, jeans, shorts, sweaters, skirts, footwear, belts, and bags) aimed at men and women ages 15–25. Virtually all of the company's products bear its private-label brand names: American Eagle Outfitters and AE. The company operates more than 900 American Eagle stores in the U.S. and Canada and plans to open more. Direct sales come from the company's Web site and its *AE Magazine*, a lifestyle magazine that doubles as a catalogue.

EXHIBIT 3   Gap Competitors

Family Clothing Retail Competitors

Company	Revenues	Gross Margin	Net Income	PE Ratio
TJX Companies, Inc. (New)	$ 17,404,637,000	24.079411	738,039,000	16.68
The Gap, Inc.	15,943,000,000	35.432478	778,000,000	22.24
Nordstrom, Inc.	8,560,698,000	37.458967	677,999,000	18.83
Abercrombie & Fitch Co.	3,318,158,000	66.573261	422,186,000	15.37
American Eagle Outfitters, Inc. (New)	2,794,409,000	47.968247	387,359,000	13.47

Source: Adapted from the companies' *Form 10-K*'s.

TJX Companies, Inc.

TJX Companies, Inc., the industry's third largest leader in sales, is considered the world's number one off-price family clothing store with operations in the United States and internationally. The company operates 799 T.J. Maxx stores, selling brand-name family apparel and accessories, women's shoes, domestic furnishings, jewelry and giftware. Marshalls, an off-price family apparel chain, operates 701 stores and HomeGoods operates 251 off-price home fashion stores. T.K. Maxx operates 197 stores in the United Kingdom and Ireland. A.J. Wright operates 152 off-price family apparel stores. The company also has 58 HomeSense stores and 174 Winners Apparel Ltd. stores in Canada.

Nordstrom, Inc.

Another industry leader is Nordstrom, Inc. Founded in 1901 by the Nordstrom family in Seattle, Washington, the company started out in the shoe business and has continued to expand, with great attention given to the quality of the store's product and customer service.

Other lesser competitors for Gap and their associated subsidiaries (Banana Republic and Old Navy) include Eddie Bauer, J. Crew, Limited Brands, Inc., Steinmart, Ann Taylor, Talbots, and Target. A summary of the major competitors and relevelant financial data is shown in Exhibit 3.

Internal Issues

Finance

Although Gap Inc. had lackluster results in 2005, Gap generated $1 billion in free cash flow, which enabled the company to repurchase $2 billion shares and double dividends to 18 cents. Due to these results, the company plans to continue the repurchasing program and also anticipates increasing the dividends to 32 cents.

Since 2002, the Gap Cooperation eliminated $2.9 billion in debt and in contrast has generated $3 billion in cash and investments. The remaining debt of just $513 million at the end of 2005 and only $188 million on October 28, 2006 helped the company to regain a high investment grade rating from Standard & Poor's and Moody's as well.

From 2001 until 2004, the company increased their net sales from $13.8 to $16.3 billion and the net earnings from a loss of $25 million to a profit of $1,150 billion in 2004, but in 2005 both figures declined. The net sales declined by 2 percent, the net earnings by 3 percent. Although the net sales declined by 2 percent; the cost of goods sold increased by 2.7 percent, which led to a decline of the gross margin by 2.6 percent. The income statement for the past three years is shown in Exhibit 4.

As of June 2007, Gap Inc. experienced a 26 percent decrease in net profits for the first quarter ended May 5. Net income also declined to $178 million from $242 million in the same period last year, while sales gained 3.5 percent to $3.56 billion from $3.44 billion. Furthermore, store sales declined 4 percent and earnings per diluted share

EXHIBIT 4 Gap Income Statement 2005–2007

As Reported Annual Income Statement	02/03/2007	01/28/2006	01/29/2005
Net sales	$ 15,943,000	16,023,000	16,267,000
Cost of goods sold & occupancy expenses	10,294,000	10,154,000	9,886,000
Gross profit	5,649,000	5,869,000	6,381,000
Operating expenses	4,475,000	4,124,000	4,296,000
Loss on early retirement of debt	–	–	(105,000)
Interest expense	41,000	45,000	167,000
Interest income	131,000	93,000	59,000
Earnings before income taxes	1,264,000	1,793,000	1,872,000
Current income taxes-federal	450,000	657,000	589,000
Current income taxes-state	64,000	63,000	73,000
Current income taxes-foreign	50,000	45,000	114,000
Total current income taxes	564,000	765,000	776,000
Deferred income taxes (benefit)-federal	(77,000)	(44,000)	(38,000)
Deferred income taxes (benefit)-state	(8,000)	4,000	(19,000)
Deferred income taxes (benefit)-foreign	7,000	(45,000)	3,000
Total deferred income taxes	(78,000)	(85,000)	(54,000)
Income taxes	486,000	680,000	722,000
Net earnings (loss)	**778,000**	**1,113,000**	**1,150,000**
Weighted average shares outstanding-basic	831,087	881,057.753	893,356.815
Weighted average shares outstanding-diluted	835,973	902,305.691	991,121.573
Year end shares outstanding	813,870	856,986	860,559.077
Net earnings (loss) per share-basic	0.94	1.26	1.29
Net earnings (loss) per share-diluted	0.93	1.24	1.21
Dividends per share	0.32	0.18	0.09
Total number of employees	154,000	153,000	152,000
Number of common stockholders	9,847	10,246	10,423

Source: http://www.mergentonline.com

dropped to 22 cents from 28 cents a year earlier. According to the annual report, sales per square foot at Gap Inc. last year were $395, down from $412 last year and $428 in 2005.[7]

Marketing

Gap's marketing strategy is to reconnect with customers across each brand through product, place, price, and promotion. Gap plans to rebuild its iconic brands, have solid operations, hire talented people, win back disappointed customers and create value for their shareholders.

Gap, Inc. owns three of the strongest apparel brands on the market today—Gap, Banana Republic, and Old Navy. All three stores have always emphasized simplicity, style, and emotion as exemplified in their well-known television commercials. Product quality has always been a paramount priority. Therefore, it focuses on creating more approachable fashion products. Gap is continuing to expand by introducing a line of personal care products through a partnership with Inter Perfumes, Inc. In 2004, Gap introduced three new women's jeans fits and launched a super soft denim line called Left Weave. Gap continued its expansion by introducing a collection of high-quality, Italian leather handbags, and launched Old Navy Special Edition denim that features better

EXHIBIT 5   Gap Inc. Balance Sheet (All numbers in thousands)

Period Ending	Feb. 03, 2007	Jan. 28, 2006	Jan. 29, 2005
Assets			
Current Assets			
Cash and Cash Equivalents	$ 2,074,000	2,090,000	3,260,000
Short-Term Investments	570,000	952,000	817,000
Net Receivables	156,000	–	–
Inventory	1,796,000	1,696,000	1,814,000
Other Current Assets	433,000	501,000	413,000
Total Current Assets	5,029,000	5,239,000	6,304,000
Long-Term Investments	–	–	–
Property, Plant and Equipment	3,197,000	3,246,000	3,376,000
Goodwill	–	–	–
Intangible Assets	–	–	–
Accumulated Amortization	–	–	–
Other Assets	131,000	336,000	368,000
Deferred Long-Term Asset Charges	187,000	–	–
Total Assets	**8,544,000**	**8,821,000**	**10,048,000**
Liabilities			
Current Liabilities			
Accounts Payable	1,947,000	1,942,000	2,242,000
Short/Current Long-Term Debt	325,000	–	–
Other Current Liabilities	–	–	–
Total Current Liabilities	2,272,000	1,942,000	2,242,000
Long-Term Debt	188,000	513,000	1,886,000
Other Liabilities	910,000	941,000	984,000
Deferred Long-Term Liability Charges	–	–	–
Minority Interest	–	–	–
Negative Goodwill	–	–	–
Total Liabilities	**3,370,000**	**3,396,000**	**5,112,000**
Stockholders' Equity			
Misc Stocks, Options, Warrants	–	–	–
Redeemable Preferred Stock	–	–	–
Preferred Stock	–	–	–
Common Stock	55,000	54,000	49,000
Retained Earnings	8,646,000	8,133,000	7,181,000
Treasury Stock	(6,235,000)	(5,210,000)	(3,238,000)
Capital Surplus	2,631,000	2,402,000	904,000
Other Stockholders' Equity	77,000	46,000	40,000
Total Stockholders' Equity	5,174,000	5,425,000	4,936,000
Total Liabilities and SE	**$ 8,544,000**	**8,821,000**	**10,048,000**

Source: http://finance.yahoo.com

EXHIBIT 6   Gap Segment Financial Data (2004–2006)

(in millions)	FY2004				
	Q1	Q2	Q3	Q4	FY2004
Gap North America	$ 1,278	$ 1,288	$ 1,432	$ 1,748	$ 5,746
Banana Republic North America	503	528	538	700	2,269
Old Navy North America	1,532	1,553	1,670	1,992	6,747
International	355	352	340	458	1,505
Total Gap Inc.	$ 3,668	$ 3,721	$ 3,980	$ 4,898	$ 16,267

(in millions)	FY2005				
	Q1	Q2	Q3	Q4	FY2005
Gap North America	$ 1,200	$ 1,214	$ 1,349	$ 1,646	$ 5,409
Banana Republic North America	512	532	537	706	2,287
Old Navy North America	1,573	1,611	1,648	2,024	6,856
International	341	359	324	439	1,463
Other (1)	–	–	2	6	8
Total Gap Inc.	$ 3,626	$ 3,716	$ 3,860	$ 4,821	$ 16,023

(in millions)	FY2006				
	Q1	Q2	Q3	Q4	FY2006
Gap North America	$ 1,121	$ 1,155	$ 1,282	$ 1,576	$ 5,134
Banana Republic North America	518	571	590	808	2,487
Old Navy North America	1,503	1,649	1,644	2,033	6,829
International (2)	296	339	335	496	1,466
Other (1)	3	2	5	17	27
Total Gap Inc.	$ 3,441	$ 3,716	$ 3,856	$ 4,930	$ 15,943

Note: Prior periods subject to adjustments for rounding purposes. Annual amounts agree to *10-K*.

1. Other includes Forth & Towne beginning August 2005, Business Direct, and Piperlime.com beginning October 2006.

2. Includes franchise business beginning September 2006.

Source: http://www.gapinc.com/public/documents/GPS_Quarterly_Sales.pdf

EXHIBIT 7   Geographic Revenues

Geographic Analysis	Revenues		
Report Date	**02/03/2007**	**01/28/2006**	**01/29/2005**
Currency	**U.S. Dollar**	**U.S. Dollar**	**U.S. Dollar**
Scale	**Thousands**	**Thousands**	**Thousands**
Europe	792,000	825,000	879,000
Asia	642,000	617,000	591,000
Other	32,000	21,000	35,000
Total	15,943,000	16,023,000	16,267,000

Source: www.gap.com

washes, details and embroidery. To reach more custumers Gap rolled out Old Navy Maternity, improved plus-size offerings, and will continue to create new brands.

Gap strives to reach new customers by expanding locally and internationally. One major area of interest is exploring opportunities in China and pursuing franchising options in more fragmented markets. Gap is testing stand-alone petite stores in Boston, Los Angeles, Seattle, St. Louis, and Washington D.C, and introduced six Banana Republic and thirteen Gap stores in Japan. The company is also seeking stronger relationships with vendors, quicker response times by optimize store fleets, and adopting more efficient inventory management systems.

Promotionally, Gap is well known for their inventive marketing using black-and-white images and celebrities in both print and visual media and sponsoring commercial projects such as Bravo Network's Project Runway and Sony Film's *Memoirs of a Geisha*. Old Navy stores were upgraded, along with their visual merchandising and supported by creative marketing. Gap stores have enhanced their lighting and added new fixtures. Another major improvement is the new online system, which was reported by the *New York Times* as one of "the best e-commerce sites in retail." The concept was quickly adopted by customers and became the largest online apparel retailer in the United States, generating $600 million in net sales in 2005. The Web sites offer more interactive experiences for shoppers, including a service that will recommend clothing choices based on an individual customer's preferences and size. Gap continues to enhance its online Web sites and launch new features.

Management

On January 23, 2007, Gap Inc. announced that it was replacing CEO Paul Pressler with Robert Fisher, interim chairman of the board during the search for a new CEO. The board's search committee is led by Adrian Bellamy, chairman of The Body Shop International and includes founder Donald Fisher. The company has focused efforts on recruiting a chief executive officer with extensive retailing and merchandising experience in apparel, who understands the creative process and can effectively execute strategies in large, complex environments while maintaining strong financial discipline. Robert Fisher stressed his personal ties and 30-year professional history in operating roles at the company and as a board member. He started with the company in 1980 as a store manager and worked his way up the company's merchandising ranks and senior executive leadership positions, including president of Banana Republic and the Gap units. Jack Calhoun, an executive vice president for marketing and merchandising has been named interim president of the Banana Republic unit. Gap, Inc. has more than 150,000 employees.

Conclusion

Interim CEO Fisher stated in June 2007 that the Gap division is now concentrating on a core customer between the ages of 24 and 34, "with the late twenties as the sweet spot." Previously, the Gap also targeted shoppers as young as 18, a spokeswoman said. Likewise, at Old Navy the company is defining its core adult customer as being "20-somethings," instead of starting at 18. Children's apparel also continues as a major focus.[8] Additionally, under pressure to bring more customers into the store, Gap has introduced their own credit card allowing customers to both purchase and earn rewards. The new card will have the VISA logo and be issued by General Electric Company.

Among the members of the board advising the company are two former retail executives with impressive track recorders: Domenico De Sole, former president and chief executive of Gucci Group, who reinvigorated the iconic luxury goods retailer, and Bob Martin, who retired from Wal-Mart in 1999 after launching the mass market chain's international wing in 1993 and rethinking the chain's logistics.

Acknowledgments

The author would like to acknowledge the contributions to this case from Brisa Arvizo, Veronika Friedrich, Hector Gonzalez, and Jörg Menke.

References

1. http://www.whitehouse.gov/cea/forecast20070606.pdf
2. http://americandemographics/
3. http://www.prnewswire.com
4. http://globaledge.msu.edu/industries/background
5. Ibid.
6. Standard & Poor's *Industry Surveys: Apparel and Footwear*, 2004.
7. Joanna Ramey, *Daily News Record*, June 11, 2007 p. 97.
8. Ibid.

20 Wendy's International — 2007

Vijaya Narapareddy
University of Denver

WEN

www.wendys.com

Wendy's is famous for its square made-to-order single-, double- or triple-hamburgers, chicken sandwiches, chili, baked potatoes, and desserts. While competitors like McDonald's were unsuccessful with their spicy chicken sandwich, Wendy's does really well with their sandwich. Millions of fast-food customers love Wendy's old-fashioned menu choices, but the company has been on a roller-coaster ride of late. Following a wave of layoffs and cost cutting, Wendy's announcement that it might be acquired sent its stock price to new heights in July 2007. Wendy's net income dropped 58 percent in 2006 to $94 million as the company closed 199 restaurants during the year.

What ails Wendy's, which annually receives accolades for the best-tasting food and is considered the highest-ranked brand in the industry?

History

Headquartered in Dublin, Ohio, Wendy's was founded by Dave Thomas in 1969 and named after his second daughter, Melinda Lou Thomas, who was fondly nicknamed "Wendy" by her older siblings. This Ohio-based restaurant chain experienced fast growth, opening more than 3,500 restaurants by 1985. As of December 31, 2006 it operates in the United States, and 20 foreign countries and territories. Its domestic and international locations are listed in Exhibit 1.

EXHIBIT 1 Wendy's Worldwide Locations

	Wendy's	
United States of America	Company	Franchise
Alabama	–	98
Alaska	–	8
Arizona	48	54
Arkansas	–	64
California	66	228
Colorado	47	82
Connecticut	5	43
Delaware	–	15
Florida	200	302
Georgia	53	243
Hawaii	7	–
Idaho	–	29
Illinois	94	87
Indiana	5	171

continued

EXHIBIT 1   Wendy's Worldwide Locations—continued

Iowa	–	47
Kansas	19	55
Kentucky	3	139
Louisiana	70	65
Maine	4	17
Maryland	–	115
Massachusetts	61	34
Michigan	30	248
Minnesota	–	69
Mississippi	8	90
Missouri	24	49
Montana	–	16
Nebraska	–	34
Nevada	–	47
New Hampshire	4	23
New Jersey	17	126
New Mexico	–	38
New York	67	156
North Carolina	40	206
North Dakota	–	8
Ohio	89	353
Oklahoma	–	41
Oregon	24	31
Pennsylvania	80	187
Rhode Island	10	12
South Carolina	–	128
South Dakota	–	9
Tennessee	–	183
Texas	84	314
Utah	61	23
Vermont	–	6
Virginia	48	164
Washington	27	46
West Virginia	22	50
Wisconsin	–	65
Wyoming	–	14
District of Columbia	–	6
Domestic Subtotal	**1,317**	**4,638**

	2006 Wendy's	
International Locations: Country/Territory	Company-owned	Franchises
Aruba	–	3
Bahamas	–	7

continued

EXHIBIT 1   Wendy's Worldwide Locations—continued

Canada	146	231
Cayman Islands	–	2
Costa Rica	–	2
Dominican Republic	–	1
El Salvador	–	12
Guam	2	-
Guatemala	–	6
Honduras	–	24
Indonesia	–	20
Jamaica	–	2
Japan	–	78
Mexico	–	17
New Zealand	–	16
Panama	–	6
Philippines	–	40
Puerto Rico	–	61
Venezuela	–	39
Virgin Islands	–	3
International Subtotal	148	570
Domestic Subtotal	1,317	4,638
Grand Total	1,465	5,208

Source: http://www.wendys-invest.com/fin/10k

Wendy's is credited with being "first" on several fronts. It was the first in the industry to introduce the convenience of a "drive-through window" in 1970, the "99 cent value menu" in 1988, and the Superbar (an all-you-can-eat salad bar) in the late 1980s. While the super value menu is a resounding success and copied by others in the industry, the Superbar had to be discontinued in most of the Wendy's restaurants by 1998. In the 1980s, Wendy's climbed to fame with its commercials, like "Where's the Beef?" and "the Soviet Fashion Show." Wendy's was also the first to demonstrate its commitment to providing healthy food choices in August 2006, when it announced that it would voluntarily switch to using healthy oils in the preparation of most of its food items, whereas industry leader McDonald's continues to fry in trans fat oils as of mid-2007.

The fast-paced growth the company experienced under the leadership of founder Dave Thomas lost steam in the late 1980s, prompting founder Dave Thomas to come out of retirement in 1989 and do commercials for the company until his death on January 8, 2002. U.S. sales declined with the occurrence of unfortunate events, such as the gay and lesbian boycott in 1997, the tragic massacre at Wendy's in 2000, and fraudulent claims filed by a customer in March 2005 claiming that she found a fingertip in her chili bought at a Wendy's restaurant in San Jose, California. As a result, Wendy's closed several of its restaurants.

As shown in Exhibit 2, Wendy's total worldwide sales decline from $2.5 billion in 2004 to $2.4 billion in 2006 was primarily fueled by revenue losses in the U.S. market. In contrast, the company's revenues increased in Canada and other international markets. In 2006, earnings from continuing operations (before taxes) increased by approximately $7.5 million overseas, but declined by approximately $102 million in the United States Details are shown in Exhibit 3.

EXHIBIT 2 Revenues by Segment

(In Thousands)	U.S.	Canada	Other International	Total
2006				
Revenues	**$2,196,949**	**$226,502**	**$15,826**	**$2,439,277**
Long-lived assets	**1,170,609**	**54,329**	**1,390**	**1,226,328**
2005				
Revenues	$2,223,030	$218,091	$14,297	$2,455,418
Long-lived assets	1,199,957	147,080	1,437	1,348,474
2004				
Revenues	$2,284,772	$203,572	$13,814	$2,502,158

Source: http://www.wendys-invest.com/fin/10k

EXHIBIT 3 Earnings from Continuing Operations Before Taxes

(In Thousands)	2006	2005	2004
Domestic	**$32,173**	$133,996	$165,891
Foreign	**10,306**	2,788	10,299
Total	**$42,479**	$136,784	$176,190

Source: http://www.wendys-invest.com/fin/10k

Restaurant Closures

In 2006, Wendy's closed 162 franchises and 37 company-owned restaurants, a total of 199 or approximately 3 percent of the 6,673 restaurants held. The number of restaurant closures during 2004, 2005, and 2006 are given in Exhibit 4.

Restaurant data displayed in Exhibit 5 shows that the number of restaurants declined in all markets, suggesting that restaurant closures extended worldwide. Furthermore, both company-owned restaurants and franchises were targeted for closures. In 2006, 34 company-owned restaurants and 29 franchises were closed in the United States, with an additional 3 company-owned and 7 franchises internationally. During the same year, a total of 122 restaurants (26 company-owned and 96 franchises) were opened, primarily in North America. No details of the new restaurant locations are available. Wendy's also plans to focus expansion of its core operations in North America by opening 80 to 110 new company-owned restaurants and franchises in 2007. In spite of the closures, Wendy's average net

EXHIBIT 4 Restaurant Closures

	2006	2005	2004
Franchise restaurants in operation—beginning of year	**5,244**	5,184	5,016
Franchises opened	**96**	155	226
Franchises closed	**(162)**	(89)	(88)
Net transfers within the system	**30**	(6)	30
Franchise restaurants in operation—end of year	**5,208**	5,244	5,184
Company-owned restaurants—end of year	**1,465**	1,502	1,487
Total system-wide restaurants—end of year	**6,673**	6,746	6,671

Source: http://www.wendys-invest.com/fin/10k

EXHIBIT 5   Restaurant Data

Other Information

Restaurant Data	2006	2005	2004*	2003	2002	2001	2000	1999	1998*	1997	1996
North American Wendy's open at year-end											
Company	**1,463**	1,497	1,482	1,460	1,316	1,223	1,148	1,082	1,021	1,186	1,306
Franchise	**4,869**	4,898	4,837	4,668	4,587	4,431	4,271	4,079	3,922	3,634	3,292
International Wendy's open at year-end											
Company	**2**	5	5	5	4	5	5	30	15	16	9
Franchise	**339**	346	347	348	346	384	368	336	375	371	326
Total Wendy's	**6,673**	6,746	6,671	6,481	6,253	6,043	5,792	5,527	5,333	5,207	4,933
Average net sales per domestic Wendy's restaurant (in thousands)											
Company	**$1,400**	1,365	1,416	1,389	1,387	1,337	1,314	1,284	1,174	1,111	1,049
Franchise	**$1,276**	1,263	1,291	1,268	1,251	1,164	1,130	1,102	1,031	1,017	978
Total domestic	**$1,303**	1,286	1,319	1,294	1,280	1,199	1,167	1,138	1,062	1,042	998

* *Fiscal year includes 53 weeks.*
Source: http://www.wendys-invest.com/fin/10k

sales per restaurant have been on an upward trend. In the United States, net sales increased from $1.37 million in 2005 to $1.4 million for each company-owned restaurant and from approximately $1.26 million in 2005 to $1.28 million per franchise. No comparable data is available for international operations.

Executive Officers

Kerrii Anderson became Wendy's CEO in November 2006 when her predecessor, Jack Schuessler, retired after six straight quarters of declining sales. Exhibit 6 provides a list of Wendy's executive officers. Note that Wendy's operates using a geographic-based divisional structure, but the division heads do not have the title of president.

EXHIBIT 6   Wendy's Executive Officers

Name	Age	Position with Company
1. Kerrii B. Anderson	49	Chief Executive Officer and President
2. David J. Near	37	Chief Operations Officer
3. Jonathan F. Catherwood	45	Executive Vice President and Treasurer
4. Jeffrey M. Cava	55	Executive Vice President
5. Leon M. McCorkle, Jr.	66	Executive Vice President, General Counsel and Secretary
6. Ian B. Rowden	47	Executive Vice President and Chief Marketing Officer
7. Brendan P. Foley, Jr.	47	Senior Vice President, General Controller and Assistant Secretary
8. Edward L. Austin		Senior Vice President, Operations – South Region
9. James C. Hartenstein		Senior Vice President, International
10. Neil G. Lester		Senior Vice President, Operations – Canada
11. John N. Peters		Senior Vice President, Operations – West Region
12. Tom Spero		Senior Vice President, Operations – North Region

continued

EXHIBIT 6   Wendy's Executive Officers—continued

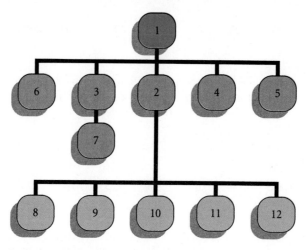

Source: http://www.wendys-invest.com/fin/10k

Financial Performance

Wendy's operates internationally with a combination of company-owned and franchised restaurants. Its total revenues declined from $2.5 million in 2004 to $2.45 million in 2005 and $2.43 million in 2006. This decline is evident in both company-owned and franchised restaurants. Exhibit 7 provides details.

However, Wendy's risk management team has fared well in managing its foreign exchange exposure. Instead of foreign currency translation losses, Wendy's saw gains from $55.9 million in 2004 to $5.4 million in 2006 as shown in Exhibit 8. Note that Wendy's has a policy forbidding trading or speculating in foreign currency and does not hedge foreign currency translation, but attempts to control the negative impact of volatility in the currency markets through the use of derivative products.

EXHIBIT 7   Revenue Declines

(In Thousands)	2006	2005	2004
Sales:			
Sales from company operated restaurants	**$2,058,454**	$2,046,592	$2,096,734
Product sales to franchisees	**96,153**	91,773	97,297
	$2,154,607	$2,138,365	$2,194,031
Franchise revenues:			
Rents and royalties	**281,072**	291,179	298,230
Franchise fees	**1,208**	4,449	4,285
Net gains on sales of properties to franchisees	**2,390**	21,425	5,612
	284,670	317,053	308,127
Total revenues	**$2,439,277**	$2,455,418	$2,502,158

Source: http://www.wendys-invest.com/fin/10k

EXHIBIT 8   Foreign Currency Translation Gains

	Years ended December 31, 2006, January 1, 2006, and January 2, 2005		
(In Thousands)	2006	2005	2004
Translation adjustments, net of tax	**5,402**	10,820	55,980

Source: http://www.wendys-invest.com/fin/10k

Wendy's consolidated income statement presented in Exhibit 9 reveals that cost of operations rose from $2.29 billion in 2004 to $2.4 billion in 2006 despite revenue decreases. General and administrative expenses also increased from $2.1 million in 2004 to $2.4 million in 2006. The company spent a total of $134.1 million in marketing and advertising in 2006, $99.5 million in 2005, and $101.3 million in 2004. Contributions for advertising and marketing are typically made to two advertising funds—one in the United States, and a second one for Canada. Contribution rates are 3 percent of restaurant retail sales for Wendy's United States and 2.75 percent for Canada. Note that restaurants in Quebec are excluded from making contributions where advertising is done locally.

In the face of declining net income and revenues, Wendy's increased its dividend payouts from 48 cents in 2004 to 60 cents in 2006 as its basic earnings from continuing operations per common share dropped from 93 cents in 2004 to 33 cents in 2006.

Wendy's recent balance sheets are presented in Exhibit 10. There has been a decline in Wendy's assets and shareholders' equity since 2002. Assets declined from $2.68 billion in 2002 to $2.06 billion in 2006. The return on average assets fell from 9.2 percent in 2002 to 2.8

EXHIBIT 9   Consolidated Statements of Income of Wendy's International, Inc.

(In thousands, except per share data)	Years ended December 31, 2006, January 1, 2006, and January 2, 2005		
	2006	2005	2004
Revenues			
Sales	$2,154,607	$2,138,365	$2,194,031
Franchise revenues	284,670	317,053	308,127
Total revenues	2,439,277	2,455,418	2,502,158
Costs and expenses			
Cost of sales	1,352,312	1,362,631	1,369,509
Company restaurant operating costs	602,298	581,869	577,294
Operating costs	46,674	20,419	21,058
Depreciation of property and equipment	122,636	127,998	109,712
General and administrative expenses	237,575	220,891	210,156
Other expense (income), net	37,468	(34,263)	(1,329)
Total costs and expenses	2,398,963	2,279,545	2,286,400
Operating income	40,314	175,873	215,758
Interest expense	(35,711)	(43,076)	(42,006)
Interest income	37,876	3,987	2,438
Income from continuing operations before income taxes	42,479	136,784	176,190
Income taxes	5,433	51,689	70,046
Income from continuing operations	37,046	85,095	106,144
Income (loss) from discontinued operations	57,266	138,972	(54,109)
Net income	$94,312	$224,067	$52,035
Basic earnings per common share from continuing operations	$0.33	$0.74	$0.93
Diluted earnings per common share from continuing operations	$0.32	$0.73	$0.92
Basic earnings (loss) per common share from discontinued operations	$0.50	$1.21	$(0.47)
Diluted earnings (loss) per common share from discontinued operations	$0.50	$1.19	$(0.47)
Basic earnings per common share	$0.83	$1.95	$0.46
Diluted earnings per common share	$0.82	$1.92	$0.45
Dividends declared and paid per common share	$0.60	$0.58	$0.48
Basic shares	114,244	114,945	113,832
Diluted shares	115,325	116,819	115,685

Source: http://www.wendys-invest.com/fin/10k

EXHIBIT 10 Wendy's International Inc. (WEN) Balance Sheet

		(All numbers in thousands)	
	Dec. 31, 2006	Jan. 1, 2006	Jan. 2, 2005
Assets			
Current Assets			
Cash and Cash Equivalents	$ 457,614	393,241	176,749
Short-Term Investments	–	–	–
Net Receivables	114,492	179,788	166,064
Inventory	30,252	62,868	56,010
Other Current Assets	54,374	120,669	60,021
Total Current Assets	**656,732**	**756,566**	**458,844**
Long-Term Investments	—	14,796	12,652
Property, Plant and Equipment	1,226,328	2,325,888	2,349,820
Goodwill	85,353	128,808	166,998
Intangible Assets	3,855	41,757	41,787
Accumulated Amortization	—	–	–
Other Assets	83,763	165,880	160,671
Deferred Long-Term Asset Charges	4,316	6,623	6,772
Total Assets	**2,060,347**	**3,440,318**	**3,197,544**
Liabilities			
Current Liabilities			
Accounts Payable	276,484	504,995	498,241
Short/Current Long-Term Debt	87,396	9,428	130,125
Other Current Liabilities	30,786	68,929	60,021
Total Current Liabilities	**394,666**	**583,352**	**688,387**
Long-Term Debt	556,102	615,833	593,607
Other Liabilities	67,682	104,338	90,187
Deferred Long-Term Liability Charges	30,220	78,206	109,674
Minority Interest	–	–	–
Negative Goodwill	–	–	–
Total Liabilities	**1,048,670**	**1,381,729**	**1,481,855**
Stockholders' Equity			
Misc Stocks, Options, Warrants	–	–	–
Redeemable Preferred Stock	–	–	–
Preferred Stock	–	–	–
Common Stock	12,955	12,549	11,809
Retained Earnings	1,241,489	1,858,743	1,700,813
Treasury Stock	(1,319,146)	(294,669)	(195,124)
Capital Surplus	1,089,825	405,588	111,286
Other Stockholders' Equity	(13,446)	76,378	86,905
Total Stockholders' Equity	**1,011,677**	**2,058,589**	**1,715,689**
Net Tangible Assets	**$ 922,469**	**$ 1,888,024**	**$ 1,506,904**
Total Liabilities and SE	$ 2,060,347	$ 3,440,318	$ 3,197,544

Source: http://finance.yahoo.com/q/bs?s=WEN&annual

percent. Shareholders' equity decreased from $1.45 billion in 2002 to $1.01 billion in 2006, whereas returns on average equity fell sharply from 17 percent in 2002 to 4.7 percent in 2006.

Competition

Wendy's operates in the highly fragmented and intensely competitive food service industry that has about 550,000 restaurants in the United States. Even though Wendy's market share is small, it holds a unique position in the industry due to the fact that it commands large brand awareness. As recently as April 2007, Wendy's was voted number 1 in consumer taste tests and brand awareness.

Wendy's direct competitors are McDonald's, Burger King, and Yum Brands, all of whom are much larger than Wendy's in the fast-food restaurant business. Exhibit 11 provides a summary of competitors' financial highlights. Note that Wendy's has the lowest earnings per share and net income and number of employees among these three competitors. In fact, in terms of number of employees, note that Wendy's has 7,000 compared to McDonald's 465,000.

Burger King (BKC)

BKC was founded in 1954 in Miami, Florida under the name "Insta Burger King" by James McLamore and David Edgerton. BKC, a subsidiary of Burger King Holdings, Inc., owns 11,184 restaurants in 66 countries and has 37,000 employees. Ninety percent of its restaurants are owned by independent franchisees. BKC became a publicly held corporation in May 2006 and in a year it reached an impressive market capitalization of $3.51 billion. With a quarterly revenue growth of 8.9 percent, profit margins of 4.69 percent, and operating margins of 11.02 percent, BKC trails only McDonald's in many categories in the fast-food industry. Its strategy appears to be similar to that of McDonald's. In addition to its famous "Whopper sandwich," BKC offers a variety of burgers, chicken sandwiches, breakfast items, and salads that compete directly with MCD. BKC, since the 1980s, has had a long-standing contract with the Army and Air Force Exchange Service. As a result of this contract, BKC restaurants are seen in every major Army and Air Force location worldwide.

EXHIBIT 11   Wendy's and Its Competitors

	Direct Competitor Comparison				
	WEN	BKC	MCD	YUM	Industry
Market Cap	$ 3.45B	3.51B	61.63B	17.48B	422.93M
Full-time Employees	7,000	37,000	465,000	53,200	5.87K
Qtrly Rev Growth	2.00%	8.90%	11.20%	6.60%	8.30%
Revenue	$ 2.45B	2.18B	22.14B	9.70B	351.17M
Gross Margin	19.12%	34.08%	32.52%	25.75%	29.76%
EBITDA	257.17M	334.00M	6.28B	1.86B	42.83M
Oper Margins	5.04%	11.02%	21.76%	12.95%	5.63%
Net Income	$57.42M	102.00M	3.06B	848.00M	14.29M
EPS	0.524	0.763	2.970	3.037	0.77
P/E	75.52	34.14	17.38	21.98	26.05
PEG (5 yr expected)	2.58	1.45	2.21	1.73	1.47
P/S	1.41	1.63	2.76	1.83	0.94

BKC = Burger King Corporation
MCD = McDonald's Corporation
YUM = Yum! Brands Inc.
Industry = Restaurants

Source: Adapted from http://finance.yahoo.com

McDonald's (MCD)

MCD is the largest player in size and global reach. With a total of about 31,700 restaurants worldwide, its sales in 2006 were $16.1 billion. Even though MCD has experienced considerable challenges overseas leading to the sale of its restaurants in Latin America, the United Kingdom, and other countries, the home country (U.S.) operations only account for one-fourth of its total revenues of $21.6 billion in 2006. As a global player, MCD seeks to follow a cost leadership strategy by aggressively expanding and saturating the marketplace through value-priced menu items. It leads the industry with 1 percent growth in number of restaurants, 9 percent growth in total worldwide revenues, and 11 percent growth in operating income in 2006. Its operating margins in 2006 stand at an impressive 22 percent!

While MCD has consistently increased its dividend payout to shareholders, the food service giant has come under increasing pressure to consolidate its operations and become more efficient. MCD is doing very well financially even though it does still use trans fat oils in an unhealthy manner.

Yum Brands (YUM)

Yum! Brands, Inc., formerly known as TRICON Global Restaurants, Inc., was founded in 1997 and is headquartered in Louisville, Kentucky. In 2002, it changed its name to YUM! Brands, Inc., YUM operates a total of about 34,000 restaurants in over 100 countries. YUM owns prominent restaurant chains, such as Kentucky Fried Chicken (KFC), Pizza Hut, Taco Bell, Long John Silver's, and A&W. These restaurants also still used trans fat oils as of June 2007. With a market cap of $17.61 billion and 53,200 employees, YUM is second in the industry in size. However, YUM is ranked 262 among the Fortune 500 companies and is considered the largest in the industry in the number of locations held worldwide. The company is on the path to building a global business through aggressive international expansion. China is viewed as the leading international market opportunity for YUM. In China alone, YUM has more than 2,600 restaurants, accounting for 15 percent of its revenues.

YUM has the unique strategy of increasing traffic at a single real estate location by offering more than one brand at a single location. Each of its flagship brands also dominates the segment consistent with the differentiation strategy it pursues. This is in contrast to Wendy's strategy of positioning itself as a niche player. For example, Taco Bell holds 60 percent of the Mexican fast-food segment, KFC holds a respectable 45 percent of the fast-food chicken business, and Pizza Hut leads the pizza business with a 15 percent market share in the pizza business segment. Since its restructuring in 2006, YUM has been pursuing aggressive expansion overseas by expanding at the rate of 700 new locations for the seventh consecutive year since 1999.

YUM is proud of its commitment to diversity and a good work environment as it continues to be recognized among "Top 50 Employers for Minorities," "Top 50 Employers for Women," "40 Best Companies for Diversity," and "30 Hottest Franchises for 2006."

The Future

On May 12, 2007, Wendy's stock price gained 79 cents, or 2 percent, to $40.58 amidst news that its largest institutional shareholder, Pelz, urged it to sell itself in an auction. Wendy's is facing the prospect of being sold to Triarc, owned by activist investor Pelz. Also under pressure from the activist shareholder, Wendy's completed the sale of Tim Horton's in 2006 even though this was a profitable company in the coffee and doughnuts business. Wendy's has recently announced a revitalization plan as outlined in Exhibit 12. Note that the company plans to sell as many as 300 to 400 restaurants annually in coming years.

EXHIBIT 12   Wendy's Revitalization Plan

1. *Revitalize Wendy's Core Brand*—The Company will re-focus on its brand essence, "Quality Made Fresh," centered on Wendy's core strength, its hamburger business.
2. *Streamline and Improve Operations*—Includes a new restaurant services group to improve system-wide restaurant operations standards, while emphasizing improved store profits and operating margins.
3. *Reclaim Innovation Leadership*—Development of new products that reinforce Wendy's "Quality Made Fresh" brand essence and drive new consumers to its restaurants. The Company believes its new product pipeline is now robust.
4. Investing approximately $60 million per year over the next five years into the upgrade and renovation of its company-operated restaurants.
5. *Strengthen Franchisee Commitment*—Providing up to $25 million per year of incentives to franchisees for reinvestments in their restaurants over the next five years, and require franchisees to meet store remodel standards.
6. Selling up to 50 in 2007 and targeting to sell up to 300 to 400 of its company operated restaurants to franchisees beginning in 2008, while improving store level profitability first.
7. *Capture New Opportunities*—Seeking to drive growth beyond its existing business. The Company is expanding breakfast and is following a disciplined process for product development and operations, as well as analyzing consumer feedback. With the QSR breakfast market estimated at $30 billion, breakfast is a high priority for the Company that could generate significant sales and profits. Also, the Company believes it has considerable opportunity to expand in the U.S. over the long-term and is making infrastructure investments to grow its International business. The Company will continue to moderate its short-term North American development until restaurant revenues and operating cash flows improve.
8. *Embrace a Performance-Driven Culture*—A redesign of its incentive compensation plan to drive future performance to better reward individual employee performance and to better align compensation with business performance in the short and longer term.
9. Maintaining its strong corporate culture based on the values established by Wendy's founder Dave Thomas.

Source: http://www.wendys-invest.com/fin/10k

Should CEO Anderson succumb to the demands of activist shareholder Pelz and sell the company? Or should she forge ahead with the new comprehensive revitalization plan instituted in October 2006 and continue her efforts to turn the company around? Or are there other alternative courses of action that Wendy's should consider? Prepare a detailed strategic analysis for Wendy's new CEO. Include in your analysis an assessment of the new revitalization plan as well as your own recommendations for the future.

References

www.biz.yahoo.com
www.burgerking.com
http://en.wikipedia.org
http://finance.yahoo.com
www.hoovers.com
www.latimes.com
www.mcdonalds.com
www.sec.gov
www.wendys.com
www.wsjonline.com
www.yum.com

21 McDonald's Corporation — 2007

Vijaya Narapareddy
University of Denver

MCD

www.mcdonalds.com

In April 2007, McDonald's (MCD) announced that 1,600 of its restaurants in Latin America and the Caribbean were being sold to a licensee, Woods Staton, CEO of RestCo Iberoamericana, Limited. This decision was part of the several steps outlined in the implementation of MCD's "Plan to Win" initiated in 2003. MCD continues to maintain its long-term goals of achieving average annual company sales and revenue growth of 3 percent to 5 percent, average annual operating income growth of 6 percent to 7 percent, and annual returns on incremental invested capital in the high teens.

The Latam Sale

The $700 million Latin American sale comes amidst MCD's strong performance in the region, known as "Latam." The Latin American division had posted double-digit sales growth in 42 consecutive months and margin improvements in 13 consecutive quarters. The region continued its strong performance with a 14.7 percent sales gain in the first quarter in 2007. MCD has grown to employ a total of 75,000 employees in 28 countries in Latin America since its first restaurant opened in Puerto Rico in 1967. MCD was recognized as the "Best Company to Work for in Latin America" by Great Place to Work Institute, Inc. in 2006.

MCD's Latin American divestiture is intended to support the company's commitment to reduce the number of restaurants it owns and minimize the volatility caused by the wild swings in the value of local currencies. "We weren't put on this earth to deal with this kind of volatility," MCD's chief financial officer, Matt Paull, comments. "It makes us nervous, and it makes some of our shareholders nervous. For Mr. Staton, who has run McDonald's restaurants in Latin America, it doesn't make him nervous." In this context, it is important to note that there has been significant pressure from MCD investor and activist William A. Ackman, managing partner of Pershing Square Capital Management, a hedge fund, to pare down restaurant ownership by consolidating them into a publicly held separate entity.

Woods Staton, with his 20 years' experience with McDonald's, is no stranger to the industry. Staton and his partners enter into a 20-year master franchise agreement to pay monthly royalties to MCD commencing at a rate of approximately 5 percent of gross sales of the restaurants. The franchisees also commit to opening approximately 150 new McDonald's restaurants over the first three years and pay an initial franchise fee for each new restaurant opened. Furthermore, under the agreement, the franchisees are obligated to commit to capital expenditures every year for existing restaurants. Thus, MCD collects royalties without investing capital. Even though the Latam sale generates about $700 million for MCD, the impact of this conversion of restaurants to franchises is an estimated decline of McDonald's consolidated revenues annually by $1.5 billion.

Organizational Structure

MCD operates in more than 100 countries and is organized into a geographical structure with five key segments: (1) McDonald's USA, (2) McDonald's Europe, (3) McDonald's AMEA (Asia, Middle East, and Africa), (4) McDonald's Latin America, and (5) McDonald's

EXHIBIT 1   Subsidiaries of the McDonald's Corporation

Domestic Subsidiaries
1. Boston Market Corporation (Delaware)
2. Franchise Realty Investment Trust—Illinois (Maryland)
3. McDonald's AMEA, LLC (Delaware)
4. McDonald's Deutschland, Inc. (Delaware)
5. McDonald's Development Italy, Inc. (Delaware)
6. McDonald's Europe, Inc. (Delaware)
7. McDonald's International Property Company, Ltd. (Delaware)
8. McDonald's Latin America, LLC (Delaware)
9. McDonald's Real Estate Company (Delaware)
10. McDonald's Restaurant Operations Inc. (Delaware)
11. McDonald's Sistemas de Espana, Inc. (Delaware)
12. McDonald's USA, LLC (Delaware)

Foreign Subsidiaries
1. Arras Comercio de Alimentos Ltda. (Brazil)
2. Alimentos Arcos Dorados de Venezuela, C.A. (Venezuela)
3. McDonald's Australia Holding Limited (Australia)
4. McDonald's Australia Limited (Australia)
5. McDonald's Comercio de Alimentos Ltda. (Brazil)
6. McDonald's Danmark A/S (Denmark)
7. McDonald's France S.A. (France)
8. McDonald's GmbH (Germany)
9. McDonald's Immobilien GmbH (Germany)
10. McDonald's LLC (Russia)
11. McDonald's Nederland B.V. (Netherlands)
12. McDonald's Polska Sp.zo.o. (Poland)
13. McDonald's Real Estate LLP (United Kingdom)
14. McDonald's Restaurants (Hong Kong) Ltd. (Hong Kong)
15. McDonald's Restaurants (New Zealand) Ltd. (New Zealand)
16. McDonald's Restaurants (Taiwan) Co., Ltd. (Taiwan)
17. McDonald's Restaurants Limited (United Kingdom)
18. McDonald's Restaurants of Canada Limited (Canada)
19. McDonald's System de Puerto Rico, Inc. (Puerto Rico)
20. McDonald's Suisse Franchise Sarl (Switzerland)
21. MDC Inmobiliaria de Mexico S. de R.L. de C.V. (Mexico)
22. Moscow—McDonald's (Russia)
23. Restaurantes McDonald's, S.A. (Spain)
24. Sistemas McDonald's Portugal Limitada (Portugal)
25. Svenska McDonald's AB (Sweden)
26. Svenska McDonald's Development AB (Sweden)

Note: This list excludes the following:
(a) 49 wholly-owned subsidiaries of McDonald's USA, LLC, each of which operates one or more McDonald's restaurants within the United States.

Source: www.mcdonalds.com (*2006 Annual Report*).

International. An additional subsidiary was created for McDonald's Ventures, which consists of non-McDonald's brands. MCD also owns Boston Market Corporation and has other domestic and foreign subsidiaries as listed in Exhibits 1 and 2. Note in Exhibit 2 that the number of McDonald's restaurants increased in every region of the world in 2006 from 2005.

MCD's performance in the global marketplace is significant. In spite of competition and challenges posed by litigation in various markets around the world, the food service giant has experienced steady growth in revenues, operating income, and assets. Exhibit 3 and Exhibit 4 contain revenues and operating margins by region, respectively. Note that MCD revenues and income are up in 2006 is every region of the world with the highest percentage increases in Latin America.

EXHIBIT 2   McDonald's Restaurants by Region

Systemwide restaurants at year end[1]

	2006	2005	2004
U.S.	**13,774**	13,727	13,673
Europe	**6,403**	6,352	6,287
AMEA	**7,822**	7,692	7,567
Latin America	**1,656**	1,617	1,607
Canada	**1,391**	1,378	1,362
Corporate & Other[2]	**621**	631	656
Total	**31,667**	31,397	31,152

[1]Includes satellite units at December 31, 2006, 2005 and 2004 as follows: U.S.–1,254, 1,268, 1,341; Europe–201, 190, 181; AMEA (primarily Japan)–1,640, 1,730, 1,819; Latin America–6, 8, 13; and Canada–411, 395, 378.
[2]Represents Boston Market restaurants.

Source: www.mcdonalds.com, sec10k filings, dt., February 26, 2007.

EXHIBIT 3   McDonald's Revenues by Region
(In $ Millions)

	Amount			Increase/(decrease)		Increase/(decrease) excluding currency translation	
	2006	2005	2004	2006	2005	2006	2005
Company-operated sales:							
U.S.	**$4,410**	$4,098	$3,828	**8%**	7%	**8%**	7%
Europe	**5,885**	5,465	5,174	**8**	6	**6**	5
AMEA	**2,674**	2,453	2,390	**9**	3	**8**	-
Latin America	**1,552**	1,237	933	**26**	33	**21**	23
Canada	**882**	765	730	**15**	5	**8**	(2)
Corporate & Other	**680**	708	700	**(4)**	1	**(4)**	1
Total	**$16,083**	$14,726	$13,755	**9%**	7%	**8%**	5%
Franchised and affiliated revenues:[1]							
U.S.	**$3,054**	$2,857	$2,697	**7%**	6%	**7%**	6%
Europe	**1,753**	1,607	1,563	**9**	3	**8**	3
AMEA	**379**	362	331	**5**	10	**7**	7
Latin America	**107**	90	75	**18**	20	**16**	15
Canada	**199**	183	168	**9**	9	**2**	1
Corporate & Other	**11**	7	5	**68**	40	**68**	40
Total	**$5,503**	$5,106	$4,839	**8%**	6%	**7%**	5%
Total revenues:							
U.S.	**$7,464**	$6,955	$6,525	**7%**	7%	**7%**	7%
Europe	**7,638**	7,072	6,737	**8**	5	**6**	5
AMEA	**3,053**	2,815	2,721	**8**	3	**8**	1
Latin America	**1,659**	1,327	1,008	**25**	32	**20**	22
Canada	**1,081**	948	898	**14**	6	**7**	(2)
Corporate & Other	**691**	715	705	**(3)**	1	**(3)**	1
Total	**$21,586**	$19,832	$18,594	**9%**	7%	**7%**	5%

[1]Includes the Company's revenues from conventional franchisees, developmental licensees, and affiliates.

Source: www.mcdonalds.com (*2006 Annual Report*).

EXHIBIT 4   Operating Income by Region (In $ Millions)

	Amount			Increase/(decrease)		Increase/(decrease) excluding currency translation		Pro forma increase/(decrease) excluding currency translation
	2006	2005	2004	**2006**	2005	**2006**	2005	2005[1]
U.S.	**$ 2,657**	$ 2,422	$ 2,182	**10%**	11%	**10%**	**11%**	15%
Europe	**1,610**	1,449	1,471	**11**	(1)	**9**	(2)	2
AMEA	**364**	345	200	**6**	72	**9**	70	92
Latin America	**55**	30	(20)	**84**	nm	**104**	nm	nm
Canada	**198**	156	178	**27**	(13)	**19**	(19)	(15)
Corporate & Other	**(439)**	(410)	(473)	**(7)**	14	**(7)**	14	27
Total	**$ 4,445**	$ 3,992	$ 3,538	**11%**	13%	**11%**	13%	21%

Nm: Not meaningful.

[1]For 2004, pro forma share-based expense as reported in the Company's year-end 2004 Form 10-K was $156 million after tax, of which $7 million of expense related to RSUs was included in net income. The remaining $149 million after tax ($241 million pretax) was disclosed in a note to the consolidated financial statements, as required, for pro forma purposes. The segments reflected the following pro forma share-based expense in 2004 (in millions): U.S.–$69; Europe –$49; AMEA–$22; Latin America–$9; Canada–$8; Corporate & Other–$84; Total–$241. The above pro forma increase/(decrease) is using an adjusted 2004 expense which is calculated by subtracting pro forma share-based expense from reported operating income.

Source: www.mcdonalds.com (*2006 Annual Report*).

CEO Skinner brought several new people on board. A total of 17 officers were listed on the executive ranks at MCD, an increase of 9 executive officers in 2006. Exhibit 5 displays a list of executive officers and their titles, as well as an organizational chart for the company.

Competitors

MCD operates in the food service industry through company-owned restaurants, franchises, and licenses worldwide, competing with international, national, regional, and local retailers of food products, including restaurants, quick-service eating establishments, pizza parlors, coffee shops, street vendors, convenience food stores, delicatessens, and supermarkets. With about 550,000 restaurants and $365 billion in sales, the U.S. market is large and highly fragmented. In spite of the intensely competitive environment, MCD's commanded an impressive 7.4 percent of the annual sales in the United States in 2006.

McDonald's competitors range from the small privately owned eateries to multinational retailers of food products, but its key competitors include Burger King, Yum Brands, and Wendy's, who directly compete with McDonald's in the fast-food restaurant business. Summary competitor financial highlights are provided in Exhibit 6.

Burger King (BKC)

Founded in Miami, Florida in 1954 under the name "Insta Burger King" by James McLamore and David Edgerton, Burger King Corporation (BKC), a subsidiary of Burger King Holdings, Inc., owns 11,184 restaurants in 66 countries and has 37,000 employees. With a market capitalization of $3.51 billion, quarterly revenue growth of 8.9 percent, profit margins of 4.69 percent, and operating margins of 11.02 percent, BKC trails only McDonald's in many categories in the fast-food industry. However, it has a P/E ratio of 34.08, twice that of MCD.

In addition to its famous "Whopper sandwich," BKC offers a variety of burgers, chicken sandwiches, breakfast items, and salads that compete directly with MCD. BKC, since the 1980s, has a long-standing contract with the Army and Air Force Exchange Service. As such, every major Army and Air Force location worldwide has a Burger King restaurant on its premises.

EXHIBIT 5   McDonald's Corporation's Executive Officers

1. Ralph Alvarez, president and chief operating officer.
2. Jose Armario, president, McDonald's Latin America.
3. Mary Dillon, corporate executive vice president–global chief marketing officer.
4. Timothy J. Fenton, president, McDonald's Asia/Pacific/Middle East/Africa.
5. Janice L. Fields, executive vice president and chief operations officer, McDonald's USA.
6. Richard Floersch, corporate executive vice president and chief human resources officer.
7. Denis Hennequin, president, McDonald's Europe.
8. Jim Johannesen, president, central division, McDonald's USA.
9. Karen King, president, McDonald's east division.
10. Andrew J. McKenna, McDonald's Corporation's non-executive chairman of the board.
11. Matthew H. Paull, corporate senior executive vice president and chief financial officer.
12. Steve Plotkin, president, west division, McDonald's USA.
13. Gloria Santona, corporate executive vice president, general counsel, and secretary.
14. James A. Skinner, vice chairman and chief executive officer.
15. Jeffrey P. Stratton, corporate executive vice president–worldwide chief restaurant officer.
16. Donald Thompson, president, McDonald's USA.
17. Fred L. Turner honorary chairman, McDonald's Corporation, also a life trustee of Ronald McDonald House Charities.

Source: http://www.mcdonalds.com/corp/about/bios

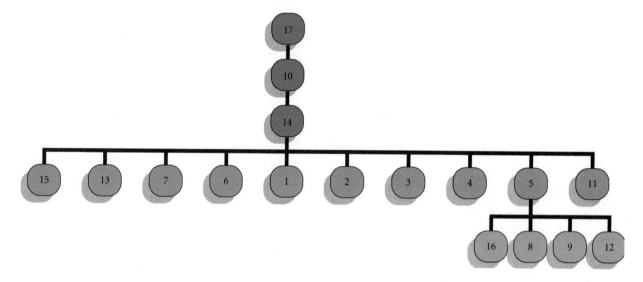

EXHIBIT 6   Direct Competitor Comparison for 2006

	McDonald's	YUM	BurKing	Wendy's	Industry
Market Cap	$61.38B	17.61B	3.51B	3.46B	422.93M
Employees	465,000	53,200	37,000	7,000	5.87K
Qtrly Rev Growth	11.20%	6.60%	8.90%	2.00%	8.30%
Revenue	$22.14B	9.70B	2.18B	2.45B	351.17M
Gross Margin	32.52%	25.75%	34.08%	19.12%	29.76%
Operating Profits	6.28B	1.86B	334.00M	257.17M	42.83M
Oper Margin	21.76%	12.95%	11.02%	5.04%	5.63%
Net Profits	$ 3.06B	848.00M	102.00M	57.42M	14.29M
EPS ratio	2.970	3.037	0.763	0.524	0.77
P/E ratio	17.31	22.13	34.08	75.73	26.05
PEG (5 yr expected):	2.21	1.73	1.45	2.61	1.47
P/S:	2.71	1.79	1.60	1.39	0.94

Source: Adapted from http://finance.yahoo.com

Yum Brands (YUM)

Yum! Brands, Inc., formerly known as TRICON Global Restaurants, Inc., was founded in 1997 and changed its name to YUM! Brands, Inc. in 2002. YUM operates 34,000 restaurants in 100 countries, including prominent restaurant chains such as Kentucky Fried Chicken (KFC), Pizza Hut, Taco Bell, Long John Silver's, and A&W. With a market cap of $17.61 billion and 53,200 employees, it is the closest competitor in size to McDonald's. Headquartered in Louisville, Kentucky, YUM is considered the largest in the industry worldwide in terms of number of locations and is ranked 262 among the Fortune 500 companies.

Offering more than one brand at a single location has helped YUM increase traffic at a single real estate location. Each of its flagship brand also dominates the segment. For example, Taco Bell holds 60 percent of the Mexican fast-food segment, KFC holds a respectable 45 percent of the fast-food chicken business, and Pizza Hut leads the pizza business with a 15 percent market share in the pizza business segment. In addition to seeking growth through acquisition of prominent brands, since its restructuring in 2006, YUM has been pursuing aggressive expansion overseas by expanding at the rate of 700 new locations for the seventh consecutive year since 1999. In China alone it has more than 2,600 restaurants, accounting for 15 percent of its revenues.

Wendy's (WEN)

Wendy's International, Inc., founded in 1969, is based in Dublin, Ohio, and operates 6,673 restaurants. With a market cap of $3.5 billion and 7,000 employees, Wendy's ranks fourth in the industry, behind McDonald's, YUM, and Burger King. However, it leads the industry with a P/E ratio of 75.73. The company is well known for its unique square single, double, or triple made-to-order burgers and fries, and alternative menu items, such as baked potatoes, chili, and salads. Its new low-priced menus directly compete for market share with MCD. In spite of its unique positioning as an old-fashioned eating place in the fast-food business, Wendy's has been struggling to prevent a severe decline in its business. In 2006, veteran CEO John Schuessler was replace by former CFO Kerrii Anderson. In spite of being recognized as the most favorite quality brand by *QSR Magazine* for the second year in a row and earning first place for customer satisfaction in the "limited service restaurants" category in this year's American Customer Satisfaction Index survey, Wendy's continues to experience financial hardship and pressure from an activist shareholder to potentially sell the company.

New Décor

At the heart of MCD's market leadership is its ability to successfully innovate and standardize products and process technologies. Embedded in this is its approach to serving customers efficiently and offering customers a variety of menu choices consistent with the changing preferences of consumers worldwide. In the United States, new products like premium roast coffee, Asian salad, snack wraps, and several premium chicken sandwiches generate revenue gains. Convenience, value-based pricing, and extended hours are an integral part of MCD's core strategy of creating value for its customers. MCD's new "Plan to Win" seeks to offer exceptional customer experience through five key drivers—people, products, place, price, and promotion. In addition to opening new restaurants, it continually upgrades its old restaurants through renovations and investments in property, plant, and equipment.

In 2006, McDonald's introduced its "Forever Young" brand by redesigning all of their restaurants, the first major redesign since the 1970s. The new design includes the traditional McDonald's yellow and red colors, but terra cotta replaces the red, and a golden "sunny" color replaces yellow. The new décor also includes contemporary earthy colors of olive and sage green. Restaurants have less plastic and more brick and wood, with modern hanging lights to produce a softer glow. Contemporary art or framed photographs hang on the walls.

New restaurants are being designed to offer three new features. The "linger" zone offers armchairs, sofas, and Wi-Fi connections. The "grab and go" zone features tall counters with bar stools for single customers who walk in alone. These new restaurants are equipped with plasma TVs. The "flexible" zone is targeted toward families and has booths featuring fabric cushions with colorful patterns and flexible seating. The plans include different music targeted to each zone.

Legal Challenges

As a large public multinational corporation, McDonald's often faces legal action from activists, consumers, labor unions, medical, and religious groups around the world. As recently as April 2007, McDonald's was faulted in China for underpaying student employees, but was cleared by the government a week later on grounds that the laws governing pay issues excluded students on the payroll.

On September 28, 2006, a California medical doctors' group sued the company and six other restaurant chains for the presence of carcinogens in the chicken menu items served. On 9th February, 2005, MCD achieved a settlement to reduce trans fatty acids (TFAs) in its cooking oil. At the heart of the litigation was the fact that in September 2002, MCD announced it was voluntarily reducing the trans fat content of its cooking oil by February 2003. But the oil was not changed. In the ensuing lawsuits, plaintiffs claimed that MCD failed to inform the public that the oil was not changed. Since that time, it has been discovered that the trans fat content of some of the products are higher than they claimed (one McDonald's large fries contains 8 grams of trans fat). As part of the settlement, the company has to inform the public that the oil was not changed. In addition, MCD will also donate $7 million to the American Heart Association for public education about the risks of consuming trans fat. Despite repeated litigation and outrage from consumer groups on health issues related to adult and child obesity and the ensuing risk of heart attacks, McDonald's has yet to make a total transition to vegetable oils.

In June 2004, MCD was thrown into the center of controversy when it distributed meal vouchers, balloons, and toys to sick children in the United Kingdom. This would have been uneventful but for the fact that it came on the heels of a local government report on the high levels of obesity among British children. In 2002, Hindu vegetarian groups in India sued MCD and won; MCD was misrepresenting French fries served at its restaurants as vegetarian.

To its credit, MCD discontinued its practice of frying French fries in beef lard as early as 1990, but it continues to add beef extract to its French fries. The French fries and biscuits served in the United States still contain beef and animal flavorings. On November 27, 2006, MCD announced plans to switch to rapeseed and sunflower oils by 2008 in making French fries, fried chicken, fried fish, and fried pies served in more than 6,300 restaurants in Europe. The initiative was expected to kick off in Denmark, Finland, Norway, and Sweden.

Financial Performance

MCD boasted of continued revenue growth, increased customer visits, and enhanced profitability as the company invested in new products, menu choices, modern restaurants, and providing attractive everyday value in the first quarter of 2007. The company also reported achieving record growth in 2006. This is consistent with the news released on January 17, 2007 indicating that it has achieved sales gains four years in a row as shown in Exhibit 7, which contains consolidated operating results. In addition to revenue gains, MCD's operating and net incomes showed a steady increase.

While total current and long-term liabilities declined, retained earnings increased from $23.5 billion in 2005 to $25.8 billion in 2006. Thus, shareholders' equity rose from $15.1 billion to $15.5 billion during this period. McDonald's consolidated balance sheets are presented in Exhibit 8.

Future Direction

On September 27, 2006, McDonald's board of directors approved a dividend payment of $1.2 billion to its shareholders. While the dividend payout was $1 per share, what was noteworthy was the increase from $0.67 to $1 per share, and that McDonald's has raised its dividend each and every year since paying its first dividend 30 years ago in 1976. MCD has more than quadrupled the dividend from 23.5 cents per share in 2002 to $1.00 per share in 2006. On this occasion, CEO Skinner notes: "Today's nearly 50 percent boost in the dividend reflects confidence in the ongoing strength of our business and the reliability

EXHIBIT 7   Consolidated Operating Results of McDonald's Corporation

Operating results

(Dollars in millions, except per share data)	2006		2005		2004
	Amount	Increase/ (decrease)	Amount	Increase/ (decrease)	Amount
Revenues					
Sales by Company-operated restaurants	**$16,083**	**9%**	$14,726	7%	$13,755
Revenues from franchised and affiliated restaurants	**5,503**	**8**	5,106	6	4,839
Total revenues	**21,586**	**9**	19,832	7	18,594
Operating costs and expenses					
Company-operated restaurant expenses	**13,542**	**8**	12,575	8	11,688
Franchised restaurants–occupancy expenses	**1,060**	**4**	1,021	2	1,003
Selling, general & administrative expenses	**2,338**	**8**	2,167	12	1,939
Impairment and other charges (credits), net	**134**	**nm**	(28)	nm	281
Other operating expense, net	**67**	**(36)**	105	(28)	145
Total operating costs and expenses	**17,141**	**8**	15,840	5	15,056
Operating income	**4,445**	**11**	3,992	13	3,538
Interest expense	**402**	**13**	356	(1)	358
Nonoperating income, net	**(123)**	**nm**	(38)	81	(21)
Income from continuing operations before provision for income taxes	**4,166**	**13**	3,674	15	3,201
Provision for income taxes	**1,293**	**19**	1,088	18	923
Income from continuing operations	**2,873**	**11**	2,586	14	2,278
Income from discontinued operations (net of taxes of $97, $11, and $1), including gain on Chipotle disposition of $653	**671**	**nm**	16	nm	1
Net income	**$3,544**	**36%**	$2,602	14%	$2,279
Income per common share–diluted					
Continuing operations	**$2.30**	**13%**	$2.03	13%	$1.79
Discontinued operations, including gain on Chipotle disposition of $0.52[1]	**0.53**	**nm**	0.01	nm	–
Net income per common share—diluted	**$2.83**	**39%**	$2.04	14%	$1.79
Weighted-average common shares outstanding–diluted	**1,251.7**		1,274.2		1,273.7

Nm: Not meaningful.

[1]During 2006, the Company disposed of its entire investment in Chipotle via public stock offerings and a tax-free exchange for McDonald's common stock and as a result, has reflected Chipotle's results of operations and transaction gains as discontinued operations. The 2006 results included $671 million of income, or $0.53 per share, related to discontinued operations. Income from continuing operations was $2.9 billion or $2.30 per share, which included impairment and other charges of $134 million ($98 million after tax or $0.07 per share), as well as net incremental tax expense of $0.01 per share primarily related to a one-time impact from a tax law change in Canada.

Source: www.mcdonalds.com (*2006 Annual Report*)

of our substantial cash flow. This confidence is driven by the success of our customer-centered Plan to Win strategy, which continues to deliver results for customers, members of the McDonald's system, and shareholders . . . This dividend increase is part of our commitment to return more cash to shareholders. We believe that cash available for dividends and share repurchases will continue to grow due to our expected strong results and stable capital expenditures over the next few years. We now expect to return at least $10 billion to shareholders through dividends and share-repurchases in 2006 through 2008 and intend to continue to reduce shares outstanding."

EXHIBIT 8 McDonald's Corporation: Consolidated Balance Sheet

(In millions, except per share data)	December 31 2006	2005
ASSETS		
Current assets		
Cash and equivalents	$2,136.4	$4,260.6
Accounts and notes receivable	904.2	793.9
Inventories, at cost, not in excess of market	149.0	144.3
Prepaid expenses and other current assets	435.7	640.2
Discontinued operations		380.0
Total current assets	3,625.3	6,219.0
Other assets		
Investment in and advances to affiliates	1,036.2	1,035.4
Goodwill, net	2,209.2	1,924.4
Miscellaneous	1,307.4	1,236.7
Total other assets	4,552.8	4,196.5
Property and equipment		
Property and equipment, at cost	31,810.2	29,482.5
Accumulated depreciation and amortization	(10,964.5)	(9,909.2)
Net property and equipment	20,845.7	19,573.3
Total assets	$29,023.8	$29,988.8
LIABILITIES AND SHAREHOLDERS' EQUITY		
Current liabilities		
Notes payable	$ –	$544.0
Accounts payable	834.1	678.0
Income taxes	250.9	569.6
Other taxes	251.4	233.1
Accrued interest	135.1	158.5
Accrued payroll and other liabilities	1,518.9	1,158.1
Current maturities of long-term debt	17.7	658.5
Discontinued operations		107.9
Total current liabilities	3,008.1	4,107.7
Long-term debt	8,416.5	8,934.3
Other long-term liabilities	1,074.9	851.5
Deferred income taxes	1,066.0	949.2
Shareholders' equity		
Preferred stock, no par value; authorized — 165.0 million shares; issued — none		
Common stock, $.01 par value; authorized — 3.5 billion shares; issued — 1,660.6 million shares	16.6	16.6
Additional paid-in capital	3,445.0	2,720.2
Retained earnings	25,845.6	23,516.0
Accumulated other comprehensive income (loss)	(296.7)	(733.1)
Common stock in treasury, at cost; 456.9 and 397.4 million shares	(13,552.2)	(10,373.6)
Total shareholders' equity	15,458.3	15,146.1
Total liabilities and shareholders' equity	$29,023.8	$29,988.8

Source: www.mcdonalds.com (*2006 Annual Report*).

Is CEO Skinner on the right path to achieve his Plan to Win? Returning large sums of money to shareholders actually has the potential of displeasing investors, who may see this as a sign of weakening commitment on the part of MCD's leadership to invest in growth avenues. Should Skinner use the excess cash that MCD is generating to grow the company using different strategies, such as acquisitions and/or diversification?

References

www.bk.com
www.mcdonalds.com
www.sec.gov
www.biz.yahoo.com
http://finance.yahoo.com
www.wendys.com
www.burgerking.com
www.wsjonline.com
www.hoovers.com
http://en.wikipedia.org

22 Compass Group PLC — 2007

Lester A. Hudson, Jr.

William Garcia
Queens University of Charlotte

CPG

www.compass-group.com

The world's leading food service company, Compass Group PLC has grown from a domestic operator in the United Kingdom to a 400,000-employee global player in the contract catering and support services industry operating in 98 countries. Since 1992, the company has grown rapidly using both acquisitions and internal growth. The London-based company increased group revenue from continuing operations 7 percent for fiscal year ending September 30, 2006, to $19.5 billion. Operating profits from continuing operations totaled $915 million, up 2.4 percent, and debt declined approximately $1.5 billion, creating a solid platform for continued growth.

The Group's mission is to develop and deliver original food and service solutions in the workplace, in schools and colleges, in hospitals, at leisure venues, and in remote environments, providing clients with the highest quality service. Its vision is to be the premium operator in the contract catering and support service market with an outstanding reputation for quality, value for money, and client and customer satisfaction.

> We are specialists who help clients either outsource or establish a food or support service, or sometimes both, to suit their needs. How we do that draws on our global resources and our understanding of different cultures and market sectors. We work in partnership with our clients, usually in their premises. And by using their facilities and equipment, we keep capital investment to an absolute minimum.[1]

Sir Roy Gardner, who was named chairman of Compass Group in July 2006, heads a ten-member board of directors consisting of six independent nonexecutive directors and four Group executives. Richard Cousins is Group CEO. As illustrated in Exhibit 1, Compass Group PLC is structured into four divisions based on geography with each division having a group managing director who reports to the group chief executive officer.

EXHIBIT 1 Compass Group PLC Organizational Chart

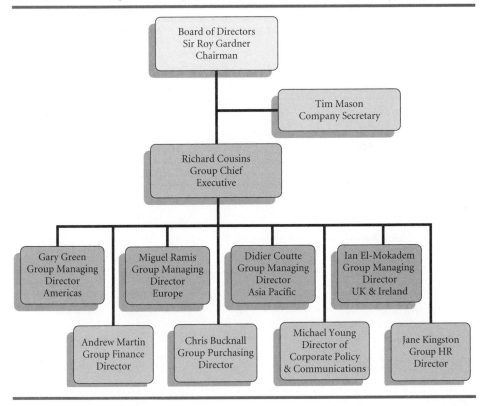

Source: Adapted from Compass Group PLC *Annual Report* 2006.

Compass' financial statements are prepared and presented in accordance with the International Financial Reporting Standards (IFRS). Income statements and balance sheets are provided in Exhibit 2 and Exhibit 3.

EXHIBIT 2 Consolidated Profit and Loss Account as of September 30, 2006

Compass Group PLC	2005 £m	2006 £m
Revenue	10,073	10,815
Operating Costs	9,685	10,309
Operating Profit	388	506
Share of profits of associates	—	2
Total operating profit	388	508
Finance income	4	15
Finance costs	(156)	(160)
Hedge accounting ineffectiveness	(3)	11
Profit before tax	233	374
Income tax expense	97	69
Profit from continuing operations	136	305
Discontinued operations	73	(10)
Profit for the year	209	295

continued

EXHIBIT 2   Consolidated Profit and Loss Account as of September 30, 2006—continued

Basic earnings per share - continued and discontinued operations	9.0p	13.3p
Diluted earnings per share - continued and discontinued operations	9.0p	13.3p

Source: Adapted from Compass Group PLC *Annual Report* 2006.

EXHIBIT 3   Consolidated Balance Sheet as of September 30, 2006

Compass Group PLC	2005 £m	2006 £m
Non-current assets		
Goodwill and other intangibles	4,388	3,603
Property, plant and equipment	1,657	756
Receivables	140	117
Other	293	307
	6,478	4,783
Current assets		
Inventories	253	212
Receivables	1,574	1,424
Cash and cash equivalents	292	867
	2,119	2,503
Total assets	8,597	7,286
Current liabilities	(2,951)	(2,533)
Non-current liabilities	(3,368)	(2,441)
Total liabilities	(6,319)	(4,974)
Net assets	(2,278)	(2,312)
Equity		
Share capital	216	210
Share premium account	94	96
Capital redemption reserve	9	15
Other reserves	4,136	4,288
Retained earnings	(4,137)	(4,288)
Total equity	2,278	2,312

Source: Adapted from Compass Group PLC *Annual Report* 2006.

Compass Group Divisions

As indicated in Exhibit 4, Compass Group North America (Compass NA) is the company's largest division, generating 40 percent of total revenues and 48 percent of operating profits in fiscal 2006. This division is also the fastest growing part of the company and has made more than 50 acquisitions during the last ten years. Continental Europe represents 26 percent of the revenue and 33 percent of operating profits, and the United Kingdom accounts for 23 percent of both revenues and profits. Australia, South America, Japan, and emerging markets such as China, India, Indonesia, and Turkey (sometimes referred to as "The Rest of the World") contribute the remaining 16 percent of revenue and 11 percent of profits.

Through a process of more than 50 acquisitions during the 10 year period 1996–2006, Compass NA entered 2007 as an $8 billion operation, with revenues targeted at $10 billion

EXHIBIT 4   Revenue and Operating Profit by Division

	Revenue (£m)		Operating Profit (£m)*	
	2006	2005	2006	2005
North America	4,290	3,761	246	218
Continental Europe	2,863	2,830	169	169
United Kingdom	1,957	1,982	115	114
Rest of World	1,705	1,500	55	53
Group Totals	10,815	10,073	508**	496**

* Before exceptional items.

** Group total Operating Profit includes adjustments and do not add.

Source: Adapted from Compass Group PLC *Annual Report* 2006.

in 2008. This company's rapid growth follows a simple mantra: *Acquire the best player in every food service sector, keep their expert management team in place, and give them the behind-the-scenes resources and support to help them excel.*

Headed by CEO Gary Green, the 123,000 employees of Compass NA generated $7.1 billion in revenue in 2005, and $8.1 billion in 2006, an increase of 14 percent, to represent 40 percent of total Group revenues. Revenue target for 2008 is $10 billion, which appears to be achievable. Operating profits increased 12 percent in 2006 to $461 million. The health care business and the sports and leisure business delivered exceptionally strong performances with revenue increases of 12 percent and 26 percent respectively.

Revenues in Continental Europe grew by 2 percent in 2006 to £2.863 billion and generated flat operating profits of £169 million, the same as in 2005. Revenues in the United Kingdom were flat in 2006 (£1.957 billion vs. £1.982 billion in 2005), and the Rest of the World division grew 13 percent in 2006 to £1.705 billion. This division completed its exit from Middle East military catering operations including the UN food logistics business, which operated principally in Africa. This contract involved some questionable activities, which resulted in lawsuits of £600 million against ESS, Compass, and ESS staff. With no admission of guilt, these suits were settled in October 2006 for less than £40 million.

The Restaurant Industry

Compass Group services the restaurant industry. As indicated in Exhibit 5, the U.S. food and drink sales were $537 billion in 2007, an increase of 66 percent during the ten-year period of 1997–2007.[2] Continued growth of 5 percent is forecasted for 2008.

About 52 percent of all meals consumed today are outside the home; that number was only 20 percent in 1970. The restaurant industry employs the largest number of people in the United States other than the government.[3] In 2007 there were 935,000 restaurant locations in the United States employing 12.8 million people. U.S. restaurant industry employment is projected to reach 14.8 million people in 2017. Eating and drinking places are labor-intensive with recent sales per employee being only $57,000, notably lower than in other industries. The industry's history of strong growth is expected to continue as U.S. citizens eat more meals outside the home.

EXHIBIT 5   U.S. Restaurant Industry Sales

Year	Sales
1970	$ 42.8
1987	$ 199.7
1997	$ 322.5
2007*	$ 536.9

*projected.

Source: Adapted from National Restaurant Association Overview, 2007.

Some of the macroeconomic factors affecting the restaurant and food services industries include job growth and unemployment rates, discretionary income, consumer confidence, and energy prices. Since the food service industry is a supplier to the restaurant industry, these macro factors overlap. For example, an aging and growing population base are favorable long-term demographics for both industries. The consolidation of the food service industry continued in 2007, especially as the prices of corn, fuel, and other materials increased and put pressure on operating margins.

Casual sit-down dining makes up about 30 percent of the restaurant business, fast foods represents another 30 percent, and family dining accounts for the remainder. Recently family dining has been losing share as consumers are trading down to fast foods. The pricing environment is stable. Menu prices increased 1–2 percent to cover higher labor costs in 2007.

Representing a cornerstone of the nation's economy, the overall economic impact of the restaurant industry way expected to exceed $1.3 trillion in 2007, including sales in related industries such as agriculture, transportation, and manufacturing. Every dollar spent by consumers in restaurants generates an additional $2.34 spent in other industries allied with the restaurant industry. Every additional $1 million in restaurant sales creates 37 jobs in the United States. The industry is expected to add two million jobs in the next decade.

In the United States, nearly half of all adults have worked in the restaurant industry at some time during their lives and 32 percent of adults got their first job experience in a restaurant. Today 55 percent of employees are female, 66 percent are single, 79 percent live in a household with two or more wage earners, and most work part-time averaging 25 hours per week.

The restaurant industry offers attractive job opportunities for women and minorities who represent 60 percent of the owners of eating and drinking establishments. Three of five first-line supervisors of food preparation and service workers are women, 16 percent are Hispanic, and 14 percent are African-American.

On a typical day, restaurant-industry sales total $1.5 billion. Fully 80 percent of consumers agree that that going out to a restaurant is a better way to use their leisure time than cooking and cleaning up. Table-service restaurants report a growing business in take-out orders and more demand for organic and healthy menu selections. Take-outs and health concerns represent two strong growth opportunities for the industry.

The Restaurant Industry Food and Drink (F&D) sales projections are categorized into three distinct groups, commercial, noncommercial, and military restaurant services, with the commercial sector representing 90 percent of the total. This sector is subdivided into eating places, managed services, lodging places, and miscellaneous. Within managed restaurant services, also referred to as onsite food service or food service contractors, the colleges and universities subcategory ranks the highest in terms of projected sales dollar volume. The primary and secondary schools sector is projected to experience the highest three-year (2004–07) compound annual growth rate (CAGR) at 11.3 percent. Colleges and universities ranked second (8.4 percent), followed by hospitals and nursing homes (7.6 percent), in terms of projected CAGR. The other managed restaurant services sectors are (listed in descending rank order of projected CAGR): recreation and sports (4.8 percent), commercial and office buildings (4.3 percent), in-transit restaurant services (4.2 percent), and manufacturing and industrial plants (4.1 percent). The Compass Group operates within the managed services sector and has a market presence in all of these managed services areas.

Competition in North America

In the fragmented U.S. market, Aramark, Sodexho, and Compass NA are the primary competitors, and all have experienced revenue growth in recent years. As indicated in Exhibit 6, during the period 2004–2006, Compass grew sales 21 percent while Sodexho and Aramark grew at rates of 9.8 and 8.7 percent respectively.

Compass consistently posts the highest margins (although decreasing) and Sodexho posts the lowest margins. These three rivals control approximately 70 percent of the U.S. contract food service market.[4] The remaining 30 percent of the market is widely dispersed among other firms, most of which are privately owned.

EXHIBIT 6   Compass versus U.S. Competitors

	Revenue (U.S. $B)			PBIT (U.S. $B)			Operating Margin (%)		
	2004	2005	2006	2004	2005	2006	2004	2005	2006
Sodexho	6.10	6.40	6.70	0.29	0.28	0.21	0.05	4.40	3.20
Aramark	6.90	7.10	7.50	0.38	0.40	0.40	0.05	5.70	5.30
Compass NA	6.70	7.10	8.10	0.40	0.41	0.46	0.06	5.80	5.70

Source: Adapted from *Foodservice Director*, March 15, 2006, and Compass Group PLC *Annual Report*, 2006.

Competition among the three main players revolves around service, quality of food, and relationships with the client. The ability to retain accounts year after year often proves to be the key element of success. Switching costs for the customer are usually low, and the change of a single customer may have a large effect on annual revenue of the food service provider. Often, these contracts are for multiple years. Other important competitive issues include variety of menu selections, attractive presentation, healthy food choices, cleanliness of facilities, refurbishment of facilities, environmental concerns, and price. Because service is directly related to individual employees, companies strive to have long-tenured employees who deliver exceptional service in a pleasant manner.

Headquartered in Philadelphia and employing 240,000 people, Aramark became a private company on January 26, 2007. It had been listed on the New York Stock Exchange (RMK) since 2001. CEO Joseph Neubauer, who controlled 40 percent of the voting power, led the buyout involving a group of private-equity firms. Exhibit 6 reveals that Aramark has lost position to Compass NA in both revenues and absolute profits, as well as operating margins. Results for fourth quarter 2006 were hurt by weak performances in sports and entertainment, causing earnings to decrease 22 percent compared to the previous fourth quarter. Now that the firm is private, information will be limited and financial comparisons will be more difficult to make.

Headquartered in Marseilles, France, Sodexho derives approximately 80 percent of its revenues outside of France. CEO Michel Landel aims to grow revenues 7 percent per year and operating profits 12 percent annually. This security is not traded in the United States, but is traded in Paris and in London. Sodexho has a strong balance sheet and is on the prowl for acquisitions. Sodexho employs 324,000 people in 80 countries and achieved overall revenues in 2005 of €11.7 billion and €12.8 billion in 2006. Exhibit 6 indicates that Sodexho has the lowest operating margin of the top three U.S. competitors. Profits in 2005 and 2006 totaled €333 million and €407 million respectively.

Overall, the 50 top contract firms grew revenues 8.3 percent in 2005 as Americans ate more and more meals away from home. Although contractors' market share of corporate dining is a high 75 percent, other sectors have considerably lower contractor shares—creating significant opportunities for continued growth. Contractors command market shares of only 18 percent for schools, 22 percent for correction facilities, and 23 percent for health care, as shown in Exhibit 7.[5] These sectors are all growing rapidly.

EXHIBIT 7   Contractor's Market Share

Corporate Dining	75%
Higher Education	57%
Recreation	36%
Health care	23%
Corrections	22%
Schools	18%
Military	10%

Source: Adapted from *Technomic Data Digest*, 2005.

Compass NA

Compass NA has grown to be the largest division in the Group and is divided into four major sectors: business and industry, health care, education, and sports and leisure. Headquartered in Charlotte, North Carolina, Compass NA's growth strategy of acquisitions continues to evolve around these principles:

- Concentrate on the fast-growth sectors of the contract catering business such as health care and athletics.
- Identify quality acquisition candidates that are well managed, highly regarded by customers, and profitable—market leaders.
- Maintain the brand and name of the target. Minimize the Compass name.
- Maintain and strengthen the relationships between the target and its customers so that customers perceive no difference in the service offered or in the processes of doing business after an acquisition is completed.
- Use incentives to retain target's key employees and to grow the business.
- Reject any target where the culture is incompatible with Compass NA.
- Pursue only friendly transactions.

Compass NA developed resources that enabled the efficient and effective implementation of its acquisition strategy. Palmer Brown, a lawyer and a CPA, began working on Compass acquisitions as an outside counsel before becoming a Compass employee devoting his full efforts to the successful consummation of acquisitions. The company developed a reputation of being a trustworthy acquisition partner with a special expertise in closing transactions efficiently. Today, more than 75 percent of proposals are closed as successful transactions.

The acquisition of Morrison gave Compass the leading position in health care; the acquisition of Chartwells created global identity for the educational sector; and the recently completed acquisition of Levy (2006), based in Chicago, gave Compass NA the premier position in the sports and leisure sector. The business and industry sector is changing rapidly as vending decreases due in part to the reduction in manufacturing positions in the United States as outsourcing increases in many industries. Emphasis is shifting to service organizations and technology firms.

Other acquisitions include Service America, Restaurants Associates, SHRM of Canada, the Patina Group, Crothall Services Group, Au Bon Pain, Bon Appetit Management Services, Select Service Partners (airports), Professional Foodservice Management, and Thompson Hospitality, a minority-owned contract foodservice company.

Realizing that the value of an acquisition in this business-to-business model is the target's relationships with its customers (other businesses), Compass NA aims to protect and enhance these relationships at all costs. Many of the targets are family-owned businesses that have become very successful. Compass approaches these targets with flexibility and an understanding of the emotional stress such a transaction may cause. To encourage the retention of key employees when an acquisition is completed, Compass attempts to make very few, if any, changes in the organization, positions, titles, salaries, and so on. Incentive plans are established where key employees can earn handsome incentives if certain performance targets are achieved over a 3- to 5-year period. This enhances the success of the acquisition, increases the compensation to the sellers, maintains customer relationships, and exploits internal growth opportunities in revenues and profits.

The timing and structure of a deal often have significant financial implications due to taxes and estate planning. Compass is receptive to all issues, is patient with the sellers, and open to arrangements where transactions are consummated over a period of years for the advantage of the seller. Compass NA has developed a reputation of being a large public company that is fair and with whom it is easy to do business. Over time, systems such as accounting, payroll, and employee benefits are standardized if desirable, but there is no rush. Compass does nothing to interfere with the customers' relationships with the company.

Lansing described his reporting relationship to Compass as being a "total pleasure" with the focus on customers, associates, culture, and win-win for everyone. The competitive advantage, he explained, is the culture among employees, which he described as family, nice people, good training, development opportunities, generous benefits, caring and concern. He sends handwritten notes to new managers and baskets of fruit and food to the homes of new employees to welcome them to the "family."

Compass is no exception to the reality that in acquisitions, the purchaser usually pays a premium to the seller. Growth via acquisition is quick, but usually expensive. How, therefore, does Compass achieve synergies and/or cost savings to pay the premium and create value for the shareholder if integration of the target is not a priority?

Because Compass NA selects only companies in growth sectors that are well managed and profitable, there is no need to overhaul operations or restructure management. Compass does create incentives among existing managers to motivate future growth. Compass does nothing to touch the relationship with the customer, but it does integrate functions that do not touch the customer. Integration of the purchasing function justifies most of the acquisitions and is done quickly.

The purchase of food represents on average 40 percent of the costs of operations, and Compass realizes savings of 10 to 15 percent when buying food in large quantities.[6] The information technology systems at Compass enables the consolidation of purchasing even though deliveries are individualized. If a particular chef feels strongly that a particular food ingredient is necessary for a recipe, Compass NA accommodates the request and does not force the use of a more universal product. The consolidation of purchasing is modified to address specific needs.

After discussions initiated by Morrison CEO Glen Davenport and that extended over a period of more than 12 months, Compass acquired Morrison, now the largest food service firm in the health care sector. Its revenue totaled $600 million at the time of the acquisition, $240 million of which represented food purchases. Annual cost savings of $24–$36 million were immediately available by consolidating purchasing. In addition, total purchases benefit from the economies of scale associated with the increased volume. The management team of Morrison stayed in place, no employees changed, payroll and benefits were consolidated after a year, and sales forces were merged after two and one-half years. No customers were lost, but several productive ideas were generated by comparing best practices of the two companies, exchanging menus and recipes, and visiting various locations.[7]

When an acquisition target is identified, usually a personal contact is made, and if there is or may be an interest, a very loose, soft-stance letter-of-intent outlining the key issues is prepared. Compass maintains a flexible position that can accommodate all issues of concern of the target. There is no pressure, no rush, and no hard sell. Sellers become partners with incentives to make the business successful. Compass imposes no managerial restrictions on the operations. Not only is there a discussion of how the business will be run after acquisition, but sellers see how this is working with similar acquisitions already concluded and, therefore, have no reservations about how they may be treated. Frequently, these new partners discover that they are treated better as a part of Compass NA than as an independent entity.[8]

The Future

Since contractors control only 18 percent of food service for schools, how can Compass exploit this opportunity and lead the industry in that market? Health care will be expanding rapidly as the elderly population in the country grows. This is a business Compass knows well and in which it can create value for clients. How should Compass proceed to exploit these opportunities? What acquisition candidates should be next for Compass?

Can Compass NA create value for prison and correctional institutions? Contractors serve only 22 percent of these facilities, and this is a growth area. How should the company proceed in this industry? Does Compass have the relationships with governmental agencies to establish itself in this sector?

But will additional growth cause complexities throughout the organization that may lead to inefficiencies? Tom recalls the paradox that often firms grow big to become more efficient, and in the process of doing so become complex and inefficient. This is especially applicable to global growth. What can Compass do to avoid this?

Even though revenue growth is important, it must be accompanied by earnings growth. Can Compass maintain its operating margin as it competes to take business from competitors? Or should the growth come from retention of existing customers and future acquisitions? What internal opportunities exist for cost reductions? Are there additional economies of scale associated with purchasing?

CEO Gary Green remarked recently that the biggest challenge going forward "is to avoid complacency. We can't rest on our laurels. We need to continue our strong sales mentality and market even more effectively. Look what we have done in 10 short years. Imagine where we will be in another decade!"

Endnotes

1. Compass Group *Annual Report* 2005, United Kingdom, inside front cover.
2. National Restaurant Association 2006 Forecast, "Restaurant Industry Food-and-Drink Sales Projected through 2006," p. 10.
3. National Restaurant Association 2006 Restaurant Industry Fact Sheet, www.restaurant.org.
4. "Contract Firms Gain Incremental Share," *FoodService Director*, March 15, 2005, p. 27; The Value Line Investment Survey, June 9, 2006, p. 3; "Contractors' Revenue Grows 8.3% in FY 05," *FoodService Director*, March 15, 2006, p. 17.
5. "Contractors' Revenue Grows 8.3% in FY 05," *FoodService Director*, March 15, 2006, www.fsdmag.com.
6. Tom Ordrof, CFO and executive vice president, Compass Group NA, interview, April 6, 2006, Compass Headquarters, Charlotte, NC.
7. Glen Davenport, CEO, Morrison, telephone interview, April 24, 2006.
8. Palmer Brown, vice president, corporate development, Compass Group NA, interview, April 19, 2006, Compass Headquarters, Charlotte, NC.

Internet Hot Links

www.compass-group.com
www.cgnad.com
www.hoovers.com/compassgroupplc
http://finance.yahoo.com/compassgroupplc
http://marketwatch.multexinvestor.com
http://moneycentral.msn.com

23 Continental Airlines Inc. — 2007

Charles M. Byles
Virginia Commonwealth University

CAL

www.continental.com

Continental Airlines launched its nonstop service between Newark Liberty International Airport and Mumbai, India on October 1, 2007, earlier than originally planned. Flights feature products and services for its Indian customers such as a Bollywood movie channel showing movies in Hindi with English subtitles. In addition, other movies have Hindi subtitles, traditional Indian music is offered on music audio channels, and safety and arrival videos and prerecorded announcements are available in Hindi. In-flight meals include Indian vegetarian and nonvegetarian choices, and no beef is served.

The new service illustrates Continental's continuing pattern of international expansion and places it as the leading airline with nonstop flights between the United States and India (it currently has service to Delhi). Given the intense rivalry in the U.S. domestic market, international markets offer excellent growth opportunities for the future. For the third quarter of 2007, Continental's net income increased 5.7 percent to $241 million, while revenues increase 3 percent to $3.8 billion.

History

In 70 years, Continental Airlines grew from a small airline flying a single-engine Lockheed Vargas carrying four passengers to the fourth largest airline in the United States and fifth largest in the world. Continental Airlines, founded by Walter Varney and Louis Mueller, began flying from El Paso, Texas to Pueblo, Colorado in 1934. The headquarters moved from El Paso to Denver in 1937 and then to Houston in 1982 following a merger with Texas International. Continental's rise to a major airline was not without problems. In 1983, the airline filed its first Chapter 11 bankruptcy. By 1987, it was the third largest U.S. airline with the consolidation of Frontier, People Express, and New York Air. A second Chapter 11 was filed by Continental in December 1990. In April 1993, it emerged from bankruptcy, and in July of the next year celebrated its 60th anniversary of service.

Immediately after the September 11 terrorist attacks, Continental reduced flights and furloughed 12,000 employees. Between 2005 and 2006, four major competitors—Delta, Northwest, United, and U.S. Airways—were under Chapter 11 bankruptcy protection. Increasing fuel costs and intense domestic competition contributed to financial losses throughout the industry. Continental had net income losses for 2001, 2002, 2004, and 2005, but in 2006 it returned to profitability with a net income of $346 million.

Internal Factors

Guiding Principles

As given in Exhibit 1, the "Go Forward Plan" unveiled in 1995 by then-CEO Gordon Bethune continues today as a guide, business plan, and basis of evaluation of accomplishment. An April 27, 2007 letter from CEO Larry Kellner and President Jeff Smisek to co-workers,

EXHIBIT 1 The Go Forward Plan

Fly to Win

- Achieve above-average profits in a changed industry environment.
- Grow the airline to where it can make money and keep improving the business/leisure mix.
- Maximize distribution channels while reducing distribution costs and eliminating non-value-added costs.

Fund the Future

- Manage company assets to maximize stockholder value and build for the future.
- Reduce costs with technology.
- Generate positive cash flow and improve financial flexibility by increasing its cash balance.

Make Reliability a Reality

- Deliver an industry-leading product the airline is proud to sell.
- Rank among the top of the industry in the key DOT measurements: on-time arrivals, baggage handling, complaints, and involuntary denied boardings.
- Keep improving the product.

Working Together

- Help well-trained employees build careers they enjoy every day. Treat each other with dignity and respect.
- Focus on safety, make employee programs easy to use, and keep improving communication.
- Keep pay and benefits competitive in a changed industry environment.

Source: Continental Airlines Company Profile (Facts), 2nd Quarter 2007. Available at the company Web site, http://www.continental.com/web/en-US/content/company/profile/default.aspx.

customers, and stockholders illustrates the role of this plan as the premier guiding principle at Continental:

> As it has in the past, and as it will in the future, our Go Forward Plan continued to guide us in 2006. It is a straightforward business plan that all our co-workers understand, with clear and measurable goals that we set and communicate each year. Our Go Forward Plan has four cornerstones—Fly to Win (our market plan), Fund the Future (our financial plan), Make Reliability a Reality (our product plan) and Working Together (our people plan).

The Go Forward Plan also serves as a means of evaluation of the airline's performance, and the letter includes an evaluation of how Continental measured up in 2006 against each of the four cornerstones.

While the Go Forward Plan provides a market plan, financial plan, and product plan, it doesn't specifically address environmental or global issues directly. Should the plan be modified in light of changes in the last 12 years in which these two areas have received greater attention in the industry in general, and Continental in particular? More discussion is given later in the sections on global issues and the natural environment.

Management and Human Resources

Continental's relatively young top management team joined the airline at about the same time in the mid-1990s. The top executive officers are Mr. Lawrence Kellner (48), chairman and CEO, and Mr. Jeffrey Smisek (52), president. Mr. Kellner joined in 1995 and became chairman of the board and chief executive officer in December 2004. Mr. Smisek joined in March 1995 and became president and board member in December 2004. Mr. Smisek oversees sales and marketing, human resources and labor relations, technology, corporate communications, global real estate and security and environmental affairs, federal affairs, and international and civic affairs. Other executive officers are Mr. Jim Compton (51), executive vice president of marketing, Mr. Jeffrey Miser (53), chief financial officer and executive vice president, and Mr. Mark Moran (51), executive vice president of operations.

EXHIBIT 2   Daily Departures

	Daily Departures
Continental Airlines	1,200
Continental Micronesia	32
Continental Express	1,371
Continental Connection	444
Total	3,047

Source: CO Facts, 2nd Quarter, 2007.

Although Continental does not make its organizational chart known, it appears to be organized along functional lines (e.g., marketing, finance, and operations). It is notable that no vice president specifically oversees international operations given its importance at Continental, although international sales are the responsibility of Mr. Compton, and international affairs are the responsibility of Mr. Smisek.

Among Continental's 44,494 employees, the largest groups are airport agents (11,310), flight attendants (8,864), management and clerical (4,671), and pilots (4,609). A unique aspect of Continental's human resource approach is its on-time arrival incentive program for employees at the managerial level and below. Employees receive incentives linked to on-time arrival targets as scored by the U.S. Department of Transportation. Eligible employees can receive $100.00 if Continental is first among six network carriers in on-time performance, $65.00 if Continental is second or third, or if the on-time performance is 80 percent or better (regardless of the on-time ranking).

It does not appear that employees have been receiving these incentives recently, however, based on Continental's poor on-time performance (see later discussion under service quality and also Exhibit 5).

Scope of Operations

Continental is the world's fifth largest airline (measured by miles flown by revenue passengers). Along with its subsidiary, Continental Micronesia Inc., and regional flights operated by Continental Express and Continental Connection, it operates more than 3,000 daily departures (see Exhibit 2) throughout the Americas, Europe, and Asia, and serves 148 domestic and 134 international destinations (see Exhibit 3). Continental serves more international destinations than other U.S. carriers. It directly serves twenty-six European cities, nine South American cities, Tel Aviv, Delhi, Hong Kong, Beijing, and Tokyo, in addition to flights to Canada, Mexico, Central America, and the Caribbean.

Continental's domestic routes are operated primarily through its hubs at Newark Liberty International Airport (New York Liberty), George Bush International Airport in Houston (Houston Bush), and Hopkins International Airport in Cleveland (Cleveland Hopkins). New York Liberty also serves 26 cities in Europe, seven in Canada, six in Mexico, eight in Central America, five in South America, 18 Caribbean destinations, Tel Aviv,

EXHIBIT 3   Airports Served

	U.S.	International	Total
Continental	17	87	104
Continental Express	41	24	65
Continental Connection	20	10	30
Combined Operation	70	13	83
Total	148	134	282

Source: CO Facts, 2nd Quarter, 2007.

Delhi, Hong Kong, Beijing, and Tokyo. Houston Bush serves 30 cities in Mexico, all seven Central American countries, nine cities in South America, six Caribbean destinations, three cities in Canada, Europe, and Tokyo.

From its hub in Guam, Continental Micronesia, Inc., provides service to eight cities in Japan (more than any U.S. carrier), Manila, Hong Kong, Cairns, Australia, and Bali. The Continental Micronesia route is linked to the U.S. market through Hong Kong, Tokyo, and Honolulu, each of which is served by nonstop flights from Guam.

Fleet

As of April 2007, Continental operates 368 jets and is one of a few all-Boeing fleets in the U.S. (others are Southwest and AirTran). In 2005, Continental retired its last MD-80 aircraft, resulting in its fleet being reduced to three Boeing aircraft types—777, 757/767, and 737. This fleet makeup allows easier training, maintenance, and savings on replacement parts. In addition, since more than 70 percent of the Continental fleet consists of common-rated Boeing 737 series aircraft, there are additional efficiencies in pilot training, crew flexibility, simplified maintenance, and savings on spare parts. Continental was one of the first to add winglets to replace the standard wingtips on its aircraft. Winglets (which reduce fuel consumption by up to 5 percent) were installed on its 737-700, 737-800, and 757-200 aircraft, and future winglet installations are planned. With an average age of 8.5 years, Continental's fleet is older than the fleets of JetBlue and AirTran, but younger than the fleets of other legacy carriers. Continental continues to add new aircraft, and as recently at March 2007, ordered 25 Boeing 787 Dreamliners to provide added fuel efficiency on international routes.

Service Quality

Service quality at Continental can be measured in two ways: first, by the Airline Quality Rating 2007 (AQR) and second by the number of awards that the airline has received. The AQR was developed in 1991 as an objective method of assessing airline quality based on four criteria: on-time arrivals, involuntary denied boardings, mishandled baggage, and a combination of 12 customer complaint categories. Data for all criteria are drawn from the U.S. Department of Transportation's *Air Travel Consumer Report*. The AQR 2007 report notes that there was a general decline in service quality in the industry for 2006 when compared to 2005. Of the 15 carriers rated in both 2005 and 2006, only Northwest and U.S. Airways showed improvement in AQR scores for 2006. Continental's AQR score has declined for the last three years even though its ranking has improved (see Exhibit 4). Details in the particular areas in which Continental's service quality has declined over the last year are given below (reproduced from the AQR 2007 report):

> Continental Airlines (CO) posted declines in performance for two of the four AQR criteria. Customer complaint rate (0.88 in 2006 versus 0.92 in 2005) and denied boarding rate (1.74 in 2006 compared to 1.92 in 2005) were the areas of improvement. Mishandled baggage rate per 1,000 passengers (4.76 in 2006 compared to 4.12 in 2005) hurt Continental's AQR score. Poorer on-time performance (73.4% in 2006 compared to 76.9% in 2005) lowered their AQR score for 2006.

A more extensive evaluation of Continental's on-time performance shows that it has not met the 80 percent or better standard for arrivals for the last four years, or for departures for the last two years (Exhibit 5). Continental's rank among airlines (Exhibit 5) is quite poor, especially given the goal in the employee incentive program (see section on management and human resources) to be in the top three rank. Another evaluation of Continental's service quality appeared in *Kiplinger.com* (May 2006), which evaluated bumping at various airlines over a three-month period. Jet Blue was commended for rarely bumping passengers, while Continental was among three airlines (the others were Comair and Atlantic Southeast) that had the worst record of overbooking and bumping. Despite these declines in service quality, Continental received numerous awards for service quality and other achievements. Some recent awards include (see the airline Web site for a full list of awards):

- Fortune's "America's Most Admired Companies 2007" (airline category)
- OAG "Best Airline in North America" 2007

EXHIBIT 4   **Airline Quality Rating Rankings**

	2006	2005	2004
AirTran	3	2	2
Alaska	9	9	5
American	10	10	8
American Eagle	17	14	13
ATA	11	11	10
Atlantic Southeast	18	17	16
Comair	16	16	15
Continental	7	8	9
Delta	12	12	11
Frontier	4	-	-
Hawaiian	1	-	-
JetBlue	2	1	1
Mesa	15	-	-
Northwest	5	7	7
SkyWest	14	13	14
Southwest	6	4	3
United	8	5	4
U.S. Airways	13	15	12

Notes:
1. Rankings for 2006 reflect the addition of Frontier, Hawaiian, and Mesa to the airlines tracked.
2. As of January 2006, data of the merged operations of U.S. Airways and America West Airlines are combined, and appear only as U.S. Airways data.
3. Rankings for 2005 reflect the removal of Independence Air from the airlines tracked.

Source: Airline Quality Rating 2007, Brent T. Bowen, University of Nebraska at Omaha, and Dean E. Headley, Wichita State University, April 2007.

- Finalist for OAG Airline of the Year 2007
- OAG "Best Business/Executive Class" 2007

EXHIBIT 5   **Percentage On-Time Performance (Domestic Flights)**

Continental	2004	2005	2006	2007	Rank
Departure	86	83	79	78	15
Arrival	79	77	73	73	12

Northwest	2004	2005	2006	2007	Rank
Departure	86	82	82	81	16
Arrival	79	75	76	72	8

Southwest	2004	2005	2006	2007	Rank
Departure	78	78	77	78	13
Arrival	80	81	80	80	18

Notes:
1. 2007 represents May 2006–April 2007.
2. 2007 ranking is for May 2006–April 2007.

Source: "Carrier Fact Sheet," Bureau of Transportation Statistics, U.S. Department of Commerce, June 10, 2007. http://www.transtats.bts.gov/printcarriers.asp?Carrier=NW

EXHIBIT 6 Selected Operating Data

Mainline Operations	2006	2005	2004
Passengers (thousands) (1)	48,788	44,939	42,743
Passenger load factor (2)	81.1%	79.5%	77.6%
Ave. yield per revenue passenger mile (cents) (3)	12.29	11.73	11.37
Cost per available seat mile (cents)	10.56	10.22	9.84
Ave. price per gallon of fuel including taxes (cents)	206.35	177.55	119.01
Ave. daily utilization of aircraft (hours) (4)	11:07	10:31	9:55
Regional Operations			
Passengers (thousands) (1)	18,331	16,076	13,739
Passenger load factor (2)	77.9%	74.7%	71.3%
Ave. yield per revenue passenger mile (cents)(3)	22.03	20.99	21.18
Comparison Data			
Industry passenger load factor	77.8%		
Northwest load factor	80.9%		
Southwest load factor	71.4%		
Northwest passenger yield	11.64		
Southwest passenger yield	11.75		
Northwest cost per available seat mile (cents)	14.37		
Southwest cost per available seat mile (cents)	7.92		

Notes:
Mainline = jets with capacity of greater than 100 seats
Regional = jets with capacity of 50 or fewer seats
1. The number of revenue passengers measured by each flight segment flown
2. Revenue passenger miles divided by available seat miles
3. The average passenger revenue received for each revenue passenger mile flown
4. The average number of hours per day that an aircraft is flown in revenue service (from gate departure to gate arrival)

Sources: Continental Airlines, Inc., 2006 *Annual Report* to Stockholders, Bureau of Transportation Statistics, U.S. Department of Commerce, 2007, http://www.transtats.bts.gov.

Operating Performance

Continental's passenger numbers and load factor have improved slightly over the last three years (see Exhibit 6). The 2006 passenger load factor (81.1 percent) was above the industry average of 77.8 percent (as reported by the Bureau of Transportation Statistics), and above the load factors of Southwest Airlines (71.4 percent) and Northwest Airlines (80.9 percent). Northwest was chosen as a comparison as it has about the same domestic market share as Continental; Southwest was chosen as a typical low-cost carrier (see Exhibit 6 for comparison data). Continental's passenger yields have risen slightly over the last two years to 12.29, and compare favorably to Northwest and Southwest. Continental's cost per available seat mile has increased from 9.84 in 2004 to 10.56 in 2006, and is lower than Northwest for 2006 (14.37) but higher than Southwest (7.72).

Exhibits 7 and 8 show a comparison of operating costs per unit for 2006 across seven carriers, including Continental, and a comparison with regional, network, and low-cost carriers. These exhibits show Continental's operating expenses to be in the middle of the group, with U.S. Airways having the highest operating expenses, and American and Alaska generally being lower than Continental. Exhibit 7 shows that Continental's operating costs are very close to the regional and national carriers, but significantly above the costs of the low-cost carriers.

EXHIBIT 7   System (Domestic and International) Airline Unit Costs (Cents per Mile)

Passenger Airlines by Group
Ranked by 4th Quarter 2006 Unit Costs
(Operating Expenses per Available Seat Mile in Cents)

2006 Rank		4th Quarter 2005	1st Quarter 2006	2nd Quarter 2006	3rd Quarter 2006	4th Quarter 2006	4th Quarter Operating Expenses $(Millions)
1	Regional Carriers	13.6	13.9	13.9	13.7	13.5	2,205
2	Network Carriers	13.7	13.5	13.4	13.3	13.2	22,475
3	Low-Cost Carriers	9.2	9.2	9.7	9.8	9.5	4,711
	21-Carrier Total	12.8	12.7	12.7	12.6	12.5	29,391

Source: Reproduced from "Fourth-Quarter 2006 System Airline Financial Data: Passenger Airlines Report Largest Fourth-Quarter Profit Margin Since 1999," Bureau of Transportation Statistics, May 14, 2007, http://www.bts.gov/press_releases/2007/bts023_07/html/bts023_07.html.

Finance

Continental reported a net income of $343 million in 2006 after two previous years of losses. Continental's income statement shows a strong increase in gross profit for 2006, and a decrease in the cost of revenue. This shows that the airline has been able to improve its operating efficiencies by improving the revenues generated per revenue passenger mile flown (see earlier operating data) while controlling its costs. As shown in Exhibit 8, the income statement does, however, show a large increase in selling, general, and administrative costs for 2006.

Exhibits 9 and 10 summarize a U.S. Department of Transportation survey of a 21-carrier group consisting of the seven largest network, low-cost, and regional carriers. Exhibit 9 shows that the group had an operating profit margin of 2.6 percent in the fourth quarter. Exhibit 10 provides a comparison of Continental's fourth-quarter profit margin (0.2 percent) to the network carrier group as a whole (1.7 percent) and to individual carriers. U.S. Airways reported the top profit margin in fourth quarter 2006. Five airlines

EXHIBIT 8   System (Domestic and International) Airline Unit Costs (Cents per Mile)

Network Carriers
Ranked by 4th Quarter 2006 Unit Costs
(Operating Expenses per Available Seat Mile in Cents)

2006 Rank	Network Carriers	4th Quarter 2005	1st Quarter 2006	2nd Quarter 2006	3rd Quarter 2006	4th Quarter 2006	4th Quarter Operating Expenses $(Millions)
1	U.S. Airways	15.6	15.6	16.1	15.7	15.4	1,808
2	Delta	14.1	14.4	13.4	13.6	13.9	4,197
3	Continental	13.5	13.3	13.6	13.4	13.6	3,126
4	Northwest	15.1	14.2	13.8	13.6	13.4	2,882
5	United	13.1	13.4	13.4	13.0	13.0	4,572
6	American	13.1	12.3	12.4	12.6	12.5	5,253
7	Alaska	11.0	13.3	11.4	12.3	11.1	637
	Seven-Carrier Total	13.7	13.5	13.4	13.3	13.2	22,475

Source: Reproduced from "Fourth-Quarter 2006 System Airline Financial Data: Passenger Airlines Report Largest Fourth-Quarter Profit Margin Since 1999," Bureau of Transportation Statistics, May 14, 2007, http://www.bts.gov/press_releases/2007/bts023_07/html/bts023_07.html.

EXHIBIT 9 **System (Domestic and International) Quarterly Operating Profit/Loss Margin (In Percent)**

Passenger Airlines by Group
Ranked by 4th Quarter 2006 Margin
(Operating Profit/Loss as Percent of Total Operating Revenue)

2006 Rank		4th Quarter 2005	1st Quarter 2006	2nd Quarter 2006	3rd Quarter 2006	4th Quarter 2006	4th Quarter Operating Profit/Loss $(Millions)
1	Regional Carriers	8.9	9.3	8.1	8.9	10.0	245
2	Low-Cost Carriers	1.8	2.5	10.8	3.3	2.7	131
3	Network Carriers	−7.3	−3.3	7.5	5.4	1.7	393
	21-Carrier Total	−4.5	−1.3	8.1	5.4	2.6	769

Source: Reproduced from "Fourth-Quarter 2006 System Airline Financial Data: Passenger Airlines Report Largest Fourth-Quarter Profit Margin Since 1999," Bureau of Transportation Statistics, May 14, 2007, http://www.bts.gov/press_releases/2007/bts023_07/html/bts023_07.html.

EXHIBIT 10 **System (Domestic and International) Quarterly Operating Profit/Loss Margin (In Percent)**

Network Carriers
Ranked by 4th Quarter 2006 Margin
(Operating Profit/Loss as Percent of Total Operating Revenue)

2006 Rank	Network Carriers	4th Quarter 2005	1st Quarter 2006	2nd Quarter 2006	3rd Quarter 2006	4th Quarter 2006	4th Quarter Operating Profit/Loss $(Millions)
1	U.S. Airways	−4.0	2.4	12.6	5.9	7.4	145
2	Northwest	−8.6	-0.2	9.2	11.1	3.7	110
3	American	−8.5	1.0	7.0	3.8	2.3	125
4	United	−4.6	−3.8	5.1	6.6	0.3	15
5	Continental	−3.7	−0.1	6.8	4.9	0.2	6
6	Delta	−12.3	−12.8	8.0	3.0	−0.1	−3
7	Alaska	−3.7	−25.1	6.3	0.5	−0.7	−5
	Seven-Carrier Total	−7.3	−3.3	7.5	5.4	1.7	393

Source: Reproduced from "Fourth-Quarter 2006 System Airline Financial Data: Passenger Airlines Report Largest Fourth-Quarter Profit Margin Since 1999," Bureau of Transportation Statistics, May 14, 2007, http://www.bts.gov/press_releases/2007/bts023_07/html/bts023_07.html.

had better fourth-quarter profit margins than Continental (U.S. Airways, Northwest, American, and United) while two had worse profit margins (Delta and Alaska).

External Factors

The end of 2006 and early 2007 saw the recovery for the U.S. airline industry after five years of losses and the bankruptcy of 21 airlines. The industry has returned to profitability, and the structure of many airlines has changed in response to the post-9/11 industry environment. Major airlines that went through Chapter 11 bankruptcy such as U.S Airways, Delta, Northwest, and United have emerged as more cost-efficient and competitive. Other changes, such as the merger of U.S. Airways and America West, have created a more efficient airline with a broader geographic coverage. However, a number of airlines have very high debt levels. For example, AMR Corp., the parent company of American Airlines, ended 2006 with total debt of $18.4 billion and negative stockholders' equity of $606 million.

EXHIBIT 11   Balance Sheet for Continental Airlines

	All numbers in thousands $		
Period Ending	Dec. 31, 2006	Dec. 31, 2005	Dec. 31, 2004
Assets			
Current Assets			
Cash and Cash Equivalents	$2,388,000	1,964,000	1,266,000
Short-Term Investments	361,000	234,000	403,000
Net Receivables	747,000	687,000	719,000
Inventory	217,000	201,000	214,000
Other Current Assets	416,000	341,000	222,000
Total Current Assets	**4,129,000**	**3,427,000**	**2,824,000**
Long-Term Investments	81,000	112,000	174,000
Property, Plant and Equipment	6,263,000	6,086,000	6,314,000
Goodwill	-	-	-
Intangible Assets	604,000	677,000	959,000
Accumulated Amortization	-	-	-
Other Assets	231,000	227,000	240,000
Deferred Long-Term Asset Charges	-	-	-
Total Assets	**11,308,000**	**10,529,000**	**10,511,000**
Liabilities			
Current Liabilities			
Accounts Payable	3,381,000	1,378,000	2,589,000
Short/Current Long-Term Debt	574,000	546,000	670,000
Other Current Liabilities	-	1,475,000	-
Total Current Liabilities	**3,955,000**	**3,399,000**	**3,259,000**
Long-Term Debt	4,859,000	5,057,000	5,167,000
Other Liabilities	1,982,000	1,693,000	1,552,000
Deferred Long-Term Liability Charges	165,000	154,000	378,000
Minority Interest	-	-	
Negative Goodwill	-	-	-
Total Liabilities	**10,961,000**	**10,303,000**	**10,356,000**
Stockholders' Equity			
Misc Stocks Options Warrants	-	-	-
Redeemable Preferred Stock	-	-	-
Preferred Stock	-	-	-
Common Stock	1,000	1,000	1,000
Retained Earnings	(11,000)	406,000	474,000
Treasury Stock	-	(1,141,000)	(1,141,000)
Capital Surplus	1,370,000	1,635,000	1,408,000
Other Stockholders' Equity	(1,013,000)	(675,000)	(587,000)
Total Stockholders' Equity	**347,000**	**226,000**	**155,000**
Total Liabilities and SE	**$11,308,000**	**$10,529,000**	**$10,511,000**

Source: Yahoo Finance, http://finance.yahoo.com/q/bs?s=CAL&annual.

EXHIBIT 12   Continental Airlines Income Statement

	All numbers in thousands $		
Period Ending	Dec. 31, 2006	Dec. 31, 2005	Dec. 31, 2004
Total Revenue	**$13,128,000**	**11,208,000**	**9,899,000**
Cost of Revenue	8,566,000	9,675,000	8,022,000
Gross Profit	**4,562,000**	**1,533,000**	**1,877,000**
Operating Expenses			
Research Development	-	-	-
Selling General and Administrative	3,676,000	1,116,000	1,700,000
Non-Recurring	27,000	67,000	-
Others	391,000	389,000	415,000
Total Operating Expenses	-	-	-
Operating Income or Loss	**468,000**	**(39,000)**	**(238,000)**
Income from Continuing Operations			
Total Other Income/Expenses Net	284,000	369,000	164,000
Earnings Before Interest and Taxes	752,000	330,000	(74,000)
Interest Expense	383,000	398,000	375,000
Income Before Tax	369,000	(68,000)	(449,000)
Income Tax Expense	-	-	(40,000)
Minority Interest	-	-	-
Net Income from Continuing Operations	369,000	(68,000)	(409,000)
Non-Recurring Events			
Discontinued Operations	-	-	-
Extraordinary Items	-	-	-
Effect of Accounting Changes	(26,000)	-	-
Other Items	-	-	-
Net Income	**343,000**	**(68,000)**	**(409,000)**
Preferred Stock and Other Adjustments	-	-	-
Net Income Applicable to Common Shares	**$343,000**	**($68,000)**	**($409,000)**

Source: Yahoo Finance, http://finance.yahoo.com/q/is?s=CAL&annual.

Competitors

American Airlines has the largest market share (15.4 percent), followed by United (12.1 percent), Southwest (11.9 percent), Delta (11.2 percent), and Continental (7.7 percent) (Exhibit 13). *Yahoo Finance* gives American, Southwest, and United as Continental's main competitors. Continental views its main competitive threats as low-cost carriers and airlines operating under, or recently emerged from, Chapter 11 bankruptcy such as Delta, Northwest, U.S. Airways, and United. A quote from its 2006 *Annual Report* gives the reasons for the threat posed by the Chapter 11 airlines:

> We are also facing stronger competition from carriers operating under bankruptcy protection, such as Delta Air Lines and Northwest Airlines, and from carriers that have emerged from bankruptcy, including U.S. Airways and United Airlines. Carriers in bankruptcy are able to achieve substantial cost reductions through, among other things, reduction or discharge of debt, lease and pension obligations and wage and benefit reductions, and may emerge from bankruptcy as more vigorous competitors with substantially lower costs than ours.

EXHIBIT 13   Airline Domestic Market Share

Airline	Share
American	15.4%
United	12.1%
Southwest	11.9%
Delta	11.2%
Continental	7.7%
Northwest	7.0%
U.S. Airways	4.7%
JetBlue	4.0%
America West	3.8%
Alaska	2.6%
Other	19.6%

Market share based on Revenue Passenger Miles March 2006–February 2007.
Top Domestic Routes March 2006–February 2007.

Source: Bureau of Transportation Statistics, U.S. Department of Transportation,
June 11, 2007, http://www.transtats.bts.gov/.

In addition to the above competitive threats, there are a number of possible future actions by competitors that that could impact Continental. For example, United Airlines has expressed interest to merge with a carrier that has a strong presence in the Northeast and a hub in the South (such as Delta). Such a merger could create a financially stronger and more efficient competitor for Continental. Other possible actions are the purchase of replacement planes by American and U.S. Airways. New aircraft would challenge Continental's lead as having the youngest, most fuel-efficient fleet among the major carriers.

In contrast to the successful JetBlue, many new entrants fail, such as Independence Airlines (failed in 2006), Mesaba Airlines (failed in 2005), and Transmeridian Airlines (failed in 2005). Some new entrants operating small jets as regional affiliates for airlines provide opportunities for larger airlines to lower costs as noted in the next section.

Regional Jets

Regional jets have transformed the industry in the last 20 years by providing a more cost-efficient component to an airline's overall route system and attracting travelers that might otherwise drive or take a bus. Regional jets offer greater range and more comfort than older turboprops, and allow airlines to offer jet service to smaller markets. Regional jets are a major cost advantage for airlines as their break-even load factor is below that of large jets (e.g., a regional jet can break-even at 50 percent versus a large jet which needs 65 percent or more).

Continental's regional jet service was at one time provided exclusively by ExpressJet (Continental Express) and gave Continental the advantage of being the only airline with a full jet service (i.e., it had no turboprops in its regional fleet). Continental also relies on its regional fleet for its domestic routes; approximately 60 percent of all departures are operated by Continental Express and Continental Connection (see Exhibit 2). In addition, of the 148 domestic airports served, 61 are exclusively by Continental Express or Continental Connection (Exhibit 3). Recently, however, because ExpressJet increased its rates, Continental reduced use of some ExpressJet aircraft offering regional service. Chautauqua Airlines was selected as a replacement and will operate fifty-four 50-seat regional jets, and Colgan was selected to operate fifteen 74-seat turboprop aircraft (as Continental Connection). Whether this disagreement with ExpressJet will affect the current service is not known, nor is the effect (from a customer satisfaction standpoint) of returning to turboprops known.

Security Measures and Internet Issues

Even with government subsidies, security costs for airlines have risen as they are required to screen all bags for explosives and ensure that each bag is matched to a passenger on the flight. A terrorist plot discovered in August 2006 resulted in more restrictions on the contents of carry-on baggage. These restrictions contributed to some reduction in bookings, primarily for those travelers who prefer to carry on baggage, and increased costs to the airlines as a result of having more checked bags.

The Internet is both an opportunity and a threat for the industry. Internet bookings have reduced the costs of ticket sales, but created a more powerful customer who can easily shop around for the best price. Many airlines now book the majority of fares online. For example, *Standard & Poors* reports that Southwest received 70 percent of its revenues from Web site bookings in 2006. In contrast, Continental was slow to adopt online bookings, and currently has about 24 percent of its revenues from its Web site. The use of electronic tickets (e-tickets) has also reduced costs as airlines or travel agents issue e-tickets and passengers then print boarding passes at home or at e-ticket machines at the airport. Electronic ticketing essentially transfers part of the traditional ticketing job to the customer and thus saves time and reduces the cost of the airline ticket counter. It also improves the speed of check-in and, as such, could improve customer satisfaction.

Fuel and Labor Costs

According to *Standard & Poors* industry surveys, fuel accounted for 25.7 percent of total expenses in 2006 at the 10 largest U.S. carriers and was the largest cost category. Fuel expenses are a function of an airline's fleet age (Continental has a relatively young fleet) and average flight length (shorter flights are less efficient as takeoffs and landings burn more fuel). Continental's fuel expenses for 2007 were 29.4 percent of operating expenses, and the average price of fuel rose by 73 percent from 2004–2006 (see Exhibit 6). For all airlines, fuel costs represent a serious market risk. *Standard & Poors* notes that fuel prices tend to be volatile and events such as a confrontation with Iran could cause prices to rise; it predicted oil would average $61.00 in 2007. Continental estimated that its 2007 fuel expenses could increase by $44 million. Many airlines, including Continental, use hedging strategies to control fuel costs.

Labor is the second largest cost for airlines and accounted for 24.5 percent of total revenues for the 10 largest carriers in 2006. Labor costs relate to various categories of employees: flight crews (pilots and engineers), flight attendants, ground service (including baggage handlers, ramp workers, and reservationists), dispatchers, maintenance, and customer service (bookings and boardings). Airline employees belong to unions such as the Association of Flight Attendants, the Airline Pilots Association, and the International Association of Machinists.

Natural Environmental Issues

Continental is committed to reducing greenhouse emissions as noted in the following statement from its Web site:

> Global climate change is an important issue and Continental recognizes that greenhouse gas emissions are everyone's concern. We recognize the importance of directly addressing this issue, even though we do not have all the answers.

Actions to protect the environmental occur primarily through fleet and ground operations. The following illustrate why Continental's fleet and operations burn less fuel and emit less carbon dioxide:

- Relatively new aircraft
- A fleet of all twin-engine aircraft (more efficient than three- or four-engine planes)
- Winglets installed on most of fleet (less drag and fuel burn)
- Regular washing of planes to reduce drag

- Purchase plan for new fuel-efficient Boeing 787 (largest order for 787s in the United States)
- Moving aircraft from the gate using ground equipment rather than aircraft engines
- Taxiing with one engine only
- Using electric ground service equipment at Houston hub

Other actions include construction of airport facilities according to the U.S. Green Building Council Leadership in Energy and Environmental Design and the Environmental Protection Agency Star standards, and the promotion of a culture that is environmentally sensitive. In recognition of its leadership in environmentally responsible actions, *Fortune* magazine named Continental one of its "10 Green Giants" in 2007.

Global Issues

Continental serves more international destinations than any other U.S. airline. An emphasis on international destinations makes strategic sense because international flights generate higher levels of revenue passenger miles than domestic flights, and revenue passenger miles are closely correlated with airline revenues. Put more simply, international service is generally more profitable and puts less wear-and-tear on the aircraft. Continental's emphasis on Asia, and China and India in particular, is astute given the importance of these economies to U.S. businesses.

The recently signed "EU-US Open Skies" treaty (which takes effect in March 2008) presents an opportunity for Continental. At present, only British Airways, Virgin Atlantic, American Airlines, and United Airlines have the right to fly between the United States and London's Heathrow airport. Under the new treaty, any U.S. or E.U. airline will be permitted to fly to any point in the United States and vice versa. The U.S. airlines that will gain from the opportunity to serve Heathrow are Delta, Continental, and U.S. Airways.

The Future

International markets are more profitable than the more competitive and less attractive domestic market. Continental plans to soon buy more Boeing 787 aircraft than any other U.S. carrier. Its modern, fuel-efficient fleet will help reduce fuel costs, which are the largest cost item in the industry. Its efforts with fuel efficiency and other environmental efforts give it high marks and enhances its reputation among customers.

Domestic competition stands out as the main challenge for Continental in the future. There are some secondary challenges in the form of service quality, but Continental must devise a strategy for competing in the domestic market against both the low-cost and the Chapter 11 airlines (i.e., those airlines that have emerged from bankruptcy with certain cost advantages).

Another broad challenge for Continental is whether it is meeting the standards set forth in the Go Forward Plan. For example, with respect to "Fly to Win," is Continental achieving above-average profits? Or, under the "Make Reliability a Reality" category, is Continental achieving the standard of ranking among the top of the industry on on-time arrivals, baggage handling, complaints, and involuntary denied boardings? Some specific summary questions to be considered in evaluating the challenges facing Continental are:

1. What strategy should Continental adopt to compete against the low-cost carriers such as AirTran, JetBlue, and Southwest? Can Continental realistically compete with these airlines on the basis of price?
2. How much of a threat are Delta, Northwest, U.S. Airways, and United, and what should be Continental's strategy to compete against these airlines?
3. Will the changes in Continental's regional jet service (i.e., moving away from the exclusive alliance with ExpressJet) affect the overall service offered by the airline? In particular, consider Continental's reliance on regional jets for domestic service.
4. Based on the service quality report by the Airline Quality Rating, what specific recommendations would you give Continental? In particular, address the criticisms about involuntary denied boardings (bumping).

5. Should Continental change its international strategy in any way? Are there destinations that it should add or remove?
6. How important are fuel costs (compared to other costs), and is Continental taking appropriate action to manage these costs now and in the future?
7. Evaluate Continental's current use of the Internet in booking tickets.
8. What should Continental's actions be in light of the EU-US Open Skies Treaty?

References

Air Travel Consumer Report, Office of Aviation Enforcement and Proceedings, Aviation Consumer Protection Division, U.S. Department of Transportation, May 2007, http://airconsumer.ost.dot.gov/reports/2007/may/200705atcr.pdf

"America's Most Admired Companies 2007," *Fortune Magazine,* 2007, http://money.cnn.com/magazines/fortune/mostadmired/2007/snapshots/2065.html

Bowen, Brent T. and Dean E. Headley, *Airline Quality Rating 2007,* April 2007, http://www.aqr.aero/

Bureau of Transportation Statistics (industry and carrier data), July 10, 2006, http://www.transtats.bts.gov

Carpenter, Dave, "United's CEO Says Merger Still a Goal," *Associated Press,* June 13, 2007.

Clark, Jane Bennett, "Win the Bumping Game," Kiplinger.com, http://www.kiplinger.com/printstory.php?pid=3628

Continental Airlines, "About Continental," company Web site, http://www.continental.com/web/en-US/content/company/default.aspx

"Continental Airlines Announces Earlier Start Date for Nonstop New York–Mumbai Service; Service from New York Liberty to Begin October 1, 2007," *PR Newswire,* 9 May, 2007.

Continental Airlines Company Profile (Facts), 2nd Quarter 2007. Available at the company Web site, http://www.continental.com/web/en-US/content/company/profile/default.aspx

Continental Airlines, Inc, 2006 Annual Report to Stockholders, http://www.continental.com/web/en-us/content/company/investor/docs/continental_ar_2006.pdf

"Direct Competitor Comparison (Continental Airlines, Inc.)," *Yahoo! Finance,* http://finance.yahoo.com/q/co?s=CAL

"Fourth-Quarter 2006 System Airline Financial Data: Passenger Airlines Report Largest Fourth-Quarter Profit Margin Since 1999," Bureau of Transportation Statistics, U.S. Department of Transportation, May 14, 2007, http://www.bts.gov/press_releases/2007/bts023_07/html/bts023_07.html

Peterson, Kyle, "U.S. Airlines Bide Their Time as Fleets' Needs Grow," *Reuters,* June 12, 2007.

Standard & Poors Industry Surveys, Airlines, May 24, 2007, http://www.netadvantage.standardandpoors.com/NASApp/NetAdvantage/showIndustrySurvey.do?code=air

"10 Green Giants, Continental," *Fortune Magazine*, http://money.cnn.com/galleries/2007/fortune/0703/gallery.green_giants.fortune/2.html

"U.S. Air Close on Boeing vs. Airbus Decision: CFO," *Reuters,* June 13, 2007.

24 Southwest Airlines Co. — 2007

Amit J. Shah
Frostburg State University

LUV

www.southwest.com

In the months following the plot to bomb U.S.-bound jets from London on August 10, 2006, new security measures, increases in liability for lost luggage, rising energy costs, and dramatic increases in labor expenses hampered major airlines' performance. In response to these issues, many major airlines cut their capacity while tapping their lines of credit and hunting for more sources of cash. Since 2000, the U.S. airline industry has not reported an annual net profit. Between 2001 and 2005, the industry posted $35 billion in cumulative net losses, according to the Air Transportation Association.

Despite recent negative trends and events, Southwest Airlines is still poised for success. For sixteen consecutive years (1991 through 2006), the Department of Transportation (DOT) Air Travel Consumer Report listed Southwest Airlines as among the top five of all major carriers for on-time performance and fewest customer complaints. In a highly competitive industry, all carriers continually strive to place first in any of these categories of the DOT report; Southwest is the only airline to ever hold the Triple Crown (first in all of the categories) for its annual performance. No other airline has earned the Triple Crown for even one month. In addition to this honor, for the tenth year in a row, Southwest was among *Fortune* magazine's most admired companies (third in 2006). Being the largest carrier in the United States by number of passengers carried in any one year, Southwest reported profits for the 34th consecutive year. In 2006, it had $499 million in net income on $9.1 billion in revenues. Southwest's low-cost structure and fuel hedging contributes to their consistent growth. In an industry that historically has been awash in red ink, where airlines continually go in and out of bankruptcy or just fail (liquidate), Southwest has an enviable record. But continued success is not guaranteed. Southwest's net income declined 41.7 percent as of September 30, 2007.

In 2006, Southwest ranked first among airlines for customer service satisfaction. In addition, Southwest was named the "Airline of the Year" by the Express Delivery & Logistics Association (XLA) for the second year in a row. Exhibit 1 presents additional awards and recognitions of Southwest.

In their best-selling book about Southwest, *Nuts*, Kevin and Jackie Freiberg point to a company with people who are committed to working hard and having fun and who avoid following industry trends. The Freibergs note that Southwest, based in Dallas, Texas, is a company that likes to keep prices at rock bottom; believes the customer comes second; runs recruiting ads that say, "Work at a place where wearing pants is optional"; paints its $30 million assets to look like killer whales and state flags; avoids trendy management programs; avoids formal, documented strategic planning; spends more time at planning parties than writing policies; and once settled a legal dispute by arm wrestling. This strategy has always worked, but will it continue to work?

History

According to Southwest folklore, the airline was conceived in 1967 on a napkin when Rollin King, an investment adviser, met with his lawyer, Herb Kelleher, to discuss his idea

EXHIBIT 1 Southwest Airlines Awards and Recognitions

- Ranked number 3 among *Fortune*'s Top Ten Most Admired companies in 2006.
- Southwest's Rapid Reward Program received the accolades as Best Program of the Year at *InsideFlyer* Magazine's 2006 annual Freddie Awards.
- For the seventh year in a row, *Business Ethics* Magazine listed Southwest in their "100 Best Corporate Citizens."
- "Most Admired Companies among Women," 2006, *Professional Women's Magazine.*
- Ranked number one among all airlines as "the most shareholder friendly company," *Institutional Investor* magazine.
- Listed among the Top 25 "Most Innovative Company," *BusinessWeek* along with the Boston Consulting Group.
- One of Top 50 Best Places to Launch a Career—*BusinessWeek.*

Source: Adapted from Southwest Airlines Fact Sheet.

for a low-fare, no-frills airline to fly between three of the major cities in Texas. At that time, King ran an unprofitable air charter service between small Texas cities. One day, his banker, John Parker, suggested that King concentrate on flying between the three biggest cities in the state. Parker suggested that the market was open for exploitation because he could never get a seat on the airlines currently flying between those cities, and besides, the fares were too high. King knew he couldn't compete with the airlines currently serving the cities, so he decided to start a bigger one. He put together a plan and a feasibility study, and then went to see Kelleher. In that meeting, King scribbled three lines on a cocktail napkin; labeled the points Houston, Dallas, and San Antonio; and muttered, "Herb, let's start our own airline." Kelleher loosened his tie and knitted his brow before replying. "Rollin, you're crazy," he said. "Let's do it!" Kelleher completed the necessary paperwork to create Air Southwest Co. (later renamed Southwest Airlines). Then the two filed for approval with the FAA; and on February 20, 1968, the Texas Aeronautical Commission approved their plans to fly between the three cities.

The very next day, the upstart airline ran into stiff opposition from several of the major carriers then doing business in Texas. On February 21, 1968, these carriers—Braniff, Texas International, and Continental—blocked approval with a temporary restraining order. They argued that Texas didn't need another carrier. For the next three years, Southwest was unable to proceed while it fought legal battles with these airlines over the right to offer flights between the three cities. In 1971, however, Southwest won the right to fly and began to offer service with a total of three planes and about two hundred employees. The efforts to squash the airline led to unbridled enthusiasm for the airline by King, Kelleher, and the other employees, which became an important part of Southwest's culture.

The outlook for Southwest, however, remained bleak. The legal battles left the airline flat broke and deep in debt. In its first year of operation, it lost $3.7 million, and it did not earn a profit for the next year and a half. But in 1973, it turned its first profit—and it never looked back. By 1978, it was one of the most profitable airlines in the country.

Southwest grew steadily and by 1975 had expanded its operations to eight more cities in Texas. By the end of the 1970s, it dominated the Texas market. Its major appeal was to passengers who wanted low prices and frequent departures. In the 1980s and 1990s, Southwest continued to expand, and by 1993, it was serving thirty-four cities in fifteen states. Southwest slowly, but methodically, moved across the Southwestern states into California, the Midwest, and the Northwest. It added new destinations in Florida and the East Coast. With its low prices and no-frills approach, it quickly dominated the markets it entered. In some markets, after Southwest entered, competitors soon withdrew, allowing the airline to expand even faster than projected. For example, when Southwest entered the California market in 1990, it quickly became the second-largest player, with over 20 percent of the intrastate market. Several competitors soon abandoned the Los Angeles–San Francisco route because they were unable to match Southwest's $59 one-way fare. Before Southwest entered this market, fares had been as high as $186 one way.

California offers a good example of the real dilemma facing competing carriers, which often referred to Southwest as a "500-pound cockroach that was too big to stamp out." While airfares were dropping, passenger traffic increased dramatically. But competitors, such as American and U.S. Airways, were losing money on several key route segments, even though they cut service drastically. In late 1994, United began to fight back by launching a low-cost, high-frequency shuttle service on the West Coast. But it found that even a shuttle could not win against Southwest in a head-to-head battle. So United repositioned its shuttle away from Southwest's routes and even abandoned some routes altogether. According to the DOT, eight airlines surrendered West Coast routes to Southwest; at the same time, one-way fares fell by over 30 percent to an average of $60, and traffic increased by almost 60 percent. The major problem for the larger airlines was the fact that many of these West Coast routes were critical for feeding traffic into their highly profitable transcontinental and transpacific routes, and Southwest was cutting into that market.

Southwest is currently the third largest carrier in the world in terms of customers boarded. The airline has transformed itself from a regional carrier operating out of Dallas into a truly national carrier. At year-end 2006, the airline served 63 cities in 32 states and operated more than 3,200 flights a day with its fleet of 483 Boeing 737s. In 2006, Southwest flew 67.7 billion revenue passenger miles (RPMs) compared with 60.2 billion RPMs in 2005. But most remarkable was its thirty-fourth year in a row of profitable operations, with total operating revenue in 2006 being $9.1 billion—a increase of 19.8 percent over 2001. Operating income in 2006 increased by 13.9 percent in 2005. Net income fell by 8.9 percent from $548 million in 2005 to $499 million in 2006 (Southwest *Form 10-K*, 2006). Southwest was the only profitable major U.S. airline in 2006. Southwest financial statements are shown in Exhibits 2–4.

EXHIBIT 2   Operating Statistics for Southwest Airlines

Consolidated Highlights

(in millions, except per-share amounts)	2006	2005	Change
Operating revenues	$9,086	$7,584	19.8%
Operating expenses	$8,152	$6,764	20.5%
Operating income	$934	$820	13.9%
Operating margin	8.7%	10.8%	(2.1)pts.
Net income	$499	$548	(8.9)%
Net margin	5.5%	7.2%	(1.7)pts.
Net income per share–basic	$0.63	$0.70	(10)%
Net income per share–diluted	$0.61	$0.67	(9)%
Stockholders' equity	$6,449	$6,675	(3.4)%
Return on average stockholders' equity	7.6%	9.0%	(1.4)pts.
Stockholders' equity per common share outstanding	$8.24	$8.32	(1)%
Revenue passengers carried	83,814,823	77,693,875	7.9%
Revenue passenger miles (RPMs) (000s)	67,691,289	60,223,100	12.4%
Available seat miles (ASMs) (000s)	92,663,023	85,172,795	8.8%
Passenger load factor	73.1%	70.7%	2.4pts.
Passenger revenue yield per RPM	12.93¢	12.09¢	6.9%
Operating revenue yield per ASM	9.81¢	8.90¢	10.2%
Operating expenses per ASM	8.80¢	7.94¢	10.8%
Employees at year end	32,664	31,729	2.9%

Source: 2006 Southwest *Form 10-K.*

EXHIBIT 3 Southwest Airlines Co. Consolidated Statement of Income

	Year ended December 31, 2006		
(in millions, except per-share amounts)	2006	2005	2004
Operating Revenues:			
Passenger	$ 8,750	$ 7,279	$ 6,280
Freight	134	133	117
Other	202	172	133
Total operating revenues	9,086	7,584	6,530
Operating Expenses:			
Salaries, wages, and benefits	3,052	2,702	2,443
Fuel and oil	2,138	1,342	1,000
Maintenance materials and repairs	468	430	457
Aircraft rentals	158	163	179
Landing fees and other rentals	495	454	408
Depreciation	515	469	431
Other operating expenses	1,326	1,204	1,058
Total operating expenses	8,152	6,764	5,976
Operating Income	934	820	554
Other Expenses (Income):			
Interest expense	128	122	88
Capitalized interest	(51)	(39)	(39)
Interest income	(84)	(47)	(21)
Other (gains) losses, net	151	(90)	37
Total other expenses (income)	144	(54)	65
Income Before Income Taxes	790	874	489
Provision for Income Taxes	291	326	176
Net Income	499	548	313
Net Income Per Share, Basic	.63	.70	.40
Net Income Per Share, Diluted	$.61	$.67	$.38

Source: 2006 Southwest *Form 10-K.*

Management

Lamar Muse led Southwest in its climb to profitability; but, in a dispute with the board, he was ousted in 1978. With Muse out, Kelleher moved into the top position and ran the airline until June 19, 2001. On that date, Kelleher was succeeded as CEO by Southwest's vice president and general counsel, James F. Parker, 54. James Parker had been the airline's top labor negotiator, making him well known to the company's employees, and, according to Herb Kelleher, he has had a say in every important decision for a "long, long time." His plan as the CEO was to stay with the blueprint—keep Southwest the low-cost, low-fare, no-frills airline it has always been. "There will be no change in our core philosophy and our basic business model," Parker had said. It was model he helped shape as general counsel for fifteen years. In 2004, Parker unexpectedly retired. Gary C. Kelly is now the vice chairman and CEO of Southwest.

Colleen C. Barrett, 56, who started her collaboration with Mr. Kelleher 34 years earlier as his legal secretary, is president and chief operating officer. Mr. Kelleher is the executive chairman of the board. Ms. Barrett, the unsung hero of Southwest, has been the keeper and crusader of Southwest's culture, and she has successfully indoctrinated thousands of new workers into Southwest's ways. Exhibit 5 shows the organizational chart of the company.

EXHIBIT 4 Southwest Airlines Co. Consolidated Balance Sheet

	Year ended December 31, 2006		
(in millions, except per-share amounts)	2006	2005	2004
ASSETS			
Current assets:			
Cash and cash equivalents	$ 1,390	$ 2,280	$ 1,048
Short-term investments	369	251	257
Accounts and other receivables	241	258	248
Inventories of parts and supplies, at cost	181	150	137
Fuel Hedge contracts	369	641	428
Prepaid expenses and other current assets	51	40	54
Total current assets	2,601	3,620	2,172
Property and equipment, at cost:			
Flight equipment	11,769	10,999	10,037
Ground property and equipment	1,356	1,256	1,202
Deposits on flight equipment purchase contracts	734	660	682
	13,859	12,915	11,921
Less allowance for depreciation	3,765	3,488	3,198
	10,094	9,427	8,723
Other assets	765	1,171	442
Total Assets	$ 13,460	$ 14,218	$ 11,337
LIABILITIES AND STOCKHOLDERS' EQUITY			
Current liabilities:			
Accounts payable	$ 643	$ 524	$ 420
Accrued liabilities	1,323	2,074	1,047
Air traffic liability	799	649	529
Current maturities of long-term debt	122	601	146
Total current liabilities	2,887	3,848	2,142
Long-term debt less current maturities	1,567	1,394	1,700
Deferred income taxes	2,104	1,896	1,610
Deferred gains from sale and leaseback of aircraft	320	136	152
Other deferred liabilities	133	269	209
Total Liabilities	7,011	7,543	5,813
Stockholders' equity:			
Common stock, $1.00 par value: 2,000,000,000 shares authorized; 807,611,634 801,641,645 and 790,181,982 shares issued in 2006, 2005, and 2004 respectively	808	802	790
Capital in excess of par value	1,142	424	299
Retained earnings	4,307	4,557	4,089
Accumulated other comprehensive income	582	892	417
Treasury stock, at cost: 24,302,215 share in 2006	(390)	–	(71)
Total stockholders' equity	6,449	6,675	5,524
Total Liabilities and SE	$ 13,460	$ 14,218	$ 11,337

Source: 2006 Southwest *Form 10-K.*

EXHIBIT 5 **Southwest Organizational Chart**

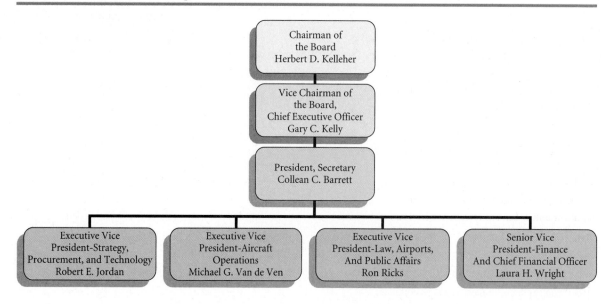

Southwest's management team drives home the feeling that all of its people are part of one big family. Southwest's Culture Committee, formerly headed by Colleen Barrett, has unique ways to preserve Southwest's underdog background and can-do spirit. She constantly reinforces the company's message that employees should be treated like customers and continually celebrates workers who went above and beyond the call of duty. Barrett also regularly visits each of the company's stations to reiterate the airline's history and to motivate employees. As keeper of the company's culture, Barrett commemorates all employee birthdays and special events with cards signed, "Herb and Colleen." Employees know the culture and expect others to live up to it. Donna Conover, another long-time Southwest employee, who also understands and supports the company's culture, will succeed Barrett as president and COO. Exhibit 6 presents the current company mission, developed in January 1988.

Strategy

Southwest's operation under Herb Kelleher has had a number of characteristics that have contributed to its success. It has always been able to quickly seize a strategic opportunity whenever one arises. Other key factors are its conservative growth pattern, its cost-containment policy, and the commitment of its employees.

Kelleher always resisted attempts to expand too rapidly. His philosophy was to expand only when there were resources available to go into a new location with ten to twelve flights per day—not just one or two. For years, he also resisted the temptation to begin transcontinental operations or to get into a head-to-head battle with the major carriers on long-distance routes. But even with a conservative approach, Southwest expanded at a vigorous pace. Its

EXHIBIT 6 **The Mission of Southwest Airlines**

The Mission of Southwest Airlines

The mission of Southwest Airlines is dedication to the highest quality of Customer Service delivered with a sense of warmth, friendliness, individual pride, and Company Spirit.

To Our Employees

We are committed to provide our Employees a stable work environment with equal opportunity for learning and personal growth. Creativity and innovation are encouraged for improving the effectiveness of Southwest Airlines. Above all, Employees will be provided the same concern, respect, and caring attitude within the organization that they are expected to share externally with every Southwest Customer.

Source: southwest.com

debt has remained the lowest among U.S. carriers, and, with an A-rating, Southwest has the highest Standard & Poor's credit rating in the industry.

Short versus Long Haul Trips

Southwest has made its mark by concentrating on flying large numbers of passengers on high frequency, short hops (usually one hour or less) at bargain fares. Southwest avoided the hub-and-spoke operations of its larger rivals, taking its passengers directly from city to city (point-to-point). Southwest also tends to avoid the more congested major airports in favor of smaller satellite fields. Kelleher revealed the niche strategy of Southwest when he noted that whereas other airlines set up hub-and-spoke systems in which passengers are shuttled to a few major hubs from which they are transferred to other planes going to their destinations, "we wound up with a unique market niche: We are the world's only short-haul, high-frequency, low-fare, point-to-point carrier. . . . We wound up with a market segment that is peculiarly ours, and everything about the airline has been adapted to serving that market segment in the most efficient and economical way possible."

However, this strategy may be changing. Southwest has begun to introduce longer, nonstop trips on such routes as Baltimore, Maryland, to Las Vegas, Nevada (2,099 miles), and Austin, Texas, to Los Angeles, California (1,234 miles). Even one-stop trips are being added through central cities such as Nashville and Kansas City for coast-to-coast travel. On November 16, 2006, Southwest Airlines added 36 new nonstop flights scheduled to begin from March to May, 2007. The prospect of Southwest going long-haul on a grand scale is what "the genie [rivals] always hoped would not come out of the bottle," says analyst Kevin C. Murphy of Morgan Stanley Dean Witter. He believes that Southwest will continue its expansion and that it "will really rewrite the economics of the airline industry." This shifting strategy is downplayed by the fact that Southwest still flies about 80 percent of its flights on route that are shorter than 750 miles. In 2006, the average flight was 622 miles and had duration of 1.53 hours. "We're built for the short-haul markets, and we know that," says Vice Chairman and CEO Gary C. Kelly. Kelleher explains the jump into routes that are one-thousand-plus miles as a way to deal with the changes in the federal ticket tax in 1997, which was pushed by the bigger carriers. The incorporation of the new tax system replaced a percentage tax with a tax that included a flat, per-segment fee, which hits low-fare carriers harder.

Competitors believe that Southwest would have moved strongly into the long-haul flights market despite the altered tax requirements. "They've dug all the shallow holes," says Rona J. Dutta, senior vice president for planning at United Airlines, Inc. He also suggests that other low-fare units are increasing the competition in Southwest's core markets. As all other major airlines have performed poorly due to recent terrorist attacks, many are expanding or developing low-fares flight programs in an effort to increase profits. Short-haul airlines such as JetBlue, Spirit, ATA, AirTran, SkyWest, and Frontier Airlines may be affecting Southwest's profitability, but with its lower costs and impressive balance sheet, Southwest still prevails. Nonetheless, some low-fare airlines have ended operations because they were unsuccessful in competing with existing low-fare firms. These include U.S. Airways' MetroJet, Shuttle by United, Vanguard, and National airlines. The newest player in the low-fare air game is Columbus, Ohio–based Skybus, which offers at least 10 seats for $10 on each of its flights. The company received the certification to fly in May 2007 and is already adding new routes. Skybus does not provide any food or drinks but will sell them to the customers. Its logic is that you should not have to pay for the items and services you do not need. With no assigned seats and only free carry-on luggage allowed, Skybus offers preboarding and checked luggage for a fee.

Southwest continues to be the lowest-cost yet profitable airline in its markets. Even when trying to match Southwest's cut-rate fares, the larger carriers could not do so without incurring substantial losses. Southwest continues to operate with the lowest cost per available seat mile (the number of seats multiplied by the distance flown) among all major airlines, with an average of 15 to 25 percent below its rivals. One of the major factors in this enviable record is that all of its planes are of a single type—Boeing 737s—which dramatically lowered the company's cost of training, maintenance, and inventory. As of January 31, 2007 Southwest operated 483 Boeing 737s. Because all Southwest crews know the 737s inside and out, they could substitute personnel rapidly from one flight to another in an emergency. In addition, Southwest recognized that planes only earn you money while they are in the air, so the company worked hard to achieve a faster turnaround time on the ground. Most airlines take up to one hour to unload passengers, clean and service the plane, and board new passengers. Southwest has a turnaround time for most flights of twenty minutes or less. Thorough knowledge of the 737s has helped in this achievement.

Southwest has also cut costs in the customer service area as well. Because its flights are usually one hour or less, it does not offer meals—only peanuts and drinks. Boarding passes are reusable plastic cards, and boarding time is saved since the airline has no assigned seating. The airline does not subscribe to any centralized reservation service. You will not find Southwest seats on Orbitz or Expedia. It will not even transfer baggage to other carriers: That is the passenger's responsibility. Even with this frugality, passengers do not seem to object, since the price is right.

This ability to turn planes around rapidly, surprisingly, has not been jeopardized by recent terrorist attacks, but this did not happen without incurring added expenses. Initially, new government-mandated security procedures did cause delays and longer check-in times. Since then, Southwest has added new automated systems and technologies that have streamlined the check-in process. This includes computer-generated baggage tags and boarding passes and self-service Rapid Check-in Kiosks. Because of these additions, Southwest check-in times are almost back to normal.

Team Spirit Approach

Southwest has achieved a team spirit that others can only envy. One of the reasons for this team spirit is that the company truly believes that employees come first, not the customers. Southwest is known for providing its employees with tremendous amounts of information that will enable them to better understand the company, its mission, its customers, and its competition. Southwest believes that information is power. It is the resource that enables employees to do their jobs better. Armed with this knowledge, they are able to serve the customer better, and customers who deal with Southwest rarely get the runaround.

Even though unionized, Southwest has been able to negotiate flexible work rules that enabled it to meet the rapid turnaround schedules. It's not unusual for pilots to help flight attendants clean the airplanes or to help the ground crew load baggage. Consequently, employee productivity is very high, and the airline is able to maintain a lean staff. In good times, Kelleher resisted the temptation to overhire, and so he avoided layoffs during lean times. Southwest has only laid off three people in twenty-five years—and it immediately hired them back. The airline industry employment level fell approximately 20 percent in the United States since the second quarter of 2001 according to the Airline Industry Council. Not only did Southwest have no layoffs, they have continued to hire employees and increased overall salaries, wages, and benefits. This was made possible by reductions in other areas: New plane deliveries were delayed, renovations to the company headquarters were scrapped—but layoffs were not considered. Previous CEO Parker had said, "We are willing to suffer some damage, even to our stock price, to protect the jobs of our people." This employee retention policy has contributed to employees' feelings of security and a fierce sense of loyalty. Southwest currently employs 32,000 employees throughout the Southwest system. The people of Southwest see themselves as crusaders whose mission is to give ordinary people the opportunity to fly.

Maximizing profitability is a major goal at Southwest. This leads to a drive to keep costs low and quality high. The airline's ideal service consists of safe, frequent, low-cost flights that get passengers to their destinations on time—and often closer to their destination than the major airlines do, because its competitors use larger airports farther from the cities. Southwest uses Dallas's Love Field, Houston's Hobby airport, and Chicago's Midway, which are closer to their respective downtown areas, are less congested, and are, therefore, more convenient for the business traveler. This also helps Southwest's on-time performance.

Marketing

In its marketing approach, Southwest always tries to set itself apart from the rest of the industry. It also plays up its fun-loving, rebel reputation. In the early years, when the big airlines were trying to run Southwest out of business by undercutting its low fares, Southwest made its customers an unprecedented offer. In response to a Braniff ad offering a $13 fare to fly between Houston and Dallas, Southwest placed an ad that read, "Nobody's going to shoot Southwest Airlines out of the sky for a lousy $13." It then offered passengers the opportunity to purchase a ticket from Southwest for the same price, which was half the normal fare, or to buy a full-fare ticket for $26 and receive a bottle of premium whiskey along with it. The response was unprecedented. Southwest's planes were full and, for a short time, Southwest was one of the top liquor distributors in the state of Texas.

Southwest's ads always try to convince the customer that what the airline offers them is of real value to them. In August 2006, the Southwest Airlines television commercial, "Flight Attendant," was named in Adweek's "Best Spots." Southwest also believes it is in the business of making flying fun. With its ads, the company wants customers to know that when they fly Southwest, they'll have an experience unlike any other. Southwest promises safe, reliable, frequent, low-cost air transportation that is topped off with outstanding service. By keeping its promises, Southwest has earned extremely high credibility in every market it serves.

E-Business

Southwest has been aggressively marketing its services on the Internet, and it was the first airline to establish a home page on the Web. When *Fortune* magazine asked the experts which businesses have Web sites that work, the answer they got was "not many." However, Southwest was one of ten cited as a business doing it right. In the Internet travel race, many observers think Southwest has lost the battle to a subsidiary of American Airlines, Travelocity. Yet while American has been getting most of the attention, Southwest has been getting the business. According to a Nielsen/NetRatings, southwest.com is the largest airline site in terms of unique visitors. The company's "look-to-book" ratio is twice that of Travelocity and higher than that of any traditional retailer on the Web. Southwest, it seems, has been a success in turning browsers into buyers. Passenger revenue generated by online bookings increased from 65 percent in 2005 to 70 percent in 2006. Southwest's cost per booking via the Internet is about $1; in comparison, the cost per booking via a travel agent is about $10.

Southwest's Web site is the number one airline Web site for online revenue according to PhoCusWright. Southwest's free online booking tool that allows business travelers to plan, purchase, and track business travel (SWABIZ) comprises 66 percent of the Fortune 500 companies. In 2005, Southwest offered a downloadable desktop application (DING!) that notifies customers about exclusive offers. Southwest was the first airline to offer this type of tool to customers.

Competitors

Since recent terrorist attacks, competition for Southwest Airlines has shifted from major airlines to low-fare airlines. This happened mainly because major airlines have been incurring losses since the start of the terrorist attacks in 2001. Before September 11, 2001, United, the fourth largest airline with over one hundred thousand employees, was one of Southwest's most formidable competitors. Since then, the company has downsized to approximately 56,000 employees. Because of financial losses, United filed for bankruptcy in December 2002. In 2006, United finally emerged from Chapter 11 bankruptcy protection, which is the largest and longest airline bankruptcy case in history.

After September 11, 2001, Delta, the second largest U.S. carrier, cut 21 percent of its workforce and in 2006 operated with approximately 47,000 employees. Delta flies to about 308 U.S. and foreign locations, and remains particularly strong throughout much of the southern tier of the United States, where two of its major hubs—Atlanta and

Dallas–Fort Worth—are located. In the summer of 2003, Delta replaced its low-fare regional carrier service, Delta Express, with Song, in an effort to better compete with low-fare airlines like Southwest. Delta has also acquired a minority stake in three regional airlines that can feed passengers into its several hubs and has established an alliance with Continental and Northwest Airlines.

A third past competitor, America West, is faring better than Southwest's above two competitors. In July 2002, America West recalled virtually all employees furloughed after the September 11, 2001 attacks. Despite net income losses of $388 million in 2002, American West expects to restructure its finances with the help of federal loan guarantees totaling $380 million. In 2005, America West merged with the U.S. Airways Group. It serves 95 cities in the United States with foreign locations in Mexico and Canada. America West has strong positions in its hubs, Phoenix and Las Vegas. These locations put it into direct competition with Southwest.

The low-fare carriers are doing better because they don't rely on high business fares and don't offer the frills the major carriers offer. They tend to gravitate toward secondary airports where less congestion and lower fees keep costs down. Many also fly point to point without stops, and in general have relied on highly efficient e-business. Most importantly, low-fare airlines have succeeded in appealing to the customer in ways that major airlines never could by using creative market strategies and promoting individualism. As a result, customers are intrigued by this new mode of transport and after trying it, are convinced that it is the new way to travel. In 1994, revenues earned by low-fare carriers represented 5 percent of the $76 billion U.S. air travel market. By 2003, their share was over 20 percent, according to *CFO* magazine, up from just 10 percent in 2000. Experts predict that low-fare airlines will continue to grow, an increase that may restructure the airline industry forever.

JetBlue is one of Southwest's most noteworthy competitors. In 2002, JetBlue was the only other airline to report profits, with $55 million on revenues of $635 million. In 2003, despite geopolitical tensions, JetBlue was hiring an average of six new employees a day to accommodate growth. With $2.3 billion in sales in 2006 and a net loss of about a million, currently Jetblue has a fleet size of 123 and flies to 54 domestic and international destinations. JetBlue's founder and longtime CEO was David Neeleman who was employed in the inner circle of Southwest for over a year. Therefore, it is no surprise that JetBlue is structured similarly to Southwest: a low-cost, low-fare airline with high employee productivity, a laid-back attitude, and a single aircraft model. It may also explain why Southwest's Gary Kelly stated, "We've got to be prepared for intense competition." In fact, Southwest ordered model JetBlue planes, which were sent to executives with a note: "Know your enemy." Currently, the two airlines don't compete out of many of the same markets, but being the only two airlines experiencing significant growth, they are certainly affecting each other's potential growth.

All of the competitors have come into head-to-head competition with Southwest on several occasions. Southwest always welcomed competition and firmly believes it can come out ahead in any of those situations. Kelleher, when asked about his thoughts on facing a competitor such as the United Shuttle head-on, stated, "I think it's good to have some real competitive activity that gets your people stirred up and renews their vigor and their energy and their desire to win."

Long-haul success for Southwest will put pressure on the profits realized by its bigger competitors. The cost advantage for Southwest includes the rapid twenty-minute gate turnarounds; an efficient all-Boeing 737 fleet, including the 737-700s that can fly cross-country nonstop; and a more productive workforce. In order to counterbalance increasing fuel expenses, Southwest has raised fares on long-haul journeys by up to $10 each way. Other major airlines have moved quickly to match Southwest's fare increases in order to remain profitable. Even though longer flights increase the costs, Southwest still realizes a significant competitive advantage. Roberts, Roach & Associates Inc., an airline consultant in Hayward, California, says that Southwest has at least a 59 percent cost advantage over bigger rivals at flights of five hundred miles, as well as a 35 percent lead for flights at fifteen hundred miles. "It's a huge threat," says a rival airline executive. Already, according to

25 Carnival Corporation — 2007

Mernoush Banton
Florida International University

CCL

www.carnivalcorp.com

Carnival is the largest and most successful cruise line in the world, carrying more passengers than any other cruise ship. But Carnival in 2007 was a vastly different company than the one started from humble beginnings more than three decades ago. Carnival was launched with a converted transatlantic ocean liner and a dream of entrepreneur Ted Arison, an Israeli immigrant and a pioneer in the modern-day cruise industry who set out to realize his vision of making a vacation experience once reserved for the very rich accessible to the average person.

"Carnival Corporation is incorporated in Panama, and Carnival PLC is incorporated in England and Wales. Carnival Corporation and Carnival PLC operate as dual listed company ("DLC"), whereby the businesses of Carnival Corporation and Carnival PLC are combined through a number of contracts and through provisions in Carnival Corporation's articles of association" (*Form 10K*, 2006). For the quarter ending August 31, 2007, Carnival's revenues increased 49 percent to $4,321 billion, while net income increased 253 percent to $1.377 billion.

History

As indicated in Exhibit 1, Carnival Cruise Lines was formed in 1972. Carnival made an initial public offering of 20 percent of its common stock in 1987. Exhibit 1 reveals that over many years Carnival has acquired companies in different market segments of the cruise industry, including premium operator Holland America Line in 1989; the Windstar Cruises and Alaskan/Canadian tour operator Holland America Tours; luxury brand Seabourn Cruise Line in 1992; contemporary operator Costa Cruises, Europe's leading cruise company, in 1997; and premium/luxury operator Cunard Line in 1998, which built the world's largest ocean liner, the 150,000-ton *Queen Mary 2*.

In 2003, Carnival acquired P & O Princess Cruises, becoming a global vacation leader with 12 brands of 66 ships and over 100,000 lower berths, creating one of the largest leisure travel companies in the world. In 2004, the Cousteau Society and Carnival Corporation PLC reached an agreement to restore the *Calipso* (a research and expedition vessel of Captain Jacques Yves Cousteau). The *Calipso* became an exhibit representing science and the environment. This was a unique opportunity for Carnival to preserve a small part of history and maintain a world-famous icon for marine research and environmental preservation. Carnival funded the restoration as a tribute to the Cousteau organization. The restored *Calipso* continues to educate the public on the importance of protecting our precious natural resources.

Internal Issues

Mission Statement

On the company's Web site, the mission statement reads, "Our mission is to deliver exceptional vacation experiences through the world's best-known cruise brands that cater to a variety of different lifestyles and budgets, all at an outstanding value unrivaled on land or at sea." The company does not have a vision statement.

EXHIBIT 1 Carnival Cruise Timeline

Year	Events
1972	Maiden voyage of Carnival's first ship, the TSS *Mardi Gras*, which runs aground on sandbar outside the Port of Miami.
1975	Carnival purchases *Empress of Britain*, enters service as the TSS *Carnivale*.
1978	The *Festivale*, formerly the *S.A. Vaal*, undergoes $30 million refurbishment, begins service for Carnival as the largest and fastest vessel sailing from Miami to the Caribbean (the ship has since been retired from the fleet).
1982	Debut of the *Tropicale*, the first new cruise ship the cruise industry has seen in many years; ship marks the beginning of an industry-wide multibillion-dollar shipbuilding boom (the ship has since been retired from the fleet).
1984	Carnival becomes first cruise line to advertise on network television with the premiere of new advertising campaign starring company spokesperson Kathie Lee Gifford (then Johnson).
1985	Debut of 46,052-ton *Holiday*.
1986	Launch of 47,262-ton *Jubilee* (the ship has since been retired from the fleet).
1987	The 47,262-ton *Celebration* enters service Carnival earns distinction as "Most Popular Cruise Line in the World," carrying more passengers than any other Carnival Cruise Lines undertakes its initial public offering on Wall Street, raising approximately $400 million to fuel future expansion; entity later becomes Carnival Corporation & PLC, a multiline worldwide cruise conglomerate.
1990	The 70,367-ton *Fantasy*—the first and namesake vessel in the highly successful "Fantasy-class"—enters service as first new ship ever placed on three- and four-day Bahamas cruise program from Miami. Eventually, Carnival would construct eight "Fantasy-class" vessels, the most cruise ships in a single class.
1991	Launch of 70,367-ton *Ecstasy*.
1993	Carnival introduces its third 70,367-ton SuperLiner, *Sensation*.
1994	Debut of 70,367-ton *Fascination*.
	Carnival's parent company renamed Carnival Corporation to distinguish between it and its flagship brand, Carnival Cruise Lines. Company is later renamed Carnival Corp. & PLC following the combination with P&O Princess Cruises, creating the world's largest cruise vacation group by far.
1995	70,367-ton *Imagination* enters service.
1996	Carnival's launches sixth "Fantasy-class" vessel, the SuperLiner *Inspiration*.
	Carnival debuts the first passenger vessel to exceed 100,000 tons, the 101,353-ton *Carnival Destiny*, at the time the world's largest cruise ship.
1998	Carnival Cruise Lines introduces seventh "Fantasy-class" vessel, the *Elation*, the first new cruise ship deployed on the West Coast.
	The eighth and last in the "Fantasy-class" series, the *Paradise*, enters service.
1999	Debut of the 102,000-ton *Carnival Triumph*, Carnival's second "Destiny-class" vessel.
2000	A third "Destiny-class" vessel, the 102,000-ton *Carnival Victory*, is launched.
2001	Carnival introduces a new class of vessel with the launch of the 88,500-ton *Carnival Spirit*, the first new "Fun Ship" ever positioned in the Alaska and Hawaii markets.
2002	A second "Spirit-class" vessel, the *Carnival Pride*, is launched.
	Carnival's third "Spirit-class" ship, *Carnival Legend*, enters service.
	Debut of the 110,000-ton *Carnival Conquest*, the largest "Fun Ship" ever constructed.
2003	Second 110,000-ton "Conquest-class" ship, the *Carnival Glory*, begins year-round seven-day cruises from Port Canaveral, Fla., July 19.
2004	*Carnival Miracle*, the fourth in Carnival's "Spirit-class," begins a series of 12 voyages from Jacksonville, Fla.—the first "Fun Ship" sailings from that port—Feb. 27, 2004.
	A third 110,000-ton "Conquest-class" ship, the *Carnival Valor*, begins year-round seven-day service from Miami Dec. 19, 2004, becoming the largest "Fun Ship" ever based at that port.
2005	A fourth 110,000-ton "Conquest-class" vessel, *Carnival Liberty*, debuts July 20, 2005, operating Carnival's first-ever Mediterranean cruises.
2007	*Carnival Freedom*, the line's fifth 110,000-ton vessel, debuts in Europe, operating by 12-day voyages to the Mediterranean, Greek Isles, and Turkey.
2008	The 113,300-ton *Carnival Splendor* is slated to debut in July 13, 2008, operating Carnival's first Northern Europe cruise program.
2009	*Carnival Dream*, a 130,000-ton vessel to be the largest "Fun Ship" ever constructed, is scheduled to enter service in October 2009, beginning a new class of vessel for the line.
2011	A second 130,000-ton SuperLiner, *Carnival Magic*, is slated to debut in June 2011.

Source: www.carnival.com

Company Objectives

The company's objectives are to use their brands to reach every tier of the cruise market. They focus on providing services to travelers regardless of the vacationers' budget, itinerary, geography, demographics or psychographics. This is part of the uniqueness of their North American cruise market, if not in the world. The company recognizes that vacationers, more than anything else, want to have fun, and Carnival offers them the ultimate fun experience. Carnival's goal is to meet the needs of vacationers seeking luxury, elegance, shorter vacations, exotic destinations or land/sea packages. A focus in their other brands— Holland America, Windstar, Seabourn, Costa, and Airtour's Sun Cruises is to provide vacation charm to virtually every potential cruise customer, a strategy that has made them the leader in every market and the most popular choice among consumers who are thinking about a cruise vacation.

Management

Key people in Carnival Corporation are Micky Arison, chairman and CEO, and Howard S. Frank, vice chairman and COO. In July 2007, the company promoted David Bernstein to chief financial officer. He has been working for Carnival since 2003. He formerly worked for Royal Caribbean Ltd. for seven years as assistant controller and assistant treasurer.

As shown in Exhibit 2, the key executives of Carnival oversee other businesses of the company, which are AIDA Cruises, Carnival Cruise Lines, Carnival Australia, Carnival

EXHIBIT 2   Organizational Chart for Carnival Corporation and PLC

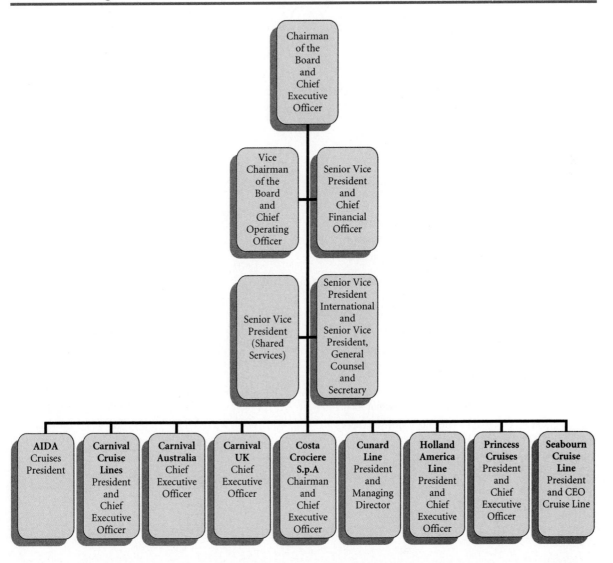

UK, Costa Crociere S.p.A., Cunard Line, Holland America Line, Princess Cruises, and Seabourn Cruise Line.

Finance

Traded on both the New York and London Stock Exchanges, Carnival is the largest cruise vacation group in the world, operating 81 cruise ships with 143,676 passenger capacity in North America, Europe, the United Kingdom, Germany, Australia, and New Zealand.

In fiscal year 2006, Carnival reported record revenues of $11.8 billion and net income of $2.2 billion. The company carried 6.8 million passengers on its ships in 2005, up from 6.3 million in 2004. Exhibits 3 and 4 demonstrate the company's consolidated financial statements for the calendar year ended 2006.

EXHIBIT 3 **Carnival Corporation and PLC, Consolidated Statements of Operations (2006) (In millions, except per share data)**

	Years Ended November 30		
	2006	2005	2004
Revenues			
Cruise			
Passenger tickets	$ 8,903	$ 8,399	$7,357
Onboard and other	2,514	2,338	2,070
Other	422	357	300
Total Revenues	11,839	11,094	9,727
Costs and Expenses			
Operating			
Cruise			
Commissions, transportation and other	1,749	1,645	1,572
Onboard and other	453	412	359
Payroll and related	1,158	1,122	1,003
Fuel	935	707	493
Food	644	613	550
Other ship operating	1,538	1,465	1,315
Other	314	254	210
Total	6,791	6,218	5,502
Selling and administrative	1,447	1,335	1,285
Depreciation and amortization	988	902	812
Total Expenses	9,226	8,455	7,599
Operating Income	2,613	2,639	2,128
Nonoperating (Expense) Income			
Interest Income	25	29	17
Interest expense, net of capitalized interest	(312)	(330)	(284)
Other expense, net	(8)	(13)	(5)
	(295)	(314)	(272)
Income Before Income Taxes	2,318	2,325	1,856
Income Tax Expense, Net	(39)	(72)	(47)
Net Income	$ 2,279	$ 2,253	$ 1,809
Earnings Per Share			
Basic	$ 2.85	$ 2.80	$ 2.25
Diluted	$ 2.77	$ 2.70	$ 2.18
Dividends Per Share	$ 1.025	$ 0.80	$ 0.525

EXHIBIT 4   **Carnival Corporation and PLC, Consolidated Balance Sheet (2006) (In millions, except per share data)**

	November 30	
ASSETS	2006	2005 (Note 2)
Current Assets		
Cash and cash equivalents	$ 1,163	$ 1,178
Trade and other receivables, net	280	430
Inventories	263	250
Prepaid expenses and other	289	263
Total current assets	1,995	2,121
Property and Equipment, Net	23,458	21,312
Goodwill	3,313	3,206
Trademarks	1,321	1,282
Other Assets	465	428
Total Assets	$30,552	$28,349
LIABILITIES AND SHAREHOLDERS' EQUITY		
Current Liabilities		
Short-term borrowings	$ 438	$ 300
Current portion of long-term debt	1,054	1,042
Convertible debt subject to current put option		283
Accounts payable	438	477
Accrued liabilities and other	1,149	1,032
Customer deposits	2,336	2,051
Total current liabilities	5,415	5,185
Long-Term Debt	6,355	5,727
Other Long-Term Liabilities and Deferred Income	572	554
Total Liabilities	12,342	11,466
Shareholders' Equity		
Common stock of Carnival Corporation; $.01 per value; 1,960 shares authorized; 641 shares at 2006 and 639 shares at 2005 issued	6	6
Ordinary shares of Carnival plc; $1.66 par value; 226 shares authorized; 213 shares at 2006 and 212 shares at 2005 issued	354	353
Additional paid-in capital	7,479	7,381
Retained earnings	11,600	10,141
Unearned stock compensation		(13)
Accumulated other comprehensive income	661	159
Treasury stock; 18 at 2006 and 2 shares at 2005 of Carnival Corporation and 42 shares at 2005 and 2005 of Carnival plc, at cost	(1,890)	(1,144)
Total shareholders' equity	18,210	16,883
Total Liabilities and SE	$30,552	$28,349

Marketing

As indicated in Exhibit 5, Carnival in 2007 has 81 cruise ships with passenger capacity of 143,676 in markets such as the United States, United Kingdom, New Zealand, Europe, and Australia. Carnival has signed agreements with shipyards for providing 20 additional cruise ships to be released between March 2007 and June 2011. These additions are expected to increase the number of passengers capacity by 49,308 (34.3 percent) to 192,984. Although the company may retire some of its older ships, combined, the company anticipates an increase in passenger capacity since they may order additional fleets.

EXHIBIT 5 Carnival Cruise Brands, Number of Ships, Passenger Capacity, Primary Market (February 2007)

Cruise Brand	Number of Cruise Ship	Passenger Capacity*	Primary Market
Carnival Cruise Liners	21	47,818	North America
Princess Cruises ("Princess")	15	32,232	North America
Costa Cruises ("Costa")	11	20,218	Europe
Holland America Line	13	18,848	North America
P&O Cruises	5	8,840	United Kingdom
AIDA Cruises ("AIDA")	4	5,378	Germany
Cunard Line ("Cunard")	2	4,380	North America and United Kingdom
P&O Cruises Australia	2	2,474	Australia and New Zealand
Ocean Village	1	1,578	United Kingdom
Swan Hellenic	1	678	United Kingdom
Seabourn Cruise Line ("Seabourn")	3	624	North America
Windstar Cruises ("Windstar")	3	608	North America
Total	81	143,676	

*In accordance with cruise industry practices, passenger capacity is calculated based on two passengers per cabin even though some cabins can accommodate three or more passengers.

Source: Carnival Corporation and PLC, *Form 10K* (2006).

The company is in the service business and, as such, invests heavily in customer service for their passengers as well as assisting travel agents. Its cruises and vacation packages are sold mainly through travel agents including wholesalers and tour operators. Other marketing activities and techniques include Web sites, seminars and videos, direct response marketing, and a variety of media such as television, magazine, newspaper, radio, and other promotional campaigns. The company also has a partnership with major airline computer reservation systems such as SABRE, Galileo, Amadeus, and Worldspan. Although the majority of their cruises are booked through travel agents, Carnival also accepts telephone and internet bookings direct from customers.

To attract customers, Carnival has an excellent interactive Web site, which offers vacationers the opportunity to scan locations, packages, prices, promotions, and so on. As an enticement to vacationers, the features offered in the Web site are discounted cruises, singles cruises, resident discounts, different departure locations, VIP savings, free personal customer service via telephone, elderly packages, special meals, holiday packages, coupons via the Web, and many other promotions.

Industry

In the 1970s, the hit television series *The Love Boat* helped revitalize the cruise industry, bringing people on board ships in larger numbers than ever before. Between 1970 and 1986 the number of people taking cruises soared from 500,000 to 2.1 million.

In recent years, the multinight cruise industry has had significant growth but still remains a small part of the wider global vacation market. Since this market is sensitive to consumers' discretionary income, consumers aggressively look for deals, discounts and other substitute vacation categories or locations. It is estimated that in 2006, the global cruise industry carried approximately 15.7 million passengers with the majority being in North America. Between 2000 and 2005, the growth in cruise travelers increased by 7.8 percent in North America and 10.0 percent in Western Europe. There is significant growth opportunity in Europe, Asia, Australia, New Zealand, and South America. It is also reported by Ocean Shipping Consultants (a London-based independent economic consultancy) that the number of cruise guests sailing in the Asia-Pacific region is projected to grow by more than 40 percent, from 1.07 million in 2005 to 1.5 million by 2010. As such, cruise ship companies are ordering and adding new fleets to their portfolio to meet the demand.

During early 2000, the cruise industry suffered drastically as the result of the events of 9/11 (fear of terrorist attack), SARS, and weak economic conditions. Since 2004, the cruise industry experienced significant increases in both capacity and net revenue, mostly for its non-Caribbean product offerings. However, there were a number of factors that have impacted the industry as well, such as hurricanes, higher fuel costs, higher interest rates (in the United States), and confidence in the U.S. economy as the result of the war in Iraq.

The cruise industry appeals to a broad range of demographic groups. The average age of cruise passengers has been falling steadily in the past ten years (56 to 44); there is a recent surge of interest from 20-year-olds; by 2005 30+ percent growth will be within the ages of 41-59. Carnival Cruises has moved toward marketing strongly to first-time (2 percent of vacationers) and repeat (only 8 percent of not applicable) customers. It is estimated that there is an untapped market of 92 percent. Based on the recent reports, the cruise ships are offering a variety of services and entertainment to their passengers such as fine dining, games, sports activities, health and beauty products and services, shows, and gambling. As reported in the company's filings with the Securities and Exchange Commission (SEC), there are approximately 127 million potential passengers for cruising in North America with a minimum household income of $40,000, headed by a person who is at least 25 years old. Moreover, about half of these individuals have expressed an interest in taking a cruise as a vacation alternative, and more than 60 percent of travelers between ages 45 and 74 is expected to increase 17 percent between 2007 and 2017.

The industry has a relatively high entry barrier but has a low penetration level. Based on a report provided by Cruise Lines International Association (CLIA), approximately 17 percent of the U.S. population has ever taken a cruise and only 10 percent has done so in the past three years. In regions such as the United Kingdom and others, the cruising industry is at an early stage of development and has far lower penetration rates.

Royal Caribbean Cruises Ltd.

Royal Caribbean, Carnival's most aggressive competitor, is a global cruise vacation company that operates Royal Caribbean International, Celebrity Cruises, Pullmantur, and Azamara Cruises. The company currently has 35 ships at sea and there are six under construction. Royal Caribbean's brand offers a range of onboard activities, services, and amenities to travelers such as swimming pools, beauty salons, exercise and spa facilities, sun decks, ice skating rinks, in-line skating, rock climbing walls, surf machines, basketball courts, bungee jumping trampolines, miniature golf courses, waterparks, gaming facilities, lounges, bars, restaurants, and cinemas. The company also offers unique land-tour vacations in Alaska, Asia, Australia, Canada, Europe, Latin America, and New Zealand.

In July 2007, Royal Caribbean announced the opening in Singapore (their Asia-Pacific headquarters) of Royal Caribbean Cruises (Asia) Pte. Ltd. This regional headquarters will support the marketing efforts of the Asia-Pacific region of three of the company's cruise brands: Royal Caribbean International, Celebrity Cruises, and Azamara Cruises. In year end 2006, Royal Caribbean's revenue surpassed $5.2 billion with net earnings of approximately $634 million. Exhibit 6 provides an overview of direct competition among Carnival Cruise, Royal Caribbean, other private cruise ships, and the industry.

Environmental and Regulatory Concerns

Environmental concerns affect the cruise line industry. For several years, the cruise industry has advocated that states enter into Memorandums of Understanding (MOUs) in an attempt to deal with discharges from cruise ships. A Memorandum of Understanding is based on trust rather than law and, therefore, it is most useful in situations where a party's word can be trusted. The cruise industry, unfortunately, has consistently demonstrated that its verbal and written promises do not correspond with its behavior and practices. The cruise industry's actions support the conclusion in a recent report from the Paris-based Organization for Economic Cooperation and Development, which questions the environmental effectiveness and economic efficiency of voluntary approaches.

EXHIBIT 6 Direct Competitor Comparison (July 2007)

	Carnival	Royal Car	Star Cruises	TUI AG	Industry
Market Cap	$ 38.75B	8.69B	N/A	N/A	554.85M
Employees	66,000	42,271	20,600[2]	53,930[2]	134
Qtrly Rev Growth	8.90%	6.70%	N/A	N/A	13.10%
Revenue	12.30B	5.31B	2.34B[2]	27.06B[2]	406.72M
Gross Margin	44.83%	61.48%	N/A	N/A	47.07%
EBITDA	3.74B	1.25B	N/A	N/A	81.44M
Oper Margins	21.36%	15.02%	N/A	N/A	−0.93%
Net Income	$ 2.32B	523.25M	17.91B[1]	−1.12B[2]	−358.05K
EPS	2.842	2.450	N/A	N/A	N/A
P/E	16.29	16.69	N/A	N/A	22.34
PEG (5 yr expected)	1.13	1.12	N/A	N/A	1.77
P/S	3.17	1.64	N/A	N/A	2.89

Industry = General Entertainment
[1] = As of 2005 [2] = As of 2006

Source: finance.yahoo.com

Cruise liners generate domestic wastewater in the course of accommodating their passengers and crew. Combined domestic wastewater, or "graywater" is comprised of galley, scullery, laundry, bath/shower, and sink Combined Domestic Wastewater drainage. It does not include sewage, or "blackwater" which is exclusively human waste from toilets and urinals, plus medical facility sink drainage. Graywater is typically collected in tanks aboard cruise ships and held for recycling, transfer, or discharge.

U.S. federal and international regulations allow discharge of graywater and properly treated blackwater virtually anywhere except in the Great Lakes, including in-port locations. However, cruise ship operators who are members of the International Council of Cruise Lines (ICCL) have voluntarily agreed to discharge graywater and treated blackwater only while ships are underway and not while in port.

The International Maritime Organization (IMO), the United States and other maritime nations have developed consistent and uniform international standards that apply to all vessels engaged in international commerce. These standards are set forth in the International Convention for the Prevention of Pollution from Ships (MARPOL).

The cruise ship industry has experienced explosive growth in terms of size and popularity in recent years. Newer, bigger, and more capable ships are coming into service to meet the demands of the cruising population. Passengers are drawn to cruising by the adventure, relaxation, and entertainment afforded by the shipboard experience and by the serenity and beauty of the cruise locales. The laws governing competition, including antitrust and consumer protection laws, have a significant impact on the cruise industry.

All ocean-going vessels engaged in international commerce must have a country of registry in order to operate in international waters. Accordingly, most countries, including the United States, provide these registration services or flags of registry. Because of the many restrictions outlined on the U.S. flag registry, nearly 90 percent of the commercial vessels calling on U.S. ports fly a non-U.S. flag. Therefore, vessels operating with international registries are not unique to the cruise industry.

Conclusion

A variety of risks and concerns could impact the industry and the company.

1. Seasonality: The demand by travelers could vary depending on a variety of factors. In general, demand for cruises has been higher during the third fiscal quarter.
2. Natural Disasters: Events such as hurricanes could impact the industry and the company when vacation packages are canceled or postponed or if the ships can't leave

the port or must return to the port. These events could impact the company's financial position.

3. Government Regulations: The industry is regulated by various international, national, state, and local laws. Each country registry conducts periodic inspections along with changes in the regulations in the areas of ports, customs, labor, immigration, gambling, security, safety, and such. Any changes to government regulations could have an impact on the company's financial position negatively.

4. Environmental and Health Concerns: The company is required to be in compliance with all the environmental concerns such as waste, pollution, and such. Furthermore, any epidemic health concerns in the regions where the company does business could prevent travelers from completing their travel plans. Accordingly, the company continuously must invest in improving its fleets which could cause an increase in expenses and have an adverse reaction on profitability.

5. Economic Condition: The travel industry, specifically cruise ships, is sensitive to economic conditions such as unemployment, reduction in discretionary income, inflation or recession, interest rates, foreign exchange, and such. Any adverse economic condition could reduce the company's revenue and profitability.

6. Internal Issues: Carnival did not suffer financially or from a public relations standpoint due to the fire on the *Ecstasy*. However, similar instances could have an increase in labor costs, food, liquor, maintenance, taxes, insurance, and other costs and expenses and could result in lower profitability than expected by the investors.

Today's competitive travel market demands progressive product differentiation. Carnival is focused on building and/or obtaining bigger ships to satisfy economies of scale and consumer preferences. However, analysts predict overcapacity in the future. Carnival's strategy is to focus on a market segmentation strategy by targeting the contemporary 20–30-year-olds, singles, married couples and honeymooners, college students, and families with teenage children. Marketing has begun targeting the premium group—aging baby boomers and luxury affluent passengers.

Carnival has signed a letter of intent for a new 116,000-ton ship for its P&O Cruises brand with a purchase price of approximately €535 million. The new vessel, scheduled for delivery in 2010, will be built by Italian shipbuilder Fincantieri at its Monfalcone yard and will have 3,076 lower passenger berths. Externally, the vessel will be similar to P&O Cruises' *Ventura*, which is scheduled to enter service in spring 2008. The interior design and new product features will be announced as part of the new campaign. Yet there are many risks and threats that the company must adhere to in order to keep its investors happy. Royal Caribbean has full wind in its sails and desires to overtake Carnival.

References

biz.yahoo.com
boards.cruisecritic.com
carnivalcruise.com
finance.yahoo.com
www.bluewaternetwork.org
www.cruising.org
www.reuters.com
www.traveldailynews.com
www.wsj.com

## 26

MGM Mirage — 2007

John K. Ross III

Sherry K. Ross
Texas State University–San Marcos

MGM

http://www.mgmmirage.com/index.asp

Lately you have begun to get a little anxious. After all, it is your final semester at State and you still do not have a good job lined up. You interviewed on campus with several companies, but none seemed right, until this last round of interviews. The first two interviews were great. You were apprehensive at first; after all, applying for a job with a Las Vegas casino had never been in your plans. But the on-campus interviewer was very professional and encouraging. The second interview two weeks later went even better, and now you are on your way to the final interview at corporate headquarters, located in the Bellagio Hotel and Casino.

Your flight was uneventful, landing as the sun was setting over the desert Southwest. The temperature has cooled to below 100° and it is dark by the time your taxi leaves McCarran Airport down the brightly lit neon road called the Strip to the Bellagio. As you gaze out the window you recall your MGM Mirage research and begin naming their properties as you pass them. First is the Four Seasons next to Mandalay Bay on your right, then the Luxor, and then the Excalibur. At the next intersection is the MGM Grand and New York-New York, which are across the street from each other. Then you pass the Monte Carlo and finally turn into the Bellagio. You know that further down the strip are more MGM Mirage properties and that these are only the ones in Las Vegas. Even though you have read about these properties, the size and scope of the casinos and resorts owned by MGM Mirage takes your breath away.

As your taxi turns into the Bellagio the dancing fountains seem to welcome you to what you hope will be your new career.

MGM Mirage

The story of the MGM Mirage parallels that of the gaming industry in the United States, and particularly that of the Las Vegas hotel/casino industry. But it is also the story of two Las Vegas gaming community giants, Kirk Kerkorian and Steven Wynn. Together, yet separately, these two men helped shape today's gaming industry and created Las Vegas as a destination resort.

Mr. Kirk Kerkorian has lived the true American rags to riches dream. Born in 1917, the son of Armenian immigrants, Mr. Kerkorian lived through the Great Depression, learned to fly, and ferried planes from Canada to England for the Royal Air Force during WWII. He then started Trans International Airlines, which he later sold, and then made investments in Las Vegas properties and in MGM Studios. Loving Las Vegas and seeing its potential for growth, he opened the first MGM Grand in 1973. With shrewd investments and a keen knowledge of the markets, Mr. Kerkorian's investment company, Tracinda Corp., now owns over 50 percent of the outstanding shares of the MGM Mirage; and he is one of the wealthiest men in America.

Steven Wynn, on the other hand, was raised in affluence and attended a military prep school and the University of Pennsylvania. He moved to Las Vegas in 1967 and through a series of astute investments gained control of the Golden Nugget in the downtown area. He took an ailing casino, turned it around, and invested the profits in land located on the Strip. Eventually he created the Mirage, followed by Treasure Island and the Bellagio. He is no longer affiliated with MGM Mirage and is currently CEO and chairman of the board of Wynn Resorts, a $2.7 billion luxury hotel and destination casino on the Strip in Las Vegas.

The MGM Mirage was created when the MGM Grand acquired Mirage Resorts in 2000. By then, the themed hotel/casino resort concept had become firmly entrenched in Las Vegas as well as in much of the remaining gaming community. The acquisition was part of a consolidation trend in the hotel/casino industry and was continued when MGM Mirage acquired Mandalay Resort Group in 2005. In 2007, MGM opened MGM Grand Detroit and MGM Grand Macan, and will open huge new resorts in Atlantic City and Abu Dhabi, UAE in 2008.

Properties

Currently MGM Mirage acts principally as a holding company and conducts operations through its wholly owned subsidiaries. Exhibit 1 provides a complete list of the properties wholly or partially owned and controlled by MGM Mirage. The list includes properties in

EXHIBIT 1   Resort and Casino Data

Name and Location	Approximate			
	Number of Guestrooms and Suites	Casino Square Footage	Slots	Gaming Tables
Las Vegas Strip, Nevada				
Bellagio	3,933	155,000	2,365	144
MGM Grand Las Vegas	5,803	156,000	2,611	174
Mandalay Bay	4,756	157,000	2,010	120
The Mirage	3,044	118,000	2,063	111
Luxor	4,404	100,000	1,589	89
Treasure Island ("TI")	2,885	87,000	1,726	68
New York-New York	2,024	84,000	1,850	75
Excalibur	3,990	90,000	1,887	73
Monte Carlo	3,002	102,000	1,612	74
Circus Circus Las Vegas	3,764	133,000	2,350	92
Subtotal	37,605	1,182,000	20,063	1,020
Other Nevada				
Primm Valley Resorts *(Primm)*	2,642	137,000	2,816	93
Circus Circus Reno	1,572	69,000	1,246	47
Silver Legacy - 50% owned	1,710	87,000	1,677	68
Gold Strike *(Jean)*	811	37,000	740	10
Nevada Landing *(Jean)*	303	36,000	727	10
Laughlin Properties *(Laughlin)*	2,524	102,000	2,199	72
Railroad Pass *(Henderson)*	120	13,000	330	6
Other Domestic Operations				
MGM Grand Detroit *(Detroit, Michigan)*	N/A	75,000	2,840	72
Beau Rivage *(Biloxi, Mississippi)*	1,740	72,000	2,048	93
Gold Strike *(Tunica, Mississippi)*	1,131	50,000	1,271	56
Borgata - 50% owned *(Atlantic City, New Jersey)*	1,971	137,000	4,068	178
Grand Victoria - 50% owned *(Elgin, Illinois)*	N/A	34,000	1,111	36
Grand Total	52,129	2,031,000	41,136	1,761

Source: 10-K, February 28, 2007.

Las Vegas as well as Jean, Laughlin, and Henderson, Nevada. Other states such as Michigan, Mississippi, and New Jersey are also well represented.

The major properties for MGM Mirage are located on the Las Vegas Strip where big, expensive, entertaining, new, and exciting are the key words for success. And MGM Mirage provides it all: mega-casinos, world-class hotels and restaurants, and some of the biggest entertainment shows in the world. And it seems to work, as evidenced by the over $7 billion in revenues and $600 million net profits in 2006. The following section gives some idea of the scope and size of some of the major MGM Mirage properties.

MGM Grand Las Vegas is one of the signature resorts and is one of the largest casino resorts in the world. Its guest rooms feature unique themes including an area offering boutique-style rooms called the West Wing, ultra-suites on the 29th floor called Skylofts, and the exclusive Mansion for premium gaming customers. World-class restaurants include two new restaurants by renowned chef Joël Robuchon, as well as Craftsteak, Nobhill, SeaBlue, Pearl, Shibuya, and Fiamma Trattoria. Other amenities include the Studio 54 nightclub, Tabu, the Ultra Lounge, Teatro, numerous retail shopping outlets, a 380,000-square-foot state-of-the-art conference center, and an extensive pool and spa complex. Entertainment by Cirque du Soleil is performed in a custom-designed theatre seating almost 2,000 guests.

The Mirage is the other signature resort, featuring a luxurious, tropically oriented theme located on a site shared with Treasure Island at the center of the Las Vegas Strip. The exterior of the resort is most recognized for its water features around a 54-foot volcano, which erupts every evening at regular intervals. Inside the front entrance is an atrium with a tropical garden and additional water features capped by a 100-foot-high glass dome designed to replicate the sights, sounds, and fragrances of the South Seas. Restaurants include Kokomos, Japonais, Fin, Stack, Cravings, and Carnegie Deli. Entertainment at the Mirage is highlighted by Cirque du Soleil and Danny Gans.

The Bellagio is one of the premier destination resorts located at the heart of the Las Vegas Strip. Bellagio is probably most famous for its eight-acre lake featuring over 1,000 fountains that come alive at regular intervals in a choreographed ballet of water, music, and lights. There is also a conservatory filled with unique botanical displays that change with the seasons, and 200,000 square feet of convention space. Restaurants include Picasso and Le Cirque, and entertainment options include *O*, produced and performed by Cirque du Soleil, the Light nightclub, and several other bars and lounges. Leisure travelers can also enjoy Bellagio's expansive pool, world-class spa, and Gallery of Fine Arts.

Mandalay Bay Resorts is the most recent addition to MGM Mirage. This South Seas–themed resort features an extensive pool and beach area, including a wave pool and a European-style "ultra" beach, as well as a 30,000-square-foot spa. Restaurants include Charlie Palmer's Aureole, Wolfgang Puck's Trattoria del Lupo, China Grill, Hubert Keller's Fleur de Lys, and Border Grill. Entertainment venues include a 12,000-seat special events arena, a 1,760-seat showroom featuring the Broadway hit *Mamma Mia!*, the House of Blues, and the Rumjungle restaurant and nightclub. In addition, Mandalay Bay features the Shark Reef, exhibiting sharks and rare sea predators. Also included within Mandalay Bay is a Four Seasons Hotel with its own lobby, restaurants, pool, and spa.

From pirates to pyramids to castles, other MGM Mirage properties follow the same general concept of themed entertainment gaming resorts covering a wide variety of locations and catering to many different types of customers. The recent acquisitions of Mirage Resorts and Mandalay Bay Resorts have provided a tremendous depth and breadth of offerings and have significantly contributed to the recent growth of MGM Mirage. These acquisitions seem to have been successfully integrated into a corporate holding organizational structure. Although MGM Mirage does not publish their actual organizational structure, Exhibit 2 might be representative based on the listing of key management. This type of structure allows operational decisions and responsibility for the MGM Grand group and the Mirage group to be located with specific individuals and further allows each to operate independently, yet coordinated. The corporate offices help provide a high degree of synergy between the two divisions and allow for shared resources to be used for future projects.

EXHIBIT 2   Possible Organizational Structure

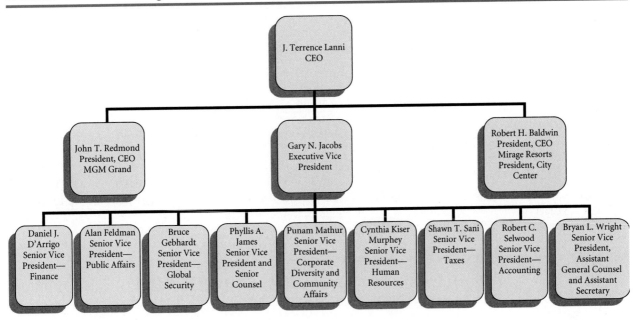

Mission

The successful integration of the many properties of MGM Mirage can, in some part, be attributed to a strong management team with a clear mission. The mission of MGM Mirage, as stated by the company, is:

> The resorts and casinos of MGM Mirage are some of the most famous in the world, widely credited for establishing a new generation of excitement in Las Vegas! Our 24 destinations are renowned for their winning combination of quality entertainment, luxurious facilities and exceptional customer service.

> Our dedicated staff of over 70,000 employees are committed to providing an unsurpassed experience for every one of our guests. We are actively expanding our presence globally, with potential developments in a number of domestic and international markets. At MGM Mirage, we are all striving together to deliver our enticing blend of entertainment to every corner of the world.

> *Source:* http://www.mgmmirage.com/missionstatement.asp

This mission has helped management remain focused on the core activities of MGM Mirage and pursue an aggressive growth strategy at the same time. The successful implementation of these strategies by management has provided substantial financial resources to peruse new venues, and the management team has been well rewarded by the company, as can be seen in Exhibit 3 and Exhibit 4.

Financials

The financial management of an organization as large as MGM Mirage could be a daunting task. From the financial data it appears that MGM Mirage is practicing solid financial statement management with even cash flow throughout the operating year.

Recent trends in revenue seem to be following the industry with casino operations becoming a smaller percentage while the revenue from rooms is growing as a percentage of total revenues. This trend has been prevalent throughout the industry for years as Las Vegas has come to depend less on gambling and more on entertainment to draw customers. However, gaming does remain some 43 percent of total revenue with food and

EXHIBIT 3   Management Compensation 2003–2005

| Name and Principal Position | Year | Annual Compensation | | Long-Term Compensation Awards | |
		Salary	Bonus	Other Annual	Shares Underlying Options	All Other Compensation
J. Terrence Lanni Chairman and Chief Executive Officer	2005	$ 2,000,000	$ 6,089,729	$ 661,857	1,200,000	$ 849,036
	2004	2,000,000	3,393,553	612,114	–	817,162
	2003	2,000,000	1,989,345	504,921	1,400,000	812,350
Robert H. Baldwin President and Chief Executive Officer — Mirage Resorts, Incorporated	2005	$ 1,500,000	$ 4,562,205	$ –	600,000	$ 461,793
	2004	1,500,000	2,542,327	25,225	–	473,554
	2003	1,500,000	1,490,345	11,345	1,200,000	500,081
John T. Redmond President and Chief Executive Officer — MGM Grand Resorts, LLC	2005	$ 1,422,308	$ 4,562,205	$ –	600,000	$ 329,607
	2004	1,300,000	2,201,837	–	–	282,219
	2003	1,300,000	1,290,745	4,981	1,000,000	300,123
James J. Murren President, Chief Financial Officer and Treasurer	2005	$ 1,315,385	$ 4,562,205	$ 100,747	700,000	$ 375,432
	2004	1,200,000	2,031,592	54,865	–	274,830
	2003	1,200,000	1,190,946	62,807	1,000,000	259,160
Gary N. Jacobs Executive Vice President, General Counsel and Secretary	2005	$ 700,000	$ 2,468,167	$ 24,972	400,000	$ 357,345
	2004	700,000	1,180,366	24,924	–	274,590
	2003	700,000	691,946	11,883	600,000	243,094

Source: Def14 A Proxy Statement Filed April 4, 2006.

entertainment revenue remaining constant. Segment data also shows that table games have shown a marked percentage increase (from 30 percent in 2004 to 40 percent in 2006) in casino revenues. This may be a reflection of the tremendous interest in table games, particularly Texas hold 'em as seen on television shows and played on home computers.

Recent acquisitions have greatly impacted the balance sheet with large increases in property, plant, and equipment as Mirage and Mandalay Bay were consolidated into the financial statements. Additionally, a seemingly large goodwill account, at over $1.3 billion, will need to be amortized in coming years. In the liabilities section of the balance sheet, the $12.0 billion in long-term debt represents some 58 percent of liabilities and stockholders' equity. Although these numbers seem large, keep in mind that MGM Mirage earned $635 million net on revenues of $7.1 billion with a market cap of $18.99 billion.

The Gaming Industry

People have undoubtedly gambled or placed wagers on the outcomes of events since before the beginning of recorded history. Today the gaming industry is a multibillion-dollar worldwide industry, which incorporates everything from massive hotel/casino destination resorts to state-run lotteries, to individuals sitting at their computer playing over the Internet. Over the past 30 years, just in the United States, we have seen gambling grow from a few destination resorts in Las Vegas and Atlantic City to some form of legalized gaming in 48 states, including the development of multistate lotteries, the proliferation of

EXHIBIT 4   Management Compensation 2006

Name	Year	Salary	Stock Awards	Option Awards	Non-Equity Incentive Plan Compensation	All Other Compensation	Total
J. Terrence Lanni Chairman and Chief Executive Officer	2006	$ 2,000,000	$ 550,458	$ 5,481,564	$ 6,567,893	$ 1,087,206	$ 15,687,121
James J. Murren President, Chief Financial Officer and Treasurer	2006	1,500,000	275,229	3,296,472	4,896,493	352,321	10,320,515
Robert H. Baldwin President and Chief Executive Officer — Mirage Resorts, Incorporated	2006	1,500,000	275,229	2,997,698	4,896,493	474,786	10,144,206
John T. Redmond President and Chief Executive Officer — MGM Grand Resorts, LLC	2006	1,500,000	275,229	2,893,368	4,896,493	335,085	$ 9,900,175
Gary N. Jacobs Executive Vice President, General Counsel and Secretary	2006	700,000	91,743	1,894,136	2,283,461	266,570	5,235,910

Source: Def14 A Proxy Statement Filed April 23, 2007.

Native American casinos, television shows promoting poker, and an explosion in Internet gambling.

The gambling industry is heavily regulated by states and by other governments. In the United States, individual states must first pass laws legalizing gambling, then they generally set up some form of regulatory commission to oversee gambling activities. The primary concern of these commissions is to ensure that games are honest and fairly run. Casino operators must provide extensive operating data to these commissions and maintain a gambling license. The U.S. government also regulates gambling through interstate commerce. Recently efforts have been aimed at slowing the growth of Internet gambling by restricting the free transfer of credit card monies to gambling sites around the world. On an international basis, each local government establishes regulations controlling gambling activities within its own borders. However, it may be necessary to go before several regulating agencies. For example, before MGM Mirage could move into Macau they needed approval from both the Macau S.A.R. government and the Nevada Gaming Commission.

United States

Even though the gaming industry is the most regulated and heavily taxed industry, there were approximately 300 public companies generating gaming revenues at the end of 2005. The American Gaming Association (http://www.americangaming.org/) and Datamonitor analysts reported that by 2005 the United States gaming industry was generating some $78.6 billion in total revenues. This was approximately an 8 percent year to year growth rate, with casinos alone generating some $49.1 billion, about 62.5 percent of the total revenues. Datamonitor predicts that by 2010 the U.S. casinos and gaming sectors' value will be approximately $109.2 billion, an increase of almost 40 percent. The ease of entry into the market for new companies adds an additional element of competition and impacts all gaming companies.

EXHIBIT 5 MGM Mirage and Subsidiaries Consolidated Balance Sheets (In thousands, except per share amounts)

	Year Ended December 31	
	2006	2005
ASSETS		
Current assets		
Cash and cash equivalents	$ 452,944	$ 377,933
Accounts receivable, net	362,921	352,673
Inventories	118,459	111,825
Income tax receivable	18,619	–
Deferred income taxes	68,046	65,518
Prepaid expenses and other	124,414	110,634
Assets held for sale	369,348	–
Total current assets	1,514,751	1,018,583
Real estate under development	188,433	–
Property and equipment, net	17,241,860	16,541,651
Other assets		
Investments in unconsolidated affiliates	1,092,257	931,154
Goodwill	1,300,747	1,314,561
Other intangible assets, net	367,200	377,479
Deposits and other assets, net	440,990	515,992
Total other assets	3,201,194	3,139,186
Total Assets	$ 22,146,238	$ 20,699,420
LIABILITIES AND STOCKHOLDERS' EQUITY		
Current liabilities		
Accounts payable	$ 182,154	$ 156,373
Construction payable	234,486	109,228
Income taxes payable	–	125,503
Current portion of long-term debt	–	14
Accrued interest on long-term debt	232,957	229,930
Other accrued liabilities	958,244	913,520
Liabilities related to assets held for sale	40,259	–
Total current liabilities	1,648,100	1,534,568
Deferred income taxes	3,441,157	3,378,371
Long-term debt	12,994,869	12,355,433
Other long-term obligations	212,563	195,976
Commitments and contingencies (Note 12)		
STOCKHOLDERS' EQUITY		
Common stock, $.01 par value: authorized 600,000,000 shares, issued 362,886,027 and 357,262,405 shares; outstanding 283,909,000 and 285,069,516 shares	3,629	3,573
Capital in excess of par value	2,806,636	2,586,587
Deferred compensation	–	(3,618)
Treasury stock, at cost (78,977,027 and 72,192,889 shares)	(1,597,120)	(1,338,394)
Retained earnings	2,635,989	1,987,725
Accumulated other comprehensive income (loss)	415	(801.00)
Total stockholders' equity	3,849,549	3,235,072
Total Liabilities and SE	$ 22,146,238	$ 20,699,420

Source: 10K February 28, 2007.

EXHIBIT 6 **MGM Mirage and Subsidiaries Consolidated Statements of Income (In thousands, except per share amounts)**

	Year Ended December 31		
	2006	2005	2004
Revenues			
Casino	$ 3,130,438	$ 2,764,546	$ 2,080,752
Rooms	1,991,477	1,634,588	889,443
Food and beverage	1,483,914	1,271,650	807,535
Entertainment	459,540	426,175	268,595
Retail	278,695	253,214	181,630
Other	452,669	339,424	184,187
	7,796,733	6,689,597	4,412,142
Less: Promotional allowances	(620,777.00)	(560,754.00)	(410,338.00)
	7,175,956	6,128,843	4,001,804
Expenses			
Casino	1,612,992	1,422,472	1,028,351
Rooms	539,442	454,082	237,837
Food and beverage	902,278	782,372	462,864
Entertainment	333,619	305,799	191,256
Retail	179,929	164,189	116,556
Other	245,126	187,956	101,780
General and administrative	1,070,942	889,806	565,387
Corporate expense	161,507	130,633	77,910
Preopening and start-up expenses	36,362	15,752	10,276
Restructuring costs (credit)	1,035	(59)	5,625
Property transactions, net	(40,980)	37,021	8,234
Depreciation and amortization	629,627	560,626	382,773
	5,671,879	4,950,649	3,188,849
Income from unconsolidated affiliates	254,171	151,871	119,658
Operating income	1,758,248	1,330,065	932,613
Non-operating income (expense)			
Interest income	11,192	12,037	5,663
Interest expense, net	(760,361)	(640,758)	(367,583)
Non-operating items from unconsolidated affiliates	(16,063)	(15,825)	(12,298)
Other, net	(15,090)	(18,434)	(9,585)
	(780,322)	(662,980)	(383,803)
Income from continuing operations before income taxes	977,926	667,085	548,810
Provision for income taxes	(341,930)	(231,719)	(203,601)
Income from continuing operations	635,996	435,366	345,209
Discontinued operations			
Income from discontinued operations, including a gain on disposal of $82,538 in 2004	18,473	11,815	101,212
Provision for income taxes	(6,205)	(3,925)	(34,089)
	12,268	7,890	67,123
Net income	$ 648,264	$ 443,256	$ 412,332

continued

EXHIBIT 6   **MGM Mirage and Subsidiaries Consolidated Statements of Income (In thousands, except per share amounts)—continued**

	Year Ended December 31		
	2006	2005	2004
Basic income per share of common stock			
Income from continuing operations	$ 2.25	$ 1.53	$ 1.24
Discontinued operations	0.04	0.03	0.24
Net income per share	$ 2.29	$ 1.56	$ 1.48
Diluted income per share of common stock			
Income from continuing operations	$ 2.18	$ 1.47	$ 1.19
Discontinued operations	0.04	0.03	0.24
Net income per share	$ 2.22	$ 1.5	$ 1.43

Source: 10K February 28, 2007.

The latest growth sector has been Internet gambling. Twenty million U.S. citizens had wagered some $4 billion by the end of 2005. It is currently illegal to use the Internet to gamble in the United States or to transfer money to an international gambling site via credit cards. However, this has not stopped or slowed this sector's growth as Western Europe, China, and India are aggressively increasing their market share. By 2009 projections are that online gambling revenues will exceed $20 billion worldwide, with a smaller percentage coming from U.S. citizens. New laws in the United Kingdom will soon draw Internet gambling dollars to that nation.

Native American reservation casinos operated in over 20 states and generated $19.4 billion in revenues during 2004. They have constantly increased their revenues, their popularity, and the number of casinos. These casinos began as small roadside slot machine casinos servicing local customers. However, the success of these ventures has led to the creation of Native American–owned mega hotel/casinos designed to serve large regions. (Visit http://www.indiangaming.org/mq/frame/index.html for a complete list of Native American casinos.)

As the gambling phenomenon swept across the nation, a few states began legalizing gambling within their borders to help keep revenue and tax dollars local. Many of these were designated as "on water" casinos to be built on rivers or the Gulf Coast. Now almost every state has some form of gambling, state-operated lotteries (generating $24.1 billion in revenues in 2004) to private casinos to Native American casinos.

EXHIBIT 7   **Segment Data**

	Year Ended December 31		
	2006	2005	2004
Casino revenue, net:			
Table games	$ 1,251,304	$ 1,107,337	$ 938,281
Slots	1,770,176	1,563,485	1,083,979
Other	108,958	93,724	58,492
Casino revenue, net	3,130,438	2,764,546	2,080,752
Non-casino revenue:			
Rooms	1,991,477	1,634,588	889,443
Food and beverage	1,483,914	1,271,650	807,535
Entertainment, retail and other	1,190,904	1,018,813	634,412
Non-casino revenue	4,666,295	3,925,051	2,331,390
	7,796,733	6,689,597	4,412,142
Less: Promotional allowances	(620,777.00)	(560,754.00)	(410,338.00)
	$ 7,175,956	$ 6,128,843	$ 4,001,804

Source: 10K February 28, 2007.

Las Vegas

"While the Las Vegas Strip is not representative of all U.S. gaming jurisdictions, it does continue to lead industry trends," reports the U.S. Commercial Casino Industry. The current trend for Las Vegas destination resorts is to have a greater portion of total revenues coming from nongaming activities such as food and beverage, hotels, entertainment, and so on. By the end of 2005, nongaming revenues were approximately 58 percent of total revenues for all casino resorts. Another trend is industry consolidation. When Harrah's Entertainment purchased Caesars for $9.4 billion, Harrah's became the world's largest gaming firm in 2006. These consolidations seem to be the norm rather than the exception with MGM Mirage and Harrah's being the clear winners in the consolidation race.

The Las Vegas Convention and Visitors Authority, in their January 2007 Hotel-Casino Development Construction Bulletin (http://www.lvcva.com/getfile/Construction Bulletin%20Mar%2006.pdf?fileID=110), listed thirteen properties to be completed in 2007, including Towers 2 and 3 of The Signature MGM Grand. The current properties to be completed include $1.75 billion in 2007, $8.39 billion by 2008, $12.7 billion by 2009, and $5.937 billion by 2010. Including future properties for MGM, there are also over 60 tentative projects without completion dates.

With this tremendous increase in hotel rooms, Las Vegas will be targeting close to 77 million American baby boomers born between 1946 and 1964. These Americans are now at their highest earnings levels, can afford expensive vacations and, as retirees, they can be expected to travel extensively and spend more during those travels.

According to the Las Vegas Visitors Profile 2006 prepared for the Las Vegas Convention and Visitors Authority (http://www.lvcva.com/getfile/VPS-2006%20 Las%20Vegas.pdf?fileID=107), visitors to Las Vegas are likely to be married (79 percent), earning $40,000 or more (78 percent), employed (70 percent), and have typically visited Las Vegas six times in the last five years. One-quarter were retired (24 percent), a decrease from previous years. The proportion of respondents who were 40 years old or older has declined from 75 percent in 2003 to 69 percent currently, and the average age has dropped from 50.2 to 48.0 over that same time span. More than one-half of visitors were from the western United States (52 percent), with the bulk of them coming from California (32 percent). Thirteen percent of visitors were foreign. Only 19 percent of 2006 visitors indicated they were first-time visitors to Las Vegas and just less than one-half of all visitors said their primary reason for visiting Las Vegas this trip was vacation or pleasure. Each average visitor stayed 4.6 days in a hotel and spent $651 if they gambled. They spent approximately $107 per night for hotel rooms, $260 for food and drink, $140 shopping and $50 for shows.

Although these statistics represent those visiting resort casinos and represents the target market for MGM Mirage, it does not necessarily portray the wide range of individuals gambling. At one end of the range are the "low rollers" that can be found in local casinos playing the penny and nickel machines. At the other end are the "whales" that are willing to gamble one million dollars at a time on the table. The larger casino companies will have suitable offerings for all levels of gamblers at different casino locations.

Global

It has been estimated that worldwide $1.4 trillion per year is generated from all forms of gambling. This includes Internet gambling as well as casinos. Globally the size of casinos is increasing and new jurisdictions are opening for development. The global casino gaming market reached a value of $298.7 billion in total revenues in 2005 and by 2010 revenues are expected to increase to $387.5 billion. The U.S gaming market is a mature market that currently comprises about 28 percent of the global market. The Asia-Pacific segment has been dominated by Japan and Australia, which have accounted for 54.7 percent of global gaming revenues. Asia is experiencing exponential growth with the legalization of gambling in Macau, the only place in China where gambling is legal, and includes the development of mega-casinos by Las Vegas Sands (Sands Macau) and Wynn Resorts (Wynn Macau). Macau's actual casino revenues exceeded Las Vegas' revenues for the first time in 2005. In 2006, according to Hoover's, Macau's gambling revenues reached $6.95 billion compared to an estimated $6.5 billion for Las Vegas. Looking forward several years, Datamonitor analysts predicts a slight deceleration in growth for the gaming segment as competition intensifies.

In an article in *USA Today* (http://www.usatoday.com/travel/destinations/2007-05-03-asia-casinos-usat_N.htm?csp=34), PricewaterhouseCoopers predicted an annual growth rate of 14 percent per year through 2010 for the Asian markets. Likely to be included in that growth will be casinos located in Singapore, South Korea, Taiwan, and Japan. However, the compound annual growth rate for global gambling is still expected to be almost 7 percent through 2010.

Competition

The gaming industry is comprised of a number of different types of venues where customers can spend their entertainment dollars. As the Las Vegas and Atlantic City casino industry began to develop, other states began approving casino gaming, and still other states began offering state-run lotteries as a source of funds.

With revenues of over $9.67 billion and profits of $523 million, Harrah's Entertainment, Inc. (http://www.harrahs.com/) is currently the largest U.S.-based casino operator. Harrah's became the largest when it acquired Caesars Entertainment in 2006. With this consolidation Harrah's now owns or manages 36 casinos under the Harrah's, Caesars, and Horseshoe brand names, which include 19 land-based casinos, 11 riverboat or dockside casinos, four managed casinos on Indian lands, one combination thoroughbred racetrack and casino, and one combination greyhound racetrack and casino.

Some of the other domestic casino operators include Las Vegas Sands Corp. (http://www.lasvegassands.com/) with revenues of $2.2 billion in 2006; Wynn Resorts (http://www.wynnresorts.com/) with revenues of $1.4 billion in 2006; privately held Columbia Sussex (http://www.columbiasussex.com/), which develops and manages some 80 hotels and casinos in about 30 states; and Trump Entertainment Resorts (http://www.trumpcasinos.com/) with $1.026 billion in revenues in 2006. Expect this list of competitors to change as mergers and acquisitions continue to change the competitive landscape. However, expect continued development of casino resorts throughout the United States by Native Americans, the opening of additional states to legalized gambling, and continued development of Las Vegas as a premier resort destination.

MGM Mirage Future Projects

Maintaining a successful corporation in the rapidly developing and changing hotel/casino/entertainment industry requires extensive strategic planning and analysis to see opportunities as well as management's willingness to pursue those opportunities. The largest project for MGM Mirage has been named CityCenter and is a $7 billion development

EXHIBIT 8   **Harrah's Properties**

Las Vegas	Atlantic City	Louisiana/Mississippi	Iowa/Missouri
Caesars Palace	Harrah's Atlantic City	Harrah's New Orleans	Harrah's St. Louis
Bally's Las Vegas	Showboat Atlantic City	Harrah's Louisiana Downs	Harrah's North Kansas City
Flamingo Las Vegas	Bally's Atlantic City	Horseshoe Bossier City	Harrah's Council Bluffs
Harrah's Las Vegas	Caesars Atlantic City	Grand Biloxi	Horseshoe Council Bluffs/
Paris Las Vegas	Harrah's Chester	Grand Tunica	Bluffs Run
Rio		Horseshoe Tunica	
Imperial Palace		Sheraton Tunica	
Illinois/Indiana	**Other Nevada**	**Managed/International/Other**	
Caesars Indiana	Harrah's Reno	Harrah's Ak-Chin	
Harrah's Joliet	Harrah's Lake Tahoe	Harrah's Cherokee	
Harrah's Metropolis	Harveys Lake Tahoe	Harrah's Prairie Band	
Horseshoe Hammond	Bill's Lake Tahoe	Harrah's Rincon	
	Harrah's Laughlin	Conrad Punta del Este	

Source: Harrah's *10Q* filed November 9, 2006.

between the Bellagio and the Monte Carlo. CityCenter will consists of a 4,000-room casino resort, two 400-room boutique hotels, 470,000 square feet of retail shops, and 2.3 million square feet of residential space in 2,700 luxury condominiums in multiple towers. Its an expected completion date is November 2009. The company reports sales of residential units have been "exceptionally strong."

In Detroit, Michigan, the MGM Grand Detroit was developed as a permanent hotel-casino complex and was expected to open in late 2007 at a cost of approximately $750 million. This property features a 400-room hotel, 100,000-square-foot casino, numerous restaurant and entertainment amenities, and spa and convention facilities.

Also being developed, in a joint ownership with MGM Grand Paradise Limited, is the MGM Grand Macau, expected to open in late 2007. This hotel-casino resort in Macau S.A.R. features at least 345 table games and 1,035 slots with room for significant expansion. At an estimated total cost of $850 million, features include approximately 600 rooms, suites and villas, a luxurious spa, convertible convention space, a variety of dining destinations, and other attractions.

Other projects include further development of MGM Mirage properties in Atlantic City, New Jersey and possible casino development in the United Kingdom. Additionally, further development of the Foxwoods Casino Resort in Ledyard, Connecticut with the Mashantucket Pequot Tribal Nation is planned. MGM Mirage will also be working with the Mubadala Development Company of Abu Dhabi, U.A.E., to develop nongaming luxury hotels targeting locations in Abu Dhabi, Las Vegas, and the United Kingdom. MGM Mirage has also signed a memorandum of understanding with the Diaoyutai State Guesthouse in Beijing, People's Republic of China, to form a joint venture to develop luxury nongaming hotels and resorts targeting locations in the People's Republic of China.

Conclusion

Although gambling has been a pastime throughout history, it has only been recently that the mega-casino/resort has developed. After a rapid growth through the 1980s and 1990s, the U.S. gambling industry has matured. However, opportunities continue to develop as local legislation opens new gaming venues and technology provides new methods of gambling. In the principle resort destination market of Las Vegas, consolidation has resulted in the market being dominated by a few very large gaming corporations. In order for these large corporations to continue high growth, they are actively searching for international gambling opportunities as well as other resort development opportunities. They also are continuing to redevelop current properties, making them bigger and better, to continue attracting customers back to their resorts. MGM Mirage is currently the second largest U.S.-based gambling company and seems to be trying to become the largest. It is also beginning to redefine itself as more than casinos as it moves into resort and land development on a global scale.

Additional Sources

There are many additional sources of information regarding the gambling casino/resort industry. Listed below are a few from the Internet:

MGM Mirage: http://www.mgmmirage.com/index.asp
Harrah's: http://www.harrahs.com/
Las Vegas Sands: http://www.lasvegassands.com/
The Trump Organization: http://www.trump.com/main.htm
American Gaming Association: http://www.americangaming.org/
Las Vegas Convention and Visitors Authority: http://www.visitlasvegas.com/vegas/index.jsp
Wynn Resorts: http://www.wynnresorts.com/
Columbia Sussex: http://www.columbiasussex.com/
National Indian Gaming Association: http://www.indiangaming.org/mq/frame/index.html
SEC Filings and Forms (EDGAR): http://www.sec.gov/edgar.shtml
Casino World News: http://www.casinoworldnews.com/
National Council on Problem Gambling: http://www.ncpgambling.org/
Macau S.A.R.: http://www.gov.mo/egi/Portal/index.jsp

## 27

Marriott International — 2007

Vijaya Narapareddy
University of Denver

MAR

www.marriott.com

Headquartered in Bethesda, Maryland, Marriott International (MAR) in 2007 and for eight years in a row has been ranked by *Fortune* as among the "100 Best Companies to Work For." Marriott has 150,600 employees worldwide and 60 percent are women and minorities. *Fortune*'s "Most Admired" rankings are based upon eight criteria: innovation; people management; use of corporate assets; social responsibility; quality of management; financial soundness; long-term investment; and quality of products/services. "Being recognized by the nation's top business leaders as the most admired lodging company is a true testament to our successful business model... We owe this honor to our experienced leaders, our great portfolio of brands, and above all, our dedicated associates," noted Marriott's chairman and chief executive officer, J.W. Marriott, Jr., on March 9, 2007.

Business Segments

Ranked number one in both market capitalization and revenues in the lodging industry, Marriott's worldwide business is divided into six segments—North American full-service lodging, North American limited-service lodging, international lodging, luxury lodging, timeshare, and synthetic fuel. Exhibit 1 provides a summary of brands held under each segment but does not include the synthetic fuel segment. Exhibit 2 reveals Marriott's revenues by business segment. Note that the North American full-service lodging segment is the largest with revenues accounting for 43.6 percent of MAR's total revenues, followed by the North American limited-service lodging (17 percent), and timeshare (15 percent). Exhibit 2 shows that revenues from the North American full-service lodging segment are steadily declining as a percentage of the total lodging business, down 2.5 percent from 46.2 percent in 2004 to 43.6 percent in 2006. In contrast, the analogous international segment percentage doubled from 6.2 percent in 2004 to approximately 12 percent in 2006. Similar trends are evident in the income from continuing operations presented in Exhibit 3. Note that income from the North American full-service lodging segment expressed as a percentage of total income declined from 37 percent in 2004 to 32 percent in 2006. Income from the timeshare segment as a percent of total income also declined, from approximately 22 percent in 2004 to 20 percent in 2006. The decline in this segment is more dramatic from 2005 (25 percent) to 2006 (20 percent). However, the international segment has the opposite trend, a growth of approximately 5 percent from 2004 to 2006.

Marriott operates or franchises 2,832 lodging properties and 2,046 furnished corporate housing rental units in 68 countries. Exhibit 4 displays the various company-operated and franchised properties by location. Its domestic operations account for over 75 percent of the 1,048 properties the company operates and over 93 percent of the 1784 properties franchised.

EXHIBIT 1   Marriott Brands by Segment

North American Full-Service Lodging Segment

- *Marriott® Hotels & Resorts*
- *Marriott Conference Centers*
- *JW Marriott® Hotels & Resorts*
- *Renaissance® Hotels & Resorts*
- *Renaissance ClubSport®*

North American Limited-Service Lodging Segment

- *Courtyard by Marriott®*
- *Fairfield Inn by Marriott®*
- *SpringHill Suites by Marriott®*
- *Residence Inn by Marriott®*
- *TownePlace Suites by Marriott®*
- *Marriott ExecuStay®*

International Lodging Segment

- *Marriott® Hotels & Resorts*
- *JW Marriott® Hotels & Resorts*
- *Renaissance® Hotels & Resorts*
- *Courtyard by Marriott®*
- *Fairfield Inn by Marriott®*
- *Residence Inn by Marriott®*
- *Ramada International*
- *Marriott Executive Apartments®*

Luxury Segment

- *The Ritz-Carlton®*
- *Bulgari Hotels & Resorts®*

Timeshare Segment

- *Marriott Vacation Club*^{SM}
- *The Ritz-Carlton Club®*
- *Grand Residences by Marriott®*
- *Horizons by Marriott Vacation Club®*

Source: www.marriott.com; SEC *Form 10K*, p. 4.

EXHIBIT 2   Revenues by Business Segment

(In $ Millions)	2006		2005		2004	
North American Full-Service Segment	$ 5,196	43.6%	$ 5,116	46.2%	$ 4,691	48.2%
North American Limited-Service Segment	2,060	17.3%	1,886	17.0%	1,673	17.2%
International Segment	1,411	11.8%	1,017	9.2%	604	6.2%
Luxury Segment	1,423	11.9%	1,333	12.0%	1,263	13.0%
Timeshare Segment	1,840	15.4%	1,721	15.5%	1,502	15.4%
Total Lodging	**11,930**	**100%**	**11,073**	**100.0%**	**9,733**	**100.0%**
Other unallocated corporate	65		56		45	
Synthetic Fuel Segment (after-tax)	165		421		321	
	$ 12,160		**$ 11,550**		**$ 10,099**	

Source: Adapted from www.marriott.com; 2006 SEC *Form 10K*, p. 32.

EXHIBIT 3   Income from Continuing Operations by Segment

(In $ Millions)	2006		2005		2004	
North American Full-Service Segment	$ 455	32.2%	$ 349	31.7%	$ 337	36.8%
North American Limited-Service Segment	380	26.9%	303	27.5%	233	25.4%
International Segment	237	16.7%	133	12.1%	109	11.9%
Luxury Segment	63	4.5%	45	4.1%	35	3.8%
Timeshare Segment	280	19.8%	271	24.6%	203	22.1%
Total Lodging	**1,415**	**100%**	**1,101**	**100.0%**	**917**	**100.0%**
Other unallocated corporate	(251)		(219)		(220)	
Synthetic Fuel Segment (after-tax)	5		125		107	
Interest income, provision for loan losses and interest expense (excluding the Synthetic Fuel Segment)	(72)		(55)		55	
Income taxes (excluding the Synthetic Fuel Segment)	(380)		(284)		(265)	
	$ 717		**$ 668**		**$ 594**	

Source: Adapted from www.marriott.com, 2006 SEC *Form 10K*, p. 32.

EXHIBIT 4 **Properties Held by Marriott International as of 2006, Excluding Timeshare Properties**

Brand	Company-Operated		Franchised	
	Properties	Rooms	Properties	Rooms
U.S. Locations				
Marriott Hotels & Resorts	145	73,621	167	51,050
Marriott Conference Centers	13	3,476	—	—
JW Marriott Hotels & Resorts	11	6,735	4	1,215
Renaissance Hotels & Resorts	35	15,881	29	9,050
Renaissance ClubSport	—	—	1	175
The Ritz-Carlton	35	11,616	—	—
Courtyard	271	42,264	379	48,962
Fairfield Inn	2	855	511	45,175
SpringHill Suites	23	3,581	129	14,103
Residence Inn	136	18,401	358	40,572
TownePlace Suites	34	3,661	89	8,707
Marriott Vacation Club [1]	36	8,673	—	—
Grand Residences by Marriott [1]	2	264	—	—
The Ritz-Carlton Club [1]	5	434	—	—
Horizons by Marriott Vacation Club [1]	2	372	—	—
Non-U.S. Locations				
Marriott Hotels & Resorts	129	34,617	29	9,095
JW Marriott Hotels & Resorts	20	7,534	1	61
Renaissance Hotels & Resorts	53	17,607	18	5,513
The Ritz-Carlton	25	7,790	—	—
Bulgari Hotels & Resorts	2	117	—	—
Marriott Executive Apartments	17	2,928	1	99
Courtyard	37	7,549	46	6,751
Fairfield Inn	—	—	5	559
SpringHill Suites	—	—	1	124
Residence Inn	1	190	16	2,123
Ramada International	2	332	—	—
Marriott Vacation Club [1]	9	1,839	—	—
The Ritz-Carlton Club [1]	2	112	—	—
Grand Residences by Marriott [1]	1	49	—	—
Total	1,048	270,498	1,784	243,334

Source: www.marriott.com; SEC *Form 10K*, p. 6.

Marriott's operations by country are listed in Exhibit 5. Note that the number of properties in the United States (2,417) account for the lion's share of its business, followed by the United Kingdom (74), Canada (52), Germany (41), China (33), and Mexico (13). However, the number of rooms is the highest in developing markets overseas. For example, the average number of rooms is 169 in the United States, 219 in Canada, 169 in the United Kingdom, 217 in Germany, 377 in China, 256 in India, and 250 in Mexico.

History

Marriott's origins date back to 1927 when J. Willard Marriott and his bride, Alice, opened a 9-seat root beer stand in Washington, D.C., called the Hot Shoppe, where hot food such as tamales, chili, and tacos were served during the winter months. In 1929, Marriott officially

EXHIBIT 5 **Marriott's Properties by Country**

Country	Properties [1]	Rooms[1]
Americas		
Argentina	1	325
Aruba	4	1,641
Bahamas	1	7
Brazil	6	1,620
Canada	52	11,397
Cayman Islands	3	883
Chile	2	485
Costa Rica	3	569
Curacao	1	247
Dominican Republic	3	574
Ecuador	1	257
Guatemala	1	385
Honduras	1	157
Jamaica	1	427
Mexico	13	3,247
Panama	2	416
Peru	1	300
Puerto Rico	4	1,322
Saint Kitts and Nevis	2	624
Trinidad and Tobago	1	119
United States	2,417	408,843
U.S. Virgin Islands	4	861
Venezuela	1	269
Total Americas	**2,525**	**434,975**
Middle East and Africa		
Armenia	1	225
Bahrain	1	264
Egypt	8	3,350
Israel	2	964
Jordan	3	609
Kuwait	2	601
Lebanon	1	174
Qatar	2	586
Saudi Arabia	3	735
Tunisia	1	221
Turkey	4	1,210
United Arab Emirates	6	1,150
Total Middle East and Africa	**34**	**10,089**
Asia		
China	33	12,435
Guam	1	357
India	6	1,534
Indonesia	5	1,511

continued

EXHIBIT 5 Marriott's Properties by Country—continued

Japan	8	2,662
Malaysia	7	2,977
Pakistan	2	509
Philippines	2	898
Singapore	2	1,002
South Korea	3	1,400
Thailand	8	2,013
Vietnam	2	874
Total Asia	**79**	**28,172**
Australia	**8**	**2,354**
Europe		
Austria	7	1,686
Belgium	4	721
Czech Republic	4	817
Denmark	1	395
France	10	2,512
Georgia	2	245
Germany	41	8,912
Greece	1	314
Hungary	2	470
Italy	8	1,706
Kazakhstan	2	322
Netherlands	3	921
Poland	2	744
Portugal	3	933
Romania	1	402
Russia	7	1,772
Spain	8	1,883
Switzerland	3	616
Total Europe	**109**	**25,371**
United Kingdom and Ireland		
Ireland	3	327
United Kingdom (England, Scotland, and Wales)	74	12,544
Total United Kingdom and Ireland	**77**	**12,871**
Total All Countries and Territories	**2,832**	**513,832**

[1] Includes timeshare resorts that are in active sales as well as those that are sold out. Products in active sales may not be ready for occupancy.

Source: www.marriott.com; SEC *Form 10K*, pp. 7–8.

incorporated in the state of Delaware as Hot Shoppes, Inc. With fast-paced growth, Hot Shoppes went public in 1953, and then in 1957, Marriott opened its first hotel, the Twin Bridges Marriott in Arlington, Virginia.

Marriott's first international expansion took place in 1966 when the company acquired an airline catering kitchen in Caracas, Venezuela. The next year, the company officially changed its name to Marriott Corporation. Marriott grew to a billion-dollar company through acquisitions—from cruise lines in 1971 to Farrell's ice cream parlors in 1972 and two theme parks near Chicago and San Francisco in 1976.

Marriott International was listed as a separate public company in March 1998 and began to focus on business and leisure lodging by selling off its senior living facilities in 2002. In 2005, Marriott divested its Ramada International Hotels and Resorts to Cendant Hotel Group and continues to diversify into the upscale lodging and management business through alliances and joint ventures. Key events in the history and development of Marriott are listed in Exhibit 6.

Leadership

Marriott's top management includes six senior executive officers and 36 corporate officers. Of these 36 corporate officers, six are ranked as executive officers per the Securities and

EXHIBIT 6 Timeline of Key Events in the History of Marriott International

1927: Newlyweds J. Willard Marriott and Alice S. Marriott open a 9-seat root beer stand in Washington, D.C. Named the Hot Shoppe, hot food such as tamales, chili, and tacos are added to attract customers during the winter months. Later they open the first drive-in Hot Shoppe restaurant in Washington, D.C.

1929: Marriott officially incorporates in the state of Delaware as Hot Shoppes, Inc.

1956: Marriott's son, J.W., is employed full-time in the family business.

1957, Jan. 19: The company enters the lodging business with the opening of its first hotel, the Twin Bridges Marriott in Arlington, Virginia.

1964: Marriott, Jr. is elected president of the company at the age of 32. The company's name changes to Marriott-Hot Shoppes, Inc. Adds ten hotels and expands in-flight services to Europe and South America.

1966: Marriott expands internationally by acquiring an airline catering kitchen in Caracas, Venezuela.

1972: J.W. Marriott, Jr. succeeds his father as CEO. Acquires Farrell's ice cream parlors.

1976: The company acquires two Great America theme parks near Chicago and San Francisco for $155 million.

1982: Acquires Host International and becomes the country's largest operator of airport terminal food, beverage, and merchandise facilities. Acquires Gino's fast-food restaurant chain, and plans to convert most units to Roy Rogers restaurants.

1983: After three years of market research, Courtyard by Marriott, a moderately priced hotel, opens near Atlanta, Georgia.

1984: Enters the vacation timesharing business with the acquisition of American Resorts Group. Sells or discontinues the Great America theme parks after they fail to make money.

1985: Acquires Gladieux Corp., a diversified food service company, and Service Systems, a contract food service company. J.W. Marriott dies at the age of 84. J.W. Marriott, Jr. is named chairman of the board. Acquires Howard Johnson Co., and sells the hotels to Prime Motor Inns, but keeps 350 restaurants and 68 turnpike units.

1986: Marriott stock splits 5 for 1. Acquires Saga Corp., a diversified food service management company, making Marriott the largest company in food service management in the United States.

1987: Enters the luxury all-suite hotel market with the first Marriott Suites hotel in Atlanta, and the economy lodging segment with the first Fairfield Inn in Atlanta. Completes expansion of its Worldwide Reservation Center in Omaha, Nebraska, making it the largest single-site reservations operation in U.S. hotel history. Acquires the Residence Inn Co., an all-suite hotel chain targeted toward extended-stay travelers.

1988: Acquires Basic American Retirement Communities of Indianapolis, Indiana, giving Marriott a major presence in the rental retirement market. Begins to test market a new restaurant called Allie's in San Diego, named after Alice Marriott. The 100th Courtyard opens.

1989: Forms a joint venture with Corporate Child Care, Inc. to provide on-site child care services for Marriott's food and services management clients. Acquires United Healthserv, Inc., a major provider of housekeeping, maintenance, and laundry services. Marriott's Senior Living Services Division opens its first "life-care" retirement community in Haverford, Pennsylvania. Completes the transfer of its airline catering division to Caterair International.

continued

EXHIBIT 6   Timeline of Key Events in the History of Marriott International—continued

1994: Opens two properties in Bangkok, the Royal Garden Riverside Hotel, and Bangkok Marriott. The Marriott Corporation is split into two entities: Host Marriott and Marriott International. Crystal Palace Resort is opened in Nassau in the Bahamas.

1995: The San Juan Marriott, a 525-room property, opens in Puerto Rico. Court rules for Marriott executives in suit brought by corporate bondholders. Buys several hotels in Mexico from Grupo Sitrer S.A. Opens a Marriott Resort and Casino on the island of Aruba. Expands its holdings in the United Kingdom. Buys New York's Vista Hotel. Marriott Corp. expanded to 1,000 properties in 1995.

1996: Beirut Marriott opens in Lebanon. Host Marriott introduces TownePlace Suites, a new line of hotels designed for long stays. Food management services and hotel restaurants account for half of Marriott's $11 billion annual revenues.

1997: Purchases Renaissance Hotel Group, based in Hong Kong. Divests 12 senior citizen units to PrimaCare One. Begins operating its Marriott Executive Residences.

1998: Acquires the share of Ritz-Carlton Hotel Co. it doesn't already own. Opens the first Marriott hotels in Israel and Armenia. Unveils SpringHill Suites, a new Marriott chain. Earnings per share rise 23 percent. Marriott adds a total of 176 properties, including 13 international hotels, and sells 17 hotels to Hospitality Prosperities Trust for $201.7 million.

1999: Acquires ExecuStay Corp., a corporate housing firm. The last remaining Hot Shoppes outlet is closed. TownePlace Suites by Marriott opens its 50th unit. Marriott announces an aggressive expansion plan to open 1,000 hotels worldwide by 2003.

2000: Alice Sheets Marriott, co-founder of Marriott Corp., dies of natural causes at the age of 92. The 500th Courtyard by Marriott is opened, in Hannover, Germany.

2005, Jan.: Marriott finalizes its sale of Ramada International Hotels & Resorts to Cendant Hotel Group.

2005, May: In a $1.45 billion deal, the company partners with Sunstone Hotel Investors and Walton Street Capital to acquire 32 hotel properties and joint-venture interests from CTF Holdings Ltd. for $1.452 billion.

2005, May: A 50-50 joint venture is formed with Whitbread PLC, the United Kingdom's largest hotel company, in which Whitbread will sell 46 upscale, franchised Marriott and Renaissance hotels and Marriott International will operate them on a long-term basis.

2005, Oct.: John W. Marriott III, executive vice president of lodging, leaves the company to become CEO of J.W.M. Family Enterprises L.P., an investment fund he founded in 1993. Marriott also accepts the position of vice chairman of the board at Marriott International.

Source: Adapted from Marriott International Inc., *Notable Corporate Chronologies,* http://galenet.galegroup.com.

Exchange Act of 1934, thus bringing the total count of executive officers at Marriott to 12. Exhibit 7 includes a list of executive and corporate officers.

Competition

With many global, national, regional, and local players, the lodging industry is fragmented. There are approximately 676 lodging management companies in the United States that compete with Marriott. Several of them operate more than 100 properties. Industry statistics show that Marriott has 8.8 percent of the domestic market share, but less than 1 percent of the market overseas based on number of rooms.

Closest competitors include Accor, a private French company, Hilton Hotels Corporation (HLT), and Intercontinental Hotels Group, Plc (IHG). Exhibit 8 contains summary competitor data and reveals that Marriott is the largest in market cap ($16.97 billion), revenues ($12.36 billion), and net income ($729 million), but Marriott lags its key competitors in quarterly revenue growth, gross margins, and expected long-term (5-year) growth. Note that Marriott's quarterly revenue growth in 2006 is 7.4 percent compared to Hilton's impressive 29.4 percent. Marriott's gross margins are 13.6 percent relative to Hilton's margins of 30 percent. IHG's gross margins at 54 percent are four times Marriott's margins!

EXHIBIT 7   Marriott's Officers

Senior Executive Officers

1. J.W. Marriott, Jr.
   Chairman of the Board and Chief Executive Officer

2. William J. Shaw
   President and Chief Operating Officer

3. Edward A. Ryan
   Executive Vice President and General Counsel

4. Arne M. Sorenson
   Executive Vice President, Chief Financial Officer and President—Continental European Lodging

5. James M. Sullivan
   Executive Vice President, Lodging Development

Corporate Officers

1. Simon F. Cooper
   President and Chief Operating Office, The Ritz-Carlton Hotel Company, L.L.C.

2. Victoria L. Dolan
   Executive Vice President—Finance and Chief Financial Officer—Marriott Vacation Club International

3. Joel M. Eisemann
   Executive Vice President, Owner and Franchise Services

4. James C. Fisher
   Senior Vice President, Owner and Franchise Services

5. Paul Foskey
   Executive Vice President, Lodging Development—Asia Pacific

6. Edwin D. Fuller
   President and Managing Director, Marriott Lodging—International

7. David J. Grissen
   Executive Vice President—Lodging Operations

8. Carolyn B. Handlon
   Executive Vice President—Finance and Global Treasurer

9. Norman K. Jenkins
   Senior Vice President, Lodging Development—North America

10. Stephen P. Joyce
    Executive Vice President Owner and Franchise Services and North American Full-Service Development

11. Kevin P. Kearney
    Executive Vice President, Lodging Development—Europe

12. Karl Kilburg
    Executive Vice President—International Operations

13. Kevin M. Kimball
    Executive Vice President—Finance

14. Thomas E. Ladd
    Senior Vice President—Government Affairs

15. Nancy C. Lee
    Senior Vice President and Deputy General Counsel

16. Kathleen Matthews
    Executive Vice President, Global Communications and Public Affairs

17. Robert J. McCarthy
    President, North American Lodging Operations and Global Brand Management

18. Amy C. McPherson
    Executive Vice President, Global Sales and Marketing

continued

EXHIBIT 7   Marriott's Officers—continued

Corporate Officers

19.	Scott E. Melby	
	Executive Vice President, Development Planning and Feasibility	
20	Robert A. Miller	
	President—Marriott Leisure	
21.	Pamela G. Murray	
	Executive Vice President, Enterprise Accounting Services	
22.	Daryl A. Nickel	
	Executive Vice President—Lodging Development, Select-Service, and Extended-Stay Brands	
23.	Laura E. Paugh	
	Senior Vice President—Investor Relations	
24.	M. Lester Pulse, Jr.	
	Executive Vice President—Taxes	
25.	David A. Rodriguez	
	Executive Vice President, Global Human Resources	
26.	Stephen P. Weisz†	
	President, Marriott Vacation Club International	
27.	Carl Wilson	
	Executive Vice President and Chief Information Officer	

Source: http://ir.shareholder.com/mar/bios.cfm

EXHIBIT 8   Summary Data for Key Competitors

	Marriott	Accor	Hilton	IHG	Industry
Market Cap	$ 16.97B	N/A	13.21B	9.08B	1.06B
Employees	150,600	168,623[1]	105,000	11,456	7.10K
Qtrly Rev Growth (yoy)	7.40%	N/A	29.40%	9.60%	7.00%
Revenue	12.36B	9.03B[1]	8.59B	1.64B	509.48M
Gross Margin	13.63%	N/A	30.04%	54.01%	38.80%
EBITDA	1.23B	N/A	1.74B	533.79M	79.24M
Oper Margin	8.17%	N/A	14.15%	24.70%	8.69%
Net Income	729.00M	394.40M[1]	552.00M	527.79M	46.24M
EPS	1.724	N/A	1.366	2.10	1.37
P/E	25.48	N/A	24.82	12.21	25.06
PEG (5 yr expected)	1.64	N/A	2.21	2.79	2.00
P/S	1.40	N/A	1.55	5.48	2.31

IHG = Intercontinental Hotels Group PLC
Industry = Lodging
[1] = As of 2005

Source: Adapted from http://finance.yahoo.com.

Accor

This French company is one of the largest employers in the lodging industry. As of 2005, it has over 168,600 employees working in 4,000 properties located in 90 countries. Accor ranks second with revenues of $9.03 billion in 2005. Accor is well known for its upscale brands, Len and Sofitel. Its mid-tier brands are Novotel, Mercure, and Suitehotel. Ibis and Formule 1 are its economy chains. In North America, Accor operates budget brands Motel 6 and Red

Roof Inns. In addition, it owns a 29 percent stake in resorts operator Club Mediterranean and 34 percent of casino hotel company Groupe Lucien Barrio. Accor also operates and/or owns stakes in several hospitality and food services. The company's Accor Services division provides outsourced benefits services to more than 340,000 corporate customers.

Hilton Hotels Corporation (HLT)

Founded in 1946 and headquartered in Beverly Hills, California, Hilton has 2,838 hotels worldwide under the brands Conrad, Doubletree, Embassy Suites, Hampton, Hilton, Hilton Garden Inn, Homewood Suites by Hilton, and Waldorf Astoria. HLT operates upscale full-service and limited service hotels in urban, airport, resort, and suburban locations. Its upscale, all-suite hotels include swimming pools, gift shops and retail facilities, meeting and banquet facilities, restaurants and lounges, room service, parking facilities, and other services. It also owns 50 percent of Windsor Casino Limited, which operates the 400-room Casino Windsor in Windsor, Canada. It ranks third in the number of employees (105,000) and revenues ($8.6 billion), but second in net income ($552 million).

Intercontinental Hotels Group PLC (IHG)

IHG, a British company, is the most profitable among the four industry leaders. Founded in 1967, it owns, manages, leases, and franchises approximately 3,741 hotels in approximately 100 countries as of 2006. It ranks number one in gross margins (54 percent), operating margins (24.7 percent), and earnings per share ($2.10) even though it is the smallest in the strategic group. As such, it appears to be a cost leader among the big four in the industry. IHG owns brand names, such as InterContinental, Crowne Plaza, Hotel Indigo, Holiday Inn, Holiday Inn Express, Staybridge Suites, and Candlewood Suites in Europe, the Middle East, Africa, the Americas, and Asia Pacific.

Finance

Marriott's revenues grow from $10.1 billion in 2004 to $12.16 billion in 2006, primarily fueled by a growth in demand for hotels worldwide. Owned and leased revenues increased dramatically from 2005 to 2006, primarily stemming from the purchase of 13 formerly managed properties from CTF Holdings Ltd., in 2005, of which 8 were sold in 2006. Operating income for 2006 includes a loss of $76 million for synthetic fuel operations, mainly caused by production suspensions in 2006 due to high oil prices. This is in addition to an operating loss of $144 million in 2005. General, administrative, and other expenses decreased by $76 million in 2006. Included in this expense category is a foreign exchange gain of $6 million in 2006, compared to $5 million foreign exchange losses in 2005.

Marriott's 20 percent growth in total revenues in 2004–2006 is accompanied by a paltry 2 percent growth in net income during this period. Note in Exhibit 9 that Marriott's net income actually declined 10 percent, from $669 million in 2005 to $608 million in 2006. This decline is partially due to a $109 million charge resulting from changes in accounting methods and principles.

Exhibit 10 includes the company's consolidated balance sheet. Marriott's current ratio decreased from approximately 1.6 in 2005 to 1.3 in 2006. Long-term debt increased by $137 million.

Marriott generates higher occupancies and revenue per available room ("RevPAR") than direct competitors in most market areas. Marriott has other things to its credit. It was the first company in the industry to serve food without any trans fat in its hotels in North America. As of September 2006, all Marriott's properties in North America are nonsmoking. The company continues to aggressively pursue growth. In 2006 alone, it added 13 managed properties with a total of 4,126 rooms and 77 franchised properties with 11,286 rooms to its worldwide system. In the same year, it opened 136 properties totaling 23,466 rooms. More than 28 percent of the new rooms were overseas, and a second Bulgari Hotels and Resorts brand property was inaugurated in Bali, Indonesia in September 2006. In 2007, approximately 100,000 rooms were under construction.

EXHIBIT 9   Consolidated Statement of Income of Marriott International, Inc.

(In $ Millions, except per share amounts)	2006	2005	2004
REVENUES			
Base management fees	$ 553	$ 497	$ 435
Franchise fees	390	329	296
Incentive management fees	281	201	142
Owned, leased, corporate housing and other revenue	1,119	944	730
Timeshare sales and services	1,577	1,487	1,247
Cost reimbursements	8,075	7,671	6,928
Synthetic fuel	165	421	321
	12,160	11,550	10,099
OPERATING COSTS AND EXPENSES			
Owned, leased and corporate housing-direct	936	778	629
Timeshare-direct	1,220	1,228	1,039
Reimbursed costs	8,075	7,671	6,928
General, administrative and other	677	753	607
Synthetic fuel	241	565	419
	11,149	10,995	9,622
OPERATING INCOME	1,011	555	477
Gains and other income	59	181	164
Interest expense	(124)	(106)	(99)
Interest income	45	79	146
Reversal of provision for (provision for) loan losses	3	(28)	8
Equity in (losses) earnings - Synthetic fuel	—	—	(28)
- Other	3	36	(14)
INCOME FROM CONTINUING OPERATIONS BEFORE INCOME TAXES AND MINORITY INTEREST	997	717	654
Provision for income taxes	(286)	(94)	(100)
Minority interest	6	45	40
INCOME FROM CONTINUING OPERATIONS	717	668	594
Cumulative effect of change in accounting principle, net of tax	(109)	—	—
Discontinued operations, net of tax	—	1	2
NET INCOME	$ 608	$ 669	$ 596
EARNINGS PER SHARE-BASIC			
Earnings from continuing operations	$ 1.77	$ 1.55	$ 1.31
Losses from cumulative effect of accounting change	(0.27)	—	—
Earnings from discontinued operations	—	—	—
Earnings per share	$ 1.50	$ 1.55	$ 1.31
EARNINGS PER SHARE-DILUTED			
Earnings from continuing operations	$ 1.66	$ 1.45	$ 1.24
Losses from cumulative effect of accounting change	(0.25)	—	—
Earnings from discontinued operations	—	—	—
Earnings per share	$ 1.41	$ 1.45	$ 1.24
DIVIDENDS DECLARED PER SHARE	$ 0.2400	$ 0.2000	$ 0.1650

Source: www.marriott.com; SEC *Form 10K,* p. 65.

EXHIBIT 10   Marriott International, Inc. Consolidated Balance Sheet (In $ Millions)

	2006	2005
ASSETS		
Current assets		
Cash and equivalents	$ 193	$ 203
Accounts and notes receivable	1,117	1,001
Inventory	1,208	1,164
Current deferred taxes, net	200	220
Assets held for sale	411	555
Other	185	247
	3,314	3,390
Property and equipment	1,238	1,134
Intangible assets		
Goodwill	921	924
Contract acquisition costs	575	466
	1,496	1,390
Cost method investments	70	233
Equity method investments	332	349
Notes receivable		
Loans to equity method investees	27	36
Loans to timeshare owners	316	311
Other notes receivable	217	282
	560	629
Other long-term receivables	178	175
Deferred taxes, net	665	545
Other	735	685
Total Assets	$ 8,588	$ 8,530
LIABILITIES AND SHAREHOLDERS' EQUITY		
Current liabilities		
Current portion of long-term debt	$ 15	$ 56
Accounts payable	658	520
Accrued payroll and benefits	615	559
Liability for guest loyalty program	384	317
Liabilities of assets held for sale	102	30
Timeshare segment deferred revenue	178	141
Other payables and accruals	570	510
	2,522	2,133
Long-term debt	1,818	1,681
Liability for guest loyalty program	847	768
Self-insurance reserves	184	180
Other long-term liabilities	599	516
Shareholders' equity		
Class A Common Stock	5	5
Additional paid-in-capital	3,617	3,562
Retained earnings	2,860	2,500
Treasury stock, at cost	(3,908)	(2,667)
Deferred compensation	—	(137)
Accumulated other comprehensive income (loss)	44	(11)
	2,618	3,252
Total Liabilities and SE	$ 8,588	$ 8,530

Source: www.marriott.com; SEC *Form 10K,* p. 66.

Conclusion

Do you feel that Marriott is continuing to rely to heavily upon the domestic market instead of the faster growing economies overseas for expansion? J.W. Marriott, Jr. has been the CEO of Marriott for the last 35 years. As noted in the Exhibit 6 timeline, for many years Mr. Marriott has used acquisition as a primary means to grow company revenues and profits. Note in Exhibit 6 that the company has entered a broad range of types of businesses from child care to cruise lines. CEO Marriott desires a strategic planning analysis for the coming three years. He wants you to include two recommended acquisition candidates in your analysis. He also wants to see a new recommended organizational chart for Marriott. Submit your strategic management analysis of Marriott International to your class for their consideration and critique.

References

http://en.wikipedia.org
www.fortune.com
www.finance.yahoo.com
www.galenet.galegroup.com
www.hilton.com
www.ihgplc.com
www.marriott.com
www.sec.gov

28 Starwood Hotels and Resorts Worldwide, Inc. — 2007

Anne M. Walsh
La Salle University

HOT

www.starwoodhotels.com

Based in White Plains, New York, Starwood Hotels and Resorts owns, manages, and franchises hotels. Starwood's portfolio includes luxury brands (St. Regis Hotel), moderately priced brands for business and leisure travel (Four Points), as well as the trendy (W Hotels) brand. Despite a recession in the travel industry and the depressed value of the dollar, Starwood has been able to expand their luxury brands in both domestic and international markets.

In 2007, Starwood had 37 properties included on the Gold List of *Conde Nast Travel* magazine. Starwood develops customer loyalty through their Starwood Preferred Guest frequent reward program. The program has no blackout dates and allows guests to redeem points for a free night or exchange points for a free airline ticket. Promoting events such as Christie's wine auction at their St. Regis hotels, or celebrity fashion shows with designer Cynthia Rowley at their W Hotels, allows Starwood to associate "upscale features" with their various hotel brands. Positioning products such as the White Tea product line as well as the Heavenly bath and bedding products in their Westin hotels also extends the company's luxury brand image.

Information on global revenues and assets of Starwood Hotels and Resorts is included in Exhibit 1. Note that revenues derived from both the United States and Italy decreased in 2006. Starwood's revenues and net income for the quarter ending June 30, 2007 were $3.0 billion and $267 million respectively. On November 8, 2007, Starwood increased its annual dividend by 7 percent.

Starwood Hotels

Starwood operations are grouped into two business segments: (1) hotels and (2) vacation ownership and residential operations. The hotel segment can further be divided into owned, managed, and franchised hotels. Revenue is derived primarily via hotel operations as well as fees earned from management contracts. Starwood recently announced plans to reduce their investment in owned real estate in order to focus on their management and franchise business. The company also plans to maximize earnings by acquiring and developing vacation ownership resorts and selling vacation ownership interests (VOIs), as well as selectively acquiring additional assets and disposing of non-core hotels.

EXHIBIT 1 **Starwood Hotels and Resorts by Geographic Region December 31, 2006**

	Revenues			Long-Lived Assets	
	2006	2005	2004	2006	2005
United States	$4,580	$4,656	$4,157	$2,765	$4,490
Italy	375	450	434	455	826
All other international	1,024	871	777	1,049	1,657
Total	$5,979	$5,977	$5,368	$4,269	$6,973

Source: Starwood *Form 10K*, 2006.

EXHIBIT 2   Starwood Hotels and Vacation Ownership Resorts

	Properties	Rooms
Managed & Unconsolidated Joint Venture Hotels	426	142,000
Franchised Hotels	360	95,800
Owned Hotels	85	27,800
Vacation Ownership Resorts & Residential	25	6,900
Total Properties by Type	**896**	**272,500**
North America	450	153,700
Europe, Africa, and Middle East	264	64,600
Asia-Pacific	124	41,800
Latin America	58	12,400
Total Properties by Region	**896**	**272,500**

Source: Starwood *Form 10K,* 2006.

Information on Starwood's hotels and the company's vacation ownership resorts is provided in Exhibit 2. At year-end 2006, Starwood owned, leased, or managed 896 properties with 272,500 rooms in more than 100 countries including Europe, Africa, and the Middle East. Plans for international expansion include the Westin Beijing in China, scheduled for completion in 2008, as well as agreements to develop three W hotels in Dubai and Doha in the Middle East.

Owned Hotels

Starwood owns 85 hotels and manages or franchises 786 other hotels. Most Starwood hotels and resorts are owned by external investment firms who have contracts with Starwood to manage their operations. Hotels owners typically pay a franchise fee for brand affiliation benefits, which can include marketing, centralized reservations, and management of the hotels.

Managed Hotels

In 2006, Starwood managed 426 hotels with 142,000 rooms worldwide. Starwood develops long-term contracts with hotel owners for the management of specific properties, and also generates additional fees through advertising and marketing of these properties. Starwood management fees are related to gross revenue generated by the property as well as incentive fees based on profits. If Starwood fails to meet performance criteria for a specific property, the contract may be terminated by the owners. Starwood assumes responsibility for routine maintenance and repair of buildings and furnishings, and may also provide equity or debt financing to owners for hotel renovations or conversion to a Starwood brand.

Management fees generated during 2006 include 43.7 percent from the United States, 17.9 percent from Europe, 15.7 percent from Asia-Pacific, 15.4 percent from the Middle East and Africa, and 7.3 percent from the Americas (Latin America and Canada).

Franchised Hotels

Sheraton, Westin, Four Points by Sheraton, Luxury Collection, Le Meridien, and Aloft are franchised brands, and include 360 properties with 96,000 rooms in 2006. Starwood receives licensing fees for these properties, and generates additional fees for associated services such as centralized reservations and marketing of these hotels. Starwood approves the location and design of all franchised properties. Franchisees may also purchase brand-specific products as well as supplies via approved vendors.

Franchise fees are based upon a fixed percentage of the franchised hotel's room revenue, as well as fees for related services such as marketing. Franchise fees generated during 2006 include 65.2 percent from the United States, 14.3 percent from Europe, 11.6 percent from the Americas, 8.0 percent from Asia-Pacific, and 0.09 percent from the Middle East and Africa.

Starwood Resorts

Starwood derives revenues from the development, ownership, and operation of vacation ownership resorts. Starwood sells VOIs (vacation ownership interests) for specific intervals in these resorts, which can be traded at other Starwood hotel properties or Starwood vacation resorts—commonly called time shares. Financing is available, in some cases, to customers who purchase ownership interests in these properties, which are marketed under the Starwood brand name. Starwood also earns revenue from the development and marketing of residential units in mixed-use hotel projects. At year-end 2006, there were 25 residential and vacation ownership resorts in the Starwood portfolio.

Starwood Brand Names

Starwood owns, franchises, or manages property through many brands including St. Regis, The Luxury Collection, Westin Hotels, Sheraton Hotels and Resorts, Four Points by Sheraton, Le Meridien, W Hotels, Aloft, and Element brands. A complete list of the Starwood brands is shown in Exhibit 3.

St. Regis Hotels & Resorts include luxury full-service hotels, resorts, and residences and are designed for high-end leisure and business travelers. St. Regis rooms are designed to capture the unique features of each location. Two distinctive properties include the St. Regis Hotel in San Francisco and The Phoenician in Scottsdale, Arizona. In late 2007, a St. Regis Hotel will open in Singapore, and additional hotels and resorts are scheduled to open in Asia-Pacific markets in the next five years.

The Luxury Collection is a group of luxury and full-service hotels and resorts offering exceptional service to elite customers. The brand is designed to preserve the brand name of the affiliate. Key international hotels include the Grand Hotel in Florence, Italy as well as the Park Tower in Buenos Aires, Argentina. These hotels feature "impeccable service, magnificent décor, and are designed to capture a sense of place as well as luxury."

Le Meridien comprises luxury and upscale full-service hotels and resorts. This is a "European brand with a French accent." In 2005, Starwood acquired 103 Le Meridien hotels, which are located in top travel destinations.

Westin Hotels and Resorts are luxury and full-service hotels and resorts acquired from the Aoki Corporation of Japan in 1994. The Westin now includes over 120 hotels in 24 countries. Westin was one of the first hotels to introduce voice mail and sells hotel products such as their White Tea fragrances and their Heavenly beds directly to consumers online at www.westinathome.com.

Westin North America includes West St. John Resort and Villas in the U.S. Virgin Islands and Westin Maui Resort in Hawaii. International resorts include the Westin Resort and Spa in Los Cabos, Mexico as well as the Westin Dublin Hotel in Ireland.

W Hotels are luxury, upscale full-service hotels, retreats, and residences. Launched in 2006 as extended-stay hotels, W Hotels are a brand extension of Westin Hotels and

EXHIBIT 3 **Starwood Hotel and Vacation Ownership Properties**

Systemwide	HOTELS		VACATION OWNERSHIP & RESIDENTIAL	
	Hotels	Rooms	Properties	Rooms
St. Regis & Luxury	60	9,500	3	100
W	21	6,000		
Westin	131	54,200	11	2,100
Le Meridien	123	32,800		
Sheraton	396	135,900	7	4,400
Four Points	126	21,900		
Independent/Other	14	5,300	4	300
Total Systemwide	**871**	**265,600**	**25**	**6900**

Source: Starwood *Form 10K*, 2006.

Resorts. The hotel features Whatever/Whenever, a signature 24-hour concierge service, designed to meet "whatever" guests desire (from a bed covered in rose petals to private jet service) "whenever" they want it. W Hotels are designed as the "hip" Starwood brand and feature a "Whappenings" home page that includes trendy events such as a New York City Junior Fashion show with designer Cynthia Rowley. In 2004, Starwood acquired Bliss Spa and launched Bliss Spas in all of their W hotels. W Hotels can be found in Times Square in New York, New Orleans, Los Angeles, and Chicago.

Sheraton Hotels and Resorts is the largest brand of the company, and was acquired along with sister brands Four Points by Sheraton, St. Regis, and The Luxury Collection by Starwood in 1998. Sheraton offers full-service hotels in major cities as well as resort locations around the world.

Four Points are moderately priced select-service hotels and are the midrange brand targeted toward business travelers and small conventions. Four Points hotels are located in diverse locations near airports as well as resort communities such as Hyannis, Massachusetts.

Aloft, moderately priced select-service hotels, was launched in 2005 and combines both brand features of W Hotels with the value of Four Points by Sheraton. The first hotel, expected to open in 2007, and was designed to offer an "effortless alternative for both business and leisure travelers." Starwood plans to open Aloft hotels in Massachusetts and Arizona as well as at the San Francisco and Philadelphia international airports. International properties will also be launched in Montreal and Toronto in Canada.

Element, an extended-stay hotel, is expected to open in 2008. The upscale hotel designed with an emphasis on nature, will be developed as an extended-stay accommodation.

Mission and Values

Starwood's mission statement reads as follows:

"A Global Branded Life Style Hospitality company that delivers branded consumer products and services in ways that are different, better and special."

> Starwood's statement of company values reads: "We succeed only when we meet and exceed the expectations of our customers, owners, and shareholders. We have a passion for excellence and will deliver the highest standards of integrity and fairness. We celebrate the diversity of people, ideas and cultures. We honor the dignity and value of individuals working as a team. We improve the communities in which we work. We encourage innovation, accept accountability, and embrace change. We seek knowledge and growth through learning. We share a sense of urgency, nimbleness, and endeavor to have fun too."

Corporate Governance

Starwood Hotels has adopted corporate governance guidelines to address issues related to board and committee composition, director share ownership, and board evaluations as well as other governance topics. The company also has a code of conduct for all employees to address legal and ethical issues confronting employees in execution of their responsibilities (www.starwoodhotels.com/corporate/investor_relations.html). There is also a Disclosure Committee, which designs and maintains policies related to preparation of periodic reports filed with the SEC.

Directors selected for the board must have no material relationships with the company either as an officer, stockholder, or partner of an organization that has a relationship with the board, and the board makes an annual determination of the independence of all nominees and board members. Starwood indemnifies "all Directors to fullest extent possible by law so they will be free from undue concern about personal liability in connection with their service to the board." Directors who are not employees of the company or subsidiaries are not considered for reelection after age 72, and directors who are employees of the company must also retire from the board upon retirement from the company.

In 2005, Starwood held 23 meetings, and each director attended at least 75 percent of the full board and committee member meetings. Starwood currently has an Audit Committee, responsible for the accounting and financial management practices of the board as well as a separate Compensation and Options Committee, which makes recommendations on executive and senior management compensation. A Capital Committee is responsible for capital plans as well as corporate acquisitions and divestitures. The Governance and Nominating Committee makes recommendations for new board members and monitors the governance policies of the company. A profile of the current members of the board of directors is available at www.starwood.com.

Top Management

In April of 2007, Steven Heyer resigned as the CEO of Starwood Hotels and Resorts Worldwide. Mr. Heyer left his position without the $35 million severance package that was part of his employment agreement. Performance was not cited as a reason for Mr. Heyer's departure, but company officials indicated that Mr. Heyer's management style often clashed with the company, and that "his style made some employees uncomfortable" (Sanders and Lubin, 2007). During Mr. Heyer's tenure, earnings increased from $440 million to more than $1 billion on sales around $6 billion. (Thomaselli, 2007).

Allegations as well as an anonymous letter to the board fueled speculation about an inappropriate relationship between Mr. Heyer and a young female employee. Mr. Heyer denied these allegations and insisted that this letter was simply a response to "structural and strategic changes" within the company. A board investigation conducted by an external law firm, however, did uncover e-mails and text messages to the employee of a suggestive nature. Complaints about favoritism in promotions of other employees were also part of the anonymous letter to the board (Sanders and Lublin, 2007).

While board members were aware of Mr. Heyer's management style prior to hiring him for the CEO position at Starwood Hotels, they also expressed concern about his absence in the company headquarters in White Plains, New York. Mr. Heyer commuted from his home in Atlanta to New York, although his contract required that the majority of his time be spent in the White Plains headquarters (Sanders and Lublin, 2007).

Steven Heyer was recruited by Barry Sternlicht, Starwood's founder, and assumed the CEO position at Starwood in October of 2004. Due to frequent clashes with Mr. Heyer, Mr. Sternlicht ultimately left his board position in 2005. Mr. Heyer's departure caused speculation of a possible sale with Barry Sternlicht and Starwood Capital identified as a possible bidder for the company (Thomaselli, 2007).

Other key company executives of Starwood are listed in Exhibit 4 and are available at www.starwood.com An organizational chart for Starwood also is provided in Exhibit 4. Note that the chart basically is divisional by geographic area.

Finance

Starwood posted revenues of $5,979 in 2006, virtually no change from 2005. Due to the seasonal nature of the industry, hotel revenues and operating income tend to be lower in the first and second quarters of the year. Starwood's 2006 net profit margin of 17.4 percent increased from the 7.1 percent net profit margin in 2005, and EPS grew from $1.88 to

EXHIBIT 4   Starwood's Top Executives and Organizational Structure

1. Bruce W. Duncan, Interim CEO and Chairman, Starwood Hotels and Resorts Worldwide
2. Raymond L. "Rip" Gellein, Jr., President, Global Development Group
3. Matt Quimet, President, Hotel Group
4. Vasant M. Prabhu, Executive Vice President and Chief Financial Officer
5. Kenneth S. Siegel, Chief Administrative Officer and General Counsel
6. Todd Thompson, Chief Information Officer
7. Geoffrey A. Ballotti, President, North American Division
8. Sue A. Brush, Senior Vice President, Westin Hotels and Resorts
9. Hoyt H. Harper, Senior Vice President, Sheraton Hotels and Resorts
10. Ross A. Klein, President, Starwood Luxury Brands Group and Aloft Hotels
11. Miquel Ko, President, Asia-Pacific
12. Osvaldo V. Libbrizzi, President, Latin America
13. Roeland Vos, President, Europe, Africa, and Middle East
14. Eva Ziegler, Senior Vice President, Le Meriden Hotels and Resorts

continued

EXHIBIT 4 **Starwood's Top Executives and Organizational Structure—continued**

Organizational Chart

$4.69. In comparison to the industry, Starwood's net profit margin of 17.4 percent exceeded the industry median of 5 percent while their debt/equity ratio was slightly above the industry median of 0.82. The stock price of the company reached a high of $68.67 in December 2006, up slightly from $65.22 in 2005.

In the third quarter of 2006, Starwood sold two hotels for approximately $84 million in cash, and recorded a loss of $36 million associated with these sales. The company also sold its 23 percent interest in a joint venture that owned the Westin La Cantera Hotel for a gain of approximately $13 million. In the first quarter of 2006, the company sold five hotels for approximately $268 million in cash and a net gain of $30 million associated with the sales. Starwood's recent income statements and balance sheets are provided in Exhibits 5 and 6 respectively.

Hotel Industry

Hotel industry profits were estimated at $25.2 billion in 2006 and were projected to increase to $29.7 billion in 2007 (Jana, 2007). Revenue gains have been attributed, in part, to an increase in national room rates from $90.95 in 2005 to $97.35 in 2006. The demand for hotels is expected to grow during 2007 due a weak dollar, which is catching the attention of foreign travelers, as well as resumption in corporate travel after September 11(newyorktimes.com, 2007). Overall, the global hotel and motel industry grew by 4.9 percent between 2002–2006, resulting in revenues of $488.6 billion in 2006 with the domestic consumer segment generating 65.8 percent of industry revenues.

New hotel construction in key global markets such as China and India is also fueling the growth of hotel rooms with 127,708 new room starts added to the existing inventory of rooms. (business weekonline.com). By 2006, the Asia-Pacific market had grown by 4.8 percent, accounting for $96 billion in the industry, while the European segment continues to play a dominant role in the industry (www.marketline.com).

Private-equity firm takeovers as well as increased demand in the industry has compelled hotel companies to focus on amenities such as docking stations for MP3 music players and high-definition televisions. Many firms such as Marriott are adding new bedding to all of their hotels to compete with Westin's Heavenly Beds and Spa products. Many existing hotels are in the process of renovations, with Hilton slated for $900 million of renovation and midrange hotels such as Hilton Garden Inn including standard 26-inch flat-screen television in their hotel rooms. Inclusion of these amenities is critical. Smith Travel Research reports that 76 percent of industry revenues are based on room sales with another 18 percent derived from food and beverage sales. As of 2006, occupancy rates in U.S hotels hovered at 71.2 percent, which reveals that most hotels were not operating at full capacity.

Condo hotels are also shaping the industry with many established companies now offering units for sale as condominiums. Many of the condo projects are new projects and account for 75 percent of industry sales, while the remaining projects are conversions,

EXHIBIT 5   Starwood's Income Statements

| | All numbers in thousands | | |
Period Ending	Dec. 31, 2006	Dec. 31, 2005	Dec. 31, 2004
Total Revenue	$5,979,000	5,977,000	5,368,000
Cost of Revenue	4,344,000	3,295,000	3,007,000
Gross Profit	1,635,000	2,682,000	2,361,000
Operating Expenses			
Research Development	–	–	–
Selling General and Administrative	470,000	1,440,000	1,314,000
Non-Recurring	20,000	13,000	(37,000)
Others	306,000	407,000	431,000
Total Operating Expenses	–	–	–
Operating Income or Loss	839,000	822,000	653,000
Income from Continuing Operations			
Total Other Income/Expenses Net	26,000	14,000	(19,000)
Earnings Before Interest and Taxes	926,000	900,000	666,000
Interest Expense	244,000	258,000	254,000
Income Before Tax	682,000	642,000	412,000
Income Tax Expense	(434,000)	219,000	43,000
Minority Interest	(1,000)	–	–
Net Income From Continuing Ops	1,115,000	423,000	369,000
Non-Recurring Events			
Discontinued Operations	(2,000)	(1,000)	26,000
Extraordinary items	–	–	–
Effect of Accounting Changes	(70,000)	–	–
Other items	–	–	–
Net Income	1,043,000	422,000	395,000
Preferred Stock and Other Adjustments	–	–	–
Net Income Applicable to Common Shares	$1,043,000	$422,000	$395,000

Source: http://finance.yahoo.com/q/is?s=HOT&annual

which account for 25 percent of sales. Owners of these hotels typically obtain higher payback from the sale of condominiums, which generate immediate sales dollars at the time of occupancy in contrast to standard nightly rates. Many firms are also divesting many of their owned properties and focusing on franchise and management fees, which provide a constant source of revenue for hotel companies

Other factors that influence success in the hotel industry include property location, geographic dispersion of firm properties, brand name recognition, management expertise, access to capital, and size. Large firms in the industry typically have scale economies that can potentially lower their costs, and their asset base as well as their brand name provides access to capital at competitive interest rates. Room prices continue to play a key role in the purchase decision for most leisure travelers with price considerations related to discretionary income and economic trends (Standard and Poor Industry Survey, 2006).

Competitors

Hilton Hotels Corporation
Founded in 1946 with corporate headquarters in Beverly Hills, California, Hilton Hotels has over 2,900 resorts in more than 80 countries with key brands including the Hilton, Hampton Inn, Doubletree, Homewood Suites by Hilton, and Embassy Suites. Most of the

EXHIBIT 6   Starwood's Balance Sheet

	All numbers in thousands		
Period Ending	31-Dec-06	31-Dec-05	31-Dec-04
Assets			
Current Assets			
Cash and Cash Equivalents	$ 512,000	1,192,000	673,000
Short-Term Investments	–	–	–
Net Receivables	593,000	642,000	482,000
Inventory	566,000	280,000	371,000
Other Current Assets	139,000	169,000	157,000
Total Current Assets	**1,810,000**	**2,283,000**	**1,683,000**
Long-Term Investments	729,000	403,000	453,000
Property, Plant and Equipment	3,833,000	7,103,000	6,997,000
Goodwill	1,711,000	1,737,000	2,157,000
Intangible Assets	591,000	526,000	387,000
Accumulated Amortization	–	–	–
Other Assets	88,000	402,000	621,000
Deferred Long-Term Asset Charges	518,000	–	–
Total Assets	**9,280,000**	**12,454,000**	**12,298,000**
Liabilities			
Current Liabilities			
Accounts Payable	1,656,000	1,660,000	1,509,000
Short/Current Long-Term Debt	805,000	1,219,000	619,000
Other Current Liabilities	-	-	-
Total Current Liabilities	**2,461,000**	**2,879,000**	**2,128,000**
Long-Term Debt	1,827,000	2,926,000	3,823,000
Other Liabilities	589,000	851,000	652,000
Deferred Long-Term Liability Charges	1,370,000	562,000	880,000
Minority Interest	25,000	25,000	27,000
Negative Goodwill	–	–	–
Total Liabilities	**6,272,000**	**7,243,000**	**7,510,000**
Stockholders' Equity			
Misc Stocks, Options, Warrants	–	–	–
Redeemable Preferred Stock	–	–	–
Preferred Stock	–	–	–
Common Stock	2,000	4,000	4,000
Retained Earnings	948,000	170,000	(68,000)
Treasury Stock	√√–	–	–
Capital Surplus	2,286,000	5,412,000	5,121,000
Other Stockholder Equity	(228,000)	(375,000)	(269,000)
Total Stockholders Equity	**3,008,000**	**5,211,000**	**4,788,000**
Net Tangible Assets	**$706,000**	**$2,948,000**	**$2,244,000**
Total Liabilities and SE	**$9,280,000**	**12,454,000**	**12,298,000**

Source: http://finance.yahoo.com/q/bs?s=HOT&annual

hotels are designed for the midrange segment of the industry with the exception of the Hilton and Conrad hotels, which are targeted toward upscale customers and designed as full-service hotels. The Homewood Suite Chain offers extended-stay services.

Over 81 percent of Hilton Hotel's 475,000 rooms are located in the Americas with sales of $8,162 million in 2006, up dramatically (84 percent) from $4,437 million in 2005. Net income for 2006 was $572 million, an increase of 24.3 percent from 2005. Hilton recently developed a joint venture with Delhi-based DLF Limited to build and own up to 75 hotels in the next seven years in India. Hilton will be primarily responsible for the management of these hotels, which will be a combination of Hilton Hotels and the Hilton Garden Inn brand, which is targeted toward the business traveler. Many hotels in India do not have restaurants; the Hilton Garden will include both Western restaurants and restaurants that serve traditional foods.

Hyatt Corporation

Founded in 1982 with corporate headquarters in Chicago, Illinois, the Hyatt Corporation is owned and operated by the Pritzker family. Since the death of Jay Pritzker in 1999, the family has considered breaking up the $20 million H Group Holding Company and taking the Hyatt public. The Pritzker portfolio also includes manufacturing conglomerate Marmon Group (Trans Union Credit Bureau), Pritzker Realty, and a stake in the Royal Caribbean cruise line.

Key Hyatt brands include Grand Hyatt and Park Hyatt, with resort destinations that include golfing and spas in over 40 countries. H Group Holdings also includes Hyatt Hotels Corporation (domestic hotels), Hyatt International and Hyatt Equities (hotel ownership), and Hyatt Vacation Ownership (timeshares). Hyatt recently acquired the Summerfield Suites chain from the Blackstone group. Hyatt reported $6.438 million in revenues in 2005, but now it is a privately held company.

Marriott International

Founded in 1971 with corporate headquarters in Washington, D.C., Marriott has more than 2,700 properties in over 65 countries. Key brands include Marriott Hotels and Resorts, Renaissance Hotels, as well as the luxury Ritz Carlton hotel chain. Extended-stay brands include the Courtyard, Residence Inn, and Fairfield Inn.

Company brands also include the Marriott Vacation Club, The Ritz-Carlton Club, Grand Residences by Marriott, and Horizons by Marriott. The Marriott Vacation Club has full-service villas and operates in 45 locations with international resorts in Aruba, France, Spain, St. Thomas, United States Virgin Islands, the West Indies, and Thailand. The Ritz-Carlton Club is a luxury-tier real estate fractional ownership and personal residence ownership, designed as a private club that gives members access to all Ritz-Carlton clubs. Marriott's 2006 revenues were $12,160 million and represented a 5.3 percent increase from 2005.

Wyndham Worldwide Corporation

Located in Parsippany, New Jersey, Wyndham has over 6,500 franchised hotels and more than 525,000 rooms. Key brands include Wyndham Hotels and Resorts, Ramada, Wingate Inns, Baymont, Days Inn, Super 8, Howard Johnson, AmeriHost Inn, Travelodge, and Knights Inn. The Wyndham also owns RCI, Global Vacation Network, which offers vacation exchange products and services to owners, and markets vacation rental properties on behalf of independent owners.

About 89 percent of Wyndham hotel rooms are located in North America with another 58,000 rooms, or 11 percent of the hotel rooms, located outside of North America. The company also provides management services to 32 hotels associated with Wyndham Hotels and Resorts. The lodging business represents 17 percent of total company net revenues with annual sales of $3,842 million for the 2006 fiscal year.

The Future

Starwood recently signed agreements to build nearly 20 large hotels in Asia, which would bring their total to over 100 hotels on that continent. The Westin Beijing will open in June 2008 in an area commonly known as the Wall Street of China. As of 2007, Starwood operated 31 hotels in China with 34 new hotels projected before the end of the decade.

In 2007, Starwood entered into a joint venture with Morgan Stanley to acquire the Sheraton Grande Tokyo Bay Hotel from the Taisei Group with Starwood owning 25.1 percent of the venture. India represents another high-growth market for the company, with a middle class of almost 300 million people. The Westin New Delhi is scheduled to open in 2008 along with a Sheraton Bangalore in 2009.

Starwood Hotels has expansion plans for the Middle East and has signed agreements for three W hotels in Dubai and Doha, as well as a Westin and Luxury Collection property in Agaba, Jordan. Should Starwood use their existing brands to expand even further into these markets, or should Starwood acquire global brands that fit with their existing portfolio of brands? Do you think a local partner should be used to expand global operations? What type of risks are typically associated with partnerships or joint ventures in both domestic and global markets?

Starwood has also developed a unique group of products and services including Bliss Spas, White Tea products, and the Heavenly Bed and Bath products. Should Starwood expand the distribution of these products and services? If yes, what type of distribution channels or additional company brands should the company consider?

The use of intermediaries such as Travelocity and Orbitz is shaping the image of many brands in the hotel industry. How can Starwood differentiate their products from competitors' products? Should they expand their Starwood Preferred Guest Program or consider other incentives to attract new customers and enter new markets?

Prepare a three-year detailed strategic plan for Mr. Bruce Duncan, the new CEO of Starwood.

References

Eistein, Aaron. "Starwood's Upside at Maximum Capacity." *Crain's New York Business,* Vol. 23(7), February 12, 2007.

Gregor, Alison. "How Long Can the Hotel Industry Stay in High Gear?" *New York Times,* January 21, 2007.

Jana, Reena. "Am I in Heaven, or Am I in My Hotel?" *Businessweekonline,* December 4, 2006.

Sanders, Peter and Lublin, Joann. "Starwood CEO's Ouster Followed Battle with Board over His Conduct." *Wall Street Journal*, April 7, 2007.

Standard and Poor's Industry Surveys, Lodging and Gaming Industry, 2006.

Thomaselli, Rich. "Why Starwood Hotels Visionary CEO Had to Go." *Advertising Age,* April 9, 2007.

Valley, Matt. "Hotel Growth Spurt Coming to India." *National Real Estate Investor*, Vol. 49(2). February, 2007.

Competitive Analysis:
   www.hoovers.com
   www.reuters.com

Industry Analysis: Global Hotels and Motels: Industry Profile (December 2006), Datamonitor: usinfo@datamonitor.com
   www.datamonitor.com

Internal Analysis: Starwood Hotels and Resorts Worldwide
   www.starwood.com

Internal Analysis: Starwood Hotels and Resorts Worldwide
   www.Marketlineinfo.com

## 29

Miami University — 2007

Joseph W. Leonard
Miami University

www.miami.muohio.edu

With new president David C. Hodge presiding over the commencement on May 5, 2007, Miami University awarded 3,291 degrees (2,921 bachelor's, 203 associate's, 157 master's, and 12 doctor of philosophy) at graduation ceremonies at the football stadium. Publications describe Miami University in a variety of ways: "a top-notch liberal education university," "J-Crew U," "21st among the top public universities in the nation," "a public Ivy League school," "a lack of diversity school," a university with "one of the most beautiful campuses," and "a school for wealthy white kids." Miami University is well known in the region and increasingly becoming better known nationwide.

Along with the main campus (14,385 undergraduates and 1,341 graduate) in Oxford, Ohio, a town with about 8,000 nonstudent residents, Miami University operates three branch campuses (two nearby in Hamilton with 2,491 students and Middletown with 1,909 students) that primarily offer two-year associate degree programs. The European campus in Luxembourg serves about 125–130 Oxford-campus students each semester. All three of the branch campuses were opened in the late 1960s. Oxford students may take courses in Luxembourg for either an academic year, one semester, or a shorter summer session. Additionally, there are a very limited number of courses offered in other regional locations in southwestern Ohio.

For the most part, this case is based primarily on the academic thrust of the main Oxford campus. Only limited information is presented about the branch campuses and the nonacademic side of the university. The Oxford campus is in southwestern Ohio, only 5 miles from the Indiana border, 30 minutes from the malls of northern Cincinnati, 45 minutes from downtown Cincinnati, 55 minutes from downtown Dayton, and one hour away from two major airports (Cincinnati and Dayton).

Main campus (Oxford) enrollment is heavily regulated by the state. If enrollment exceeds 16,000 undergraduate students, the state of Ohio penalizes the university by reducing the state subsidy.

There has always been some confusion between Miami University and the University of Miami. Around campus you will occasionally see a T-shirt or a bumper sticker that says, "Miami was a university when Florida still belonged to Spain." And most of Miami's 155,000 alumni don't like the way Miami is often referred to as "Miami of Ohio" or "Miami of Ohio University" or "Miami (Ohio) University." But during nearly all college football seasons, the University of Miami located in Coral Gables, Florida, gets much more attention on ESPN and the nation's newspaper sports pages.

History

Miami University was officially established in 1809 after a series of governmental actions beginning with the U.S. Congress in 1792. President George Washington signed legislation creating and naming the university and setting aside about 36 square miles of land in the old Northwest Territory. Named after an Indian tribe, Miami University maintains close relations and exchanges with the Miami Nation of Oklahoma. Many faculty/staff and students visit the tribe's headquarters, and many tribal leaders visit the Oxford campus. Over the past few years, student projects have included environmental science, education, language and culture, architecture, business, and anthropology. In the fall of 2007, about 20 tribal members attended the Oxford campus as full-time students.

In the beginning, the course of study at Miami University was strictly classical. Over the years, new academic divisions were added to meet the changing needs of students and society: education in 1902, business in 1927, fine arts in 1929, graduate programs in 1947, applied science (which became engineering) in 1959, and interdisciplinary studies in 1974.

Miami University is recognized as the "Cradle of Coaches," with several former players and coaches now within professional and NCAA Division I ranks. More recently, the university is beginning to be recognized for its many successful entrepreneurs.

Noted alumni include one U.S. president (Benjamin Harrison) and three professional athletes: Ron Harper, 1987, who has five NBA championship rings; Wally Szczerbiak, 1999, former NBA all-star now playing for the Boston Celtics; and Ben Roethlisberger, 2004, youngest winning quarterback in Super Bowl history with the Pittsburgh Steelers.

Physical Facilities—Buildings and Grounds

The campus is known for its red bricks and Georgian architecture. Nearly all buildings look alike, except for the Art Museum and a few others. The campus has been described as peaceful and supportive of learning. There are many trees on campus and wooded areas nearby. After years of debate, the first parking garage opened in 2007. Campuswide wireless Internet access is available on the Oxford campus. Off-campus housing exists within the city limits of the town. Most students live within a mile from campus, and a university bus system has been in place for nearly 20 years. The Hamilton and Middletown campuses are nonresidential and primarily target local/regional commuter first- and second-year students.

The Oxford campus (about 2,000 acres) has residence and dining halls, health services, libraries, museums, public safety, athletic facilities and recreation center, student center and student services, fine arts performance halls, administrative and maintenance buildings.

From the mid-1980s until a couple of years ago, several buildings were renovated, but there was not much new building construction on campus. However, over the last two years, Miami has been in a rapid capital ($309 million) construction period with a new psychology building, new student apartments, the Goggin Ice Center, Miami's first parking garage, a new engineering building, and a new Farmer Business School under construction, and plans for a new performing arts center.

It is generally thought that Miami University does a very good job of maintaining the buildings and grounds. Some within the university community have said that the university spends too much on maintenance and related functions.

Organization Structure, Control, and Governance

Miami University is organized into seven academic divisions (rank ordered by number of students from largest to smallest): arts and science, business, education, engineering, fine arts, graduate school, and interdisciplinary, (which will become downgraded to a program within arts and science beginning in 2008). The Farmer School of Business (named for Richard T. Farmer, '56 alumnus and chairman of the board of Cintas Corporation) has the stated objective of preparing young men and women of character and intellectual ability for positions in business, government, and other complex organizations. Bachelor's degree majors are offered in nine areas: accountancy, business, economics, decision sciences, finance, interdisciplinary business management, management information systems, marketing, and supply chain and operations management. Additionally, minors are available in arts management, business legal studies, decisions sciences, economics, entrepreneurship, finance, international business, management, management information systems, management of information technologies, marketing, risk management and insurance, and supply chain management. The Farmer School of Business (FSB) has been accredited by the Association to Advance Collegiate Schools of Business at the undergraduate level since 1932 and at the graduate level since 1961. The FSB is organized into six departments and has more than 125 full-time faculty. Information about the other divisions of Miami University is readily available at the university's Web site.

Over the past decade, Miami University has been moving toward a more decentralized structure and decision-making style, with each of the academic divisions more directly participating in their own fund-raising, dealing with alumni, and operational and strategic decision making.

On the academic side, the university is administered by department chairs and program directors, deans (with associate and assistant deans), the provost (with associate and assistant provost, and the division of admission), and the president (with a staff). Additionally, there are several nonacademic divisions including finance and business affairs, student affairs, and intercollegiate athletics. There are a number of other support functions.

In addition to the administration, the university has an 11-member board of trustees appointed by the governor, and including two students. Over the past several years, many have said that the board has participated more in the strategic management of the university. For the most part, the public universities (and colleges) within Ohio operate fairly autonomously of each other. In recent years however, there has been increasing discussion about a state-controlled system that would create more coordination and cooperation among the universities.

The university mission statement is long and is available online. The three-paragraph mission statement and also the "Statement Asserting Respect for Human Diversity" are at www.miami.muohio.edu/edu/about_miami/mission. The university is reviewing the mission statement and probably will come out with a revised statement in 2008. Additionally, most of the academic divisions and individual departments and other aspects of the university have their own mission and/or vision statements.

Miami University's value statement as approved by the board of trustees in February 2002 is as follows:

> Miami University is a scholarly community whose members believe that a liberal education is grounded in qualities of character as well as of intellect. We respect the dignity of other persons, the rights and property of others, and the right of others to hold and express disparate beliefs. We believe in honesty, integrity, and the importance of moral conduct. We defend the freedom in inquiry that is the heart of learning and combine that freedom with the exercise of judgment and the acceptance of personal responsibility.

Academic Affairs

Miami University has a typical academic structure and system of achieving the university's mission and strategy. Miami follows a traditional approach to course and classroom instruction and offers online courses. There are more than 840 full-time faculty. According to princetonreview.com, 75 percent of full-time and part-time faculty have PhDs; the student/faculty ratio is 16:1; in the sciences the most frequent class size is 20–29 and lab and subsection size is 10–19; and universitywide 10 percent of classes are taught by teaching assistants. Miami offers more than 120 undergraduate major degree programs and more than 80 undergraduate minors, and offers 11 doctoral programs and more than 50 master's programs (including MBA, master's of accountancy, and master of arts in economics degrees).

Called the Miami Plan, university requirements to fulfill a bachelor's degree are based on four basic goals: thinking critically, understanding contexts, engaging with other learners, and reflecting and acting. These requirements require a minimum of 36 semester credit hours of foundations courses, 9 hours of a thematic sequence (sometimes called a mini-minor), and 3 hours of a senior capstone course. Business majors are required to complete the thematic sequence from a field of study outside of business. The minimum requirement for graduation from Miami's main campus is 128 hours.

Miami University consistently ranks among the top U.S. universities for the number of students studying abroad; about 1,000 students each year earn academic credit abroad. Nearly 30 percent of Miami students study abroad before they graduate. In the summer of 2007, the Farmer Business School offered seven overseas programs in Asia (2), Europe (4), and Latin America (1). Five of these programs are six weeks long and require 8 semester credit hours; Costa Rica is four weeks long and requires 6 credit hours; and Russia is three weeks long and 5 credit hours. All of the summer programs require orientation and regular classes during the spring semester before students go overseas. The programs are taught by full-time tenured Miami University business school faculty. Additionally there are many overseas summer programs from the divisions of arts and science and education, and a few from fine arts and engineering. The Luxembourg campus offers spring/fall/summer courses. Miami University has exchange agreements in five countries and has access to more than 130 universities worldwide through the International Student Exchange Program.

The Miami University Libraries contain an extensive collection of information including 2.8 million books and 20,000 journals/magazines/newspapers, and provides access to over 40 million library items from the state network (OhioLINK) library consortium. The main library is open 24 hours, five days per week and has 24/7 Internet research availability, electronic reserves, and many online databases available, which business students can use to find financial information and SWOT analysis for their business courses. The main library has been recently updated and now has a coffee shop.

The university offers academically superior students unique and challenging opportunities. Miami has three honors and scholars programs that accept a select number of students with records of outstanding achievement: Harrison Scholars, University Honors, and University Scholars. Also, departmental and divisional honors programs are available in many departments or divisions on the Oxford campus. For example, the Farmer School of Business has a special Business Honors Program for its students. This program admits about 40 students per year and offers an opportunity for intensive work under the guidance of a faculty mentor(s).

Finance Issues

All of the university's financial statements and data can be found at www.miami.muohio.edu.

Universities have high scholarship and personnel costs including salaries and wages with benefits that consume the vast majority of operating expenses. As a non-profit organization, Miami's financial statements and information are somewhat different from those of a profit-oriented company. Miami tries to operate a financially smooth and efficient organization, holding back some funds for emergencies and unforeseen expenses as surpluses.

As seen in the exhibits, the 2006–07 Miami University budget shows total revenues of $626.6 million, an increase of 6.0 percent over the prior year: 83.7 percent ($524.5 million) is from E&G (educational and general) and 16.3 percent from auxiliary enterprises. Of the E&G revenues, 75.8 percent comes from students (tuition, fees, and other student charges), 14.3 percent comes directly from state of Ohio appropriations, and the remaining 9.9 percent comes from grants, contracts, gifts, and other sources. For the "auxiliary enterprises" ($102.1 million) revenues, 60.1 percent comes from residence and dining halls, 18.0 percent from the student center operations, 5.1 percent from intercollegiate athletics, and the remaining 16.7 percent from other support sources. On the expenditures side of E&G, the budget calls for 33.8 percent to scholarships and fellowships, 29.7 percent for instruction and departmental research, 10.4 percent for academic support, 8.4 percent for institutional support, 6.5 percent for plant operations and maintenance, and 11.1 percent for other expenditures. For the auxiliary enterprises ($107.1 million), the budget calls for 50.8 percent for residence and dining halls, 17.9 percent for the student center, and 16.1 percent for intercollegiate athletics.

Many students wonder where their general fee money goes. At Miami University's main campus, students paid about $1,629 for the 2006–07 year. Of this $1,629 per student, the budget called for 46.4 percent to go to intercollegiate athletics, 19.3 percent for the Recreational Sports Center, 9.0 percent for Goggin Ice Arena, 5.2 percent for the student health service, 3.5 percent for the student center, 3.4 percent for student organizations, 1.5 percent for Millett Assembly Hall (used for basketball, performing arts, and other events), 1.2 percent for lectures and artists, 0.9 percent for the student affairs council, 0.7 percent for the equestrian center, 0.6 percent for music organizations, 0.3 percent for parking, 1.3 percent for other student activities, and 6.9 percent held back for contingencies. Miami

University's 2006 endowment was $281 million, a ranking of #168 among U.S. and Canadian universities. This was an increase of 12.2 percent from 2005 ($250.5 million), which was an increase of 16.4 percent from 2004 ($215.2 million).

Student Facts and Student Affairs

It is said that Miami University places more emphasis on student affairs outside of the classroom than does most other universities. There are more than 300 student organizations, which present opportunities for students to become involved in a wide range of interests from academic to recreation to social interests. Nearly all main campus students (with few exceptions) are required to live on campus during their first years. For the 2006–07 year, 98 percent of first-year students lived on campus. In a few years, it is expected that Miami University will require students to live on campus for the first two years. Now, about 48 percent of Oxford students live on campus, about 50 percent live within two miles of campus, and about 2 percent are commuters. Students from Ohio make up 64 percent of the undergraduate students. Other geographic areas that are significantly represented include the greater Chicago area and lower Michigan. Despite the university's location five miles from the Indiana border, relatively few students are from Indiana. During the first year, all students are part of a living-learning community. Living-learning communities are designed to create and extend learning opportunities outside the classroom to heighten students' intellectual and personal growth. These communities are purposeful attempts to integrate curricular and co-curricular experiences that complement and extend classroom learning. Student resident assistants lead students who participate in a range of activities surrounding the particular living-learning theme. Recent living-learning communities have celebrated the arts, emerging community leaders, the Chinese and Spanish languages, RedHawks traditions, the Scholastic Enhancement Program, courses in common, student-created programming, technology and science, the environmental awareness program, technology and society, the French and German language programs, women in science/engineering/math, health enhancement and lifestyle management, honors and scholars, and the international living-learning community.

Miami's main campus has very few nontraditional students. Nearly all undergraduate students are age 18–23; 55.5 percent are female; fewer than 10 percent self-identify into one of the classification categories of students of color. University-provided information for 2006 incoming first-year students on the main campus reports that 8.2 percent of the students were ethnically diverse, 15.9 percent were first-generation college (neither parent attended college), 4.3 percent were low income (as determined by student's adjusted family income from FAFSA), and 20 percent were "first generation *or* low income *or* ethnically diverse." Nearly all of these numbers indicate that Miami University's diversity is significantly below that of most other universities within the state and the region. The breakdown for the entering 2006 class was 3.4 percent African-American, 2.0 percent Asian-American, 1.9 percent Latino, 0.8 percent Native American and Pacific Islander, 0.7 percent international, 4.3 percent unknown, and 86.8 percent white. Asian-Americans were down from 2.9 percent in 2005 to 2.0 percent in 2006; in general the other percentages have been fairly stable for the past five years. Retention rates (to sophomore year) are 89.6 percent for the total Oxford campus. Most component numbers are about the same (near 89.6 percent); 89.6 percent female, 89.5 percent male, African-American 78.8 percent, Latino 84.1 percent, Asian-American 92.6 percent, Native American 94.7 percent, and minority 85.9 percent and nonminority 89.9 percent. Graduation rates (based on within six years) show about the same trend as retention into sophomore year, with African-American and Latino lagging behind and Asian-American and Native American a little ahead of the composite graduation rate. Aggregate numbers for incoming students indicate 42.2 percent Protestant, 39.1 percent Catholic, 12.5 percent none, 3.9 percent Jewish, and all others totaling 2.3 percent. Reported student disabilities total 6.3 percent at Miami, 2.4 percent learning disabilities, all other categories are under 1.0 percent. (Note: Most of these percentages are based on students' self-reported data.)

Faculty ethnicity numbers are higher than the student numbers. For 2006, out of 50 new hire faculty, 11 were classified as diverse ethnicity. In 2006, faculty ethnic diversity was reported to be 14.9 percent (6.7 percent Asian-American, 5.6 percent African-American, 2.1 percent Hispanic, and 0.5 percent Native American.)

The fall 2006 freshmen academic profile included an overall average SAT of about 1240 and average ACT of 26, high school GPA of 3.66 and 38 percent in the top 10 percent of high school class and 98 percent in the top 50 percent of high school class. Freshman admission statistics reveal that 78 percent of total applicants were accepts and 30 percent of accepted students enrolled. Other demographics of the 2006 incoming class show that 21 percent graduated from a private high school, 10 percent have a parent who attended Miami University, 12 percent have a sibling who attended Miami, over 50 percent were members of their high school National Honor Societies, 4 percent were athletes, 2 percent had enough transfer hours to be classified as either a sophomore or junior. Reported family income indicates that many Miami students are from high-income households: 18 percent $200K and greater, 13 percent between $150–200K, 28 percent between $100–150K, 29 percent between $50–100K, and 11 percent less than $50K. For Miami University, 28.1 percent indicate that home is within 100 miles, 84.7 percent home within 500 miles; 83.0 percent report both parents alive and living together; 2.0 percent English not native language, 80.0 percent father with minimum bachelor's, and 73.5 percent mother with minimum bachelor's. These numbers show some differences with "highly selective public universities" where 49.3 percent home is within 100 miles, 89.0 percent home within 500 miles, 76.8 percent both parents alive and living together, 12.1 percent English not native language; 66.9 percent father with minimum bachelor's, and 64.0 percent mother with minimum bachelor's. Fewer Miami students have major concerns about their ability to finance their college education than students at other high selectivity public universities (5.6 percent vs. 10.4 percent). Concerning political attitudes, values and beliefs, Miami students report themselves to be 2.2 percent far left (vs. 3.6 percent for high selectivity public universities), 19.9 percent liberal (vs. 34.3 percent), 38.9 percent middle-of-the-road (vs. 41.0 percent), 36.0 percent conservative (vs. 19.8 percent), and 2.9 percent far right (vs. 1.3 percent). In general, Miami freshmen come from well-educated, high-income, "traditional" family environments and have high academic expectations.

Miami's graduation rates are at 81 percent within six years and 68 percent graduate within four years. As of July 2006, 89.6 percent of Miami freshmen returned for the sophomore year.

Because of changes in Ohio high schools over the past several years, more and more students are starting their first year with college credit earned during high school. Many incoming Miami students earn credit through advance placement (AP), CLEP testing and International Baccalaureate Programs (IB), postsecondary courses (available to qualified Ohio high school students), and departmental proficiency exams.

According to Farmer Business School information, the average class size in the business school is 34 students. More than 92 percent of business school graduates secure employment within months, while 5 percent continue with graduate education. More than 2,000 Miami business graduates are president, CEOs, or owners of companies. Nearly one-fourth of all business school students study abroad. The business school invites many business leaders to visit classes each semester. The school's Business Advisory Council, 45 men and women, meets on campus twice each year. Additionally, the business school sponsors an executive speaker series each semester. For spring 2007, four executives (Bill Nutti, CEO and president, NCR; Phil Francis, chairman and CEO, PetSmart; Dennis Nally, U.S. chairman and senior partner, PriceWaterhouseCoopers; and Robert Johnson, CEO, Dubai Aerospace Enterprise) presented their ideas at talks open to the public.

With 36 residence halls, 5 dining halls, and several *à la carte* locations, housing and dining is a large support function at Miami University. Each residence hall has cable TV and assess to Internet, e-mail, and Miami computer systems. An academic advisor lives in each first-year residence hall to provide personal support and assistance in scheduling classes and exploring majors. Some dining halls offer traditional "buffet" meals, but many offer other options such as create your own stir-fry. Miami has won many awards for the quality and variety of the dining and food options. But in spite of a recent survey that 97 percent of users gave high ratings to both food and service, it is not uncommon to hear students complain about the dining halls. All but one of the residence halls is more than 20 years old. And although the university has added some new features and other improvements, quite a few students seem to feel that many residence hall rooms are too small. The standard room accommodates two students.

Miami University is known as the "Mother of Fraternities" and has an active Greek life. In 1833 Alpha Delta Phi was founded and five social fraternities began at Miami. The impact of social fraternities and sororities on campus promotes the university's rich heritage of traditions, history, and pride. About a third of undergraduate students are members of the Greek community. The Interfraternity Council (IFC), the Panhellenic Association, and the National Pan-Hellenic Council are the governing organizations and help coordinate many community service projects in the Oxford community. Students involved in the social Greek system report that they have benefited in leadership development and experiences, strong friendships, service, and in other ways.

The Recreation Center is a popular place on campus for student recreation and socializing. Additionally, it serves faculty/staff and community members who pay a users fee. A portion of student fees support the facility, which includes courts for basketball, volleyball, indoor soccer, and racquetball; two swimming pools with diving center; aerobic rooms, an indoor $1/8$-mile jogging track; a climbing wall; and a two-story fitness center. The Goggin Ice Center (which opened in fall 2006) is the home of Miami hockey games, and contains two ice rinks available for public skating, summer resident programs, and private lessons. The Outdoor Pursuit Center loans equipment and sponsors trips for camping, kinking, canoeing, and rafting. There is an intramural sports and club sports program involving many activities with about 1,800 teams in 45 sports. The RedHawks sports teams compete in NCAA Division I Mid-American Conference, the Central Collegiate Hockey Association, and the U.S. Figure Skating Association.

Many arts and entertainment events on campus are sponsored by a number of different organizations.

Miami's Student Health Service (SRS) provides comprehensive medical to all Oxford campus students who have paid the general fee. The Student Counseling Service is a campus mental health resource that offers a variety of services, including individual and group counseling and other programs.

The Miami University Police Department is a full-service police agency. Other safety practices include a nighttime door-to-door escort service.

A summer orientation for incoming first-year students takes place during June. The orientation's 16 sessions are attended by more than 95 percent of the incoming first-years. Many parents and families also participate in this program.

The university offers many other support services including a student newspaper (three issues per normal week in fall and spring semesters), a conference center and inn, a detailed Web site, an award-winning National Public Radio station, a Women's Center, academic advising, a student court and judicial system, student government, university senate, privacy and student records policies, Career Services (job placement), Office of Admission, Office of the Bursar, student financial assistance, university communications, information technology and computing policies, parking services and policies, and many more supporting activities.

Marketing and Competition and the Future

Miami University is very well known within its geographic region and is striving toward becoming more nationally known and recognized. In 2007, the *U.S. News & World Report* college rankings listed Miami University 21st among the top public universities in the nation. *Kiplinger's* annual list of the "100 Best Values in Public Colleges" ranked Miami University as "the top bargain in Ohio and 38th nationally" (2007). The *Fiske Guide to Colleges 2007* praised Miami as "one of the rising stars among state universities" for its "strong emphasis on liberal arts and its opportunities for research, travel abroad, and leadership." But despite these and other examples of positive recognition, the university's reach beyond the region remains limited.

A few years ago, Miami University formally developed benchmarking with peer institutions. This was done for a variety of reasons but especially to expand Miami's image outside its region. Initial peer institutions included Syracuse, Clemson, the University of Connecticut, SUNY-Binghampton, and the University of Delaware. At present, Miami continues to benchmark with these institutions but is now putting more emphasis on competing with "aspirational peers" including Notre Dame, the College of William and Mary, Duke University, UNC-Chapel Hill, and the University of Virginia. Overlap school include Vanderbilt, Indiana University, the University of Michigan, and Washington University.

Miami University has the highest tuition and fees of any public-supported university or college in the region (Ohio, Indiana, and Kentucky), including the flagship Ohio State University. Miami University fees for the 2006–07 year (assuming no summer school or excess student hours) were an average of $10,029 for in-state students and $22,543 for out-of-state students. These fees do not include room and board, summer school, parking, excess hours, lab and other minor fees. For 2006–07 other state-supported Ohio universities' tuition averaged about $9,000 for in-state and $19,900 for out-of-state students. Ohio State University tuition for 2006–07 was $8,767 for in-state and 20,562 for out-of-state.

The Miami University Alumni Association supports the university financially and in many other ways. The Alumni Association is committed to preserving the university's heritage and cultivating the relationship that connects it to the university. It has a mission statement, vision statement, and value statement. The alumni board of directors is composed of 20 volunteers who provide support with programs, planning, and focusing the efforts of the Alumni Association. While many alumni events center or are related to intercollegiate athletics, at Miami University there is less of an emphasis on athletics performance than at most other universities that are NCAA Division I in revenue-producing sports. The university-paid compensation for the athletic director, head football coach, and head men's basketball coach are very near the low end of Division I. It has been said that Miami University's location and the power and influence of Ohio State University, especially in football, lessen Miami's ability to sustain a huge following in athletics. Others have said that Miami's rural setting is a negative. While there are a number of people who think Miami is located out in the middle of nowhere with no easy access, it is relative close to the major interstate highway system that serves Cincinnati and Dayton. Also, some say that people in Cincinnati think that Miami University is in the Dayton TV and media market, while people in Dayton think that Miami is in the Cincinnati TV and media market. Sports fans sometimes assume that with Miami's high academic standards, it is very difficult to recruit athletes for revenue sports who are highly qualified both on the field and in the classroom.

The university is in the middle of a major fundraising effort called "Love and Honor for Miami." As of May 1, 2007, $271 million had been pledged out of a goal of $500 million by the end of the 2009–10 school year.

State funding support is another issue for Miami University. The state's former governor and new governor, along with the legislature, seem to be focusing higher education toward technology, science/math, and engineering with the idea of developing a professional workforce that meets the needs of maintaining the state's economy. In his inaugural address, Governor Ted Strickland surprised university administrators around the state when he mentioned a tuition freeze for higher education. At the time this case was being written, it was not yet clear what the governor meant by tuition freeze. For the past decade, Miami University has had annual tuition increases of as much as 9.9 percent, with several years exceeding 6 percent. Thus, Miami's cost for students has increased at a rate significantly higher than the national inflation rate.

Miami University is perceived as a liberal arts university that is less than compatible with the state's vision of what higher education should be. All of the countywide elected officeholders and the state senator and state representative are Republicans. The city of Oxford is often the only city in the county that supports the Democratic Party's candidates in county and state legislative elections. Some have expressed their opinion that this hampers state funding. One senior administrator remarked, "What might be best [in higher education] for the state of Ohio as a whole, may not be best for Miami."

Miami University continues to be on the receiving end of jokes and stereotypic remarks such as "too white, too rich, and too traditional." Quite a few people seem to think Miami is a place full of North Face jackets, Hummers and SUVs, and a country club lifestyle.

Uncertain funding, changing demographics and student profiles are two issues for the university to cope with. Miami University faces many challenges as it prepares to enter its third century in February 2009.

EXHIBIT 1 Educational and General Funds Revenues, Expenditures and Transfers

	Budget 2005–2006	Actual 2005–2006	Budget 2006–2007
I. REVENUES			
Tuition, Fees, and Other Student Charges			
Instructional fee	$ 333,345,700	$ 334,566,911	$ 350,417,400
General fee	25,515,100	25,813,562	26,624,900
Tuition surcharge	8,408,600	9,490,741	10,394,800
Other fees and charges	4,212,200	3,983,288	9,982,200
Total Tuition, Fees, and Other student charges	371,481,600	373,854,502	397,419,300
State Appropriations			
Instructional subsidies	68,219,300	68,300,085	66,286,500
Other state appropriation	8,735,500	9,270,016	8,536,300
Total State Appropriations	76,954,800	77,570,101	74,822,800
Federal Grants and Contracts	13,428,400	16,737,176	14,555,200
State Grants and Contracts	3,844,500	5,304,008	4,091,600
Local Grants and Contracts	650,600	637,908	670,400
Private Gifts	11,600,000	12,067,230	10,934,500
Private Grants and Contracts	2,228,300	3,705,141	2,108,600
Endowment Income	4,610,800	5,093,905	4,600,800
Sales and Services of Educational Activities	4,748,200	5,482,811	4,812,000
Temporary Investment Income	5,610,000	15,156,307	7,795,000
Other Sources	1,558,500	2,505,701	2,668,100
Total Educational and General Revenues	**496,715,700**	**518,114,790**	**524,478,300**
II. EXPENDITURES			
Instruction and Departmental Research	$ 145,254,000	$ 161,315,153	$ 155,074,100
Separately Budgeted Research	7,609,300	12,246,331	9,172,100
Public Service	1,987,300	2,925,869	2,453,400
Academic Support	50,173,200	54,644,033	54,646,900
Student Services	21,587,400	21,240,638	23,018,700
Institutional Support	42,852,900	37,839,823	44,100,600
Plant Operation and Maintenance	31,481,500	32,857,747	34,023,200
Scholarships and Fellowships	172,676,500	165,509,596	177,233,900
Total Educational and General Expenditures	**473,622,100**	**488,579,190**	**499,722,900**
III. TRANSFERS-OUT/(IN)			
General Fee	$ 20,141,200	$ 20,413,828	$ 20,408,300
Allocated Fund Balance	-	2,014,962	-
Other	2,952,400	7,195,760	4,347,100
Total Educational & General Transfers	**23,093,600**	**29,624,550**	**24,755,400**
Net Increase(Decrease) in E&G Fund Balance	**$ —**	**$ (88,950)**	**$ —**

Source: www.miami.muohio.edu

EXHIBIT 2   2006–2007 Operating Budget

	General Funds	Designated Funds	Restricted Funds	Total
I. REVENUES				
A. Educational and General				
Oxford Campus	$ 443,094,300	$ 12,067,700	$ 25,700,000	$ 480,862,000
Hamilton Campus	18,442,300	290,000	3,200,000	21,932,300
Middletown Campus	16,649,000	585,000	4,450,000	21,684,000
Total Educational and General	478,185,600	12,942,700	33,350,000	524,478,300
B. Auxiliary Enterprises	100,220,400	902,000	972,700	102,095,100
Total Revenues	**578,406,000**	**13,844,700**	**34,322,700**	**626,573,400**
II. EXPENDITURES AND TRANSFERS				
A. Educational and General				
Oxford Campus				
President's Office	$ 6,328,300	$ –	$ –	$ 6,328,300
Academic Affairs	332,761,400	–	–	332,761,400
Finance & Business Services	38,989,800	–	–	38,989,800
Student Affairs	11,145,700	–	–	11,145,700
University Advancement	5,900,500	–	–	5,900,500
Information Technology	18,700,000	–	–	18,700,000
Miami University, division non-specific	4,680,200	–	–	4,680,200
Designated and Restricted Funds	–	12,067,700	25,700,000	37,767,700
General Fee and Other Transfers	24,588,400	–	–	24,588,400
Total Oxford Campus Educational and General	443,094,300	12,067,700	25,700,000	480,862,000
Hamilton Campus	18,442,300	290,000	3,200,000	21,932,300
Middletown Campus	16,649,000	585,000	4,450,000	21,684,000
Total Non-Auxiliary Expenditures & Transfers	**478,185,600**	**12,942,700**	**33,350,000**	**524,478,300**
B. Auxiliary Enterprises				
Aviation Services	$ 118,100	$ –	$ –	$ 118,100
Equestrian Center	305,000	–	800	305,800
Goggin Ice Arena	2,411,100	74,000	7,200	2,492,300
Intercollegiate Athletics	3,787,800	650,000	774,200	5,212,000
Marcum Conference Center & Inn	2,861,000	30,000	4,200	2,895,200
Miami Metro	1,445,600	–	–	1,445,600
Millett Assembly Hall	–	–	–	–
Network Operations Auxiliary	1,364,000	–	–	1,364,000
Network Services Enterprise	1,855,000	–	–	1,855,000
Parking Program—Oxford	2,065,500	–	700	2,066,200
Recreational Sports Center	1,506,800	5,000	30,000	1,541,800
Residence and Dining Halls	61,253,600	9,000	115,000	61,377,600
Shriver Center	18,207,100	134,000	39,200	18,380,300
Telecommunications	2,920,300	–	400	2,920,700
Utility Enterprise				
Recoveries	(22,338,000)	–	–	(22,338,000)
Expenditures & Transfers Out	22,338,000	–	–	22,338,000
Hamilton–Wilks Conference Center	90,000	–	–	90,000
Hamilton–Parking Program	7,000	–	–	7,000
Hamilton–Student Center	7,500	–	500	8,000
Middletown–Parking Program	10,000	–	–	10,000
Middletown–Student Center	5,000	–	500	5,500
Total Auxiliary Expenditures & Transfers	**100,220,400**	**902,000**	**972,700**	**102,095,100**
TOTAL EDUCATIONAL & GENERAL AND AUXILIARY EXPENDITURES & TRANSFERS	**$ 578,406,000**	**$ 13,844,700**	**$ 34,322,700**	**$ 626,573,400**

Source: www.miami.muohio.edu

EXHIBIT 3 Educational and General Funds Revenues, Expenditures and Transfers

	2006–2007 Budget			
	Oxford Campus	Hamilton Campus	Middletown Campus	Total
I. REVENUES				
Tuition, Fees, and Other Student Charges				
Instructional fee	$ 331,512,200	$ 10,262,700	$ 8,642,500	$ 350,417,400
General fee	25,136,900	805,900	682,100	26,624,900
Tuition surcharge	10,109,800	254,800	30,200	10,394,800
Other fees and charges	9,001,000	456,000	525,200	9,982,200
Total Tuition, Fees, and Other student charges	375,759,900	11,779,400	9,880,000	397,419,300
State Appropriations				
Instructional subsidies	54,498,700	5,789,300	5,998,500	66,286,500
Other state appropriation	6,510,700	945,100	1,080,500	8,536,300
Total State Appropriations	61,009,400	6,734,400	7,079,000	74,822,800
Federal Grants and Contracts	9,717,000	2,242,000	2,596,200	14,555,200
State Grants and Contracts	2,804,200	477,000	810,400	4,091,600
Local Grants and Contracts	440,000	114,400	116,000	670,400
Private Gifts	10,256,500	248,000	430,000	10,934,500
Private Grants and Contracts	1,740,000	98,800	269,800	2,108,600
Endowment Income	4,508,000	12,800	80,000	4,600,800
Sales and Services of Educational Activities	4,442,000	103,300	266,700	4,812,000
Temporary Investment Income	7,700,000	45,000	50,000	7,795,000
Other Sources	2,485,000	77,200	105,900	2,668,100
Total Educational and General Revenues	**480,862,000**	**21,932,300**	**21,684,000**	**524,478,300**
II. EXPENDITURES AND TRANSFERS				
Instruction and Departmental Research	$ 136,891,800	$ 8,869,600	$ 9,312,700	$ 155,074,100
Separately Budgeted Research	8,024,100	152,000	996,000	9,172,100
Public Service	1,885,400	315,000	253,000	2,453,400
Academic Support	50,638,400	1,959,200	2,049,300	54,646,900
Student Services	18,761,300	2,166,700	2,090,700	23,018,700
Institutional Support	38,551,900	3,373,400	2,175,300	44,100,600
Plant Operation and Maintenance	30,238,600	2,164,600	1,620,000	34,023,200
Scholarships and Fellowships	171,282,100	2,913,800	3,038,000	177,233,900
Total Educational and General Expenditures	**456,273,600**	**21,914,300**	**21,535,000**	**499,722,900**
Mandatory Transfers Out (Debt Service)	3,282,500	–	–	3,282,500
Non-Mandatory Transfers (In)/Out				
General Fee and Other	21,305,900	18,000	149,000	21,472,900
Unallocated Fund Balance	–	–	–	–
Total Educational and General Transfers	24,588,400	18,000	149,000	24,755,400
Total Educational and General Expenditures & Transfers	**480,862,000**	**21,932,300**	**21,684,000**	**524,478,300**

Source: www.miami.muohio.edu

## 30

Wesley United Methodist Church — 2007

William James
Francis Marion University

www.wesleyhartsville.com

"A jewel in the center of Hartsville" is how members think of Wesley United Methodist Church, located in Hartsville, South Carolina, and there is certainly enough beautiful stained glass to dignify the statement. Small-town churches such as Wesley are a source of spiritual support and activity for their communities. Wesley is not one of the super-churches where services take place in stadium-like facilities. It has a membership of only 459 and its sanctuary is over 100 years old. Still, Wesley opens its doors to the Hartsville community by extending a warm welcome to resident students from neighboring schools, by actively participating in downtown life, and by reaching out to Hartsville's less fortunate through its Hartsville Soup Kitchen Mission. Countless small churches just like Wesley do the same each and every week.

Even though Wesley is essentially a small-town church, it still has the backing of the United Methodist Church, a church with a North American presence of 35,102 local churches that boast a combined membership of 8,251,000 people. The United Methodist Church is America's third largest denomination behind the Catholic Church and the Southern Baptist Convention. Things are changing, however. A recent study found that the total number of adults in the United States increased nearly 19 percent, while the number of adults who classify themselves as Christian increased only 5 percent and the number of adults who identify themselves as Methodist declined .17 percent over the same period.[1]

In the United States today, over 47 percent of the populace are Christian church adherents.[2] Still, theological conflicts and scandals have left many disillusioned with the leaders of Christian churches and organized religion in general. It is no wonder that nondenominational, evangelical, and independent churches have seen the greatest levels of growth. Meanwhile, non-Christian followings, including religions such as Wicca, Hinduism, and Buddhism, have reported an overall increase of 32 percent while the number of people claiming no religious affiliation at all has increased by over 105 percent.[3]

Today, the question being faced by small churches like Wesley is: How does a local church compete in an environment of skepticism of virtually all Christian organizations and deal with the rising tide of theologically opposing religions and the overtly nonreligious? Christian churches still have much to offer the modern world, but many churches like Wesley are facing an identity crisis. When there are so many needs within the church itself, the local community, and the entire globe, what do these relatively small churches do? How do they reach out to those in need of spiritual and physical help when they are essentially fighting for their own survival? Wesley needs a clear strategic plan.

Wesley's Mission Statement

Wesley Church shall be a spiritual center for community life through Christian, social, health, and service ministries.

History

Wesley was established in 1893 and was the first Methodist church in the newly incorporated town of Hartsville—a decade later its sanctuary became the first brick church in town. In 1928, Wesley's McNabb Education Building was called model of modern church architecture by the *Southern Christian Advocate*.

During the 1960s, a growing membership and a visionary pastor led the church to purchase nearly half of a city block that included the former Segars automotive dealership property and two houses. A fourth property owned by the Wiggins family would have had to be purchased in order for the church to gain complete ownership of the entire end of the block. The plan was to expand the church campus to include a new, larger sanctuary along with more modern and spacious facilities. The minister was transferred to another church and the plans never materialized. The Segars Building was converted for use as a youth center, then a Boy Scout hut, and was most recently used as a Sunday-school classroom for some of the church's elderly members (for many years this was the only building that could be accessed without navigating stairs). The Segars Building currently houses Wesley's Hartsville Soup Kitchen Mission. The church has also retained the two houses and uses them as rental property; these two houses currently generate $13,200 of revenue per year for the church.

St. Luke United Methodist Church

In the late 1960s, after Wesley's failed expansion attempt, a group of Wesley members left the church to form St. Luke United Methodist Church in a suburban neighborhood on the opposite side of town. In the 1990s, another group of families left Wesley, many moving their memberships to St. Luke. Because most of these were families with young children, attendance at Wesley's children and youth programs became unstable and has remained so ever since. Between the two churches, St. Luke's congregation is made up of more young families with children, while Wesley is increasingly the church home of retirees. In many cases, the parents and grandparents of St. Luke members go to Wesley. The two churches' staffs collaborate often, but there remains a sense of competition between the two congregations.

The Hartsville Soup Kitchen

The Hartsville Soup Kitchen is a mission that was begun in 1996 by Wesley members, though it has maintained only a loose affiliation with the church. Volunteers and donations come from throughout the Hartsville community, including 14 participating churches, and administrative duties are still carried out by Wesley members. Housed in Wesley's Segars Building, the Hartsville Soup Kitchen serves over 20,000 hot meals annually.

The 2002 Building Project

Wesley continued its progressive history with the construction of its Family Life Center in 2002, but the construction project brought additional problems with finances and parking. At a total cost of $1.3 million, the church added a spacious new office complex, a fellowship hall, and an elevator connecting the new facility to the three existing floors of the McNabb Education Building. Since its construction, this building has been the model for comparable building projects in the area. The project has not been without its downsides and conflicts, however. Since constructing the Family Life Center, Wesley has faced budget shortfalls for the first time in its history, and parking has become more of a problem for church services and events.

Parking Issues

Years of development have left Wesley, a downtown church, virtually landlocked. Church leaders were faced with the choice of either razing the Segars Building or constructing the new Family Life Center in the church's largest parking lot behind the Sanctuary and McNabb Education Building. They chose to construct in the parking lot, leaving only six parking spaces in the church's largest area. Many members protested the location of the new building because of the parking situation. In 2003, the church was able to purchase an adjoining property with an abandoned building. At a cost of approximately $30,000, the church razed this building and constructed a small parking lot with fifteen more parking spaces. Still, Wesley has problems with parking. Sunday mornings find all of the parking areas filled, with cars lining the streets and overflowing into a city parking lot on College Avenue and the Coker College parking lot on the opposite side of Fourth Street.

In order to ease parking problems many members would like to raze the Segars Building—a building viewed by many as an eyesore and a money pit—and construct a parking lot in its place. Others are adamant that the building can still serve a purpose for the church, pointing out that more Christian outreach ministries have originated in that building than in the prettier buildings across the street. Currently, half of the Segars Building stands empty, but demolition of the building would mean the Hartsville Soup Kitchen would have to move.

The Campus

The church campus, as it currently exists, can be seen in Exhibit 1. The Segars Building and other properties originally purchased for expansion are on the right side of College Avenue, and the church's primary buildings—the Sanctuary, McNabb Education Building, and Family Life Center—are on the left.

Hartsville, South Carolina (www.hartsvillesc.com)

Hartsville is the kind of town that comes to mind when thinking of "small town America," a National Civic League "All-America City" award winner with tree-lined streets and lots of small family-owned shops and restaurants. Wesley is located right on the edge of Hartsville's historic downtown business district—a vibrant, diverse, arts-oriented environment. Hartsville has a population of 7,556 within its city limits, with 29,803 people living in the greater Hartsville area.[4] Hartsville is also home to some noteworthy institutions, including the international headquarters of Sonoco Products Company, Inc., a Fortune 1000 company founded in Hartsville in 1899; Coker College, a small liberal arts college with a student population of just over 1,100; and the South Carolina Governor's School for Science and Mathematics, which is a magnet school that draws gifted high school students from around the state.

Placed firmly in the "Bible Belt," the Hartsville area is also home to 107 churches of all denominations, including 10 other United Methodist churches. Therefore, Wesley's primary competition is from other Protestant Christian churches. Though Wesley's leaders are

EXHIBIT 1 Wesley Campus Map

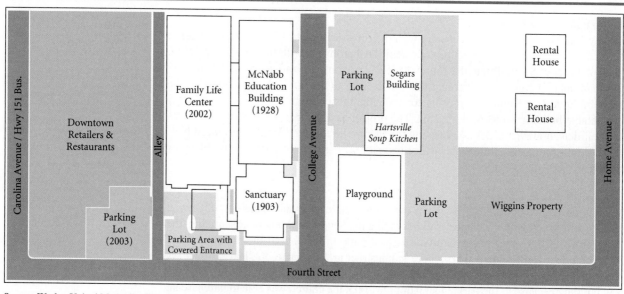

Source: Wesley United Methodist Church.

EXHIBIT 2   Wesley United Methodist Church Membership

Year	Church Membership	Average Worship Attendance	Sunday School Membership	Attendance
2006	459	150	198	80
2005	469	153	212	77
2004	466	160	206	88
2003	465	162	195	90
2002	464	186	212	90
2001	456	180	144	89
2000	446	160	389	75
1999	453	189	201	111
1998	434	191	219	111
1997	420	176	176	101

Source: Wesley United Methodist Church.

apprehensive about using the word "competitors" to describe its relationship with other churches who are also in the business of promoting the teachings of Jesus Christ, if Wesley is to thrive for the next one hundred years, it must be competitive with other Hartsville area churches.

Membership

With a membership of 459, Wesley is one of the top ten largest Methodist congregations in the Hartsville district. Demographically, Wesley's congregation is segmented as follows:

- By racial identification: 100 percent Caucasian
- By gender: 35 percent male and 65 percent female
- By age group: 7 percent under age 18, 27 percent age 18–30, 44 percent age 30–65, and 22 percent over age 65

During 2006, Wesley received four new members, while losing six to other United Methodist churches, two to other denominations, and six to death—a net loss of ten. As can be seen in Exhibit 2, Wesley's overall membership and Sunday School membership have grown in the past ten years, but average weekly attendance has actually decreased.

Contributions

Each year Wesley asks its members to submit pledge cards indicating how much they intend to give during the year ahead. In 2006, Wesley received 172 pledges from 459 members. While some members do not contribute financially, pledges to the operating fund for 2006 were nearly $260,000. Actual receipts exceeded pledges by over $55,000. The difference reflects gifts that were given in excess of pledges and gifts from individuals who did not fill out pledge cards. Stock gifts are also an important part of Wesley's contributions, totaling approximately 22 percent of all contributions for 2006. An analysis of actual receipts indicates a typical pyramidal giving structure; an illustration of Wesley's giving structure for 2006 is shown in Exhibit 3.

Church Organization

Church Staff

Wesley employs a staff of twelve. The entire staff is managed by the Committee on Pastor/Staff–Parish Relations (the PSPRC), and answers directly to the PSPRC chairperson. Within this structure, the pastor's position at Wesley can be likened to that of a chief operating officer in the corporate world; he is the clearinghouse for all of the ministries and

EXHIBIT 3 Wesley United Methodist Church—2006 Giving Analysis

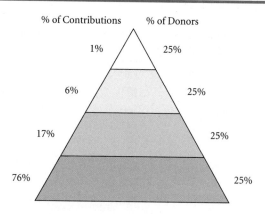

% of Contributions   % of Donors

1%   25%

6%   25%

17%   25%

76%   25%

	Receipts	Expenses	Net
2006	$ 317,988	$ 344,170	–$ 26,182
2005	323,718	333,719	–10,001
2004	342,635	342,205	+430

Source: Wesley United Methodist Church.

activities that take place within the church and the church's link to the larger United Methodist Church.

Wesley's administrative and financial functions are performed by the church administrator and the financial secretary. The church administrator directs all the administrative functions for the church and is responsible for all membership records, cash receipts, publication of the weekly newsletter, publication of worship programs, scheduling for church buildings and events, and oversight of the two church sextons. Historically, Wesley's church administrators serve through multiple pastoral appointments, orienting new pastors to Wesley's people, organization, and schedule. A new part-time financial secretary position was created in 2005 to lighten the workload of the church's volunteer treasurer. Under the supervision of the church treasurer, this position is responsible for the maintenance of an accounting system, all cash expenditures, and financial reporting.

Working alongside the pastor to shape the church's ministries and activities are the director of children, youth, and young adults; the director of nurture and missions; the church hostess; and the director of music. Formerly, Wesley had an associate pastor or youth minister. Because of difficulties in finding and retaining a suitable employee for such a position, the PSPRC split the job into two positions: the director of nurture and missions, and the director of children, youth, and young adults. The church also employs a hostess, who is responsible for all events where meals are served in the church. Wesley's director of music is in charge of the chancel choir's performances and rehearsals. Working with the director of music are an organist who plays at the traditional 10:30 A.M. service, and an early service music coordinator, a pianist, who plays during the early service at 8:30 A.M.

Volunteer Structure

While Wesley is fortunate to have talented and dedicated staff, volunteers are responsible for much of the life of the church. Most of Wesley's volunteer positions are on committees that are led by a chairperson and typically alternate duties among the committee members on a monthly basis. In addition to leading their particular committee, chairpersons also serve on the church's administrative board, the committee that directs the entire church. Administrative committees typically meet quarterly, and work committees typically meet monthly.

EXHIBIT 4   Wesley United Methodist Church—Organizational Chart

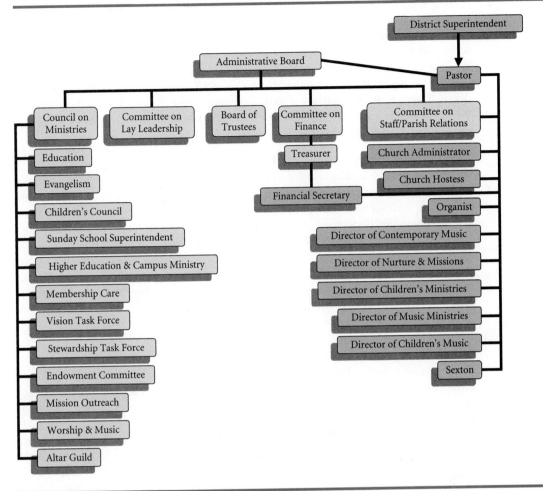

Source: Wesley United Methodist Church.

Organizational Chart

The organizational chart shown in Exhibit 4 depicts the interlaced structure of Wesley's paid staff and volunteer committees.

Church Services and Events

The life of Wesley revolves around a busy schedule of weekly, monthly, and annual events. Wesley's traditional Sunday schedule is as follows:

- 8:30 A.M.—Early Worship Service
- 9:30 A.M.—Sunday School for all ages
- 10:30 A.M.—Traditional Worship Service
- 6:00 P.M.—United Methodist Youth Fellowship (UMYF)

In addition to these events on Sunday, Wesley holds a monthly family night supper, charging $4 for adults and $2 for children, and has regularly scheduled monthly meetings for nearly all of its committees and social organizations, including AMITY (a large senior group that has attracted many members from outside the church), the United Methodist Men, the United Methodist Women, the Women of Wesley, the Rosa Lee Circle, and the Tincie Y. Crouch Circle. A new monthly event was also launched in 2006, the 1st Monday Café, which has been successful in attracting members and downtown workers to the church for lunch on the first Monday of each month.

Wesley also has some annual events that have become traditional. The most notable of these events include the Renofest gospel sing, part of a weekend-long bluegrass festival sponsored by the Hartsville Downtown Development Association that draws crowds from South Carolina's Pee Dee and coastal regions (www.renofest.com); the joint Sunday service with Centenary United Methodist Church (a primarily African-American church) in honor of Martin Luther King's birthday; the Valentine Banquet and Silent Auction; the October "Pumpkin Patch" that offers pumpkins of all shapes and sizes, photo opportunities, and story times for students at local preschools; the Fall Food Fair; and the Taste of Wesley, which is a large community social event at which Wesley members volunteer to prepare their favorite appetizers and hors d'ouevres.

The 8:30 A.M. Early Worship Service

Wesley began its 8:30 A.M. worship service in 2000 as an attempt to serve the spiritual needs of current members and prospective members who were interested in a more contemporary style of worship. The resulting Early Worship Service is certainly more informal than the 10:30 service, but is also far from contemporary. The service has a free-flowing, old-time-hymn-singing, rural church feeling. Average attendance at this service is 33 and seems to be growing. The service generates no additional costs, and many find it convenient to be able to attend Sunday School and a church service all before 10:30 A.M. Still, some of the originators of the contemporary worship service idea would like to see yet another service added to cater to those who prefer that style of worship.

Marketing and Communications

Since Wesley's Vision Task Force completed a vision plan for the church in 2005, new efforts have been put forth to create awareness of church activities among both the existing membership and the Hartsville community. Wesley's primary source of communication with its membership and visitors who provide their mailing addresses is its weekly newsletter, "The Bulletin." "The Bulletin" is received by 260 households. The usual contents are a note from the pastor or one of the staff members, a weekly calendar of events at the church, notes about upcoming events, a section of "Children's Notes" and "Youth News" from the director of children, youth, and young adults, updates about hospitalized members, prayer requests, attendance reports, a list of guests who attended the previous Sunday, and staff contact information. "The Bulletin" is mailed out each Wednesday and usually received by members in Hartsville on Friday.

Completely new marketing efforts at Wesley include small signs placed around town that include the church's name and worship times. Also, Wesley's director of nurture and missions has begun to utilize connections with the Hartsville Chamber of Commerce as a marketing tool for Wesley events, and Wesley's director of children, youth, and young adults has produced short articles about church events that have appeared in several local publications, including *Hartsville Today* (www.hvtd.com) and Hartsville's local newspaper, *The Messenger* (www.hartsvillemessenger.com). Wesley also runs regular ads in *The Messenger*'s worship section, and larger ads are purchased for special events.

In spite of these new marketing efforts, concerns have been raised that Wesley is viewed in the Hartsville community as "a church for rich people, a church for seniors, or a church for white people." All of these stereotypes have some basis in reality—the church does have a large budget considering its membership, the senior 25 percent of the church membership are the most active, and the congregation is entirely Caucasian. Still, the leaders of Wesley United Methodist Church wish to follow the mission of the United Methodist Church by reaching out to all residents of the Hartsville community.

Wesley's Finances

The committee on finance is responsible for Wesley's finances. Day-to-day financial activities are conducted by the church administrator and financial secretary, both whom are supervised by the church treasurer. Wesley's committee on finance has adopted several financial controls and constraints. As a control on cash flows, there is a mandatory separation and duplication of duties—the church administrator is only allowed to deal with cash receipts, the financial secretary is only allowed to manage cash expenditures. Moreover, all cash receipt counts and expense invoices must be approved by a designee of the committee on finance before deposits can be made or checks can be written. The committee has also set budgeting constraints that states, in brief, only current year revenues can be used to pay current year expenses and local church expenses must be paid first. This set of constraints was enacted in 2002, when for the first time in its history Wesley could not fund its entire budget. Consequently, when contributions fall short of the budget, the first budget item to be cut is the church apportionment, which is paid to the South Carolina Annual Conference of the United Methodist Church. Also since 2002, a debate has accompanied the annual budgeting process regarding whether or not pledges should be considered when creating the budget; currently they are not.

A detailed statement of Wesley's operating fund budget and actual expenses for 2005 and 2006 are shown in Exhibit 5. Consistent with Wesley's budgeting constraint, the "Apportionment" went underfunded even when local expenses exceeded their budgeted amounts.

Exhibit 6 shows receipts and expenses for Wesley's operating fund. It is important to note that receipts for specific funds, such as the building fund or missions funds, are not

EXHIBIT 5   Wesley United Methodist Church—Operating Fund

Account	2006		2005	
	Budget	Actual	Budget	Actual
General Ministry	2,000	991	2,700	1,777
Worship Expense	500	433	1,800	530
Stewardship	350	0	1,000	211
Evangelism/Church Growth	1,100	923	750	1,143
Family Life Center Activities	4,000	7,497	3,500	4,749
Education	6,500	7,366	6,500	7,255
Youth Ministry	2,000	2,279	2,000	2,136
Children's Ministry	1,000	651	500	1,066
General Music	1,400	1,282	1,500	1,271
Children's Music	150	250	300	(109)
Annual Conference Expense	750	750	750	750
Library Expense	50	0	100	5
Office Supplies & Expense	2,750	1,703	2,500	3,056
Office Machine Expense	5,000	4,571	4,500	5,568
Accounting Expense	9,600	9,800	0	0
Postage	3,500	3,211	3,500	4,142
Janitorial Supplies & Expense	4,000	2,584	4,000	5,273
Telephone	6,500	7,360	6,000	6,847
Utilities	22,000	22,934	21,000	23,612
Church Maintenance	7,000	7,201	7,000	21,415
Parsonage Maintenance	1,500	7,694	1,000	4,043
Organ Tuning & Maintenance	1,250	1,506	1,500	1,345
Van Maintenance	500	169	500	638
Insurance	10,500	10,354	10,000	10,359
Damascus Cemetery Maintenance	50	0	200	0

continued

EXHIBIT 5 Wesley United Methodist Church—Operating Fund—continued

Pastor	75,825	69,696	73,012	73,247
Youth Coordinator	25,500	16,177	22,496	20,593
Administrator	26,883	28,380	26,100	26,262
Financial Secretary	2,400	2,228	0	0
Director of Nurture & Missions	8,000	8,000	0	0
Director of Music	12,675	12,783	12,305	12,413
Organist	12,500	13,126	8,250	8,696
Contemporary Music Coordinator	2,600	2,600	2,600	2,650
Children's Choir Director	3,350	3,404	3,250	3,250
Sexton	17,082	16,345	14,500	14,857
Hostess	5,438	5,674	5,280	5,355
Nursery Workers	250	0	1,700	1,218
Pulpit Substitute	300	0	300	75
Secretary Substitute	300	200	300	250
Organist Substitute	500	100	500	1,650
Payroll Tax Expense	8,357	7,945	6,897	6,829
Workman's Compensation Expense	1,500	1,794	1,500	1,459
Apportionment	53,124	33,505	43,785	23,822
Insurance Assessment	4,896	8,604	25,224	13,727
Pension Assessment	10,095	9,671	17,707	9,629
United Methodist Center Assessment	1,199	695	1,199	652
Pastor Relocation Expense	0	1,731	0	0

Source: Wesley United Methodist Church.

reported as receipts to the operating fund. However, the committees responsible for these funds can and sometimes do elect to transfer money to the church operating fund, and this is what happened in the instances since 2002 where actual receipts are reported as less than actual expenses. Exhibit 7 shows the church's total assets and debt. "Other Assets" shown in Exhibit 7 are cash and equivalents, and the debt is directly related to the church's 2002 building project.

EXHIBIT 6 Wesley United Methodist Church Operating Fund

Year	Pledges	Actual Receipts	Budgeted Expenses	Actual Expenses
2006	$ 259,921	$ 317,988	$ 366,724	$ 344,170
2005	268,000	323,718	348,448	333,719
2004	238,426	342,635	345,664	342,205
2003	301,882	320,933	324,848	320,933
2002	229,768	302,548	304,544	299,567
2001	206,180	270,413	273,814	283,729
2000	199,798	292,734	239,725	259,067
1999	190,430	239,214	254,575	229,701
1998	177,416	238,701	245,319	252,080
1997	134,730	215,729	237,436	223,813

Source: Wesley United Methodist Church.

lorikeets, reptiles, and fish native to Australia. There is a large free flight aviary for the lorikeets. Visitors can enter the aviary where they can purchase and feed cups of nectar to the lorikeets.

The zoo actively participates in the Species Survival Plan (SSP) of the AZA to ensure the survival of endangered species. Many zoos participate in the program. For example, in Texas, the Houston Zoological Gardens hatched two critically endangered species, the prairie chicken and the Hawaiian thrush. Riverbanks focuses on 28 of the 155 SSP animals including the golden lion tamarin, Siberian tiger, palm cockatoo, African penguin, and Bali mynah.

Riverbanks has received awards for successfully breeding the black howlers and the white-faced sakis, and the zoo has the honor of being the first zoo to breed in captivity two rare birds, the toco toucan and the crimson seedcracker, and the first zoo in the Western hemisphere to breed milky eagle owls, blue-billed weavers, and cinereous vultures. Riverbanks has the only pair of cinereous vultures raising their own chicks, and it has successfully bred the endangered pine barrens tree frogs in captivity, a first for this species. Riverbanks received the 2002 International Conservation Award that recognizes support of kangaroo conservation in Papua New Guinea and the 2002 Exhibits Significant Achievement Award for the Avian Center (Bird Conservation Center, Birdhouse, and outdoor aviaries).

Riverbanks uses the Zoological Park for a variety of activities such as Migratory Bird Day with hands-on activities, lorikeet feeding, giraffe feeding, pony rides, and 3-D Action Theatre. On Migratory Bird Day, visitors learn about bird banding, making birdhouses and feeders, and satellite tracking. Visitors get up close during lorikeet feedings and sometimes the birds land on the guests. Visitors have the opportunity to pet giraffes as they feed them. Children enjoy brief trail rides. Guests view 3-D action movies while learning about plants and animals and the importance of preserving the planet.

Botanical Garden

The Botanical Garden includes a visitors' center, a walled garden, an amphitheater, a river walk, woodland trails, and an outdoor classroom. The Botanical Garden's historic ruins from the 1800s earned Riverbanks a listing on the National Register of Historic Places.

The well-designed Lexington County entrance on the left bank of the Saluda River has an elaborately landscaped parking lot large enough for 250 cars, a landscaped entrance gate, and a boardwalk/bridge leading to the Botanical Garden. Visitors passing through the Lexington County side entrance walk past the Bog Garden in the entrance plaza, along a short path through woodlands, and over a wooden bridge above a brook bordered by plants and flowers toward the entrance to the walled garden, which is larger than a football field. Visitors entering the original gate on the Richland County side walk or ride the tram up from the zoo to the Botanical Garden.

The Saluda Factory Interpretive Center is a rough-hewn log cabin located near the mill ruins. It features exhibits to assist in the interpretation of the mill ruins and the flora and fauna of the area. There is also an outdoor classroom for educational programs.

The garden is a leading source of horticultural and botanical information in the area. Through a cooperative effort with Clemson Extension Service, the public can access information by talking with an extension agent or by using the Internet in the Visitors Center. The garden also provides facilities for related activities. The Mid-Carolina Daylily Society holds its annual show and the SC Native Plant Society its annual symposium in the garden. The Community Concert Band continues to hold its annual show in the amphitheater.

Signature Events

Riverbanks has several special attractions including "Lights Before Christmas" and "Boo at the Zoo." The *"Lights Before Christmas"* special attraction enhances Riverbanks in December with over one million colorful lights along walkways, in trees, on shrubbery, and in other locations. At the entrance, visitors are greeted with lighted trees containing large stars and the sound of Christmas music. There are colorful lighted images of animals.

Some of the animals appear to be in motion. For example, there is an elephant spraying water over its back, an ostrich running through the woods, and bears ice skating in the Rhino Camp. Visitors on their way to the bridge pass under an arch artfully decorated with colorful lights and view numerous decorated trees and shrubs, as well as a group of frogs that appear to be playing. There is a marshmallow-roasting pit where guests can warm themselves and a Holiday Village where children can visit with Santa.

Riverbanks is one of a number of zoos that is presenting attractions of this kind. The Winnipeg, Canada, Assiniboine Park Zoo features "The Lights of the Wild" and reindeer sleigh rides. The Fort Worth Zoo presents a "Zoobilee of Lights," which increased its December attendance from only 10,000 to 12,000 visitors to over 75,000 visitors.

"Lights Before Christmas" is a major event each year. In addition to gate receipts, this event generates revenue from concessions, carousel rides, and from additional membership purchases. "Lights Before Christmas" has been named one of the Top Twenty Events in the Southeast by the Southeast Tourism Society and one of the Top 100 Events in North America by the American Bus Association.

"Boo at the Zoo" is a Halloween program with enjoyable, safe activities. Kids and parents wander the Trick-or-Treat trail and find candy stations, storytellers, glow-in-the-dark tattoos, face painting, major prizes, and more. Costumed kids may wander into caves, ride the Crazy Carousel and the Hobgoblin Express, and see the 3-D Haunted Mine Ride movie. Little boys and girls may watch the magic show and dance at the DJ dance party "Monster Mash" style.

Riverbanks hosts a wine tasting event in May. Society members' tickets are $40, and nonmember tickets are $50. In addition to the hundreds of local and international vintages, there is a jazz band, wine experts, and vintners in the gardens. Proceeds support Riverbanks' conservation and educational programs. The zoo has teamed up with a local Embassy Suites Hotel to offer a weekend package that includes a suite, two wine glasses, a reception before the wine tasting, and transportation to the event.

"Brew at the Zoo" is a beer tasting event. Live bands play as patrons wander the park and sample the works of the brewmasters. Each patron is given a 4-ounce tasting cup and beer stations are set up throughout the park. In addition, beer-flavored food and various appetizers and desserts are available at food carts located throughout the park. Society members' tickets are only $25, and nonmembers' tickets are $35.

Rental of Zoo and Garden

Riverbanks provides the opportunity to rent various portions of the property and facilities for activities such as birthday parties, weddings, and business meetings. Total revenue from all rentals has decreased from approximately $124,735 in 2005 to $112,985 in 2006 (Exhibit 3 and Exhibit 4).

The zoo offers facilities for meetings, parties, weddings, receptions, and other activities for up to 500 people with prices ranging up to $2,500. Daytime rentals are available in the Magnolia Room, Safari Camp, and the Ndoki Lodge. The Magnolia Room in the Botanical Garden accommodates up to 200 for a theatre-style meeting or up to 150 for a seated luncheon. The Safari Camp accommodates up to 300 for picnic table seating. The Ndoki Lodge accommodates 350 for a theatre-style meeting or up to 250 for a seated luncheon. In the evening additional rentals are available in the Riverbanks Theatre, Aquarium Reptile Complex, Birdhouse of Riverbanks, Gorilla Base Camp, and Botanical Gardens. Rental of Riverbanks property and facilities promotes attendance by more individuals and organizations who benefit from an enjoyable and educational experience.

EXHIBIT 3   Riverbank's Income Statement

	2006	2005	2004
Revenues			
Property Taxes	$ 2,413,523	$ 2,194,998	$ 2,135,947
State Government Contribution	112,000	110,000	166,191
Accommodations & Hospitality Taxes	220,000	167,500	150,000
General Admission Fees	2,637,897	2,640,913	2,640,105
Concession Fees	–	757,459	765,538
Concessionaire Commissions on Sales	728,273	–	–
Concession Upkeep Contribution	–	–	–
Riverbanks Society Contibutions	1,002,800	1,293,249	1,000,000
Classes and Program Fees	318,233	274,859	276,670
Net Revenues–Rides, Shows, and Promotions	995,339	974,989	640,565
Facilty Rental and Corporate Sales Initiative	112,985	124,735	107,668
Sponsorships	–	80,000	80,662
Federal Grant	–	–	56,250
Non-Federal Grants and Donations	134,100	57,339	58,070
Dispute Settlement with Architect	–	–	–
Insurance Settlement–Property Damage	13,408	35,082	6,954
Investment Earnings		9,141	4,917
Interest Revenue	26,747	–	–
Miscellaneous Revenues	19,361	11,839	32,621
Total Revenues	**8,734,666**	**8,732,103**	**8,122,158**
Expenditures			
Current			
Administrative	1,000,501	926,975	826,824
Animal Care	2,393,803	2,340,063	2,299,940
Education	193,365	205,297	197,739
Botancial	662,311	609,317	627,088
Facility Management	555,424	462,279	512,441
Utilities	705,478	632,244	628,447
Marketing and Public Relations	835,337	663,484	562,714
Guest Services	1,160,076	1,126,623	1,075,941
Rides, Shows, and Promotions	625,068	604,307	455,744
Classes and Programs	191,312	186,635	167,248
Litigation	–	–	–
Debt Service			
Principal	360,143	486,633	265,174
Interest	39,373	59,715	64,069
Capital Outlay			
General Operations–Equipment & Improvements	80,685	179,988	68,293
Major Repairs	68,684	113,100	49,750
Rides, Shows and Promotions	5,198	11,500	423,102
Total Expenditures	**8,876,758**	**8,608,160**	**8,224,514**
Excess of Revenues Over (Under) Expenditures	**(142,092)**	**(123,943)**	**(102,356)**

continued

EXHIBIT 3   Riverbank's Income Statement—continued

	2006	2005	2004
Other Financing Sources (Uses)			
Advance of Commissions	–	–	–
Loan Proceeds–3D Theater	–	–	349,700
Proceeds of 2003 General Obligation Bonds Issued	–	–	–
Refunding of 1991 General Obligation Bonds Issued	–	–	–
2003 Bonds Premium	–	–	–
2003 Bonds Accured Interest	–	–	–
Return on Sinking Fund	–	–	–
Transfers In	–	–	–
Transfers Out	(33,132)	(34,291)	(36,152)
Total Other Financing Sources (Uses)	**(33,132)**	**(34,291)**	**313,548**
Excess of Revenues and Other Financing Sources Over (Under) Expenditures and Other Financing Uses	–	**89,652**	**211,192**
Net Change in Fund Balances	**(175,224)**	–	–
Fund Balance (Deficit), Beginning of Year	**956,128**	**866,476**	**655,284**
Fund Balance (Deficit), End of Year	**780,904**	**956,128**	**866,476**

EXHIBIT 4   Riverbank's Balance Sheets (fiscal year ends in June)

Assets	2005	2006
Current Assets		
Cash and Cash Equivalents	$ 1,206,879	$ 689,811
Cash Held by Fiscal Agent	891,842	–
Cash Held by Fiscal Agent for Debt Service	–	457,541
Cash Held by Fiscal Agent for Future Operations	–	692,986
Receivables	387,806	379,986
Unconditional Promises to Give Restricted	–	–
Prepaid Expense	–	20,000
Inventory	–	77,966
Supplies Inventories and Prepaid Expense	83,516	–
Other Assets	–	76,950
Total Current Assets	2,570,043	2,395,240
Non Current Assets		
Capital Assets	43,782,950	43,497,218
Less: Accumulated Depreciation	(10,392,547)	(11,343,012)
Total Capital Assets	33,390,403	32,154,206
Other Assets	–	–
Long Term Unconditional Promises to Give-Restricted Net of Allowance	–	–
Total Noncurrent Assets	33,390,403	32,154,206
Total Assets	35,960,446	34,549,446
Current Liabilities		
Accounts and Retainage Payable	421,545	266,481
Accrued Salaries	126,994	147,647
Accrued Admissions and Use Taxes Payable	11,359	11,721

continued

EXHIBIT 4 Riverbank's Balance Sheets (fiscal year ends in June)—continued

Retirement Contributions Payable	36,328	56,739
Accrued Interest Payable	258,974	249,977
Unearned Revenue	789,285	–
Deferred Revenue	–	817,459
Current Portion Compensated Absences–Accrued Vacation Leave Payable	–	133,000
Current Portion of Long-Term Debt	1,290,144	1,196,612
Total Current Liabilities	2,934,829	2,879,636
Noncurrent Liabilities		
Compensated Absences—Accrued Vacation Leave Payable	193,223	75,130
General Obligation Bonds Payable	15,475,000	14,550,000
Notes Payable	562,726	291,115
Total Noncurrent Liabilities	16,230,949	14,916,245
Total Liabilities	19,165,578	17,795,881
Net Assets		
Invested in Capital Assets, Net of Related Debt	16,612,740	16,540,913
Restricted Donations—Purpose Not Yet Satisfied	–	–
Unrestricted	182,128	212,652
Total Net Assets	16,794,868	16,753,565
Total Liabilities and Net Assets	35,960,446	34,549,446

Source: www.riverbanks.org/planvisit/.

Riverbanks Education Department

The Education Department works to interpret animal exhibits and plants, and assist in learning about animal and plant worlds. The primary facility of the Education Department is the Education Center, which has two classrooms, an auditorium, and a library. Other facilities available for education programs include a classroom in the Aquarium Reptile Complex, another in the Riverbanks Farm, an outdoor classroom at the Saluda Factory Interpretive Center, and the amphitheater adjacent to the Botanical Garden.

During the week, Riverbanks offers classes to groups ranging from preschool through college (Exhibit 5). On weekends and in the summer Riverbanks offers classes and special programs for students, scouts, teachers, and family members. Special programs include Home School Mondays, zoo ventures, zoo camp, overnights, day camp, after-school programs, zoo teens, educational excursions, and guided garden tours.

EXHIBIT 5 Examples of Riverbanks Education Programs

Single-Grade Programs

Special Education • Close Encounters • Animal Around the World Tour	**Grade 3** • Animal Kingdom • Zoo-vivor • History of Riverbanks
Preschool and Kindergarten • Critters That Crawl • Lions, Tigers and Bears, OH MY! • Animals in Winter	**Grade 4** • Zoo-vivor • A Place to Call Their Own
Grade 1 • Flower Power	**Grade 5** • Populations & Ecosystems • Who's Eating Who?

continued

EXHIBIT 5   Examples of Riverbanks Education Programs—continued

Single-Grade Programs

Grade 2	**Grade 6**
• Circle of Life	• Animal Enrichment
• Wild World	• Sea of Uncertainty

Multi-Grade Programs

Grades 7–12
• Biodiversity

College Level Programs

Contact Education Department at 803-779-8717 x1113

Source: http://www.riverbanks.org

Financing

Individuals, businesses, and government have funded the original construction, major renovations and expansions, and the annual operating budget. The Riverbanks Zoological Park and Botanical Garden has an annual operating budget of over $10 million. The 2006 *Annual Report* stated, "During fiscal year 2005–06 admissions revenue, concessionaire commissions on retail sales, other charges for services and the Riverbanks Society operating contribution (collectively 'earned revenues') amounted to $6,369,467, or 56% of total revenues, which is down from 62% for the previous fiscal year. Property taxes amounted to 38% of total revenues, up from 34% last fiscal year. Contributions by the State of South Carolina, other grants and contributions, and other revenues were 6% of total revenues, up from 4% for the previous fiscal year. Nationally, governments provide approximately 54 percent of the support for zoos."

A nonprofit organization, the zoo uses fund accounting to report its financial position and results of operations. The basic financial statements for the years ending June 30, 2005 to 2006 are shown in Exhibits 3 and 4.

Admission revenues are impacted by weather conditions because most of the attractions are outdoors. Riverbanks earns admissions revenue directly from visitors who pay per visit or indirectly from Riverbanks Society members who pay per year for one of several different memberships. General admission fees are small. A single admission is $9.75 for adults and $7.25 for children ages 3–12. Special prices of $8.50 are available for military members, and $8.25 for senior citizens. Discounts are available for groups, special activities, or special days. Free classes are provided for Lexington and Richland County schools. Charges for special activities vary.

Attendance is a critical issue for the zoo. The financial performance is directly related to attendance. Zoo patrons also purchase food and drinks at the concessions, pay to ride the carousel, and feed the birds. Attendance decreased from a total of 869,499 in 2005 to 852,993 in 2006. While most of this shortfall was from a reduction in "free admissions," visits by Riverbanks society members also continue to decrease. In fiscal year 2004 there were over 348,000 society visits. They dropped to nearly 327,000 in 2005 and were only slightly more than 303,000 in 2006. Given that society memberships make up a large portion of the zoo's operating budget, a decrease in attendance may portend a decrease in memberships.

Attendance peaked in the 2002 fiscal year when attendance surpassed 1 million visitors. This was primarily due to the Zoo 2002 Campaign's major expansion. The drop in attendance the following few years was in line with what was experienced by similar operations. There is a large increase in attendance the year of the changes, followed by a decline to a level that is below the peak, but above the level of attendance prior to the expansion.

The Magnolia Room in the Botanical Gardens, the Ndoki Lodge, and the Palmetto Plaza in the Aquarium are available for rental for corporate meetings and weddings. Packages are available for as little as $150 to use the facilities after hours to propose, or to have a photographer prepare engagement and bridal portraits. Riverbanks can accommodate the rehearsal dinner on Friday night, the wedding Saturday afternoon, and the reception Saturday night. Programs are available to host corporate parties of from 100 to 500 guests. Revenue from this source of operations was budgeted to be $175,000 in fiscal 2006. However, this level of funding was only $112,985. That $62,000 budget shortfall was even below the prior years' earnings of $124,735.

Other funding issues faced by Riverbanks were not unique to zoos. Just as for all consumers electricity, natural gas, and sewer costs were significantly higher in 2006 than in 2005. This resulted in the zoo being overbudget by $54,000 in this area.

Additional information concerning zoo and aquarium industry financing is available at the AZA Web site, www.aza.org.

Riverbanks Society

Consisting of over 28,000 households, the Riverbanks Society is one of the largest zoo societies per capita in the United States. The society provides funds for operations, construction and renovations, new exhibits, and special activities. Many of the exhibits and portions of the gardens were provided by individual donations. For example, the Old Rose Garden established in the Botanical Garden, and the new bird house and gorilla exhibits in the zoo were funded by private contributions, as were other projects in previous years. An endangered species carousel, funded by a local business, is a focal point of the children's play area. The carousel has 22 endangered species that children can ride and a scenic mural of other endangered species in their natural habitats.

The society offers reasonable annual membership fees for individuals or family members. A variety of memberships for individuals and families range from $34 to $125 for a standard membership, and from $250 to $1,000 for benefactor memberships. Types of memberships, associated benefits, and costs are shown in Exhibit 6. Society members enjoy benefits in addition to those in the exhibit. For example, Riverbanks sends society members a bimonthly newsletter and a quarterly magazine. The magazine contains a feature article, timely information on zoo and garden activities, and pages devoted to younger members. Some issues of the magazine have pictures of children with their zoo art, word puzzles, and special children's programs and activities. This is especially appropriate since many children visit Riverbanks. Riverbanks also arranges tours to Africa, Australia, Peru, South America, and other places across the globe. The members get the opportunity to learn from a Riverbanks professional as they tour the natural habits of the animals.

EXHIBIT 6   Riverbanks Society Memberships

Individual—$34

 FREE admission for 1 adult named on card PLUS 4 guest passes
 One free admission to "Lights Before Christmas"
 Free admission to 100 other zoos, Riverbanks magazine and newsletter, discounts in gift shops and education programs, members-only events, preview of exhibits

Individual Plus—$49

 Benefits of Individual Membership PLUS permanent guest option, 6 guest passes

Family/Grandparent—$59

 Benefits of Individual Membership PLUS admission for children/grandchildren 18 years and under, 6 free passes

Family Plus—$74

 Benefits of Family/Grandparent Membership PLUS 12 free passes, early bird enrollment in Wild Weeks Summer Camp, unlimited free admission to "Lights Before Christmas," and 4 free activity tokens (good for carousel, lorikeet, or giraffe)

Patron—$125

 Benefits of Family Plus Membership PLUS permanent guest option, duplicate membership card, subscription to *Wildlife Conservation*

continued

EXHIBIT 6   Riverbanks Society Memberships—continued

Curators Membership—$250
  Benefits of Patron Membership PLUS 16 free passes and private Gold Circle events

Director Membership—$500
  Same benefits as Curators' Circle PLUS escorted behind-the-scenes tours, *Satch's Scoop* newsletter, 25% discount on facility rentals

Benefactor Membership—$1,000
  Same benefits as Director's Circle PLUS VIP tours and events

Source: http://www.riverbanks.org/support/membership.shtml

The Future

The zoo and botanical garden industry always face issues such as health of the animals and plants, uncertainty of the economy, and competition. High gas prices in 2006–2007 were an issue. The recent downturn in the economy has reduced tax receipts of many states leading to budget cuts.

Other attractions in South Carolina compete with Riverbanks Zoo for tourists' dollars and time. Myrtle Beach, a popular entertainment and shopping destination, is home to Ripley's Aquarium located at Broadway at the Beach and many other forms of entertainment. Charleston, famous for its historic district, is home to the South Carolina State Aquarium, the CSS *Hunley* (the Confederate submarine credited with being the first submarine to sink a ship), and Patriot's Point (museum site of the aircraft carrier USS *Yorktown* and several other naval vessels). Columbia, the capital city, is home to the SC State Museum and other attractions.

In the face of declining attendance numbers, the zoo needs a clear strategic plan for the coming three years. Do you feel the zoo should add covered walkways to accommodate visitors during bad weather? Should the zoo begin developing a prehistoric animal exhibit since fossil collecting is gaining in popularity nationwide? Develop a new marketing campaign for the zoo. Develop a questionnaire that could be administered to zoo visitors and nonvisitors to determine how the zoo could best attract new customers.